LEARNING OFFICE ACCOUNTING PROFESSIONAL 2008

Terri E. Brunsdon, CPA, CITP, JD

Prentice Hall

Upper Saddle River, NJ 07458

Library of Congress Cataloging-in-Publication Data
Brunsdon, Terri E.
Learning Office accounting professional 2008 / Terri E. Brunsdon,.
p. cm.
Includes index.
ISBN-13: 978-0-13-606342-1 (pbk.)
ISBN-10: 0-13-606342-X (pbk.)
1. Accounting--Computer programs. 2. Small business--Accounting--Software. I. Title.
HF5679.B66335 2010
657.0285'53--dc22
2008048915

VP/Publisher: Natalie E. Anderson
AVP/Executive Editor: Jodi McPherson
Director, Product Development: Pamela Hersperger
Product Development Manager: Eileen Bien Calabro
Editorial Project Manager: Melissa Arlio
AVP/Executive Editor, Media: Richard Keaveny
Editorial Media Project Manager: Ashley Lulling
Production Media Project Manager: Lorena Cerisano
Marketing Manager: Maggie Moylan
Marketing Assistant: Ian Gold
Senior Managing Editor: Cynthia Zonneveld
Associate Managing Editor: Camille Trentacoste
Production Project Manager: Rhonda Aversa
Manager of Rights & Permissions: Charles Morris
Senior Operations Specialist: Nick Sklitsis
Operations Specialist: Natacha St. Hill Moore
Senior Art Director: Jonathan Boylan
Cover Design: Jonathan Boylan
Cover Illustration/Photo: © Kimball Stock
Manager, Cover Visual Research & Permissions: Karen Sanatar
Composition: GEX Publishing Services
Full-Service Project Management: GEX Publishing Services
Printer/Binder: Webcrafters
Typeface: 12/14 Calibri

Credits and acknowledgments borrowed from other sources and reproduced, with permission, in this textbook appear on appropriate page within text.

Pearson Education LTD.
Pearson Education Singapore, Pte. Ltd
Pearson Education, Canada, Ltd
Pearson Education–Japan
Pearson Education Australia PTY, Limited
Pearson Education North Asia Ltd
Pearson EducaciÛn de Mexico, S.A. de C.V.
Pearson Education Malaysia, Pte. Ltd.

Prentice Hall
is an imprint of

www.pearsonhighered.com

10 9 8 7 6 5 4 3 2 1
ISBN-13: 978-0-13-606342-1
ISBN-10: 0-13-606342-X

TABLE OF CONTENTS

PREFACE

A Special Note to Students and Instructors from Terri Brunsdon
How This Textbook Teaches Office Accounting Pro 2008

Learning Microsoft Office Accounting Professional 2008 is a comprehensive approach to teaching accounting concepts in a software environment. The text includes sample databases designed to simulate real-world businesses so that students gain "hands-on" experience with initiating transactions, performing accounting activities, producing financial statements, and analyzing company performance.

This text uses a "WHoW" approach to teaching software by explaining ***why*** a task is performed, illustrating ***how*** to perform the task, and then explaining ***what*** the task affected. Chapters begin with an introduction to **Manual Accounting Procedures *("MAPS")*** before illustrating transaction posting in the software. MAPS topics expose students to the subsidiary journals, accounting ledgers, and audit trail concepts necessary to understanding why and how transaction posting impacts financial data. MAPS topics also provide insight for illustrations in ***Behind the Keys*** topics where students trace the audit trail for posted transactions. With MAPS and Behind the Keys, students learn to conceptualize accounting transactions and to correct posting errors.

The text provides step-by-step illustrations that guide students through posting transactions and performing other accounting activities. On occasion, students will be asked to complete a ***You Try*** exercise following a guided illustration to reinforce skills previously covered. Solutions for these exercises are located in Appendix E.

Office Accounting Professional (OAP) is new to the area of accounting software, but you will find that it functions similar to comparably priced general ledger products on the market. In addition, OAP is part of Microsoft's Office Suite so it fully integrates with Excel, Word, and Outlook. OAP runs over top Microsoft's MSDE SQL Server, meaning that data files must be attached to the SQL Server before opening. Comprehensive instructions for performing this task are illustrated in the text.

How Chapters Are Organized

- **Chapter 1** begins by explaining the role of accounting software and illustrates activities such as opening, closing, attaching and detaching, and backing up and restoring company data files. It also covers using OAP help and shortcut keys and navigating the OAP interface.
- **Chapter 2** illustrates customizing OAP preferences, reviewing the chart of accounts, printing, customizing, and exporting reports, emailing documents, and locating information using find, drilldown, and hyperlink features.
- **In Chapter 3,** students post basic and complex journal entries and then print financial statements. This chapter is intended to give students a comfort level with posting basic transactions, printing reports, and locating information before tackling more complicated tasks involving sales, purchasing, and payroll transactions. After this chapter, the text branches into two distinct tracts that present accounting activities for a service based business and then a merchandising business.
- **Chapters 4 through 7** use a cycle based approach to illustrating accounting activities for a service based business using job costing. This tract begins by processing sales activities and then proceeds to separate chapters illustrating purchasing and payroll activities. The tract concludes by reviewing postings, recording adjusting entries, printing financial statements, and closing the accounting period. After completing this series of chapters, students have worked with job costing and have completed an entire accounting cycle for a serviced based business. The text then presents a comprehensive project covering cycle activities for a different service based business that can be assigned to test student skills.
- **In Chapters 8 through 11**, the cycle based approach is repeated for a merchandising business. After completing this tract, students have worked with inventory and have completed an entire accounting cycle for a merchandising company. The text then presents a comprehensive project covering cycle activities for a different merchandising business that can be assigned to test student skills.
- **Chapter 12** provides an opportunity for students to create a merchandising business from scratch and then record a month of transactions for the new business.
- **Appendix A** includes detailed instructions for installing OAP. **Appendix B** includes comprehensive instructions for correcting posting errors. **Appendix C** provides data file backup and restore procedures that make data portable between school and home. **Appendix D** contains the IRS Circular E tax tables used in the text to illustrate calculating employee payroll deductions. **Appendix E** contains solutions for *You Try* exercises that appear throughout the text.

***Note: The author recommends that readers complete Chapters 1 through 3 before embarking on either the service based business or merchandising business tracts. In addition, students should complete the Practice Set at the end of Chapter 1 where students load sample data files, customize with their initials, and backup the files for use in later chapters.*

Where Student Data Files Are Found and How They Are Named and Used in the Text

The sample data files located on the accompanying CD labeled **Student Data** are named and used in the text as follows:

Data File Name	**When to use**
Practice TEK Business	While reading Chapters 3
Graded TEK Business	End of chapter exercises in Chapter 3
Practice Astor Landscaping	While reading Chapters 4 through 7
Graded Astor Landscaping	End of chapter exercises in Chapters 4 through7
Practice Baxter Garden Supply	While reading Chapters 1 and 2 and 8 through 11
Graded Baxter Garden Supply	End of chapter exercises in Chapters 8 through 11
Eragon Electrical Contracting Project	Service based company for completing Project 1
Olsen Office Furniture Project	Merchandising company for completing Project 2

*** Note: There is NO data file for Chapter 12 because the student will create the data file while reading the chapter.*

Features That Help Readers Really Learn the Software AND Accounting

The following marginal icons are placed alongside topics and exercises to signal:

Step-by-step instructions for performing a task with illustrated solutions.

You Try exercises with solutions in Appendix E.

Manual Accounting Procedures (*MAPS*) illustration.

Behind the Keys procedures for tracing posted entries.

New feature for Office Accounting 2008.

Web-based video tutorial available to illustrate the topic.

LEARNING RESOURCES FOR STUDENTS

Companion Website located at www.prenhall.com/compaccounting

The book's Website contains updates for the text and a link to instructor resources.

Accompanying CD

A Student CD accompanies the text and contains sample data files used with the text.

TEACHING RESOURCES FOR INSTRUCTORS

Instructors Manual

The Instructors Manual provides teaching tips and solutions. The Instructors CD contains solution databases by chapter for tasks performed while reading the text and while completing end-of-chapter practice sets.

Web-based Tutorials

- Tutorial videos demonstrating and explaining particular tasks illustrated in the text. These tutorials are perfect for implementing an online course.

Online Instructors Resource Center located at www.prenhall.com/irc

- The Instructor Website contains links to instructor resource materials. Contact your local sales representative for access to this password-protected area.

Course Management Solutions

- WebCT Course Management
- Blackboard Course Management

Author Website located at www.terribrunsdon.com

This companion site contains information on text updates and other news.

About the Author

Terri Brunsdon is a Certified Public Accountant with undergraduate degrees in accounting and computer programming. She also has a Juris Doctorate in Law and a Masters in Tax. Terri has over twenty years of accounting experience and specializes in recommending and implementing accounting software solutions. In addition, Terri has six years of higher education teaching experience in accounting information systems and computer software applications. She is a member of the American Institute of Certified Public Accountants (AICPA) and an AICPA Certified Information Technology Professional (CITP).

More Computerized Accounting Software Texts by Terri Brunsdon

If you like the teaching and learning approach of this text, don't forget to review these other Prentice Hall textbooks by Terri Brunsdon.

- *Learning QuickBooks Pro 2008*
- *Learning Microsoft Office Accounting Professional 2008*
- *Introduction to Microsoft Great Plains 8.0: Focus on Internal Controls*
- *Coming Soon – Introduction to Microsoft Great Plains 10.0: Focus on Internal Controls*

Dedicated to my husband and best friend, Bill Brunsdon.

Chapter 1 GET READY FOR OFFICE ACCOUNTING 2008

LEARNING OBJECTIVES

This chapter introduces Office Accounting Professional 2008 (OAP) by covering:

1. An introduction to accounting software
2. Copying sample data files and attaching to the software
3. Launching OAP and opening and closing sample data files
4. Learning basic OAP features and keyboard shortcuts
5. Customizing sample company names
6. Using OAP help
7. Backing up and restoring sample data files

INTRODUCTION TO ACCOUNTING SOFTWARE

Accounting software simplifies capturing and posting accounting transactions. Although basic accounting procedures remain the same, accounting software eliminates tedious processes such as typing documents, manually posting and calculating transactions, and documenting the audit trail.

Manual Accounting System	Computerized Accounting System
1. Business transaction occurs and is manually entered onto a source document.	1. Business transaction occurs and is entered into the accounting software.
2. Source document manually posted to subsidiary journal, account ledger, and general ledger while documenting audit trail.	2. Accounting software posts transaction to subsidiary journal, account ledger, and general ledger and records the audit trail.
3. Manually prepare trial balance.	3. Print computerized trial balance.
4. Record adjusting entries on general journal and post entries to general ledger.	4. Record adjusting entries to general journal and software posts to general ledger.
5. Manually prepare adjusted trial balance.	5. Reprint trial balance with adjusting entries.
6. Manually calculate and post closing entries.	6. Computer posts closing entries.
7. Manually prepare financial statements.	7. Print computerized financial statements.

Computerized accounting minimizes posting errors, thus protecting data validity. After correctly capturing a transaction, the software coordinates posting, reporting, and the audit trail. In addition, the accountant can quickly monitor transactions and analyze financial performance.

Naturally you need computer hardware and operating software to use computerized accounting software. Computer hardware encompasses the physical components such as keyboard, screen, hard drive, CD-ROM, mouse, memory, and printers. Operating software is the system software that translates user instructions to hardware components and application software. Microsoft's Windows XP, Windows 2000, and Vista as well as Linux and UNIX are examples of operating software.

Application Software

Application software serves specific user needs and is installed over operating software. There are a wide variety of application software packages on the market and the following table outlines a few of the more familiar packages alongside its purpose.

Application	Purpose
Microsoft Word	Word processing
Microsoft Excel	Financial analysis
Microsoft Access	Database
Microsoft Explorer	Internet browser
Microsoft Outlook	Email and contact manager
Microsoft Office Accounting Professional	Accounting software

Application software must match the computer operating system. Therefore, you will often find multiple versions of the same software for installation with particular operating software.

Accounting Software

Accounting software is application software that automates manual accounting procedures. This software is normally organized by activities with each activity representing a specific functional area of accounting such as customer activities or vendor activities. OAP segregates accounting activities into company (general journal entries), customer (sales, accounts receivable, and cash receipts), vendor (purchases, accounts payable, and cash disbursements), employee (payroll), and banking (deposits and checks) activities. A visual depiction of these activities is illustrated in Chapter 3 under the topic that discusses data integration.

Copy Sample Data Files

To cover concepts presented in this text, you will work with the sample company databases designed by the author and located on the **Student CD** accompanying the text. Before launching OAP, you will need to copy these files located onto your computer's hard drive.

The following table lists the data files stored on the CD and describes when a data file is used in the text. (Note: Each sample company requires two data files.) The description also explains that companies containing **Graded** in the data file name are duplicates of companies containing **Practice** in the data file name. This design lets you practice tasks while reading a chapter then complete graded tasks at the end of the chapter without having to learn a new accounting structure for a different company.

Company Name	Data Files	Description
Practice TEK Business	practicetekbusiness.sbd practicetekbusiness.sbl	Service based consulting business used while reading Chapter 3.
Graded TEK Business	gradedtekbusiness.sbd gradedtekbusiness.sbl	Duplicate of Practice TEK Business used when completing the Practice Set at the end of Chapter 3.
Practice Astor Landscaping	practiceastorlandscaping.sbd practiceastorlandscaping.sbl	Service based landscaping business used when reading Chapters 4 through 7.
Graded Astor Landscaping	gradedastorlandscaping.sbd gradedastorlandscaping.sbl	Duplicate of Practice Astor Landscaping used when completing Practice Sets at the end of Chapters 4 through 7.
Practice Baxter Garden Supply	practicebaxtergardensupply.sbd practicebaxtergardensupply.sbl	Home and garden merchandiser used when reading Chapters 1 and 2 and 8 through 11.
Graded Baxter Garden Supply	gradedbaxtergardensupply.sbd gradedbaxtergardensupply.sbl	Duplicate of Practice Baxter Garden Supply used while completing Practice Sets at the end of Chapters 8 through 11.
Eragon Electrical Contracting Project	eragonelectricalcontractingproject.sbd eragonelectricalcontractingproject.sbl	Service based electrical contracting business used when completing Project 1.
Olsen Office Furniture Project	olsenofficefurnitureproject.sbd olsenofficefurnitureproject.sbl	Wholesale merchandising business used when completing Project 2.

Complete the next steps to copy these data files onto your machine.

STEPS TO COPY COMPANY DATA FILES

1. Insert the CD labeled **Student CD** into your computer CD drive. Using the mouse, right click Window's **Start** menu and select **Explore** to open the My Computer window illustrated in Figure 1:1.

   Verify that the **Folders** icon is depressed so that the Folder pane appears on the left and then click to select the **My Computer** folder on the left. The contents of the folder will now be listed to the right. *(Note: Your folder's contents may be different from the illustration.)*

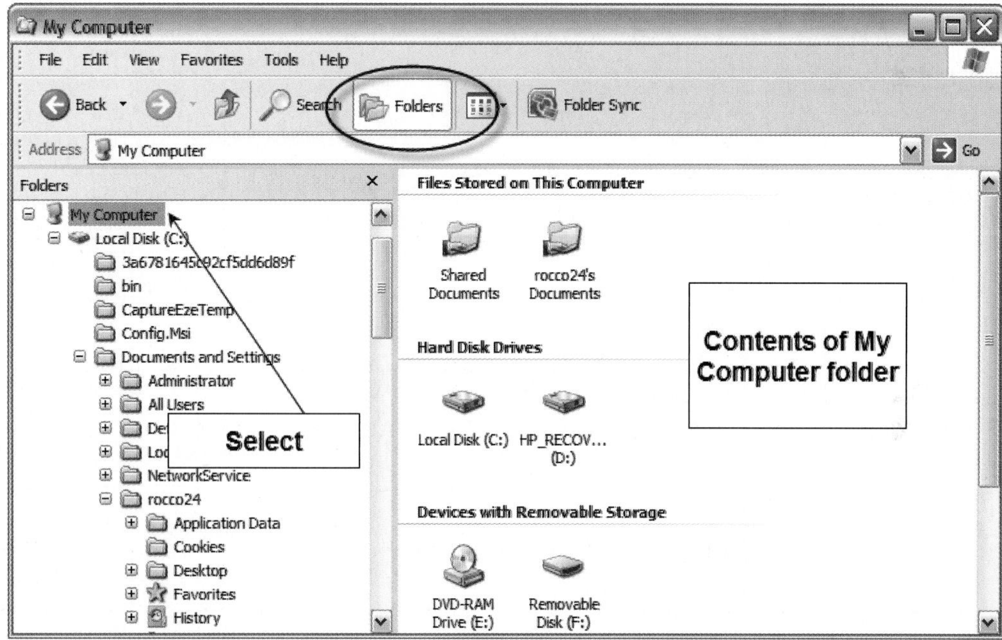

Figure 1:1

2. Right click the drive letter containing a CD icon and select **Explore**. This drive is normally labeled **D**.

   Double click the **Assets** folder and then double click the **Data Files** folder.

   Right click zipped **Student_Data_Files** folder and select **Explore**. Double click the **Student Data Files** folder.

   From the menu select ***View>>Tiles*** and the data files will appear as illustrated in Figure 1:2.

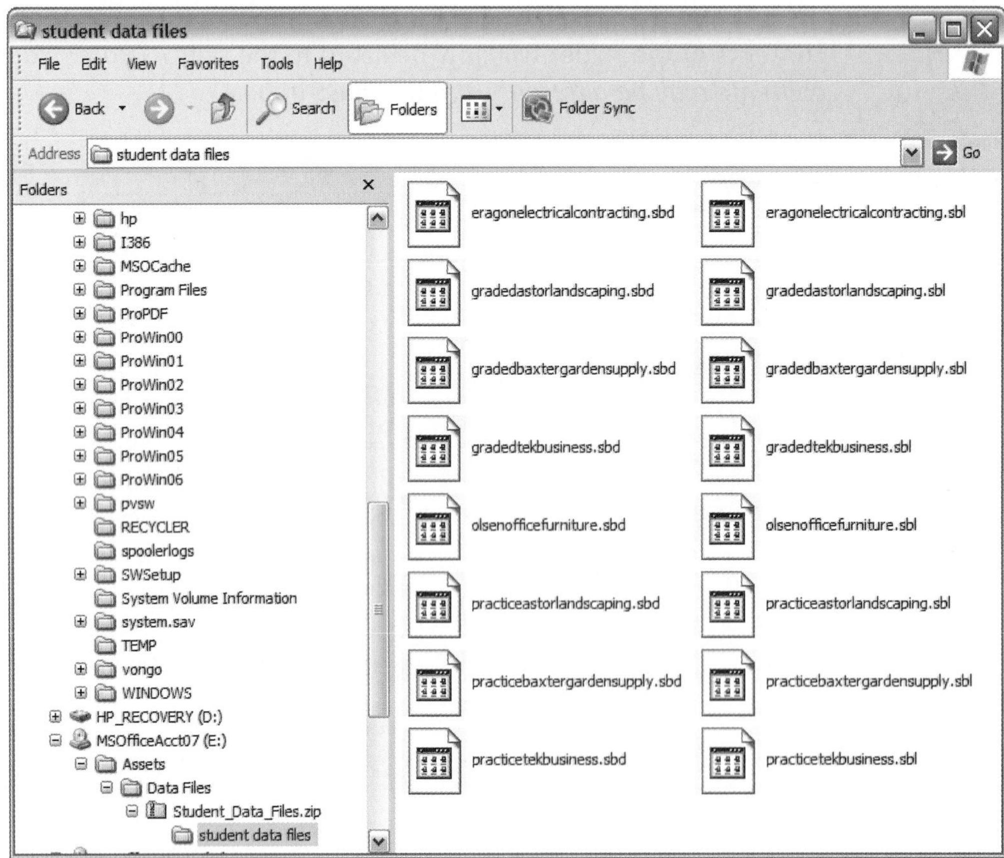

Figure 1:2

3. You will now locate the folder on your computer where the data files will be stored.

   Scroll up the Folder pane on the left and locate the **Program Files** folder. Click the **plus** symbol to open this folder (Figure 1:3).

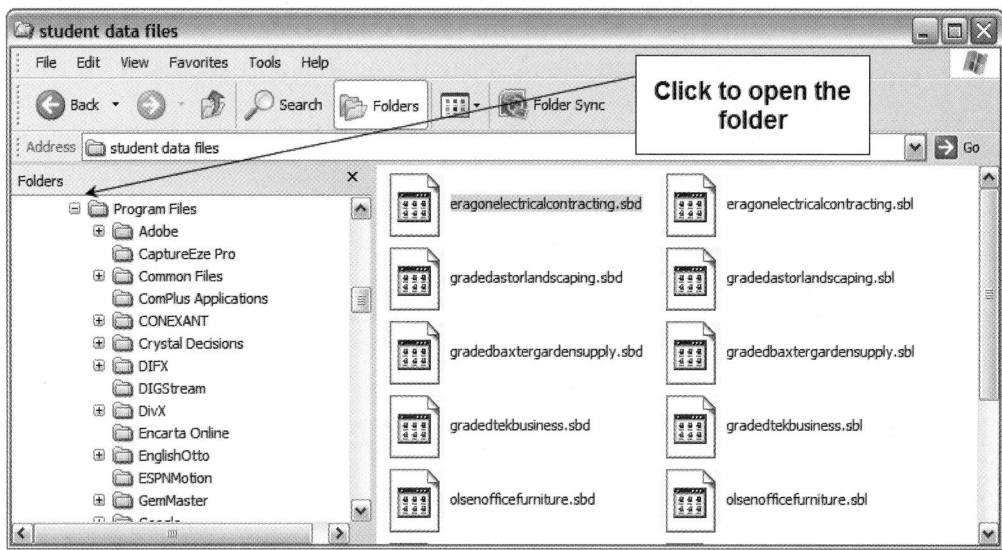

Figure 1:3

Scroll down the Program Files folder and locate the **Microsoft SQL Server** folder. Click the **plus** symbol to open the folder. Next, click the plus symbol on the **MSSQL.1** folder and the **plus** symbol on the **MSSQL** folder. You will now see a folder named **Data**.

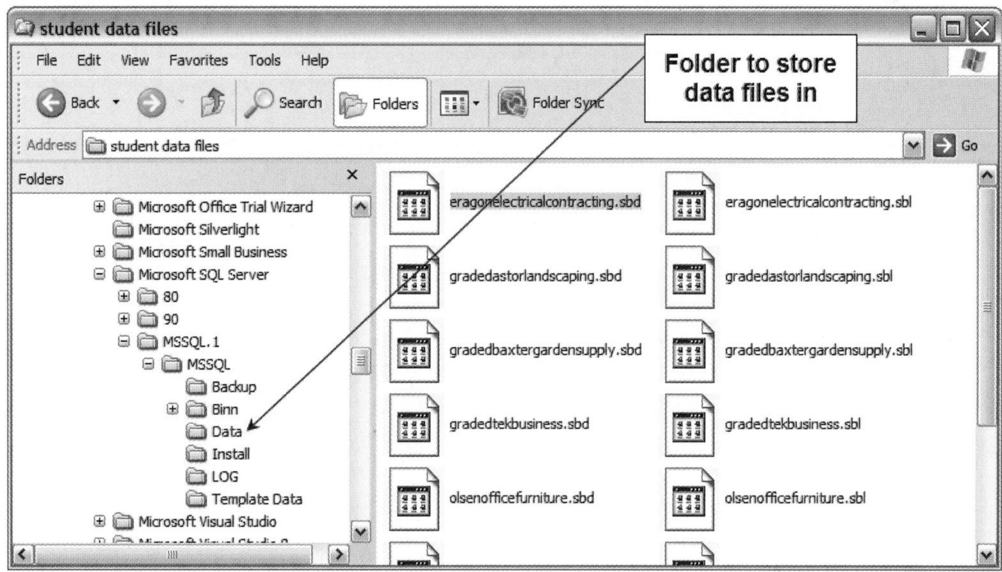

Figure 1:4

4. Click to select the first data file listed in the right pane and, while pressing the **Ctrl** key on your keyboard, press the letter A to select all the data files. Now drag these files onto the folder named **Data** and your computer will begin copying the data files into the folder.

5. When copying is complete, click the plus symbol on the Data folder to verify the contents. On the menu select ***View>>Arrange Icons by>>Type*** and the folder will contain the files illustrated in Figure 1:5. Click **X** to close the Explorer window.

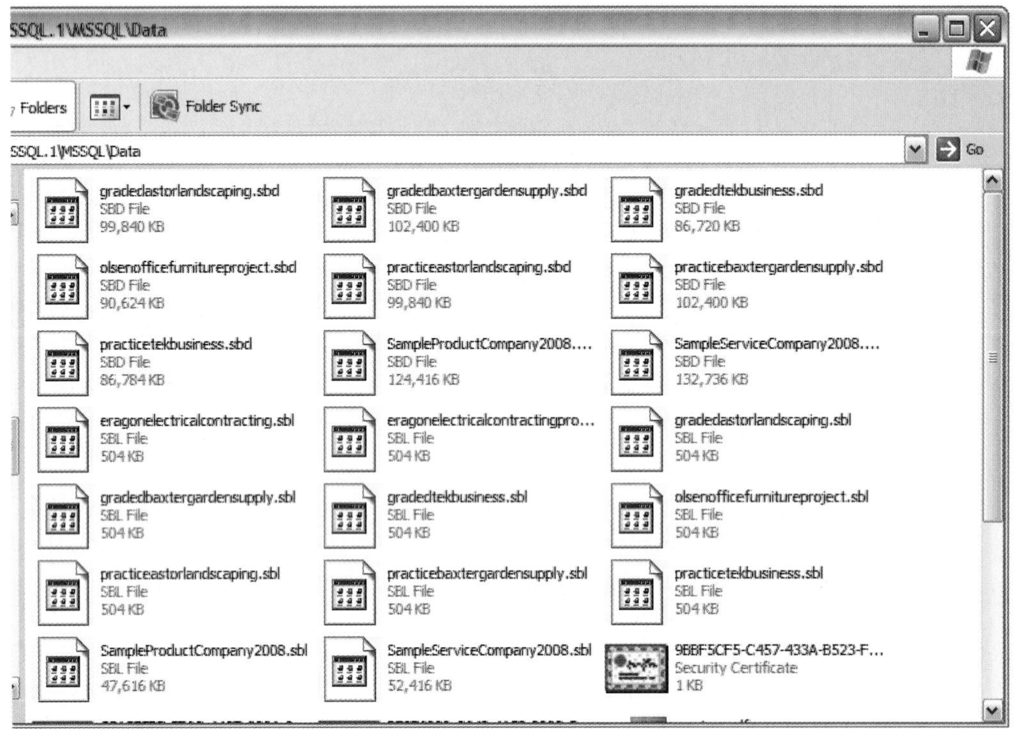

Figure 1:5

Attach Sample Data Files

After copying data files onto your computer you must then attach the files to the software. Complete the next steps to attach the sample data files.

If Microsoft Office Accounting Professional 2008 is not installed on your computer, Appendix A will guide you through installation.

Steps to Attach Sample Data Files

1. Click Window's Start menu and select **Programs** or **All Programs**. Point to ***Microsoft Office>>Microsoft Office Accounting 2008 Tools*** and click Data Tools to open the Data Utilities window (Figure 1:6).

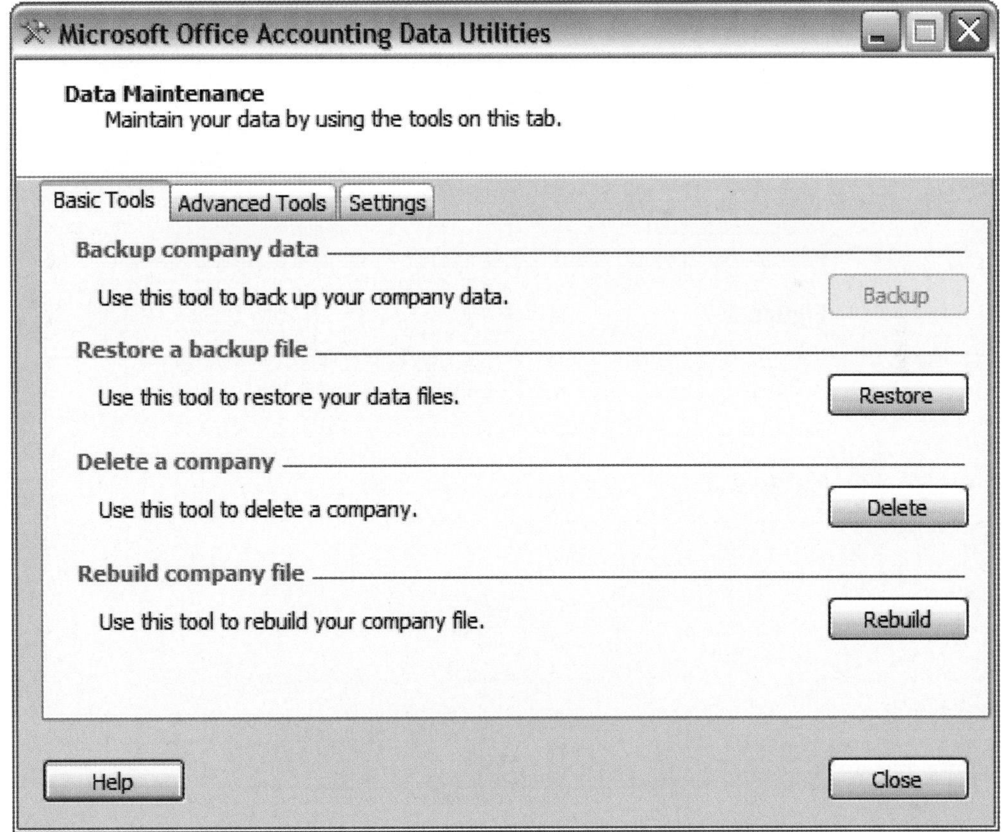

Figure 1:6

2. Click the **Advanced Tools** tab to access the utilities used to attach and detach data files to the software (Figure 1:7). Click **Attach**.

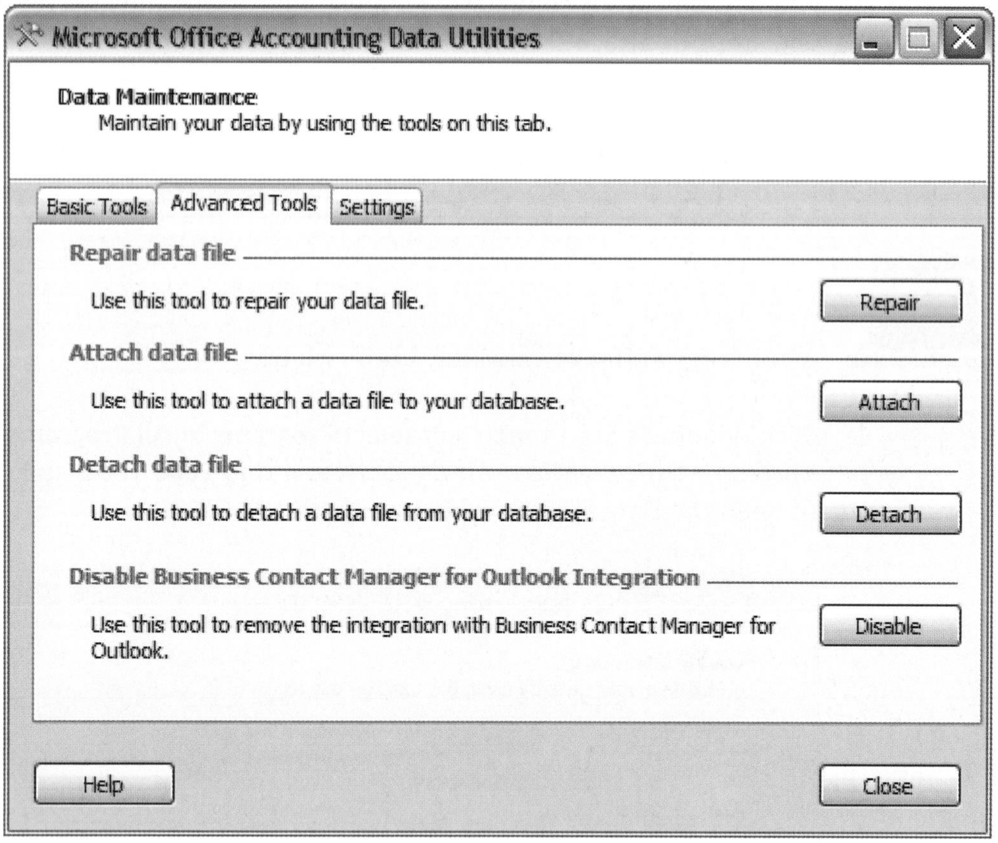

Microsoft Office Accounting Data Utilities

Data Maintenance
Maintain your data by using the tools on this tab.

Basic Tools | Advanced Tools | Settings

Repair data file
Use this tool to repair your data file. Repair

Attach data file
Use this tool to attach a data file to your database. Attach

Detach data file
Use this tool to detach a data file from your database. Detach

Disable Business Contact Manager for Outlook Integration
Use this tool to remove the integration with Business Contact Manager for Outlook. Disable

Help Close

Figure 1:7

3. Click the **Browse** button (Figure 1:8).

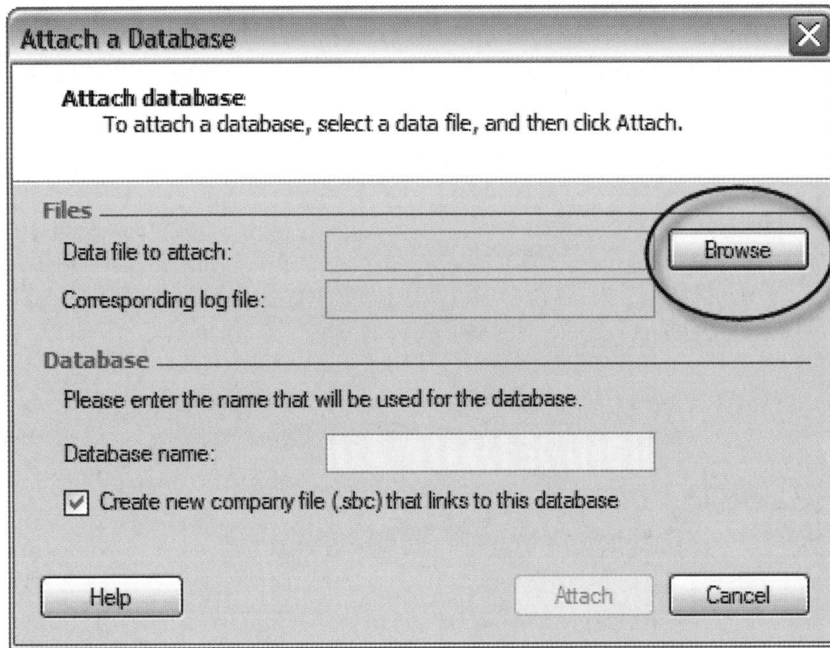

Figure 1:8

4. You will be attaching the Practice Baxter Garden Supply data file so click to select "practicebaxtergarden.sbd" and then click **Open** (Figure 1:9).

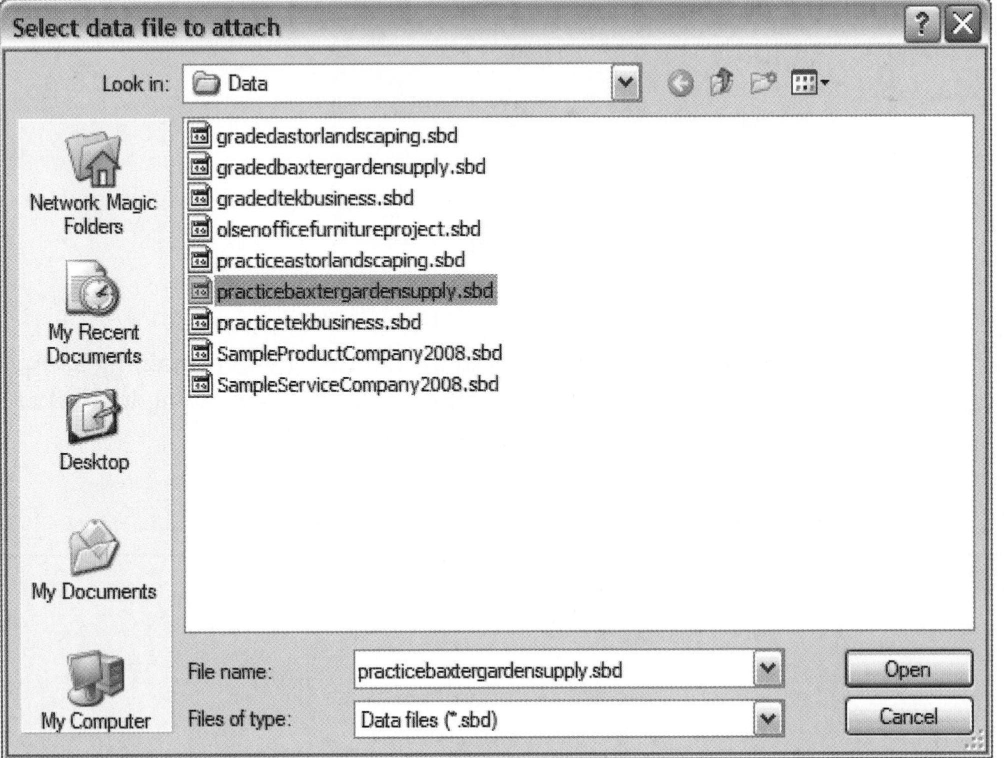

Figure 1:9

5. Keep the **Database name** of "practicebaxtergardensupply" and confirm that the **Create new company file** option is selected (Figure 1:10). Click **Attach.**

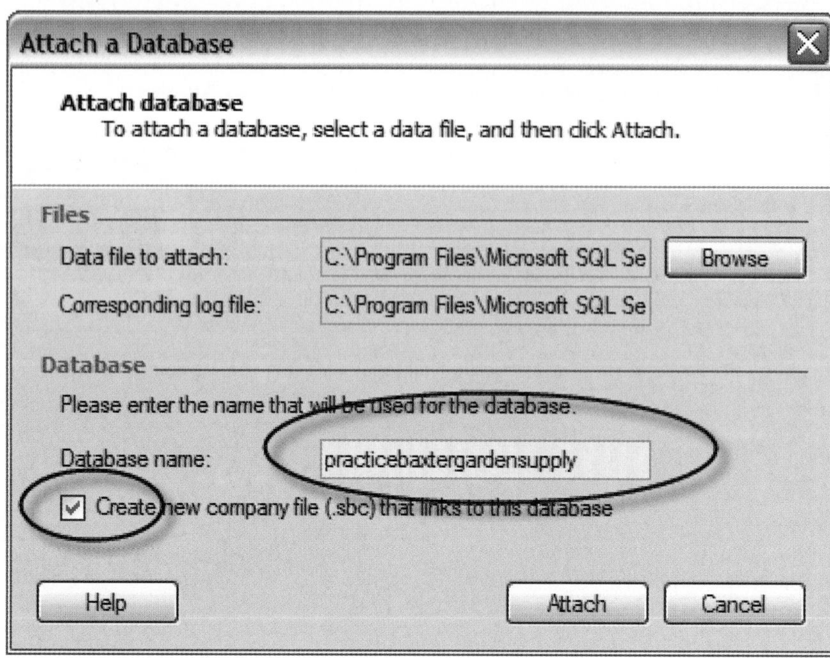

Figure 1:10

6. Click **OK** when OAP notifies you that the data file has been attached (Figure 1:11).

Figure 1:11

7. **Repeat Steps 2 through 6 to attach the seven remaining sample companies. For Step 4 select the file name of the data file being loaded and for Step 5 accept the default database name provided**.

8. Click **Close** to exit the data utilities window.

9. Now verify that the data files are attached. Double click the **My Documents** folder on your desktop. Double click to open the **Small Business Accounting** folder and then double click the **Companies** folder. Your folder should contain the company files illustrated in Figure 1:12. *(Note: These icons also function as shortcuts to opening a company in OAP.)* Click **X** to close the folder.

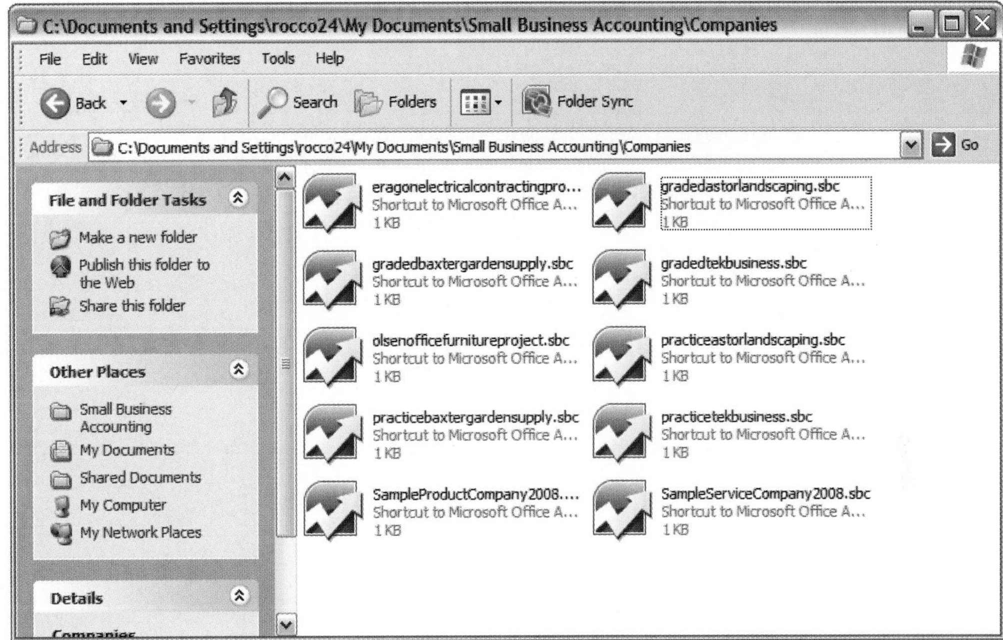

Figure 1:12

Detach Sample Data Files

After attaching a data file to the software you cannot copy or move it without first detaching it. Data files are detached when you want to physically move files from one computer to another.

Note: Do not use these procedures to restore work from a backup file; instead refer to the Restoring Company Data Files topic that appears later in the chapter or the restoring data files topic in Appendix C.

The next steps illustrate detaching a data file.

STEPS TO DETACH A COMPANY FILE

1. Point to Window's Start menu and select **Programs** or **All Programs**. Point to ***Microsoft Office>>Microsoft Office Accounting 2008 Tools*** and click **Data Tools** to open the data utilities window (Figure 1:13). Click the **Advanced Tools** tab.

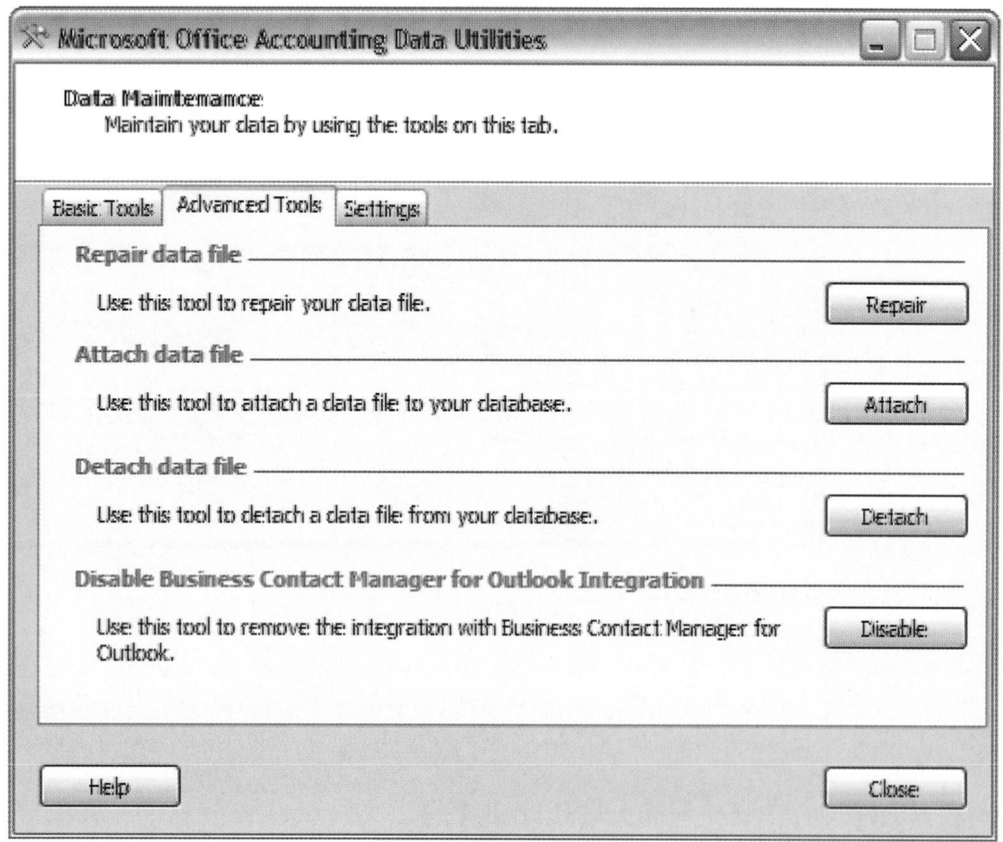

Figure 1:13

2. Click **Detach** to open the window illustrated in Figure 1:14. This window lists data files attached to the software. *(Note: If you have updated the software, your Version number will differ from the illustration.)*

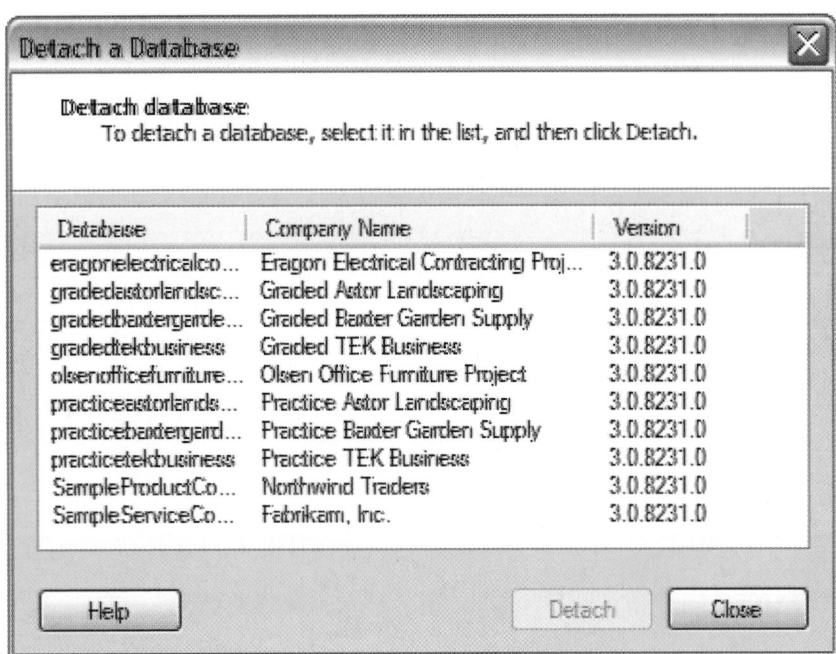

Figure 1:14

3. Highlight any of the files and click **Detach**.

4. To move the data file to another computer use Windows Explorer to open the C:/Program Files/Microsoft SQL Server/MSSQL.1/MSSQL/Data folder and copy the data files onto a removable storage disk. *(Note: Refer to Step 3 in the Copy Sample Data Files topic for help on locating this folder.)*

Open Sample Data Files

After attaching the data files you are ready to open them in the software. First, launch OAP by either clicking the shortcut link on the desktop or clicking the **Start** menu and pointing to **Programs or All Programs** and then point to **Microsoft Office** to click **Microsoft Office Accounting 2008**.

The **Start** window illustrated in Figure 1:15 will open each time OAP needs instruction for selecting a data file to open. Click **Open an existing company**.

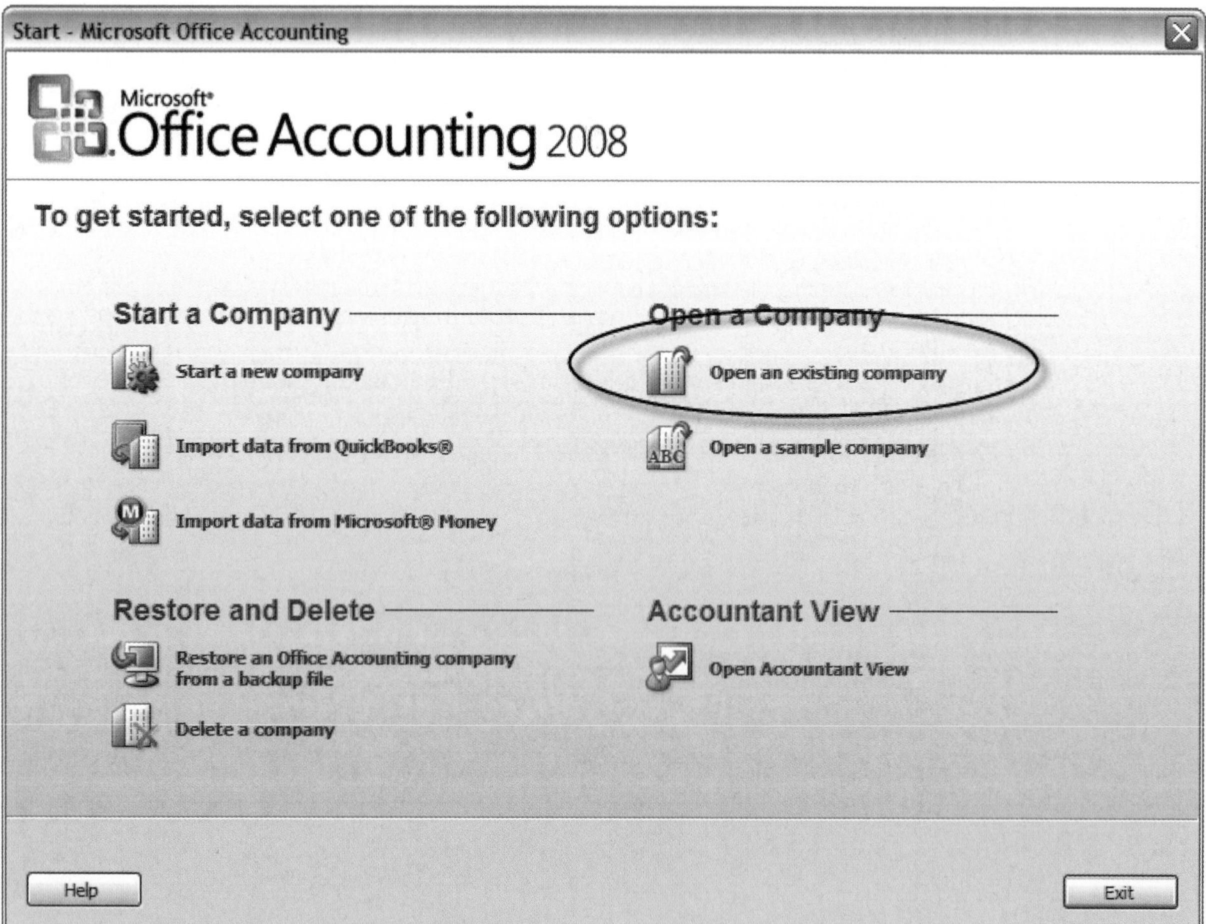

Figure 1:15

Highlight **practicebaxtergardensupply** and click **Open.** (See Figure 1:16.)

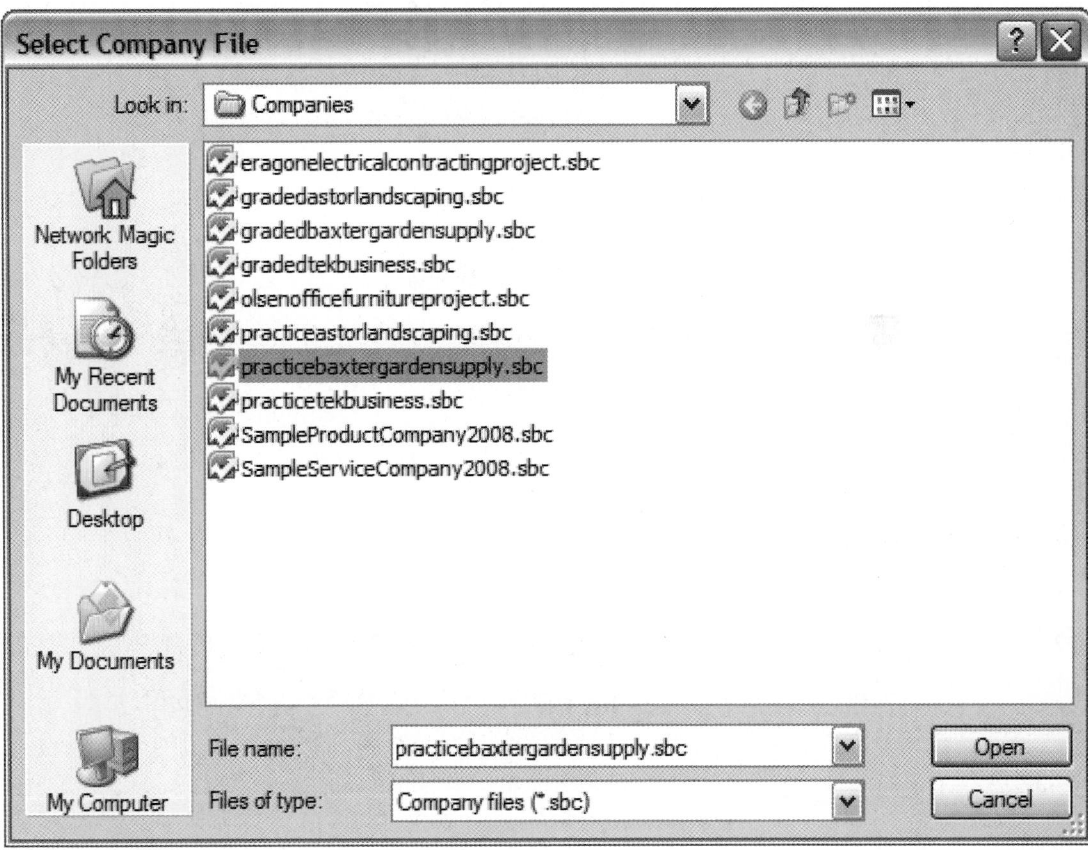

Figure 1:16

The Quick Start window (Figure 1:17) appears the first time you open a data file. Mark the option illustrated and click **Close**.

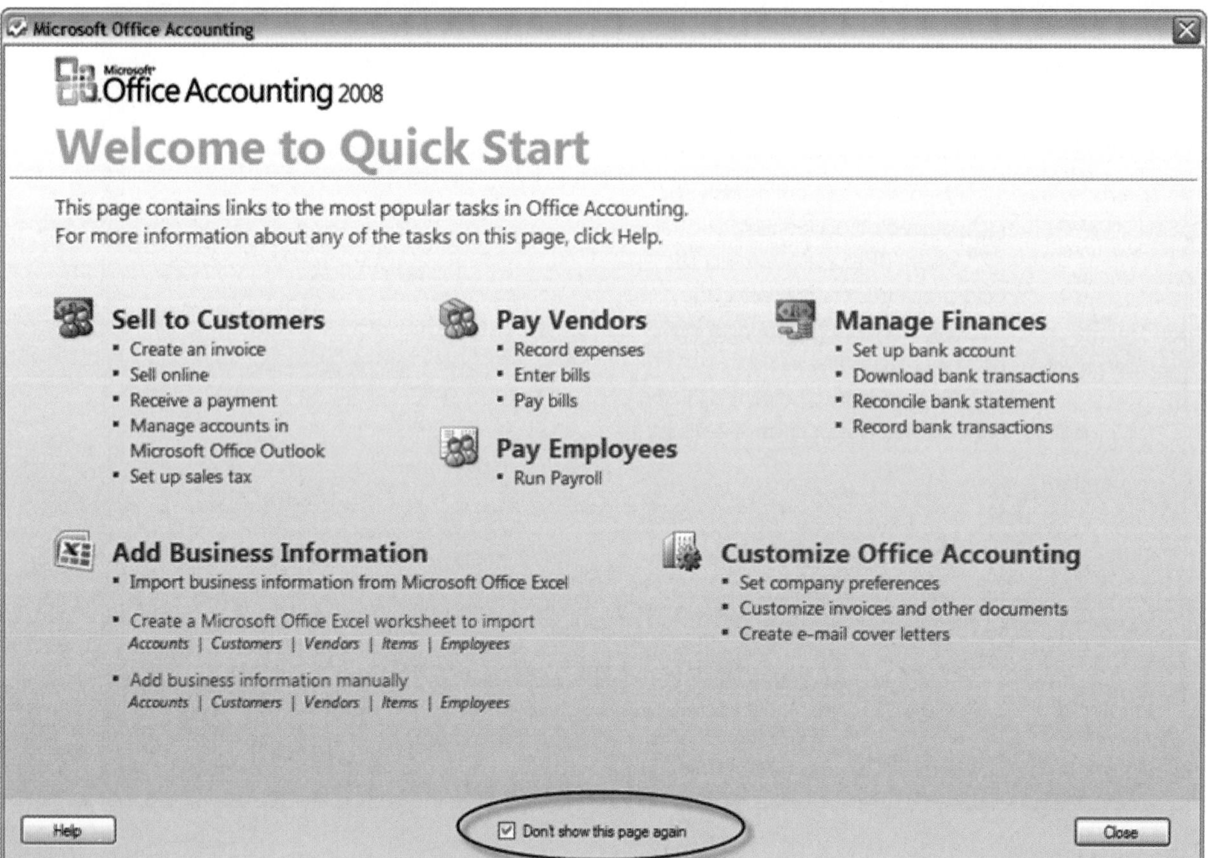

Figure 1:17

Click **OK** when OAP prompts that you have chosen to not open this window in the future (Figure 1:18).

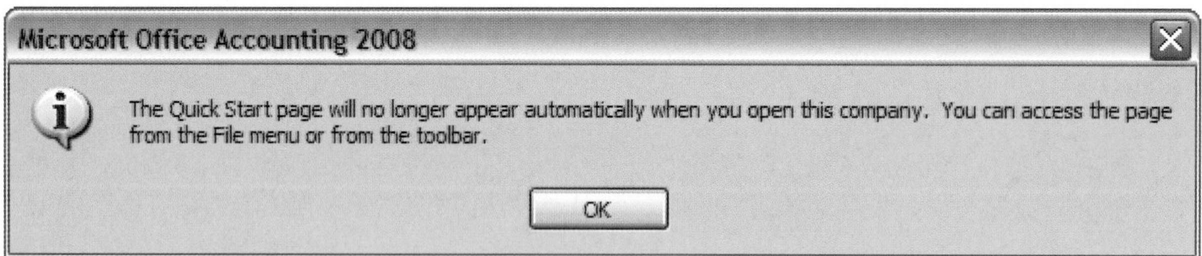

Figure 1:18

After opening a company you have two options for opening a different company. First, you can select ***File>>Close Company*** on the main menu to reopen the Start screen illustrated in Figure 1:15. Second, you can select ***File>>Open Company*** on the main menu, which closes the current company and bypasses the Start screen to open the Select Company File window illustrated in Figure 1:16. Keep Practice Baxter Garden Supply as the open company. The next topic explains using the OAP desktop.

Office Accounting Desktop

Baxter's desktop is illustrated in Figure 1:19 with the **Company Home** page active. This home page is activated by clicking the **Company** button on the bottom left.

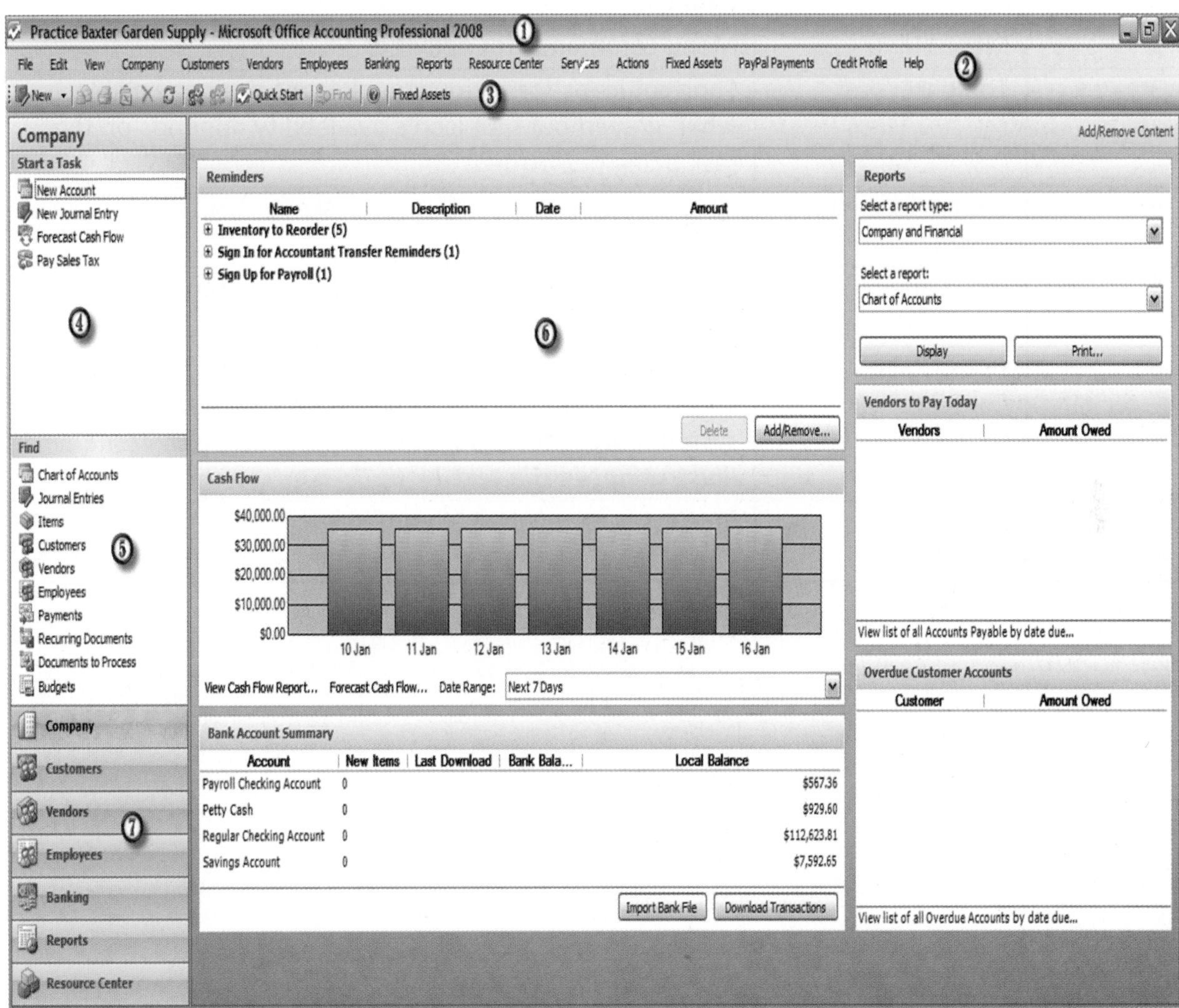

Figure 1:19

The desktop illustration above has been labeled so that you can identify its elements and the table that follows explains these elements.

OFFICE ACCOUNTING DESKTOP ELEMENTS		
Labels	**Desktop Element**	**Description**
1	Title Bar	Displays the name of the open company. Always check the title bar to verify you are working in the correct data file.
2	Main Menu	Menu commands for activities.
3	Toolbar	Shortcut icons for various tasks. Icons are unavailable when grayed out. An icon's availability depends on the task being performed.
4	Start a Task Pane	Links to frequently performed tasks for the active home page.
5	Find Pane	Links to lists of posted transactions and accounts. Links vary by home page.
6	Home Page Contents	Content pane of the active home page. ***(Note: Data displayed in this section is based on your computer's system date; therefore, your display may vary from illustrations in the text.)***
7	Home Page Buttons	Buttons for activating a home page.

You will also need to become familiar with locating menu commands so the next table provides information on menu categories.

MENU COMMANDS	
Main Menu Category	**Description**
File	Submenus for basic operations such as opening and closing companies, data backup and recovery utilities, printing, and printer setup.
Edit	Submenus for data manipulation actions such as cut, copy, paste, delete, and undo. The active status of a submenu depends on the task being performed.
View	Submenus for customizing a home page and filtering or sorting account lists.
Company	Submenus for company related tasks such as entering company identifying information, closing accounting periods, establishing budgets, entering general journal entries, and opening company support lists.
Customers	Submenus for customer related tasks such as invoicing, receiving payments, and printing customer statements.
Vendors	Submenus for vendor related tasks such as entering billings, remitting payment, and managing inventory activities.
Employees	Submenus for employee related tasks such as creating paychecks and entering time sheets.
Banking	Submenus for banking related activities such as making deposits, writing checks, and reconciling bank statements.
Reports	Submenus for printing a variety of reports that analyze company performance.
Actions	Submenus for finding transactions and exporting data.
Help	OAP help files, license agreement, and software version.

Office Accounting Home Pages

In this topic you will practice working with home pages. The Company Home page (Figure 1:20) is the active home page whenever you open a company. With this home page, you can view a snapshot of current financial information. In addition, you will find shortcut links under Start a Task for creating general journal entries and adding general ledger accounts as well as links under Find for viewing lists of account data and posted transactions.

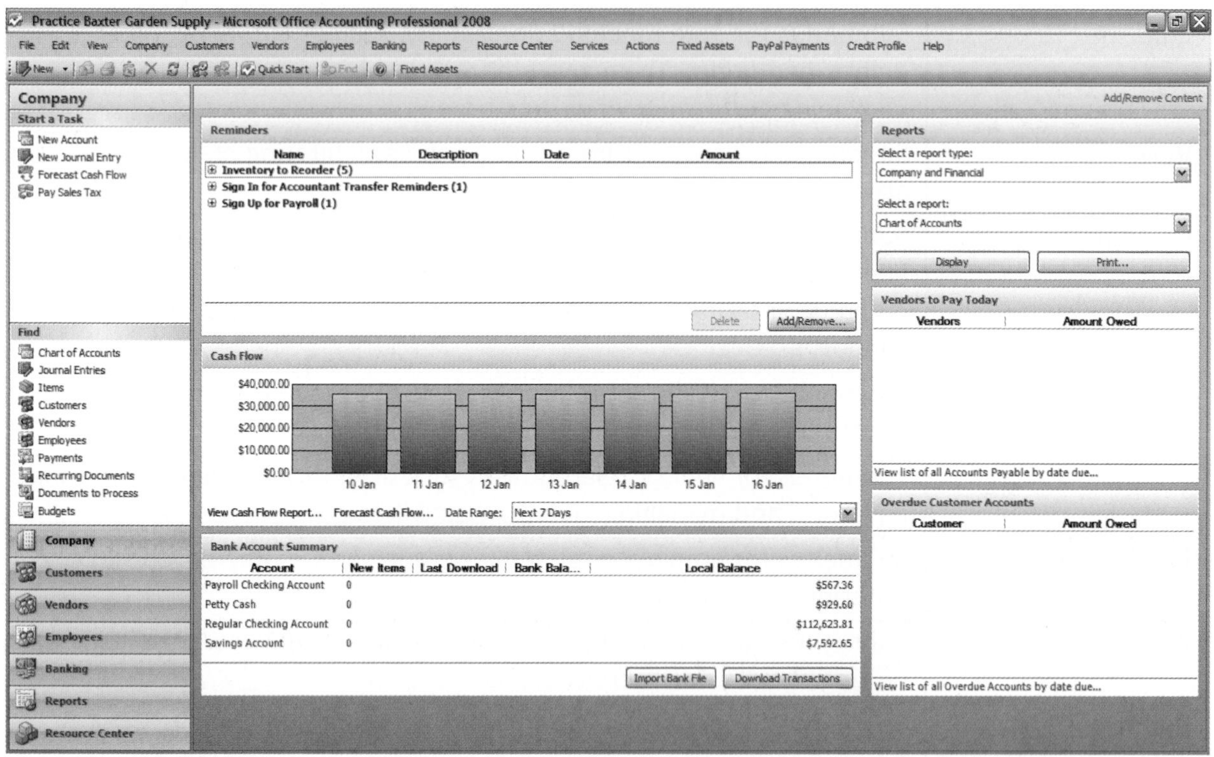

Figure 1:20

You will now customize the Company Home page. Click the **Add/Remove Content** link located on the top right corner of the home page to open the window illustrated in Figure 1:21.

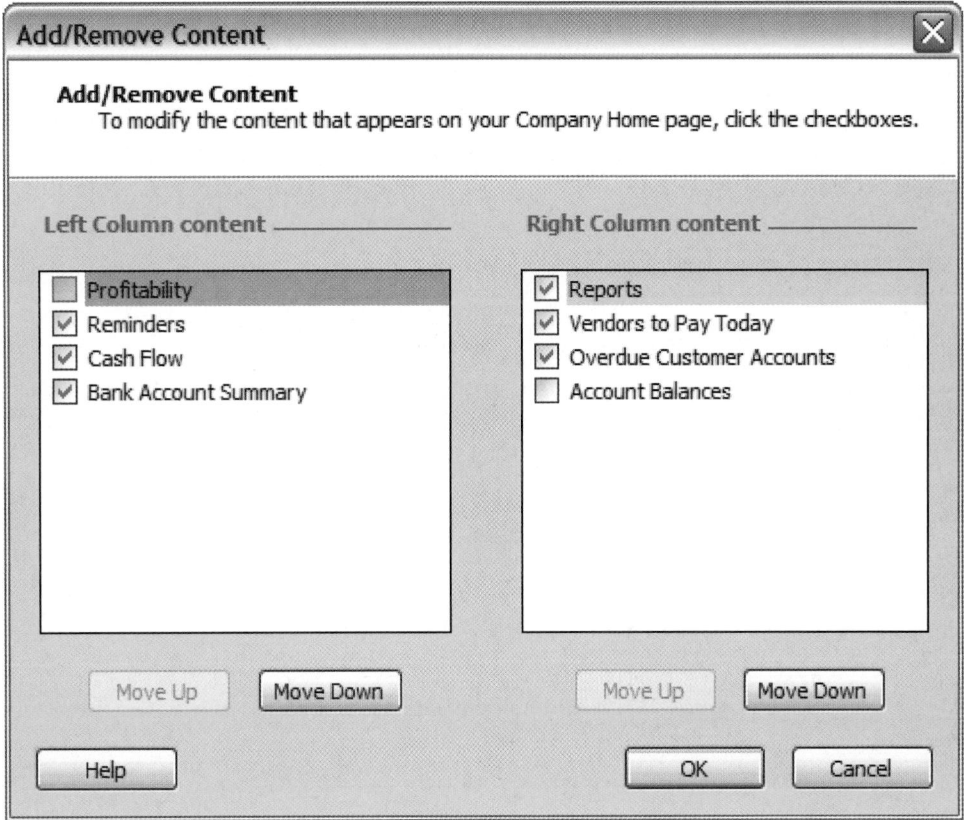

Figure 1:21

Content is added and removed by double clicking an item to change its selection. You can also rearrange home page content by highlighting an item and clicking Move Up or Move Down.

Double click **Reminders** to turn off this content and then double click **Profitability** and **Account Balances** to turn on this content. (See Figure 1:22.)

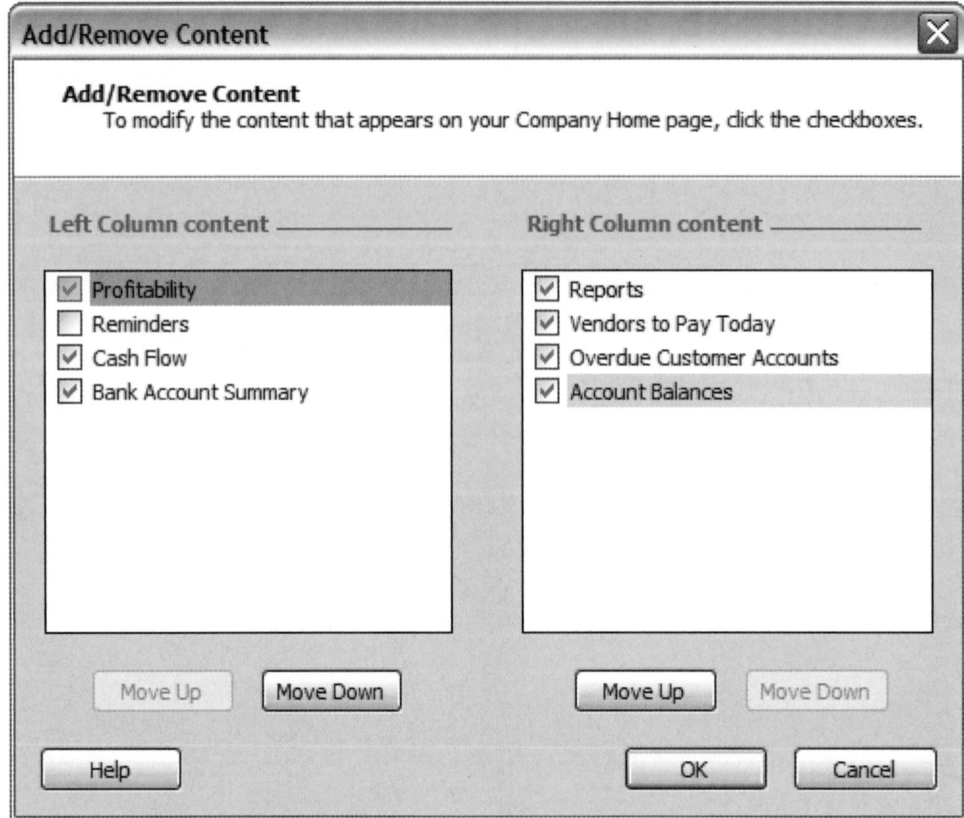

Figure 1:22

Click **OK** and the Company Home page changes as illustrated in Figure 1:23.

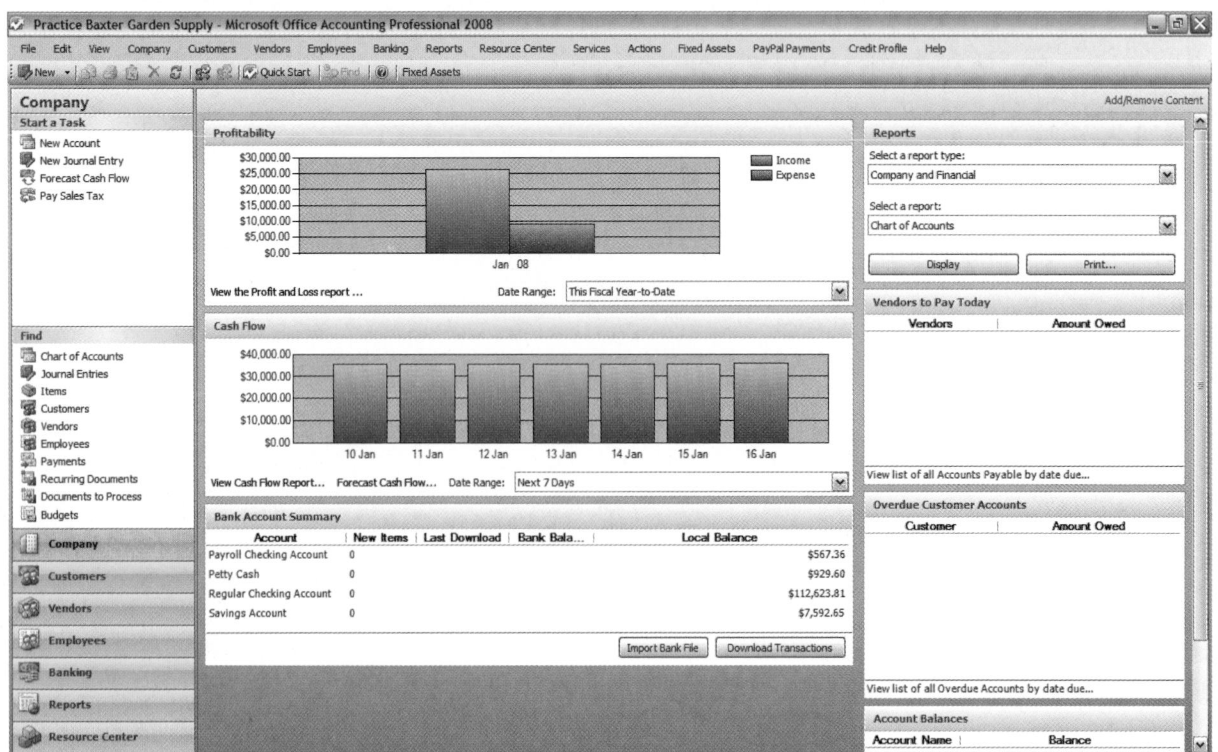

Figure 1:23

(Note: The appearance of graphs and data in financial lists are determined by your computer's system date; therefore, your desktop may not be identical to the desktop illustrated.)

The Reports section (Figure 1:24) of the Company Home page provides shortcuts for printing financial information. To print a particular report, click the **Select a report type** dropdown list to choose a report category and then click the dropdown list on **Select a report** to choose the report name.

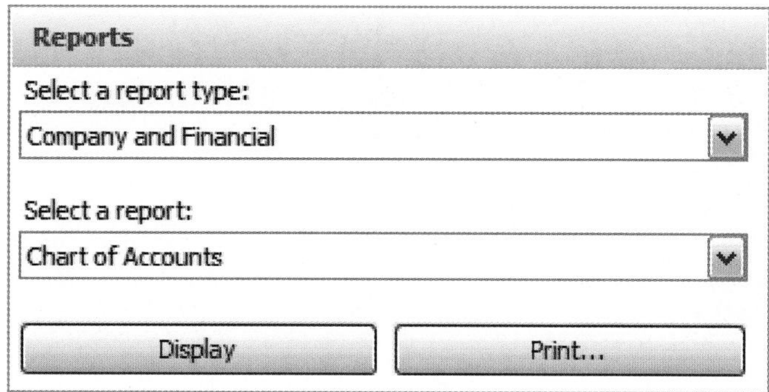

Figure 1:24

OAP provides separate home pages for performing different tasks. Each home page focuses tasks to particular accounting activities, thus, contains task and report links unique to that activity. As you navigate to new areas in OAP the home page buttons remain docked in the lower left corner so you can quickly shift focus to a different activity.

Click the **Customers Home** page (Figure 1:25) to find task icons for processing sales transactions. In addition, the Reports section for this home page focuses on customer activity reports and the **Start a Task** and **Find** panes contain links specific to customer activities.

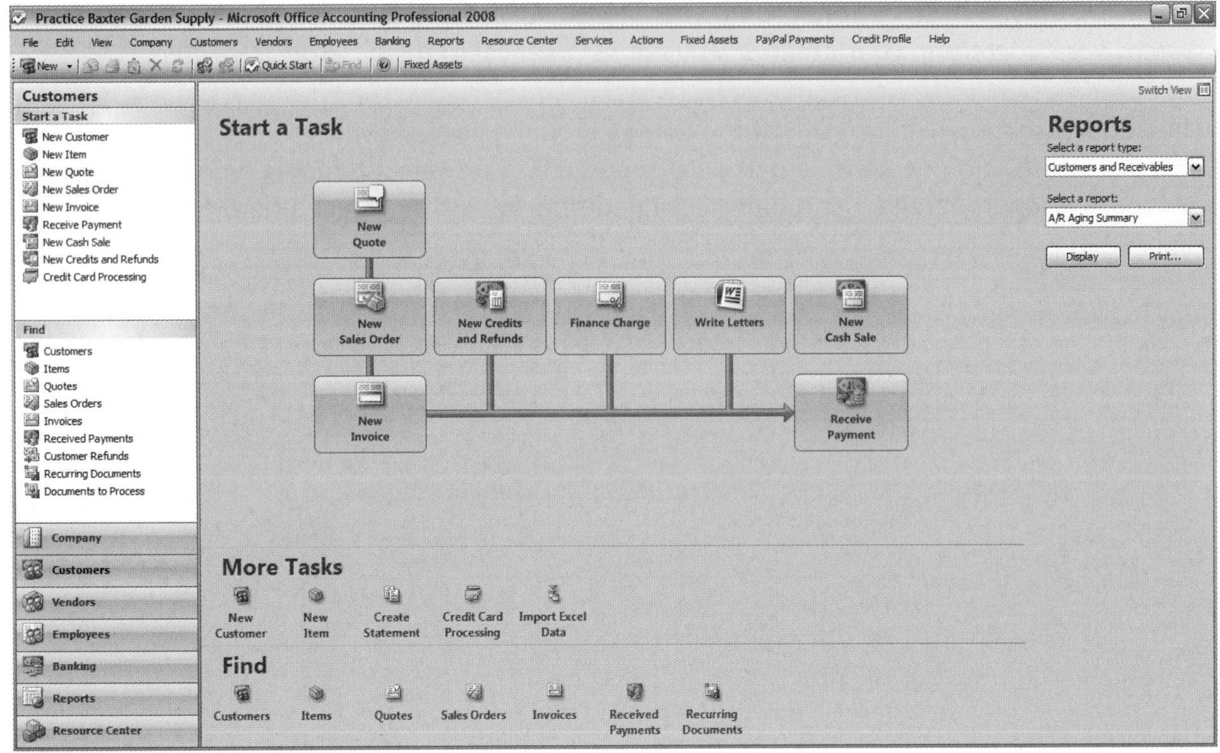

Figure 1:25

You will fully explore each home page in subsequent chapters. For now, practice locating information on the Company Home page by completing the next exercise.

PRACTICE NAVIGATING THE COMPANY HOME PAGE

1. Click the **Company Home** page to activate it. You will first practice opening a task window using the links under **Start a Task**. Click the **New Journal Entry** link to open the Journal Entry window illustrated in Figure 1:26. This window is used to post general journal entries.

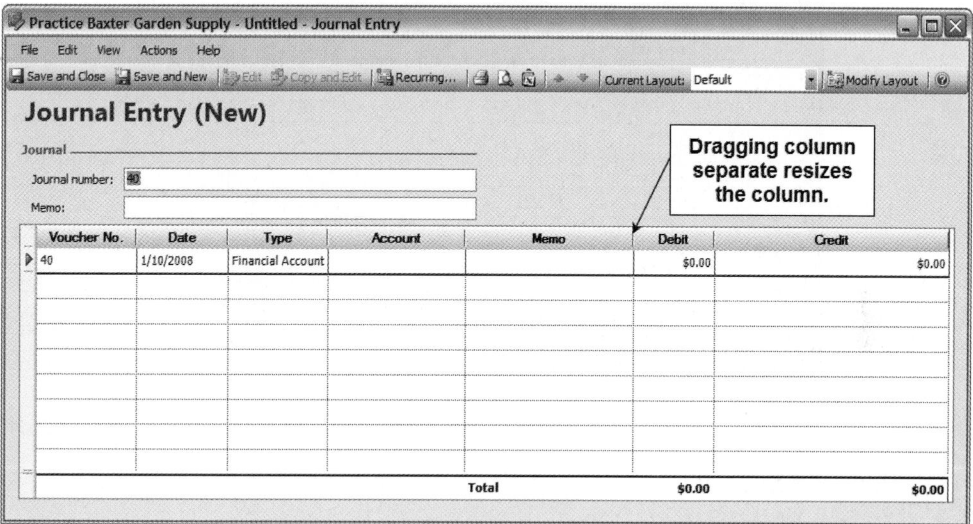

Figure 1:26

You can resize columns in a task window by clicking the column separator and dragging it.

(Note: OAP will default the transaction date to your computer's system date; therefore, your date will differ from the date illustrated above.)

Leave the transaction window open and complete the next step.

2. The **Find** pane on a home page contains links for listing accounts and posted transactions. Click the **Chart of Accounts** link under this pane to view Baxter's Chart of Accounts list (Figure 1:27).

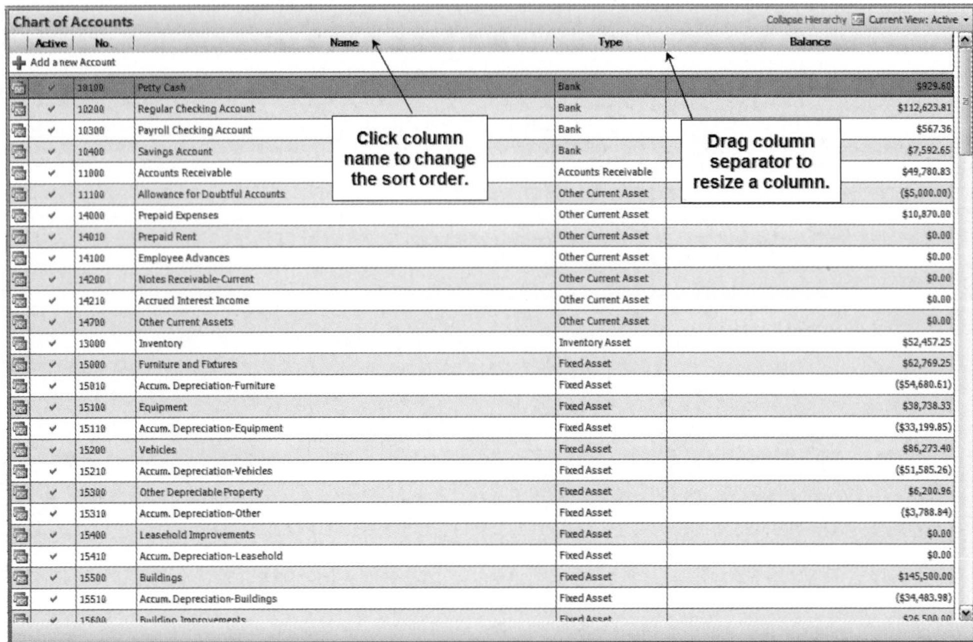

Figure 1:27

The Chart of Accounts (COA) list displays account numbers and names, account types, and current balances. List columns can be resized by dragging the column separator bar. You can also click a column name to change the sort order.

The COA list view is currently set to **Active**. You can change the view to **Inactive** or **All** by choosing one of these options from the dropdown list under Current View.

You can also add new general ledger accounts from the COA list by clicking the **Add a new Account** link at the top of the list. You can edit existing accounts by right clicking an account and selecting **Open Selected Items**.

These data manipulation icons Quick Start | Find are activated after opening the list and can be used to print the list and copy, delete, or find an account.

3. Click the **Company** button to close the list by redisplaying the home page. Now click the Journal Entries link to view a list of posted general journal entries.

   You will now customize this list. Select ***View>>Add/Remove Content*** on the main menu to open the window illustrated in Figure 1:28. Highlight the **Created By** field and then click **Remove**.

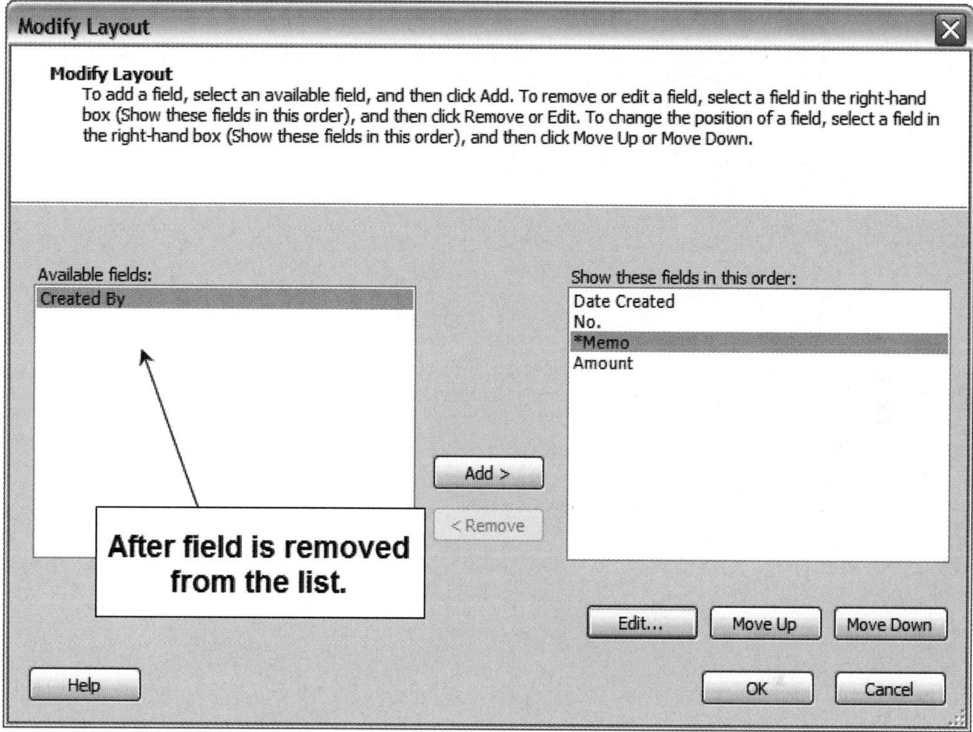

Figure 1:28

Click **OK** to redisplay the list (Figure 1:29). Notice that the lists contain a link at the top for entering new journal entries.

Journal Entry List — Current View: Non Voided

+ Add a new Journal Entry

Date Created	No.	Memo	Amount
1/3/2008	1	Beginning Balances	$505,353.37
1/3/2008	2	Reverse Accrual Entries	$5,342.85
1/3/2008	3	Employer Unemployment Taxes and 401K Contributions	$446.19
1/3/2008	4	Transfer to cover payroll	$9,100.00
1/3/2008	5	Transfer to cover payroll	$9,100.00
1/3/2008	6	Transfer to cover payroll	$9,100.00
1/3/2008	7	Transfer to cover payroll	$9,100.00
1/3/2008	8	Transfer to cover payroll	$9,200.00
1/3/2008	9	Employer Unemployment Taxes and 401K Contributions	$446.19
1/3/2008	10	Employer Unemployment Taxes and 401K Contributions	$446.19
1/3/2008	11	Employer Unemployment Taxes and 401K Contributions	$446.19
1/3/2008	12	Employer Unemployment Taxes and 401K Contributions	$426.40
1/3/2008	13	Accrued interest	$75.00
1/3/2008	14	Amortize organization costs	$83.00

Figure 1:29

Note: The Date Created column on the Journal Entry List is not the transaction date for an entry. Instead, it is the date the entry was posted by the user.

To view the transaction date for a transaction you must double click to open the entry. Figure 1:30 illustrates the location of the transaction date on a journal entry.

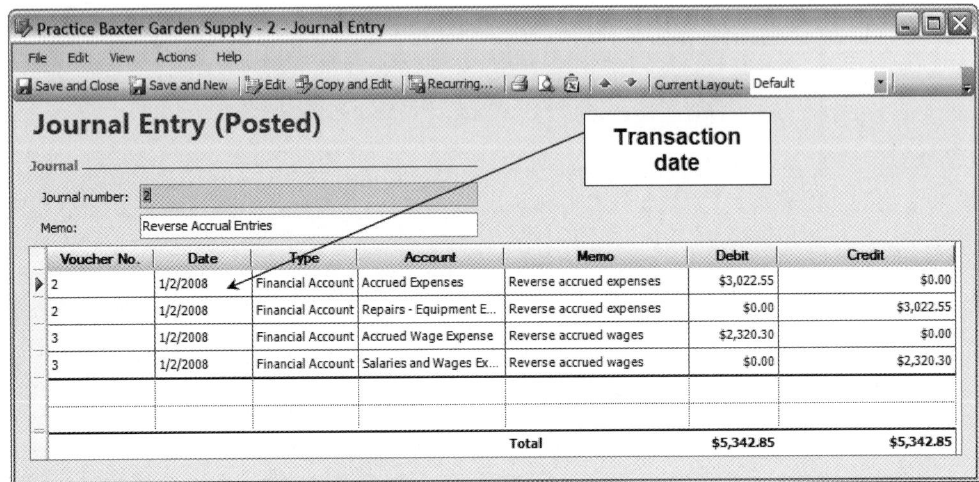

Figure 1:30

4. Click the **Company** button to redisplay the home page. We will now display the Income Statement. Keep the Select a report type field set to **Company and Financial** and then lookup and choose **Profit and Loss** in the Select a report field. Click Display to view the report.

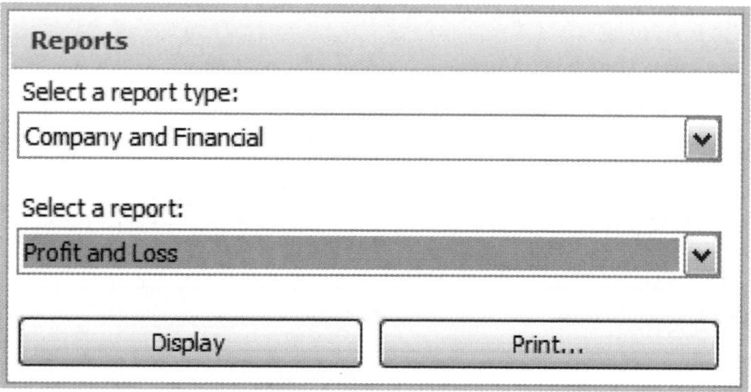

Figure 1:31

Now focus your attention to the computer task bar (Figure 1:32) where you will find three active OAP tasks.

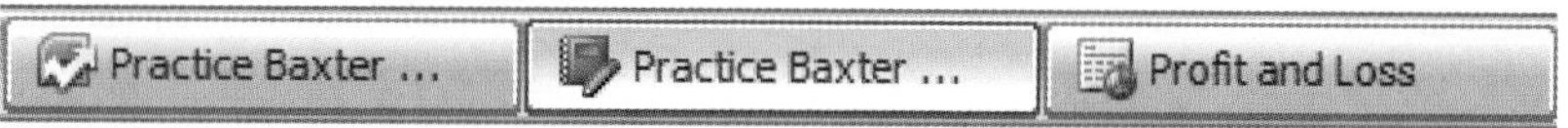

Figure 1:32

Click to select the second task to reactivate the journal entry window. Click **X** to close the entry.

5. Now activate the Profit and Loss report by clicking it on the task bar. Click the **Minimize** button (Figure 1:33) and the report shrinks to the task bar.

Figure 1:33

Click the report again on the task bar and click **X** to close it. You are now returned to the Company Home page.

We have just illustrated using the task bar to multitask in OAP.

Customize Company Names

Before using a sample data file, you need to customize the company name so that reports and assignments will be identified as yours. In this topic you will customize the company name for Practice Baxter Garden Supply. ***You will customize the names for remaining sample companies in the Practice Set at the end of the chapter.***

Select ***Company>>Company Information*** on the main menu to open the window illustrated in Figure 1:34 and type your initials at the end of the **Company name** and **Legal name**.

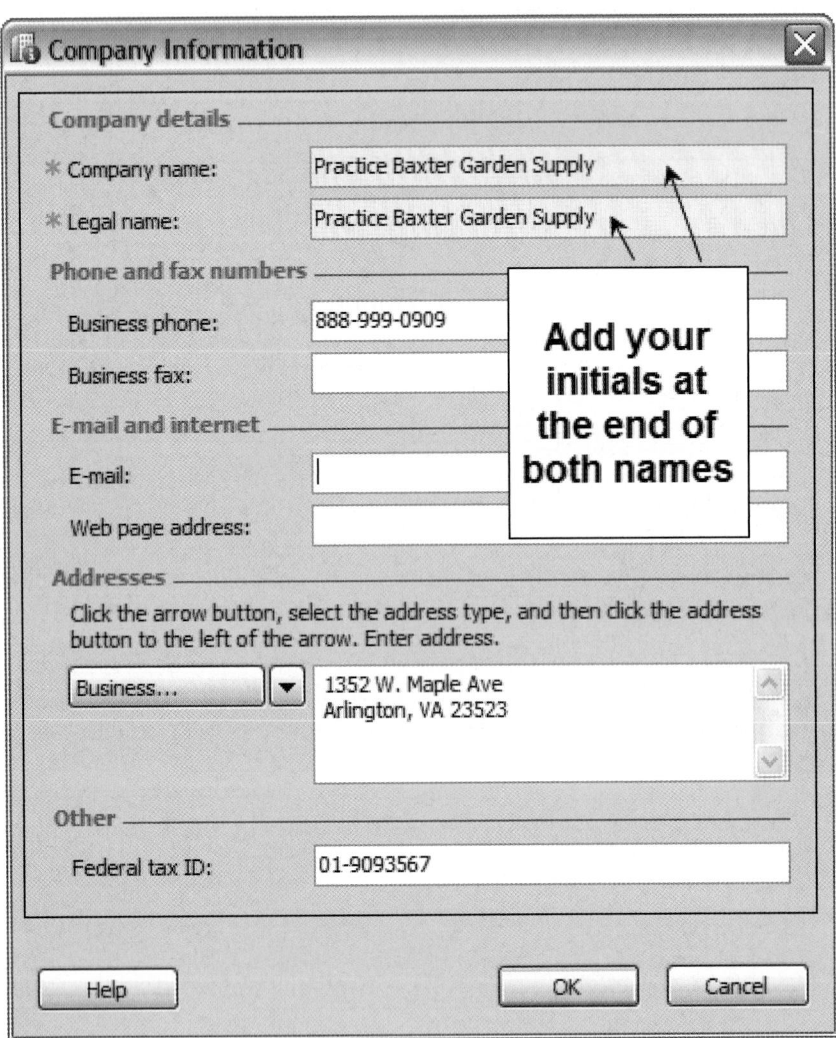

Figure 1:34

Before saving the changes, click the dropdown list on the **Business** button. You are viewing options that will toggle the label description to a different address. After selecting to a new label you can enter additional addresses for the company. Click **OK** to close this window and save your changes.

OFFICE ACCOUNTING KEYBOARD SHORTCUTS

Keyboard shortcuts are methods of executing software commands without selecting a command from the menu. You may already be familiar with these shortcuts from using other software applications. OAP sometimes list the keyboard shortcut for a menu command alongside the menu choice. For instance, click **Edit** on the main menu and notice that the keyboard shortcut for the **Delete** command is **Ctrl+D**. To execute this shortcut, you first highlight the item to be deleted and next press and hold the Ctrl key on your keyboard before pressing the letter "D." The table that follows lists frequently used OAP keyboard shortcuts.

General Category	**Key**	**Item Lists**	**Key**
Open the Help table of contents	F1	Chart of Accounts	Ctrl+Shift+A
Get Help for the current page	Alt+F1	Bills and Item Receipts	Ctrl+Shift+B
Licensing information on OAP	F2	Customers	Ctrl+Shift+C
Refresh the screen display	F5	Employees	Ctrl+Shift+E
		Invoices	Ctrl+Shift+I
Activate Home Page		Jobs	Ctrl+Shift+J
Go to Company Home page	Ctrl+1	Payments	Ctrl+Shift+M
Go to Customers Home page	Ctrl+2	Purchase Orders	Ctrl+Shift+P
Go to Vendors Home page	Ctrl+3	Quotes	Ctrl+Shift+Q
Go to Employees Home page	Ctrl+4	Sales Orders	Ctrl+Shift+S
Go to Banking Home page	Ctrl+5	Time Entries	Ctrl+Shift+T
Go to Online Sales Home page	Ctrl+6	Items	Ctrl+Shift+U
Go to Reports Home page	Ctrl+7	Vendors	Ctrl+Shift+V
Exit OAP	Alt+F4	Journal Entries	Ctrl+Shift+Y

OFFICE ACCOUNTING HELP

OAP help is only one click away. Open the **Company Home** page and then press **F1**. Click to activate the **Contents** pane and help for the Company Home page is displayed. (See Figure 1:35.) *Note: You can also select the main menu command of **Help>>Help with this Window**.*

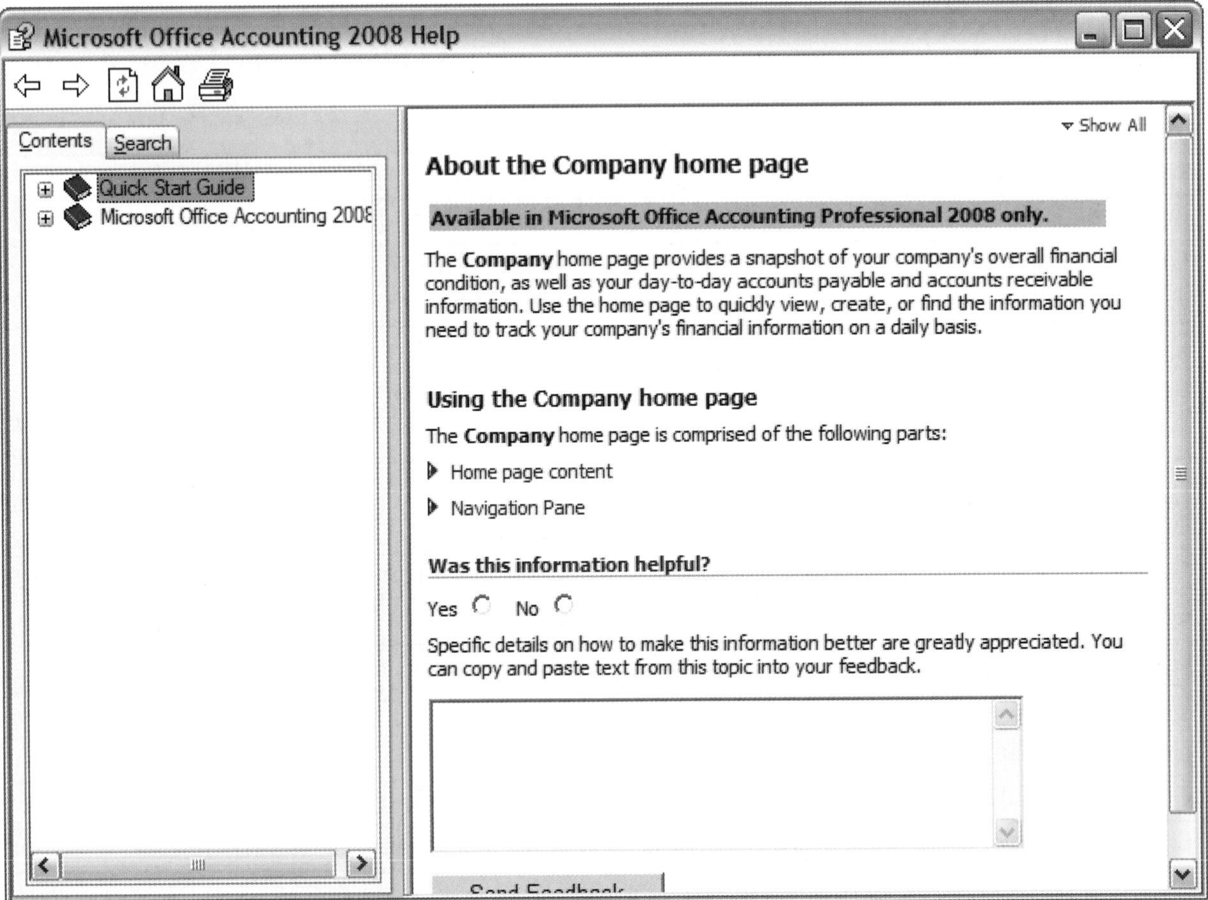

Figure 1:35

The **Contents** pane on the left of the Help window provides help information by topic. You can click the plus symbol preceding a topic to expand its contents. This pane is useful for reading broad overviews on a topic.

You can also click any hyperlinks displayed in a topic on the right to view additional information on a topic. For instance, the **Home page content** hyperlink in the current topic contains additional information and hyperlinks. (See Figure 1:36.)

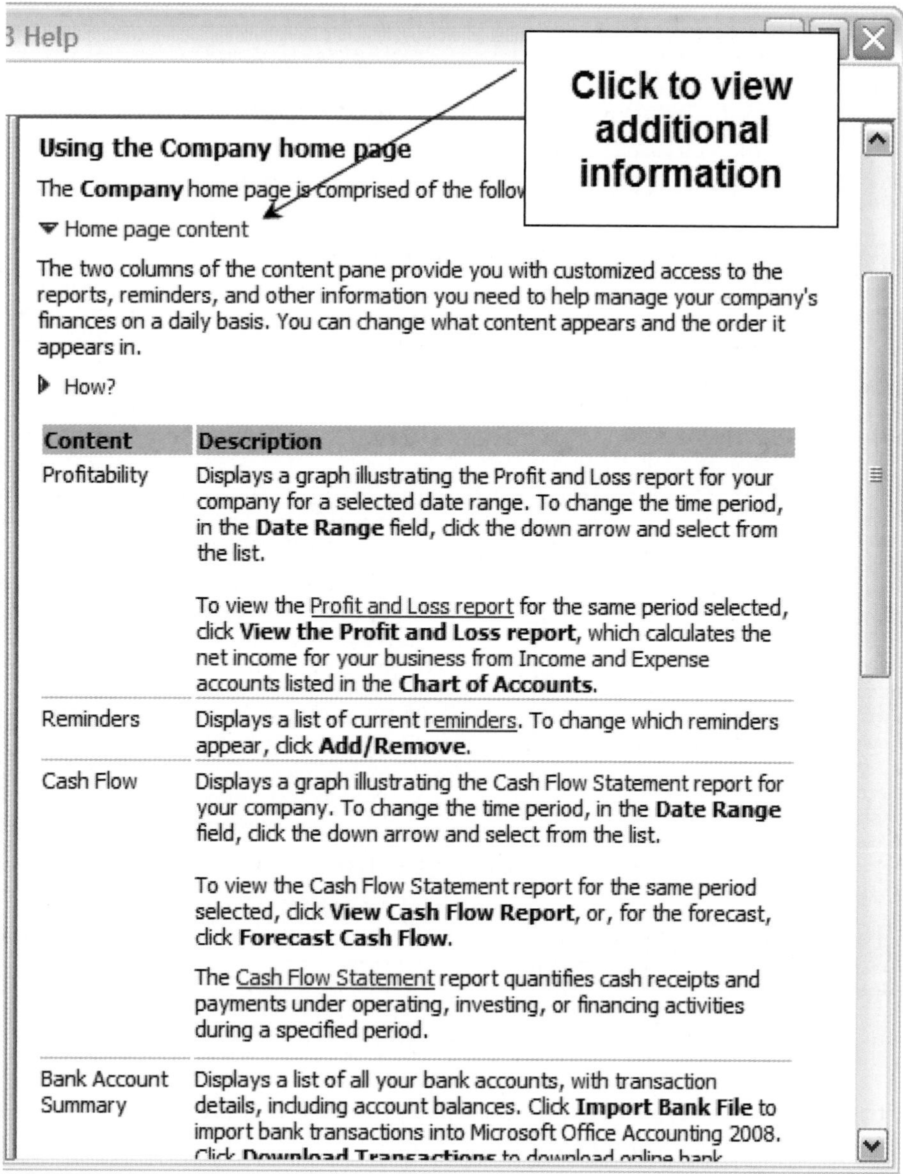

Figure 1:36

Next, click to select the **Search** tab. This tab contains a field for entering words or phrases to search for in a topic. Type "posting invoices" in the search field and click **List Topics** to display a list of topics containing these terms (Figure 1:37).

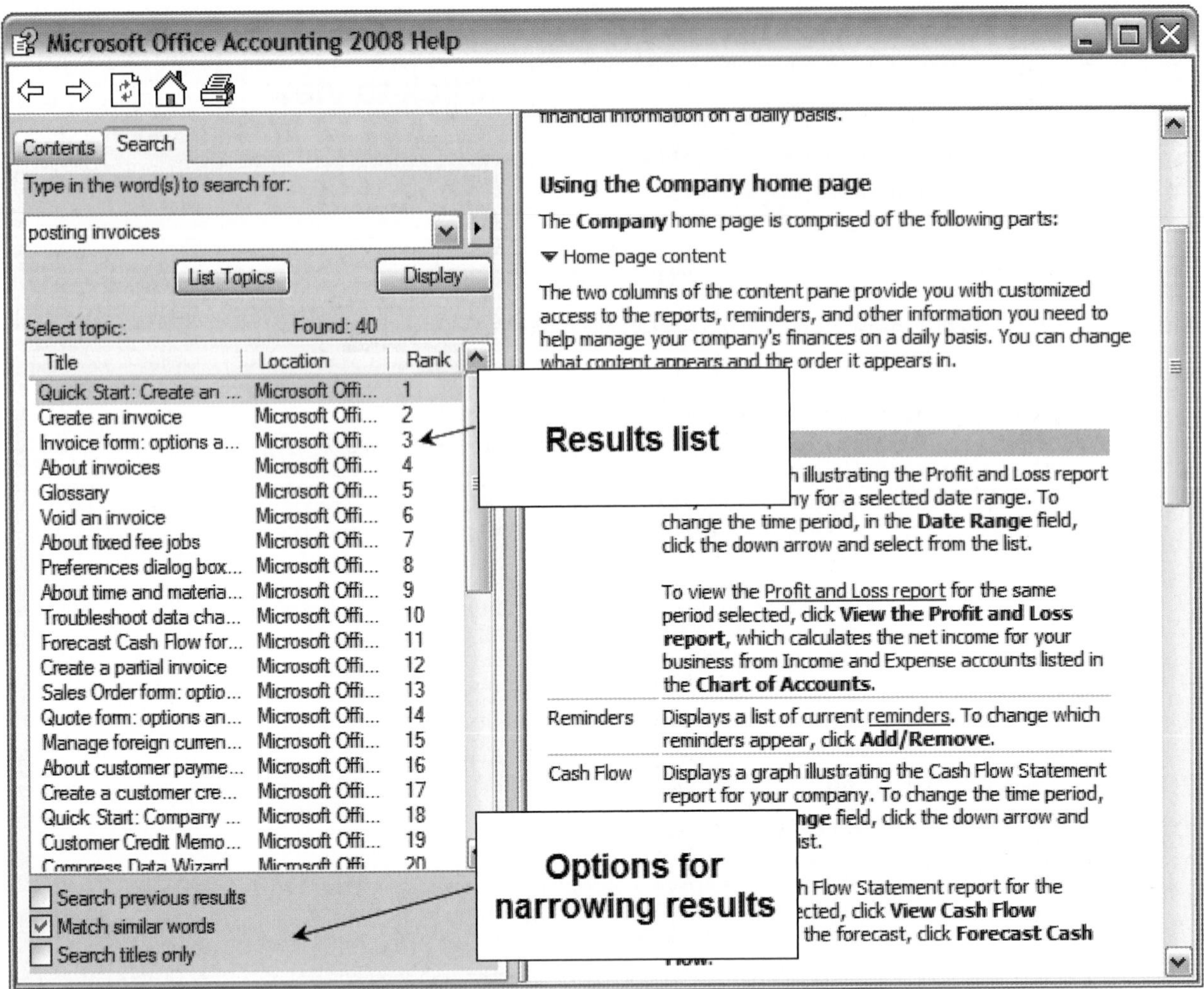

Figure 1:37

Double click the **Create an invoice** result and the right pane displays the contents for this topic with the search terms highlighted. (See Figure 1:38.)

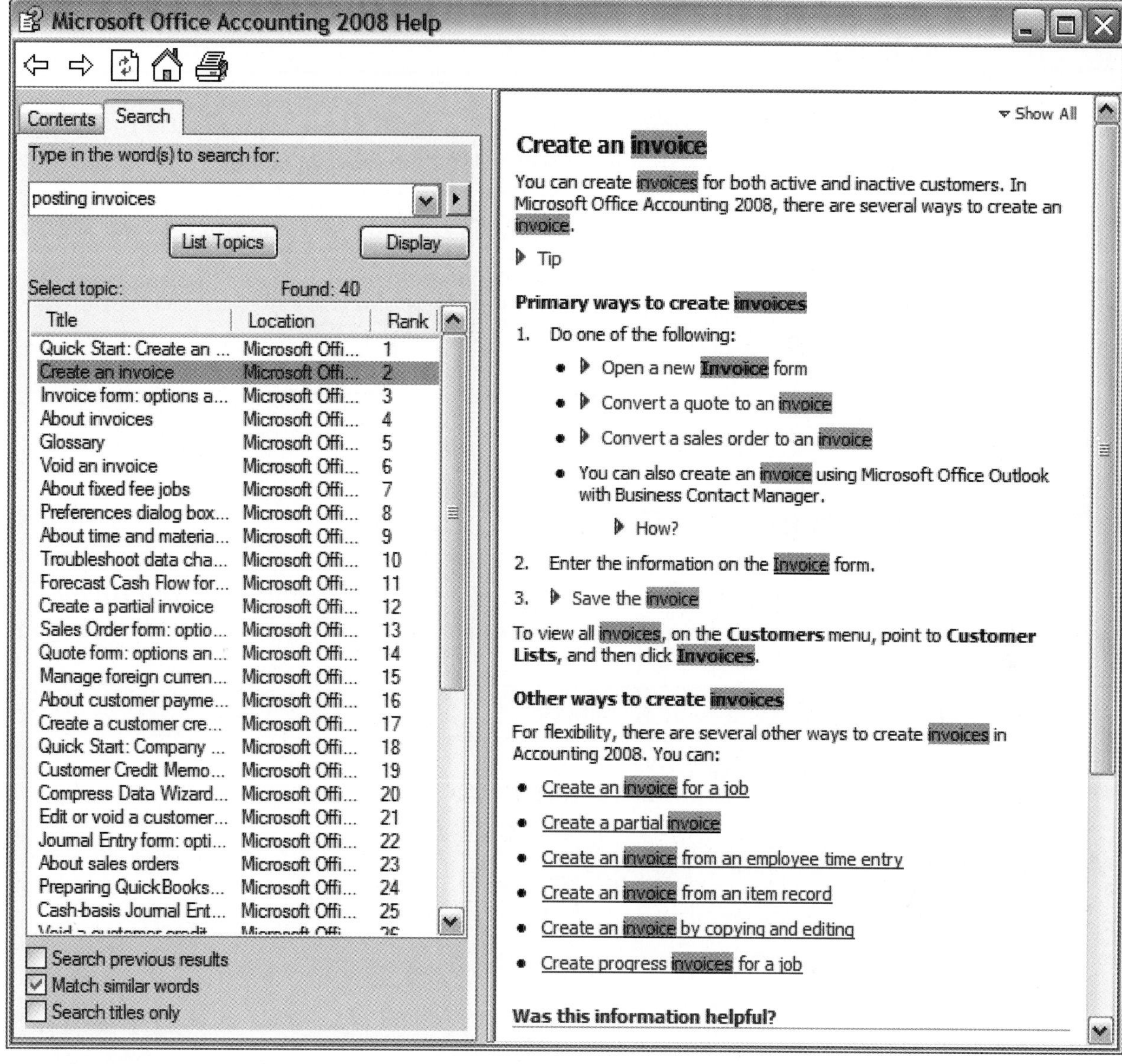

Figure 1:38

Recall that your search phrase was "posting invoices" but highlighted terms in the current topic include any variation of invoices even when the word "posting" is not present. This result occurred because the option of **Match similar words** is marked. You can narrow search results by changing this option.

Finally, Help window icons provide additional functionality, for instance these icons ⇦ ⇨ move between topics and this icon 🖨 prints the topic currently displayed on the right.

Click **X** to close the Help window.

Backing Up Data Files

Data files should be backed up each time you finish working in a company because the backup file can be used to restore your work should a problem occur with your computer.

OAP's backup utility performs a backup on the company currently open in the software and, because this company is now Practice Baxter Garden Supply, the steps to follow back up this company. You will create backups for remaining sample companies in the Practice Set at the end of the chapter.

Steps to Back Up Company Data Files

1. Open the company to be backed up and select ***File>>Utilities>>Data Utilities*** on the main menu to open the window illustrated in Figure 1:39. Click **Backup**.

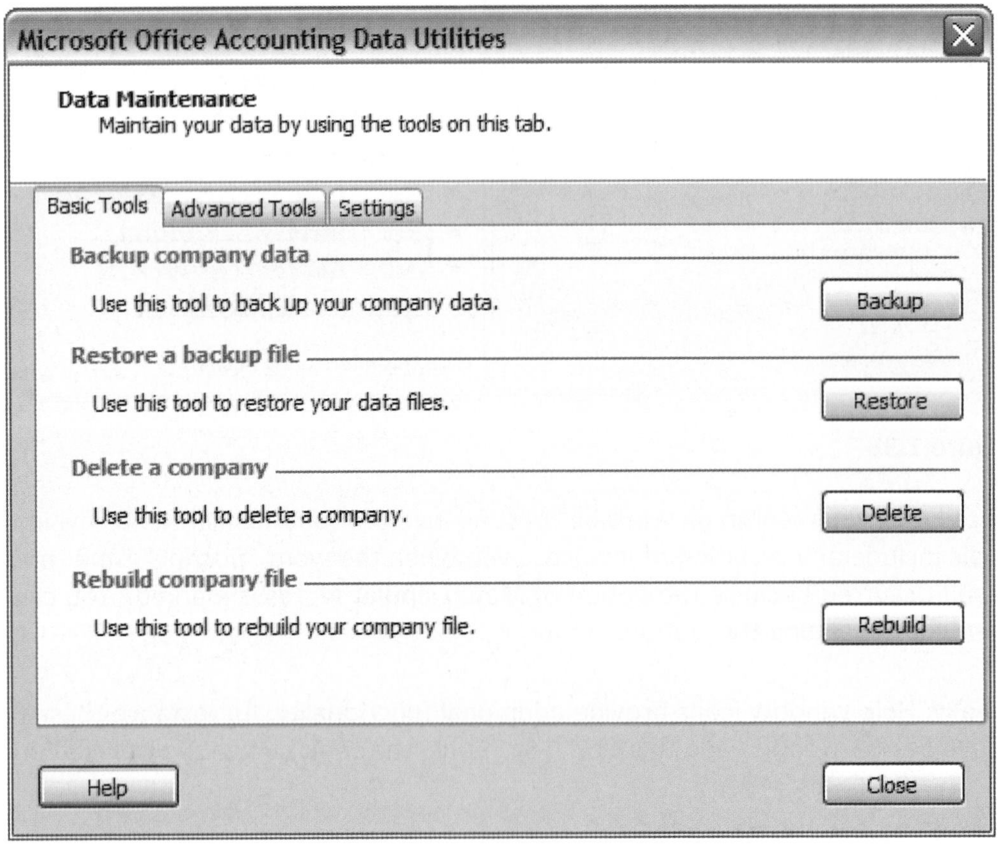

Figure 1:39

2. The Backup window opens with the **Backup file name** defaulted to the company name plus the computer's system date (Figure 1:40).

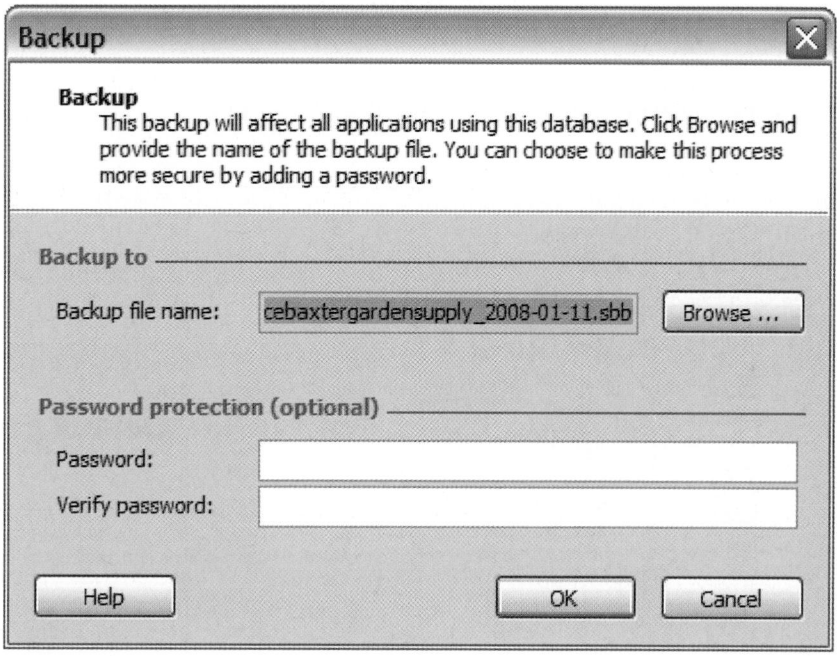

Figure 1:40

3. Click **Browse** so that you can select a path for storing the backup file and change the name of the backup file. OAP stores backups in the default path of ***Desktop>>My Documents>>Small Business Accounting>>Backups***. You can trace this path by clicking the dropdown list on the **Save in box** (Figure 1:41).

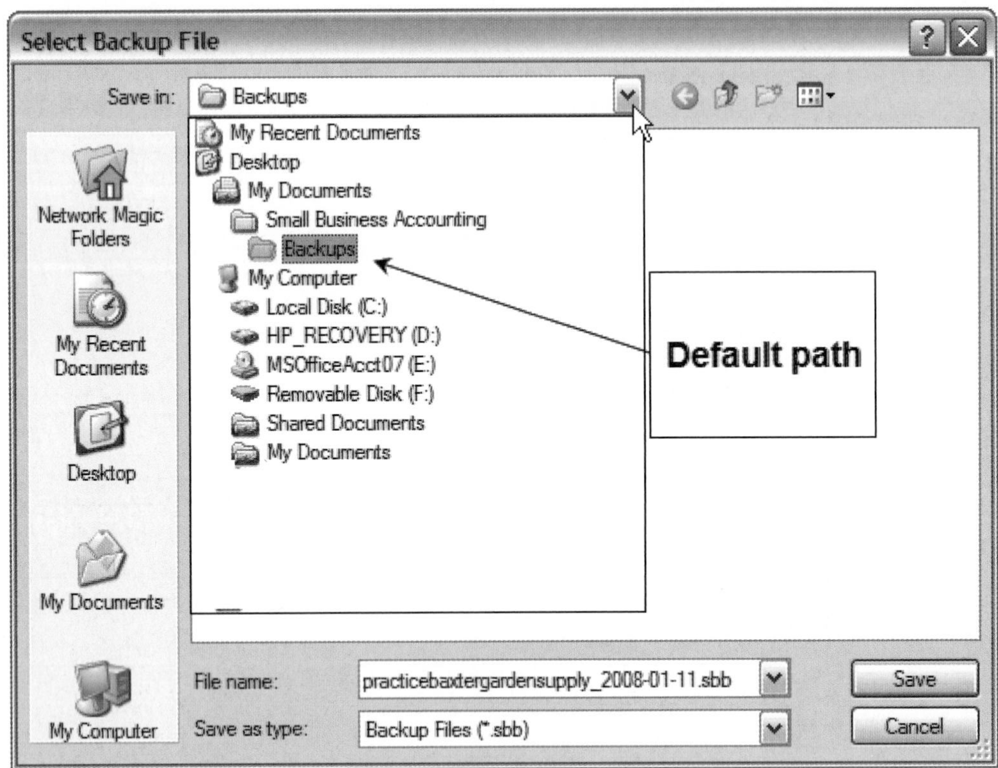

Figure 1:41

Note: You can copy data files to a removable storage drive by changing the path to that location. A CD drive is normally labeled "D" and a USB drive normally labeled "E." Just remember where you stored the backup file should you need to restore it later.

4. Keep the current path but you will change the backup file name. We recommend that you replace the date portion of the file name with the chapter name you are currently working on. Thus, change the **File name** to ***practicebaxtergardensupply Chpt 1*** (Figure 1:42) and click **Save**.

Figure 1:42

5. You have returned to the Backup window (Figure 1:43). Click **OK** to create the backup file.

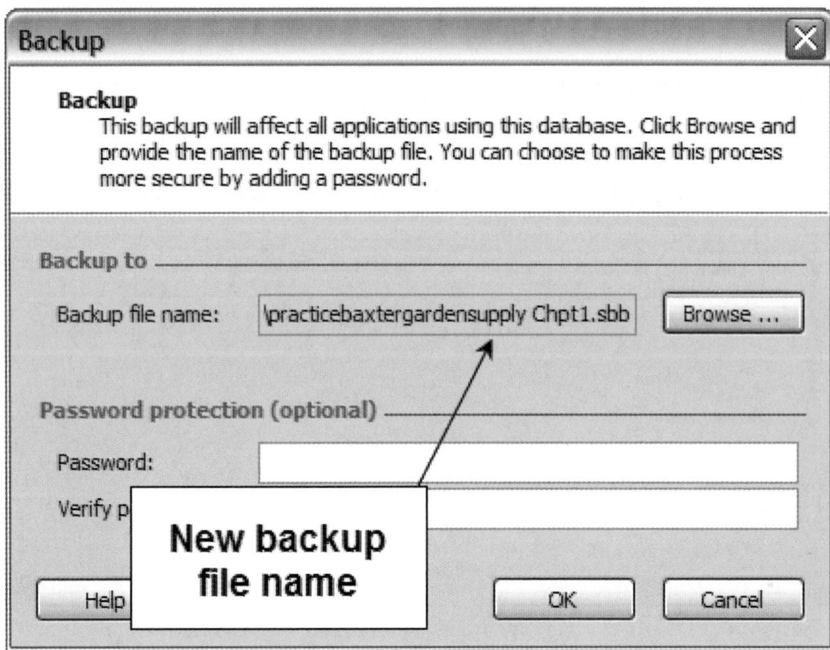

Figure 1:43

6. Click **OK** when OAP prompts that backup is complete and then click **Close** to exit the utility window.

RESTORING DATA FILES

This topic illustrates restoring a backup file. You will need these instructions should you need to restore previous work due to a computer problem or want to move data files between school and home.

Note: You cannot restore previous work unless you have created a backup file; however, you can always reload the original data from the Student CD.

Note: Restoring a backup file overwrites all existing data. Therefore, you should back up the current data to a unique file name before restoring a backup file.

Steps to Restore a Company Data File

1. The easiest method for restoring data is to restore a backup file while in the software. First, you have to close the current company or open a different company from the one you want to restore. We will close the current company so click ***File>>Close Company*** on the main menu to open the **Start** window and click the icon marked in Figure 1:44.

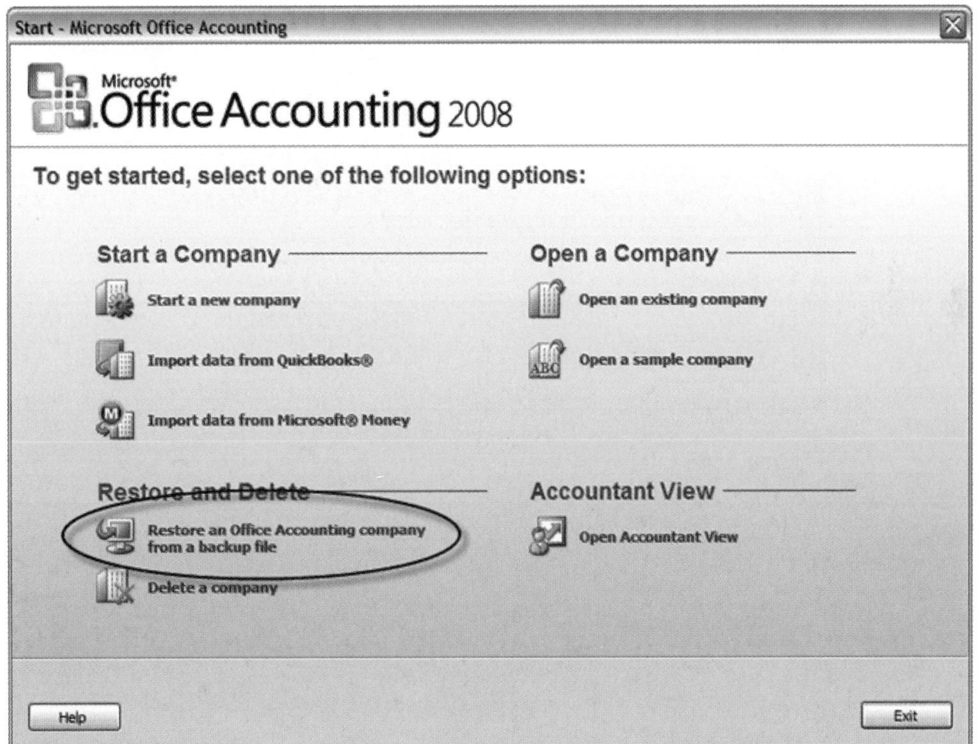

Figure 1:44

2. When the **Database Restore** window opens (Figure 1:45), click **Browse** on the **Backup filename** to select the location and name of the backup file to restore.

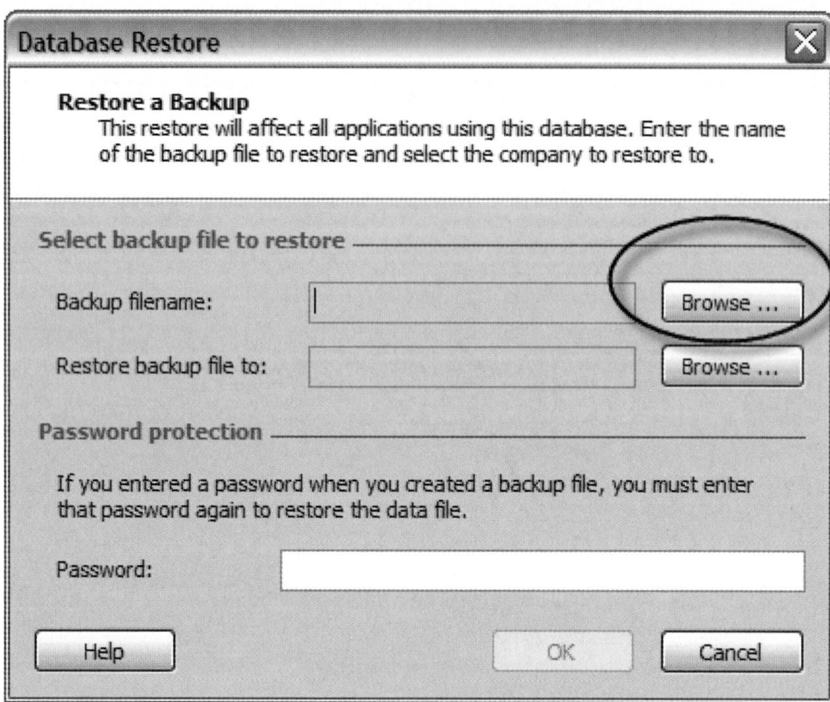

Figure 1:45

3. Highlight the backup file created in the previous topic and click **Open** (Figure 1:46).

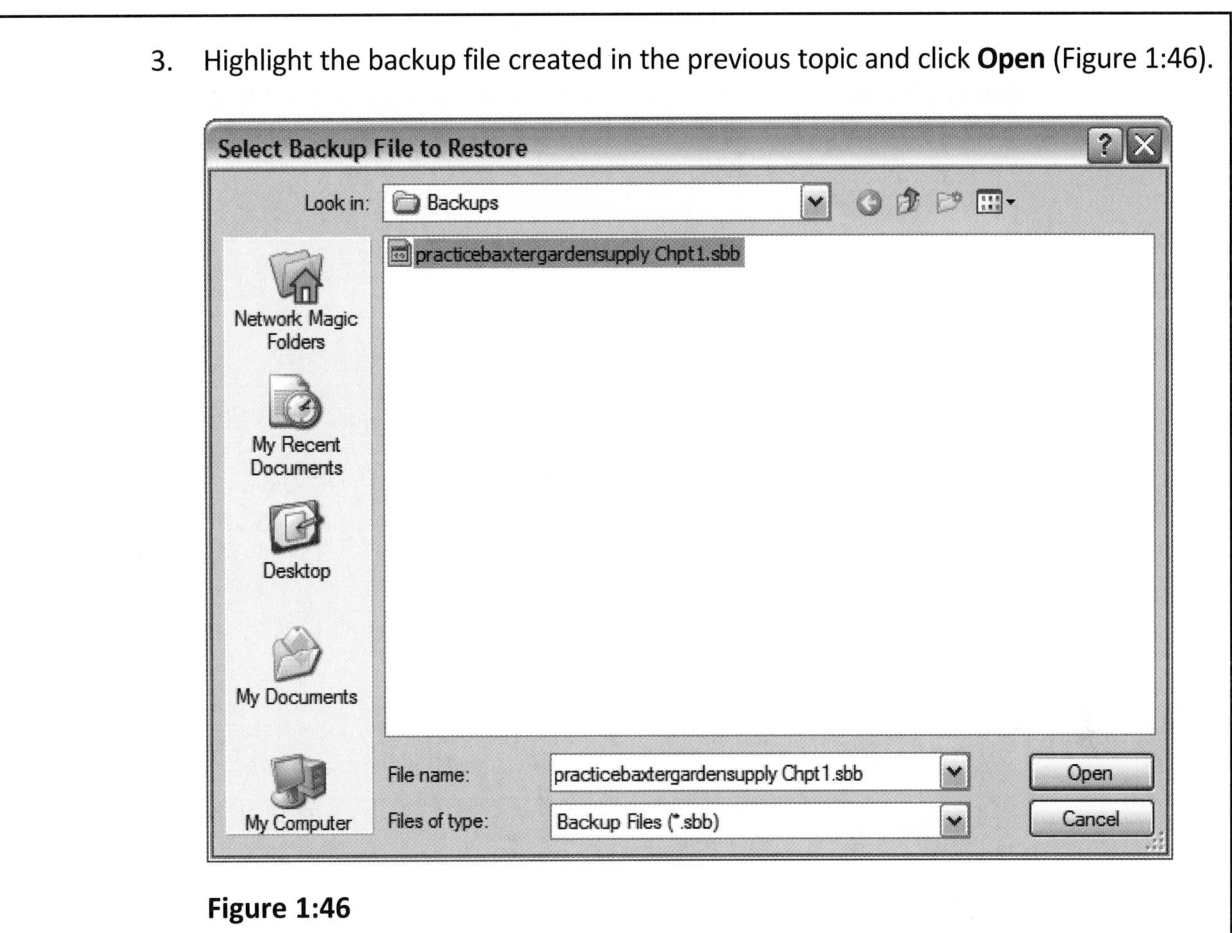

Figure 1:46

4. When you return to the Database Restore window, click **Browse** on **Restore backup file to**. Highlight the company name being restored (Figure 1:47) and click **Save**. Click **Yes** to confirm replacing the file.

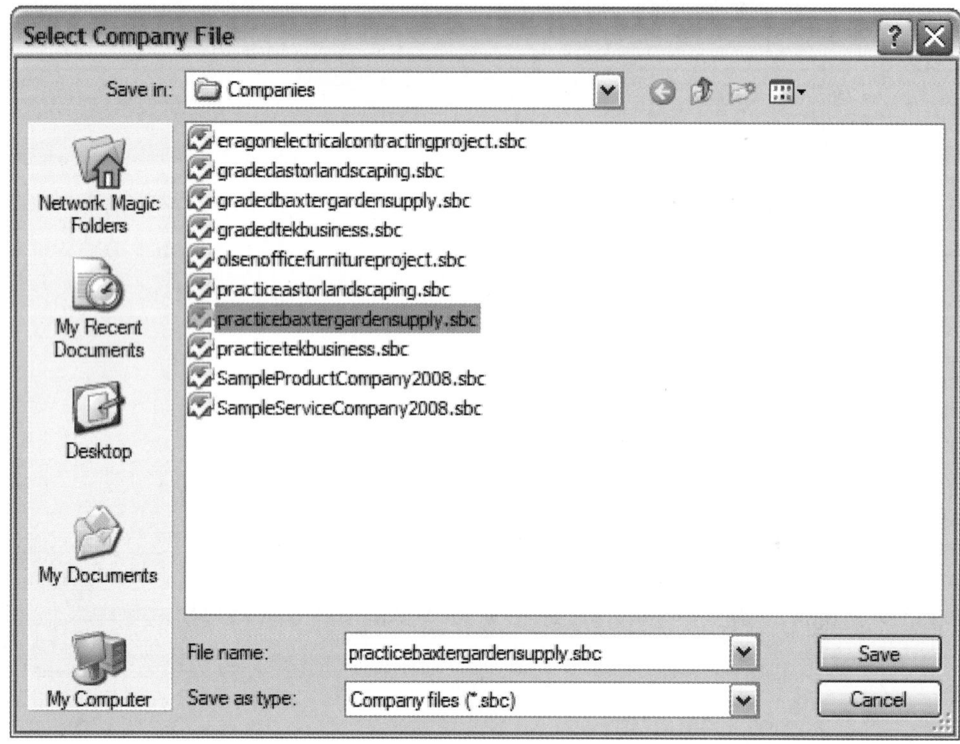

Figure 1:47

5. When returned to the Database Restore window, click **OK** and OAP overwrites the existing file with the backup file. Click **OK** when the restore completes.

6. Click **Open an existing company** on the Start window to reopen the Practice Baxter Garden Supply data file.

You can also restore a data file by selecting ***File>>Utilities>>Data Utilities*** on OAP's main menu; however, you must make sure to open a different company file from the one you are restoring.

Moving Data Files Between School and Home

You can use the backup and restore procedures previously illustrated to copy work between school and a home computer by following the next steps.

1. On the current machine, open the company to be copied to the new machine and follow the steps listed in the *Backing Up Data Files* topic. For Backup Step 3, change the Look in location to your USB or CD drive.

2. On the second machine, follow the steps outlined in the *Restoring Data Files* topic. *(Note: You must have previously attached the data file to the software.)* In Restore Step 3, change the Look in location to your USB or CD drive.

Exiting Office Accounting Professional

To exit OAP select **File** and then **Exit**. The next time you launch OAP, the company that was open when exiting the software will reopen. To close a company before exiting the software select ***File>>Close Company*** on the main menu and click the **Exit** button on the Start window.

Summary

In this chapter, you copied sample data files to your computer and attached them to the software. You customized the Practice Baxter Garden Supply company name with your initials and will customize the names of remaining sample companies in the Practice Set that follows. In addition, you worked with OAP's home pages and learned to multi-task in the software. Finally, you practiced using help, keyboard shortcuts, and backing up and restoring a company data file.

Congratulations! You are now ready to move on to other tasks. In the next chapter, you will focus on working with additional OAP features that prepare you for entering transactions.

END-OF-CHAPTER QUESTIONS

TRUE/FALSE

_____ 1. You do not need a backup file to restore a company file.

_____ 2. Each home page contains a Find section with quick links to account and posted transaction lists.

_____ 3. OAP help is accessed by pressing the F1 key.

_____ 4. You must close a company before exiting OAP.

_____ 5. You only need to use OAP's restore utility to copy data files to a new computer.

MULTIPLE CHOICE

_____ 1. You can identify the open company in OAP by looking at the _____.
   a. Menu Bar
   b. Title Bar
   c. Toolbar
   d. Window Bar

_____ 2. While on the Company Home page, invoking OAP "Help with this Window" opens the help topic of _____.
   a. About the Chart of Accounts
   b. How to get help
   c. About the Company Home page
   d. Check for updates

_____ 3. Customizing a company name is performed using the _____ menu.
   a. ***File>>Company Information***
   b. ***File>>Company***
   c. ***Company>>Company Information***
   d. ***Edit>>Company Information***

_____ 4. OAP's default location for storing a company backup file is _____
   a. Desktop\Small Business Accounting
   b. Desktop\My Documents\Small Business Accounting\Backups
   c. Desktop\Small Business Accounting\Backups
   d. Desktop\My Documents\Backups

_____ 5. OAP includes a _____ home page.
   a. Vendors
   b. Employees
   c. Reports
   d. All of the above

PRACTICE SET

Open each of the sample companies listed below and add your initials to the company name. *(Note: You will be instructed to add your initials to project data files when completing these assignments.)* Remember that the company name is found under ***Company>>Company Information*** on the main menu.

After adding your initials, back up the company using the backup file names listed.

Sample Company	Backup File Name
gradedbaxtergardensupply	gradedbaxtergardensupply Chpt 1
practiceastorlandscaping	practiceastorlandscaping Chpt 1
gradedastorlandscaping	gradedastorlandscaping Chpt 1
practicetekbusiness	practicetekbusiness Chpt 1
gradedtekbusiness	gradedtekbusiness Chpt 1

Chapter 2 OFFICE ACCOUNTING BASICS

LEARNING OBJECTIVES

This chapter works with the **Practice Baxter Garden Supply** data file from Chapter 1. ***When this data file is not loaded on your computer, restore it using the "practicebaxtergarden Chpt 1" backup file created after reading Chapter 1.***

In this chapter you will review OAP settings and options that affect transaction posting and learn features that help you print reports and locate posted transactions. The chapter covers:

1. The chart of accounts and general ledger framework
2. OAP posting control preferences
3. Printing and customizing reports
4. Exporting and emailing reports
5. Report drilldown features
6. Accounting periods

You are probably ready to jump in and begin recording transactions. But accounting is more than posting entries. Accountants determine the "where and when" of transaction posting, for example, where a rent bill should post (i.e., prepaid asset or expense account) and when revenue should be recognized (i.e., upon taking an order or shipping the goods). Understanding the where and when of accounting software lets the accountant know when human intervention is required to ensure that financial statements are correct.

To understand the where and when in accounting software, you must know how OAP behaves behind the keys. Therefore, this chapter looks at settings and options that control transaction posting and reporting. In addition, subsequent chapters will take you *Behind the Keys* after posting transactions. Before that, you need to become familiar with the basic foundation for all accounting entries, namely, the chart of accounts (COA). The COA lists the general ledger accounts and framework that form a company's accounting system.

Launch OAP and open **Practice Baxter Garden Supply**.

CHART OF ACCOUNTS LIST

Before discussing general ledger accounts, open the Chart of Accounts list by activating the Company Home page and clicking the **Chart of Accounts** link under **Find** or selecting ***Company>>Company Lists>>Chart of Accounts*** on the main menu.

The list that follows displays Baxter's general ledger accounts along with current account balances and account types. Use the scroll bar to view accounts toward the bottom.

Chart of Accounts — Collapse Hierarchy — Current View: Active

Add a new Account

Active	No.	Name	Type	Balance
✓	10100	Petty Cash	Bank	$929.60
✓	10200	Regular Checking Account	Bank	$112,623.81
✓	10300	Payroll Checking Account	Bank	$567.36
✓	10400	Savings Account	Bank	$7,592.65
✓	11000	Accounts Receivable	Accounts Receivable	$49,780.83
✓	11100	Allowance for Doubtful Accounts	Other Current Asset	($5,000.00)
✓	14000	Prepaid Expenses	Other Current Asset	$10,870.00
✓	14010	Prepaid Rent	Other Current Asset	$0.00
✓	14100	Employee Advances	Other Current Asset	$0.00
✓	14200	Notes Receivable-Current	Other Current Asset	$0.00
✓	14210	Accrued Interest Income	Other Current Asset	$0.00
✓	14700	Other Current Assets	Other Current Asset	$0.00
✓	13000	Inventory	Inventory Asset	$52,457.25
✓	15000	Furniture and Fixtures	Fixed Asset	$62,769.25
✓	15010	Accum. Depreciation-Furniture	Fixed Asset	($54,680.61)
✓	15100	Equipment	Fixed Asset	$38,738.33
✓	15110	Accum. Depreciation-Equipment	Fixed Asset	($33,199.85)
✓	15200	Vehicles	Fixed Asset	$86,273.40
✓	15210	Accum. Depreciation-Vehicles	Fixed Asset	($51,585.26)
✓	15300	Other Depreciable Property	Fixed Asset	$6,200.96
✓	15310	Accum. Depreciation-Other	Fixed Asset	($3,788.84)
✓	15400	Leasehold Improvements	Fixed Asset	$0.00
✓	15410	Accum. Depreciation-Leasehold	Fixed Asset	$0.00
✓	15500	Buildings	Fixed Asset	$145,500.00
✓	15510	Accum. Depreciation-Buildings	Fixed Asset	($34,483.98)
✓	15600	Building Improvements	Fixed Asset	$26,500.00

Scroll Bar

Figure 2:1

Account balances that appear in parentheses mean that the balance in the account is opposite the normal balance for that account type. For example, Allowance for Doubtful Accounts carries Other Current Asset as the account type and this type normally carries a debit balance. However, the allowance account's balance is shown in parenthesis, indicating that the balance in the account is a credit. If you scroll down to Accounts Payable you will see that this account carries the Current Liability type and this type normally carries a credit balance. The balance in Accounts Payable is not displayed in parenthesis, indicating that the account balance is a credit.

The accounts displayed on the COA list will be used when posting Baxter's accounting transactions. Furthermore, the balances in these accounts will appear on financial statements and other reports. After reading the topics to follow, you will be familiar with Baxter's COA and ready to post company transactions.

Print the Chart of Accounts

You will now print the COA to begin familiarizing yourself with Baxter's COA. Click ***Reports>>Company and Financial>>Chart of Accounts*** on the main menu and the report opens (Figure 2:2). Use the scroll bar to view accounts toward the bottom. You can resize report columns by selecting the column separator and dragging.

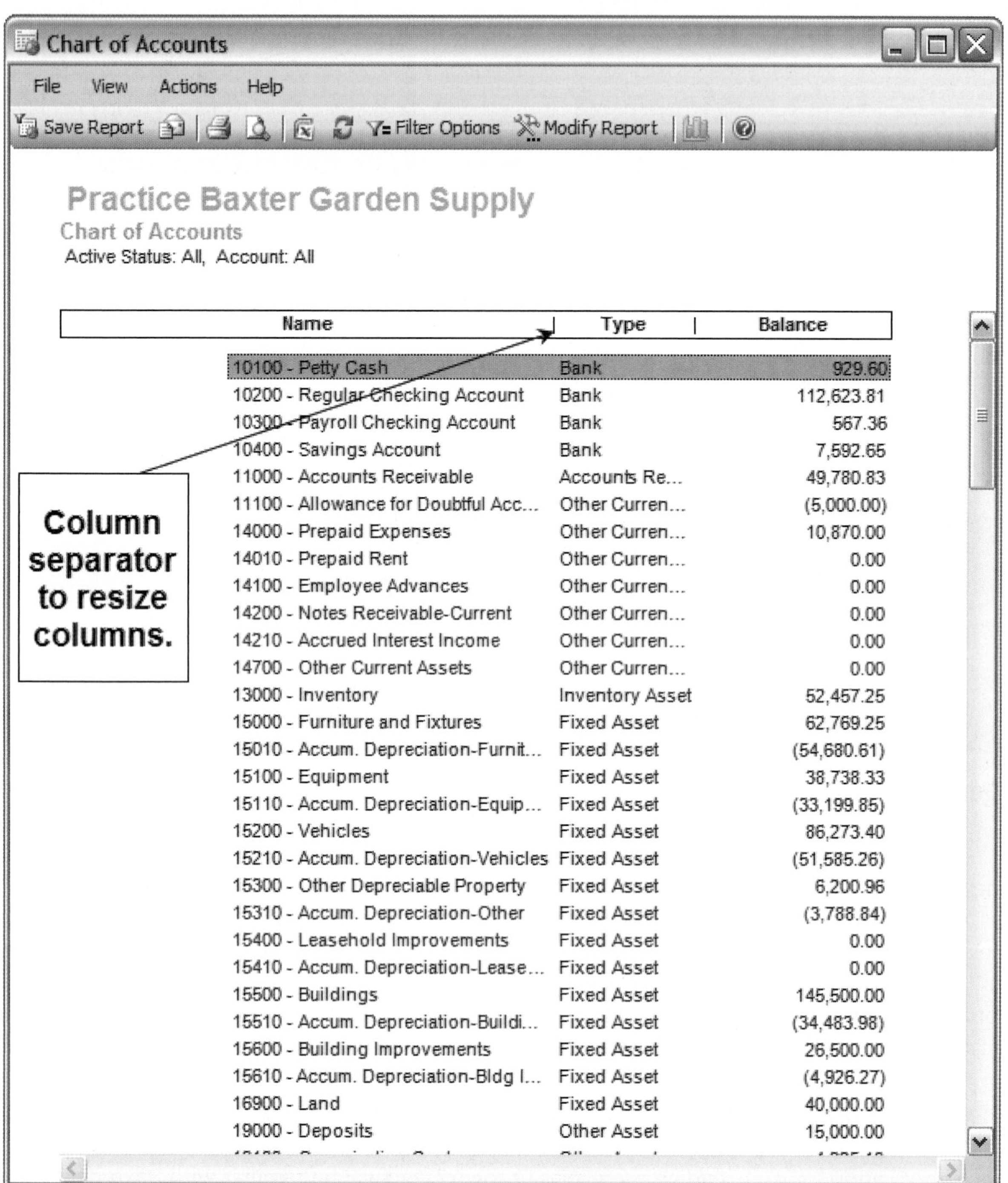

Name	Type	Balance
10100 - Petty Cash	Bank	929.60
10200 - Regular Checking Account	Bank	112,623.81
10300 - Payroll Checking Account	Bank	567.36
10400 - Savings Account	Bank	7,592.65
11000 - Accounts Receivable	Accounts Re...	49,780.83
11100 - Allowance for Doubtful Acc...	Other Curren...	(5,000.00)
14000 - Prepaid Expenses	Other Curren...	10,870.00
14010 - Prepaid Rent	Other Curren...	0.00
14100 - Employee Advances	Other Curren...	0.00
14200 - Notes Receivable-Current	Other Curren...	0.00
14210 - Accrued Interest Income	Other Curren...	0.00
14700 - Other Current Assets	Other Curren...	0.00
13000 - Inventory	Inventory Asset	52,457.25
15000 - Furniture and Fixtures	Fixed Asset	62,769.25
15010 - Accum. Depreciation-Furnit...	Fixed Asset	(54,680.61)
15100 - Equipment	Fixed Asset	38,738.33
15110 - Accum. Depreciation-Equip...	Fixed Asset	(33,199.85)
15200 - Vehicles	Fixed Asset	86,273.40
15210 - Accum. Depreciation-Vehicles	Fixed Asset	(51,585.26)
15300 - Other Depreciable Property	Fixed Asset	6,200.96
15310 - Accum. Depreciation-Other	Fixed Asset	(3,788.84)
15400 - Leasehold Improvements	Fixed Asset	0.00
15410 - Accum. Depreciation-Lease...	Fixed Asset	0.00
15500 - Buildings	Fixed Asset	145,500.00
15510 - Accum. Depreciation-Buildi...	Fixed Asset	(34,483.98)
15600 - Building Improvements	Fixed Asset	26,500.00
15610 - Accum. Depreciation-Bldg I...	Fixed Asset	(4,926.27)
16900 - Land	Fixed Asset	40,000.00
19000 - Deposits	Other Asset	15,000.00

Figure 2:2

Select ***File>>Page Setup*** on the report menu to view the page orientation for the report. The report is currently set to print in Landscape. Change the orientation to **Portrait** and click **OK** (Figure 2:3).

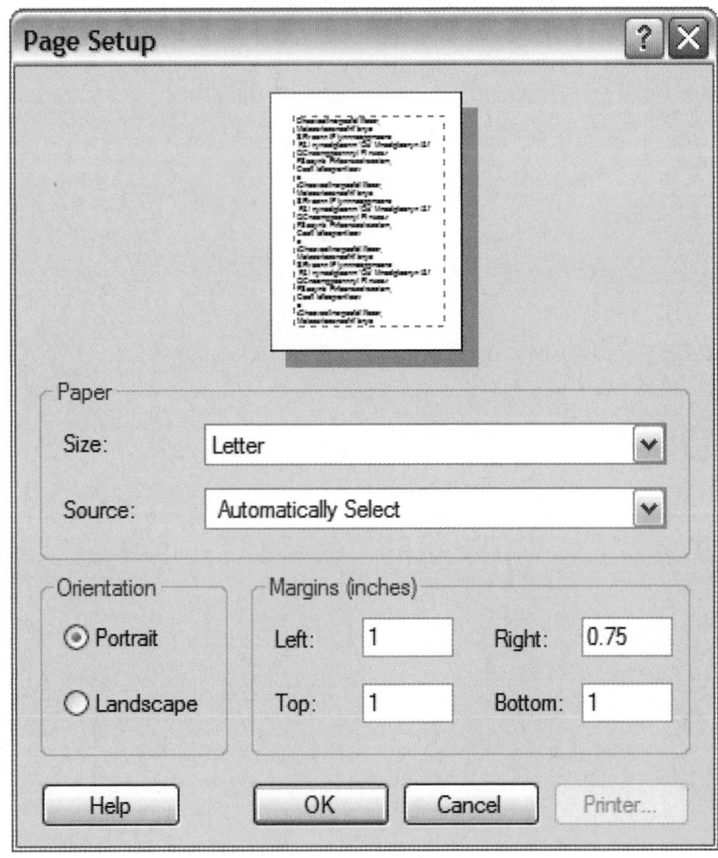

Figure 2:3

Next, select ***File>>Print*** from the report menu and the printer dialog window in Figure 2:4. opens for you to choose a printer. *(Note: The Printer icon on the report will bypass the printer selection window and send the report to your default printer.)*

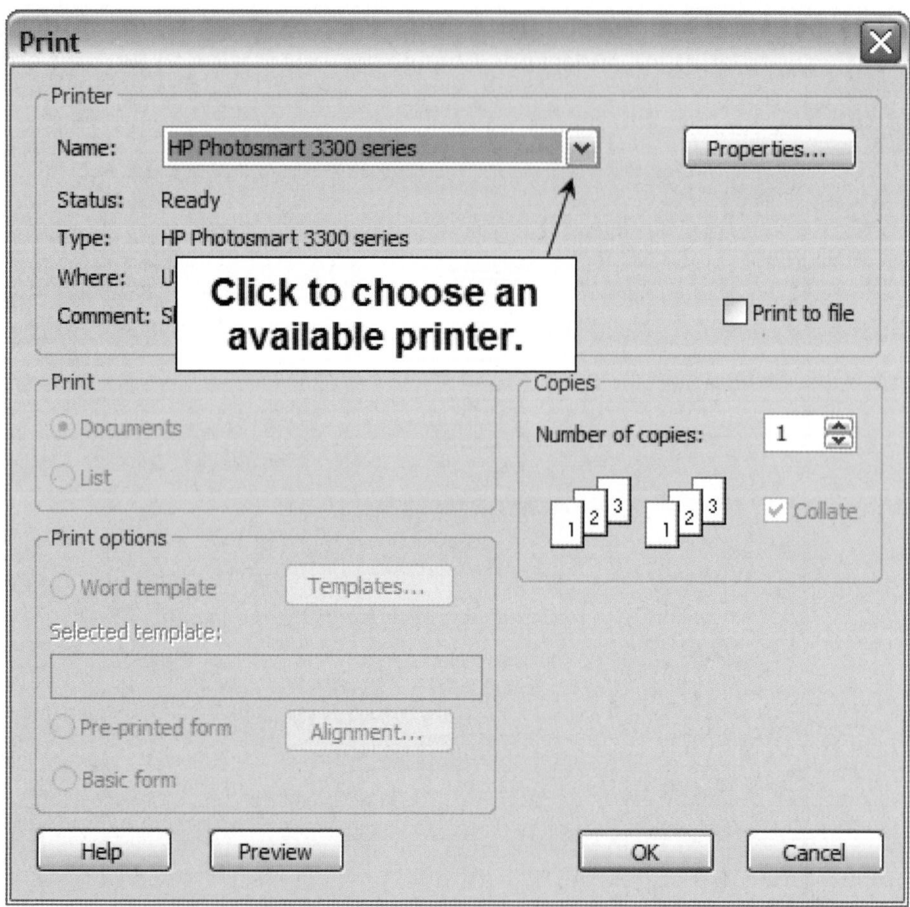

Figure 2:4

The **Name** dropdown list is where you select a different printer. *(Note: Your printer name will vary from the printer illustrated.)*

Click the **Preview** button to open a preview of the report. (See Figure 2:5.)

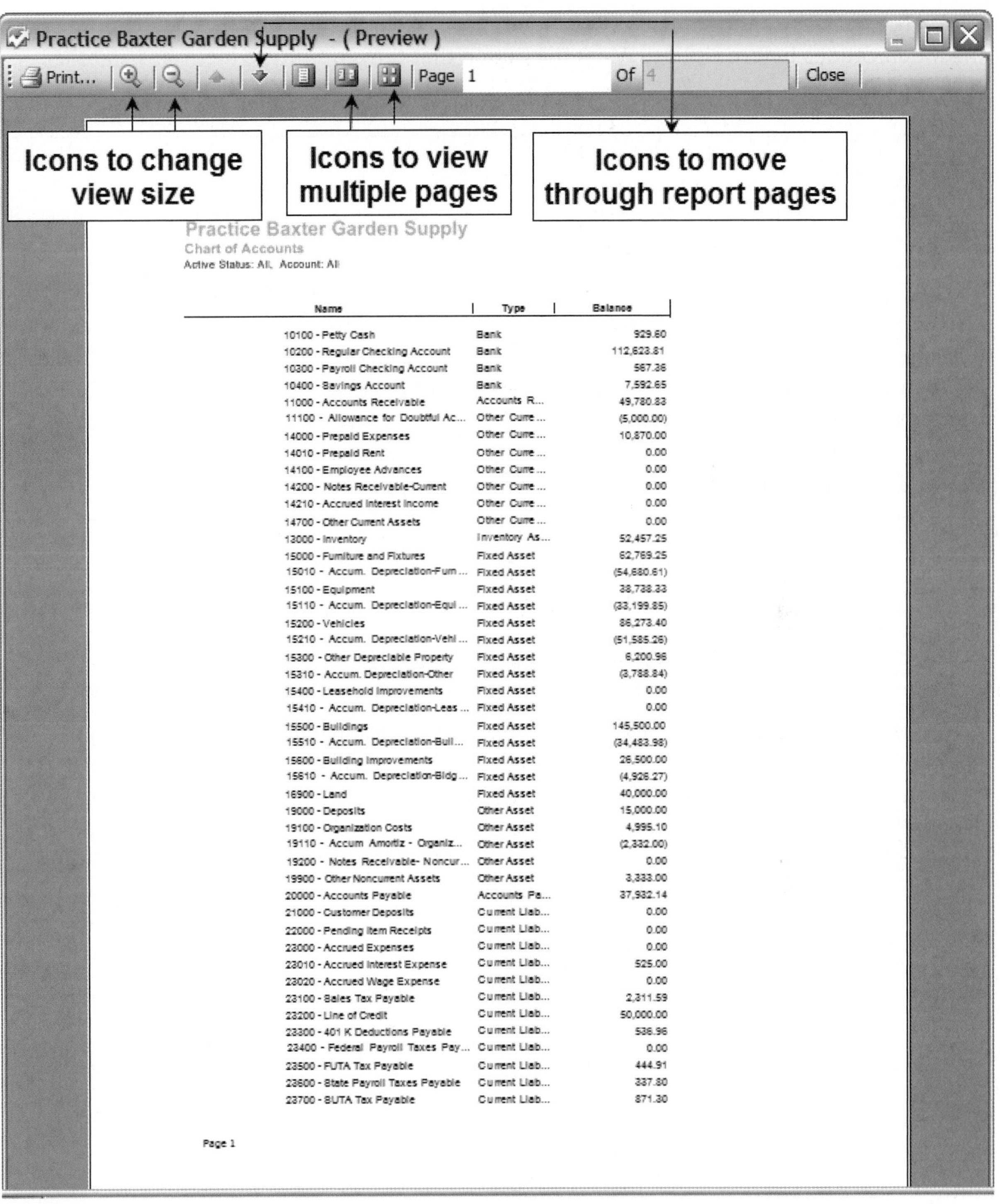

Practice Baxter Garden Supply
Chart of Accounts
Active Status: All, Account: All

Name	Type	Balance
10100 - Petty Cash	Bank	929.60
10200 - Regular Checking Account	Bank	112,623.81
10300 - Payroll Checking Account	Bank	567.36
10400 - Savings Account	Bank	7,592.65
11000 - Accounts Receivable	Accounts R...	49,780.83
11100 - Allowance for Doubtful Ac...	Other Curre...	(5,000.00)
14000 - Prepaid Expenses	Other Curre...	10,870.00
14010 - Prepaid Rent	Other Curre...	0.00
14100 - Employee Advances	Other Curre...	0.00
14200 - Notes Receivable-Current	Other Curre...	0.00
14210 - Accrued Interest Income	Other Curre...	0.00
14700 - Other Current Assets	Other Curre...	0.00
13000 - Inventory	Inventory As...	52,457.25
15000 - Furniture and Fixtures	Fixed Asset	62,769.25
15010 - Accum. Depreciation-Furn...	Fixed Asset	(54,680.61)
15100 - Equipment	Fixed Asset	38,738.33
15110 - Accum. Depreciation-Equi...	Fixed Asset	(33,199.85)
15200 - Vehicles	Fixed Asset	86,273.40
15210 - Accum. Depreciation-Vehi...	Fixed Asset	(51,585.26)
15300 - Other Depreciable Property	Fixed Asset	6,200.96
15310 - Accum. Depreciation-Other	Fixed Asset	(3,788.84)
15400 - Leasehold Improvements	Fixed Asset	0.00
15410 - Accum. Depreciation-Leas...	Fixed Asset	0.00
15500 - Buildings	Fixed Asset	145,500.00
15510 - Accum. Depreciation-Buil...	Fixed Asset	(34,483.98)
15600 - Building Improvements	Fixed Asset	26,500.00
15610 - Accum. Depreciation-Bldg...	Fixed Asset	(4,926.27)
16900 - Land	Fixed Asset	40,000.00
19000 - Deposits	Other Asset	15,000.00
19100 - Organization Costs	Other Asset	4,995.10
19110 - Accum Amortiz - Organiz...	Other Asset	(2,332.00)
19200 - Notes Receivable- Noncur...	Other Asset	0.00
19900 - Other Noncurrent Assets	Other Asset	3,333.00
20000 - Accounts Payable	Accounts Pa...	37,932.14
21000 - Customer Deposits	Current Liab...	0.00
22000 - Pending Item Receipts	Current Liab...	0.00
23000 - Accrued Expenses	Current Liab...	0.00
23010 - Accrued Interest Expense	Current Liab...	525.00
23020 - Accrued Wage Expense	Current Liab...	0.00
23100 - Sales Tax Payable	Current Liab...	2,311.59
23200 - Line of Credit	Current Liab...	50,000.00
23300 - 401 K Deductions Payable	Current Liab...	536.96
23400 - Federal Payroll Taxes Pay...	Current Liab...	0.00
23500 - FUTA Tax Payable	Current Liab...	444.91
23600 - State Payroll Taxes Payable	Current Liab...	337.80
23700 - SUTA Tax Payable	Current Liab...	871.30

Page 1

Figure 2:5

Previewing a report gives you the opportunity to view whether the report needs to be changed to landscape or columns need to be resized before sending it to the printer.

Click **Print**, which again opens the printer selection window. Choose a printer and click **OK**. Retain this report as a reference for posting transactions in subsequent chapters.

Click **X** to close the report. If you resized the report's columns, then OAP will prompt to save the modifications before closing. Mark the option that turns off future messages and then click **No**.

PRINTING THE CHART OF ACCOUNTS FOR OTHER SAMPLE COMPANIES

When you have the time, print the COA report for Practice Astor Landscaping and Practice TEK Business. You do not need to print the COAs for graded companies because these data files are identical to practice companies. Keep these reports as a reference for posting transactions in subsequent chapters.

(Note: The solution for this exercise is not provided in Appendix E.)

General Ledger Account Framework

Return to the Chart of Accounts list. The COA displays individual general ledger accounts identified by account numbers. Baxter has numbered its general ledger accounts using five digits. The first digit denotes whether the account is an asset, liability, equity, income, or expense account based on the following table.

First Digit	Type of Account
1	Asset
2	Liability
3	Equity
4	Income
5	Cost of Goods Sold
6/7	Operating Expense
8	Other Income
9	Other Expense

The second digit indicates when an asset account is current or noncurrent or a liability account current or long-term. Current assets and current liabilities are numbered 0 through 4. Noncurrent assets and long-term liabilities are numbered 5 through 9.

Review through the COA list to better understand the use of account numbering to identify the type of account. Once you begin entering transactions, understanding a company's account numbering scheme helps identify the account to select on the transaction. In the real world, you will find that many companies use a similar general ledger framework for numbering its general ledger accounts.

General Ledger Accounts

After reviewing Baxter's general ledger framework, it is now a good time to discuss creating and managing general ledger accounts. On the **Chart of Accounts** list highlight "10100 Petty Cash" and right click to select **Open Selected Items**.

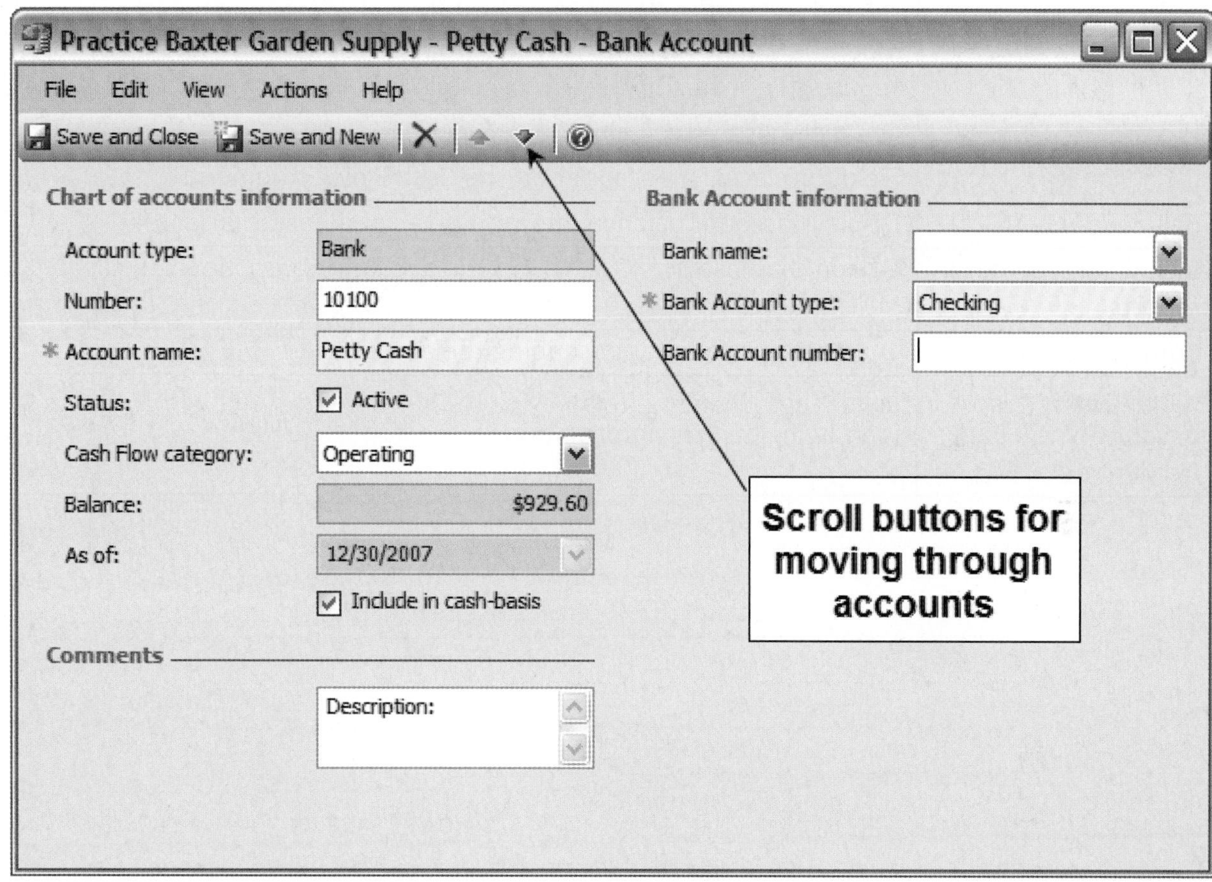

Figure 2:6

The following table describes the fields stored on an account. Fields marked by an asterisk will be required. In addition, fields on the account vary by account type.

Field	Description
Account type	Determines an account's normal balance (debit or credit) and the account's placement on financial reports. Account types are explained in the next table. You cannot change the account type after creating the account.
Account no	Unique number used for implementing the general ledger account framework.
Account name	Unique name to describe the account. The name should be concise and properly spelled and capitalized because this description appears on financial reports. This is a required field.
Status	Changes an account from active to inactive. OAP only permits posting transactions to accounts marked as Active.
Subaccount of	Field available on particular account types that are used to group related accounts with a main account. Linked accounts appear indented on the COA list and are grouped together on financial reports. For example, Baxter uses this option on sales accounts.
Hierarchy	OAP establishes the value for this field.
Cash Flow category	Field for placing an account on the Cash Flow Statement.
Balance / As of	Displays account balance information as of a particular date.
Include in cash-basis reports	Option that instructs OAP to include account transactions on cash-basis reports.
Comments	Optional text field for describing the account.
Bank name / Bank Account type / Bank Account no	Fields that appear on Bank account types that are used for identifying banking information.

Click **X** to close the Petty Cash account. In the exercise that follows you create a new general ledger account. Before performing this task go through the following accounting refresher.

The table that follows lists OAP account types alongside the accounting categories introduced in accounting courses. The table also lists an account category's normal balance. With this table you can see that asset, expense, and withdrawal accounts carry a normal balance of debit whereas liability, equity, and revenue accounts carry a normal balance of credit.

OAP Account Type	Accounting Category	Normal Balance
Cash	Asset	Debit
Bank	Asset	Debit (Note: This type interfaces with the account reconciliation window.)
Accounts Receivable	Asset	Debit (Note: OAP creates this account type and permits only one account to have type.)
Inventory Asset	Asset	Debit
Other Current Assets	Asset	Debit
Fixed Asset	Asset	Debit
Other Asset	Asset	Debit
Accounts Payable	Liability	Credit (Note: OAP creates this account type and permits only one account to have this type.)
Credit Card	Liability	Credit (Note: This type works with the account reconciliation window.)
Payroll Liability	Liability	Credit
Current Liability	Liability	Credit
Long-term Liability	Liability	Credit
Equity	Equity	Credit
Income	Revenue	Credit
Cost of Goods Sold	Cost of Sales	Debit
Expense	Expense	Debit
Other Income	Income	Credit
Other Expense	Expense	Debit

Steps for Adding a New General Ledger Account

1. Under Start a Task on the Company Home page, click New Account. *(Note: You can also click the **Add a new Account** link located at the top of the COA list.)*

2. You must first select one of the account types outlined in the previous table. You will be creating a new expense account for equipment rentals so click **Expense** (Figure 2:7) and click OK.

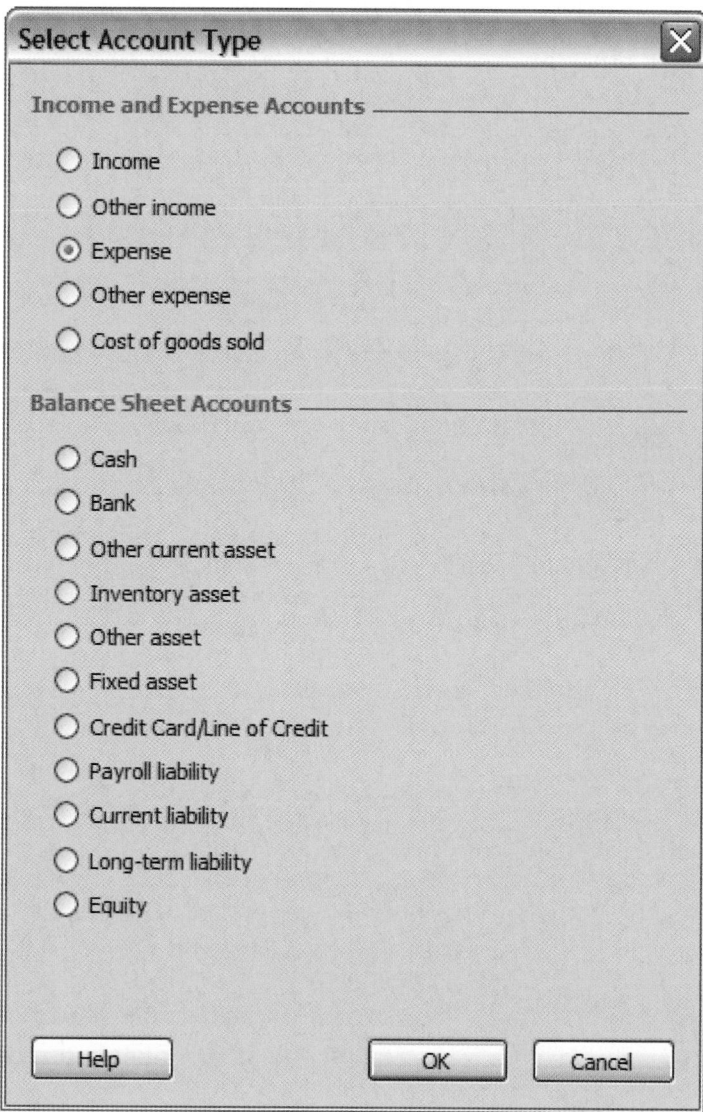

Figure 2:7

3. This account will be grouped with existing rent expense accounts so enter "71120" as the **Account no** (Figure 2:8).

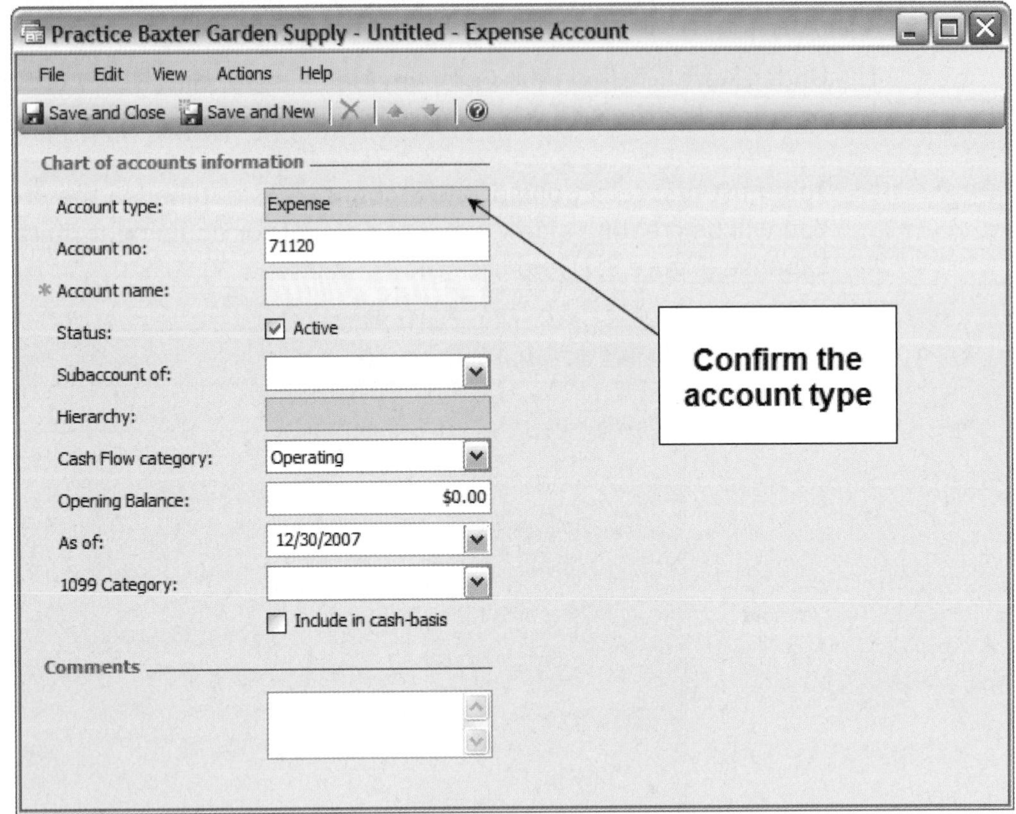

Figure 2:8

Note: If you selected the wrong Account Type in Step 2 click **X** and click **No** to saving your changes. Then start over at Step 1. You cannot change an account type after selecting it.

4. Tab to **Account name** and enter "Rent - Equipment."

5. Click the dropdown list on **Subaccount of** and select account "71000 Rent Expense." When finished the new account appears as illustrated in Figure 2:9.

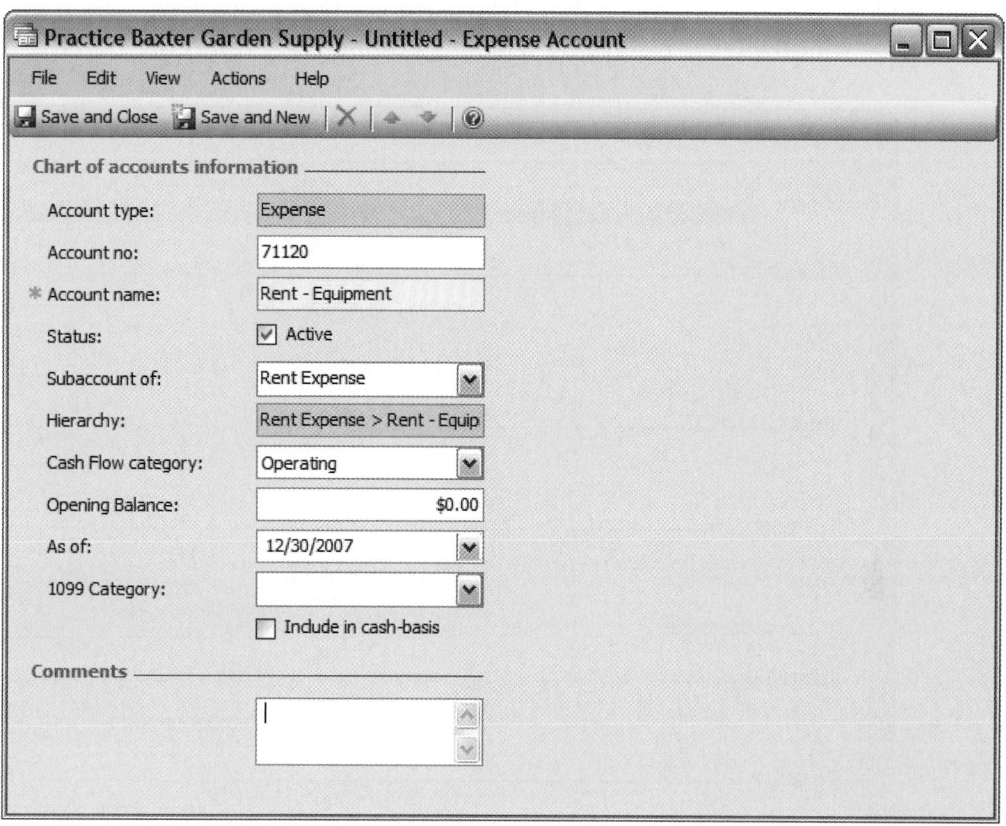

Figure 2:9

6. Click **Save and Close**. When OAP returns you to the COA list, scroll down to verify that the new account was added.

Company Preferences

In this topic you manage options that control transaction processing. Open the Company Preferences window (Figure 2:10) by selecting ***Company>>Preferences*** on the main menu.

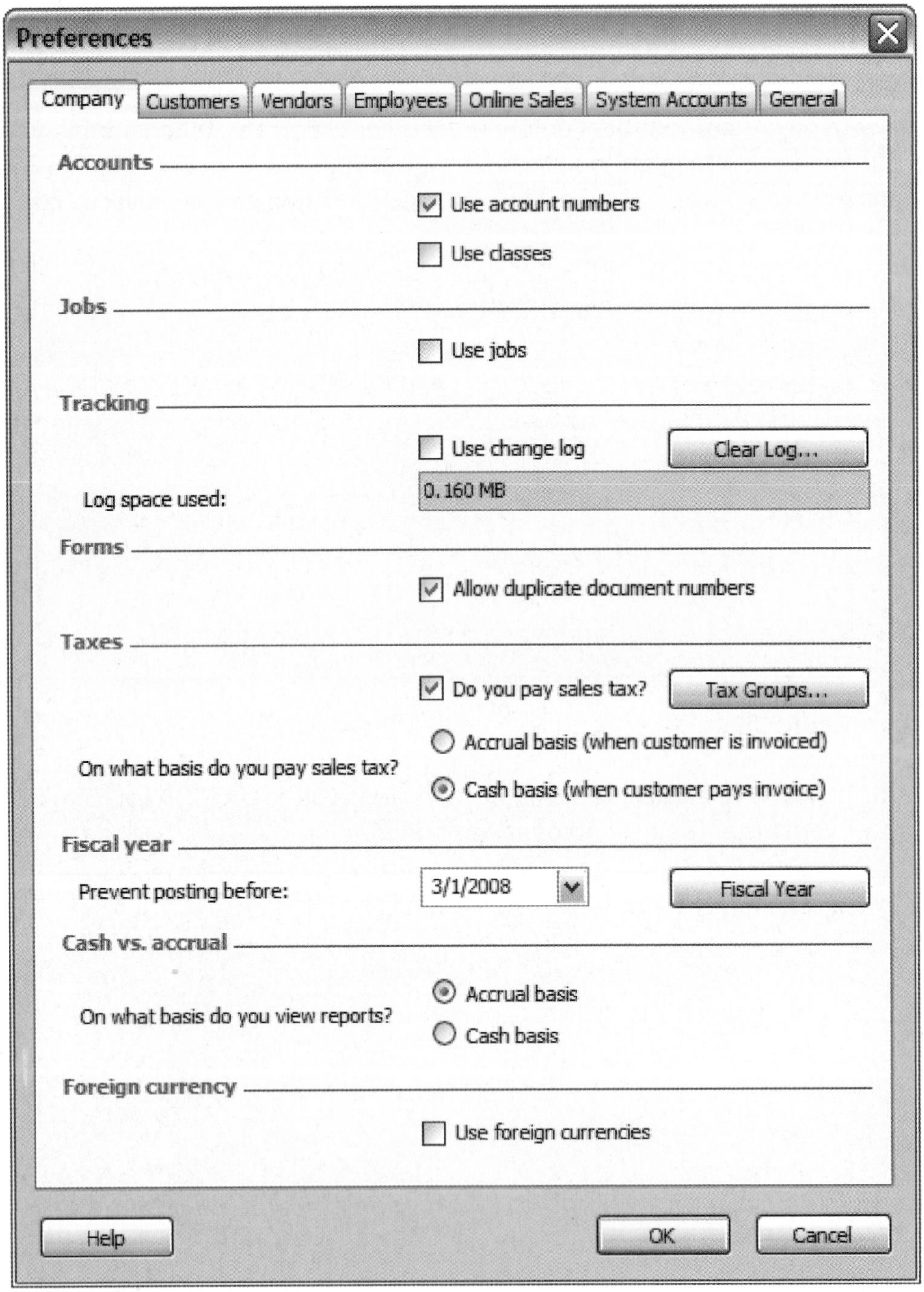

Preferences

Company | Customers | Vendors | Employees | Online Sales | System Accounts | General

Accounts

Use account numbers

Use classes

Jobs

Use jobs

Tracking

Use change log Clear Log...

Log space used: 0.160 MB

Forms

Allow duplicate document numbers

Taxes

Do you pay sales tax? Tax Groups...

On what basis do you pay sales tax? Accrual basis (when customer is invoiced) Cash basis (when customer pays invoice)

Fiscal year

Prevent posting before: 3/1/2008 Fiscal Year

Cash vs. accrual

On what basis do you view reports? Accrual basis Cash basis

Foreign currency

Use foreign currencies

Help OK Cancel

Figure 2:10

The Company Preferences window contains several tabs of options. The following explains relevant options.

Company Tab

Use account numbers activates the general ledger account numbering field. **Use classes** activates account classes that can be used to group accounts by department for producing departmental or regional financial reports.

Use jobs activates job costing. You will find this option selected on the Practice Astor Landscaping data file.

Allow duplicate document numbers enforces document controls. When not marked, you cannot reuse duplicate document numbers on transactions. This means that you could not enter the same vendor invoice number twice, thus, preventing paying a bill twice.

Taxes options activate sales tax features and the **Tax Groups** button establishes the government taxing agencies for remitting sales taxes.

Prevent posting before closes an accounting period and prevents posting transactions to a period prior to the date appearing in the field. Baxter's current accounting period is March because 3/1/2008 is the date in this field. Accounting periods should be closed after reporting financial results for the period.

Click the **Fiscal Year** button to open the Manage Fiscal Year window illustrated in Figure 2:11.

Figure 2:11

This window opens and closes fiscal years, which is different from closing the accounting period. The **New Fiscal Year** button will create a new fiscal year, which must be done before you can post transactions in a new year. The **Close Fiscal Year** button closes a fiscal year, causing OAP to post closing entries to Retained Earnings. Click **Close** to exit this window.

Finally, **Cash vs. accrual** sets the company's accounting method. Remember that the accrual basis of accounting means revenues are recognized when earned and expenses when incurred. In OAP terms this means that revenue is recognized when posting a sales invoice and expenses when posting a vendor bill or receipt.

Customers Tab

Customer preferences affect customer activities. This tab (Figure 2:12) is used to set default shipping terms and finance charge calculations on past due invoices.

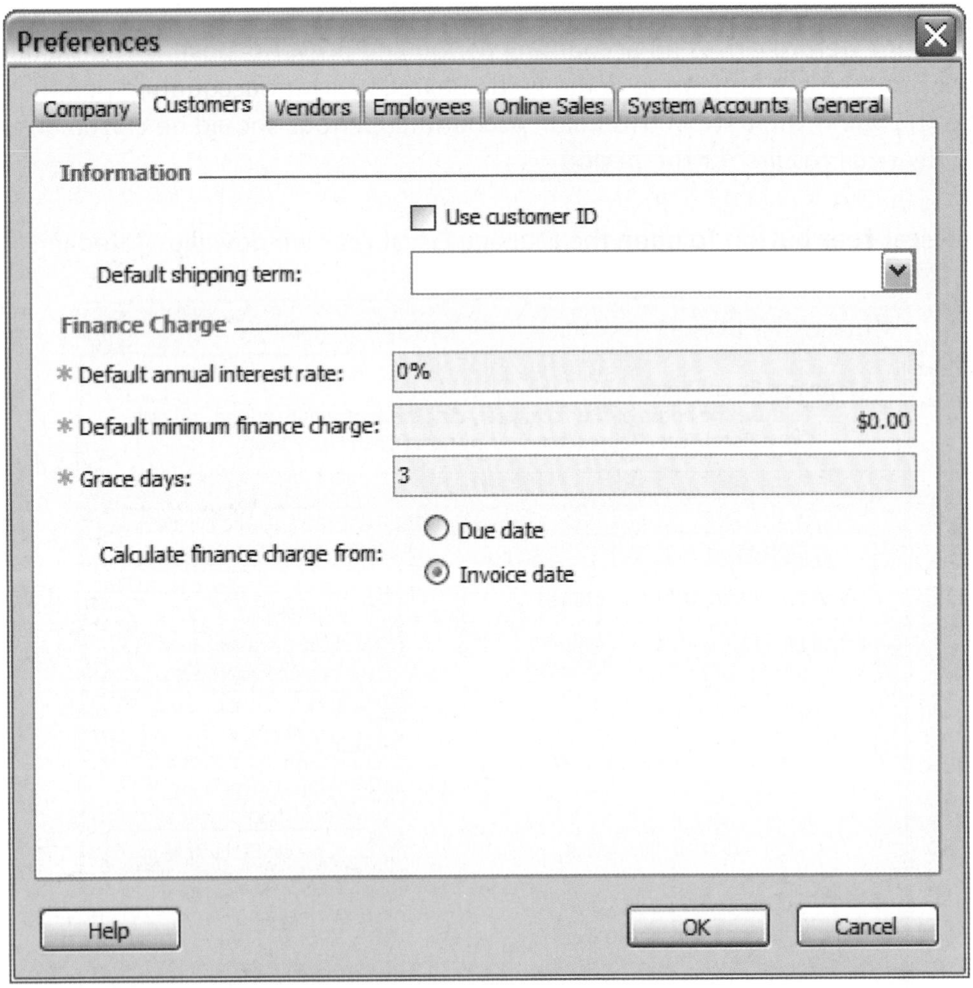

Figure 2:12

Vendors and Employees Tabs

Vendor preferences (Figure 2:13) affect vendor and inventory activities. **Check for item quantity on hand** instructs OAP to warn when entering a sales transaction for out-of-stock inventory. **Update cost automatically** updates inventory item purchase costs when a vendor bill is higher than the last cost paid for the item.

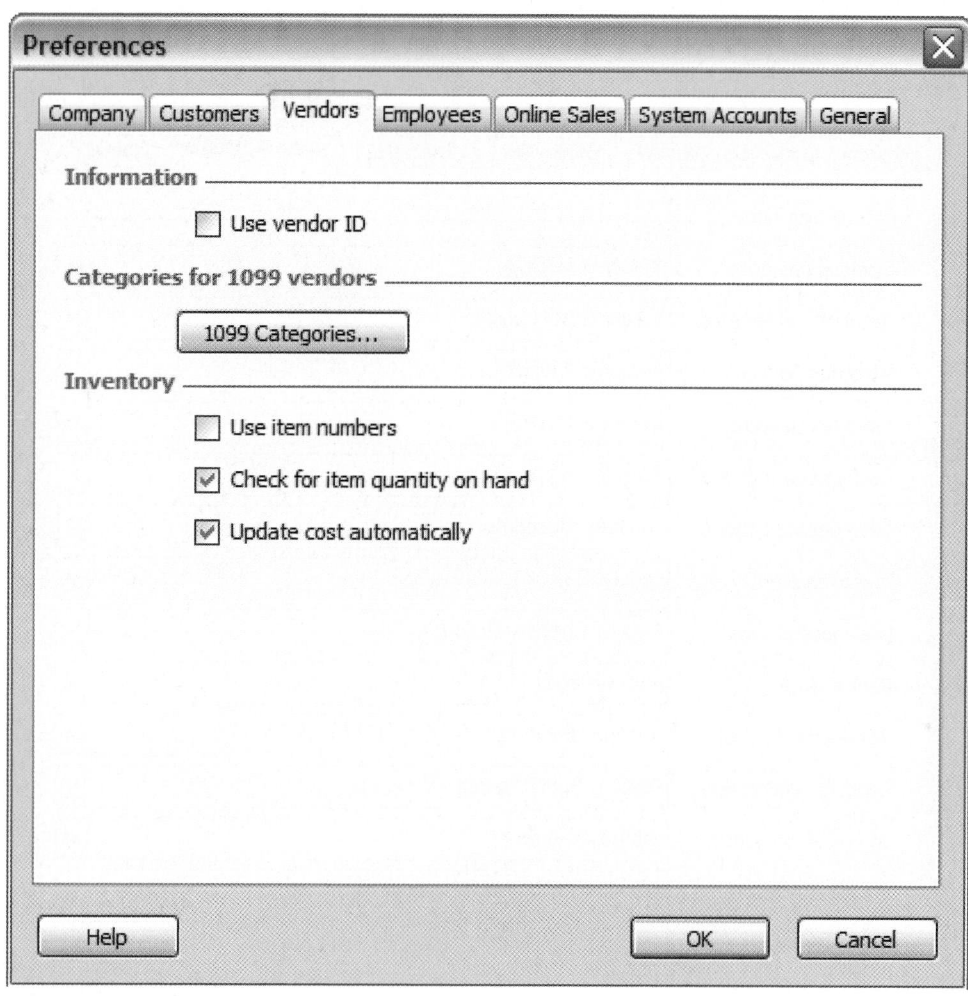

Figure 2:13

Employee preferences (not illustrated) affect employee activities and activate payroll options.

Online Sales preferences (not illustrated) activate features for selling merchandise online.

System Accounts Tab

This tab (Figure 2:14) stores important links to general ledger accounts that function as the default account for posting certain transactions. Click the dropdown list on the **Accounts receivable** option to find that the default general ledger account for these transactions is 11000 Accounts Receivable. OAP will use this link to debit the account for sales invoices and credit the account for customer payments or credit memos.

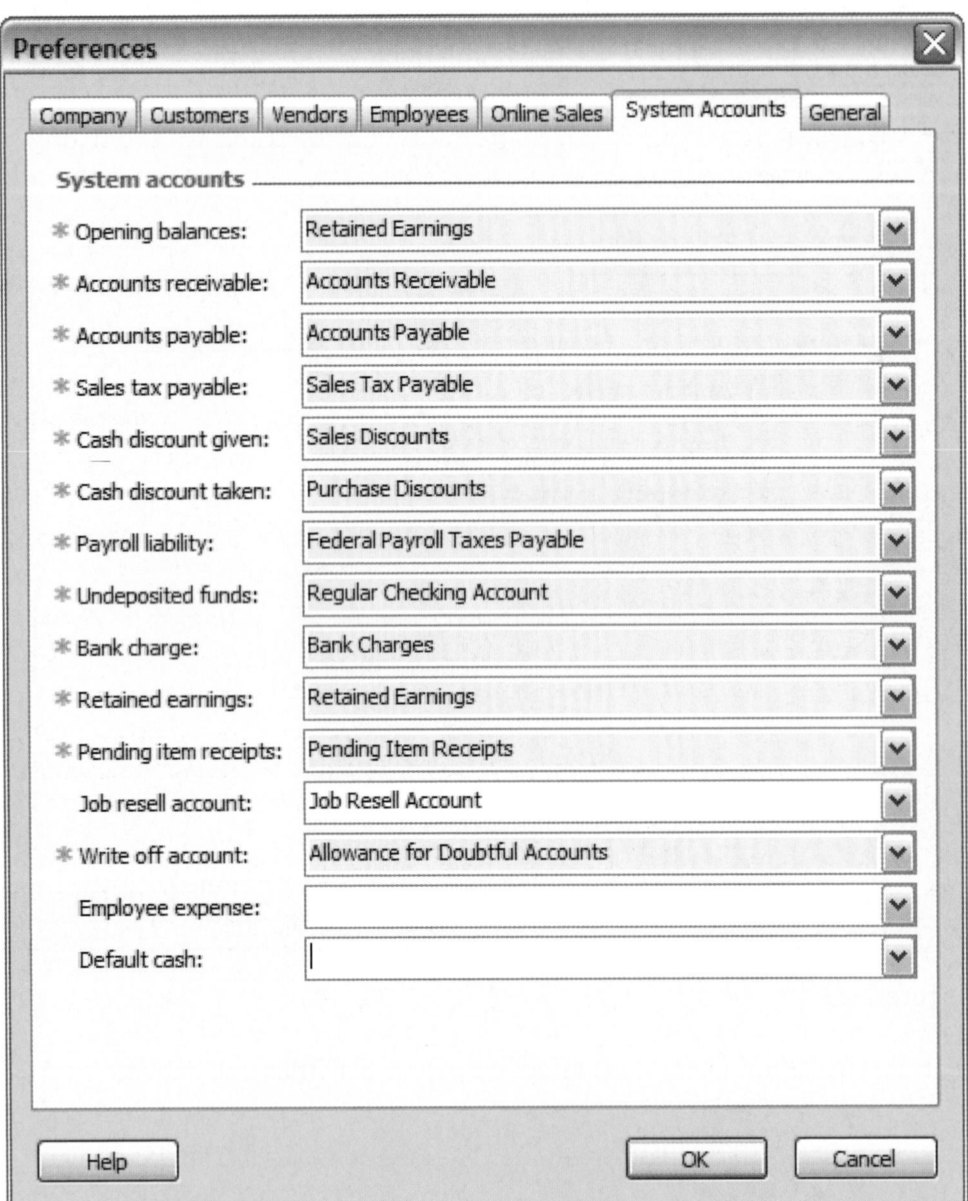

Figure 2:14

The next table explains the role played by each system account linked to an account in the above illustration. Accounts marked by an asterisk are required.

System Account	Account Used by Baxter	Purpose
Opening balances	39100 Retained Earnings	Equity account to use when posting a company's beginning account balances.
Accounts receivable	11000 Accounts Receivable	Asset account to debit when posting sales invoices and credit when posting customer payments and credit memos.
Accounts payable	20000 Accounts Payable	Liability account to credit when posting vendor bills and debit when posting vendor payments or credit memos.
Sales tax payable	23100 Sales Tax Payable	Liability account to credit when posting sales invoices that carry sales tax and debit when posting sales tax payments and customer credit memos.
Cash discount given	49000 Sales Discounts	Contra-sales account to debit when posting customer payments on invoices carrying early payment discounts.
Cash discount taken	59500 Purchase Discounts	Contra-purchasing account to credit when paying vendors for bills carrying an early payment discount.
Payroll liability	23400 Federal Payroll Taxes Payable	Liability account to credit when posting employee payroll tax withholdings.
Undeposited funds	10200 Regular Checking Account	Cash account to debit when posting cash receipts. OAP will deposit cash to an intermediate account so it can then be transferred into a bank account when the deposit is actually made at the bank. Because this feature is often confusing and does little to enhance bank reconciliation, it will not be illustrated.
Bank charge	73000 Bank Charges	Expense account to debit when posting bank fees during bank reconciliation.

System Account	Account Used by Baxter	Purpose
Retained earnings	39100 Retained Earnings	Equity account OAP uses for posting closing entries when a company's fiscal year is closed.
Pending item receipts	22000 Pending Item Receipts	Liability account to credit when posting inventory receipts.
Job resell account	45000 Job Resell Account	Income account to credit for job-related expenses such as travel that are subsequently billed to a customer.
Write off account	11100 Allowance for Doubtful Accounts	Account to debit when writing off a customer invoice.

Office Accounting Drilldown Features

Software drilldown features offer a significant advantage to manual systems. Instead of sorting though general journal sheets, account ledgers and other paperwork, you need only locate a transaction on a report or an account and click to reopen the details. Let's begin by learning to use drilldown features on a report.

Select ***Reports>>Company and Financial>>Chart of Accounts*** on the main menu. Place your cursor on **11000 Accounts Receivable** and double click. This action opens the **Transaction Detail by Account** report illustrated in Figure 2:15.

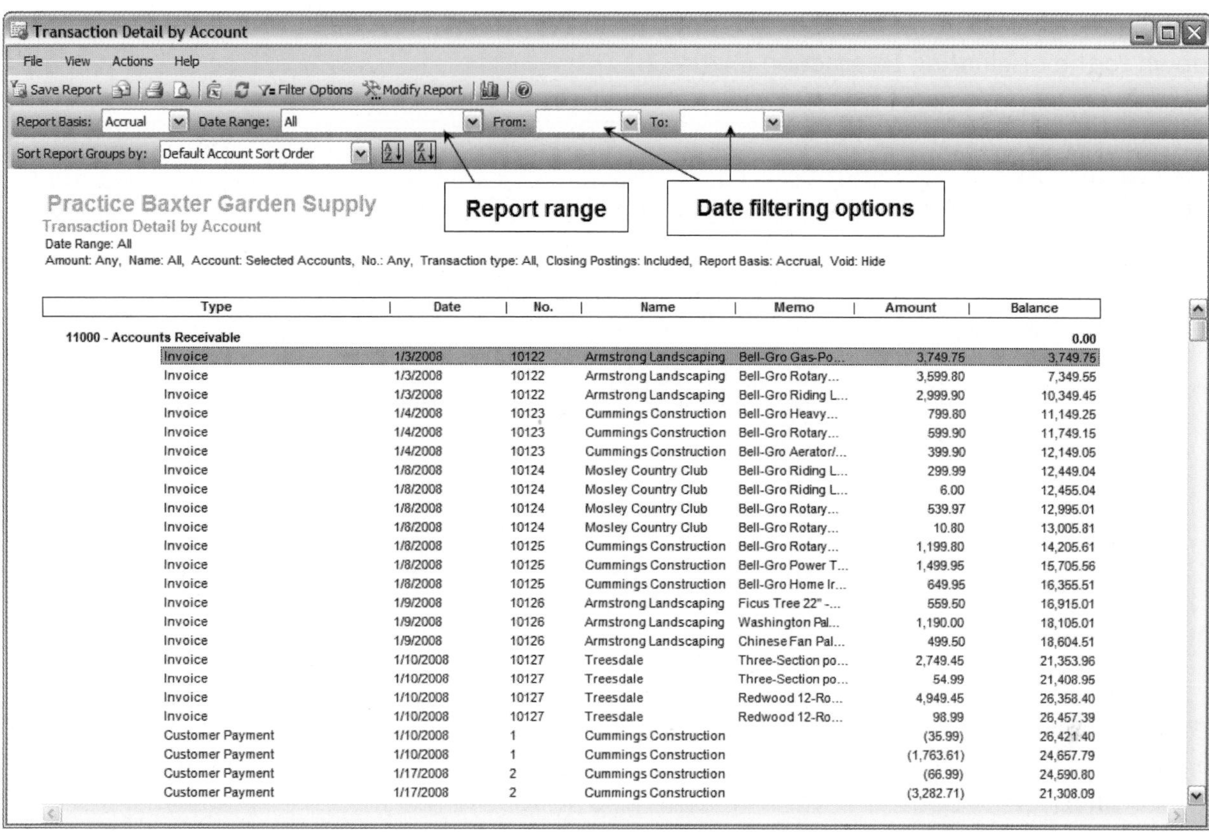

Practice Baxter Garden Supply
Transaction Detail by Account
Date Range: All
Amount: Any, Name: All, Account: Selected Accounts, No.: Any, Transaction type: All, Closing Postings: Included, Report Basis: Accrual, Void: Hide

Type	Date	No.	Name	Memo	Amount	Balance
11000 - Accounts Receivable						0.00
Invoice	1/3/2008	10122	Armstrong Landscaping	Bell-Gro Gas-Po...	3,749.75	3,749.75
Invoice	1/3/2008	10122	Armstrong Landscaping	Bell-Gro Rotary...	3,599.80	7,349.55
Invoice	1/3/2008	10122	Armstrong Landscaping	Bell-Gro Riding L...	2,999.90	10,349.45
Invoice	1/4/2008	10123	Cummings Construction	Bell-Gro Heavy...	799.80	11,149.25
Invoice	1/4/2008	10123	Cummings Construction	Bell-Gro Rotary...	599.90	11,749.15
Invoice	1/4/2008	10123	Cummings Construction	Bell-Gro Aerator/...	399.90	12,149.05
Invoice	1/8/2008	10124	Mosley Country Club	Bell-Gro Riding L...	299.99	12,449.04
Invoice	1/8/2008	10124	Mosley Country Club	Bell-Gro Riding L...	6.00	12,455.04
Invoice	1/8/2008	10124	Mosley Country Club	Bell-Gro Rotary...	539.97	12,995.01
Invoice	1/8/2008	10124	Mosley Country Club	Bell-Gro Rotary...	10.80	13,005.81
Invoice	1/8/2008	10125	Cummings Construction	Bell-Gro Rotary...	1,199.80	14,205.61
Invoice	1/8/2008	10125	Cummings Construction	Bell-Gro Power T...	1,499.95	15,705.56
Invoice	1/8/2008	10125	Cummings Construction	Bell-Gro Home Ir...	649.95	16,355.51
Invoice	1/9/2008	10126	Armstrong Landscaping	Ficus Tree 22" -...	559.50	16,915.01
Invoice	1/9/2008	10126	Armstrong Landscaping	Washington Pal...	1,190.00	18,105.01
Invoice	1/9/2008	10126	Armstrong Landscaping	Chinese Fan Pal...	499.50	18,604.51
Invoice	1/10/2008	10127	Treesdale	Three-Section po...	2,749.45	21,353.96
Invoice	1/10/2008	10127	Treesdale	Three-Section po...	54.99	21,408.95
Invoice	1/10/2008	10127	Treesdale	Redwood 12-Ro...	4,949.45	26,358.40
Invoice	1/10/2008	10127	Treesdale	Redwood 12-Ro...	98.99	26,457.39
Customer Payment	1/10/2008	1	Cummings Construction		(35.99)	26,421.40
Customer Payment	1/10/2008	1	Cummings Construction		(1,763.61)	24,657.79
Customer Payment	1/17/2008	2	Cummings Construction		(66.99)	24,590.80
Customer Payment	1/17/2008	2	Cummings Construction		(3,282.71)	21,308.09

Figure 2:15

The report is currently filtered to display **All** transactions. Enter "3/1/2008" in the **From** field and "3/31/2008" in the **To** field then press Tab to refresh the report (Figure 2:16).

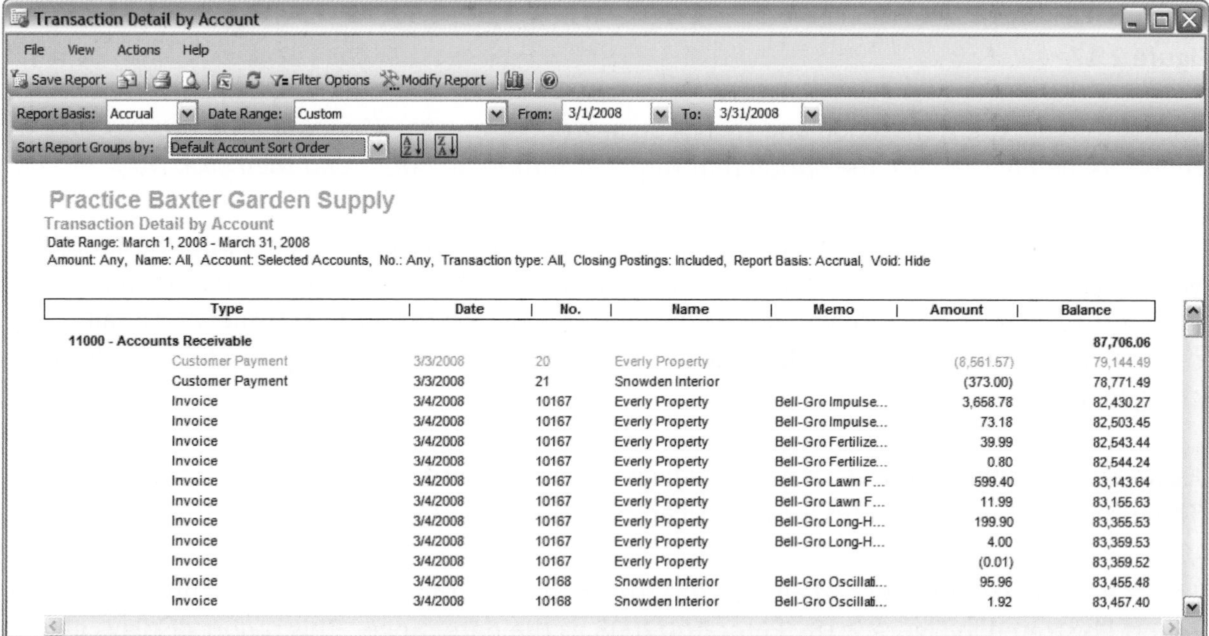

Practice Baxter Garden Supply
Transaction Detail by Account
Date Range: March 1, 2008 - March 31, 2008
Amount: Any, Name: All, Account: Selected Accounts, No.: Any, Transaction type: All, Closing Postings: Included, Report Basis: Accrual, Void: Hide

Type	Date	No.	Name	Memo	Amount	Balance
11000 - Accounts Receivable						87,706.06
Customer Payment	3/3/2008	20	Everly Property		(8,561.57)	79,144.49
Customer Payment	3/3/2008	21	Snowden Interior		(373.00)	78,771.49
Invoice	3/4/2008	10167	Everly Property	Bell-Gro Impulse...	3,658.78	82,430.27
Invoice	3/4/2008	10167	Everly Property	Bell-Gro Impulse...	73.18	82,503.45
Invoice	3/4/2008	10167	Everly Property	Bell-Gro Fertilize...	39.99	82,543.44
Invoice	3/4/2008	10167	Everly Property	Bell-Gro Fertilize...	0.80	82,544.24
Invoice	3/4/2008	10167	Everly Property	Bell-Gro Lawn F...	599.40	83,143.64
Invoice	3/4/2008	10167	Everly Property	Bell-Gro Lawn F...	11.99	83,155.63
Invoice	3/4/2008	10167	Everly Property	Bell-Gro Long-H...	199.90	83,355.53
Invoice	3/4/2008	10167	Everly Property	Bell-Gro Long-H...	4.00	83,359.53
Invoice	3/4/2008	10167	Everly Property		(0.01)	83,359.52
Invoice	3/4/2008	10168	Snowden Interior	Bell-Gro Oscillati...	95.96	83,455.48
Invoice	3/4/2008	10168	Snowden Interior	Bell-Gro Oscillati...	1.92	83,457.40

Figure 2:16

Double click Invoice **10167** to **Everly Property** issued on March 4, 2008. You have just drilled down to the originating transaction (Figure 2:17).

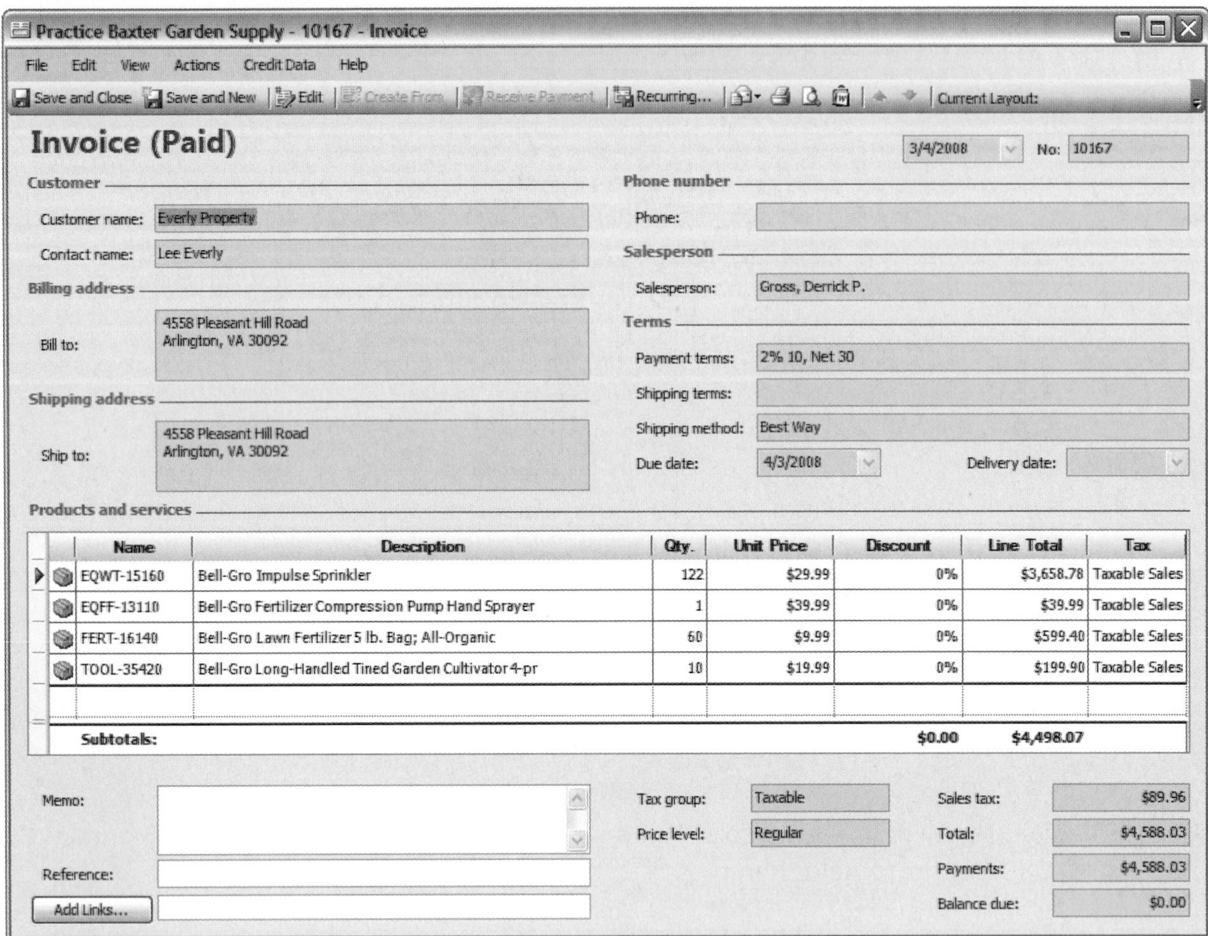

Practice Baxter Garden Supply - 10167 - Invoice

File Edit View Actions Credit Data Help

Save and Close | Save and New | Edit | Create From | Receive Payment | Recurring... | Current Layout:

Invoice (Paid) 3/4/2008 No: 10167

Customer

Customer name: Everly Property

Contact name: Lee Everly

Billing address

Bill to: 4558 Pleasant Hill Road Arlington, VA 30092

Shipping address

Ship to: 4558 Pleasant Hill Road Arlington, VA 30092

Phone number

Phone:

Salesperson

Salesperson: Gross, Derrick P.

Terms

Payment terms: 2% 10, Net 30

Shipping terms:

Shipping method: Best Way

Due date: 4/3/2008 Delivery date:

Products and services

Name	Description	Qty.	Unit Price	Discount	Line Total	Tax
EQWT-15160	Bell-Gro Impulse Sprinkler	122	$29.99	0%	$3,658.78	Taxable Sales
EQFF-13110	Bell-Gro Fertilizer Compression Pump Hand Sprayer	1	$39.99	0%	$39.99	Taxable Sales
FERT-16140	Bell-Gro Lawn Fertilizer 5 lb. Bag; All-Organic	60	$9.99	0%	$599.40	Taxable Sales
TOOL-35420	Bell-Gro Long-Handled Tined Garden Cultivator 4-pr	10	$19.99	0%	$199.90	Taxable Sales
Subtotals:				$0.00	$4,498.07	

Memo:

Reference:

Add Links...

Tax group: Taxable

Price level: Regular

Sales tax: $89.96

Total: $4,588.03

Payments: $4,588.03

Balance due: $0.00

Figure 2:17

Click **X** to close the transaction and then **X** on any open reports. *(Note: If prompted to save a report, remember to click the option that turns off future messages and then click No.)*

You just used a report to drilldown and locate an original transaction. What information did you gain by drilling down to the invoice? First, you know that the transaction debited accounts receivable because you drilled down to the invoice from the Transaction Detail report for the accounts receivable account. You also know the inventory items sold, sales tax charged, and invoice total.

However, you cannot tell which general ledger accounts were credited by the transaction. The next report demonstrates locating all accounts affected by a sales invoice transaction.

Select ***Reports>>Company and Financial>>Transaction Journal*** on the main menu to open the report illustrated in Figure 2:18. Enter 3/4/2008 as the date range. This report displays all transactions posted on March 4 and the general ledger accounts affected by those transactions. *(Note: You will learn to filter this report for specific transaction types in a subsequent topic.)*

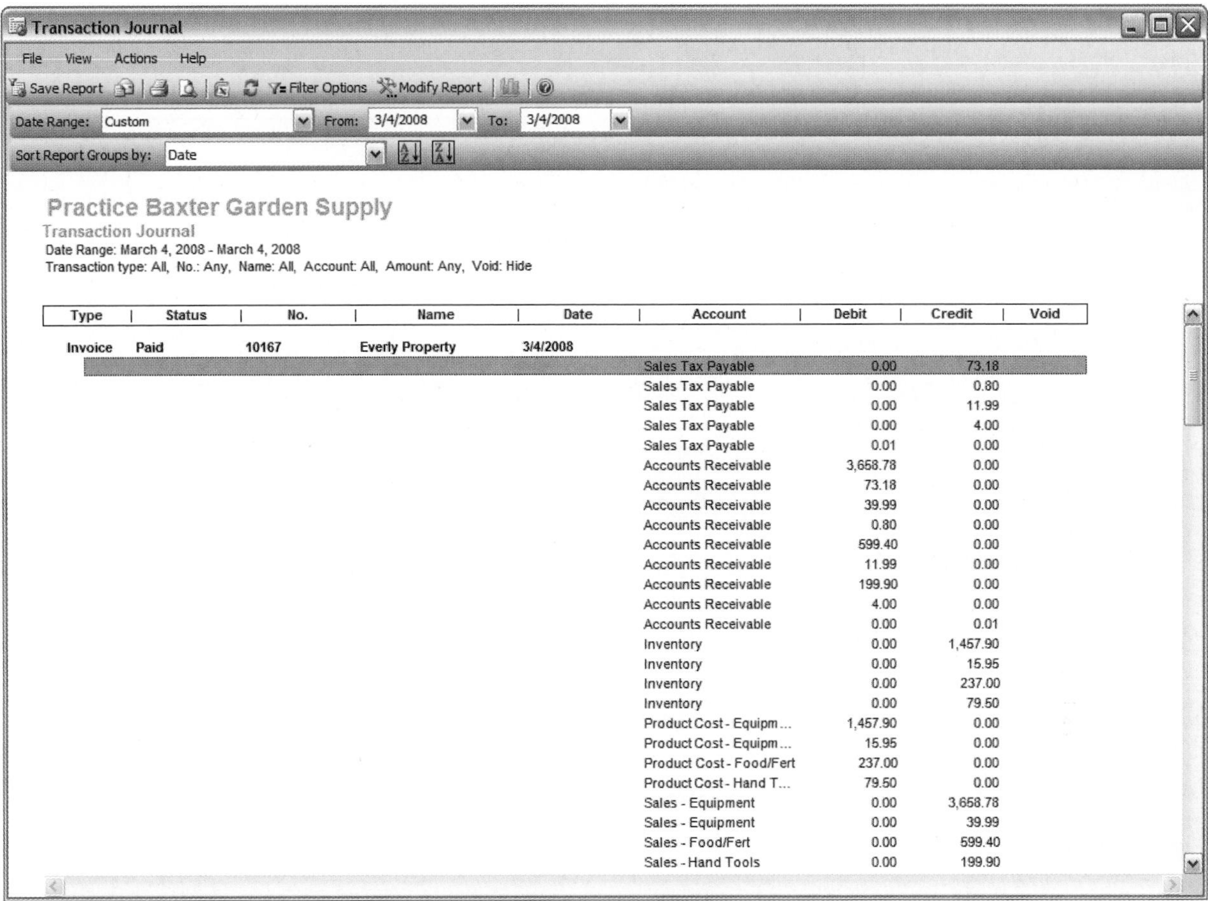

Type	Status	No.	Name	Date	Account	Debit	Credit	Void
Invoice	Paid	10167	Everly Property	3/4/2008				
					Sales Tax Payable	0.00	73.18	
					Sales Tax Payable	0.00	0.80	
					Sales Tax Payable	0.00	11.99	
					Sales Tax Payable	0.00	4.00	
					Sales Tax Payable	0.01	0.00	
					Accounts Receivable	3,658.78	0.00	
					Accounts Receivable	73.18	0.00	
					Accounts Receivable	39.99	0.00	
					Accounts Receivable	0.80	0.00	
					Accounts Receivable	599.40	0.00	
					Accounts Receivable	11.99	0.00	
					Accounts Receivable	199.90	0.00	
					Accounts Receivable	4.00	0.00	
					Accounts Receivable	0.00	0.01	
					Inventory	0.00	1,457.90	
					Inventory	0.00	15.95	
					Inventory	0.00	237.00	
					Inventory	0.00	79.50	
					Product Cost - Equipm...	1,457.90	0.00	
					Product Cost - Equipm...	15.95	0.00	
					Product Cost - Food/Fert	237.00	0.00	
					Product Cost - Hand T...	79.50	0.00	
					Sales - Equipment	0.00	3,658.78	
					Sales - Equipment	0.00	39.99	
					Sales - Food/Fert	0.00	599.40	
					Sales - Hand Tools	0.00	199.90	

Figure 2:18

Click **X** to close the report.

There is another way to locate transactions. Assume you already know the customer and invoice number and want a quick way to open the invoice without running a report. Click to activate the **Customers Home** page and then click **Invoices** under Find. You have opened the Invoice List and the Current View is set to Open invoices (Figure 2:19).

Invoice List Current View: Open

Add a new Invoice

Type	Date	No.	Customer Name	Phone	Due Date	Total Price	Balance
Invoice	2/28/2008	10164	Snyder Securities		3/29/2008	$285.56	$285.56
Invoice	2/28/2008	10165	Thurman Golf Course		3/29/2008	$3,108.45	$3,108.45
Invoice	3/4/2008	10169	Holland Properties		4/3/2008	$7,096.40	$7,096.40
Invoice	3/5/2008	10171	Holland Properties		4/4/2008	$162.59	$162.59
Invoice	3/5/2008	10172	Armstrong Landscaping		4/4/2008	$59.90	$59.90
Invoice	3/6/2008	10176	Kenton Golf		4/5/2008	$7,137.17	$7,137.17
Invoice	3/6/2008	10177	Stevenson Leasing		4/5/2008	$1,784.64	$1,784.64
Invoice	3/11/2008	10179	Snowden Interior		4/10/2008	$177.34	$177.34
Invoice	3/12/2008	10180	Stevenson Leasing		4/11/2008	$7,496.44	$7,496.44
Invoice	3/13/2008	10182	Cummings Construction		4/12/2008	$159.97	$159.97
Invoice	3/17/2008	10188	Mosley Country Club		4/16/2008	$7,254.33	$7,254.33
Invoice	3/17/2008	10189	Franklin Botanical		4/16/2008	$1,889.40	$1,889.40
Invoice	3/17/2008	10190	Tacoma Park Golf		4/16/2008	$1,009.42	$1,009.42
Invoice	3/17/2008	10191	Franklin Botanical		4/16/2008	$1,259.82	$1,259.82
Invoice	3/17/2008	10192	Cannon Healthcare		4/16/2008	$611.91	$611.91
Invoice	3/17/2008	10193	Mosley Country Club		4/16/2008	$7,837.24	$7,837.24
Invoice	3/18/2008	10194	Chapple Law		4/17/2008	$2,276.95	$2,276.95
Invoice	3/20/2008	10195	Holland Properties		4/19/2008	$173.30	$173.30

Current view

Figure 2:19

You will recall from Figure 2:17 that Everly Property's invoice is paid. Therefore, to see it on the Invoice List you must change the View to **All**. Next, click the **No.** column header until the sort indicator points up (Figure 2:20), meaning the list is sorted in ascending invoice order. Scroll down to Everly's paid invoice. After locating it, you can double click to reopen.

Invoice List Current View: All

Add a new Invoice

Type	Date	No.	Customer Name	Phone	Due Date	Total Price	Balance
Invoice	2/22/2008	10160	Archer Scapes		3/23/2008	$6,957.25	$0.00
Invoice	2/26/2008	10161	Gordon Park		3/27/2008	$1,753.69	$0.00
Invoice	2/26/2008	10162	Tacoma Park Golf		3/27/2008	$2,497.93	$0.00
Invoice	2/27/2008	10163	Armstrong Landscaping		3/28/2008	$6,957.25	$0.00
Invoice	2/28/2008	10164	Snyder Securities		3/29/2008	$285.56	$285.56
Invoice	2/28/2008	10165	Thurman Golf Course		3/29/2008	$3,108.45	$3,108.45
Invoice	2/28/2008	10166	Saia's Neighborhood		3/29/2008	$7,257.10	$0.00
Invoice	3/4/2008	10167	Everly Property		4/3/2008	$4,588.03	$0.00
Invoice	3/4/2008	10168	Snowden Interior		4/3/2008	$373.00	$0.00
Invoice	3/4/2008	10169	Holland Properties		4/3/2008	$7,096.40	$7,096.40
Invoice	3/4/2008	10170	Freemond Country Club		4/3/2008	$7,137.17	$0.00
Invoice	3/5/2008	10171	Holland Properties		4/4/2008	$162.59	$162.59

Sort indicator

Figure 2:20

Lists also have a Find feature that assists in locating posted transactions and this feature is the subject of our next topic.

FINDING TRANSACTIONS IN OFFICE ACCOUNTING

After using the software for a while, you will find so many transactions on a transaction list that scrolling through a list to search for a specific transaction is inefficient. This is where the Find feature is useful. We will use this feature to locate Invoice 10167 issued to Everly Property on March 4, 2008.

With the Invoice List open, click this Find icon on the toolbar or use the **Ctrl + F** keyboard shortcut. The Find fields illustrated in Figure 2:21 are now open at the top of the list.

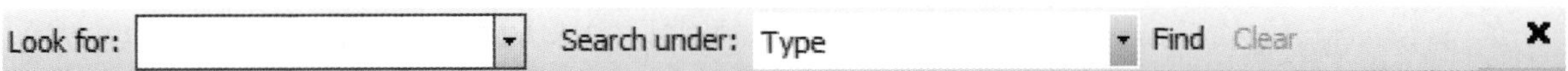

Figure 2:21

Use the **Search under** dropdown list to select **Customer Name** and then begin typing "Ev" in the **Look for** field. The list narrows to customer names containing these letters (Figure 2:22) and you can easily locate Invoice 10167. Clicking **Clear** will redisplay all invoices.

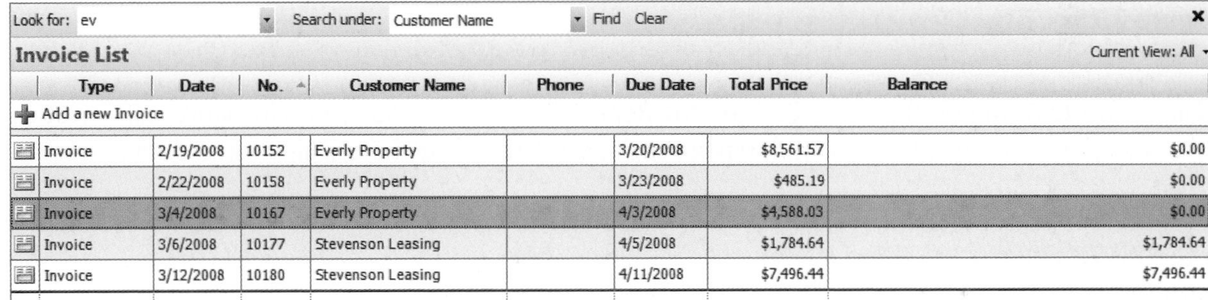

Type	Date	No.	Customer Name	Phone	Due Date	Total Price	Balance
Invoice	2/19/2008	10152	Everly Property		3/20/2008	$8,561.57	$0.00
Invoice	2/22/2008	10158	Everly Property		3/23/2008	$485.19	$0.00
Invoice	3/4/2008	10167	Everly Property		4/3/2008	$4,588.03	$0.00
Invoice	3/6/2008	10177	Stevenson Leasing		4/5/2008	$1,784.64	$1,784.64
Invoice	3/12/2008	10180	Stevenson Leasing		4/11/2008	$7,496.44	$7,496.44

Figure 2:22

The Reports Menu and Home Page

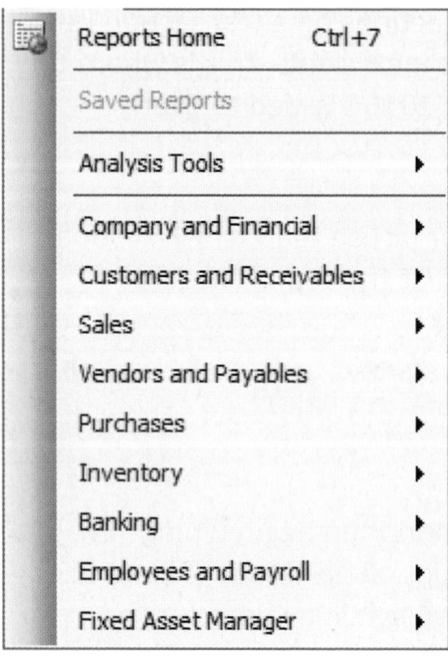

Figure 2:23

In this topic you learn to work with reports. Click ***Reports*** on the main menu to view the menu items illustrated in Figure 2:24. The arrow indicator on a menu item means submenus exist.

Reports are categorized by activities; therefore, you can generally find a report by identifying the reporting activity. For instance, financial statements are submenus under the Company and Financial menu whereas accounts receivable reports are found under the Customers and Receivables menu. Reports that have been customized and saved will be found under the Saved Reports category. *(Note: The menu is currently grayed out because there are no customized reports.)*

Click **Reports Home** on the menu to open the Reports Home page illustrated in Figure 2:24. Notice that categories on the left of the home page correspond to menu choices illustrated above.

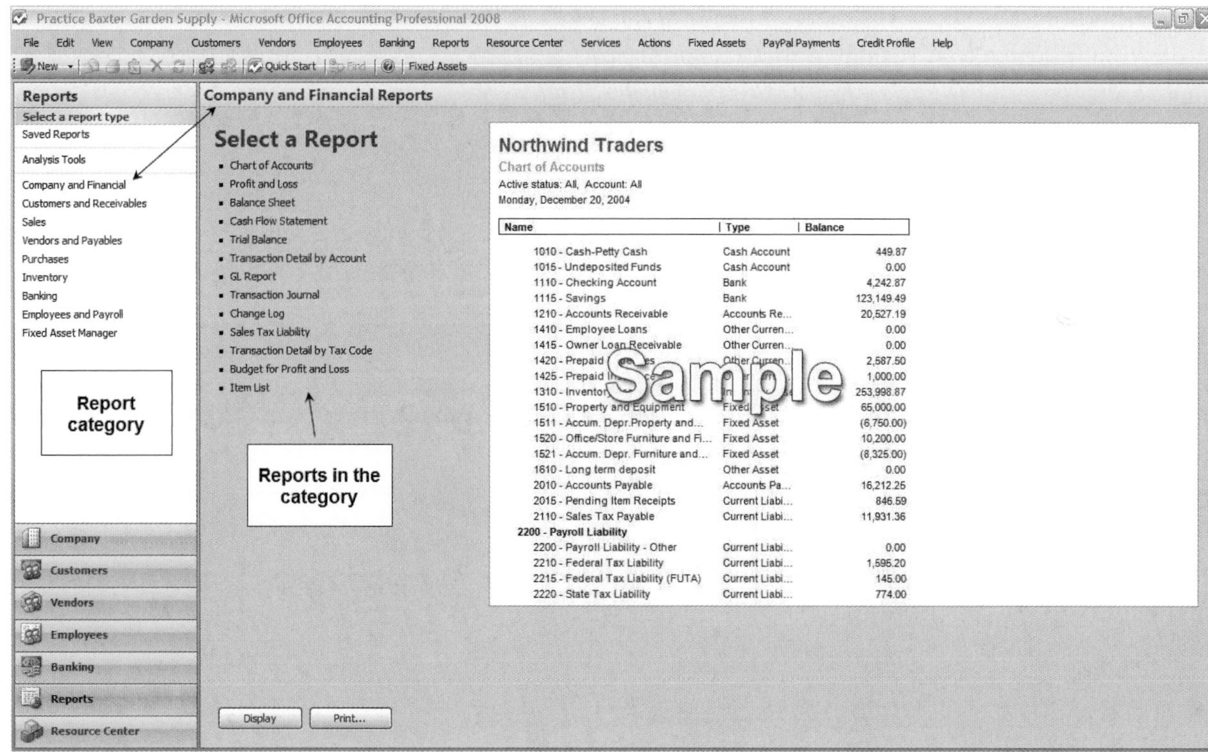

Figure 2:24

Reports found under the **Company and Financial** category of the home page correspond to submenus found under the Company and Financial menu (Figure 2:25).

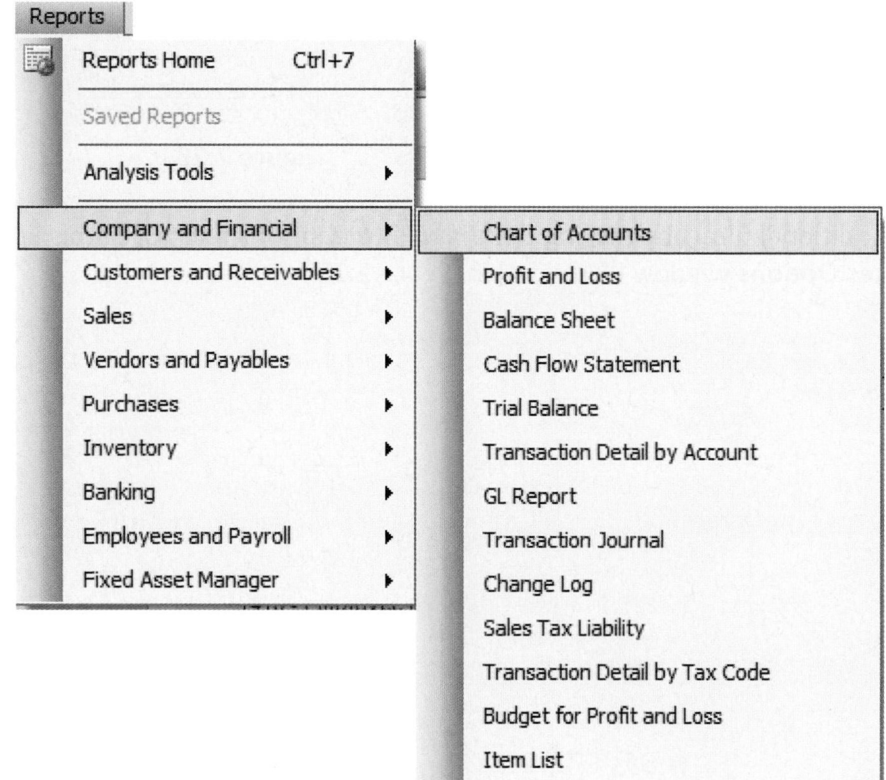

Figure 2:25

Thus, the Reports Home page is a descriptive version of the Reports menu because it contains additional feature that display a report's appearance and also gives you immediate access to any report category. Keep this home page open for the next topic where you learn to customize reports.

CUSTOMIZING REPORTS

With the Reports Home page active and the Company and Financial category selected, double click the **Chart of Accounts** to open the COA report.

You will now customize the report to list only active accounts. Click the **Modify Report** button on the report's toolbar to open the **Modify Report** pane illustrated in Figure 2:26.

The active filters on a report are displayed at the top of it above the report date. The **Predefined filter options** section of the Modify Panes window lists OAP filters that can be instantly applied by clicking the filter name. For the COA report, these filters are **All Balance Sheet A/cs**. (i.e., display only Balance Sheet accounts) and **All Income & Expense A/cs**. (i.e., display only Income Statement accounts).

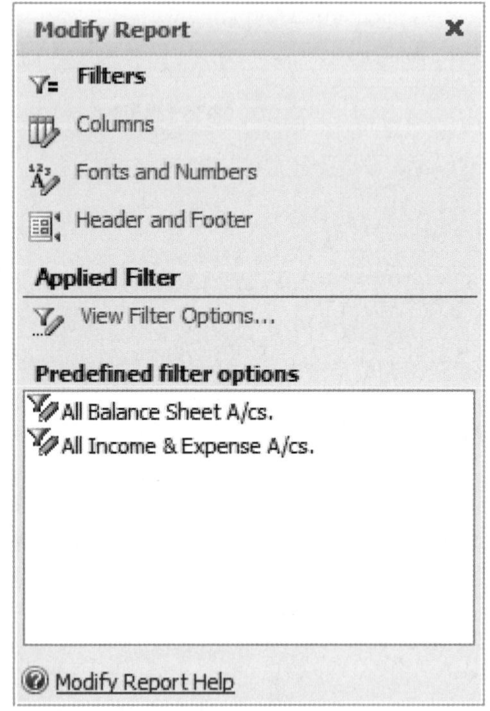

Figure 2:26

You can add additional filters by clicking the **View Filter Options** link. Click this link to open the **Select Filter Options** window illustrated in Figure 2:27.

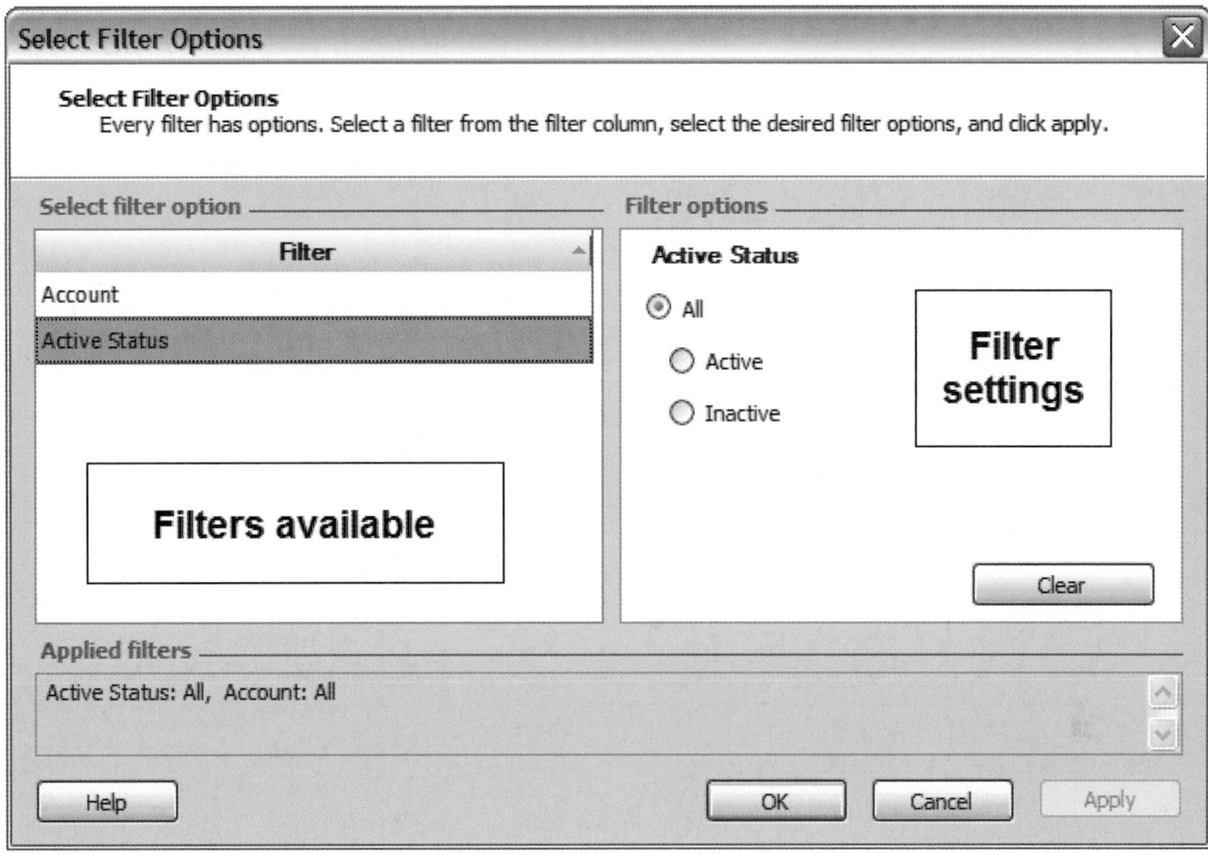

Figure 2:27

This window lists available filters on the left and the highlighted filter's current settings on the right. Filters vary by report and options vary by filter.

With the Active Status filter highlighted, click to select the **Active** option on the right and then click **OK**. The report refreshes to display only active general ledger accounts. Figure 2:28 shows the filters currently applied to the COA report.

Figure 2:28

Return to the **Modify Report** pane so we can discuss additional report-customizing features. There are options for changing a report columns, fonts, and headers (Figure 2:29).

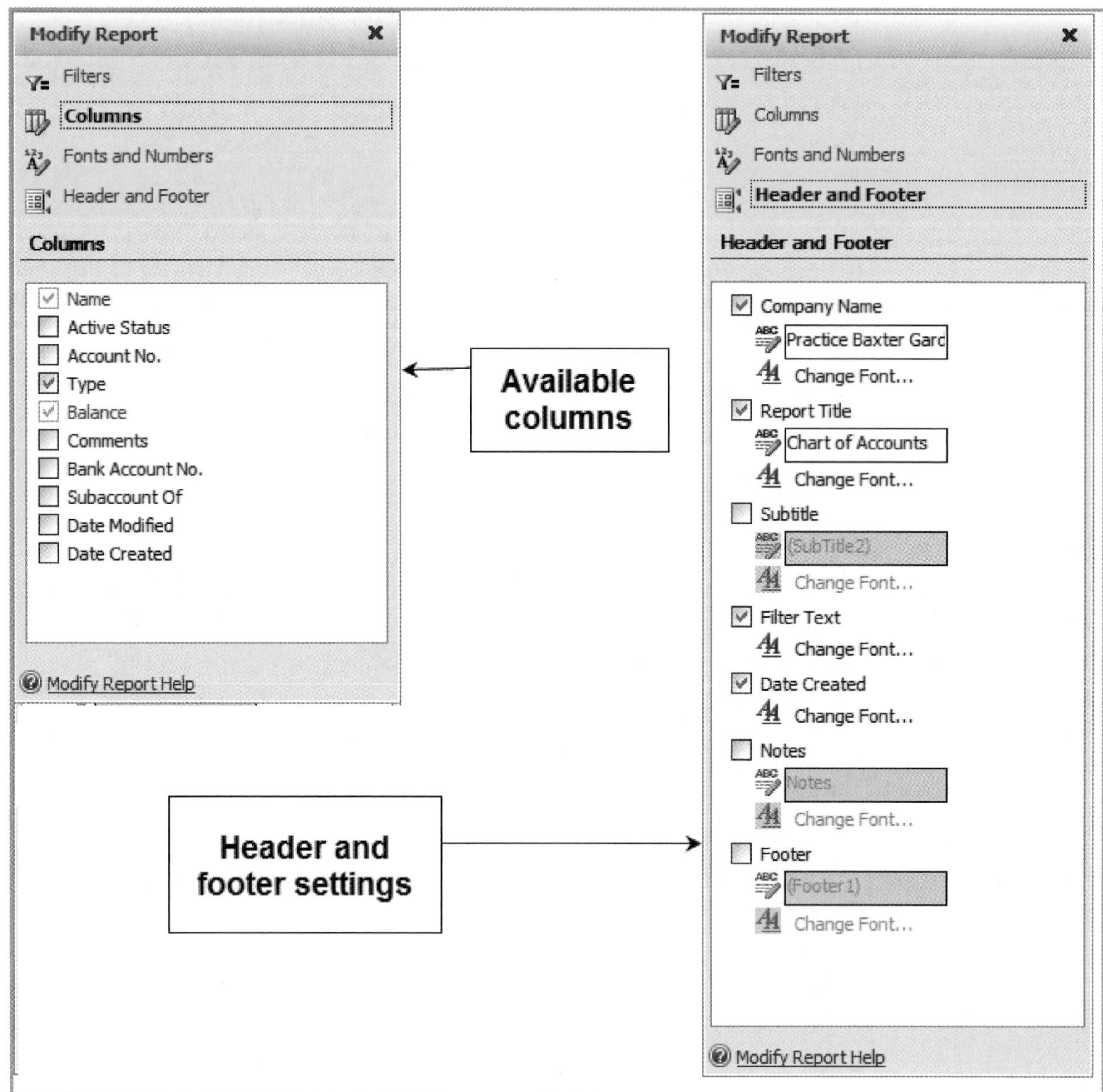

Figure 2:29

Click **Columns** to view data columns that can be added to the COA report. Columns vary by report and fields that are grayed out cannot be removed from the report. Columns are added and removed by clicking the column name to change its selection.

Click **Header and Footer** to view options for changing information appearing at the top and bottom of a report. You can click the **Date Created** option to stop printing the date of running a report.

You will next save the customized COA. Close the Modify Report pane by clicking **X** at the top of the pane. Click the **Save Report** button on the report toolbar and the **Save Report** window opens (Figure 2:30). Enter the report name illustrated and click **OK**. Click **X** to close the customized report.

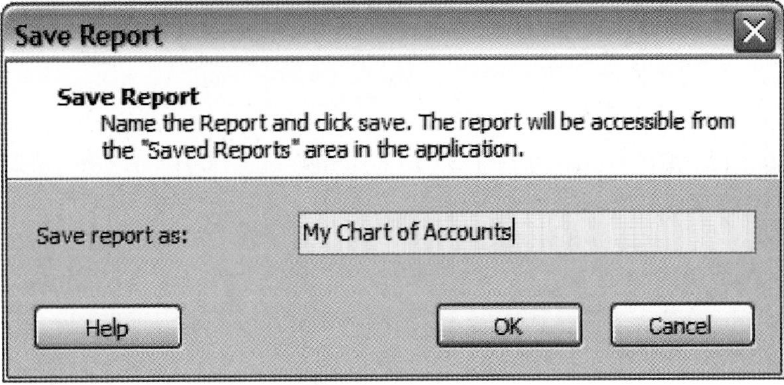

Figure 2:30

From the Reports Home page select the **Saved Reports** category to find your customized report. In addition, this report now appears under ***Reports>>Saved Reports*** on the main menu.

When you no longer need a customized report, delete it by highlighting the report name on the Reports Home page and pressing **Delete** on your keyboard or clicking **X** on the toolbar.

Double click to reopen **My Chart of Accounts**. In the next topic you will learn to email and export reports.

Exporting and Emailing Reports

Your professor may want you to export reports to Excel and then email the workbook. *(Note: You must have Microsoft's Excel software installed on the machine to complete this exercise.)*

With your customized COA report open, click the Excel icon on the report toolbar and the report opens in Excel. *(See Figure 2:31, illustrating the workbook in Excel 2007. We will also provide commands for earlier versions of the software.)* Scroll to the bottom of the report. *(Hint: Using the shortcut key of **Ctrl+End** will jump to the end of the report.)*

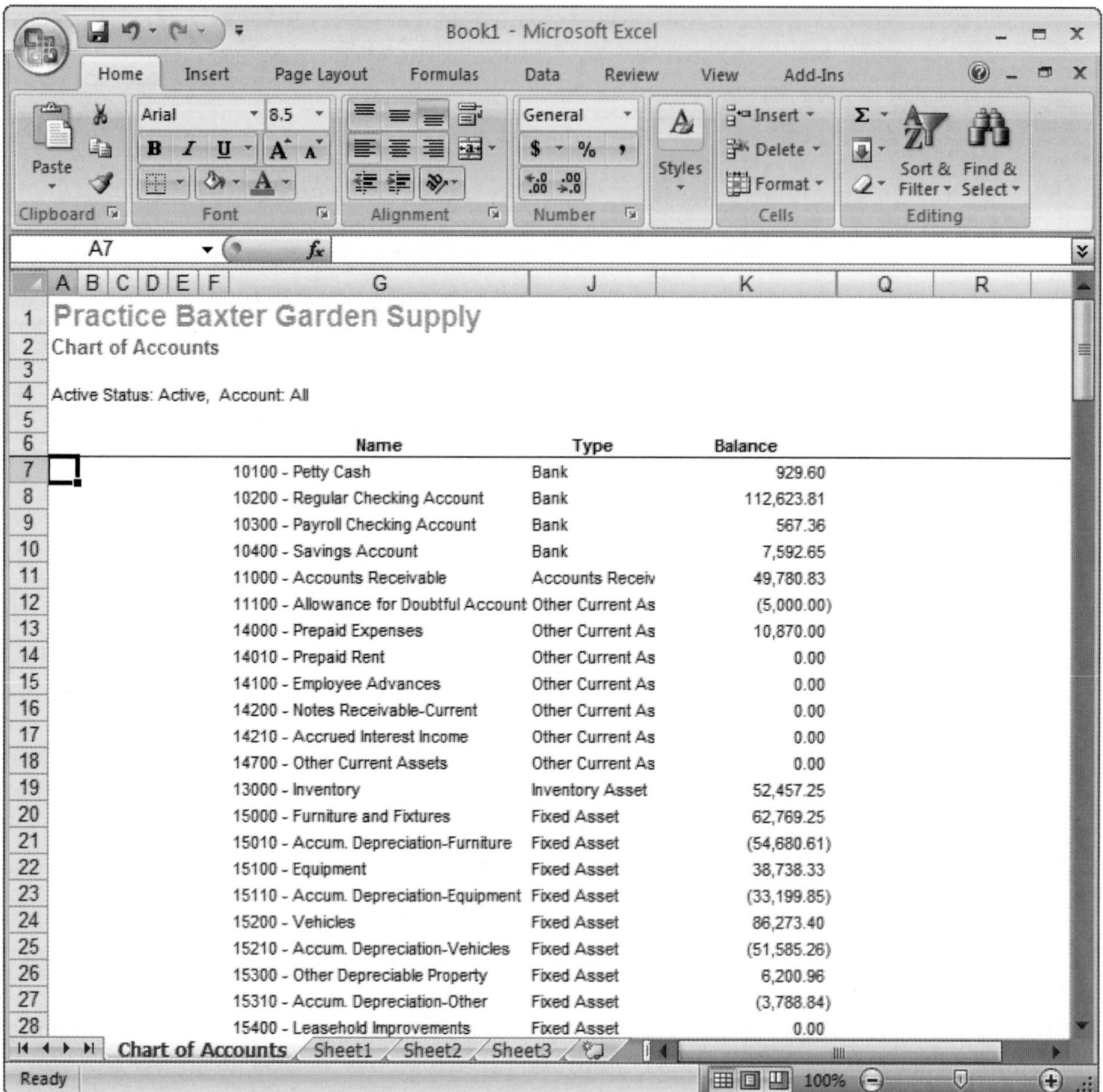

Practice Baxter Garden Supply
Chart of Accounts

Active Status: Active, Account: All

Name	Type	Balance
10100 - Petty Cash	Bank	929.60
10200 - Regular Checking Account	Bank	112,623.81
10300 - Payroll Checking Account	Bank	567.36
10400 - Savings Account	Bank	7,592.65
11000 - Accounts Receivable	Accounts Receiv	49,780.83
11100 - Allowance for Doubtful Account	Other Current As	(5,000.00)
14000 - Prepaid Expenses	Other Current As	10,870.00
14010 - Prepaid Rent	Other Current As	0.00
14100 - Employee Advances	Other Current As	0.00
14200 - Notes Receivable-Current	Other Current As	0.00
14210 - Accrued Interest Income	Other Current As	0.00
14700 - Other Current Assets	Other Current As	0.00
13000 - Inventory	Inventory Asset	52,457.25
15000 - Furniture and Fixtures	Fixed Asset	62,769.25
15010 - Accum. Depreciation-Furniture	Fixed Asset	(54,680.61)
15100 - Equipment	Fixed Asset	38,738.33
15110 - Accum. Depreciation-Equipment	Fixed Asset	(33,199.85)
15200 - Vehicles	Fixed Asset	86,273.40
15210 - Accum. Depreciation-Vehicles	Fixed Asset	(51,585.26)
15300 - Other Depreciable Property	Fixed Asset	6,200.96
15310 - Accum. Depreciation-Other	Fixed Asset	(3,788.84)
15400 - Leasehold Improvements	Fixed Asset	0.00

Figure 2:31

Save the Excel workbook. Click the **Office Icon** and select ***Save As>>Excel Workbook***. *(Note: In earlier versions you select **File>>Save As** on the menu.)* Choose **My Documents** as the folder and type “Baxter COA” as the file name (Figure 2:32). Click **Save**.

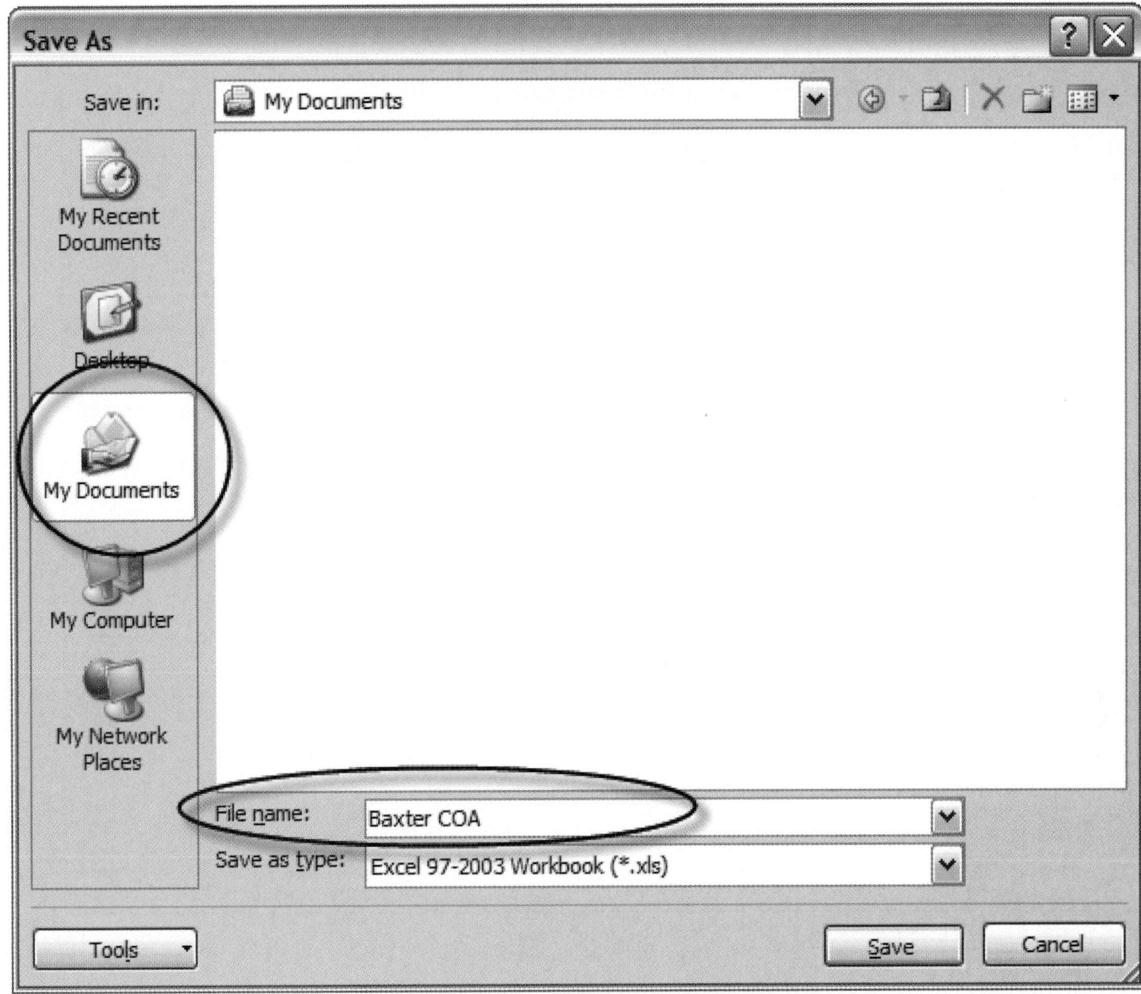

Figure 2:32

Now practice emailing the workbook. First, connect to the Internet and open your email software.

From within Excel, click the **Office Icon** and select ***File>>Send>>Email***. *(Note: If using an earlier version, select **File>>Send To** and choose **Mail Recipient (as Attachment)**).* When the message opens (Figure 2:33) enter your email address in the **To** field and click **Send**. Check your email later to verify delivery.

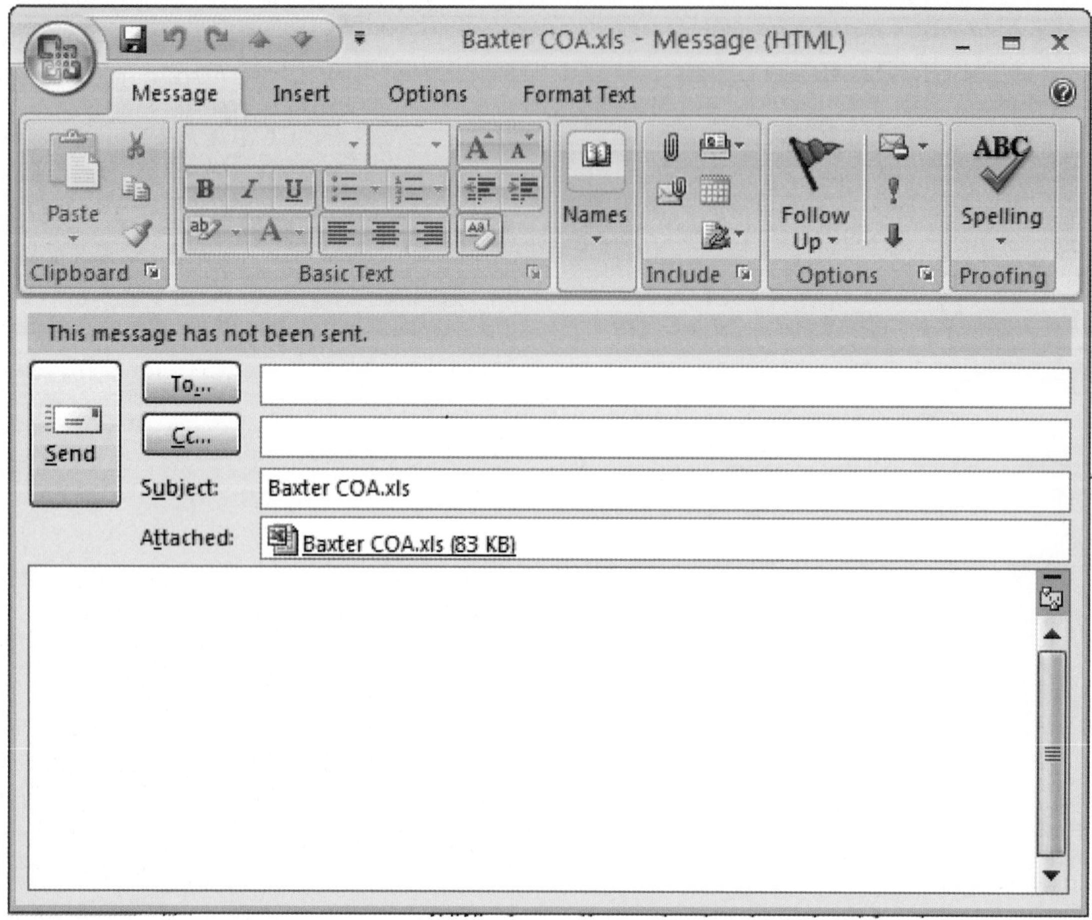

Figure 2:33

Close the Excel workbook and return to the COA report.

You can also email the report directly from OAP. Click the Email icon on the report toolbar and OAP opens the same email window previously illustrated.

Close all open reports and complete the next topic that discusses accounting periods.

Managing Accounting Periods

One final topic and you have covered OAP basics. Accounting transactions can only be posted to open accounting periods. Recall from an earlier topic, information on the accounting period is stored under ***Company>>Preferences*** on the main menu. Make this menu selection and focus your attention to the **Prevent posting before** field on the Company tab. (See Figure 2:34.)

Fiscal year

Prevent posting before: 3/1/2008 Fiscal Year

Figure 2:34

Baxter's books are closed as of 2/28/2008 because OAP is set to prevent posting prior to 3/1/2008. To close an accounting period you merely enter a different date in the **Prevent posting before** field.

Click **Cancel** to exit this window.

You should always close an accounting period after finalizing transactions and issuing financial reports. Closing the period protects the integrity of reported data by preventing erroneous postings to the reported period. However, there is another key point to keep in mind. While you can prevent posting to prior months, you cannot prevent posting to future months. Therefore, be very careful to enter correct dates on transactions.

You have now completed this chapter so ***make a backup of Practice Baxter Garden Supply data file to a backup file named "practicebaxtergardensupply Chpt 2." In the next chapter, you build on the work completed in this chapter.***

SUMMARY

You began the chapter by reviewing and printing the chart of accounts. You then reviewed Baxter's general ledger framework used to define the company's general ledger accounts. With this information, you were able to create a new general ledger account.

You next looked *Behind the Keys* to OAP options that control transaction processing. You worked with drilldown features on reports and the Find feature on lists to locate posted transactions. You also worked with reports and learned to customize, export, and email reports. You ended by learning to recognize the open accounting period and the method used to close a period.

Make sure that you feel comfortable with these topics before moving on to subsequent chapters. The background information covered in this chapter forms the basis for many of the tasks performed later in the text.

END-OF-CHAPTER QUESTIONS

TRUE/FALSE

_____ 1. An accounting period is closed by clicking the Fiscal Year button on the Company tab of the Company Preferences window.

_____ 2. Sales tax reporting is activated under the Company Preferences window.

_____ 3. After closing a year, you can reopen it and make adjusting entries.

_____ 4. OAP uses system accounts to set default general ledger accounts used when posting transactions.

_____ 5. The Cash Discount Taken system account is used for posting discounts taken by customers.

_____ 6. Customized reports are saved under the Saved Reports category.

_____ 7. Reports from any category are available on the Reports Home page.

_____ 8. You can add new general ledger accounts using a link located at the top of the COA list.

_____ 9. For Baxter, the first digit of the general ledger account number identifies the account category.

_____ 10. The COA list and the Trial Balance contain the same information.

MULTIPLE CHOICE

_____ 1. For Baxter, the general ledger account linked to the Retained Earnings system account is _____.

a. 39003
b. 39100
c. 30000
d. 39008

_____ 2. The _____ menu is used for entering sales invoices.
   a. Customers
   b. Company
   c. Banking
   d. Vendors

_____ 3. Financial statements are printed from the _____ menu.
   a. Company
   b. Reports
   c. Employees
   d. Customers

_____ 4. The COA list can be viewed using _____.
   a. the Find segment on the Company Home page
   b. the ***Company>>Company Lists*** menu
   c. the keyboard shortcut **Ctrl+Shift+A**
   d. all of the above

_____ 5. Baxter's general ledger account for recording accounts payable transactions is _____.
   a. 23200
   b. 20000
   c. 23700
   d. 23000

_____ 6. To print a range of accounts on the COA report, select _____.
   a. the Filter Options link at the top of the report
   b. the Columns link on the Modify Report pane
   c. the Header and Footer link on the Modify Report pane
   d. none of the above

_____ 7. To print a report's creation date, you activate the Date Created option found under the _____.
   a. Filter Options link at the top of the report
   b. Columns link contained under the Modify Report window
   c. Header and Footer link contained under the Modify Report window
   d. none of the above

CHAPTER 3 GENERAL JOURNAL TRANSACTIONS AND REPORTS

LEARNING OBJECTIVES

This chapter introduces OAP general journal entries and works the **Practice TEK Business** data file customized with your initials at the end of Chapter 1. ***When this data file is not loaded on your computer, restore it using the "practicetekbusiness Chpt1" backup file created in the Practice Set at the end of Chapter 1.***

In the chapter you will:

1. Learn manual accounting procedures (*MAPS)* for recording general journal entries before posting entries in OAP
2. Post basic and complex general journal entries
3. Look *Behind the Keys* at posted transactions
4. Enter adjusting entries
5. Print general journal and general ledger reports
6. Print the trial balance and financial statements
7. Close an accounting period

Launch OAP and open **Practice TEK Business**.

MANUAL ACCOUNTING PROCEDURES

TEK is a start-up company that began business on January 1, 2008. The company provides technology consulting services and made its first cash sale on January 2, 2008.

Before attempting to record this transaction, refresh your memory on using the T-Account method for balancing accounting entries. This method applied to TEK's cash sale is illustrated next.

Regular Checking Account

Dr.	Cr.
$1,000	

Consulting Income

Dr.	Cr.
	$1,000

Accountants with years of experience still rely on this method to visualize entries before recording a complicated transaction. You should also rely on this method when encountering new and complicated exercises in the text.

You will now become acquainted with the manual accounting procedures (*MAPS*) for recording a sale using general journal entries. With *MAPS*, the accountant would record the journal entry on the general journal illustrated in Figure 3:1.

Audit trail

TEK Business
General Journal **Page 2**

Date	Account Post Ref.	Description	Debit	Credit
1/02/2008	10100	Regular Checking Account	1,000.00	
	40000	Consulting Income		1,000.00

To record cash sale.

Figure 3:1

The entry lists the transaction date, general ledger account numbers and descriptions, and the debit and credit amount. The entry balances and the account number forms part of the audit trail documenting this transaction. Finally, the transaction was recorded on the second page of general journal and this page number becomes part of the audit trail in the next illustration.

After posting this entry on the general journal, the accountant next posts it to the general ledger accounts listed on the entry. These postings are illustrated in Figure 3:2.

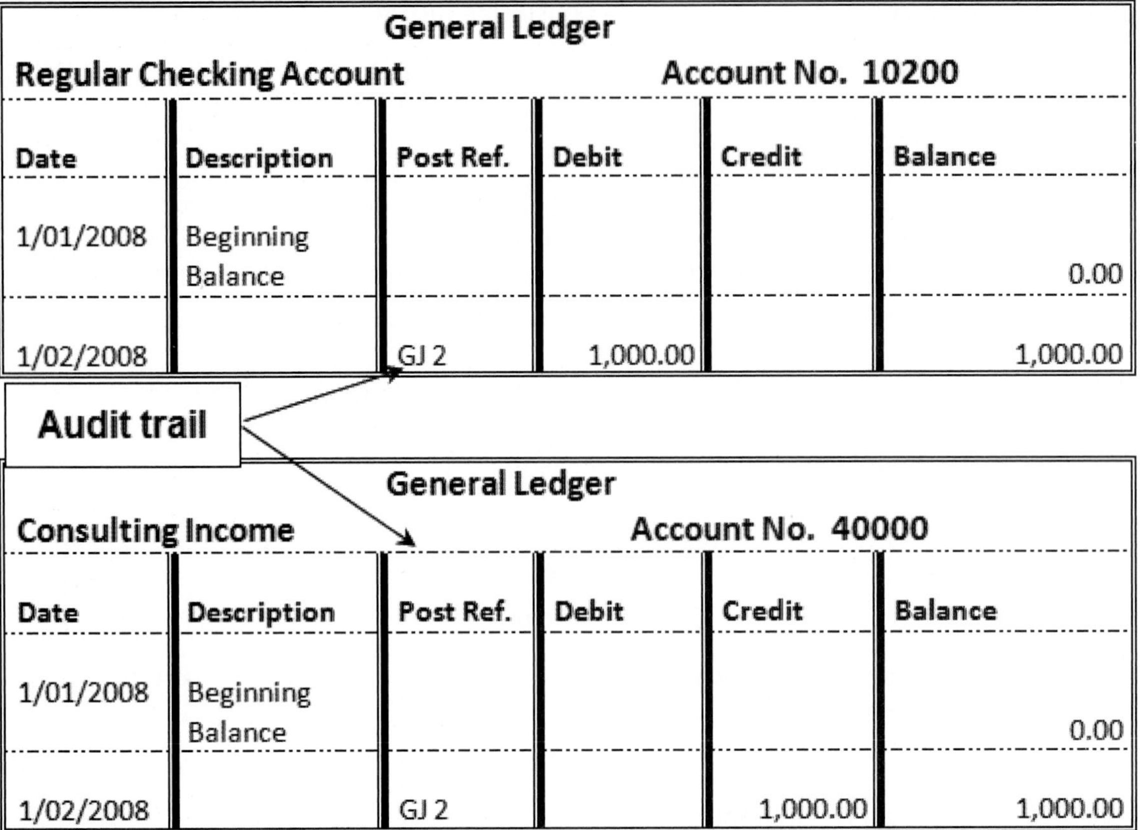

General Ledger

Regular Checking Account — **Account No. 10200**

Date	Description	Post Ref.	Debit	Credit	Balance
1/01/2008	Beginning Balance				0.00
1/02/2008		GJ 2	1,000.00		1,000.00

General Ledger

Consulting Income — **Account No. 40000**

Date	Description	Post Ref.	Debit	Credit	Balance
1/01/2008	Beginning Balance				0.00
1/02/2008		GJ 2		1,000.00	1,000.00

Figure 3:2

While posting entries on the general ledger, an audit trail is entered to cross-reference originating entry on the general journal. GJ 2 means that the entry originated on General Journal page 2. The audit trail becomes the path for tracing entries between the general journal and the general ledger.

Basic Journal Entries

In this topic you learn to post general journal entries in OAP. In the exercise that follows you post TEK's cash sale journal entry illustrated in the *MAPS* topic. Before starting the exercise read the following data entry tips.

Data Entry Tips	
Data manipulation	You can copy and cut text in a transaction window by highlighting it and clicking the Edit menu on the transaction window. You can also paste text or undo changes using this menu.
Deleting and inserting transaction lines	Highlight the row, right click, and select Delete to delete transaction lines. If you select Insert, a blank transaction line is inserted above the highlighted transaction line. Voucher No. Date Type Delete 1/2/2008 Financial Account Insert 1/2/2008 Financial Account **Figure 3:3**
Save and Close	Saves the transaction and exits the transaction window.
Save and New	Saves the transaction and clears the window for entering the next transaction.
	Prints the transaction.
	Close the transaction window. If you click **X** on an unsaved transaction OAP prompts to save the entry. When answering the prompt, choosing **Yes** closes the window and **saves** the entry; **No** closes the window **without saving** the entry; and **Cancel** returns you to the transaction window.

Steps to Posting a Journal Entry

1. From the Company Home page, click the **New Journal Entry** link under **Start a Task** to open the Journal Entry window (Figure 3:4). *(Note: You can also select **Company>>New Journal Entry** on the main menu.)*

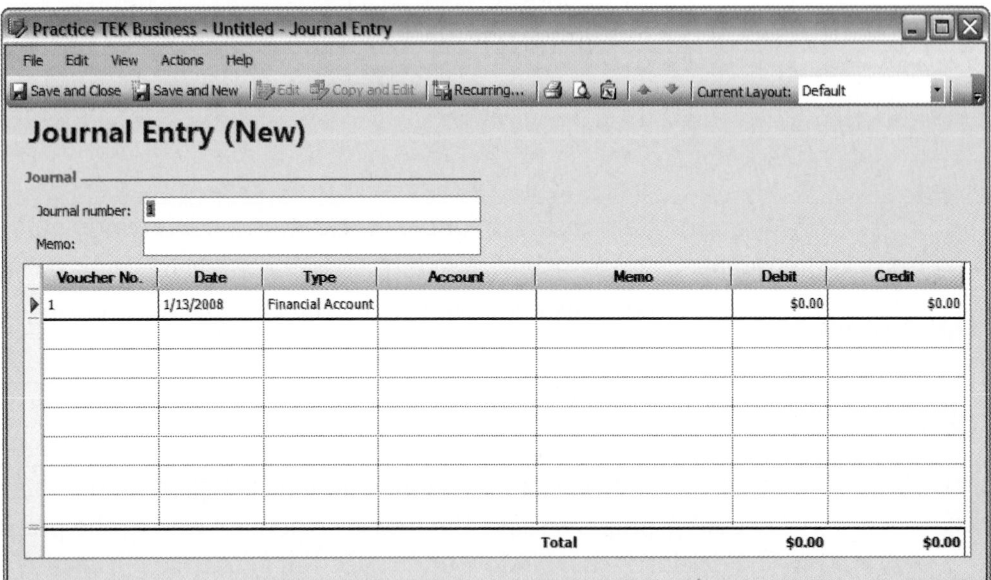

Figure 3:4

Notice that **Journal number** contains a "1" meaning this is the first journal entry in the data file. OAP automatically increments journal numbers each time you post an entry.

2. Tab to the **Memo** field and enter "Cash fees earned" to document the transaction. Then tab to the **Voucher No.** field. These numbers can be used for referring to external documentation supporting the entry. When working exercises in the text accept the default Voucher No. supplied by OAP.

3. Tab to the **Date** field and enter "1/02/2008." This is the posting date of the transaction. When opening a transaction window OAP enters your computer's system date. ***You must always check the transaction date to verify that transactions will be posted to the correct accounting period.***

4. Tab to the **Type** field. This field determines whether the transaction posts to a Financial Account (general ledger account) or Vendor, Customer, or Tax Code account. Always keep the Financial Account selection when posting journal entries in the text.

5. Tab to the **Account** field. Click the dropdown list and select "Regular Checking Account" or type "re" to advance the dropdown list to the checking account. Tab to the **Memo** field and enter "Cash sale" as additional text to describe this transaction.

6. Tab to the **Debit** field and enter "1000." Press Tab and OAP enters the decimal point, changing the value to 1,000.00. When entering whole dollar amounts you can omit typing in the decimal point and cents. However, when a transaction involves cents (i.e., $5,123.25), you must enter the amount by including the decimal point (i.e., 5123.25).

7. Your cursor is now in the **Credit** field. Press Tab to open the next transaction line and OAP enters the same Voucher No. and Date as the previous line. OAP allows entering multiple transactions for different dates on the same journal entry; however, each transaction must balance before you can enter a different date or voucher number.

8. Tab to **Account** and select "Consulting Income."

9. Press Tab and OAP supplies the 1,000.00 **Credit** needed to balance the entry. OAP will not post an out-of-balance entry. The completed transaction appears in Figure 3:5.

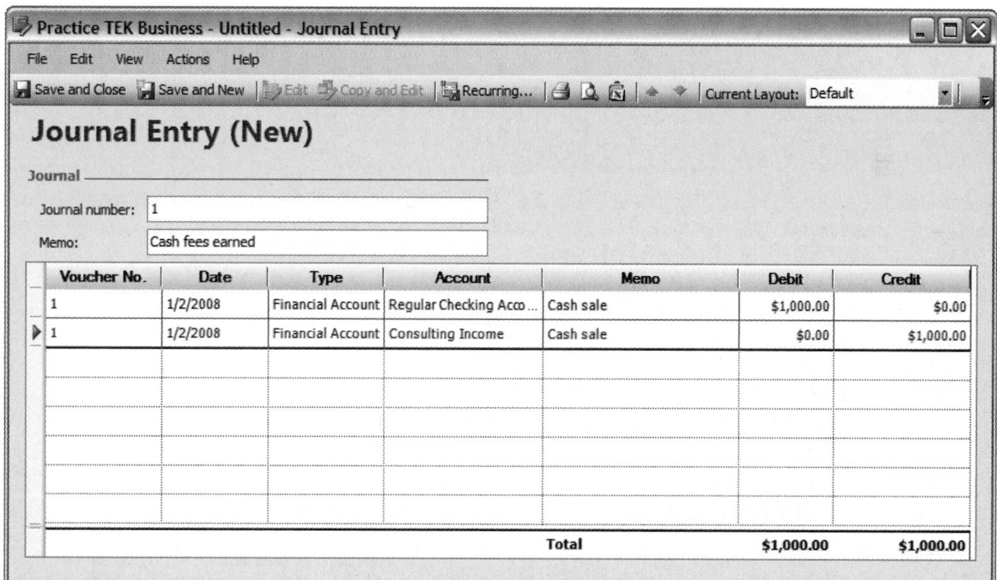

Figure 3:5

10. Click **Save and Close** to post the entry and exit the transaction entry window.

Upon returning to the Company Home page, click this refresh icon on the Toolbar to update the balance in the checking account. (See Figure 3:6.)

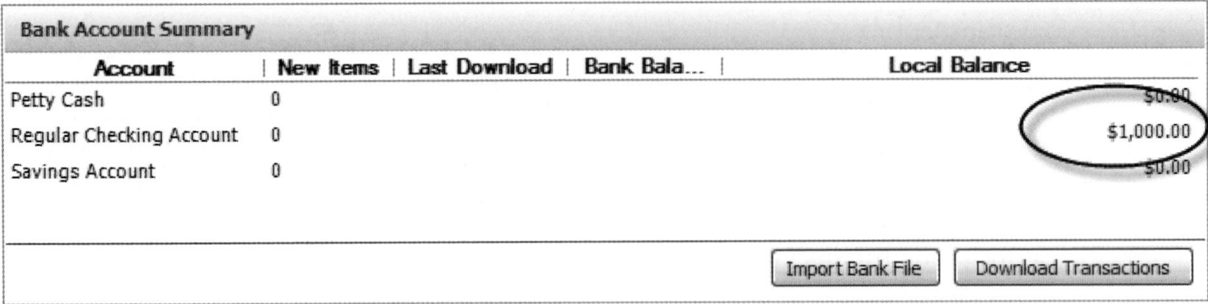

Bank Account Summary				
Account	New Items	Last Download	Bank Bala...	Local Balance
Petty Cash	0			$0.00
Regular Checking Account	0			$1,000.00
Savings Account	0			$0.00

Import Bank File | Download Transactions

Figure 3:6

Behind the Keys of a Posted Journal Entry

In this topic, you trace the *Behind the Keys* Sentries for the cash sale posted in the previous topic. Select ***Reports>>Company and Financial>>Transaction Journal*** on the main menu. Enter the reporting date range of **From 1/2/2008** and **To 1/2/2008**.

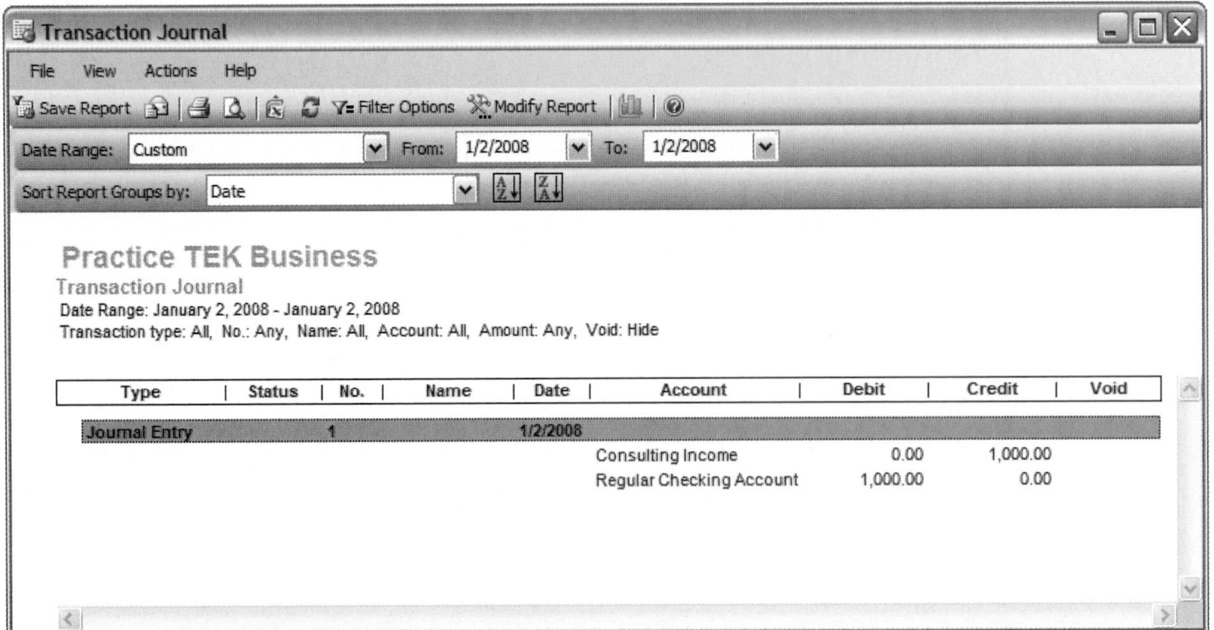

Type	Status	No.	Name	Date	Account	Debit	Credit	Void
Journal Entry		1		1/2/2008				
					Consulting Income	0.00	1,000.00	
					Regular Checking Account	1,000.00	0.00	

Figure 3:7

Figure 3:7 is OAP's version of the general journal illustrated in the *MAPS* topic. The audit trail code is listed under the No. column. You can highlight the Journal Entry line and double click to reopen the posted transaction.

To view OAP's postings to the general ledger, select ***Reports>>Company and Financial>> Transaction Detail by Account*** on the main menu and enter the same date range of "1/2/2008." The report (Figure 3:8) lists the two accounts affected by the transaction and the No. column displays the same audit trail code as the previous report.

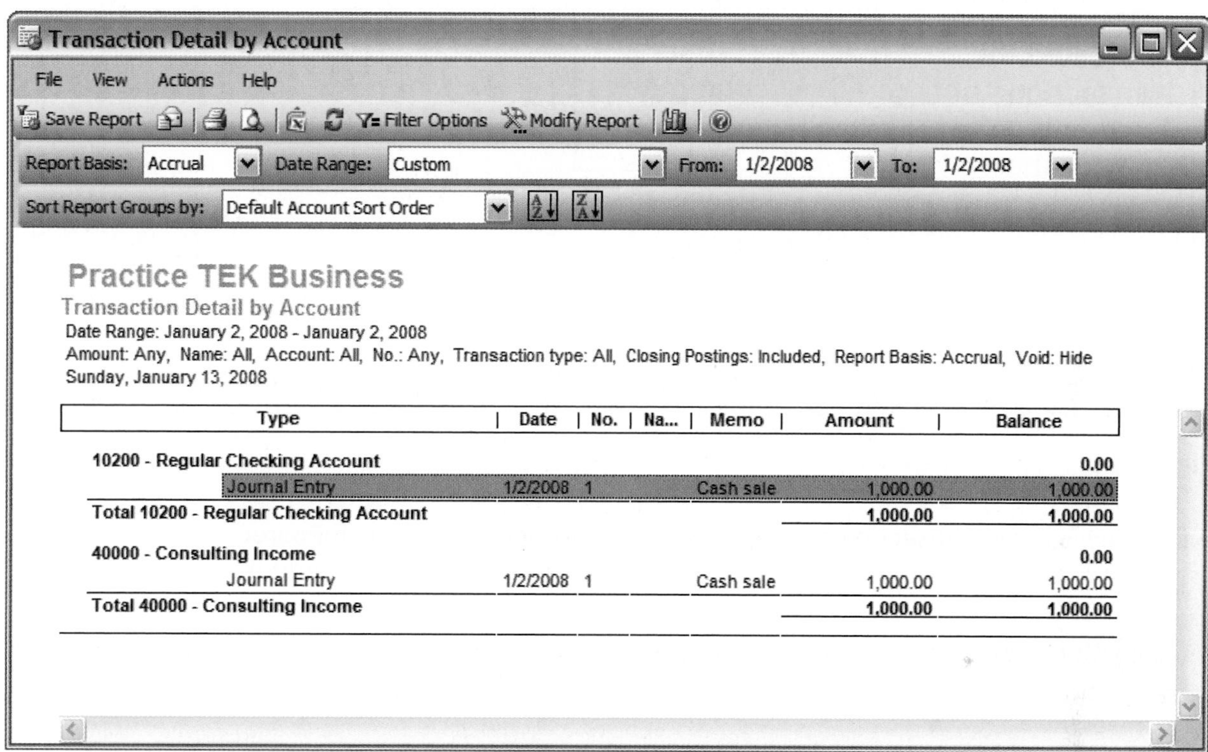

Practice TEK Business
Transaction Detail by Account
Date Range: January 2, 2008 - January 2, 2008
Amount: Any, Name: All, Account: All, No.: Any, Transaction type: All, Closing Postings: Included, Report Basis: Accrual, Void: Hide
Sunday, January 13, 2008

Type	Date	No.	Na...	Memo	Amount	Balance
10200 - Regular Checking Account						**0.00**
Journal Entry	1/2/2008	1		Cash sale	1,000.00	1,000.00
Total 10200 - Regular Checking Account					**1,000.00**	**1,000.00**
40000 - Consulting Income						**0.00**
Journal Entry	1/2/2008	1		Cash sale	1,000.00	1,000.00
Total 40000 - Consulting Income					**1,000.00**	**1,000.00**

Figure 3:8

Keep these reports open to complete the next topic.

Correcting a Posted Journal Entry

It is easy to correct a posted journal entry in OAP. First, you locate the posted journal entry using either a report or the Journal Entry List (Figure 3:9). Open this list by clicking **Journal Entries** under **Find** on the Company Home page.

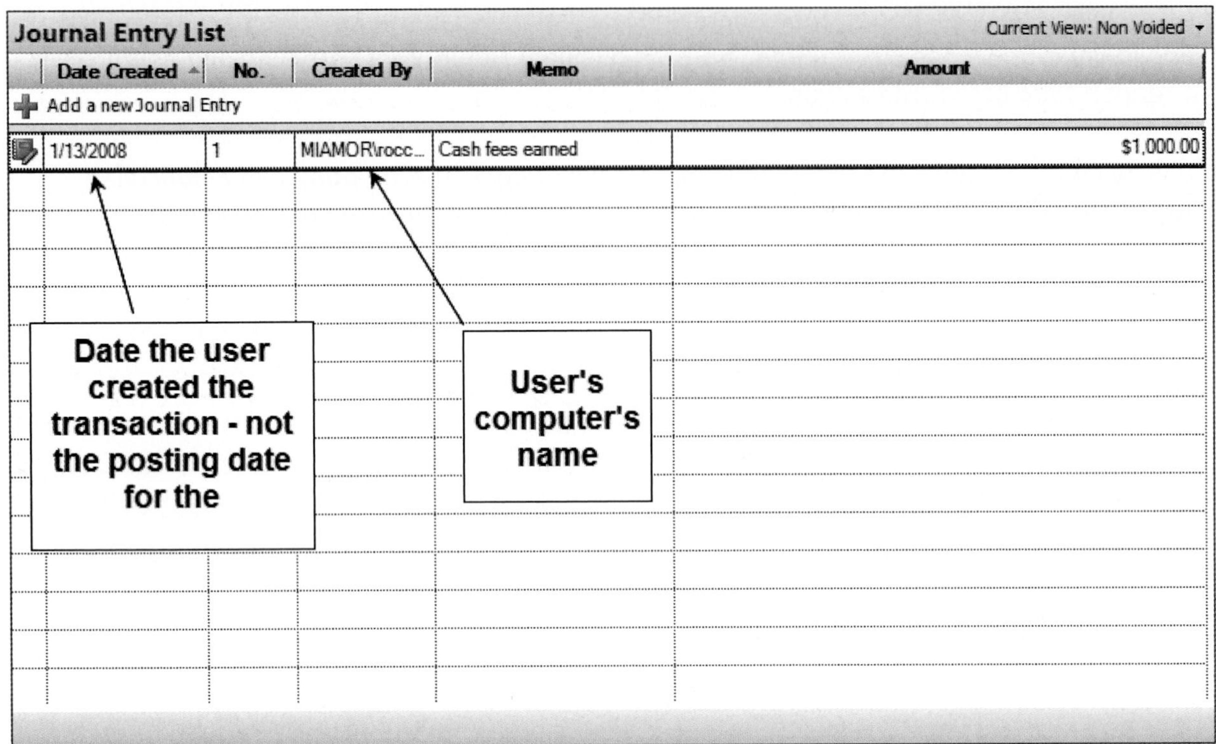

Figure 3:9

Double click the transaction to reopen it. The transaction is marked **Posted** and data fields are grayed out (not illustrated). You must reopen the transaction to edit it.

Click **Edit** on the toolbar to reopen the transaction. Click the **Memo** field for the second transaction line and change the description to "Cash fees" (Figure 3:10).

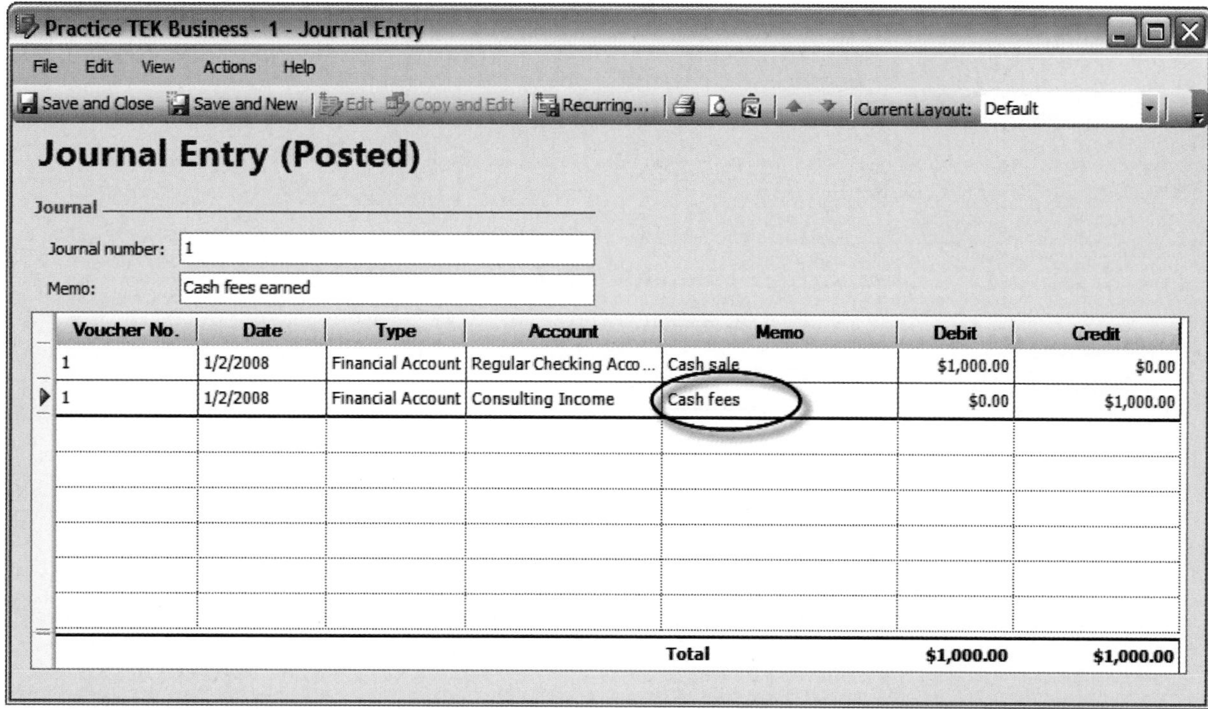

Figure 3:10

Click **Save and Close** to repost the entry.

Return to the **Transaction Journal** report that remained open from the previous topic and click **Yes** to refresh the report. Click the **Filter Options** button and highlight the **Void** filter. Select the **Show** option (Figure 3:11) and click **OK**.

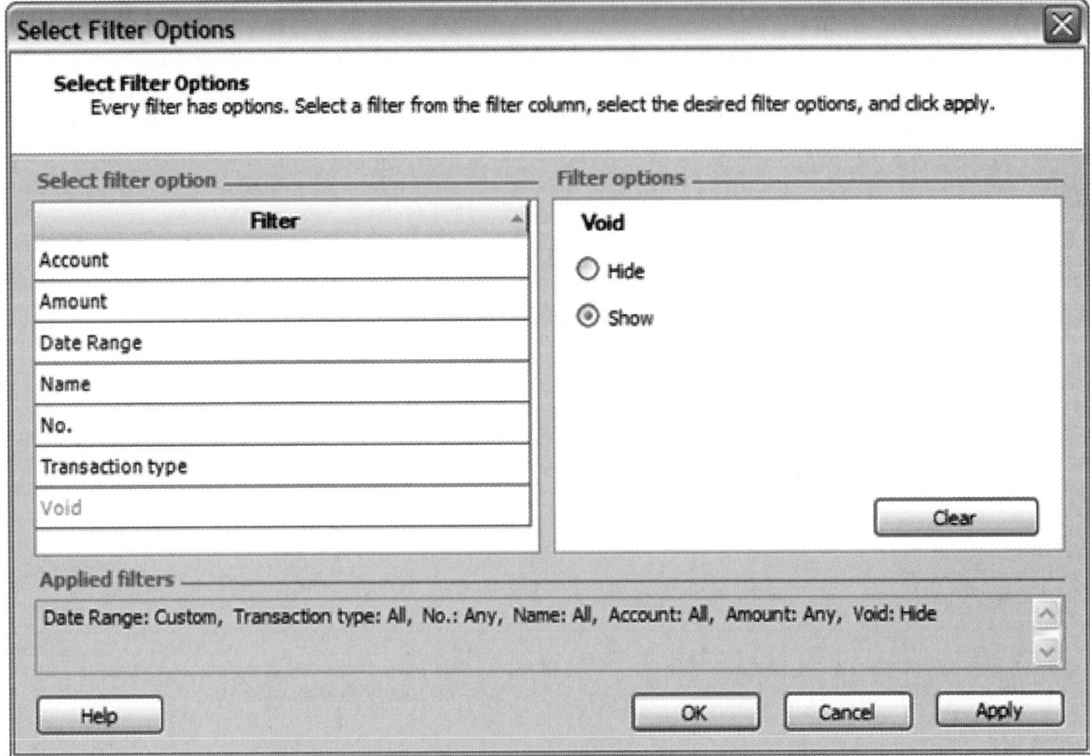

Figure 3:11

Notice that OAP voided the original transaction by creating a transaction that reversed it (Figure 3:12). Click **X** to close the report. Select the option to turn off future warnings for saving changes to a report and click **No**.

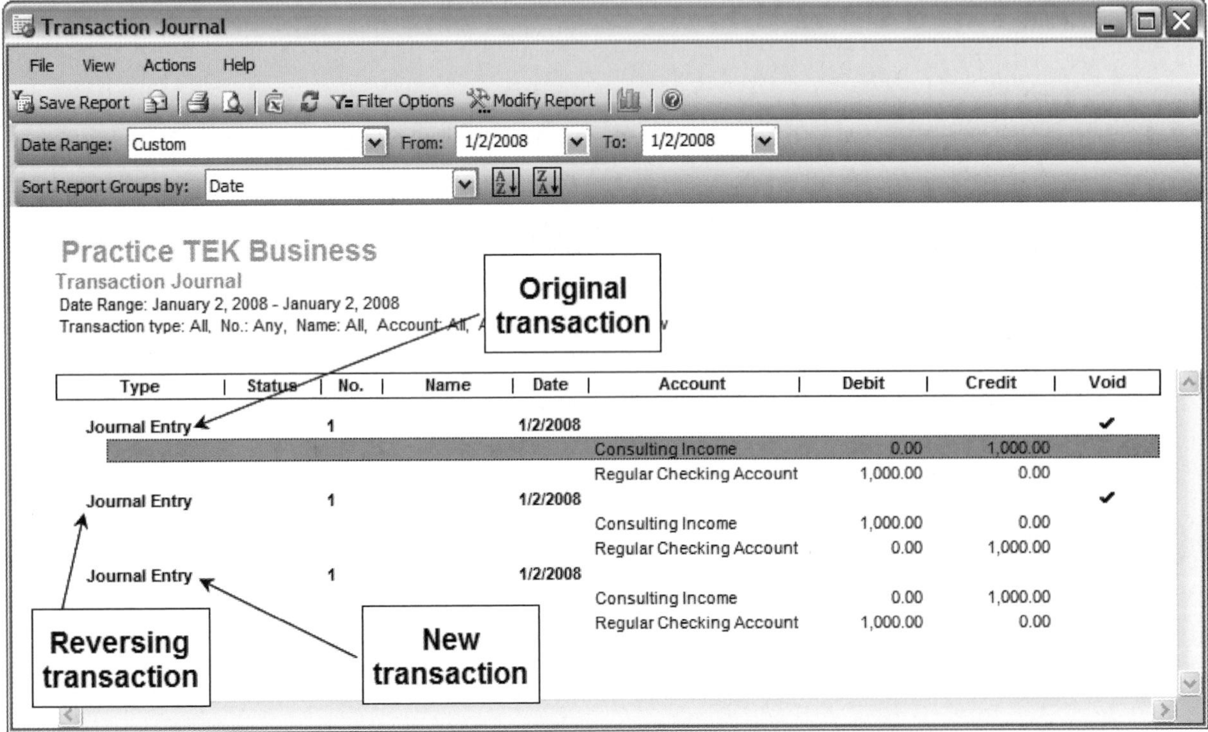

Figure 3:12

Return to the **Transaction Detail by Account** report opened in the previous topic and click **Yes** to refresh it. Use the Filter Options to again show voided transactions.

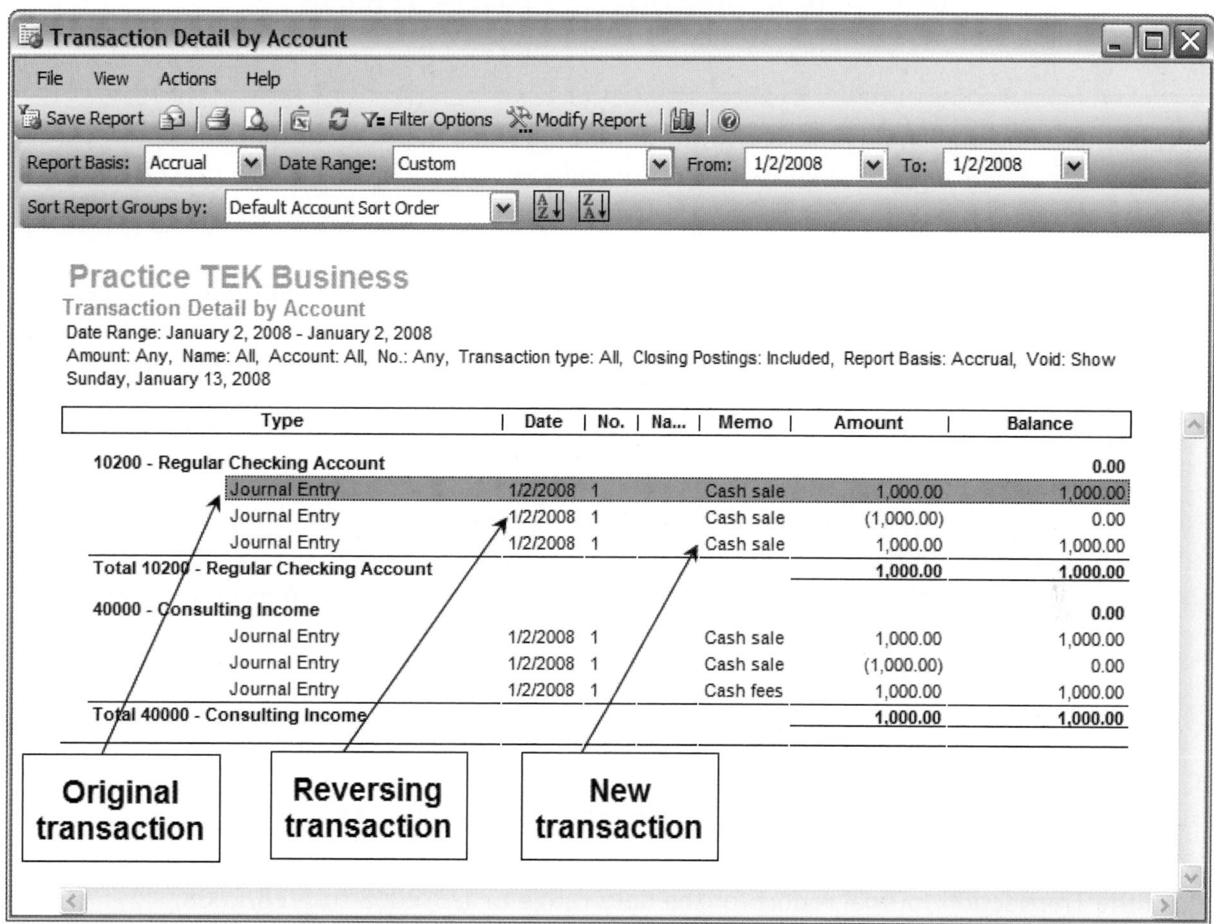

Figure 3:13

Figure 3:13 again shows that OAP posted an entry reversing the original transaction to void the original transaction.

In the future you may want to remove a posted journal entry instead of correcting it. Posted transactions are removed by voiding. The easiest method for voiding is highlighting a transaction on the Journal Entry list, right clicking, and selecting **Void**.

Close the Transaction Detail by Account report and then complete the next exercise.

RECORD TEK'S JANUARY TRANSACTIONS

Record the following January entries on the general journal. Remember that you can record multiple transactions in the same Journal Entry window, but each transaction must balance before entering the next.

You can use "January transactions" for the Memo field at the top of the entry and then enter a unique Memo description for transaction lines. When the transaction lists a check number, include this number in the description. All entries affect the Regular Checking Account.

2008 Jan.	
3	Owner deposit to open Regular Checking Account, $5,000.
4	Check number 171 for office supplies expense, $250.
7	Check number 172 for two months of rent, $500. (Hint: Use prepaid expense account)
9	Cash received for fees earned, $1,375.
15	Owner cash withdrawal from checking, $700.
21	Cash received for fees earned, $625.
23	Check number 173 for telephone bill, $195.
28	January salaries paid from Regular Checking Account, $975.

Print the Transaction Journal report for the date range of 1/3/2008 to 1/28/2008.

COMPOUND JOURNAL ENTRIES

Thus far you have recorded simple journal entries using only two accounts. Often accountants record transactions affecting multiple accounts.

For instance, on January 30, 2008, TEK's owner made an additional investment in the company. She invested $7,000 in cash, a car valued at $10,000, and computer equipment valued at $12,000. Follow the next steps to record this transaction.

Steps to Record a Compound Journal Entry

1. Open a new journal entry.

2. Enter “Owner investment” as the Memo.

3. Tab to **Date** on the first line and enter “1/30/2008.” Tab to **Account** and select “Regular Checking Account.” Tab to **Memo** and enter “Owner cash contribution.” Tab to **Debit** and enter “7000.”

4. Tab to **Account** on the second line and select “Vehicle.” Tab to **Memo** and enter “Owner car contribution.” Tab to **Debit** and enter “10000.” (Note: You will be overriding OAP’s entry in the Credit field.)

5. Tab to **Account** on the third line and select “Office Equipment.” Tab to **Memo** and enter “Owner computer contribution.” Tab to the **Debit** field and enter “12000.”

6. Tab to **Account** on the fourth line and select “Owners Contribution.” OAP has entered “29,000.00” as the Credit amount. *(Note: If you do not have this amount, check your previous entries.)*

7. Tab to **Memo** and enter "Owner contribution cash, car, computer." The completed entry is illustrated below.

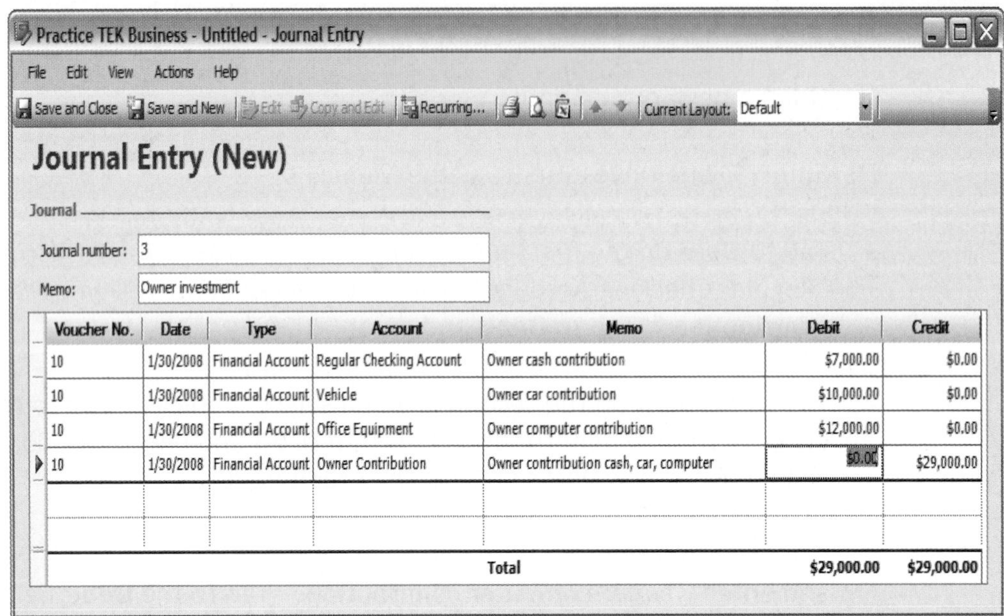

Practice TEK Business - Untitled - Journal Entry

File Edit View Actions Help

Save and Close | Save and New | Edit | Copy and Edit | Recurring... | Current Layout: Default

Journal Entry (New)

Journal

Journal number: 3

Memo: Owner investment

Voucher No.	Date	Type	Account	Memo	Debit	Credit
10	1/30/2008	Financial Account	Regular Checking Account	Owner cash contribution	$7,000.00	$0.00
10	1/30/2008	Financial Account	Vehicle	Owner car contribution	$10,000.00	$0.00
10	1/30/2008	Financial Account	Office Equipment	Owner computer contribution	$12,000.00	$0.00
10	1/30/2008	Financial Account	Owner Contribution	Owner contrribution cash, car, computer	$0.00	$29,000.00
				Total	$29,000.00	$29,000.00

Figure 3:14

8. Click **Save and New** and complete the next exercise.

RECORD ADDITIONAL JOURNAL ENTRIES

Record the following journal entries and remember to enter a memo description.

2008

Jan.

29 Check number 174 for six months of vehicle insurance, $1,200. *(Hint: Use prepaid expense account.)*

29 Check number 175 for office supplies expense of $210 and four desks for $3,250 recorded as office furniture.

29 Check number 176 for electricity expense (utilities expense), $375.

30 Cash received for fees earned, $2,376.

Print the Transaction Journal report for the date range of 1/29/2008 to 1/30/2008.

Adjusting Journal Entries

Adjusting entries are journal entries that adjust account balances in accounts such as prepaid expense or record non-cash expenses such as depreciation expense. After reviewing TEK's January transactions, the accountant asks you to post the following adjusting entries.

RECORD JANUARY'S ADJUSTING ENTRIES

Open the Journal Entry window and record the following adjusting entries for January 31, 2008.

a. Expense one month of prepaid rent, $250.
b. Post January depreciation expense of $235 posted as follows.

Office equipment, $120
Office furniture, $30
Vehicles, $85

Print the Transaction Journal report for January 31, 2008.

Print the Trial Balance

The Trial Balance report differs from the Chart of Accounts report illustrated in Chapter 2 because it totals columns by debits and credits to verify that general ledger accounts are "in balance." In a manual system, proving that the trial balance "balances" is critical because it forms the basis for preparing financial statements.

In a computerized system entries automatically balance. You have already seen that OAP will not post an out-of-balance entry. Therefore, accountants now use the trial balance to review account balances and to reconcile balances to external documents such as bank statements and asset reports.

Complete the following steps to print TEK's January Trial Balance report.

STEPS TO PRINT THE TRIAL BALANCE

1. Select ***Reports>>Company and Financial>>Trial Balance*** on the main menu. Enter 1/31/2008 as the date (Figure 3:15).

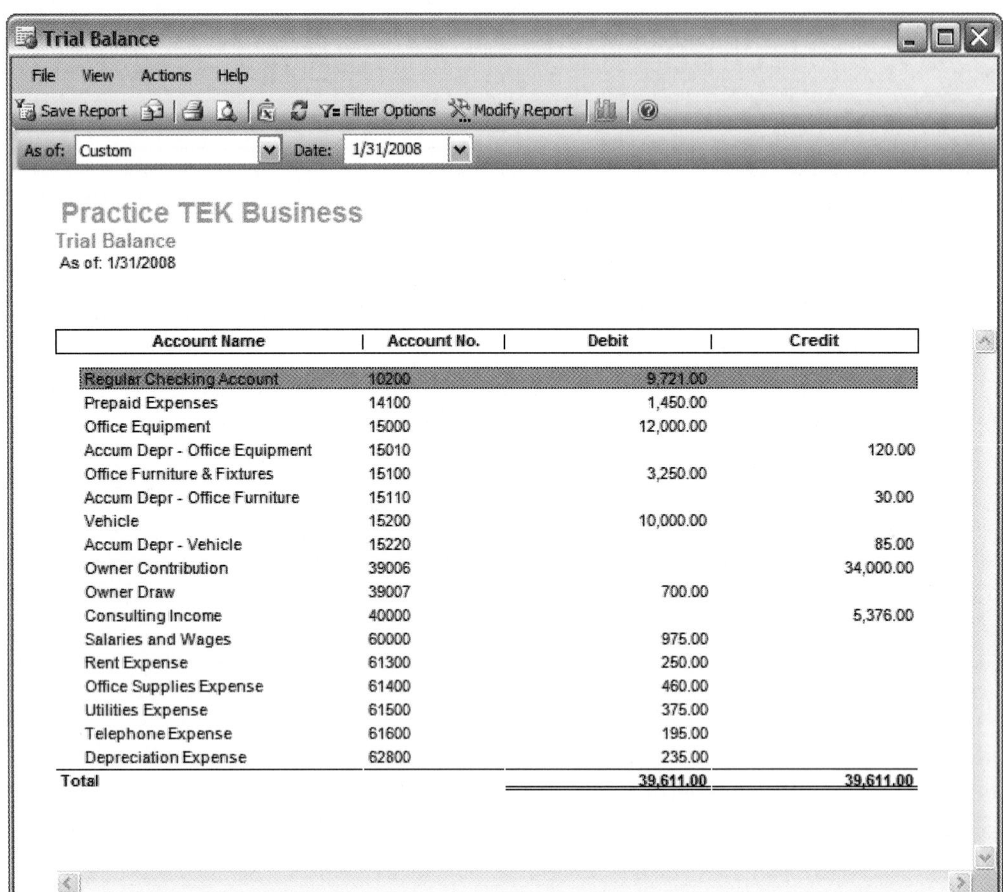

Account Name	Account No.	Debit	Credit
Regular Checking Account	10200	9,721.00	
Prepaid Expenses	14100	1,450.00	
Office Equipment	15000	12,000.00	
Accum Depr - Office Equipment	15010		120.00
Office Furniture & Fixtures	15100	3,250.00	
Accum Depr - Office Furniture	15110		30.00
Vehicle	15200	10,000.00	
Accum Depr - Vehicle	15220		85.00
Owner Contribution	39006		34,000.00
Owner Draw	39007	700.00	
Consulting Income	40000		5,376.00
Salaries and Wages	60000	975.00	
Rent Expense	61300	250.00	
Office Supplies Expense	61400	460.00	
Utilities Expense	61500	375.00	
Telephone Expense	61600	195.00	
Depreciation Expense	62800	235.00	
Total		39,611.00	39,611.00

Figure 3:15

2. Click the **Printer** icon, choose a printer, and click **OK** to print a hardcopy of the report.

3. Click **X** to close the report.

PRINT FINANCIAL STATEMENTS

Financial statements include the Income Statement and Balance Sheet as well as the Cash Flow Statement. *(Note: OAP refers to the Income Statement as the Profit and Loss Statement.)* In a manual system, the Income Statement is prepared first because net income or loss from this statement is needed to create the remaining statements.

With a computerized system financial statements may be printed in any order because the computer internally calculates the net income or loss used by other statements. Perform the next steps and print TEK's January Income Statement and Balance Sheet.

STEPS TO PRINT FINANCIAL STATEMENTS

1. Select ***Reports>>Company and Financial>>Profit and Loss*** on the main menu. Enter the date range of **From** 1/1/2008 **To** 1/31/2008 (Figure 3:16). Click **Print** to send the report to a printer. *(Note: Recall from Chapter 2 that you can also email and export reports.)* Close the report after noting January Net Income.

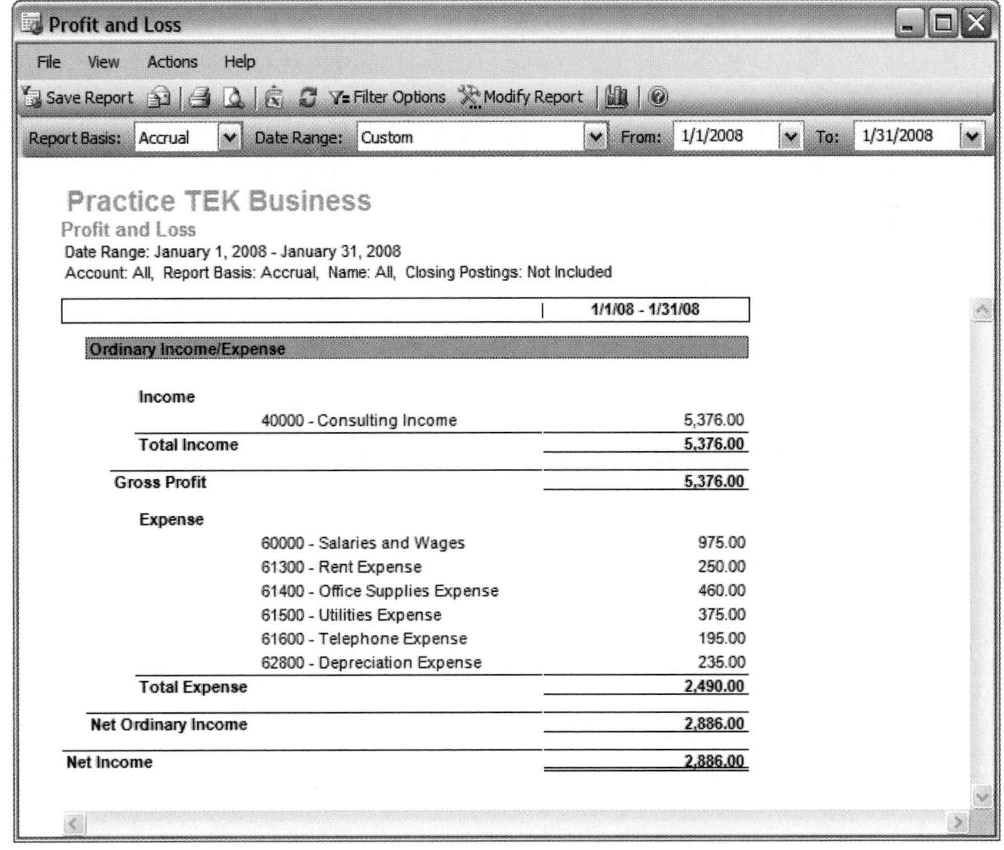

Profit and Loss
File View Actions Help
Save Report Filter Options Modify Report
Report Basis: Accrual Date Range: Custom From: 1/1/2008 To: 1/31/2008
Practice TEK Business
Profit and Loss
Date Range: January 1, 2008 - January 31, 2008
Account: All, Report Basis: Accrual, Name: All, Closing Postings: Not Included
1/1/08 - 1/31/08
Ordinary Income/Expense
Income
40000 - Consulting Income 5,376.00
Total Income 5,376.00
Gross Profit 5,376.00
Expense
60000 - Salaries and Wages 975.00
61300 - Rent Expense 250.00
61400 - Office Supplies Expense 460.00
61500 - Utilities Expense 375.00
61600 - Telephone Expense 195.00
62800 - Depreciation Expense 235.00
Total Expense 2,490.00
Net Ordinary Income 2,886.00
Net Income 2,886.00

Figure 3:16

2. Select ***Reports>>Company and Financial>>Balance Sheet*** on the main menu. Enter 1/31/2008 as the date. Close the report after noting net income on the statement.

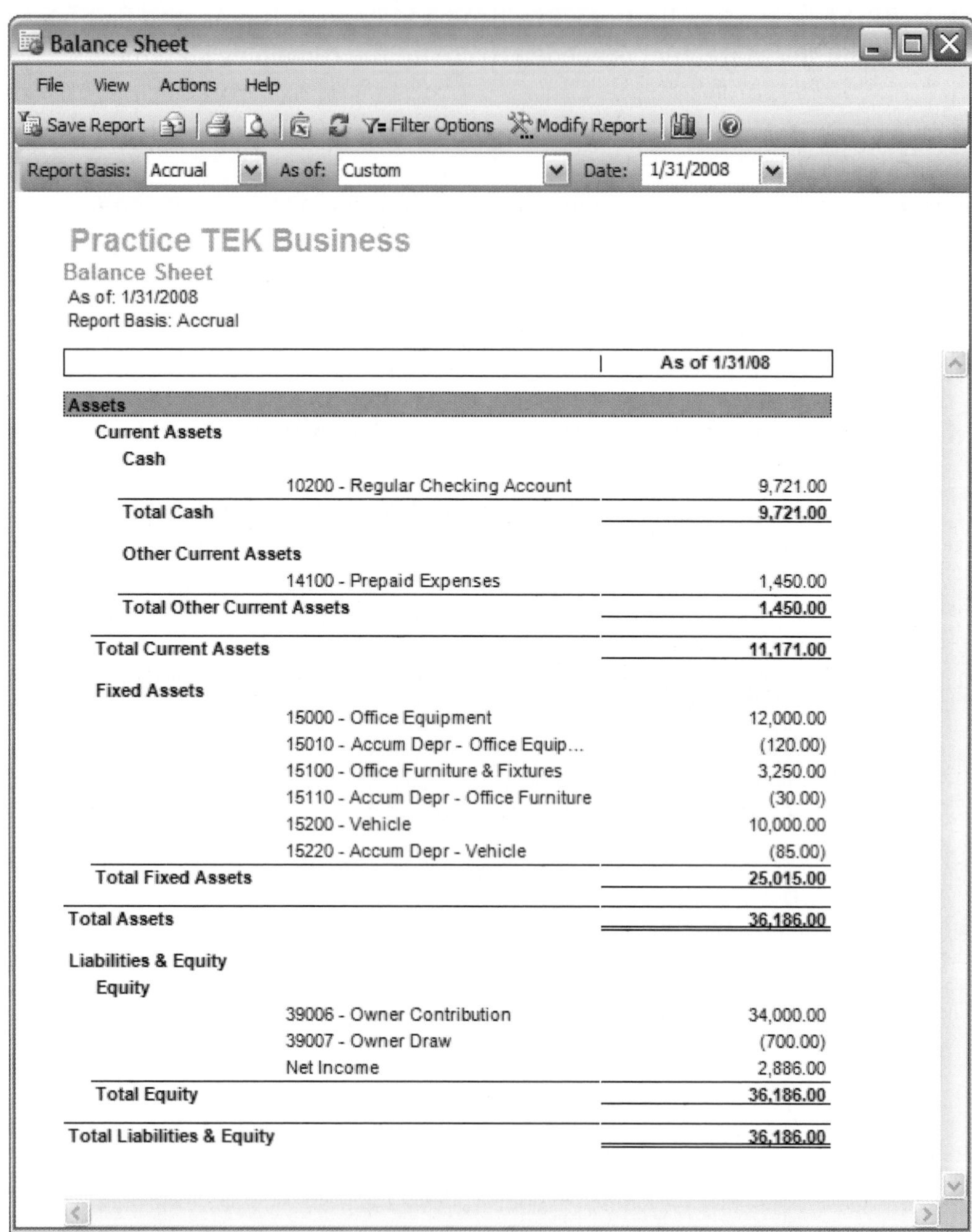

Practice TEK Business
Balance Sheet
As of: 1/31/2008
Report Basis: Accrual

	As of 1/31/08
Assets	
Current Assets	
Cash	
10200 - Regular Checking Account	9,721.00
Total Cash	**9,721.00**
Other Current Assets	
14100 - Prepaid Expenses	1,450.00
Total Other Current Assets	**1,450.00**
Total Current Assets	**11,171.00**
Fixed Assets	
15000 - Office Equipment	12,000.00
15010 - Accum Depr - Office Equip...	(120.00)
15100 - Office Furniture & Fixtures	3,250.00
15110 - Accum Depr - Office Furniture	(30.00)
15200 - Vehicle	10,000.00
15220 - Accum Depr - Vehicle	(85.00)
Total Fixed Assets	**25,015.00**
Total Assets	**36,186.00**
Liabilities & Equity	
Equity	
39006 - Owner Contribution	34,000.00
39007 - Owner Draw	(700.00)
Net Income	2,886.00
Total Equity	**36,186.00**
Total Liabilities & Equity	**36,186.00**

Figure 3:17

Close the Accounting Period

You should always close the accounting period after issuing financial statements to protect the integrity of printed reports. After closing, OAP will deny posting additional entries to the closed period.

With TEK's January reports issued, you are now ready to close the January accounting period. Before closing, you should always make a backup of the company's data file.

Perform a backup of the Practice TEK Business data file to a backup file named "practicetekbusiness Chpt 3."

You will now close the January accounting period.

Steps to Close an Accounting Period

1. Click ***Company>>Preferences*** on the main menu.

2. On the Company tab enter "2/1/2008" in the **Prevent posting before** field (Figure 3:18).

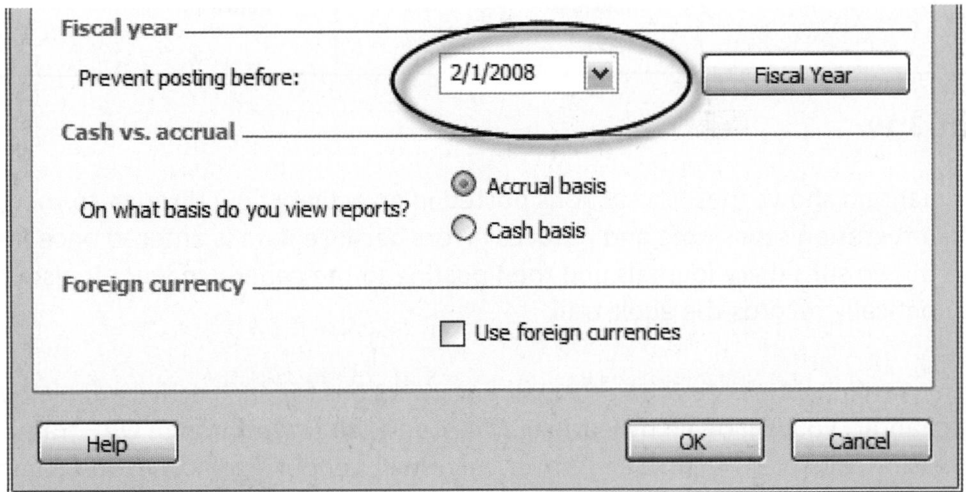

Figure 3:18

3. Click **OK.** You can no longer post transactions in January 2008.

Office Accounting Data Integration

Data integration explains why OAP simultaneously posts transactions to general ledger accounts and customer, vendor, employee, and banking accounts. Figure 3:19 visually depicts data integration.

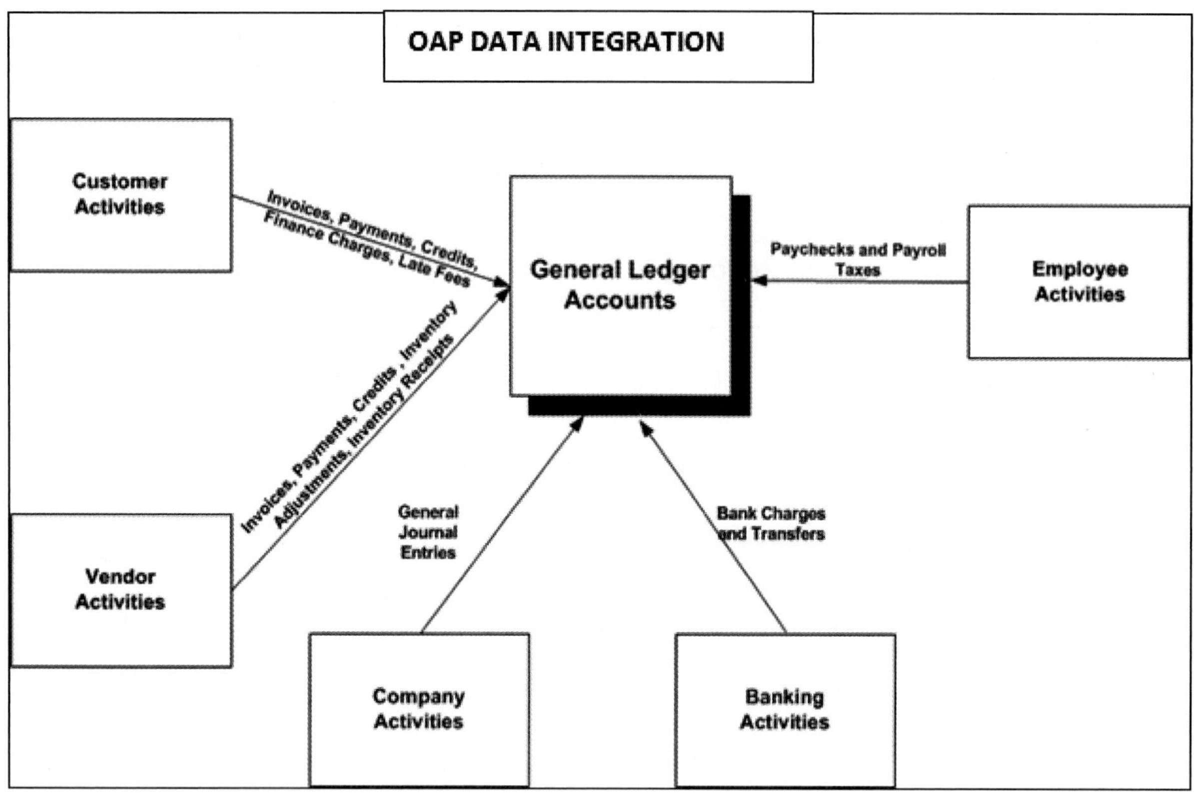

Figure 3:19

This diagram shows that transactions posted in an activity flow through to the general ledger. Data integration saves time and reduces errors because data is entered once instead of entering on subsidiary journals and then posting to the general ledger. It also means that OAP automatically records the audit trail.

Subsequent chapters focus on processing transactions for each activity depicted above. As in this chapter, you will begin by learning *MAPS* and then step through OAP transaction processing. Chapters 4 through 7 cover customer, vendor, employee, and company/banking activities for a service based business. Chapters 8 through 11 will focus on the same activities for a merchandising business.

SUMMARY

You began the chapter by looking at T-Accounts and *MAPS* for posting general journal entries. You then posted a general journal entry in OAP and looked *Behind the Keys* of the posted transaction to trace the audit trail. You also posted complex journal entries and adjusting entries. You learned to correct entries and print the Trial Balance, Income Statement, and Balance Sheet. You finalized the accounting period by backing up TEK's data file and closing the January accounting period. Finally, you looked at OAP data integration, which explains how computerized accounting saves time and reduces errors.

After completing the end-of-chapter materials you can branch off and explore either the service based business or merchandising business tracks.

END-OF-CHAPTER QUESTIONS

TRUE/FALSE

_____ 1. You should always back up a company's data file before closing the accounting period.

_____ 2. A list of journal entries can be viewed by selecting Chart of Accounts under Find.

_____ 3. OAP will let you drilldown to open original transactions using the Trial Balance report.

_____ 4. You can open a new journal entry using the Company menu.

_____ 5. The Save and New button on a journal entry posts the transaction.

_____ 6. OAP will let you delete a posted journal entry.

_____ 7. The printer icon on the Trial Balance report opens the printer selection window so you can select a printer.

_____ 8. You can restore a company's data file using a backup file for the company.

_____ 9. OAP will let you reopen a posted journal entry to correct data on the entry.

_____ 10. The Company Information menu is used to close an accounting period.

MULTIPLE CHOICE

_____ 1. Which report is used to document the audit trail for entries posted from the general journal to general ledger accounts?

   a. Transaction Journal
   b. Balance Sheet
   c. Transaction Detail by Account
   d. Trial Balance

_____ 2. The __________ is used for printing the Transaction Journal report.

   a. Customer and Receivables menu
   b. Report Home page
   c. Company and Financials menu
   d. both b and c

_____ 3. OAP will let you change the layout of a report by using the _________.
   a. Reports menu
   b. Modify Report button on a report
   c. Filter Options button on a report
   d. Date range on a report

_____ 4. Adjusting journal entries are used to record _________.
   a. depreciation expense
   b. the expired portion of prepaid expenses
   c. both a and b
   d. none of the above

_____ 5. Given TEK's Chart of Accounts, you would post a check for repairing a furnace to the _________ account.
   a. Repairs and Maintenance
   b. Equipment Repairs
   c. Vehicle Expenses
   d. Rent Expense

_____ 6. Which of the following will let you enter a range of dates for reporting financial results?
   a. Balance Sheet
   b. Profit and Loss
   c. Trial Balance
   d. Both a and c

_____ 7. Which report is also called the Income Statement?
   a. Balance Sheet
   b. Chart of Accounts
   c. Profit and Loss
   d. Trial Balance

Practice Set

This exercise uses the **Graded TEK Business** data file customized with your initials at the end of Chapter 1. ***When this data file is not loaded on your computer, restore it using the "gradedtekbusiness Chpt 1" backup file created in the Practice Set at the end of Chapter 1.***

1. Open **Graded TEK Business** and enter TEK's January accounting entries that follow. Remember to enter a description on all transactions. All entries affect the Regular Checking Account.

<u>**2008**</u>

Jan 2	Owner initial investment of $24,000: Cash, $3,000 Office equipment, $12,000 Office furniture, $4,000 Vehicles, $5,000
Jan 3	Check number 178 for office supplies expense, $380.
Jan 4	Check number 179 for six months of prepaid rent, $2,400.
Jan 7	Check number 180 for advertising expense, $980. Check number 181 to vehicle repairs and maintenance, $1,700.
Jan 10	Cash received for fees earned, $7,625.
Jan 15	Paid office salaries, $1,200.
Jan 17	Cash received for fees earned, $3,300.
Jan 18	Check number 182 for donation to local charity, $300. Check number 183 to owner, $1,300.
Jan 28	Check number 184 for electricity expense, $350. Paid office salaries, $1,200.

2. Record the following January 31 adjusting entries.

   a. Expense one month of prepaid rent.
   b. January depreciation expense of $355 posted as follows.
      Office equipment, $170
      Office furniture, $65
      Vehicles, $120

3. Print the following January reports.

   a. Transaction Journal
   b. Trial Balance
   c. Profit and Loss
   d. Balance Sheet

4. Back up the Graded TEK Business data file to a backup file named "gradedtekbusiness Chpt 3." Close the January accounting period.

CHAPTER 4 Customer Activities for a Service Based Business

Learning Objectives

This chapter works with the **Practice Astor Landscaping** data file customized with your initials at the end of Chapter 1. ***When this data file is not loaded on your computer, restore it using the "practiceastorlandscaping Chpt 1" backup file created in the Practice Set at the end of Chapter 1.***

The chapter focuses on using OAP to process customer activities for a service based business and covers:

1. Learning manual accounting procedures (*MAPS*) for customer transactions before recording transactions in OAP
2. Using the Customer Home page to perform customer tasks
3. Recording customer job invoices, payments, and credits
4. Looking *Behind the Keys* of posted transactions
5. Managing customer accounts and jobs and inventory service items
6. Correcting and voiding transactions
7. Analyzing sales and job reporting
8. Preparing customer statements
9. Reconciling customer activities to the accounts receivable control account

Launch OAP and open **Practice Astor Landscaping.**

The following is background information on Astor's business operations. The company provides landscaping and lawn maintenance services to residential and commercial customers. Customers are not invoiced until services are provided. Astor uses OAP inventory features to track job material purchases and service pricing. Service labor costs are incurred by paying Astor employees or subcontractors and the accountant use job costing to analyze job performance. The company's current accounting period is March 2008.

MANUAL ACCOUNTING PROCEDURES

Before processing sales transactions in OAP, become familiar with a manual accounting system. This topic walks through manual accounting procedures (*MAPS*) for processing customer sales transactions. We begin at the point where the customer initiates a transaction.

On March 24, 2008, John Chester contacts Astor salesperson, Jan Folse, requesting seasonal lawn maintenance. John has used the company in the past. Jan quoted John a price of $80.00 plus tax and the service is scheduled for March 27, 2008.

In a manual system, Jan writes up a service ticket, which an employee performing the service takes to the job. These tickets are not entered into the accounting records because the sale is not recognized until after performing the services. Recall that accrual accounting does not recognize revenue until earned and Astor does not earn revenue until the service is provided.

On March 27, Jeff Henderson picks up the service ticket and heads to John's home. After completing the service, Jeff has John sign the service ticket to acknowledge completion and returns the signed ticket to Jan. Jan then forwards the ticket to the accountant, Judy White, who prepares the following invoice.

Astor Landscaping 1505 Pavilion Place, Suite C Arlington, VA 30093 Customer: Mr. John Chester 2404 Pleasant Hill Danville, VA 30096 Date: 3/27/2008 INVOICE No. 1020	
Seasonal Lawn Maintenance March 27, 2008	$ 80.00
Sales Tax	4.00
Total	$ 84.00
Please remit balance within 30 days	

Figure 4:1

Judy next records the invoice, along with other invoices for that day, in the Sales Journal. Her entries to the Sales Journal for March 27 appear next.

Astor Landscaping
Sales Journal

Date: 3/27/2008 **Page 15**

Customer	Post Ref	Description	Accounts Receivable (Debit)	Maint. Services (Credit)	Hardscape Sales (Credit)	Sales Tax Payable (Credit)
John Chester	CHES001	Seasonal Maint. INV1020	84.00	80.00		4.00
DBH Enterprises	DBHE001	Landscaping / Maint. INV1021	3,383.15	290.00	2,916.78	176.37
Yango Software	YANG001	Seasonal Maint. INV 1022	290.13		275.00	15.13
Totals:	**Audit Trail**		$3,757.28	$370.00	$3,191.78	$195.50
		Acct Ref:	(11000)	(45000)	(42000)	(22000)

Figure 4:2

You see that Judy entered John's invoice as a debit to accounts receivable and as credits to maintenance services and sales tax payable. At the end of the day, Judy totals Sales Journal columns and cross-foots totals to verify that entries balance (i.e., debits equal credits). She then posts each invoice to the customer's account and posts column totals to the general ledger accounts noted at the bottom.

Figure 4:3 shows Judy's entry to John's customer account. *(Note: Entries for other customer accounts are not illustrated.)*

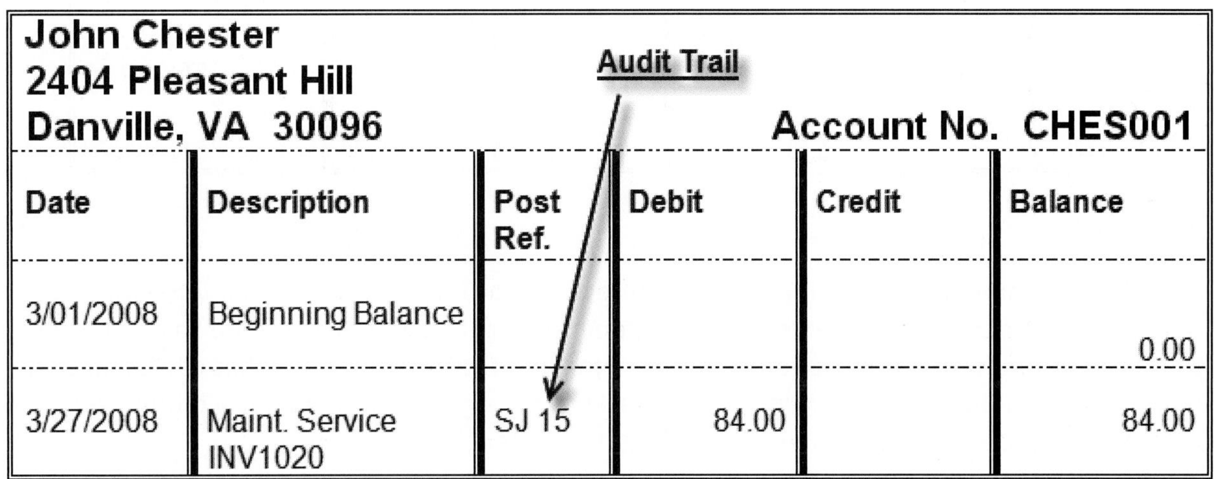

John Chester
2404 Pleasant Hill
Danville, VA 30096

Audit Trail

Account No. CHES001

Date	Description	Post Ref.	Debit	Credit	Balance
3/01/2008	Beginning Balance				0.00
3/27/2008	Maint. Service INV1020	SJ 15	84.00		84.00

Figure 4:3

Judy's entries to general ledger accounts are illustrated next. *(Note: The entry to the sales tax payable account is not shown.)*

General Ledger

Accounts Receivable — **Account No. 11000**

Date	Description	Post Ref.	Debit	Credit	Balance
3/26/2008	Balance Forward				96,273.96
3/27/2008		SJ 15	3,757.28		100,031.24

Audit trail

General Ledger

Maintenance Services — **Account No. 45000**

Date	Description	Post Ref.	Debit	Credit	Balance
3/26/2008	Balance Forward				22,240.00
3/27/2008		SJ 15		370.00	22,610.00

Audit trail

General Ledger

Hardscape Sales — **Account No. 42000**

Date	Description	Post Ref.	Debit	Credit	Balance
3/26/2008	Balance Forward				55,290.00
3/27/2008		SJ 15		3,191.78	58,481.78

Figure 4:4

As Judy posts, she is also entering posting references that form the audit trail. An audit trail documents entries from the Sales Journal to general ledger accounts, from the Sales Journal to customer accounts, and vice versa. You can imagine the posting errors that can occur in a manual system. Judy could record an entry backwards (e.g., enter a debit as a credit), record an out-of-balance entry, omit an entry, or forget to enter the audit trail.

On the same day that Judy posts invoices she also posts customer payments for outstanding invoices. These entries are recorded in a separate journal called the Cash Receipts Journal. Entries to the Cash Receipts Journal are illustrated next.

Astor Landscaping Cash Receipts Journal						
Date: 3/27/2008						**Page 3**
Customer	**Check No.**	**Post Ref**	**Invoice No.**	**Regular Checking (Debit)**	**Accounts Receivable (Credit)**	**Payment Discounts (Debit)**
O'Hara Homes	993	OHAR001	993	1,000.00	1,000.00	
Sycamore Homes	9832	SYCA001	1012	$20,291.72	20,681.95	390.23
Totals:				$21,291.72	$21,681.95	$ 390.23
Audit trail →		Acct Ref:		(10200)	(11000)	(49000)

Figure 4:5

As with postings on the Sales Journal, Judy posts each check to the customer's account and column totals to the general ledger accounts. This time she will use the posting reference of CRJ (Cash Receipts Journal) along with the page number. *(Note: These postings are not illustrated.)*

With OAP most of the posting errors are eliminated. You will see in subsequent topics that sales invoices and customer payments are posted when saving. In addition, OAP automatically posts entries recorded to the Sales and Cash Receipts Journals to customer accounts and general ledger accounts. OAP also enters the audit trail and will not post out of balance entries.

We will now focus our attention to processing customer transactions in OAP.

Customers Menu and Home Page

Before processing customer activities, become familiar with locating the commands that initiate activities. The first command on the **Customers** menu illustrated to the right opens the **Customers Home** page. The **New** menu opens submenus for creating customer accounts, jobs, quotes, and invoices. Finally, there are separate menus for receiving payments, creating statements, and viewing customer lists.

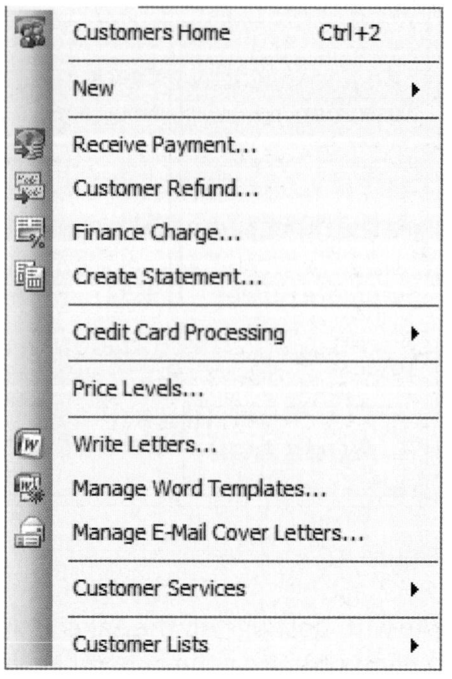

Figure 4:6

Click **Customers Home** on the menu to open the Customers Home page illustrated in Figure 4:7. This home page serves as central command for customer activities.

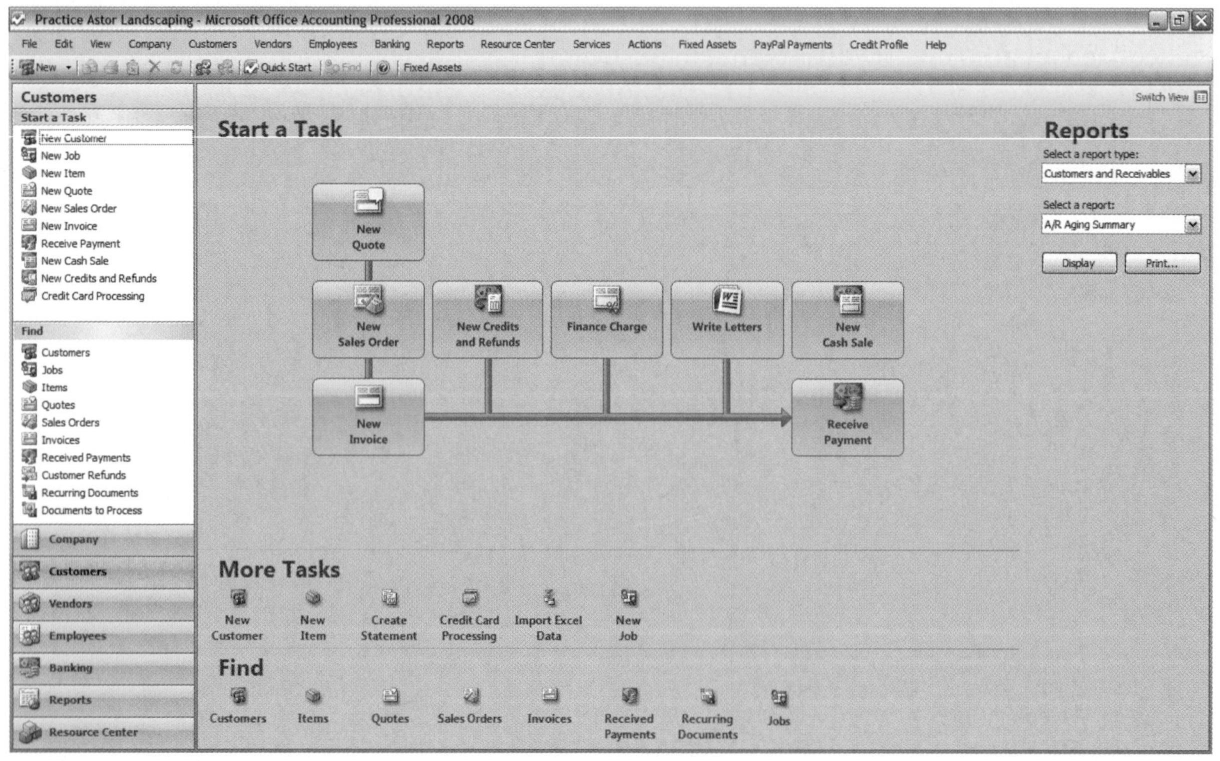

Figure 4:7

On this page are links to many of the commands located on the Customers menu. *(Note: The Switch View link located on the top right changes the home page view. Click this link if your view does not match the illustration.)*

Start a Task icons in the center of the page depict the normal flow of customer activities. These icons show that customer activities can originate as quotes (proposed sales), sales orders (pending sales), or invoices (completed sales). Moreover, sales quotes and sales orders will transfer to create sales invoices and invoices are the transactions that receive payments. Credit memos, finance charges, and customer letters can occur anytime after creating the invoice. Finally, cash sales are self-contained transactions that include both sale and payment.

Beneath Start a Task icons are the icons for performing **More Tasks** and for opening lists that **Find** transactions. The activities found on the home page are repeated as links under the **Start a Task** and **Find** headings to the left of the home page.

Now that you are familiar with the Customers menu and home page, let's begin recording customer transactions.

Entering Sales Quotes

You now return to John Chester's transaction illustrated in the *MAPS* and capture his initial inquiry as an OAP sales quote. Sales quotes are an integral part of job costing because these documents store estimated job revenues and expenses. Astor will only record sales quotes on the jobs it wants to analyze by comparing actuals to estimates.

Read the following tips on entering data in a transaction window before creating John's quote in the exercise that follows.

Data Entry Tips

Tip 1: The **Customer name** field links the transaction to a customer account. The **Name** field under **Products and services** links the transaction to service and non-inventory items. The **Job name** field links the transaction to a customer job. These fields link to what is called a master record. You will recognize a master record field in a transaction window because it contains a lookup for selecting records.

Tip 2: Customers, jobs, and items can be selected using the field lookup. You can also begin typing the name of the account or item to advance the lookup list.

Tip 3: If you select the wrong customer, job, or item then return to the field and change the selection. Remember that the Edit menu contains data manipulation commands such as cut, copy, and paste.

Tip 4: When you want to remove a line item on a transaction, highlight the row, right click, and select Delete. (See Figure 4:8.) You can also insert lines using this method.

Name	Description	Qty.	Unit Price	Discount	Line Total	
BLUE FLAG	1.5 Ton Pallet Blues Flagstone	1	$242.00	0%	$242.00	N(
		1	$0.00	0%	$0.00	

Delete
Insert

Figure 4:8

Tip 5: You can create new master records "on the fly," meaning to add a new customer, job, or item while entering a transaction. For instance, if you want to add a new customer named XYZ Company begin by typing the company name in the Customer name field and press tab for OAP to prompt to create the new account.

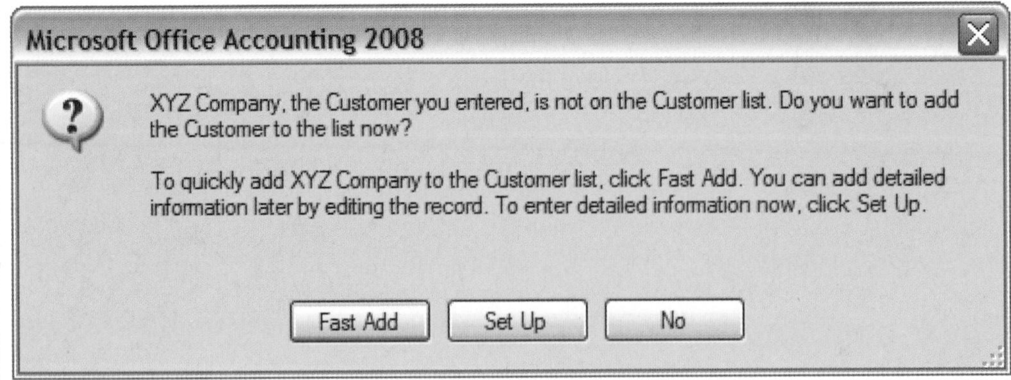

Figure 4:9

You should always click **Set Up** so you can enter all information for the new account. If you select **No**, OAP returns to the Customer name field for you to change the customer selection.

Steps for Entering Sales Quotes

1. Click **New Quote** on the Customer Home page to open a quote transaction (Figure 4:10). Enter "3/24/2008" as the transaction date. *(Note: You can also choose a date by clicking the dropdown list to access the calendar feature.)*

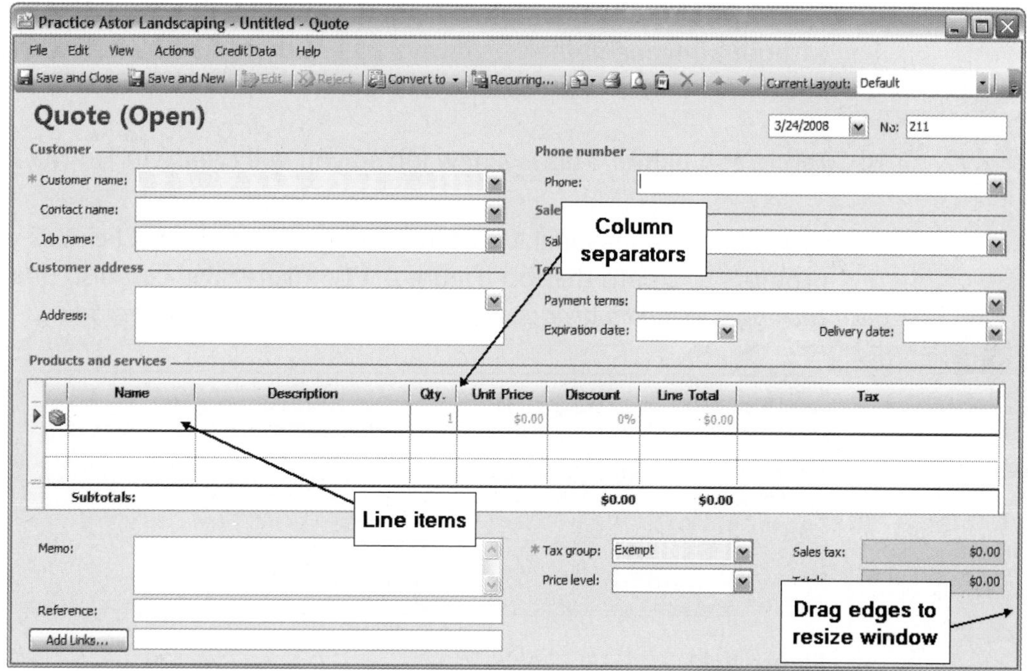

Figure 4:10

Note: You can resize a transaction window by dragging its edges with the mouse. You can also resize line item columns by dragging a column separator.

2. Place your cursor in **Customer name** and begin typing "ch" to advance the lookup to John's account and then press Tab. (*Note: You can also use the field's dropdown list to select the account.)* The form autofills with the customer's information.

   OAP has supplied the **No.** value (i.e., quote number). These numbers are sequentially incremented for each quote so keep the current value.

   The **Payment terms** defaulted from the customer account and can be changed without affecting defaults. Always accept the default when working exercises in the text unless instructed to change.

3. Tab to **Job name**. This is a new job so you will create it "on the fly."

   Type "Chester Seasonal Maintenance" and press Tab. Click **Yes** when OAP prompts to create the Job (Figure 4:11). *(Note: You can also add a new job by clicking the field's dropdown list and selecting **Add a new job**.)*

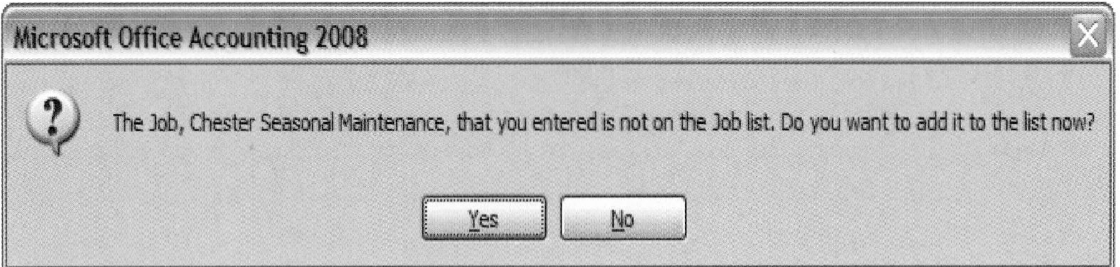

Figure 4:11

4. The Job name transferred to the Job window from the data entered on the quote. (See Figure 4:12.) You can make corrections if needed.

   OAP tracks both Fixed fee and Time and materials jobs. A job marked **Fixed fee** means that the customer is charged a single fee regardless of the time and materials required to provide the service. **Time and materials** jobs are those jobs that invoice a customer for actual time and materials used to complete the service. ***Astor uses only Time and materials jobs so always mark this option when creating a job.***

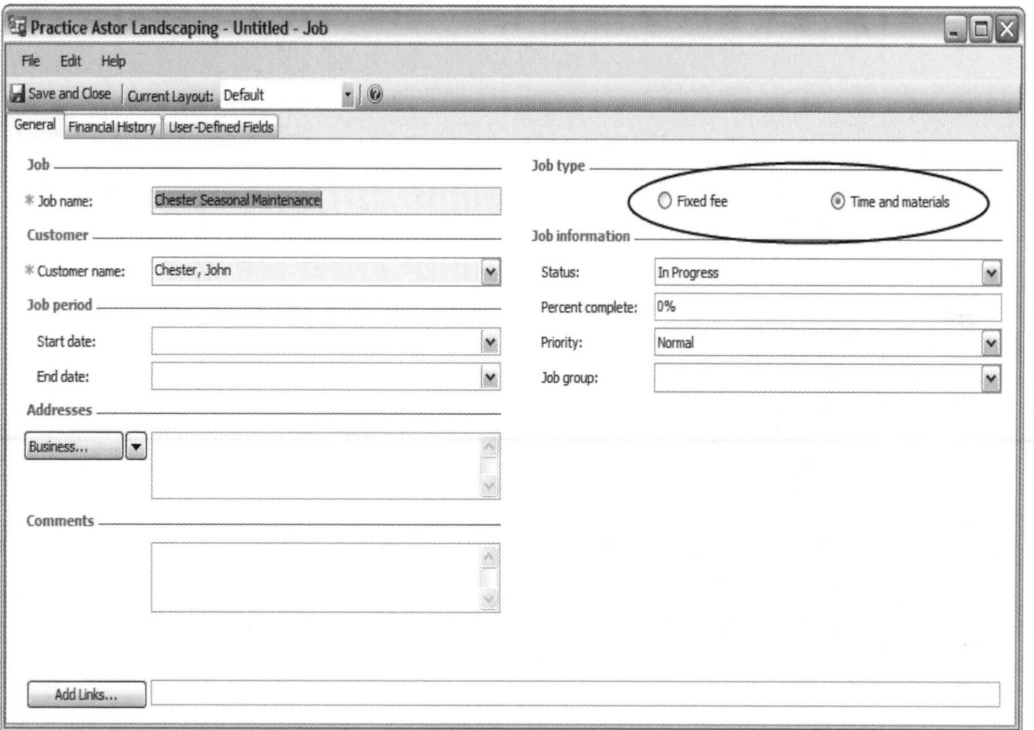

Figure 4:12

5. Complete remaining job information by referring to Figure 4:13. Click **Save and Close**.

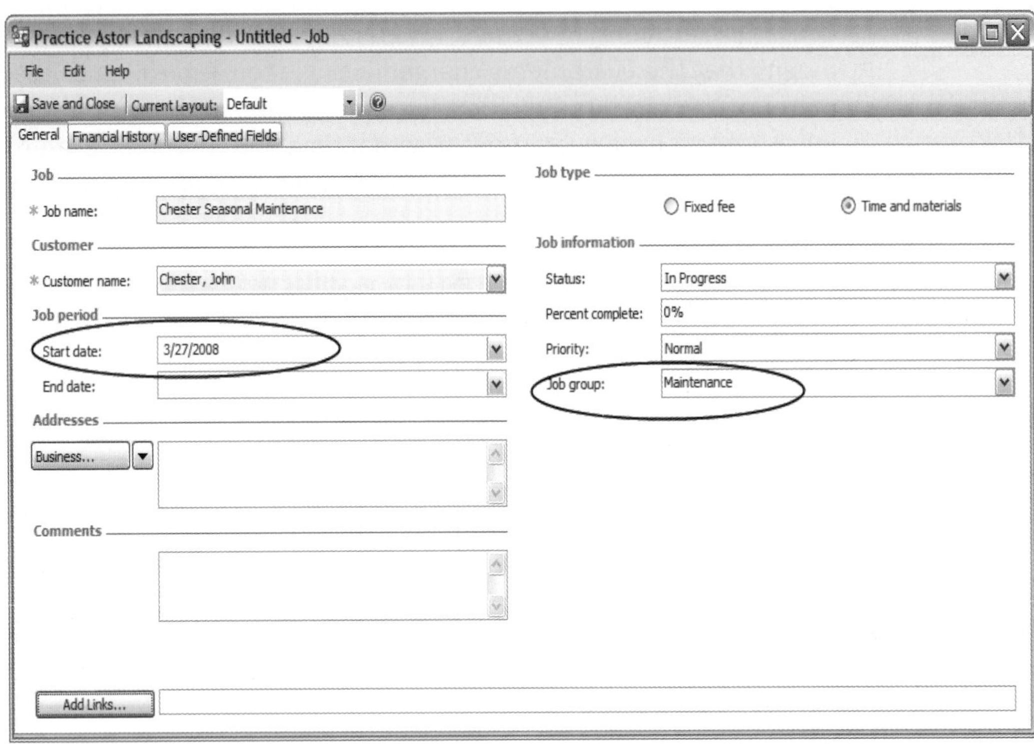

Figure 4:13

6. Upon returning to the quote, the top portion appears as shown in Figure 4:14.

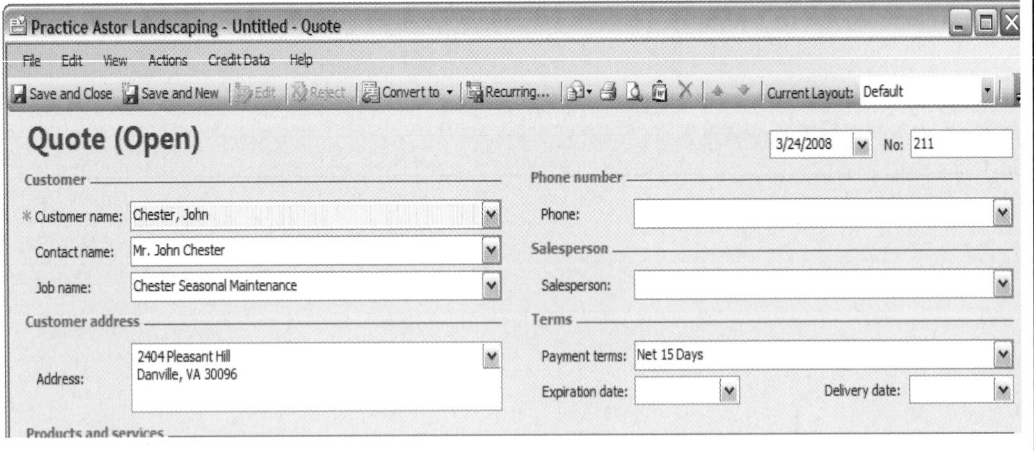

Figure 4:14

7. Tab to the **Products and services** section and, upon reaching the line item icon, OAP lists line item types. (See Figure 4:15.)

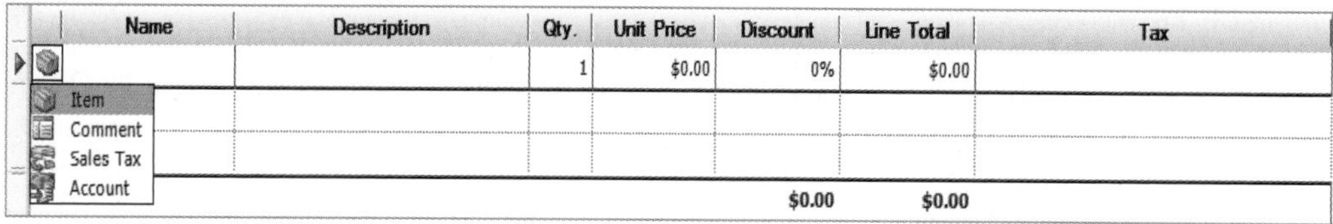

Figure 4:15

These icons determine the type of information to be entered on the line item. The following explains line item types.

- **Item** is selected when entering sales of services, inventory, and non-inventory. After choosing, you can look up items in the inventory table.
- **Comment** is selected when adding text to convey information to a customer.
- **Sales Tax** is selected when implementing complicated sales tax schemes. You will not use this type because Astor assesses sales taxes using the Tax fields on the line item and the tax field on the customer account. The sales tax charged on the sale will appear in the **Sales tax** field at the bottom of the transaction.
- **Account** is selected when posting sales directly to a general ledger account. After choosing, you can look up general ledger accounts and record a sale that bypasses items in the inventory table.

8. Select **Item** and press Tab. Tab to **Name** and use the lookup to select "SEASONAL MAINT: RESIDENTIAL." *(Note: You can type "sea" to advance the list.)*

   (Note: The lookup on this field signals it as master record.)

9. Tab to **Qty** and enter "2." Figure 4:16 shows the completed quote.

   Astor charges $40 as the unit price for this service so the Line Total is $80. In addition, the service is **Taxable** and the customer is taxable (i.e., Tax group equals VA SALES TAX). Thus, the **Sales tax** field displays $4.00, making the **Total** quote equal to $84.00.

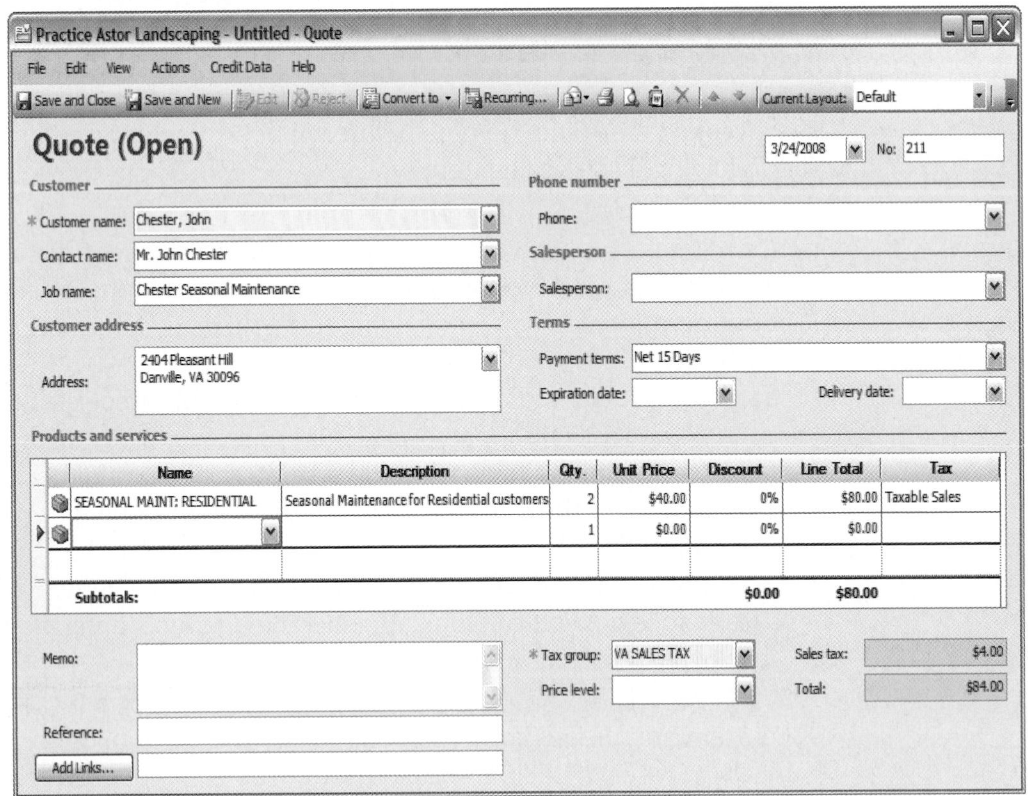

Figure 4:16

Notes:
OAP always computes tax on a transaction by referring to the tax code on line items and the tax code on the customer. If a line item is taxed but the customer is not then the transaction is not tax.

OAP opens a blank line item when you tab to the next line. You do not need to delete this line because it will be disregarded when saving the transaction.

*The **Add Links** button at the bottom of a transaction lets you link a transaction to external documents stored in Word or Excel.*

10. Click the Print Preview icon on the toolbar to preview the invoice before printing (Figure 4:17). These icons enlarge and shrink the view.

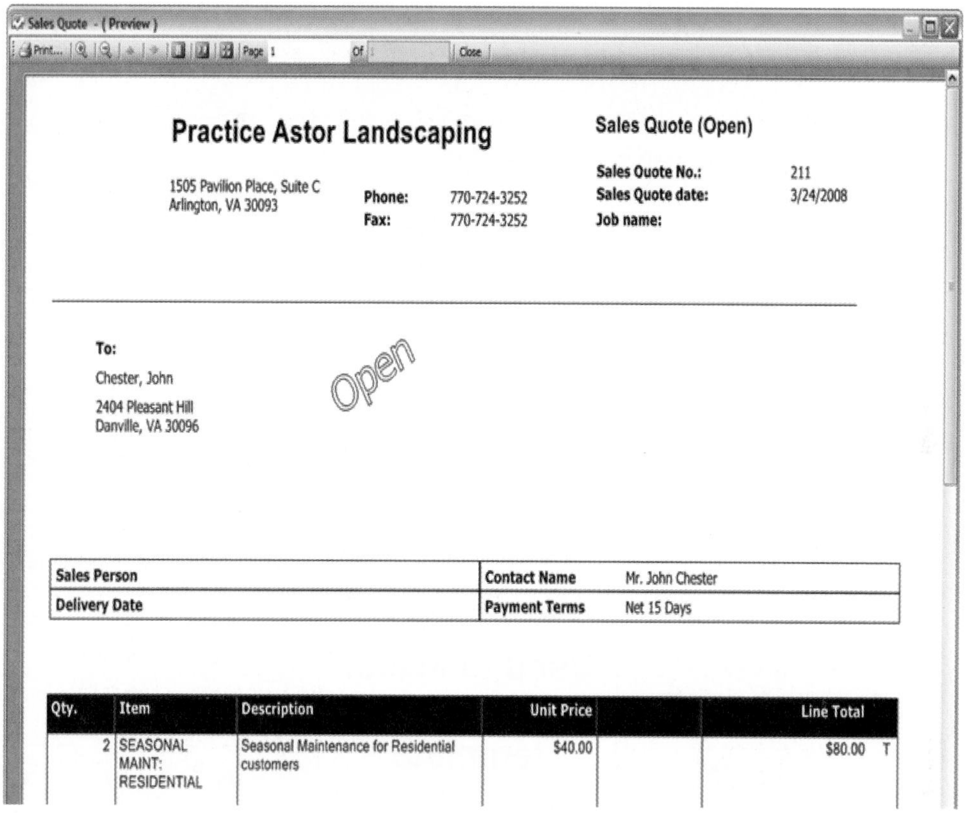

Sales Quote - (Preview)

Print... Page 1 Of Close

Practice Astor Landscaping

1505 Pavilion Place, Suite C
Arlington, VA 30093

Phone: 770-724-3252
Fax: 770-724-3252

Sales Quote (Open)

Sales Quote No.: 211
Sales Quote date: 3/24/2008
Job name:

To:
Chester, John
2404 Pleasant Hill
Danville, VA 30096

Open

Sales Person		Contact Name	Mr. John Chester
Delivery Date		Payment Terms	Net 15 Days

Qty.	Item	Description	Unit Price		Line Total
2	SEASONAL MAINT: RESIDENTIAL	Seasonal Maintenance for Residential customers	$40.00		$80.00 T

Figure 4:17

11. Click the **Print** icon on the toolbar and click **OK** to save the quote. Also click Yes to save the billing address on the job. Select a printer (Figure 4:18) and click **OK** to send a hardcopy to the printer.

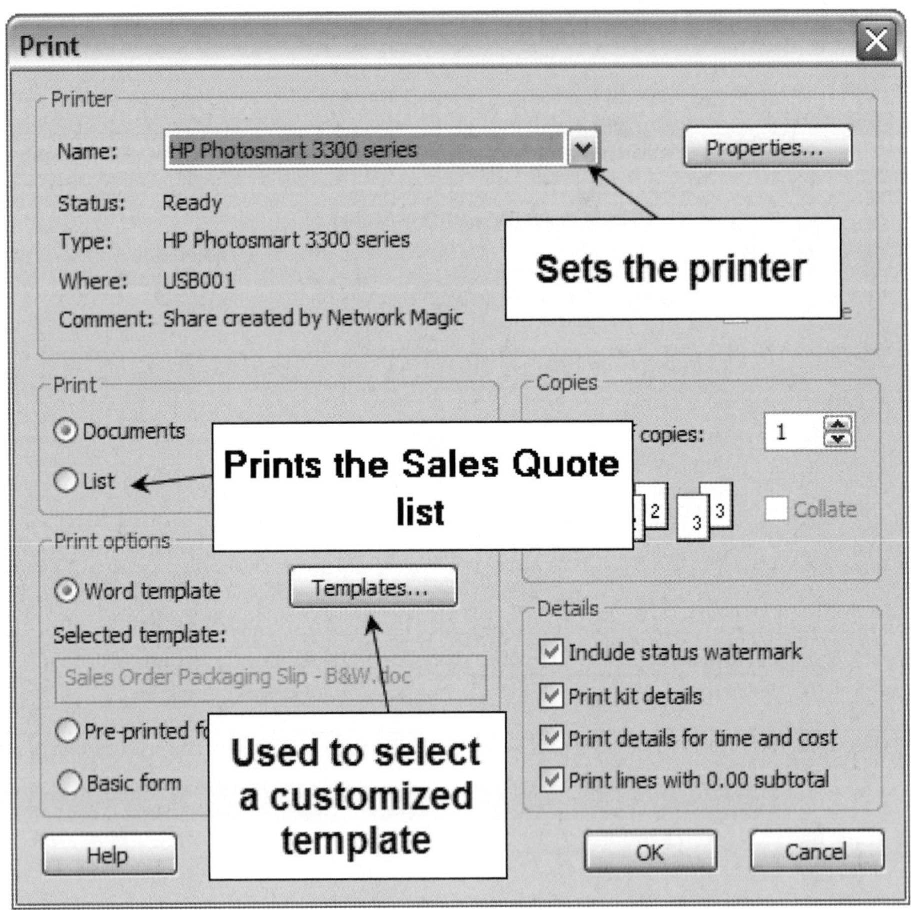

Figure 4:18

12. Click **Save and Close** to exit the transaction window.

John's quote is now stored and can be monitored by clicking the **Quotes** link under **Find** to open the Quote List illustrated in Figure 4:19.

Quote List — Current View: Open

Date	No.	Customer Name	Job Name	Phone	Sales Person	Exp. Date	Delivery Date	Total Price
Add a new Quote								
1/2/2008	198	Crawford, Shelly	Crawford Side Gardens					$10,077.50
1/3/2008	199	Fairbanks Construction	Fairbanks Backyard Patio					$5,340.00
1/5/2008	200	Gibson, Robert	Gibson New Deck					$8,437.50
1/5/2008	201	Hutcheon, Brian	Hutcheon Backyard Landscaping					$13,489.40
1/15/2008	202	O'Hara Homes	O'Hara Patios and Walks					$70,948.75
1/15/2008	203	Pleasantdale Luxury Apartments	Pleasantdale Common Areas					$3,584.00
1/15/2008	204	Sallens Property Management	Sallens New Deck					$16,200.00
2/15/2008	205	Sycamore Homes	Sycamore Plantings					$33,975.00
2/15/2008	206	O'Hara Homes	O'Hara Redesign Gardens					$56,502.50
2/15/2008	207	Peck, Oliver	Peck Front Yard					$4,593.75
2/15/2008	208	Silver Homes	Silver Plantings					$20,432.50
2/15/2008	209	White and Associates	White Redesign Gardens					$17,268.50
3/5/2008	210	Zara Apartment Homes	Zara Redesign Common Areas					$11,025.00
3/24/2008	211	Chester, John	Chester Seasonal Maintenance					$84.00

Figure 4:19

Correcting Sales Quotes

You can easily modify an **Open** sales quote. Remember that these documents are potential sales transactions so entries are not posted to general ledger accounts.

First, view the Quote List illustrated in the previous topic. Double click to reopen John's quote (Figure 4:20).

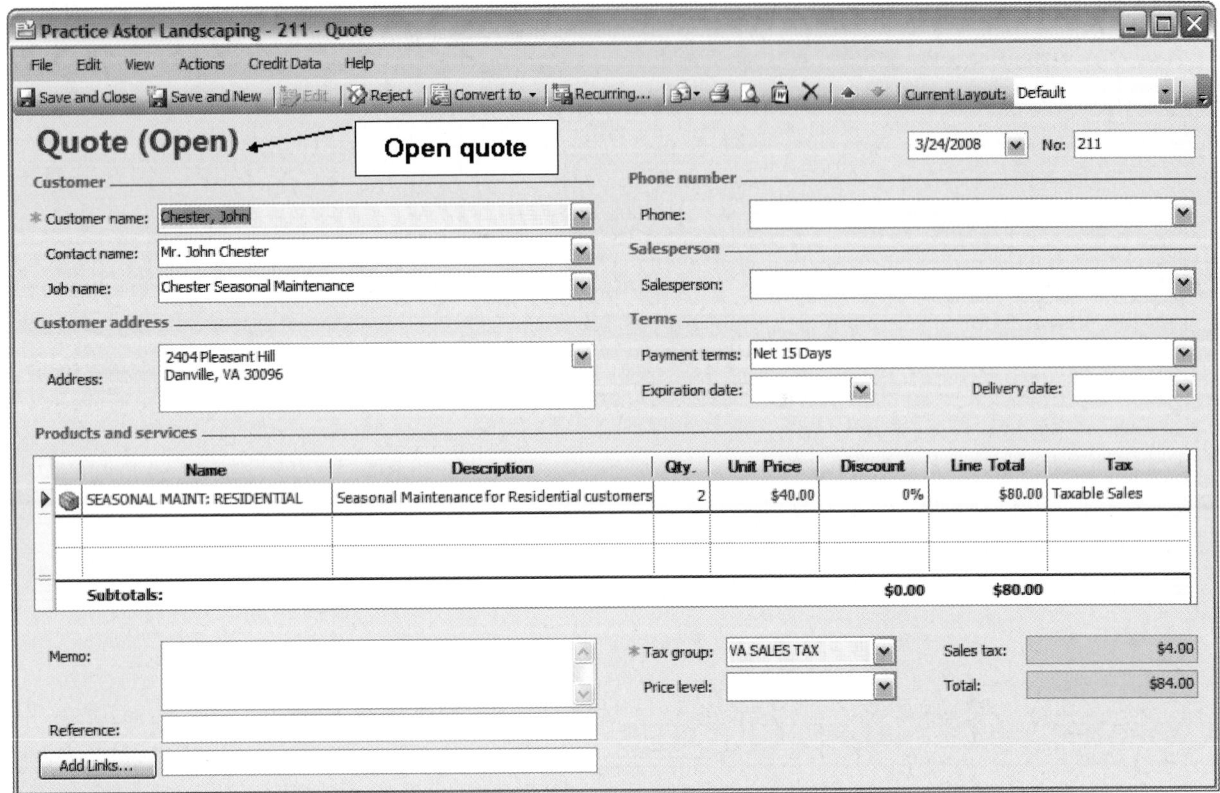

Figure 4:20

After reopening, you can change data, reprint, and resave. You can also delete by clicking the delete ✕ icon on the toolbar.

Click **X** to close the quote and return to the Quote List.

You can also highlight a quote on the list and right click to select a task.

Quote List — Current View: Open

+ Add a new Quote

Date	No.	Customer Name	Job Name	Phone	Sales Person	Exp. Date	Delivery Date	Total Price
1/2/2008	198	Crawford, Shelly	Crawford Side Gardens					$10,077.50
1/3/2008	199	Fairbanks Construction	Fairbanks Backyard Patio					$5,340.00
		...bert	Gibson New Deck					$8,437.50
		...Brian	Hutcheon Backyard Landscaping					$13,489.40
		...mes	O'Hara Patios and Walks					$70,948.75
		...le Luxury Apartments	Pleasantdale Common Areas					$3,584.00
		...perty Management	Sallens New Deck					$16,200.00
		...Homes	Sycamore Plantings					$33,975.00
		...mes	O'Hara Redesign Gardens					$56,502.50
		...er	Peck Front Yard					$4,593.75
		...es	Silver Plantings					$20,432.50
		...Associates	White Redesign Gardens					$17,268.50
		...nent Homes	Zara Redesign Common Areas					$11,025.00
3/24/2008	211	Chester, John	Chester Seasonal Maintenance					$84.00

Open Selected Items
Print...
Select All
Reject Quote
Convert To Sales Order...
Convert to Invoice...
Progress Invoice...
Recurring...
E-Mail Quote
Delete

Figure 4:21

Notice that besides deleting, you can convert a quote to an order or invoice and reject a quote. Rejecting causes OAP to retain quote information and removes the quote from the list of open quotes. The quote is then viewed by changing the Current View to Rejected or All.

EMAILING QUOTES AND EXPORTING THE QUOTE LIST

Unlike a manual system, accounting software tracks sales orders so you can analyze potential sales and enhance customer service. We will now review features that add value when it comes to servicing customers.

Note: To perform this exercise, you must be connected to the Internet and have an E-mail software package installed on your computer. In addition, your machine must have Microsoft Word® and Excel® installed.

OAP 2008 comes with improved email features that supply the option of emailing documents as PDF or XPS attachments. However, an add-in for the software must be downloaded from the Internet and installed before you can use this feature.

Open the Quote List and highlight John's order. Click the E-mail icon and select **Send as Word Attachment**. *(Note: You can also select **Actions>>E-Mail Quote>>As Word Attachment** on the main menu.)* The Select Word Templates window opens (Figure 4:22). Highlight **Quote – B&W.doc** and click **Select**.

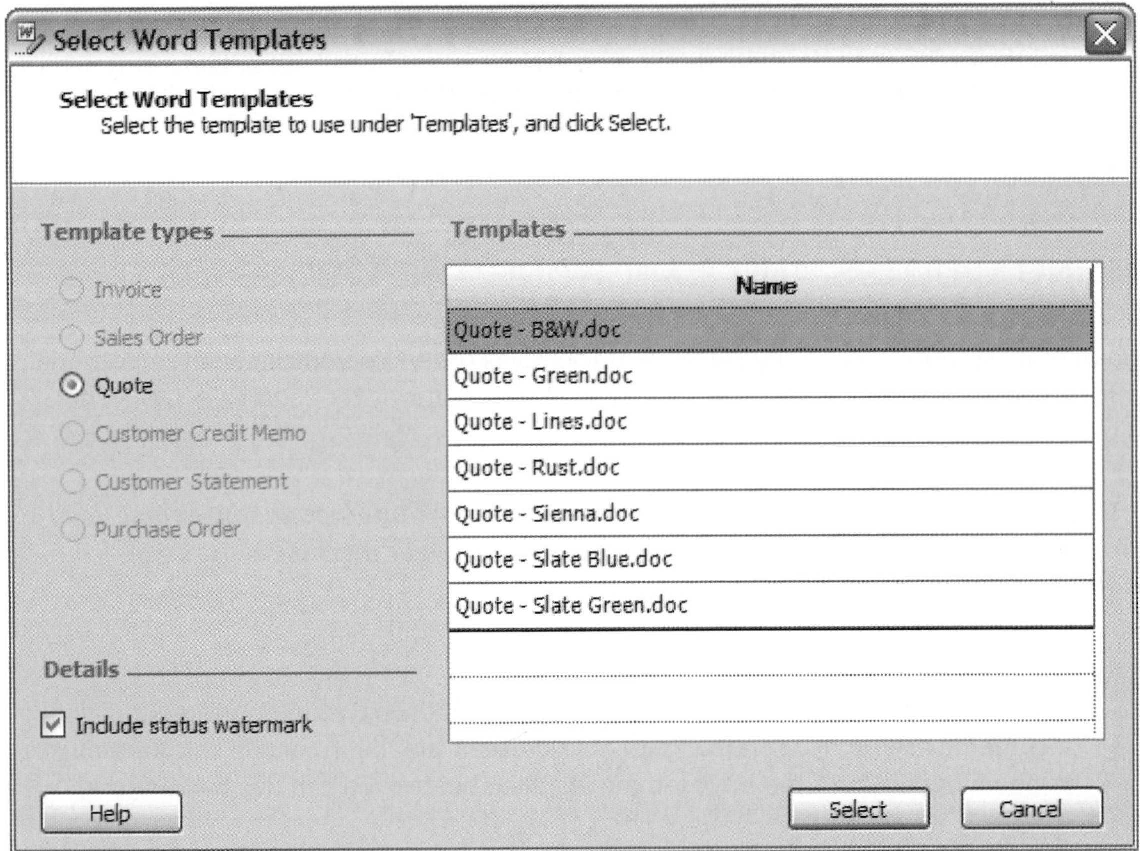

Figure 4:22

An email message opens with the quote attached (Figure 4:23). Enter your email address in the **To** field and click **Send**. *(Note: The illustration uses Outlook® 2007. When not using this E-mail software or version, click the command on the window that sends a message.)* Check your email later to verify delivery.

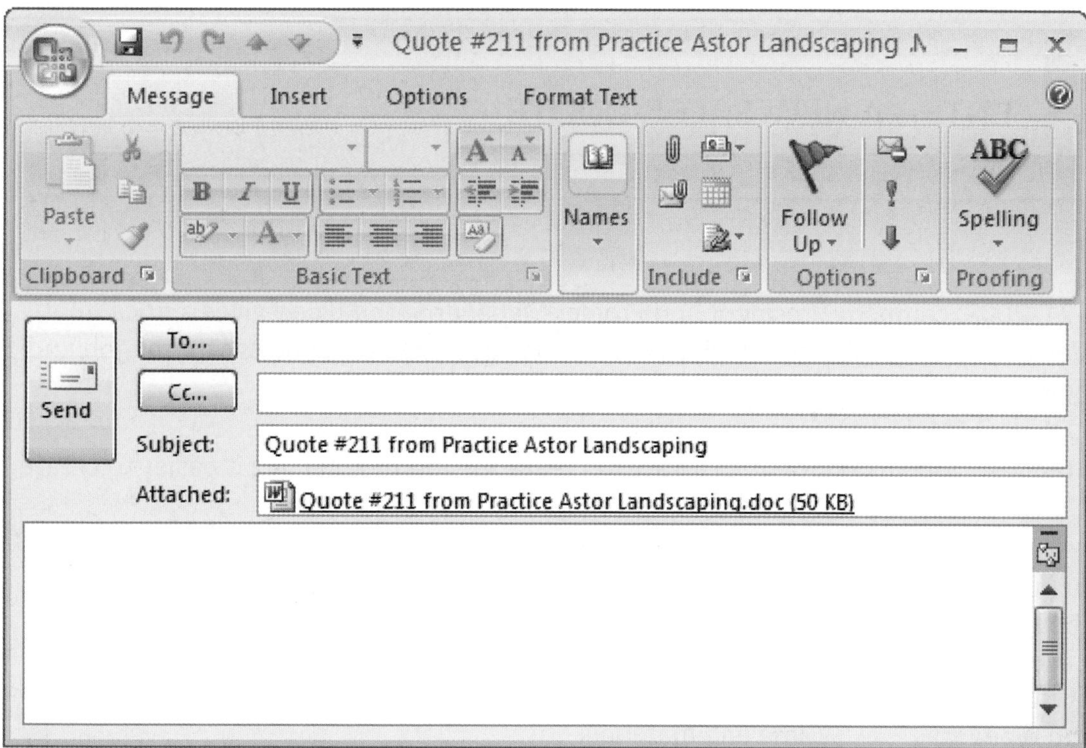

Figure 4:23

You can also use OAP to analyze quotes by exporting information to an Excel workbook. While viewing the Quote List click the Excel icon on the toolbar. *(Note: You can also select **Actions>>Export to Excel** on the main menu.)*

After exporting the list (not illustrated) you can save the workbook and use spreadsheet tools to analyze quotes. Click **X** on the Excel window and select **No** when prompted to save the workbook.

One final note, just like the manual system, quotes are not posted to general ledger accounts because these documents are only potential sales and accrual accounting recognizes sales revenue when earned (i.e., service is performed). In OAP terms, this means that revenue is posted when invoicing the customer after performing the work and invoicing is the subject of our next topic.

ENTER A NEW SALES QUOTE

On March 21, 2008, company President and Project Manager Seth Ruland gives a price quote for the redesign of Sugar Hill Tennis Club's gardens. He now asks that you create the job and prepare the quote.

Hint: Use the New Job link under Start a Task to create the job first making it easier to create the quote.

Information for the job:

Job name:	Sugar Hill Garden Design
Customer name:	Sugar Hill Tennis Club
Start date:	3/25/2008
Job type:	Time and materials
Job group:	Landscaping

Items on the quote dated March 21, 2008 are as follows.

QTY	ITEM	Line Total
1	DESIGN – COMMERCIAL	350.00
40	INSTL HARD – COMMERCIAL	2,400.00
1	INSTL SPRINK – COMMERCIAL	1,575.00
30	INSTL LAND – COMMERCIAL	1,500.00

Print the quote for the customer. Remember solutions to *You Try* exercises are found in Appendix E.

Creating a Sales Invoice Using a Quote

In this topic, you will transfer John Chester's quote to an invoice. Although we are demonstrating this method of invoicing, it is the only time you will use the method because time and materials jobs are normally invoiced by transferring job costs. *(Note: You will learn to invoice job costs in a later topic.)*

Steps to Create an Invoice Using a Quote

1. View the Quote List and highlight John's quote. Click the **Convert to** button on the toolbar and select **Convert to Invoice**. *(Note: An alternative method is opening the quote and clicking the **Convert to** button on the Quote window toolbar.)*

2. First, change the template for the Current Layout to Service because this changes the field display. (See Figure 4:24.)

   John's services were completed on March 27, 2008 so enter this as the invoice date. The invoice **No.** is 1018. Leave this unchanged because OAP automatically increments and assigns these numbers. However, note that the invoice number differs from the quote number.

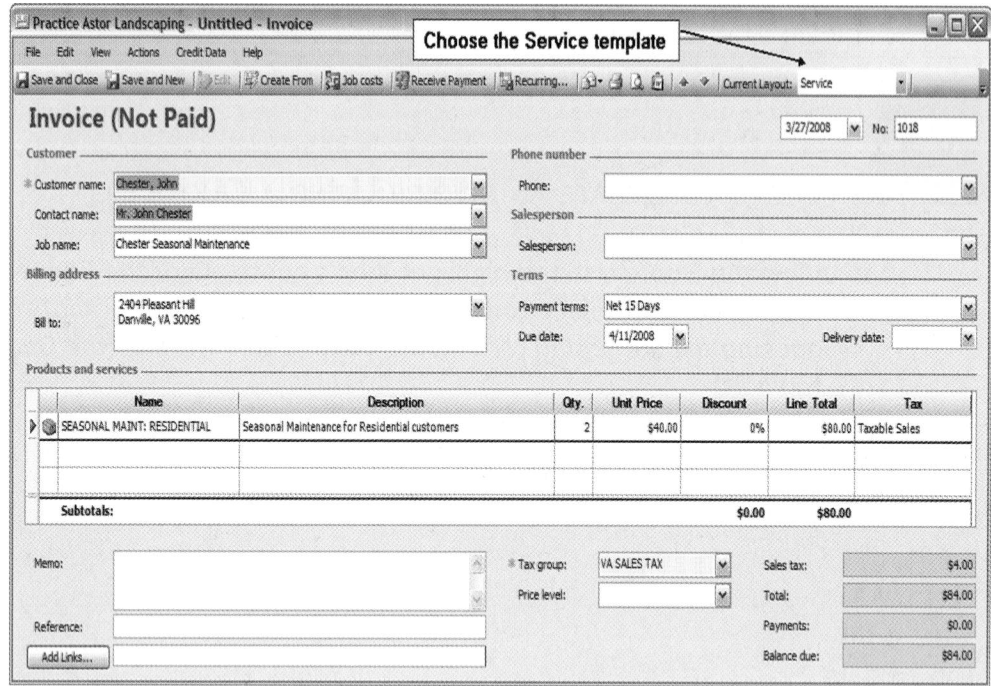

Figure 4:24

3. Click the **Print Preview** icon on the toolbar to view the invoice. Notice that the document appears similar to the quote previewed in a previous topic except that the document is now entitled "Invoice."

   Click **Close** to exit the Preview window without printing the document.

4. Click **Save and Close** on the transaction window.

Now check the status of John's quote. Return to the Quote list to find that John's quote is no longer displayed. Click the dropdown list on **Current View** to choose **Accepted**.

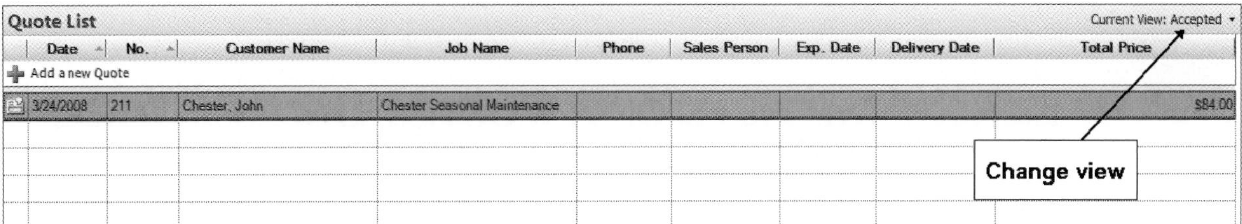

Figure 4:25

This shows that after invoicing a quote OAP changes the quote status to Accepted. Double click to reopen the quote to view its status (Figure 4:26). Click **X** to close the quote. Change the view on the Quote List back to Open.

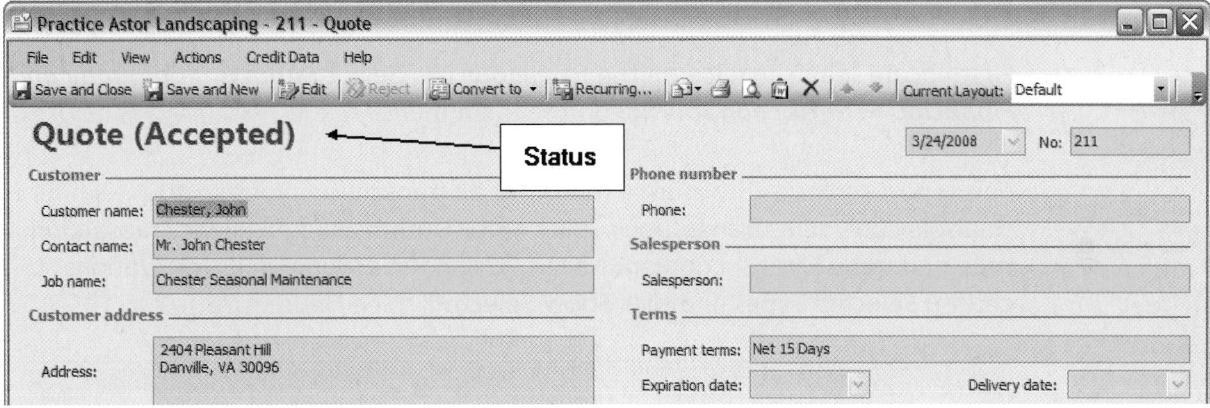

Figure 4:26

Printing Multiple Sales Invoices

Thus far we have only illustrated printing a transaction document while creating the transaction. Normally you will want to enter several transactions before printing.

After creating multiple sales invoices you can print them altogether using the Invoice List. First, open the list. Next, select the invoices to print by holding down the **Ctrl** key on the keyboard and clicking each invoice with the mouse to highlight it. After selecting the invoices, right click one of the selected invoices and select **Print**. When the Printer window opens, mark the option that prints Documents (Figure 8:25) and click **OK**. *(Note: Selecting the List option prints the Sales Invoice list.)*

Figure 4:27

You will next trace the entries made when posting John Chester's invoice.

BEHIND THE KEYS OF A POSTED SALES INVOICE

In this topic you trace OAP's audit trail to locate the entries made when posting John's invoice.

TRACE THE AUDIT TRAIL OF A POSTED SALES INVOICE

1. First, locate John's invoice on the Sales Journal. Select ***Reports>>Company and Financial>>Transaction Journal*** on the main menu.

   This report serves as the journal report for all transaction types so you will filter it to display only sales transactions. Click **Filter Options** and highlight **Transaction type** under the Filter section on the left. Using the dropdown list on Options, choose **Selected Types** and click **Show Selected**. (See Figure 4:28.)

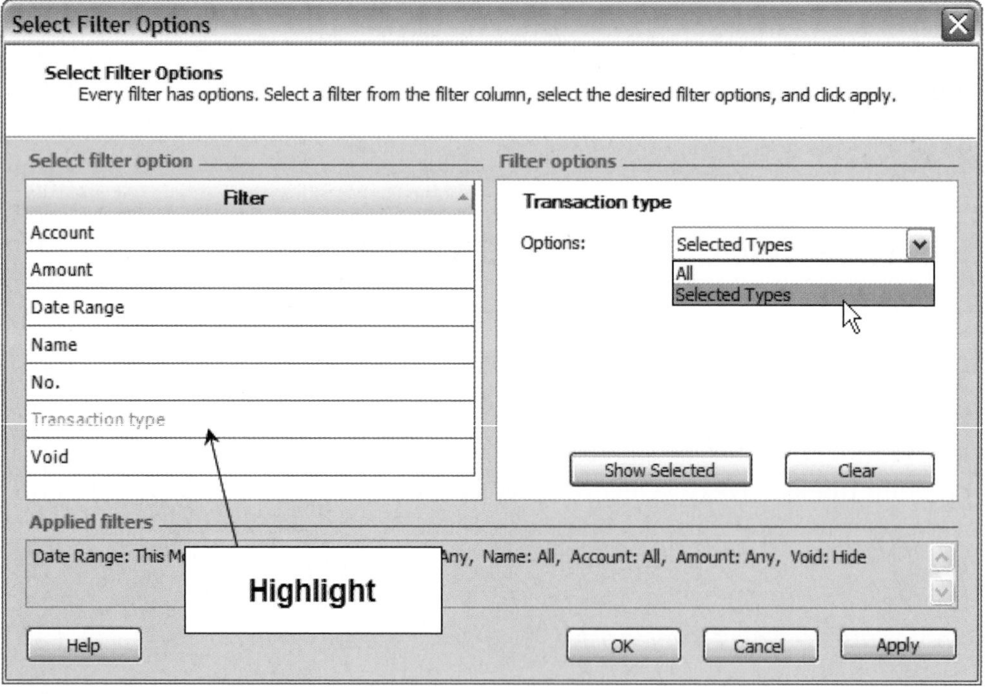

Figure 4:28

2. In the Select Transaction Types window add the Transaction Types illustrated in Figure 4:29 by highlighting each type on the left and clicking **Add**. After adding click **OK** and **OK** again.

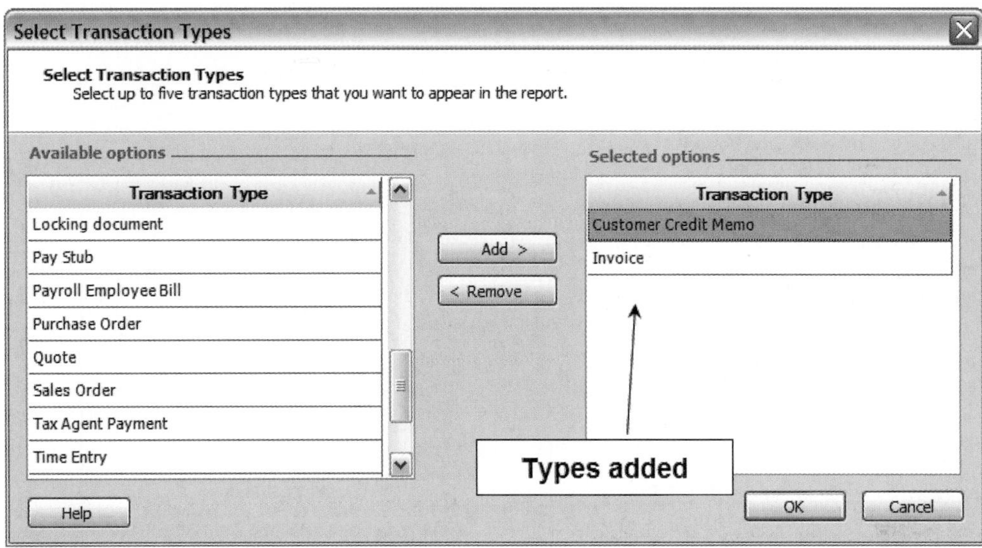

Figure 4:29

3. Next, change the name of the report. Click **Modify Report** and click **Header and Footer**. Change the **Report Title** to Sales Journal (Figure 4:30) and click **X** to close the pane.

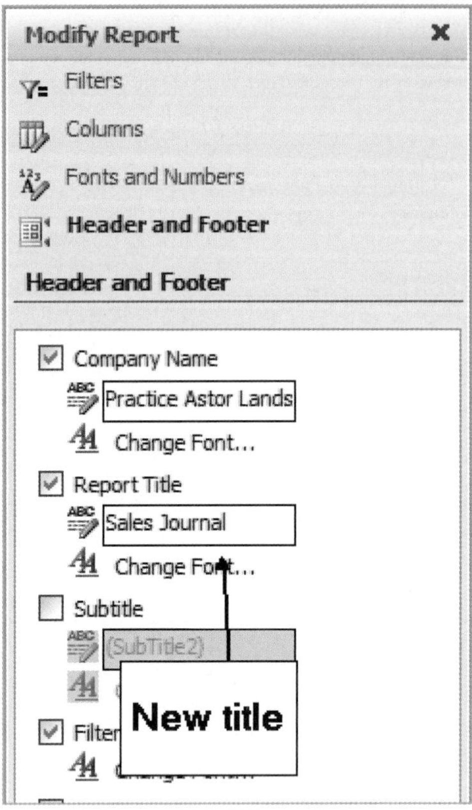

Figure 4:30

4. Click **Save Report** and click **OK** to save the report as the Sales Journal. This report will now appear under ***Reports>>Saved Reports*** on the main menu.

5. Enter the date range of **From** 3/27/2008 and **To** 3/27/2008. Figure 4:31 shows the Sales Journal for March 27.

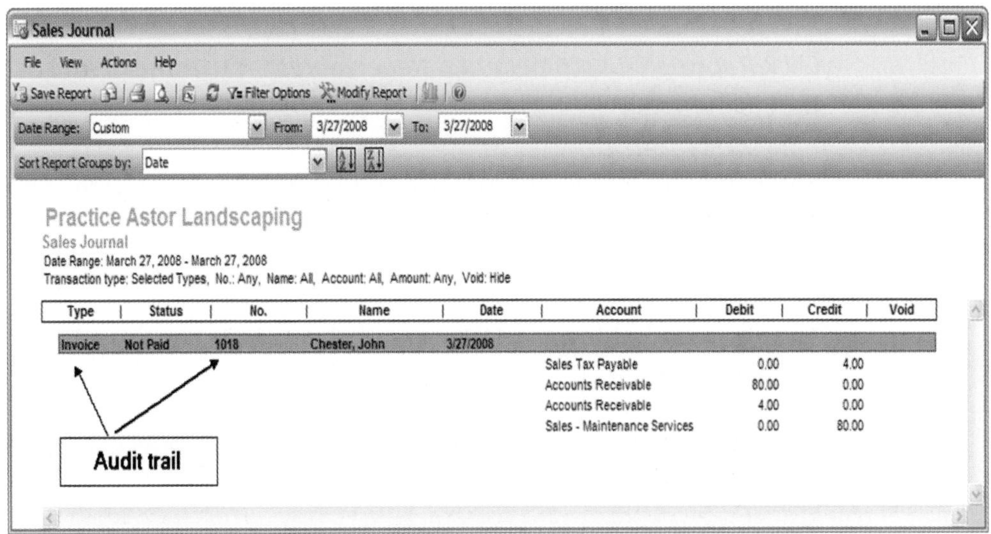

Figure 4:31

OAP's audit trail codes are displayed under the Type and No. columns; thus, the audit trail for John's transaction is Invoice 1018.

Recall that John's invoice entries on the manual Sales Journal debited Accounts Receivable for $84.00, credited Sales - Maintenance Services for $80.00, and credited Sales Taxes Payable for $4.00. This is exactly what OAP shows as the entries.

(Hint: You can reopen the original entry by double clicking the invoice.)

Close this report.

6. You will next locate OAP's entries to John's customer account. Recall in the *MAPS* topic that after posting an invoice on the Sales Journal the transaction was then posted to the customer's account.

   Click ***Reports>>Customers and Receivables>>Customer Transaction History*** on the main menu.

   Enter the date range of **From** 3/27/2008 and **To** 3/27/2008. Using the same method for filtering the Sales Journal report, click Filter Options to set the Customer name filter to John Chester.

   The audit trail of Invoice 1015 (Figure 4:32) matches the audit trail viewed on the Sales Journal. Close this report.

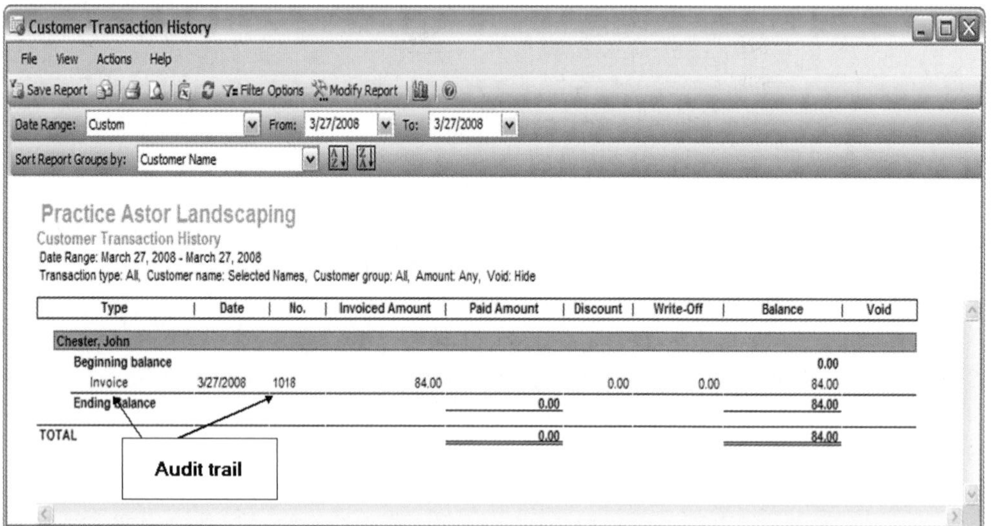

Figure 4:32

7. All that remains is tracing entries made to the general ledger. Select ***Reports>>Company and Financial>>Transaction Detail by Account*** on the main menu. Enter the date range of "3/27/2008." You will find several transactions on that date. Look for the entries highlighted in Figure 4:33. Close this report.

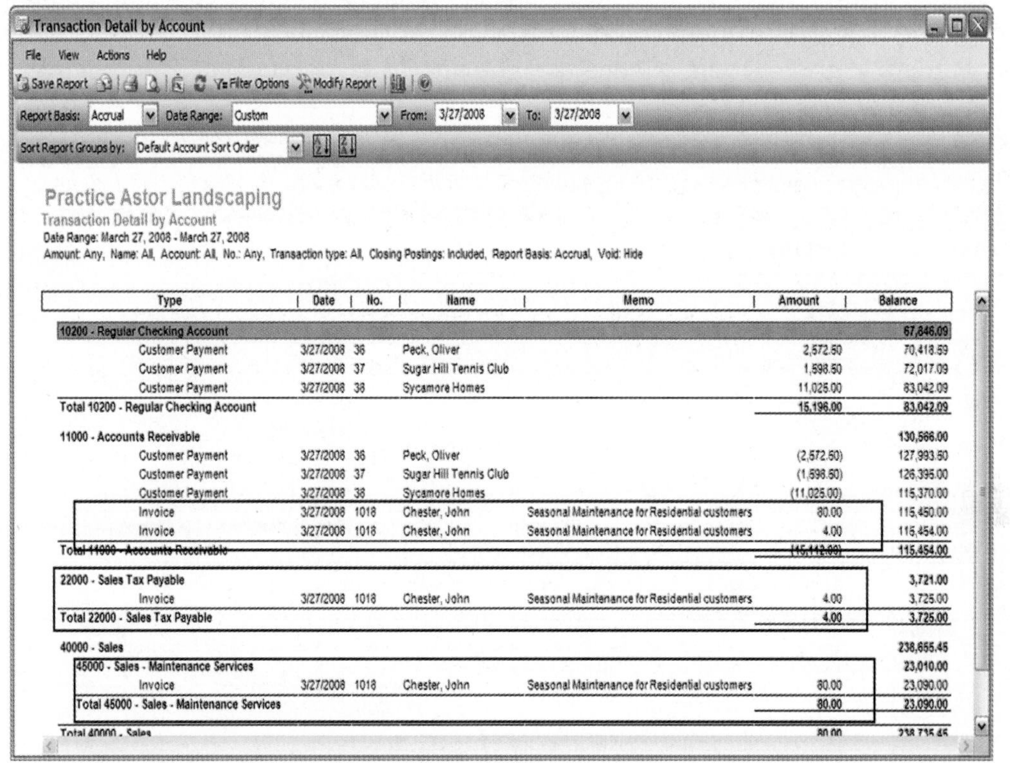

Practice Astor Landscaping
Transaction Detail by Account
Date Range: March 27, 2008 - March 27, 2008
Amount: Any, Name: All, Account: All, No.: Any, Transaction type: All, Closing Postings: Included, Report Basis: Accrual, Void: Hide

Type	Date	No.	Name	Memo	Amount	Balance
10200 - Regular Checking Account						67,846.09
Customer Payment	3/27/2008	36	Peck, Oliver		2,572.50	70,418.59
Customer Payment	3/27/2008	37	Sugar Hill Tennis Club		1,598.50	72,017.09
Customer Payment	3/27/2008	38	Sycamore Homes		11,025.00	83,042.09
Total 10200 - Regular Checking Account					15,196.00	83,042.09
11000 - Accounts Receivable						130,566.00
Customer Payment	3/27/2008	36	Peck, Oliver		(2,572.50)	127,993.50
Customer Payment	3/27/2008	37	Sugar Hill Tennis Club		(1,598.50)	126,395.00
Customer Payment	3/27/2008	38	Sycamore Homes		(11,025.00)	115,370.00
Invoice	3/27/2008	1018	Chester, John	Seasonal Maintenance for Residential customers	80.00	115,450.00
Invoice	3/27/2008	1018	Chester, John	Seasonal Maintenance for Residential customers	4.00	115,454.00
Total 11000 - Accounts Receivable					(15,112.00)	115,454.00
22000 - Sales Tax Payable						3,721.00
Invoice	3/27/2008	1018	Chester, John	Seasonal Maintenance for Residential customers	4.00	3,725.00
Total 22000 - Sales Tax Payable					4.00	3,725.00
40000 - Sales						238,655.45
45000 - Sales - Maintenance Services						23,010.00
Invoice	3/27/2008	1018	Chester, John	Seasonal Maintenance for Residential customers	80.00	23,090.00
Total 45000 - Sales - Maintenance Services					80.00	23,090.00
Total 40000 - Sales					80.00	238,735.45

Figure 4:33

You have now followed OAP's audit trail and see the advantages to using a computerized accounting system. You were able to create a sales quote and then transfer the quote to an invoice. When saving the invoice, OAP posted entries to the Sales Journal, customer account, and general ledger accounts and entered the audit trail. In addition, the accountant is better equipped to answer customer inquiries, provide customer support, manage company sales, and analyze profitability.

Correcting and Voiding Sales Invoices

This topic explains the procedures for voiding invoices and correcting errors on **unpaid** invoices. *(Note: Refer to the instructions in Appendix B before correcting paid invoices.)* First, locate the invoice by opening the Invoice List. For this illustration reopen John's invoice created in an earlier topic. Notice that the invoice is marked **Not Paid** (Figure 4:34).

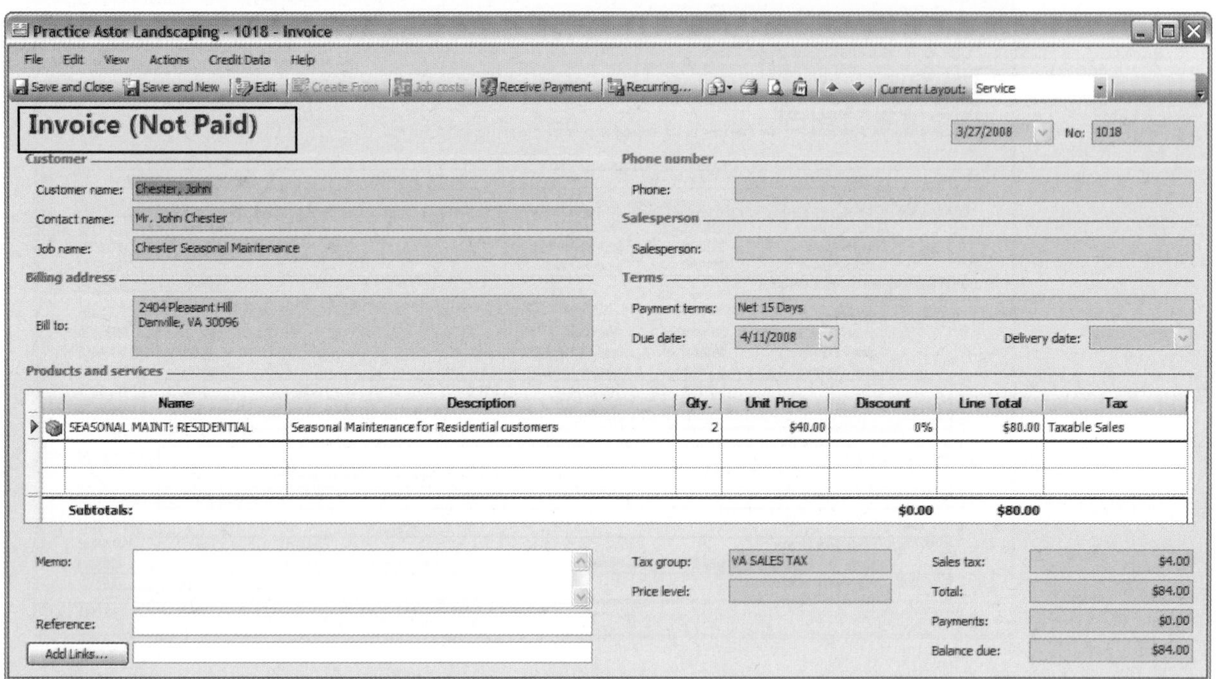

Figure 4:34

The fields on a posted invoice are locked so to make changes you must click the **Edit** button on the toolbar or select ***Action>>Edit*** on the menu. After making changes, click Save and Close for OAP to reverse the original transaction and post a new transaction.

OAP does not permit deleting invoices. Therefore, if you want to remove an invoice it must be voided. To void, you select ***Action>>Void*** on the Invoice menu. *(Note: You can also void an invoice without reopening it by highlighting the transaction on the Invoice List, right clicking, and selecting Void.)*

Voiding an invoice causes OAP to reverse the transaction and reinstate the Quote to again invoice the customer. Voided transactions are listed on account registers with this symbol.

Click **X** to close John's invoice.

CREATE A SALES INVOICE USING A QUOTE

On March 31, 2008, Astor completed Sugar Hill Tennis Club's landscaping job. Turn this quote into an invoice. Verify that you are using the Service template.

Remember to enter the correct invoicing date. You can assume that all other fields are correct. Click Yes when prompted to exceed the customer's credit limit.

Print the invoice. Return to the job and enter "3/31/2008" as the End date and change the Status to Complete.

CUSTOMER ACCOUNTS

This topic explains creating, editing, and deleting customer accounts. Begin by opening the Customer List. Click the **Customers** link under **Find**.

The Current View is set to Active customers. The list displays customer names and current account balances with the sum of outstanding balances listed at the bottom. (See Figure 4:35.)

Customer List Current View: Active

+ Add a new Customer

Active	Customer Name	Address	City	State	Zip Code	Phone	Fax	Balance
✓	Ashford Hill Apartments	3466 Ashford Hill	Danbury	VA	30097	770-555-4466	770-555-44...	$4,116.00
✓	Chester, John	2404 Pleasant Hill	Danville	VA	30096	770-555-4086	770-555-40...	$84.00
✓	Crawford, Shelly	5440 Jimmy Carter Boulevard	Navarre	VA	30093	770-555-4492	770-555-44...	$0.00
✓	DBH Enterprises	1500 Corporate Way	Navarre	VA	30010	770-555-4599	770-555-45...	$2,143.50
✓	Elkorn Apartments	302 Pavillion Ct	Marshville	VA	30069	770-555-8852	770-555-88...	$0.00
✓	Fairbanks Construction	3466 Old Alabama Road	Arlington	VA	30004	770-555-4463	770-555-44...	$0.00
✓	Gibson, Robert	2809 Roswell Road	Arlington	VA	30328	770-555-0989		$9,768.75
✓	Hobbs Web Design	1923 Cobblestone Drive	Danville	VA	30033	770-555-4569	770-555-45...	$0.00
✓	Hutcheon, Brian	3526 Spaulding Road.	Narvarre	VA	30093	770-555-8223		$10,573.35
✓	Jenke, Lynda	688 Spring Street	Narvarre	VA	30093	770-555-4599		$0.00
✓	O'Hara Homes	2551 Canton Road	Canton	VA	30115	770-555-4455	770-555-44...	$15,220.00
✓	Peck, Oliver	1945 Golden Circle	Lancaster	VA	30045	770-555-4720		$1,102.50
✓	Pleasantdale Luxury Apa...	3515 Pleasantdale Road	Danbury	VA	30340	770-555-4726	770-555-47...	$1,609.50
✓	Reynolds Court Subdivis...	1045 Reynolds Place	Arlington	VA	30033	770-555-4597	770-555-45...	$4,924.50
✓	Sallens Property Manag...	1849 Aurum Avenue	Arlington	VA	30533	770-555-4426	770-555-44...	$9,540.00
✓	Silver Homes	1800 Clarkes Bridge Road	Blacksburg	VA	30519	770-555-8852	770-555-88...	$12,127.50
✓	Sugar Hill Tennis Club	2500 Sugar Hill Drive	Sugar Hill	VA	30518	770-555-5598	770-555-55...	$5,843.40
✓	Sycamore Homes	562 Copernicus Way	Arlington	VA	30213	770-555-0001	770-555-00...	$21,826.00
✓	White and Associates	1999 Old Augusta Road	Arlington	VA	30334	770-555-4637	770-555-46...	$12,495.00
✓	Yango Software	2504 Chastain Road	Kennelsworth	VA	30144	770-555-6952	770-555-69...	$0.00
✓	Zara Apartment Homes	6311 Satellite Blvd.	Blacksburg	VA	30096	770-555-8564	770-555-85...	$9,922.50

Viewing active customers

Outstanding balance

Total outstanding balance: $121,296.50

Figure 4:35

Double click **Chester, John** to open his account and then follow below as we describe the tabs of the customer account.

General Tab

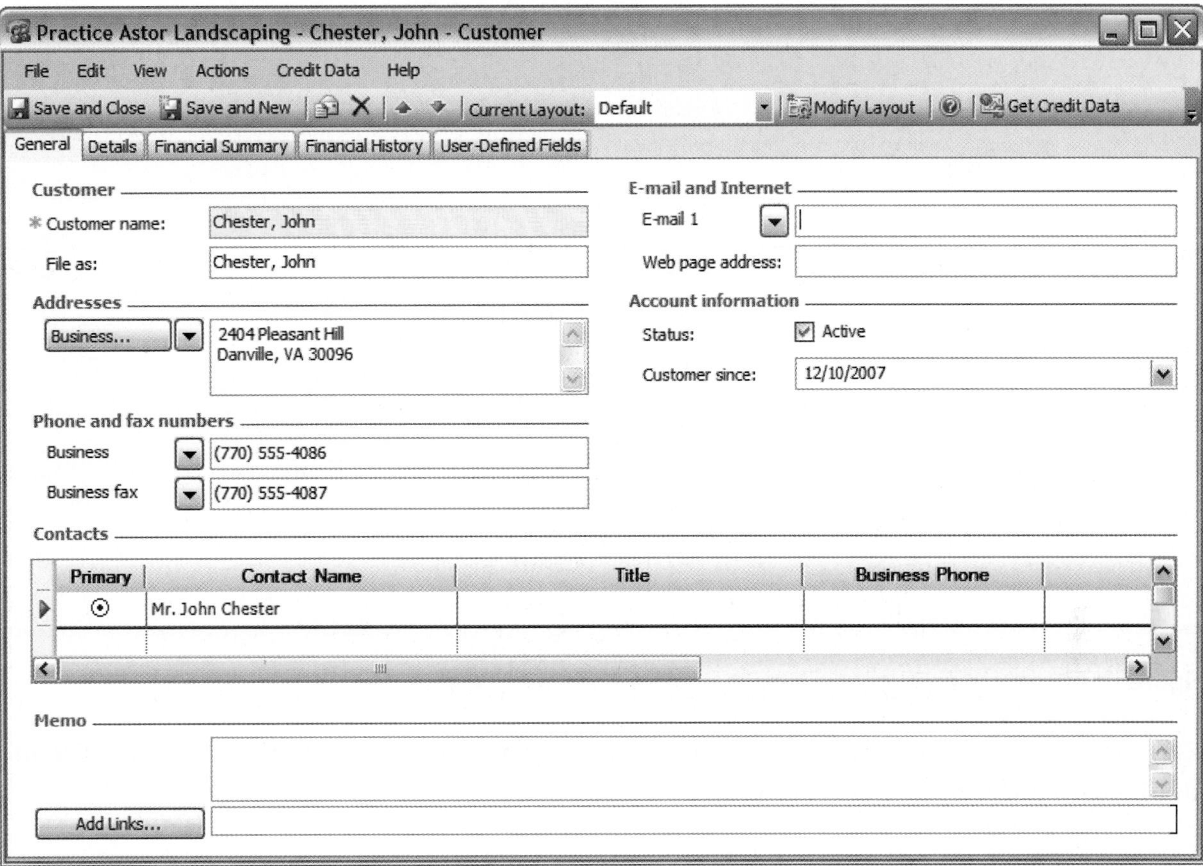

Figure 4:36

This tab stores basic customer information such as address, phone numbers, and email address. The dropdown symbol on a field means you can toggle the field to enter additional data. For instance, the dropdown symbol on Business can be changed to Ship To for storing a separate shipping address.

Details Tab

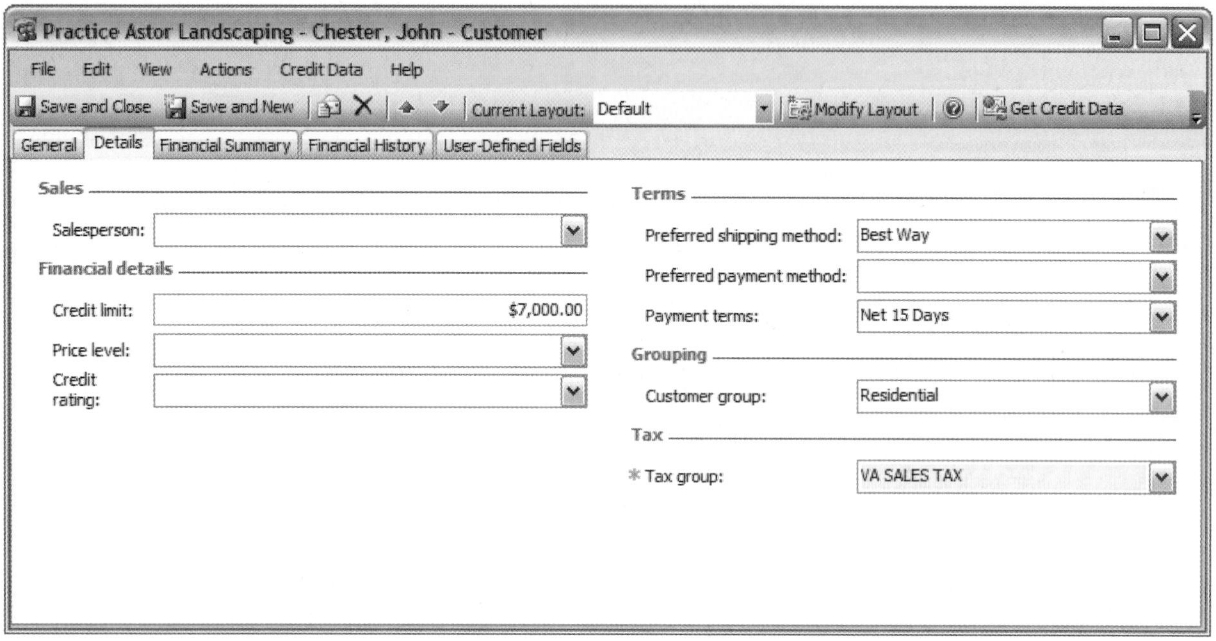

Figure 4:37

This tab sets customer defaults used during transaction entry, including the customer's **Credit limit**, **Payment terms**, and **Tax group**.

Salesperson is used to assign an employee sales representative for tracking sales commissions and sales performance.

Credit limit is an important option for managing bad debt. OAP will warn before saving a new invoice that causes the customer's outstanding balance to exceed the credit limit.

Price level is used when companies implement tiered sales pricing. Tiered pricing means that a company can sell the same service or inventory item at different prices. This feature is discussed in Chapter 8.

Customer group is optional and will differentiate sales by customer characteristics. Astor uses the Commercial and Residential types. A wholesale customer does not pay sales tax.

Click the dropdown list on **Payment terms** to view options for determining invoice due dates and payment discount terms (Figure 4:38).

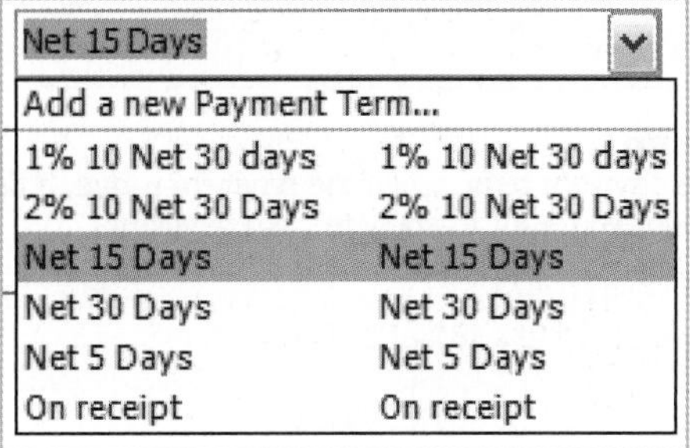

Figure 4:38

Terms are created by selecting ***Company>>Manage Support Lists>>Payment Terms List*** on the main menu. The Net 15 Days term (Figure 4:39) means an invoice is due 15 days from the invoice date.

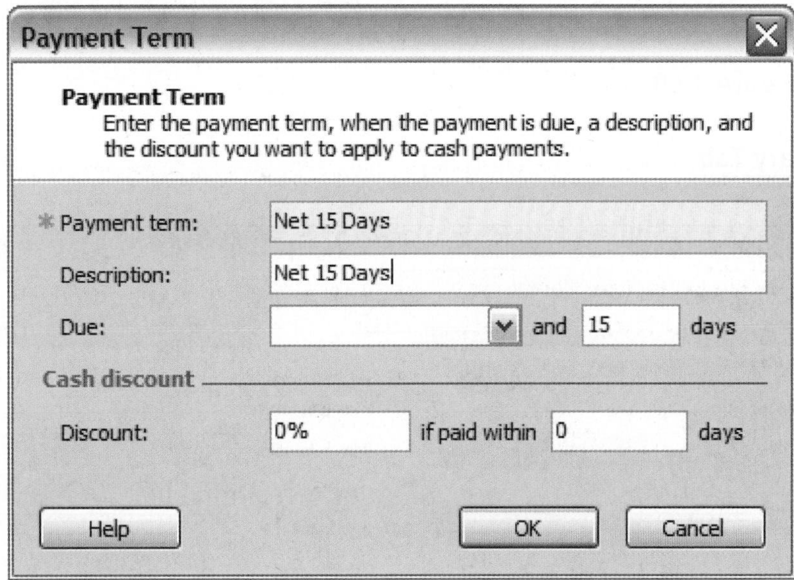

Figure 4:39

The 2% 10 Net 30 Days term (Figure 4:40) means an invoice is due 30 days from the invoice and the customer will receive a 2 percent discount if paying the invoice within 10 days of the invoice date. *(Note: Discounts do not apply to sales tax.)*

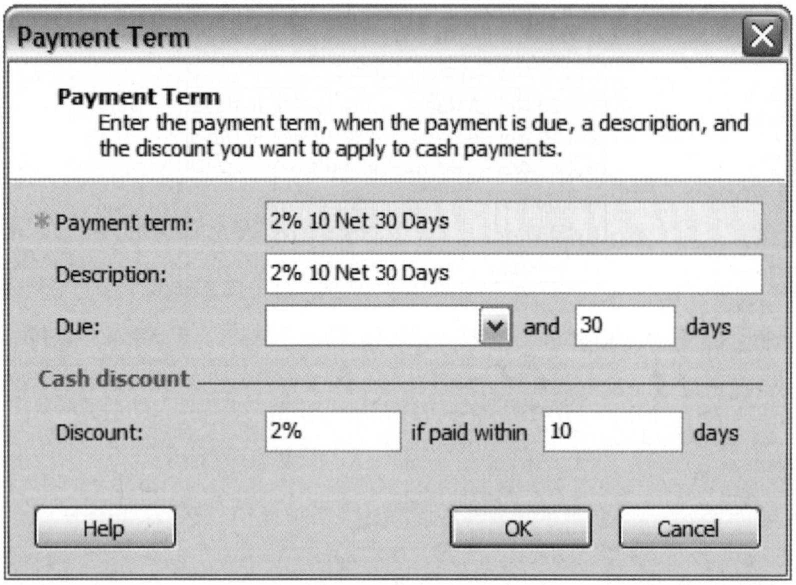

Payment Term

Payment Term
Enter the payment term, when the payment is due, a description, and the discount you want to apply to cash payments.

* Payment term: 2% 10 Net 30 Days

Description: 2% 10 Net 30 Days

Due: and 30 days

Cash discount

Discount: 2% if paid within 10 days

Help OK Cancel

Figure 4:40

Financial Summary Tab

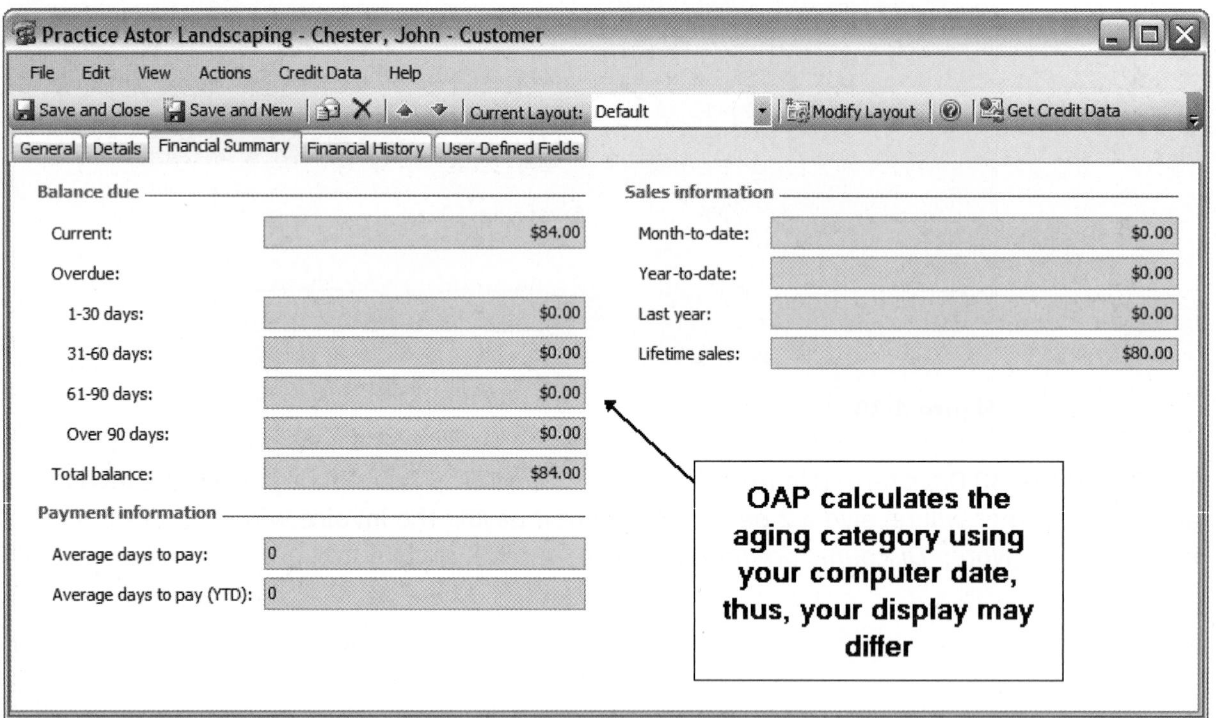

Figure 4:41

This tab displays a quick snapshot of customer activity, including aging information, sales history totals, and average days to pay information.

Financial History Tab

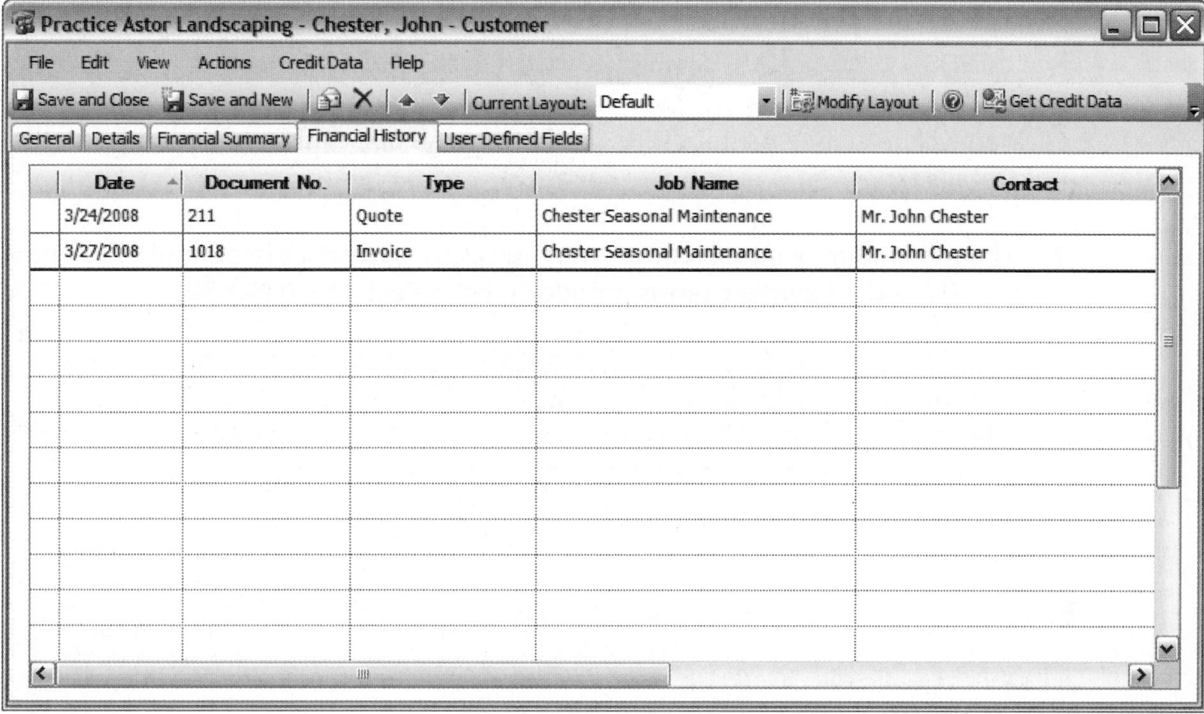

Figure 4:42

This tab lists customer transactions. You can drill down to original entries by double clicking a transaction, which facilitates answering customer account inquiries.

Click **X** to close John's account. The next exercise illustrates editing a customer account.

Steps to Edit Customer Account Information

1. You will be editing Ashford Hill's credit terms so open this account and click the **Details** tab.

2. The accountant wants to offer Ashford an early payment discount of 1/10 net 30. Using the **Payment terms** dropdown list, select **1% 10 Net 30**.

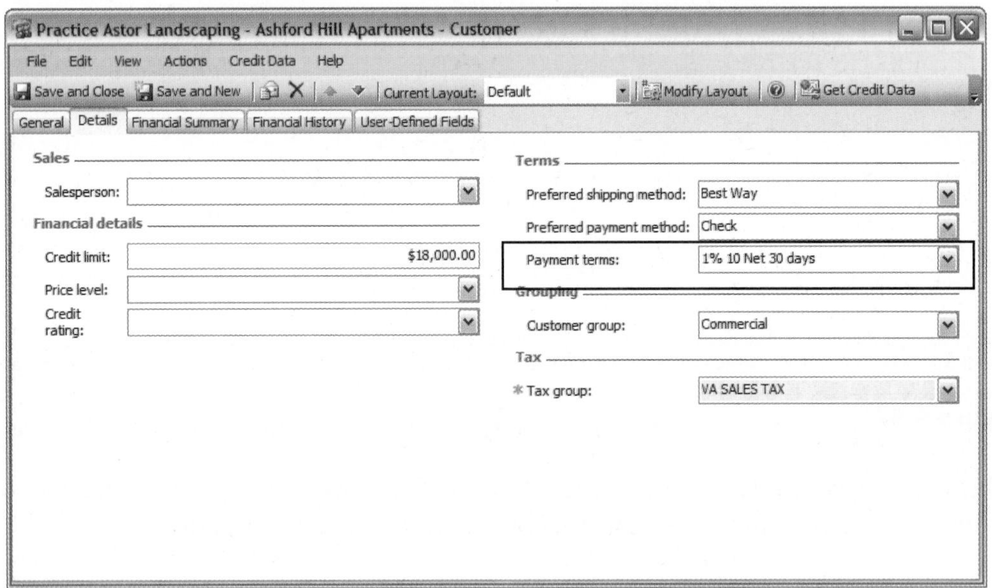

Figure 4:43

Ashford will now receive a 1 percent discount when paying an invoice in full within 10 days of the invoice date. Ashford is still required to pay the invoice in full within 30 days of the invoice date.

3. Click **Save and Close** to save the changes.

You will next walk through creating a new customer.

Steps to Create a Customer Account

1. Click **New Customer** under **Start a Task**. *(Note: You can also click the Add a new Customer link at the top of the Customer List.)*

2. Now enter the following information.

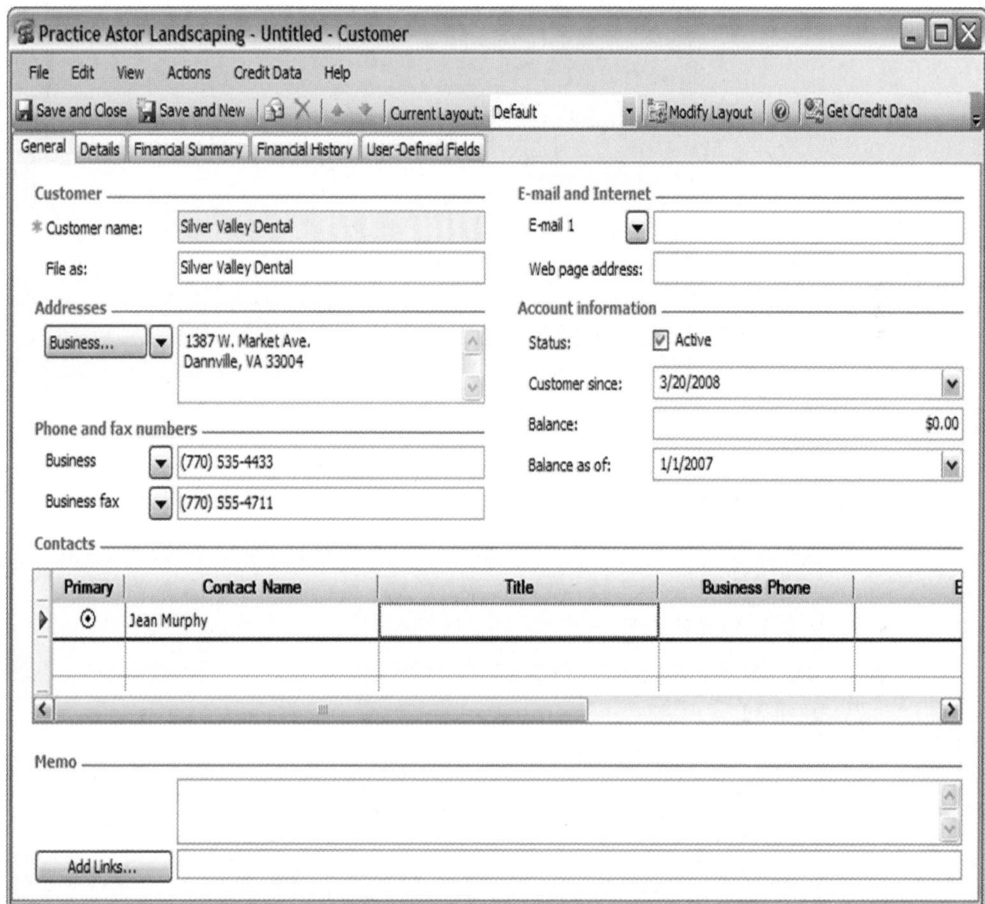

Figure 4:44

3. Click the dropdown list on the **Business** address and toggle the field to **Bill to**. Click the Bill to button to enter an address using a different method. Enter the information illustrated in Figure 4:45 and click **OK**.

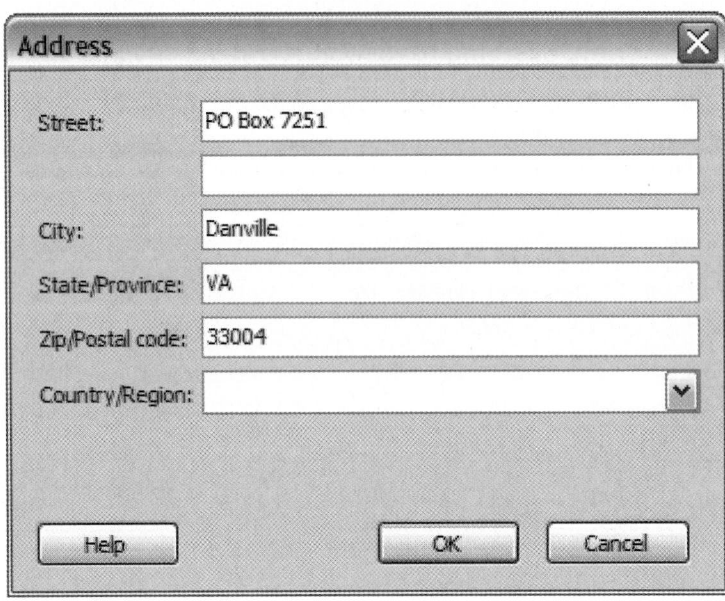

Figure 4:45

4. Click **Details** and enter the information in Figure 4:46.

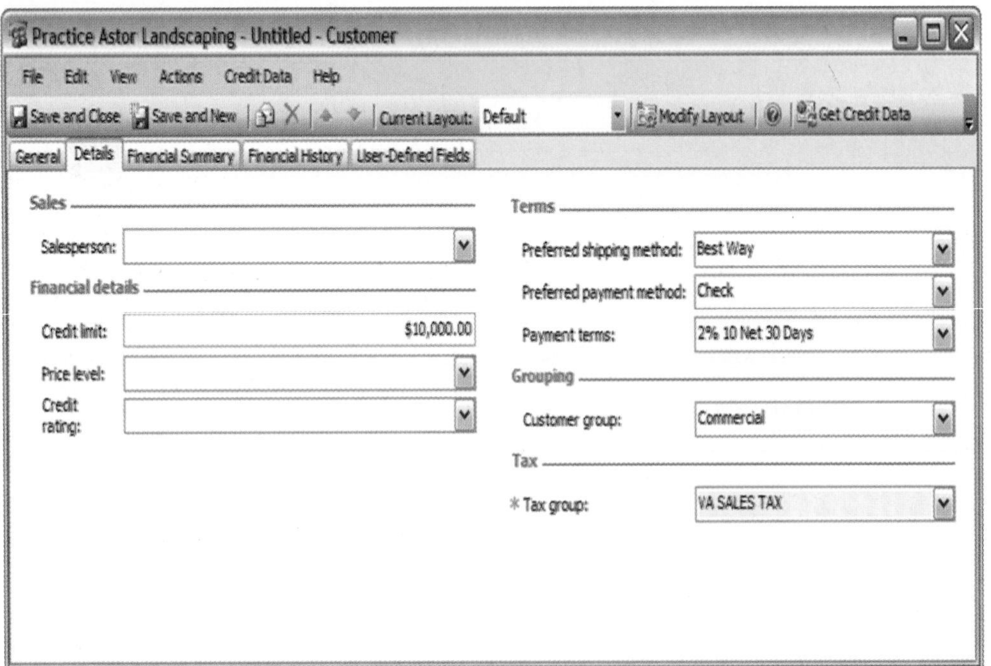

Figure 4:46

5. Click **Save and Close**.

What happens when you try to delete an account with transaction history?

Highlight **Ashford Hill Apartments'** account on the Customer List and select ***Edit>>Delete*** on the main menu.Click **Yes** when OAP prompts to confirm deletion. You receive the warning message illustrated in Figure 8:45 stating that the customer account cannot be deleted so consider marking it inactive.

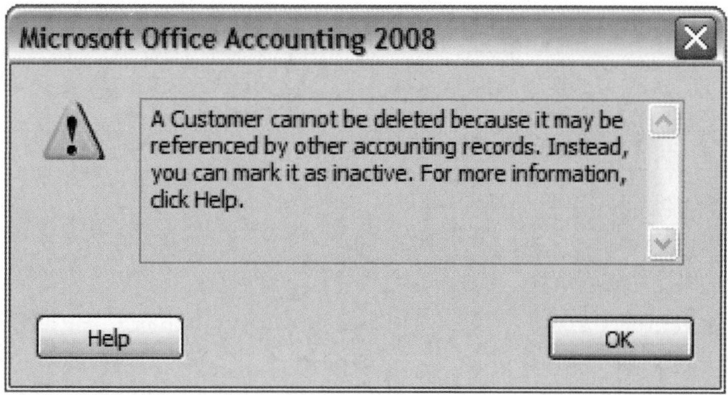

Figure 4:47

Inactivating an account denies future transactions for the account while retaining account history. Click **OK**. You can mark an account inactive by turning off this Status: ☑ Active option on the General tab of the customer account.

CREATE A NEW CUSTOMER ACCOUNT

On March 1, 2008, Astor gained a new commercial customer with the following information.

Graphic Printing Services	Phone:	701 555-1515
127 Technology Way	Fax:	701 555-1518
Arlington, VA 30097	Contact:	Jeffrey Davis
	Email:	davis@graphic.net

Credit limit: $5,000.00
Preferred payment method: Check

The customer pays "VA" sales tax and will be offered net 30 terms. Create this account.

UNDERSTANDING SERVICE AND NON-INVENTORY ITEMS

Service and non-inventory items differ from the traditional inventory items used by a merchandising business discussed in Chapter 8. Unlike goods sold by a merchandiser, services and job materials are not purchased until the work is performed. Thus, service based businesses do not hold inventory. *(Note: Astor's inventory balance is zero.)*

Service Item types are used for invoicing labor costs and store service sales prices. These items do not interact with inventory by tracking quantities on hand or purchasing costs. This also means that cost of goods sold does not post when invoicing. Recall that John Chester's invoice traced in a previous exercise recorded only sales revenue. Since cost of goods sold does not post at the time of sale, Astor must post these costs through another activity, namely, employee or vendor activities.

Non-inventory items are used for invoicing job material purchases. Again, these items do not interact with inventory by tracking quantities on hand or purchasing costs so cost of goods sold does not post when invoicing. Cost of goods sold posts only after recording a vendor receipt or bill for material purchases.

It is important to understand the posting of cost of goods sold; otherwise, you might prepare financial statements that do not match revenues with expenses. The following table explains the inventory, non-inventory, and service items used in this text. After reviewing this table, you will better understand when an item interacts with inventory and when the item posts cost of goods sold at the time of sale.

Item Class	Purpose
Inventory Item	Used on goods purchased and held for resale. Tracks quantities and purchase costs. Cost of goods sold posts at the time of invoicing and calculates under the FIFO costing method, meaning the first item purchased will be the first item sold and expensed to cost of goods sold.
Non-Inventory Item	Used on goods purchased for customer jobs and not tracked as inventory. These are normally job material items. Cost of goods sold posts when posting vendor bills or receipts for the materials purchased.
Service Item	Used on services provided by company employees or subcontractors. When provided by subcontractors, cost of goods sold posts when paying the contractor. When provided by employees, cost of goods sold posts when paying employees.
Kit	Used for grouping inventory items sold together.

Now review a list of Astor's items. Click the **Items** link under **Find** to open the Item List illustrated in Figure 4:48, paying particular attention to the Type column.

Item List

Current View: Active

Active	Item Name	Description	Type	Price	On Hand	Reorder
Add a new Item						
✓	BLUE FLAG	1.5 Ton Pallet Blues Flagstone	Non-Inventory Item	$242.00		
✓	BW COPY	Black and white copy of Scale Plan	Service Item	$35.00		
✓	CEMENT	2 Ton Bag Cement	Non-Inventory Item	$17.00		
✓	CLR COPY	Color copy of Scale Plan	Service Item	$45.00		
✓	COBBLESTONE	Pallet 8"x4"x4X Cobblestone	Non-Inventory Item	$1.75		
✓	DELIVERY CHARGES	Delivery Charges	Service Item	$30.00		
✓	DESIGN - COMMERCIAL	Planning and Design	Service Item	$350.00		
✓	DESIGN - RESIDENTIAL	Planning and Design	Service Item	$175.00		
✓	FERTILIZER	2G Fertilizer	Non-Inventory Item	$21.26		
✓	INSTL HARD - COMMERCIAL	Install Hardscape Materials	Service Item	$60.00		
✓	INSTL HARD - RESIDENTIAL	Install Hardscape Materials	Service Item	$55.00		
✓	INSTL LAND - COMMERCIAL	Install Landscape Materials	Service Item	$50.00		
✓	INSTL LAND - RESIDENTIAL	Install Landscape Materials	Service Item	$45.00		
✓	INSTL SPRINK - COMMERCIAL	Installation of sprinkler system for commercial customer.	Service Item	$1,575.00		
✓	INSTL SPRINK - RESIDENTIAL	Installation of sprinkler system forresidential customer	Service Item	$600.00		
✓	LAWN SOD	St Augistine Sod 1x1 Sq Ft	Non-Inventory Item	$0.38		
✓	MULCH	6 Cu Ft. Bags Mulch	Non-Inventory Item	$14.25		
✓	PAVERS	2'x2'x1" Granite Pavers (Gray)	Non-Inventory Item	$6.75		
✓	PLANTS:AZALEA AMY	1G Amy Azalea	Non-Inventory Item	$12.15		
✓	PLANTS:AZALEA PINK	1G Gumbo Pink Azalea	Non-Inventory Item	$14.85		
✓	PLANTS:BOXWOOD	2G Wintergreen Boxwood	Non-Inventory Item	$30.35		
✓	PLANTS:CAMELLIAS	1G Sparkling Burgundy Camellias	Non-Inventory Item	$16.20		
✓	PLANTS:CYPRESS	1G Cypress Trees	Non-Inventory Item	$33.70		
✓	PLANTS:DAYLILLY PANDORA	1G Pandora's Box Daylilly	Non-Inventory Item	$14.85		
✓	PLANTS:TULIP	Tulip Bulbs	Non-Inventory Item	$3.70		

Figure 4:48

We next provide an overview of these items.

Service Items

Highlight **SEASONAL MAINT: RESIDENTIAL** and double click to open the item. (See Figure 4:49.)

While explaining this item, we will refer back to the *Creating Sales Invoices Using a Quote* topic where you invoiced John Chester for two units of this item. We will also refer back to the *Behind the Keys of a Posted Sales Invoice* topic where you traced the entries made after posting John's invoice.

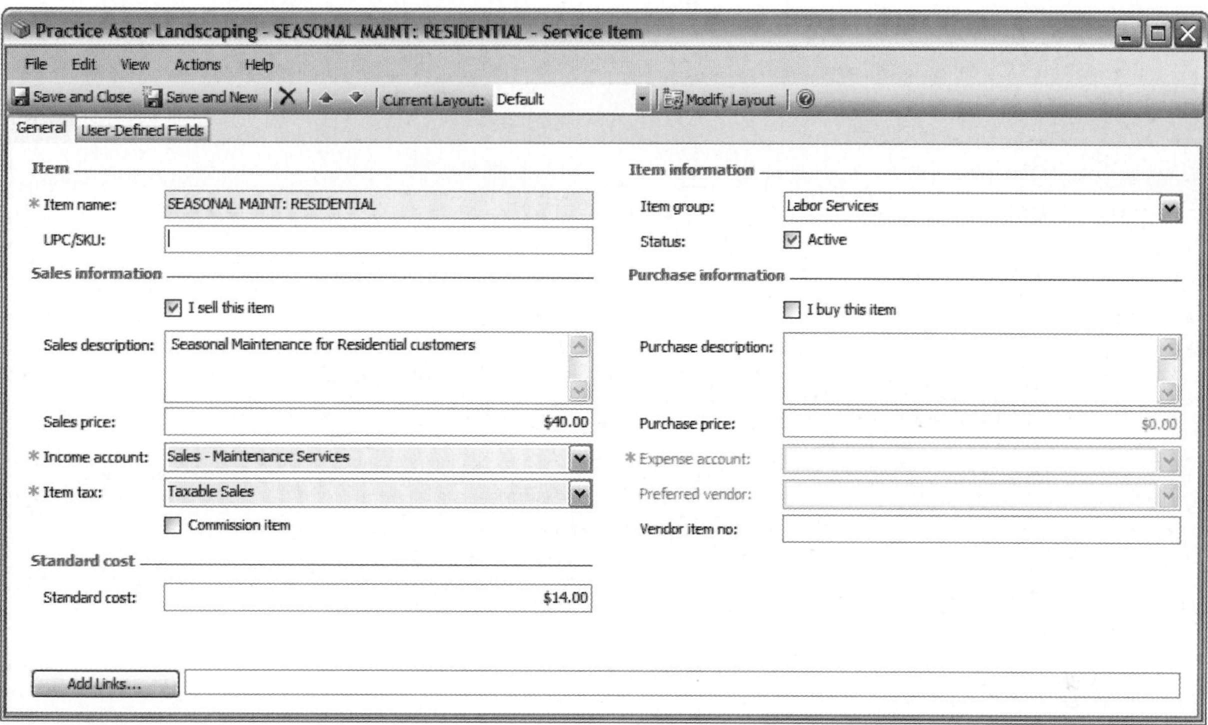

Figure 4:49

Item name is a required field that serves as the record's primary key, meaning also that the value must be unique on each item.

Sales description is the description appearing on customer quotes and invoices.

This is a service item with the labor provided by company employees because "I buy this item" is not selected. In addition, the **Item group** is Labor Services. Item groups are optional fields for grouping sales report information.

Sales price is the fee charged for performing this service, explaining why John was charged $80.00 for two units.

Item tax shows that sales of this service are taxable. However, OAP also looks to the tax default on a customer's account to determine the overall taxability of a sale.

Income account is the general ledger account OAP will use for posting sales revenue, explaining why John's invoice posted revenue to 45000 Sales - Maintenance Services.

Notice that the item does not list a cost of goods sold or inventory general ledger account because services are not inventoried and cost of goods sold does not post at the time of sale. This explains why John's invoice posted only revenue entries.

The item does list $14.00 as the **Standard cost** for providing this service. This cost is an estimate of Astor's wages and benefits for employees providing the service and is used on job costing reports to compare standard to actual cost.

Close the item and open **INSTL SPRINK – COMMERCIAL**.

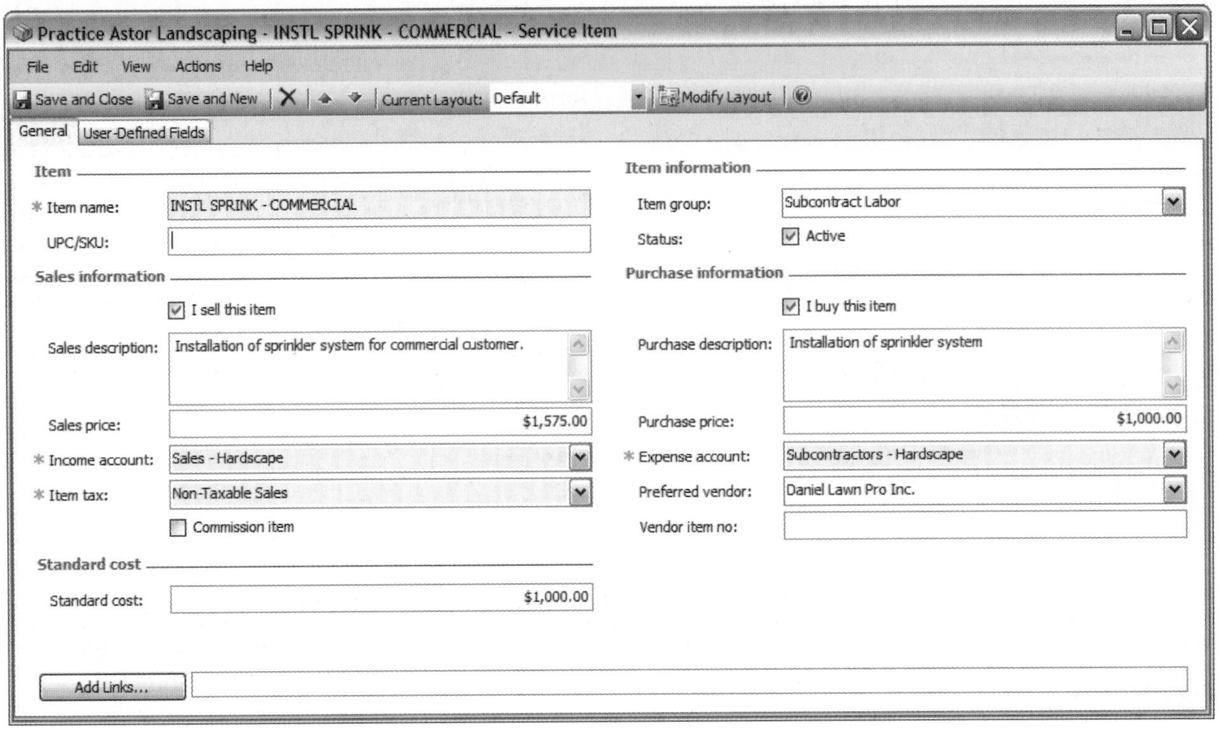

Figure 4:50

This is also a service item but labor for this service is provided by subcontractors so **I buy this item** is selected to open purchasing information fields.

Purchase price is the amount Astor pays subcontractors supplying this service. This price will update after posting a vendor bill with a different price because Astor has chosen the company preference option that updates cost automatically. *(Note: This option was illustrated in Chapter 2.)*

Expense account is the general ledger account for posting vendor bills for this service. This is also the cost of goods sold account for the service.

Preferred vendor stores the name of the subcontractor that normally supplies the service. This field is linked to Astor's vendor accounts.

Non-Inventory Items

Close the item and open **REDWOOD CAPS**.

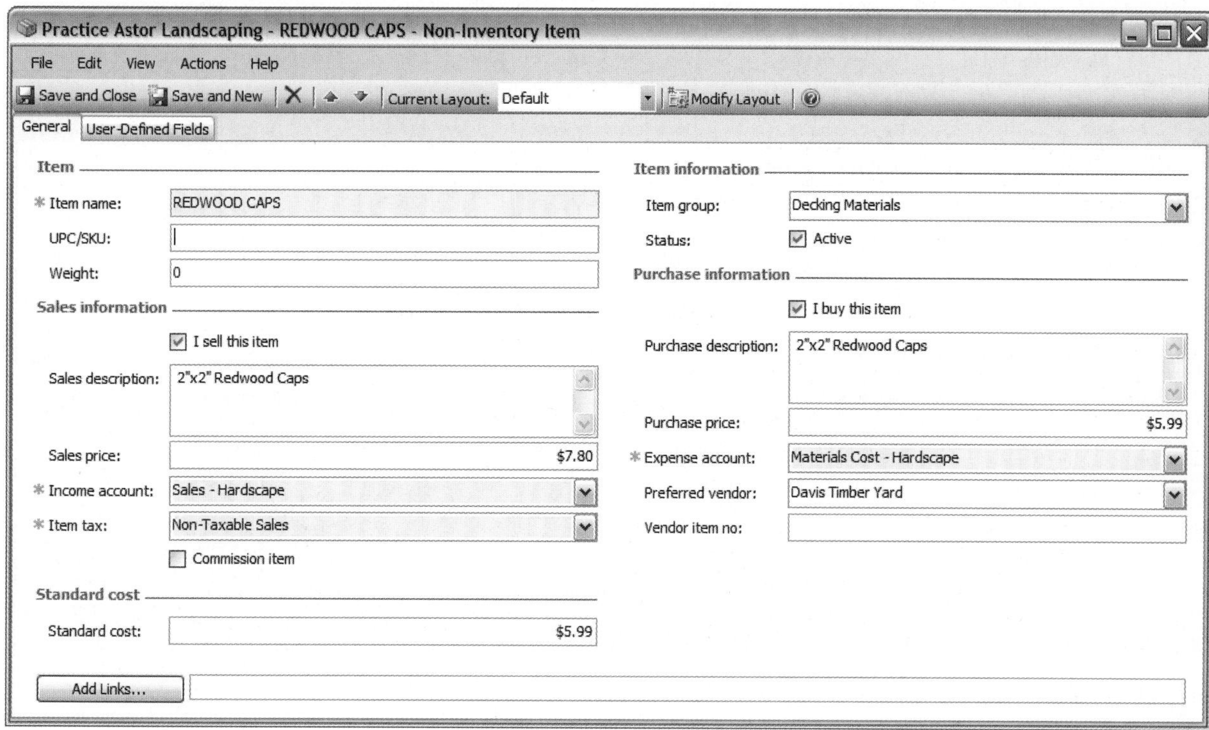

Figure 4:51

This is a non-inventory item used to track job material purchases. Astor buys these caps from Davis Timber Yard (i.e., Preferred vendor) and the vendor charges $5.99 each (i.e., Purchase price). Astor then charges the customer $7.80 each (i.e., Sales price).

Sales revenue will post to 42000 Sales – Hardscape (i.e., Income account). Davis's bills for the item will post to the cost of goods sold account 52000 Materials Cost – Hardscape (i.e., Expense account).

Close this item.

When Astor wants to adjust sales pricing, OAP provides an efficient means for performing the task. Click the **Change Item Prices** button on the toolbar to open the **Change Item Price** window illustrated in Figure 4:52. *(Note: You cannot use this window to change standard or purchase costs. Instead, you must enter these changes on each item.)*

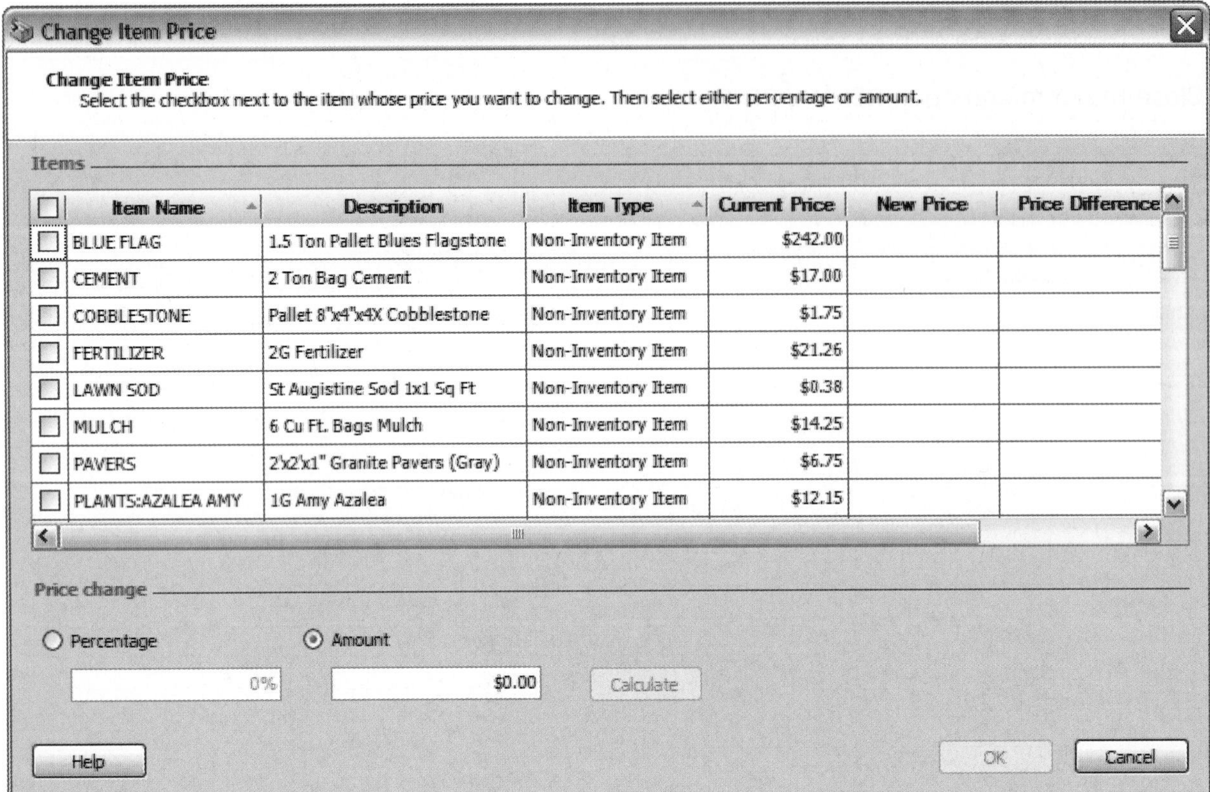

Figure 4:52

Current prices are changed by first selecting the items to adjust. *(Note: Clicking the box in the column header selects all items.)* You next choose whether to calculate new sales prices by applying a fixed percentage or a fixed dollar amount to current prices. After setting the option, the **Calculate** button activates and clicking this button computers the new sales prices.

Chapter 8 demonstrates using this feature to adjust sales prices so click **Cancel** to close the window.

You are now ready to begin invoicing customer jobs.

UNDERSTANDING CUSTOMER JOBS

Astor assigns sales quotes, sales invoices, vendor bills, and employee hours to jobs to take advantage of job costing. Recall in a previous exercise that you assigned John's quote to a job. Click the **Jobs** link under Find to open the Job List illustrated in Figure 4:53. Verify that the Current View is Open jobs.

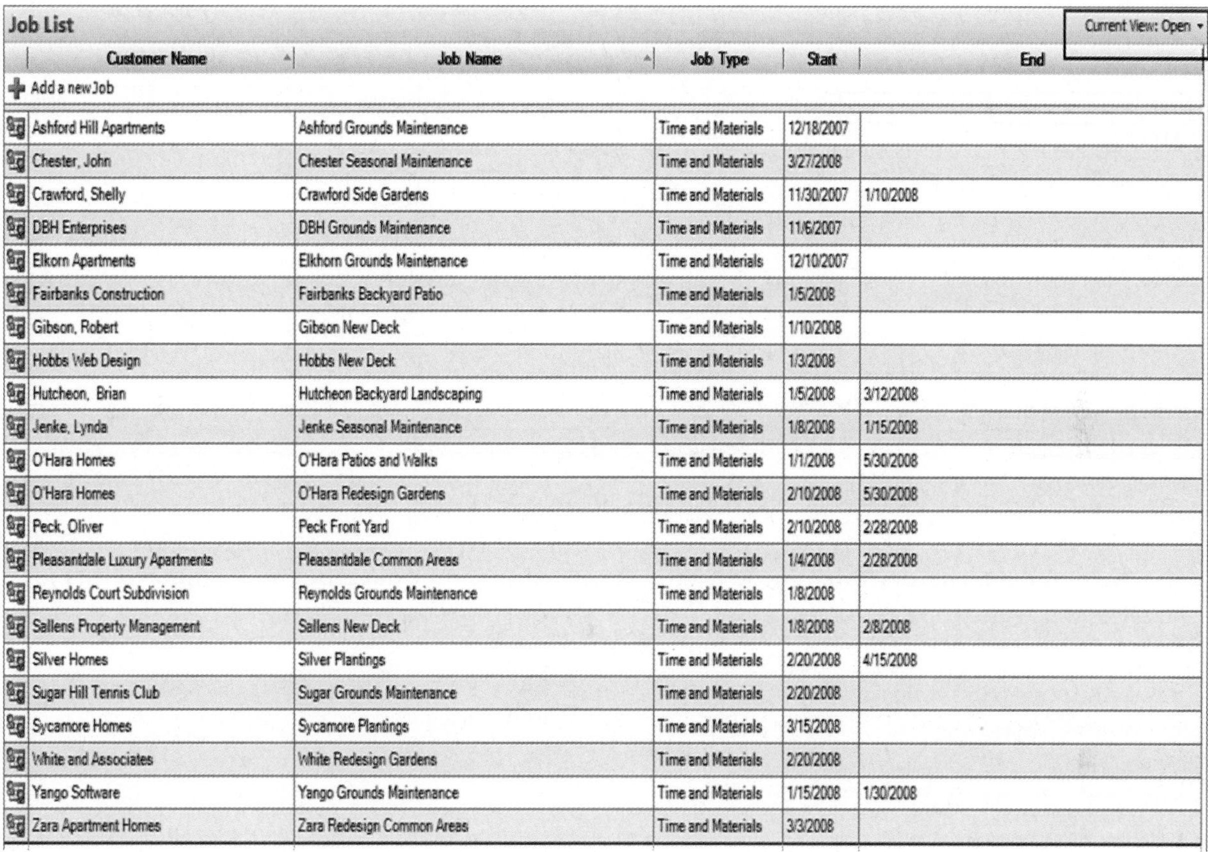

Job List — Current View: Open

Customer Name	Job Name	Job Type	Start	End
Add a new Job				
Ashford Hill Apartments	Ashford Grounds Maintenance	Time and Materials	12/18/2007	
Chester, John	Chester Seasonal Maintenance	Time and Materials	3/27/2008	
Crawford, Shelly	Crawford Side Gardens	Time and Materials	11/30/2007	1/10/2008
DBH Enterprises	DBH Grounds Maintenance	Time and Materials	11/6/2007	
Elkorn Apartments	Elkhorn Grounds Maintenance	Time and Materials	12/10/2007	
Fairbanks Construction	Fairbanks Backyard Patio	Time and Materials	1/5/2008	
Gibson, Robert	Gibson New Deck	Time and Materials	1/10/2008	
Hobbs Web Design	Hobbs New Deck	Time and Materials	1/3/2008	
Hutcheon, Brian	Hutcheon Backyard Landscaping	Time and Materials	1/5/2008	3/12/2008
Jenke, Lynda	Jenke Seasonal Maintenance	Time and Materials	1/8/2008	1/15/2008
O'Hara Homes	O'Hara Patios and Walks	Time and Materials	1/1/2008	5/30/2008
O'Hara Homes	O'Hara Redesign Gardens	Time and Materials	2/10/2008	5/30/2008
Peck, Oliver	Peck Front Yard	Time and Materials	2/10/2008	2/28/2008
Pleasantdale Luxury Apartments	Pleasantdale Common Areas	Time and Materials	1/4/2008	2/28/2008
Reynolds Court Subdivision	Reynolds Grounds Maintenance	Time and Materials	1/8/2008	
Sallens Property Management	Sallens New Deck	Time and Materials	1/8/2008	2/8/2008
Silver Homes	Silver Plantings	Time and Materials	2/20/2008	4/15/2008
Sugar Hill Tennis Club	Sugar Grounds Maintenance	Time and Materials	2/20/2008	
Sycamore Homes	Sycamore Plantings	Time and Materials	3/15/2008	
White and Associates	White Redesign Gardens	Time and Materials	2/20/2008	
Yango Software	Yango Grounds Maintenance	Time and Materials	1/15/2008	1/30/2008
Zara Apartment Homes	Zara Redesign Common Areas	Time and Materials	3/3/2008	

Figure 4:53

Although you have experience working with jobs from previous exercises we want to spend a little more time explaining jobs.

The Sugar Hill Tennis Club job you created in a previous *You Try* exercise does not appear on the above list because the job's status was changed to Complete. Toggle the Current View to Completed to see this job. You can no longer assign sales, purchasing, or employee transactions to completed jobs.

Change the view back to Open and then double click Brian Hutcheon's job to open it. (See Figure 4:54.) This job is projected to end on March 12, 2008 but remains open for assigning costs because the status is not marked complete.

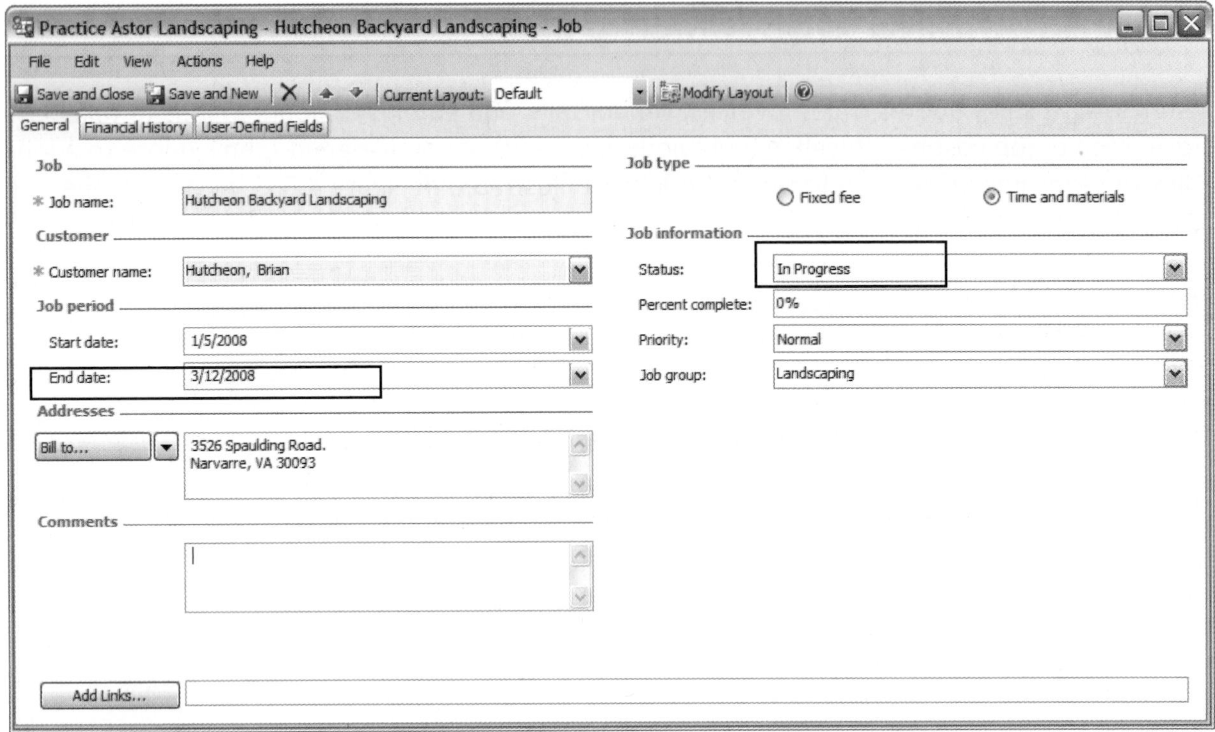

Figure 4:54

Click the **Financial History** tab. These are the transactions that have been assigned to this job. Click **X** to close the job.

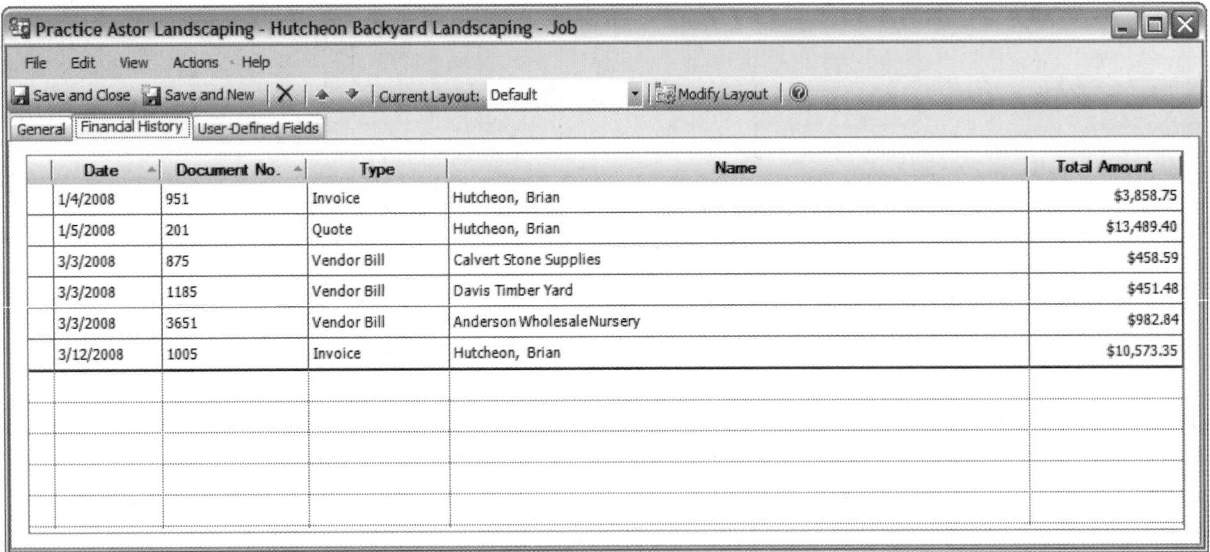

Date	Document No.	Type	Name	Total Amount
1/4/2008	951	Invoice	Hutcheon, Brian	$3,858.75
1/5/2008	201	Quote	Hutcheon, Brian	$13,489.40
3/3/2008	875	Vendor Bill	Calvert Stone Supplies	$458.59
3/3/2008	1185	Vendor Bill	Davis Timber Yard	$451.48
3/3/2008	3651	Vendor Bill	Anderson Wholesale Nursery	$982.84
3/12/2008	1005	Invoice	Hutcheon, Brian	$10,573.35

Figure 4:55

In the next topic you will learn to invoice job costs for time and materials jobs.

Invoicing Jobs

In an earlier topic you created John Chester's invoice by transferring a quote and invoiced the job before recording Astor's costs to perform the service. These are the normal steps for invoicing fixed fee jobs but remember that Astor charges customers time plus materials.

With time and materials jobs you invoice customers after recording time and material expenses and the invoice is created by transferring job costs. The drawback to invoicing by transferring job costs is that costs must be recorded before invoicing can occur so it is important to record these costs in a timely manner to invoice as early as possible. The earlier an invoice is created the sooner the company collects the cash.

Let's now learn to invoice job costs. On March 31, 2008, Astor invoices Silver Homes for job costs incurred to date. Follow the next steps to create the invoice.

STEPS TO INVOICING JOBS

1. Open a new sales invoice and enter "3/31/2008" as the date. Select "Silver Homes" as the **Customer name**.

   OAP will open the Create From window illustrated in Figure 4:56 so you can create the invoice using an existing quote. Remember that Astor enters quotes to record estimated revenues and expenses used on job cost reports but not to invoice job costs. Click **Cancel**.

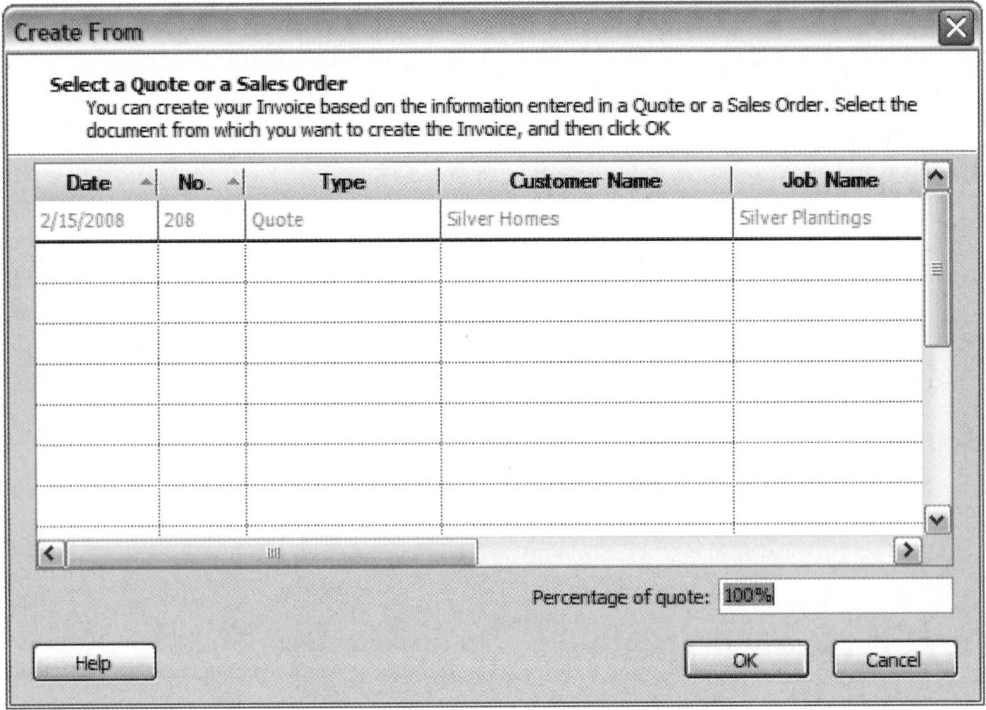

Figure 4:56

2. In **Job name**, look up and select "Silver Plantings."

3. Click **Job Costs** on the toolbar to open the window shown in Figure 4:57. This window lists job costs waiting to be invoiced. Upon opening the window costs on all tabs will be marked for invoicing.

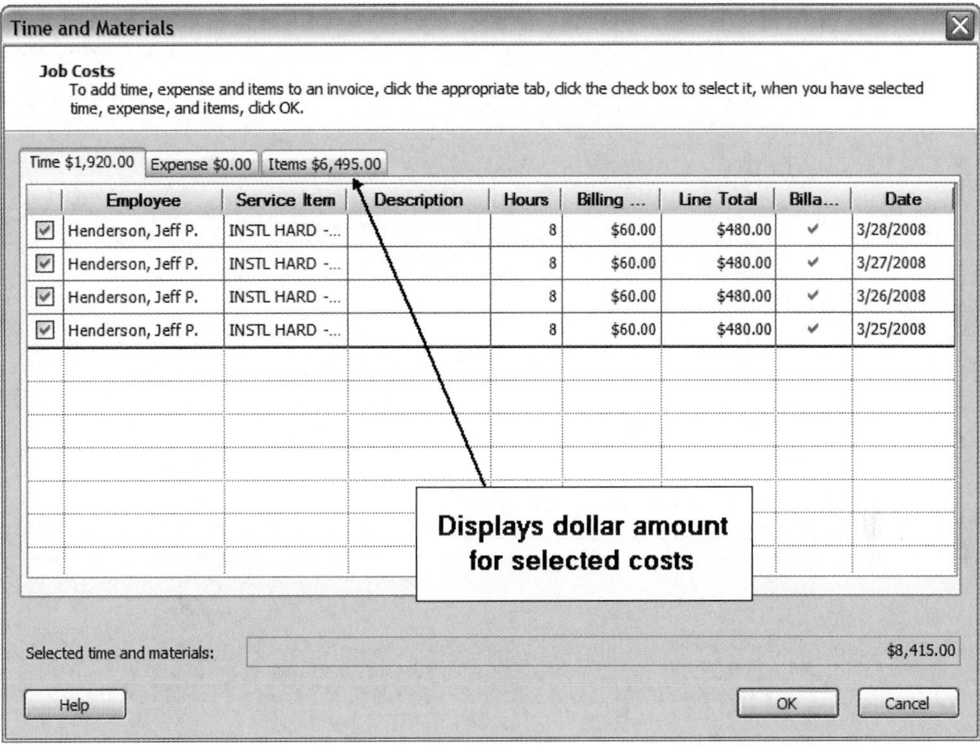

Figure 4:57

We now explain the types of costs for each tab.

Time

This tab displays employee hours assigned to the job. In Chapter 6 you will learn to assign employee time to jobs.

Expense

This tab displays reimbursable expenses assigned to the job. These are for costs such as employee meals.

Items

This tab displays vendor bills assigned to the job. In Chapter 5 you will learn to assign these costs to jobs.

4. Keep all employee time selected for invoicing and then click the **Items** tab (Figure 4:58). All costs are also selected for invoicing.

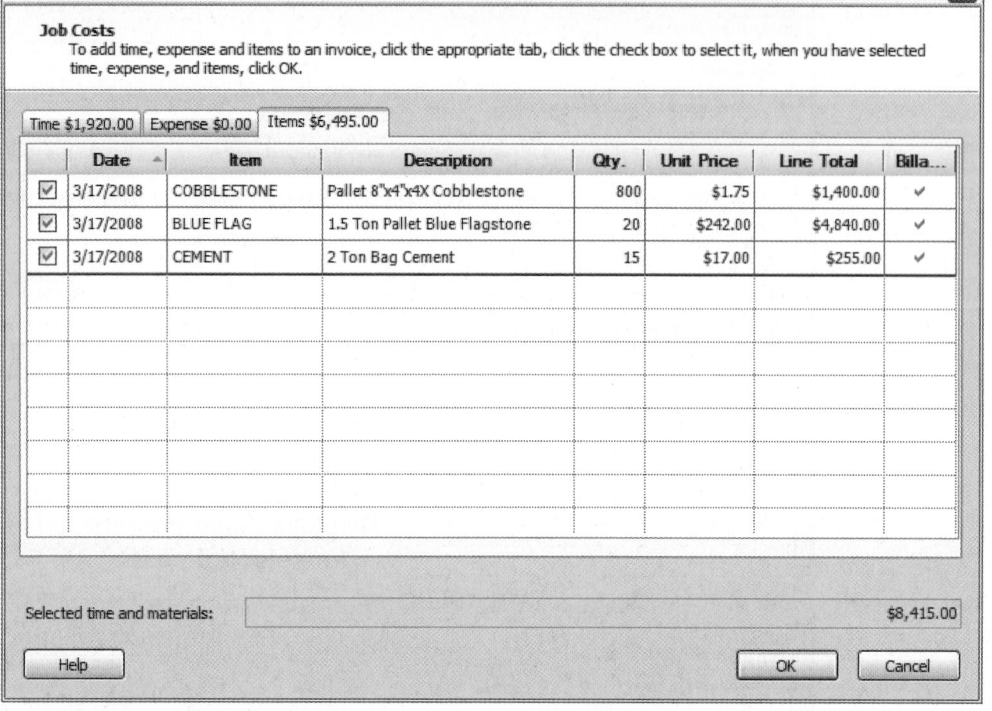

Figure 4:58

5. Click **OK** to create the invoice illustrated in Figure 4:59.

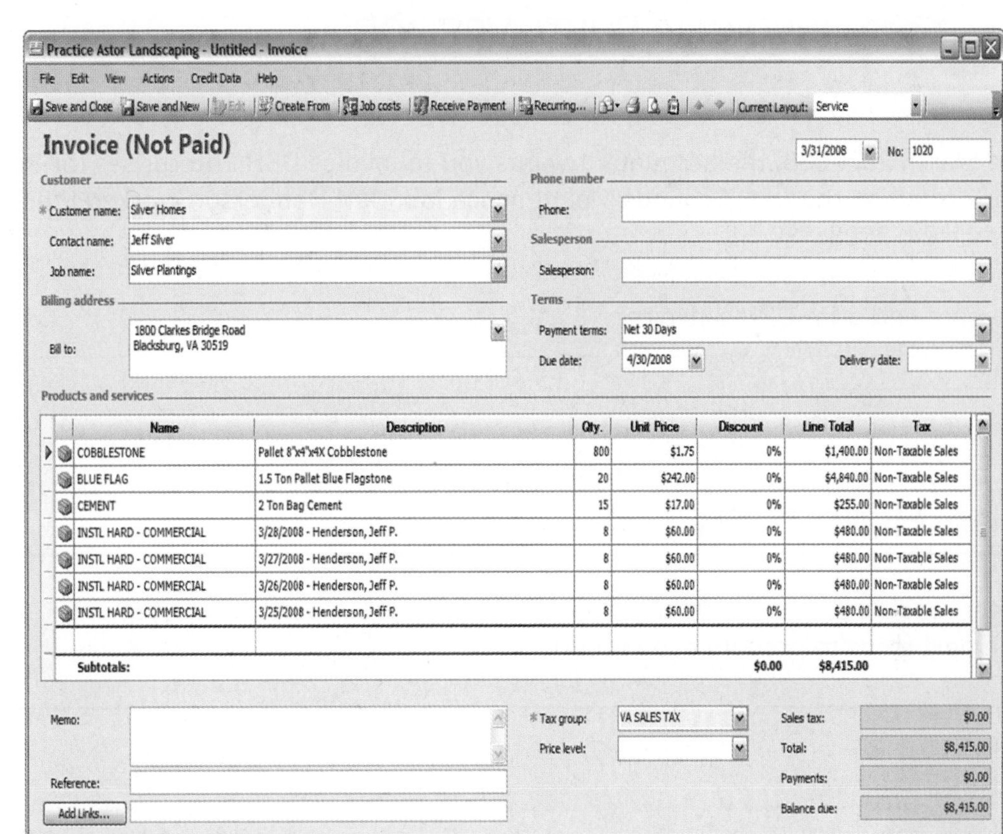

Figure 4:59

If you made a mistake on selecting billable costs click the **Job Costs** icon to change the selection.

A word of caution: After saving this invoice, you cannot transfer these costs again unless you void the invoice.

6. Click **Save and Close** and click **Yes** to exceed the customer's credit limit. *(Note: The credit limit warning illustrates OAP's feature of notifying when saving an invoice causes a customer's outstanding balance to exceed the credit limit on the account.)*

Let's now spend a few minutes discussing the importance of invoice dates. OAP posts entries to the general ledger as of the date on invoice. It is important to use correct dates so that transactions post in the proper accounting period; otherwise, financial statements will be misstated.

Invoice dates also affect due dates and due dates affect the number of days an invoice is outstanding, which then affects a customer's credit history and early payment discount. **Always pay careful attention to transaction dates.**

INVOICE A CUSTOMER JOB

On March 26, 2008, the accountant wants you to invoice DBH Enterprises for 8 hours of work performed on the DBH Grounds Maintenance job. Jeff Henderson worked these hours on March 24, 2008.

Prepare and print DBH's invoice.

JOB REPORTING

After reading this topic you will understand using job reports to analyze profitability. Follow the next steps to prepare a job report.

STEPS TO CREATE A JOB ESTIMATES VERSUS ACTUALS REPORT

1. We will first analyze job estimates versus job actuals. Select ***Reports>>Jobs and Time>>Job Estimates vs. Actuals Detail*** on the main menu.

2. Click **Filter Options** and filter the **Customer name** to show only John Chester and White and Associates.

3. Click **OK** to close the filter window. Verify that the **Date Range** displays **All** and your report will match the next illustration.

Practice Astor Landscaping
Job Estimates vs. Actuals Detail
Date Range: All
Customer name: Selected Names, Item: All

Type	Date	No.	Customer Name	Item Name	Qty.	Cost	Revenue
Chester Seasonal Maintenance							
Estimates							
Quote	3/24/20...	211	Chester, John	SEASONAL MAINT: RESIDEN...	2.00	28.00	80.00
Total Estimates						28.00	80.00
Actuals							
Invoice	3/27/20...	1018	Chester, John	SEASONAL MAINT: RESIDEN...	2.00	28.00	80.00
Total Actuals						28.00	80.00
Total Chester Seasonal Maintena...						0.00	0.00
White Redesign Gardens							
Estimates							
Quote	2/15/20...	209	White and Associates	DESIGN - COMMERCIAL	30.00	2,700.00	10,500.00
Quote	2/15/20...	209	White and Associates	INSTL HARD - COMMERCIAL	60.00	960.00	3,600.00
Quote	2/15/20...	209	White and Associates	LAWN SOD	3,300.00	891.00	1,254.00
Quote	2/15/20...	209	White and Associates	PLANTS:DAYLILLY PANDORA	20.00	219.80	297.00
Quote	2/15/20...	209	White and Associates	PLANTS:VERBENA	25.00	397.50	537.50
Quote	2/15/20...	209	White and Associates	PLANTS:TULIP	150.00	412.50	555.00
Total Estimates						5,580.80	16,743.50
Actuals							
Invoice	2/22/20...	989	White and Associates	DESIGN - COMMERCIAL	6.00	540.00	2,100.00
Invoice	2/22/20...	989	White and Associates	DESIGN - COMMERCIAL	7.00	630.00	2,450.00
Invoice	2/22/20...	989	White and Associates	DESIGN - COMMERCIAL	7.00	630.00	2,450.00
Invoice	2/22/20...	989	White and Associates	DESIGN - COMMERCIAL	7.00	630.00	2,450.00
Invoice	2/22/20...	989	White and Associates	DESIGN - COMMERCIAL	7.00	630.00	2,450.00
Time Entry	3/26/20...	345	White and Associates	INSTL HARD - COMMERCIAL	8.00	0.00	
Time Entry	3/27/20...	351	White and Associates	INSTL HARD - COMMERCIAL	8.00	0.00	
Time Entry	3/28/20...	357	White and Associates	INSTL HARD - COMMERCIAL	8.00	0.00	
Time Entry	4/2/2008	369	White and Associates	INSTL LAND - COMMERCIAL	8.00	0.00	
Time Entry	4/3/2008	374	White and Associates	INSTL LAND - COMMERCIAL	8.00	0.00	
Time Entry	4/4/2008	379	White and Associates	INSTL LAND - COMMERCIAL	8.00	0.00	
Vendor Bill	4/15/20...	9351	Anderson Wholesale...	LAWN SOD	3,300.00	891.00	
Vendor Bill	4/15/20...	9351	Anderson Wholesale...	PLANTS:AZALEA PINK	15.00	164.85	
Vendor Bill	4/15/20...	9351	Anderson Wholesale...	PLANTS:VERBENA	25.00	397.50	
Vendor Bill	4/15/20...	9351	Anderson Wholesale...	PLANTS:TULIP	150.00	412.50	
Total Actuals						4,925.85	11,900.00
Total White Redesign Gardens						654.95	(4,843.50)
Total Difference($)						654.95	(4,843.50)

Figure 4:60

Estimated cost and revenue come from quotes. Actual revenues are derived from the item price on the invoice price. Actual costs for labor hours (i.e., Time Entry) are the service item's standard cost. Actual costs for job materials (i.e., Vendor Bill) are the actual prices paid to vendors.

This report analyzes job pricing by comparing estimated revenue and expenses with actual revenues and expenses. Companies monitor the report to gauge the ability to quote jobs for customers and evaluate job performance.

White and Associates was invoiced by transferring job costs whereas John Chester was invoiced using a quote.

For the White job, unbilled job costs are listed as either a Time Entry or a Vendor Bill. Time entries do not carry a cost because the standard cost will be used and will be listed on the Invoice line after invoicing the time. Vendor bills show the cost paid for the materials.

On the other hand, John's job costs display differently because you invoiced John Chester before recording job costs. Notice that the Cost column under Actuals shows $28.00 despite the fact that job costs have yet to be recorded and, like White's job, is the standard cost for the labor item.

However, when actual costs are finally posted, the labor costs for Actuals will be listed twice (i.e., the standard cost on the Invoice line as well as a standard cost on the Time Entry). This occurs even when such costs are marked non-billable. Figure 4:61 shows how the report will appear after posting John's actual job costs. Remember that these actual costs will never be invoiced because you already invoiced the customer using the quote. Thus, you see the effect on reporting when invoicing from a quote.

Type	Date	No.	Customer Name	Item Name	Qty.	Cost	Revenue
Chester Seasonal Maintenance							
Estimates							
Quote	3/24/2008	211	Chester, John	SEASONAL MAINT: RESIDENTIAL	2.00	28.00	80.00
Total Estimates						28.00	80.00
Actuals							
Time Entry	3/27/2008	388	Chester, John	SEASONAL MAINT: RESIDENTIAL	2.00	28.00	
Invoice	3/27/2008	1018	Chester, John	SEASONAL MAINT: RESIDENTIAL	2.00	28.00	80.00
Vendor Bill	3/27/2008	8923	Anderson Wholesale Nursery	PLANTS:AZALEA AMY	1.00	8.99	
Total Actuals						64.99	80.00
Total Chester Seasonal Maintenance						(36.99)	0.00

Figure 4:61

Now contrast this report with the job profitability report.

STEPS TO CREATE A JOB PROFITABILITY REPORT

1. Select ***Reports>>Jobs and Time>>Profitability by Job Detail*** on the main menu.

2. Click **Filter Options** to again filter the report for viewing **Chester, John** and **White and Associates**. Figure 4:62 shows the report.

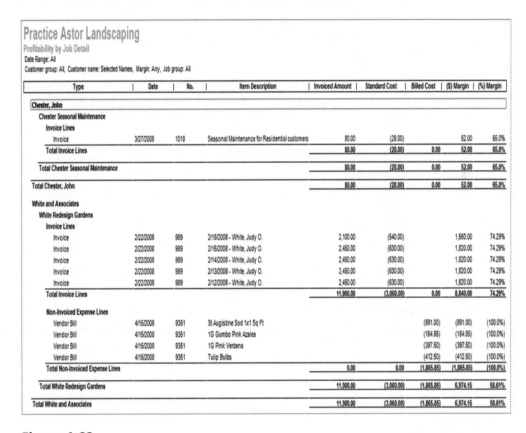

Practice Astor Landscaping
Profitability by Job Detail
Date Range: All
Customer group: All, Customer name: Selected Names, Margin: Any, Job group: All

Type	Date	No.	Item Description	Invoiced Amount	Standard Cost	Billed Cost	($) Margin	(%) Margin
Chester, John								
Chester Seasonal Maintenance								
Invoice Lines								
Invoice	3/27/2008	1018	Seasonal Maintenance for Residential customers	80.00	(28.00)		52.00	65.0%
Total Invoice Lines				80.00	(28.00)	0.00	52.00	65.0%
Total Chester Seasonal Maintenance				80.00	(28.00)	0.00	52.00	65.0%
Total Chester, John				80.00	(28.00)	0.00	52.00	65.0%
White and Associates								
White Redesign Gardens								
Invoice Lines								
Invoice	2/22/2008	989	2/18/2008 - White, Judy O.	2,100.00	(540.00)		1,560.00	74.29%
Invoice	2/22/2008	989	2/15/2008 - White, Judy O.	2,450.00	(630.00)		1,820.00	74.29%
Invoice	2/22/2008	989	2/14/2008 - White, Judy O.	2,450.00	(630.00)		1,820.00	74.29%
Invoice	2/22/2008	989	2/13/2008 - White, Judy O.	2,450.00	(630.00)		1,820.00	74.29%
Invoice	2/22/2008	989	2/12/2008 - White, Judy O.	2,450.00	(630.00)		1,820.00	74.29%
Total Invoice Lines				11,900.00	(3,060.00)	0.00	8,840.00	74.29%
Non-Invoiced Expense Lines								
Vendor Bill	4/15/2008	9351	St Augistine Sod 1x1 Sq Ft			(891.00)	(891.00)	(100.0%)
Vendor Bill	4/15/2008	9351	1G Gumbo Pink Azalea			(164.85)	(164.85)	(100.0%)
Vendor Bill	4/15/2008	9351	1G Pink Verbena			(397.50)	(397.50)	(100.0%)
Vendor Bill	4/15/2008	9351	Tulip Bulbs			(412.50)	(412.50)	(100.0%)
Total Non-Invoiced Expense Lines				0.00	0.00	(1,865.85)	(1,865.85)	(100.0%)
Total White Redesign Gardens				11,900.00	(3,060.00)	(1,865.85)	6,974.15	58.61%
Total White and Associates				11,900.00	(3,060.00)	(1,865.85)	6,974.15	58.61%

Figure 4:62

This report focuses on comparing standard and billed costs to invoiced amounts. It also sets out costs needing to be invoiced.

For White and Associates, invoice lines listing employee names are invoices for employee hours. You see that the customer still needs to be invoiced for vendor bills. After invoicing, the expense is moved to an invoice line and the cost will appear under the Billed Cost column.

As for John Chester's job invoiced using a quote, when actual expenses are entered these costs will appear as non-invoiced expenses even when marked non-billable. Figure 4:63 shows how the report will appear after entering actual costs.

Type	Date	No.	Item Description	Invoiced Amount	Standard Cost	Billed Cost	($) Margin	(%) Margin
Chester, John								
Chester Seasonal Maintenance								
Invoice Lines								
Invoice	3/27/2008	1018	Seasonal Maintenance for Residential customers	80.00	(28.00)		52.00	65.0%
Total Invoice Lines				80.00	(28.00)	0.00	52.00	65.0%
Non-Invoiced Expense Lines								
Vendor Bill	3/27/2008	8923	1G Amy Azalea			(8.99)	(8.99)	(100.0%)
Time Entry	3/27/2008	388			(28.00)		(28.00)	(100.0%)
Total Non-Invoiced Expense Lines				0.00	(28.00)	(8.99)	(36.99)	(100.0%)
Total Chester Seasonal Maintenance				80.00	(56.00)	(8.99)	15.01	18.76%
Total Chester, John				80.00	(56.00)	(8.99)	15.01	18.76%

Figure 4:63

CREATE A JOB REPORT

Print the Profitability by Job Detail and the Job Estimates vs. Actuals Detail reports for Silver Homes. Analyze these reports.

CUSTOMER PAYMENTS

Sales must be realized in cash before a company can pay employees and vendors or invest in the business. This topic focuses on processing receipts of customer payments on account.

On March 25, 2008, Ashford Hill Apartments remitted check number 1786 for $1,764.00, paying Invoices 985 and 990 in full. Follow the next steps to record this payment.

STEPS TO POST A CUSTOMER PAYMENT

1. Click **Receive Payment** on the Customers Home page to open the transaction window. Change the date to **3/25/2008** and select **Ashford Hill Apartments** as the **Received from**. Ashford's outstanding invoices are listed at the bottom of the window illustrated in Figure 4:64.

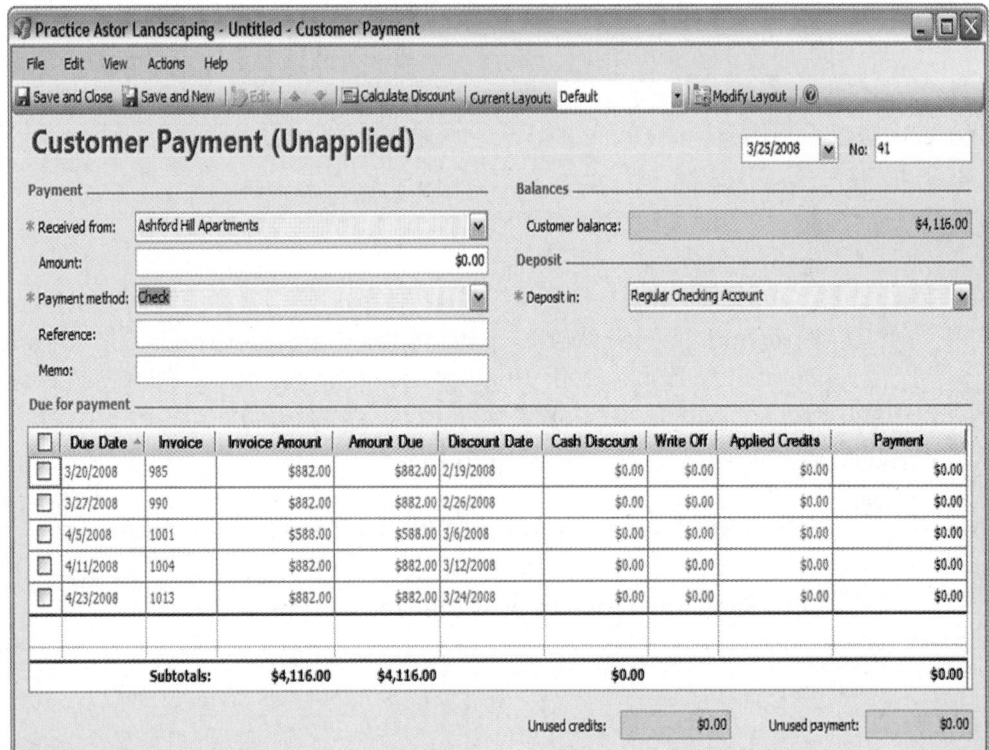

Figure 4:64

2. Tab to **Amount** and enter "1,764.00" and the first two invoices are marked for payment. *(Note: OAP will always apply a payment to the oldest invoices. You can override OAP selections by changing the check box.)*

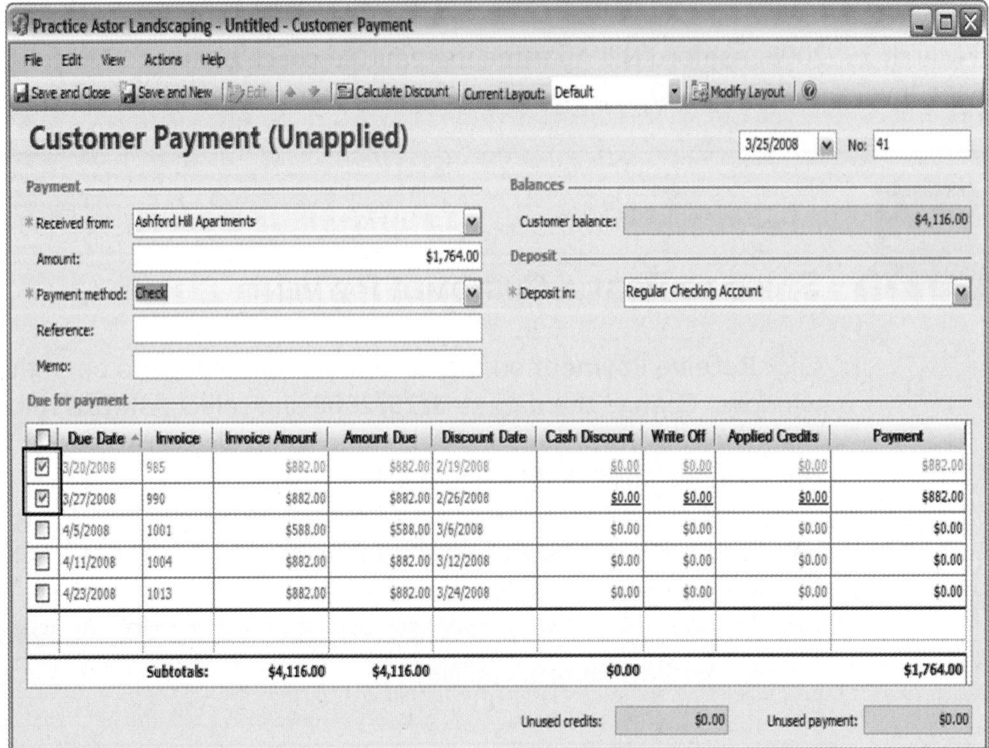

Figure 4:65

3. You should always verify that the **Payment method** is correct and that the **Deposit in** displays the Regular Checking Account. *(Note: A cash receipt transaction debits the Deposit in account and credits the Accounts Receivable account.)*

4. Tab to **Reference** and enter "1786" as the check number.

5. Click **Save and Close** to post the transaction.

BEHIND THE KEYS OF A POSTED CUSTOMER PAYMENT

Now trace the audit trail for the receipt posted in the previous topic. Select ***Reports>>Company and Financial>>Transaction Journal*** on the main menu. Filter the report for the date range of "3/25/2008."

Click **Modify Report** and filter the **Transaction type** to list the types illustrated in Figure 4:66. Also rename the report **Cash Receipts Journal** and save it for future use.

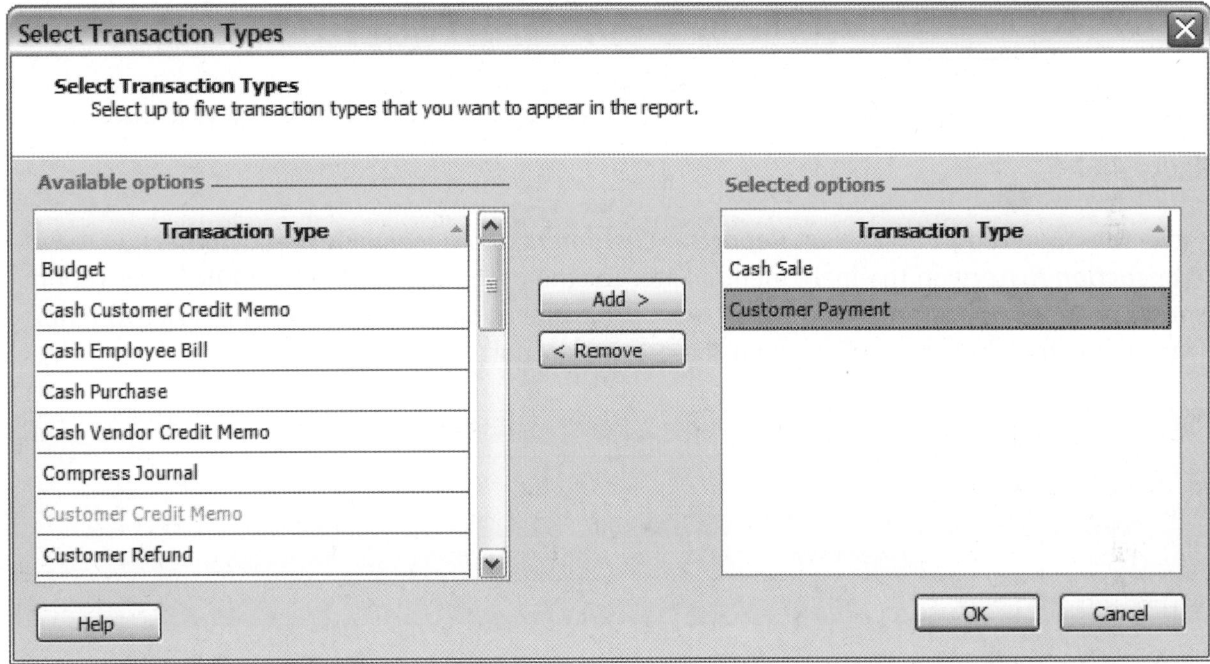

Figure 4:66

Click **OK** and then **OK**. Figure 4:67 illustrates the Cash Receipts Journal. Note that the audit trail displays in the Type and No. columns.

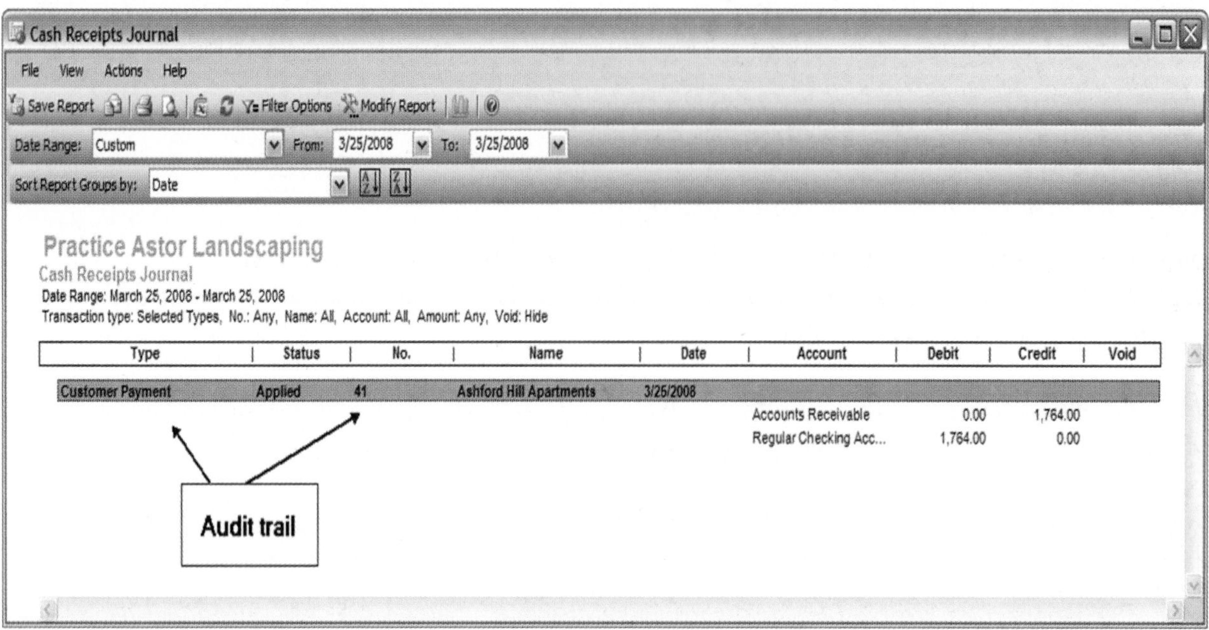

Figure 4:67

Close the open report and select ***Reports>>Customers and Receivables>>Customer Transaction History*** on the main menu. Filter for the date range of "3/25/2008." This report shows postings to customer accounts. Notice that the audit trail on Ashford Hill Apartments' transaction matches the audit trail on the previous report.

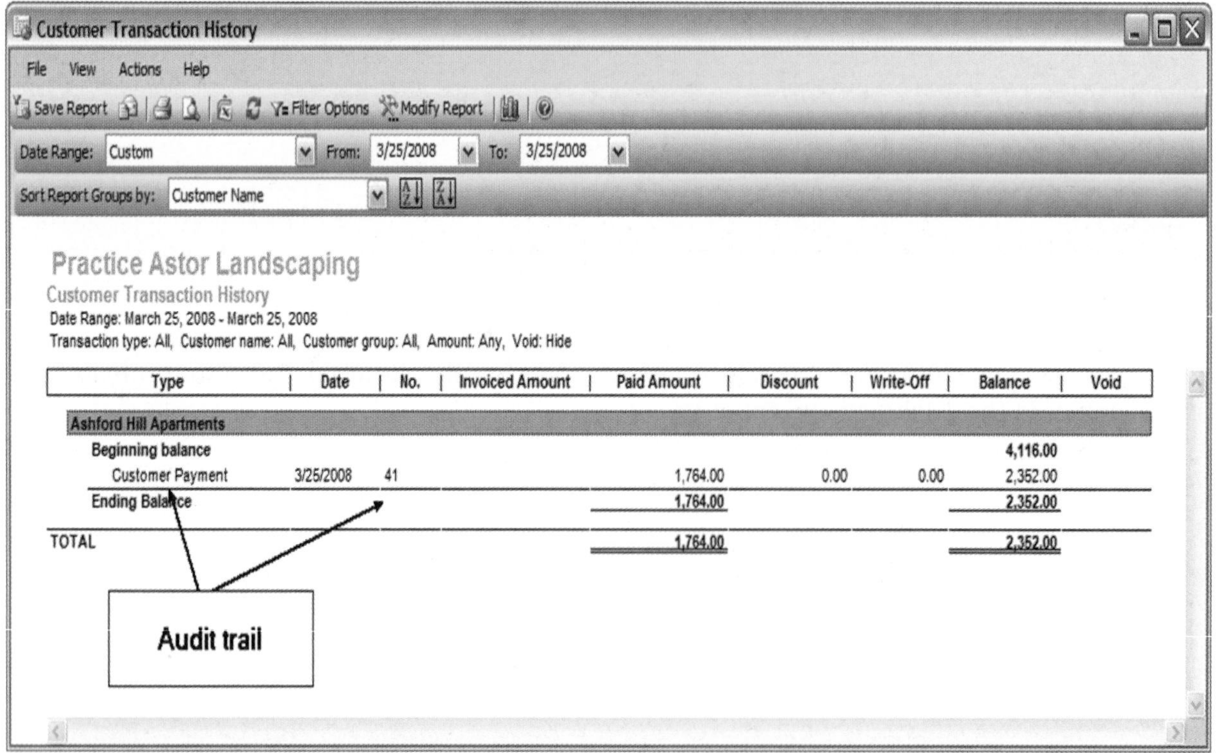

Figure 4:68

Close this report and complete tracing entries by opening the **Transaction Detail by Account** report. Locate your entries in accounts 10200 Regular Checking Account and 11000 Accounts Receivable (not illustrated).

CUSTOMER PAYMENTS WITH A DISCOUNT

In this topic you continue posting customer payments. This time the customer is paying within the discount period. O'Hara Homes remitted payment on March 22 for Invoices 993, 999, and 1007. Complete the next exercise to record the transaction.

STEPS TO POST A CUSTOMER PAYMENT WITH A DISCOUNT

1. Click **Receive Payment**, change the date to "3/22/2008" and select "O'Hara Homes" in **Received from**.

   Recheck the date because OAP uses it to determine when the customer is paying within the discount period.

2. Click **Calculate Discount** so that discount amounts are listed under the Cash Discount column. ***Note: You should click this button each time a payment is entered or OAP will not apply available discounts.***

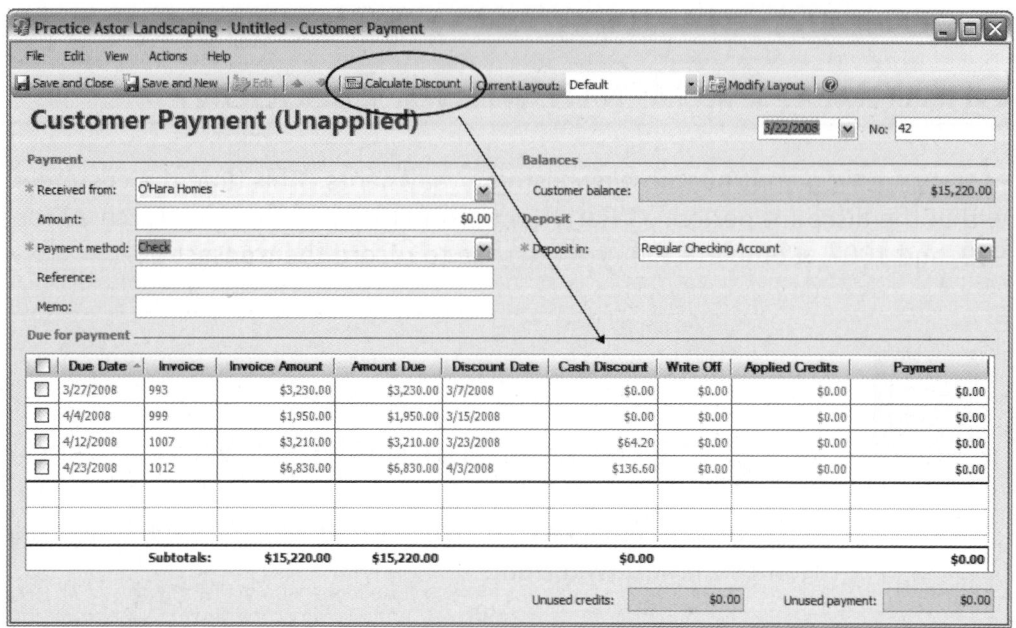

Figure 4:69

3. Tab to **Amount** and enter "8,325.80" and then enter "8213" in **Reference**. Notice that the three invoices are fully paid and Invoice 1007 carries a $64.20 discount. (See Figure 4:70.)

   (Note: If you forget to calculate discounts then click Calculate Discount after entering the amount and click Yes on the prompt asking to redistribute the payment.)

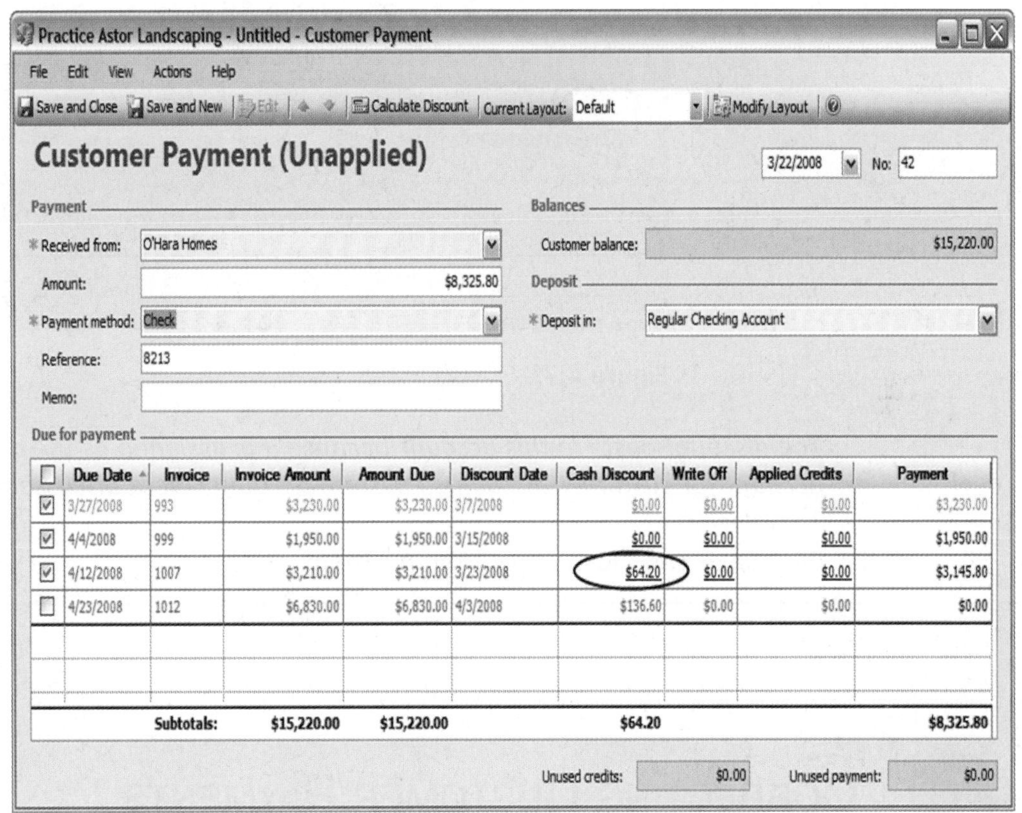

Figure 4:70

4. Click the hyperlinked discount amount to open the Cash Discount window illustrated in Figure 4:71. This window shows that the discount will post (i.e., debit) the Sales Discounts account. Click **Cancel**.

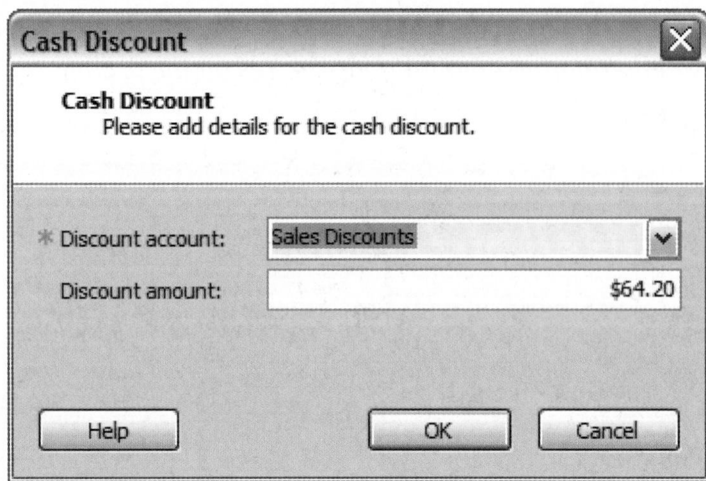

Figure 4:71

The discount posts to this account because it is assigned as the default system account for customer discounts. System accounts were discussed in Chapter 2.

5. Click **Save and Close** to post the payment.

Correcting Customer Payments

OAP will not permit editing or deleting payments. Instead, you must void a payment and reenter a new payment transaction. We will now demonstrate this.

Click **Received Payments** under Find to open the Received Payment List illustrated in Figure 4:72.

Received Payment List Current View: All

Payment Date	No.	Customer Name	Payment Method	Amount Paid
Add a new Payment				
1/4/2008	1	DBH Enterprises	Check	$2,601.20
1/8/2008	2	Ashford Hill Apartments	Check	$1,772.40
1/25/2008	3	Fairbanks Construction	Check	$6,082.10
1/25/2008	4	O'Hara Homes	Check	$2,360.25
2/1/2008	5	Ashford Hill Apartments	Check	$882.00
2/1/2008	6	Crawford, Shelly	Check	$5,129.95
2/6/2008	7	Sallens Property Management	Check	$3,390.00
2/12/2008	8	Ashford Hill Apartments	Check	$882.00
2/12/2008	9	Reynolds Court Subdivision	Check	$1,764.00
2/14/2008	10	DBH Enterprises	Check	$322.50
2/14/2008	11	DBH Enterprises	Check	$857.60
2/20/2008	12	Jenke, Lynda	Check	$336.00
2/20/2008	13	Pleasantdale Luxury Apartments	Check	$2,507.65
2/27/2008	14	Ashford Hill Apartments	Check	$588.00
2/27/2008	15	Reynolds Court Subdivision	Check	$588.00
2/27/2008	16	O'Hara Homes	Check	$2,620.00
2/27/2008	17	Ashford Hill Apartments	Check	$882.00
2/27/2008	18	Reynolds Court Subdivision	Check	$882.00
2/27/2008	19	Yango Software	Check	$1,260.00
3/3/2008	20	Hutcheon, Brian	Check	$3,858.75
3/3/2008	21	Fairbanks Construction	Check	$5,280.00
3/5/2008	22	Pleasantdale Luxury Apartments	Check	$1,956.00
3/5/2008	23	O'Hara Homes	Check	$20,694.50
3/5/2008	24	Sugar Hill Tennis Club	Check	$1,324.25
3/5/2008	39	Sugar Hill Tennis Club	Check	$1,323.35
3/6/2008	40	Gibson, Robert	Check	$9,768.75

Figure 4:72

OAP prompts with the warning illustrated in Figure 4:73 informing you that editing the payment voids the current transaction. Click **No** and then click **X** to close the payment.

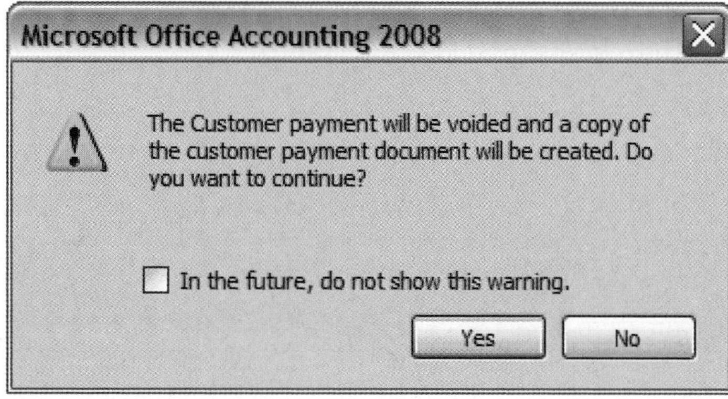

Figure 4:73

You can also void a payment without reopening it by highlighting the transaction on the list, right clicking, and selecting Void. After voiding a payment you can then reenter the transaction and apply the payment to the same invoices as on the voided payment or to different invoices.

RECORD CUSTOMER PAYMENTS

On April 3, 2008, the following customer payments were received. Post the payments.

Reynolds Court Subdivision, check number 7856 for $2,352.00 paying Invoice 988, 992, and 998.

O'Hara Homes, check number 1092 for $6,693.40 paying Invoice 1012.

Pleasantdale Luxury Apartments, check number 7672 for 1,609.40 paying Invoice 997. *(Note: The customer is not paying the invoice in full and you will learn to write off the invoice balance in a later topic.)*

Print the Cash Receipts Journal you created earlier in the chapter, filtered for 4/3/2008.

Customer Credits

Occasionally Astor may need to issue a credit against a customer invoice. In the exercise that follows Astor issues a credit to Sugar Hill Tennis Club for 3 of the Amy Azalea plants billed on Invoice 991. Follow the next steps to record the credit.

Steps to Enter a Customer Credit Memo

1. From the Customer Home page, click **New Credits and Refunds**.

2. Select "Sugar Hill Tennis Club" as the **Customer name**. Click **Create From** on the toolbar and select Invoice 991 before clicking **OK**. Enter "3/31/2008" as the date.

   The transaction window (Figure 4:74) displays items on the original invoice.

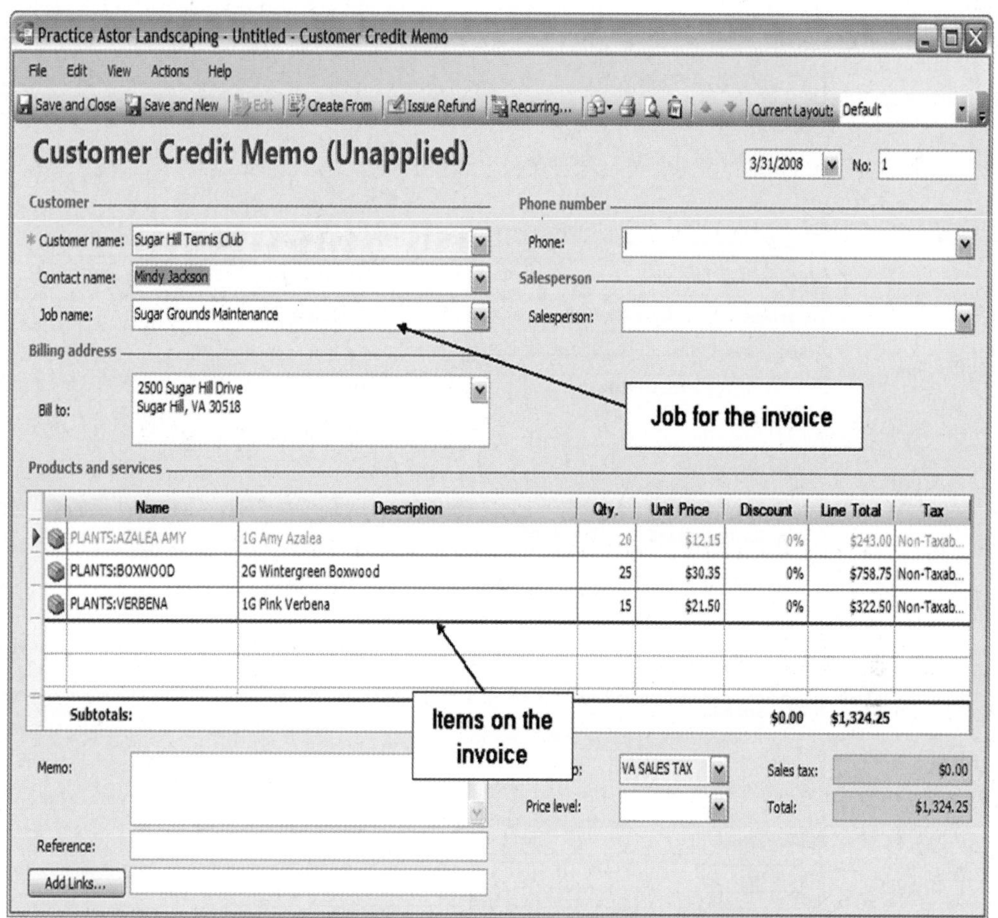

Figure 4:74

3. Enter "3" as the quantity for Amy Azaleas and then right click the remaining line items and select delete. The complete credit memo is illustrated in Figure 4:75.

Note: When creating a credit memo from the invoice, you must always delete line items not being credited because OAP does not permit entering zero as the returned quantity. In Chapter 8 you use the alternative method of creating credit memos, which is to not create it from the invoice.

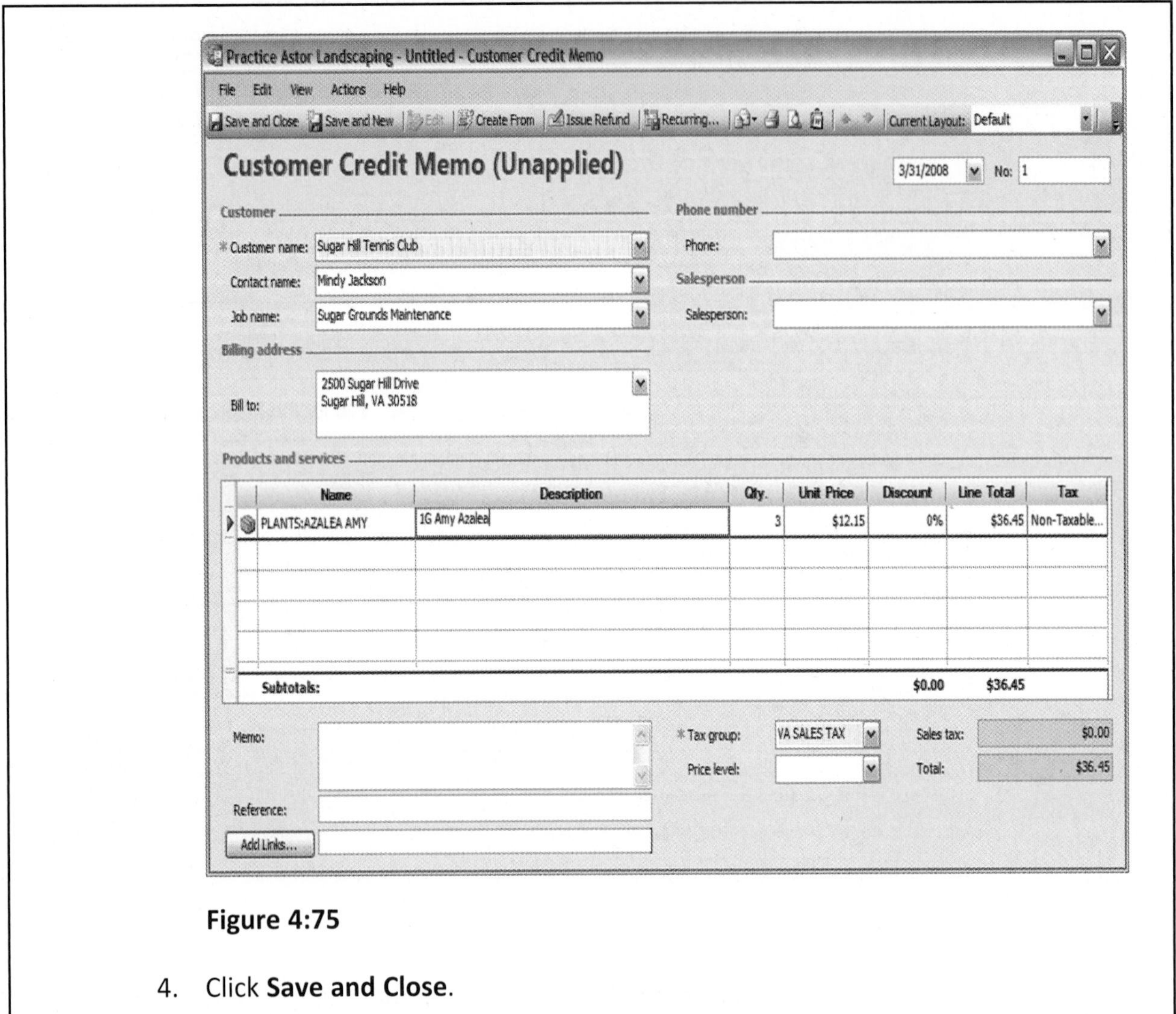

Figure 4:75

4. Click **Save and Close**.

The credit memo just created is linked to Invoice 1019 so let us see what happens when Sugar Hill Tennis Club remits its next payment.

STEPS FOR APPLYING A CUSTOMER CREDIT MEMO

1. Click **Receive Payment** and enter the information illustrated in Figure 4:76. Notice the unused credits amount listed at the bottom.

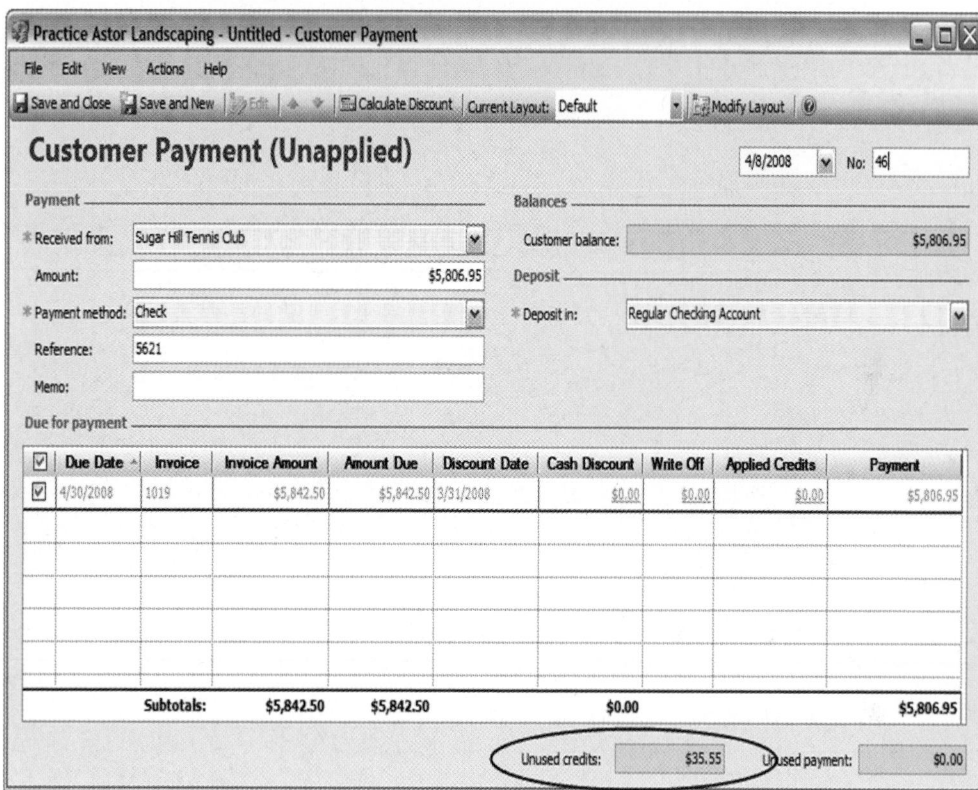

Figure 4:76

2. Click the **Applied Credits** hyperlink on Invoice 1019 to open the window illustrated in Figure 4:75. Click to select the credit memo and then click **Adjust** to apply the credit to the invoice.

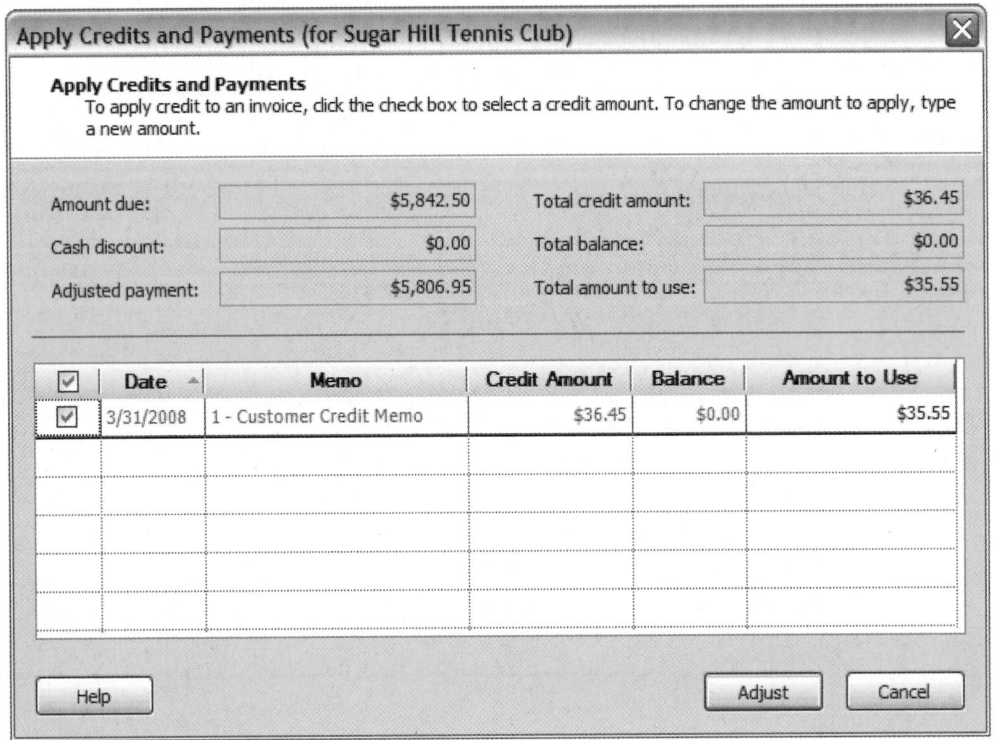

Figure 4:77

3. The completed payment is illustrated next.

Figure 4:78

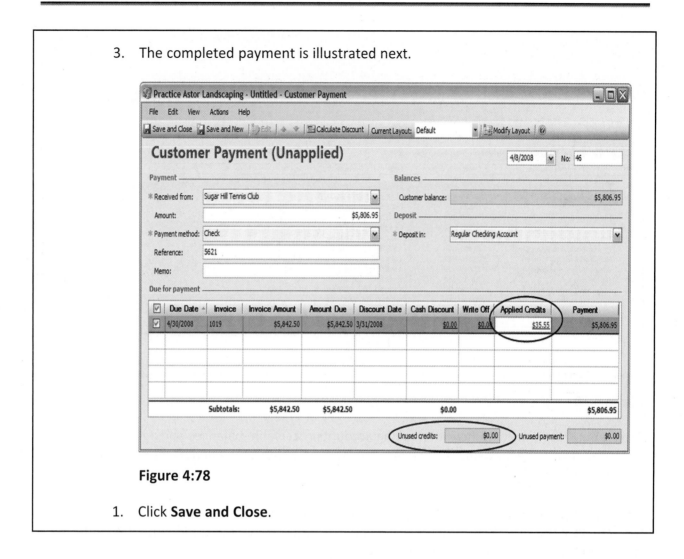

1. Click **Save and Close**.

Customer Reporting and Reconciling Customer Activities

OAP offers a variety of customer and sales reports. These reports can be run from the ***Reports>>Sales*** *and* ***Reports>>Customers and Receivables*** menus. In addition, you can run these reports from the Reports section on the Customer Home page (Figure 4:79).

Figure 4:79

Let's run the A/R Aging Summary report first because this is the current report in **Select a report**. Click **Display**. Filter the report for "3/31/2008." (See Figure 4:80.)

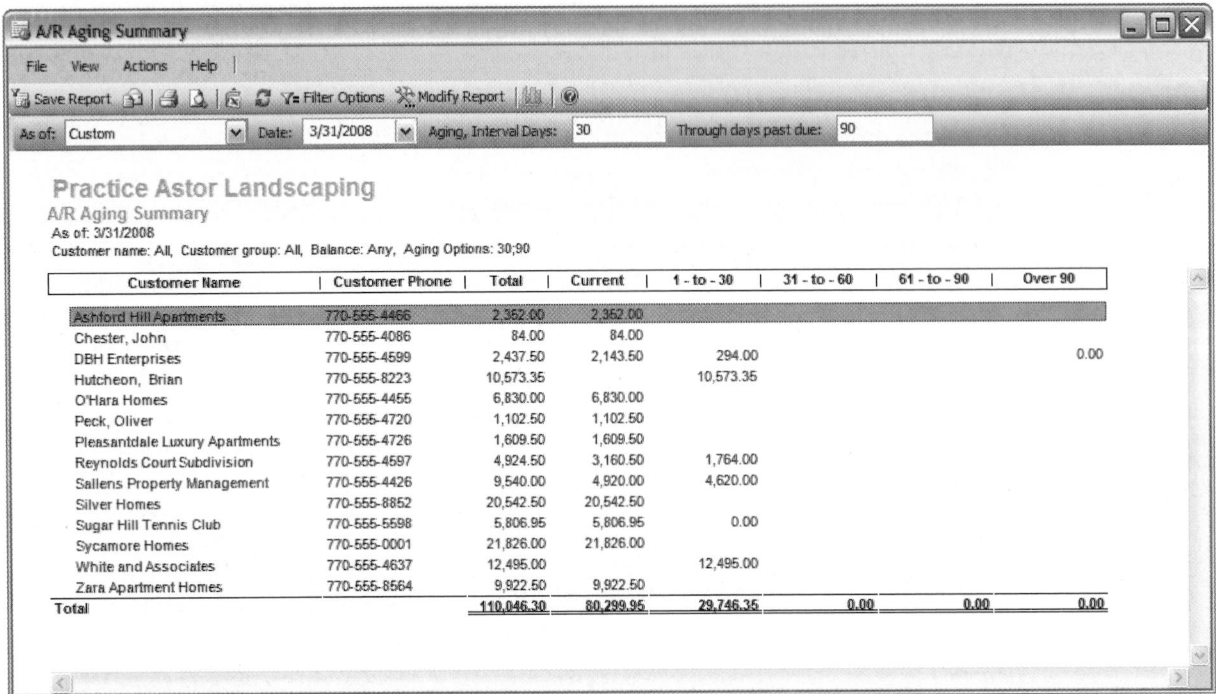

Practice Astor Landscaping
A/R Aging Summary
As of: 3/31/2008
Customer name: All, Customer group: All, Balance: Any, Aging Options: 30;90

Customer Name	Customer Phone	Total	Current	1 - to - 30	31 - to - 60	61 - to - 90	Over 90
Ashford Hill Apartments	770-555-4466	2,362.00	2,362.00				
Chester, John	770-555-4086	84.00	84.00				
DBH Enterprises	770-555-4599	2,437.50	2,143.50	294.00			0.00
Hutcheon, Brian	770-555-8223	10,573.35		10,573.35			
O'Hara Homes	770-555-4455	6,830.00	6,830.00				
Peck, Oliver	770-555-4720	1,102.50	1,102.50				
Pleasantdale Luxury Apartments	770-555-4726	1,609.50	1,609.50				
Reynolds Court Subdivision	770-555-4597	4,924.50	3,160.50	1,764.00			
Sallens Property Management	770-555-4426	9,540.00	4,920.00	4,620.00			
Silver Homes	770-555-8852	20,542.50	20,542.50				
Sugar Hill Tennis Club	770-555-5598	5,806.95	5,806.95	0.00			
Sycamore Homes	770-555-0001	21,826.00	21,826.00				
White and Associates	770-555-4637	12,495.00		12,495.00			
Zara Apartment Homes	770-555-8564	9,922.50	9,922.50				
Total		110,046.30	80,299.95	29,746.35	0.00	0.00	0.00

Figure 4:80

This report displays customer outstanding accounts receivable balances and age of the balance. *(Note: Your balances will differ from those illustrated if you have not completed all chapter exercises.)*

The report serves two important purposes. First, Astor uses it to monitor customer payments and mitigate the risk of performing future services for customers that fail to pay. Monitoring the report also manages company cash flow.

Second, this report is used to reconcile customer activities with the accounts receivable control account. This task is performed by comparing the aging report total with the March ending balance in account 11000 Accounts Receivable.

Compare your balance in Accounts Receivable to the report by selecting ***Reports>>Company and Financial>>Trial Balance*** on the main menu and filtering the report for 3/31/2008. Scroll to the balance in account 11000 Accounts Receivable and compare this amount to your report total. These amounts must agree to verify proper recording of customer activities.

The amounts can become out of balance when you improperly correct customer transactions. Therefore, always refer to instructions in this chapter or Appendix B when correcting customer transactions. You should reconcile the aged receivables report to the accounts receivable balance at the end of every month and prior to issuing financial reports.

Close this report and open the **Detail A/R Aging** report (not illustrated). This time enter "4/30/2008" as the date. This report is a variation on the summary aging report because it lists total outstanding accounts receivable along with invoice details. In addition, the Amount column displays the original invoice amount and the Total column displays the remaining invoice balance.

Scroll down to Pleasantdale Luxury Apartments' Invoice 994. Recall that in a previous *You Try* exercise an outstanding balance of $0.10 was left on this invoice. You will write off this balance in the next topic. Close the report.

WRITING OFF CUSTOMER INVOICES

You will find in business that customers do not always pay. Furthermore, like Pleasantdale Luxury Apartments, customers sometimes pay the wrong amount. Instead of calling this error to the customer's attention, Astor has decided to write off the invoice balance.

The instructions that follow illustrate writing off an invoice balance after posting the payment. The instructions in Chapter 8 illustrate writing off the balance while recording the payment.

(Note: To complete this exercise, you must have completed the previous You Try exercise named Record Customer Payments.)

STEPS TO WRITE OFF A CUSTOMER'S INVOICE

1. Open the Customer List under **Find**.
2. Double click Pleasantdale Luxury Apartments to open the customer account.
3. Select ***Actions>>Write off*** on the customer window menu.

4. Complete the window as illustrated in Figure 4:81.

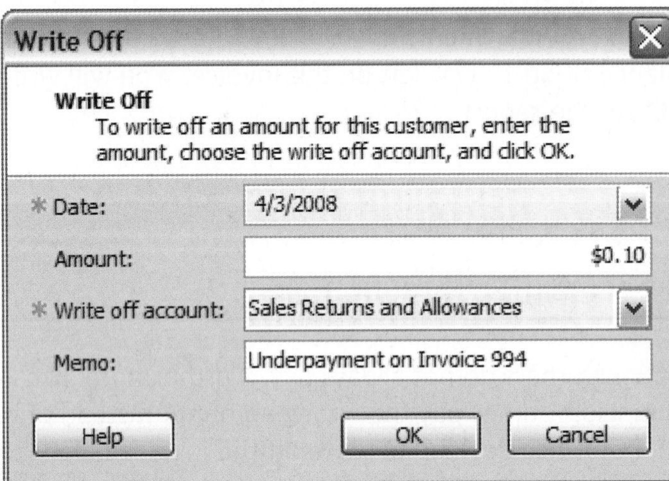

Figure 4:81

Notice that the balance is being written off to the Sales Returns and Allowances account because the write-off is an underpayment error by the customer and Astor has decided to forgo the balance.

When writing off a bad debt invoice, you would post the write-off amount to the Allowance for Doubtful Accounts because Astor uses the allowance method for estimating bad debt.

5. Click **OK** and then click **X** to close the customer's account.

Customer Statements

Astor mails customer statements once a month. These statements list invoice and payment activity and prompt customers to pay.

Select ***Customers>>Create Statement*** on the main menu to open the window illustrated in Figure 4:82.

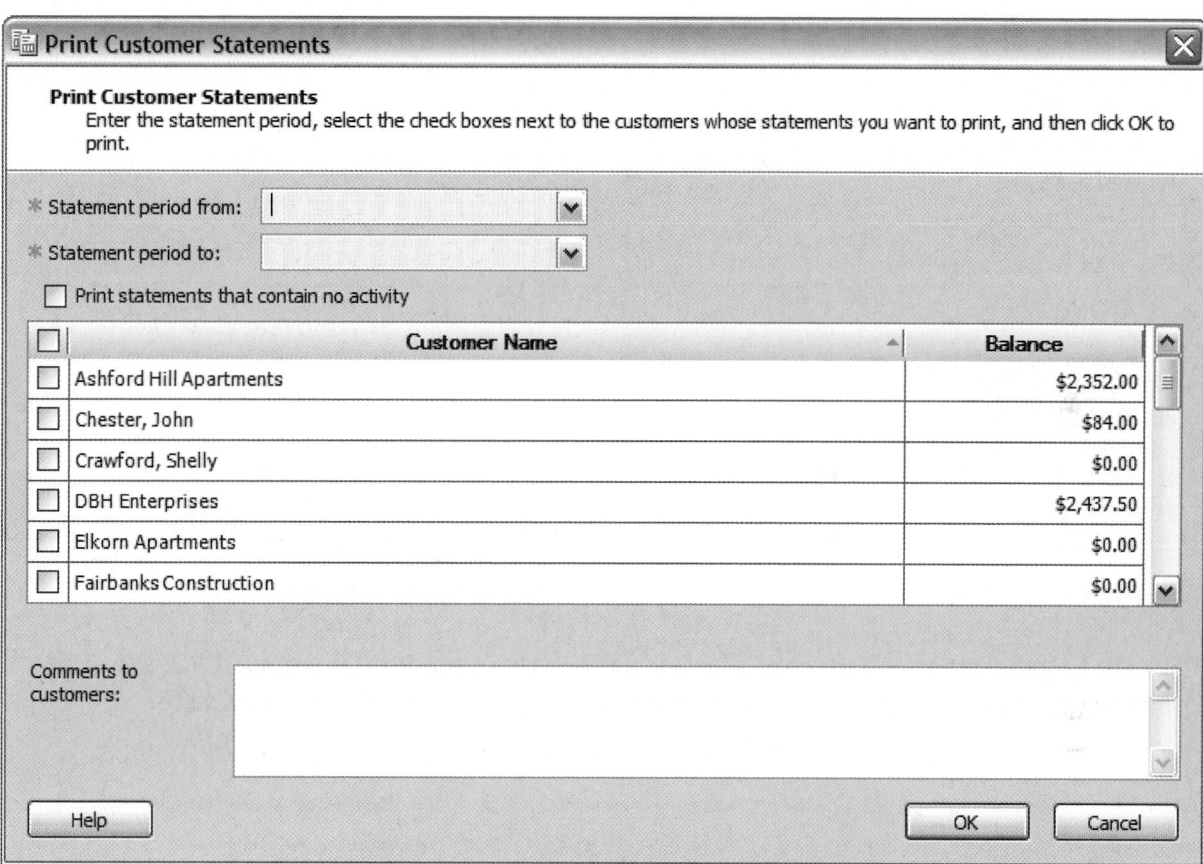

Figure 4:82

Enter "3/1/2008" in the **Statement period from** field and "3/31/2008" in the **Statement period to** field. Click the selection box for Ashford Hill Apartments. The completed window is illustrated in Figure 4:83.

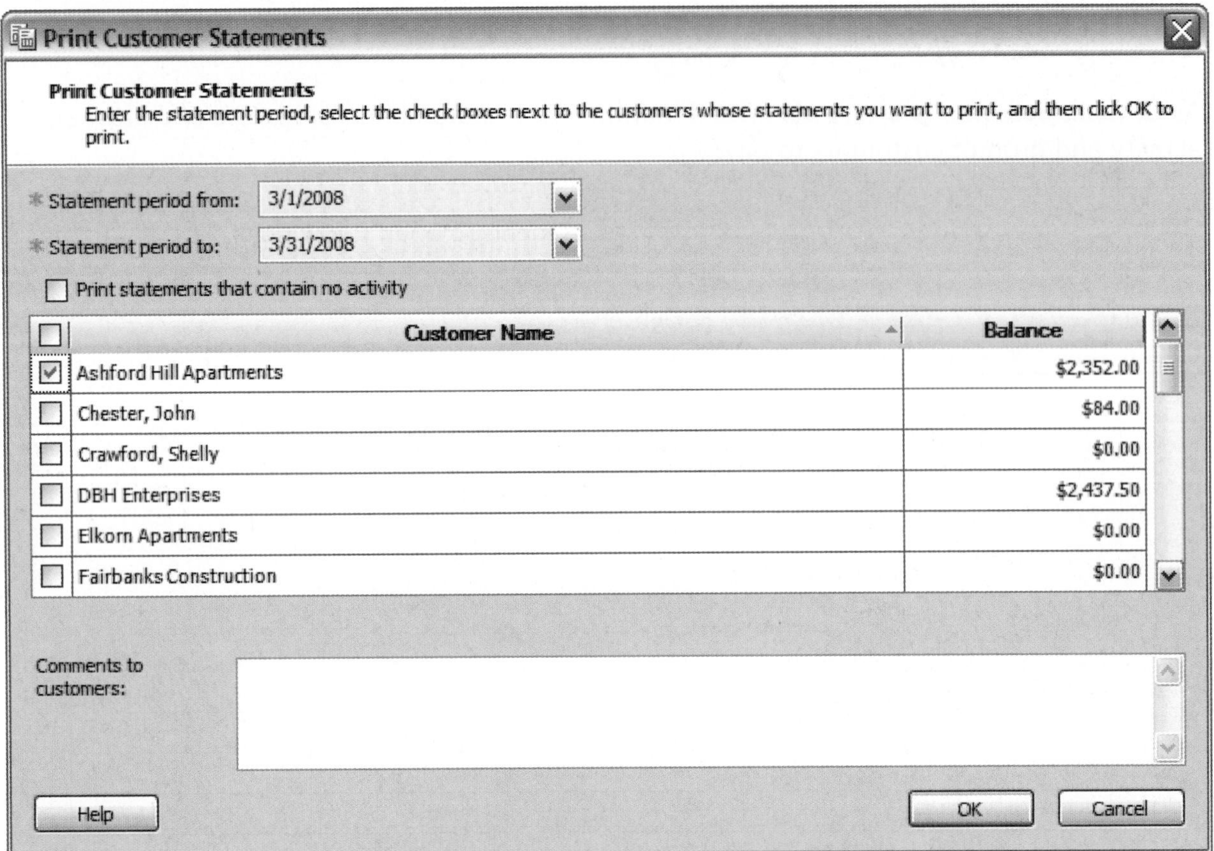

Figure 4:83

Click **OK** to generate the statement and select a printer in the Print window. Click **OK**. The printed statement is illustrated in Figure 4:84. Close the window by clicking **Cancel**.

Practice Astor Landscaping **Statement**

1505 Pavilion Place, Suite C
Arlington, VA 30093

Phone: 770-724-3252
Fax: 770-724-3252

Statement period: 3/1/2008 - 3/31/2008
Statement date:

To:

Ashford Hill Apartments

3466 Ashford Hill
Danbury, VA 30097

Date	Transaction				Amount	Balance
2/29/2008	Balance forward					$3,234.00
3/6/2008	Invoice	1001	- Due 4/5/2008	Not Paid	$588.00	$3,822.00
3/7/2008	Customer Payment	25		Applied	($882.00)	$2,940.00
3/12/2008	Invoice	1004	- Due 4/11/2008	Not Paid	$882.00	$3,822.00
3/19/2008	Customer Payment	31		Applied	($588.00)	$3,234.00
3/24/2008	Invoice	1013	- Due 4/23/2008	Not Paid	$882.00	$4,116.00
3/25/2008	Customer Payment	41		Applied	($1,764.00)	$2,352.00

Ending Balance: $2,352.00

Comments:

Page 1 of 1

Figure 4:84

You have now completed the chapter. ***Make a backup of the Practice Astor Landscaping data file to a backup file named "practiceastorlandscaping Chpt 4." In the next chapter, you will build on the work completed in this chapter.***

SUMMARY

In this chapter you learned the *MAPS* procedures for posting customer transactions before recording transactions in OAP. By understanding manual entries, you were able to anticipate OAP's *Behind the Keys* postings. Understanding a transaction's effect on financial accounts is critical to posting transactions correctly and to tracing the audit trail of a posted transaction.

After completing this chapter, you are skilled in recording customer invoices, payments, and credit memos for a service based business. You can manage the master accounts linked to transactions (i.e., customer accounts, jobs, and items). You understand job reporting as well as other reports that let you monitor and document customer activities. With firm knowledge on processing customer activities, you are now ready to take on Astor's vendor activities in the next chapter.

END-OF-CHAPTER QUESTIONS

TRUE/FALSE

_____ 1. The audit trail lets accountants trace entries from a source journal to a general ledger.

_____ 2. Like the manual system, OAP's Sales Journal report lists general ledger accounts affected by sales transactions.

_____ 3. You can transfer a sales quote for a time and billing job to a customer invoice.

_____ 4. You can create a customer account "on the fly" while entering a sales invoice.

_____ 5. You can use the Item icon on the invoice window to enter a comment on a customer invoice.

_____ 6. OAP marks a quote as accepted when you transfer it to an invoice.

_____ 7. Quotes and invoices can be emailed to customers.

_____ 8. You can delete a customer account that has transaction history.

_____ 9. The Invoice List can be exported to Excel.

_____ 10. You can modify a posted customer payment.

MULTIPLE CHOICE

_____ 1. Which menu will print a Sales Journal?

a. ***Reports>>Sales>>Sales by Item Detail***
b. ***Reports>>Customers and Receivables>>A/R Aging Detail***
c. ***Reports>>Customers and Financial>>Transaction Journal***
d. none of the above

_____ 2. The _____ menu item will print the details of sales transactions posted to the general ledger.

a. Trial Balance
b. Transaction Journal
c. Transaction Detail by Account
d. both b and c

_____ 3. OAP items are categorized as _____.
   a. Service Item
   b. Inventory Item
   c. Inventoried Item
   d. both a and b

_____ 4. Which report analyzes estimated revenues versus actual revenue?
   a. Job Estimates vs. Actuals Detail
   b. Profitability by Job Detail
   c. both a and b
   d. none of the above

_____ 5. An accounts receivable aging report is used for _____.
   a. monitoring the age of customer invoices
   b. reconciling customer activities with the general ledger
   c. managing cash flow
   d. all of the above

_____ 6. Customer statements are printed from the _____.
   a. Reports menu
   b. Customers menu
   c. both a and b
   d. none of the above

_____ 7. You can print a report for analyzing profitability by customer using the _____ menu.
   a. ***Reports>>Customers and Receivables***
   b. ***Reports>>Sales***
   c. ***Reports>>Jobs and Time***
   d. both a and c

PRACTICE SET

In this Practice Set you will be using the **Graded Astor Landscaping** data file customized with your initials at the end of Chapter 1. ***When this data file is not loaded on your computer, restore it using the "gradedastorlandscaping Chpt 1" backup file created in the Practice Set at the end of Chapter 1.***

1. Open **Graded Astor Landscaping** and enter Astor's April customer activities listed below. All reports will be printed in Step 2.

2008

Apr. 2 Received check number 1087 for $21,826.00 from Sycamore Homes paying Invoice 1011.

Apr. 3 Invoice 1018 to O'Hara Homes on Redesign Gardens job for $5,600.00. Transfer 96 hours from time tickets dated March 24 to March 31, 2008. *(Note: Remember to click Cancel on the Quote selection window.)*

Apr 7 Create the following invoices.

Invoice 1019 to Reynolds Court Subdivision for $1,120.00 plus tax for Grounds Maintenance job. Transfer 32 hours from time tickets dated March 25 to March 31, 2008.

Create Invoice 1020 to White and Associates for $1,440.00 on Redesign Gardens job. Transfer 24 hours from time tickets dated March 26 to March 31, 2008. Click OK to exceed the customer's credit limit.

Apr. 9 Received the following checks.

Check number 763 for $5,180.00 from O'Hara Homes paying Invoices 993 and 999.

Check number 3253 for $4,620.00 from Sallens Property Management paying Invoice 994.

Apr. 11 Received check number 7577 for $2,352.00 from Ashford Hill Apartments paying Invoices 995, 990, and 1001.

Apr. 17 Create the following invoices.

Invoice 1021 to Ashford Hill Apartments for $1,960.00 plus tax for Grounds Maintenance job. Transfer 56 hours from all time tickets on file.

Invoice 1022 to DBH Enterprises for $1,680.00 for Grounds Maintenance job. Transfer 48 hours from all time tickets on file.

Invoice 1023 to Reynolds Court Subdivision for $1,120.00 plus tax for Grounds Maintenance job. Transfer 32 hours from all time tickets on file. Owner has approved customer exceeding the credit limit.

Apr. 23 Received the following checks.

Check number 2363 for $1,555.50 from DBH Enterprises paying Invoices 995, 1000, 1006, and 1010.

Check number 6785 for $10,573.00 from Brian Hutcheon paying Invoice 1005. Write off any difference needed to pay the invoice in full to the Sales Returns and Allowances account.

Check number 567 for $4,116.00 from Reynolds Court Subdivision paying Invoices 988, 992, 998, 1003, and 1008.

Check number 7345 for $10,040.00 from O'Hara Homes paying Invoices 1007 and 1012.

Apr. 25 Create the following invoices.

Invoice 1024 to O'Hara Homes for $9,702.50 for Redesign Gardens job. Transfer 64 hours from all remaining time tickets on file and all item costs.

Invoice 1025 to Sugar Hill Tennis Club for $560.00 plus tax for Grounds Maintenance job. Transfer 16 hours from all time tickets on file.

Invoice 1026 to Silver Homes for $8,415.00 for Plantings job. Transfer 32 hours from all time tickets on file and all item costs. The owner has approved exceeding the customer credit limit.

Invoice 1027 to White and Associates for $3,769.25 for Redesign Gardens job. Transfer 24 hours from all time tickets on file and all item costs. The owner has approved exceeding the customer's credit limit.

Apr. 28 Received the following checks.

Check number 9099 for $12,127.50 from Silver Homes paying Invoice 1002.

Check number 526 for $12,495.00 from White and Associates paying Invoice 989.

Check number 7355 for $15,108.45 from O'Hara Homes paying Invoices 1018 and 1024 with a discount.

Create the following new customer.

Jordan Industries
575 N. Main Street
Arlington, VA 30022
(701) 555-8723

Contact:	April Raines
Customer Group:	Commercial
Preferred Payment Method:	Check
Payment Terms:	Net 30 Days
Tax Group:	VA SALES TAX
Credit Limit:	$10,000

Create the following job for this customer.

Job name:	Jordan New Deck
Start date:	5/1/2008
Job Group:	Landscaping

Create and print Quote 211 for this customer totaling $7,241.50 for the following items.

Items	Qty	Unit Price	Line Total
REDWOOD DECKING	100	$ 12.15	$1,215.00
REDWOOD RAILS	10	$114.85	$1,148.50
REDWOOD CAPS	10	$ 7.80	$ 78.00
INSTL HARD – COMMERCIAL	80	$ 60.00	$4,800.00

2. Print the following reports.

   a. Transaction Journal for April 1 to April 30, 2008, filtered to display the transaction types of Customer Payment and Invoice.

   b. Job Profitability Summary report for January 1 to April 30, 2008.

   c. A/R Aging Detail report at April 30, 2008. Explain how this report is used.

   d. Customer statement for DBH Enterprises showing activity for April 1 to April 30, 2008.

3. ***Back up the Graded Astor Landscaping data file to a backup file named "gradedastorlandscaping Chpt 4." The Practice Set for the next chapter will build on the work completed in this chapter.***

CHAPTER 5 VENDOR ACTIVITIES FOR A SERVICE BASED BUSINESS

LEARNING OBJECTIVES

This chapter uses the Practice Astor Landscaping data file from Chapter 4. ***When this data file is not loaded on your computer, restore it using the "practiceastorlandscaping Chpt 4" backup file created after reading Chapter 4.***

In this chapter you continue processing Astor's accounting activities with the focus now on vendors. Vendor activities include placing orders for goods and services, entering vendor bills for receipts of goods and services, and remitting vendor payments. While performing these activities, you will:

1. Learn *MAPS* for recording vendor transactions before posting transactions in OAP
2. Use the Vendors Home page to perform vendor tasks
3. Record vendor purchase orders, bills, payments, and credits
4. Look *Behind the Keys* at posted transactions
5. Memorize vendor transactions
6. Assign vendor costs to jobs
7. Correct and void vendor transactions
8. Print and analyze vendor reports
9. Reconcile vendor activities to the general ledger

Launch OAP and open **Practice Astor Landscaping**.

Manual Accounting Procedures

As in the previous chapter, you begin by learning manual accounting procedures (*MAPS*) for posting vendor activities before using OAP. These procedures help you to understand OAP transaction posting.

Before continuing, it helps to explain that Astor sometimes uses a purchase order (PO) to order job materials. POs authorize purchases and document quantities ordered and vendor prices. An Astor employee with authorization to order materials creates and signs the PO before sending it to the vendor. Thereafter, an employee either picks up the materials at the vendor's location or the vendor delivers the materials to a job site.

The vendor's bill is normally included with the materials. This bill is then forwarded to the accounting department. Before recording the bill, the accountant matches it with the PO. This matching process verifies that the purchase was authorized and confirms that billed quantities and prices equal PO terms.

On March 21, 2008, Seth Ruland issues a PO for materials to be used on John Chester's job created in Chapter 4. He manually prepares the document, signs it, and then faxes it to Clooney Chemical Supply. A copy of the PO is sent to Judy in accounting, who files the document for matching with the vendor bill. POs do not trigger accounting recognition because the liability does not occur until receipt of the materials.

On March 24, 2008, Jeff Henderson picks up the materials with the vendor bill. At the end of the day, the bill is dropped off to Judy in accounting. Judy matches the PO with the bill illustrated in Figure 5:1.

Clooney Chemical Supply
3099 Weston Blvd.
Arlington, VA 30312

Customer: Date: 3/24/2008
Astor Landscaping
1505 Pavilion Place
Arlington, VA 30093

INVOICE **No. 1157**

Qty	Item	Price Each	
3	2G Fertilizer	$15.75	$ 47.25
		Total	$ 47.25

Please remit within 30 days.

Figure 5:1

Judy then records the transaction on the March 24 Purchases Journal illustrated in Figure 5:2.

Astor Landscaping
Purchases Journal

Date: 3/24/2008 **Page 5**

Vendor	Post Ref	Description	Accounts Payable (Credit)	Materials Cost Landscape (Debit)	Office Supplies Expense (Debit)	Utilities (Debit)
Clooney Chemical Supply	CLOO001	Maintenance Job INV 1157	47.25	47.25		
Georgia Gas Co.	GEOR002	March Utilities	143.17			143.17
Office Maxters	OFFI001	Office Supplies INV 7631	237.25		237.25	
Totals:	↑		$ 427.67	$ 47.25	$237.25	$143.17
Audit trail →		Acct Ref:	(20000)	(51000)	(63000)	(71100)

Figure 5:2

Like the procedures used to enter transactions on the Sales Journal in Chapter 4, Judy totals journal columns and cross-foots totals to verify that entries balance (i.e., debits equal credits). Judy then posts each invoice to the vendor's account and posts column totals to the general ledger accounts listed at the bottom.

Judy's entry to Clooney's account is illustrated in Figure 5:3. *(Note: Entries for other vendor accounts are not illustrated.)*

Clooney Chemical Supply
3099 Weston Blvd.
Arlington, VA 30312

Audit Trail

Account No. CLOO001

Date	Description	Post Ref.	Debit	Credit	Balance
3/1/2008	Beginning Balance				0.00
3/24/2008	John Chester Maintenance Job INV1157	PJ 5	47.25		47.25

Figure 5:3

Judy's entries to general ledger accounts are illustrated in Figure 5:4. *(Note: The entry for utilities is not shown.)*

General Ledger					
Accounts Payable					**Account No. 20000**
Date	**Description**	**Post Ref.**	**Debit**	**Credit**	**Balance**
3/23/2008	Balance Forward				18,158.82
3/24/2008		PJ 5		427.67	18,586.49

Audit trail

General Ledger					
Materials Cost – Landscape					**Account No. 51000**
Date	**Description**	**Post Ref.**	**Debit**	**Credit**	**Balance**
3/23/2008	Balance Forward				1,250.12
3/24/2008		PJ 5	47.25		1,297.37

Audit trail

General Ledger					
Office Supplies Expense					**Account No. 63000**
Date	**Description**	**Post Ref.**	**Debit**	**Credit**	**Balance**
3/23/2008	Balance Forward				253.40
3/24/2008		PJ 5	237.25		490.65

Figure 5:4

The next day, Judy reviews vendor bills and prepares checks for bills that are due. Judy also prepares a check to buy postage. These checks are recorded on the Cash Disbursements Journal illustrated in Figure 5:5.

Date: 3/25/2008		Astor Landscaping Cash Disbursements Journal				Page 7
Vendor	**Check No.**	**Post Ref**	**Invoice No.**	**Regular Checking (Credit)**	**Accounts Payable (Debit)**	**Postage (Debit)**
Neighbors Telephone	440	PAIN001	March Phone	262.43	262.43	
Calvert Stone	441	CALV01	32532	4,937.35	4,937.35	
Clooney Chemical Supply	442	CLOO001	1157	10.00	10.00	
Postmaster	443	POST001	March Postage	150.00		150.00
Totals:				$5,359.78	$5209.78	$ 150.00
Audit trail →		Acct Ref:		(10200)	(20000)	(63100)

Figure 5:5

Like on the Purchases Journal, columns are totaled and cross-footed. Each check is then posted to a vendor account and column totals are posted to general ledger accounts. This time, Judy will use CDJ (Cash Disbursements Journal) along with the page number as the posting reference. *(Note: These postings are not illustrated.)*

As discussed in Chapter 4, the manual method is fraught with opportunities for making posting errors. Judy could enter an amount incorrectly, post an entry backwards, or forget to post it altogether.

With an understanding of *MAPS* for vendor activities, you are now ready to use OAP for recording vendor transactions. The topic that follows will introduce you to the home page focused on these activities.

Vendors Menu and Home Page

Before processing vendor activities become familiar with the menus that initiate activities. The Vendors menu is illustrated to the right. The first item opens the Vendors Home page. The New menu opens submenus for creating vendors, inventory items, and purchase orders. There are separate menus for receiving inventory and paying bills.

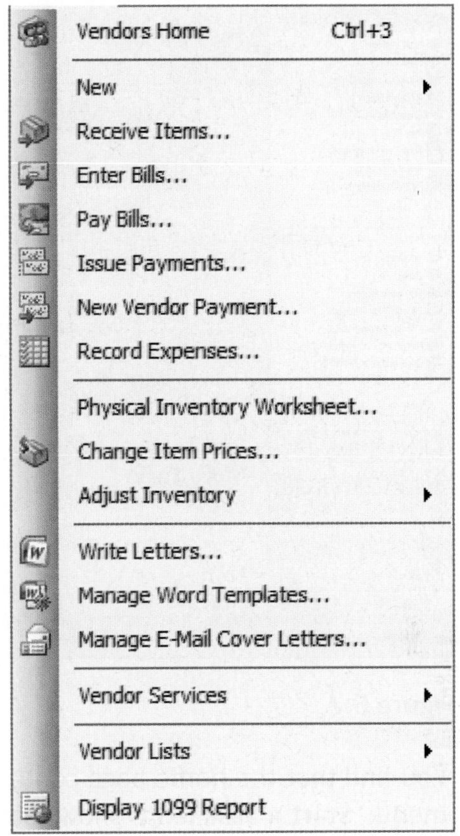

Figure 5:6

Click **Vendors Home** on the menu to open the Vendors Home page illustrated in Figure 5:7. This home page serves as central command for vendor activities. You can also click the Vendors Home page button to activate the page.

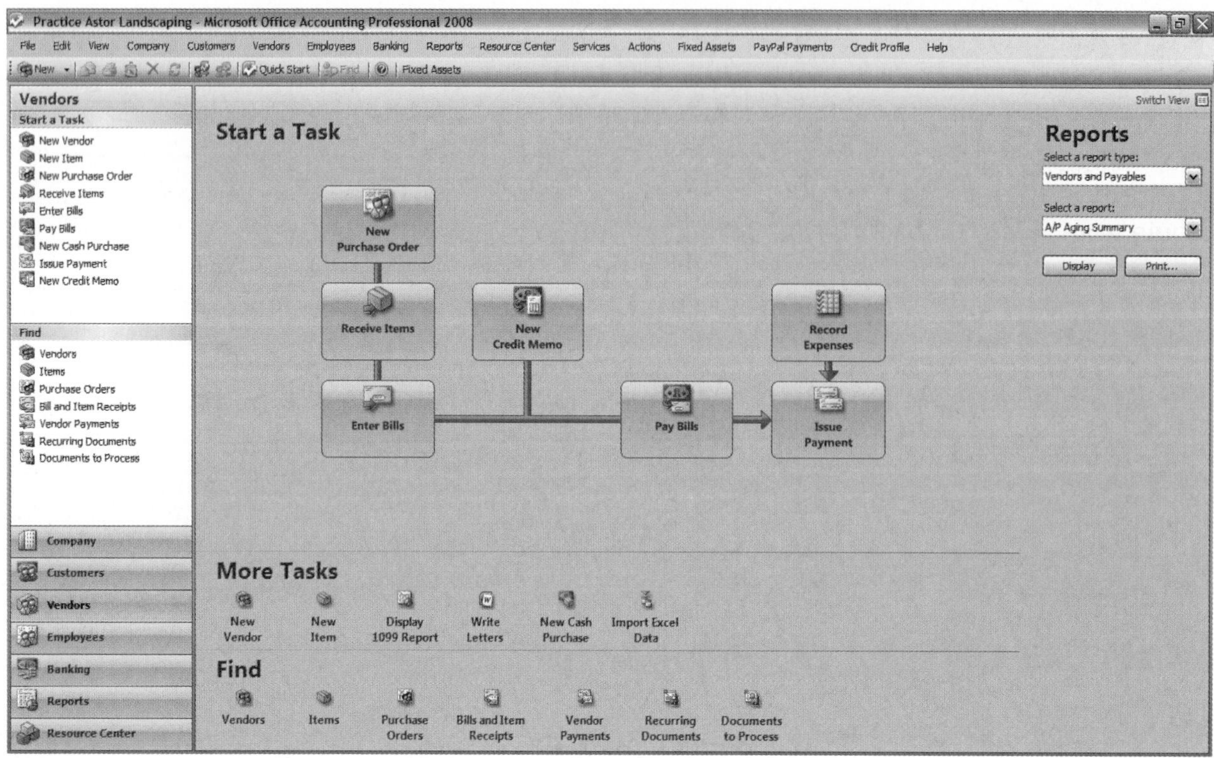

Figure 5:7

You find that the home page contains links to many of the commands found on the Vendors menu. **Start a Task** icons show that vendor activities can originate as purchase orders (purchase commitments), item receipts (goods received and awaiting a vendor bill), or vendor bills. Moreover, these icons demonstrate that purchase orders and item receipts will transfer to vendor bills and bills are the transactions that get paid. Credit memos can occur anytime before payment. Finally, Record Expenses are self-contained transactions that allow you to record an expense for payment transactions issued outside the software such as credit card payments.

Beneath Start a Task icons are icons for performing **More Tasks** and opening lists that **Find** posted transactions. The activities found on the center of the page are replicated under the **Start a Task** and **Find** links located to the left of the page.

Now that you are familiar with the Vendors menu and home page, let's begin recording vendor transactions.

Purchase Orders

As previously discussed, POs authorize vendor purchases. Recall from the *MAPS* topic that Seth created a PO for John Chester's landscape maintenance job. Follow the next steps to capture the transaction in OAP.

Steps to Create a Purchase Order

1. On the **Vendors Home** page, click either the **New Purchase Order** link under **Start a Task** or the **New Purchase Order** icon on the home page.

2. Enter "3/21/2008" as the transaction date. Leave the PO **No.** unchanged. OAP sequentially increments this number for each PO issued.

3. Tab to **Vendor name** and select "Clooney Chemical Supply" and OAP completes the top portion of the PO using the information on this vendor's account. (See Figure 5:8.)

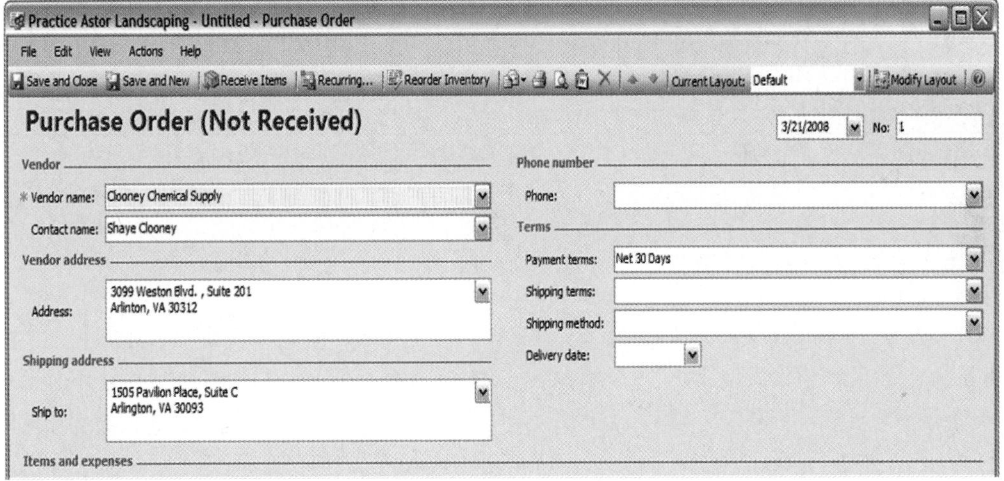

Figure 5:8

4. Tab to the icon symbol on the first line item and OAP opens a list of line item types. (See Figure 5:9.)

Name	Description	On Hand	Qty.	Unit Price	Line Total	Job Name	Billable
			1	$0.00	$0.00		☐
Expense							
Item							
Comment							

Figure 5:9

The following explains these types:

- **Expense** is used when entering vendor expenses directly to a general ledger account. Normally these will be for vendor transactions such as utilities, rent, or insurance. After selecting this icon you can look up general ledger accounts in the Name field and bypass items in the inventory table.
- **Item** is used when entering purchases of services or non-inventory items because it lets you look up items in the inventory table.
- **Comment** is for adding text to convey information to the vendor.

Select the **Item** icon.

5. In **Name**, look up and select "Fertilizer." Tab to **Qty.** and enter "3."

6. Tab to **Job Name** and select "Chester Seasonal Maintenance." Uncheck **Billable** because you already invoiced John Chester's in Chapter 4. *(Note: The Billable option is marked when the customer will be invoiced for the expense.)* The completed PO is illustrated in Figure 5:10.

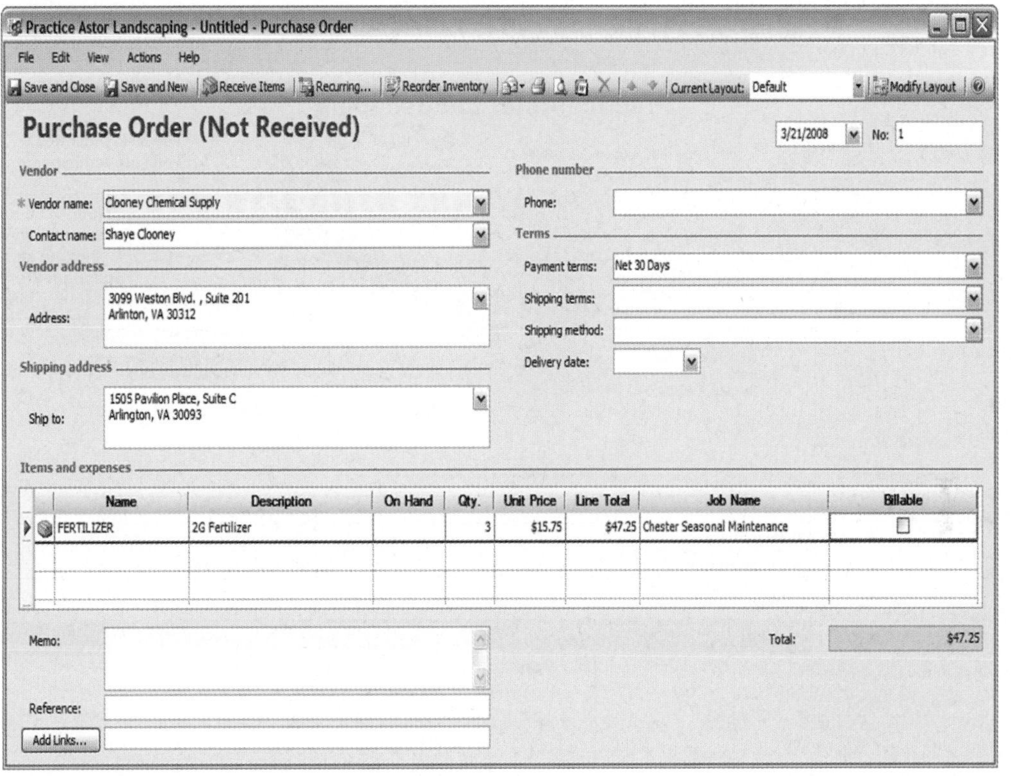

Figure 5:10

7. Print the PO by selecting ***File>>Print*** on the menu and click **OK** when prompted to save the PO. When the Printer Selection window opens, choose a printer and click **OK**. (*Note: You can also click the Printer icon on the toolbar and bypass the Printer Selection window.)*

   Figure 5:11 is the printed PO.

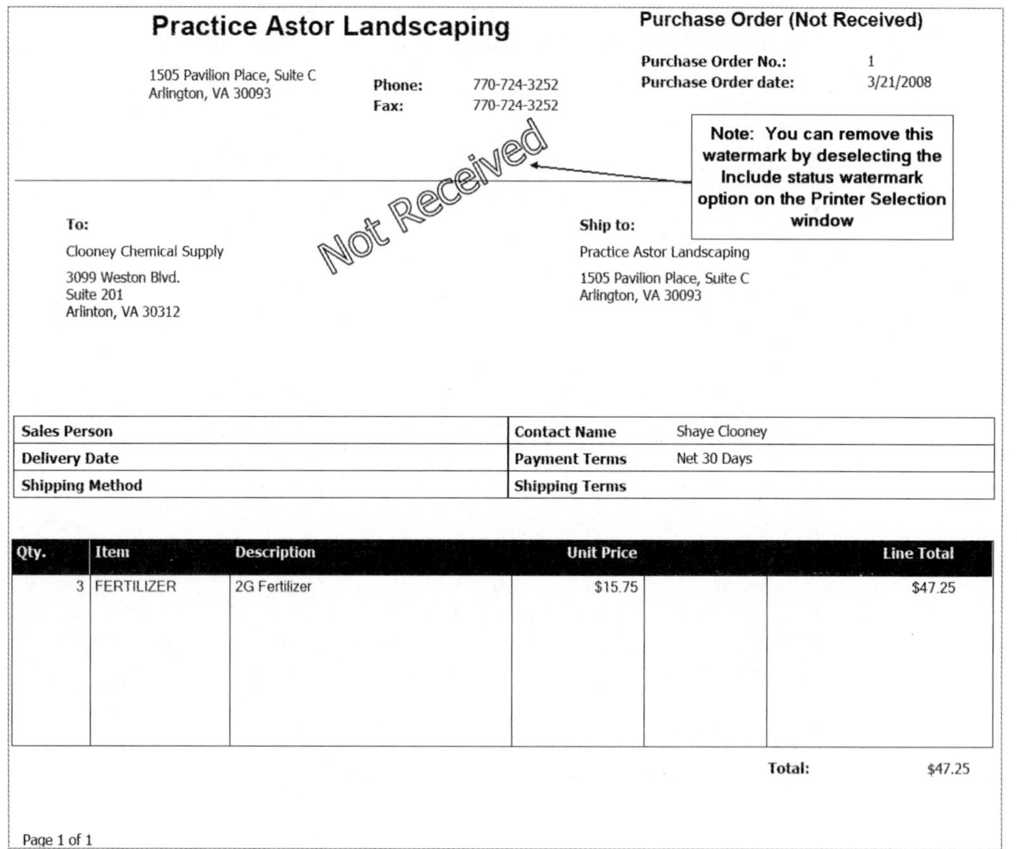

Practice Astor Landscaping

1505 Pavilion Place, Suite C
Arlington, VA 30093

Phone: 770-724-3252
Fax: 770-724-3252

Purchase Order (Not Received)

Purchase Order No.: 1
Purchase Order date: 3/21/2008

To:
Clooney Chemical Supply
3099 Weston Blvd.
Suite 201
Arlinton, VA 30312

Ship to:
Practice Astor Landscaping
1505 Pavilion Place, Suite C
Arlington, VA 30093

Sales Person		**Contact Name**	Shaye Clooney
Delivery Date		**Payment Terms**	Net 30 Days
Shipping Method		**Shipping Terms**	

Qty.	Item	Description	Unit Price		Line Total
3	FERTILIZER	2G Fertilizer	$15.75		$47.25

Total: $47.25

Page 1 of 1

Figure 5:11

8. Click **Save and New** so you can enter the next PO.

9. Now enter the following information.

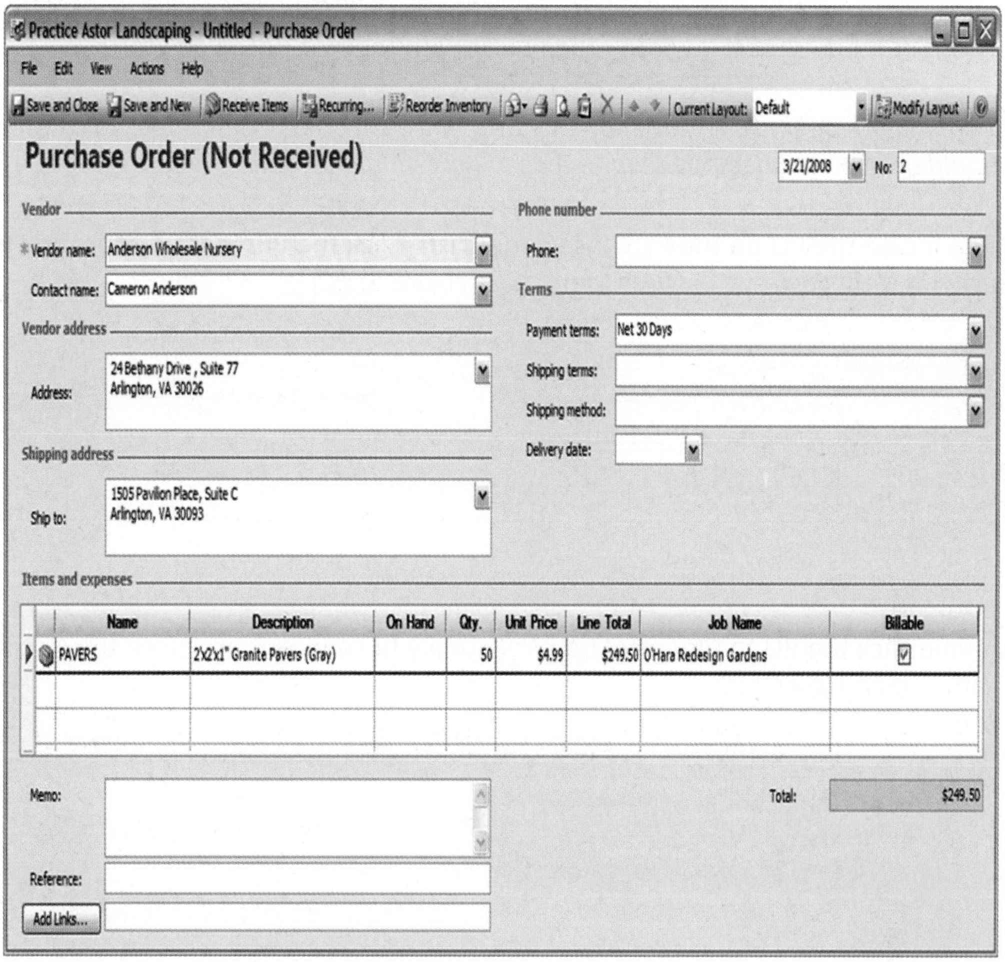

Figure 5:12

10. Click the **Printer** icon on the toolbar and click **OK** to save the PO. Click **Save and Close** to exit the transaction window.

    POs do not post entries to general ledger accounts because these documents are merely purchase commitments. Accounting recognition occurs when posting the vendor bill or receipt for the goods in a subsequent topic.

Correcting a Purchase Order

You can correct information on a saved PO as long as Astor has not received items on the order. In other words, you can modify POs with the **Not Received** status.

(Note: Keep in mind that, in the real world, once a PO has been released to the vendor it should not be changed. Instead, released POs should be voided and reissued.)

First, locate the PO on the Purchase Order List. Click the **Purchase Orders** link under **Find** and verify that the Current View is **Open**. (See Figure 5:13.)

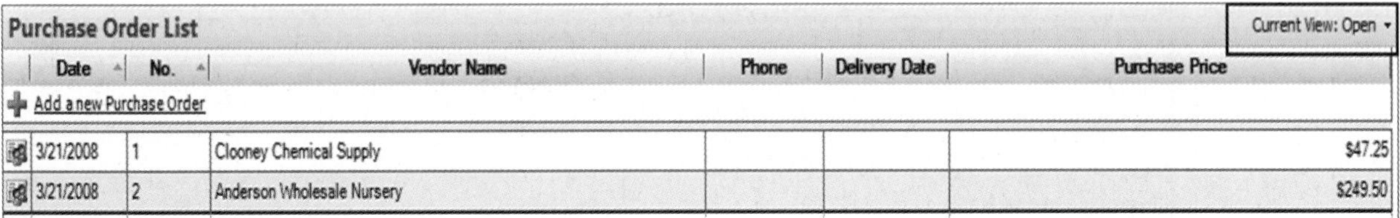

Figure 5:13

Double click the PO to Clooney Chemical Supply to reopen it and note the Not Received status. (See Figure 5:14.)

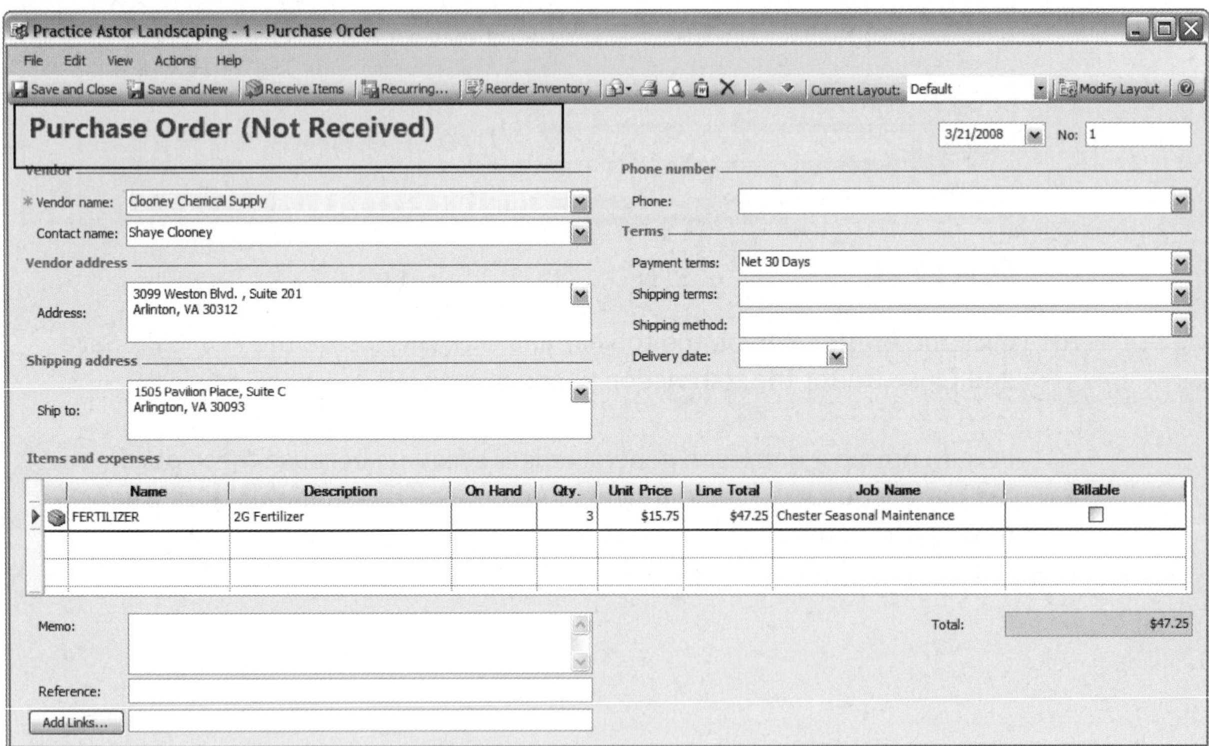

Figure 5:14

When the order is Not Received you can change information and then reprint and resave the transaction. You can delete it by clicking X on the toolbar. *(Note: You can also delete a PO without opening it by right clicking the transaction on the Purchase Order List and selecting Delete.)*

Once items on a PO have been received (i.e., a receipt or vendor bill has been posted) the PO status changes to Received or Partially Received and the list view must be changed to All or Received to view these POs. You can no longer modify line items containing items that have been received unless you void the vendor bill or receipt but you can modify items that remain outstanding.

Click **X** to close the PO. Now try the next exercise.

ENTER PURCHASE ORDERS

On March 25, 2008, Astor issued the POs listed below for items needed to complete Sugar Hill Tennis Club's grounds maintenance job. Two POs were required because materials were ordered from separate vendors. Enter the POs and then exit the transaction window. Remember to use correct transaction dates.

PO 3 for $199.60 is issued to Calvert Stone Supplies consisting of the following billable materials.

Item	Qty	Unit Price	Job
MULCH	40	$ 4.99	Sugar Grounds Maintenance

PO 4 for $764.60 is issued to Southern Garden Wholesale consisting of the following billable materials.

Item	Qty	Unit Price	Job
PLANTS: BOXWOOD	30	$ 22.49	Sugar Grounds Maintenance
PLANTS: AZALEA AMY	10	$ 8.99	Sugar Grounds Maintenance

Print the POs. Multiple POs are printed using the Purchase Order List. First, highlight one of the POs and next press and hold the Ctrl key as you click with the mouse to highlight remaining POs. After selecting all POs to print, right click a highlighted PO and select Print.

VENDOR BILLS AND RECEIPTS FOR PURCHASE ORDERS

You will recall from the *MAPS* topic that Jeff picked up the chemicals and the vendor bill from Clooney Chemical Supply on March 24. Jeff then turned the bill over to Judy, who matched it with the PO before posting the bill to the Purchases Journal.

Judy now uses OAP to perform this matching process as she enters the vendor bill. Complete the following exercise to record the bill from Clooney Chemical Supply.

STEPS TO RECORD A VENDOR BILL FOR ITEMS ON A PURCHASE ORDER

1. On the Vendors Home page, click the **Enter Bills** link under **Start a Task** or the **Enter Bills** icon on the home page. Click **Create From** on the toolbar to open the PO selection window illustrated in Figure 5:15.

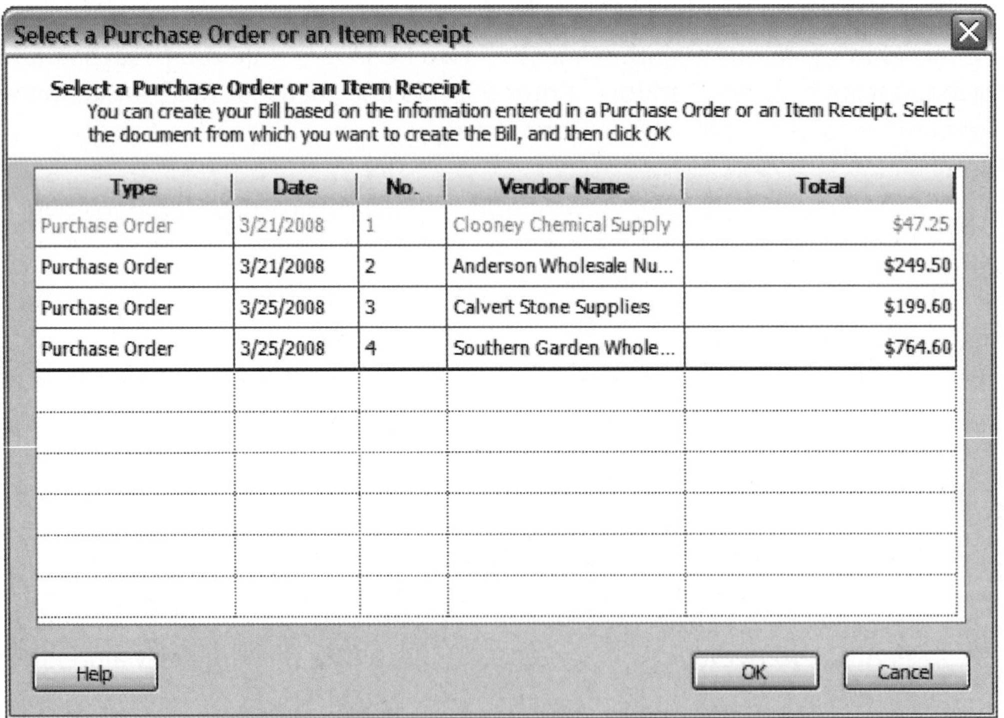

Figure 5:15

2. Highlight the PO to Clooney Chemical Supply and click **OK**.

3. Enter "3/24/2008" as the transaction date. Enter Clooney's invoice number of "78265" in the **No.** field.

   The completed entry is illustrated in Figure 5:16.

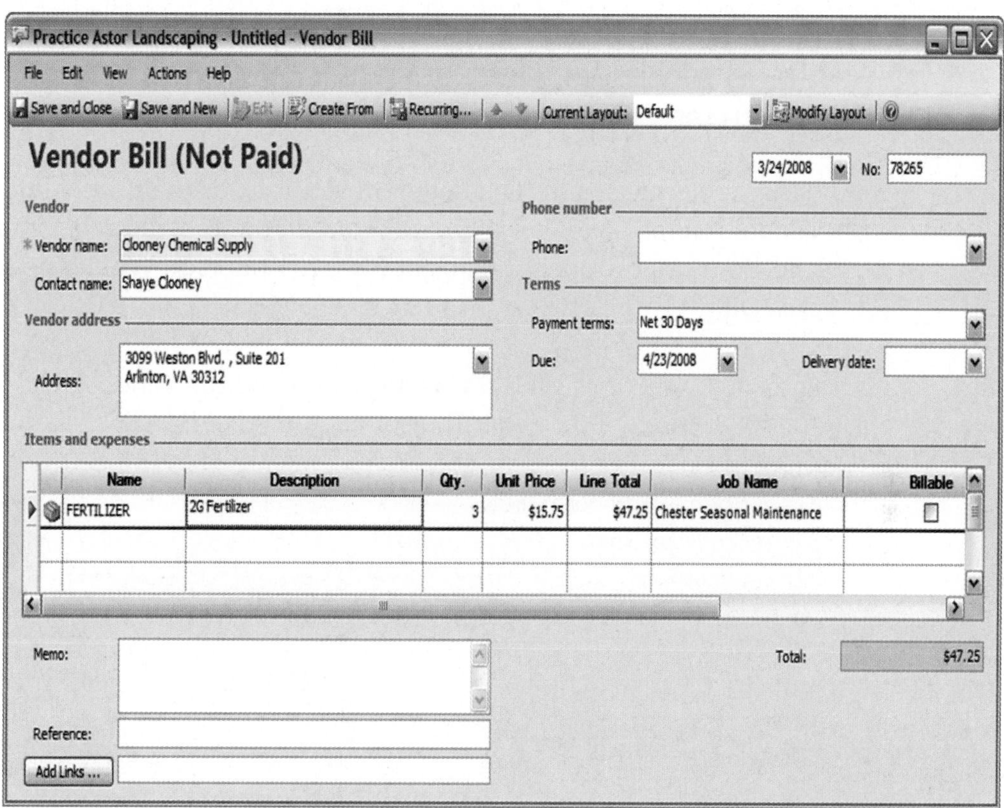

Figure 5:16

Review the following information on line item fields before saving the transaction.

Qty. stores the number of items received from the vendor. OAP automatically fills all quantities on the order; therefore, you may have to adjust to the number of items actually received. Furthermore, you delete the line item when none of the item has been received. Adjusting the quantity of items received changes the PO status to Partially Received after posting.

Billable marks a bill for invoicing to the customer. However, in Chapter 4 you already invoiced John Chester so verify that this option is not marked.

4. Click Save and Close.

We will cover one last thing before leaving this topic. You may sometimes receive items on a PO prior to receiving a vendor's bill. Remember that the liability is recognized upon receipt of the goods because this is when the obligation to pay arises. Therefore, you need to be able to post a receipt of inventory prior to receiving the bill.

The next exercise illustrates recording a vendor receipt for PO items.

STEPS TO RECORD A VENDOR RECEIPT FOR ITEMS ON A PURCHASE ORDER

1. Click the **Receive Items** link under **Start a Task** or the **Receive Items** icon on the Vendors Home page. Click **Create From** on the toolbar and, when the PO selection window opens, highlight PO 2 to Anderson Wholesale Nursery and click **OK**.

2. Enter "3/24/2008" as the transaction date and the vendor's receipt number of "RCT0886" in the **No.** field. The completed receipt is illustrated in Figure 5:17.

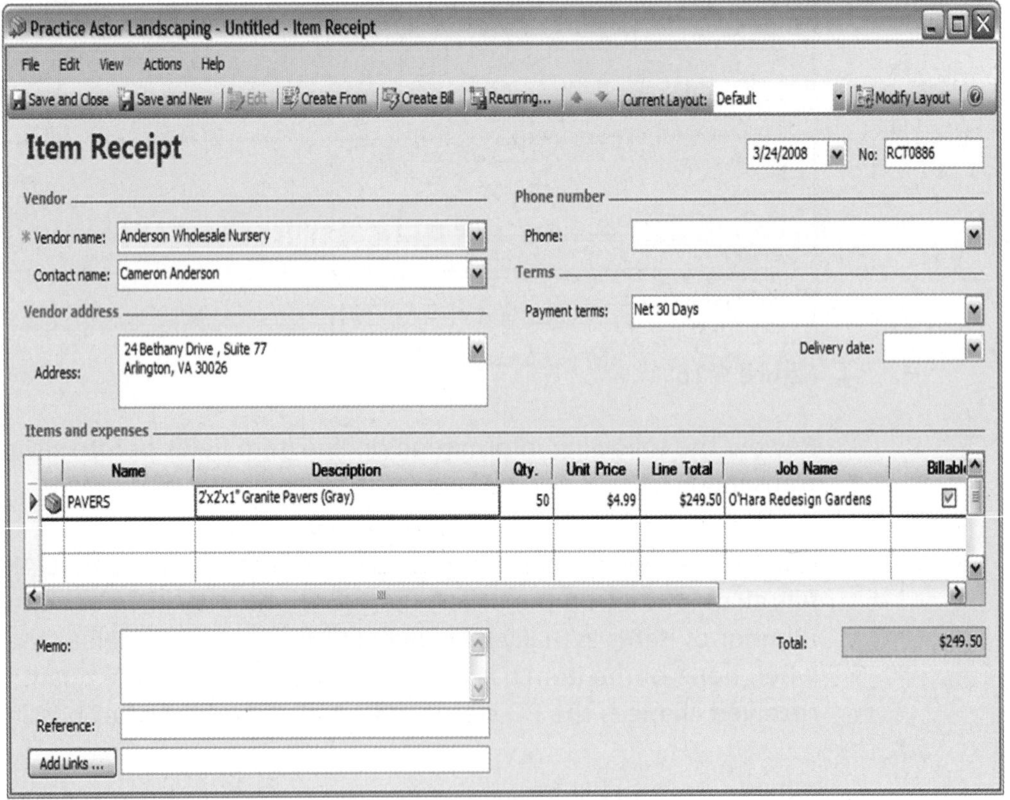

Figure 5:17

3. Click **Save and Close**.

Behind the Keys of a Posted Vendor Bill and Receipt

The transactions recorded in the previous topic posted entries to the Purchases Journal, to vendor accounts, and to the general ledger. Follow the next steps to trace those entries.

Steps to Trace Entries for a Vendor Bill and Receipt

1. First, open the Transaction Journal report by selecting ***Reports>>Company and Financial>>Transaction Journal*** on the main menu.

2. Next, customize the Transaction Journal to display only purchasing transactions. Click **Modify Report** on the toolbar and select **View Filter Options**. Highlight **Transaction Type** and then select the types shown in Figure 5:18.

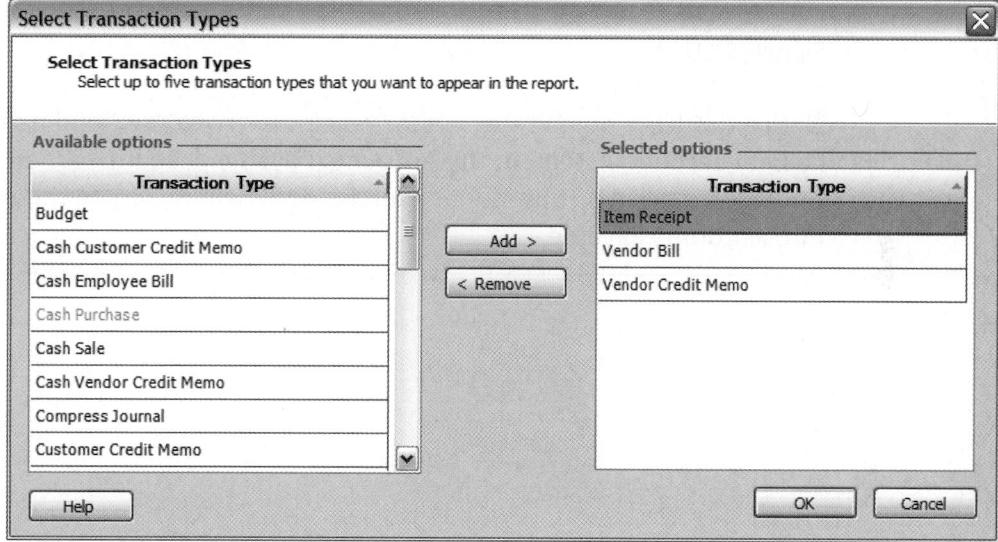

Figure 5:18

Click **OK** and **OK**. Now change the **Header Report Title** to "Purchases Journal." Click **X** to close the Modify Report pane.

Click **Save Report** on the toolbar. Click **OK** to accept the report name and save the report.

3. Enter the date range of **From** "3/24/2008 and **To** "3/24/2008"and the report displays as illustrated next.

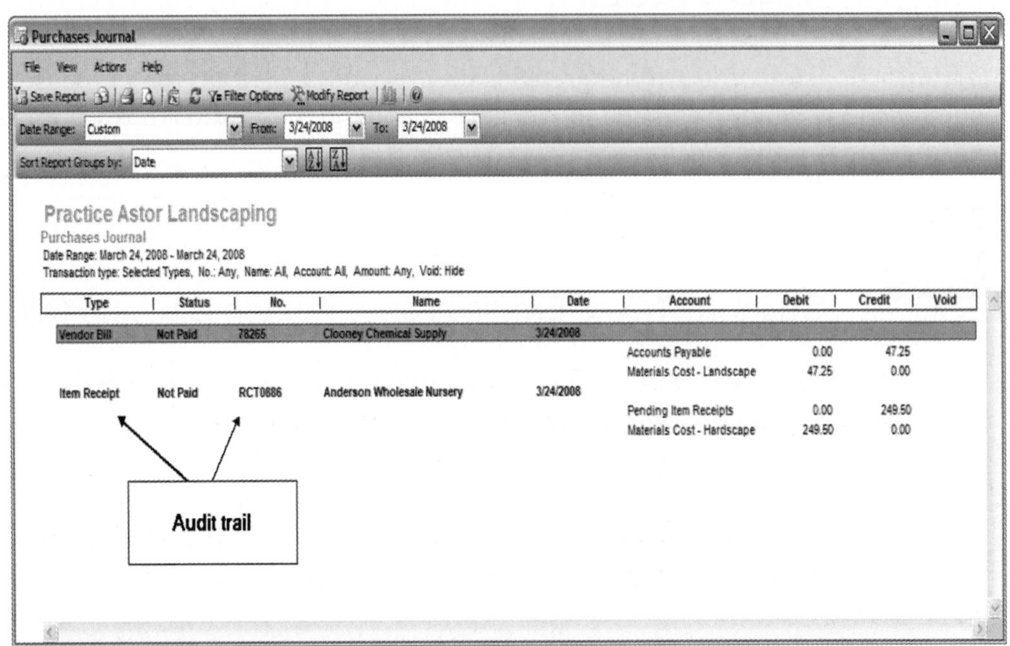

Figure 5:19

Notice that OAP posted the vendor receipt entry to the Pending Item Receipts liability account instead of the Accounts Payable account. When you post Anderson's bill in a subsequent exercise, OAP will reclassify the receipt liability into Accounts Payable.

4. Close the report to next trace entries on the vendor accounts.

   Select ***Reports>>Vendors and Payables>>Vendor Transaction History*** on the main menu. Enter the date range of **From** "3/24/2008" and **To** "3/24/2008."

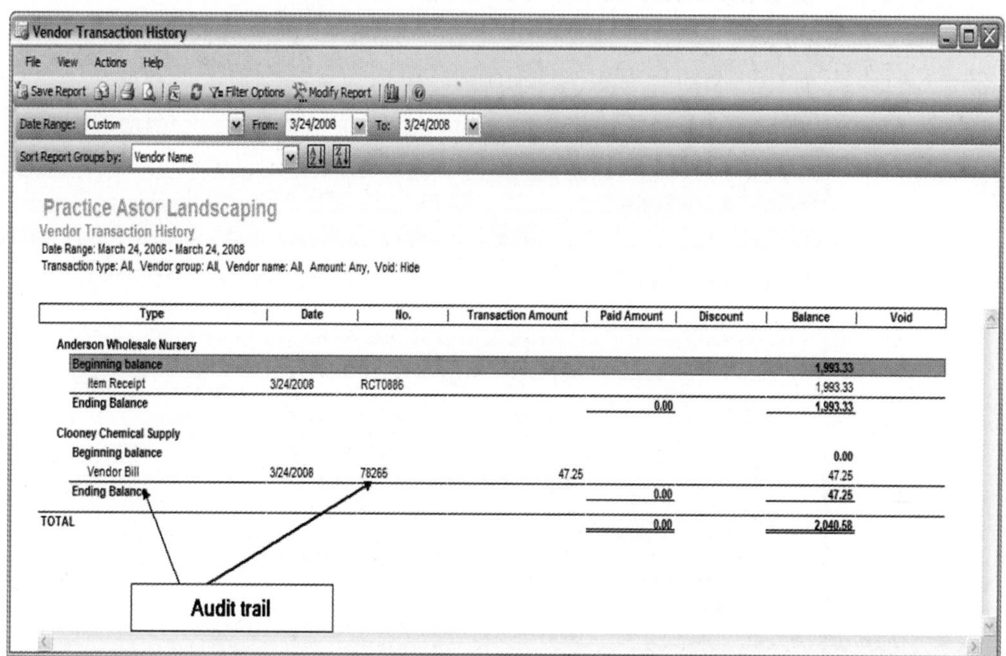

Figure 5:20

Notice that Anderson's receipt has no entry under the Transaction Amount column and the account balance remains unchanged, explaining why OAP did not post Anderson's receipt to Accounts Payable. Anderson cannot be paid for this transaction until the bill arrives so the transaction is not an account that is payable. Furthermore, you will see later in the chapter that the Accounts Payable account must reconcile to the total outstanding balance on vendor accounts so OAP had to record the receipt transaction to a liability account other than Accounts Payable.

Close this report.

5. Finally, verify OAP's entries to the general ledger.

   Select ***Reports>>Company and Financial>>Transaction Detail by Account*** on the main menu. Enter "3/24/2008" as the date range. By now you are able to trace the audit trail to locate the accounts affected by these transactions. Scroll down to the cost of goods sold accounts. (See Figure 5:21.)

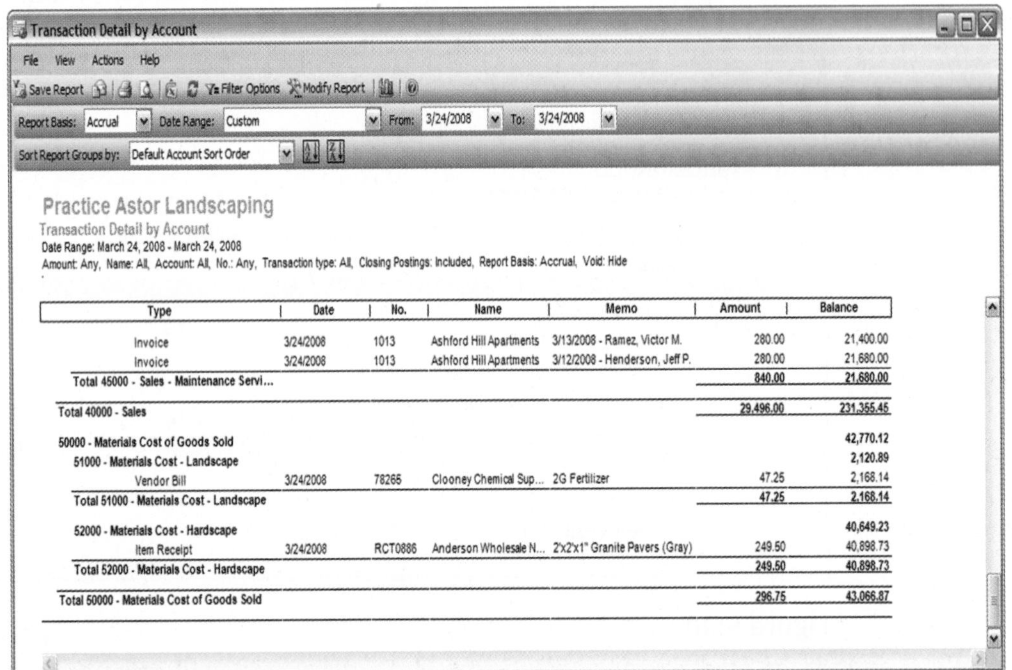

Practice Astor Landscaping
Transaction Detail by Account
Date Range: March 24, 2008 - March 24, 2008
Amount: Any, Name: All, Account: All, No.: Any, Transaction type: All, Closing Postings: Included, Report Basis: Accrual, Void: Hide

Type	Date	No.	Name	Memo	Amount	Balance
Invoice	3/24/2008	1013	Ashford Hill Apartments	3/13/2008 - Ramez, Victor M.	280.00	21,400.00
Invoice	3/24/2008	1013	Ashford Hill Apartments	3/12/2008 - Henderson, Jeff P.	280.00	21,680.00
Total 45000 - Sales - Maintenance Servi...					840.00	21,680.00
Total 40000 - Sales					29,496.00	231,355.45
50000 - Materials Cost of Goods Sold						42,770.12
51000 - Materials Cost - Landscape						2,120.89
Vendor Bill	3/24/2008	78265	Clooney Chemical Sup...	2G Fertilizer	47.25	2,168.14
Total 51000 - Materials Cost - Landscape					47.25	2,168.14
52000 - Materials Cost - Hardscape						40,649.23
Item Receipt	3/24/2008	RCT0886	Anderson Wholesale N...	2'x2'x1" Granite Pavers (Gray)	249.50	40,898.73
Total 52000 - Materials Cost - Hardscape					249.50	40,898.73
Total 50000 - Materials Cost of Goods Sold					296.75	43,066.87

Figure 5:21

You finally see cost of goods sold entries. Recall that when explaining service and non-inventory items in Chapter 4 we stated that service based businesses post cost of goods sold when paying employees and posting vendor bills or receipts.

Close the report. You have completed tracing the entries.

CORRECTING A VENDOR RECEIPT AND BILL

You can modify vendor receipts and ***unpaid*** vendor bills. Vendor receipts and bills with the **Not Paid** status are listed on the Open view of the Bill/Item Receipt List. Click the **Bill and Item Receipts** link under **Find** and verify that the Current View reads Open (Figure 5:22).

Bill/Item Receipt List — Current View: Open

Type	Due Date	No.	Vendor Name	Original Amount	Balance
Add a new Bill					
Vendor Bill	3/27/2008	3628	Anderson Wholesale Nursery	$9.98	$9.98
Vendor Bill	3/29/2008	3675	Anderson Wholesale Nursery	$980.55	$980.55
Vendor Bill	4/2/2008	1185	Davis Timber Yard	$451.48	$451.48
Vendor Bill	4/2/2008	3651	Anderson Wholesale Nursery	$982.84	$982.84
Vendor Bill	4/4/2008	3793	Anderson Wholesale Nursery	$9.98	$9.98
Vendor Bill	4/5/2008	MarTeleph	Neighbors Telephone Company	$262.43	$262.43
Vendor Bill	4/11/2008	3807	Anderson Wholesale Nursery	$9.98	$9.98
Vendor Bill	4/16/2008	901	Calvert Stone Supplies	$4,679.15	$4,679.15
Vendor Bill	4/23/2008	78265	Clooney Chemical Supply	$47.25	$47.25
Item Receipt	4/23/2008	RCT0886	Anderson Wholesale Nursery	$249.50	$249.50
Vendor Bill	5/7/2008	3253	Anderson Wholesale Nursery	$4,782.75	$4,782.75
Vendor Bill	5/15/2008	9351	Anderson Wholesale Nursery	$1,865.85	$1,865.85

Figure 5:22

There are several unpaid bills as well as the Item Receipt from Anderson Wholesale Nursery. Double click the Vendor Bill from Davis Timber Yard to reopen it. (See Figure 5:23.)

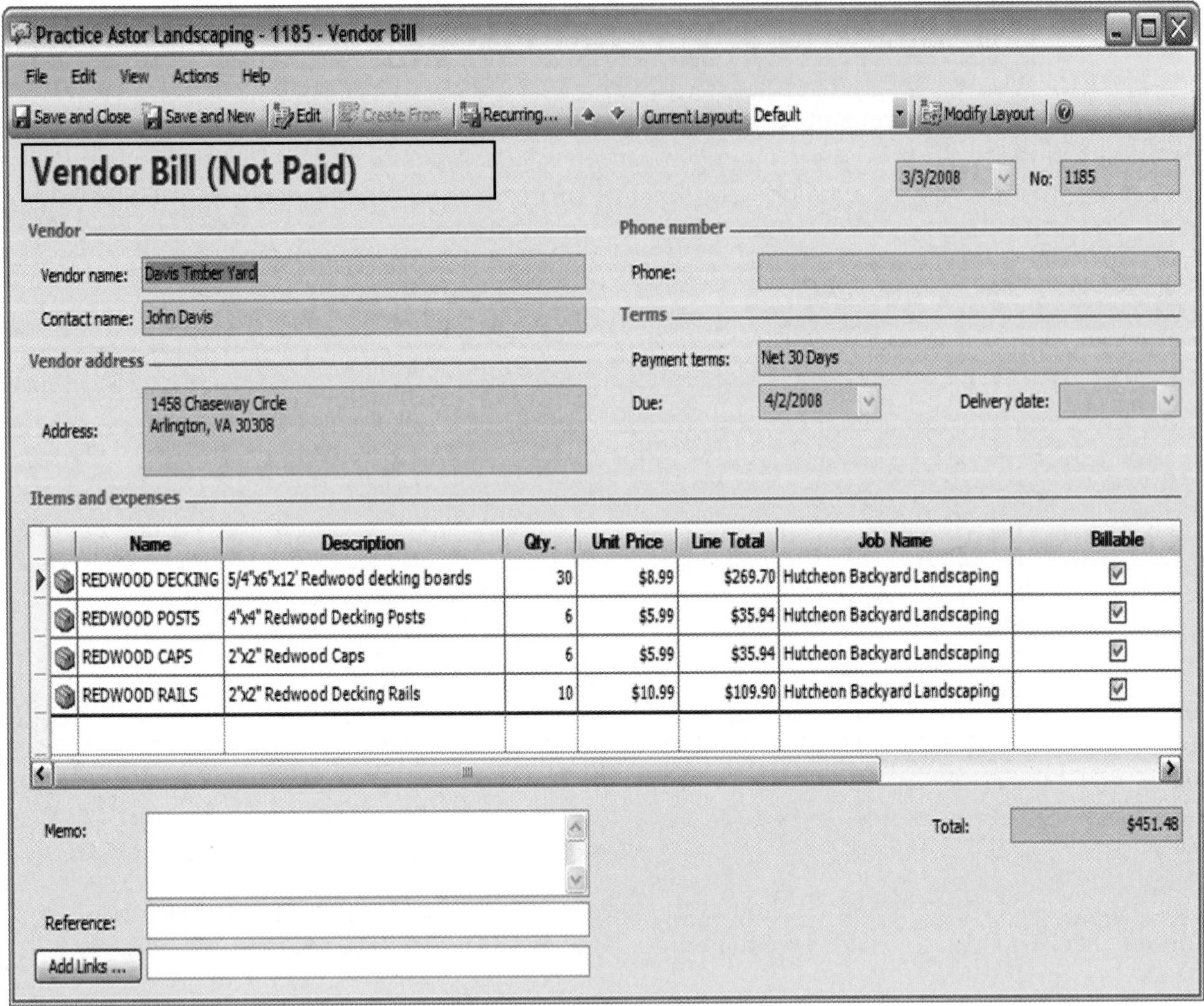

Figure 5:23

This bill is Not Paid so it can be modified. Clicking **Edit** on the toolbar will reopen the bill for editing. After changing, **Save and Close** causes OAP to void the original transaction by posting reversing entries for the original transaction and new entries for modified transaction.

You cannot delete vendor bills or receipts. Instead, you must void these transactions by selecting ***Actions>>Void*** on the menu. *(Note: This menu selection is not available if you already clicked Edit. Exit the transaction to make the menu available. You can then right click the transaction on the list and select Void.)* After voiding a transaction OAP releases the PO used to create the transaction so you can again receive the items.

Click **X** to close Davis' transaction.

A bill's status changes to **Paid** after paying the bill. Toggle the Current View on the Bill/Item Receipt List to All (Figure 5:24). Bills with zero under the Balance column are paid.

Bill/Item Receipt List Current View: All

Type	Due Date	No.	Vendor Name	Original Amount	Balance
Add a new Bill					
Vendor Bill	12/29/2007	8261	Paris Brothers Tree Surgeons	$199.99	$0.00
Vendor Bill	12/29/2007	DEC Electr...	Southern Power Co.	$105.22	$0.00
Vendor Bill	1/7/2008	JanRent	General Leasing Corp.	$2,500.00	$0.00
Vendor Bill	1/13/2008	0235	Anderson Wholesale Nursery	$9.98	$0.00
Vendor Bill	1/13/2008	8425	Jackson Advertising Company	$585.27	$0.00
Vendor Bill	1/19/2008	825	Molly Maid Cleaning Services	$300.00	$0.00
Vendor Bill	1/19/2008	PRTaxes	Nations Bank	$3,457.16	$0.00
Vendor Bill	1/23/2008	Janelec	Southern Power Co.	$102.04	$0.00
Vendor Bill	1/23/2008	JanWater	Arlington City Water	$210.57	$0.00
Vendor Bill	1/25/2008	JanPostage	Postmaster	$150.00	$0.00
Vendor Bill	2/1/2008	00801	Clooney Chemical Supply	$157.50	$0.00
Vendor Bill	2/1/2008	3112	Anderson Wholesale Nursery	$9.98	$0.00
Vendor Bill	2/2/2008	PRTaxes	Nations Bank	$3,535.38	$0.00
Vendor Bill	2/2/2008	StPRTaxes	VA Department of Taxation	$815.78	$0.00
Vendor Bill	2/3/2008	7569	Miles Maintenance & Repair	$1,416.56	$0.00
Vendor Bill	2/3/2008	JanInsur	Safe State Insurance Company	$422.10	$0.00
Vendor Bill	2/6/2008	FebRent	General Leasing Corp.	$2,500.00	$0.00
Vendor Bill	2/7/2008	3178	Anderson Wholesale Nursery	$9.98	$0.00
Vendor Bill	2/8/2008	0230	Fast Track Couriers	$64.99	$0.00
Vendor Bill	2/9/2008	JanTeleph	Neighbors Telephone Company	$276.18	$0.00
Vendor Bill	2/14/2008	3204	Anderson Wholesale Nursery	$9.98	$0.00
Vendor Bill	2/15/2008	JanHealth	Medi Benefits Adminstrators	$600.00	$0.00
Vendor Bill	2/16/2008	125002	Daniel Lawn Pro Inc.	$3,000.00	$0.00
Vendor Bill	2/16/2008	PRTaxes	Nations Bank	$3,537.50	$0.00
Vendor Bill	2/20/2008	2763	Molly Maid Cleaning Services	$300.00	$0.00
Vendor Bill	2/20/2008	FebElec	Southern Power Co.	$117.32	$0.00

Figure 5:24

Double click to open General Leasing Corp's bill for January rent (Figure 5:25).

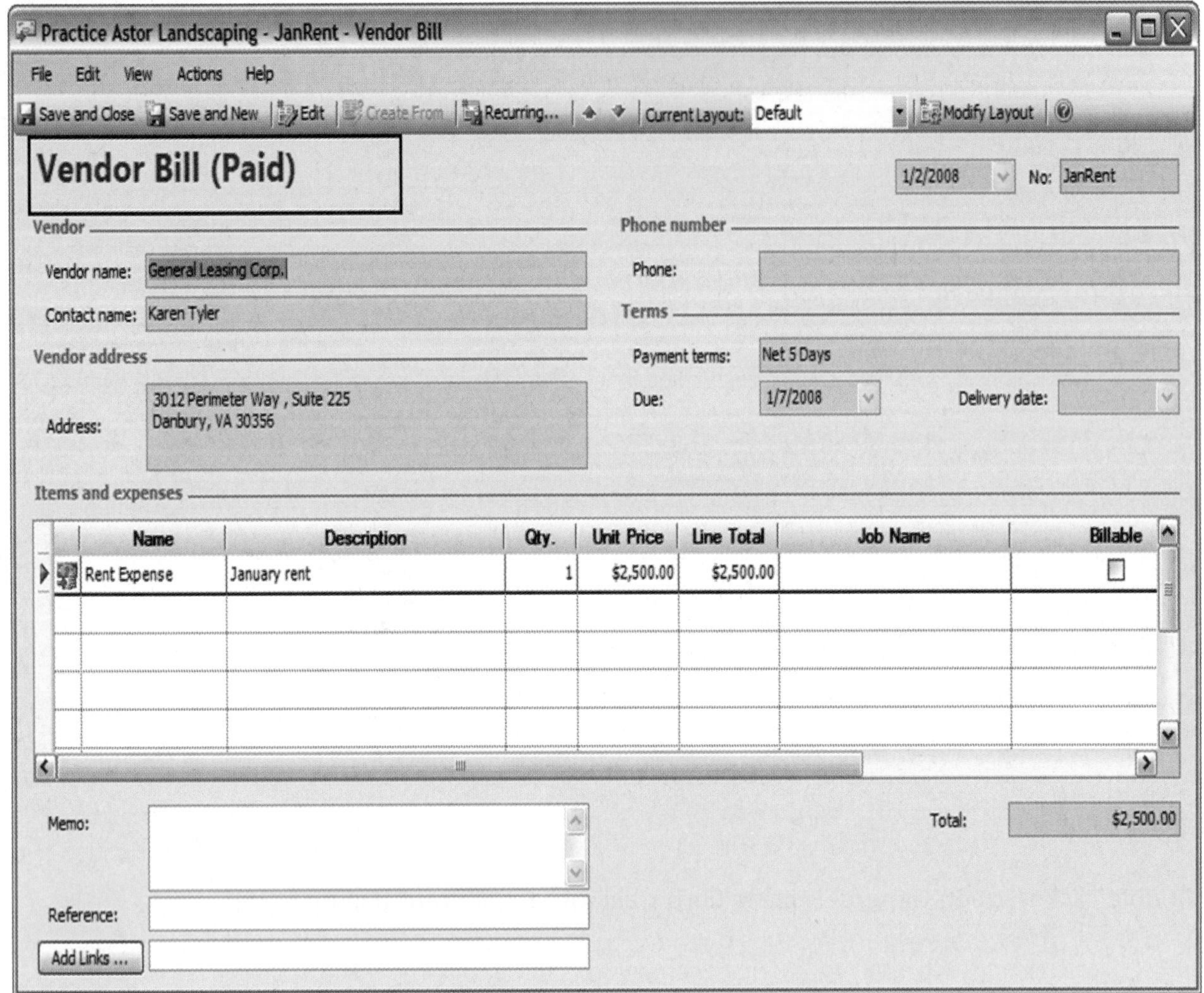

Figure 5:25

This bill is Paid and, although OAP will let you Edit it, the bill should not be modified because the payment will no longer match the bill. Instead, you should void the payment before modifying the bill. We will illustrate voiding a vendor payment later in the chapter. In addition, Appendix B provides complete instructions on correcting transactions.

Click **X** to close the transaction.

ENTER VENDOR RECEIPTS AND BILLS FOR PURCHASE ORDERS

On March 27, 2008, the following items were received for previously issued POs. Post these transactions and click **Yes** if prompted to exceed a vendor's credit limit.

Calvert Stone Supplies Invoice 2346 for all items on PO 3.

Southern Garden Wholesale Receipt RCT5132 for 30 Boxwoods on PO 4. Note: Delete the Amy Azalea Plant line item because this item was not received. The PO status will then be Partially Received.

Print the Purchases Journal for March 27, 2008.

VENDOR BILLS FOR VENDOR RECEIPTS

You still need to post the vendor bill for Anderson Wholesale Nursery's receipt recorded on March 24. The next instructions illustrate turning a receipt into a bill so you can pay the vendor.

STEPS TO RECORD A VENDOR BILL FOR A VENDOR RECEIPT

1. Click the **Bill and Item Receipts** link under **Find** and toggle the list to **Open**. Double click **RCT0886** from **Anderson Wholesale Nursery** to reopen the transaction. (See Figure 5:26.)

   (Note: This is one method for entering a bill for receipt. You can also open a new bill transaction, click the Create From icon, and select the receipt transaction just as you selected POs in an earlier topic.)

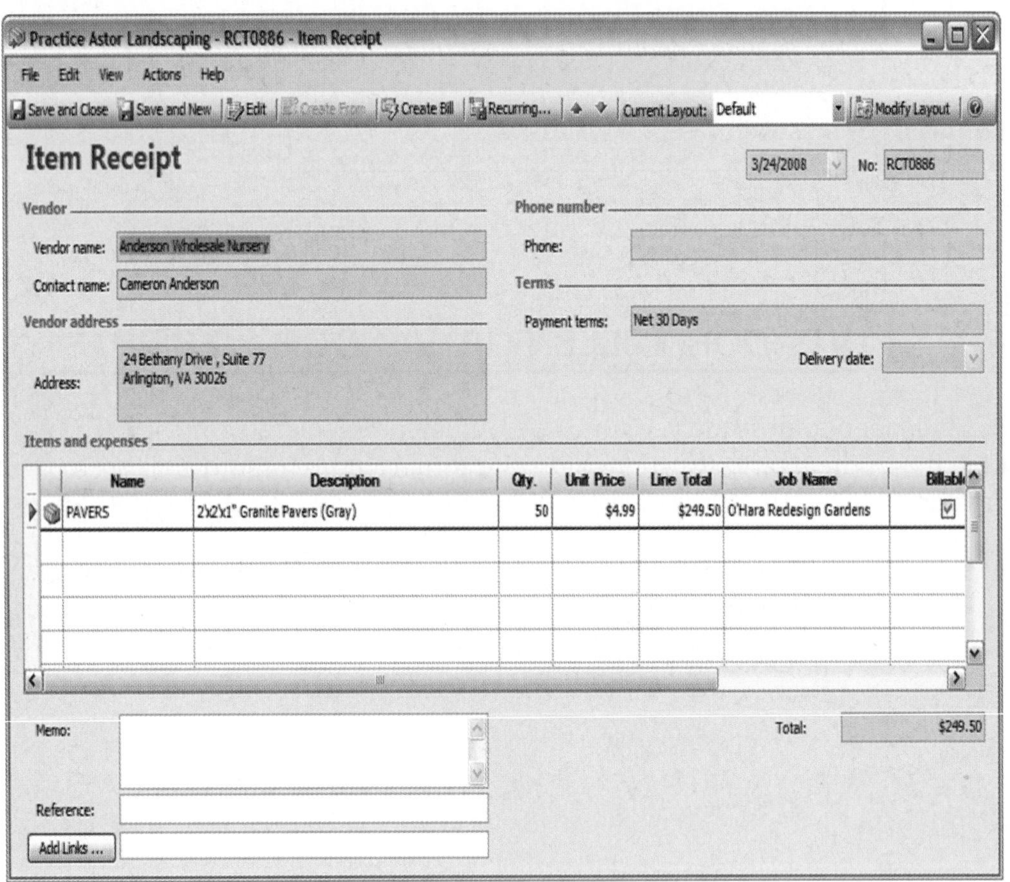

Figure 5:26

2. Click **Create Bill** on the toolbar, change the transaction date to "3/26/2008," and enter Anderson's invoice number of "8213."

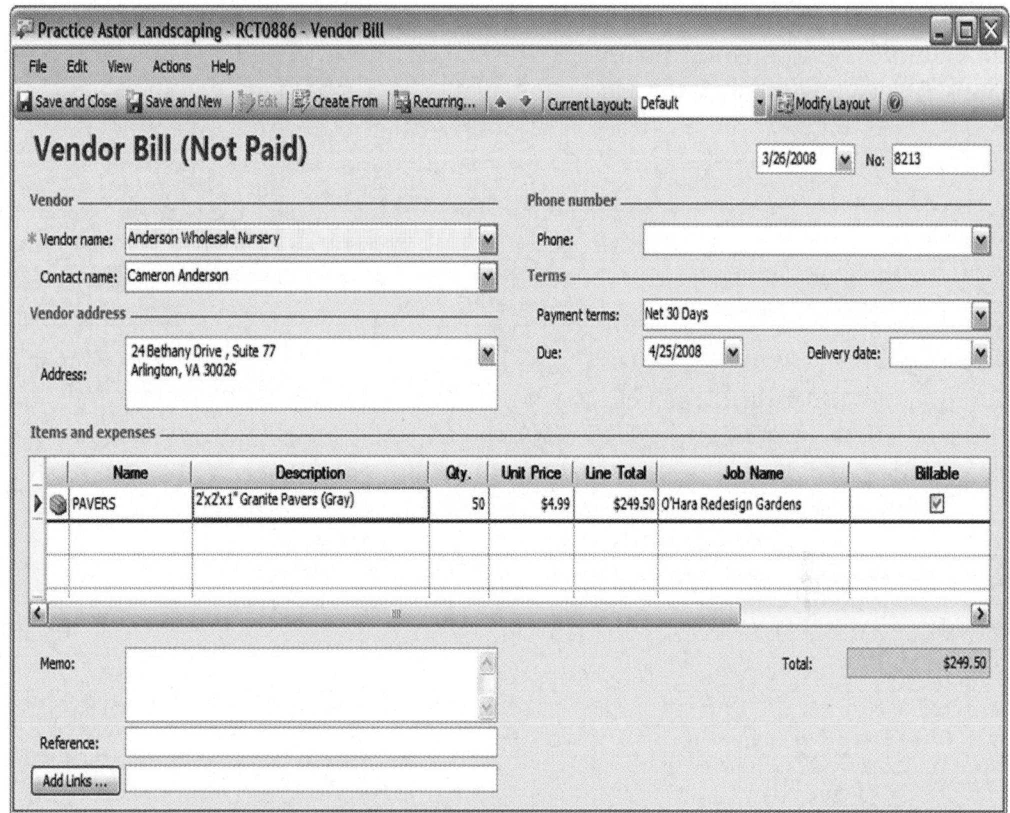

Figure 5:27

3. Click **Save and Close**. Return to the Bill/Item Receipt List and note that the Type has changed to Vendor Bill.

ENTER VENDOR BILL FOR VENDOR RECEIPT

Invoice 7631 for $674.70 arrives from Southern Garden Wholesale for RCT5132. The invoice is dated March 28, 2008.

Record this transaction and print the Purchases Journal for the date of the transaction.

Vendor Accounts

This topic explains creating, editing, and deleting vendor accounts.

Click **Vendors** under **Find** to open the Vendor List. As on the Customer list, OAP reports the total outstanding balance for accounts payable at the bottom.

Vendor List — Current View: Active

Active	Vendor Name	Address	City	State	Zip Code	Phone	Fax	Balance
Add a new Vendor								
✓	Anderson Wholesale Nurs...	24 Bethany Drive	Arlington	VA	30026	678-555-1279	770-555-77...	$8,891.43
✓	Arlington City Water	Box 4551	Arlington	VA	30044	770-555-0177	770-555-01...	$0.00
✓	Arlington Gas Company	1304 Sheridan Road	Arlington	VA	30329	404-555-3144	404-555-12...	$0.00
✓	Calvert Stone Supplies	554 Ashford Ctr. N	Arlington	VA	30301	404-555-5264	404-555-57...	$4,878.75
✓	Clooney Chemical Supply	3099 Weston Blvd.	Arlinton	VA	30312	404-555-0899	404-555-10...	$47.25
✓	Daniel Lawn Pro Inc.	5150 Arc Way	Blacksburg	VA	30093	770-555-1126	770-555-11...	$0.00
✓	Davis Timber Yard	1458 Chaseway Circle	Arlington	VA	30308	404-555-6885	404-555-68...	$451.48
✓	Eddison Builders Supplies	111 Main St.	Arlington	VA	30188	770-555-5827	770-555-58...	$0.00
✓	Fast Track Couriers	5611 Medlock Bridge Road	Arlington	VA	30099	770-555-0136	770-555-01...	$0.00
✓	Gary Wilson Jones & Smith	One Tower Square	Arlington	VA	30302	404-555-8000	404-555-81...	$0.00
✓	General Leasing Corp.	3012 Perimeter Way	Danbury	VA	30356	770-555-1901	404-555-19...	$0.00
✓	Jackson Advertising Comp...	1458 Chaseway Circle	Arlington	VA	30308	404-555-5855	404-555-57...	$0.00
✓	Medi Benefits Adminstrators	PO Box 7902	Arlington	VA	30311			$0.00
✓	Miles Maintenance & Repair	2536 Satellite Road	Arlington	VA	30093	770-555-7117	770-555-70...	$0.00
✓	Molly Maid Cleaning Servi...	1121 Praxter St	Arlington	VA	30097	770-724-0001		$0.00
✓	Nations Bank	11000 Main Street	Arlington	VA	30022	770-555-8821	770-555-63...	$0.00
✓	Neighbors Telephone Com...	PO Box 9010	Arlington	VA	30301	404-555-1022	404-555-10...	$262.43
✓	Office Maxtors	3173 W. Salem	Arlington	VA	30003			$0.00
✓	Paris Brothers Tree Surge...	8572 Halcyon Way	Blacksburg	VA	30044	770-555-4154	770-555-21...	$0.00
✓	Postmaster							$0.00
✓	Safe State Insurance Com...	311 State Bridge Road	Arlington	VA	30097	770-555-1136	770-555-86...	$0.00
✓	Southern Garden Wholesale	4555 Oakland Park Blvd.	Arlington	VA	30312	404-555-9668	404-555-15...	$674.70
✓	Southern Power Co.	Box 2199	Arlington	VA	30301	404-555-0799	404-555-08...	$0.00
✓	VA Department of Taxation	PO Box 789	Arlington	VA	30313			$0.00
✓	VA Employment Commissi...	PO Box 7878	Arlington	VA	30313			$0.00
✓	VA Sales Tax Department	PO Box 2351	Arlington	VA	30235			$3,756.50

Total outstanding balance: $18,962.54

Figure 5:28

Double click **Anderson Wholesale Nursery** to open the account and follow below as we describe the tabs on the vendor account.

General Tab

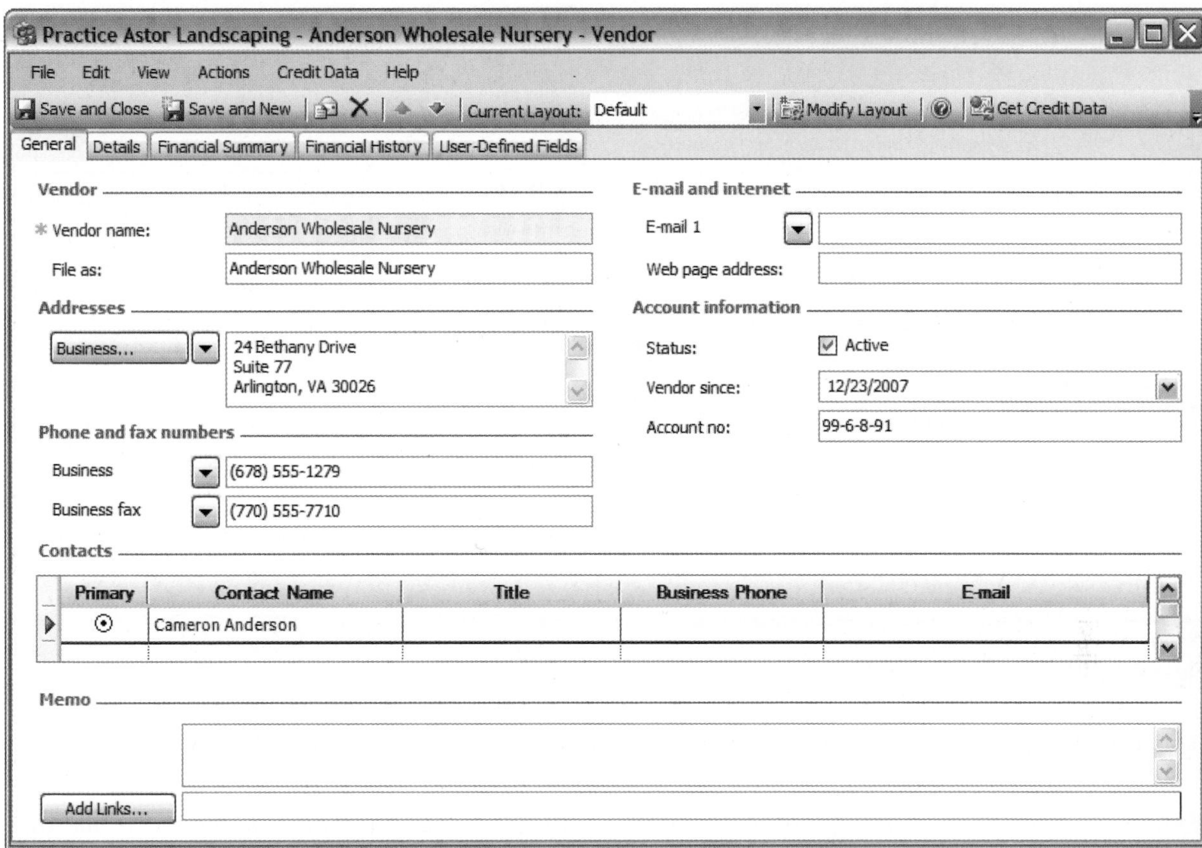

Figure 5:29

This tab stores basic information such as address, phone numbers, and contacts. When **Active** is not checked, OAP denies posting future purchases and bills for the vendor. This option is important when companies need to control purchases for reasons such as poor vendor performance but cannot delete the account because it contains transaction history.

Details Tab

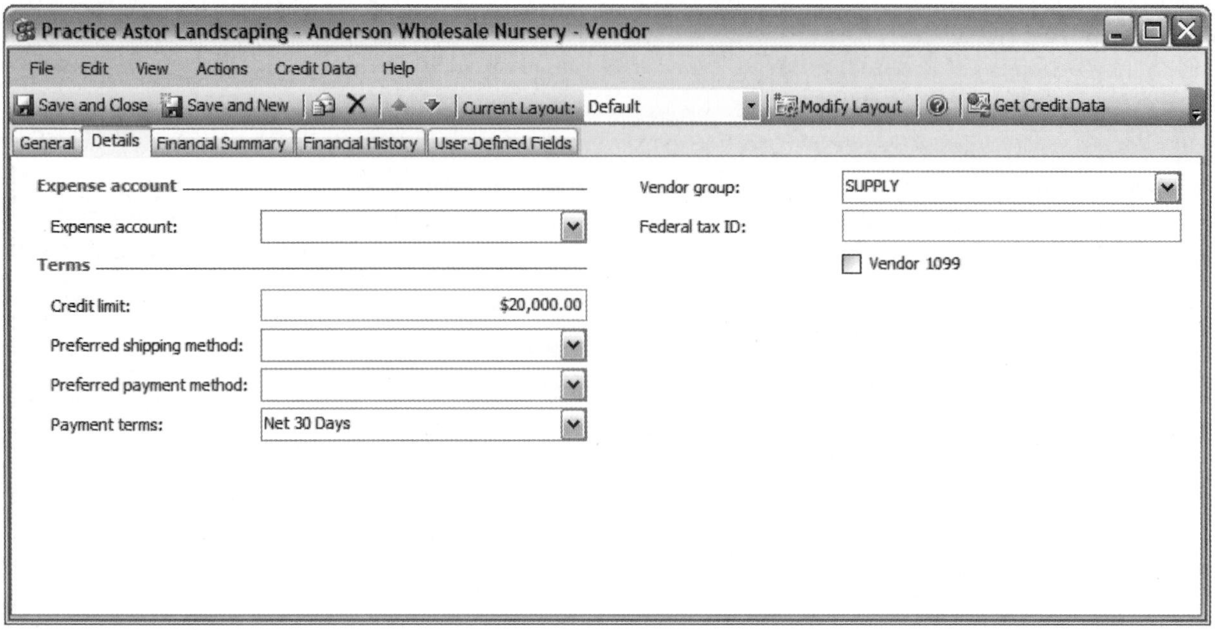

Figure 5:30

This tab stores defaults to be used on vendor transactions and reporting.

Expense account stores the general ledger account to be used when posting a vendor bill for expenses (i.e., line items using the expense icon). Vendors that are non-inventory suppliers will not have an account in this field because purchases from these vendors are for non-inventory items (i.e., line items with the inventory icon) and OAP posts the transaction to the general ledger expense account stored on the item.

Credit limit instructs OAP to warn when saving a vendor bill that causes the account balance to exceed the credit limit.

Payment terms function like customer payment terms by controlling vendor bill due dates and early payment discount terms.

Vendor group is optional and used on reports to analyze purchases by vendor characteristics. You can click the dropdown list to view the types used by Astor.

Federal tax ID stores a vendor's social security number or federal ID number used when preparing Form 1099.

Vendor 1099 triggers a vendor account for IRS tax reporting. If selected, OAP tracks annual payments to the vendor for reporting on Form 1099. *(Note: The IRS requires an annual filing of Form 1099 for payments made to subcontractors that exceed $600. Information on 1099 reporting requirements is available at www.irs.gov.)*

Financial Summary Tab

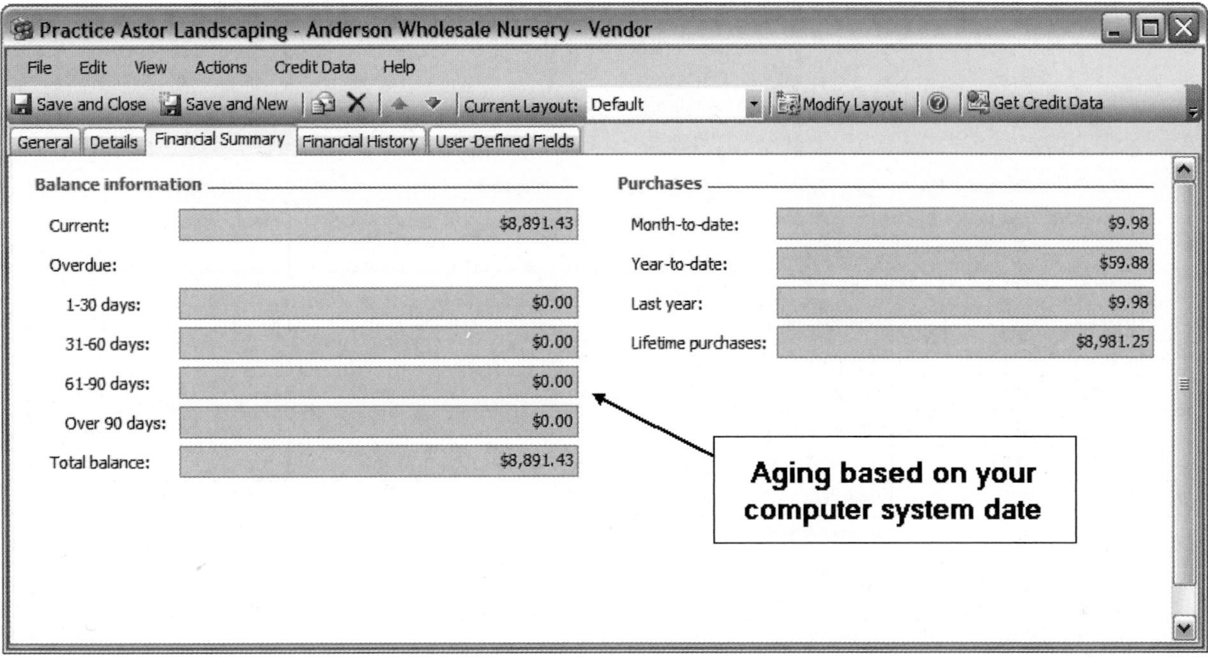

Figure 5:31

This tab provides a quick snapshot on the age of the vendor balance and purchasing totals. OAP uses your computer's system date to calculate aging categories.

Financial History Tab

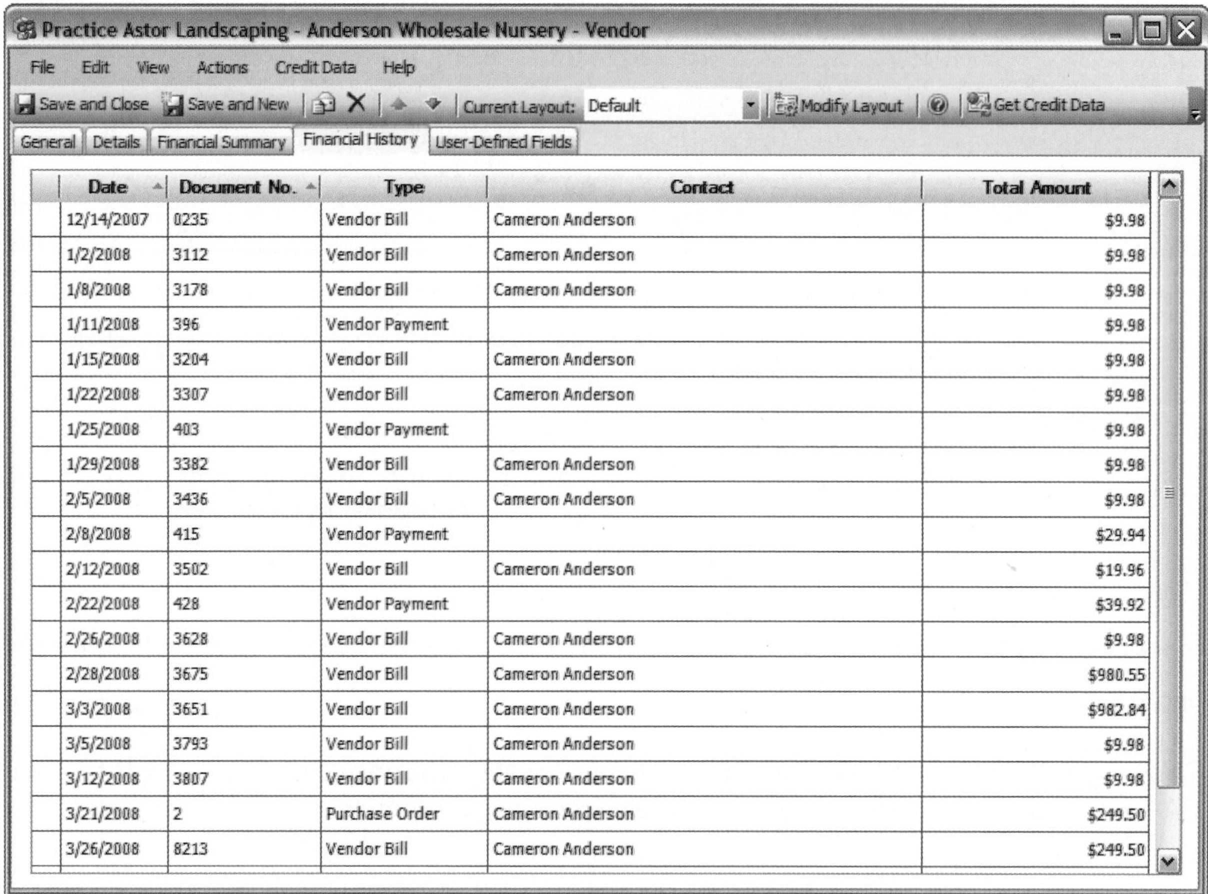

Date	Document No.	Type	Contact	Total Amount
12/14/2007	0235	Vendor Bill	Cameron Anderson	$9.98
1/2/2008	3112	Vendor Bill	Cameron Anderson	$9.98
1/8/2008	3178	Vendor Bill	Cameron Anderson	$9.98
1/11/2008	396	Vendor Payment		$9.98
1/15/2008	3204	Vendor Bill	Cameron Anderson	$9.98
1/22/2008	3307	Vendor Bill	Cameron Anderson	$9.98
1/25/2008	403	Vendor Payment		$9.98
1/29/2008	3382	Vendor Bill	Cameron Anderson	$9.98
2/5/2008	3436	Vendor Bill	Cameron Anderson	$9.98
2/8/2008	415	Vendor Payment		$29.94
2/12/2008	3502	Vendor Bill	Cameron Anderson	$19.96
2/22/2008	428	Vendor Payment		$39.92
2/26/2008	3628	Vendor Bill	Cameron Anderson	$9.98
2/28/2008	3675	Vendor Bill	Cameron Anderson	$980.55
3/3/2008	3651	Vendor Bill	Cameron Anderson	$982.84
3/5/2008	3793	Vendor Bill	Cameron Anderson	$9.98
3/12/2008	3807	Vendor Bill	Cameron Anderson	$9.98
3/21/2008	2	Purchase Order	Cameron Anderson	$249.50
3/26/2008	8213	Vendor Bill	Cameron Anderson	$249.50

Figure 5:32

This tab lists vendor transactions. You can drill down to original entries by double clicking a transaction, which facilitates answering vendor inquiries.

Click **X** to close Anderson's account and **No.** if prompted to save changes. Now practice editing vendor accounts by completing the next exercise.

STEPS TO EDIT VENDOR ACCOUNT INFORMATION

1. Open Davis Timber Yard's account. You will change the account terms to calculate a 1 percent discount when paying invoices within 10 days of the invoice date.

2. Select the **Details** tab and change the **Payment terms** to those illustrated next.

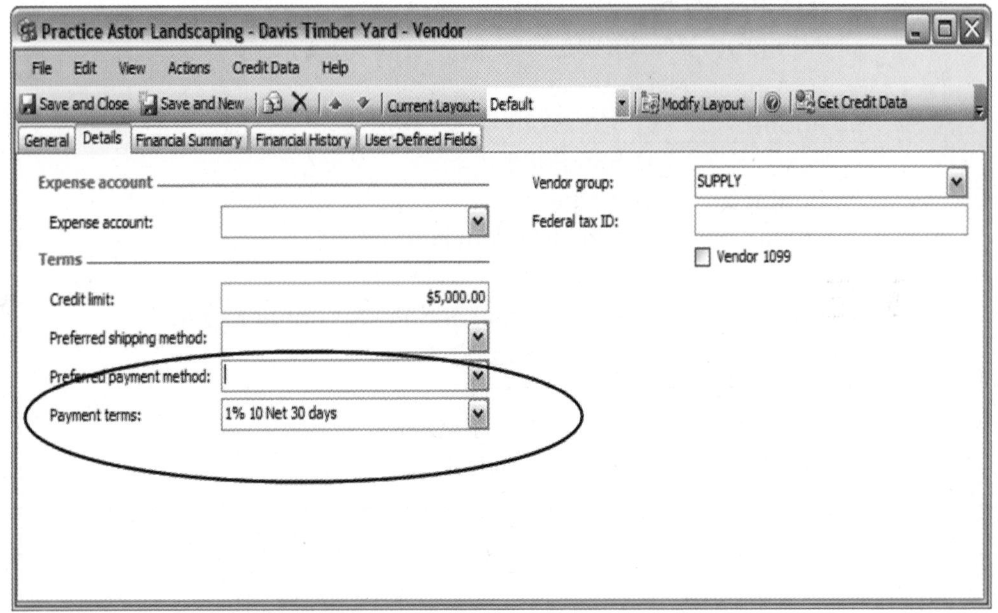

Figure 5:33

3. Click **Save and Close**.

You can delete a vendor by highlighting the account on the list and clicking X on the toolbar. Like customers, you cannot delete accounts with transaction history so change the Active option to deny future transactions.

Adding vendors is similar to adding customers. Practice creating a new vendor in the exercise that follows.

CREATE A NEW VENDOR

On March 27, Astor opened a new vendor account with the following information. Create the vendor account.

Jackson Hyland Tax Service
P.O. Box 8276
Arlington, VA 30010

Phone:	701 555-8723
Fax:	701 555-9083
Contact:	Sam Calper
Email:	calper@jacksonhyland.net

Expense account:	Legal and Professional Expense
Credit limit:	$5,000
Preferred payment:	Check
Payment terms:	Net 15 Days
Vendor group:	ADMIN

Vendor Bills for Expenses

Astor also receives vendor bills for expenses not originating on POs. These bills are normally for expenses such as office supplies, utilities, and insurance.

On March 24, Astor receives a bill for office supplies. Complete the next exercise to record this transaction.

STEPS FOR ENTERING VENDOR BILLS FOR EXPENSES

1. Click **Enter Bills** and enter "3/24/2008" as the transaction date. Enter the vendor's invoice **No.** of "364" and look up "Office Maxtors" as the **Vendor name**.

   Figure 5:34 points out that the **Icon** defaulted to **Expense** because this vendor's account stores **Office Supplies Expense** as the default transaction account.

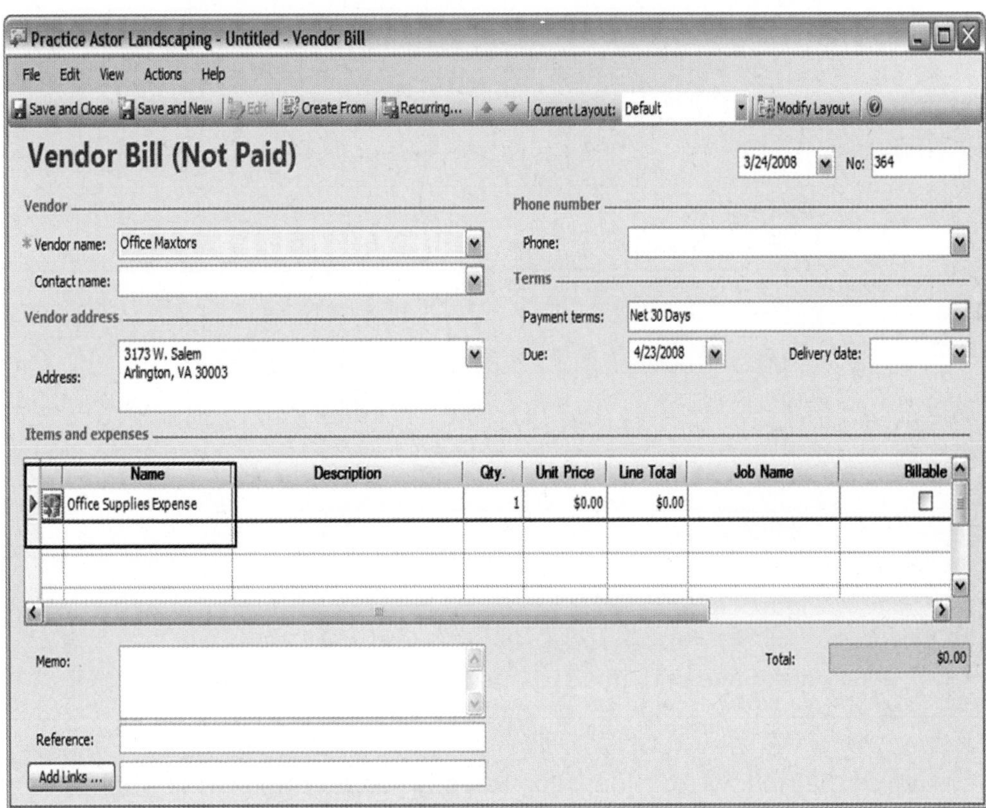

Figure 5:34

2. Tab to **Description** and type "Paper supplies." Then tab to **Unit Price** and enter "125.76." Expense bills are not usually assigned to a job so the completed transaction is shown in Figure 5:35.

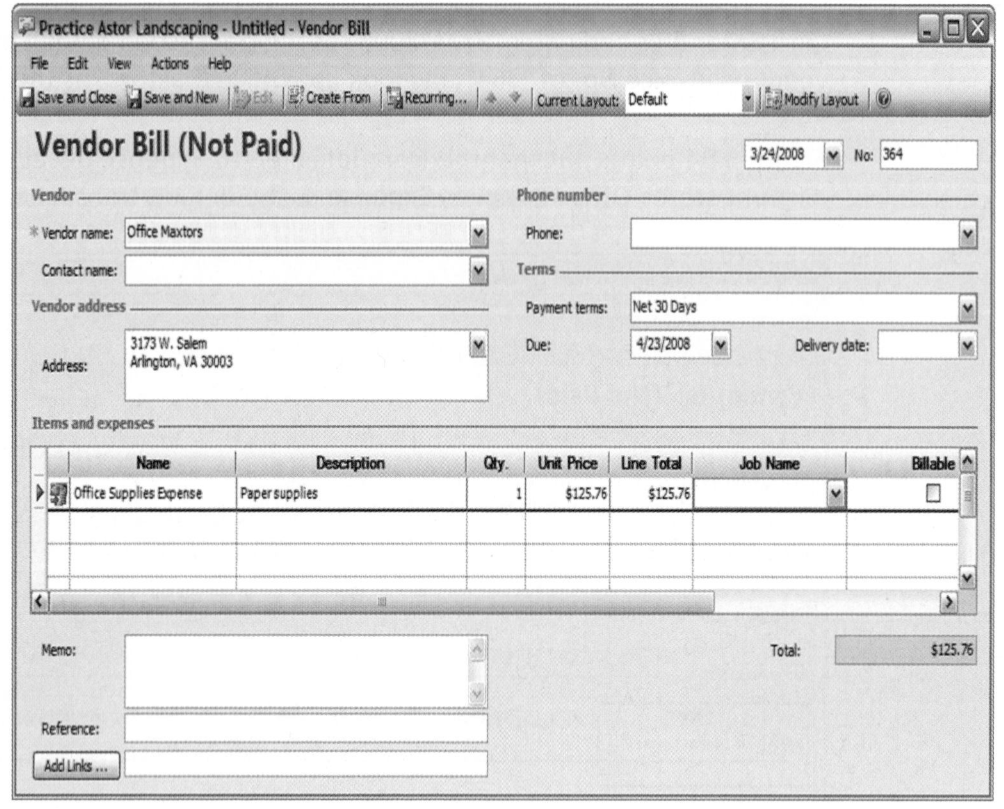

Figure 5:35

3. Click **Save and Close** to post the bill.

The exercise that follows provides more practice on entering vendor bills for expenses.

ENTER VENDOR BILLS FOR EXPENSES

On March 27, Astor received a bill dated March 20, 2008, from Jackson Hyland Tax Service. This is the vendor you created in a previous *You Try* exercise. The bill for $762.00 is for first quarter tax advice and is posted to Legal and Professional Expense. Record this bill.

Hints:
There are a couple of points to this exercise. First, the invoice date, not the date you received the bill, is always the transaction date. Generally, bills will not be received on the same date as the invoice date.

Second, Jackson Hyland's transaction did not provide an invoice number. You will often encounter bills without an invoice number, particularly bills for utility and professional service expense. Therefore, you must create an invoice number and create it in such a way as to later identify the transaction. For instance, you can use "MarElec" as the invoice number for March electricity.

RECURRING VENDOR BILLS

OAP will memorize vendor bills, which is especially useful for repeating bills such as rent. You can memorize bills while posting a new bill or open a posted bill to memorize it.

The accountant received a bill for monthly advertising. In the following exercise, you enter this bill and turn it into a recurring bill.

STEPS TO CREATE A RECURRING VENDOR BILL

1. Click **Enter Bills** on the home page and enter the information shown in Figure 5:36.

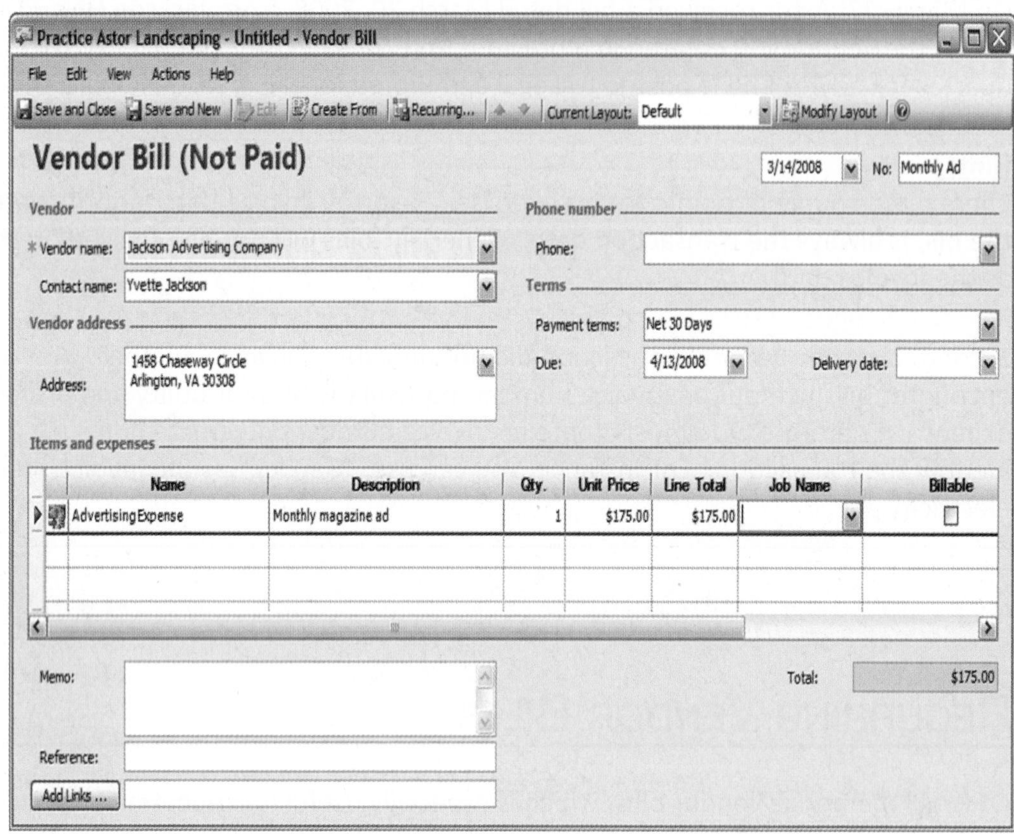

Figure 5:36

2. Click **Recurring** on the toolbar and complete the window as illustrated next.

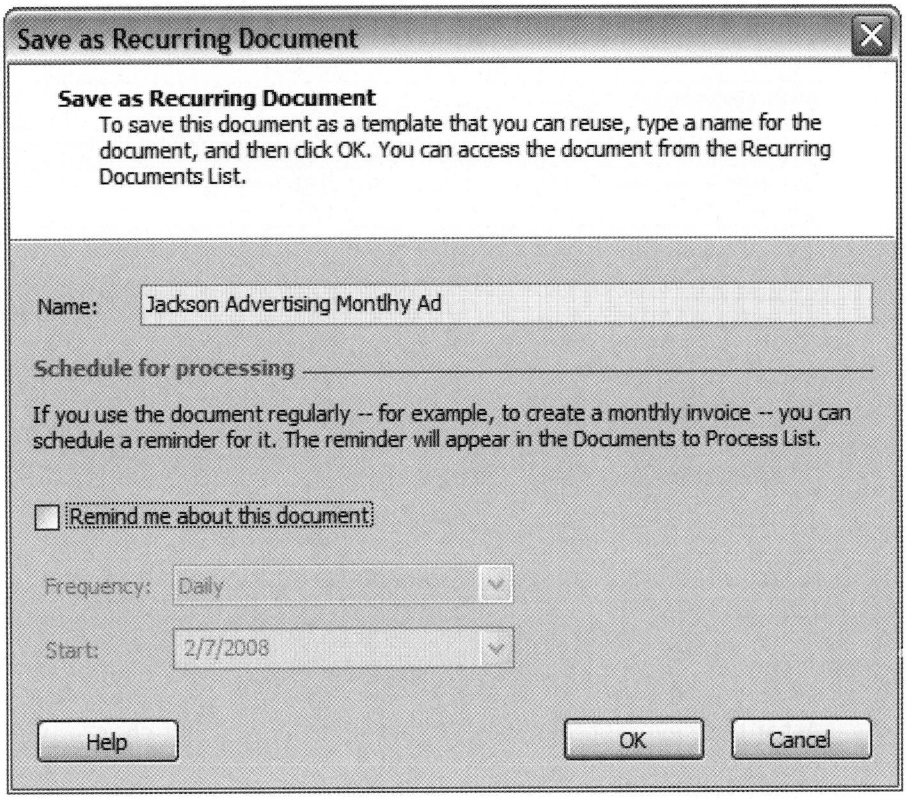

Save as Recurring Document

Save as Recurring Document
To save this document as a template that you can reuse, type a name for the document, and then click OK. You can access the document from the Recurring Documents List.

Name: Jackson Advertising Montlhy Ad

Schedule for processing

If you use the document regularly -- for example, to create a monthly invoice -- you can schedule a reminder for it. The reminder will appear in the Documents to Process List.

☐ Remind me about this document

Frequency: Daily

Start: 2/7/2008

Help | OK | Cancel

Figure 5:37

Note: Normally you would choose the Remind me about this document option and set the Frequency to Monthly. OAP would then remind you to post this transaction every month; however; these reminders would pile up considering you are working exercises months after the company's current accounting period.

Click **OK** to save the recurring transaction. Click **Save and Close** to post the March transaction.

3. You will now locate the recurring transaction. Click the **Recurring Documents** link under **Find** or select ***Company>>Company Lists>>Recurring Documents*** on the main menu. Click the Type column to sort the list (Figure 5:38).

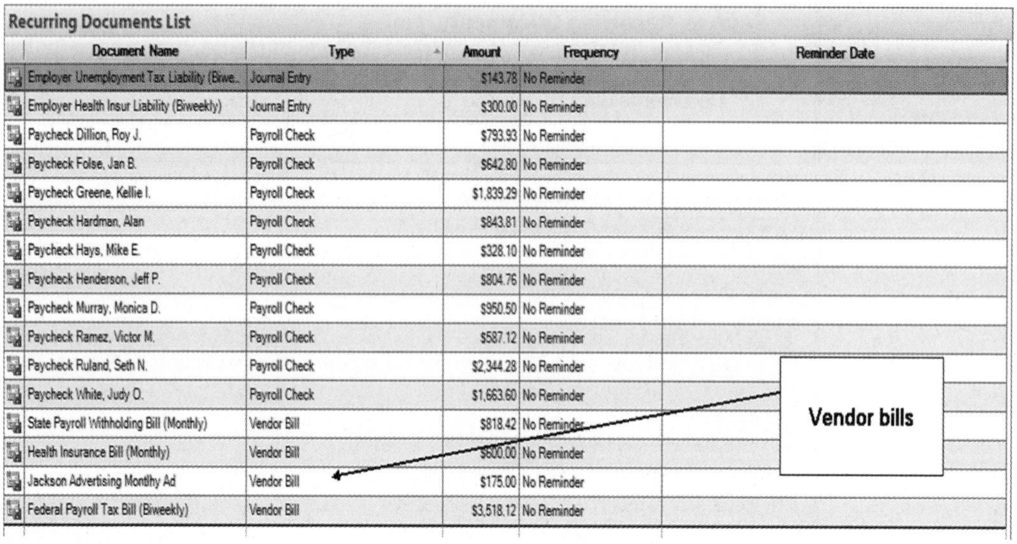

Recurring Documents List

Document Name	Type	Amount	Frequency	Reminder Date
Employer Unemployment Tax Liability (Biwe...	Journal Entry	$143.78	No Reminder	
Employer Health Insur Liability (Biweekly)	Journal Entry	$300.00	No Reminder	
Paycheck Dillion, Roy J.	Payroll Check	$793.93	No Reminder	
Paycheck Folse, Jan B.	Payroll Check	$642.80	No Reminder	
Paycheck Greene, Kellie I.	Payroll Check	$1,839.29	No Reminder	
Paycheck Hardman, Alan	Payroll Check	$843.81	No Reminder	
Paycheck Hays, Mike E.	Payroll Check	$328.10	No Reminder	
Paycheck Henderson, Jeff P.	Payroll Check	$804.76	No Reminder	
Paycheck Murray, Monica D.	Payroll Check	$950.50	No Reminder	
Paycheck Ramez, Victor M.	Payroll Check	$587.12	No Reminder	
Paycheck Ruland, Seth N.	Payroll Check	$2,344.28	No Reminder	
Paycheck White, Judy O.	Payroll Check	$1,663.60	No Reminder	
State Payroll Withholding Bill (Monthly)	Vendor Bill	$818.42	No Reminder	
Health Insurance Bill (Monthly)	Vendor Bill	$600.00	No Reminder	
Jackson Advertising Monthly Ad	Vendor Bill	$175.00	No Reminder	
Federal Payroll Tax Bill (Biweekly)	Vendor Bill	$3,518.12	No Reminder	

Vendor bills

Figure 5:38

Astor has several recurring transactions. In the next chapter you will use the paycheck transactions to pay employees.

Recurring transactions are posted by double clicking a transaction to reopen, making any necessary changes, and then saving the transaction.

You can modify the scheduling and name of the transaction by right clicking it and selecting **Edit Recurring Document**.

4. Let's post the advertising bill for April. Double click **Jackson Advertising Monthly Ad**. Enter "4/14/2008" as the transaction date and "Monthly Ad" as the **No**. Click **Save and Close** to post the transaction.

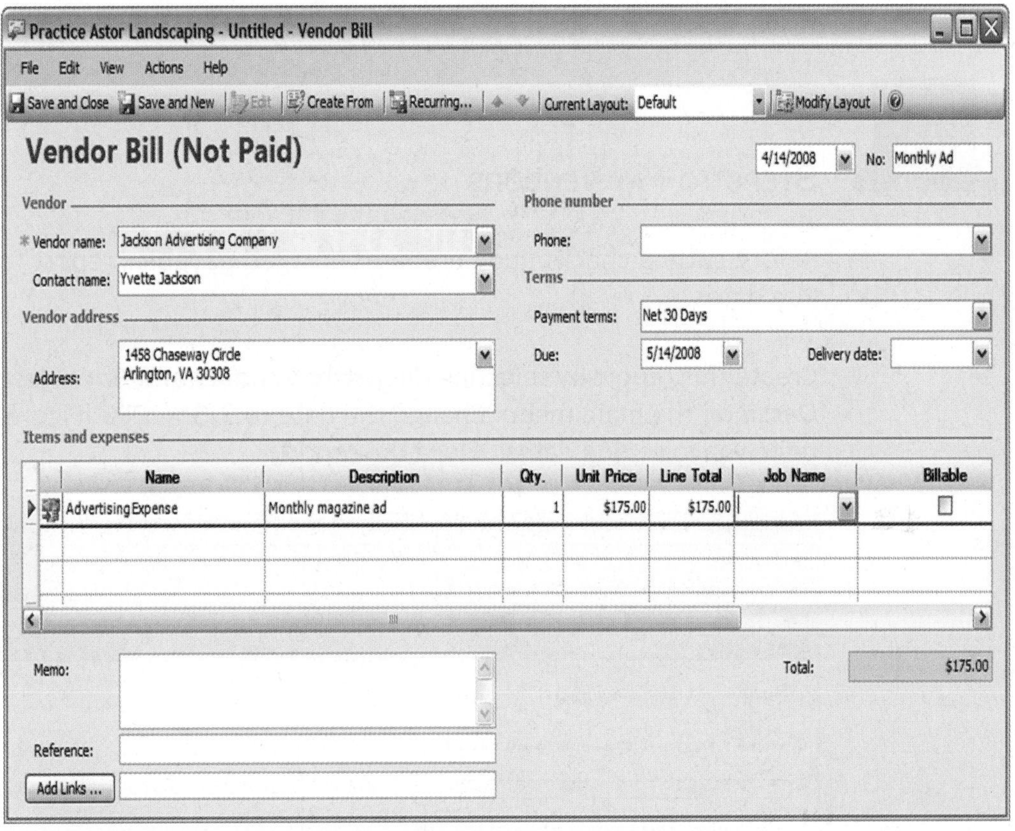

Figure 5:39

Vendor Payments

In this topic you focus on paying vendor bills. In the following exercise you create checks dated March 21, 2008 to pay vendor bills due by April 5, 2008.

Steps to Pay Vendors

1. Before cutting checks, Judy prepares an aged payables report to review bill due dates.

   Create this report by selecting ***Reports>>Vendors and Payables>>A/P Aging Detail*** on the main menu. Change the date to 3/31/2008 (Figure 5:40) and review invoice due dates. Close the report.

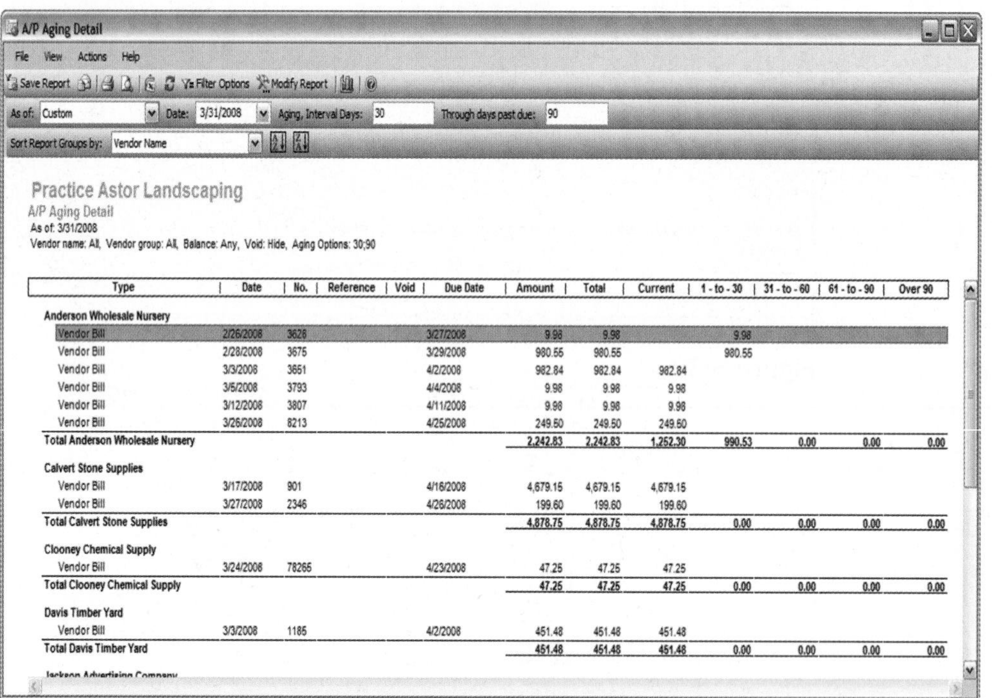

Practice Astor Landscaping
A/P Aging Detail
As of: 3/31/2008
Vendor name: All, Vendor group: All, Balance: Any, Void: Hide, Aging Options: 30;90

Type	Date	No.	Reference	Void	Due Date	Amount	Total	Current	1 - to - 30	31 - to - 60	61 - to - 90	Over 90
Anderson Wholesale Nursery												
Vendor Bill	2/26/2008	3626			3/27/2008	9.98	9.98		9.98			
Vendor Bill	2/28/2008	3675			3/29/2008	980.55	980.55		980.55			
Vendor Bill	3/3/2008	3651			4/2/2008	982.84	982.84	982.84				
Vendor Bill	3/5/2008	3793			4/4/2008	9.98	9.98	9.98				
Vendor Bill	3/12/2008	3807			4/11/2008	9.98	9.98	9.98				
Vendor Bill	3/26/2008	8213			4/25/2008	249.50	249.50	249.50				
Total Anderson Wholesale Nursery						2,242.83	2,242.83	1,252.30	990.53	0.00	0.00	0.00
Calvert Stone Supplies												
Vendor Bill	3/17/2008	901			4/16/2008	4,679.15	4,679.15	4,679.15				
Vendor Bill	3/27/2008	2346			4/26/2008	199.60	199.60	199.60				
Total Calvert Stone Supplies						4,878.75	4,878.75	4,878.75	0.00	0.00	0.00	0.00
Clooney Chemical Supply												
Vendor Bill	3/24/2008	78265			4/23/2008	47.25	47.25	47.25				
Total Clooney Chemical Supply						47.25	47.25	47.25	0.00	0.00	0.00	0.00
Davis Timber Yard												
Vendor Bill	3/3/2008	1185			4/2/2008	451.48	451.48	451.48				
Total Davis Timber Yard						451.48	451.48	451.48	0.00	0.00	0.00	0.00
Jackson Advertising Company												

Figure 5:40

2. Click **Pay Bills** under **Start a Task** and enter the following information on the top of the form.

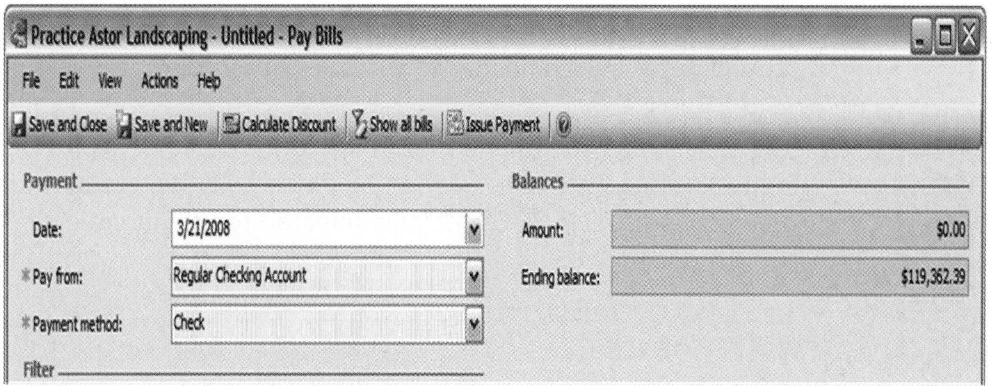

Figure 5:41

Date is the date that will print on checks. **Pay from** is the general ledger account to be credited by the payments.

3. You will now go through two steps to select bills for payment. First, select all bills with a due date on or before April 5, 2008 by entering the following information on the form.

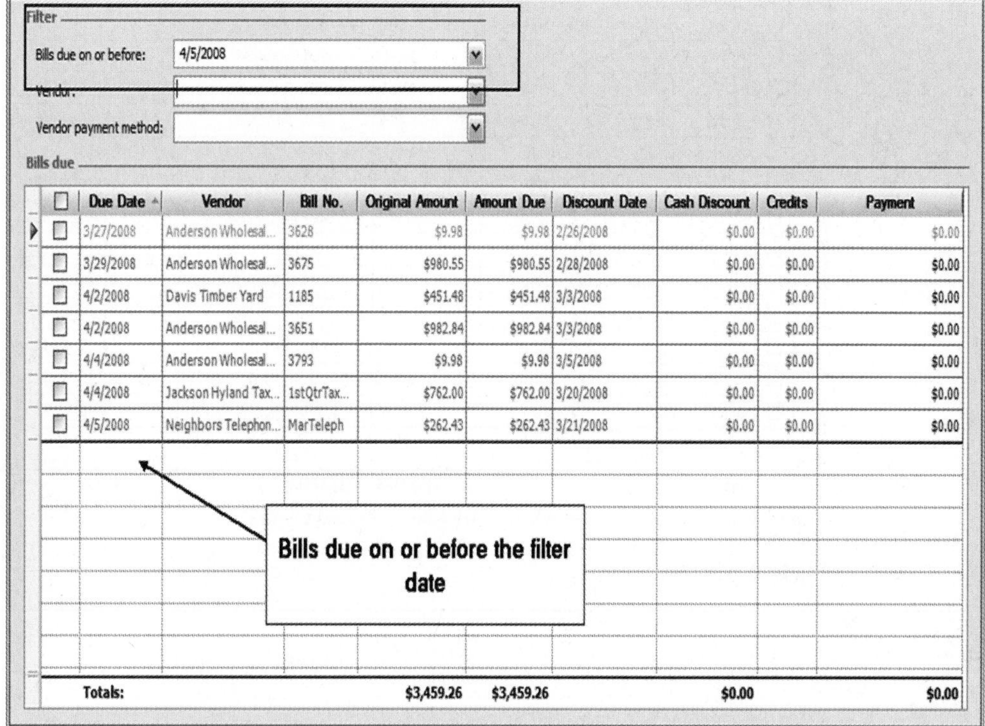

Due Date	Vendor	Bill No.	Original Amount	Amount Due	Discount Date	Cash Discount	Credits	Payment
3/27/2008	Anderson Wholesal...	3628	$9.98	$9.98	2/26/2008	$0.00	$0.00	$0.00
3/29/2008	Anderson Wholesal...	3675	$980.55	$980.55	2/28/2008	$0.00	$0.00	$0.00
4/2/2008	Davis Timber Yard	1185	$451.48	$451.48	3/3/2008	$0.00	$0.00	$0.00
4/2/2008	Anderson Wholesal...	3651	$982.84	$982.84	3/3/2008	$0.00	$0.00	$0.00
4/4/2008	Anderson Wholesal...	3793	$9.98	$9.98	3/5/2008	$0.00	$0.00	$0.00
4/4/2008	Jackson Hyland Tax...	1stQtrTax...	$762.00	$762.00	3/20/2008	$0.00	$0.00	$0.00
4/5/2008	Neighbors Telephon...	MarTeleph	$262.43	$262.43	3/21/2008	$0.00	$0.00	$0.00
Totals:			$3,459.26	$3,459.26		$0.00		$0.00

Figure 5:42

4. The list sorts to view bills meeting the filter criteria. Click the selection box in the header row to select these bills payment.

5. For the second step, you will select bills carrying a discount that expire by April 5, 2008.

   Click **Show all bills** on the toolbar and then click **Calculate Discount**. Click the **Discount Date** column header to sort the list by this date.

   Figure 5:43 shows the one bill with a discount that will expire if not paid with this check run. Click the selection box for the bill. The total at the bottom should display $8,044.83 as the bills selected for payment.

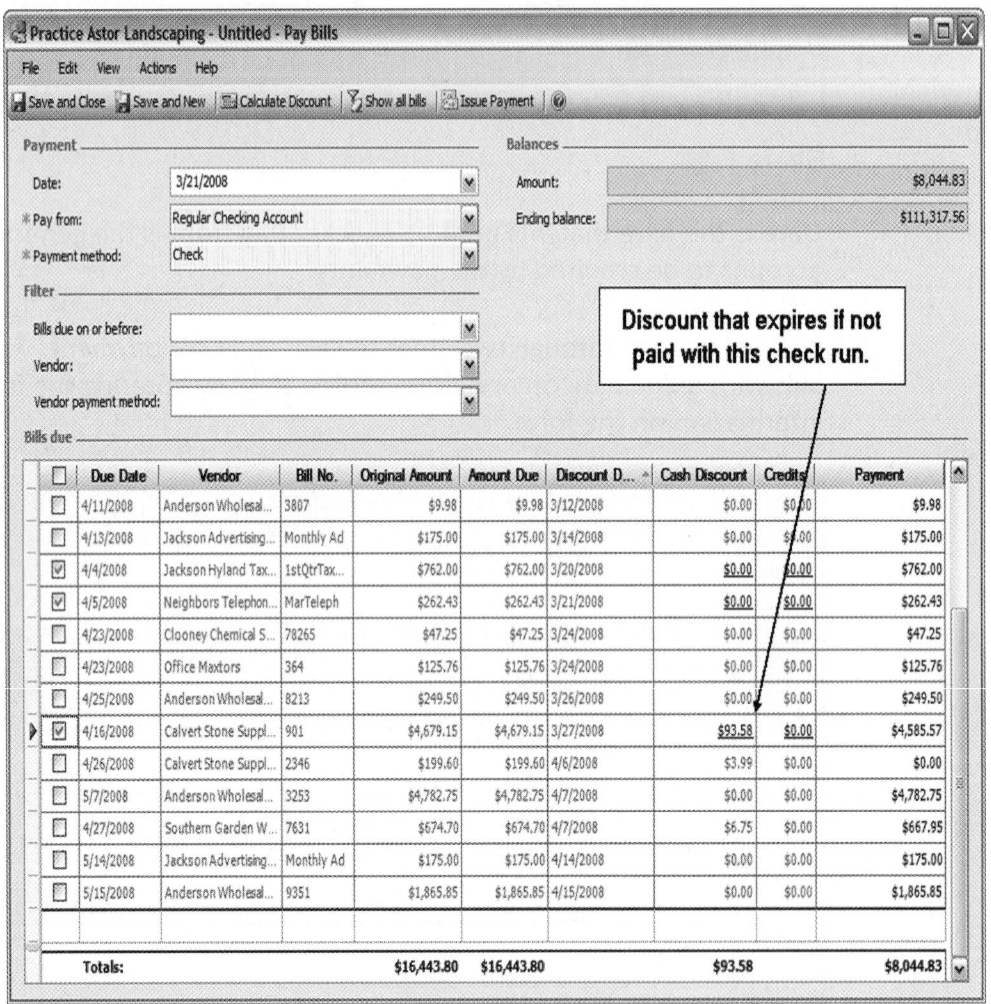

Figure 5:43

6. Click **Issue Payment** on the toolbar and click **OK** to save your selections. *(Note: You can also click Save and Close to keep your selections and then use the Issue Payment icon on the home page to return to printing checks.)*

   Figure 5:44 shows the checks that will print and the total payments. The first check will print on check number 436.

   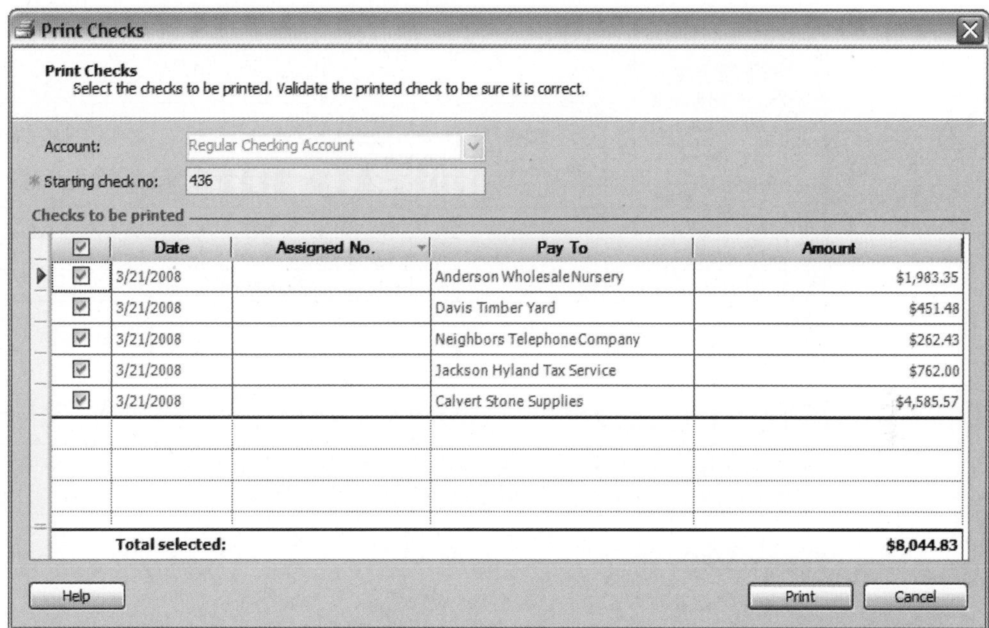

   Figure 5:44

   Note: You can click Cancel at this step and return to printing checks later by using the Issue Payments icon on the home page.

7. Click **Print** and the printer selection window opens. Select a printer and click **OK.**

8. OAP returns to the Print Checks window to confirm that checks printed correctly. Click **Close** and OAP assigns the check numbers and post the payments.

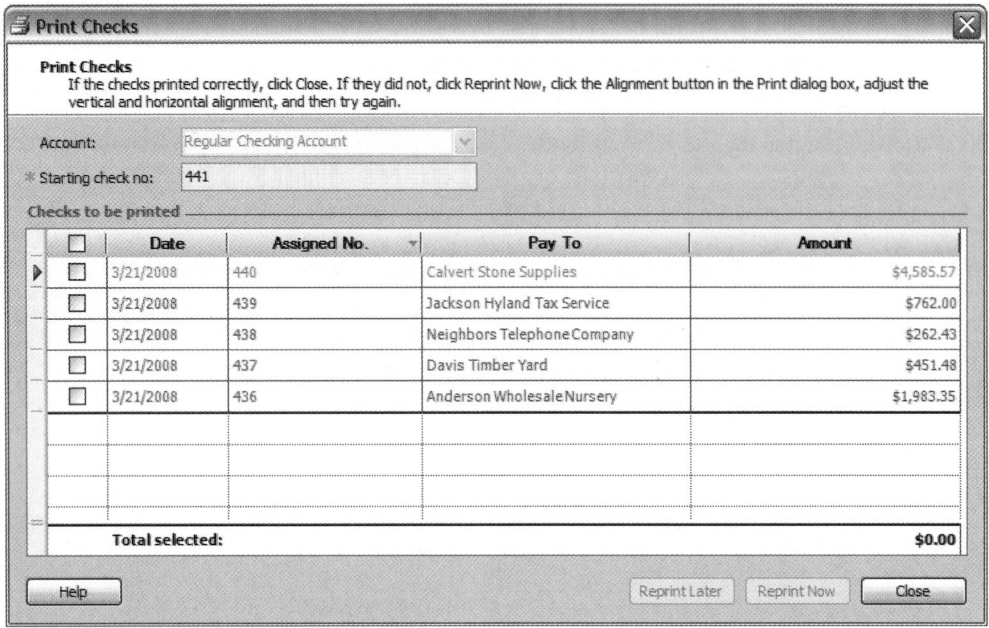

Figure 5:45

Note: If a printer error occurs, click the selection box on checks with errors and the Reprint Later and Reprint Now buttons activate. You can then reprint the checks by clicking one of the buttons.

9. OAP next confirms that five payments were issued. Click **OK** and then click **X** to close the Pay Bills window.

Behind the Keys of a Posted Vendor Payment

Now trace the audit trail for the checks printed in the last topic. On the main menu, select ***Reports>>Company and Financial>>Transaction Journal***. Change the date range to "3/21/2008" and filter the report for the **Vendor Payment** transaction type. Finally, change the report title to Cash Disbursements Journal and save the report.

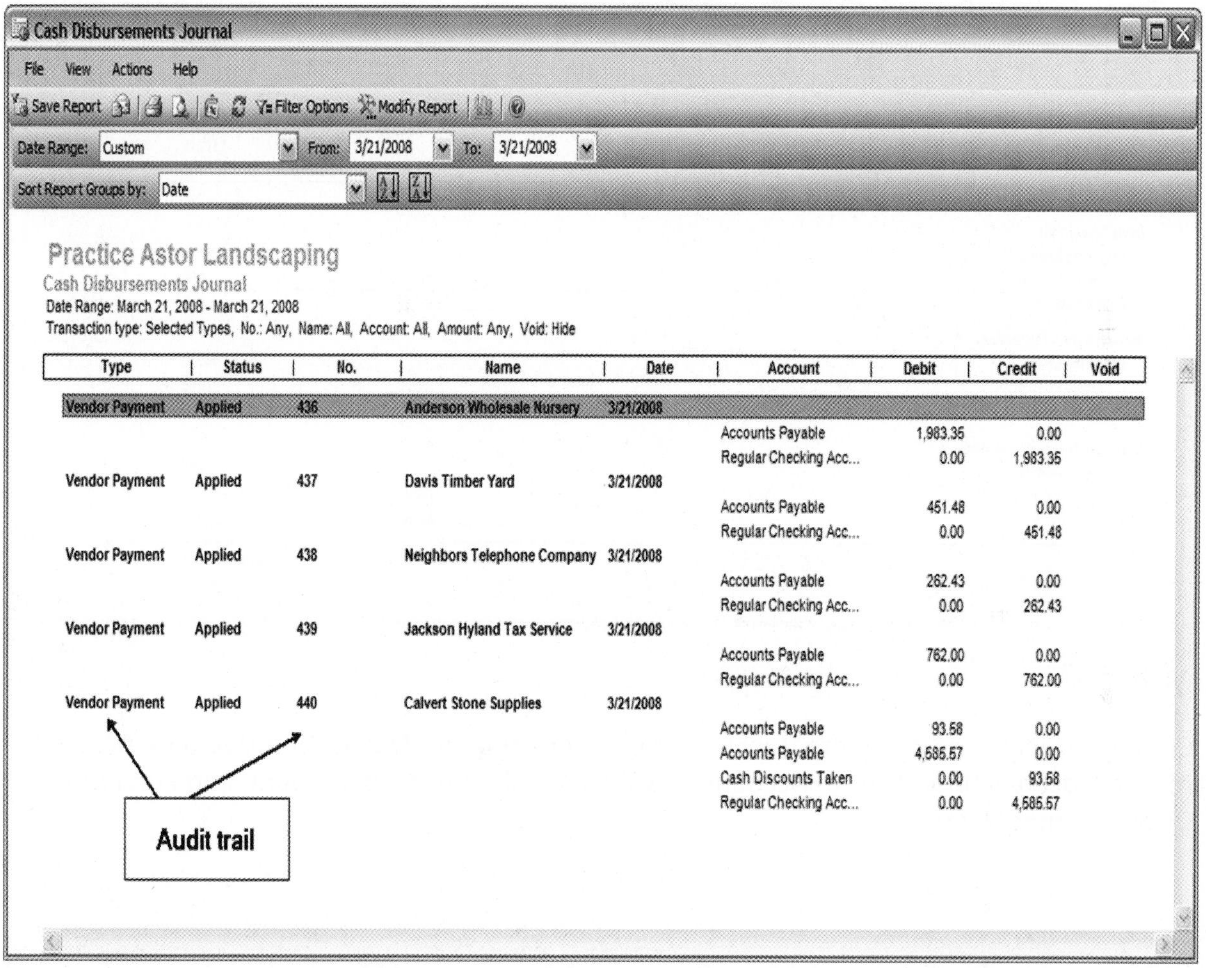

Cash Disbursements Journal

File View Actions Help

Save Report | Filter Options | Modify Report

Date Range: Custom From: 3/21/2008 To: 3/21/2008

Sort Report Groups by: Date

Practice Astor Landscaping
Cash Disbursements Journal
Date Range: March 21, 2008 - March 21, 2008
Transaction type: Selected Types, No.: Any, Name: All, Account: All, Amount: Any, Void: Hide

Type	Status	No.	Name	Date	Account	Debit	Credit	Void
Vendor Payment	Applied	436	Anderson Wholesale Nursery	3/21/2008				
					Accounts Payable	1,983.35	0.00	
					Regular Checking Acc...	0.00	1,983.35	
Vendor Payment	Applied	437	Davis Timber Yard	3/21/2008				
					Accounts Payable	451.48	0.00	
					Regular Checking Acc...	0.00	451.48	
Vendor Payment	Applied	438	Neighbors Telephone Company	3/21/2008				
					Accounts Payable	262.43	0.00	
					Regular Checking Acc...	0.00	262.43	
Vendor Payment	Applied	439	Jackson Hyland Tax Service	3/21/2008				
					Accounts Payable	762.00	0.00	
					Regular Checking Acc...	0.00	762.00	
Vendor Payment	Applied	440	Calvert Stone Supplies	3/21/2008				
					Accounts Payable	93.58	0.00	
					Accounts Payable	4,586.57	0.00	
					Cash Discounts Taken	0.00	93.58	
					Regular Checking Acc...	0.00	4,586.57	

Audit trail

Figure 5:46

The report shows that checks debited Accounts Payable and credited the Regular Checking Account. In addition, bills carrying a discount posted the discount amount as a credit to Purchase Discounts. Close the report.

Select ***Reports>>Vendors and Payables>>Vendor Transaction History*** on the main menu to trace payments to the vendor accounts. Enter "3/21/2008" as the date range and filter the report to display the transaction type of **Vendor Payment**. (See Figure 5:47.)

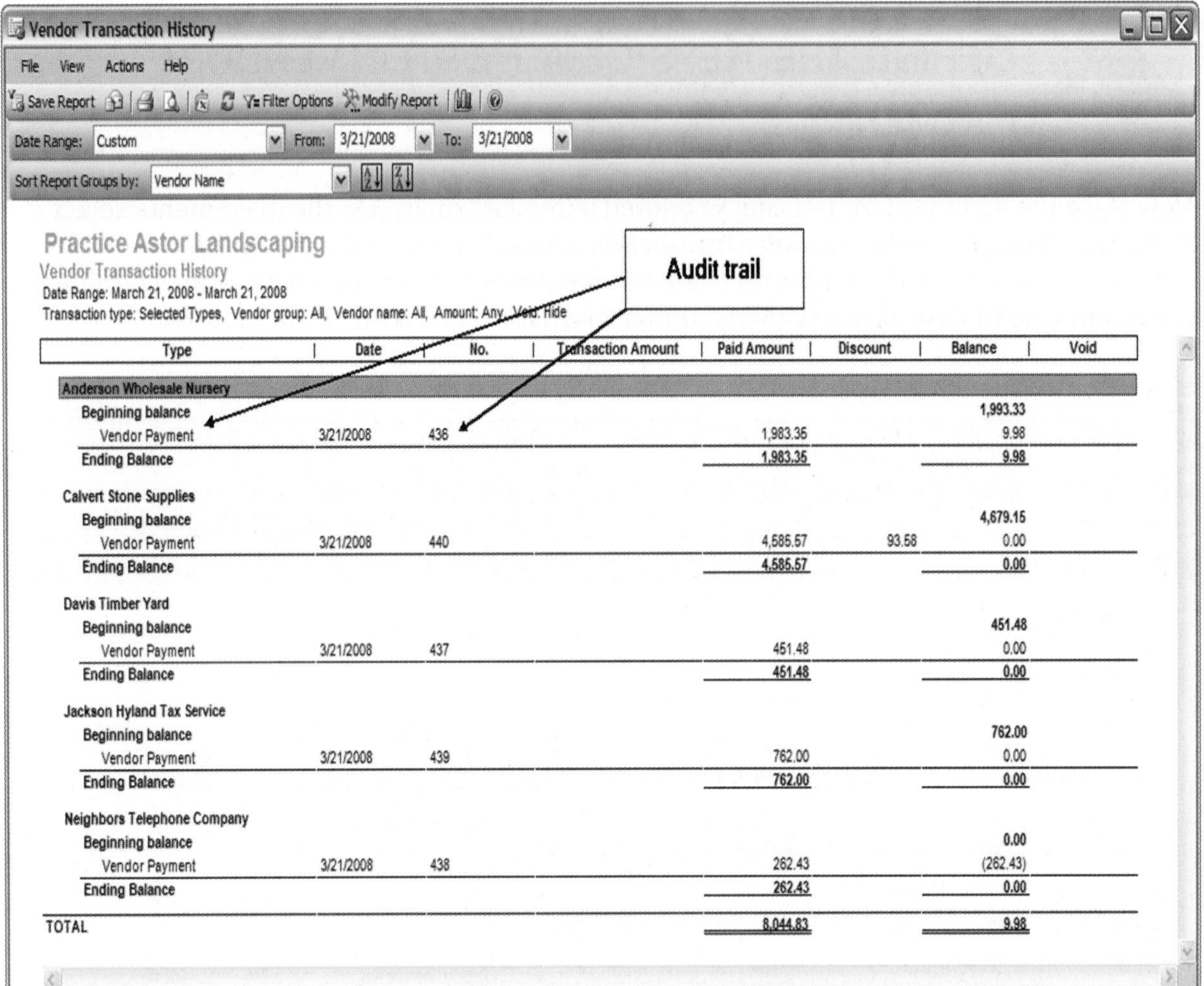

Practice Astor Landscaping
Vendor Transaction History
Date Range: March 21, 2008 - March 21, 2008
Transaction type: Selected Types, Vendor group: All, Vendor name: All, Amount: Any, Void: Hide

Type	Date	No.	Transaction Amount	Paid Amount	Discount	Balance	Void
Anderson Wholesale Nursery							
Beginning balance						**1,993.33**	
Vendor Payment	3/21/2008	436		1,983.35		9.98	
Ending Balance				**1,983.35**		**9.98**	
Calvert Stone Supplies							
Beginning balance						**4,679.15**	
Vendor Payment	3/21/2008	440		4,585.57	93.58	0.00	
Ending Balance				**4,585.57**		**0.00**	
Davis Timber Yard							
Beginning balance						**451.48**	
Vendor Payment	3/21/2008	437		451.48		0.00	
Ending Balance				**451.48**		**0.00**	
Jackson Hyland Tax Service							
Beginning balance						**762.00**	
Vendor Payment	3/21/2008	439		762.00		0.00	
Ending Balance				**762.00**		**0.00**	
Neighbors Telephone Company							
Beginning balance						**0.00**	
Vendor Payment	3/21/2008	438		262.43		(262.43)	
Ending Balance				**262.43**		**0.00**	
TOTAL				**8,044.83**		**9.98**	

Figure 5:47

Close this report and complete tracing entries by opening the **Transaction Detail by Account** report. Locate your entries to Accounts Payable, Regular Checking Account, and Purchase Discounts (not illustrated).

Writing Checks Without a Vendor Bill

OAP also allows you to write checks without entering a vendor bill first. For instance, you may need to write a check to a local grocer for office party food. Sometimes the vendor account is new so it needs to be added "on the fly." *(Note: Remember "on the fly" means creating a new account while entering a transaction.)*

Complete the next exercise to write a check for office party food.

STEPS TO ADD A VENDOR ON THE FLY WHILE WRITING A CHECK WITHOUT A VENDOR BILL

1. Select ***Banking>>Write Checks*** on the main menu. Select "Regular Checking Account" as the **Bank account** and enter "3/31/2008" as the **Date**.

2. The vendor is not on file so place your cursor in **Pay to** and type "Joe's Grocery." Press Tab and, when prompted to add the payee, click **Yes**.

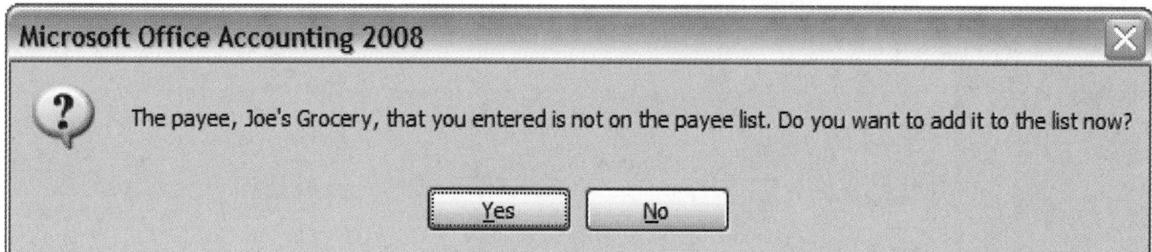

Figure 5:48

Select **Vendor** and click **OK**.

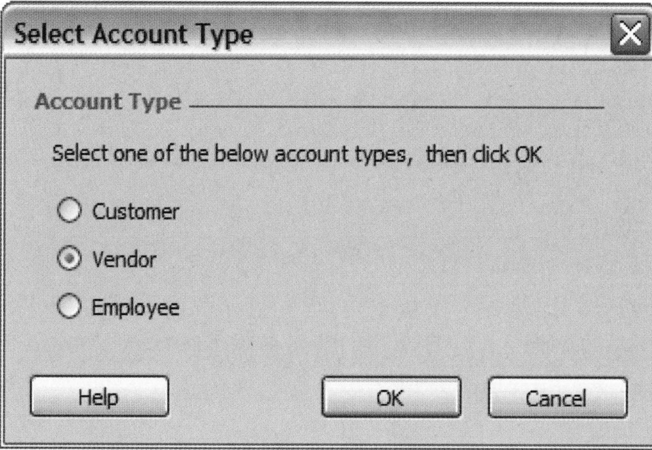

Figure 5:49

3. Use the information that follows to create the vendor account.

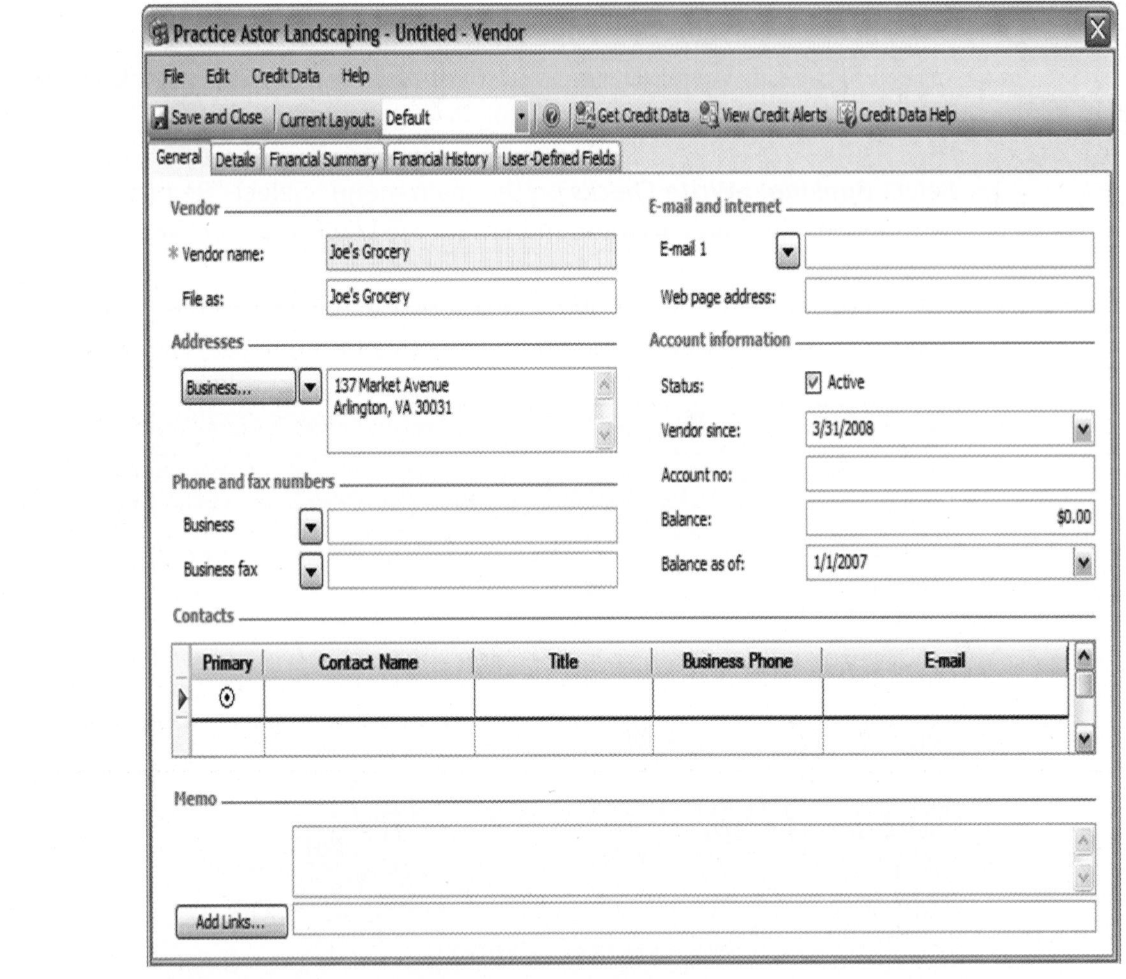

Figure 5:50

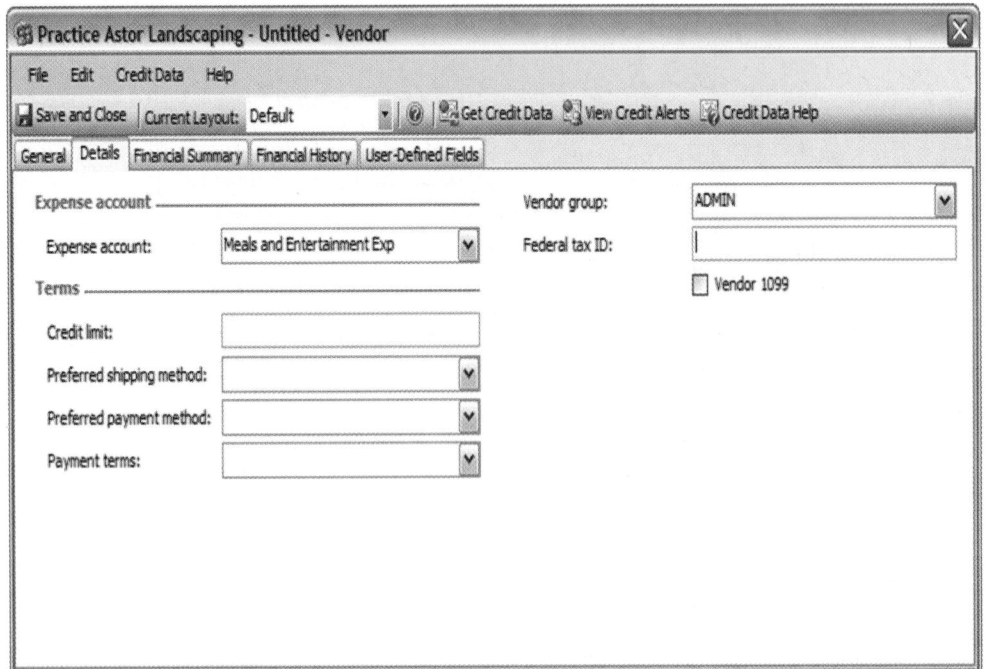

Figure 5:51

Click **Save and Close** and you have just added a vendor "on the fly."

4. Now complete the check as illustrated in Figure 5:52.

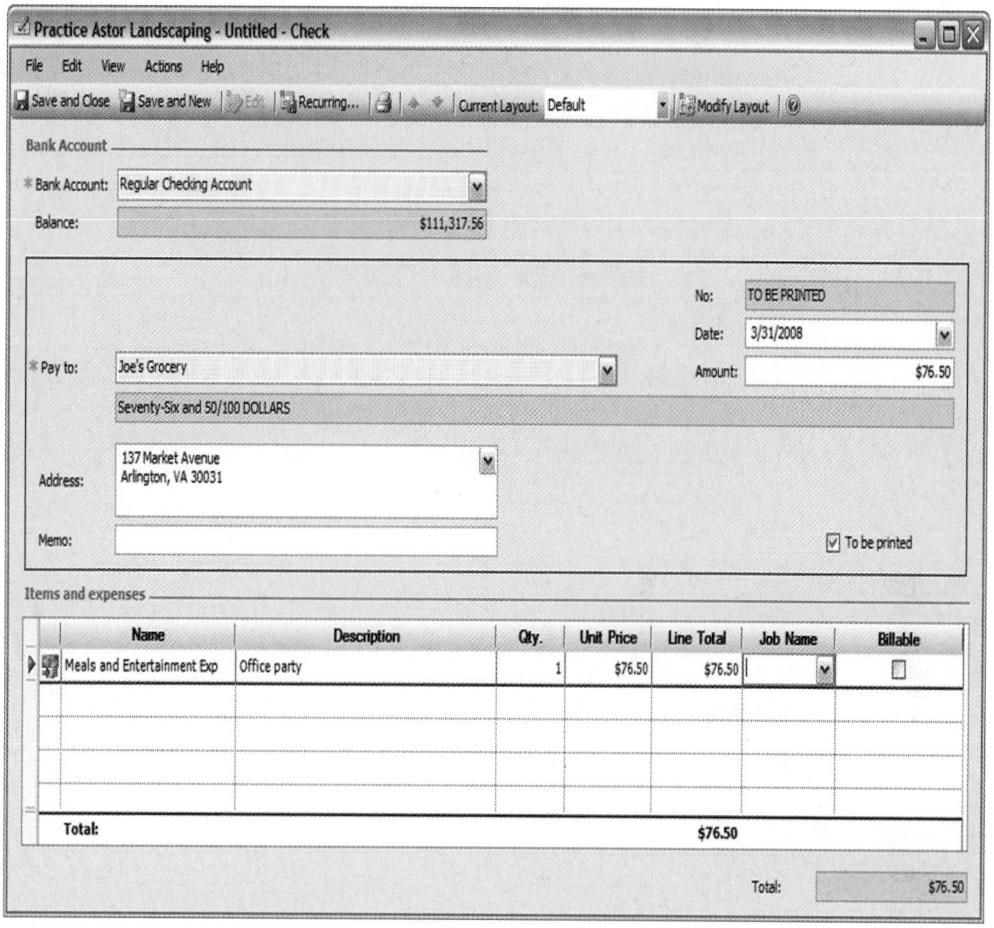

Figure 5:52

5. Click the **Printer** icon on the toolbar and click **OK** to save the transaction. When the Print Checks window opens, click **Print** and then click **OK** in the printer selection window.

   Return to the Print Checks window and click **Close**.

6. Return to the transaction window and notice that the check number has been assigned. (See Figure 5:53.) Click **Save and Close.**

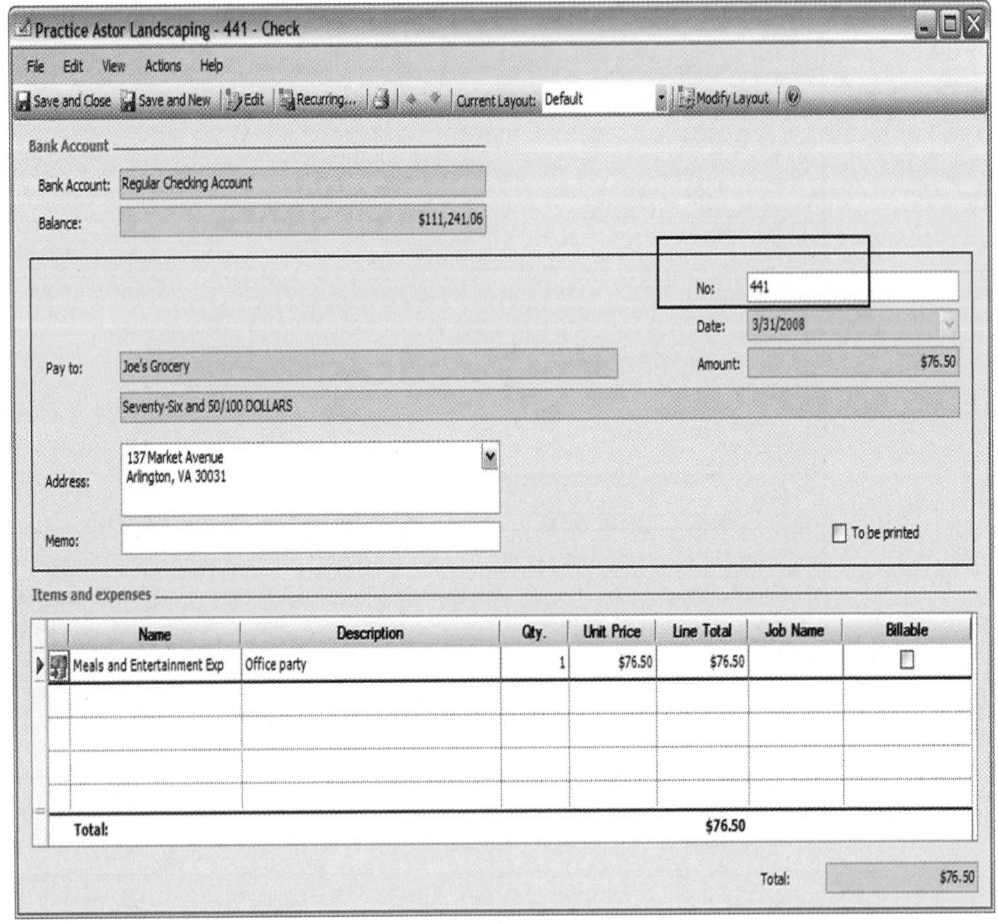

Figure 5:53

Voiding Vendor Payments

OAP does not permit editing payments; therefore, you must void checks and reissue the payments to make corrections. Practice by performing the next steps.

Steps to Voiding a Vendor Payment

1. In this exercise you will void check number "436" cut to Anderson Wholesale Nursery on March 21.

   First, locate the payment by clicking the **Vendor Payments** link under **Find**. Verify that the **Current View** is **Issued** and scroll to the bottom to locate the transaction by referring to the Payment No. or Payment Date column. *(Note: The Issue Date column is the user date of printing checks.)*

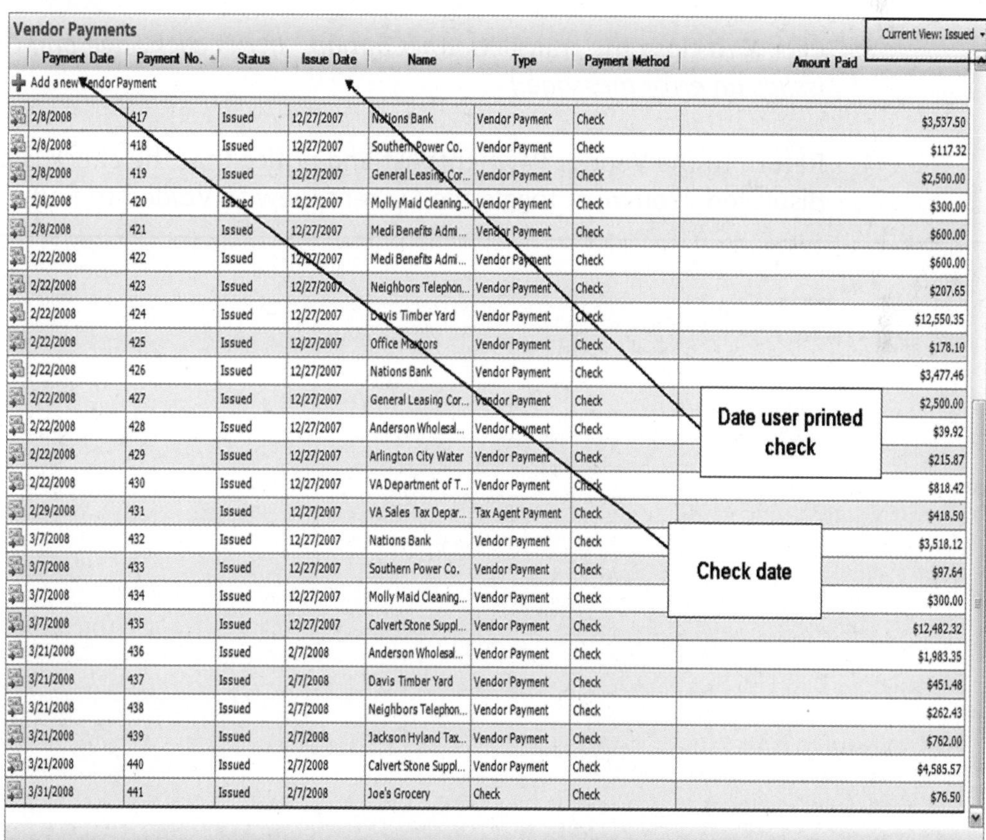

Vendor Payments — Current View: Issued

Add a new Vendor Payment

Payment Date	Payment No.	Status	Issue Date	Name	Type	Payment Method	Amount Paid
2/8/2008	417	Issued	12/27/2007	Nations Bank	Vendor Payment	Check	$3,537.50
2/8/2008	418	Issued	12/27/2007	Southern Power Co.	Vendor Payment	Check	$117.32
2/8/2008	419	Issued	12/27/2007	General Leasing Cor...	Vendor Payment	Check	$2,500.00
2/8/2008	420	Issued	12/27/2007	Molly Maid Cleaning...	Vendor Payment	Check	$300.00
2/8/2008	421	Issued	12/27/2007	Medi Benefits Admi...	Vendor Payment	Check	$600.00
2/22/2008	422	Issued	12/27/2007	Medi Benefits Admi...	Vendor Payment	Check	$600.00
2/22/2008	423	Issued	12/27/2007	Neighbors Telephon...	Vendor Payment	Check	$207.65
2/22/2008	424	Issued	12/27/2007	Davis Timber Yard	Vendor Payment	Check	$12,550.35
2/22/2008	425	Issued	12/27/2007	Office Mentors	Vendor Payment	Check	$178.10
2/22/2008	426	Issued	12/27/2007	Nations Bank	Vendor Payment	Check	$3,477.46
2/22/2008	427	Issued	12/27/2007	General Leasing Cor...	Vendor Payment	Check	$2,500.00
2/22/2008	428	Issued	12/27/2007	Anderson Wholesal...	Vendor Payment	Check	$39.92
2/22/2008	429	Issued	12/27/2007	Arlington City Water	Vendor Payment	Check	$215.87
2/22/2008	430	Issued	12/27/2007	VA Department of T...	Vendor Payment	Check	$818.42
2/29/2008	431	Issued	12/27/2007	VA Sales Tax Depar...	Tax Agent Payment	Check	$418.50
3/7/2008	432	Issued	12/27/2007	Nations Bank	Vendor Payment	Check	$3,518.12
3/7/2008	433	Issued	12/27/2007	Southern Power Co.	Vendor Payment	Check	$97.64
3/7/2008	434	Issued	12/27/2007	Molly Maid Cleaning...	Vendor Payment	Check	$300.00
3/7/2008	435	Issued	12/27/2007	Calvert Stone Suppl...	Vendor Payment	Check	$12,482.32
3/21/2008	436	Issued	2/7/2008	Anderson Wholesal...	Vendor Payment	Check	$1,983.35
3/21/2008	437	Issued	2/7/2008	Davis Timber Yard	Vendor Payment	Check	$451.48
3/21/2008	438	Issued	2/7/2008	Neighbors Telephon...	Vendor Payment	Check	$262.43
3/21/2008	439	Issued	2/7/2008	Jackson Hyland Tax...	Vendor Payment	Check	$762.00
3/21/2008	440	Issued	2/7/2008	Calvert Stone Suppl...	Vendor Payment	Check	$4,585.57
3/31/2008	441	Issued	2/7/2008	Joe's Grocery	Check	Check	$76.50

Figure 5:54

2. Double click to reopen the payment and select ***Actions>>Void*** on the menu. When OAP confirms the action, click **Yes**.

   (Note: You can also void the payment without reopening it by right clicking the transaction on the Vendor Payments list and selecting Void.)

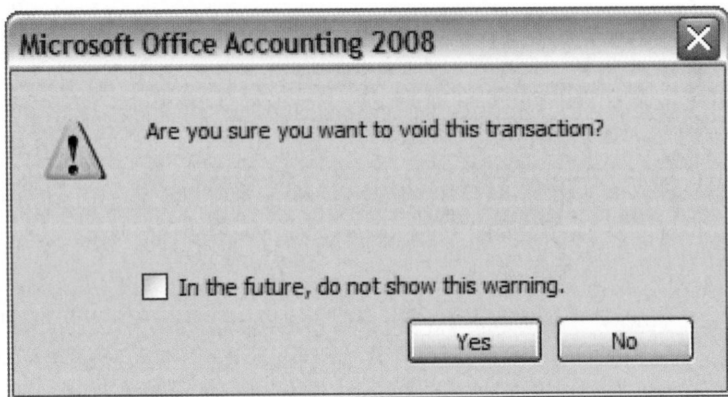

Figure 5:55

3. Click **X** to close the transaction. *(Caution: If you click Save and Close, OAP issues an error message.)*

4. Return to the Vendor Payments list and notice that the check is no longer displayed. You must toggle the Current View to Voided to find it.

5. Now view the entries posted by your action. Select ***Reports>>Company and Financial>>Transaction Detail by Account*** on the main menu. Filter the report to Show void transactions and display only the Regular Checking Account and Accounts Payable account. Enter "3/21/2008" (i.e., date on the check) as the date range.

   Notice that OAP voided the check as of the check date. Close the report.

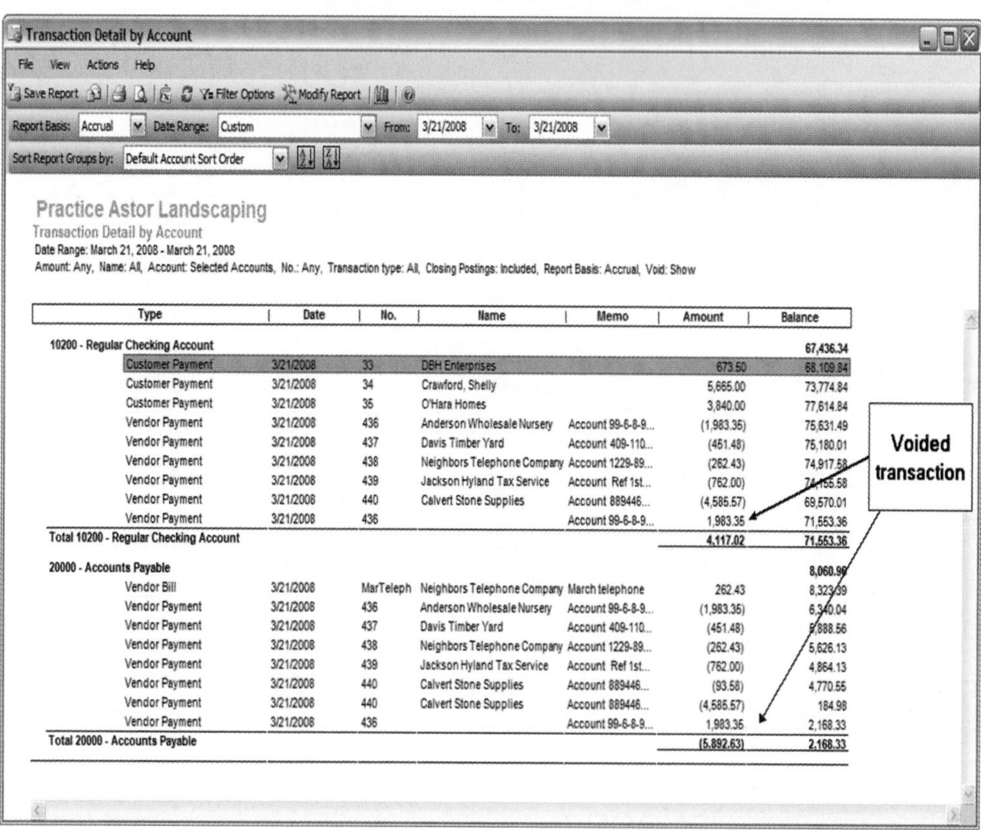

Practice Astor Landscaping
Transaction Detail by Account
Date Range: March 21, 2008 - March 21, 2008
Amount: Any, Name: All, Account: Selected Accounts, No.: Any, Transaction type: All, Closing Postings: Included, Report Basis: Accrual, Void: Show

Type	Date	No.	Name	Memo	Amount	Balance
10200 - Regular Checking Account						**67,436.34**
Customer Payment	3/21/2008	33	DBH Enterprises		673.50	68,109.84
Customer Payment	3/21/2008	34	Crawford, Shelly		5,665.00	73,774.84
Customer Payment	3/21/2008	35	O'Hara Homes		3,840.00	77,614.84
Vendor Payment	3/21/2008	436	Anderson Wholesale Nursery	Account 99-6-8-9...	(1,983.35)	75,631.49
Vendor Payment	3/21/2008	437	Davis Timber Yard	Account 409-110...	(451.48)	75,180.01
Vendor Payment	3/21/2008	438	Neighbors Telephone Company	Account 1229-89...	(262.43)	74,917.58
Vendor Payment	3/21/2008	439	Jackson Hyland Tax Service	Account Ref 1st...	(762.00)	74,155.58
Vendor Payment	3/21/2008	440	Calvert Stone Supplies	Account 889446...	(4,585.57)	69,570.01
Vendor Payment	3/21/2008	436		Account 99-6-8-9...	1,983.35	71,553.36
Total 10200 - Regular Checking Account					**4,117.02**	**71,553.36**
20000 - Accounts Payable						**8,060.96**
Vendor Bill	3/21/2008	MarTeleph	Neighbors Telephone Company	March telephone	262.43	8,323.39
Vendor Payment	3/21/2008	436	Anderson Wholesale Nursery	Account 99-6-8-9...	(1,983.35)	6,340.04
Vendor Payment	3/21/2008	437	Davis Timber Yard	Account 409-110...	(451.48)	5,888.56
Vendor Payment	3/21/2008	438	Neighbors Telephone Company	Account 1229-89...	(262.43)	5,626.13
Vendor Payment	3/21/2008	439	Jackson Hyland Tax Service	Account Ref 1st...	(762.00)	4,864.13
Vendor Payment	3/21/2008	440	Calvert Stone Supplies	Account 889446...	(93.58)	4,770.55
Vendor Payment	3/21/2008	440	Calvert Stone Supplies	Account 889446...	(4,585.57)	184.98
Vendor Payment	3/21/2008	436		Account 99-6-8-9...	1,983.35	2,168.33
Total 20000 - Accounts Payable					**(5,892.63)**	**2,168.33**

Figure 5:56

6. Now open the Vendor List and double click to open Anderson's account. Click the **Financial History** tab. The voided payment released the March bill so that it can be repaid. You will pay this bill in the next exercise.

   Close the vendor's account.

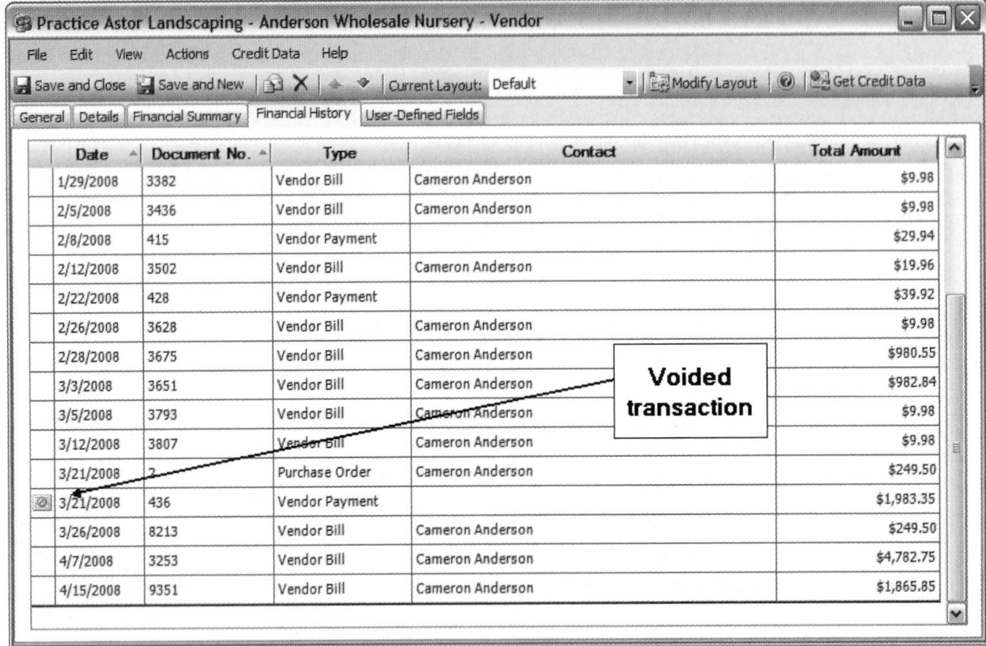

Practice Astor Landscaping - Anderson Wholesale Nursery - Vendor
File Edit View Actions Credit Data Help
Save and Close Save and New Current Layout: Default Modify Layout Get Credit Data
General Details Financial Summary Financial History User-Defined Fields
Date Document No. Type Contact Total Amount
1/29/2008 3382 Vendor Bill Cameron Anderson $9.98
2/5/2008 3436 Vendor Bill Cameron Anderson $9.98
2/8/2008 415 Vendor Payment $29.94
2/12/2008 3502 Vendor Bill Cameron Anderson $19.96
2/22/2008 428 Vendor Payment $39.92
2/26/2008 3628 Vendor Bill Cameron Anderson $9.98
2/28/2008 3675 Vendor Bill Cameron Anderson $980.55
3/3/2008 3651 Vendor Bill Cameron Anderson $982.84
3/5/2008 3793 Vendor Bill Cameron Anderson $9.98
3/12/2008 3807 Vendor Bill Cameron Anderson $9.98
3/21/2008 2 Purchase Order Cameron Anderson $249.50
3/21/2008 436 Vendor Payment $1,983.35
3/26/2008 8213 Vendor Bill Cameron Anderson $249.50
4/7/2008 3253 Vendor Bill Cameron Anderson $4,782.75
4/15/2008 9351 Vendor Bill Cameron Anderson $1,865.85
Voided transaction

Figure 5:57

PAY VENDORS

Create vendor checks dated April 4, 2008. Select all bills with a due date before 4/14/2008. Also select all bills with a discount that expires by 4/14/2008.

Click the Payment field for Anderson Wholesale Supplies' Invoice 3651 and reduce the payment to $900.00.

Payments total $2,949.05. Print the checks on starting check number 442.

Select ***Reports>>Banking>>Payments*** on the main menu and enter "4/4/2008" as the date range. Remove the Issue date, Status detail, Reference number, and Void columns. Print the report to document the payments.

Paying Sales Tax

At the end of every month Astor must remit the sales tax collected from customers. OAP tracks the sales tax collected and the following shows you how to remit the tax.

Steps to Paying Sales Tax

1. First, we will view the Sales Tax Liability report. Select ***Company>>Sales Tax>>View Sales Tax Liability*** on the main menu. Enter the date range of "3/1/2008" to "3/31/2008."

   Astor owes sales tax on the cash basis, meaning the company owes the tax after collecting it from the customer (i.e., the customer pays the invoice). Therefore, change the **Report Basis** to **Cash** and the total in the Tax Collected column reports the sales tax due by April 15, 2008 (Figure 5:58). *(Note: Your report will differ if you have not completed all previous exercises.)*

   Close the report.

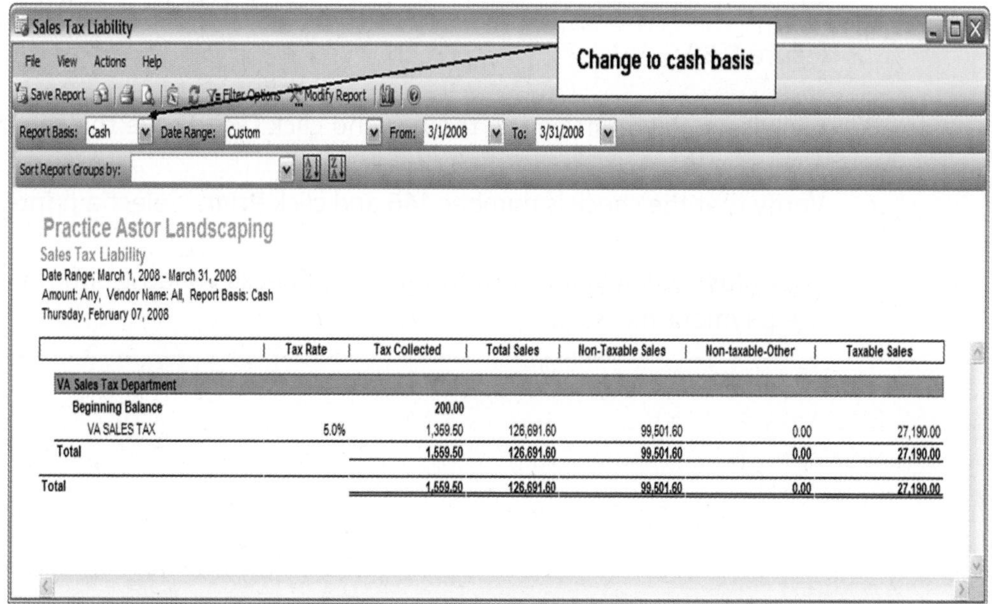

Figure 5:58

2. Now select ***Company>>Sales Tax>>Pay Sales Tax*** on the main menu and enter the information illustrated in Figure 5:59. Remember to click the selection box on the Tax Agency.

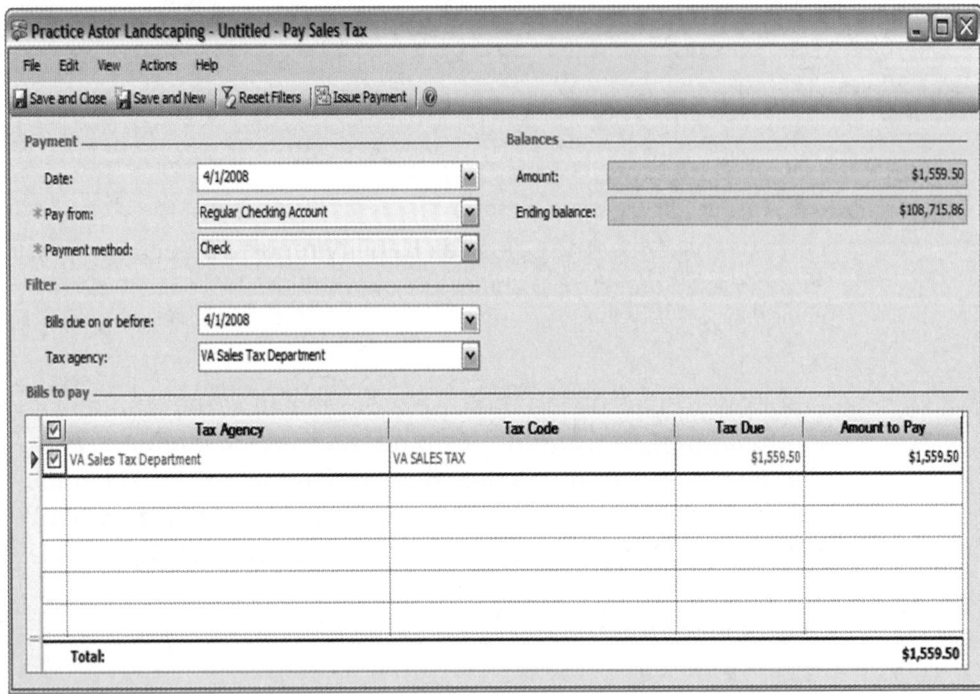

Figure 5:59

3. Click **Issue Payment** on the toolbar and click **OK** to save the selected payment.

4. Verify that the check is number 446 and click **Print.** Select a printer and click **OK**.

5. Click **Close** when you return to the Print Checks window and then click **OK** on the payment message.

Vendor Credits

Just as Astor issues credits to customers, vendors issue credits to Astor. Follow the next steps to record a credit on March 26 for returning 10 granite pavers to Anderson Wholesale Nursery that were billed on Invoice 8213.

Steps to Enter a Vendor Credit Memo

1. Click **New Credit Memo** under **Start a Task** or on the home page. Enter the following information on the credit memo.

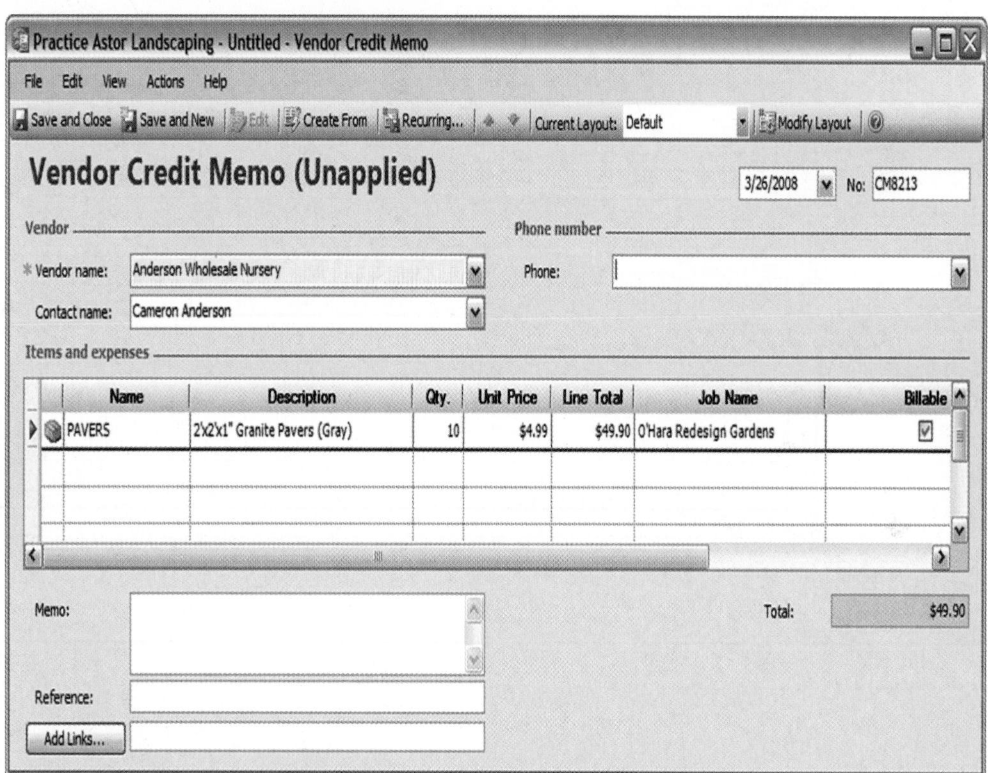

Figure 5:60

2. Click **Save and Close**.

3. Now see what happens the next time you pay Anderson. Click **Pay Bills** and enter "4/4/2008" as the check date.

   Click the selection box for Anderson's Invoice 8213. (See Figure 5:61.)

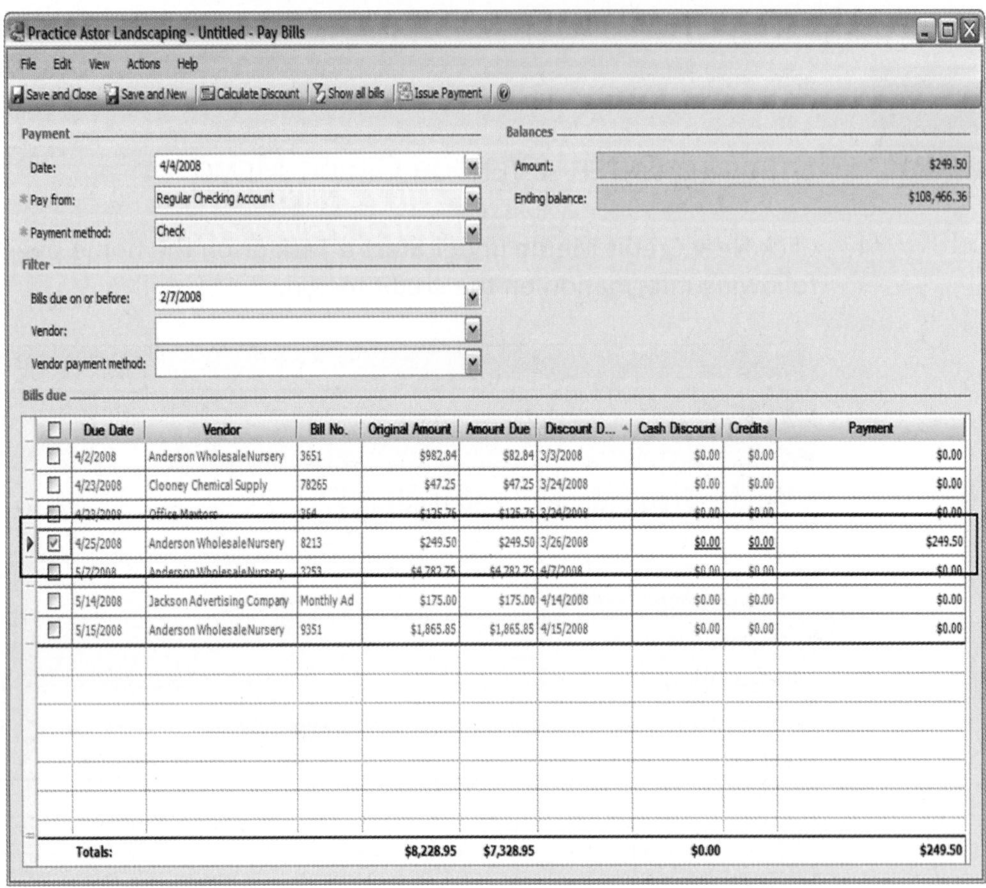

Figure 5:61

4. Click the hyperlink in the **Credits** column of this invoice to open the following window. Click the selection box to apply the credit memo and then click **Adjust**.

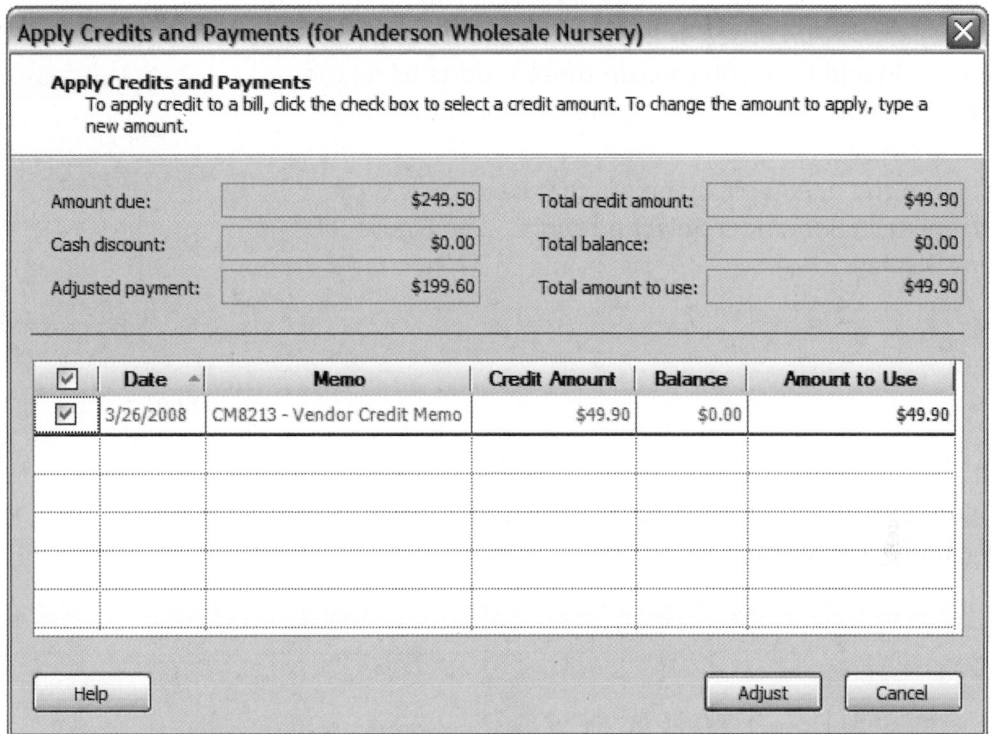

Figure 5:62

5. The payment is now reduced to $199.60. Click **Issue Payment** and complete the remaining steps that process the check.

Vendor Reporting and Reconciling Vendor Activities

OAP offers a variety of vendor reports that can be run from the ***Reports>>Purchases*** or ***Reports>>Vendors and Payables*** menus. In addition, you can run these reports using the Reports section on the right of the Vendors Home page.

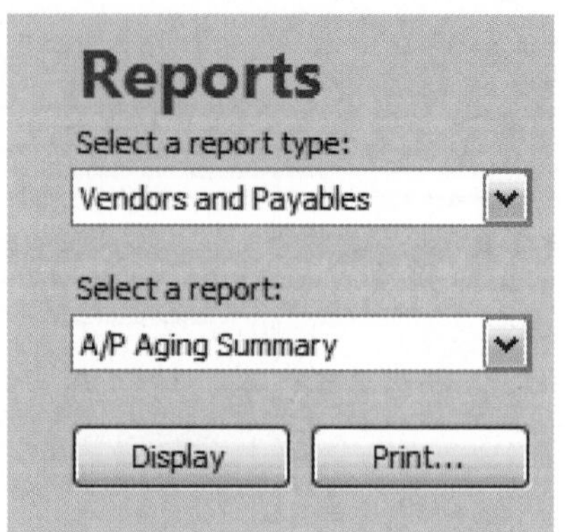

Figure 5:63

Let's run the A/P Aging Summary first because it is the current selection under **Select a report**. (See Figure 5:63) Click **Display**.

Filter the report for "3/31/2008" to display the age of accounts payable at the end of March (Figure 5:64). *(Note: Your balance will differ from the illustration if you have not completed all chapter exercises.)*

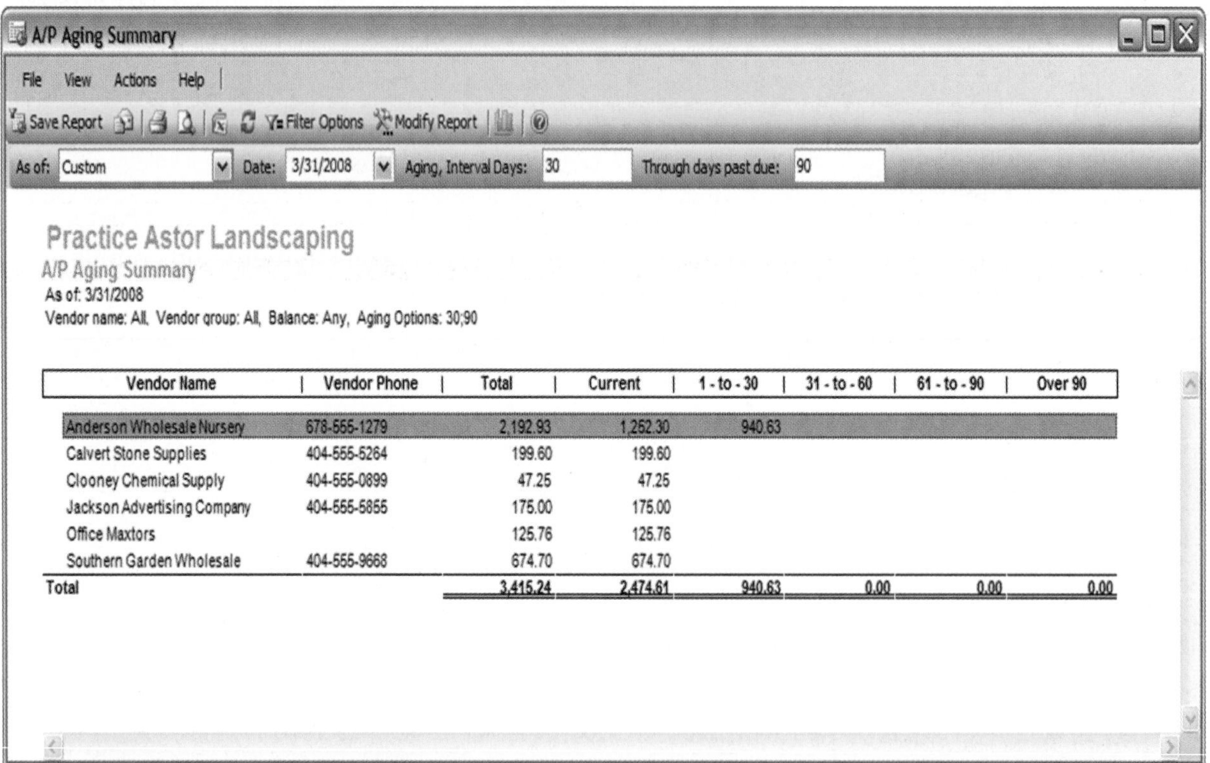

Practice Astor Landscaping
A/P Aging Summary
As of: 3/31/2008
Vendor name: All, Vendor group: All, Balance: Any, Aging Options: 30;90

Vendor Name	Vendor Phone	Total	Current	1 - to - 30	31 - to - 60	61 - to - 90	Over 90
Anderson Wholesale Nursery	678-555-1279	2,192.93	1,252.30	940.63			
Calvert Stone Supplies	404-555-5264	199.60	199.60				
Clooney Chemical Supply	404-555-0899	47.25	47.25				
Jackson Advertising Company	404-555-5855	175.00	175.00				
Office Maxtors		125.76	125.76				
Southern Garden Wholesale	404-555-9668	674.70	674.70				
Total		3,415.24	2,474.61	940.63	0.00	0.00	0.00

Figure 5:64

This report is a condensed version of accounts payable and serves several purposes. First, Astor can quickly monitor the age of vendor balances to manage cash flow. The report can also point out unapplied credit memos or other vendor balance issues.

Second, the report is used to reconcile vendor activities with the accounts payable control account. This task is performed by comparing the aging report Total with the March ending balance in accounts payable. You can view your March ending balance in accounts payable by selecting ***Reports>>Company and Financial>>Trial Balance*** on the main menu and filtering the report for 3/31/2008 (not illustrated). Scroll to the Accounts Payable account and compare the balance on this report with the total on your aging report. The two amounts must agree to confirm proper recording of vendor activities.

Vendor activities can become out of balance when you improperly correct vendor transactions. Therefore, you should always refer to the instructions in this chapter or Appendix B when correcting transactions. You should reconcile the aged payables report to the accounts payable balance at the end of every month and prior to issuing financial reports.

Close this report and open the **Detail A/P Aging** report filtered for "3/31/2008" (Figure 5:65). This report provides more detail on outstanding accounts payable, for instance, you can see individual bill due dates.

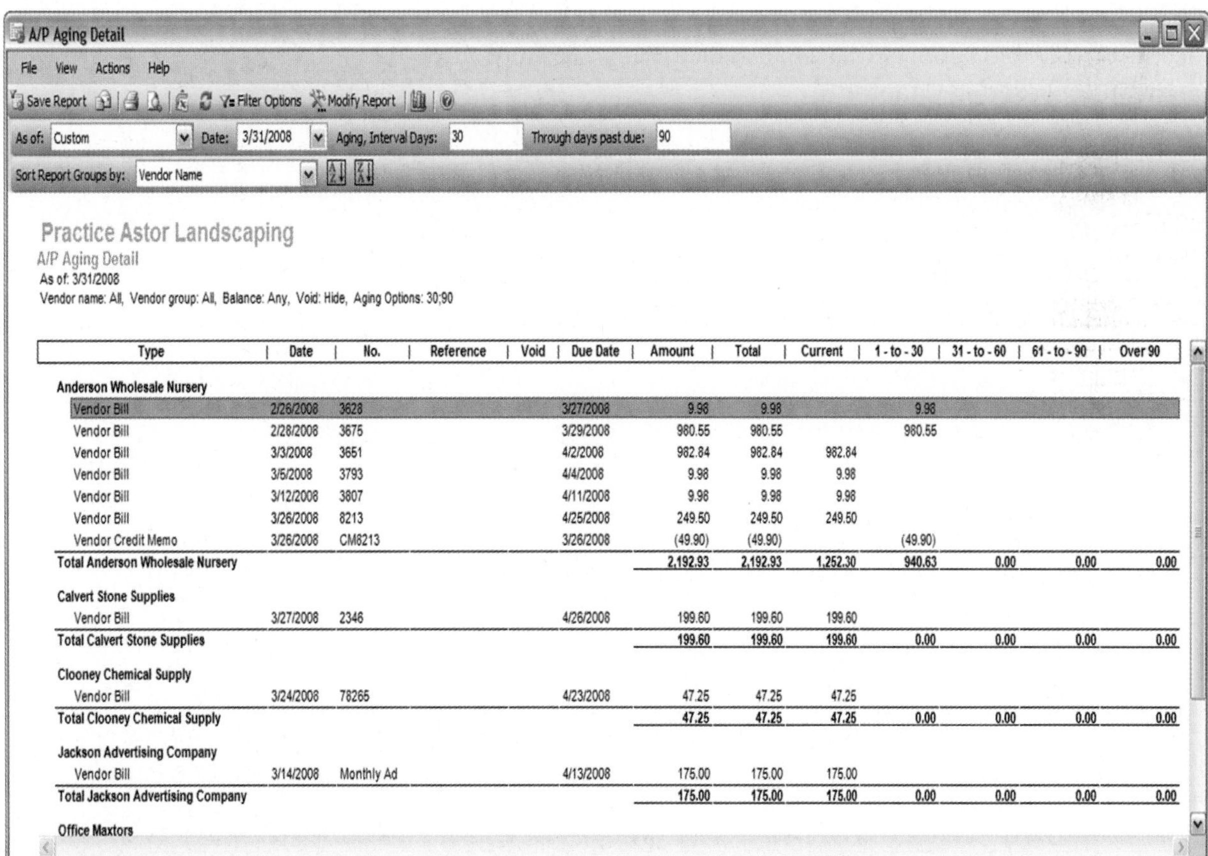

Practice Astor Landscaping
A/P Aging Detail
As of: 3/31/2008
Vendor name: All, Vendor group: All, Balance: Any, Void: Hide, Aging Options: 30;90

Type	Date	No.	Reference	Void	Due Date	Amount	Total	Current	1 - to - 30	31 - to - 60	61 - to - 90	Over 90
Anderson Wholesale Nursery												
Vendor Bill	2/26/2008	3628			3/27/2008	9.98	9.98		9.98			
Vendor Bill	2/28/2008	3675			3/29/2008	980.55	980.55		980.55			
Vendor Bill	3/3/2008	3651			4/2/2008	982.84	982.84	982.84				
Vendor Bill	3/5/2008	3793			4/4/2008	9.98	9.98	9.98				
Vendor Bill	3/12/2008	3807			4/11/2008	9.98	9.98	9.98				
Vendor Bill	3/26/2008	8213			4/25/2008	249.50	249.50	249.50				
Vendor Credit Memo	3/26/2008	CM8213			3/26/2008	(49.90)	(49.90)		(49.90)			
Total Anderson Wholesale Nursery						2,192.93	2,192.93	1,252.30	940.63	0.00	0.00	0.00
Calvert Stone Supplies												
Vendor Bill	3/27/2008	2346			4/26/2008	199.60	199.60	199.60				
Total Calvert Stone Supplies						199.60	199.60	199.60	0.00	0.00	0.00	0.00
Clooney Chemical Supply												
Vendor Bill	3/24/2008	78265			4/23/2008	47.25	47.25	47.25				
Total Clooney Chemical Supply						47.25	47.25	47.25	0.00	0.00	0.00	0.00
Jackson Advertising Company												
Vendor Bill	3/14/2008	Monthly Ad			4/13/2008	175.00	175.00	175.00				
Total Jackson Advertising Company						175.00	175.00	175.00	0.00	0.00	0.00	0.00
Office Maxtors												

Figure 5:65

Close the aging report and open the **1099 Summary** report (not illustrated). This report will list payments to vendors marked for 1099 reporting when payments to the vendor equal or exceed the $600 reporting threshold. Remember 1099 reporting requirements are set by the IRS. Close the report.

You have now completed the chapter. ***Make a backup of the Practice Astor Landscaping data file to a backup file named "practiceastorlandscaping Chpt 5." In the next chapter, you will build on the work completed in this chapter.***

SUMMARY

You began the chapter by learning to post transactions in a manual accounting system. You then posted *MAPS* transactions in OAP. You also learned to use the Vendor Home page to process vendor activities.

You have recorded POs and receipts of items on a PO. You posted vendor bills for receipts and vendor bills for expenses. You also paid vendors, voided payments, and recorded vendor credits.

Finally, you reconciled vendor transactions to the general ledger and worked with a variety of accounts payable reports that analyze activities. You are now ready to focus on the payroll activities covered in Chapter 6.

END-OF-CHAPTER QUESTIONS

TRUE/FALSE

_____ 1. You can toggle the view on the Purchase Orders List using the View menu.

_____ 2. You can create vendor bills from a purchase order.

_____ 3. Line items on vendor bills for expenses are entered using the Item icon.

_____ 4. Job materials can be billed to a customer job after posting a vendor bill.

_____ 5. Purchase orders are used to verify item quantities and prices on a vendor's receipt.

_____ 6. OAP changes a PO status to Received after matching it with a vendor receipt.

_____ 7. POs and payments can be emailed to vendors.

_____ 8. You can delete a vendor account with transaction history.

_____ 9. The Vendor List can be exported to Excel.

_____ 10. You can enter corrections to a vendor payment.

MULTIPLE CHOICE

_____ 1. Which menu will open a report that can be customized as the Purchases Journal report?

a. ***Reports>>Purchases>>Purchases by Item Detail***
b. ***Reports>>Vendors and Payables>>Transaction Journal***
c. ***Reports>>Company and Financial>>Transaction Journal***
d. ***Reports>>Company and Financial>>Transaction Detail by Account***

_____ 2. The only difference between the GL Report and the Transaction Detail by Account report is that _____.

a. the GL Report adds Debit and Credit columns
b. the GL Report does not show account ending balances
c. the GL Report only lists asset and liability accounts
d. all of the above

_____ 3. Reconciling vendor activities means that the balance on the aged payables report equals the balance(s) in the _____.

a. Accounts Payable account
b. Accrued Liabilities account
c. both a and b
d. none of the above

_____ 4. You can use the _____ report to analyze transactions on a vendor's account, including payments.

a. Vendor Transaction History
b. Purchases by Vendor Detail
c. Purchases by Vendor Summary
d. both a and b

_____ 5. To reduce the payment on a vendor bill you reduce the payment amount in the _____ window.

a. Payments
b. Pay Bills
c. Print Checks
d. all of the above

_____ 6. The _____ menu prints checks without entering a vendor bill.

a. Banking
b. Vendors
c. both a and b
d. none of the above

_____ 7. Which icon(s) will initiate a new vendor transaction?

a. New Purchase Order
b. Receive Items
c. Enter Bills
d. Both a and c

PRACTICE SET

In this Practice Set you will be using the **Graded Astor Landscaping** data file that includes the Practice Set completed in Chapter 4. ***When this data file is not loaded on your computer, restore it using the "gradedastorlandscaping Chpt 4" backup file created after completing the Chapter 4 Practice Set.***

1. Enter Astor's April vendor activities listed below. Unless otherwise instructed, you will print information in Step 2. In addition, accept transaction defaults assigned from the vendor account unless instructed otherwise.

<u>2008</u>

Apr 2 Post Safe State Insurance Company bill for $1,200.00 for six months of prepaid liability insurance.

Apr 4 Add the following Non-Inventory Item. *(Note: Click always update when prompted to set default accounts.)*

Item name:	PLANTS: ARBORVITAE
Sales description:	2G Arborvitae
Sales price:	$52.00
Income account:	Sales - Landscape
Item tax:	Non-Taxable Sales
Item group:	Plants
Purchase description:	2G Arborvitae
Purchase price:	$40.00
Expense account:	Materials Cost - Landscape
Preferred vendor:	Anderson Wholesale Nursery
Standard cost:	$40.00

Record the following vendor bills for job materials.

Anderson Wholesale Nursery Invoice 7383 dated April 3, $2,318.00, for O'Hara Redesign Gardens job.

Qty	Item	Cost
20	PLANTS: VERBENA	$ 15.90
50	PLANTS: ARBORVITAE	$ 40.00

Paris Brothers Tree Surgeons Invoice 4263 dated April 2, $1,020.00, for O'Hara Redesign Gardens job.

Qty	Item	Cost
12	TREE REMOVAL	$ 85.00

Apr 9 Record Davis Timber Yard Invoice 9033 dated April 7, $3,775.70 for White Redesign Gardens job.

Qty	Item	Cost
400	REDWOOD DECKING	$ 8.99
15	REDWOOD POSTS	$ 5.99
15	REDWOOD CAPS	$ 5.99

Apr 11 Pay vendors for bills with a due date or discount date before April 20. Remember to Calculate Discount. First check number is 436 and bills total $8,406.39.

Apr 16 Record Miles Maintenance & Repair Invoice 1762 for $275.00 dated April 11 for auto repairs.

Apr 17 Issue PO 1 for $449.50 to Davis Timber Yard for White Redesign Gardens job for the following item. **Print the PO.**

Qty	Item	Cost
50	REDWOOD DECKING	$ 8.99

Record Anderson Wholesale Nursery Invoice 3766 for $9.98 dated April 16 for the following item used on the DBH Grounds Maintenance job.

Qty	Item	Cost
2	MULCH	$ 4.99

Apr 18 Record the following bills for expenses dated April 18.

Arlington City Water	April water	$110.00
Neighbors Telephone Co.	April phone	$230.00
Arlington Gas Company	April gas	$175.80
Southern Power Co.	April electricity	$162.50

Apr 21 Write and print check number 441 to Postmaster for postage expense, $150.00.

Record Davis Timber Yard Invoice 9037, $449.50, dated April 18 for all items on PO 1 issued April 17.

Apr 22 Create the following new vendor.

Metropolitan Supplies
672 N. Main Street
Arlington, VA 30010
(701) 555-7023

Contact:	Shannon Wilson
Expense account:	Office Supplies Expense
Payment terms:	Net 30 Days
Vendor group:	ADMIN

Record Metropolitan Supplies Invoice 6565 dated April 21 for office supply expense, $137.20.

Apr 28 Record Anderson Wholesale Nursery Credit memo CM7383, $80.00, dated April 22 for returning 2 Arborvitae on Invoice 7383 for O'Hara Redesign Gardens job.

Apr 30 Pay vendors for bills with a due date or discount date before May 4, 2008. Make sure to apply Anderson's credit memo and to Calculate Discount. First check number is 442 and payments total $4,116.30.

Write and print check number 448 for $1,853.50 for sales tax due on May 1.

2. Print the following reports to document April vendor transactions.

   a. Transaction Journal listing April 1 through April 30 transactions filtered for the transaction types of Vendor Bill, Vendor Credit Memo, and Vendor Payment.

   b. Detailed A/P Aging report as of April 30, 2008. Explain how you would use this report.

   c. Profitability by Job Summary report listing April transactions.

   d. Vendor Payments report for April 1 through April 30 modified to remove the Issue Date, No., Status Detail, Memo, Reference number, and Void columns.

3. ***Back up the Graded Astor Landscaping data file to a backup file named "gradedastorlandscaping Chpt 5." The Practice Set for the next chapter will build on the work completed in this chapter.***

CHAPTER 6 PAYROLL ACTIVITIES FOR A SERVICE BASED BUSINESS

LEARNING OBJECTIVES

This chapter uses the Practice Astor Landscaping data file containing the tasks completed in Chapter 5. ***When this data file is not loaded on your computer, restore it using the "practiceastorlandscaping Chpt 5" backup file created after reading Chapter 5.***

In this chapter you process Astor's payroll and:

1. Learn *MAPS* for employee paychecks before processing paychecks in OAP
2. Use the Employee Home page to manage employees and process paychecks
3. Record employee time
4. Calculate, print, and post employee paychecks
5. Go *Behind the Keys* of posted paychecks
6. Correct a posted paycheck
7. Remit payroll tax liabilities to government taxing agencies

Launch OAP and open **Practice Astor Landscaping**.

MANUAL ACCOUNTING PROCEDURES

Astor pays employees biweekly (every two weeks). Employees are paid either an hourly wage or an annual salary. Salaried employees are paid the same amount each pay period. Hourly employees are paid for the total hours worked during the pay period and document these hours by filling out timesheets and noting the hours worked on jobs so Astor can invoice customers.

You will soon learn that payroll in a manual accounting system is tedious and time consuming. You must first calculate each hourly employee's gross pay by totaling timesheet hours for the pay period and multiplying total hours by the hourly pay rate. The gross pay for salaried employees is calculated by dividing the annual salary by the number of pay periods in the year. For Astor the number of pay periods is 26.

After calculating gross pay, you must then calculate the employee's net pay. Net pay equals gross pay minus total payroll tax withholdings and total voluntary deductions. The following tables explain payroll tax withholdings and voluntary deductions.

Employee Tax Withholdings	**Description**
Federal Income Tax	Employee federal income taxes withheld on taxable wages. Taxable wages exclude employee contributions to a 401K or IRA retirement plan. IRS Circular E sets the guidelines for withholding federal income taxes (explained below).
Social Security (FICA)	Employee taxes withheld on gross wages and paid to the federal government to fund Social Security retirement. Gross wages include employee contributions to a 401K or IRA retirement plan. The IRS currently taxes gross wages at 6.2 percent (0.062) until wages paid during the year exceed an annual cap. For 2007, the annual cap was $97,500. This cap is increased each year and the 2008 cap was not available at the time of publishing the text.
Medicare	Employee taxes withheld on gross wages and paid to the federal government to fund Medicare health insurance. Gross wages include employee contributions to a 401K or IRA retirement plan. The IRS taxes gross wages at 1.45 percent (0.0145) and there is no annual wage cap.
State Income Tax	Employee state income taxes withheld on taxable wages (i.e., gross wages minus contributions to a 401K or IRA retirement plan). Each state publishes guidelines for withholding state income taxes. ***Astor withholds 3 percent (0.03) of gross wages.***

Employee Voluntary Deductions	**Description**
Retirement Plans	Employee voluntary contributions to an employer-sponsored retirement plan. Retirement plans include 401K and IRA plans. These contributions are deducted from gross wages to determine federal and state taxable wages. ***Astor does not sponsor a retirement plan.***
Health Insurance	Health insurance premiums deducted from net pay when the employer requires its employees to pay for a portion of health insurance costs. ***Astor does not require employees to share this cost.***
Contributions	Deductions from net pay for charitable contributions made by the employee.

Astor also pays taxes on employee compensation and provides additional compensation by providing health insurance. The next tables explain typical employer tax liabilities and other forms of employee compensation.

Employer Payroll Taxes	**Description**
Social Security (FICA) and Medicare	Employer portion of Social Security and Medicare taxes paid on gross wages. The employer tax equals the tax paid by employees.
Federal Unemployment (FUTA)	Employer tax on gross wages paid to the federal government for subsidizing state unemployment compensation funds. Typically, employers pay 0.08 percent (0.008) on the first $7,000 of annual gross wages paid to each employee.
State Unemployment (SUTA)	Employer tax on gross wages paid to the state for funding compensation for unemployed workers. Typically the tax rate is based on an employer's unemployment history and/or business type and will be capped after reaching an annual limit on gross wages. ***For Astor the rate is 1.5 percent (0.015) of the first $8,000 of annual wages paid to each employee.***
Worker's Compensation	Employer tax paid to the state to fund compensating injured workers. Typically, states set the tax rates based on risk factors in an employee's job. ***The text does not illustrate worker's compensation tax.***

Additional Compensation	**Description**
Retirement Plans	Employer contributions to a company-sponsored 401K or IRA retirement plan. Typically companies match contributions based on employee participation in the plan. ***Astor does not sponsor a retirement plan.***
Health Insurance	Employer premiums for health insurance. Employers may pay all premiums or require employees to share in this cost. ***Astor pays all health insurance premiums for employees eligible to participate in the plan.***

Each pay period the accountant prepares an Excel spreadsheet called the Payroll Register to calculate employee net pay. The register illustrated in Figure 6:1 covers the pay period of February 25 to March 9, 2008.

	A	B	C	D	E	F	G	H	I	J	K	L	M	N
1	**Astor Landscaping**													
2	**Pay Period 2/25/2008 thru 3/09/2008**													
3														
4	**Check No.**	**Employee**	**Filing Status**	**Allow.**	**Pay Type**	**Pay Rate**	**Regular Hrs**	**O.T. Hours**	**Gross Pay**	**Federal Income Tax**	**Soc. Sec. (FICA) Tax**	**Medicare Tax**	**VA State Tax**	**Net Pay**
5	721	Dillion, Roy J.	Single	1	Hourly Wage	12.00	80.00		996.00	96.00	61.75	14.44	29.88	793.93
6	722	Folse, Jan B.	Single	1	Hourly Office	10.00	80.00		800.00	72.00	49.60	11.60	24.00	642.80
7	723	Greene, Kellie I.	Married	1	Salary	2,346.15			2,346.15	257.00	145.46	34.02	70.38	1,839.29
8	724	Hardman, Alan	Single	2	Hourly Wage	12.00	78.00		1,044.00	89.00	64.73	15.14	31.32	843.81
9	725	Hayes, Mike E	Single	1	Hourly Wage	12.00	32.00		384.00	15.00	23.81	5.57	11.52	328.10
10	726	Henderson, Jeff P.	Married	1	Hourly Wage	12.00	80.00		960.00	53.00	59.52	13.92	28.80	804.76
11	727	Murray, Monica D.	Single	1	Salary	1,211.54			1,211.54	132.00	75.12	17.57	36.35	950.50
12	728	Ramez, Victor M.	Single	0	Hourly Wage	10.00	75.00		750.00	83.00	46.50	10.88	22.50	587.12
13	729	Ruland, Seth N.	Married	0	Salary	3,103.85			3,103.85	429.00	192.44	45.01	93.12	2,344.28
14	730	White, Judy O.	Married	2	Salary	2,084.62			2,084.62	199.00	129.25	30.23	62.54	1,663.60
15														
16		**Totals**					**425.00**	**0.00**	**13,680.16**	**1,425.00**	**848.18**	**198.38**	**410.41**	**10,798.19**
17														
18		**Tax Basis**								**Circular E**	**6.20%**	**1.45%**	**3.00%**	
19														
20		**G/L Accounts**							**57000 / 60000**	**23400**	**23400**	**23400**	**23600**	**10300**

Figure 6:1

The Payroll Register shows that Kellie Greene claims the Married (M) federal filing status with one withholding allowance. To calculate Kellie's federal income tax withholding for this pay period look to the 2007 IRS Circular E tax table in Figure 6:2. *(Note: IRS tables for 2008 were not available at the time of publishing the text. The 2007 tables are also provided in Appendix D.)*

MARRIED Persons—BIWEEKLY Payroll Period

(For Wages Paid in 2007)

If the wages are–		And the number of withholding allowances claimed is—										
At least	But less than	0	1	2	3	4	5	6	7	8	9	10
		The amount of income tax to be withheld is—										
$1,380	$1,400	$133	$113	$94	$74	$56	$43	$30	$17	$4	$0	$0
1,400	1,420	136	116	97	77	58	45	32	19	6	0	0
1,420	1,440	139	119	100	80	60	47	34	21	8	0	0
1,440	1,460	142	122	103	83	63	49	36	23	10	0	0
1,460	1,480	145	125	106	86	66	51	38	25	12	0	0
1,480	1,500	148	128	109	89	69	53	40	27	14	1	0
1,500	1,520	151	131	112	92	72	55	42	29	16	3	0
1,520	1,540	154	134	115	95	75	57	44	31	18	5	0
1,540	1,560	157	137	118	98	78	59	46	33	20	7	0
1,560	1,580	160	140	121	101	81	62	48	35	22	9	0
2,280	2,300	268	248	229	209	189	170	150	131	111	91	72
2,300	2,320	271	251	232	212	192	173	153	134	114	94	75
2,320	2,340	274	254	235	215	195	176	156	137	117	97	78
2,340	2,360	277	257	238	218	198	179	159	140	120	100	81
2,360	2,380	280	260	241	221	201	182	162	143	123	103	84
2,380	2,400	283	263	244	224	204	185	165	146	126	106	87
2,400	2,420	286	266	247	227	207	188	168	149	129	109	90
2,420	2,440	289	269	250	230	210	191	171	152	132	112	93
2,440	2,460	292	272	253	233	213	194	174	155	135	115	96
2,460	2,480	295	275	256	236	216	197	177	158	138	118	99
2,480	2,500	298	278	259	239	219	200	180	161	141	121	102
2,500	2,520	301	281	262	242	222	203	183	164	144	124	105
2,520	2,540	304	284	265	245	225	206	186	167	147	127	108
2,540	2,560	307	287	268	248	228	209	189	170	150	130	111
2,560	2,580	310	290	271	251	231	212	192	173	153	133	114
2,580	2,600	313	293	274	254	234	215	195	176	156	136	117
2,600	2,620	316	296	277	257	237	218	198	179	159	139	120
2,620	2,640	319	299	280	260	240	221	201	182	162	142	123
2,640	2,660	322	302	283	263	243	224	204	185	165	145	126
2,660	2,680	325	305	286	266	246	227	207	188	168	148	129
2,680	2,700	328	308	289	269	249	230	210	191	171	151	132
$2,700 and over		Use Table 2(b) for a **MARRIED person** on page 37. Also see the instructions on page 35.										

Figure 6:2

Figure 6:2 is the IRS table for employees paid biweekly and claiming the Married (M) filing status. There are separate IRS tables for employees claiming the Single (S) filing status and separate tables for married and single employees paid on a weekly or monthly basis

Kellie's $257.00 federal income tax withholding amount is found at the point where her taxable pay of $2,346.15 intersects with her one claimed withholding allowance. Because Kellie does not contribute to a 401K or IRA retirement plan, her taxable pay equals her gross pay.

Kellie's FICA tax withholding of $145.46 equals her gross pay times 6.2 percent (0.062). Her Medicare tax withholding of $34.02 equals gross pay times 1.45 percent (0.0145).

The state tax withholding of $70.38 is 3 percent (0.03) of her taxable pay.

Kellie has no deductions for health insurance premiums, retirement plan contributions, or charitable contributions. In fact, premiums are not deducted from any employee's paycheck because Astor pays the full cost of health insurance. There are no deductions for retirement plans because Astor does not sponsor a plan. Finally, there are no employees making charitable contributions through payroll.

Accordingly, Kellie's net pay of $1,839.29 equals her gross pay minus the sum of her total tax withholdings.

The accountant has also computed the employer payroll tax liabilities for the pay period, illustrated in Figure 6:3.

	P	Q	R	S	T	U
1	**Astor Landscaping**					
2	**Employer Costs for Period 2/25/2008 thru 3/9/2008**					
3						
4	**Employee**	**ER Soc Sec FICA**	**ER Medicare**	**ER FUTA**	**ER SUTA**	**Health Insurance**
5	Dillion, Roy J.	61.75	14.44	7.97	14.94	0.00
6	Folse, Jan B.	49.60	11.60	6.40	12.00	60.00
7	Greene, Kellie I.	145.46	34.02	0.00	0.00	60.00
8	Hardman, Alan	64.73	15.14	8.35	15.66	0.00
9	Hayes, Mike E	23.81	5.57	5.51	5.76	0.00
10	Henderson, Jeff P.	59.52	13.92	7.68	14.40	0.00
11	Murray, Monica D.	75.12	17.57	9.69	18.17	60.00
12	Ramez, Victor M.	46.50	10.88	6.00	11.25	0.00
13	Ruland, Seth N.	192.44	45.01	0.00	0.00	60.00
14	White, Judy O.	129.25	30.23	0.00	0.00	60.00
15						
16	**Totals**	**848.18**	**198.38**	**51.60**	**92.18**	**300.00**
17						
18	**Tax Basis**	**6.20%**	**1.45%**	**0.8%**	**1.50%**	
19						
20	**G/L Accounts**	**23400 / 61000**	**23400 / 61000**	**23500 / 61000**	**23700 / 61000**	**23800 / 60600**

Figure 6:3

After computing employee pay and employer payroll tax liabilities, the accountant creates paychecks and records the general journal entries illustrated in Figure 6:4. *(Note: General ledger accounts are listed on the worksheets. The expense recorded to 57000 Direct Labor is the gross pay for employees paid by Hourly Wage.)*

Audit Trail

Astor Landscaping
General Journal **Page 5**

Date	Account Post Ref.	Description	Debit	Credit
3/10/2008	57000	Direct Labor	4,134.00	
	60000	Salaries Expense	9,546.16	
	23400	Federal Payroll Tax Liabilities		2,471.56
	23600	State Payroll Taxes Payable		410.41
	10300	Payroll Checking Account		10,798.19
To record employee paychecks				
3/10/2008	61000	Payroll Tax Expense	1,190.34	
	60600	Employee Benefit Expense	300.00	
	23400	Federal Payroll Tax Liabilities		1,046.56
	23500	FUTA Tax Payable		51.60
	23700	SUTA Tax Payable		92.18
	23800	Medical Insurance Payable		300.00
To record employer payroll tax expense				

Figure 6:4

The journal entries are then posted to the general ledger accounts affected by the transactions (Figure 6:5). *(Note: Only two general ledger accounts are illustrated.)*

General Ledger					
Payroll Checking Account			Account No. 10300		
Date	Description	Post Ref.	Debit	Credit	Balance
3/09/2008	Balance Forward				15,574.80
3/10/2008		GJ 5		10,798.19	4,776.61

Audit Trail

General Ledger					
Federal Payroll Tax Liabilities			Account No. 23400		
Date	Description	Post Ref.	Debit	Credit	Balance
3/09/2008	Balance Forward				0.00
3/10/2008		GJ 5		2,471.56	2,471.56
3/10/2008		GJ 5		1,046.56	3,518.12

Figure 6:5

As explained in previous chapters, the audit trail is recorded while posting to general ledger accounts.

With an understanding of *MAPS* for paycheck activities, you are now ready to perform these activities in OAP.

Employees Menu and Home Page

Before processing employee activities become familiar with the commands that initiate activities. The Employees menu is illustrated in Figure 6:6. The first menu choice opens the Employees Home page. There are separate menus for creating employees and timesheets and for entering manual payroll.

Click **Employees Home** on the menu to open the Employees Home page illustrated in Figure 6:7. This page serves as central command for processing employee activities. You can also click the Employees Home page icon to activate this page.

Figure 6:6

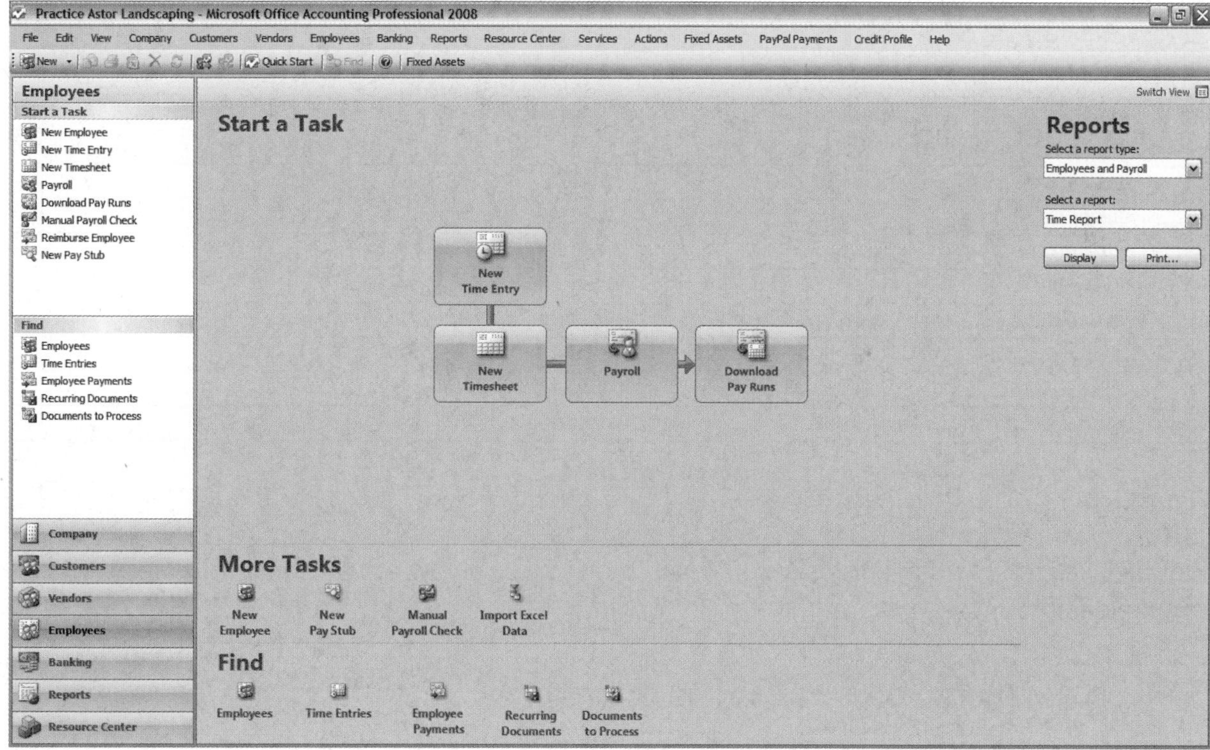

Figure 6:7

You will find that the home page contains links to many of the commands located on the Employees menu. **Start a Task** icons show that employee hours are entered through timesheets and can then be uploaded to ADP's online payroll service. Thereafter, ADP calculates paychecks and sends back pay information for downloading into OAP.

Unfortunately, you will not be able to use this service because it is fee based. However, you will be able to enter manual paycheck information to print paychecks.

Beneath Start a Task icons are the icons for **More Tasks** and opening lists that **Find** posted transactions. The activities located in the center of the home page are replicated under the **Start a Task** and **Find** links located to the left of the page.

Now that you are familiar with the Employees menu and home page let's begin recording employee transactions.

MANAGING EMPLOYEES

Click the **Employees** link under **Find** to create the following Employee List.

Employee List — Current View: Active

Active	Employee Name	Job Title	Home Phone	Business Phone	Mobile Phone
Add a new Employee					
✓	Dillion, Roy J.	Laborer	(770) 555-1225		
✓	Folse, Jan B.	Sales	(404) 555-0754		
✓	Greene, Kellie I.	Landscaper	(770) 555-8411		
✓	Hardman, Alan	Laborer	(770) 555-6424		
✓	Hayes, Mike E.	Laborer	(770) 555-8754		
✓	Henderson, Jeff P.	Laborer	(404) 555-3729		
✓	Murray, Monica D.	Admin	(404) 555-8112		
✓	Ramez, Victor M.	Laborer	(770) 555-9133		
✓	Ruland, Seth N.	Owner	(770) 555-0791		
✓	White, Judy O.	Accountant	(770) 555-1392		

Figure 6:8

Double click to open Jan Folse's account and then follow below as we explain the fields on an employee account.

General Tab

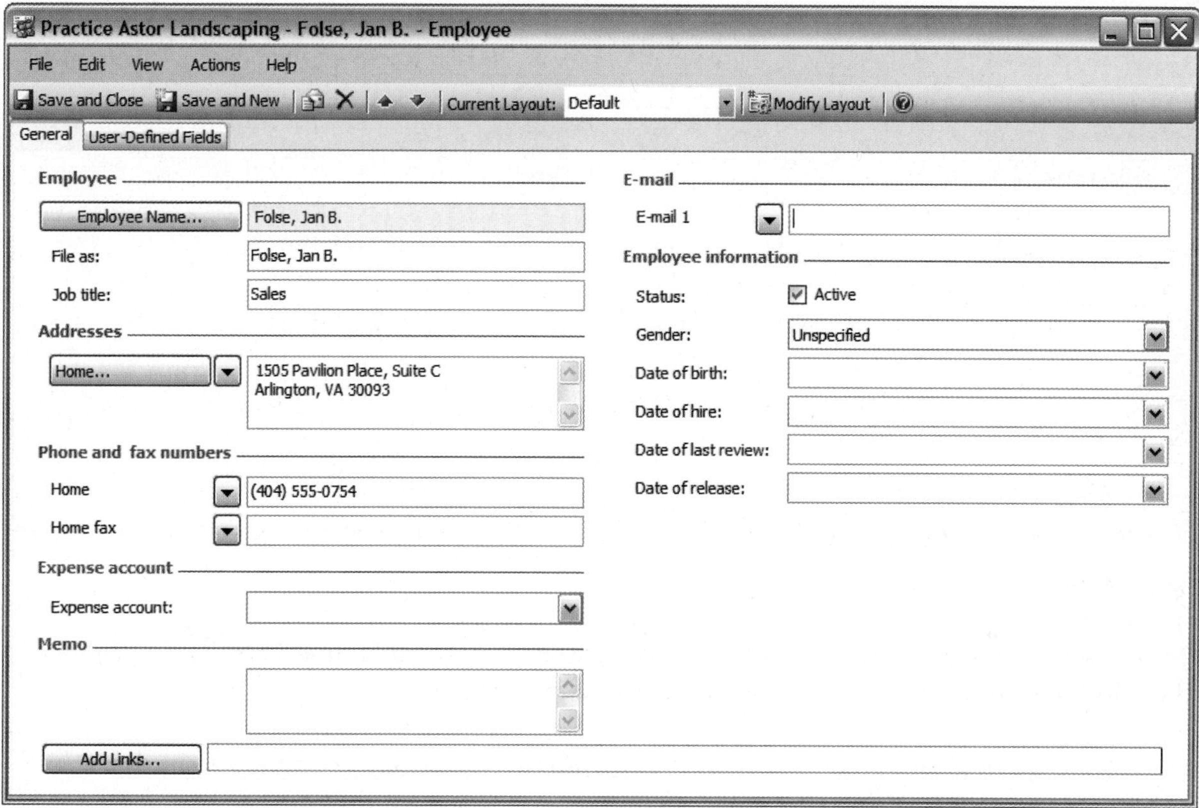

Figure 6:9

This tab store employee contact information as well as hire, review, and release dates.

User-Defined Fields

After selecting this tab, click the dropdown list on **Current Layout** to select **Employee Form**. This is a customized form that changes the appearance of information on the tab. (See Figure 6:10.)

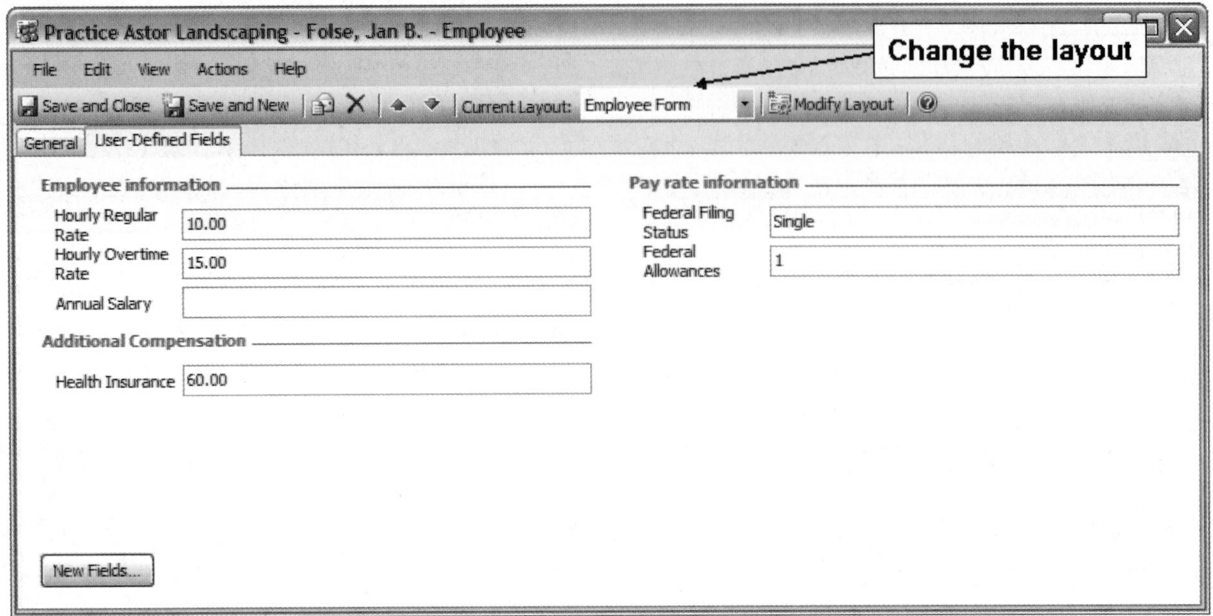

Figure 6:10

These fields are user defined and have been created to store additional payroll information that OAP does not provide for storing on the employee account.

The tab shows that Jan is paid a regular hourly rate of $10.00 and $15.00 per hour for overtime. She claims the Single federal filing status with one allowance and receives employer health insurance benefits.

Click **X** to close Jan's account and click **No** to saving changes. OAP always issues this prompt even when no changes were made to the account.

Next, open Seth Ruland's account and activate the User-Defined Fields tab (Figure 6:11).

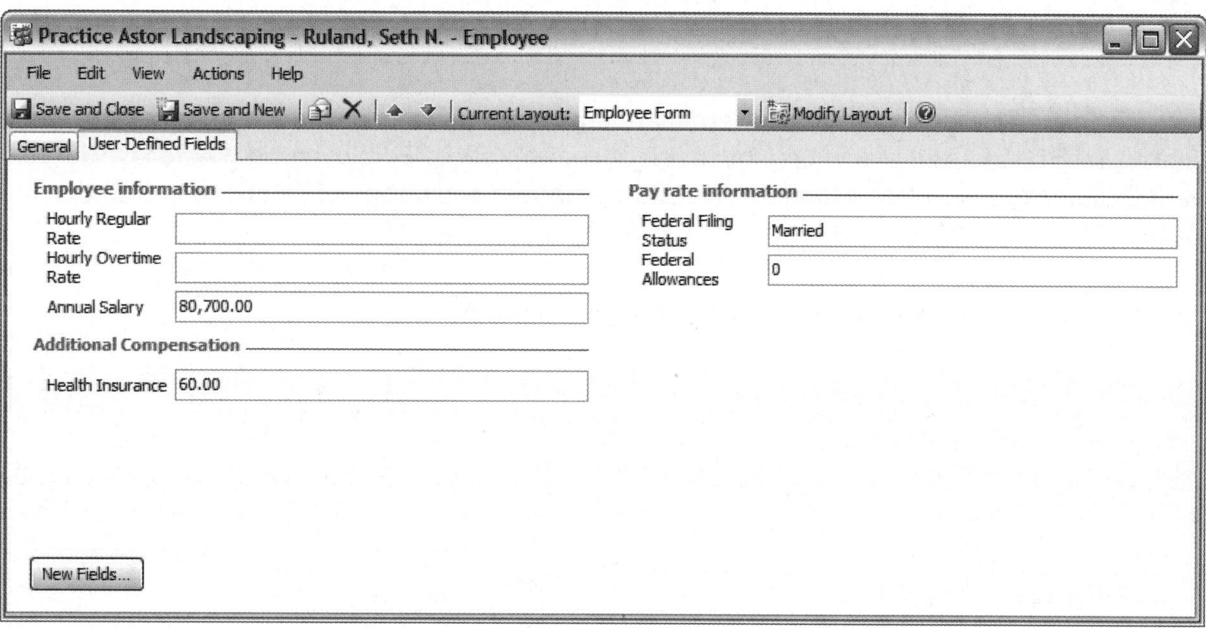

Figure 6:11

The tab shows that Seth is a salaried employee and claims the Married federal filing status with zero allowances. Click **X** to close the account and **No** to saving changes.

You can delete employee accounts by highlighting an account on the Employee List and clicking on the toolbar; however, you cannot delete employees with transaction history. If attempting to delete an employee account with history, you will receive the message in Figure 6:12 reminding you to change the account's active status in lieu of deleting.

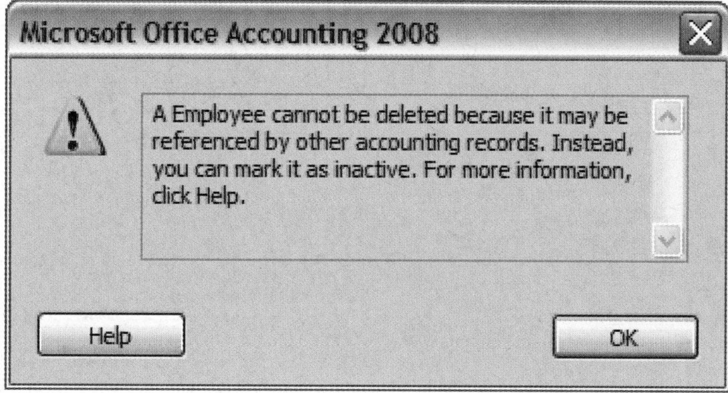

Figure 6:12

Managing Employees

In this topic you learn to create and terminate employees. Click the **New Employee** link under Start a Task or the **Add a new Employee** link at the top of the Employee List. Astor has hired Jack Zickefoose to work as a laborer on customer jobs. Follow the next steps to create the account.

Complete the **General** information by referring to Figure 6:13.

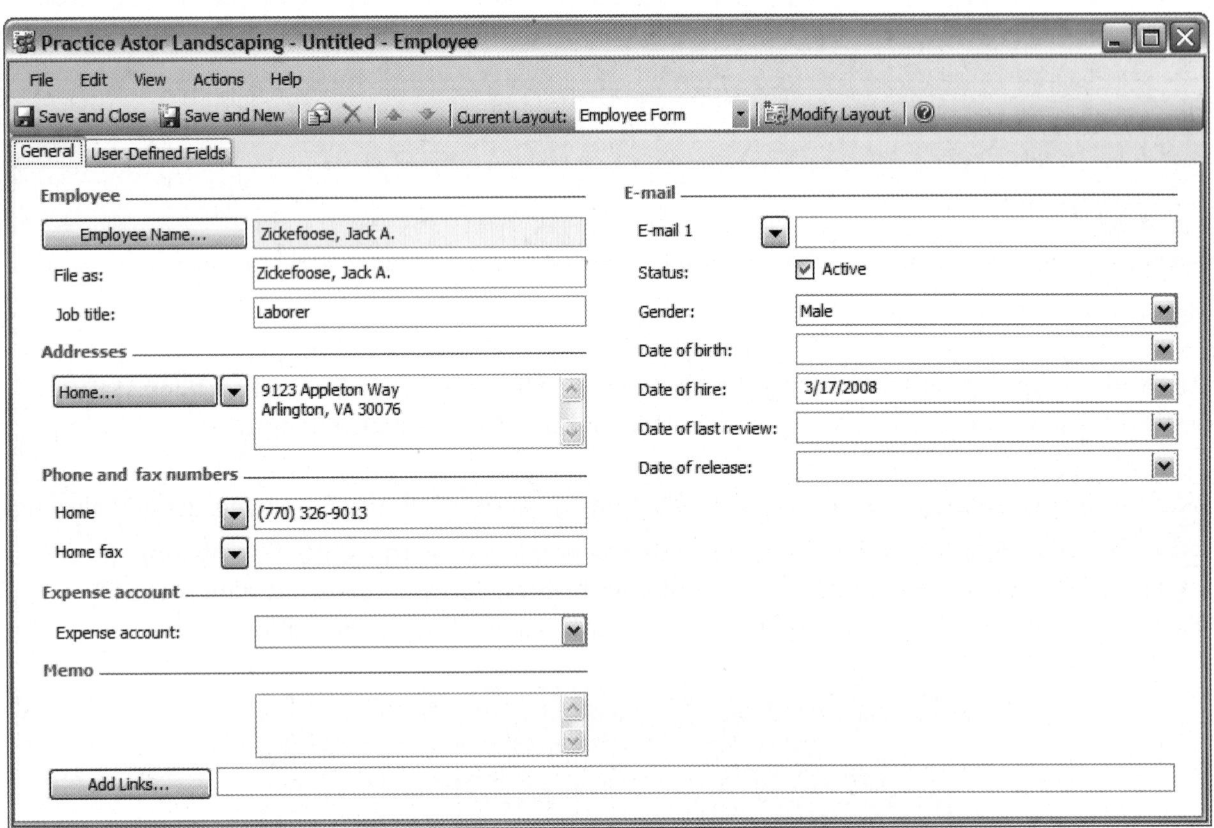

Figure 6:13

Refer to the next illustration to enter information on the **User-Defined Fields** tab.

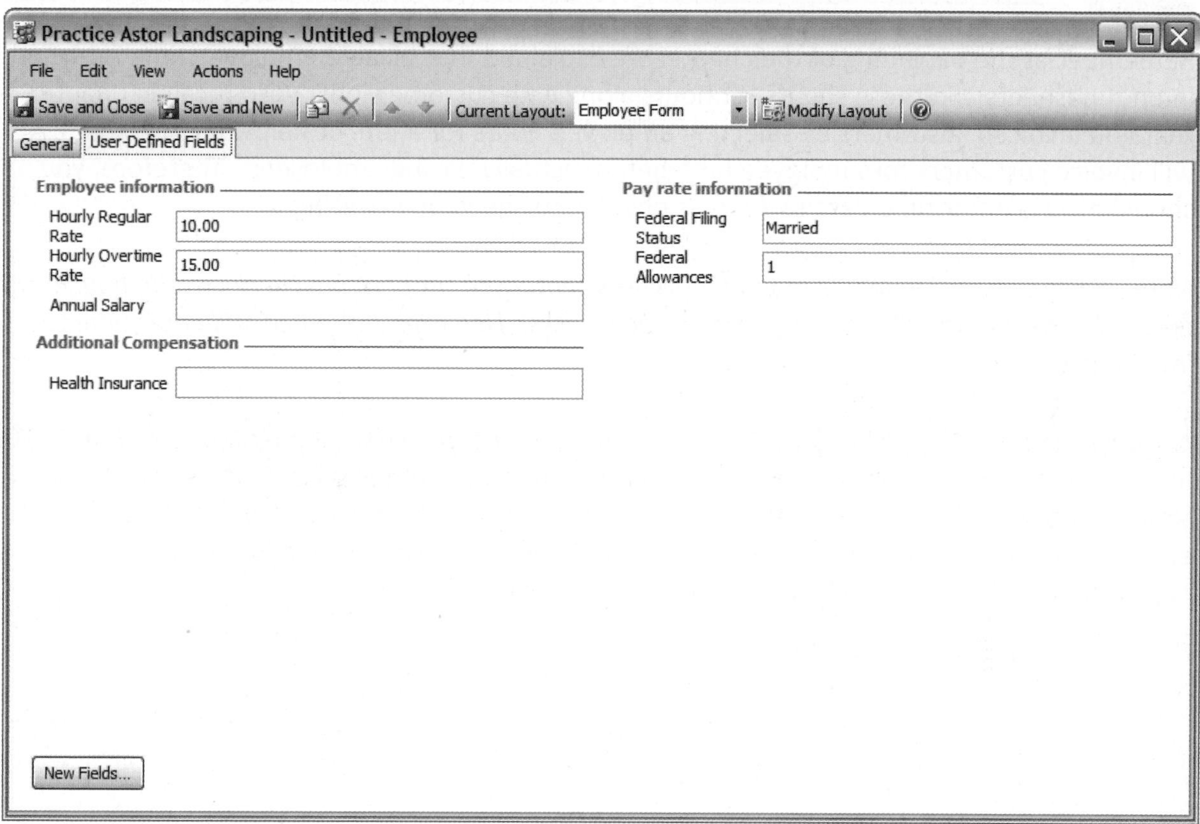

Figure 6:14

Click **Save and Close**.

You also need to know the procedures for terminating employees because you cannot delete employee accounts with paycheck history. You can termination an employee by opening the account and entering a date in the **Date of Release** field. Also, click to turn off the **Active** option.

Now that you understand managing employee accounts, you are ready to begin paying employees.

EMPLOYEE TIME

Remember at the beginning of the chapter we explained that billable employee time is turned in on timesheets and these sheets list hours along with customer jobs. Also recall in Chapter 4 that you invoiced customers by selecting employee hours for a job. It helps to know that OAP will invoice customers for employee time before actually paying employees. Therefore, you should always enter time data as soon as possible to speed up invoicing.

Note: You will be using OAP's manual paycheck feature to prepare paychecks so the hours entered in this topic will not interface with paychecks. However, you must still enter time to invoice customers.

Astor's next pay date is March 24, 2008, covering the two weeks beginning Monday, March 10 and ending Sunday, March 23. Before the accountant enters timesheets, Seth verifies these sheets, reviewing for accuracy. Seth then gives the timesheets to Judy who has already entered most of the time data for this pay period. In the next exercise and the *You Try* exercise that follows, you will finish entering time for this pay period

Steps to Recording Employee Time Data

1. On the Employees Home page, click **New Timesheet**. In **Employee name**, look up Hardman, Alan. Type "3/17/2008" in **Select week**. *(Note: You can select this date by using the calendar feature on the dropdown list.)*

   The following displays Alan's hours already entered for the week. Notice how the columns for hours are headed by the date and day. You can resize columns by dragging the column separator.

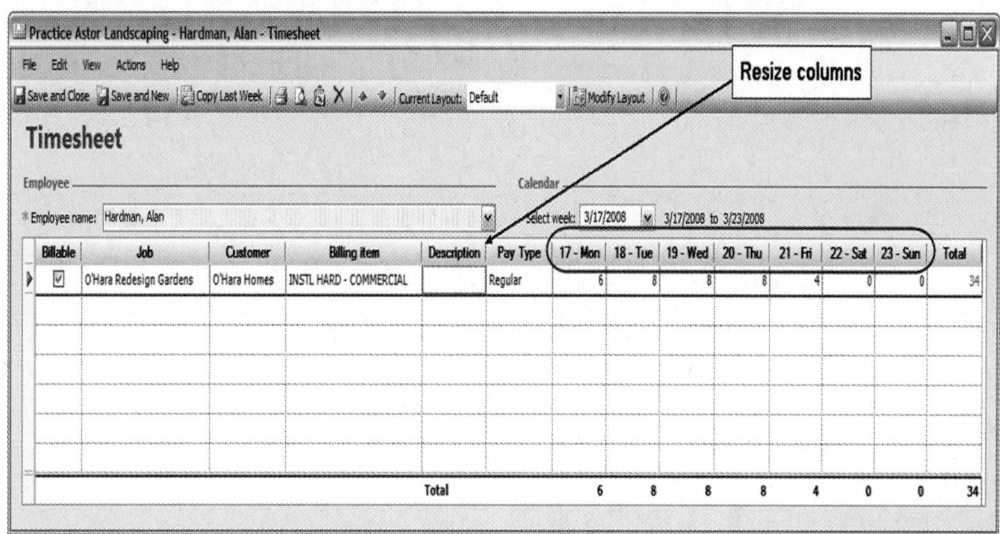

Figure 6:15

2. Alan worked 6 additional hours on Friday for a different customer job. Place your cursor in **Job** on the second line and look up **Ashford Grounds Maintenance.**

3. The Customer field autofills based on the job selection. Tab to **Billing Item** and look up the inventory service item of **WKLY MNTNCE - COMMERCIAL**.

4. Tab to **Pay Type** and select **Regular**. *(Note: You select Overtime when employee hours are for overtime.)*

5. Place your cursor in the Friday column (**21-Fri**) and enter "6." *(Note: Alan has no overtime hours despite working 10 hours on Friday because he still worked only 40 hours for the pay week.)*

   Press Tab and Alan's timesheet for the week is complete (Figure 6:16) with the new hours marked **Billable** to the customer.

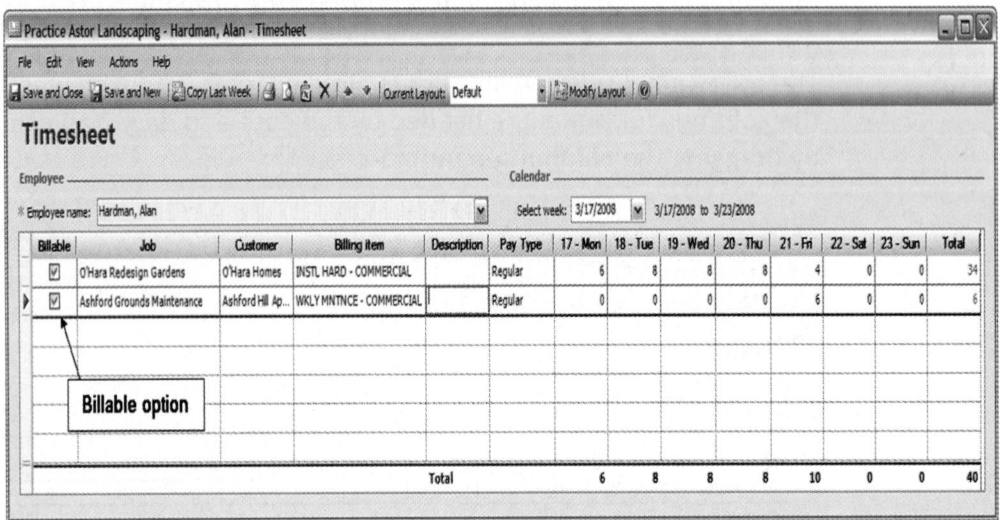

Billable	Job	Customer	Billing item	Description	Pay Type	17 - Mon	18 - Tue	19 - Wed	20 - Thu	21 - Fri	22 - Sat	23 - Sun	Total
☑	O'Hara Redesign Gardens	O'Hara Homes	INSTL HARD - COMMERCIAL		Regular	6	8	8	8	4	0	0	34
☑	Ashford Grounds Maintenance	Ashford Hill Ap...	WKLY MNTNCE - COMMERCIAL		Regular	0	0	0	0	6	0	0	6
				Total		6	8	8	8	10	0	0	40

Figure 6:16

6. Click **Save and New** so you can enter Jack's timesheet for the same work week. Refer to the following information and verify that all hours are marked Billable.

   Name: Zickefoose, Jack A.

   Line 1:
   Job: O'Hara Redesign Gardens
   Billing item: INSTL LAND – COMMERCIAL
   Pay Type: Regular
   Mon through Fri: Enter 8 for each day

   Line 2:
   Job: O'Hara Redesign Gardens
   Billing item: INSTL LAND – COMMERCIAL
   Pay Type: Overtime
   Fri: 2

   Figure 6:17 shows the completed timesheet.

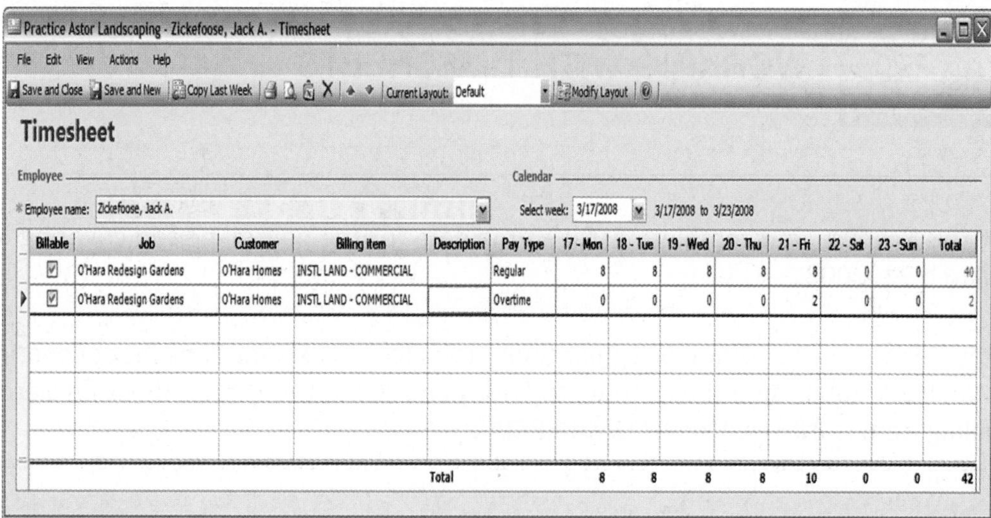

Practice Astor Landscaping - Zickefoose, Jack A. - Timesheet

File Edit View Actions Help

Save and Close | Save and New | Copy Last Week | Current Layout: Default | Modify Layout

Timesheet

Employee — Employee name: Zickefoose, Jack A.

Calendar — Select week: 3/17/2008 3/17/2008 to 3/23/2008

Billable	Job	Customer	Billing item	Description	Pay Type	17 - Mon	18 - Tue	19 - Wed	20 - Thu	21 - Fri	22 - Sat	23 - Sun	Total
☑	O'Hara Redesign Gardens	O'Hara Homes	INSTL LAND - COMMERCIAL		Regular	8	8	8	8	8	0	0	40
☑	O'Hara Redesign Gardens	O'Hara Homes	INSTL LAND - COMMERCIAL		Overtime	0	0	0	0	2	0	0	2
				Total		8	8	8	8	10	0	0	42

Figure 6:17

We want to point out other information before leaving this window.

Clicking these icons on the toolbar will scroll though the selected employee's existing timesheets.

The Copy Last Week icon transfers time data from the selected employee's previous timesheet onto the new timesheet. This can save data entry time; however, we have found that transferring timesheet data produces unexpected results because OAP internally assigns the computer's system date to transferred timesheets causing time to sort out of order in the invoicing window and the wrong date to appear for unbilled hours on job reports.

You can delete a timesheet by clicking this delete icon on the toolbar. However, you cannot delete time that has been invoiced to customers.

7. Click **Save and Close**.

WORKING WITH TIMESHEETS

In this exercise you complete Astor's time data for the payroll period covering March 10 to March 23, 2008.

Roy Dillion has 2 additional regular time hours for his existing timesheet covering March 17 to March 23, 2008. Add these hours to Friday and bill to the White Redesign Gardens job. The billing item is INSTL LAND – COMMERCIAL.

Employee Time Reports

After recording employee time, Judy prints an employee time report to verify that hours and job information were entered correctly. Follow the next steps to create the report.

Steps to Create an Employee Time Report

1. Select ***Reports>>Employee and Payroll>>Time Report*** on the main menu.

2. Enter the date range of 3/10/2008 to 3/23/2008 (i.e., the biweekly pay period).

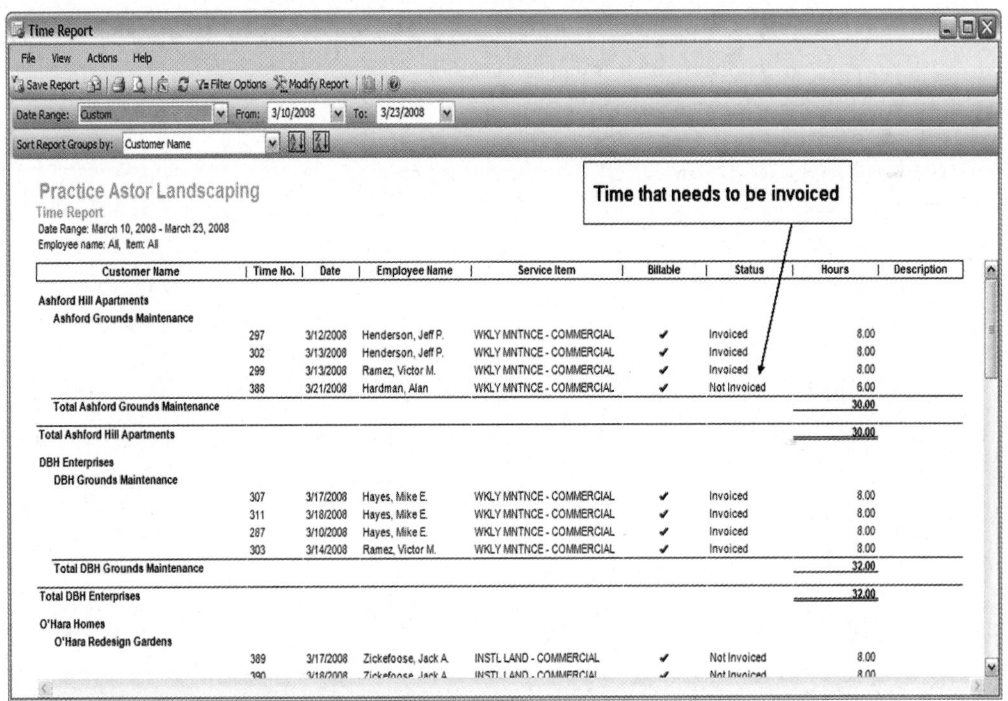

Practice Astor Landscaping
Time Report
Date Range: March 10, 2008 - March 23, 2008
Employee name: All, Item: All

Customer Name	Time No.	Date	Employee Name	Service Item	Billable	Status	Hours	Description
Ashford Hill Apartments								
Ashford Grounds Maintenance								
	297	3/12/2008	Henderson, Jeff P.	WKLY MNTNCE - COMMERCIAL	✔	Invoiced	8.00	
	302	3/13/2008	Henderson, Jeff P.	WKLY MNTNCE - COMMERCIAL	✔	Invoiced	8.00	
	299	3/13/2008	Ramez, Victor M.	WKLY MNTNCE - COMMERCIAL	✔	Invoiced	8.00	
	388	3/21/2008	Hardman, Alan	WKLY MNTNCE - COMMERCIAL	✔	Not Invoiced	6.00	
Total Ashford Grounds Maintenance							30.00	
Total Ashford Hill Apartments							30.00	
DBH Enterprises								
DBH Grounds Maintenance								
	307	3/17/2008	Hayes, Mike E.	WKLY MNTNCE - COMMERCIAL	✔	Invoiced	8.00	
	311	3/18/2008	Hayes, Mike E.	WKLY MNTNCE - COMMERCIAL	✔	Invoiced	8.00	
	287	3/10/2008	Hayes, Mike E.	WKLY MNTNCE - COMMERCIAL	✔	Invoiced	8.00	
	303	3/14/2008	Ramez, Victor M.	WKLY MNTNCE - COMMERCIAL	✔	Invoiced	8.00	
Total DBH Grounds Maintenance							32.00	
Total DBH Enterprises							32.00	
O'Hara Homes								
O'Hara Redesign Gardens								
	389	3/17/2008	Zickefoose, Jack A.	INSTL LAND - COMMERCIAL	✔	Not Invoiced	8.00	

Figure 6:18

Note: OAP does not provide a report for grouping time by employee; however, you can filter the report multiple times to select each employee. The report also does not provide a grand total for time but you can export the report to Excel to calculate a total.

Check your previous entries and then close the Time Report. You are now ready to pay employees.

Paying Employees

With employee time tickets entered and verified the time has come to pay employees. Because payroll data cannot be uploaded to ADP for calculating paychecks you are going to create paychecks by entering information calculated in Excel. Although this takes additional time, there are benefits to knowing the manual method of paying employees because not all companies subscribe to ADP's payroll service.

Figure 6:19 is the Excel paycheck register for Astor's next pay period ending on March 23, 2008. The spreadsheet that follows is the Excel payroll register for employer costs (Figure 6:20). You will use both of these worksheets to complete the next exercise.

Astor Landscaping													
Pay Period 3/10/2008 thru 3/23/2008													
Check No.	Employee	Filing Status	Allow.	Pay Type	Pay Rate	Regular Hrs	O.T. Hours	Gross Pay	Federal Income Tax	Soc. Sec. (FICA) Tax	Medicare Tax	VA State Tax	Net Pay
731	Dillion, Roy J.	Single	1	Hourly Wage	12.00	75.00		900.00	87.00	55.80	13.05	27.00	717.15
732	Folse, Jan B.	Single	1	Hourly Office	10.00	80.00		800.00	72.00	49.60	11.60	24.00	642.80
733	Greene, Kellie I.	Married	1	Salary	2,346.15			2,346.15	257.00	145.46	34.02	70.38	1,839.29
734	Hardman, Alan	Single	2	Hourly Wage	12.00	78.00		936.00	71.00	58.03	13.57	28.08	765.32
735	Hayes, Mike E	Single	1	Hourly Wage	12.00	54.00		648.00	48.00	40.18	9.40	19.44	530.98
736	Henderson, Jeff P.	Married	1	Hourly Wage	12.00	72.00		864.00	43.00	53.57	12.53	25.92	728.98
737	Murray, Monica D.	Single	1	Salary	1,211.54			1,211.54	132.00	75.12	17.57	36.35	950.50
738	Ramez, Victor M.	Single	0	Hourly Wage	10.00	78.00		780.00	89.00	48.36	11.31	23.40	607.93
739	Ruland, Seth N.	Married	0	Salary	3,103.85			3,103.85	429.00	192.44	45.01	93.12	2,344.28
740	White, Judy O.	Married	2	Salary	2,084.62			2,084.62	199.00	129.25	30.23	62.54	1,663.60
741	Zickefoose, Jack A.	Married	1	Hourly Wage	10.00	40.00	2.00	430.00	0.00	26.66	6.24	12.90	384.20
	Totals					477.00	2.00	14,104.16	1,427.00	874.47	204.53	423.13	11,175.03
	Tax Basis								Circular E	6.20%	1.45%	3.00%	
	G/L Accounts							57000 / 60000	23400	23400	23400	23600	10300

Figure 6:19

Astor Landscaping					
Employer Costs For Period 3/10/2008 thru 3/23/2008					
Employee	ER Soc Sec FICA	ER Medicare	ER FUTA	ER SUTA	Health Insurance
Dillion, Roy J.	55.80	13.05	7.20	13.50	0.00
Folse, Jan B.	49.60	11.60	6.40	12.00	60.00
Greene, Kellie I.	145.46	34.02	0.00	-	60.00
Hardman, Alan	58.03	13.57	7.49	14.04	0.00
Hayes, Mike E	40.18	9.40	5.18	9.72	0.00
Henderson, Jeff P.	53.57	12.53	6.91	12.96	0.00
Murray, Monica D.	75.12	17.57	7.55	18.17	60.00
Ramez, Victor M.	48.36	11.31	6.24	11.70	0.00
Ruland, Seth N.	192.44	45.01	0.00	-	60.00
White, Judy O.	129.25	30.23	0.00	-	60.00
Zickefoose, Jack A.	26.66	6.24	3.44	6.45	0.00
Totals	**874.47**	**204.53**	**50.41**	**98.54**	**300.00**
Tax Basis	**6.20%**	**1.45%**	**0.8%**	**1.50%**	
G/L Accounts	**23400 / 61000**	**23400 / 61000**	**23500 / 61000**	**23700 / 61000**	**23800 / 60600**

Figure 6:20

STEPS TO CREATE EMPLOYEE PAYCHECKS

1. The accountant has already created recurring employee paychecks so click **Recurring Documents** under Find.

Recurring Documents List

Document Name	Type	Amount	Frequency	Reminder Date
Employer Unemployment Tax Liability (Biweekly)	Journal Entry	$143.78	No Reminder	
Employer Health Insur Liability (Biweekly)	Journal Entry	$300.00	No Reminder	
Paycheck Dillion, Roy J.	Payroll Check	$793.93	No Reminder	
Paycheck Folse, Jan B.	Payroll Check	$642.80	No Reminder	
Paycheck Greene, Kellie I.	Payroll Check	$1,839.29	No Reminder	
Paycheck Hardman, Alan	Payroll Check	$843.81	No Reminder	
Paycheck Hayes, Mike E.	Payroll Check	$328.10	No Reminder	
Paycheck Henderson, Jeff P.	Payroll Check	$804.76	No Reminder	
Paycheck Murray, Monica D.	Payroll Check	$950.50	No Reminder	
Paycheck Ramez, Victor M.	Payroll Check	$587.12	No Reminder	
Paycheck Ruland, Seth N.	Payroll Check	$2,344.28	No Reminder	
Paycheck White, Judy O.	Payroll Check	$1,663.60	No Reminder	
State Payroll Withholding Bill (Monthly)	Vendor Bill	$818.42	No Reminder	
Health Insurance Bill (Monthly)	Vendor Bill	$600.00	No Reminder	
Jackson Advertising Montlhy Ad	Vendor Bill	$175.00	No Reminder	
Federal Payroll Tax Bill (Biweekly)	Vendor Bill	$3,518.12	No Reminder	

Figure 6:21

2. Double click **Paycheck Dillion, Roy J.** to open his recurring paycheck.

   Change the **Date** to "3/24/2008" and the **Amount** to $717.15.

   Enter "Pay period Mar 10 to Mar 23, 2008" in **Memo** and click the **To be printed** option.

   Figure 6:22 illustrates the top portion of the check.

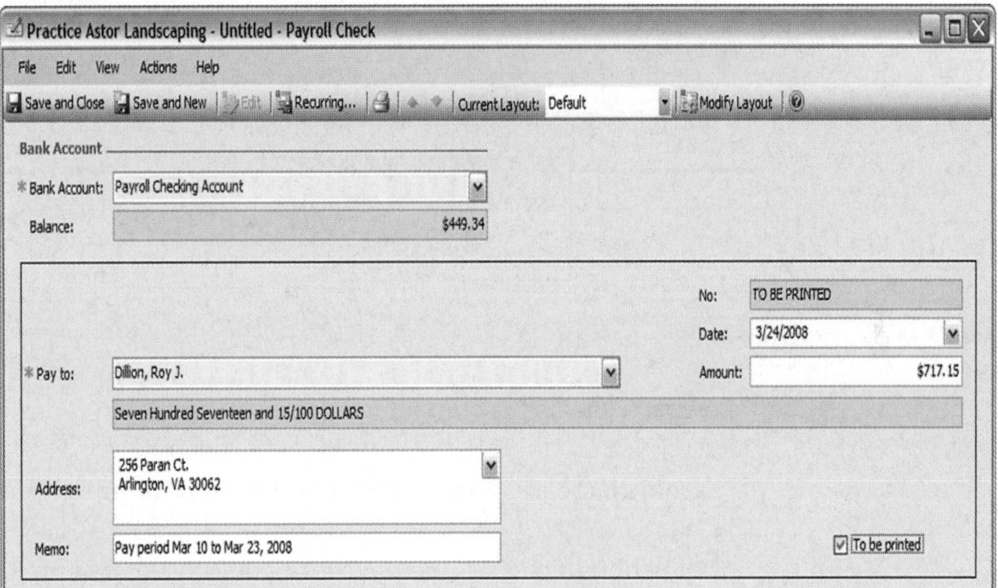

Figure 6:22

3. You will now change information on the bottom. Remember the data are gathered from the Excel spreadsheet. Complete the fields as illustrated in Figure 6:23.

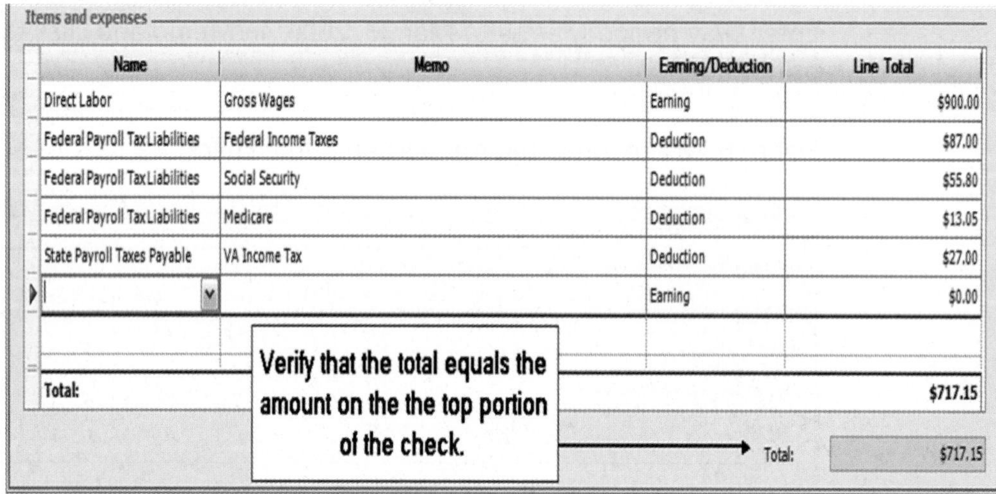

Name	Memo	Earning/Deduction	Line Total
Direct Labor	Gross Wages	Earning	$900.00
Federal Payroll Tax Liabilities	Federal Income Taxes	Deduction	$87.00
Federal Payroll Tax Liabilities	Social Security	Deduction	$55.80
Federal Payroll Tax Liabilities	Medicare	Deduction	$13.05
State Payroll Taxes Payable	VA Income Tax	Deduction	$27.00
		Earning	$0.00
Total:			$717.15

Figure 6:23

The following explains the function of Earning/Deduction types.

Earning increases the paycheck and is used for employee gross pay.

Deduction decreases the paycheck and is used for employee tax withholdings and other deductions.

Total must agree with **Amount** at the top.

4. Click **Save and Close**. You will print the check in a later step. If prompted that the check exceeds the bank balance, mark the option to turn off future messages and click Yes. You will transfer money to this account later in the text. Also, if prompted to link an employee account to an address, click the option to turn off future messages and click Yes.

5. Continue opening recurring paychecks and finish creating paychecks for this pay period by referring to the payroll register illustrated previously and the next series of paycheck illustrations. Some employees will receive the same pay amount as on the recurring check so you need only change the top portion of the check.

   Always remember to change the check date to "3/24/2008" and to confirm the amount. Also change the Memo description to "Pay period Mar 10 to Mar 23, 2008" and mark the **To be printed** option. *(Hint: You can copy and paste the memo description.)*

Paycheck Folse, Jan B.

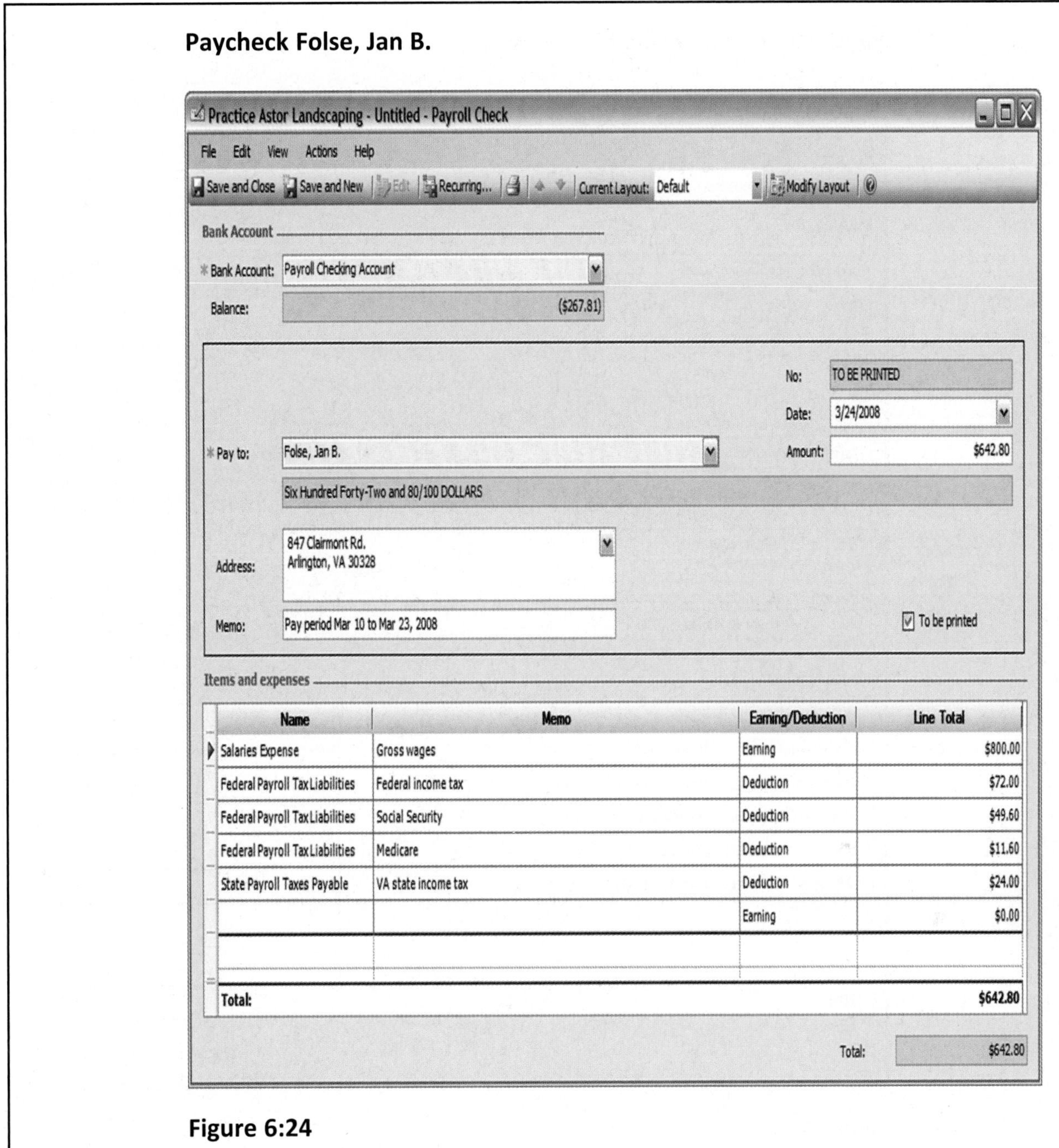

Name	Memo	Earning/Deduction	Line Total
Salaries Expense	Gross wages	Earning	$800.00
Federal Payroll Tax Liabilities	Federal income tax	Deduction	$72.00
Federal Payroll Tax Liabilities	Social Security	Deduction	$49.60
Federal Payroll Tax Liabilities	Medicare	Deduction	$11.60
State Payroll Taxes Payable	VA state income tax	Deduction	$24.00
		Earning	$0.00
Total:			**$642.80**

Figure 6:24

Paycheck Greene, Kellie I.

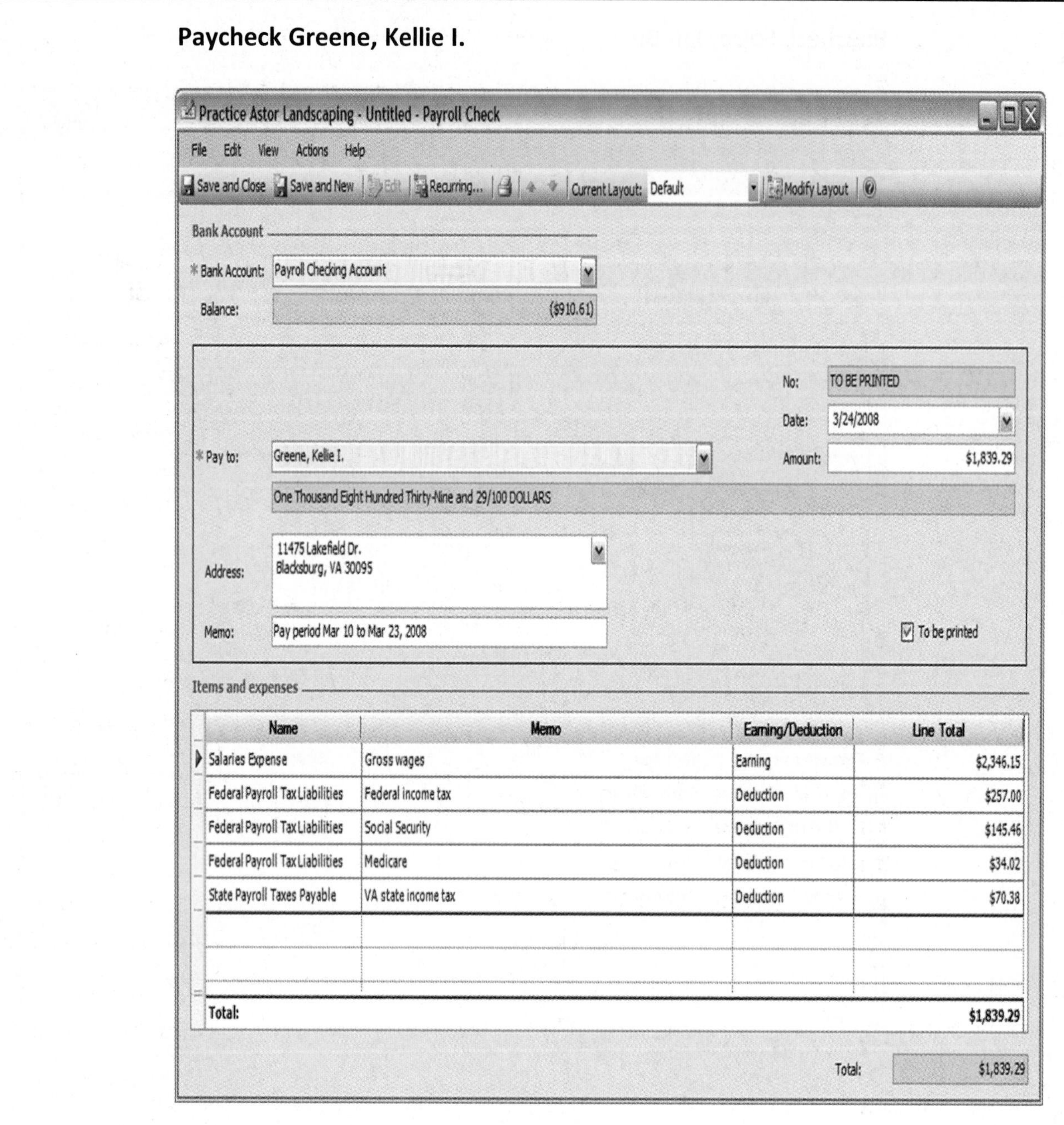

Name	Memo	Earning/Deduction	Line Total
Salaries Expense	Gross wages	Earning	$2,346.15
Federal Payroll Tax Liabilities	Federal income tax	Deduction	$257.00
Federal Payroll Tax Liabilities	Social Security	Deduction	$145.46
Federal Payroll Tax Liabilities	Medicare	Deduction	$34.02
State Payroll Taxes Payable	VA state income tax	Deduction	$70.38
Total:			$1,839.29

Figure 6:25

Paycheck Hardman, Alan

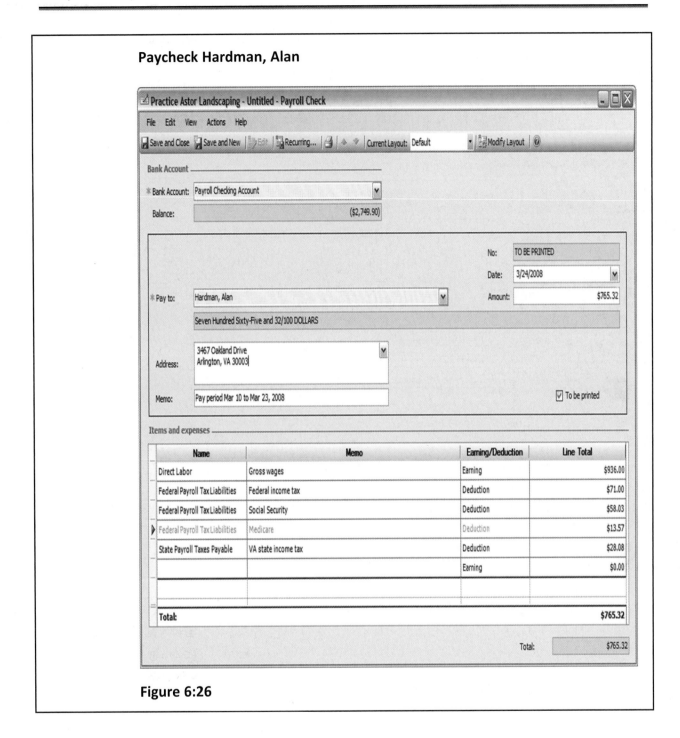

Practice Astor Landscaping - Untitled - Payroll Check

File Edit View Actions Help

Save and Close | Save and New | Edit | Recurring... | Current Layout: Default | Modify Layout

Bank Account

* Bank Account: Payroll Checking Account

Balance: ($2,749.90)

No: TO BE PRINTED

Date: 3/24/2008

* Pay to: Hardman, Alan

Amount: $765.32

Seven Hundred Sixty-Five and 32/100 DOLLARS

Address: 3467 Oakland Drive
Arlington, VA 30003

Memo: Pay period Mar 10 to Mar 23, 2008

☑ To be printed

Items and expenses

Name	Memo	Earning/Deduction	Line Total
Direct Labor	Gross wages	Earning	$936.00
Federal Payroll Tax Liabilities	Federal income tax	Deduction	$71.00
Federal Payroll Tax Liabilities	Social Security	Deduction	$58.03
Federal Payroll Tax Liabilities	Medicare	Deduction	$13.57
State Payroll Taxes Payable	VA state income tax	Deduction	$28.08
		Earning	$0.00
Total:			**$765.32**

Total: $765.32

Figure 6:26

Paycheck Hayes, Mike E.

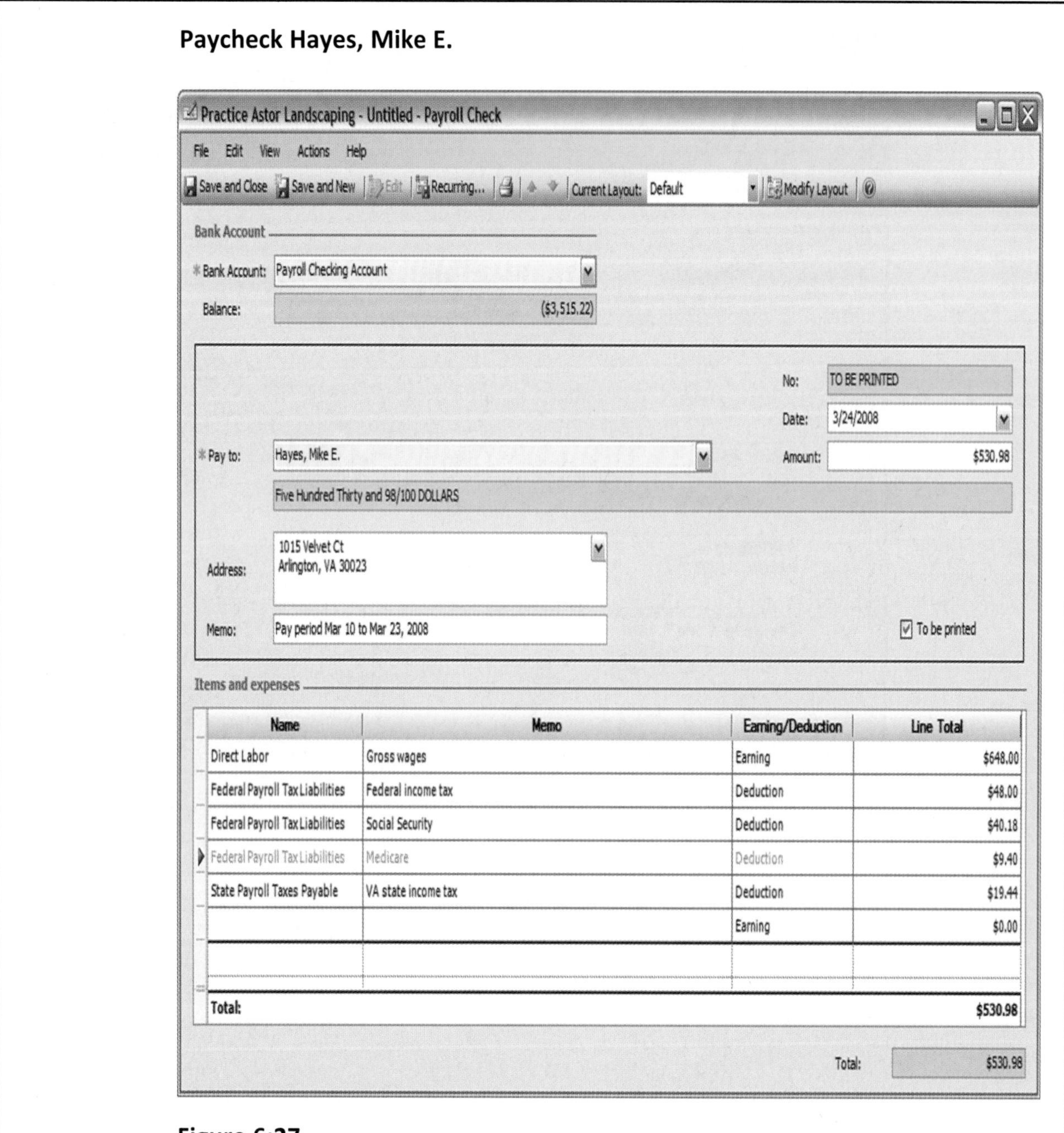

Name	Memo	Earning/Deduction	Line Total
Direct Labor	Gross wages	Earning	$648.00
Federal Payroll Tax Liabilities	Federal income tax	Deduction	$48.00
Federal Payroll Tax Liabilities	Social Security	Deduction	$40.18
Federal Payroll Tax Liabilities	Medicare	Deduction	$9.40
State Payroll Taxes Payable	VA state income tax	Deduction	$19.44
		Earning	$0.00
Total:			**$530.98**

Figure 6:27

Paycheck Henderson, Jeff P.

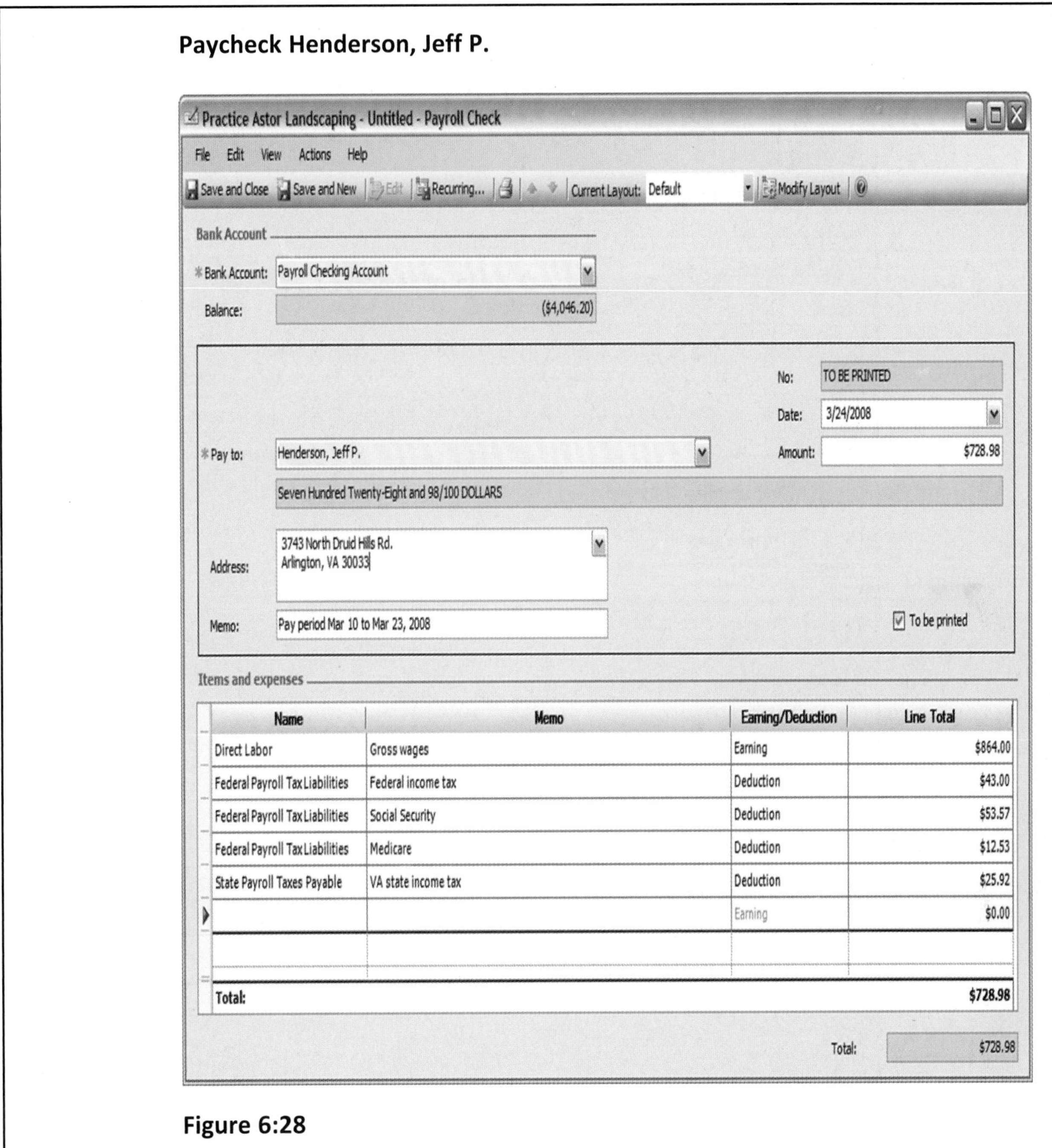

Name	Memo	Earning/Deduction	Line Total
Direct Labor	Gross wages	Earning	$864.00
Federal Payroll Tax Liabilities	Federal income tax	Deduction	$43.00
Federal Payroll Tax Liabilities	Social Security	Deduction	$53.57
Federal Payroll Tax Liabilities	Medicare	Deduction	$12.53
State Payroll Taxes Payable	VA state income tax	Deduction	$25.92
		Earning	$0.00
Total:			**$728.98**

Figure 6:28

Paycheck Murray, Monica D.

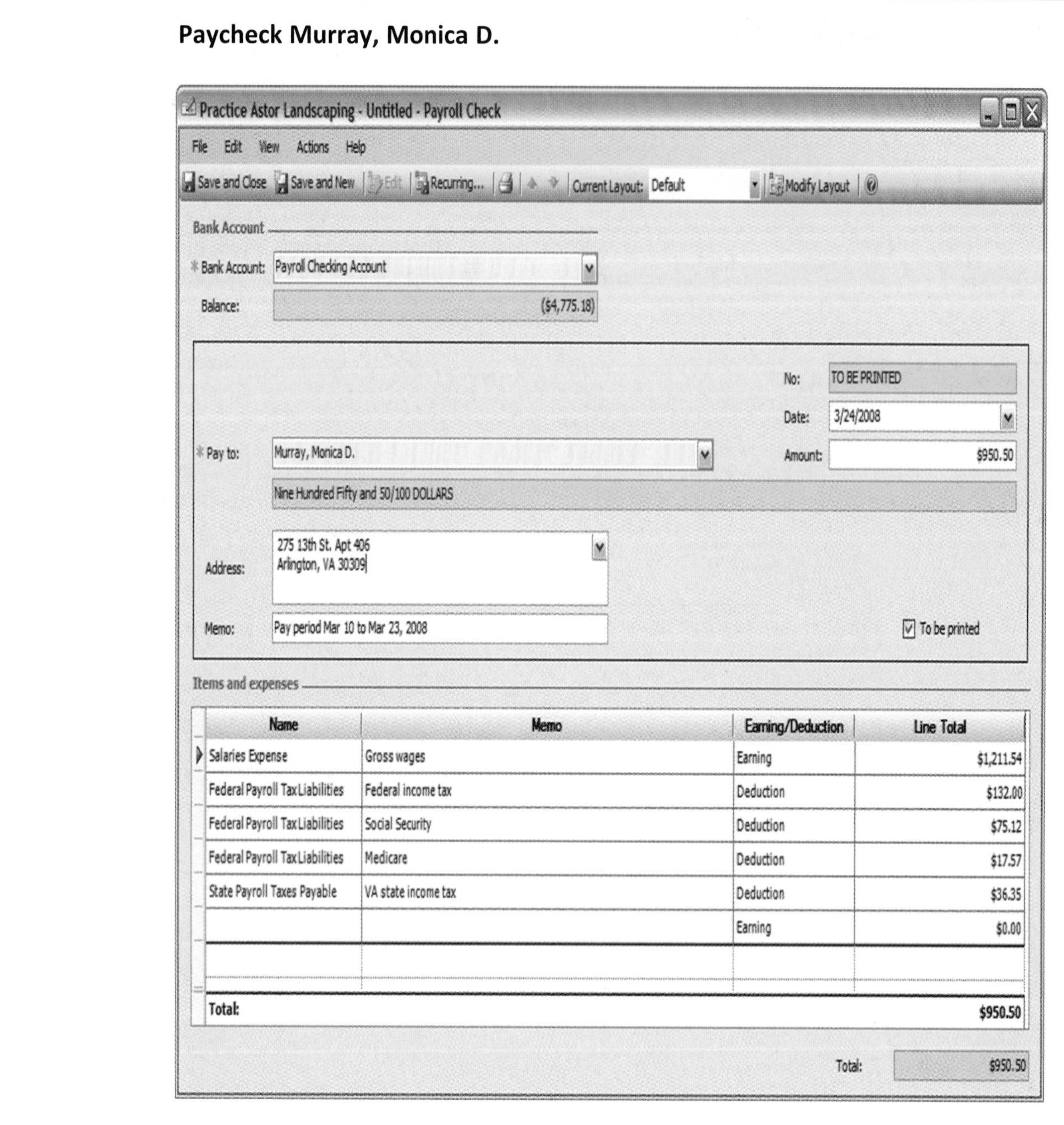

Figure 6:29

Paycheck Ramez, Victor M.

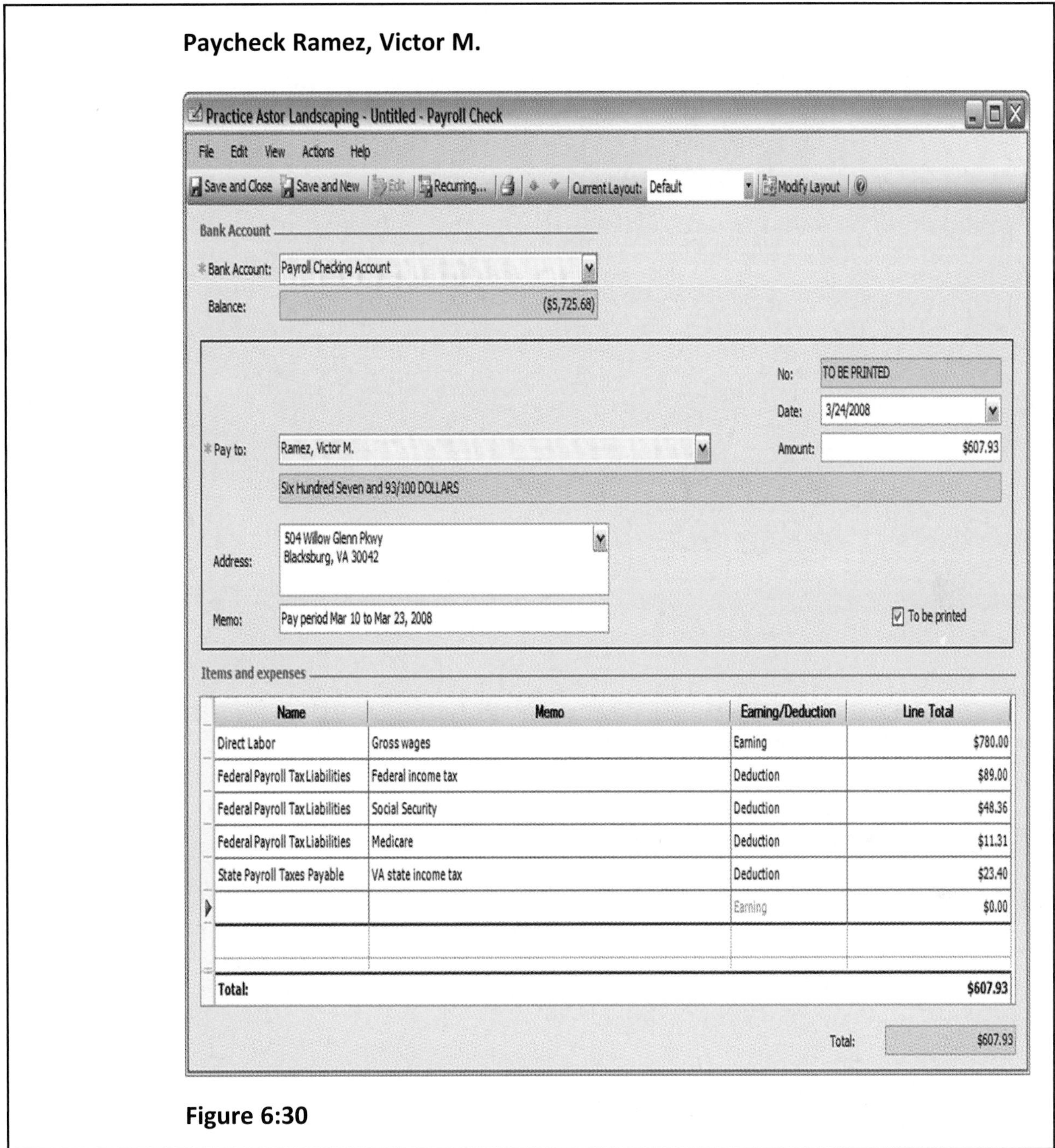

Name	Memo	Earning/Deduction	Line Total
Direct Labor	Gross wages	Earning	$780.00
Federal Payroll Tax Liabilities	Federal income tax	Deduction	$89.00
Federal Payroll Tax Liabilities	Social Security	Deduction	$48.36
Federal Payroll Tax Liabilities	Medicare	Deduction	$11.31
State Payroll Taxes Payable	VA state income tax	Deduction	$23.40
		Earning	$0.00
Total:			**$607.93**

Figure 6:30

Paycheck Ruland, Seth N.

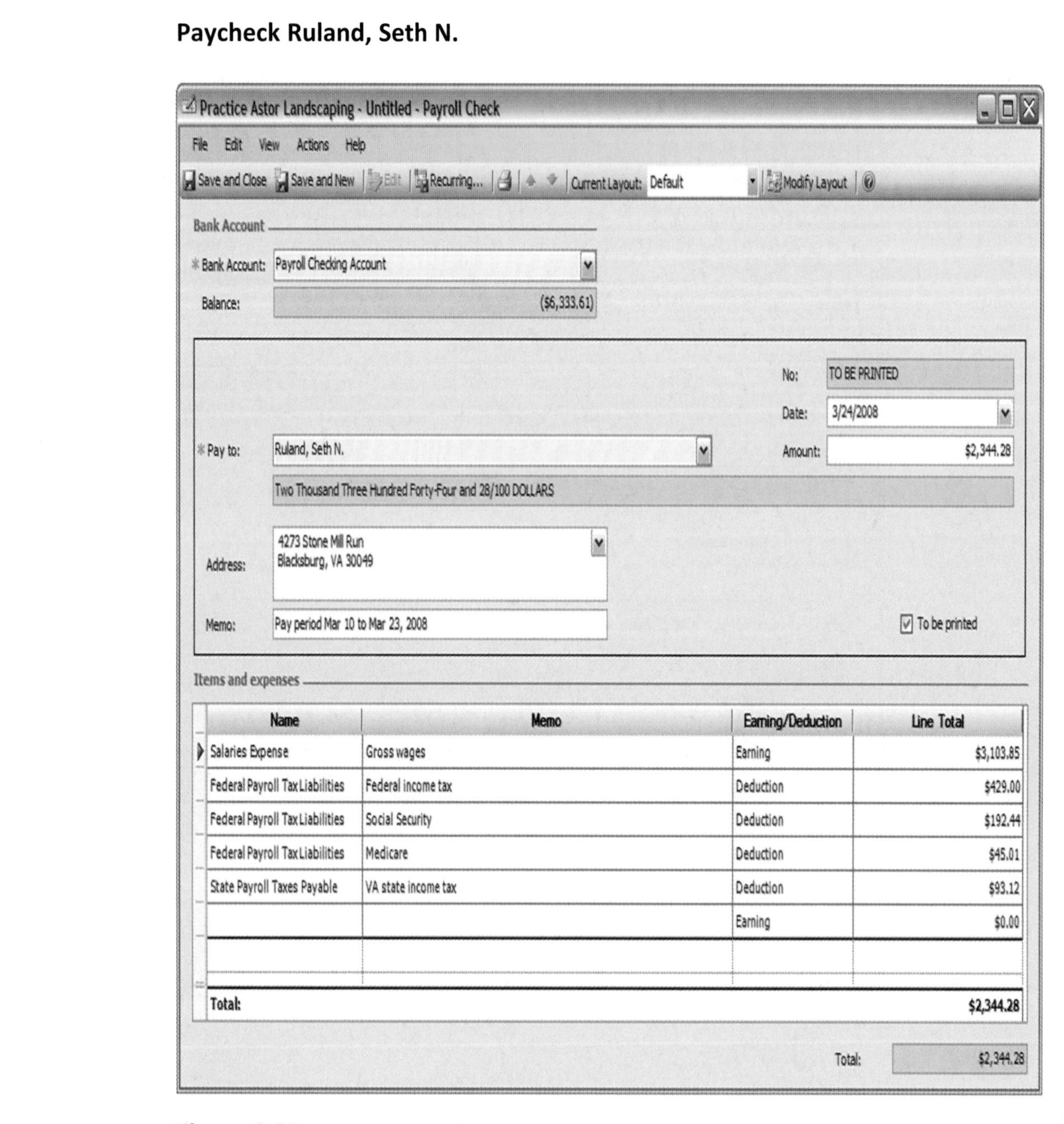

Figure 6:31

Paycheck White, Judy O.

Practice Astor Landscaping - Untitled - Payroll Check

File Edit View Actions Help

Save and Close | Save and New | Edit | Recurring... | Current Layout: Default | Modify Layout

Bank Account

*Bank Account: Payroll Checking Account

Balance: ($8,677.89)

No: TO BE PRINTED

Date: 3/24/2008

*Pay to: White, Judy O.

Amount: $1,663.60

One Thousand Six Hundred Sixty-Three and 60/100 DOLLARS

Address: 1264 Oak Lane
Blacksburg, VA 30045

Memo: Pay period Mar 10 to Mar 23, 2008

☑ To be printed

Items and expenses

Name	Memo	Earning/Deduction	Line Total
Salaries Expense	Gross wages	Earning	$2,084.62
Federal Payroll Tax Liabilities	Federal income tax	Deduction	$199.00
Federal Payroll Tax Liabilities	Social Security	Deduction	$129.25
Federal Payroll Tax Liabilities	Medicare	Deduction	$30.23
State Payroll Taxes Payable	VA state income tax	Deduction	$62.54
		Earning	$0.00
Total:			**$1,663.60**

Total: $1,663.60

Figure 6:32

6. You will now create a paycheck for the new employee. Click **Manual Payroll Check** under **Start a Task** and enter the following information. Be sure to select the Payroll Checking Account. *(Note: Gross wages are intentionally posted to Salaries Expense so that we can illustrate correcting the error in Chapter 7.)*

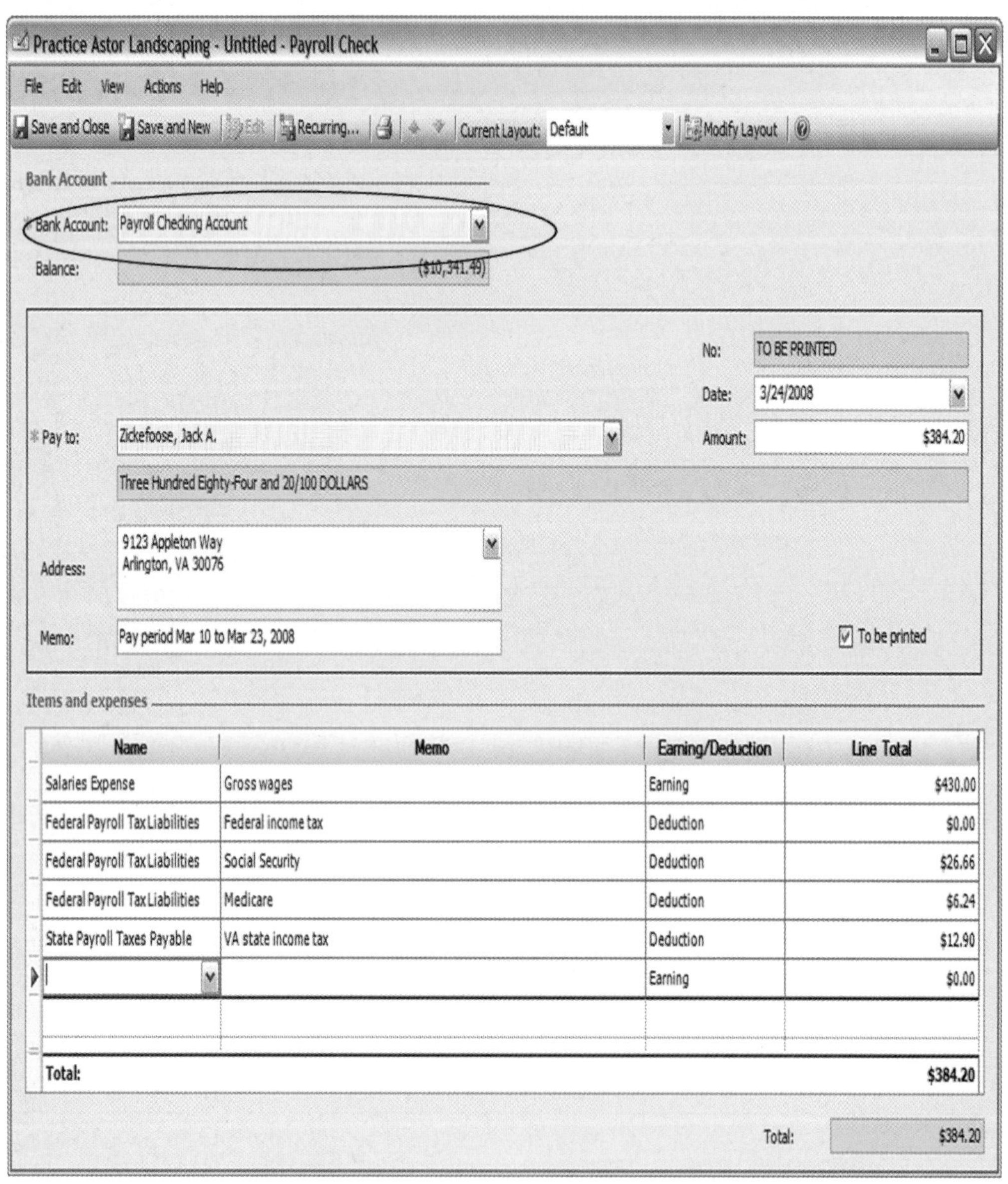

Figure 6:33

7. Click **Recurring** on the toolbar, causing OAP to save the transaction and prompt to store the address. Click **Yes**.

   Enter the recurring transaction name as illustrated in Figure 6:34 and click **OK**.

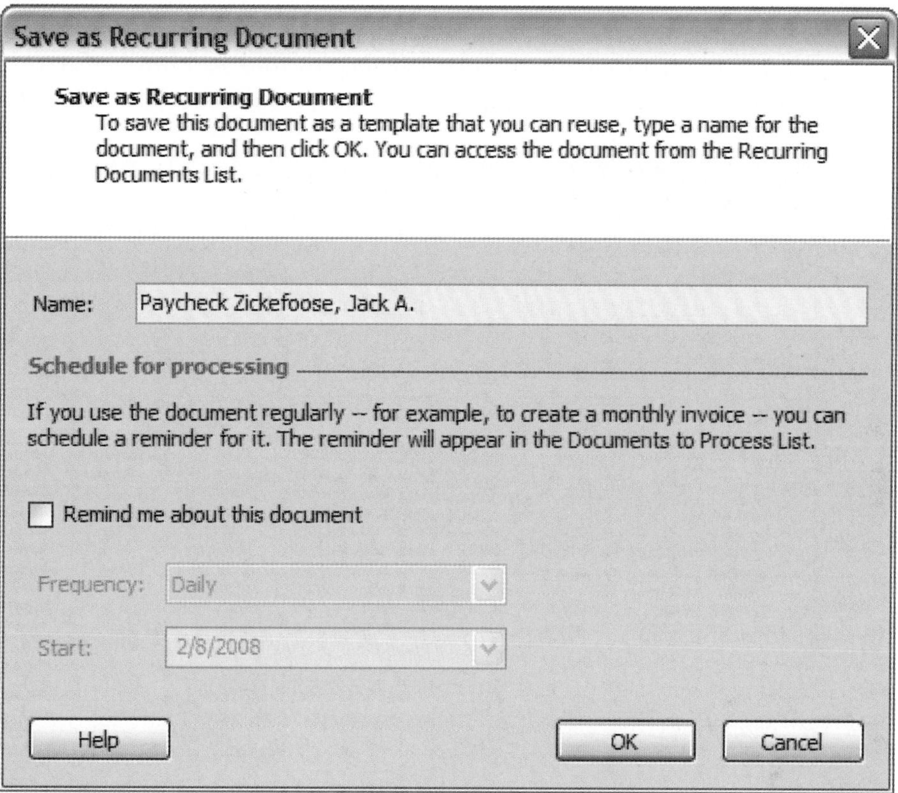

Figure 6:34

Click **Save and Close** to post the paycheck transaction.

8. You will next print the paychecks, but first verify your entries. Select ***Reports>>Employees and Payroll>>Employee Payments*** on the main menu. Filter the report for "3/24/2008" and remove the Issue date, No., Status detail, Memo, and Reference number columns (Figure 6:35).

   You can export the report to Excel to total the amount and compare to the Payroll Register illustrated previously. Should you find an error on a check, double click to reopen it, make changes, and resave the transaction.

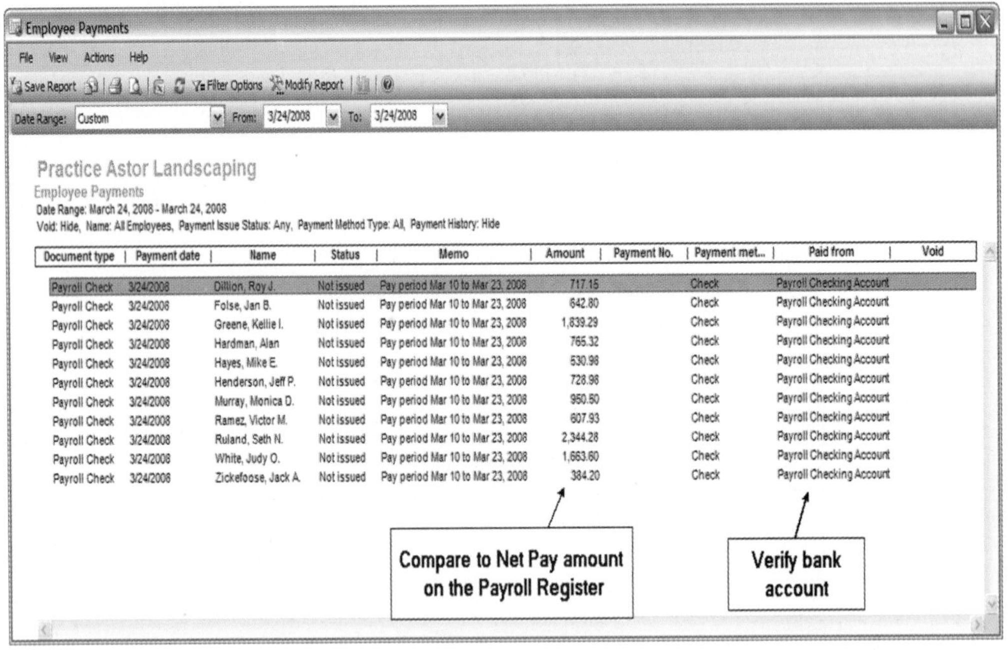

Practice Astor Landscaping
Employee Payments
Date Range: March 24, 2008 - March 24, 2008
Void: Hide, Name: All Employees, Payment Issue Status: Any, Payment Method Type: All, Payment History: Hide

Document type	Payment date	Name	Status	Memo	Amount	Payment No.	Payment met...	Paid from	Void
Payroll Check	3/24/2008	Dillion, Roy J.	Not issued	Pay period Mar 10 to Mar 23, 2008	717.15		Check	Payroll Checking Account	
Payroll Check	3/24/2008	Folse, Jan B.	Not issued	Pay period Mar 10 to Mar 23, 2008	642.80		Check	Payroll Checking Account	
Payroll Check	3/24/2008	Greene, Kellie I.	Not issued	Pay period Mar 10 to Mar 23, 2008	1,839.29		Check	Payroll Checking Account	
Payroll Check	3/24/2008	Hardman, Alan	Not issued	Pay period Mar 10 to Mar 23, 2008	765.32		Check	Payroll Checking Account	
Payroll Check	3/24/2008	Hayes, Mike E.	Not issued	Pay period Mar 10 to Mar 23, 2008	530.98		Check	Payroll Checking Account	
Payroll Check	3/24/2008	Henderson, Jeff P.	Not issued	Pay period Mar 10 to Mar 23, 2008	728.98		Check	Payroll Checking Account	
Payroll Check	3/24/2008	Murray, Monica D.	Not issued	Pay period Mar 10 to Mar 23, 2008	950.50		Check	Payroll Checking Account	
Payroll Check	3/24/2008	Ramez, Victor M.	Not issued	Pay period Mar 10 to Mar 23, 2008	607.93		Check	Payroll Checking Account	
Payroll Check	3/24/2008	Ruland, Seth N.	Not issued	Pay period Mar 10 to Mar 23, 2008	2,344.28		Check	Payroll Checking Account	
Payroll Check	3/24/2008	White, Judy O.	Not issued	Pay period Mar 10 to Mar 23, 2008	1,663.60		Check	Payroll Checking Account	
Payroll Check	3/24/2008	Zickefoose, Jack A.	Not issued	Pay period Mar 10 to Mar 23, 2008	384.20		Check	Payroll Checking Account	

Figure 6:35

9. Close the report and print the paychecks. Select ***Employees>>Manual Payroll>>Print Payroll Checks*** on the main menu.

   Complete the window as illustrated in Figure 10:33. The total amount to pay should be $11,175.03, which agrees to the Net Pay total on the Payroll Register.

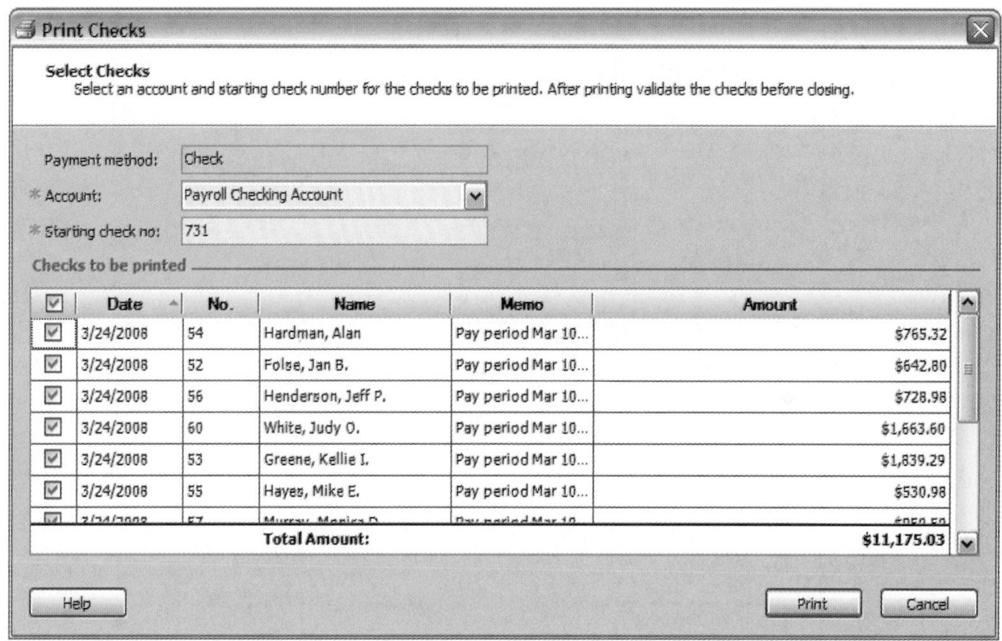

Figure 6:36

10. Click **Print**, select a printer, and click **OK**.

11. Click **Close** to exit the Print Checks window. Click **OK** when OAP displays payment information.

12. The last step is posting employer payroll tax liabilities. Astor enters a bill for federal income tax withholdings and Social Security and Medicare taxes each pay date. The accountant has created a recurring vendor bill for this payment.

    Click **Recurring Documents** and open the **Federal Payroll Tax Bill (Biweekly)** recurring document. Enter the information illustrated in Figure 6:37. Again, this information comes from the Excel spreadsheets previously illustrated.

    Click **Save and Close** to post the bill.

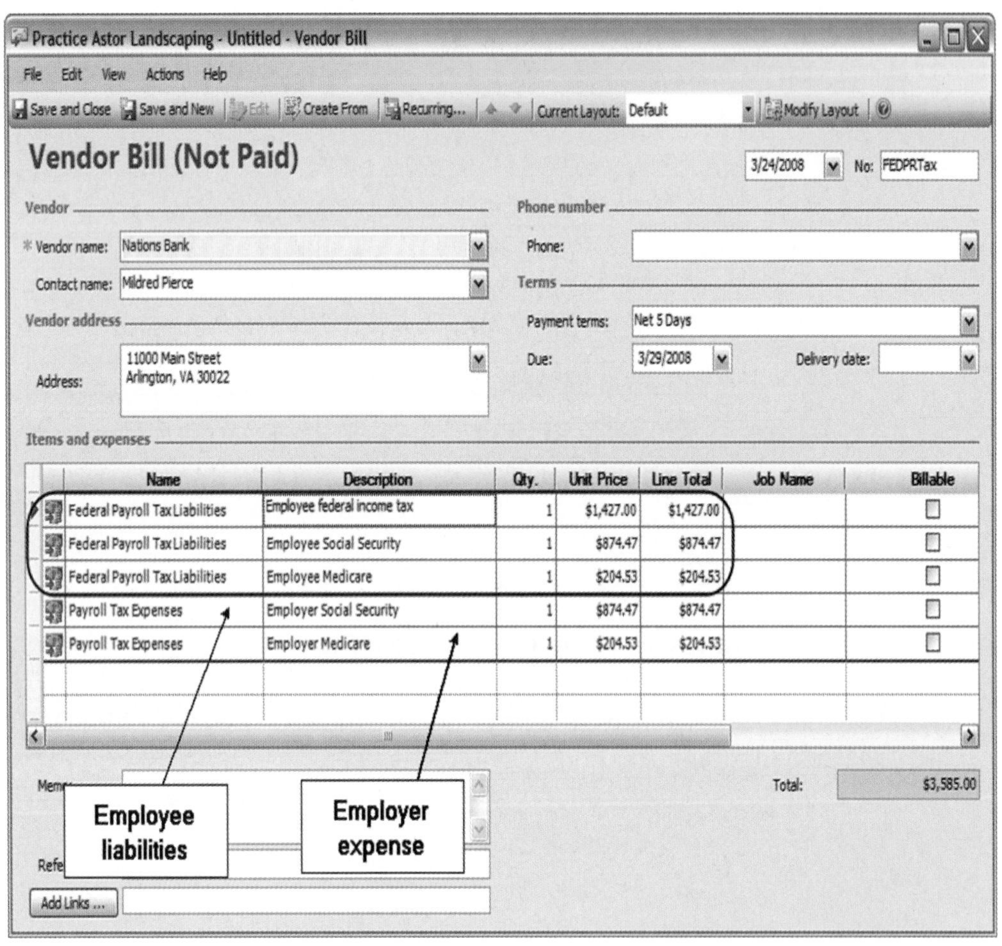

Figure 6:37

13. Next post journal entries for health insurance and unemployment tax liabilities. First, open the **Employer Health Insurance Liability (Biweekly)** recurring document and complete as illustrated (Figure 6:38). Click **Save and Close**.

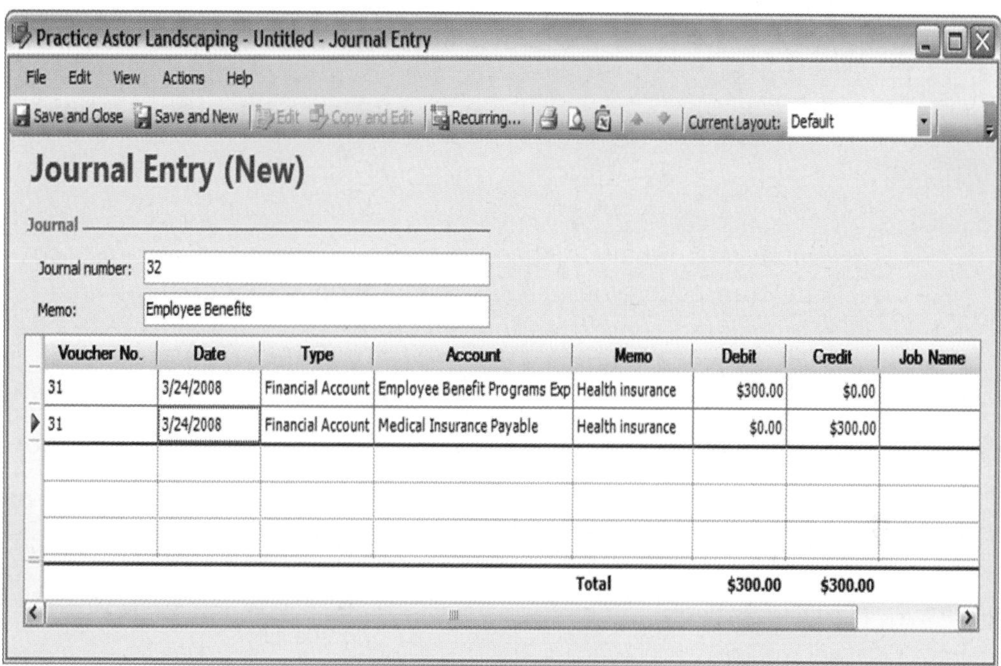

Figure 6:38

Open the **Employer Unemployment Tax Liability (Biweekly)** recurring document and complete as illustrated (Figure 6:39). Click **Save and Close**.

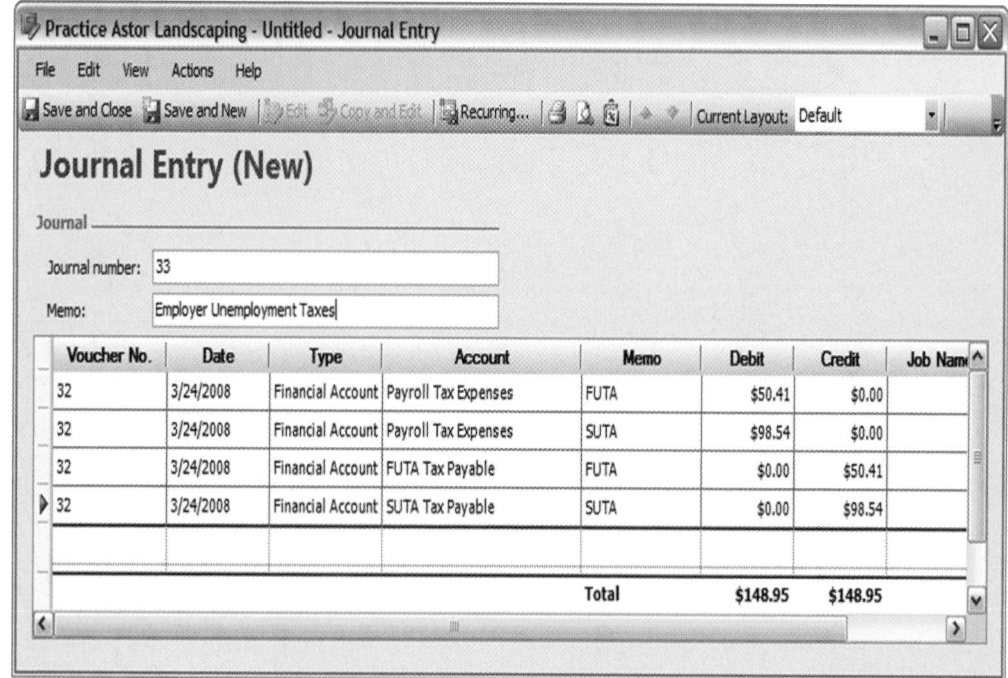

Figure 6:39

Behind the Keys of a Posted Paycheck

You will now trace the entries made when printing paychecks by following the next steps.

Steps to Tracing Paycheck Entries

1. You will find that OAP has limited payroll reporting. You can trace entries on the Transaction Journal by selecting ***Reports>>Company and Financial>>Transaction Journal*** on the main menu. Filter the report for 3/24/2008 and the **Transaction Type** of Cash Employee Bill.

   Scroll down the report illustrated in Figure 6:40 to view additional paychecks and then close it.

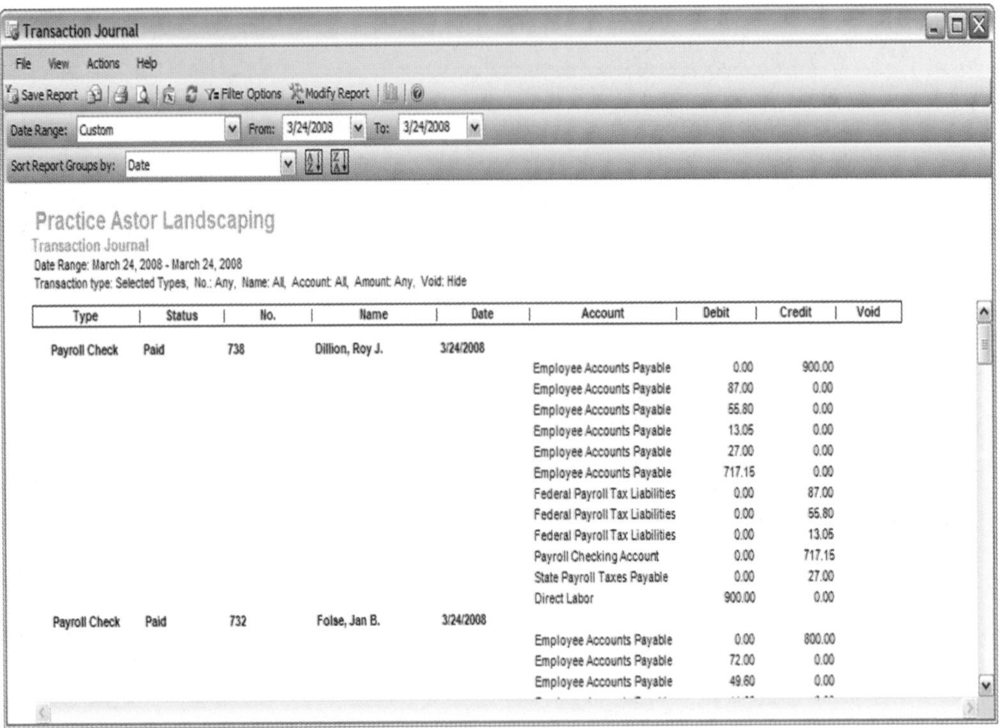

Figure 6:40

2. You can also print the ***Reports>>Employees and Payroll>>Employee Payments*** report printed earlier. Filter the report for "3/24/2008" and notice that this time the Status is Issued and the check number is listed under the Payment No column. (See Figure 6:41.) Close the report.

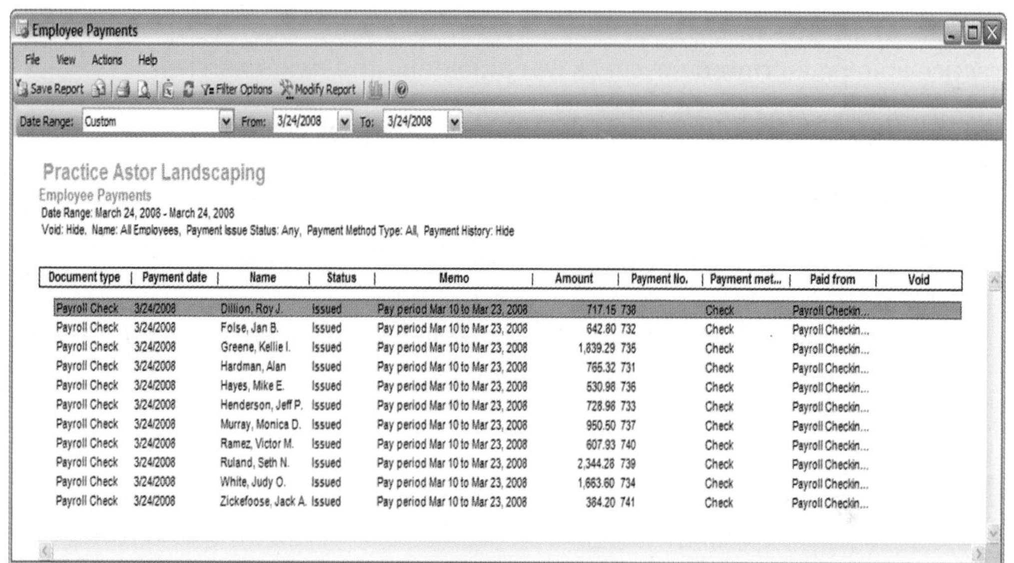

Employee Payments

File View Actions Help

Save Report Filter Options Modify Report

Date Range: Custom From: 3/24/2008 To: 3/24/2008

Practice Astor Landscaping

Employee Payments

Date Range: March 24, 2008 - March 24, 2008

Void: Hide, Name: All Employees, Payment Issue Status: Any, Payment Method Type: All, Payment History: Hide

Document type	Payment date	Name	Status	Memo	Amount	Payment No.	Payment met...	Paid from	Void
Payroll Check	3/24/2008	Dillion, Roy J.	Issued	Pay period Mar 10 to Mar 23, 2008	717.15	738	Check	Payroll Checkin...	
Payroll Check	3/24/2008	Folse, Jan B.	Issued	Pay period Mar 10 to Mar 23, 2008	642.80	732	Check	Payroll Checkin...	
Payroll Check	3/24/2008	Greene, Kellie I.	Issued	Pay period Mar 10 to Mar 23, 2008	1,839.29	735	Check	Payroll Checkin...	
Payroll Check	3/24/2008	Hardman, Alan	Issued	Pay period Mar 10 to Mar 23, 2008	765.32	731	Check	Payroll Checkin...	
Payroll Check	3/24/2008	Hayes, Mike E.	Issued	Pay period Mar 10 to Mar 23, 2008	530.98	736	Check	Payroll Checkin...	
Payroll Check	3/24/2008	Henderson, Jeff P.	Issued	Pay period Mar 10 to Mar 23, 2008	728.98	733	Check	Payroll Checkin...	
Payroll Check	3/24/2008	Murray, Monica D.	Issued	Pay period Mar 10 to Mar 23, 2008	950.50	737	Check	Payroll Checkin...	
Payroll Check	3/24/2008	Ramez, Victor M.	Issued	Pay period Mar 10 to Mar 23, 2008	607.93	740	Check	Payroll Checkin...	
Payroll Check	3/24/2008	Ruland, Seth N.	Issued	Pay period Mar 10 to Mar 23, 2008	2,344.28	739	Check	Payroll Checkin...	
Payroll Check	3/24/2008	White, Judy O.	Issued	Pay period Mar 10 to Mar 23, 2008	1,663.60	734	Check	Payroll Checkin...	
Payroll Check	3/24/2008	Zickefoose, Jack A.	Issued	Pay period Mar 10 to Mar 23, 2008	384.20	741	Check	Payroll Checkin...	

Figure 6:41

3. You can also trace entries to the general ledger by printing the **Transaction Detail by Account** report (not illustrated).

VOIDING EMPLOYEE PAYCHECKS

When you were entering paycheck data we explained correcting a paycheck before printing it. What happens when you find an error after printing? The only solution is to void the paycheck and reissue it.

Practice voiding a printed paycheck by completing the next exercise.

STEPS TO VOIDING A PRINTED PAYCHECK

1. Click the **Employee Payments** link under Find and toggle the **Current View** to **Issued**. Click the Payment Date column to sort the list by descending paycheck date.

   Scroll to the top and highlight check number 735 issued to Kellie Greene on March 24. (See Figure 6:42.) Right click the transaction and select **Void**. Click **Yes** to confirm.

Figure 6:42

2. Now reissue her paycheck. Click **Recurring Documents** under Find. Reopen Kellie's recurring paycheck and enter the following information.

Practice Astor Landscaping - Untitled - Payroll Check

File Edit View Actions Help

Save and Close | Save and New | Edit | Recurring... | Current Layout: Default | Modify Layout

Bank Account

Bank Account: Payroll Checking Account

Balance: ($8,886.40)

No: TO BE PRINTED

Date: 3/24/2008

Pay to: Greene, Kellie I.

Amount: $1,839.29

One Thousand Eight Hundred Thirty-Nine and 29/100 DOLLARS

Address: 11475 Lakefield Dr.
Blacksburg, VA 30095

Memo: Pay period Mar 10 to Mar 23, 2008

To be printed

Items and expenses

Name	Memo	Earning/Deduction	Line Total
Salaries Expense	Gross wages	Earning	$2,346.15
Federal Payroll Tax Liabilities	Federal income tax	Deduction	$257.00
Federal Payroll Tax Liabilities	Social Security	Deduction	$145.46
Federal Payroll Tax Liabilities	Medicare	Deduction	$34.02
State Payroll Taxes Payable	VA state income tax	Deduction	$70.38
Total:			**$1,839.29**

Total: $1,839.29

Figure 6:43

3. Click the **Printer** icon on the toolbar and click **OK** to save the entry.

   Enter **Starting check no** "742", click **Print**, select a printer and click **OK**.

   Click **Close** to exit the Print Checks window.

4. Click **Save and Close** on Roy's paycheck.

Paying Employer and Employee Payroll Taxes

In this topic you remit employee tax withholdings and employer payroll tax liabilities. Payroll taxes are due on the dates set by the taxing agency. Normally federal tax, FICA, and Medicare taxes are due within three to five days after paying employees. State income taxes for the current month are normally due the first of the following month. Health insurance premiums are also due the first of every month. Federal and state unemployment taxes are due at the end of every quarter.

You will now create bills for these liabilities. Before creating these bills, you should prepare a trial balance report to view balances in the liability accounts. Select ***Reports>>Company and Financial>>Trial Balance*** on the main menu. Filter the report for 3/31/2008 and scroll down to the accounts illustrated in Figure 6:44.

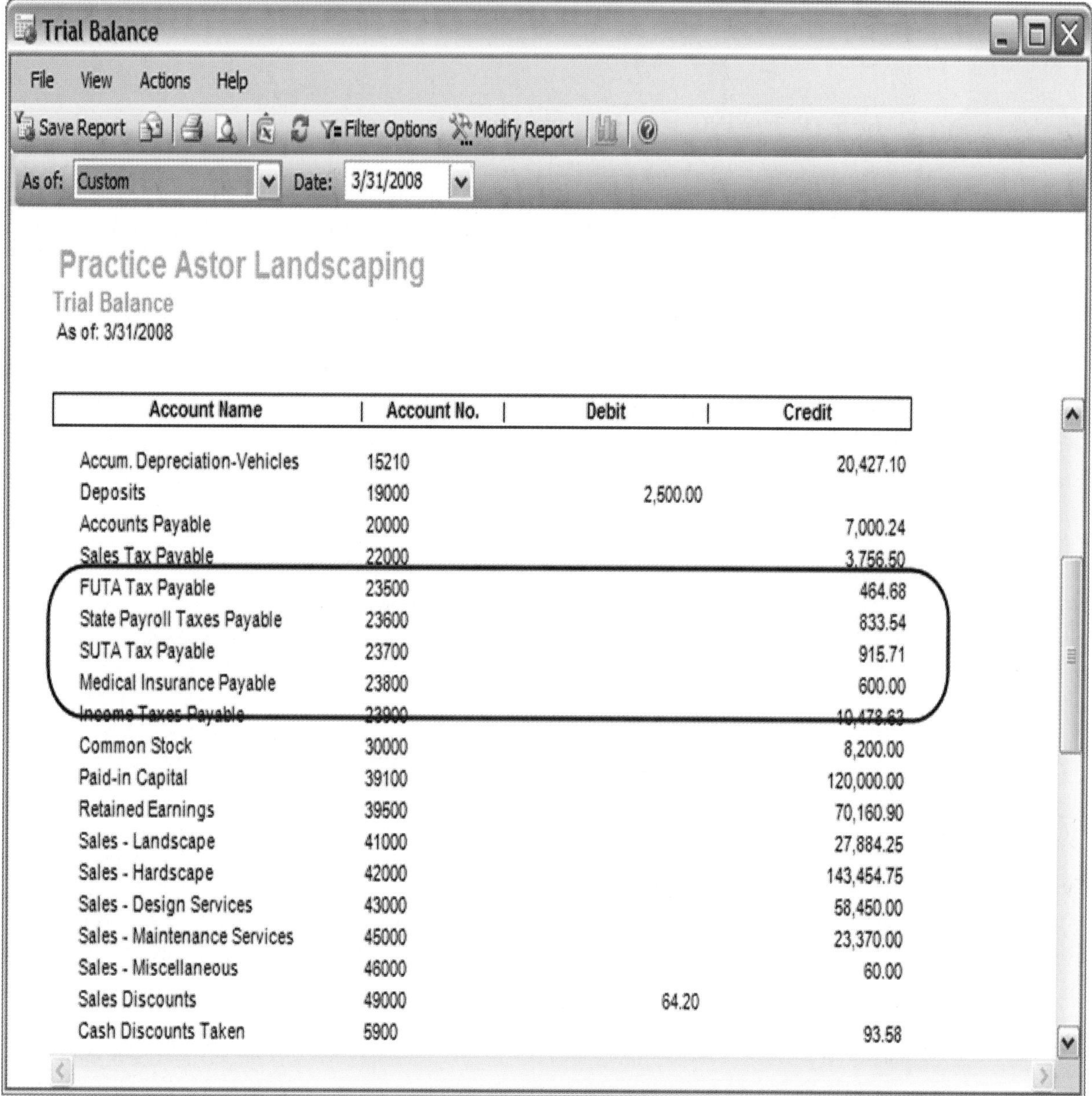

Practice Astor Landscaping
Trial Balance
As of: 3/31/2008

Account Name	Account No.	Debit	Credit
Accum. Depreciation-Vehicles	15210		20,427.10
Deposits	19000	2,500.00	
Accounts Payable	20000		7,000.24
Sales Tax Payable	22000		3,756.50
FUTA Tax Payable	23500		464.68
State Payroll Taxes Payable	23600		833.54
SUTA Tax Payable	23700		915.71
Medical Insurance Payable	23800		600.00
Income Taxes Payable	23900		10,478.63
Common Stock	30000		8,200.00
Paid-in Capital	39100		120,000.00
Retained Earnings	39500		70,160.90
Sales - Landscape	41000		27,884.25
Sales - Hardscape	42000		143,454.75
Sales - Design Services	43000		58,450.00
Sales - Maintenance Services	45000		23,370.00
Sales - Miscellaneous	46000		60.00
Sales Discounts	49000	64.20	
Cash Discounts Taken	5900		93.58

Figure 6:44

In the next exercise you create bills for employer health insurance and unemployment liabilities. In the *You Try* that follows you create a bill paying state income taxes.

Steps to Paying Payroll Taxes

1. You will first pay the monthly health insurance bill. Click **Recurring Documents** under Find and open the **Health Insurance Bill (Monthly)** recurring document. Complete the bill using the following information and click **Save and Close**.

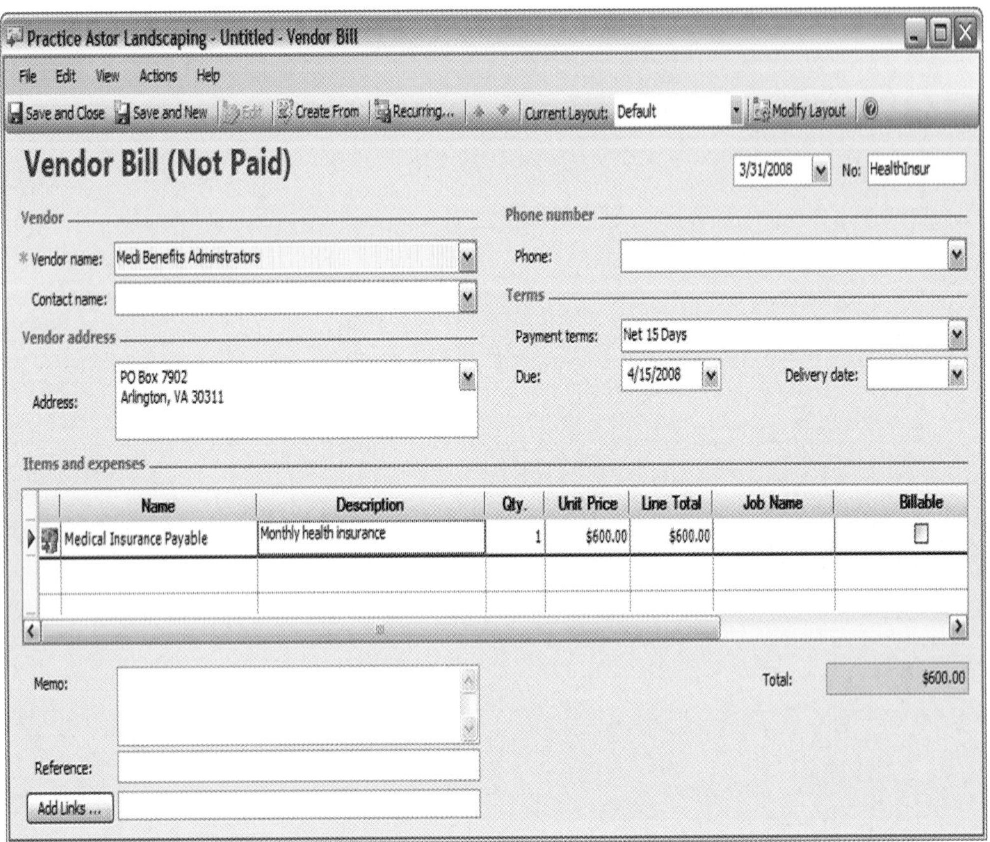

Figure 6:45

2. Now pay the unemployment taxes. The accountant has not created recurring documents for these bills so select ***Vendors>>Enter Bills*** on the main menu and enter the information illustrated in Figure 6:46.

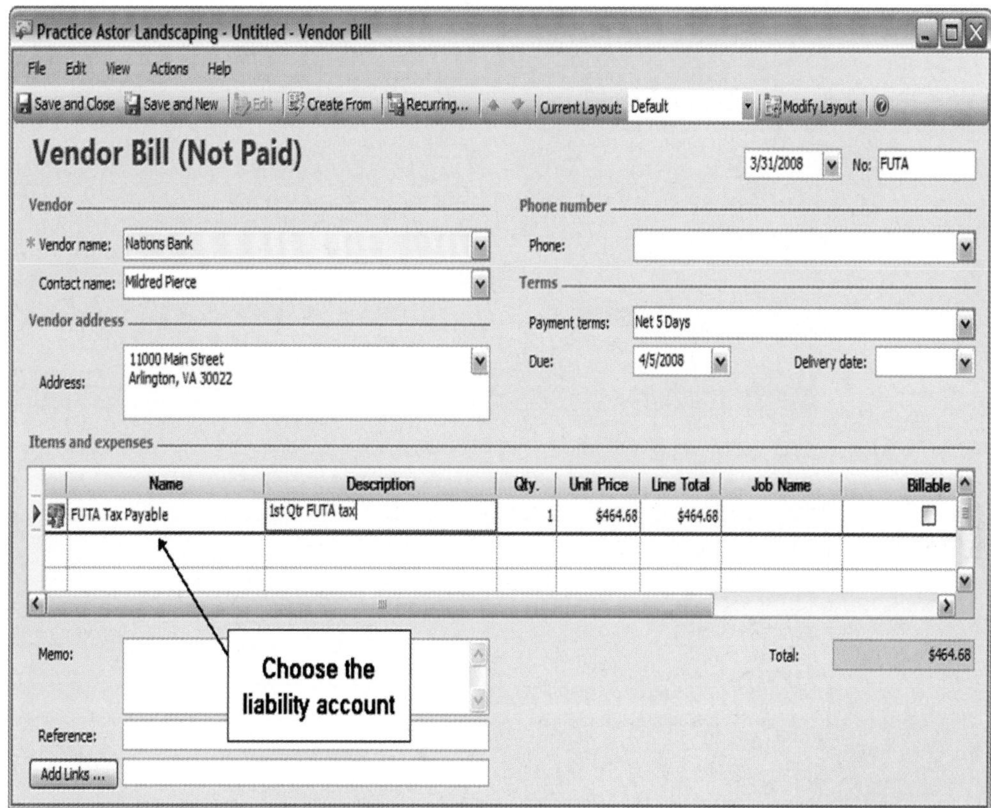

Figure 6:46

3. Click **Recurring** and name the document as shown in Figure 6:47. Click **OK.**

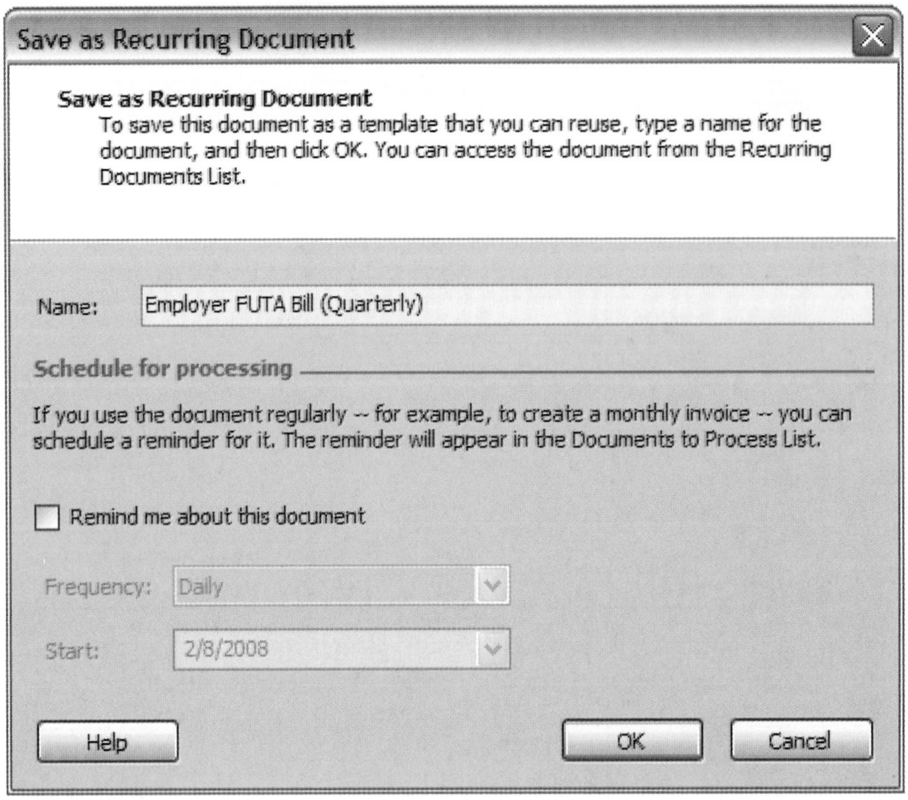

Save as Recurring Document

Save as Recurring Document
To save this document as a template that you can reuse, type a name for the document, and then click OK. You can access the document from the Recurring Documents List.

Name: Employer FUTA Bill (Quarterly)

Schedule for processing

If you use the document regularly -- for example, to create a monthly invoice -- you can schedule a reminder for it. The reminder will appear in the Documents to Process List.

☐ Remind me about this document

Frequency: Daily

Start: 2/8/2008

Help | OK | Cancel

Figure 6:47

4. Click **Save and New** on the Vendor Bill window and create the bill for SUTA taxes as illustrated in Figure 6:48.

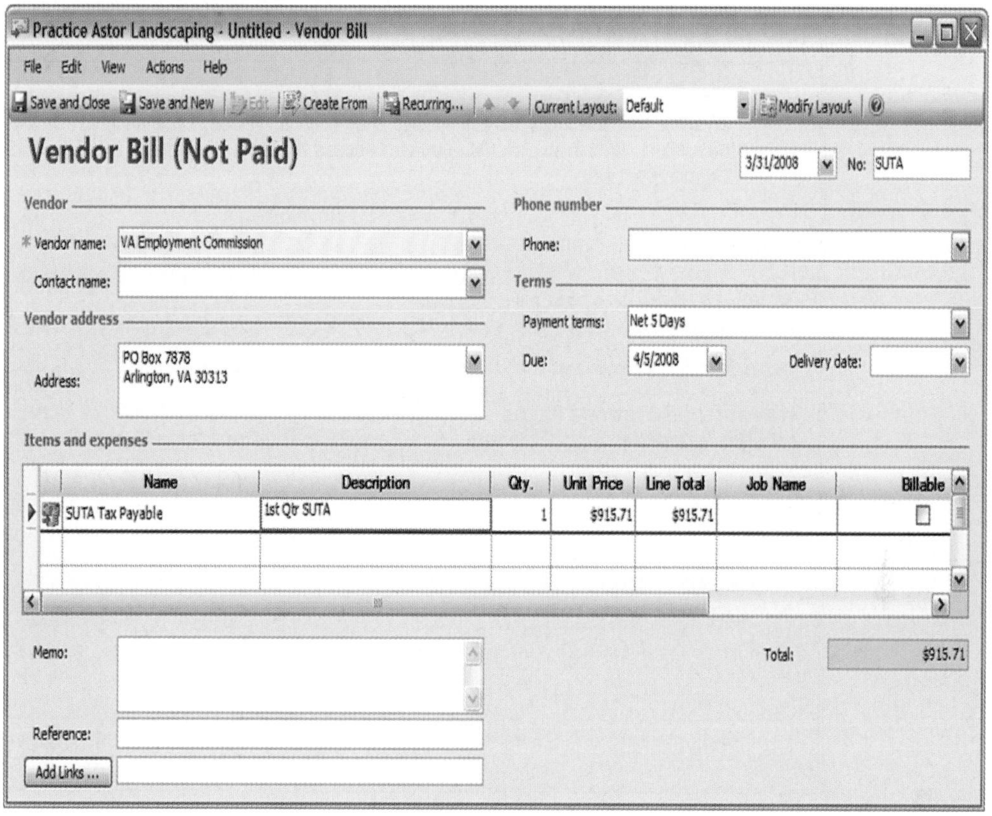

Figure 6:48

5. Click **Recurring** and save the document as illustrated in Figure 6:49. Click **OK** and then click **Save and Close** on the Vendor Bill window.

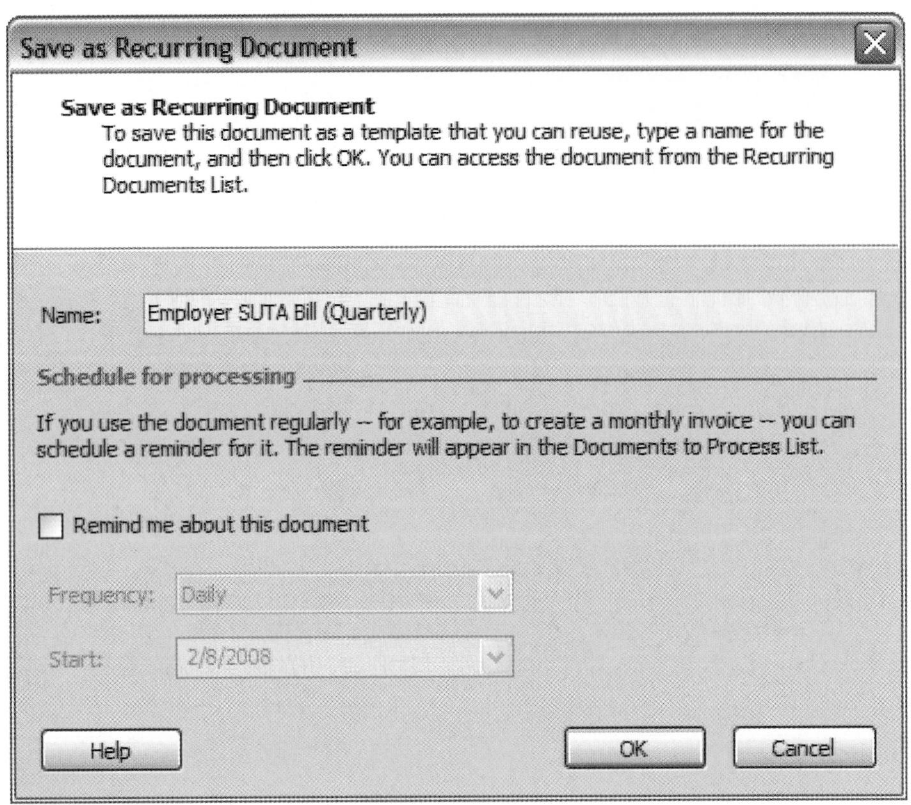

Figure 6:49

6. Now cut checks to the vendors. Click **Pay Bills** on the Vendors Home page. Enter 3/31/2008 as the payment date and select the four bills illustrated in Figure 6:50.

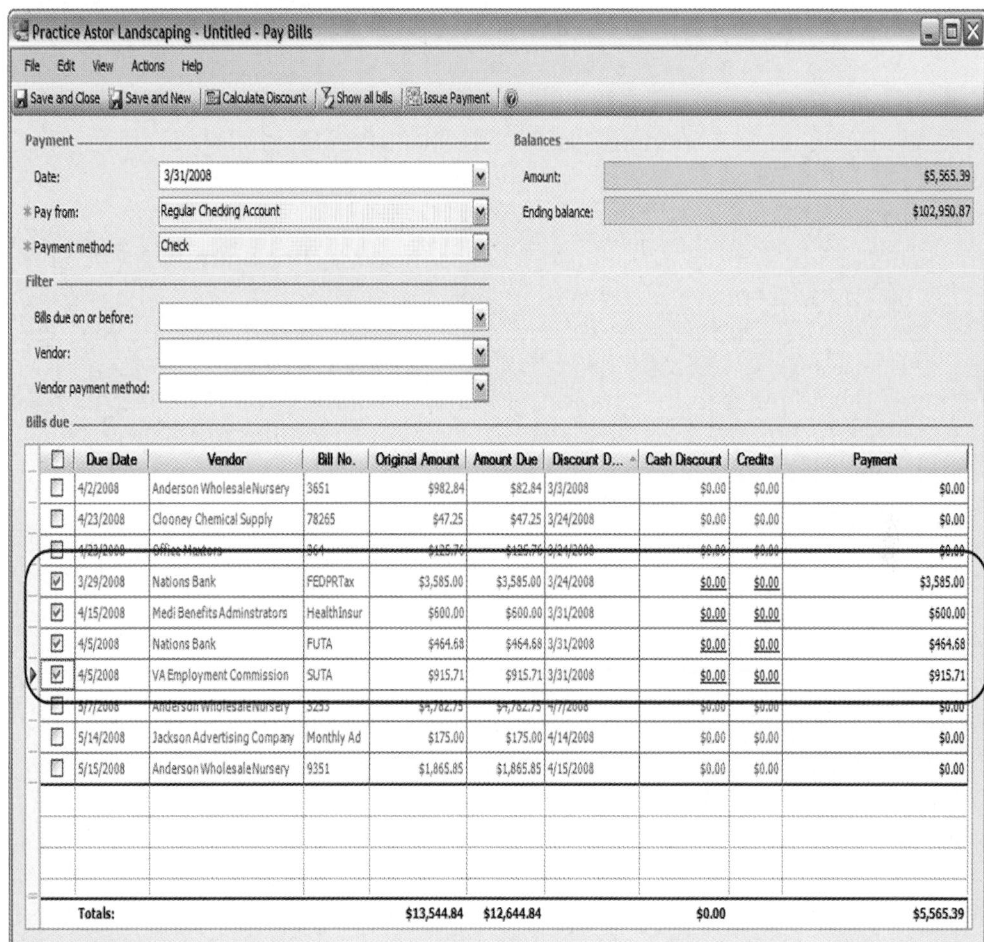

Figure 6:50

7. Click **Issue Payment** and complete the steps that process the checks. The first check number is 448.

Now complete the next exercise where you pay state tax liabilities for March.

CREATE CHECKS FOR PAYROLL TAXES

In this exercise you create a bill to pay March state income tax liabilities. Create the bill using the recurring documents named State Payroll Withholding Bill (Monthly). The bill is dated March 31, 2008.

Print a check dated April 2, 2008 using 451 as the first check number. Also print the Payment report for April 2, 2008.

You have now completed the chapter. ***Make a backup of the Practice Astor Landscaping data file to a backup file named "practiceastorlandscaping Chpt 6." In the next chapter, you will build on the work completed in this chapter.***

SUMMARY

You began this chapter with a *MAPS* overview of payroll processing. We first explained the types of employee withholdings and voluntary deductions as well as the types of employer payroll taxes and other forms of compensation. You also learned to calculate payroll tax withholdings.

You created a new employee and learned the procedures for terminating an employee. With this knowledge, you were ready to process paychecks. You entered employee time and verified time data entries. You used recurring transactions to create employee paychecks and then printed the checks. After printing, you went *Behind the Keys* to trace entries posted to the general ledger. Finally, you recorded payroll tax liabilities and printed checks for these liabilities.

In the next chapter, you will focus on finalizing Astor's March accounting period by recording adjusting entries, printing financial statements, and closing the period.

End-of-Chapter Questions

TRUE/FALSE

_____ 1. OAP can send employee timesheets to ADP to calculate paychecks.

_____ 2. Employers and employees pay Social Security and Medicare taxes.

_____ 3. Payroll tax liabilities are paid through the Employees menu.

_____ 4. You can change information on a saved paycheck if the check has not been printed.

_____ 5. Memorizing employee paychecks as recurring documents saves time because general ledger accounts are saved with the transaction.

_____ 6. FUTA tax is withheld from employee paychecks.

_____ 7. You cannot delete an employee in OAP.

_____ 8. You can calculate an employee's tax withholdings in OAP.

MULTIPLE CHOICE

_____ 1. Which menu creates a report that displays employee paychecks for the pay period?
   a. ***Employees>>Manual Payroll>>Print Payroll Checks***
   b. ***Reports>>Employees and Payroll>>Time Report***
   c. ***Reports>>Banking>>Payments***
   d. None of the above

_____ 2. The _____ link will display a list of employee paychecks that are saved to speed data entry.
   a. Download Pay Runs
   b. Time Entries
   c. Employees
   d. Memorized Documents

_____ 3. Social Security withholdings are calculated as _____ of an employee's wages.
   a. 1.45 percent
   a. 6.2 percent
   c. both a and b
   d. none of the above

______ 4. Per the IRS tax table, the withholding amount for a biweekly paid employee with gross wages of $960 claiming Married with 4 allowances will be ______. *(Note: See Appendix D for complete payroll tax withholding tables.)*

a. 12
b. 14
c. 1
d. Either a or b

______ 5. An employee with gross pay of $830 will have a net pay of ______. Assume the employee is paid biweekly, claims Married with 3 exemptions, and pays state taxes of 2 percent of taxable pay.

a. 800.40
b. 788.36
c. 736.90
d. 748.94

PRACTICE SET

In this Practice Set you will be using the **Graded Astor Landscaping** data file containing the Practice Set completed in Chapter 5 ***When this data file is not loaded on your computer, restore it using the "gradedastorlandscaping Chpt 5" backup file created after completing the Chapter 5 Practice Set.***

1. Open **Graded Astor Landscaping**. Complete the March and April payroll activities that follow.

<u>**2008**</u>

Mar 24 Add 8 hours of billable time to Victor Ramez's timesheet for the week of March 17 to March 23. These hours were worked on Monday on the Sycamore Plantings job and the billing item is INSTL HARD – Commercial.

Create the following paychecks for the Pay Period ending 3/23/2008. *(Note: Recurring paychecks are already created.)* Print the paychecks on starting check number 731.

Astor Landscaping

Pay Period 3/10/2008 thru 3/23/2008

Check No.	Employee	Filing Status	Allow	Pay Type	Pay Rate	Reg Hrs	OT Hrs	Gross Pay	Federal Income Tax	Soc. Sec. (FICA) Tax	Medicare Tax	VA State Tax	Net Pay
731	Dillion, Roy J.	Single	1	Hrly Wage	12.00	73.00		876.00	81.00	54.31	12.70	26.28	701.71
732	Folse, Jan B.	Single	1	Hrly Office	10.00	80.00		800.00	72.00	49.60	11.60	24.00	642.80
733	Greene, Kellie I.	Married	1	Salary	2,346.15			2,346.15	257.00	145.46	34.02	70.38	1,839.29
734	Hardman, Alan	Single	2	Hrly Wage	12.00	72.00		864.00	62.00	53.57	12.53	25.92	709.98
735	Hayes, Mike E	Single	1	Hrly Wage	12.00	54.00		648.00	48.00	40.18	9.40	19.44	530.98
736	Henderson, Jeff P.	Married	1	Hrly Wage	12.00	72.00		864.00	43.00	53.57	12.53	25.92	728.98
737	Murray, Monica D.	Single	1	Salary	1,211.54			1,211.54	132.00	75.12	17.57	36.35	950.50
738	Ramez, Victor M.	Single	0	Hrly Wage	10.00	78.00		780.00	89.00	48.36	11.31	23.40	607.93
739	Ruland, Seth N.	Married	0	Salary	3,103.85			3,103.85	429.00	192.44	45.01	93.12	2,344.28
740	White, Judy O.	Married	2	Salary	2,084.62			2,084.62	199.00	129.25	30.23	62.54	1,663.60
	Totals					**429.00**	**0.00**	**13,578.16**	**1,412.00**	**841.86**	**196.90**	**407.35**	**10,720.05**
	Tax Basis								Circular E	6.20%	1.45%	3.00%	

Mar 24 Post recurring journal entries for the following FUTA, SUTA, and health insurance liabilities.

Post the recurring bill to Nations Bank for the following employer FICA and Medicare taxes plus employee federal, FICA, and Medicare tax withholdings. Print check 449 for $3,489.52.

Astor Landscaping					
Employer Costs for 3/10/2008 thru 3/23/2008					
Employee	ER Soc Sec FICA	ER Medicare	ER FUTA	ER SUTA	Health Insurance
Dillion, Roy J.	54.31	12.70	7.01	13.14	0.00
Folse, Jan B.	49.60	11.60	6.40	12.00	60.00
Greene, Kellie I.	145.46	34.02	0.00	0.00	60.00
Hardman, Alan	53.57	12.53	6.91	12.96	0.00
Hayes, Mike E	40.18	9.40	5.18	9.72	0.00
Henderson, Jeff P.	53.57	12.53	6.91	12.96	0.00
Murray, Monica D.	75.12	17.57	7.55	18.17	60.00
Ramez, Victor M.	48.36	11.31	6.24	11.70	0.00
Ruland, Seth N.	192.44	45.01	0.00	0.00	60.00
White, Judy O.	129.25	30.23	0.00	0.00	60.00
Totals	**841.86**	**196.90**	**46.20**	**90.65**	**300.00**
Tax Basis	**6.20%**	**1.45%**	**0.8%**	**1.50%**	
G/L Accounts	**23400 / 61000**	**23400 / 61000**	**23500 / 61000**	**23700 / 61000**	**23800 / 60600**

2008

Apr 2 Post recurring bills for the following payroll liabilities. All bills affect liability accounts.

Medicare Benefits	March health insurance	$600.00
VA Department of Taxation	March state taxes	$817.76

Create bills for the following payroll liabilities.

Nations Bank	First Qtr. FUTA taxes	$460.47
VA Employment Commission	First Qtr. SUTA taxes	$907.82

Print checks for these bills totaling $2,786.05 on starting check number 450.

Apr 7 Enter the following timesheet for Alan Hardman. All hours are billable.

Employee ID: Hardman, Alan **Mar 31 to Apr 6, 2008**

Job	Customer	Billing Item	Pay Type	M 31	Tu 1	W 2	Th 3	F 4	Sa 5	Su 6	Totals
O'Hara Redesign Gardens	O' Hara Homes	INSTL HARD - COMMERCIAL	Regular	8.00	8.00	8.00	8.00	8.00			40.00
O'Hara Redesign Gardens	O' Hara Homes	INSTL HARD - COMMERCIAL	Overtime	2.00							2.00
			Totals	**10.00**	**8.00**	**8.00**	**8.00**	**8.00**			**42.00**

Apr 7 Create the following paychecks for the Pay Period ending 4/6/2008. Print the paychecks on starting check number 741.

Astor Landscaping
Pay Period 3/24/2008 thru 4/6/2008

Check No.	Employee	Filing Status	Allow.	Pay Type	Pay Rate	Reg Hrs	OT Hrs	Gross Pay	Federal Income Tax	Soc. Sec. (FICA) Tax	Medicare Tax	VA State Tax	Net Pay
741	Dillion, Roy J.	Single	1	Hrly Wage	12.00	80.00		960.00	96.00	59.52	13.92	28.80	761.76
742	Folse, Jan B.	Single	1	Hrly Office	10.00	80.00		800.00	72.00	49.60	11.60	24.00	642.80
743	Greene, Kellie I.	Married	1	Salary	2,346.15			2,346.15	257.00	145.46	34.02	70.38	1,839.29
744	Hardman, Alan	Single	2	Hrly Wage	12.00	80.00	2.00	996.00	80.00	61.75	14.44	29.88	809.93
745	Hayes, Mike E	Single	1	Hrly Wage	12.00	80.00		960.00	96.00	59.52	13.92	28.80	761.76
746	Henderson, Jeff P.	Married	1	Hrly Wage	12.00	80.00		960.00	53.00	59.52	13.92	28.80	804.76
747	Murray, Monica D.	Single	1	Salary	1,211.54			1,211.54	132.00	75.12	17.57	36.35	950.50
748	Ramez, Victor M.	Single	0	Hrly Wage	10.00	64.00		640.00	68.00	39.68	9.28	19.20	503.84
749	Ruland, Seth N.	Married	0	Salary	3,103.85			3,103.85	429.00	192.44	45.01	93.12	2,344.28
750	White, Judy O.	Married	2	Salary	2,084.62			2,084.62	199.00	129.25	30.23	62.54	1,663.60
	Totals					**464.00**	**2.00**	**14,062.16**	**1,482.00**	**871.86**	**203.91**	**421.87**	**11,082.52**
	Tax Basis								Circular E	6.20%	1.45%	3.00%	

Apr 7 Post recurring journal entries for the following FUTA, SUTA, and health insurance liabilities.

Post the recurring bill to Nations Bank for the following employer FICA and Medicare taxes plus employee federal, FICA, and Medicare tax withholdings.
Print check 454 to Nations Bank for $3,633.54.

Astor Landscaping					
Employer Costs for 3/24/2008 thru 4/6/2008					
Employee	ER Soc Sec FICA	ER Medicare	ER FUTA	ER SUTA	Health Insurance
Dillion, Roy J.	59.52	13.92	7.68	14.40	0.00
Folse, Jan B.	49.60	11.60	6.40	12.00	60.00
Greene, Kellie I.	145.46	34.02	0.00	0.00	60.00
Hardman, Alan	61.75	14.44	7.97	14.94	0.00
Hayes, Mike E	59.52	13.92	7.68	14.40	0.00
Henderson, Jeff P.	59.52	13.92	7.68	14.40	0.00
Murray, Monica D.	75.12	17.57	0.00	10.98	60.00
Ramez, Victor M.	39.68	9.28	5.12	9.60	0.00
Ruland, Seth N.	192.44	45.01	0.00	0.00	60.00
White, Judy O.	129.25	30.23	0.00	0.00	60.00
Totals	**871.86**	**203.91**	**42.53**	**90.72**	**300.00**
Tax Basis	**3.00%**	**0.00%**	**0.8%**	**1.50%**	
G/L Accounts	**23400 / 61000**	**23400 / 61000**	**23500 / 61000**	**23700 / 61000**	**23800 / 60600**

Apr 14 Enter the timesheets that follow. Print a Time Report and compare it to the following results.

Ashford Grounds Maintenance	16 hours
DBH Grounds Maintenance	24 hours
O'Hara Redesign Gardens	40 hours
Reynolds Grounds Maintenance	24 hours
Silver Plantings	32 hours
Sugar Grounds Maintenance	16 hours
White Redesign Gardens	40 hours

Employee ID: Dillion, Roy **Apr 7 to Apr 13, 2008**

Job	Customer	Billing item	Pay Type	M 7	Tu 8	W 9	Th 10	F 11	Sa 12	Su 13	Totals
O'Hara Redesign Gardens	O'Hara Homes	INSTL LAND - COMMERCIAL	Regular	8.00	8.00	8.00	8.00	8.00			**40.00**

Employee ID: Hardman, Alan **Apr 7 to Apr 13, 2008**

Job	Customer	Billing item	Pay Type	M 7	Tu 8	W 9	Th 10	F 11	Sa 12	Su 13	Totals
Sugar Grounds Maintenance	Sugar Hill Tennis Club	WKLY MNTNCE - COMMERCIAL	Regular	8.00			8.00				16.00
Reynolds Grounds Maintenance	Reynolds Court Subdivision	WKLY MNTNCE - COMMERCIAL	Regular		8.00	8.00		8.00			24.00
			Totals	**8.00**	**8.00**	**8.00**	**8.00**	**8.00**			**40.00**

Employee ID: Hayes, Mike **Apr 7 to Apr 13, 2008**

Job	Customer	Billing item	Pay Type	M 7	Tu 8	W 9	Th 10	F 11	Sa 12	Su 13	Totals
White Redesign Gardens	White and Associates	INSTL LAND - COMMERCIAL	Regular	8.00	8.00	8.00	8.00	8.00			**40.00**

Employee ID: Henderson, Jeff **Apr 7 to Apr 13, 2008**

Job	Customer	Billing item	Pay Type	M 7	Tu 8	W 9	Th 10	F 11	Sa 12	Su 13	Totals
Silver Plantings	Silver Homes	INSTL HARD - COMMERCIAL	Regular	8.00	8.00	8.00	8.00				**32.00**

Employee ID: Ramez, Victor **Apr 7 to Apr 13, 2008**

Job	Customer	Billing item	Pay Type	M 7	Tu 8	W 9	Th 10	F 11	Sa 12	Su 13	Totals
Ashford Grounds Maintenance	Ashford Hill Apartments	WKLY MNTNCE - COMMERCIAL	Regular	8.00	8.00						16.00
DBH Grounds Maintenance	DBH Enterprises	WKLY MNTNCE - COMMERCIAL	Regular			8.00	8.00	8.00			24.00
			Totals	**8.00**	**8.00**	**8.00**	**8.00**	**8.00**			**40.00**

Apr 14 Add a new employee. Remember to choose the Employee Form.

Name:	David R. Bellows
Address:	873 Trumpet St., Arlington, VA 30026
Telephone:	777-325-0909
Job Title:	Laborer
Hired:	4/14/2008
Fed Filing Status:	Single
Federal Allowances:	0
Regular Wage:	$12.00
Overtime:	$18.00

Apr 14 Terminate Alan Hardman. Termination date is April 14, 2008.

Apr 21 Enter the timesheets that follow. Print a Time Report and compare it to the following results:

Ashford Grounds Maintenance	16 hours
DBH Grounds Maintenance	22 hours
O'Hara Redesign Gardens	40 hours
Reynolds Grounds Maintenance	16 hours
Silver Plantings	40 hours
Sugar Grounds Maintenance	24 hours
White Redesign Gardens	37 hours

Employee ID: Bellows, David **Apr 14 to Apr 20, 2008**

Job	Customer	Billing item	Pay Type	M 7	Tu 8	W 9	Th 10	F 11	Sa 12	Su 13	Totals
Sugar Grounds Maintenance	Sugar Hill Tennis Club	WKLY MNTNCE - COMMERCIAL	Regular	8.00	8.00	8.00					24.00
Reynolds Grounds Maintenance	Reynolds Court Subdivision	WKLY MNTNCE - COMMERCIAL	Regular				8.00	8.00			16.00
			Totals	**8.00**	**8.00**	**8.00**	**8.00**	**8.00**			**40.00**

Employee ID: Dillion, Roy **Apr 14 to Apr 20, 2008**

Job	Customer	Billing item	Pay Type	M 7	Tu 8	W 9	Th 10	F 11	Sa 12	Su 13	Totals
O'Hara Redesign Gardens	O'Hara Homes	INSTL LAND - COMMERCIAL	Regular	8.00	8.00	8.00	8.00	8.00			**40.00**

Employee ID: Hayes, Mike **Apr 14 to Apr 20, 2008**

Job	Customer	Billing item	Pay Type	M 7	Tu 8	W 9	Th 10	F 11	Sa 12	Su 13	Totals
White Redesign Gardens	White and Associates	INSTL HARD - COMMERCIAL	Regular	8.00	8.00	8.00	8.00	5.00			**37.00**

Employee ID: Henderson, Jeff **Apr 14 to Apr 20, 2008**

Job	Customer	Billing item	Pay Type	M 7	Tu 8	W 9	Th 10	F 11	Sa 12	Su 13	Totals
Silver Plantings	Silver Homes	INSTL HARD - COMMERCIAL	Regular	8.00	8.00	8.00	8.00	8.00			**40.00**

Employee ID: Ramez, Victor **Apr 14 to Apr 20, 2008**

Job	Customer	Billing item	Pay Type	M 7	Tu 8	W 9	Th 10	F 11	Sa 12	Su 13	Totals
Ashford Grounds Maintenance	Ashford Hill Apartments	WKLY MNTNCE - COMMERCIAL	Regular	8.00	8.00						16.00
DBH Grounds Maintenance	DBH Enterprises	WKLY MNTNCE - COMMERCIAL	Regular			8.00	6.00	8.00			22.00
			Totals	**8.00**	**8.00**	**8.00**	**6.00**	**8.00**			**38.00**

Apr 21 Create the following paychecks for the Pay Period ending 4/20/2008. Print the paychecks on starting check number 751.

Note: When creating David Bellows' check, wages are expensed to Direct Labor. Also verify that the Bank Account is Payroll Checking Account.

Astor Landscaping													
Pay Period 4/7/2008 thru 4/20/2008													
Check No.	Employee	Filing Status	Allow.	Pay Type	Pay Rate	Reg Hrs	OT Hrs	Gross Pay	Federal Income Tax	Soc. Sec. (FICA) Tax	Medicare Tax	VA State Tax	Net Pay
751	Bellows, David R	Single	0	Hrly Wage	12.00	40.00		480.00	43.00	29.76	6.96	14.40	385.88
752	Dillion, Roy J.	Single	1	Hrly Wage	12.00	80.00		960.00	96.00	59.52	13.92	28.80	761.76
753	Folse, Jan B.	Single	1	Hrly Office	10.00	78.00		780.00	89.00	48.36	11.31	23.40	607.93
754	Greene, Kellie I.	Married	1	Salary	2,346.15			2,346.15	257.00	145.46	34.02	70.38	1,839.29
755	Hardman, Alan	Single	2	Hrly Wage	12.00	40.00		480.00	12.00	29.76	6.96	14.40	416.88
756	Hayes, Mike E	Single	1	Hrly Wage	12.00	77.00		924.00	90.00	57.29	13.40	27.72	735.59
757	Henderson, Jeff P.	Married	1	Hrly Wage	12.00	72.00		864.00	43.00	53.57	12.53	25.92	728.98
758	Murray, Monica D.	Single	1	Salary	1,211.54			1,211.54	132.00	75.12	17.57	36.35	950.50
759	Ramez, Victor M.	Single	0	Hrly Wage	10.00	78.00		780.00	89.00	48.36	11.31	23.40	607.93
760	Ruland, Seth N.	Married	0	Salary	3,103.85			3,103.85	429.00	192.44	45.01	93.12	2,344.28
761	White, Judy O.	Married	2	Salary	2,084.62			2,084.62	199.00	129.25	30.23	62.54	1,663.60
	Totals					465.00	0.00	14,014.16	1,479.00	868.89	203.22	420.43	11,042.62
	Tax Basis								Circular E	6.20%	1.45%	3.00%	

Apr 21 Post recurring journal entries for the following FUTA, SUTA, and health insurance liabilities.

Post the recurring bill to Nations Bank for the following employer FICA and Medicare taxes plus employee federal, FICA, and Medicare tax withholdings. Print check 455 to Nations Bank for $3,623.22.

Astor Landscaping
Employer Costs for 4/7/2008 thru 4/20/2008

Employee	ER Soc Sec (FICA)	ER Medicare	ER FUTA	ER SUTA	Health Insurance
Bellows, David R	29.76	6.96	3.84	7.20	0.00
Dillion, Roy J.	59.52	13.92	7.68	14.40	0.00
Folse, Jan B.	48.36	11.31	0.00	11.70	60.00
Greene, Kellie I.	145.46	34.02	0.00	0.00	60.00
Hardman, Alan	29.76	6.96	2.72	7.20	0.00
Hayes, Mike E	57.29	13.40	7.39	13.86	0.00
Henderson, Jeff P.	53.57	12.53	3.01	12.96	0.00
Murray, Monica D.	75.12	17.57	0.00	0.00	60.00
Ramez, Victor M.	48.36	11.31	6.24	11.70	0.00
Ruland, Seth N.	192.44	45.01	0.00	0.00	60.00
White, Judy O.	129.25	30.23	0.00	0.00	60.00
Totals	**868.89**	**203.22**	**30.88**	**79.02**	**300.00**
Tax Basis	**6.20%**	**1.45%**	**0.8%**	**1.50%**	
G/L Accounts	**23400 / 61000**	**23400 / 61000**	**23500 / 61000**	**23700 / 61000**	**23750 / 60300**

Apr 30 Post recurring bills for the following payroll liabilities. All bills affect liability accounts.

Medicare Benefits	April health insurance	$600.00
VA Department of Taxation	April state taxes	$842.30

2. Print the following reports to document activities.

   a. Time Report filtered for 4/7/2008 to 4/13/2008 and filtered for 4/14/2008 to 4/20/2008.

   b. Employee Payments report filtered for 3/24/2008 to 4/21/2008. Modify the report to remove the Issue date, No., Status detail, Reference number, and Void columns. Sort by Payment No.

   c. Check Detail report filtered for 3/24/2008 to 4/30/2008 and the following vendors.

      Medicare Benefits Administrators
      Nations Bank
      VA Department of Taxation
      VA Employment Commission

3. ***Back up the Graded Astor Landscaping data file to a backup file named "gradedastorlandscaping Chpt 6." The Practice Set for the next chapter will build on the work completed in this chapter.***

CHAPTER 7 CLOSE THE ACCOUNTING PERIOD FOR A SERVICE BASED BUSINESS

LEARNING OBJECTIVES

This chapter uses the Practice Astor Landscaping data file containing the tasks completed in Chapter 6. ***When this data file is not loaded on your computer, restore it using the "practiceastorlandscaping Chpt 6" backup file created after reading Chapter 6.***

In this chapter you complete Astor's accounting transactions for March 2008 by:

1. Analyzing transactions posted in March
2. Posting adjusting entries
3. Reconciling bank statements
4. Printing financial reports
5. Closing the accounting period

Launch OAP and open **Practice Astor Landscaping**.

ANALYZE TRANSACTIONS

In Chapter 3, you learned to post general journal entries. In this chapter, you use journal entries to adjust account balances and accrue expenses. You will then print financial statements for March and close the accounting period.

It is important to analyze posted transactions before closing an accounting period. You begin this analysis by reviewing the **GL Report**.

Open the report by selecting ***Reports>>Company and Financial>>GL Report*** on the main menu. *(Note: You can also select this report from the Reports section on the Company Home page and from the Reports Home page.)*

Enter the date range of 3/1/2008 to 3/31/2008 (Figure 7:1).

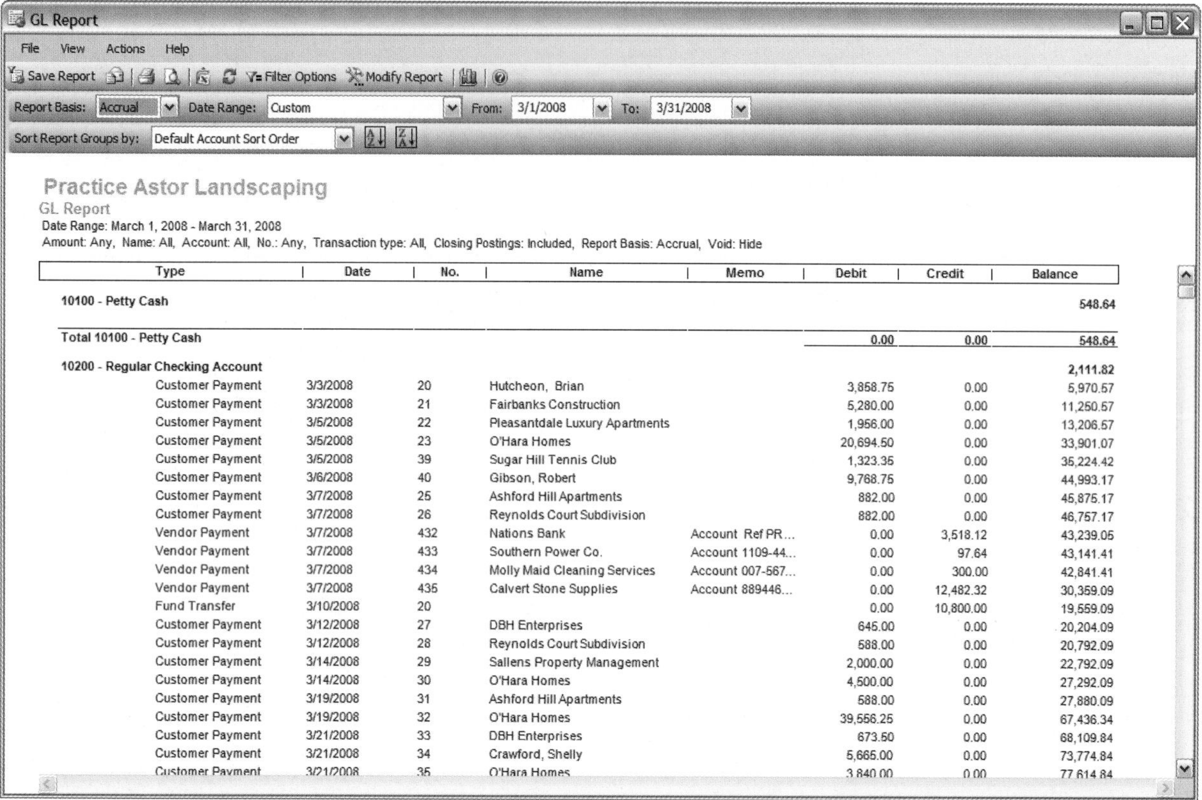

Practice Astor Landscaping
GL Report
Date Range: March 1, 2008 - March 31, 2008
Amount: Any, Name: All, Account: All, No.: Any, Transaction type: All, Closing Postings: Included, Report Basis: Accrual, Void: Hide

Type	Date	No.	Name	Memo	Debit	Credit	Balance
10100 - Petty Cash							548.64
Total 10100 - Petty Cash					0.00	0.00	548.64
10200 - Regular Checking Account							2,111.82
Customer Payment	3/3/2008	20	Hutcheon, Brian		3,858.75	0.00	5,970.57
Customer Payment	3/3/2008	21	Fairbanks Construction		5,280.00	0.00	11,250.57
Customer Payment	3/5/2008	22	Pleasantdale Luxury Apartments		1,956.00	0.00	13,206.57
Customer Payment	3/5/2008	23	O'Hara Homes		20,694.50	0.00	33,901.07
Customer Payment	3/5/2008	39	Sugar Hill Tennis Club		1,323.35	0.00	35,224.42
Customer Payment	3/6/2008	40	Gibson, Robert		9,768.75	0.00	44,993.17
Customer Payment	3/7/2008	25	Ashford Hill Apartments		882.00	0.00	45,875.17
Customer Payment	3/7/2008	26	Reynolds Court Subdivision		882.00	0.00	46,757.17
Vendor Payment	3/7/2008	432	Nations Bank	Account Ref PR...	0.00	3,518.12	43,239.05
Vendor Payment	3/7/2008	433	Southern Power Co.	Account 1109-44...	0.00	97.64	43,141.41
Vendor Payment	3/7/2008	434	Molly Maid Cleaning Services	Account 007-567...	0.00	300.00	42,841.41
Vendor Payment	3/7/2008	435	Calvert Stone Supplies	Account 889446...	0.00	12,482.32	30,359.09
Fund Transfer	3/10/2008	20			0.00	10,800.00	19,559.09
Customer Payment	3/12/2008	27	DBH Enterprises		645.00	0.00	20,204.09
Customer Payment	3/12/2008	28	Reynolds Court Subdivision		588.00	0.00	20,792.09
Customer Payment	3/14/2008	29	Sallens Property Management		2,000.00	0.00	22,792.09
Customer Payment	3/14/2008	30	O'Hara Homes		4,500.00	0.00	27,292.09
Customer Payment	3/19/2008	31	Ashford Hill Apartments		588.00	0.00	27,880.09
Customer Payment	3/19/2008	32	O'Hara Homes		39,556.25	0.00	67,436.34
Customer Payment	3/21/2008	33	DBH Enterprises		673.50	0.00	68,109.84
Customer Payment	3/21/2008	34	Crawford, Shelly		5,665.00	0.00	73,774.84
Customer Payment	3/21/2008	35	O'Hara Homes		3,840.00	0.00	77,614.84

Figure 7:1

This report differs from the Transaction Detail by Account report because it breaks transactions into Debit and Credit columns along with listing ending account balances. The following explains steps to perform when analyzing this report.

First, scroll through looking for transactions that may indicate a posting error. In particular, scroll to 60000 Salaries Expense and notice that Jack Zickefoose's gross pay of $430.00 posted as salaries and wages instead of direct labor. *(Note: In Chapter 6, we had you post this transaction to the wrong account so you could learn to correct it in this chapter.)*

You will now reclassify the expense. Double click the entry to reopen it and then click **Edit**. OAP warns that you should not change payments that have already been issued; however, you are only going to change the posting account so click **Yes**.

In **Name,** change the Salaries Expense account to Direct Labor. (See Figure 7:2.)

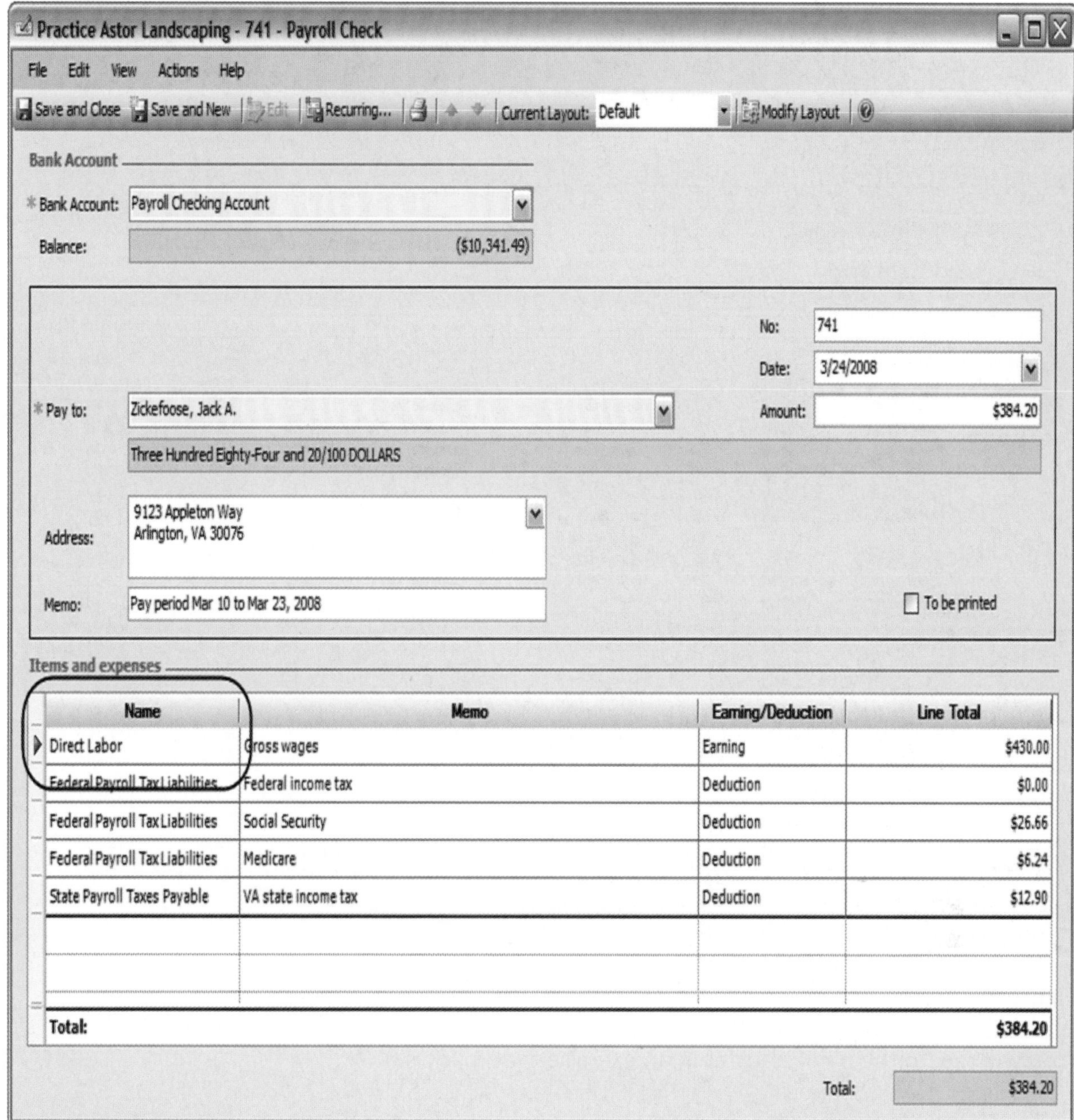

Name	Memo	Earning/Deduction	Line Total
Direct Labor	Gross wages	Earning	$430.00
Federal Payroll Tax Liabilities	Federal income tax	Deduction	$0.00
Federal Payroll Tax Liabilities	Social Security	Deduction	$26.66
Federal Payroll Tax Liabilities	Medicare	Deduction	$6.24
State Payroll Taxes Payable	VA state income tax	Deduction	$12.90
Total:			$384.20

Figure 7:2

Click **Save and Close**.

Return to the GL Report and refresh. Scroll to 57000 Direct Labor to note that Jack's salary now appears in this account. That is how easy it is to reclassify a posting error to the wrong account.

The next step involves reviewing the report for missing transactions. In particular, scroll to account 10300 Payroll Checking to find that the March 24 bank transfer covering payroll checks has not been recorded. (See Figure 7:3.)

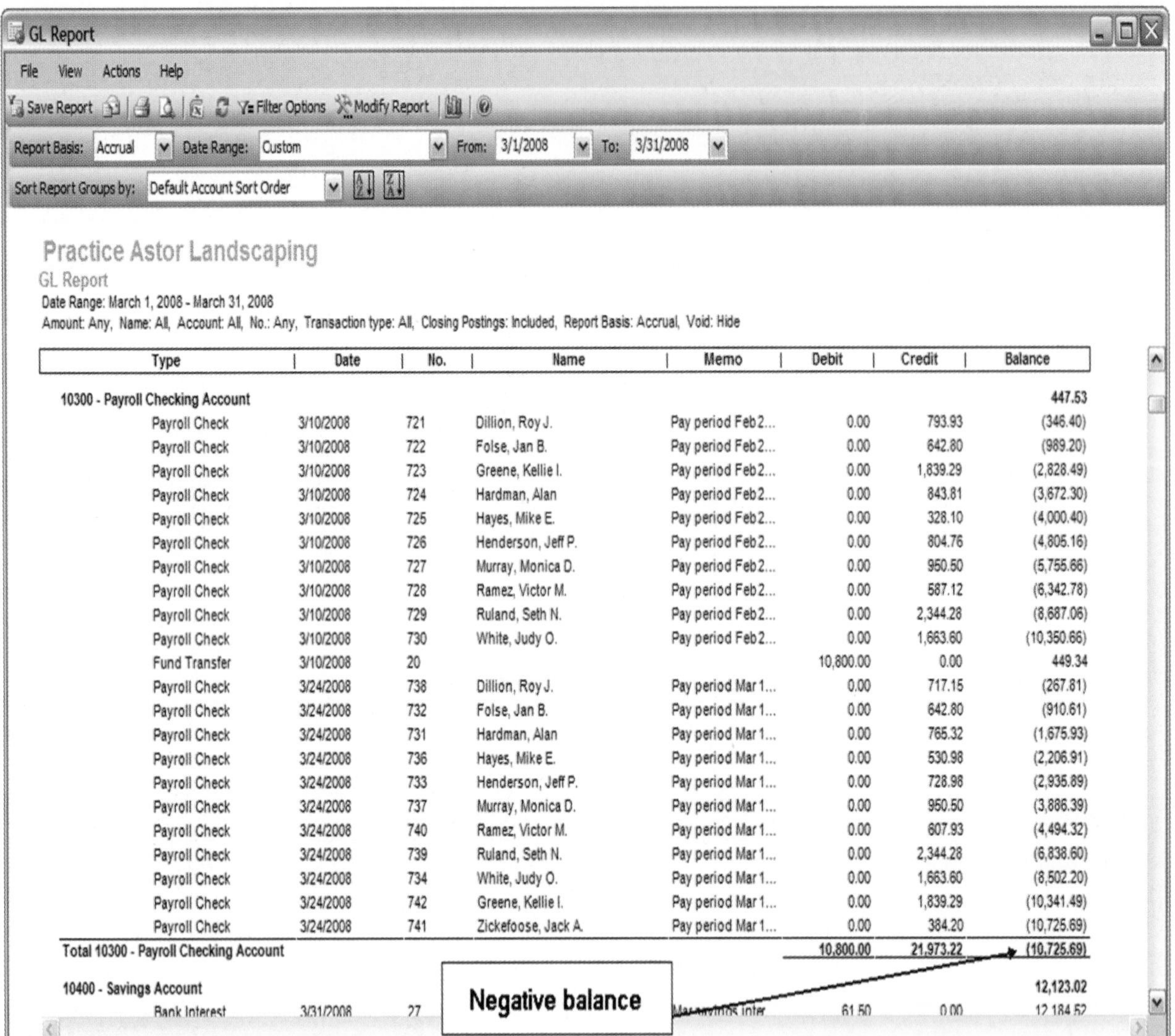

Practice Astor Landscaping
GL Report
Date Range: March 1, 2008 - March 31, 2008
Amount: Any, Name: All, Account: All, No.: Any, Transaction type: All, Closing Postings: Included, Report Basis: Accrual, Void: Hide

Type	Date	No.	Name	Memo	Debit	Credit	Balance
10300 - Payroll Checking Account							447.53
Payroll Check	3/10/2008	721	Dillion, Roy J.	Pay period Feb2...	0.00	793.93	(346.40)
Payroll Check	3/10/2008	722	Folse, Jan B.	Pay period Feb2...	0.00	642.80	(989.20)
Payroll Check	3/10/2008	723	Greene, Kellie I.	Pay period Feb2...	0.00	1,839.29	(2,828.49)
Payroll Check	3/10/2008	724	Hardman, Alan	Pay period Feb2...	0.00	843.81	(3,672.30)
Payroll Check	3/10/2008	725	Hayes, Mike E.	Pay period Feb2...	0.00	328.10	(4,000.40)
Payroll Check	3/10/2008	726	Henderson, Jeff P.	Pay period Feb2...	0.00	804.76	(4,805.16)
Payroll Check	3/10/2008	727	Murray, Monica D.	Pay period Feb2...	0.00	950.50	(5,755.66)
Payroll Check	3/10/2008	728	Ramez, Victor M.	Pay period Feb2...	0.00	587.12	(6,342.78)
Payroll Check	3/10/2008	729	Ruland, Seth N.	Pay period Feb2...	0.00	2,344.28	(8,687.06)
Payroll Check	3/10/2008	730	White, Judy O.	Pay period Feb2...	0.00	1,663.60	(10,350.66)
Fund Transfer	3/10/2008	20			10,800.00	0.00	449.34
Payroll Check	3/24/2008	738	Dillion, Roy J.	Pay period Mar 1...	0.00	717.15	(267.81)
Payroll Check	3/24/2008	732	Folse, Jan B.	Pay period Mar 1...	0.00	642.80	(910.61)
Payroll Check	3/24/2008	731	Hardman, Alan	Pay period Mar 1...	0.00	765.32	(1,675.93)
Payroll Check	3/24/2008	736	Hayes, Mike E.	Pay period Mar 1...	0.00	530.98	(2,206.91)
Payroll Check	3/24/2008	733	Henderson, Jeff P.	Pay period Mar 1...	0.00	728.98	(2,935.89)
Payroll Check	3/24/2008	737	Murray, Monica D.	Pay period Mar 1...	0.00	950.50	(3,886.39)
Payroll Check	3/24/2008	740	Ramez, Victor M.	Pay period Mar 1...	0.00	607.93	(4,494.32)
Payroll Check	3/24/2008	739	Ruland, Seth N.	Pay period Mar 1...	0.00	2,344.28	(6,838.60)
Payroll Check	3/24/2008	734	White, Judy O.	Pay period Mar 1...	0.00	1,663.60	(8,502.20)
Payroll Check	3/24/2008	742	Greene, Kellie I.	Pay period Mar 1...	0.00	1,839.29	(10,341.49)
Payroll Check	3/24/2008	741	Zickefoose, Jack A.	Pay period Mar 1...	0.00	384.20	(10,725.69)
Total 10300 - Payroll Checking Account					10,800.00	21,973.22	(10,725.69)
10400 - Savings Account							12,123.02
Bank Interest	3/31/2008	27		...savings inter	61.50	0.00	12,184.52

Figure 7:3

You will record the bank transfer in an exercise that follows.

Now scroll to 14000 Prepaid Insurance. The accountant has already posted the adjusting entry recognizing this month's expired insurance. Double click the $400 entry to open the transactions. (See Figure 7:4.)

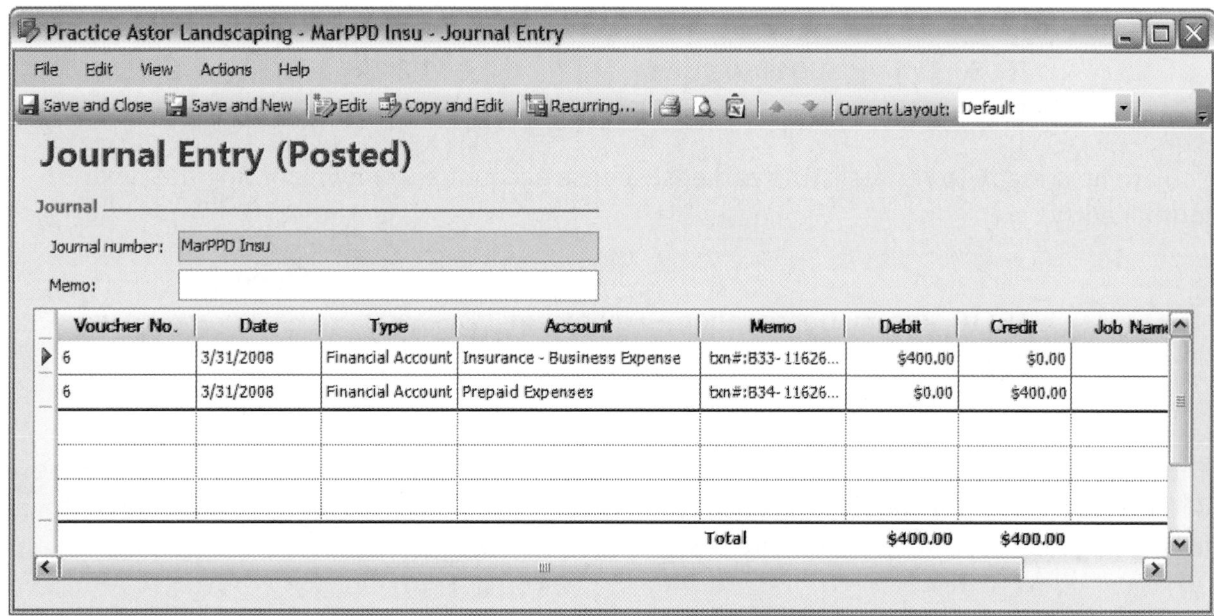

Figure 7:4

This is how you will record adjusting entries in the exercises that follow. Click **X** to close the window.

As you scroll past prepaid expenses notice that March entries for accumulated depreciation have not been recorded so you will book depreciation in an exercise that follows.

You have now finished reviewing the report so close it. Now is a good time to talk about the suspense account and how it is used. Click **Company** to activate the home page and then select **Chart of Accounts** under Find.

Now is a good time to talk about using a suspense account. Scroll to the bottom of the General Ledger report to locate the **99999 Suspense** account. This account is used when you need to post an entry but do not have all the information necessary to complete it.

For instance, assume the company sold equipment costing $15,000 and received $8,500 in cash. You cannot delay recording cash on the sale; however, you do not have final depreciation on the equipment to finalize gain or loss on the sale. This is where the entry can be posted using the suspense account. The following illustrates the journal entry to post the transaction using the suspense account.

		Debit	Credit
10200	Regular Checking Account	$8,500	
99999	Suspense	$6,500	
15100	Equipment		$15,000

When you later calculate that $8,000 was previously posted to the accumulated equipment depreciation account and that final depreciation is $9,200, the following journal entry records the depreciation adjustment.

	Debit	Credit
75000 Depreciation Expense	$1,200	
15110 Accum. Depreciation – Equipment		$ 1,200

You are now ready to reclassify the earlier suspense account entry by recording the next journal entry.

	Debit	Credit
15110 Accum. Depreciation – Equipment	$9,200	
90000 Gain/Loss on Sale of Assets		$2,700
99999 Suspense		$6,500

Thus, the suspense account becomes a useful tool for recording entries when you are unsure of all the accounts affected by a transaction. However, you must diligently review the balance in the suspense account to make sure entries are finalized.

You have finished reviewing the GL Report so close it.

There are a variety of procedures to be followed before closing an accounting period. Some of these were explained in previous chapters. Additional procedures vary based on a company's accounting transactions. It is not possible to simulate the variety of reconciling procedures you may encounter in practice. Instead, we have prepared the following preclosing checklist to help guide you in the future.

Preclosing Checklist	
Review Pending Transactions	Review pending sales to verify all sales income has been recognized.
	Review pending purchases to verify all expenses have been recognized.
	Review payroll tax liability accounts to ensure timely payment.
Reconciliation Procedures	Reconcile all bank statements.
	Reconcile the A/R aging report to the accounts receivable control account. (Performed in Chapters 4 and 8.)
	Reconcile the inventory valuation report to the inventory control account. (Performed in Chapter 8.)
	Reconcile fixed asset reports to fixed asset control accounts. Often fixed asset costs and depreciation will be tracked outside the software. OAP can track fixed asset costs and calculate depreciation but this feature is not illustrated.
	Reconcile the A/P aging report to the accounts payable control account. (Performed in Chapter 5 and 9.)
Adjusting Entries	Post petty cash transactions.
	Review prepaid expenses for expired costs.
	Review accrued liability accounts such as wages and taxes payable.
	Review expenses in the prior period to identify expenses that need to be recognized in the current period. For example, missing utility bills or recurring rent transactions.
	Review posted expenses for prepaid costs and for fixed assets expensed to office supplies.

POST ADJUSTING ENTRIES

In this topic you post Astor's remaining adjusting entries for March. The accountant has already posted expired prepaid expense. All that remains are an entry transferring funds to the Payroll Checking Account and entries that post depreciation and accrued wage expense.

In the next exercise you post the bank transfer and depreciation entries. In the *You Try* exercise that follows you post accrued wages. When posting depreciation, keep in mind that this is an estimate of expense based on ending assets held in the prior year. The estimate may be revised during the year for current year acquisitions or dispositions and any difference between estimated and actual expense is adjusted in December.

STEPS TO ENTER ADJUSTING ENTRIES

1. You will record the payroll transfer first. Select ***Banking>>Transfer Funds*** on the main menu and enter the following information. Click **Transfer** to post the entry.

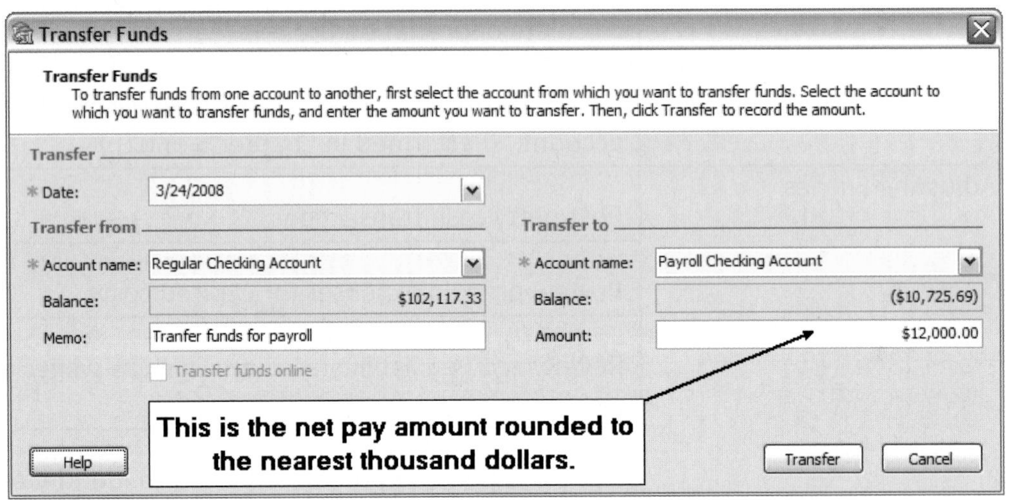

Figure 7:5

2. You next post the depreciation entry. First, let us turn an existing depreciation transaction into a recurring transaction. Open the **Chart of Accounts** by clicking this link under Find. Double click **15010 Accum. Depreciation-Furniture** to open the account and then double click the February 28 entry to open it. (See Figure 7:6.)

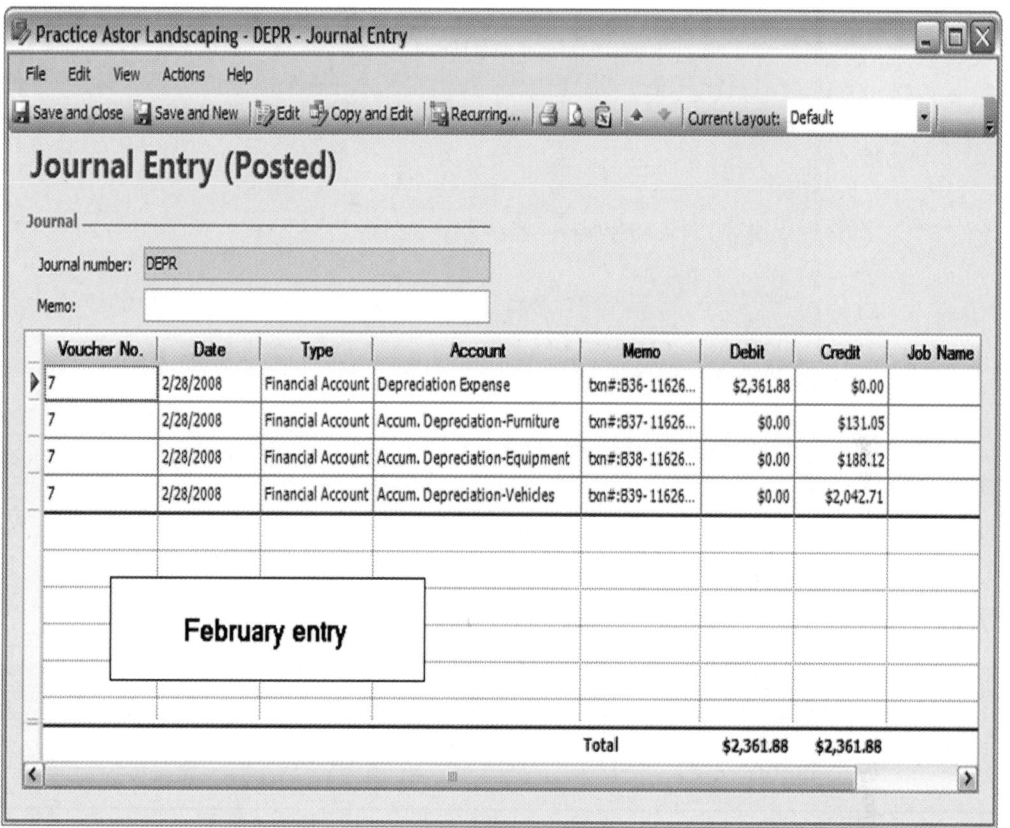

Figure 7:6

3. Click **Recurring** and enter the following information. Click **OK** and then click **X** to close the February transaction and the accumulated depreciation Account Register window.

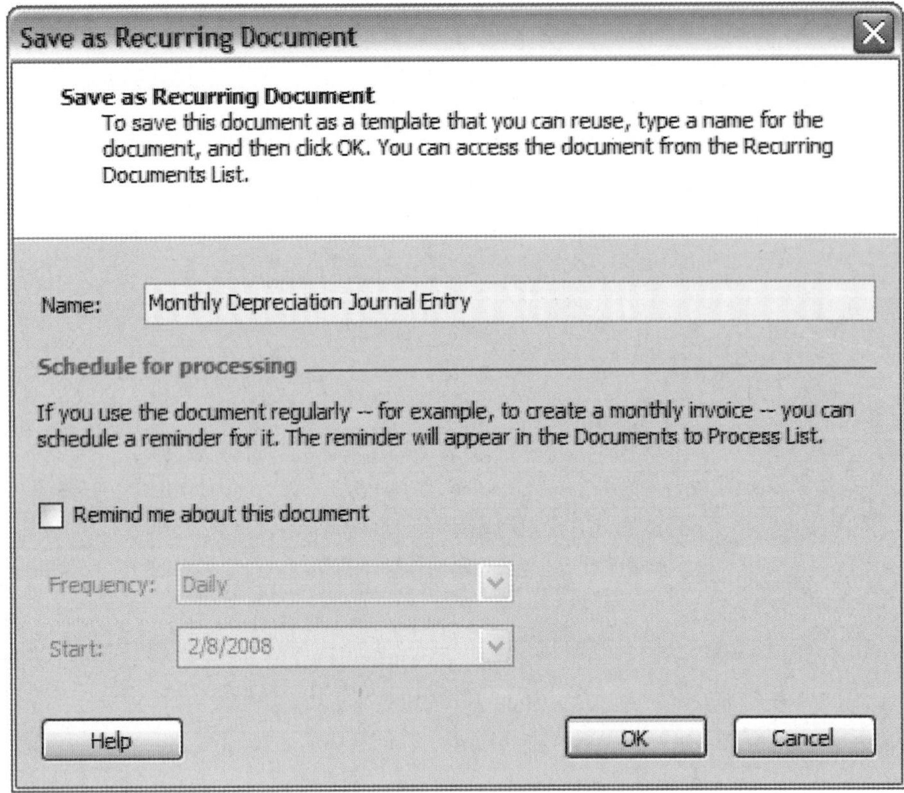

Figure 7:7

4. View the Recurring Document List to open the depreciation entry and make the following changes. Remember to change the posting date to March 31.

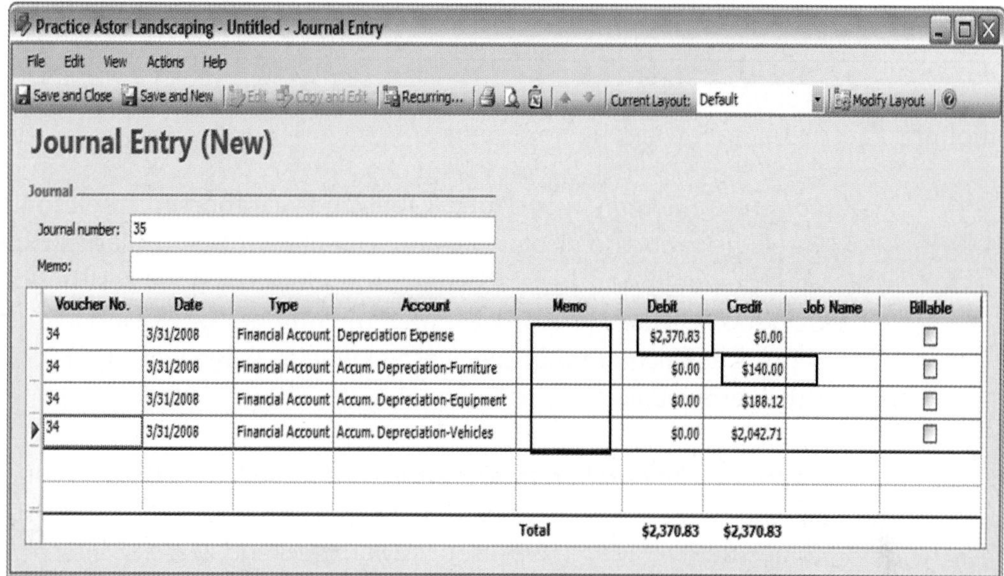

Figure 7:8

5. Before you post this entry replace the existing memorized transaction.

   Click **Recurring** on the toolbar and select **Replace**.

6. Now click Save and Close.

Finish Recording March Adjusting Entries

You will be recording accrued wages for March in this exercise. First, you must calculate the amount to accrue by following the next steps.

a. ***Compute the daily wage rate:*** Open the GL report for the month of March. Filter the report to display only the Direct Labor and Salaries Expense accounts. The total debit for these accounts, rounded to the nearest hundred dollars, is $27,800. Divide the total by 4 (i.e., the number of weeks covered by the report) to calculate that the average weekly wage was $6,950. This then makes the average daily wage rate equal to $1,390 (i.e., $6,950 / 5).

b. ***Compute the number of days to accrue:*** The last pay period ended on March 23 and there are 31 days in March. This means that there are 6 days of wages to accrue (i.e., March 24 through March 28 and March 31).

c. ***Multiply the daily wage rate by the number of dates to accrue:*** The daily wage multiplied by the number of accrual days makes the accrued wage amount equal to $8,340 (i.e., $1,390 times 6 days).

Now post a journal entry for Astor's March accrued wages to 60000 Salaries Expense and 23200 Accrued wages. Also post a journal entry to reverse this amount as of April 1.

Reconcile Bank Accounts

After posting adjusting entries, you are ready to reconcile Astor's bank accounts. The accountant has already reconciled the savings account. Astor received the March bank statement for the Regular Checking Account (Figure 7:9). You will next reconcile this account in the exercise that follows.

Astor Landscaping
Bank Statement March 31, 2008

Beginning Balance from February Statement				$ 3,348.74
March Deposits				
	March 3, 2008		3,858.75	
	March 3, 2008		5,280.00	
	March 5, 2008		1,956.00	
	March 5, 2008		20,694.50	
	March 5, 2008		1,323.35	
	March 6, 2008		9,768.75	
	March 7, 2008		882.00	
	March 7, 2008		882.00	
	March 12, 2008		645.00	
	March 12, 2008		588.00	
	March 14, 2008		2,000.00	
	March 14, 2008		4,500.00	
	March 19, 2008		588.00	
	March 19, 2008		39,556.25	
	March 21, 2008		673.50	
	March 21, 2008		5,665.00	
	March 21, 2008		3,840.00	
	March 22, 2008		8,325.80	
	March 25, 2008		1,764.00	
	March 27, 2008		2,572.50	
	March 27, 2008		1,598.50	
	March 27, 2008		11,025.00	
Total Deposits for March				127,986.90
March Checks Cleared				
	Feb 22, 2008	430	818.42	
	Feb 29, 2008	431	418.50	
	Mar 7, 2008	432	3,518.12	
	Mar 7, 2008	433	97.64	
	Mar 7, 2008	434	300.00	
	Mar 7, 2008	435	12,482.32	
	Mar 21, 2008	437	451.48	
	Mar 21, 2008	438	262.43	
	Mar 21, 2008	439	762.00	
Total Cleared Checks for March				19,110.91
Less Bank Transfers				
	Mar 10, 2008		10,800.00	
	Mar 24, 2008		12,000.00	
Total March Transfers				22,800.00
March Service Charges				67.50
Ending Bank Balance March 31, 2008				$ 89,357.23

Figure 7:9

Steps to Reconcile the Checking Account

1. Click **Banking** to open the Banking Home page and then click **Reconcile Account.** *(Note: You can also select **Banking>>Reconcile Account** on the main menu.)*

   Select the **Regular Checking Account**. Enter the **Statement date** and **Ending balance** listed on the bank statement.

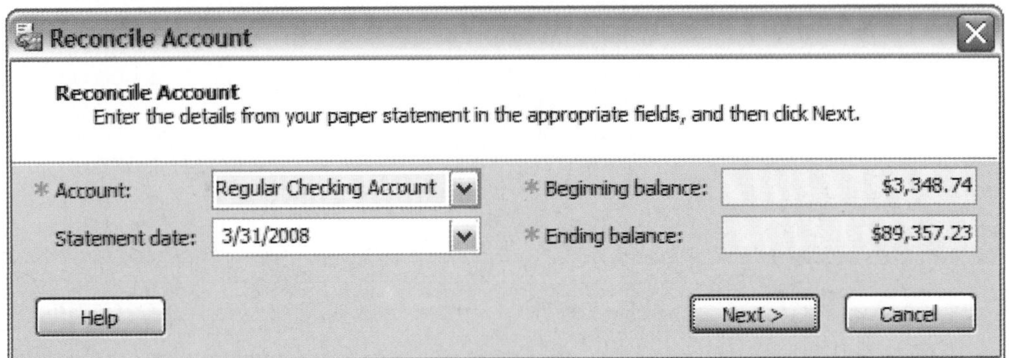

Figure 7:10

2. Click **Next** to open the window for selecting deposits and checks that have cleared the March bank statement (Figure 7:11).

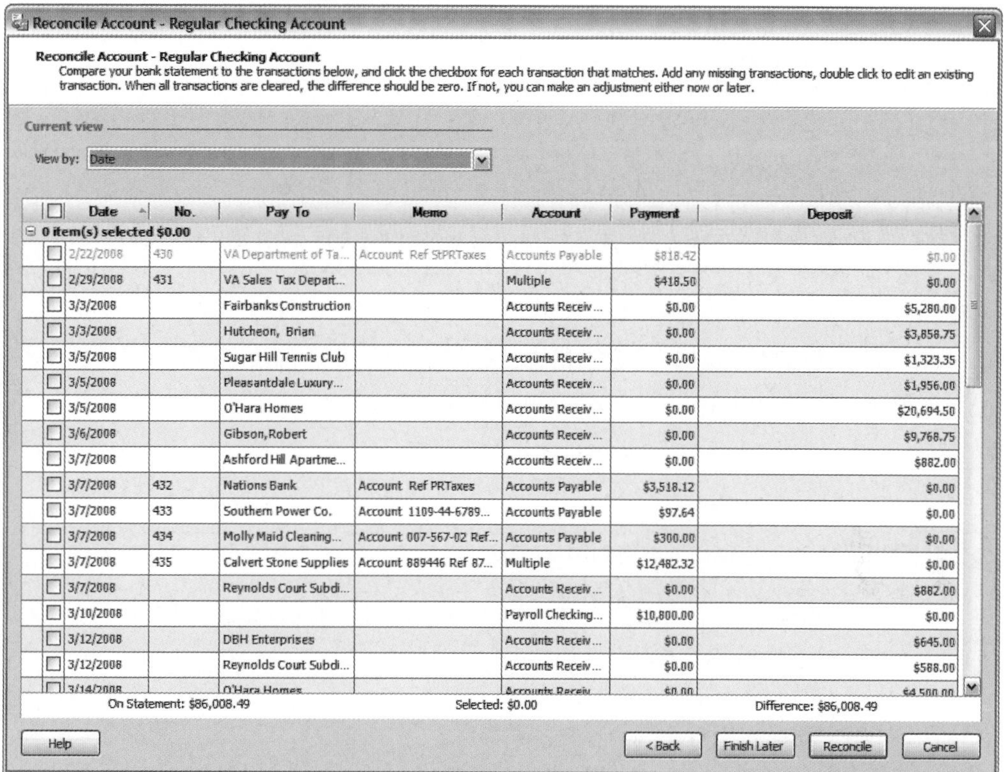

Figure 7:11

3. The following explanations help identify and select transactions in the window.

   Individual items are selected by clicking the item's selection box. Clicking the box in the header row selects all items.

   Outstanding checks display a check number in the No. column and an amount under the Payment column.

   Outstanding deposits display an amount under the Deposit column.

   Bank transfers display a bank account name in the Account column.

   The list can be sorted by clicking a column header. You can also change the view by selecting an option from the dropdown list on View by.

4. You will first enter the bank service charge for March. Scroll to the bottom of the list and click the link **Click here to add a new Transaction**.

   Select **Enter bank fee** and click **OK**. Enter the following information and click **OK**.

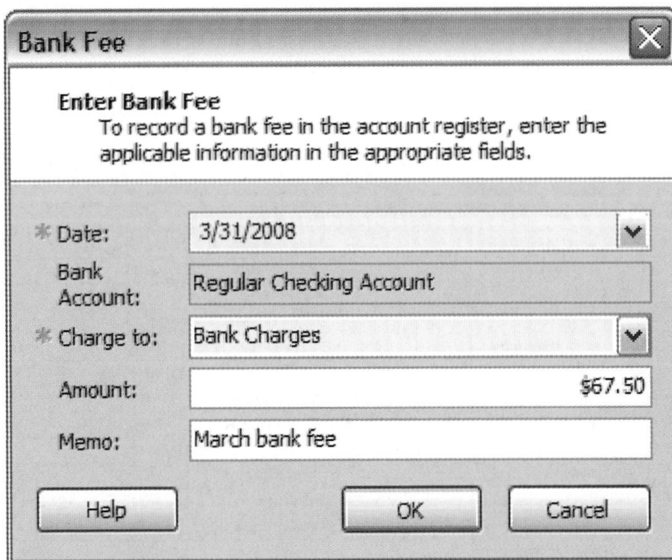

Figure 7:12

5. Click the selection box in the header row to select all items. It is often easier to mark all items as cleared and then scroll through to remove uncleared items.

6. Refer back to the bank statement and click to deselect checks that have not cleared in March. *(Note: All deposits have cleared.)* You can click the **No.** column header to sort by check number. When finished, the reconciliation window appears as illustrated in Figure 7:13.

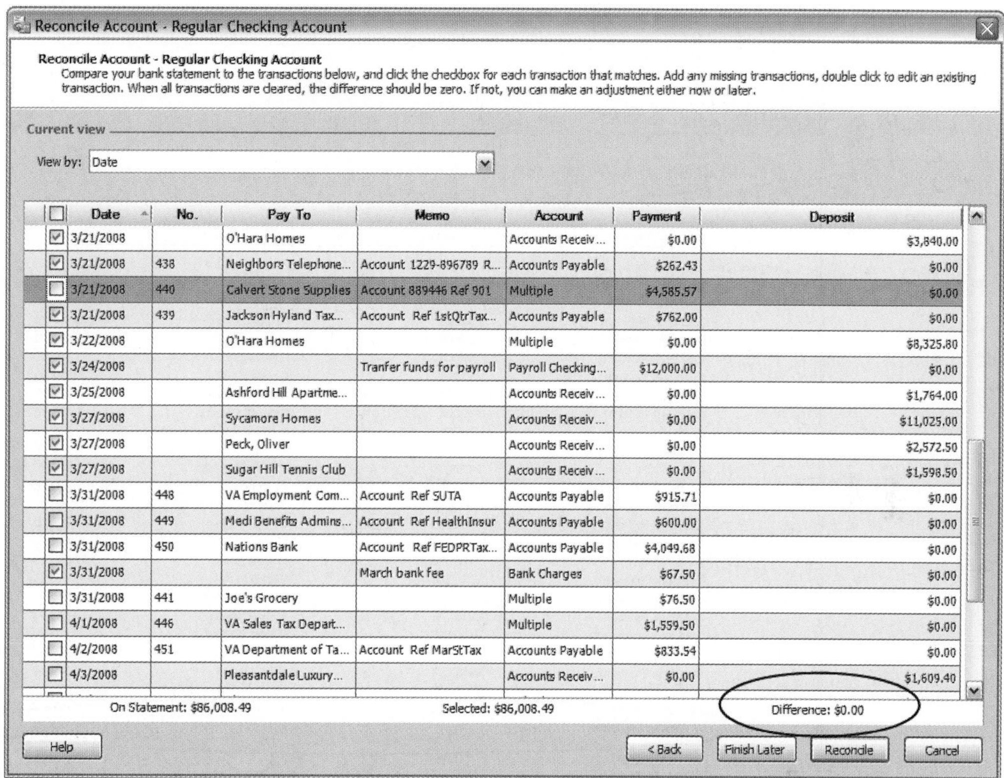

☐	Date	No.	Pay To	Memo	Account	Payment	Deposit
☑	3/21/2008		O'Hara Homes		Accounts Receiv...	$0.00	$3,840.00
☑	3/21/2008	438	Neighbors Telephone...	Account 1229-896789 R...	Accounts Payable	$262.43	$0.00
☐	3/21/2008	440	Calvert Stone Supplies	Account 889446 Ref 901	Multiple	$4,585.57	$0.00
☑	3/21/2008	439	Jackson Hyland Tax...	Account Ref 1stQtrTax...	Accounts Payable	$762.00	$0.00
☑	3/22/2008		O'Hara Homes		Multiple	$0.00	$8,325.80
☑	3/24/2008			Tranfer funds for payroll	Payroll Checking...	$12,000.00	$0.00
☑	3/25/2008		Ashford Hill Apartme...		Accounts Receiv...	$0.00	$1,764.00
☑	3/27/2008		Sycamore Homes		Accounts Receiv...	$0.00	$11,025.00
☑	3/27/2008		Peck, Oliver		Accounts Receiv...	$0.00	$2,572.50
☑	3/27/2008		Sugar Hill Tennis Club		Accounts Receiv...	$0.00	$1,598.50
☐	3/31/2008	448	VA Employment Com...	Account Ref SUTA	Accounts Payable	$915.71	$0.00
☐	3/31/2008	449	Medi Benefits Admins...	Account Ref HealthInsur	Accounts Payable	$600.00	$0.00
☐	3/31/2008	450	Nations Bank	Account Ref FEDPRTax...	Accounts Payable	$4,049.68	$0.00
☑	3/31/2008			March bank fee	Bank Charges	$67.50	$0.00
☐	3/31/2008	441	Joe's Grocery		Multiple	$76.50	$0.00
☐	4/1/2008	446	VA Sales Tax Depart...		Multiple	$1,559.50	$0.00
☐	4/2/2008	451	VA Department of Ta...	Account Ref MarStTax	Accounts Payable	$833.54	$0.00
☐	4/3/2008		Pleasantdale Luxury...		Accounts Receiv...	$0.00	$1,609.40

Figure 7:13

You cannot complete the next step until the **Difference** equals zero.

When you have difficulty reconciling an account, the Finish Later button will save your work and close the reconciliation window. You can then return later to complete the reconciliation.

7. Click **Reconcile** and then click **Display Report**.

   Total Cleared Deposits will equal the total deposits on the bank statement (Figure 7:14).

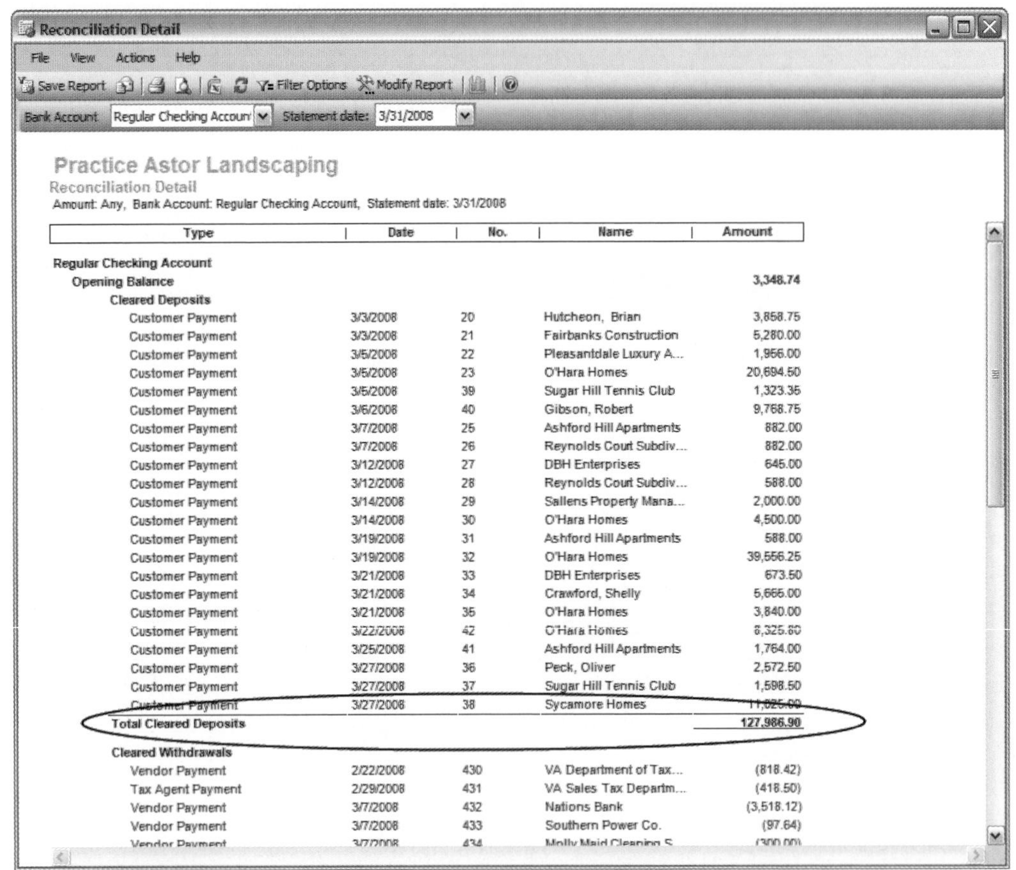

Practice Astor Landscaping
Reconciliation Detail
Amount: Any, Bank Account: Regular Checking Account, Statement date: 3/31/2008

Type	Date	No.	Name	Amount
Regular Checking Account				
Opening Balance				**3,348.74**
Cleared Deposits				
Customer Payment	3/3/2008	20	Hutcheon, Brian	3,858.75
Customer Payment	3/3/2008	21	Fairbanks Construction	5,280.00
Customer Payment	3/5/2008	22	Pleasantdale Luxury A...	1,956.00
Customer Payment	3/5/2008	23	O'Hara Homes	20,694.50
Customer Payment	3/5/2008	39	Sugar Hill Tennis Club	1,323.35
Customer Payment	3/6/2008	40	Gibson, Robert	9,768.75
Customer Payment	3/7/2008	25	Ashford Hill Apartments	882.00
Customer Payment	3/7/2008	26	Reynolds Court Subdiv...	882.00
Customer Payment	3/12/2008	27	DBH Enterprises	645.00
Customer Payment	3/12/2008	28	Reynolds Court Subdiv...	588.00
Customer Payment	3/14/2008	29	Sallens Property Mana...	2,000.00
Customer Payment	3/14/2008	30	O'Hara Homes	4,500.00
Customer Payment	3/19/2008	31	Ashford Hill Apartments	588.00
Customer Payment	3/19/2008	32	O'Hara Homes	39,556.25
Customer Payment	3/21/2008	33	DBH Enterprises	673.50
Customer Payment	3/21/2008	34	Crawford, Shelly	5,666.00
Customer Payment	3/21/2008	35	O'Hara Homes	3,840.00
Customer Payment	3/22/2008	42	O'Hara Homes	8,325.80
Customer Payment	3/25/2008	41	Ashford Hill Apartments	1,764.00
Customer Payment	3/27/2008	36	Peck, Oliver	2,572.50
Customer Payment	3/27/2008	37	Sugar Hill Tennis Club	1,598.50
Customer Payment	3/27/2008	38	Sycamore Homes	[illegible]
Total Cleared Deposits				**127,986.90**
Cleared Withdrawals				
Vendor Payment	2/22/2008	430	VA Department of Tax...	(818.42)
Tax Agent Payment	2/29/2008	431	VA Sales Tax Departm...	(418.50)
Vendor Payment	3/7/2008	432	Nations Bank	(3,518.12)
Vendor Payment	3/7/2008	433	Southern Power Co.	(97.64)
Vendor Payment	3/7/2008	434	Molly Maid Cleaning S...	(300.00)

Figure 7:14

Total Cleared Withdrawals will match the sum of total cleared checks, bank transfers, and bank fees on the bank statement. The Reconciled Balance As Of Statement Date will match the ending balance on the bank statement. (See Figure 7:15.)

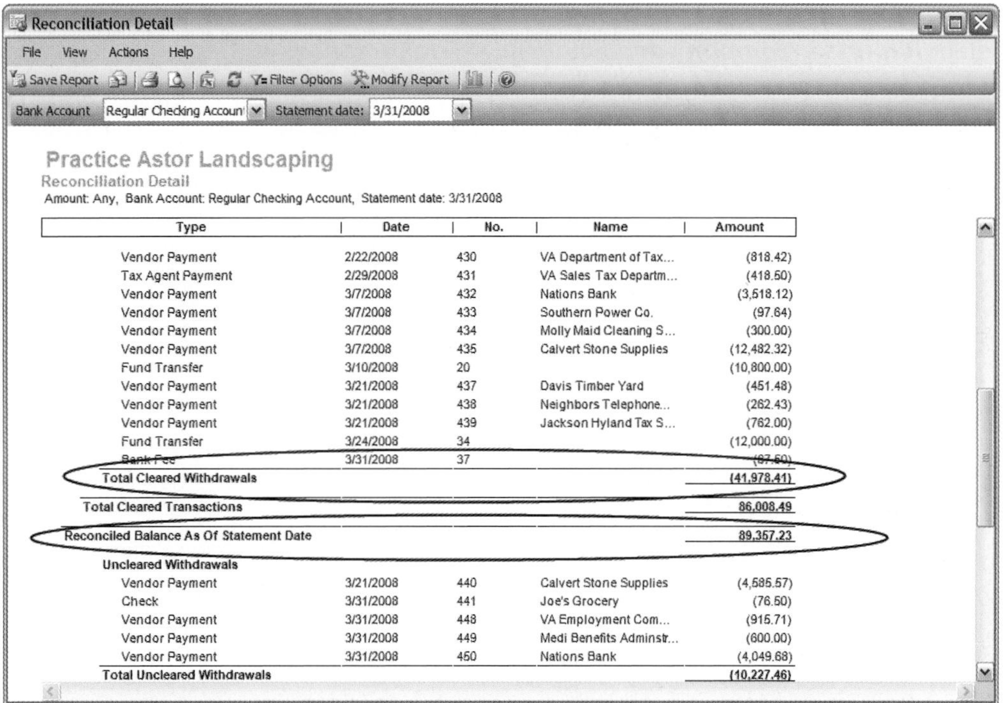

Reconciliation Detail

File View Actions Help

Save Report | Filter Options | Modify Report

Bank Account: Regular Checking Account | Statement date: 3/31/2008

Practice Astor Landscaping

Reconciliation Detail

Amount: Any, Bank Account: Regular Checking Account, Statement date: 3/31/2008

Type	Date	No.	Name	Amount
Vendor Payment	2/22/2008	430	VA Department of Tax...	(818.42)
Tax Agent Payment	2/29/2008	431	VA Sales Tax Departm...	(418.60)
Vendor Payment	3/7/2008	432	Nations Bank	(3,518.12)
Vendor Payment	3/7/2008	433	Southern Power Co.	(97.64)
Vendor Payment	3/7/2008	434	Molly Maid Cleaning S...	(300.00)
Vendor Payment	3/7/2008	435	Calvert Stone Supplies	(12,482.32)
Fund Transfer	3/10/2008	20		(10,800.00)
Vendor Payment	3/21/2008	437	Davis Timber Yard	(451.48)
Vendor Payment	3/21/2008	438	Neighbors Telephone...	(262.43)
Vendor Payment	3/21/2008	439	Jackson Hyland Tax S...	(762.00)
Fund Transfer	3/24/2008	34		(12,000.00)
Bank Fee	3/31/2008	37		[illegible]
Total Cleared Withdrawals				**(41,978.41)**
Total Cleared Transactions				**86,008.49**
Reconciled Balance As Of Statement Date				**89,357.23**
Uncleared Withdrawals				
Vendor Payment	3/21/2008	440	Calvert Stone Supplies	(4,585.57)
Check	3/31/2008	441	Joe's Grocery	(76.50)
Vendor Payment	3/31/2008	448	VA Employment Com...	(915.71)
Vendor Payment	3/31/2008	449	Medi Benefits Adminstr...	(600.00)
Vendor Payment	3/31/2008	450	Nations Bank	(4,049.68)
Total Uncleared Withdrawals				**(10,227.46)**

Figure 7:15

8. Print the report by clicking the Printer icon and then click **X** to close it.

Note: You can reprint the Reconciliation Detail Report by selecting ***Reports>>Banking >>Reconciliation Detail*** on the main menu.

Reconcile the Payroll Checking Account

The March bank statement for the Payroll Checking Account has arrived. All paychecks and deposits have cleared. Bank charges for March are $28.30 and the ending bank statement balance is $1,246.01.

Reconcile the statement and print the Reconciliation Detail report.

FINANCIAL REPORTS

You have now completed the preclosing checklist and are ready to print the trial balance and financial statements.

The trial balance is printed first so that you can perform one final check of account balances. Select ***Reports>>Company and Financial>>Trial Balance*** on the main menu. Enter 3/31/2008 as the date. (See Figure 7:16.)

Practice Astor Landscaping
Trial Balance
As of: 3/31/2008

Account Name	Account No.	Debit	Credit
Petty Cash	10100	548.64	
Regular Checking Account	10200	79,129.77	
Payroll Checking Account	10300	1,246.01	
Savings Account	10400	12,184.52	
Accounts Receivable	11000	110,046.30	
Allowance for Doubtful Accounts	11500		5,000.00
Prepaid Expenses	14000	400.00	
Furniture and Fixtures	15000	11,007.96	
Accum. Depreciation-Furniture	15010		1,980.31
Equipment	15100	35,802.41	
Accum. Depreciation-Equipment	15110		16,366.78
Vehicles	15200	102,562.64	
Accum. Depreciation-Vehicles	15210		22,469.81
Deposits	19000	2,500.00	
Accounts Payable	20000		4,248.78
Sales Tax Payable	22000		3,756.50
Accrued Wages	23200		8,340.00
Income Taxes Payable	23900		10,478.63
Common Stock	30000		8,200.00
Paid-in Capital	39100		120,000.00
Retained Earnings	39500		70,160.90
Sales - Landscape	41000		27,884.25
Sales - Hardscape	42000		143,454.75
Sales - Design Services	43000		58,450.00
Sales - Maintenance Services	45000		23,370.00
Sales - Miscellaneous	46000		60.00
Sales Discounts	49000	64.20	
Cash Discounts Taken	5900		93.58
Materials Cost - Landscape	51000	2,842.84	
Materials Cost - Hardscape	52000	41,048.43	
Subcontractors - Landscaping	57400	3,000.00	
Direct Labor	57000	24,980.00	
Purchase Discounts	59500		457.17
Salaries Expense	60000	65,616.96	
Employee Benefit Programs Exp	60600	1,800.00	
Payroll Tax Expenses	61000	7,673.20	
Office Supplies Expense	63000	379.16	
Postage Expense	63100	282.83	
Advertising Expense	64000	175.00	
Legal and Professional Expense	65000	762.00	
Insurance - Business Expense	66100	800.00	
Insurance - Auto Expense	66200	822.10	
Rent Expense	71000	7,500.00	
Utilities Expense	71100	743.44	
Telephone Expense	71200	746.26	
Repairs - Auto Expenses	72300	1,416.56	
Cleaning Expense	72500	900.00	
Bank Charges	73000	290.22	
Depreciation Expense	75000	7,094.59	
Travel Expense	76000	279.82	
Meals and Entertainment Exp	76100	304.90	
Interest Income	80000		179.30
Total		524,950.76	524,950.76

Figure 7:16

In a manual accounting system this report was critical to proving that debits equaled credits (i.e., general ledger accounts balance) before preparing financial statements. You will recall Chapter 4 illustrations on cross-footing manual Sales Journal transactions before posting Sales Journal totals to general ledger accounts. This calculation was performed to prove that transactions balanced before posting column totals to general ledger accounts. However, this calculation did not prevent posting a total backwards (i.e., a debit as a credit) on the account or transposing numbers when posting.

Remember that a manual system not only involved posting entries from the Sales Journal but also the Purchase Journal illustrated in Chapter 5, Payroll Register illustrated in Chapter 6, and General Journal illustrated in Chapter 3. Imagine how easy it would be to post a transaction incorrectly, thus causing general ledger accounts to be out of balance. You now understand how the "trial" balance garnered its name. Imagine the number of trials it could take before the books balanced in a manual system. In fact, accounts would prepare a preclosing trial balance before posting adjusting entries and then a post closing trial balance before preparing financial statements.

All that work is eliminated with accounting software. Although a computerized trial balance still verifies that general ledger accounts balance, this report more likely functions as a tool for reconciling account balances to external source documents and other software reports. In fact, you used this report in Chapter 5 to tie the balance on the A/P aging report back to the balance in Accounts Payable to prove that vendor activities reconciled to the general ledger.

Close the trial balance so we can now focus on financial statements.

Select ***Reports>>Company and Financial>>Profit and Loss*** on the main menu and filter the report for 1/1/2008 to 3/31/2008 (Figure 7:17).

Practice Astor Landscaping
Profit and Loss
Date Range: January 1, 2008 - March 31, 2008
Account: All, Report Basis: Accrual, Name: All, Closing Postings: Not Included

	1/1/08 - 3/31/08
Ordinary Income/Expense	
Income	
40000 - Sales	
41000 - Sales - Landscape	27,884.25
42000 - Sales - Hardscape	143,454.75
43000 - Sales - Design Services	58,450.00
45000 - Sales - Maintenance Services	23,370.00
46000 - Sales - Miscellaneous	60.00
Total 40000 - Sales	**253,219.00**
49000 - Sales Discounts	(64.20)
Total Income	**253,154.80**
Cost of Goods Sold	
5900 - Cash Discounts Taken	(93.58)
50000 - Materials Cost of Goods Sold	
51000 - Materials Cost - Landscape	2,842.84
52000 - Materials Cost - Hardscape	41,048.43
Total 50000 - Materials Cost of Goods Sold	**43,891.27**
57400 - Subcontractors - Landscaping	3,000.00
Total COGS	**46,797.69**
Gross Profit	**206,357.11**
Expense	
57000 - Direct Labor	24,980.00
59500 - Purchase Discounts	(457.17)
60000 - Salaries Expense	65,616.96
60600 - Employee Benefit Programs Exp	1,800.00
61000 - Payroll Tax Expenses	7,673.20
63000 - Office Supplies Expense	379.16
63100 - Postage Expense	282.83
64000 - Advertising Expense	175.00
65000 - Legal and Professional Expense	762.00
66000 - Insurance Expense	
66100 - Insurance - Business Expense	800.00
66200 - Insurance - Auto Expense	822.10
Total 66000 - Insurance Expense	**1,622.10**
71000 - Rent Expense	7,500.00
71100 - Utilities Expense	743.44
71200 - Telephone Expense	746.26
72000 - Repairs and Maintenance Expense	
72300 - Repairs - Auto Expenses	1,416.56
Total 72000 - Repairs and Maintenance Expense	**1,416.56**
72500 - Cleaning Expense	900.00
73000 - Bank Charges	290.22
75000 - Depreciation Expense	7,094.59
76000 - Travel Expense	279.82
76100 - Meals and Entertainment Exp	304.90
Total Expense	**122,109.87**
Net Ordinary Income	**84,247.24**
Other Income/Expense	
Other Income	
80000 - Interest Income	179.30
Total Other Income	**179.30**
Net Other Income	**179.30**
Net Income	**84,426.54**

Figure 7:17

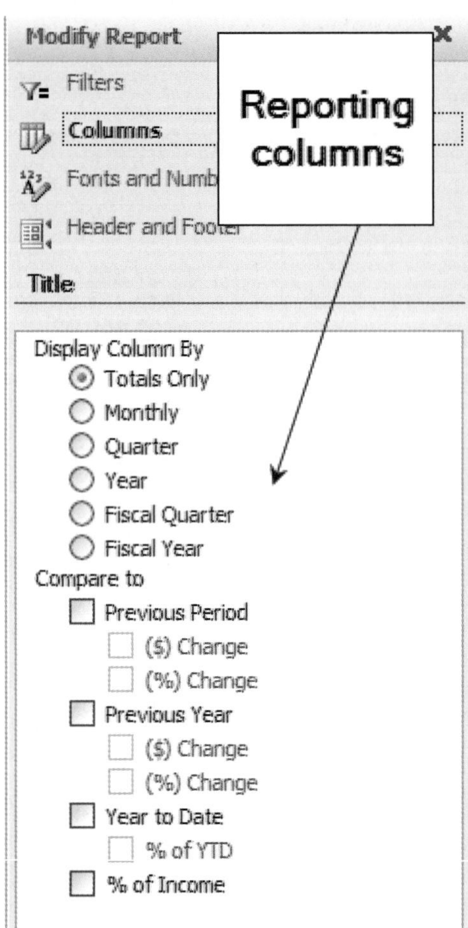

Figure 7:17 is also called the Income Statement and we will refer to it as such. The Income Statement you produced displays only year-to-date net income. We will next modify it to display financial results that compare multiple time periods.

Click **Modify Report** and select **Columns** (Figure 7:18). Select the **Monthly** column and close the Modify Report pane. Scroll to the bottom to view Net Income by month (Figure 7:19).

Figure 7:18

Practice Astor Landscaping
Profit and Loss
Date Range: January 1, 2008 - March 31, 2008
Account: All, Report Basis: Accrual, Name: All, Closing Postings: Not Included

Time periods

	1/1/08 - 1/31/08	2/1/08 - 2/29/08	3/1/08 - 3/31/08	TOTAL
72000 - Repairs and Maintenance Expense				
72300 - Repairs - Auto Expenses	1,416.56	0.00	0.00	1,416.56
Total 72000 - Repairs and Maintenance Expense	1,416.56	0.00	0.00	1,416.56
72500 - Cleaning Expense	300.00	300.00	300.00	900.00
73000 - Bank Charges	96.15	98.27	95.80	290.22
75000 - Depreciation Expense	2,361.88	2,361.88	2,370.83	7,094.59
76000 - Travel Expense	172.08	107.74	0.00	279.82
76100 - Meals and Entertainment Exp	103.10	125.30	76.50	304.90
Total Expense	39,049.32	37,006.72	46,053.83	122,109.87
Net Ordinary Income	10,762.97	44,971.96	28,512.31	84,247.24
Other Income/Expense				
Other Income				
80000 - Interest Income	60.00	57.80	61.50	179.30
Total Other Income	60.00	57.80	61.50	179.30
Net Other Income	60.00	57.80	61.50	179.30
Net Income	10,822.97	45,029.76	28,573.81	84,426.54

Figure 7:19

You already know that the Income Statement paints a company's financial picture over a period of time and this report tells Astor's owners that February produced the highest net income and

March was approximately 34 percent of year-to-date income. Therefore, the time period comparison revealed better information on company performance.

OAP uses general ledger account types to create the Income Statement. You will recall choosing an account type when creating general ledger accounts. You will now see how types are mapped to the Income Statement.

Press **Ctrl + Shift + A** on the keyboard to open the **Chart of Accounts** and refer back to the Income Statement illustrated in Figure 7:17 as we discuss the account types displayed on the Chart of Accounts.

Scroll down the Chart of Accounts until you reach account 40000 Sales. This account is assigned the Income type; therefore, it appears under the Income category of the Income Statement. Cost of Goods Sold account types appear under Cost of Goods Sold and so forth. Individual account balances are listed within each category and subaccounts are grouped with the main account.

Account types serve the same purpose on the Balance Sheet. Close the Income Statement and open the **Balance Sheet** filtered for 3/31/2008 (Figure 7:20).

Practice Astor Landscaping
Balance Sheet
As of: 3/31/2008
Report Basis: Accrual

	As of 3/31/08
Assets	
Current Assets	
Cash	
10100 - Petty Cash	548.64
10200 - Regular Checking Account	79,129.77
10300 - Payroll Checking Account	1,246.01
10400 - Savings Account	12,184.52
Total Cash	**93,108.94**
Accounts Receivable	
11000 - Accounts Receivable	110,046.30
Total Accounts Receivable	**110,046.30**
Other Current Assets	
11500 - Allowance for Doubtful Acco...	(5,000.00)
14000 - Prepaid Expenses	400.00
Total Other Current Assets	**(4,600.00)**
Total Current Assets	**198,555.24**
Fixed Assets	
15000 - Furniture and Fixtures	11,007.96
15010 - Accum. Depreciation-Furniture	(1,980.31)
15100 - Equipment	35,802.41
15110 - Accum. Depreciation-Equip...	(16,366.78)
15200 - Vehicles	102,562.64
15210 - Accum. Depreciation-Vehicles	(22,469.81)
Total Fixed Assets	**108,556.11**
Other Assets	
19000 - Deposits	2,500.00
Total Other Assets	**2,500.00**
Total Assets	**309,611.35**
Liabilities & Equity	
Liabilities	
Current Liabilities	
Accounts Payable	
20000 - Accounts Payable	4,248.78
Total Accounts Payable	**4,248.78**
Other Current Liabilities	
22000 - Sales Tax Payable	3,756.50
23200 - Accrued Wages	8,340.00
23900 - Income Taxes Payable	10,478.63
Total Other Current Liabilities	**22,575.13**
Total Current Liabilities	**26,823.91**
Total Liabilities	**26,823.91**
Equity	
30000 - Common Stock	8,200.00
39100 - Paid-in Capital	120,000.00
39500 - Retained Earnings	70,160.90
Net Income	84,426.54
Total Equity	**282,787.44**
Total Liabilities & Equity	**309,611.35**

Figure 7:20

Unlike the Income Statement, the Balance Sheet reports a company's financial position as of a specific point in time. Take the time to scroll through the Balance Sheet and the Chart of Accounts to understand type mapping on the statement.

Close all open reports and open the **Cash Flow Statement**. Enter the date range of 3/1/2008 to 3/31/2008 (Figure 7:21).

Practice Astor Landscaping
Cash Flow Statement
Date Range: March 1, 2008 - March 31, 2008
Closing Postings: Not Included

	3/1/08 - 3/31/08
OPERATING ACTIVITIES	
Net Income	**28,573.81**
Adjustments to reconcile net income to net cash provided by Operating Activities	
11000 - Accounts Receivable	32,018.70
14000 - Prepaid Expenses	400.00
20000 - Accounts Payable	5,758.25
22000 - Sales Tax Payable	1,504.00
23200 - Accrued Wages	8,340.00
23500 - FUTA Tax Payable	(362.67)
23700 - SUTA Tax Payable	(724.99)
Net Cash provided by Operating Activities	**75,507.10**
INVESTING ACTIVITIES	
15010 - Accum. Depreciation-Furniture	140.00
15110 - Accum. Depreciation-Equipment	188.12
15210 - Accum. Depreciation-Vehicles	2,042.71
Net Cash provided by Investing Activities	**2,370.83**
Net cash change for the Period	**77,877.93**
Cash at beginning of the period	**15,231.01**
Cash at end of the Period	**93,108.94**

Figure 7:21

This may be your first exposure to the Cash Flow Statement so we will spend some time explaining its importance. This statement reports changes in cash produced by operating, investing, and financing activities. Net Cash provided by Operating Activities is cash generated by day-to-day activities such as selling collecting accounts receivable and reducing accounts payable. Net Cash provided by Investing Activities is the cash effect of buying or selling company assets such as equipment or buildings. Finally, Net Cash provided by Financing Activities is the cash effect of borrowing or repaying loans. *(Note: Astor does not have any financing activities for March.)*

After reviewing the report, the accountant notices that accumulated depreciation accounts are appearing under financing activities and should appear under operating activities because depreciation is a noncash activity added back to Net Income to determine cash from operations.

Return to the Chart of Accounts. Scroll to **15010 Accum. Depreciation-Furniture** and right click to select **Open Selected Items**. Change the **Cash Flow category** to **Operating** (Figure 7:22).

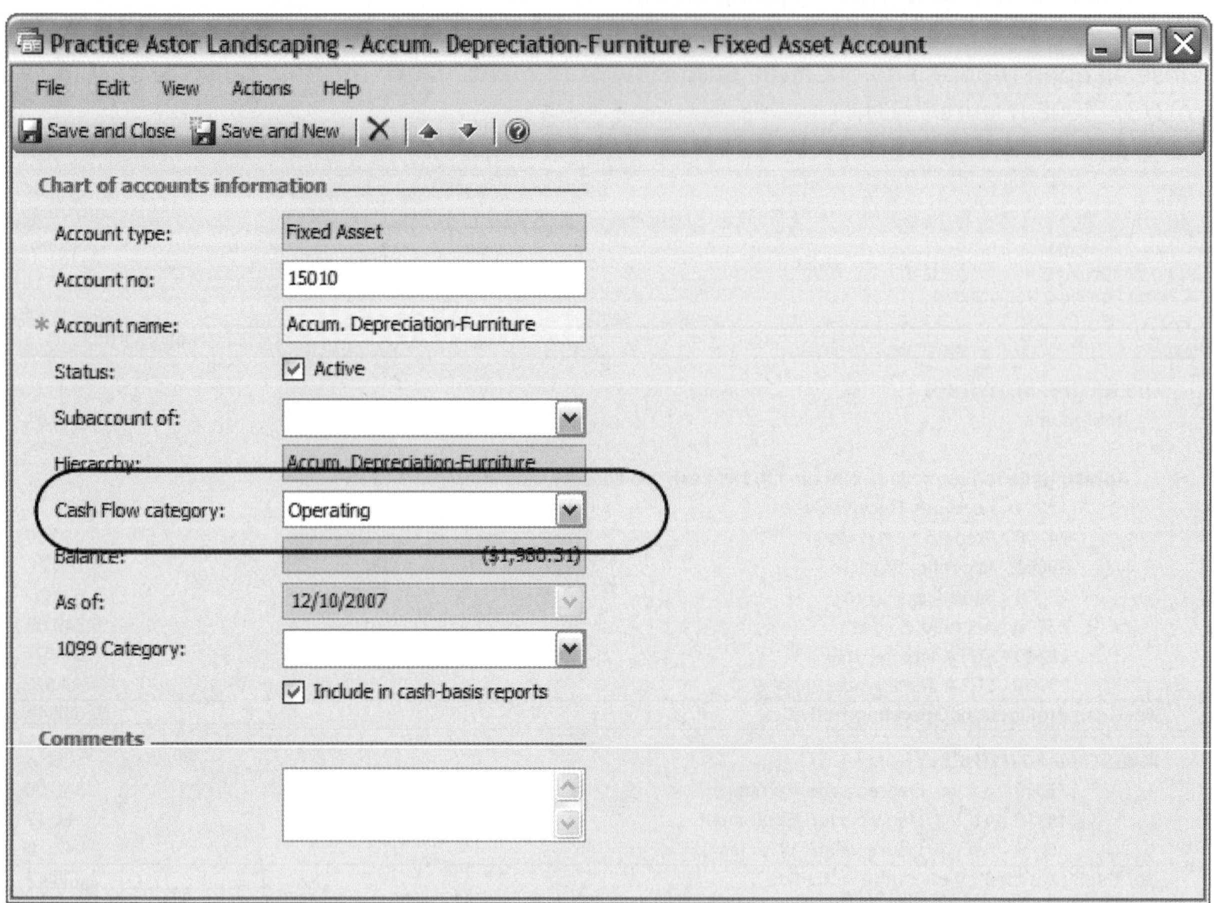

Figure 7:22

Use this record scroll button to move to the next accumulated depreciation account, clicking **OK** when prompted to save changes. Continue changing the cash flow category on remaining accumulated depreciation accounts. When finished, return to the Cash Flow Statement and click **Yes** to refresh the report (Figure 7:23).

Practice Astor Landscaping
Cash Flow Statement
Date Range: March 1, 2008 - March 31, 2008
Closing Postings: Not Included

	3/1/08 - 3/31/08
OPERATING ACTIVITIES	
Net Income	**28,573.81**
Adjustments to reconcile net income to net cash provided by Operating Activities	
11000 - Accounts Receivable	32,018.70
14000 - Prepaid Expenses	400.00
15010 - Accum. Depreciation-Furniture	140.00
15110 - Accum. Depreciation-Equipment	188.12
15210 - Accum. Depreciation-Vehicles	2,042.71
20000 - Accounts Payable	5,758.25
22000 - Sales Tax Payable	1,504.00
23200 - Accrued Wages	8,340.00
23500 - FUTA Tax Payable	(362.67)
23700 - SUTA Tax Payable	(724.99)
Net Cash provided by Operating Activities	**77,877.93**
Net cash change for the Period	**77,877.93**
Cash at beginning of the period	**15,231.01**
Cash at end of the Period	**93,108.94**

Figure 7:23

We will now focus on interpreting this statement. The statement begins with **Net Income** from the March Income Statement and adjusts this number to arrive at income on a cash basis.

Noncash items (i.e., depreciation) are added back to net income and cash increases and decreases for operating assets and liabilities (i.e., accounts receivable, accounts payable, etc.) are factored in to obtain **Net Cash provided by Operating Activities**. Positive net cash flow from operations is a critical point of analysis. Companies that continually fail to generate cash from operations will eventually need to borrow to fund day-to-day operations, such as paying employees and vendors. Continued borrowing eventually places a company in the position of closure when they no longer have the cash flow to pay back the debt.

The Net Cash provided by Operating Activities is then adjusted for any cash increases and decreases in investing or financing activities to arrive at the **Net cash change for the Period**. Notice that Astor has a large positive net cash increase for the period whereas its net income was significantly less. This result, in large part, was due to collecting more cash from accounts receivable and using less cash to pay accounts payable.

Focus now on cash at the beginning and ending of the period. **Cash at the beginning of the period** equals the total for all cash accounts listed on the Balance Sheet for February 29. (See Figure 7:24.)

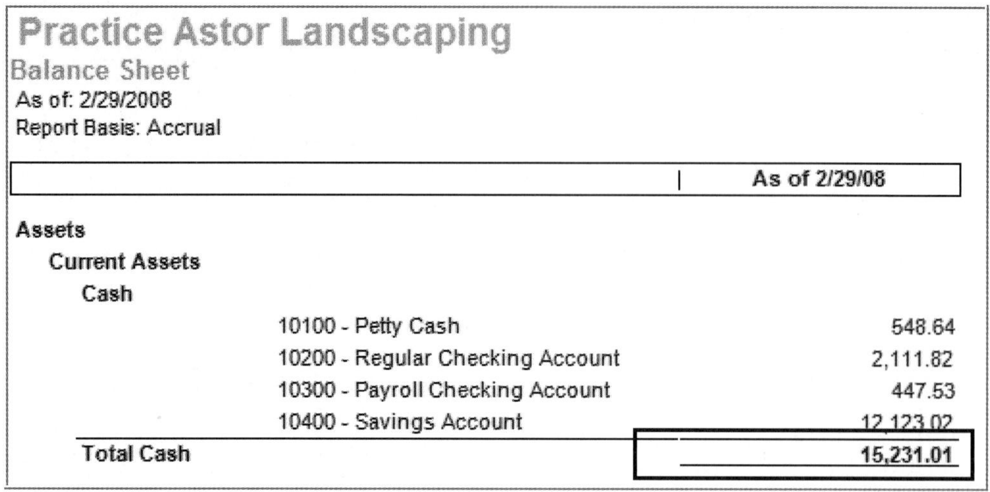

Practice Astor Landscaping
Balance Sheet
As of: 2/29/2008
Report Basis: Accrual

	As of 2/29/08
Assets	
Current Assets	
Cash	
10100 - Petty Cash	548.64
10200 - Regular Checking Account	2,111.82
10300 - Payroll Checking Account	447.53
10400 - Savings Account	12,123.02
Total Cash	**15,231.01**

Figure 7:24

Cash at the end of Period equals the total for all cash accounts listed on the Balance Sheet for March 31.

Practice Astor Landscaping
Balance Sheet
As of: 3/31/2008
Report Basis: Accrual

	As of 3/31/08
Assets	
Current Assets	
Cash	
10100 - Petty Cash	548.64
10200 - Regular Checking Account	79,129.77
10300 - Payroll Checking Account	1,246.01
10400 - Savings Account	12,184.52
Total Cash	**93,108.94**

Figure 7:25

The difference between the two matches the **Net cash change for the Period**.

Close this statement. After printing financial statements, you are ready to close the accounting period.

Close the Accounting Period

Closing the accounting period is important to prevent posting transactions that affect issued financial statements. You do not want to send March financial statements to owners or the bank and subsequently have an entry erroneously posted to March.

Before closing the March accounting period, create a ***backup of Astor's data file to a backup file named "practiceastorlandscaping Chpt 7."***

Now select ***Company>>Preferences*** on the main menu and enter "4/1/2008" in the **Prevent posting before** field (Figure 7:26).

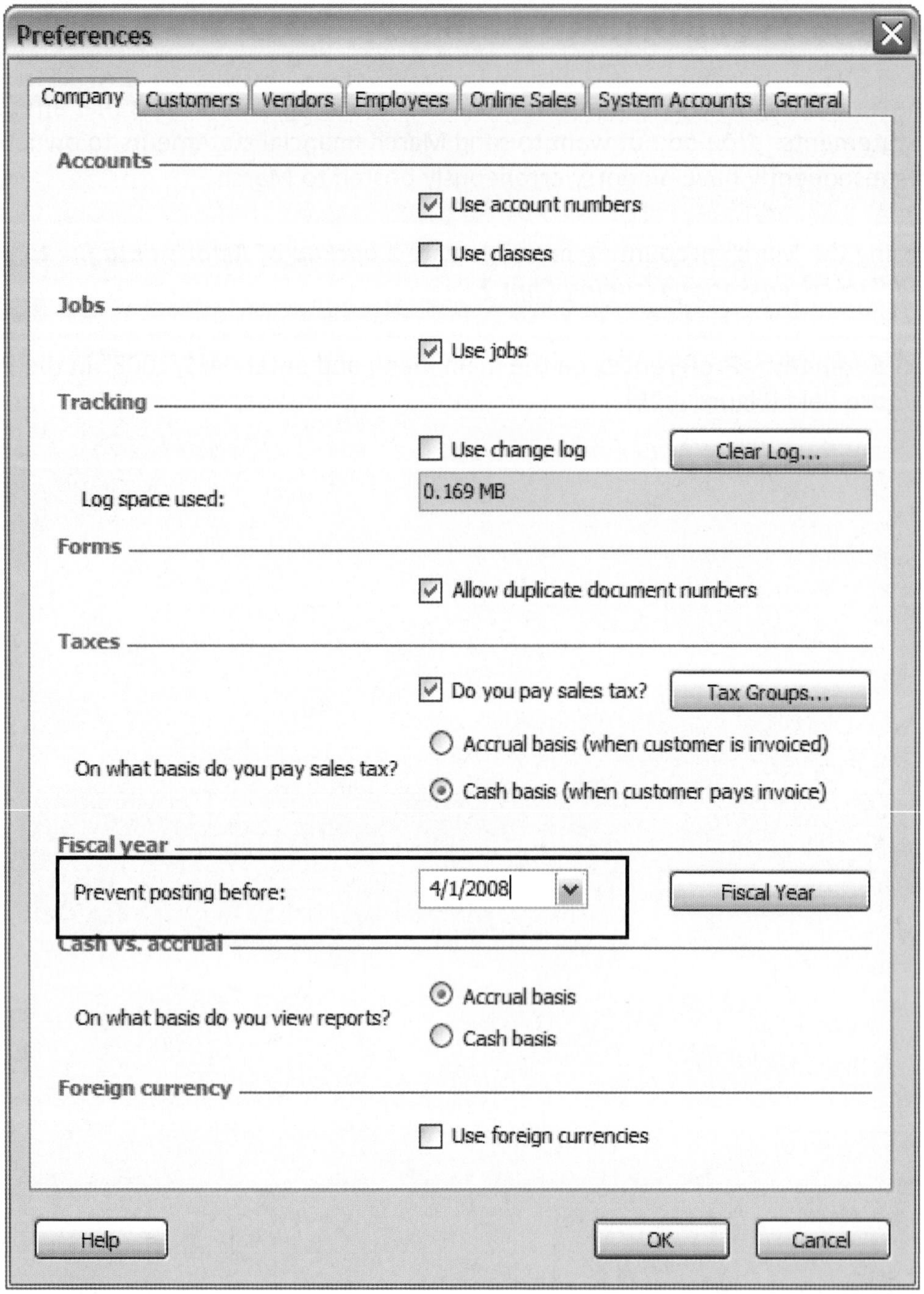

Figure 7:26

Click **OK** to save the changes and close the window.

Closing the year is different from closing the period. When closing the year, you click the **Fiscal Year** button on the Preferences window or select ***Company>>Manage Fiscal Year*** on the main menu.

Figure 7:27

You then highlight the year to close and the **Close Fiscal Year** button activates. When closing a year, OAP posts closing entries. Closing entries zero out balances in income and expense accounts by posting these balances into retained earnings.

Click **X** to close the Manage Fiscal Year window. You have completed the chapter and have already backed up the data file.

SUMMARY

In this chapter, you finalized Astor's March accounting period. You reviewed the GL Report for missing transactions and posting errors. You corrected posting errors and posted adjusting entries. You then reconciled bank statements and printed financial statements.

Finally, you backed up the Practice Astor Landscaping data file and then closed the March accounting period.

Congratulations! You have completed an entire accounting cycle for a service based business. The next chapter presents a comprehensive project for a service based business. Thereafter, Chapters 8 through 11 illustrate the activities completed in Chapters 4 through 7 for a merchandising business.

END-OF-CHAPTER QUESTIONS

TRUE/FALSE

______ 1. Closing the accounting period prevents posting to a closed month.

______ 2. Adjusting entries are used to correct posting errors.

______ 3. The Cash Flow Statement at the end of a month will tie back to the ending cash account balances for that month.

______ 4. Adjusting entries are routine, so these transactions are memorized to save data entry time.

______ 5. The GL Report lets you analyze the details of transactions made to general ledger accounts.

MULTIPLE CHOICE

______ 1. Which menu can be used to enter bank charges?

a. ***Banking>>Make Deposit***
b. ***Banking>>Transfer Funds***
c. ***Banking>>Reconcile Account***
d. Both b and c

______ 2. The ending balance in the Reconcile Account window comes from the ______.

a. Checking account balance in the general ledger
b. Bank statement
c. both a and b
d. none of the above

______ 3. Which financial report(s) accept(s) a range of dates?

a. Balance Sheet
b. Income Statement
c. Trial Balance
d. Both b and c

______ 4. Adjusting entries can be entered using the menu ______.

a. ***Banking>>Make Deposit***
b. ***Banking>>Reconcile Account***
c. ***Company>>New Journal Entry***
d. none of the above

______ 5. Which menu closes the accounting period?

a. ***Company>>Company Information***
b. ***Company>>Manage Fiscal Periods***
c. ***Company>>Preferences***
d. Both b and c

PRACTICE SET

In this Practice Set you will be using the **Graded Astor Landscaping** data file with the tasks completed in the Practice Set at the end of Chapter 6. ***When this data file is not loaded on your computer, restore it using the "gradedastorlandscaping Chpt 6" backup file created after completing the Chapter 6 Practice Set.***

1. Open **Graded Astor Landscaping** and perform the accounting activities that follow to close the March accounting period.

2008

Mar 24 Transfer $11,000 from Regular Checking to Payroll Checking to cover the March 24 paychecks.

Mar 31 Reconcile the Regular Checking Account for March 31 using the statement that follows. *(Note: This statement is different from the statement illustrated in the chapter.)* Print the Reconciliation Detail report.

Reconcile the Payroll Checking Account for March 31. The March ending statement balance is $702.29. All March checks and deposits have cleared and the March monthly bank charge is $27.00. Print the Reconciliation Detail report. *(Remember that April paychecks are in this account.)*

Post depreciation journal entry based on February depreciation. Save the transaction as a recurring document.

Accrue $6,500 for Salaries expense and reverse the entry on April 1.

Print the Trial Balance, Balance Sheet, Profit and Loss, and Cash Flow Statement for March. *(Note: Your professor may have you change the cash flow category on accumulated depreciation accounts.)*

Create a backup file named "gradedastorlandscaping March Close" and then close the March accounting period.

Astor Landscaping
Bank Statement March 31, 2008

Beginning Balance from February Statement				$ 3,348.74
March Deposits				
	Mar 3, 2008		3,858.75	
	Mar 3, 2008		5,280.00	
	Mar 5, 2008		1,956.00	
	Mar 5, 2008		20,694.50	
	Mar 5, 2008		1,323.35	
	Mar 6, 2008		9,768.75	
	Mar 7, 2008		882.00	
	Mar 7, 2008		882.00	
	Mar 12, 2008		645.00	
	Mar 12, 2008		588.00	
	Mar 14, 2008		2,000.00	
	Mar 14, 2008		4,500.00	
	Mar 19, 2008		588.00	
	Mar 19, 2008		39,556.25	
	Mar 21, 2008		673.50	
	Mar 21, 2008		5,665.00	
	Mar 21, 2008		3,840.00	
	Mar 27, 2008		2,572.50	
	Mar 27, 2008		1,598.50	
	Mar 27, 2008		11,025.00	
Total Deposits for March				117,897.10
March Checks Cleared				
	Feb 22, 2008	430	818.42	
	Feb 29, 2008	431	418.50	
	Mar 7, 2008	432	3,518.12	
	Mar 7, 2008	433	97.64	
	Mar 7, 2008	435	12,482.32	
	Mar 24, 2008	449	3,489.52	
Total Cleared Checks for March				20,824.52
Less Bank Transfers				
	Mar 10, 2008		10,800.00	
	Mar 24, 2008		11,000.00	
Total March Transfers				21,800.00
March Service Charges				73.20
Ending Bank Balance March 31, 2008				$ 78,548.12

2. Perform the activities that follow to close the April accounting period.

2008

Apr 7 Transfer $11,000.00 from the Regular Checking Account to the Payroll Checking Account to cover paychecks printed on April 7.

Apr 21 Transfer $11,000.00 from the Regular Checking Account to the Payroll Checking Account to cover paychecks printed on April 21.

Apr 24 Post a journal entry for the following equipment sale.

Equipment cost:	$2,300.00
Accumulated depreciation on equipment:	$1,100.00
Cash deposited to Regular Checking Account:	$ 750.00

Write and print check number 456 to Petty Cash for $175.86, expensed as follows. *(Note: Add vendor on the fly.)*

Meals	$125.86
Travel	$ 50.00

Apr 30 Post the following adjusting journal entries.

Accrue 8 days of salaries and reverse on May 1	$11,230.00
Expense prepaid business insurance	$ 200.00
Expense prepaid auto insurance	$ 400.00

Post the recurring depreciation transaction after adjusting equipment depreciation to $178.12. Replace the previous recurring transaction.

Reconcile the Regular Checking Account for April 30 using the statement that follows. Print the Reconciliation Detail report.

Reconcile the Payroll Checking Account for April 30. The April ending statement balance is $550.65. All April checks and deposits have cleared and the monthly bank charge is $26.50. Print the Reconciliation Detail report.

Reconcile the Savings Account for April 30. Interest income is $61.74 and the ending balance is $12,246.26. Do not print the reconciliation report.

Print the Trial Balance, Balance Sheet, Profit and Loss, and Cash Flow Statement for April.

Create a backup file named "gradedastorlandscaping April Close" and then close the April accounting period.

Astor Landscaping
Bank Statement April 30, 2008

Beginning Balance from March Statement				$ 78,548.12
April Deposits				
	Apr 2, 2008		21,826.00	
	Apr 9, 2008		5,180.00	
	Apr 9, 2008		4,620.00	
	Apr 11, 2008		2,352.00	
	Apr 23, 2008		1,555.50	
	Apr 23, 2008		10,573.00	
	Apr 23, 2008		4,116.00	
	Apr 23, 2008		10,040.00	
	Apr 24, 2008		750.00	
	Apr 28, 2008		12,127.50	
	Apr 28, 2008		12,495.00	
	Apr 28, 2008		15,108.45	
Total Deposits for April				100,743.45
April Checks Cleared				
	Mar 7, 2008	434	300.00	
	Apr 2, 2008	450	817.76	
	Apr 2, 2008	451	907.82	
	Apr 2, 2008	452	600.00	
	Apr 2, 2008	453	460.47	
	Apr 7, 2008	454	3,633.54	
	Apr 11, 2008	436	1,993.33	
	Apr 11, 2008	437	1,020.00	
	Apr 11, 2008	438	451.48	
	Apr 11, 2008	439	262.43	
	Apr 11, 2008	440	4,679.15	
	Apr 21, 2008	441	150.00	
	Apr 21, 2008	455	3,623.22	
	Apr 24, 2008	456	175.86	
Total Cleared Checks for April				19,075.06
Less Bank Transfers				
	Apr 7, 2008		11,000.00	
	Apr 21, 2008		11,000.00	
Total March Transfers				22,000.00
March Service Charges				83.20
Ending Bank Balance April 30, 2008				$ 138,133.31

PROJECT 1 COMPREHENSIVE EXAM FOR A SERVICE BASED BUSINESS

You begin this exam by opening the **eragonelectricalcontractingproject** sample company. *(Note: This file was copied to your computer and attached to the software in Chapter 1.)* Add your initials to the **Company name** and **Legal name** using the main menu path of ***Company>>Company Information***.

The following are February 2008 transactions for Eragon Electrical Contracting. This is a service based business that designs and installs electrical systems for new construction and older buildings under renovation. Eragon focuses primarily on commercial buildings although they will also perform residential work on large projects. You will be entering all transactions for the month of February including adjusting entries at month end.

All checks received on account are deposited into the regular checking account.

Feb 1

Issue and print the following Purchase Orders (POs).

PO 1803 to Parcells Electric for $797.40 for the following items.

Qty	Item	Rate	Job
2	Switch 30 Amp	218.95	TAM Alamo
10	Breaker 30 Amp	35.95	Jackson Property Red Bird

PO 1804 to RJM Electric for $1,678.00 for the following item.

Qty	Item	Rate	Job
40	Wire 100 Ft.	41.95	Fox and Hound

PO 1805 to Spade Hardware for $244.40 for following items.

Qty	Item	Rate	Job
5	Timer Outdoor	18.96	Mendez Home
10	Timer Air Condition	14.96	Mendez Home

Enter a bill for $1,100 to Brays Property Management for February office and warehouse rental. Print the rent check on check number 1217.

<table>
<tr><td>Feb 4</td><td>Invoiced for the following job materials.
All items on PO 1800 to Parcells Electric. Invoice 8901 for $1,408.75 dated Feb 1. Assign to River Run Housing job.

All items on PO1801 to RJM Electrical Supplies. Invoice 23890 for $582.75 dated Feb. 1. Assign to Fox and Hound job.

Only 5 rolls of wire on PO 1802 to Spade Hardware. Invoice 109 for $209.75 dated Feb. 1. Assign to Thompson Home job.</td></tr>
<tr><td rowspan="5">Feb 5</td><td>Received the remaining job materials on PO 1802 to Spade Hardware. Invoice 121 for $209.75 dated Feb. 4. Assign to Thompson Home job.</td></tr>
<tr><td>Issue and print PO 1806 to RJM Electric for $2,517.00 for the following item.

<table><tr><th>Qty</th><th>Item</th><th>Rate</th><th>Job</th></tr><tr><td>60</td><td>Wire 100 Ft.</td><td>41.95</td><td>Jackson Property Wellington</td></tr></table></td></tr>
<tr><td>Received the following checks. (Note: Verify that checks will post to the Regular Checking Account.)

Check number 1395 for $839.00 from Fox and Hound Apartments paying Invoice 1205.

Check number 151 for $6,700.26 from Jessie Johnson paying Invoice 1203.</td></tr>
<tr><td>Pay all bills due on or before Feb. 15. Print the checks on starting check number 1218.</td></tr>
<tr><td>Hired the following electrician. Set the Current Layout to the Employee Form.

James Munson
321 Park Springs Blvd.
Arlington, TX 76017
Job title: Labor
Filing status: Married with 2 allowances
Pay rate: $35.00 per hour for regular time, $52.50 per hour for overtime</td></tr>
</table>

<table>
<tr><td rowspan="2">Feb 6</td><td>
Issue and print the following POs.
PO 1807 to Spade Hardware for $674.55 for following items. Note the price change.
<table>
<tr><th>Qty</th><th>Item</th><th>Rate</th><th>Job</th></tr>
<tr><td>20</td><td>Switch Beach</td><td>14.99</td><td>Mendez Home</td></tr>
<tr><td>25</td><td>Switch Granite</td><td>14.99</td><td>Mendez Home</td></tr>
</table>
PO 1808 to Parcells Electric for $1,148.50 for following items.
<table>
<tr><th>Qty</th><th>Item</th><th>Rate</th><th>Job</th></tr>
<tr><td>10</td><td>Breaker 50 Amp</td><td>42.95</td><td>TAM Alamo</td></tr>
<tr><td>20</td><td>Breaker 30 Amp</td><td>35.95</td><td>TAM Alamo</td></tr>
</table>
</td></tr>
<tr><td>
Create invoices for all customers with activity during the week of Jan 28 to Feb 3. Perform the following steps to identify customers for billing.
<ol type="a">
<li>For labor hours, print the Time Report and bill all transactions marked Not Invoiced.</li>
<li>For material costs, print the Profitability by Job Detail report and bill all transactions marked Non-Invoiced Expenses Lines.</li>
</ol>
Verify that the invoice Current Layout is set to Service.
Print these invoices using starting invoice number 1215.
</td></tr>
<tr><td>Feb 8</td><td>
Received bills for the following job materials.
All items on PO 1804 to RJM Electric. Invoice 24803 for $1,678.00 dated Feb. 8.
All items on PO 1805 to Spade Hardware. Invoice 137 for $244.40 dated Feb. 7
All items on PO 1803 to Parcells Electric. Invoice 8975 for $797.40 dated Feb. 8.
</td></tr>
</table>

<table>
<tr><td rowspan="3">Feb 11</td><td>Record credit memo CM8975 for $359.50 from Parcells Electric dated Feb. 8 for the return of 10 items of Breaker 30 Amp on Invoice 8975 for Jackson Property Red Bird job.</td></tr>
<tr><td>Enter James Munson's time ticket for the week of Feb. 4 to Feb. 10. All hours are for regular time and are billable.
<table>
<tr><th>Billing Item</th><th>Job</th><th>Hours</th></tr>
<tr><td>Residential Remodel</td><td>Mendez Home</td><td>8 hours Wed. through Fri.</td></tr>
</table>

Add the following hours to Vu Tran's time ticket for the week of Feb. 4 to Feb. 10. Hours are billable.
<table>
<tr><th>Billing Item</th><th>Job</th><th>Hours</th></tr>
<tr><td>Commercial Installation</td><td>Fox and Hound</td><td>4 hours of overtime on Sunday</td></tr>
</table>
</td></tr>
<tr><td>Create paychecks for the biweekly pay period of Jan. 28 to Feb. 10 by referring to the spreadsheets that follow. Recurring paychecks exist for all employees except James Munson. Create a recurring paycheck for James while creating his paycheck. Also, James' gross wages are expensed to the direct labor account.

Print the paychecks on beginning check number 847.

Post the recurring vendor bill for employee federal withholding, Medicare, and Social Security taxes and company Medicare and Social Security taxes. Print on check number 1222 from the Regular Checking Account.

Post the recurring journal entry for FUTA and SUTA taxes listed on the spreadsheet.

Transfer $12,268.18 from the Regular Checking Account to the Payroll Checking Account to cover the Net Pay amount listed on the spreadsheet.</td></tr>
</table>

Eragon Electrical Contracting
Pay Period 1/28/2008 thru 2/10/2008

Employee	Filing Status	Allow	Pay Type	Pay Rate	Regular Hrs	OT Hrs	Gross Pay	Federal Income Tax	Soc. Sec. (FICA) Tax	Medicare Tax	Net Pay
Eragon, Ernest	Married	5	Salary	3,000.00			3,000.00	443.00	186.00	43.50	2,327.50
Hardisty, Warren	Married	2	Salary	2,500.00			2,500.00	262.00	155.00	36.25	2,046.75
Jameson, Mike	Married	2	Hourly	25.75	80.00		2,060.00	196.00	127.72	29.87	1,706.41
Munson, James	Married	2	Hourly	35.00	24.00		840.00	28.00	52.08	12.18	747.74
Rodriguez, Jamie	Married	3	Hourly	25.75	80.00		2,060.00	176.00	127.72	29.87	1,726.41
Tran, Vu	Single	1	Hourly	35.00	80.00	4.00	3,010.00	685.00	186.62	43.65	2,094.73
Wilson, Chuck	Single	1	Hourly	28.00	80.00		2,240.00	450.00	138.88	32.48	1,618.64
Totals					**344.00**	**4.00**	**15,710.00**	**2,240.00**	**974.02**	**227.80**	**12,268.18**
Tax Basis								**Circular E**	**6.20%**	**1.45%**	
G/L Accounts							**57000 / 60000**	**23400**	**23400**	**23400**	**10300**

Eragon Electrical Contracting
Employer Costs for Period 1/28/2008 thru 2/10/2008

Employee	ER Soc. Sec. (FICA)	ER Medicare	ER FUTA	ER SUTA
Eragon, Ernest	186.00	43.50	16.00	90.00
Hardisty, Warren	155.00	36.25	20.00	75.00
Jameson, Mike	127.72	29.87	16.48	61.80
Munson, James	52.08	12.18	6.72	25.20
Rodriguez, Jamie	127.72	29.87	16.48	61.80
Tran, Vu	186.62	43.65	24.08	90.30
Wilson, Chuck	138.88	32.48	17.92	67.20
Totals	**974.02**	**227.80**	**117.68**	**471.30**
Tax Basis	**6.20%**	**1.45%**	**0.8%**	**3.0%**
G/L Accounts	**23400 / 61000**	**23400 / 61000**	**23500 / 61000**	**23700 / 61000**

<table>
<tr><td>Feb 11</td><td>Received the following checks.

Check number 1087 for $2,280.00 from River Run Housing paying Invoice 1206.
Check number 131 for $10,104.00 from TAM Apartments paying Invoice 1204.
Check number 803 for $960.00 from Fred Thompson paying Invoice 1202.</td></tr>
<tr><td></td><td>Pay all bills due on or before Feb. 22. Remember to apply Parcells Electric's credit memo. Print checks on beginning check number 1223.</td></tr>
<tr><td>Feb 13</td><td>Received check number 3247 for $10,915.30 from TMI Properties paying Invoices 1201.</td></tr>
<tr><td></td><td>Issue and print PO 1809 to Spade Hardware for $149.90 for following item.
<table><tr><td>Qty</td><td>Item</td><td>Rate</td><td>Job</td></tr><tr><td>10</td><td>Switch Beach</td><td>14.99</td><td>Fox and Hound</td></tr></table></td></tr>
<tr><td></td><td>Create invoices for customers with activity during the week of Feb. 4 to Feb. 10. Identify customers for invoicing by printing the reports previously illustrated.

After checking with the owner for approval, you allow Fox and Hound to exceed its credit limit.

Print these invoices using starting invoice number 1219.</td></tr>
<tr><td>Feb 15</td><td>Received bills for the following job materials.
All items on PO 1806 to RJM Electric. Invoice 24897 for $2,517.00 dated Feb. 14.
All items on PO 1807 to Spade Hardware. Invoice 135 for $674.55 dated Feb. 15.</td></tr>
<tr><td></td><td>Issue and print PO 1810 to RJM Electric for $629.25 for following item.
<table><tr><td>Qty</td><td>Item</td><td>Rate</td><td>Job</td></tr><tr><td>15</td><td>Wire 100 Ft.</td><td>41.95</td><td>Jackson Property Red Bird</td></tr></table></td></tr>
<tr><td></td><td>Create the following vendor.
Barts Automotive
3318 Pioneer Parkway
Arlington, TX 76019
Terms: Net 30
Expense account: 72300 Repairs – Auto Expenses

Enter Invoice 5663 dated Feb. 15 for $573.95 from Barts Automotive for auto repairs.</td></tr>
</table>

<table>
<tr><td rowspan="3">Feb 19</td><td>Enter James Munson's time ticket for the week of Feb. 11 to Feb 17. All hours are for regular time and are billable.
<table><tr><td>Billing Item</td><td>Job</td><td>Hours</td></tr><tr><td>Residential Remodel</td><td>Mendez Home</td><td>8 hours, Mon. through Fri.</td></tr></table></td></tr>
<tr><td>Received all items on PO 1810 to RJM Electric. Invoice 25002 for $629.25 dated Feb. 19.</td></tr>
<tr><td>Create invoices for customers with activity during the week of Feb. 11 to Feb. 17. Identify customers for invoicing by printing the reports previously provided.

After checking with the owner for approval, you allow Jackson Property Management to exceed its credit limit.

Print these invoices using starting invoice number 1226.</td></tr>
<tr><td rowspan="2">Feb 22</td><td>Received check number 1192 for $7,323.95 from River Run Housing paying Invoice 1210.</td></tr>
<tr><td>Signed a contract for a new residential remodeling job for David White to begin on March 3.

Create a customer using the following information.
David White
3851 Southpark Drive
Arlington, TX 76011
Type: RESID
Terms: Net 30

Create a job using the following information.
Job Name: White Residential Remodel
Start date: 2/25/2008</td></tr>
</table>

<table>
<tr><td>Feb 25</td><td>Enter the following timesheets for the week of Feb. 18 to Feb. 24. All employees worked 40 hours and all hours are billable.

<table>
<tr><td>Employee</td><td>Billing Item</td><td>Job</td><td>Hours</td></tr>
<tr><td>Mike Jameson</td><td>Design Labor</td><td>Jackson Property Wellington</td><td>8 hours Mon. through Fri.</td></tr>
<tr><td rowspan="2">Jamie Rodriguez</td><td>Commercial Remodel</td><td>Jackson Property Red Bird</td><td>8 hours Mon. through Thur.</td></tr>
<tr><td>Commercial Installation</td><td>Jackson Property Wellington</td><td>8 hours on Fri.</td></tr>
<tr><td>Vu Tran</td><td>Commercial Installation</td><td>River Run Housing</td><td>8 hours Mon. through Fri.</td></tr>
<tr><td>Chuck Wilson</td><td>Commercial Installation</td><td>Fox and Hound</td><td>8 hours Mon. through Fri.</td></tr>
<tr><td>James Munson</td><td>Residential Remodel</td><td>Mendez Home</td><td>8 hours Mon. through Fri.</td></tr>
</table>
</td></tr>
<tr><td></td><td>Create paychecks for the biweekly pay period ending on Feb. 24 by referring to the spreadsheets that follow. Print the paychecks on beginning check number 854.

Post the recurring bill for federal withholding, Medicare, and Social Security taxes and company Medicare and Social Security taxes. Print on check number 1225 from the Regular Checking Account.

Post the recurring journal entry for FUTA and SUTA taxes listed on the spreadsheet.

Transfer $13,514.31 from the Regular Checking Account to the Payroll Checking Account to cover the Net Pay amount listed on the spreadsheet.</td></tr>
</table>

Eragon Electrical Contracting
Pay Period 2/11/2008 thru 2/24/2008

Employee	Filing Status	Allow	Pay Type	Pay Rate	Regular Hrs	OT Hrs	Gross Pay	Federal Income Tax	Soc. Sec. (FICA) Tax	Medicare Tax	Net Pay
Eragon, Ernest	Married	5	Salary	3,000.00			3,000.00	443.00	186.00	43.50	2,327.50
Hardisty, Warren	Married	2	Salary	2,500.00			2,500.00	262.00	155.00	36.25	2,046.75
Jameson, Mike	Married	2	Hourly	25.75	80.00		2,060.00	196.00	127.72	29.87	1,706.41
Munson, James	Married	2	Hourly	35.00	80.00		2,800.00	460.00	173.60	40.60	2,125.80
Rodriguez, Jamie	Married	3	Hourly	25.75	80.00		2,060.00	176.00	127.72	29.87	1,726.41
Tran, Vu	Single	1	Hourly	35.00	80.00		2,800.00	623.00	173.60	40.60	1,962.80
Wilson, Chuck	Single	1	Hourly	28.00	80.00		2,240.00	450.00	138.88	32.48	1,618.64
Totals					**400.00**	**0.00**	**17,460.00**	**2,610.00**	**1,082.52**	**253.17**	**13,514.31**
Tax Basis								**Circular E**	**6.20%**	**1.45%**	
G/L Accounts							**57000 / 60000**	**23400**	**23400**	**23400**	**10300**

Eragon Electrical Contracting
Employer Costs for Period 2/11/2008 thru 2/24/2008

Employee	ER Soc. Sec. (FICA)	ER Medicare	ER FUTA	ER SUTA
Eragon, Ernest	186.00	43.50	0.00	0.00
Hardisty, Warren	155.00	36.25	4.00	45.00
Jameson, Mike	127.72	29.87	0.27	61.80
Munson, James	173.60	40.60	22.40	84.00
Rodriguez, Jamie	127.72	29.87	16.48	61.80
Tran, Vu	173.60	40.60	1.84	36.90
Wilson, Chuck	138.88	32.48	17.92	67.20
Totals	**1,082.52**	**253.17**	**62.91**	**356.70**
Tax Basis	**6.20%**	**1.45%**	**0.8%**	**3.0%**
G/L Accounts	**23400 / 61000**	**23400 / 61000**	**23500 / 61000**	**23700 / 61000**

Feb 25	Pay all bills due on or before March 8. Print checks on beginning check number 1226.
Feb 27	Received the following checks. Check number 3302 for $1,397.50 from TMI Properties paying Invoice 1213. Check number 842 for $4,800.00 from Fred Thompson paying invoice 1212. Check number 181 for $2,880.00 from Jessie Johnson paying Invoice 1209.
	The owner asks that you increase the credit limits for Jackson Property Management to $40,000 and for River Run Housing and Fox and Hound Apartments to $30,000.
	Create invoices for customers with activity during the week of Feb. 18 to Feb. 24. Identify customers for invoicing by printing the reports previously provided. You have received approval for any customers that will exceed the credit limit. Print these invoices using starting invoice number 1231.
Feb 28	Received the following checks. Check number 6387 for $9,768.75 from Jackson Property Management paying Invoices 1208 and 1214. Check number 1237 for $8,918.00 from Fox and Hound Apartments paying Invoice 1207.
	Enter the following bills dated Feb. 28. Arlington Utilities — Feb Water — $265.00 Southwestern Bell Telephone — Feb Phone — $450.00 TXU Electric — Feb Elect — $775.00

<table>
<tr><td>EOM</td><td>Prepare the following end of month adjusting entries.

Refer to the Jan. 31 entry and record February depreciation expense.

Refer to the Jan. 31 entry and adjust prepaid expenses for expired February insurance.

Accrue 5 days of wages. Calculate the accrual amount using the gross pay from the last pay period. Reverse this entry on Mar. 1.

Write and print check number 1229 to Cash for $141.40 to replenish petty cash fund for the following expenses.
Office Supplies Expense $38.95
Meals and Entertainment $84.50
Postage $17.95

Prepare the following bank reconciliations and print the detail reconciliation report.

Regular Checking Account statement provided below.

Payroll Checking Account. The ending statement balance is $171.00. Monthly service charge is $25.00. All checks and transfers have cleared.

Print a February General Ledger Trial Balance report and review for accuracy.

Print the Aged Receivables and Aged Payables reports and reconcile Accounts Receivable and Accounts Payable account balances to the trial balance.

Print the Job Profitability Summary for February.

Print the following February financial statements.
Profit & Loss
Balance Sheet
Cash Flow Statement</td></tr>
<tr><td colspan="2">Back up the company data file using the backup file name of Eragon Proj1.QBB.</td></tr>
</table>

Eragon Electrical Contracting
Bank Statement February 29, 2008

Beginning Balance from January Statement				$ 92,398.83
February Deposits				
	Feb 5, 2008		6,700.26	
	Feb 5, 2008		839.00	
	Feb 11, 2008		2,280.00	
	Feb 11, 2008		10,104.00	
	Feb 11, 2008		960.00	
	Feb 13, 2008		10,915.30	
	Feb 22, 2008		7,323.95	
	Feb 27, 2008		1,397.50	
	Feb 27, 2008		4,800.00	
	Feb 27, 2008		2,880.00	
	Feb 28, 2008		9,768.75	
	Feb 28, 2008		8,918.00	
Total Deposits for February				66,886.76
February Checks Cleared				
	Jan 31, 2008	1209	412.50	
	Jan 31, 2008	1210	4,392.98	
	Jan 31, 2008	1211	450.00	
	Jan 31, 2008	1212	2,127.25	
	Jan 31, 2008	1213	789.46	
	Jan 31, 2008	1214	1,679.45	
	Jan 31, 2008	1215	173.85	
	Jan 31, 2008	1216	100.00	
	Feb 1, 2008	1217	1,100.00	
	Feb 5, 2008	1218	1,048.65	
	Feb 5, 2008	1219	3,145.00	
	Feb 5, 2008	1220	372.25	
	Feb 5, 2008	1221	1,048.75	
	Feb 11, 2008	1222	4,643.64	
	Feb 11, 2008	1223	3,404.75	
	Feb 11, 2008	1224	1,243.95	
	Feb 25, 2008	1228	1,048.75	
	Feb 25, 2008	1225	5,281.38	
Total Cleared Checks for February				32,462.61
Less Bank Transfers				
	Feb 11, 2008		12,268.18	
	Feb 25, 2008		13,514.31	
Total February Transfers				25,782.49
February Service Charges				75.00
Ending Bank Balance February 29, 2008				$ 100,965.49

CHAPTER 8 CUSTOMER ACTIVITIES FOR A MERCHANDISING BUSINESS

LEARNING OBJECTIVES

This chapter works with the Practice Baxter Garden Supply data file containing the tasks completed in Chapter 2. ***When this data file is not loaded on your computer, restore it using the "practicebaxtergardensupply Chpt 2" backup file created after reading Chapter 2.***

The chapter focuses on using OAP to process customer activities for a merchandising business and covers:

1. Learning manual accounting procedures (*MAPS*) for customer transactions before recording transactions in OAP
2. Using the Customer Home page to perform customer tasks
3. Recording customer invoices, payments, and credits
4. Looking *Behind the Keys* of posted transactions
5. Managing customer accounts and inventory items
6. Correcting and voiding transactions
7. Analyzing sales and inventory reporting
8. Preparing customer statements
9. Reconciling customer activities to the accounts receivable control account

Launch OAP and open **Practice Baxter Garden Supply.**

The following is background information on Baxter's business operations. The company sells garden supplies to retail and wholesale customers and uses OAP to track inventory and invoice customers. The current accounting period is March 2008.

Manual Accounting Procedures

Before illustrating OAP sales transactions, we want to cover the accounting procedures for a manual accounting system so that you will better understand processing these transactions in the software. Manual accounting procedures (*MAPS*) for processing a customer sales transaction begins at the point where a customer initiates a transaction.

On March 21, 2008, Knight Brothers contacts Baxter salesperson, Brandee Nunnley, requesting shipment of 10 Bell-Gro hose end sprayers and 15 Bell-Gro fan head sprayers. Brandee quoted Knight a total price of $384.35.

In a manual system, Brandee writes up a sales order and sends a copy of the order to the customer and the company accountant, Melvin Frost. She also sends a picking ticket to Al Duke in the company warehouse. Al then fills and ships the order, indicating the quantities filled on the picking ticket.

Al filled Knight's order on March 24 and forwarded the picking ticket to Melvin. Melvin matched the ticket with the sales order and prepared the invoice illustrated in Figure 8:1.

Baxter Garden Supply
1305 W. Maple Ave
Arlington, VA 23523

Customer:
Knight Brothers
5682 Main Street
Arlington, VA 30004

Date: 3/24/2008

INVOICE **No. 10346**

Qty	Description		
10	Bell-Gro Hose End Sprayers		$ 129.50
15	Bell-Gro Fan Head Sprayers		254.85
		Subtotal	$ 384.35
		Sales Tax	0.00
		Total	$ 384.35

Terms: Net 30

Figure 8:1

Melvin then records the invoice, along with other invoices issued that day, on the Sales Journal for March 24 (Figure 8:2).

Baxter Garden Supply
Date: 3/24/2008 **Sales Journal** **Page 8**

Customer	Post Ref.	Description	Accounts Receivable (Debit)	Sales Equipment (Credit)	Sales Tax Payable (Credit)
Knight Brothers	KNIG001	Invoice 10196	384.35	384.35	
Cummings Construction	CUMM001	Invoice 10197	3,768.25	3,504.47	263.78
Dash Business Systems	DASH001	Invoice 10198	4,326.00	4,023.18	302.82
Totals:			$ 8,478.60	$ 7,912.00	$ 566.60
Audit trail		Acct Ref:	(11000)	(40003)	(23100)

Figure 8:2

Melvin entered Knight's invoice as a debit to accounts receivable and as a credit to sales. At day's end, Melvin totals Sales Journal columns and cross-foots totals to verify that entries balance (i.e., debits equal credits). He then posts each invoice to the customer's account and posts column totals to the general ledger accounts noted at the bottom.

Melvin's entry to Knight's customer account is illustrated in Figure 8:3. *(Note: Entries for other customer accounts are not illustrated.)*

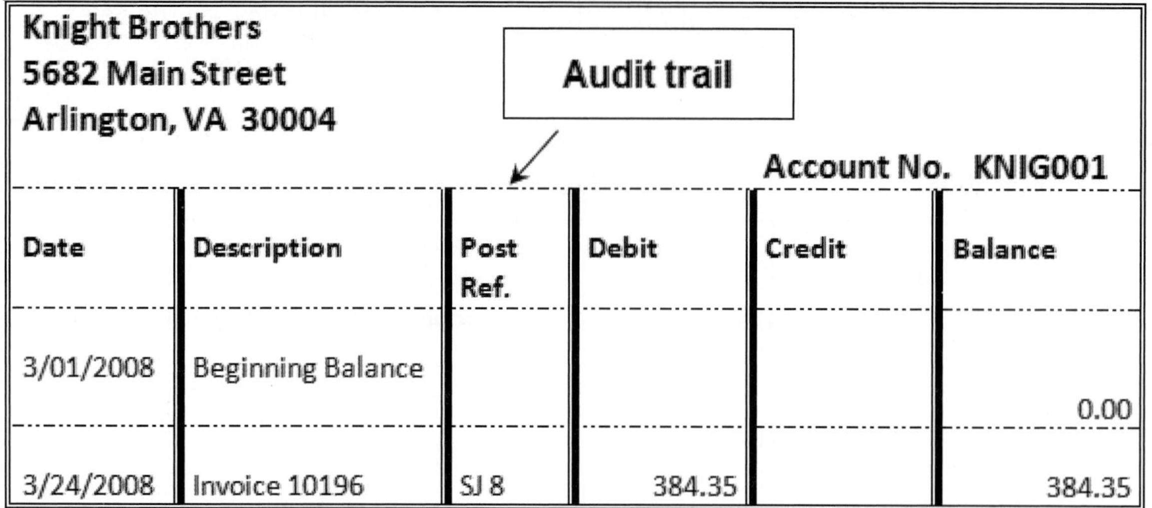

Knight Brothers
5682 Main Street
Arlington, VA 30004

Account No. KNIG001

Date	Description	Post Ref.	Debit	Credit	Balance
3/01/2008	Beginning Balance				0.00
3/24/2008	Invoice 10196	SJ 8	384.35		384.35

Figure 8:3

Melvin's entries to the general ledger accounts are illustrated in Figure 8:4.

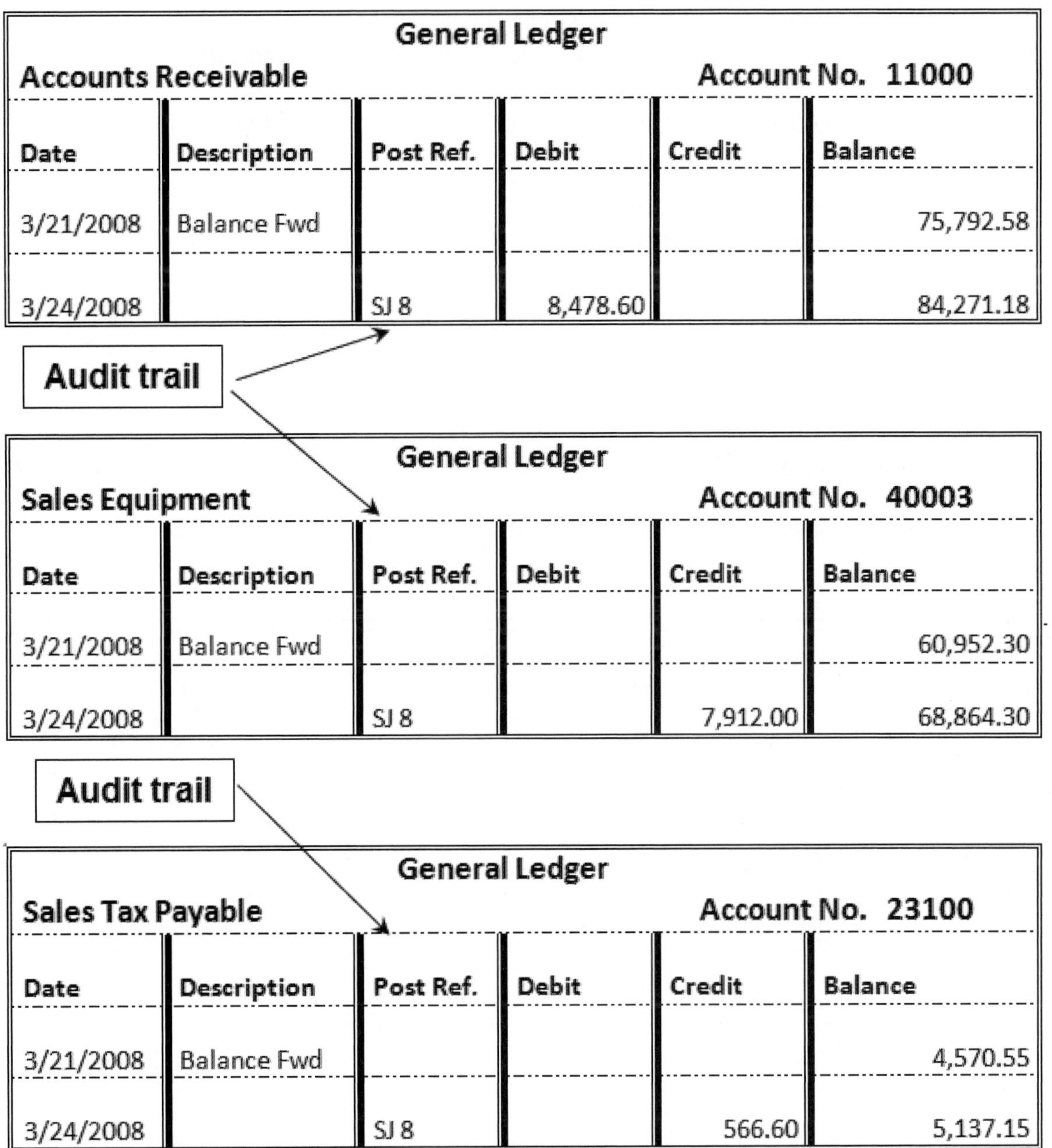

General Ledger

Accounts Receivable — **Account No. 11000**

Date	Description	Post Ref.	Debit	Credit	Balance
3/21/2008	Balance Fwd				75,792.58
3/24/2008		SJ 8	8,478.60		84,271.18

Audit trail

General Ledger

Sales Equipment — **Account No. 40003**

Date	Description	Post Ref.	Debit	Credit	Balance
3/21/2008	Balance Fwd				60,952.30
3/24/2008		SJ 8		7,912.00	68,864.30

Audit trail

General Ledger

Sales Tax Payable — **Account No. 23100**

Date	Description	Post Ref.	Debit	Credit	Balance
3/21/2008	Balance Fwd				4,570.55
3/24/2008		SJ 8		566.60	5,137.15

Figure 8:4

As Melvin posts, he is also entering the posting references that form the audit trail. An audit trail documents entries from the Sales Journal to general ledger accounts, from the Sales Journal to customer accounts, and vice versa. You can imagine the posting errors that could occur in a manual system. Melvin could record an entry backwards (e.g., enter a debit as a credit), record an out-of-balance entry, omit an entry, or forget to enter the audit trail.

Notice that Melvin did not post an entry for costs of goods sold and inventory when recording Knight's invoice because he does not know the specific cost for the items sold. In a manual system, inventory purchases are recorded to the purchases account instead of the inventory account. Only after conducting a physical inventory count to determine the cost of quantities on hand does the accountant post a general journal entry to adjust the inventory and purchases account. The example that follows illustrates calculating an inventory adjusting entry.

1/1/2007	Beginning Inventory		$ 17,856.00
	Purchases in 2007	+	30,765.00
	Total Inventory Available		$ 48,621.00
12/31/2007	Ending Inventory	–	$ 16,375.00
12/31/2007	COGS		$ 32,246.00

The above calculation shows that a credit of $1,481.00 ($17,856 minus $16,375) needs to be posted to the inventory account to adjust begging inventory to the physical count taken on December 31, 2007. Figure 8:5 illustrates the adjusting entry that will be recorded on the general journal.

Baxter Garden Supply
General Journal **Page 17**

Date	Account Post Ref.	Description	Debit	Credit
12/31/2007	45100	Purchases	1,481.00	
	13000	Inventory		1,481.00

To record COGS.

Figure 8:5

After reading the inventory topic, you will discover that OAP automatically posts inventory and cost of goods sold entries at the time of sale (i.e., when saving an invoice).

On the same day as posting sales invoices, Melvin posts customer payment receipts on outstanding invoices. These transactions are recorded on the Cash Receipts Journal shown in Figure 8:6.

Baxter Garden Supply
Date: 3/24/2008 Cash Receipts Journal Page 4

Customer	Check No.	Post Ref.	Invoice No.	Regular Checking (Debit)	Accounts Receivable (Credit)	Payment Discounts (Debit)
Franklin Botanical Garden	1983	FRANK001	10326	1,800.00	2,000.00	200.00
Tacoma Park Golf Course	2351	TACO001	10212	300.00	300.00	
Totals:				$ 2,100.00	$ 2,300.00	$ 200.00
Audit trail → Acct Ref:				(10200)	(11000)	(49000)

Figure 8:6

As with the Sales Journal, Melvin posts each check to a customer account and column totals to general ledger accounts. This time he will use the posting reference of CRJ (Cash Receipts Journal) along with the page number. *(Note: These postings are not illustrated.)*

With OAP most of the posting errors are eliminated. You will see in subsequent topics that sales invoices and customer payments are posted when saving. In addition, OAP posts entries recorded on the Sales and Cash Receipts Journals to the customer's account and general ledger accounts. OAP also enters the audit trail and will not post entries that are out of balance.

We next focus your attention on processing customer transactions in OAP.

Customers Menu and Home Page

Before processing customer activities, become familiar with locating the commands that initiate activities. The first command on the **Customers** menu illustrated to the right opens the **Customers Home** page. The **New** menu opens submenus for creating customer accounts, jobs, quotes, and invoices. Finally, there are separate menus for receiving payments, creating statements, and viewing customer lists.

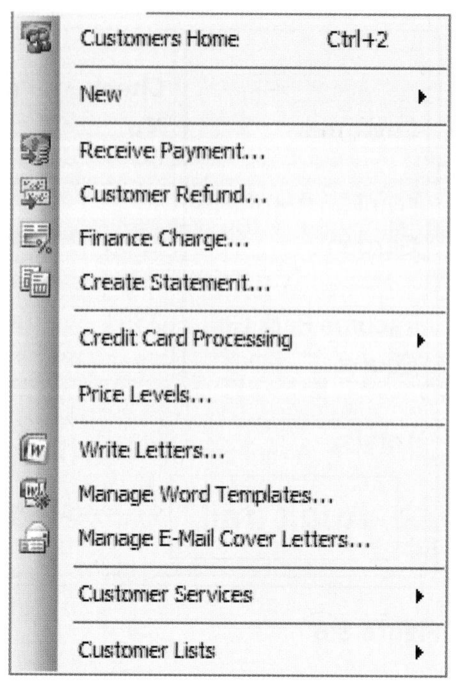

Figure 8:7

Click **Customers Home** on the menu to open the Customers Home page illustrated in Figure 8:8. This home page serves as central command for customer activities.

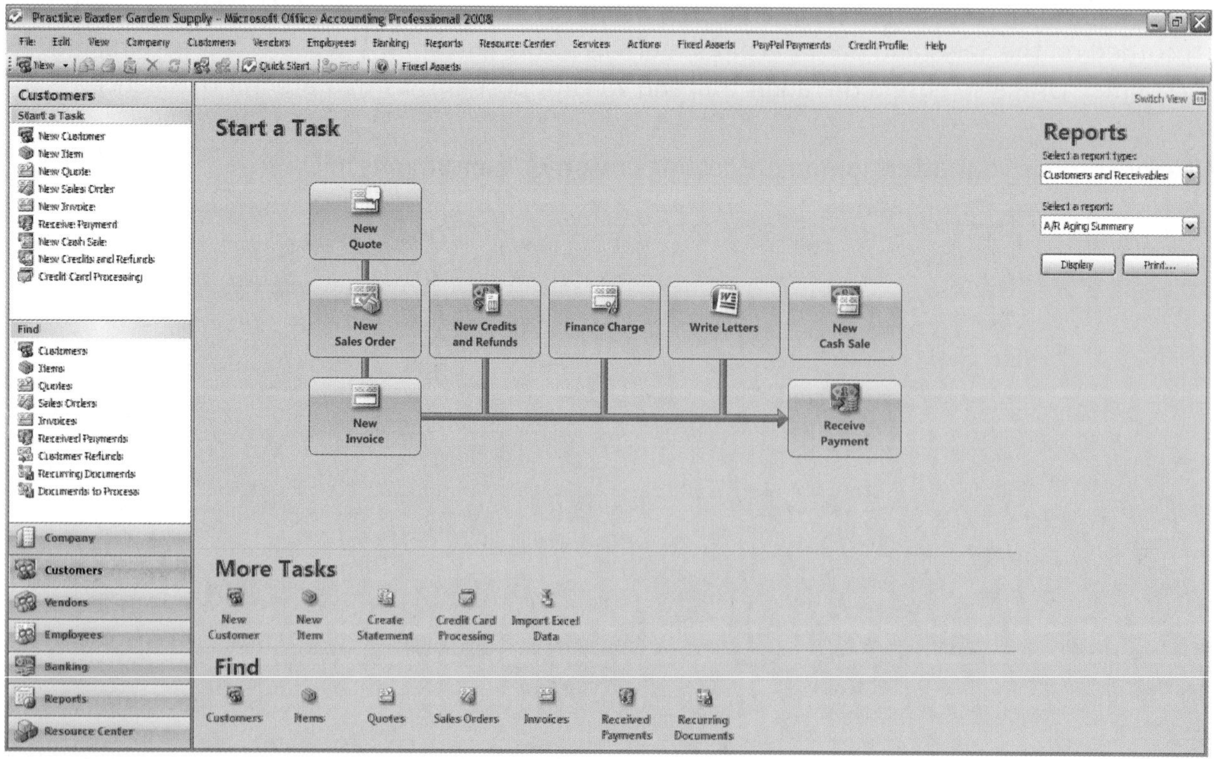

Figure 8:8

On this page are links to many of the commands located on the Customers menu. (Note: The ***Switch View*** link located on the top right changes the home page view. Click this link if your view does not match the illustration.)

Start a Task icons in the center of the page depict the normal flow of customer activities. These icons show that customer activities can originate as quotes (proposed sales), sales orders (pending sales), or invoices (completed sales). Moreover, sales quotes and sales orders will transfer to create sales invoices and invoices are the transactions that receive payments. Credit memos, finance charges, and customer letters can occur anytime after creating the invoice. Finally, cash sales are self-contained transactions that include both sale and payment.

Beneath Start a Task icons are the icons for performing **More Tasks** and for opening lists that **Find** transactions. The activities found on the home page are repeated as links under the **Start a Task** and **Find** headings to the left of the home page.

Now that you are familiar with the Customers menu and home page, let's begin recording customer transactions.

ENTERING SALES ORDERS

You now return to Knight Brothers' transaction illustrated in the *MAPS* topic and capture the transaction in the exercise that follows. Before that - read the data entry tips that follow.

Data Entry Tips

Tip 1: The **Customer name** field links the transaction to a customer account. The **Name** field under **Products and services** links the transaction to inventory items. Customer accounts and inventory items are also called master records. You will recognize a master record field in a transaction window because it contains a lookup for selecting records.

Tip 2: Customers and items can be selected using the field lookup. You can also begin typing the name of the account or item to advance the lookup list.

Tip 3: If you select the wrong customer or item then return to the field and change the selection. Remember that the Edit menu contains data manipulation commands such as cut, copy, and paste.

Tip 4: When you want to remove a line item on a transaction, highlight the row, right click, and select Delete. (See Figure 8:9.) You can also insert lines using this method.

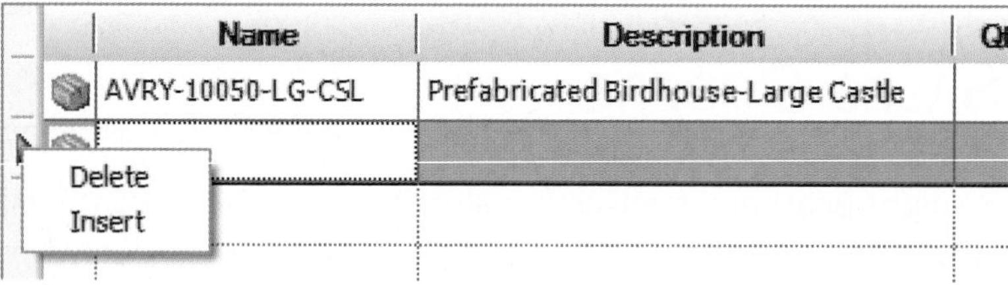

Figure 8:9

Tip 5: You can create new master records "on the fly," meaning to add a new customer or item while entering a transaction. For instance, if you want to add a new customer named XYZ Company begin by typing the company name in the Customer name field and press tab for OAP to prompt to create the new account.

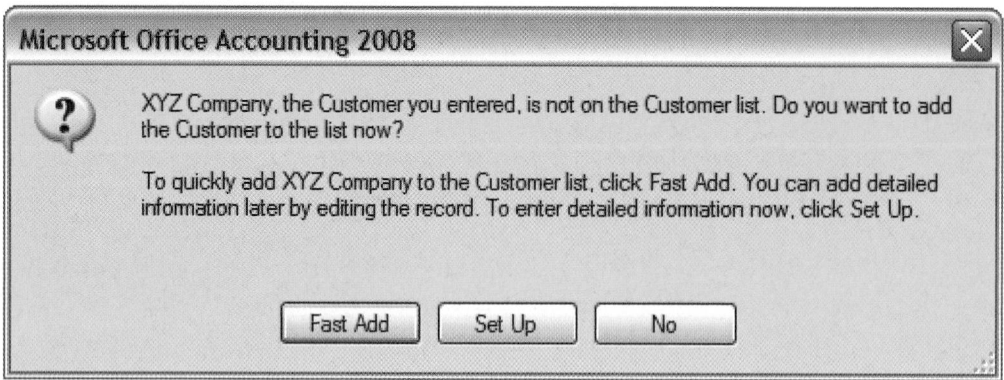

Figure 8:10

You should always click **Set Up** so you can enter all information for the new account. If you select **No**, OAP returns to the Customer name field for you to change the customer selection.

Steps for Entering a Sales Order

1. Click **New Sales Order** on the Customer Home page to open a sales order transaction (Figure 8:11). Enter "3/21/2008" as the transaction date. *(Note: You can either type the date or select it by clicking the dropdown list to open the calendar feature.)*

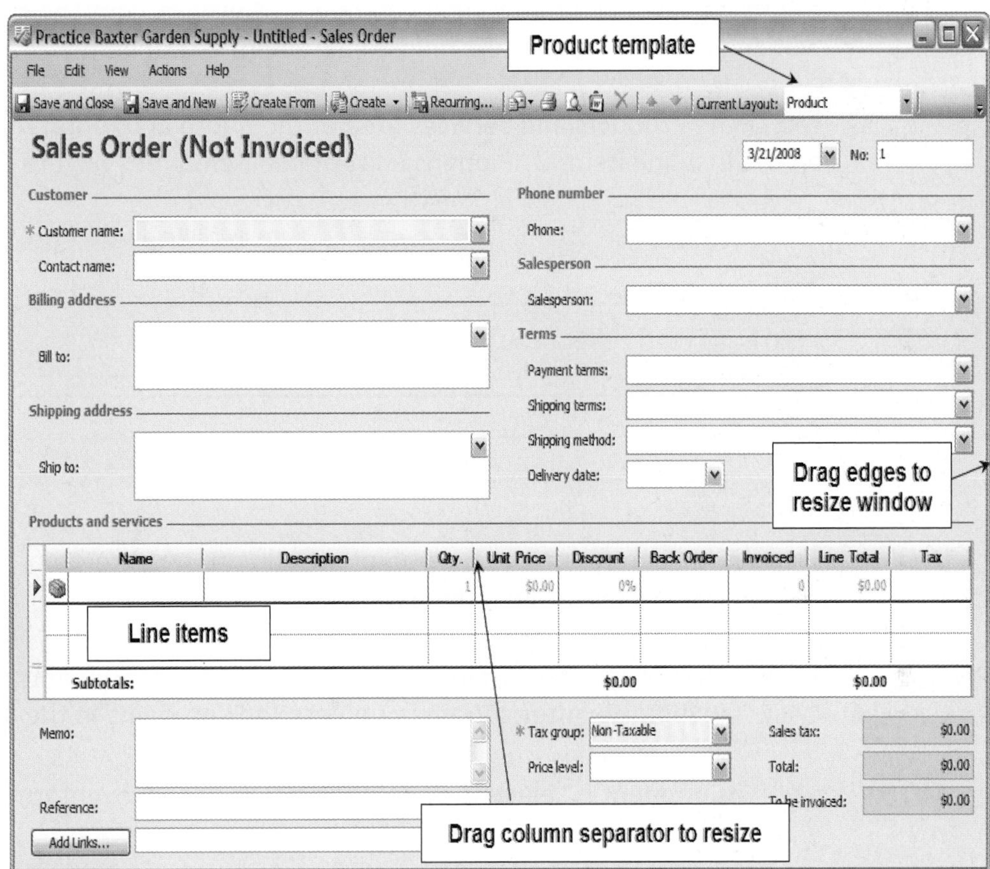

Figure 8:11

Note: You can resize a transaction window by dragging its edges with the mouse. You can also resize line item columns by dragging a column separator.

2. Place your cursor in **Customer name** and begin typing "kn" to advance the lookup to Knight's account and then press Tab. *(Note: You can also use the field's dropdown list to select the account.)* The form autofills with the customer's information.

   OAP has supplied the **No.** value (i.e., sales order number). These numbers are sequentially incremented for each order so keep the current value.

   The **Payment terms** and **Salesperson** defaulted from the customer account and can be changed without affecting defaults. Always accept the default when working exercises in the text unless instructed to change.

3. Tab to the **Products and services** area of the quote and, upon reaching the icon on the first line item, OAP opens a list of line item types (Figure 8:12).

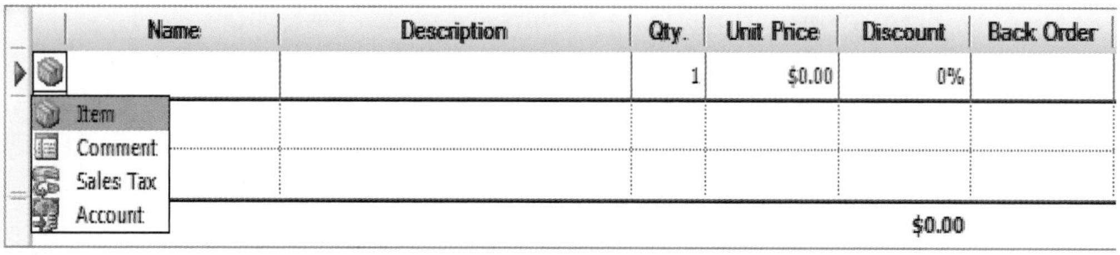

Name	Description	Qty.	Unit Price	Discount	Back Order
		1	$0.00	0%	

Item
Comment
Sales Tax
Account

$0.00

Figure 8:12

These icons determine the type of information to be entered on the line item. The following explains line item types.

- **Item** is selected when entering sales of services, inventory, and non-inventory. After choosing, you can look up items in the inventory table.

- **Comment** is selected when adding text to convey information to a customer.

- **Sales Tax** is selected when implementing complicated sales tax schemes. You will not use this type because Baxter assesses sales taxes using the Tax fields on the line item and the tax field on the customer account. The sales tax charged on the sale will appear in the **Sales tax** field at the bottom of the transaction.

- **Account** is selected when posting sales directly to a general ledger account. After choosing, you can look up general ledger accounts and record a sale that bypasses items in the inventory table.

4. Select **Item** and press Tab. Use the lookup on **Name** to select inventory item "EQFF-13130." *(Note: You can type "eqff" to advance the list.)*

   (Note: The lookup on this field signals it as a master record.)

5. Tab to **Qty.** and enter "10."

6. Tab to **Name** on the second line item and select "EQWT-15150." Tab to **Qty.** and enter "15."

7. The completed order appears in Figure 8:13. Although line items are taxable, Knight is a wholesale customer that does not pay sales tax. Therefore, the customer's **Tax group** at the bottom is Non-Taxable and the order is not taxed.

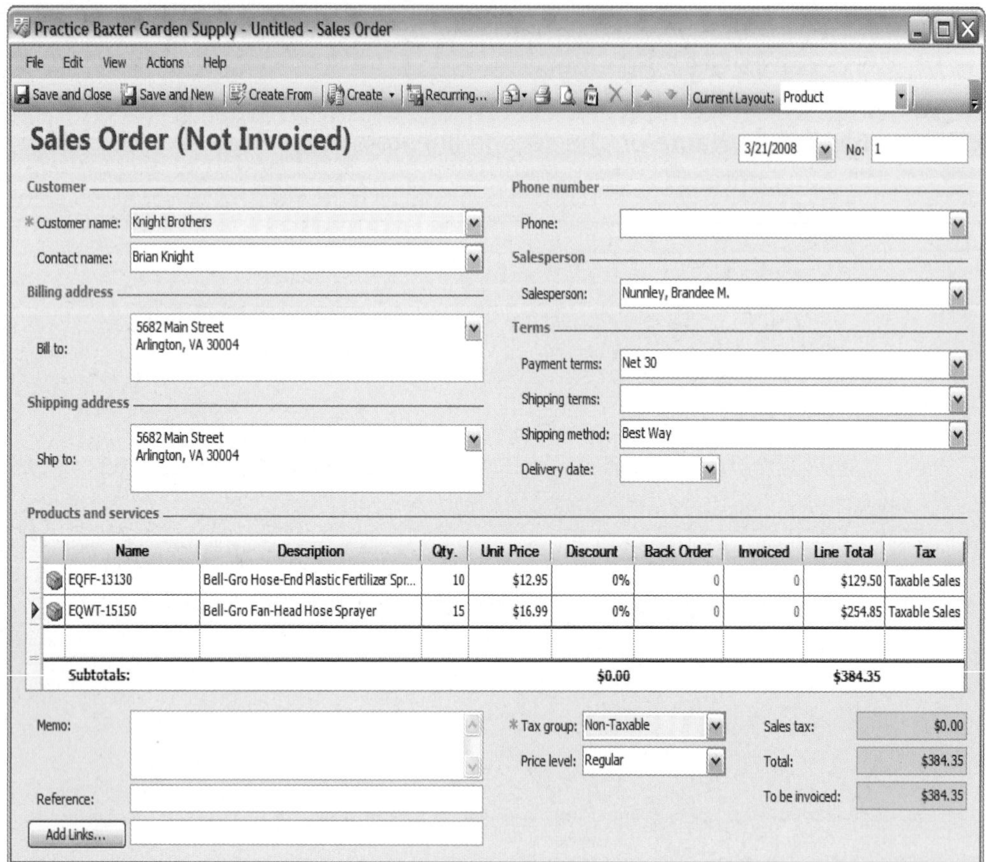

Figure 8:13

Notes:

OAP always computes tax on a transaction by referring to the tax code on line items and the tax code on the customer. If a line item is taxed but the customer is not then the transaction is not tax.

When you tab to the next line, OAP opens a blank line item. This line will be disregarded when saving the transaction.

*The **Add Links** button at the bottom of a transaction will let you link a transaction to an external document stored in Word or Excel.*

8. Click the Print Preview icon on the toolbar to preview the invoice before printing (Figure 8:14). These icons enlarge and shrink the view.

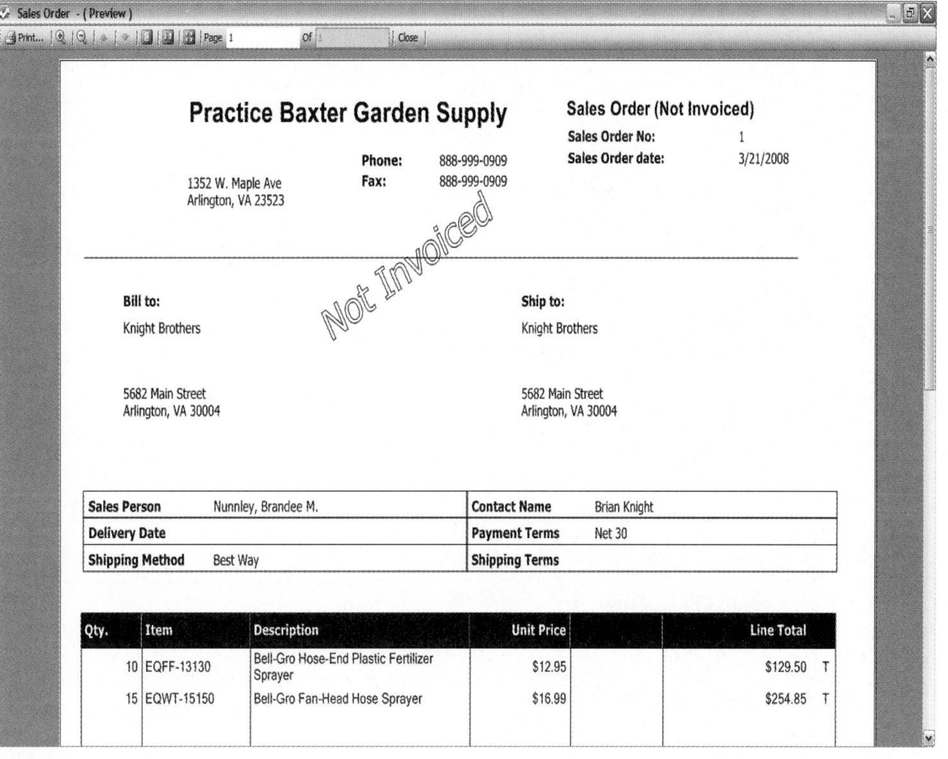

Sales Order - (Preview)

Print... Page 1 Of 1 Close

Practice Baxter Garden Supply

1352 W. Maple Ave
Arlington, VA 23523

Phone: 888-999-0909
Fax: 888-999-0909

Sales Order (Not Invoiced)
Sales Order No: 1
Sales Order date: 3/21/2008

Not Invoiced

Bill to:
Knight Brothers

5682 Main Street
Arlington, VA 30004

Ship to:
Knight Brothers

5682 Main Street
Arlington, VA 30004

Sales Person	Nunnley, Brandee M.	**Contact Name**	Brian Knight
Delivery Date		**Payment Terms**	Net 30
Shipping Method	Best Way	**Shipping Terms**	

Qty.	Item	Description	Unit Price		Line Total	
10	EQFF-13130	Bell-Gro Hose-End Plastic Fertilizer Sprayer	$12.95		$129.50	T
15	EQWT-15150	Bell-Gro Fan-Head Hose Sprayer	$16.99		$254.85	T

Figure 8:14

9. Click the **Print** icon and click **OK** to save the order. Select a printer (Figure 8:15) and click **OK** to send a hardcopy to the printer.

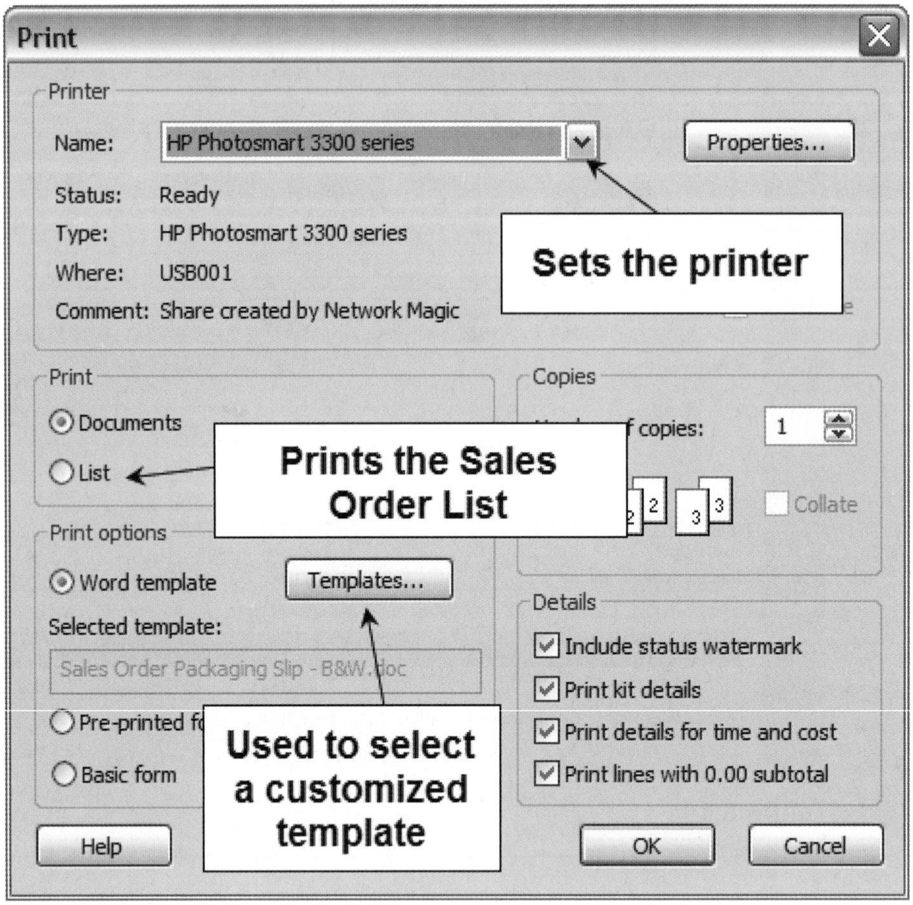

Print

Printer

Name: HP Photosmart 3300 series Properties...

Status: Ready

Type: HP Photosmart 3300 series

Where: USB001

Comment: Share created by Network Magic

Sets the printer

Print

Documents

List

Prints the Sales Order List

Copies

f copies: 1

Collate

Print options

Word template Templates...

Selected template:

Sales Order Packaging Slip - B&W.doc

Pre-printed f

Basic form

Used to select a customized template

Details

Include status watermark

Print kit details

Print details for time and cost

Print lines with 0.00 subtotal

Help OK Cancel

Figure 8:15

10. Click **Save and Close** to exit the transaction window.

Knight's order is now stored and can be monitored by clicking the **Sales Orders** link under **Find** to open Sales Order List (Figure 8:16).

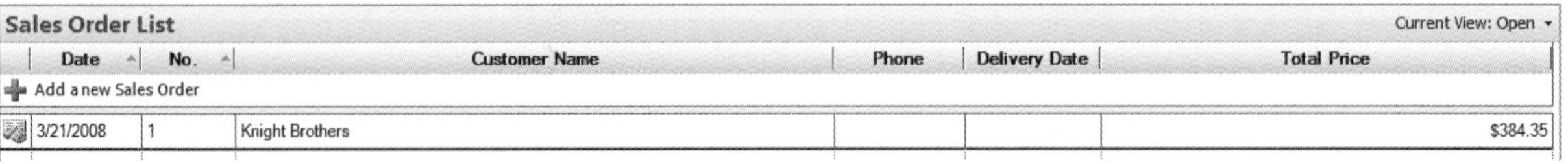

Sales Order List — Current View: Open

Date	No.	Customer Name	Phone	Delivery Date	Total Price
Add a new Sales Order					
3/21/2008	1	Knight Brothers			$384.35

Figure 8:16

Correcting Sales Orders

With OAP, you can easily modify sales orders that have not been invoiced. First, view the Sales Order list by clicking **Sales Orders** under Find and then double click to reopen Knight's order (Figure 8:17).

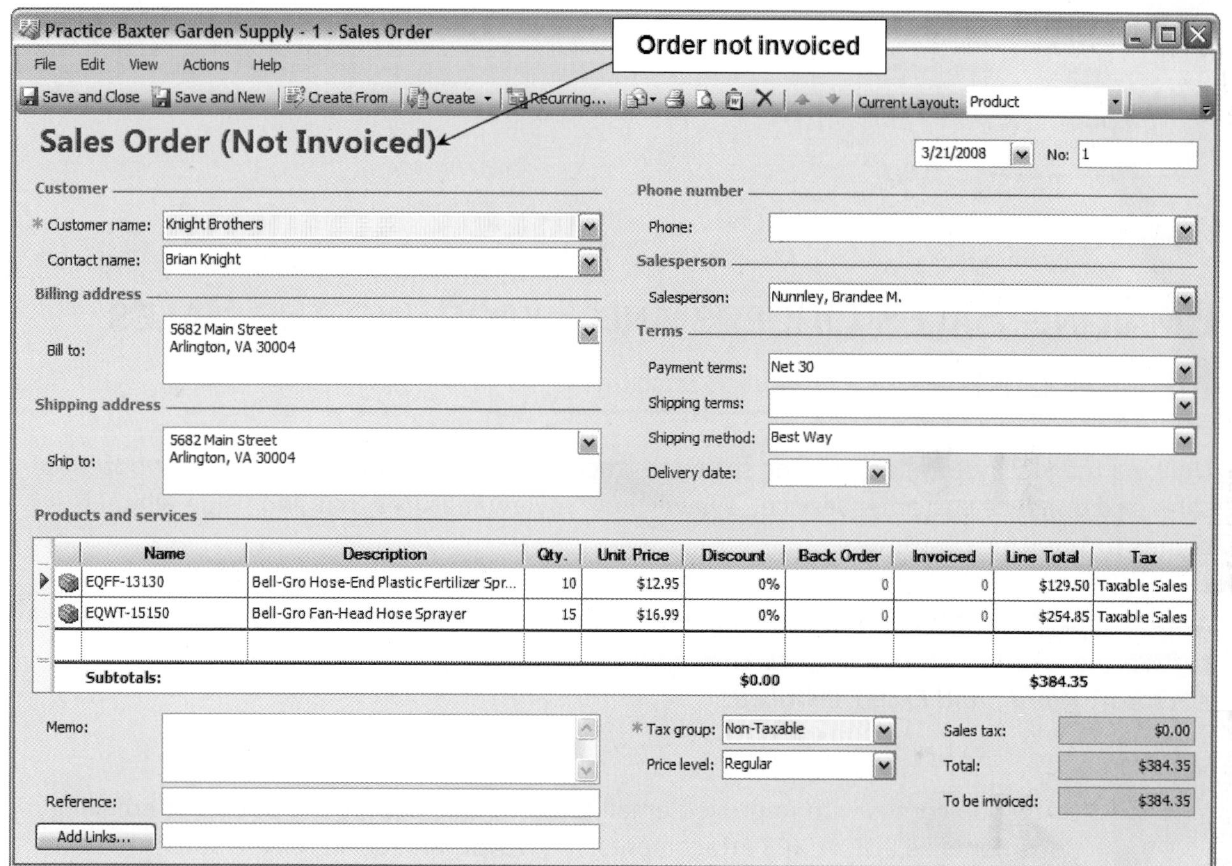

Figure 8:17

After reopening, you can change data, reprint, and resave. You can also delete by clicking the delete X icon on the toolbar. You cannot delete or change orders after transferring an order to an invoice. *(Note: Appendix B provides complete instructions on correcting transactions.)*

Click **X** to close the order and return to the Sales Order List.

You can also highlight an order on the list and right click to select a task.

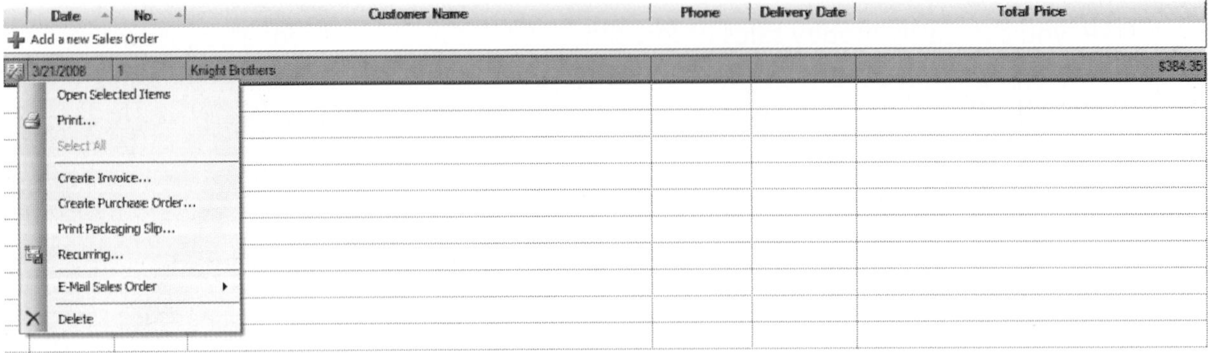

Figure 8:18

Emailing Sales Orders and Exporting the Sales Order List

Unlike a manual system, accounting software tracks sales orders so you can analyze potential sales and enhance customer service. We will now review features that add value when it comes to servicing customers.

Note: To perform this exercise, you must be connected to the Internet and have an E-mail software package installed on your computer. In addition, your machine must have Microsoft Word® and Excel® installed.

OAP 2008 comes with improved email features that supply the option of emailing documents as PDF or XPS attachments. However, an add-in for the software must be downloaded from the Internet and installed before you can use this feature.

Open the Sales Order List and highlight Knight's order. Click the E-mail icon and select **Send as Word Attachment**. *(Note: You can also select **Actions>>E-Mail Sales Order>>As Word Attachment** on the main menu.)* The Select Word Templates window opens (Figure 8:19). Highlight Sales Order – **B&W.doc** and click **Select**.

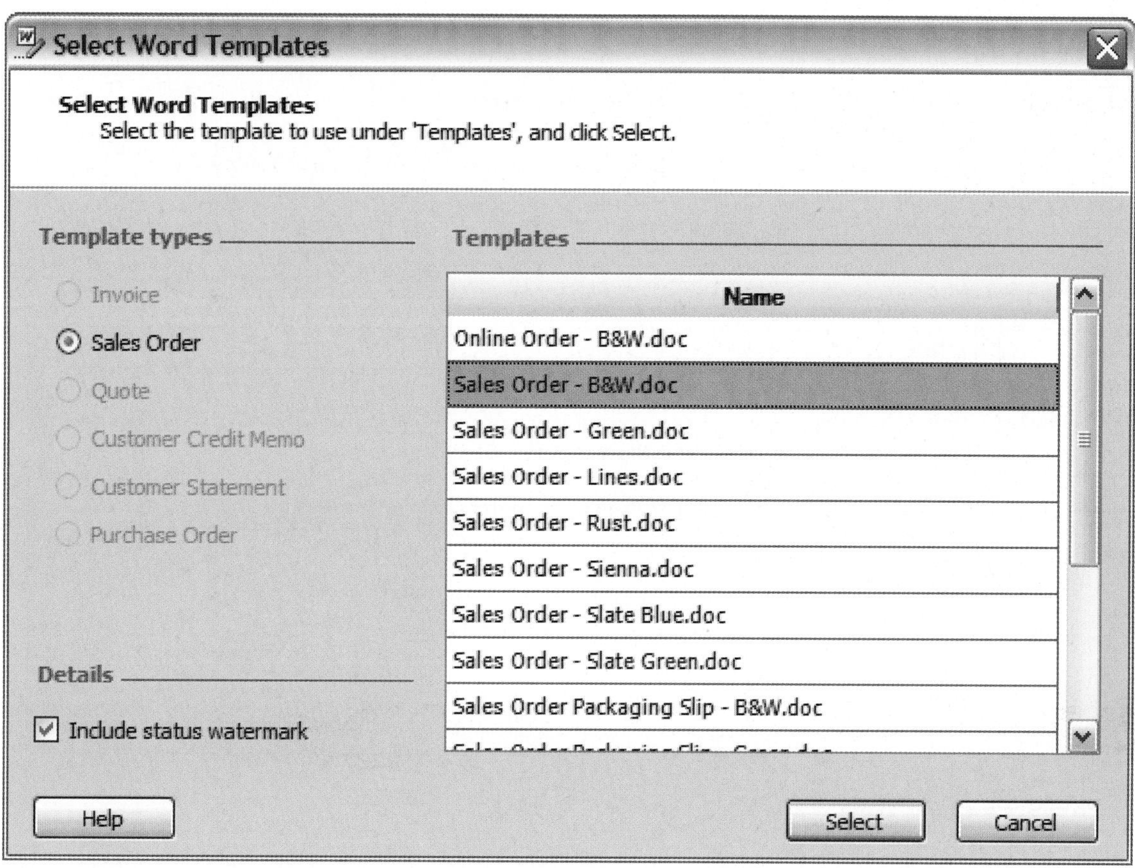

Figure 8:19

An email message opens with the sales order attached (Figure 8:20). Enter your email address in the **To** field and click **Send**. *(Note: The illustration uses Outlook® 2007. When not using this E-mail software or version, click the command on the window that sends a message.)* Check your email later to verify delivery.

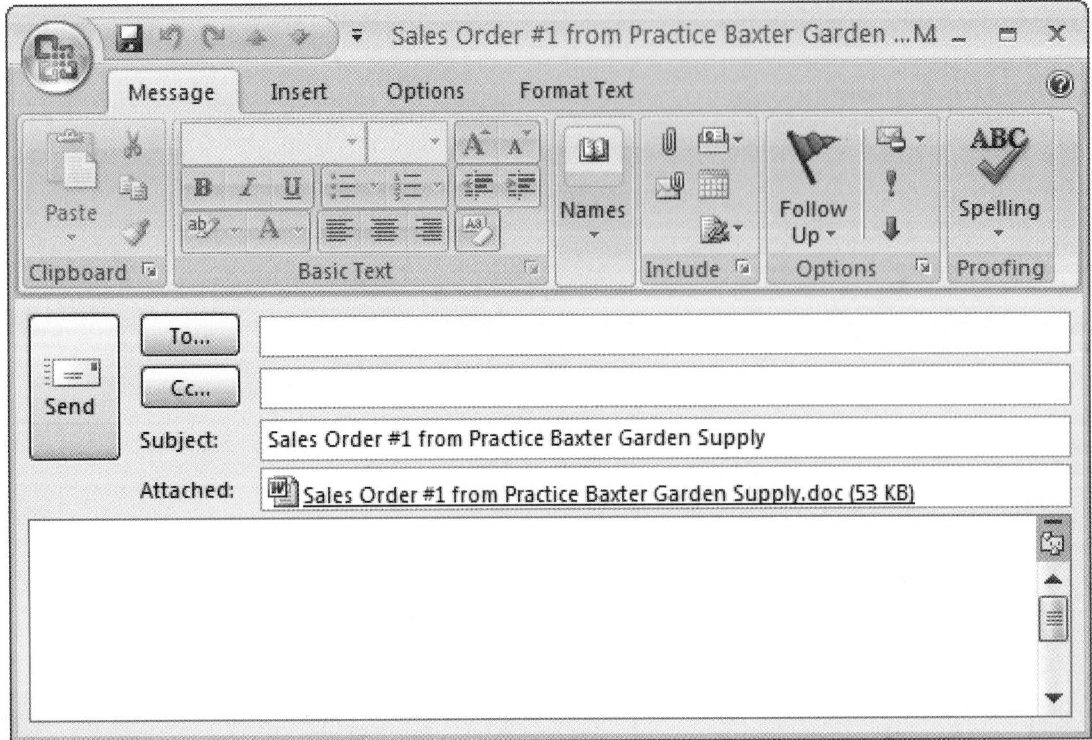

Figure 8:20

You can also use OAP to analyze orders by exporting information to an Excel workbook. While viewing the Sales Order List click the Excel icon on the toolbar. *(Note: You can also select **Actions>>Export to Excel** on the main menu.)*

After exporting the list (not illustrated) you can save the workbook and use spreadsheet tools to analyze orders. Click **X** on the Excel window and select **No** when prompted to save the workbook.

One final note, just like the manual system, sales orders are not posted to general ledger accounts because orders are only potential sales and accrual accounting recognizes sales revenue when earned (i.e., merchandise is shipped). In OAP terms, this means that revenue is posted when invoicing the customer after shipping merchandise and invoicing is the subject of our next topic.

ENTER A NEW SALES ORDER

On March 26, 2008, Chapple Law contacts salesperson Brandee Nunnley to order the following items from the company.

QTY	ITEM	Description	Amount
15	POTS-30100	Bell-Gro 10 in. planters	29.85
8	NURS-24010	Chinese Fan Palm trees	976.00

The order totals $1,005.85 with tax.

Record this order, remembering to use the correct transaction date. Print the order for the customer. Check your work by referring to Appendix E.

Creating a Sales Invoice Using a Sales Order

Most companies ship orders before invoicing the customer. Furthermore, a company's shipping department is often separate from the accounting department so there are procedures for notifying accounting that an order is ready for invoicing.

When Al Duke fills Baxter's customer orders he pulls the inventory by referring to the picking ticket sent to him by the sales department. *(Note: OAP's Word templates can be customized to print these tickets.)* As he fills the order picked quantities are entered onto the ticket. Al then ships the inventory and forwards the completed picking ticket to Melvin in accounting.

Upon receiving the ticket, Melvin creates a sales invoice by transferring the sales order. Processing a sales invoice in OAP correlates to the point in the *MAPS* topic where Melvin typed the invoice and posted it to the Sales Journal, customer account, and general ledger.

We now return to the *MAPS* illustration to invoice Knight's order in OAP. Recall that Al shipped Knight's order on March 24 and notified Melvin to invoice the customer. Complete the next steps to prepare Knight's invoice.

Steps to Create an Invoice Using a Sales Order

1. Open the Sales Order List. Double click Knight's sales order to reopen it and click **Create Invoice** on the toolbar. The order changes into an invoice.

   Verify that the **Current Layout** is "Product" (Figure 8:21). This is a customized form template that determines the layout of the sales invoice window. The template is changed by making a selection on the dropdown list.

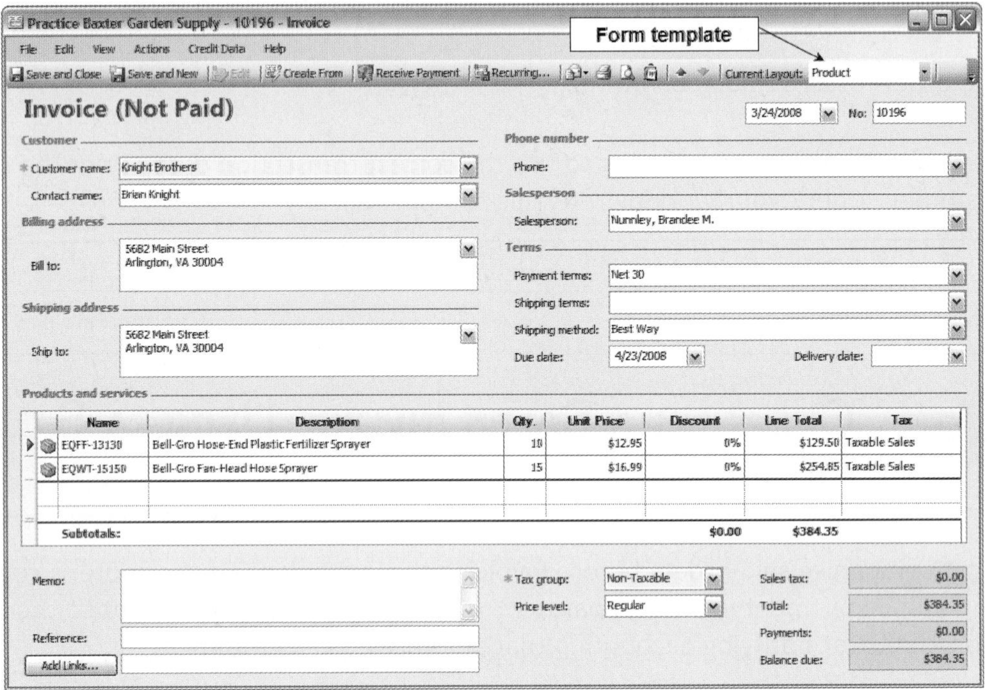

Figure 8:21

Alternative Invoicing Methods

You can invoice a sales order without reopening the order by highlighting it on the Sales Order List, right clicking, and selecting Create Invoice.

You can open a new invoice and select the customer for OAP to prompt to select a sales order for invoicing. If you previously entered the transaction date, reenter it because OAP changes the date on the window after selecting the order.

You can open a new invoice and click the Create From icon on the toolbar to select a sales order for invoicing. Again, verify the transaction date because OAP changes it after selecting the order.

2. Enter the transaction date of "3/24/2008" because this is the date of shipping. Accept "10196" as the invoice number.

3. Now focus on the line items (Figure 8:22). OAP has filled in all quantities assuming all were shipped. If this is not the case, you must manually enter the shipped quantity.

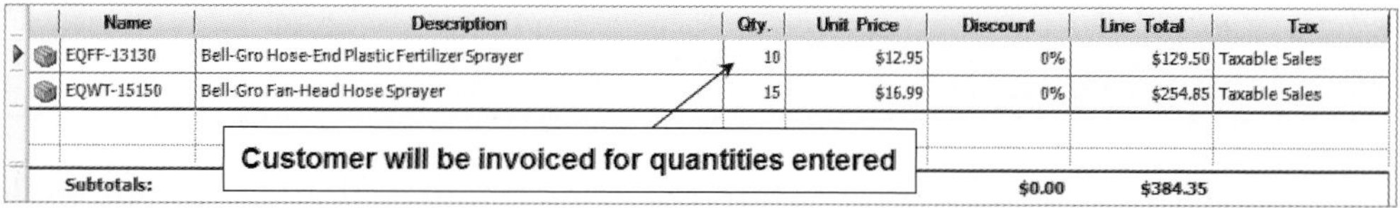

Figure 8:22

4. The invoice is complete so click **Save and Close** and return to the Sales Order List. Knight's order has disappeared from the list. To view it, toggle the list's Current View to Fully Invoiced (Figure 8:23).

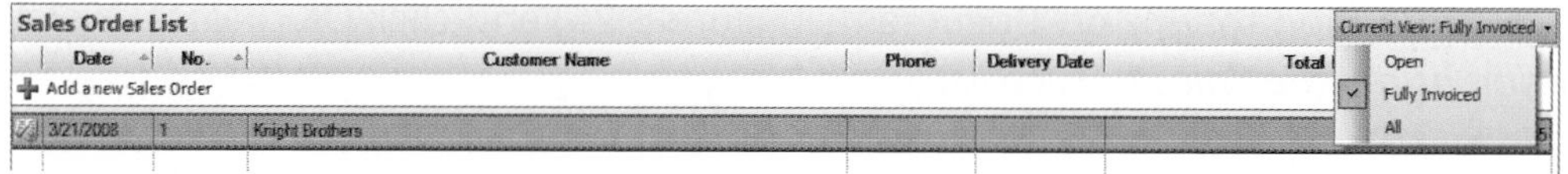

Figure 8:23

5. Double click to reopen the order and note that the status has changed from Sales Order (Not Invoiced) to Sales Order (Invoiced).

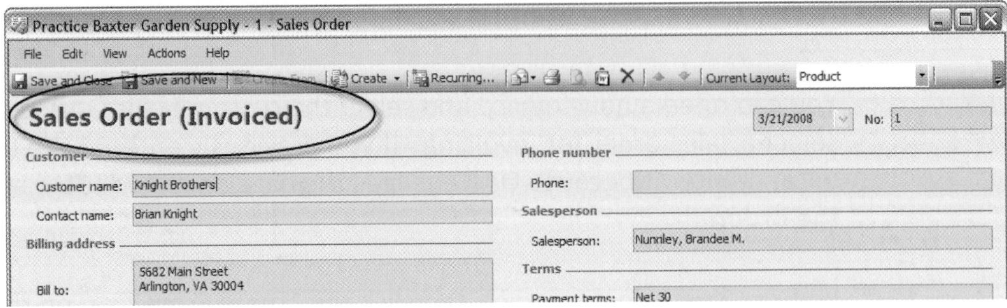

Figure 8:24

Click **X** to close the window and toggle the Sales Order List back to Open.

6. Click the **Invoices** link under **Find** to view the Sales Invoice List. You will find Invoice 10196 to Knight Brothers listed.

PRINTING MULTIPLE SALES INVOICES

In the Sales Order exercise, we illustrated printing a transaction document while creating the transaction. Normally you will want to enter several transactions before printing.

After creating multiple sales invoices you can print them altogether using the Invoice List. First, open the list. Next, select the invoices to print by holding down the **Ctrl** key on the keyboard and clicking each invoice with the mouse to highlight it. After selecting the invoices, right click one of the selected invoices and select **Print**. When the Printer window opens, mark the option that prints Documents (Figure 8:25) and click **OK**. *(Note: Selecting the List option prints the Sales Invoice list.)*

Figure 8:25

You will next trace the entries made when posting Knight's invoice.

BEHIND THE KEYS OF A POSTED SALES INVOICE

In this topic you trace OAP's audit trail to locate the entries made when posting Knight's invoice.

TRACE THE AUDIT TRAIL OF A POSTED SALES INVOICE

1. First, locate Knight's invoice on the Sales Journal. Select ***Reports>> Company and Financial>>Transaction Journal*** on the main menu.

   This report serves as the journal report for all transaction types so you will filter it to display only sales transactions. Click **Filter Options** and highlight **Transaction type** under the Filter section on the left. Using the dropdown list on Options, choose **Selected Types** and click **Show Selected** (Figure 8:26).

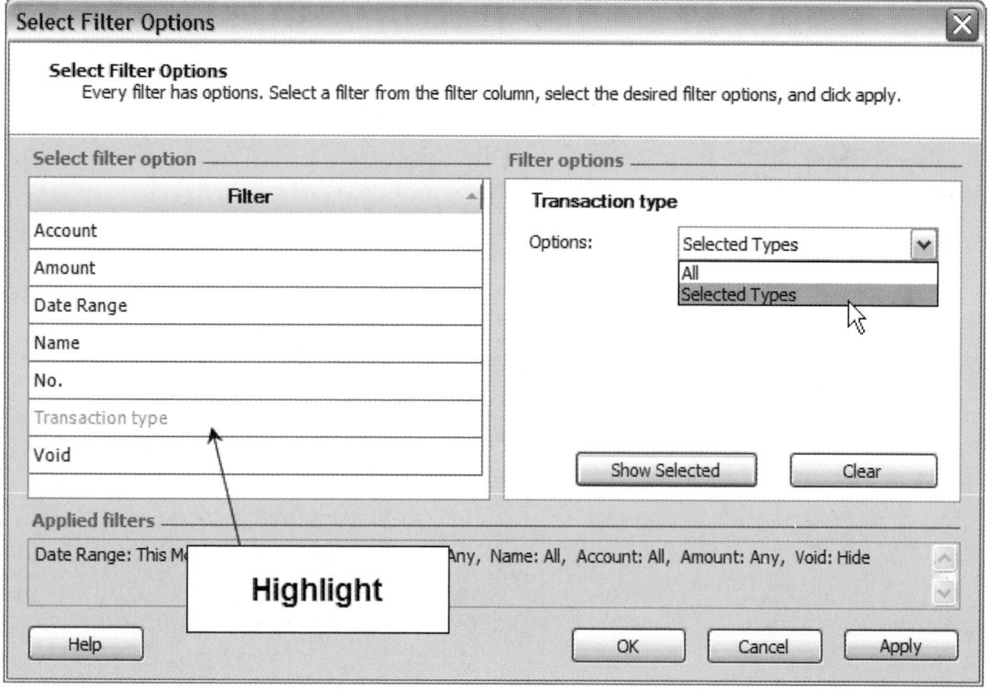

Figure 8:26

2. In the Select Transaction Types window add the Transaction Types illustrated in Figure 8:27 by highlighting each type on the left and clicking **Add**. After adding click **OK** and **OK** again.

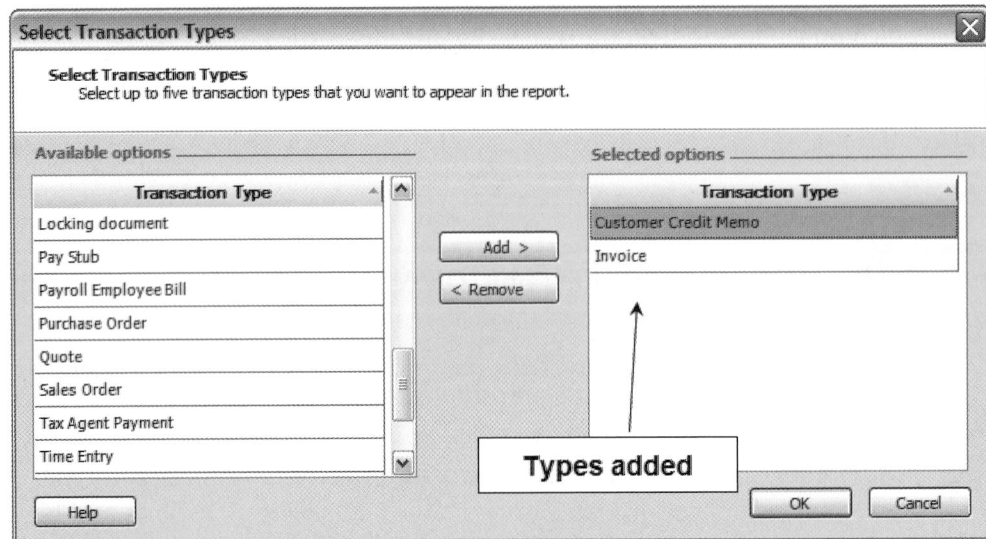

Figure 8:27

3. Next, change the name of the report. Click **Modify Report** and click **Header and Footer**. Change the **Report Title** to Sales Journal (Figure 8:28) and click **X** to close the pane.

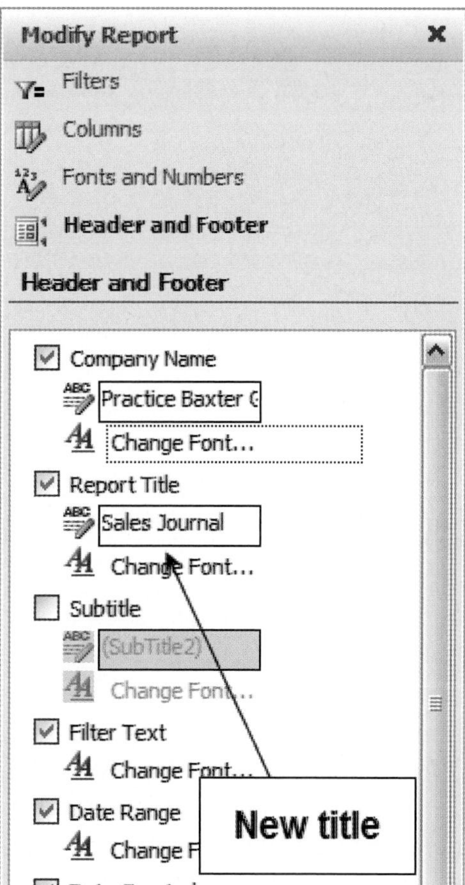

Figure 8:28

4. Click **Save Report** and click **OK** to save the report as the Sales Journal. This report will now appear under ***Reports>>Saved Reports*** on the main menu.

5. Enter the date range of **From** 3/24/2008 and **To** 3/24/2008. Figure 8:29 shows the report for this date.

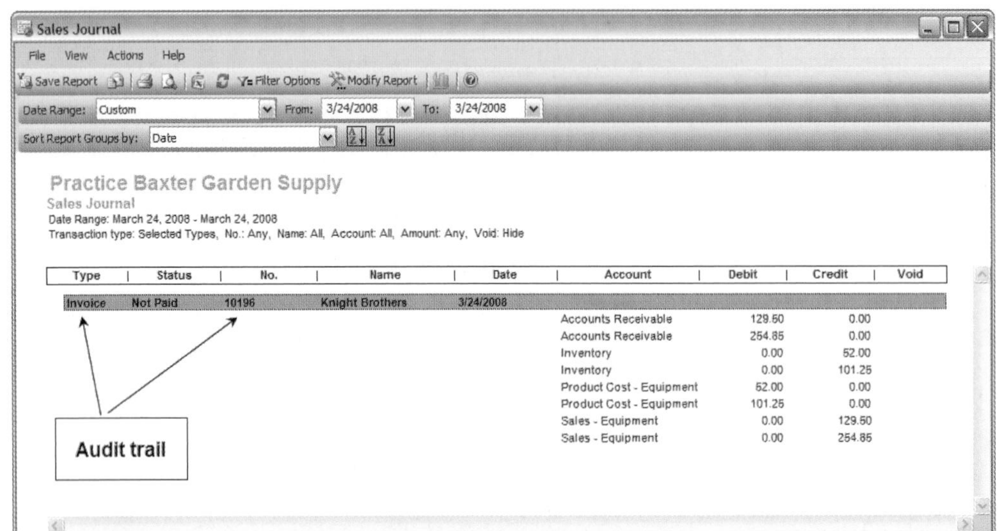

Figure 8:29

OAP's audit trail codes are displayed under the Type and No. columns; thus, the audit trail for Knight's transaction is Invoice 10196.

Recall that Knight's invoice entries illustrated on the manual Sales Journal debited Accounts Receivable for $384.35 and credited Sales - Equipment for $384.35. While OAP recorded sales entries to the same accounts, it posted each line item as a separate entry. OAP also posted cost of goods sold and inventory entries for the items sold.

As explained in the *MAPS* topic, cost of goods sold entries are not recorded in a manual system because companies do not have the resources to identify inventory costs at the time of sale. Instead, cost of goods sold is recorded after taking a physical count of quantities on hand. Thus, companies using a manual system do not have immediate access to accurate quantities on hand.

You will see in the inventory topic that follows that OAP tracks item costs and quantities on hand. As a result, companies have more timely financial information because cost of goods sold and quantities on hand adjust when invoicing.

Close this report.

(Hint: You can reopen the original invoice by double clicking any of the entries listed on the report.)

6. You will now locate OAP's entries to Knight's customer account. Recall in the *MAPS* topic that after posting an invoice on the Sales Journal the entry was then posted to the customer's account.

   Click ***Reports>>Customers and Receivables>>Customer Transaction History*** on the main menu.

   Enter the date range of **From** 3/24/2008 **To** 3/24/2008. Using the same method for filtering the Sales Journal report, click Filter Options to set the Customer name filter to Knight Brothers.

   The audit trail on Knight's account is Invoice 10196, which matches the audit trail on the Sales Journal. Close this report.

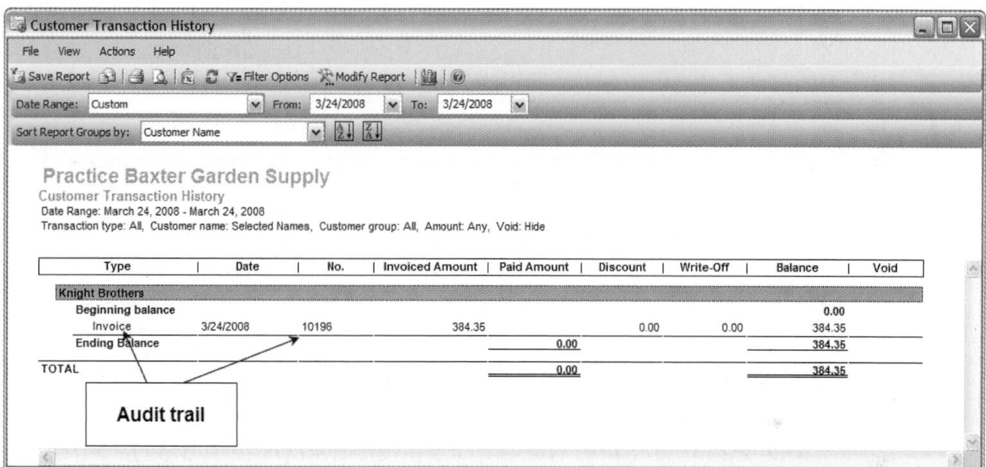

Figure 8:30

7. All that remains is tracing entries made to the general ledger. Select ***Reports>>Company and Financial>>Transaction Detail by Account*** on the main menu. Enter the date range of "3/24/2008." You will find several transactions on that date. Scroll down the account 11000 Accounts Receivable.

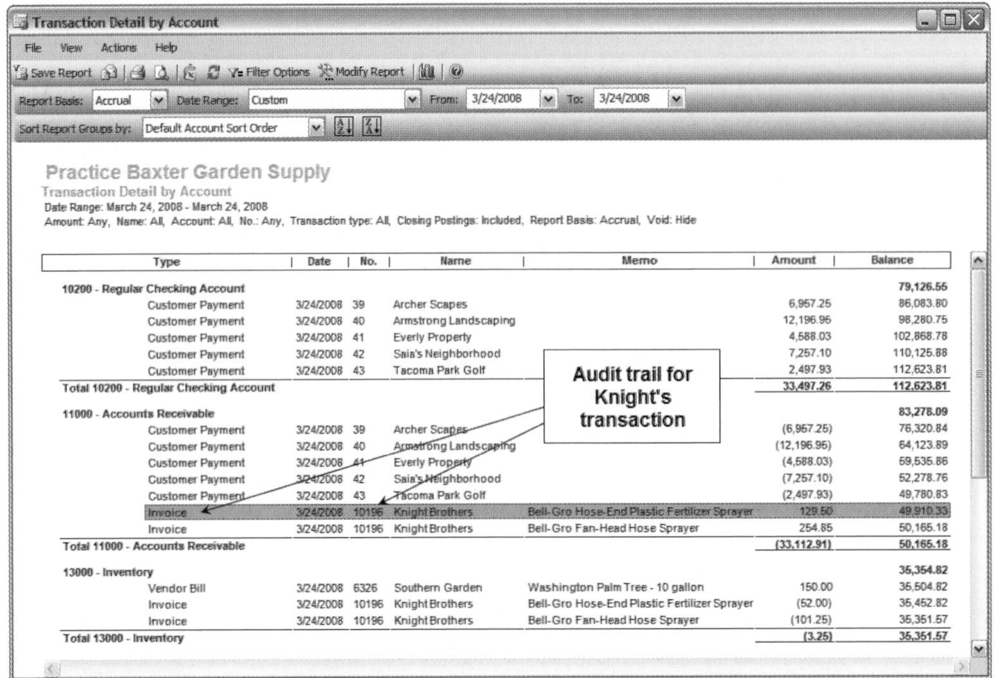

Practice Baxter Garden Supply
Transaction Detail by Account
Date Range: March 24, 2008 - March 24, 2008
Amount: Any, Name: All, Account: All, No.: Any, Transaction type: All, Closing Postings: Included, Report Basis: Accrual, Void: Hide

Type	Date	No.	Name	Memo	Amount	Balance
10200 - Regular Checking Account						**79,126.55**
Customer Payment	3/24/2008	39	Archer Scapes		6,957.25	86,083.80
Customer Payment	3/24/2008	40	Armstrong Landscaping		12,196.95	98,280.75
Customer Payment	3/24/2008	41	Everly Property		4,588.03	102,868.78
Customer Payment	3/24/2008	42	Saia's Neighborhood		7,257.10	110,125.88
Customer Payment	3/24/2008	43	Tacoma Park Golf		2,497.93	112,623.81
Total 10200 - Regular Checking Account					33,497.26	112,623.81
11000 - Accounts Receivable						**83,278.09**
Customer Payment	3/24/2008	39	Archer Scapes		(6,957.25)	76,320.84
Customer Payment	3/24/2008	40	Armstrong Landscaping		(12,196.95)	64,123.89
Customer Payment	3/24/2008	41	Everly Property		(4,588.03)	59,535.86
Customer Payment	3/24/2008	42	Saia's Neighborhood		(7,257.10)	52,278.76
Customer Payment	3/24/2008	43	Tacoma Park Golf		(2,497.93)	49,780.83
Invoice	3/24/2008	10196	Knight Brothers	Bell-Gro Hose-End Plastic Fertilizer Sprayer	129.50	49,910.33
Invoice	3/24/2008	10196	Knight Brothers	Bell-Gro Fan-Head Hose Sprayer	254.85	50,165.18
Total 11000 - Accounts Receivable					(33,112.91)	50,165.18
13000 - Inventory						**35,354.82**
Vendor Bill	3/24/2008	6326	Southern Garden	Washington Palm Tree - 10 gallon	150.00	35,504.82
Invoice	3/24/2008	10196	Knight Brothers	Bell-Gro Hose-End Plastic Fertilizer Sprayer	(52.00)	35,452.82
Invoice	3/24/2008	10196	Knight Brothers	Bell-Gro Fan-Head Hose Sprayer	(101.25)	35,351.57
Total 13000 - Inventory					(3.25)	35,351.57

Figure 8:31

Once again you find the entry's audit trail (Figure 8:31). Scroll to the bottom to trace all the entries.

Close the report.

You have now followed OAP's audit trail and see the advantages to using a computerized accounting system. You were able to create a sales order and then transfer the order to an invoice. When saving the invoice, OAP posted entries to the Sales Journal, customer account, and general ledger accounts and entered the audit trail. In addition, the accountant is better equipped to answer customer inquiries, provide customer support, manage company sales, and analyze profitability.

CORRECTING AND VOIDING SALES INVOICES

This topic explains the procedures for voiding invoices and correcting errors on **unpaid** invoices. *(Note: Refer to the instructions in Appendix B before correcting paid invoices.)* First, locate the invoice by opening the Invoice List. For this illustration reopen Knight Brothers' invoice created in an earlier topic. Notice that the invoice is marked **Not Paid** (Figure 8:32).

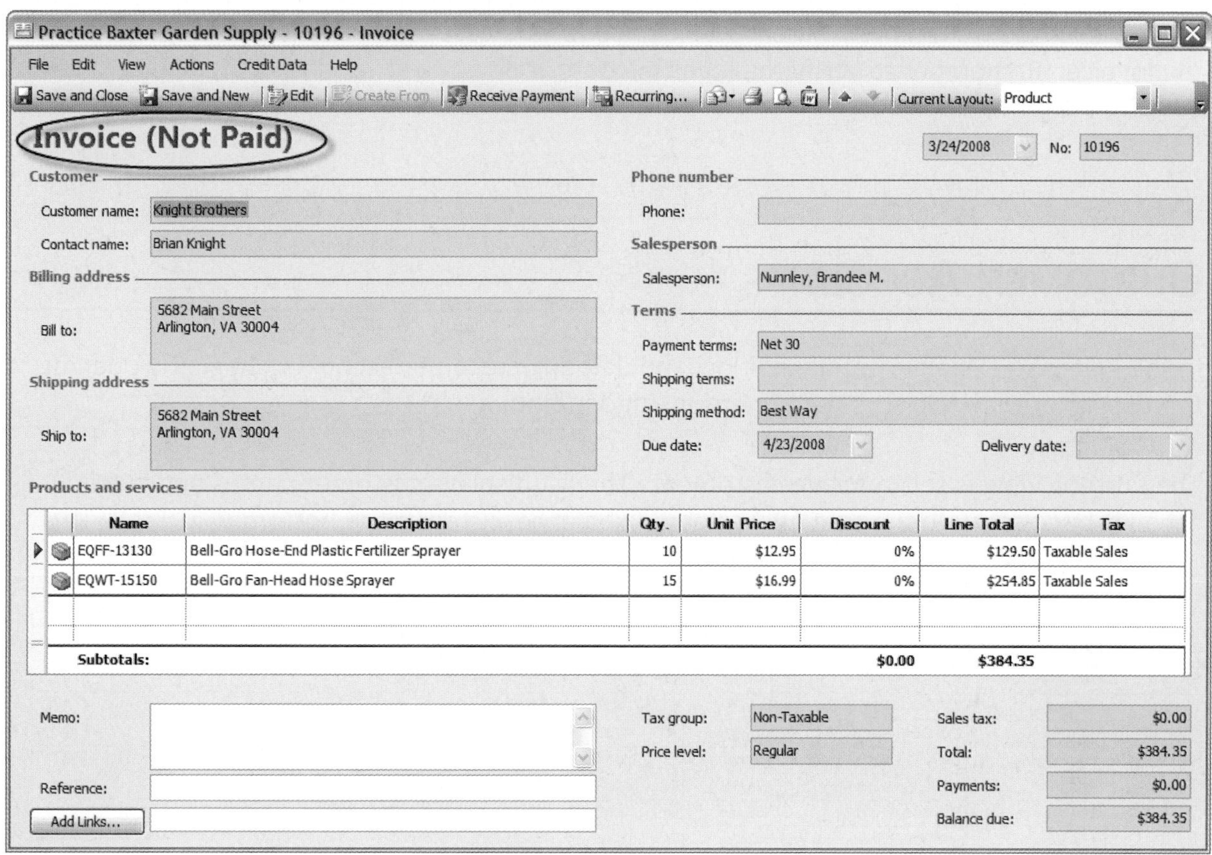

Figure 8:32

The fields on a posted invoice are locked so to make changes you must click the **Edit** button on the toolbar or select ***Action>>Edit*** on the menu. After making changes, click Save and Close for OAP to reverse the original transaction and post a new transaction.

OAP does not permit deleting invoices. Therefore, if you want to remove an invoice it must be voided. To void, you select ***Action>>Void*** on the Invoice menu. *(Note: You can also void an invoice without reopening it by highlighting the transaction on the Invoice List, right clicking, and selecting Void.)*

Voiding an invoice causes OAP to reverse the transaction and reinstate the Sales Order to again invoice the customer. Voided transactions are listed on account registers with this symbol.

Click **X** to close Knight's invoice.

CREATE A SALES INVOICE USING A SALES ORDER

On March 27, 2008, all merchandise on the sales order to Chapple Law created in the previous *You Try* exercise was shipped. Create an invoice for the customer using this order and print the invoice. Remember to verify the invoicing date.

Customer Accounts

In this topic we explain creating, editing, and deleting customer accounts. Begin by opening the Customer List. Click the **Customers** link under **Find**.

The Current View is set to Active customers. The list displays customer names and current account balances with the sum of outstanding balances listed at the bottom.

Customer List — Current View: Active (Current view)

Active	Customer Name	Address	City	State	Zip Code	Phone		Balance
Add a new Customer								
✓	Aldred Builders	412 Sever Rd	Arlington	VA	30092	770-555-0654	770-555-06...	$0.00
✓	Archer Scapes	778 Oakland Parkway	Arlington	VA	30092	770-555-4660	770-555-46...	$0.00
✓	Armstrong Landscaping	2300 Club Drive	Blacksburg	VA	30093	770-555-8824	770-555-88...	$59.90
✓	Cannon Healthcare	2300 Club Drive	Arlington	VA	30093	770-555-4128	770-555-41...	$611.91
✓	Chapple Law	12554 Lawrenceville Hwy.	Blacksburg	VA	30095-1120	770-555-8858	770-555-88...	$3,302.92
✓	Cummings Construction	4785 Satellite Road	Arlington	VA	30093	770-555-1147	770-555-11...	$159.97
✓	Dash Business	1448 Steve Reynolds Blvd.	Arlington	VA	30093	770-555-9988	770-555-99...	$0.00
✓	Everly Property	4558 Pleasant Hill Road	Arlington	VA	30092	770-555-6660	770-555-66...	$0.00
✓	Franklin Botanical	4589 East Jefferson Blvd.	Arlington	VA	30004	770 555-9598	770 555-8772	$3,149.22
✓	Freemond Country Club	9845 Willow Trail Dr	Blacksburg	VA	30093	770-555-8967	770-555-89...	$0.00
✓	Frost Technology	1492 Indian Trail	Arlington	VA	30093	770-555-4153	770-555-41...	$0.00
✓	Golden Gardens	9861 Hidden Valley Trail	Arlington	VA	30018	404 555-7763	404 555-4445	$0.00
✓	Gordon Park	4318 Simms Rd	Blacksburg	VA	30093	770-555-0014	770-555-00...	$0.00
✓	Henton Park	15560 Harrison Road	Arlington	VA	30344	404-555-2025	404-555-20...	$0.00
✓	Holland Properties	1577 Johnson Ferry Road	Arlington	VA	30062	770-555-9927	770-555-99...	$7,432.29
✓	Kenton Golf	1969 Fort Solitude Circle	Centerville	VA	31028	770-555-4469	770-555-44...	$7,137.17
✓	Knight Brothers	5682 Main Street	Arlington	VA	30004	770 555-6772		$384.35
✓	Mason Office Park	4501 Peachtree Industrial	Blacksburg	VA	30329	770-555-3311	770-555-33...	$0.00
✓	McKay Construction	4556 Piedmont Road	Arlington	VA	30344	404-555-4225	404-555-42...	$0.00
✓	Mosley Country Club	1 Howell Walk	Dunvy	VA	30096	770-555-6948	770-555-69...	$15,091.57
✓	Pierce Properties	313 Abbots Bridge Rd	Arlington	VA	30093	770-555-3765	770-555-37...	$0.00
✓	Retail Cash Sales							$0.00
✓	Roberts Learning	573 Crestview Lane	Napier	VA	30092	770-555-6178	770-555-51...	$0.00
✓	Rose University	4444 Parsons Road NE	Arlington	VA	30333	404-555-7202	404-555-72...	$0.00
✓	Saia's Neighborhood	8520 Ronald Reagan Pkwy	Arlington	VA	30093	770-555-1684	770-555-16...	$0.00
✓	Seawright Sod	1505 Ponce De Leon	Blacksburg	VA	30311	404-555-2246	404-555-22...	$0.00

Total outstanding balance: $51,191.15

Outstanding balance for accounts receivable

Figure 8:33

Double click **Knight Brothers** to open the account and follow below as we describe the tabs on the customer account.

General Tab

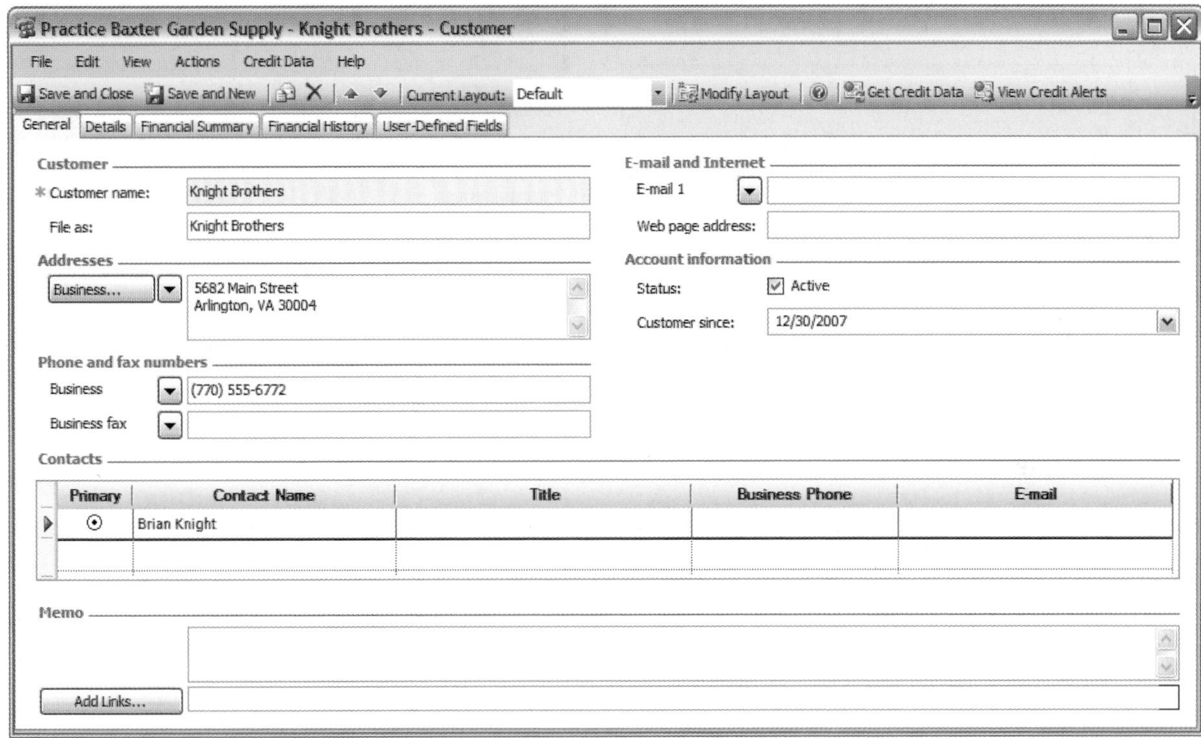

Figure 8:34

This tab stores basic customer information such as address, phone numbers, and email address. The dropdown symbol on a field means you can toggle the field to enter additional data. For instance, the dropdown symbol on Business can be changed to Ship To for storing a separate shipping address.

Details Tab

Figure 8:35

This tab sets customer defaults used during transaction entry, including the customer's **Credit limit**, **Payment terms**, and **Tax group**.

Salesperson is used to assign an employee sales representative for tracking sales commissions and sales performance.

Credit limit is an important option for managing bad debt. OAP will warn before saving a new invoice that causes the customer's outstanding balance to exceed the credit limit.

Price level is used when companies implement tiered sales pricing. Tiered pricing means that a company can sell the same service or inventory item at different prices. This feature is discussed later in the chapter.

Customer group is optional and will differentiate sales by customer characteristics. Baxter uses the Wholesale and Retail types. A wholesale customer does not pay sales tax.

Click the dropdown list on **Payment terms** to view options for determining invoice due dates and payment discount terms (Figure 8:36).

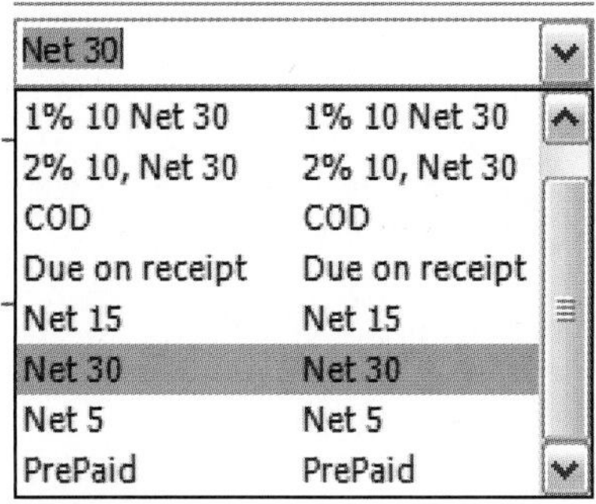

Figure 8:36

Terms are created by selecting ***Company>>Manage Support Lists>>Payment Terms List*** on the main menu. The Net 15 term (Figure 8:37) means an invoice is due 15 days from the invoice date.

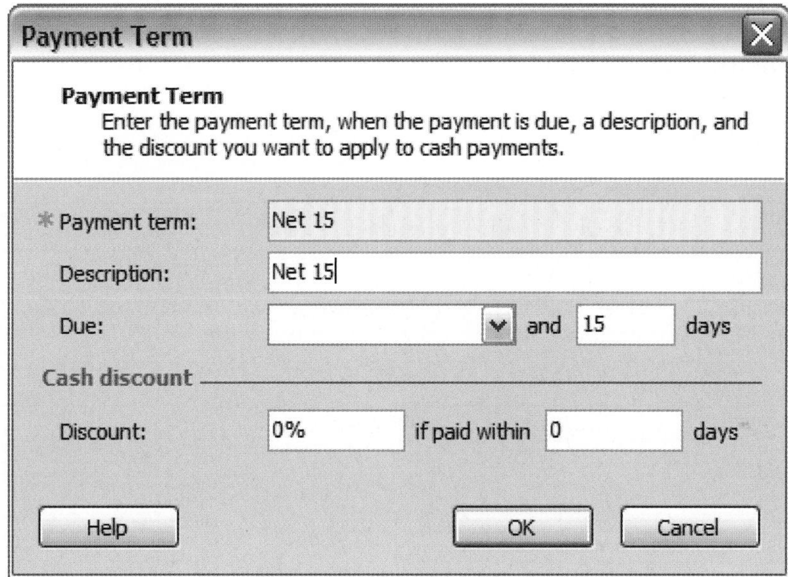

Figure 8:37

The 1% 10 Net 30 term (Figure 8:38) means an invoice is due 30 days from the invoice and the customer will receive a 1 percent discount if paying the invoice within 10 days of the invoice date. *(Note: Discounts do not apply to sales tax.)*

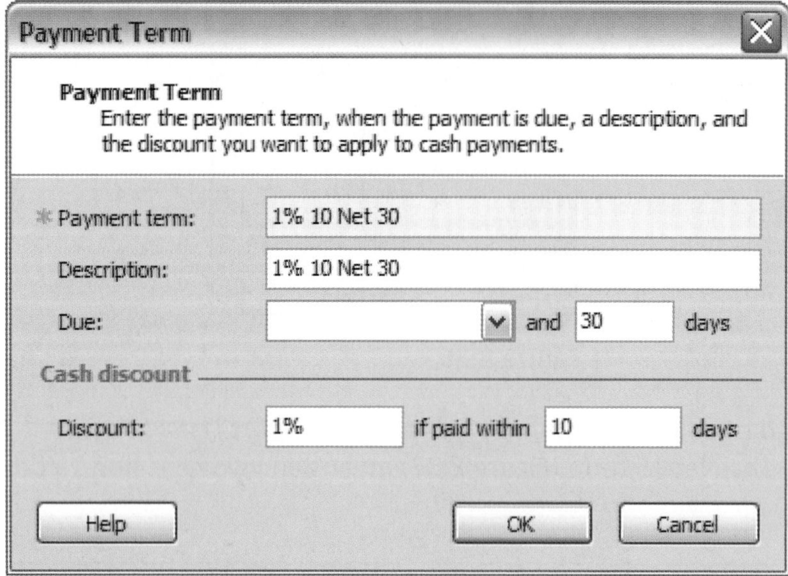

Figure 8:38

Financial Summary Tab

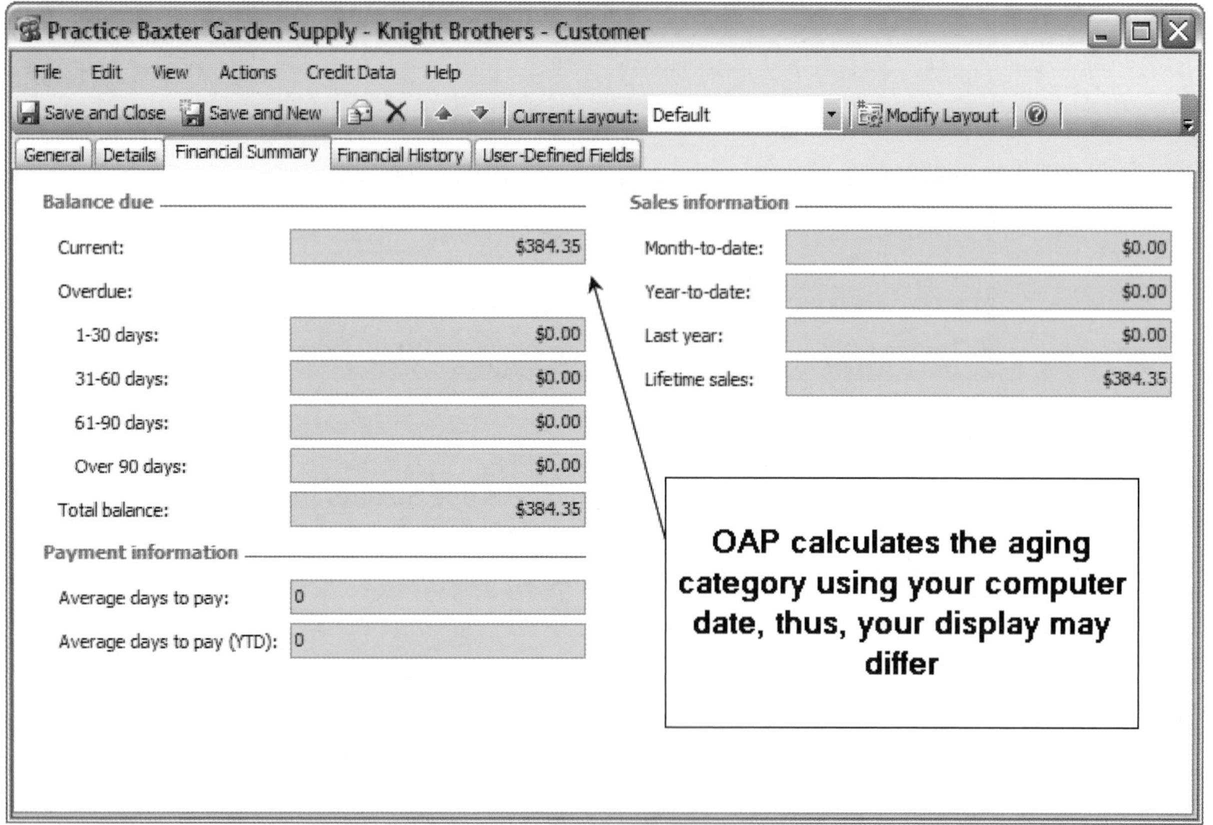

Figure 8:39

This tab displays a quick snapshot of customer activity, including aging information, sales history totals, and average days to pay information.

Financial History Tab

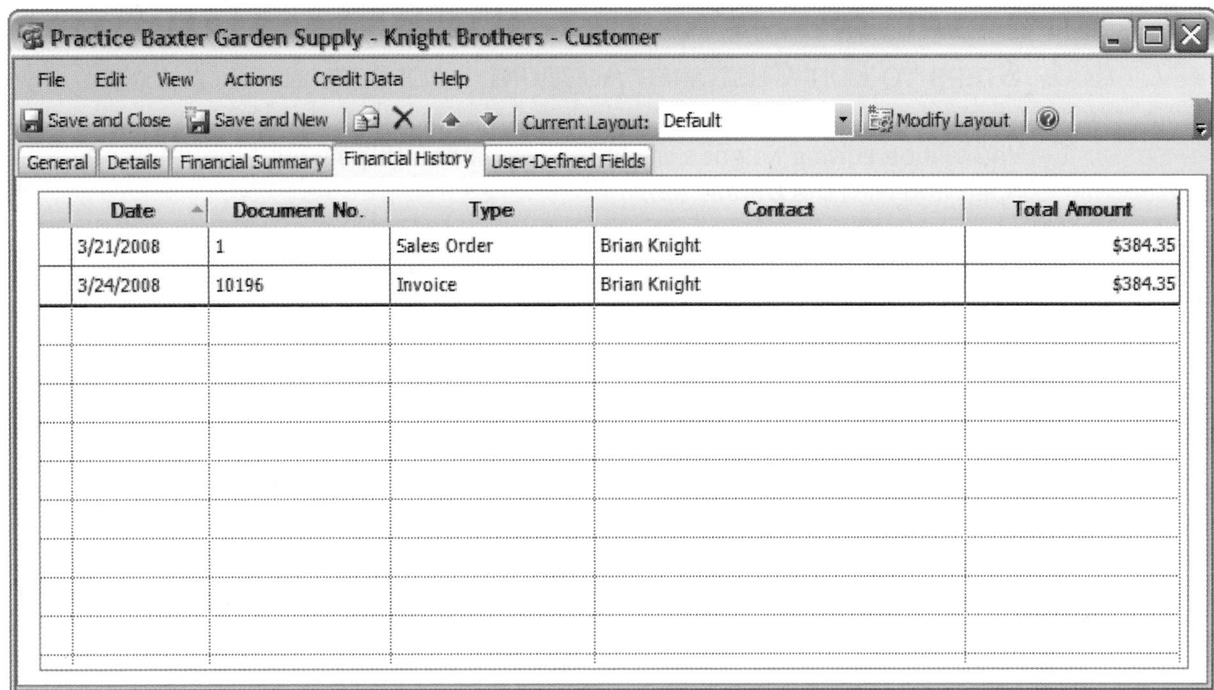

Figure 8:40

This tab lists customer transactions. You can drill down to original entries by double clicking a transaction, which facilitates answering customer account inquiries.

The next exercise illustrates editing a customer account.

Steps to Edit Customer Account Information

1. You will be editing Knight's credit terms so open this account if not already open and click the **Details** tab.

2. The accountant wants to offer Knight an early payment discount of 2/10 net 30. Using the **Payment terms** dropdown list select the **2% 10 Net 30** terms.

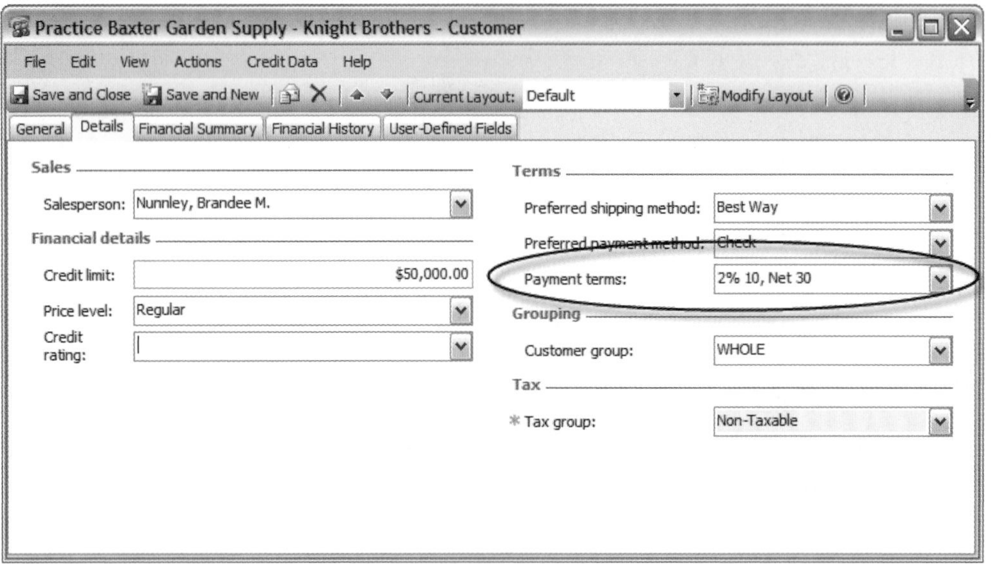

Figure 8:41

Knight will now receive a 2 percent discount on future invoices (not existing) when paying the invoice within 10 days of the invoice date. Knight must still pay the invoice in full within 30 days of the invoice date.

3. Click **Save and Close** to save the changes.

You will now walk through creating a new customer account.

STEPS TO CREATE A CUSTOMER ACCOUNT

1. Click **New Customer** under **Start a Task**. *(Note: You can also click the Add a new Customer link at the top of the Customer List.)*

2. Now enter the information illustrated in Figure 8:42.

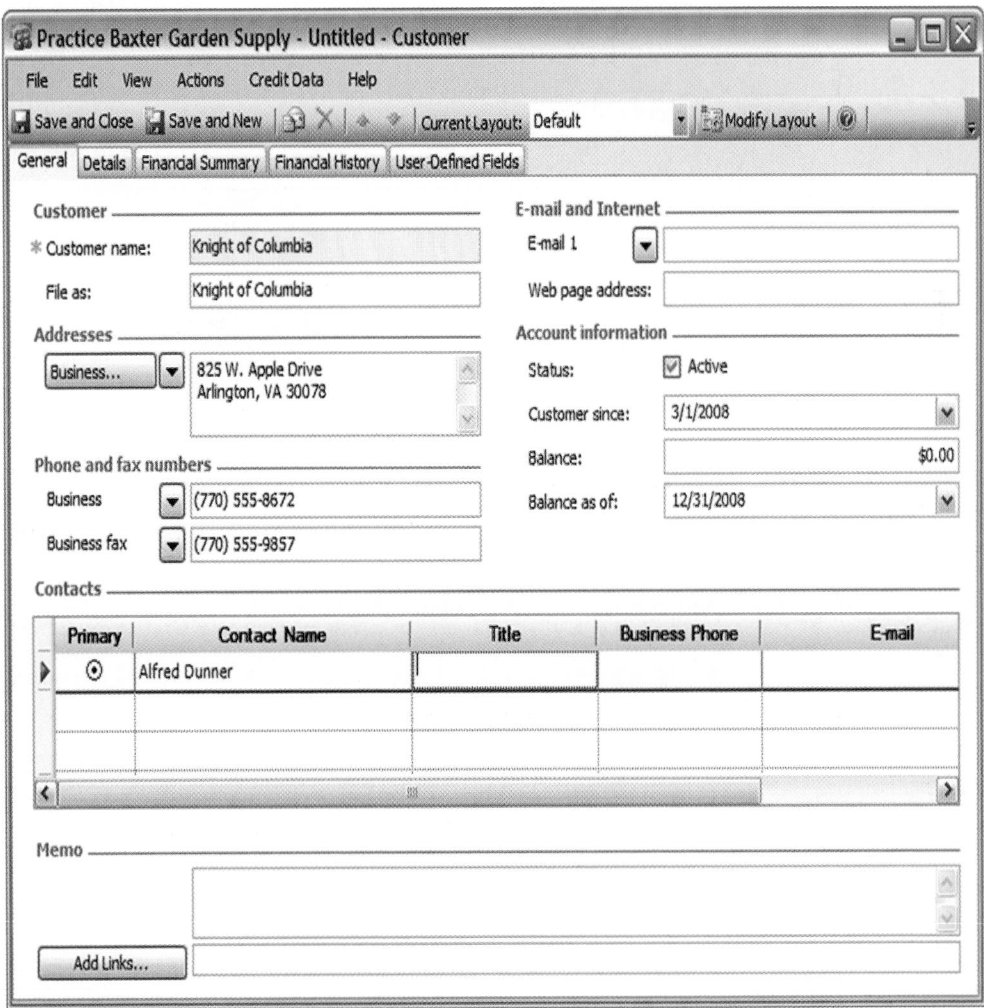

Figure 8:42

3. Click the dropdown list on the **Business** address and toggle the field to **Bill to**. Click the Bill to button to enter an address using a different method. Enter the information illustrated in Figure 8:43 and click **OK**.

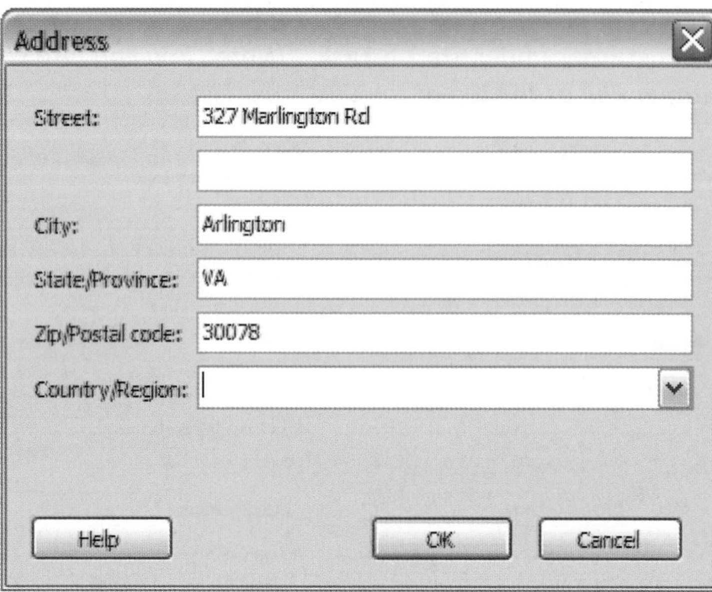

Figure 8:43

4. Click the **Details** tab and enter the information in Figure 8:44. *Note: The customer is a not-for-profit organization so the* ***Tax group*** *is Non-Taxable.*

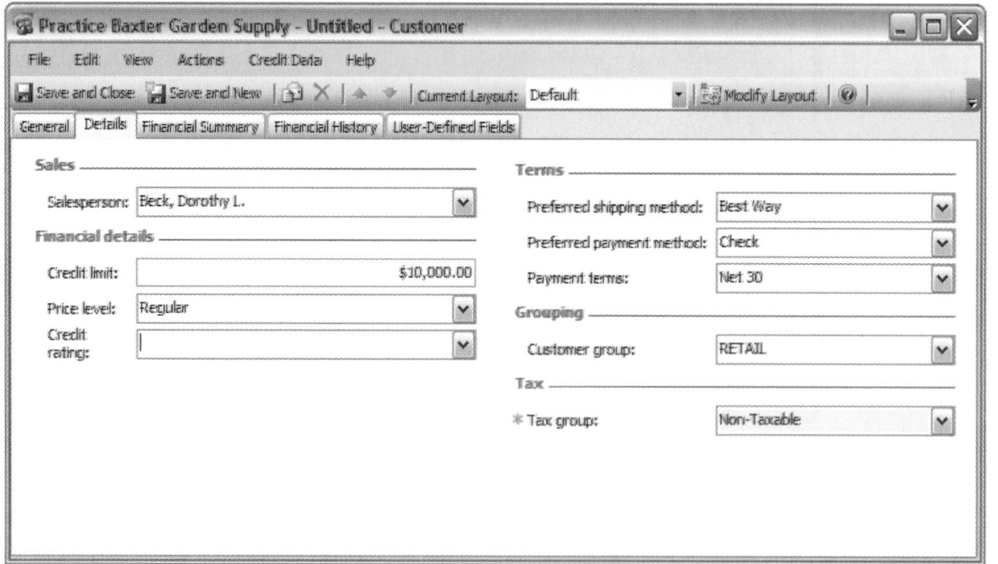

Figure 8:44

5. Click **Save and Close**.

What happens when you try to delete an account with transaction history?

Highlight **Knight Brothers'** account on the Customer List and select ***Edit>>Delete*** on the main menu. Click **Yes** when OAP prompts to confirm deletion. You receive the warning message illustrated in Figure 8:45 stating that the customer account cannot be deleted so consider marking it inactive.

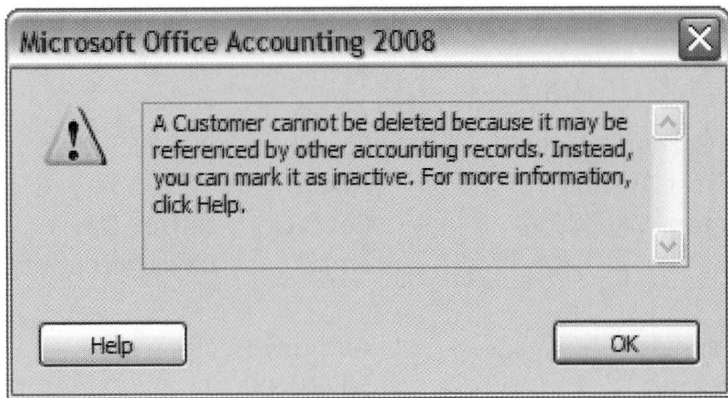

Figure 8:45

Inactivating an account denies future transactions for the account while retaining account history. Click **OK**. You can mark an account inactive by turning off this Status: ☑ Active option on the General tab of the customer account.

CREATE A NEW CUSTOMER ACCOUNT

On March 1, 2008, Baxter gained a new wholesale customer with the following information. Create the new account.

Frost Garden Center	Phone:	701 555-1515
127 Frost Avenue	Fax:	701 555-1518
Arlington, VA 30097	Contact:	Jeffrey Davis
	Email:	davis@frost.net

Salesperson	Anthony Hecter
Credit limit	$8,000.00
Price level	Regular
Preferred shipping method	Best Way
Payment terms	Net 30
Customer group	Wholesale
Tax group	Non-Taxable

UNDERSTANDING INVENTORY ITEMS

Inventory items differ from the service and non-inventory items discussed in Chapter 4. Remember that service based businesses pay for services and purchase job materials at the time of performing the work so these businesses do not hold inventory. On the other hand, merchandising businesses purchase goods in advance of sales so track on-hand quantities and purchase costs of inventory.

OAP's Inventory Item type stores item sales prices, on-hand quantities, and purchase costs. Purchase costs are posted to the inventory account and tracked in layers. When posting sales invoices, OAP posts cost of goods sold for items on the invoice using the FIFO (first-in, first-out) method. Recall that Knight's invoice traced in a previous exercise posted cost of goods sold.

With FIFO, inventory layers are tracked by the cost paid for the items and the first items purchased are the first items sold (i.e., the first items expensed to cost of goods sold). It just so happened that at the time of invoicing Knight Baxter had only one cost layer for the items sold.

However, let us assume that Baxter had 30 hoses on hand with 15 purchased at $5.20 and 15 subsequently purchased at $5.30. This item now has two cost layers. When Baxter sells 16 hoses the cost of goods sold would equal $83.30, calculated as follows:

Layer 1:	15 hoses * $5.20 =	$ 78.00
Layer 2:	1 hose * $5.30 =	$ 5.30
Total COGS		$ 83.30

It is important to understand the posting of cost of goods sold; otherwise, you might prepare financial statements that do not match revenues with expenses. The following table explains the inventory, non-inventory, and service items used in this text. After reviewing this table, you will better understand when an item interacts with inventory so that OAP posts cost of goods sold at the time of sale.

Item Class	**Purpose**
Inventory Item	Used on goods purchased and held for resale. Tracks quantities and purchase costs. Cost of goods sold posts at the time of invoicing and calculates under the FIFO costing method, meaning the first item purchased will be the first item sold and expensed to cost of goods sold.
Non-Inventory Item	Used on goods purchased for customer jobs and not tracked as inventory. These are normally job material items. Cost of goods sold posts when posting vendor bills or receipts for the materials purchased.
Service Item	Used on services provided by company employees or subcontractors. When provided by subcontractors, cost of goods sold posts when paying the contractor. When provided by employees, cost of goods sold posts when paying employees.
Kit	Used for grouping inventory items sold together.

Now review a list of Baxter's inventory items. Click the **Items** link under **Find** to open the Item List illustrated in Figure 8:46, paying particular attention to the Type column.

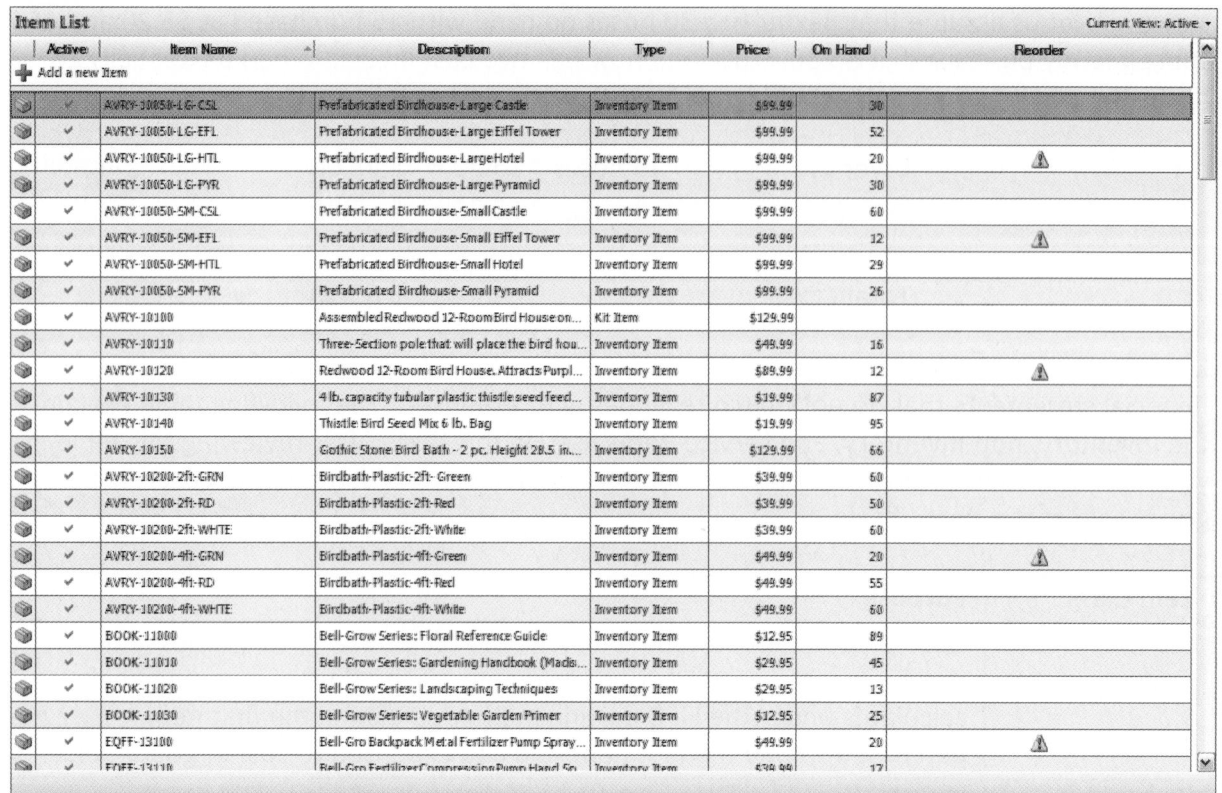

Item List — Current View: Active

Active	Item Name	Description	Type	Price	On Hand	Reorder
✓	AVRY-10050-LG-CSL	Prefabricated Birdhouse-Large Castle	Inventory Item	$99.99	30	
✓	AVRY-10050-LG-EFL	Prefabricated Birdhouse-Large Eiffel Tower	Inventory Item	$99.99	52	
✓	AVRY-10050-LG-HTL	Prefabricated Birdhouse-Large Hotel	Inventory Item	$99.99	20	
✓	AVRY-10050-LG-PYR	Prefabricated Birdhouse-Large Pyramid	Inventory Item	$99.99	30	
✓	AVRY-10050-SM-CSL	Prefabricated Birdhouse-Small Castle	Inventory Item	$99.99	60	
✓	AVRY-10050-SM-EFL	Prefabricated Birdhouse-Small Eiffel Tower	Inventory Item	$99.99	12	
✓	AVRY-10050-SM-HTL	Prefabricated Birdhouse-Small Hotel	Inventory Item	$99.99	29	
✓	AVRY-10050-SM-PYR	Prefabricated Birdhouse-Small Pyramid	Inventory Item	$99.99	26	
✓	AVRY-10100	Assembled Redwood 12-Room Bird House on...	Kit Item	$129.99		
✓	AVRY-10110	Three-Section pole that will place the bird hou...	Inventory Item	$49.99	16	
✓	AVRY-10120	Redwood 12-Room Bird House. Attracts Purpl...	Inventory Item	$89.99	12	
✓	AVRY-10130	4 lb. capacity tubular plastic thistle seed feed...	Inventory Item	$19.99	87	
✓	AVRY-10140	Thistle Bird Seed Mix 6 lb. Bag	Inventory Item	$19.99	95	
✓	AVRY-10150	Gothic Stone Bird Bath - 2 pc. Height 28.5 in...	Inventory Item	$129.99	66	
✓	AVRY-10200-2ft-GRN	Birdbath-Plastic-2ft- Green	Inventory Item	$39.99	60	
✓	AVRY-10200-2ft-RD	Birdbath-Plastic-2ft-Red	Inventory Item	$39.99	50	
✓	AVRY-10200-2ft-WHTE	Birdbath-Plastic-2ft-White	Inventory Item	$39.99	60	
✓	AVRY-10200-4ft-GRN	Birdbath-Plastic-4ft-Green	Inventory Item	$49.99	20	
✓	AVRY-10200-4ft-RD	Birdbath-Plastic-4ft-Red	Inventory Item	$49.99	55	
✓	AVRY-10200-4ft-WHTE	Birdbath-Plastic-4ft-White	Inventory Item	$49.99	60	
✓	BOOK-11000	Bell-Grow Series: Floral Reference Guide	Inventory Item	$12.95	89	
✓	BOOK-11010	Bell-Grow Series: Gardening Handbook (Madis...	Inventory Item	$29.95	45	
✓	BOOK-11020	Bell-Grow Series: Landscaping Techniques	Inventory Item	$29.95	13	
✓	BOOK-11030	Bell-Grow Series: Vegetable Garden Primer	Inventory Item	$12.95	25	
✓	EQFF-13100	Bell-Gro Backpack Metal Fertilizer Pump Spray...	Inventory Item	$49.99	20	
✓	EQFF-13110	Bell-Gro Fertilizer Compression Pump Hand Sp...	Inventory Item	$39.99	17	

Figure 8:46

We next provide an overview of these items.

Inventory Item Type

Highlight **EQFF-13130** and double click to open (Figure 8:47).

While explaining this item, we will refer back to the *Creating a Sales Invoice from a Sales Order* topic where you sold 10 of these items to Knight Brothers. We will also refer back to the *Behind the Keys of a Posted Sales Invoice* topic where you traced the entries made after posting Knight's invoice.

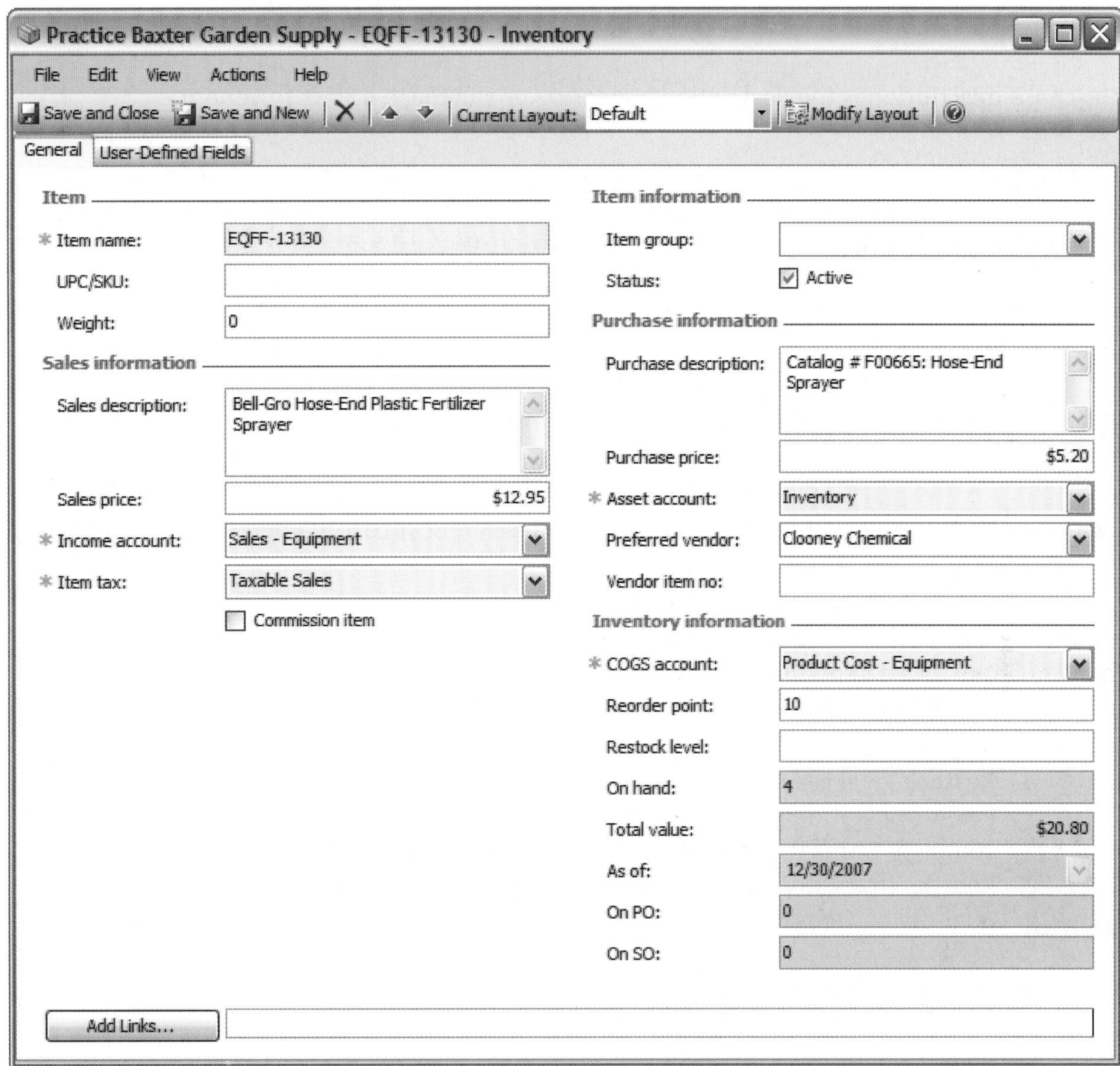

Figure 8:47

Item name is a required field that serves as the record's primary key, meaning also that the value must be unique for each item.

Sales description is the description appearing on customer orders and invoices.

Sales price is the price charged to customers, explaining why Knight was charged $129.50 for 10 of these items.

Income account is the general ledger account OAP will use for posting sales revenue, explaining why Knight's invoice posted revenue to 40003 Sales – Equipment.

Item tax shows that sales of this item are normally taxable. However, OAP also looks to the tax default on a customer's account to determine the overall taxability of a sale.

Item group is an optional field for grouping items to report sales information.

Purchase description is the description appearing on purchase orders to vendors.

Purchase price is the amount Baxter pays vendors to restock the item. This price updates after posting a vendor bill with a price increase because Baxter has chosen the company preference option that updates cost automatically. *(Note: This option was illustrated in Chapter 2.)*

Asset account is the general ledger inventory account for tracking purchase costs.

Preferred vendor is the name of the vendor that normally supplies the item. This field is linked to Baxter's vendor accounts.

COGS account is the general ledger account OAP uses to post cost of goods sold when posting an invoice.

Reorder point is the minimum quantity the company wants to keep on hand. When the **On hand** quantity for an item is less than or equal to the **Reorder point**, OAP places this ⚠ symbol on the Inventory List, indicating time to reorder.

Restock level is a new field added to OAP 2008 and works with the new Reorder Inventory feature explained in Chapter 9. The field stores the maximum quantity a company wants to have on hand. If a quantity is entered in this field then the Reorder Inventory feature places a purchase order to the Preferred Vendor for the quantity of items needed to bring the On hand quantity up to the Restock level.

On hand, **Total value**, **On PO**, and **On SO** are internally generated stock status information.

Kit Item Type

Close the previous item and open **AVRY-10100** (Figure 8:48).

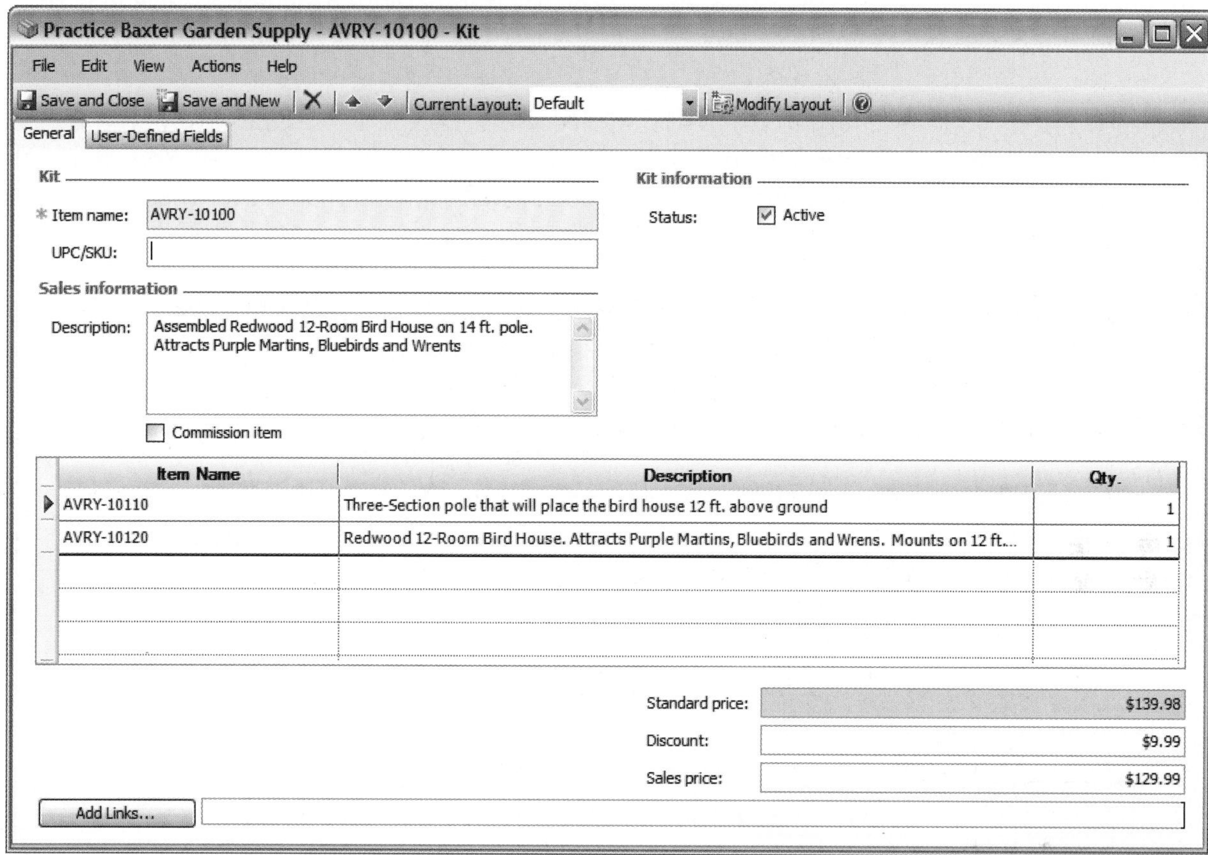

Figure 8:48

This inventory type groups individual inventory items together to sell as a kit. The individual items are chosen at the bottom and the quantity of the items per kit is entered.

Standard price is the sum of the sales price if the items were sold individually.

Discount is the amount deducted from the standard price when sold as a kit.

Sales price is the price charged customers buying this kit, which is the standard price minus the discount.

Close this item. We will next explain inventory pricing and price levels.

INVENTORY PRICING AND PRICE LEVELS

Item sales prices can be changed individually by opening each item and entering a new price. But what if you wanted to change the prices for several items? OAP provides a quick way to accomplish this task.

With the Item List open, click the **Change Item Prices** button on the toolbar to open the **Change Item Price** window illustrated in Figure 8:49. *(Note: You cannot use this window to change standard or purchase costs. Instead, you must enter these changes on each item.)*

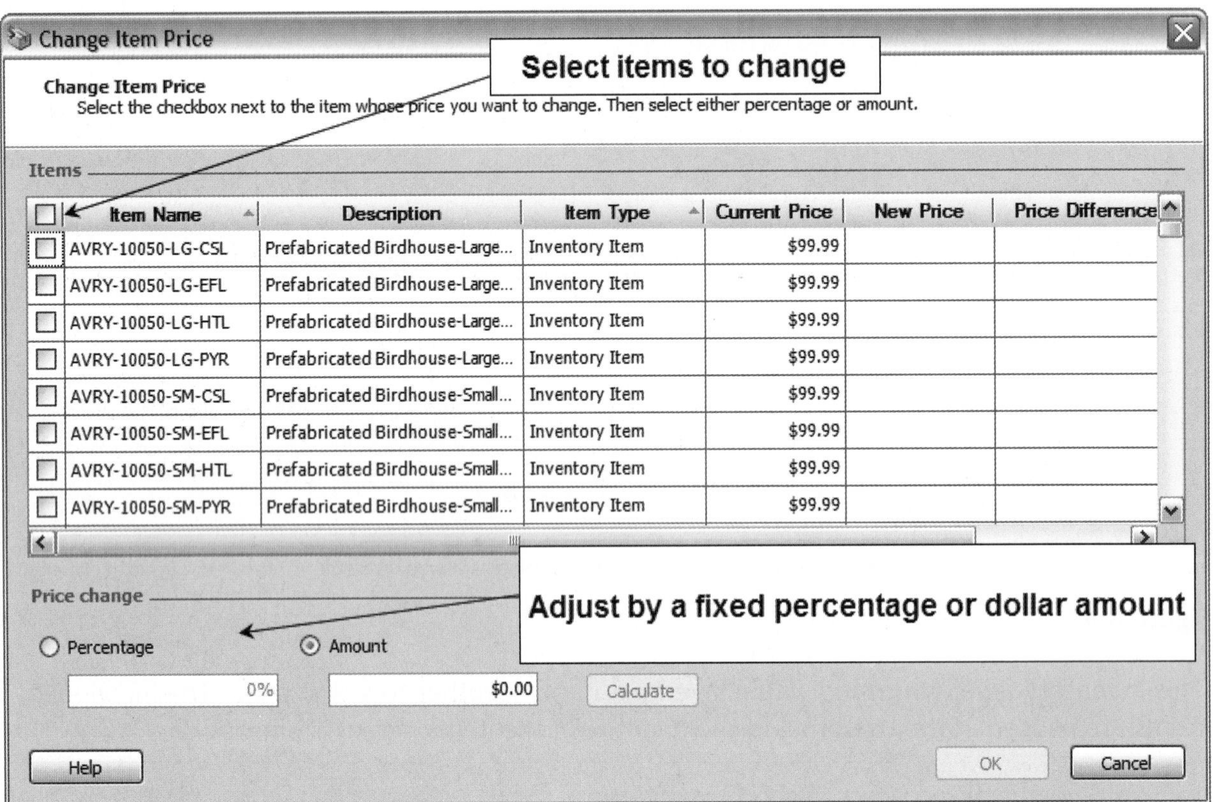

Figure 8:49

First, you select the items to adjust. *(Note: Clicking the box in the column header selects all items.)* Next, you choose whether to calculate new sale prices by applying a fixed percentage or a fixed dollar amount to current prices. After setting the option, the **Calculate** button activates and clicking this button computes the new sales price.

We will now illustrate this feature by increasing the current selling price on items EQLW-14160 and EQLW-14170 by 10 percent.

First, scroll the window and select items EQLW-14160 and EQLW-14170. Next, enter the price setting option illustrated in Figure 8:50.

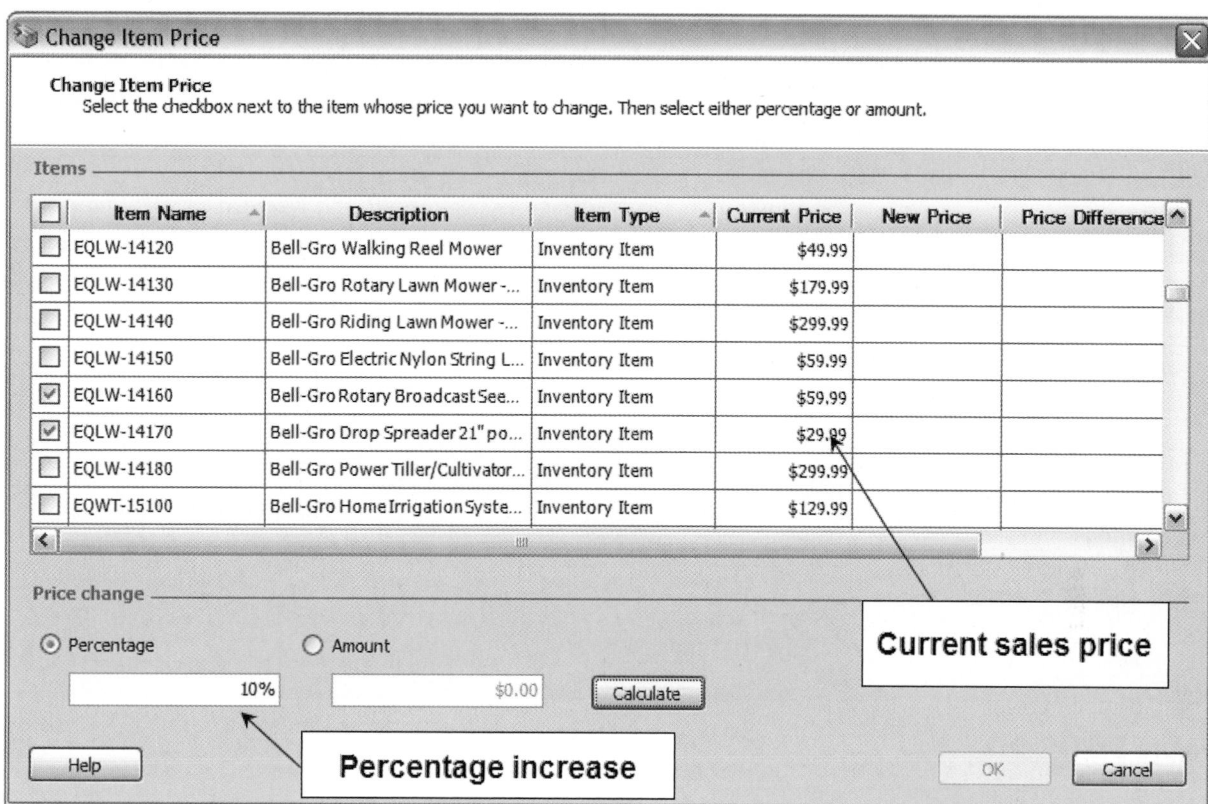

Figure 8:50

Now click **Calculate** and scroll back to the items to view the increased prices.

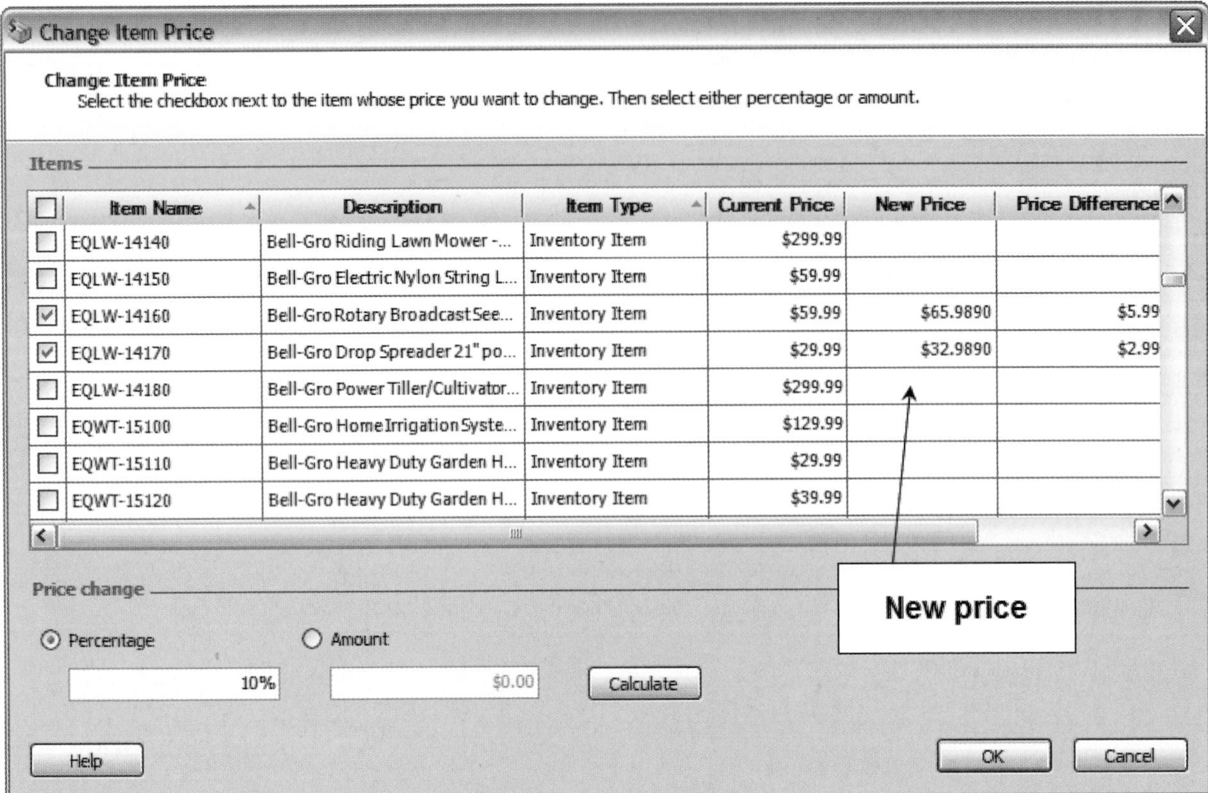

Figure 8:51

Click **OK** to save the new prices.

Now open EQLW-14160 to verify the sales price increase (Figure 8:52).

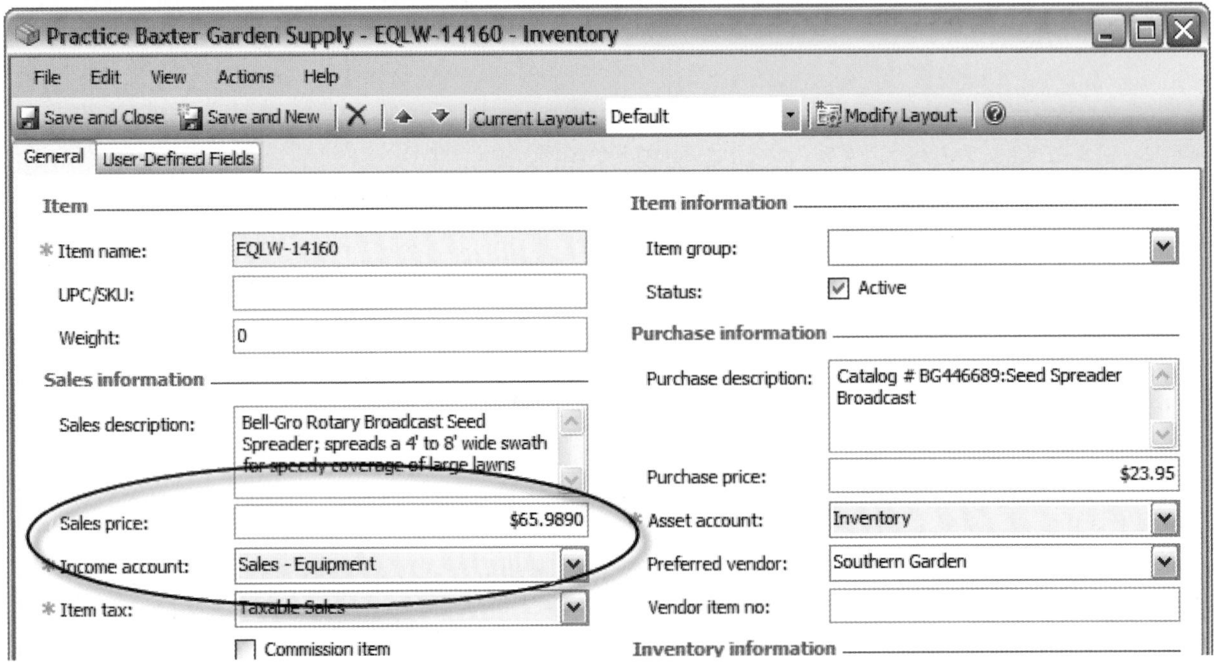

Figure 8:52

Notice that the new price is not rounded to the nearest cent. This is one of the drawbacks to using a fixed percentage. Close the item.

We now explain inventory pricing levels. Recall that customer accounts contain a field for assigning price levels. Baxter has two price levels, namely, Regular and Discounted.

Select ***Company>>Manage Support Lists>>Price Level List*** to view Baxter's price levels (Figure 8:53).

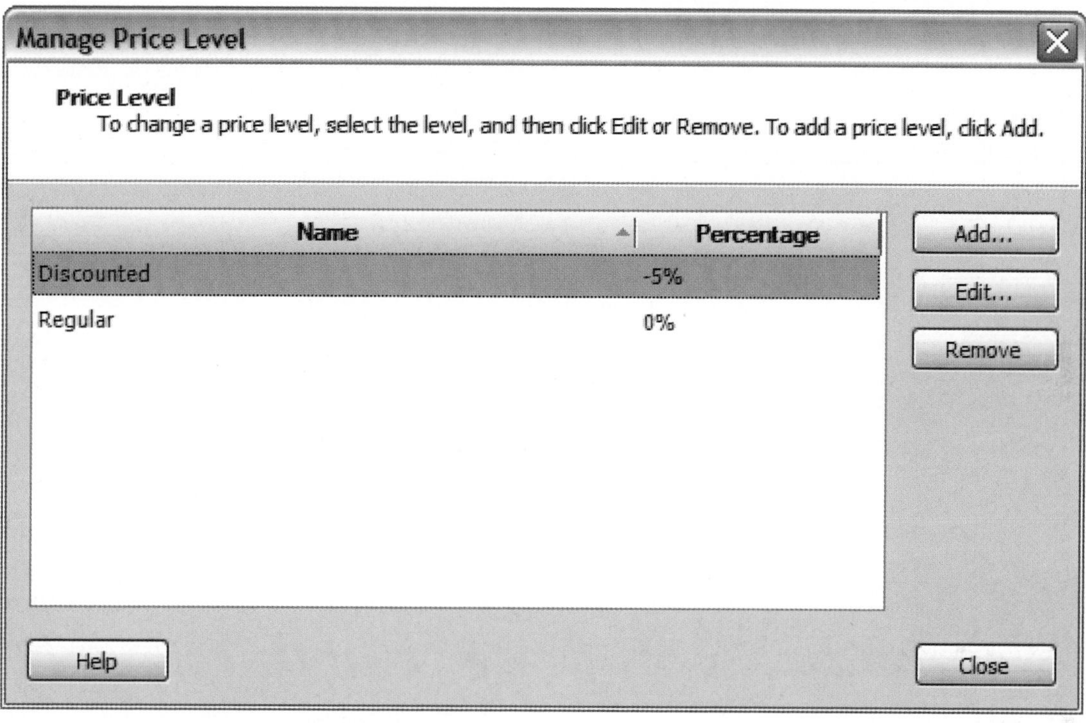

Figure 8:53

The Regular price level charges customers the current sales price stored on the item. Highlight the **Discounted** price level and click **Edit** (Figure 8:54).

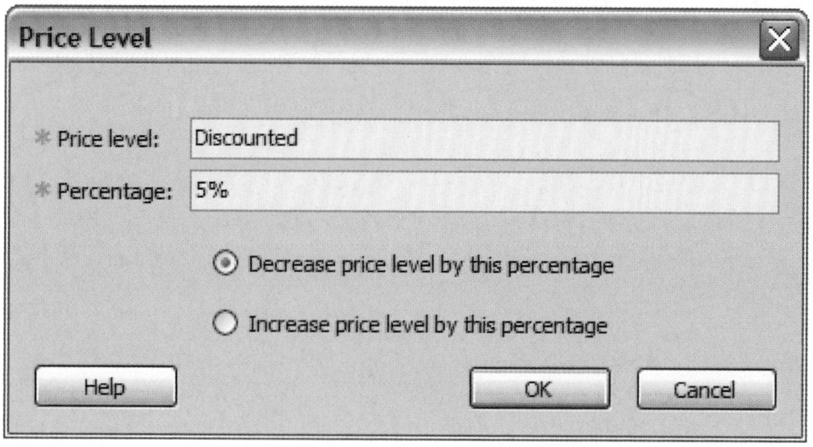

Figure 8:54

This level charges customers 5 percent less than the item's selling price. Click **Cancel** and then click **Close** to exit the Manage Price Level window.

You will now test these price levels. Click the **New Sales Order** link under Start a Task and complete the transaction using Figure 8:55.

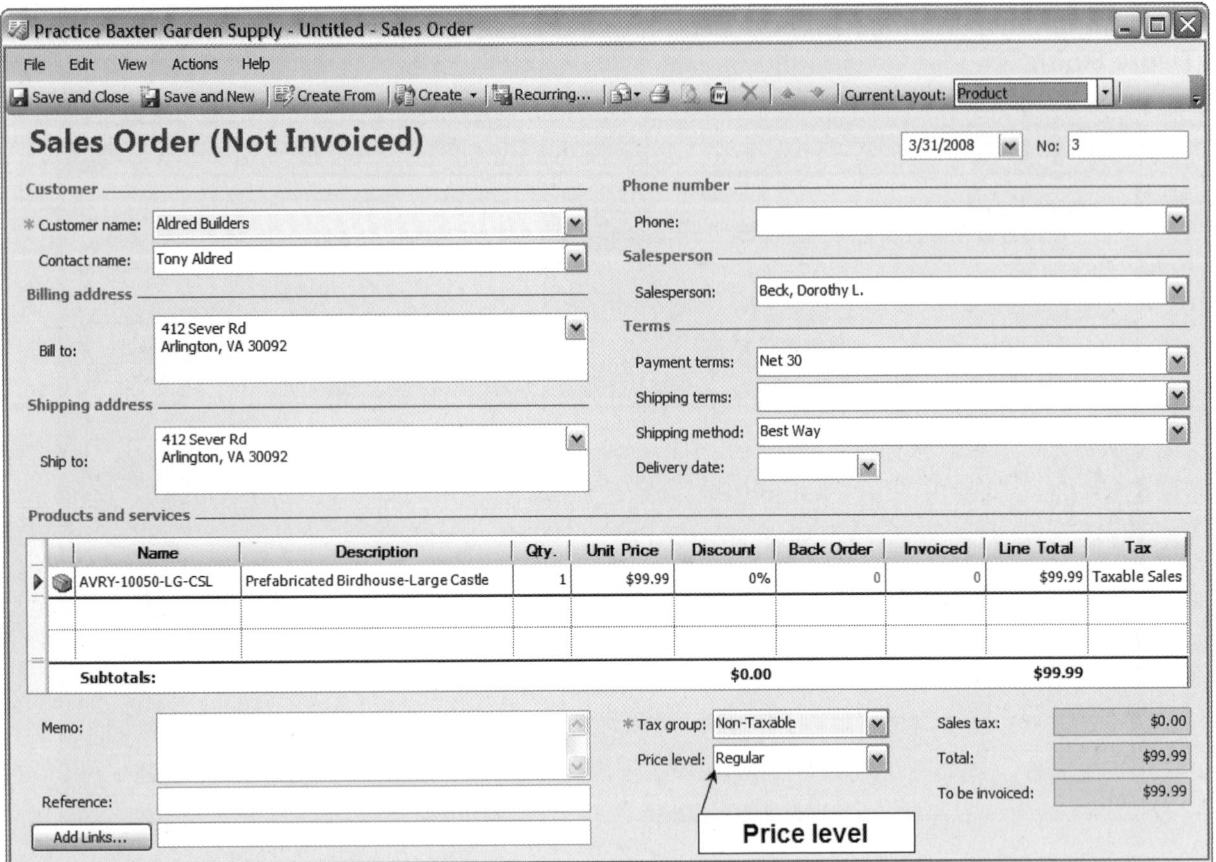

Figure 8:55

Notice that the **Price level** is currently **Regular** and the item selling price is $99.99. Use the **Price level** dropdown to select **Discounted** (Figure 8:56) and the selling price adjusts to $94.9905 (i.e., 10 percent less than the regular selling price).

Click **X** to close the transaction and then **No** to saving your changes.

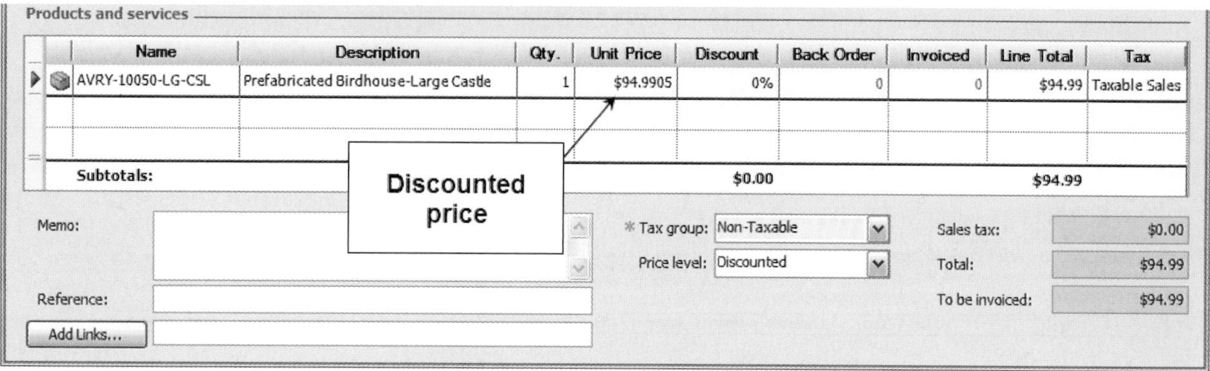

Figure 8:56

INVENTORY REPORTING

Inventory reports are located under the ***Reports>>Inventory*** main menu and on the **Reports** section of the **Customers Home** page. Using the home page, change the report category to **Inventory** and select the **Inventory Valuation** report (Figure 8:57).

Click **Display** to view the report and enter the filtering date range of "3/31/2008" (Figure 8:58). Scroll to the bottom and locate the total under the Balance Value column.

Figure 8:57

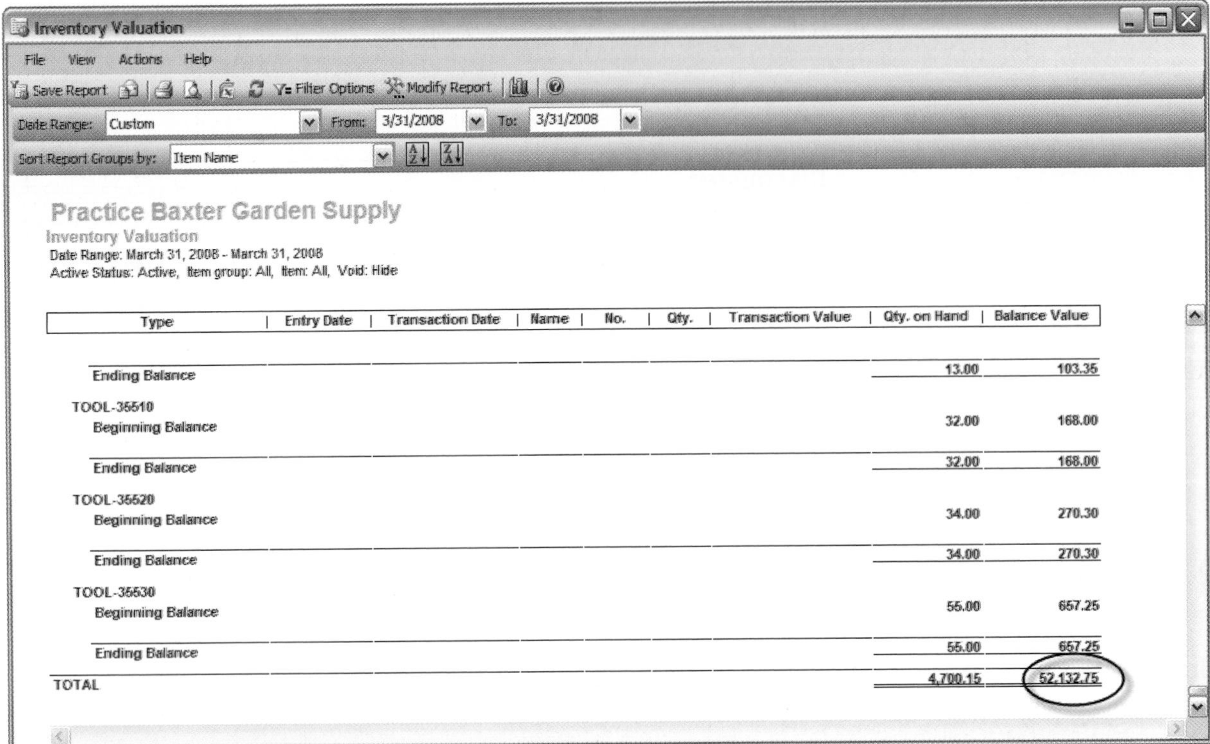

Figure 8:58

This report lists inventory quantities on-hand and costs by item as well as the total quantities and cost. The total value should reconcile to the inventory control account on the general ledger. *(Note: Your report total will differ if you have not completed all chapter exercises.)*

Let us now locate the total in the inventory control account. Open the Trial Balance report and filter for "3/31/2008." Locate the ending balance in account 13000 Inventory and verify that your balance agrees with your report total.

Close the Inventory Valuation and Trial Balance reports and display the **Item Profitability** report for the date range of "1/1/2008" to "3/31/2008." (See Figure 8:59.)

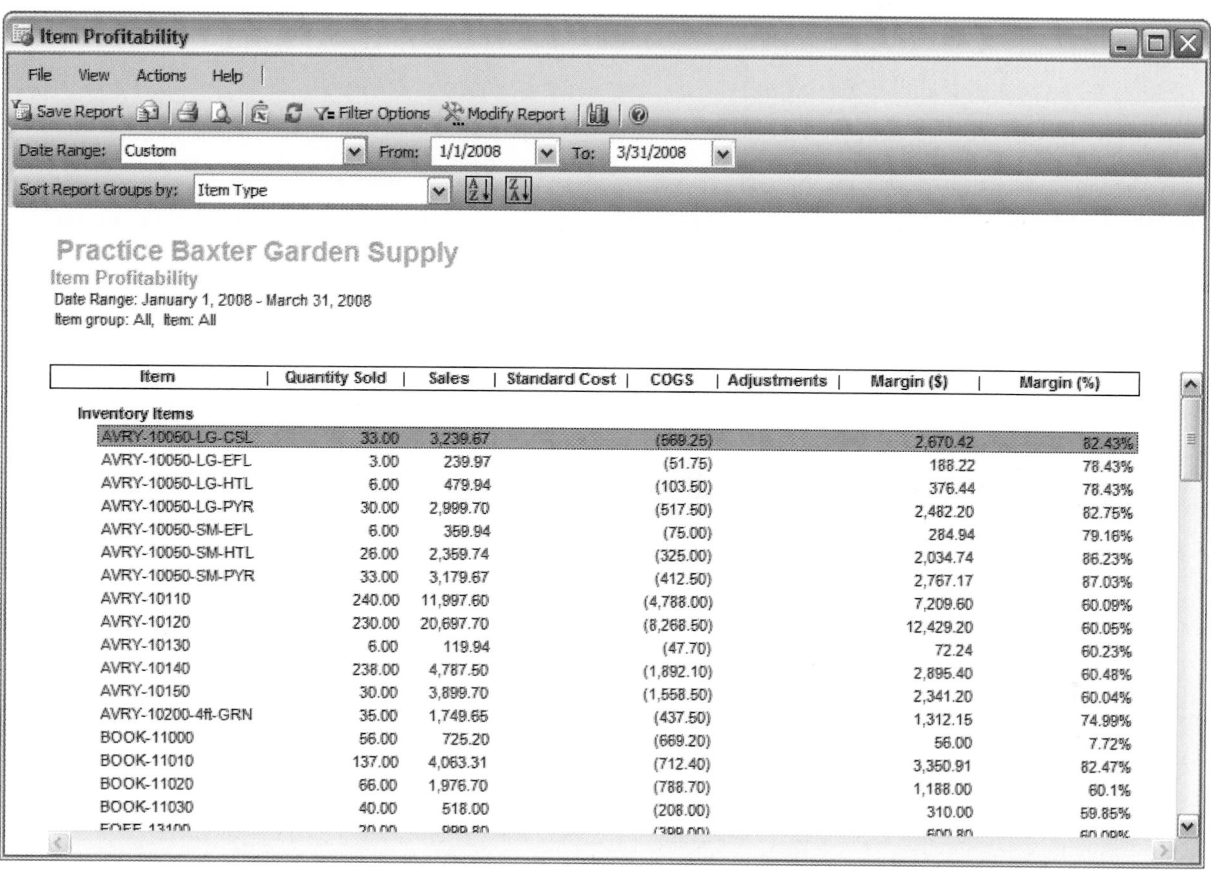

Practice Baxter Garden Supply
Item Profitability
Date Range: January 1, 2008 - March 31, 2008
Item group: All, Item: All

Item	Quantity Sold	Sales	Standard Cost	COGS	Adjustments	Margin ($)	Margin (%)
Inventory Items							
AVRY-10050-LG-CSL	33.00	3,239.67		(569.25)		2,670.42	82.43%
AVRY-10050-LG-EFL	3.00	239.97		(51.75)		188.22	78.43%
AVRY-10050-LG-HTL	6.00	479.94		(103.50)		376.44	78.43%
AVRY-10050-LG-PYR	30.00	2,999.70		(517.50)		2,482.20	82.75%
AVRY-10050-SM-EFL	6.00	359.94		(75.00)		284.94	79.16%
AVRY-10050-SM-HTL	26.00	2,359.74		(325.00)		2,034.74	86.23%
AVRY-10050-SM-PYR	33.00	3,179.67		(412.50)		2,767.17	87.03%
AVRY-10110	240.00	11,997.60		(4,788.00)		7,209.60	60.09%
AVRY-10120	230.00	20,697.70		(8,268.50)		12,429.20	60.05%
AVRY-10130	6.00	119.94		(47.70)		72.24	60.23%
AVRY-10140	238.00	4,787.50		(1,892.10)		2,895.40	60.48%
AVRY-10150	30.00	3,899.70		(1,558.50)		2,341.20	60.04%
AVRY-10200-4ft-GRN	35.00	1,749.65		(437.50)		1,312.15	74.99%
BOOK-11000	56.00	725.20		(669.20)		56.00	7.72%
BOOK-11010	137.00	4,063.31		(712.40)		3,350.91	82.47%
BOOK-11020	66.00	1,976.70		(788.70)		1,188.00	60.1%
BOOK-11030	40.00	518.00		(208.00)		310.00	59.85%

Figure 8:59

This report analyzes Baxter's profitability by item. The report shows sales and costs by item and provides the dollar and percentage margins for each item. From this report, you see that Baxter realizes a high gross profit margin on items.

Close the report and display the **Inventory Stock Status by Item** report (not shown). Enter "3/31/2008" as the date. This report lists the reorder point along with current quantities on hand and quantities on POs (purchase orders) and SOs (sales orders). The Place Order column contains a checkmark when stocking levels fall below the reorder point. Baxter employees monitor this report to make sure that current stock levels meet anticipated sales needs.

Close the report and display the **Physical Inventory Worksheet** illustrated in Figure 8:60. Enter "3/31/2008" as the date.

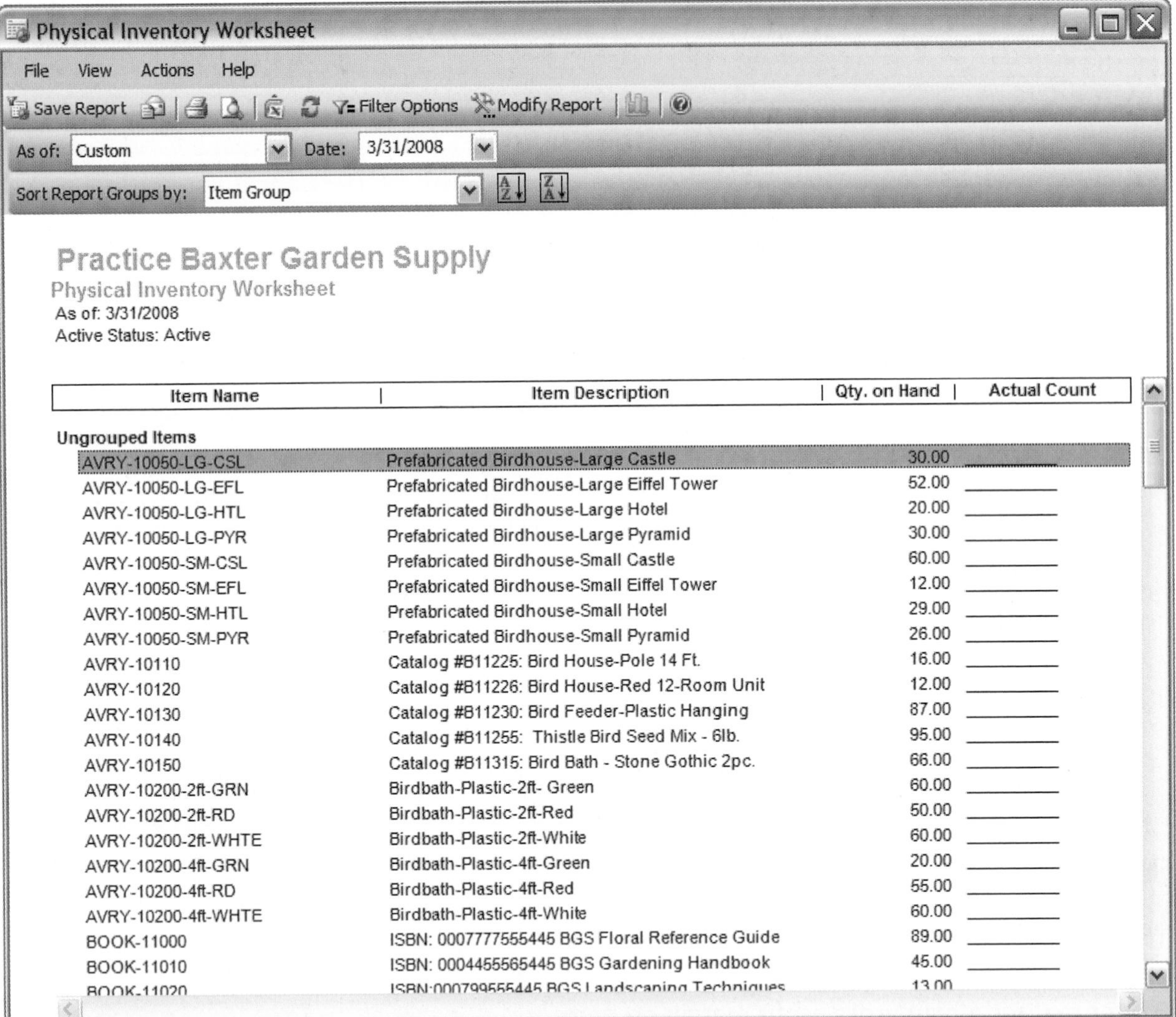
Physical Inventory Worksheet

File View Actions Help

Save Report | Filter Options | Modify Report

As of: Custom Date: 3/31/2008

Sort Report Groups by: Item Group

Practice Baxter Garden Supply
Physical Inventory Worksheet
As of: 3/31/2008
Active Status: Active

Item Name	Item Description	Qty. on Hand	Actual Count
Ungrouped Items			
AVRY-10050-LG-CSL	Prefabricated Birdhouse-Large Castle	30.00	________
AVRY-10050-LG-EFL	Prefabricated Birdhouse-Large Eiffel Tower	52.00	________
AVRY-10050-LG-HTL	Prefabricated Birdhouse-Large Hotel	20.00	________
AVRY-10050-LG-PYR	Prefabricated Birdhouse-Large Pyramid	30.00	________
AVRY-10050-SM-CSL	Prefabricated Birdhouse-Small Castle	60.00	________
AVRY-10050-SM-EFL	Prefabricated Birdhouse-Small Eiffel Tower	12.00	________
AVRY-10050-SM-HTL	Prefabricated Birdhouse-Small Hotel	29.00	________
AVRY-10050-SM-PYR	Prefabricated Birdhouse-Small Pyramid	26.00	________
AVRY-10110	Catalog #B11225: Bird House-Pole 14 Ft.	16.00	________
AVRY-10120	Catalog #B11226: Bird House-Red 12-Room Unit	12.00	________
AVRY-10130	Catalog #B11230: Bird Feeder-Plastic Hanging	87.00	________
AVRY-10140	Catalog #B11255: Thistle Bird Seed Mix - 6lb.	95.00	________
AVRY-10150	Catalog #B11315: Bird Bath - Stone Gothic 2pc.	66.00	________
AVRY-10200-2ft-GRN	Birdbath-Plastic-2ft- Green	60.00	________
AVRY-10200-2ft-RD	Birdbath-Plastic-2ft-Red	50.00	________
AVRY-10200-2ft-WHTE	Birdbath-Plastic-2ft-White	60.00	________
AVRY-10200-4ft-GRN	Birdbath-Plastic-4ft-Green	20.00	________
AVRY-10200-4ft-RD	Birdbath-Plastic-4ft-Red	55.00	________
AVRY-10200-4ft-WHTE	Birdbath-Plastic-4ft-White	60.00	________
BOOK-11000	ISBN: 0007777555445 BGS Floral Reference Guide	89.00	________
BOOK-11010	ISBN: 0004455565445 BGS Gardening Handbook	45.00	________
BOOK-11020	ISBN:000799555445 BGS Landscaping Techniques	13.00	

Figure 8:60

This report is distributed to employees conducting a physical inventory count. Notice that it lists the quantities on hand and provides a space for entering counted quantities. Before distributing this report, the Qty. on Hand column should be removed to protect the integrity of the count by ensuring that employees independently count items.

Close the report. The next topic discusses the tasks performed when conducting a physical count.

Physical Inventory

Although OAP tracks inventory quantities, Baxter still conducts a physical count to confirm that actual quantities on hand agree with OAP quantities. To conduct a physical count of inventory, management distributes the Physical Inventory Worksheet illustrated in the previous topic to employees conducting the count. These employees enter the actual quantities counted on the worksheet and return the completed report to the accounting department for reconcilement with OAP data.

Select ***Vendors>>Adjust Inventory>>Adjust Quantity*** on the main menu to open the window illustrated in Figure 8:61, which is the window used to enter counted quantities. Set the date to "3/31/2008" and click **Yes**.

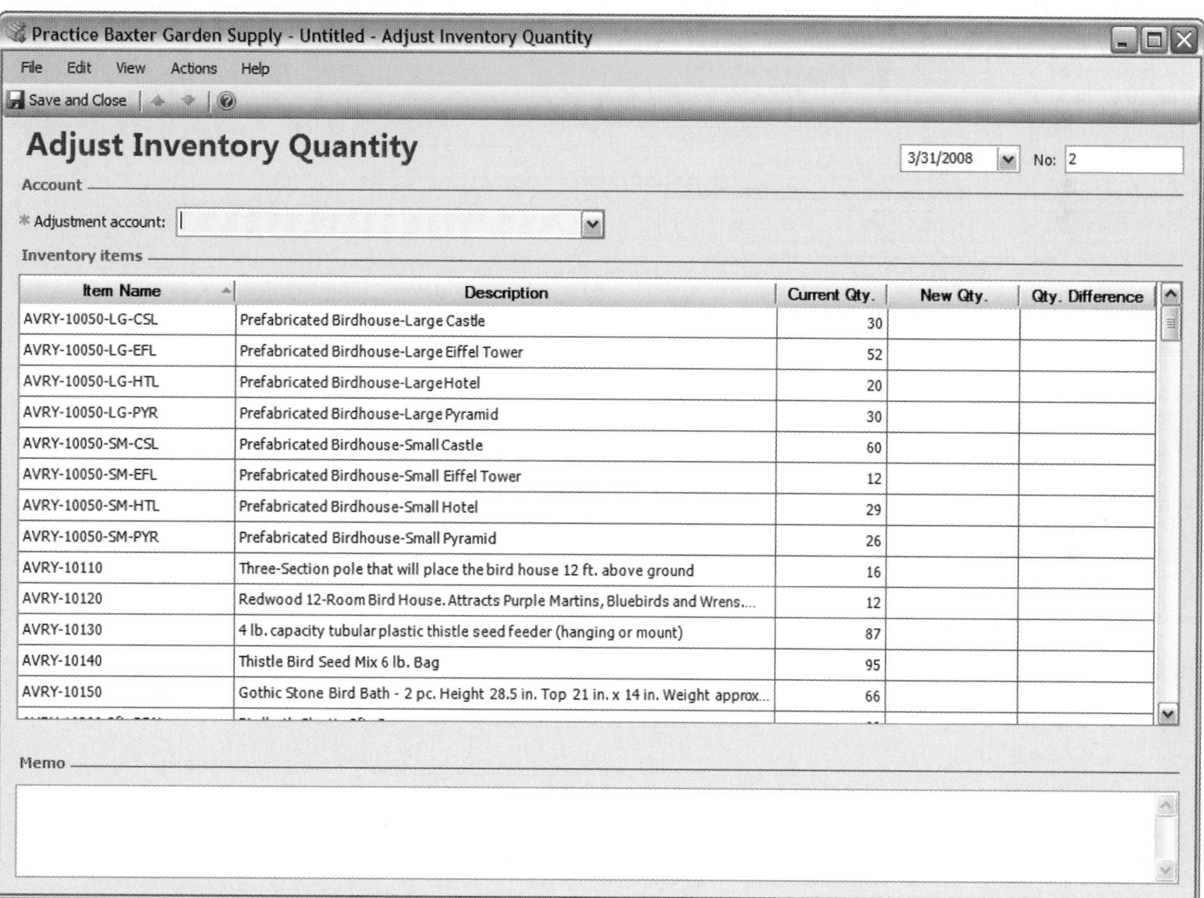

Practice Baxter Garden Supply - Untitled - Adjust Inventory Quantity

File Edit View Actions Help

Save and Close

Adjust Inventory Quantity

3/31/2008 No: 2

Account

* Adjustment account:

Inventory items

Item Name	Description	Current Qty.	New Qty.	Qty. Difference
AVRY-10050-LG-CSL	Prefabricated Birdhouse-Large Castle	30		
AVRY-10050-LG-EFL	Prefabricated Birdhouse-Large Eiffel Tower	52		
AVRY-10050-LG-HTL	Prefabricated Birdhouse-Large Hotel	20		
AVRY-10050-LG-PYR	Prefabricated Birdhouse-Large Pyramid	30		
AVRY-10050-SM-CSL	Prefabricated Birdhouse-Small Castle	60		
AVRY-10050-SM-EFL	Prefabricated Birdhouse-Small Eiffel Tower	12		
AVRY-10050-SM-HTL	Prefabricated Birdhouse-Small Hotel	29		
AVRY-10050-SM-PYR	Prefabricated Birdhouse-Small Pyramid	26		
AVRY-10110	Three-Section pole that will place the bird house 12 ft. above ground	16		
AVRY-10120	Redwood 12-Room Bird House. Attracts Purple Martins, Bluebirds and Wrens....	12		
AVRY-10130	4 lb. capacity tubular plastic thistle seed feeder (hanging or mount)	87		
AVRY-10140	Thistle Bird Seed Mix 6 lb. Bag	95		
AVRY-10150	Gothic Stone Bird Bath - 2 pc. Height 28.5 in. Top 21 in. x 14 in. Weight approx...	66		

Memo

Figure 8:61

The accountant has found that the actual quantity for AVRY-10140 Thistle Bird Seed is 93 whereas OAP shows 95. It is not unusual for minor quantity discrepancies to occur, particularly if items were discarded due to damage or obsolescence. However, large discrepancies in physical counts indicate a problem with control over inventory and should be investigated.

You will now adjust the quantity for AVRY-10140 to reflect the actual quantity counted. Enter the new quantity for this item as illustrated in Figure 8:62. Make sure to select the expense account for the adjustment and to enter a description that documents the write off.

Click **Save and Close** to post the adjustment.

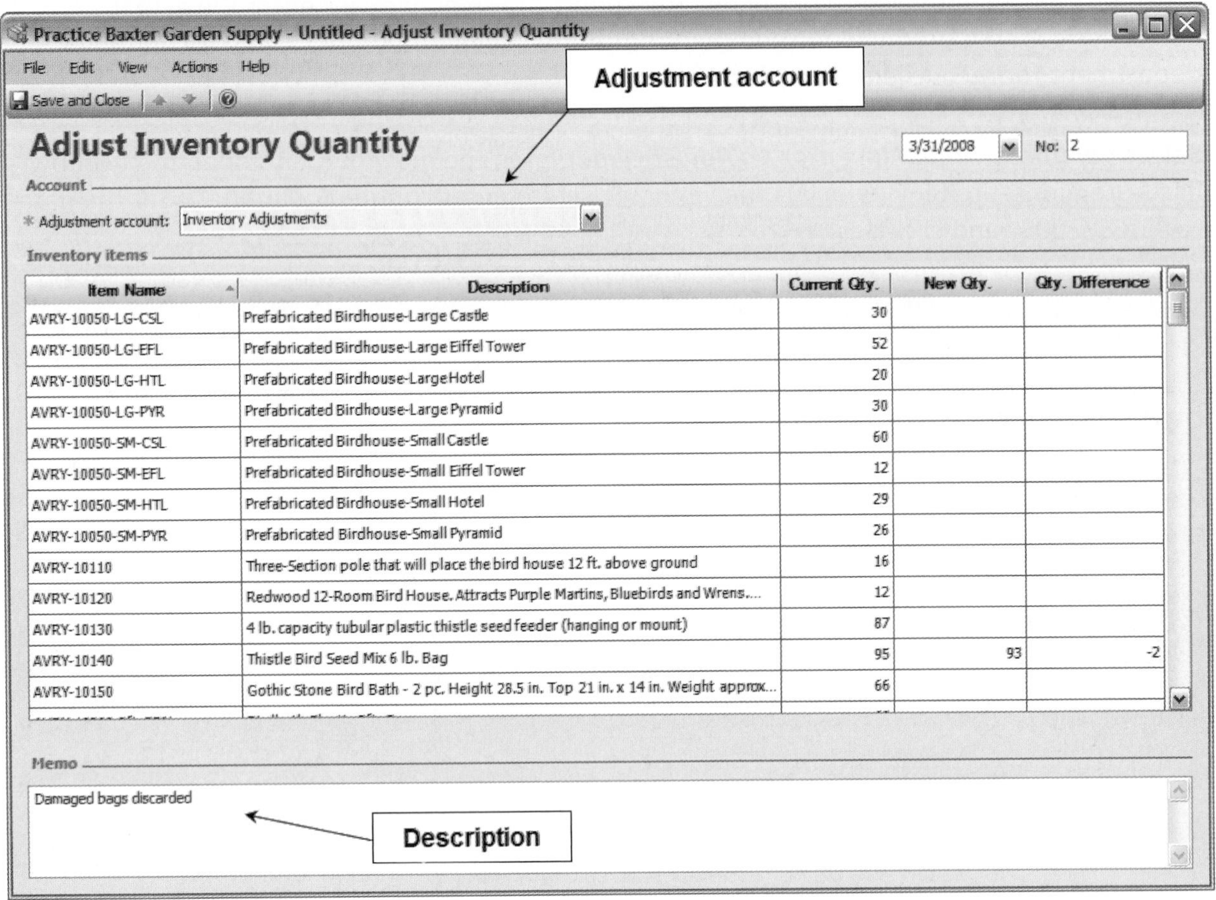

Item Name	Description	Current Qty.	New Qty.	Qty. Difference
AVRY-10050-LG-CSL	Prefabricated Birdhouse-Large Castle	30		
AVRY-10050-LG-EFL	Prefabricated Birdhouse-Large Eiffel Tower	52		
AVRY-10050-LG-HTL	Prefabricated Birdhouse-Large Hotel	20		
AVRY-10050-LG-PYR	Prefabricated Birdhouse-Large Pyramid	30		
AVRY-10050-SM-CSL	Prefabricated Birdhouse-Small Castle	60		
AVRY-10050-SM-EFL	Prefabricated Birdhouse-Small Eiffel Tower	12		
AVRY-10050-SM-HTL	Prefabricated Birdhouse-Small Hotel	29		
AVRY-10050-SM-PYR	Prefabricated Birdhouse-Small Pyramid	26		
AVRY-10110	Three-Section pole that will place the bird house 12 ft. above ground	16		
AVRY-10120	Redwood 12-Room Bird House. Attracts Purple Martins, Bluebirds and Wrens....	12		
AVRY-10130	4 lb. capacity tubular plastic thistle seed feeder (hanging or mount)	87		
AVRY-10140	Thistle Bird Seed Mix 6 lb. Bag	95	93	-2
AVRY-10150	Gothic Stone Bird Bath - 2 pc. Height 28.5 in. Top 21 in. x 14 in. Weight approx...	66		

Figure 8:62

CREATE A NEW INVENTORY ITEM

Baxter Garden Supply is adding the following new inventory item on March 1, 2008.

Item name:	EQWT-15175
Sales description:	Bell-Gro Drip Sprinkler
Sales price:	$22.00
Income account:	Sales – Equipment *(Do not make this the default account.)*
Item tax:	Taxable Sales
Purchase description:	Bell-Gro Drip Sprinkler
Purchase price:	$10.00
Asset account:	You determine this account
Preferred vendor:	Southern Garden
COGS account:	Product Cost – Equipment *(Do not make this the default account.)*
Reorder point:	6

Create the item and print an Inventory Stock Status by Item report filtered to display only the new item.

STOREFRONT SALES OF MERCHANDISE

On March 25, 2008, Baxter made a storefront sale of merchandise. With these sales, customers usually come into the store and pay for items at the time of sale. Therefore, these transactions are recorded using the **New Cash Sale** icon.

Follow the next steps and record this sale.

STEPS TO RECORD A STOREFRONT SALE OF MERCHANDISE

1. On the **Customers Home** page click **New Cash Sale** and enter the information illustrated in Figure 8:63.

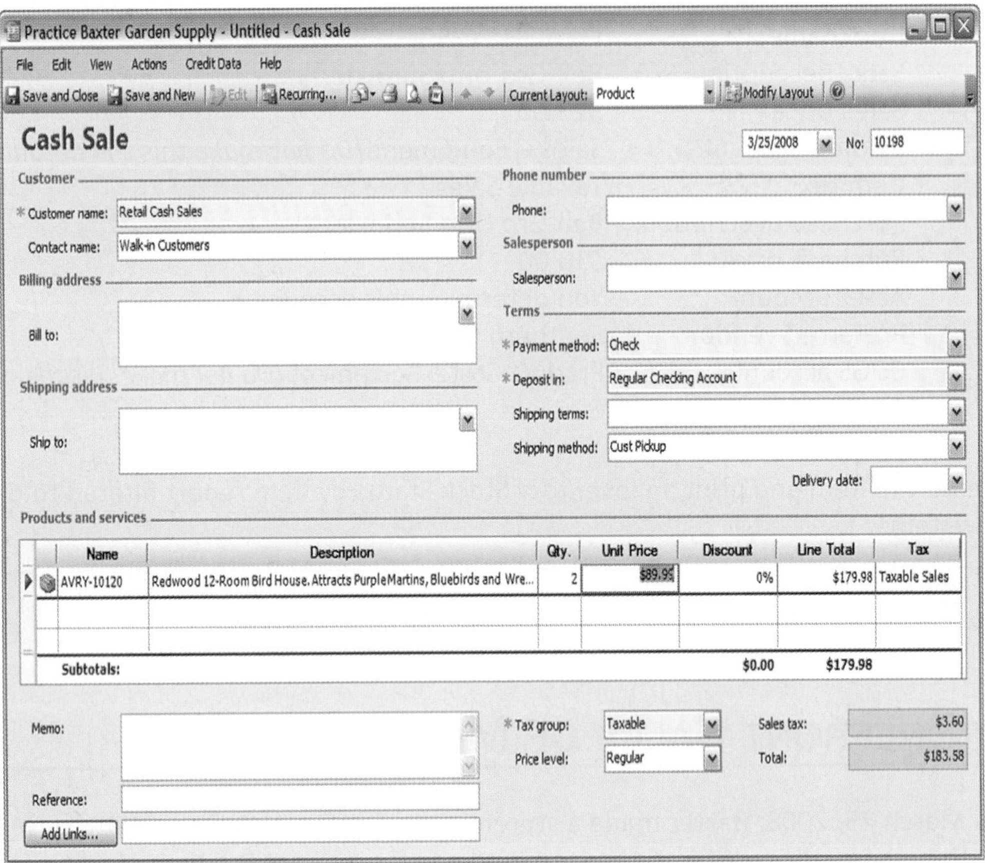

Figure 8:63

2. Click the **Printer** icon to give the customer a receipt. Click **OK** to save the transaction. Click **Save and Close** to exit the transaction window.

   Because this is not a sale on account, the debit will post to the Regular Checking Account instead of the Accounts Receivable account.

ENTER A STOREFRONT SALE OF MERCHANDISE

On March 27, 2008, Freemond Country Club picked up 30 bags of topsoil (SOIL-34120). The customer paid $213.89 by check at the time of sale. Record the transaction and print Freemond's receipt.

Invoices for Out-of-Stock Merchandise

OAP will warn when quantities of inventory on a sales invoice exceed quantities on hand. *(Note: The warning does not occur on sales orders.)* You can override the warning and save the invoice. We will now test the warning.

Open a new sales invoice, enter "3/27/2008" as the transaction date, and select Pierce Properties as the customer.

On the first line item, select "EQFF-13130" and enter "30" as the quantity. Click **Save and Close**.

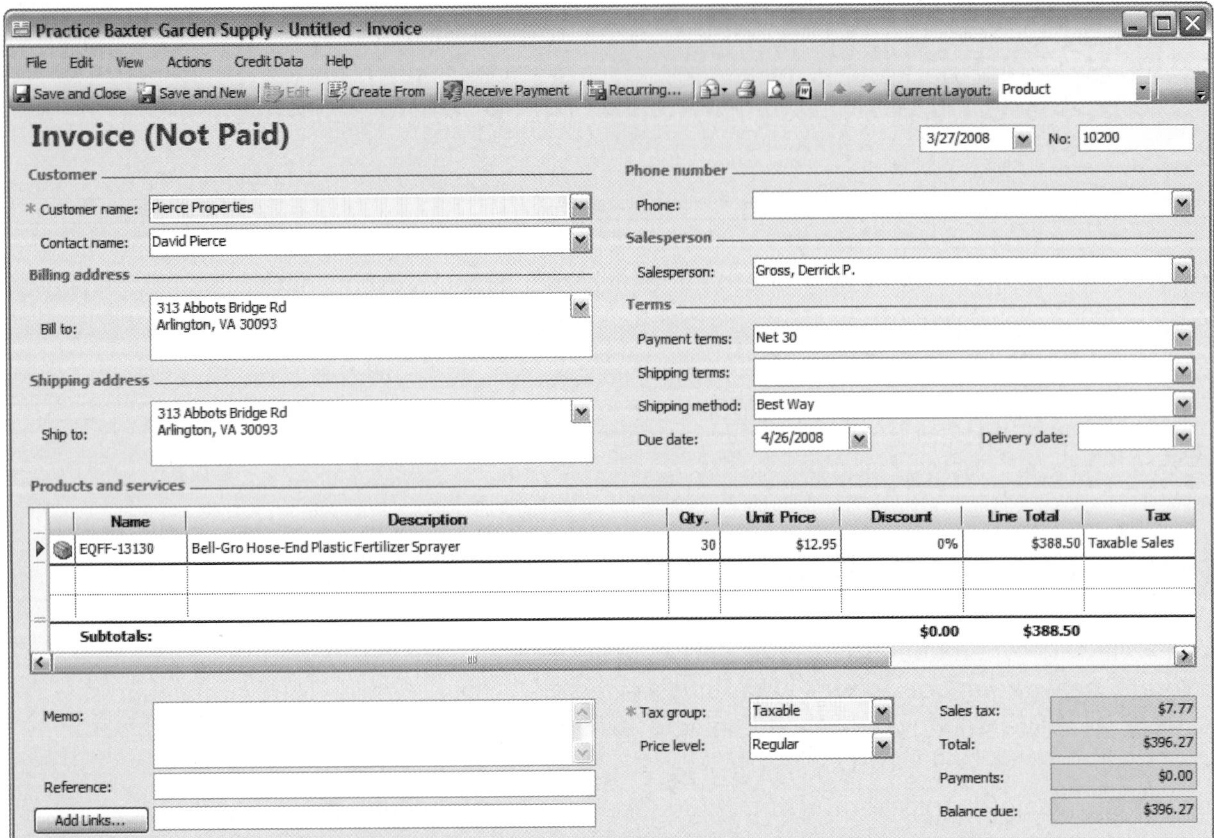

Figure 8:64

OAP issues the warning in Figure 8:65. Click Yes will override the message and save the invoice; however, you would be invoicing the customer without shipping the merchandise.

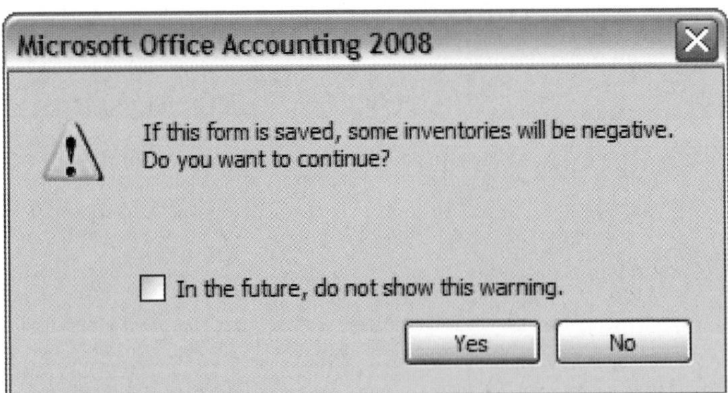

Figure 8:65

Click **No**. Click **X** on the transaction window and then click **No** to saving the invoice.

Customer Payments

Companies can have thousands of dollars in sales and collecting those sales is critical to continuing operations. In other words, sales must be realized in cash before the company can pay employees and vendors or invest in the business. This topic focuses on processing customer payments on account.

On March 27, 2008, Cannon Healthcare remitted check number 875 for $917.91, paying Invoice 10329 in full. Follow the next steps to record the payment.

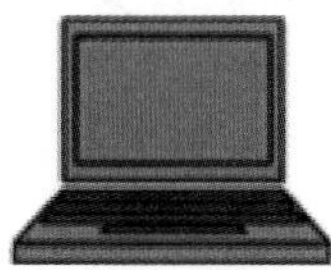

Steps to Post a Customer Payment

1. Click **Receive Payment** on the Customers Home page to open the window illustrated in Figure 8:66. Change the date to "3/28/2008" and select "Cannon Healthcare" as **Received from**. Cannon's outstanding invoices are listed at the bottom of the window.

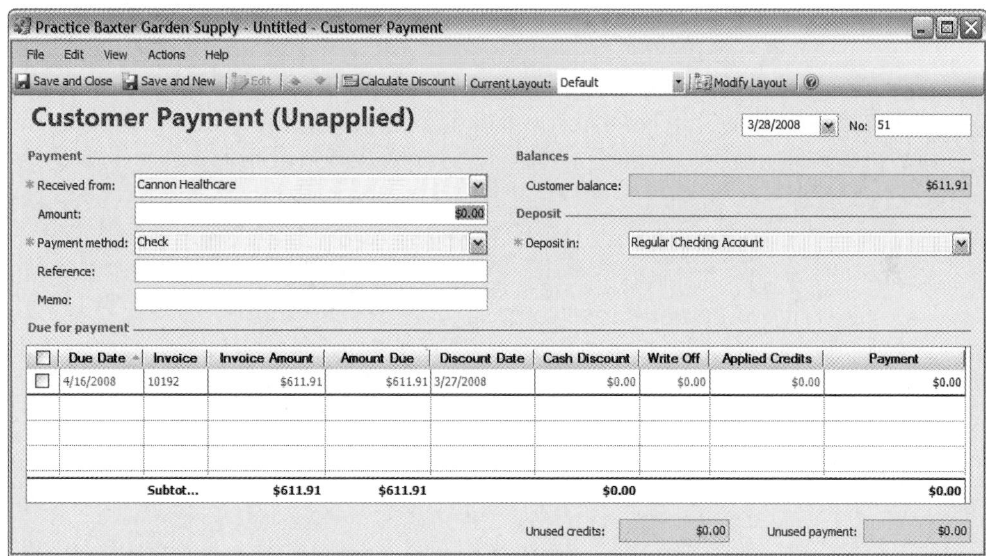

Figure 8:66

2. Tab to **Amount** and enter "611.91." OAP applies the payment to Invoice 10192. When there are multiple invoices, OAP will always select the oldest invoice and continue applying the payment to subsequent invoices. You can override OAP selections by changing the check box.

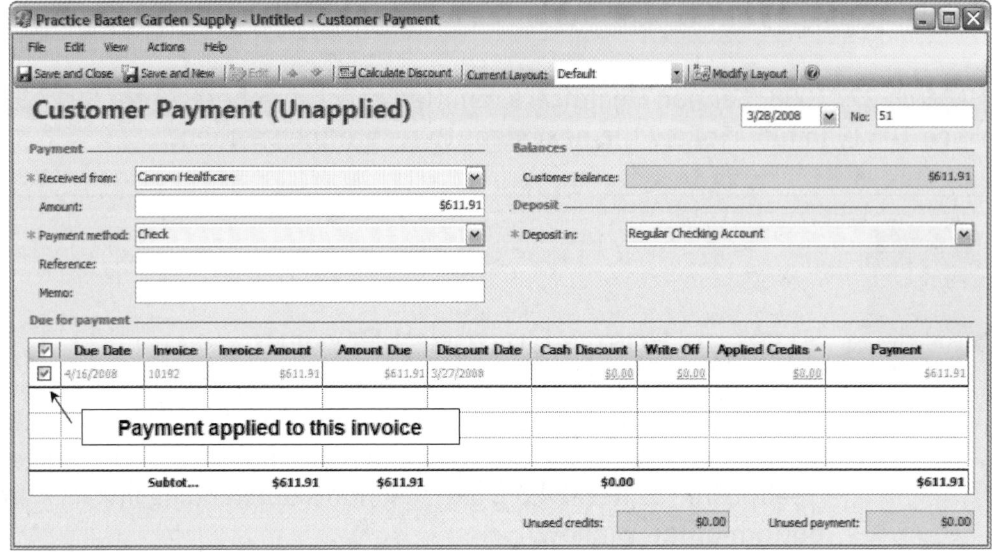

Figure 8:67

3. Verify that the **Payment method** is check and that the **Deposit in** field is set to Regular Checking Account (i.e., the general ledger account to debit). The credit will automatically post to Accounts Receivable.

4. Tab to **Reference** and enter "875" as the check number.

5. Click **Save and Close** to post the transaction.

Behind the Keys of a Posted Customer Payment

Now trace the audit trail for this receipt. Select ***Reports>>Company and Financial>> Transaction Journal*** on the main menu. Filter the report for the date range of "3/28/2008."

You will now turn this into a Cash Receipts Journal report. Click **Filter Options** and filter the **Transaction Type** to list Cash Sale and Customer Payment transactions (Figure 8:68).

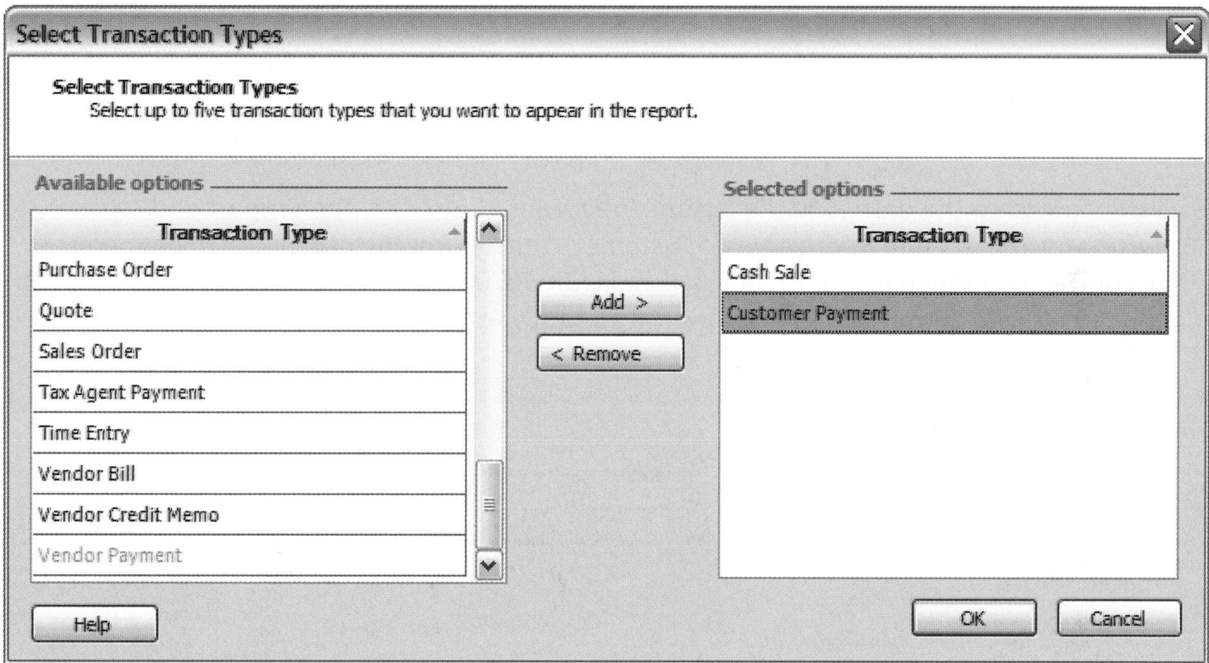

Figure 8:68

Click **OK** and then **OK**.

Click **Modify Report** and select the **Header and Footer** link. Change the **Report Title** to **Cash Receipts Journal**. (Not illustrated.) Save the report.

The Cash Receipts Journal is illustrated in Figure 8:69. Note that the audit trail codes displays in the Type and No. columns.

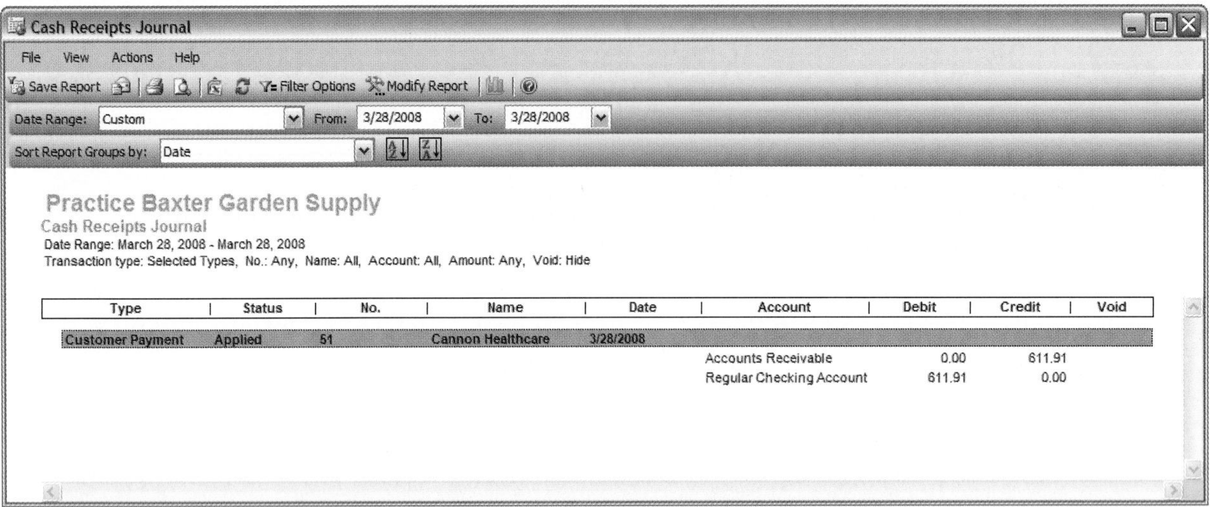

Figure 8:69

You will now trace the entries to the customer account. Close the open report and select ***Reports>>Customers and Receivables>>Customer Transaction History*** on the main menu. Filter for the date range of "3/28/2008." (See Figure 8:70.) Again, note that the audit trail on Cannon Healthcare's transaction matches the audit trail on the previous report.

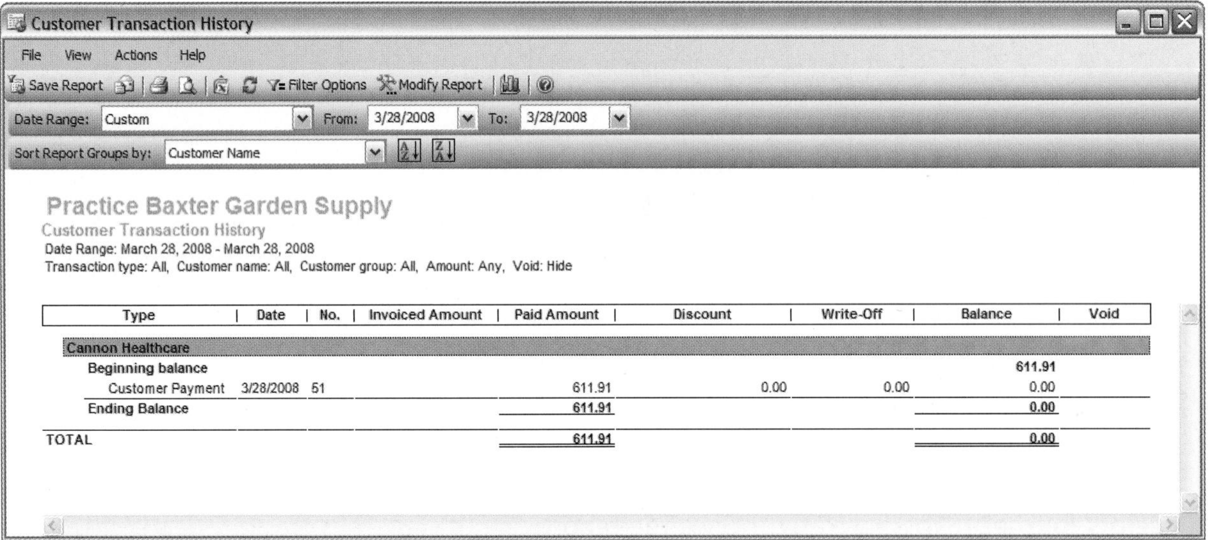

Figure 8:70

Close this report and complete tracing entries to the general ledger by opening the **Transaction Detail by Account** report. Locate your entries in accounts 10200 Regular Checking Account and 11000 Accounts Receivable (not illustrated).

CUSTOMER PAYMENTS WITH A DISCOUNT

In this topic, you continue posting customer payments. This time the customer is paying within the discount period. On March 24, 2008, Franklin Botanical paid Invoices 10189 and 10191 with check number 1983 for $3,117.73. Record this transaction.

STEPS TO POST A CUSTOMER PAYMENT WITH A DISCOUNT

1. Click **Receive Payment**, change the date to "3/24/2008" and select "Franklin Botanical" in **Received from**.

   Recheck the date because OAP uses it to determine whether the customer is paying within the discount period.

2. Click Calculate Discount so that discount amounts are listed under the Cash Discount column. ***Note: You should click this button each time a payment is entered or OAP will not apply available discounts.***

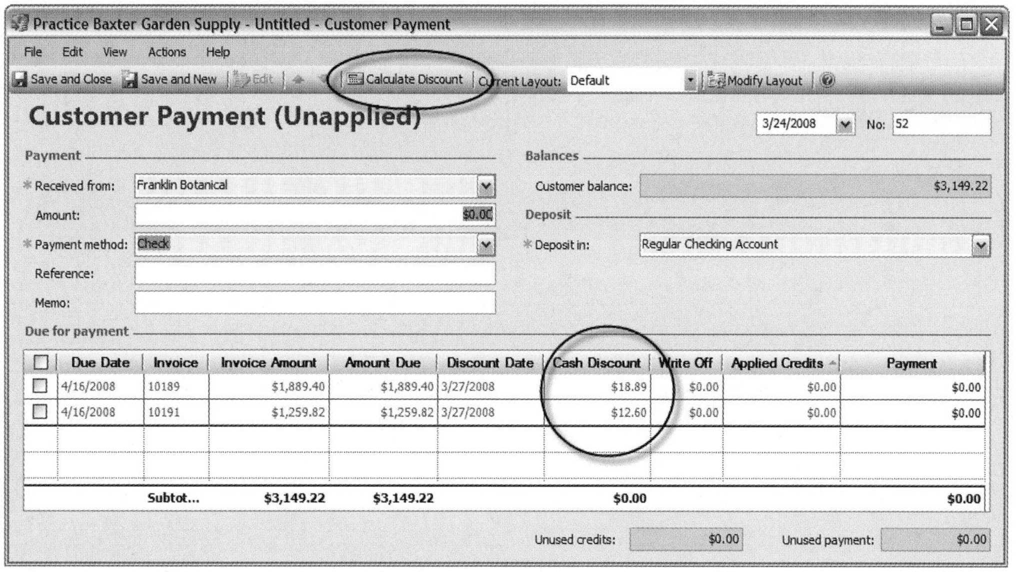

Figure 8:71

3. Tab to **Amount** and enter "3,117.73" and then enter "1983" as the check **Reference**.

4. Click the hyperlinked discount of $18.89 on the first invoice to open the Cash Discount window showing that the discount will post (i.e., debit) the Sales Discounts account. Click **Cancel**.

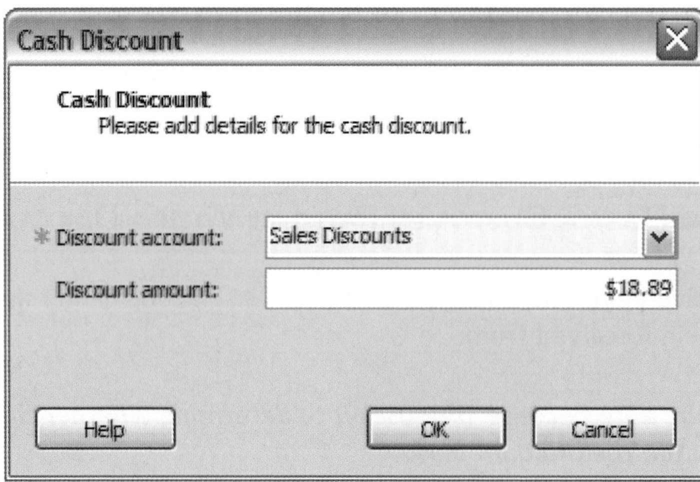

Figure 8:72

The discount posts to this account because it is assigned as the default system account for customer discounts. System accounts were discussed in Chapter 2.

5. Figure 8:73 shows the completed transaction. Click **Save and Close** to post the payment.

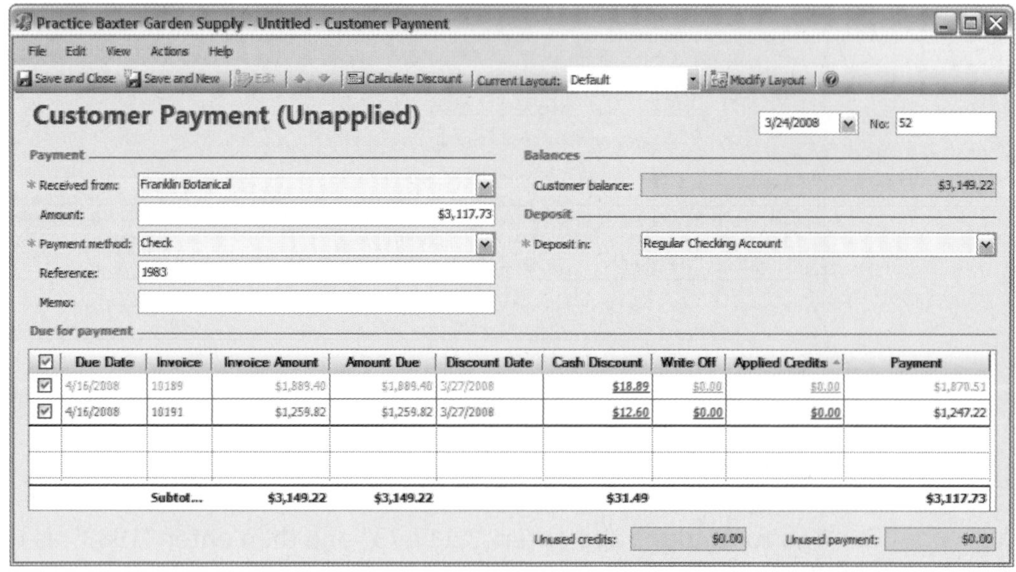

Figure 8:73

CORRECTING CUSTOMER PAYMENTS

OAP will not permit editing or deleting payments. Instead, you must void a payment and reenter a new payment transaction. We will now demonstrate this.

Click **Received Payments** under Find to open the Received Payment List illustrated in Figure 8:74.

Received Payment List — Current View: Fully Applied

Payment Date	No.	Customer Name	Payment Method	Amount Paid
Add a new Payment				
1/10/2008	1	Cummings Construction	Check	$1,763.61
1/17/2008	2	Cummings Construction	Check	$3,282.71
1/25/2008	3	Retail Cash Sales	Check	$74.31
1/29/2008	4	Retail Cash Sales	Check	$166.48
1/29/2008	5	Retail Cash Sales	Check	$411.23
1/29/2008	6	Retail Cash Sales	Check	$1,322.27
1/30/2008	7	Retail Cash Sales	Check	$344.51
1/31/2008	8	McKay Construction	Check	$2,579.86
2/1/2008	9	Armstrong Landscaping	Check	$7,050.31
2/1/2008	10	Armstrong Landscaping	Check	$10,349.45
2/11/2008	11	Treesdale	Check	$7,852.88
2/12/2008	12	Archer Scapes	Check	$21,637.00
2/14/2008	13	McKay Construction	Check	$4,038.61
2/14/2008	48	Cannon Healthcare	Check	$149.69
2/15/2008	14	Saia's Neighborhood	Check	$6,505.19
2/15/2008	15	Snowden Interior	Check	$187.58
2/18/2008	16	Mosley Country Club	Check	$856.76
2/21/2008	44	Retail Cash Sales	Check	$3,500.64
2/22/2008	17	Dash Business	Check	$1,243.34
2/25/2008	18	Holland Properties	Check	$826.13
2/25/2008	19	Williams Industries	Check	$377.28
3/3/2008	20	Everly Property	Check	$8,561.57
3/3/2008	21	Snowden Interior	Check	$373.00
3/5/2008	45	Retail Cash Sales	Cash	$539.13
3/5/2008	49	Chapple Law	Cash	$38.73
3/5/2008	50	Williams Industries	Check	$210.02

Figure 8:74

Double click to open the first payment and then click **Edit**. OAP prompts with the warning illustrated in Figure 8:75 informing you that editing the payment voids the current transaction. Click **No** and then click **X** to close the payment.

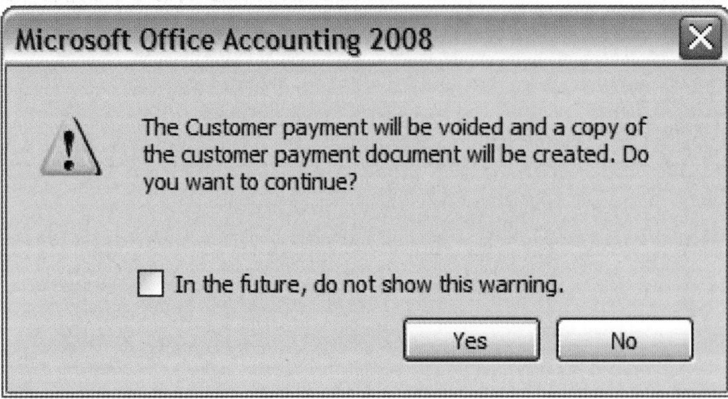

Figure 8:75

You can also void a payment without reopening it by highlighting the transaction on the list, right clicking, and selecting Void. After voiding a payment you can then reenter the transaction and apply the payment to the same invoices as on the voided payment or to different invoices.

RECORD CUSTOMER PAYMENTS

On March 31, 2008, the following customer payments were received. Post the payments.

Holland Properties check number 3533 for $7,258.99 paying Invoices 10169 and 10171.

Snyder Securities check number 7634 for $285.56 paying Invoices 10164.

Print the Cash Receipts Journal you created earlier in the chapter, filtered for 3/30/2008.

CUSTOMER CREDITS

Occasionally Baxter will issue credits to customers for returned inventory. On March 28, 2008, Baxter issues a credit to Mosley Country Club for the return of 3 Bell-Gro cedar planter boxes on Invoice 10193. Follow the next steps to record this credit.

STEPS TO ENTER A CUSTOMER CREDIT MEMO

1. From the Customer Home page, click **New Credits and Refunds**. Enter "3/28/2008" as the date and select "Mosley Country Club" as the **Customer name**.

2. Under **Products and services**, select "POTS-30200" and enter the quantity of "3." Figure 8:76 is the completed credit memo.

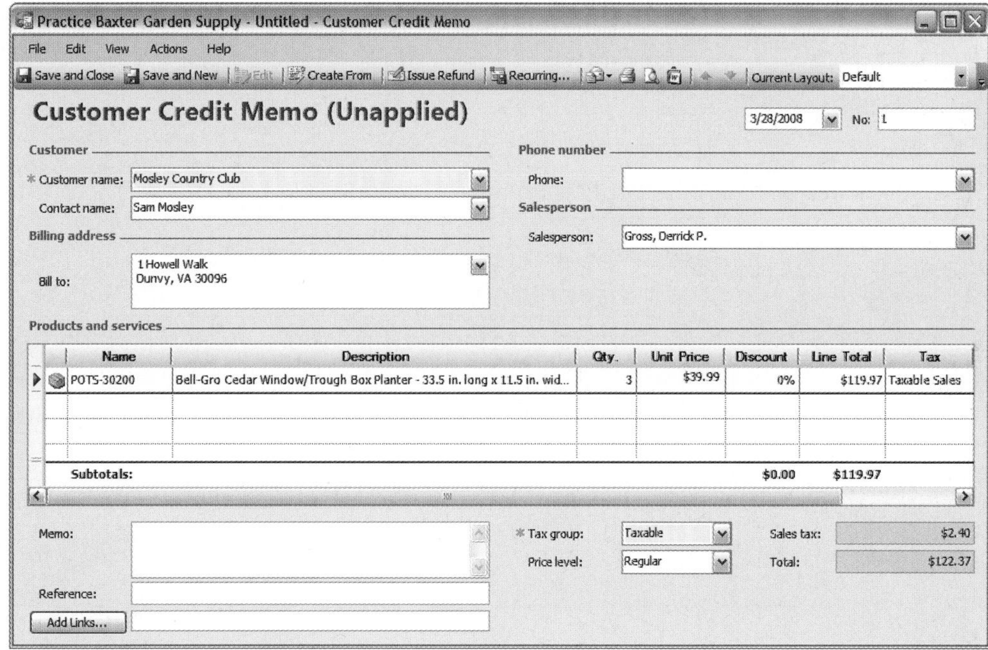

Figure 8:76

Note: The Create From icon on the window lets you choose an outstanding invoice for creating the credit memo. This method is illustrated in Chapter 4. With the create from method, the credit memo lists all items and quantities on the invoice and you have to manually delete items not being credited because OAP does not permit entering zero as the quantity. Therefore, the Create From method is generally not used for crediting invoices with multiple line items.

3. Click **Save and Close**.

The credit memo just created is not linked to an invoice so let us see what happens when Mosley Country Club remits its next payment.

Steps for Applying a Customer Credit Memo

1. Click **Receive Payment** and enter the information illustrated in Figure 8:77. Notice the unused credits amount listed at the bottom.

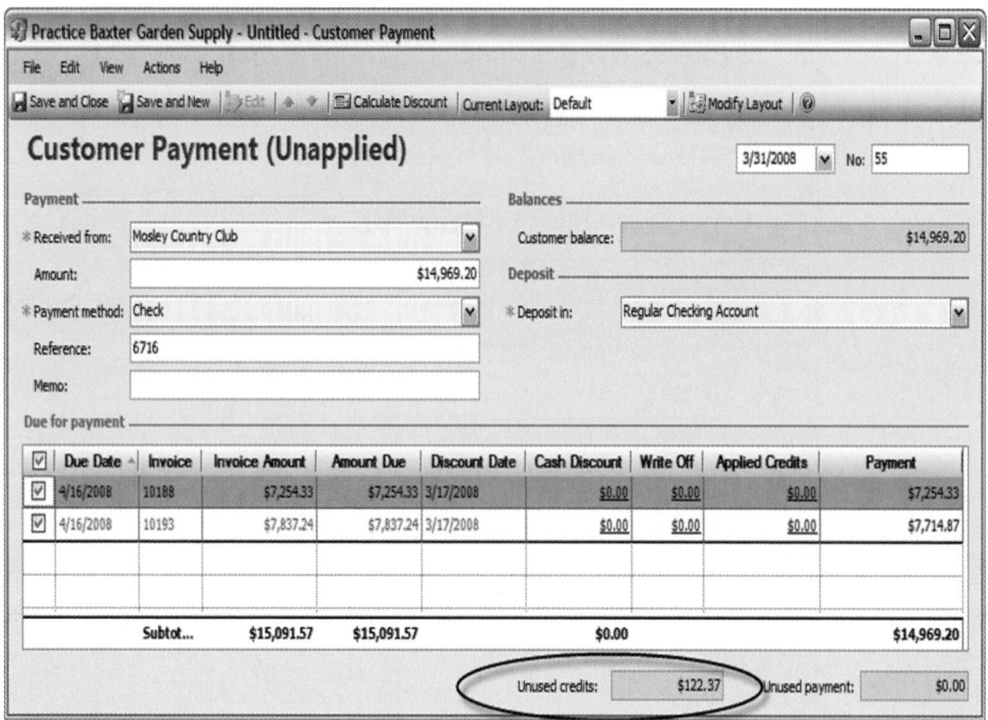

Figure 8:77

2. Click the **Applied Credits** hyperlink on Invoice 10193 to open the window illustrated in Figure 8:78. Click to select the credit memo and then click **Adjust** to apply the credit to the invoice.

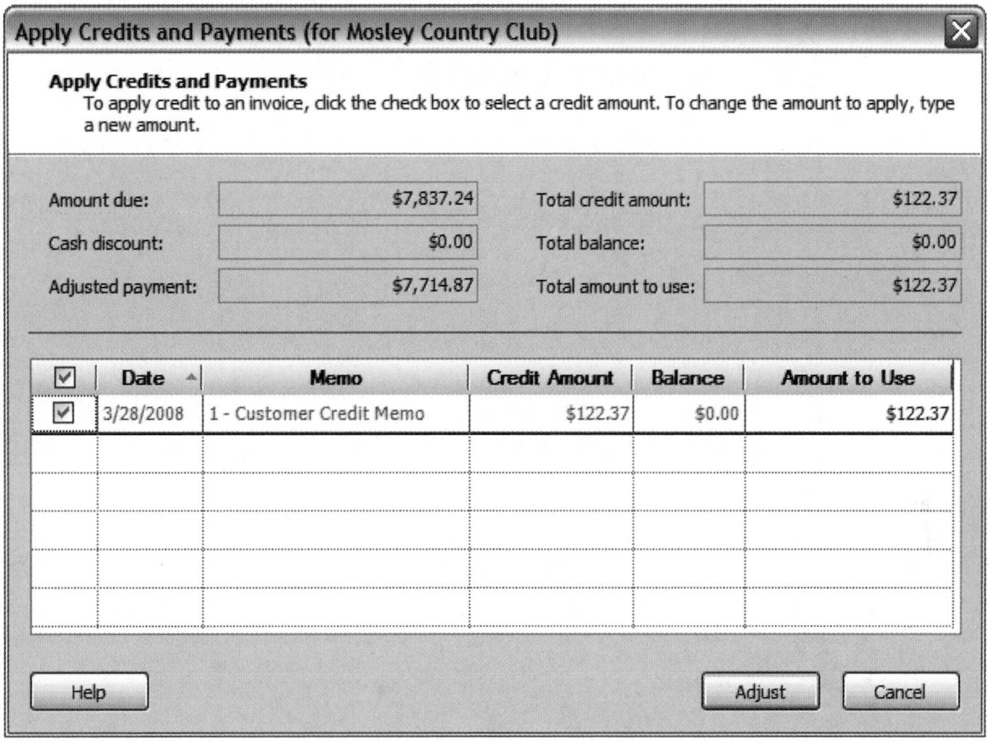

Apply Credits and Payments (for Mosley Country Club)

Apply Credits and Payments
To apply credit to an invoice, click the check box to select a credit amount. To change the amount to apply, type a new amount.

Amount due:	$7,837.24	Total credit amount:	$122.37
Cash discount:	$0.00	Total balance:	$0.00
Adjusted payment:	$7,714.87	Total amount to use:	$122.37

✓	Date	Memo	Credit Amount	Balance	Amount to Use
✓	3/28/2008	1 - Customer Credit Memo	$122.37	$0.00	$122.37

Help Adjust Cancel

Figure 8:78

3. Figure 8:79 shows the completed payment with the credit applied.

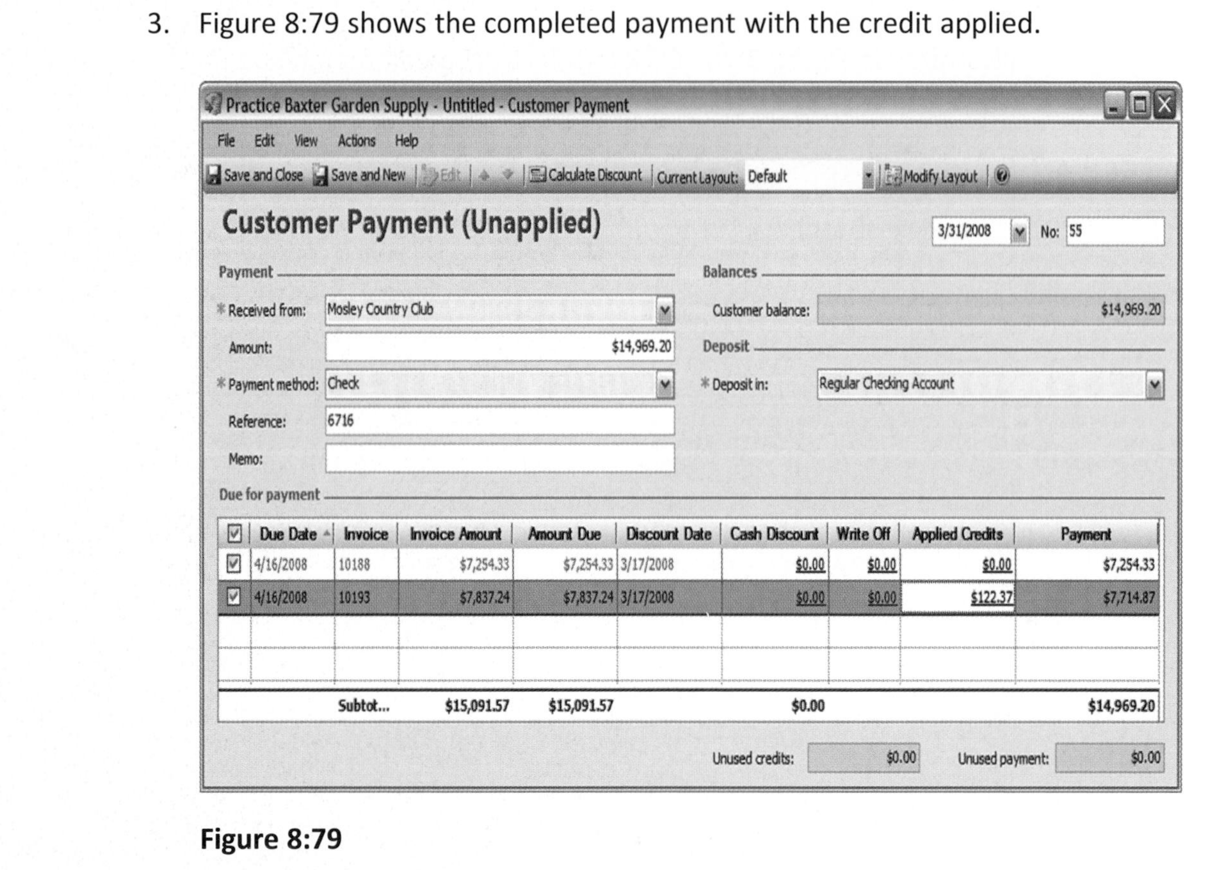

Figure 8:79

4. Click **Save and Close**.

Customer Reporting and Reconciling Customer Activities

OAP offers a variety of customer and sales reports. These reports can be run from the ***Reports>>Sales*** *and* ***Reports>>Customers and Receivables*** menus. In addition, you can run these reports from the Reports section on the Customer Home page (Figure 8:80).

Figure 8:80

Let's run the A/R Aging Summary report first because this is the current report in **Select a report**. Click **Display**. Filter the report for "3/31/2008." (See Figure 8:81.)

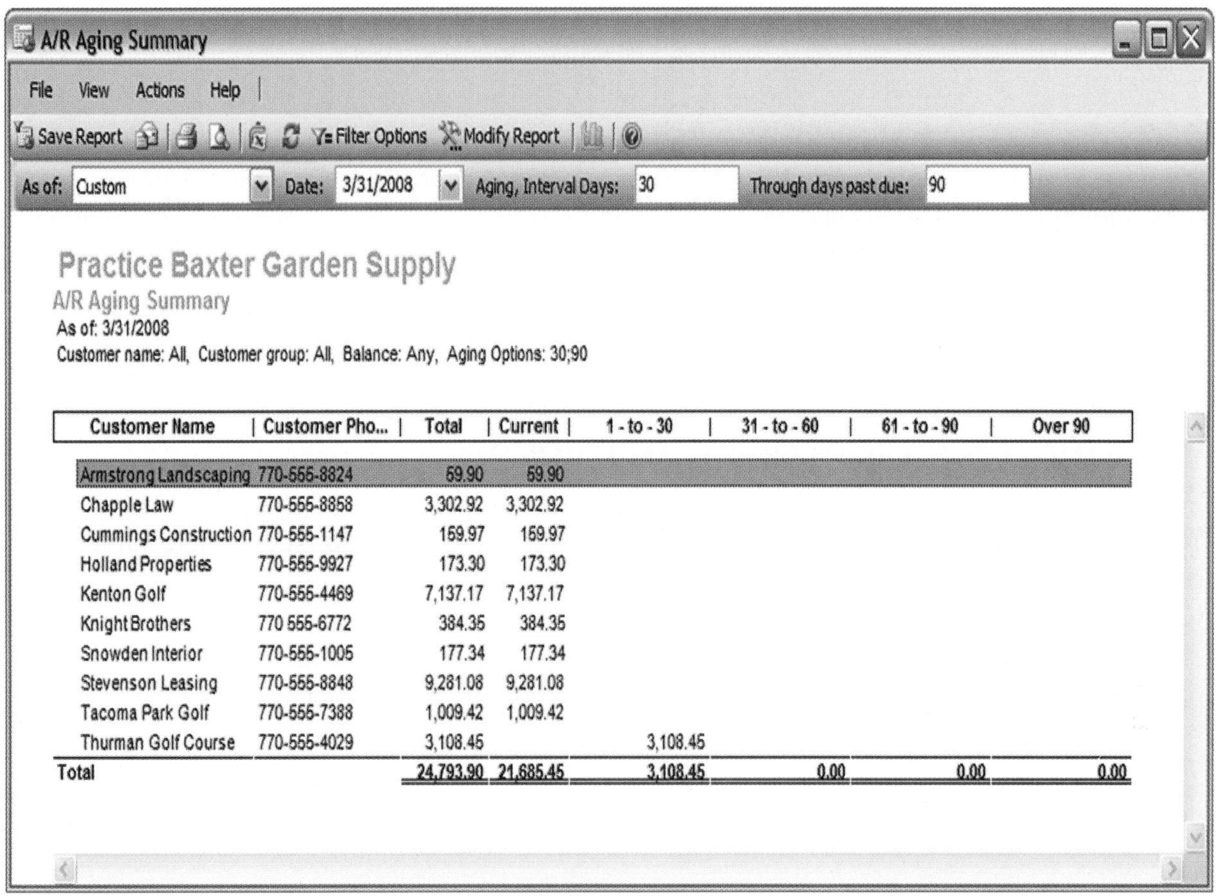

A/R Aging Summary

File View Actions Help

Save Report | Filter Options | Modify Report

As of: Custom | Date: 3/31/2008 | Aging, Interval Days: 30 | Through days past due: 90

Practice Baxter Garden Supply

A/R Aging Summary

As of: 3/31/2008

Customer name: All, Customer group: All, Balance: Any, Aging Options: 30;90

Customer Name	Customer Pho...	Total	Current	1 - to - 30	31 - to - 60	61 - to - 90	Over 90
Armstrong Landscaping	770-555-8824	69.90	69.90				
Chapple Law	770-555-8858	3,302.92	3,302.92				
Cummings Construction	770-555-1147	159.97	159.97				
Holland Properties	770-555-9927	173.30	173.30				
Kenton Golf	770-555-4469	7,137.17	7,137.17				
Knight Brothers	770 555-6772	384.35	384.35				
Snowden Interior	770-555-1005	177.34	177.34				
Stevenson Leasing	770-555-8848	9,281.08	9,281.08				
Tacoma Park Golf	770-555-7388	1,009.42	1,009.42				
Thurman Golf Course	770-555-4029	3,108.45		3,108.45			
Total		24,793.90	21,685.45	3,108.45	0.00	0.00	0.00

Figure 8:81

This report displays customer outstanding accounts receivable balances and age of the balance. *(Note: Your balances will differ from those illustrated if you have not completed all chapter exercises.)*

The report serves two important purposes. First, Baxter uses it to monitor customer payments and mitigate the risk of performing future services for customers that fail to pay. Monitoring the report also manages company cash flow.

Second, this report is used to reconcile customer activities with the accounts receivable control account. This task is performed by comparing the aging report total with the March ending balance in account 11000 Accounts Receivable.

Compare your balance in Accounts Receivable to the report by selecting ***Reports>>Company and Financial>>Trial Balance*** on the main menu and filtering the report for 3/31/2008. Scroll to the balance in account 11000 Accounts Receivable and compare this amount to your report total. These amounts must agree to verify proper recording of customer activities.

The amounts can become out of balance when you improperly correct customer transactions. Therefore, always refer to instructions in this chapter or Appendix B when correcting customer transactions. You should reconcile the aged receivables report to the accounts receivable balance at the end of every month and prior to issuing financial reports.

Close this report and open the **Detail A/R Aging** report (not illustrated). Enter "3/31/2008" as the date. This report is a variation on the summary aging report because it lists total outstanding accounts receivable along with invoice details. In addition, the Amount column displays the original invoice amount and the Total column displays the remaining invoice balance. Close the report.

Writing Off Customer Invoices

You will find in business that customers do not always pay. In addition, customers sometimes pay the wrong amount, leaving a few cents on the invoice.

The instructions that follow illustrate writing off an invoice balance while posting the payment. In Chapter 4 we illustrated writing off a balance after posting a payment.

Steps to Write Off a Customer Invoice

1. Click **Receive Payment** and enter the information in Figure 8:82.

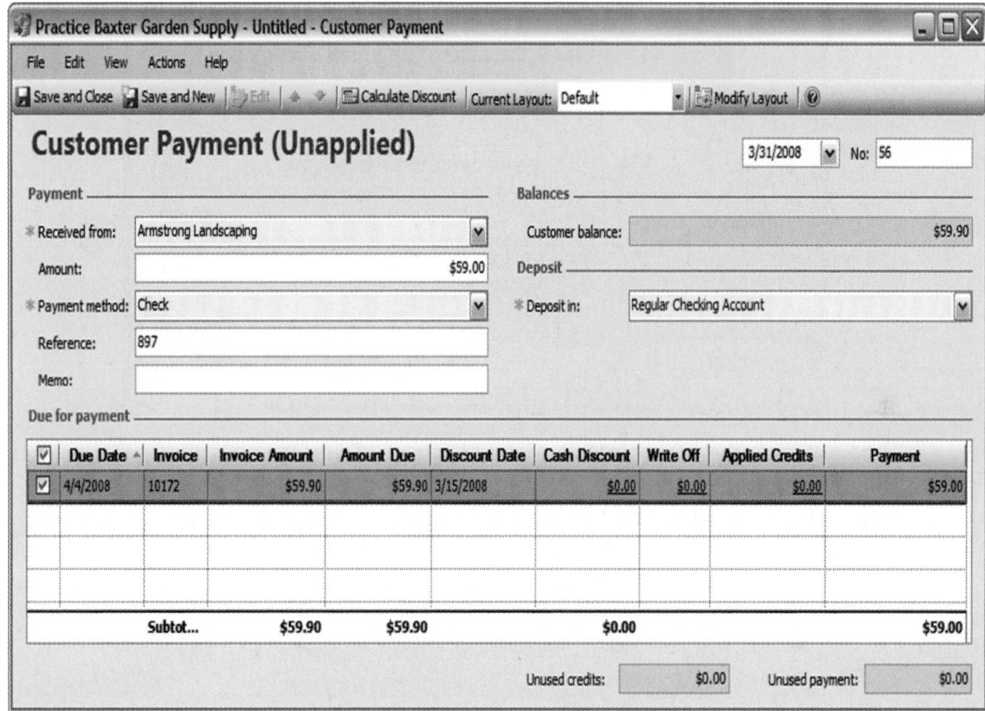

Figure 8:82

2. Click the hyperlink in the **Write Off** column to open this window.

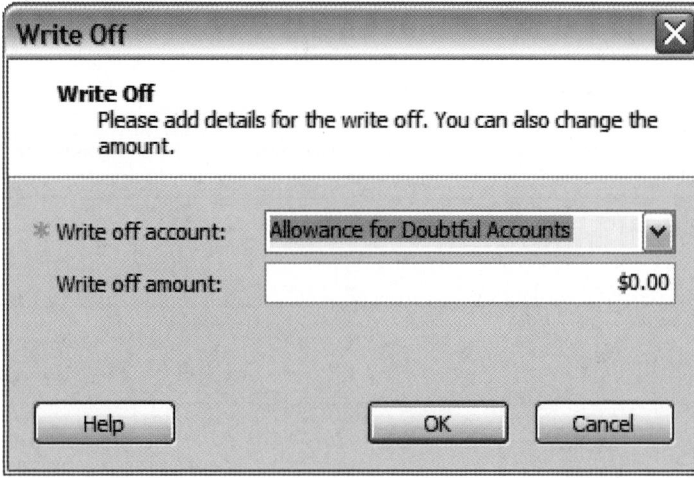

Figure 8:83

3. Baxter does not want to record the write-off to the Allowance for Doubtful Accounts because this is not a bad debt write-off. Change the account to Sales Returns and Allowances and enter "0.90" cents as the write off amount (Figure 8:84). Click **OK**.

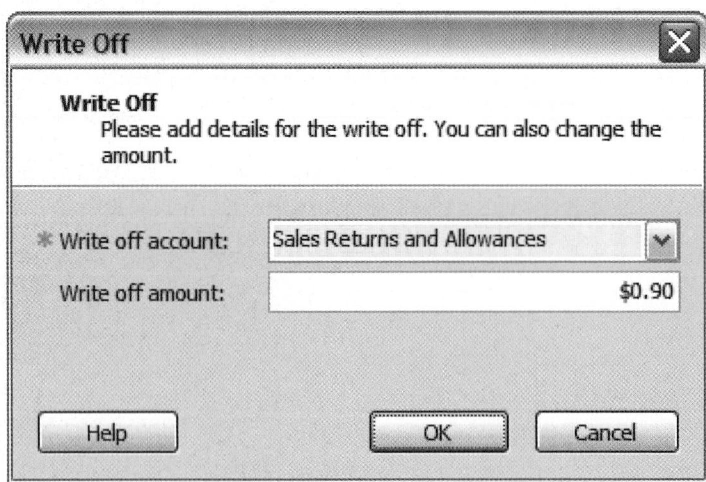

Figure 8:84

4. Figure 8:85 shows the completed payment. Click **Save and Close**.

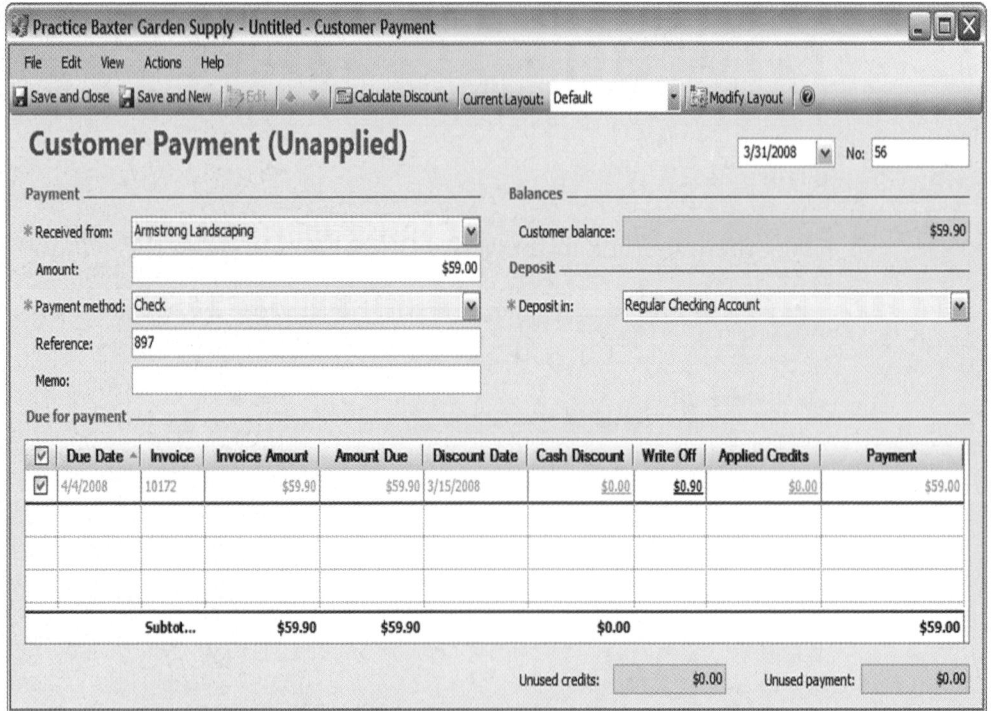

Figure 8:85

CUSTOMER STATEMENTS

Baxter mails customer statements once a month. These statements list invoice and payment activity and prompt customers to pay.

Select ***Customers>>Create Statement*** on the main menu to open the window illustrated in Figure 8:86.

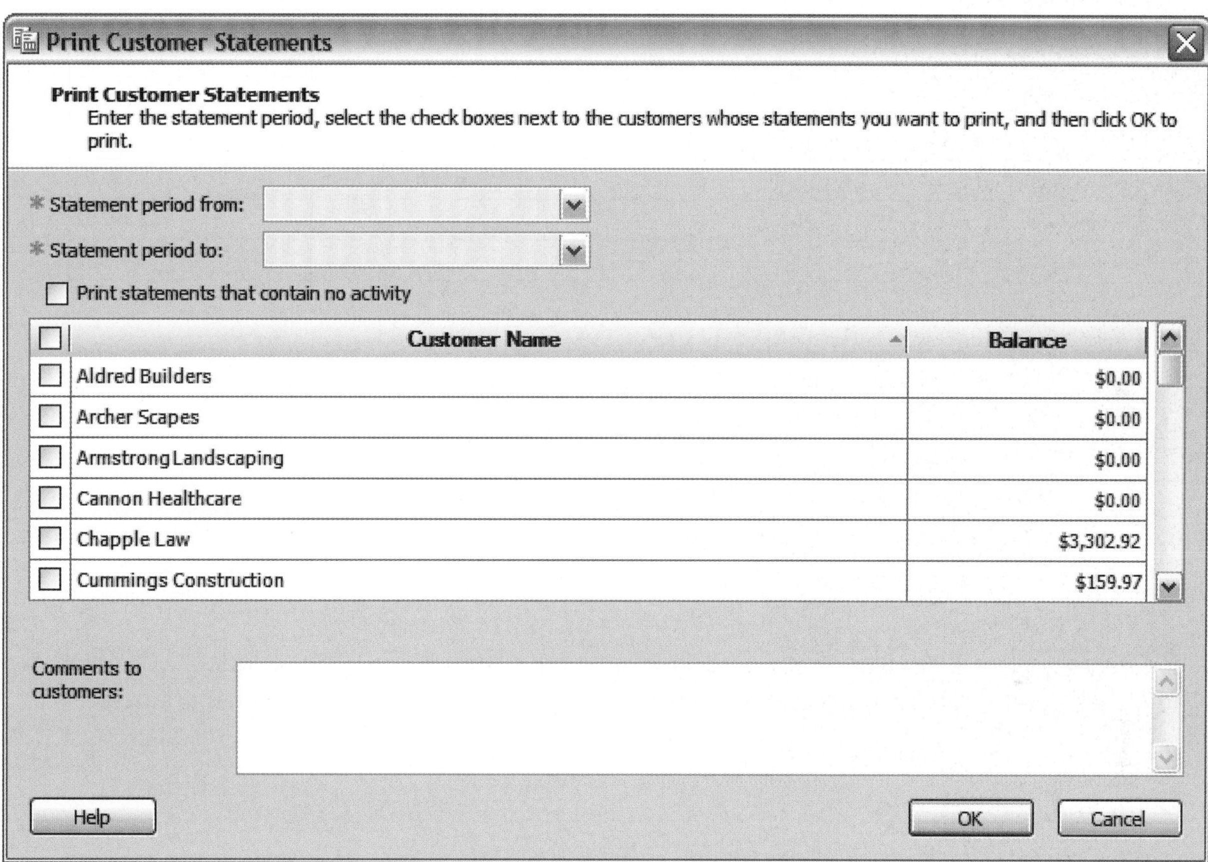

Figure 8:86

Enter "3/1/2008" in the **Statement period from** field and "3/31/2008" in the **Statement period to** field. Click the selection box on Chapple Law to print only this statement. The completed window is illustrated in Figure 8:87.

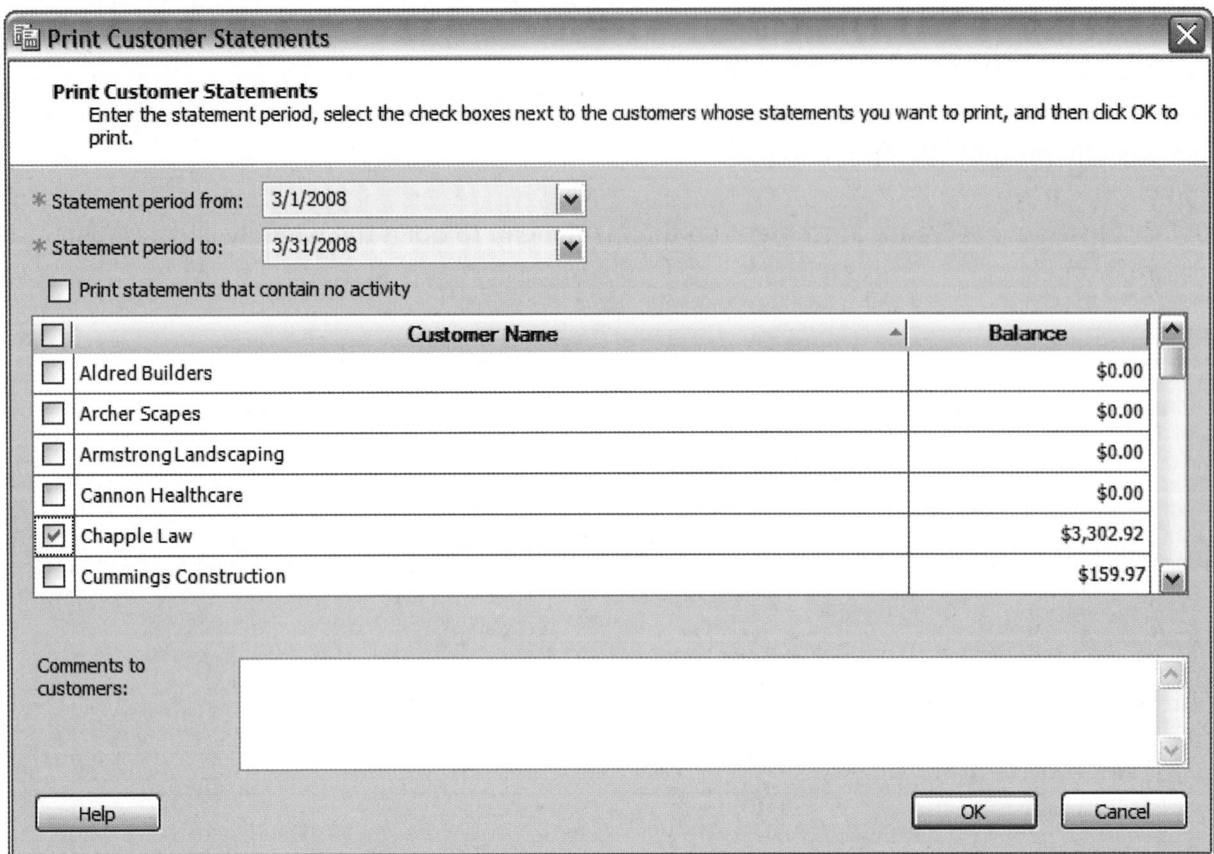

Figure 8:87

Click **OK** to generate the statement and then select a printer in the Print window. Click **OK**. The printed statement is illustrated in Figure 8:88. Close the window by clicking **Cancel**.

Practice Baxter Garden Supply

Statement

1352 W. Maple Ave
Arlington, VA 23523

Phone: 888-999-0909
Fax: 888-999-0909

Statement period: 3/1/2008 - 3/31/2008
Statement date:

To:

Chapple Law

12554 Lawrenceville Hwy.
Blacksburg, VA 30095-1120

Date	Transaction				Amount	Balance
2/29/2008	Balance forward					$0.00
3/5/2008	Invoice	10175		Paid	$38.73	$38.73
3/5/2008	Customer Payment	49		Applied	($38.73)	$0.00
3/18/2008	Invoice	10194	- Due 4/17/2008	Not Paid	$2,276.95	$2,276.95
3/27/2008	Invoice	10197	- Due 4/26/2008	Not Paid	$1,025.97	$3,302.92

Ending Balance: $3,302.92

Comments:

Figure 8:88

You have now completed the chapter. ***Make a backup of the Practice Baxter Garden Supply data file to a backup file named "practicebaxtergardensupply Chpt 8." In the next chapter, you will build on the work completed in this chapter.***

SUMMARY

In this chapter, you learned *MAPS* for customer transactions before entering transactions in OAP. By understanding manual accounting entries you were able to anticipate OAP's *Behind the Keys* entries. It is important to understand each transaction's effect on financial accounts so that you know when a transaction posts correctly. In addition, you are better equipped to trace the audit trail and to correct transactions.

After completing this chapter, you are skilled in recording customer orders, invoices, payments, and credit memos for a merchandising business. You can manage the master accounts linked to transactions (i.e., customer accounts and inventory items). You understand customer and sales reporting that let you monitor and document customer activities. With firm knowledge on processing customer activities, you are now ready to take on Baxter's vendor activities in the next chapter.

END-OF-CHAPTER QUESTIONS

TRUE/FALSE

_____ 1. OAP will post the cost of goods sold entry at the time of saving a sales order.

_____ 2. The Sales by Customer Detail report displays general ledger accounts used when posting a customer invoice.

_____ 3. Sales invoices can be transferred to sales orders.

_____ 4. You would post a journal entry to adjust quantities of on-hand merchandise.

_____ 5. Companies do not need to conduct a physical inventory count because OAP tracks the quantities of on-hand inventory.

_____ 6. OAP uses the transaction date on a customer payment to determine whether the customer has remitted payment within the discount period.

_____ 7. Sales orders and invoices can be emailed to customers.

_____ 8. When a customer pays for inventory at the time of sale, OAP will post entries to the inventory account but not to accounts receivable.

_____ 9. You can export a customer list to Excel.

_____ 10. You must delete the original transaction and reenter it to correct the transaction date on a customer payment.

MULTIPLE CHOICE

_____ 1. Saving a sales order will post entries to the _____ accounts.
   a. sales and accounts receivable
   b. sales, accounts receivable, and cost of goods sold
   c. sales, accounts receivable, cost of goods sold, and inventory
   d. none of the above

_____ 2. Saving a cash sale of merchandise will post entries to the _____ accounts.
   a. cash, accounts receivable, and sales
   b. cash, accounts receivable, inventory, and cost of goods sold
   c. cash, sales, inventory, and cost of goods sold
   d. none of the above

_____ 3. Saving a credit memo will post entries to the _____ accounts.
   a. cash and accounts receivable
   b. sales, accounts receivable, and cost of goods sold
   c. sales, accounts receivable, cost of goods sold, and inventory
   d. cash, sales, cost of goods sold, and inventory

_____ 4. Which report will let you analyze the profit margin on inventory?
   a. Inventory Valuation
   b. Item Profitability
   c. Item Price List
   d. Both a and b

_____ 5. An Inventory Valuation report can be used to_____.
   a. show quantities sold by item for a range of dates
   b. reconcile inventory values to the general ledger
   c. show the quantity on hand as of a specific date
   d. all of the above

_____ 6. The Sales by Item Detail report filtered for 3/1/2008 to 3/31/2008 shows_____.
   a. March cost of goods sold by item
   b. March sales by item
   c. both a and b
   d. none of the above

_____ 7. Price levels let you _____.
   a. offer customers a discount on inventory sales prices
   b. offer multiple prices on the same item
   c. receive discounts on purchases from vendors
   d. both a and b

PRACTICE SET

In this Practice Set you will be using the **Graded Baxter Garden Supply** data file customized with your initials at the end of Chapter 1. ***When this data file is not loaded on your computer, restore it using the "gradedbaxtergardensupply Chpt 1" backup file created in the Practice Set at the end of Chapter 1.***

1. Open **Graded Baxter Garden Supply** and enter the following April customer activities. Print transactions only if instructed. Reports will be printed in Step 2. Transactions use the payment terms and tax rates that default from the customer account.

<u>2008</u>

Apr 2 Post check number 1077 for $59.90 from Armstrong Landscaping paying Invoice 10172.

Create and print Sales order number 1 for $1,979.82 to Franklin Botanical for the following items.

QTY	Item	Unit Price
10	EQLW-14110	$ 149.99
8	EQLW-14160	59.99

Apr 4 Create Sales order number 2 for $7,599.10 to Knight Brothers for the following items.

QTY	Item	Unit Price
30	AVRY-10130	$ 19.99
50	EQWT-15100	129.99
10	TOOL-35300	49.99

Apr 8 Create the following invoices.

Invoice 10196 for $1,979.82 to Franklin Botanical for Sales Order 1.

Invoice 10197 for $7,599.10 to Knight Brothers for Sales Order 2.

Apr 9 Post the following checks from customers.

Check number 463 for $15,091.57 from Mosley Country Club paying Invoices 10188 and 10193.

Check number 255 for $3,108.45 from Thurman Golf Course paying Invoice 10165.

Apr 11 Create Invoice 10198 for $12,137.15 to Smith Family Garden for the following items.

QTY	Item	Unit Price
25	EQLW-14140	$ 299.99
40	NURS-21900	55.95
60	POTS-30200	39.99

Apr 17 Create Invoice 10199 for $4,499.10 to Saia's Neighborhood for the following items.

QTY	Item	Unit Price
60	SOIL-34160	$ 6.99
30	NURS-21810	16.99
30	NURS-23010	119.00

Post retail cash sale 10200 for 10 EQWT-15130 for $203.90 with tax, paid by check.

Apr 21 Post the following checks from customers.

Check number 234 for $7,137.17 from Kenton Golf paying Invoice 10176.

Check number 6725 for $2,276.95 from Chapple Law paying Invoices 10194.

Check number 735 for $5,129.04 from Franklin Botanical paying Invoices 10189, 10191, and 10196.

Create sales order number 3 for $13,069.18 to Golden Gardens for the following items.

QTY	Item	Unit Price
30	EQLW-14180	$ 299.99
20	EQWT-15150	16.99
17	EQWT-15170	23.99
35	FERT-16100	8.99
30	NURS-21820	16.99
50	NURS-22000	49.95

Apr 22 Post the following checks from customers.

Check number 685 for $159.97 from Cummings Construction paying Invoice 10182.

Check number 9925 for $7,432.29 from Holland Properties paying Invoices 10169, 10171, and 10195.

Check number 7155 for $9,281.08 from Stevenson Leasing paying Invoices 10177 and 10180.

Apr 23 Create the following invoices.

Invoice 10201 for $1,325.90 with tax to Cannon Healthcare for 10 AVRY-10150.

Invoice 10202 for $10,369.27 to Golden Gardens for following items on Sales Order 3. *(Note: Not all items were shipped.)*

QTY	Item	Unit Price
21	EQLW-14180	$ 299.99
20	EQWT-15150	16.99
17	EQWT-15170	23.99
35	FERT-16100	8.99
30	NURS-21820	16.99
50	NURS-22000	49.95

Apr 25 Create the following new customer.

Rose Gardens Supply
603 W. Arndale Street
Blacksburg, VA 30004
(701) 555-8144

Contact: Jeffrey Campbell, e-mail: jeffrey@rose.com
Salesperson: Dorothy Beck

Price level:	Regular
Credit limit:	$20,000
Preferred shipping:	Best Way
Preferred payment:	Check
Payment terms:	Net 30
Customer group:	Wholesale
Tax group:	Non-Taxable

Apr 28 Create sales order number 4 for $149.85 to Rose Gardens for the following item.

QTY	Item	Unit Price
15	EQFF-13120	$ 9.99

Apr 29 Post a credit memo for $69.90 to Saia's Neighborhood for returning 10 items of SOIL-34160 on Invoice 10199.

Apr 30 Post the following checks.

Check number 566 for $1,911.29 from Cannon Healthcare paying Invoices 10192 and 10201 with discount.

Check No. 248 for $4,429.20 from Saia's Neighborhood paying Invoice 10199 in full with credit.

2. Print the following reports.

    a. Transaction Journal for April 1 to April 30, 2008, filtered to display the transaction types of Cash Sale, Customer Credit Memo, Customer Payment, Invoice, and Sales Order.

    b. Inventory Valuation report for April 30, 2008. Explain how this report is used.

    c. A/R Aging Detail report as of April 30, 2008. Explain how this report is used.

    d. Customer statement for Cannon Healthcare showing activity for April 1 to April 30, 2008.

3. ***Back up the Graded Baxter Garden Supply data file to a backup file named "gradedbaxtergardensupply Chpt 8." The Practice Set for the next chapter will build on the work completed in this chapter.***

CHAPTER 9 VENDOR ACTIVITIES FOR A MERCHANDISING BUSINESS

LEARNING OBJECTIVES

This chapter works with the Practice Baxter Garden Supply data file with the tasks completed in Chapter 8. ***When this data file is not loaded on your computer, restore it using the "practicebaxtergardensupply Chpt 8" backup file created after reading Chapter 8.***

In this chapter, you continue processing Baxter's accounting activities by focusing on vendor activities. These activities include ordering goods, entering vendor bills for receipt of goods, and remitting vendor payments. While performing these activities, you will:

1. Learn *MAPS* for posting vendor transactions before processing transactions in OAP
2. Work with the Vendors Home page to process vendor transactions
3. Record vendor purchase orders, bills, payments, and credits
4. Look *Behind the Keys* of posted transactions
5. Manage vendor accounts and memorize vendor transactions
6. Correct and void vendor transactions
7. Print and analyze vendor reports
8. Reconcile vendor activities to the general ledger

Launch OAP and open **Practice Baxter Garden Supply**.

MANUAL ACCOUNTING PROCEDURES

As in the previous chapter, you begin by learning the manual accounting procedures (*MAPS*) for posting vendor activities before using OAP. These procedures help you to understand OAP transaction posting.

Before continuing it will help to explain that Baxter uses purchase orders (POs) to order inventory. POs authorize inventory purchases and document purchased quantities and prices. A Baxter employee, with authorization to order, creates and signs the PO before sending it to the vendor. Thereafter, the vendor ships the order to Baxter's warehouse, enclosing a packing receipt. This receipt is then forwarded to the accounting department and filed until Baxter receives a vendor bill.

When the bill arrives, the accountant matches it with the PO and receipt. This matching process verifies that the purchase was authorized and that billed quantities and prices agree to PO terms. The accountant then records the transaction.

On March 19, 2008, Sam Prather issues a PO to restock Baxter's supply of drip sprinklers. He orders 20 EQWT-15100 drip sprinklers at $59.95 each from Southern Garden Wholesale. Sam manually writes up the PO and signs it before sending it to Southern Garden. A copy of the PO is also sent to Melvin in accounting, who files the document for matching with the vendor bill. POs do not trigger accounting recognition because the liability does not occur until receipt of the goods.

The vendor's shipment arrives on March 20. Inventory clerk, Al Duke, inspects the merchandise before placing items on warehouse shelves. Al then sends Southern Garden's packing receipt to Melvin, who files it with the PO until Southern Garden's bill arrives.

On March 24, Melvin receives the following bill.

Southern Garden
4555 Oakland Park Blvd.
Arlington, VA 30312

Customer: **Date: 3/20/2008**
Baxter Garden Supply
1352 W. Maple Ave
Arlington, VA 23523

INVOICE **No. 97325**

Qty	Item	Item Price	
20	EQWT-15100 Drip sprinkler	$59.95	$ 1,199.00
		Total	$ 1,199.00

Terms Net 30.

Figure 9:1

Melvin matches the bill with the receipt and the PO and then enters the bill in the Purchases Journal. Melvin's entries to the Purchases Journal for March 24 appear in Figure 9:2.

Note: Technically the liability to Southern Garden was incurred on March 20 (i.e., the day the merchandise was received). However, manual accounting procedures do not accommodate such semantics. It would be tedious to record the receipt and then to record the bill. Instead, bills are recorded to the Purchases Journal on the date of receiving the bill.

Date: 3/24/2007		**Baxter Garden Supply** **Purchases Journal**			**Page 4**
Vendor	**Post Ref.**	**Description**	**Accounts Payable (Credit)**	**Purchases (Debit)**	**Utilities Expense (Debit)**
Southern Garden	SOUT001	Invoice 97325	1,199.00	1,199.00	
Neighbors Telephone	NEIGH001	March Phone	237.05		237.05
Hubbard Wholesale	HUBB001	Invoice 877	677.00	677.00	
Totals:			$ 2,113.05	$ 1,876.00	$ 237.05
Audit trail →		Acct Ref:	(20000)	(50000)	(71100)

Figure 9:2

Like the procedures used to enter transactions on the Sales Journal in Chapter 8, Melvin totals journal columns and cross-foots totals to verify that entries balance (i.e., debits equal credits). He then posts each invoice to the vendor's account and posts column totals to general ledger accounts listed at the bottom.

Melvin's entry to Southern Garden's vendor account is illustrated in Figure 9:3. *(Note: Entries for other vendor accounts are not illustrated.)*

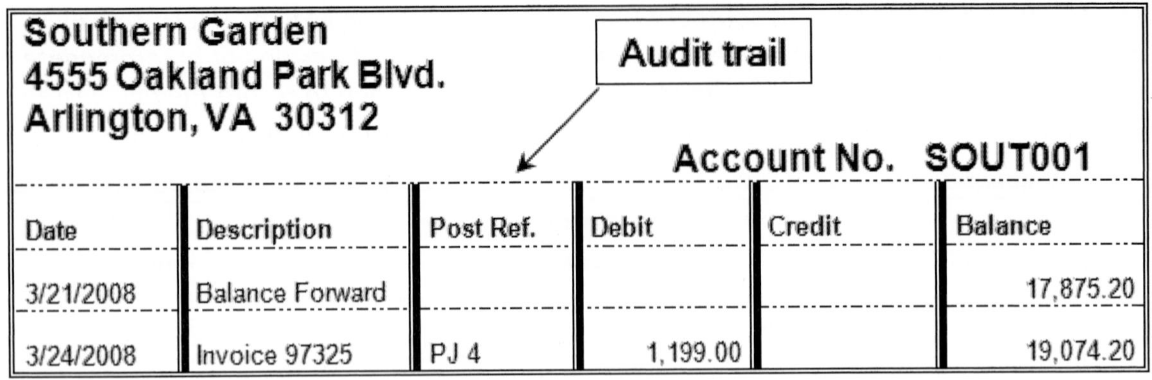

Southern Garden
4555 Oakland Park Blvd.
Arlington, VA 30312

Audit trail

Account No. SOUT001

Date	Description	Post Ref.	Debit	Credit	Balance
3/21/2008	Balance Forward				17,875.20
3/24/2008	Invoice 97325	PJ 4	1,199.00		19,074.20

Figure 9:3

Melvin's entries to general ledger accounts follow. *(Note: The entry for utilities is not shown.)*

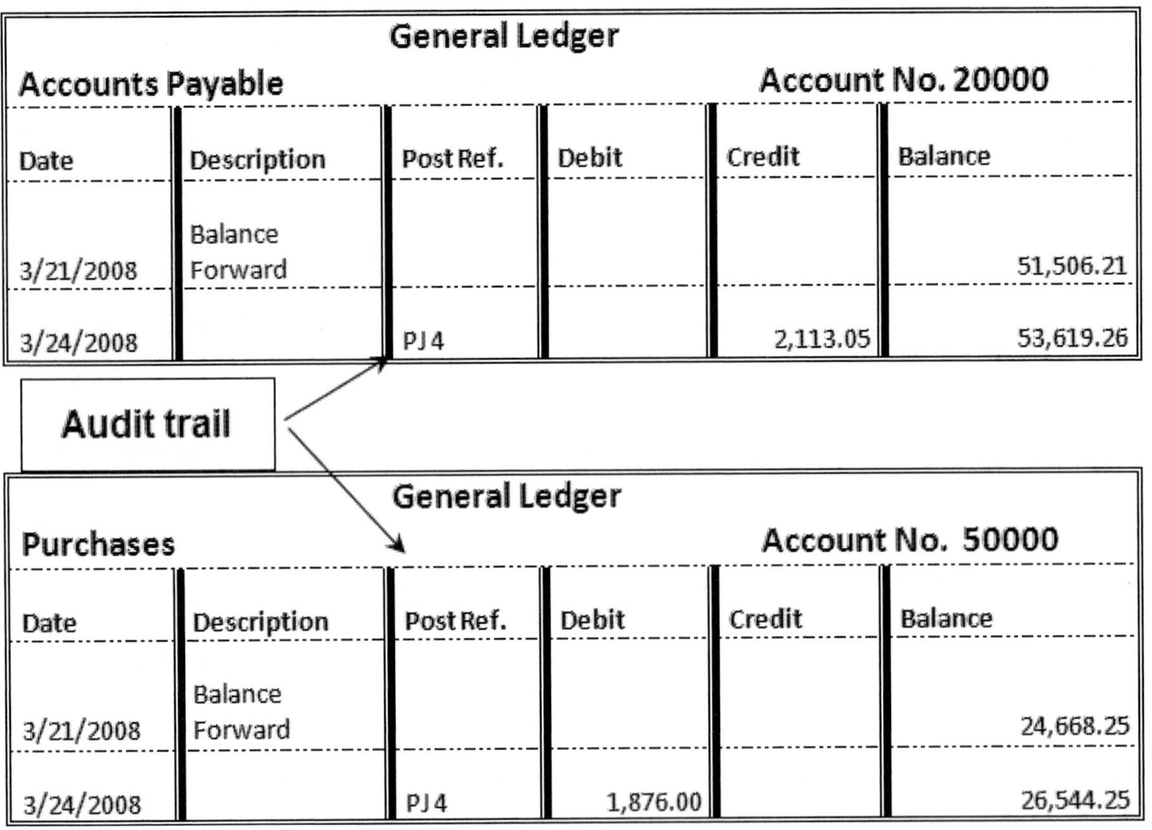

General Ledger

Accounts Payable — Account No. 20000

Date	Description	Post Ref.	Debit	Credit	Balance
3/21/2008	Balance Forward				51,506.21
3/24/2008		PJ 4		2,113.05	53,619.26

General Ledger

Purchases — Account No. 50000

Date	Description	Post Ref.	Debit	Credit	Balance
3/21/2008	Balance Forward				24,668.25
3/24/2008		PJ 4	1,876.00		26,544.25

Figure 9:4

The next day Melvin reviews vendor bills and prepares checks for bills that are due. He also prepares a check to buy postage. Melvin records these checks on the Cash Disbursements Journal shown in Figure 9:5.

Baxter Garden Supply						
Date: 3/25/2008		Cash Disbursements Journal			Page 3	
Vendor	Check No.	Post Ref.	Invoice No.	Regular Checking (Credit)	Accounts Payable (Debit)	Postage Expense (Debit)
Aker Distribution	10247	AKER001	4	5,179.20	5,179.20	
Daniel Lawn Pro, Inc.	10248	DANI001	3253	7,532.00	7,532.00	
US Post Office	10249		March Postage	150.00		150.00
Totals:				$ 12,861.20	$ 12,711.20	$ 150.00
Audit trail →		Acct Ref:		(10200)	(20000)	(63100)

Figure 9:5

As with the Purchases Journal, Melvin posts each check to a vendor's account and column totals to general ledger accounts. He will use the posting reference of CDJ (Cash Disbursements Journal) along with the page number. *(Note: These postings are not illustrated.)*

As discussed in Chapter 8, the manual method is fraught with opportunities to make posting errors. Melvin could enter an amount incorrectly, post an entry backwards, or forget to post it altogether.

With an understanding of *MAPS* for vendor activities, you are now ready to use OAP for processing vendor transactions. The topic that follows will introduce you to the home page and menu for these activities.

VENDORS MENU AND HOME PAGE

Before processing vendor activities become familiar with the menus that initiate activities. The Vendors menu is illustrated to the right. The first item opens the Vendors Home page. The New menu opens submenus for creating vendors, inventory items, and purchase orders. There are separate menus for receiving inventory and paying bills.

Click **Vendors Home** on the menu to open the Vendors Home page illustrated in Figure 9:7. This home page serves as central command for vendor activities. You can also click the Vendors Home page button to activate the page.

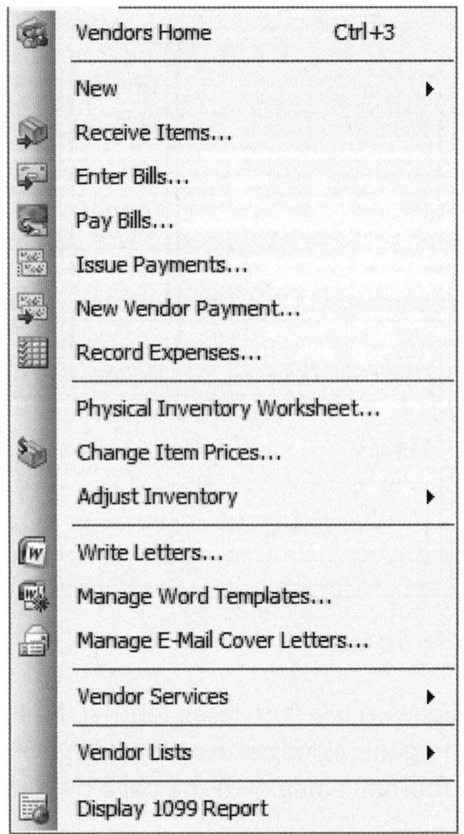

Figure 9:6

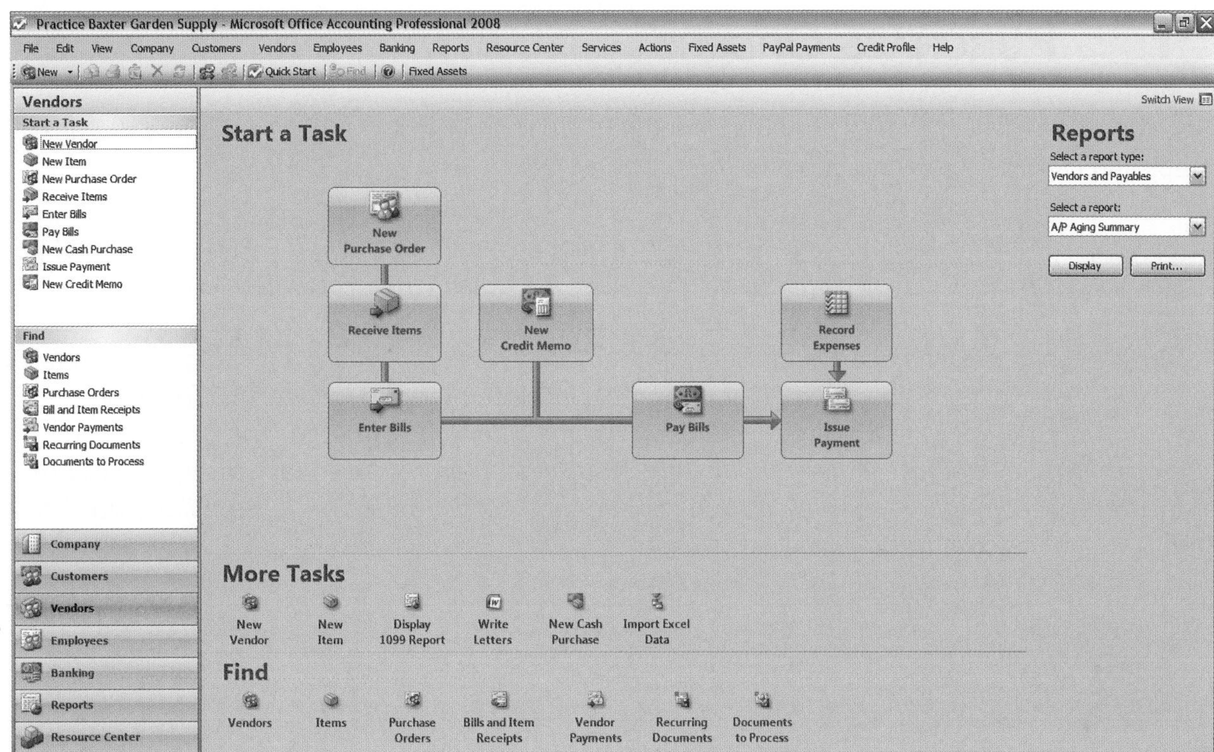

Figure 9:7

You find that the home page contains links to many of the commands found on the Vendors menu. **Start a Task** icons show that vendor activities can originate as purchase orders (purchase commitments), item receipts (merchandise received and awaiting a vendor bill), or vendor bills. Moreover, these icons demonstrate that purchase orders and item receipts will transfer to vendor bills and bills are the transactions that get paid. Credit memos can occur anytime before payment. Finally, Record Expenses are self-contained transactions that allow you to record an expense for payment transactions issued outside the software such as credit cards payments.

Beneath Start a Task icons are icons for performing **More Tasks** and opening lists that **Find** posted transactions. The activities found on the center of the page are replicated under the **Start a Task** and **Find** links located to the left of the page.

Now that you are familiar with the Vendors menu and home page, let's begin recording vendor transactions.

Purchase Orders

Recall from the *MAPS* topic that Sam created a PO to restock drip sprinklers. Follow the next steps and capture this transaction in OAP.

As previously discussed POs authorize vendor purchases and OAP 2008 significantly improves the way companies can issue these documents. You will recall from Chapter 8 that a new field (Restock level) was added to the Item window and that the Item List places an indicator in the Reorder column when on hand quantities fall below the reorder point. This list now contains a Reorder Inventory button for creating POs to preferred vendors for items below the reorder point. This feature also opens in the Purchase Order window after you select a preferred vendor that supplies any of the items needing to be reordered. You will see the Reorder Inventory feature illustrated in Step 3 of the exercise that follows.

Steps to Create a Purchase Order

1. On the **Vendors Home** page, click either the **New Purchase Order** link under **Start a Task** or the **New Purchase Order** icon on the home page.

2. Enter "3/19/2008" as the transaction date. Keep the PO **No.** supplied by OAP. The software sequentially increments this number for each PO issued.

3. Tab to **Vendor name** and select "Southern Garden." The window in Figure 9:8 opens because this preferred vendor supplies items where the On Hand quantities have fallen below the reorder point.

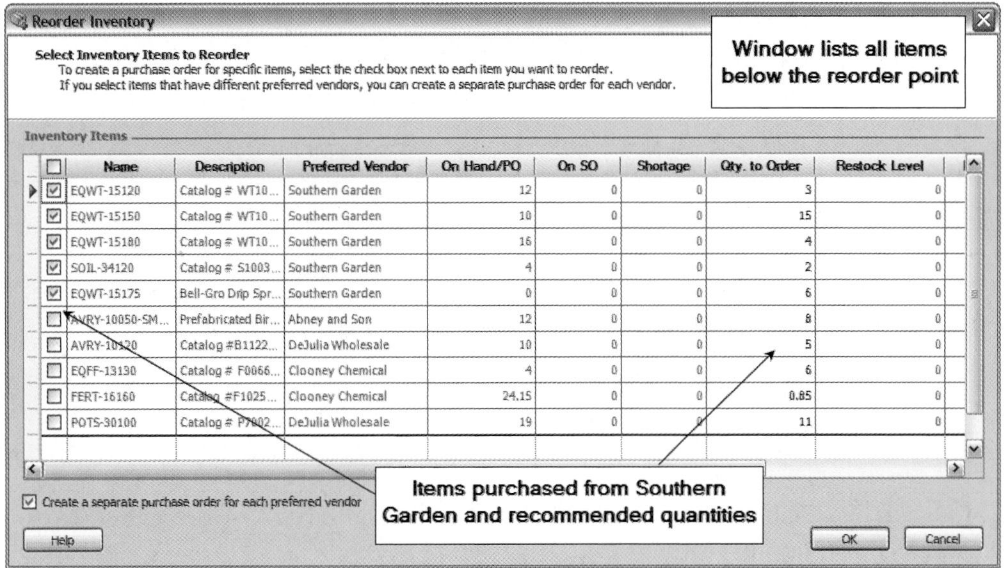

Figure 9:8

You can save time issuing POs with this window because it lists all items where stock levels are below the reorder point. By marking the checkbox on all items and selecting the Create a separate purchase order for each preferred vendor option at the bottom, OAP will create separate POs to the vendors listed using the recommended quantities under the Qty. to Order column.

Recommended ordering quantities are determined by looking at fields on the item record. If the item stores a Restock level quantity then the recommended ordering quantity equals the Restock level quantity minus the On Hand quantity; otherwise, the recommended ordering quantity equals the Reorder point quantity minus the On Hand quantity. Baxter has not entered Restock level quantities on its items so the second method will be used.

The item we are ordering is not listed in the window so click **Cancel** and we will enter the item to order in Step 6.

4. OAP has completed the top portion of the PO using the information on the vendor account (Figure 9:9).

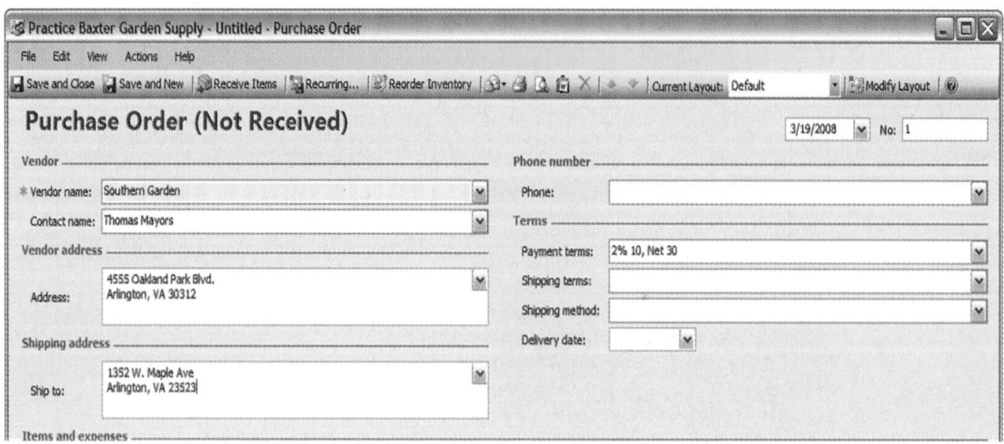

Figure 9:9

5. Tab to the icon symbol on the first line item of the PO and OAP opens a list of line item types.

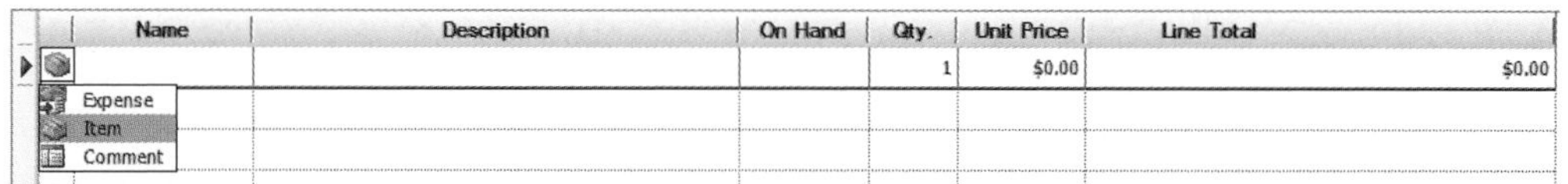

Figure 9:10

The following explains these types:

- **Expense** is used when entering vendor expenses directly to a general ledger account. Normally these will be for vendor transactions such as utilities, rent, or insurance. After selecting this icon you can look up general ledger accounts in the Name field and bypass items in the inventory table.

- **Item** is used when entering purchases of inventory or non-inventory items because it lets you look up items in the inventory table.

- **Comment** is for adding text to convey information to the vendor.

Select the **Item** icon.

6. In **Name** look up and select "EQWT-15100." Tab to **Qty.** and enter "20." Figure 9:11 shows the completed PO. Notice that the On Hand field displays the current item quantities in stock.

Practice Baxter Garden Supply - Untitled - Purchase Order

File Edit View Actions Help

Save and Close | Save and New | Receive Items | Recurring... | Reorder Inventory | Current Layout:

Purchase Order (Not Received) 3/19/2008 No: 1

Vendor
- Vendor name: Southern Garden
- Contact name: Thomas Mayors

Vendor address
- Address: 4555 Oakland Park Blvd. Arlington, VA 30312

Shipping address
- Ship to: 1352 W. Maple Ave Arlington, VA 23523

Phone number
- Phone:

Terms
- Payment terms: 2% 10, Net 30
- Shipping terms:
- Shipping method:
- Delivery date:

Items and expenses

Name	Description	On Hand	Qty.	Unit Price	Line Total
EQWT-15100	Catalog # WT1005225: Drip Irrigation System	66	20	$59.95	$1,199.00

Memo:

Total: $1,199.00

Reference:

Add Links...

Figure 9:11

7. Print the PO by selecting ***File>>Print*** on the menu and click **OK** when prompted to save the PO. When the Printer Selection window opens, select a printer and click **OK**. (*Note: You can also click the Printer icon on the toolbar and bypass the Printer Selection window.)*

   Figure 9:12 is the printed PO.

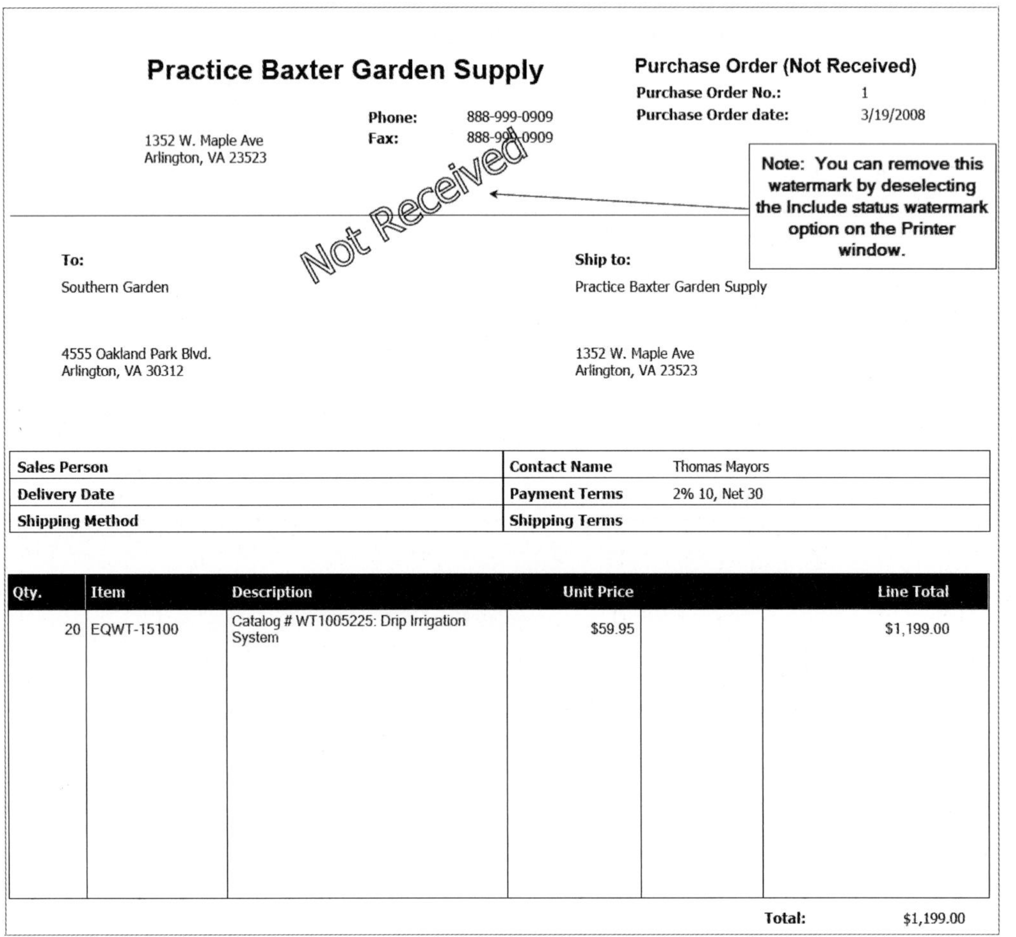

Practice Baxter Garden Supply

1352 W. Maple Ave
Arlington, VA 23523

Phone: 888-999-0909
Fax: 888-999-0909

Purchase Order (Not Received)

Purchase Order No.: 1
Purchase Order date: 3/19/2008

Not Received

Note: You can remove this watermark by deselecting the Include status watermark option on the Printer window.

To:
Southern Garden

4555 Oakland Park Blvd.
Arlington, VA 30312

Ship to:
Practice Baxter Garden Supply

1352 W. Maple Ave
Arlington, VA 23523

Sales Person		Contact Name	Thomas Mayors
Delivery Date		Payment Terms	2% 10, Net 30
Shipping Method		Shipping Terms	

Qty.	Item	Description	Unit Price		Line Total
20	EQWT-15100	Catalog # WT1005225: Drip Irrigation System	$59.95		$1,199.00
				Total:	$1,199.00

Figure 9:12

8. Click **Save and New** so you can enter the next PO.

9. This time click the **Reorder Inventory** button on the toolbar to reopen the Reorder Inventory window. Mark the two items ordered from Clooney Chemical and click **OK** (Figure 9:13).

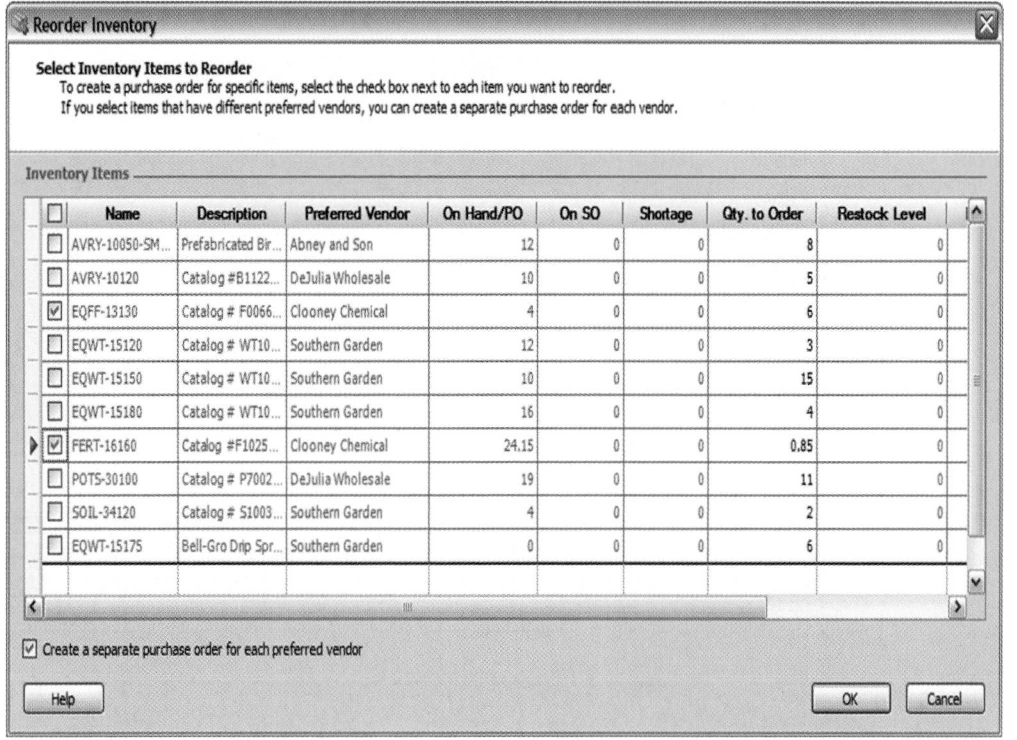

Figure 9:13

10. Adjust the quantity for item EQFF-13130 to 30 and for FERT-16160 to 30.85. The complete PO appears in Figure 9:14.

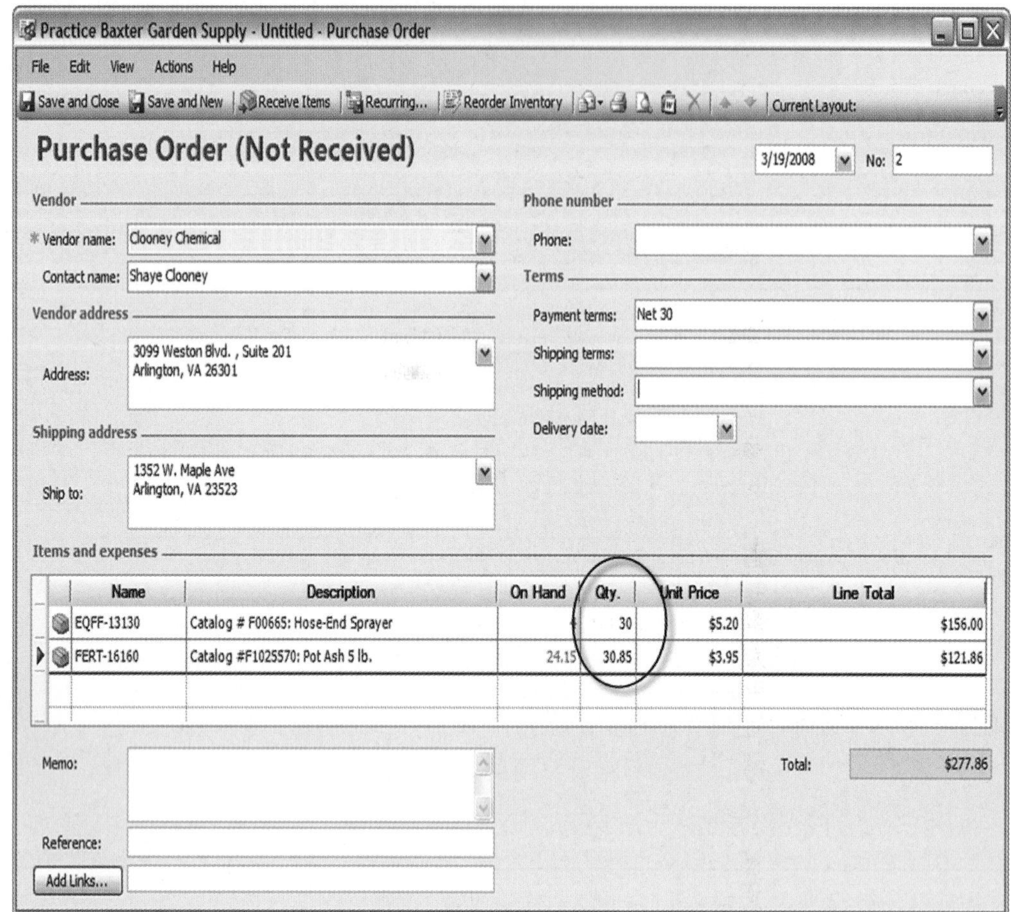

Figure 9:14

11. Click the **Printer** icon on the toolbar to print the PO and click **OK** to save the PO. Click **Save and Close** to exit the transaction window.

POs do not post entries to general ledger accounts because these documents are merely purchase commitments. Accounting recognition occurs when posting a vendor bill or receipt for the merchandise in a subsequent topic.

CORRECTING A PURCHASE ORDER

Information on saved POs can be changed as long as Baxter has not received items on the order. In other words, you can modify POs with the **Not Received** status.

(Note: Keep in mind that, in the real world, once a PO has been released to the vendor it should not be changed. Instead, released POs should be voided and reissued.)

First, locate the PO using the Purchase Order List. Click the **Purchase Orders** link under **Find** and verify that the Current View is **Open** (Figure 9:15) because this view displays POs with the Not Received status.

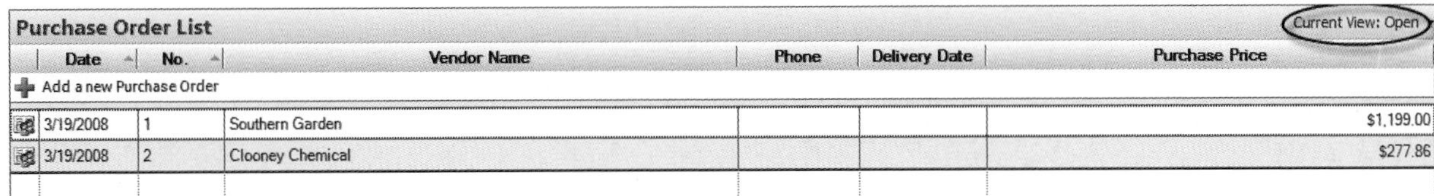

Figure 9:15

Double click to reopen the PO issued to Clooney Chemical and note the Not Received status (Figure 9:16).

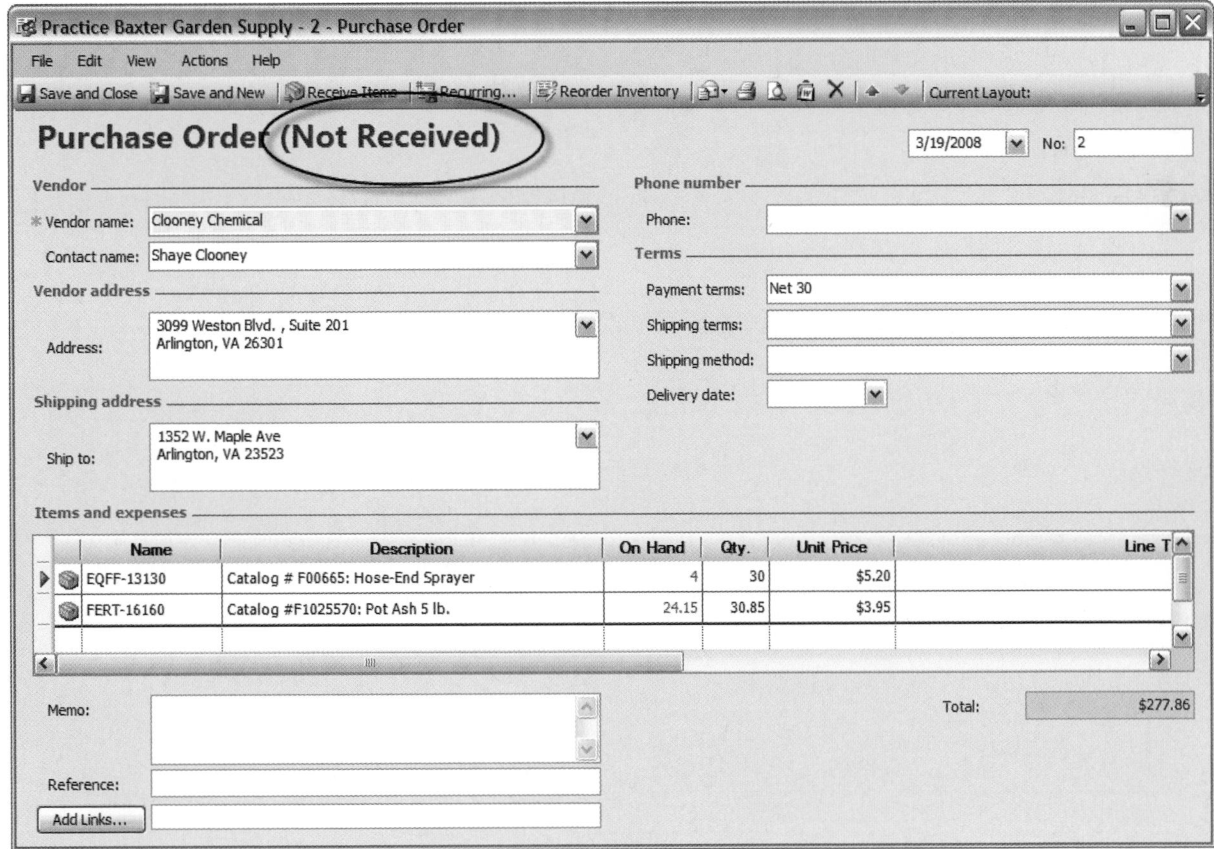

Figure 9:16

When the order is Not Received you can change information and then reprint and resave the transaction. You can delete it by clicking X on the toolbar. *(Note: You can also delete a PO without opening it by right clicking the transaction on the Purchase Order List and selecting Delete.)*

Once items on a PO have been received (i.e., a receipt or vendor bill has been posted) the PO status changes to Received or Partially Received and the list view must be changed to All or Received to view these POs. You can no longer modify line items containing items that have been received unless you void the vendor bill or receipt but you can modify items that remain outstanding.

Click **X** to close the PO. Now try the next exercise.

ENTER PURCHASE ORDERS

On March 21, 2008, Baxter is issuing POs for all items below the reorder point.

Step 1:
Open the Item List and, using the Reorder Inventory button, issue POs to the following vendors. Verify that the option to Create a separate purchase order for each preferred vendor is marked.

Step 2:
You will have three POs open after making selections and clicking OK. Activate each PO from the task bar and enter the transaction date. Enter the PO number specified below and confirm items and quantities on each PO before saving. Do not print individual POs because you will print them in the next step.

PO 3 for $188.00 to DeJulia Wholesale for the following items.

Item	Qty	Short Description	Unit Price
AVRY-10120	5	Bird House-Red	$35.95
POTS-30100	11	Planter Basket	$ 0.75

PO 4 for $100.00 to Abney and Son for the following item.

Item	Qty	Short Description	Unit Price
AVRY-10050-SM-EFL	8	Prefab Birdhouse-Small Eiffel	$12.50

PO 5 for $235.68 to Southern Garden for the following items.

Item	Qty	Short Description	Unit Price
EQWT-15120	3	Garden Hose	$15.95
EQWT-15150	15	Fan Head Sprayer	$ 6.75
EQWT-15180	4	Watering Can	$ 5.25
EQWT-15175	6	Bell-Gro Drip Sprinkler	$10.00
SOIL-34120	4	Topsoil	$ 2.79

Step 3:
Print the POs. Multiple POs are printed using the Purchase Order List. First, highlight one of the POs and next press and hold the Ctrl key as you click with the mouse to highlight remaining POs. After selecting all POs to print, right click a highlighted PO and select Print.

Vendor Bills and Receipts for Purchase Orders

You will recall from the *MAPS* topic that vendors ship orders to Baxter's warehouse, enclosing a packing receipt with the merchandise. Furthermore, once Southern Garden Wholesale's order arrived, Al inspected the merchandise and sent the packing receipt to Melvin in accounting. Melvin then filed the receipt until the vendor bill arrived.

With OAP, Melvin now records the packing receipt as a receipt of inventory. Two benefits flow from immediately recording the receipt. First, inventory assets are recorded when possession takes place and the liability is recognized when the obligation to pay arises. Second, quantities of on hand inventory are immediately updated and available for sale to customers.

In the next exercise you record Baxter's receipt of merchandise on PO 1 issued to Southern Garden.

STEPS TO RECORD A VENDOR RECEIPT FOR ITEMS ON A PURCHASE ORDER

1. Click the **Receive Items** link under **Start a Task** or the **Receive Items** icon on the Vendors Home page. Click **Create From** on the window toolbar to open the Select A Purchase Order window (Figure 9:17). Highlight the PO to Southern Garden and click **OK**.

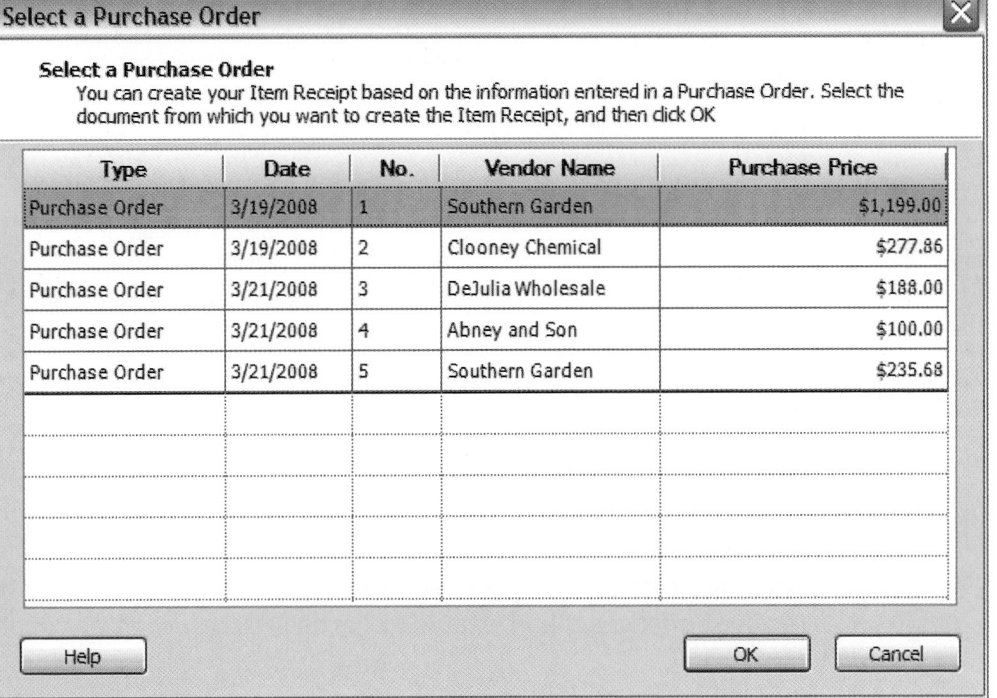

Type	Date	No.	Vendor Name	Purchase Price
Purchase Order	3/19/2008	1	Southern Garden	$1,199.00
Purchase Order	3/19/2008	2	Clooney Chemical	$277.86
Purchase Order	3/21/2008	3	DeJulia Wholesale	$188.00
Purchase Order	3/21/2008	4	Abney and Son	$100.00
Purchase Order	3/21/2008	5	Southern Garden	$235.68

Figure 9:17

2. Enter "3/20/2008" as the transaction date. In **No.**, enter the vendor's receipt number of "RCT3271." (See Figure 9:18.)

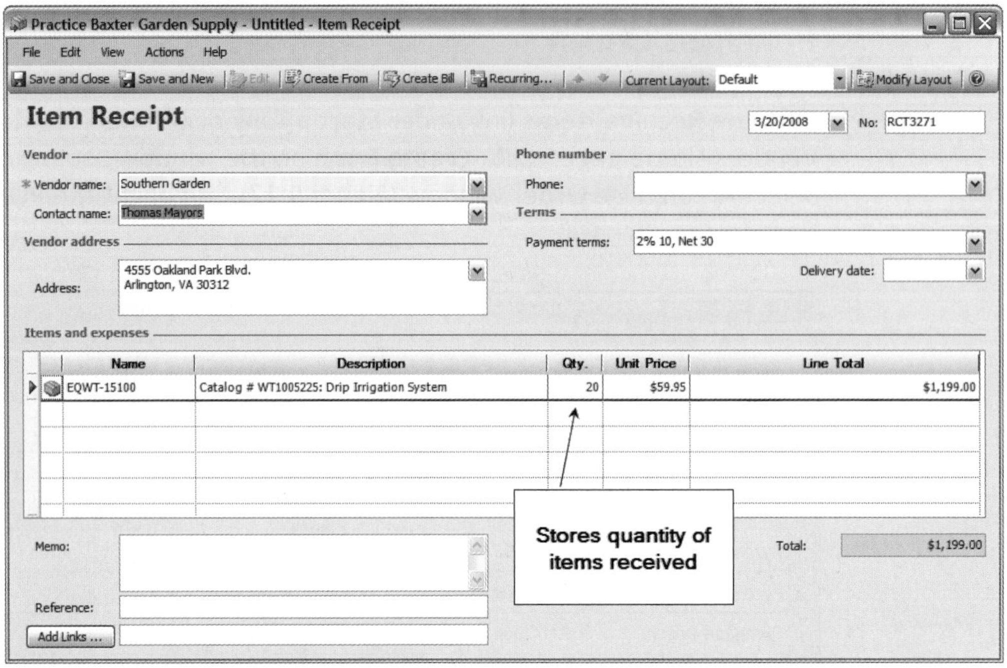

Figure 9:18

Qty. stores the number of items received from the vendor. OAP automatically fills all quantities on the order; therefore, you may have to adjust to the number of items actually received. Furthermore, you delete the line item when none of the item has been received. Adjusting the quantity of items received changes the PO status to Partially Received after posting.

3. Click **Save and Close**.

The previous transaction posted entries to the inventory and pending item receipts accounts. You will trace those entries in the next topic.

Unlike the manual system where Southern Garden's bill was recorded to the Purchases Journal on the date the bill arrived (March 24), Baxter now recognizes the transaction on the date the liability was actually incurred, March 20.

We have one last task before leaving this topic. Vendors sometimes enclose a bill with the merchandise instead of a packing receipt. When this occurs, you record the bill and bypass recording a receipt so the next exercise illustrates recording vendor bills for PO items.

STEPS TO RECORD A VENDOR BILL FOR ITEMS ON A PURCHASE ORDER

1. Click the **Enter Bills** link under **Start a Task** or the **Enter Bills** icon on the Vendors Home page. Click **Create From** on the window toolbar and the PO selection window opens (Figure 9:19).

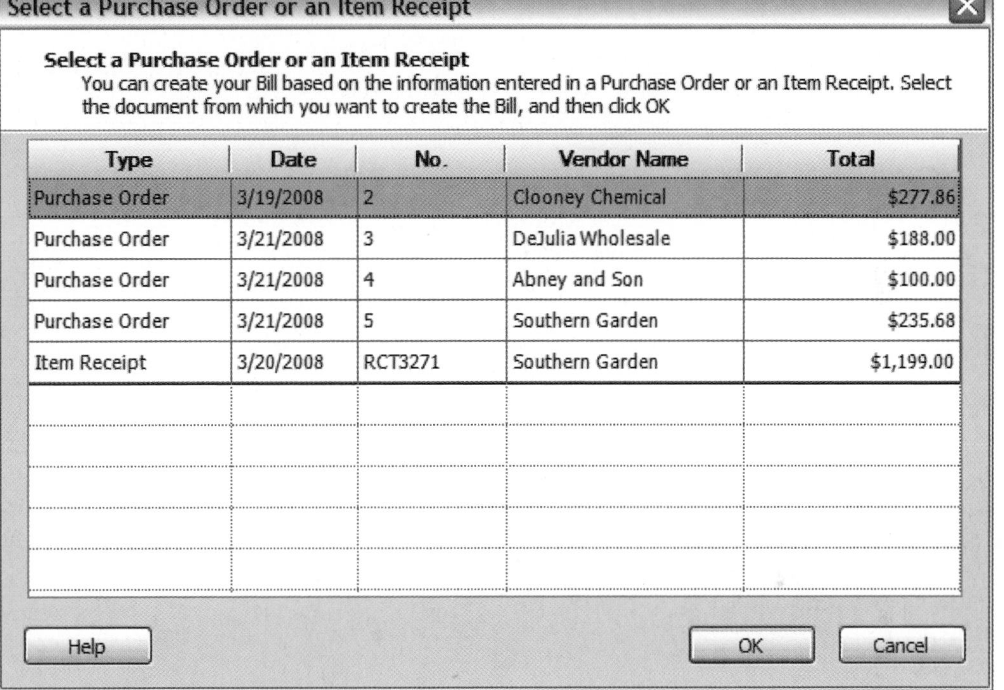

Select a Purchase Order or an Item Receipt

Select a Purchase Order or an Item Receipt
You can create your Bill based on the information entered in a Purchase Order or an Item Receipt. Select the document from which you want to create the Bill, and then click OK

Type	Date	No.	Vendor Name	Total
Purchase Order	3/19/2008	2	Clooney Chemical	$277.86
Purchase Order	3/21/2008	3	DeJulia Wholesale	$188.00
Purchase Order	3/21/2008	4	Abney and Son	$100.00
Purchase Order	3/21/2008	5	Southern Garden	$235.68
Item Receipt	3/20/2008	RCT3271	Southern Garden	$1,199.00

Help OK Cancel

Figure 9:19

2. Highlight PO 2 issued to Clooney Chemical and click **OK**.

3. Enter "3/20/2008" as the transaction date and enter Clooney's invoice number of "1265" into the **No.** field (Figure 9:20).

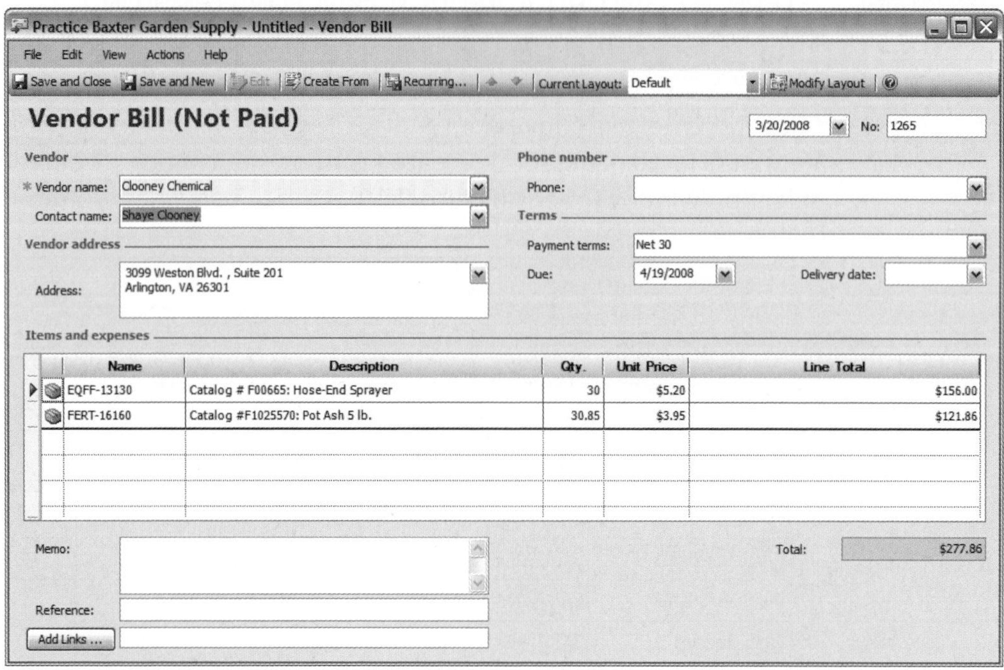

Figure 9:20

4. Click **Save and Close**.

BEHIND THE KEYS OF A POSTED VENDOR BILL AND RECEIPT

The transactions recorded in the previous topic posted entries on the Purchases Journal, vendor accounts, and general ledger accounts. Follow the next steps to trace those entries.

STEPS TO TRACE ENTRIES FOR A VENDOR BILL AND RECEIPT

1. First, open the Transaction Journal report by selecting ***Reports>>Company and Financial>>Transaction Journal*** on the main menu.

2. Next, customize the Transaction Journal to display only purchasing transactions. Click **Modify Report** on the toolbar and select **View Filter Options**. Highlight **Transaction Type** and then select the types shown in Figure 9:21.

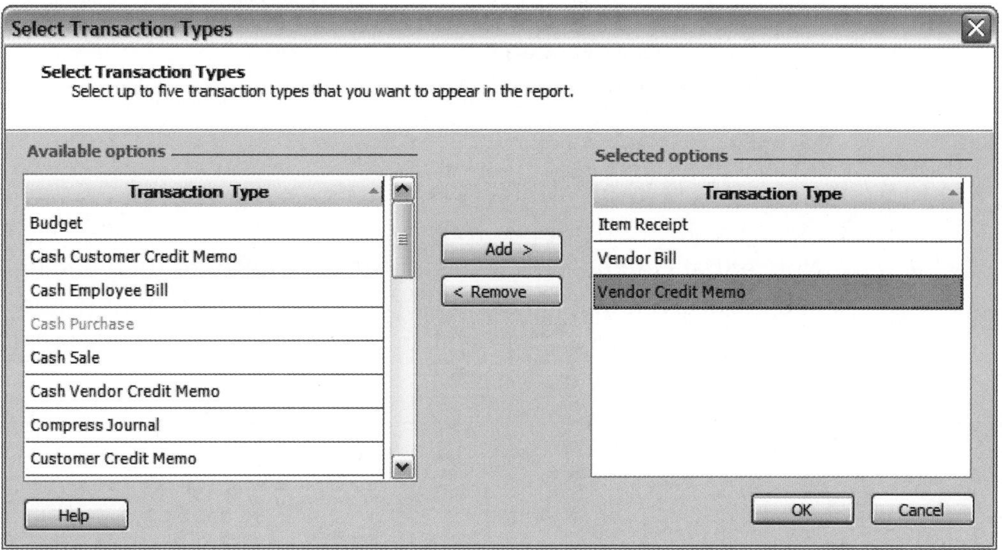

Figure 9:21

Click **OK** and **OK**. Now change the **Header Report Title** to “Purchases Journal.” Click **X** to close the Modify Report pane.

Click **Save Report** on the toolbar. Click **OK** to accept the report name and save the report.

3. Filter the report for the date range of **From** "3/20/2008" **To** "3/20/2008." *(Note: There are two other transactions posted on this date.)*

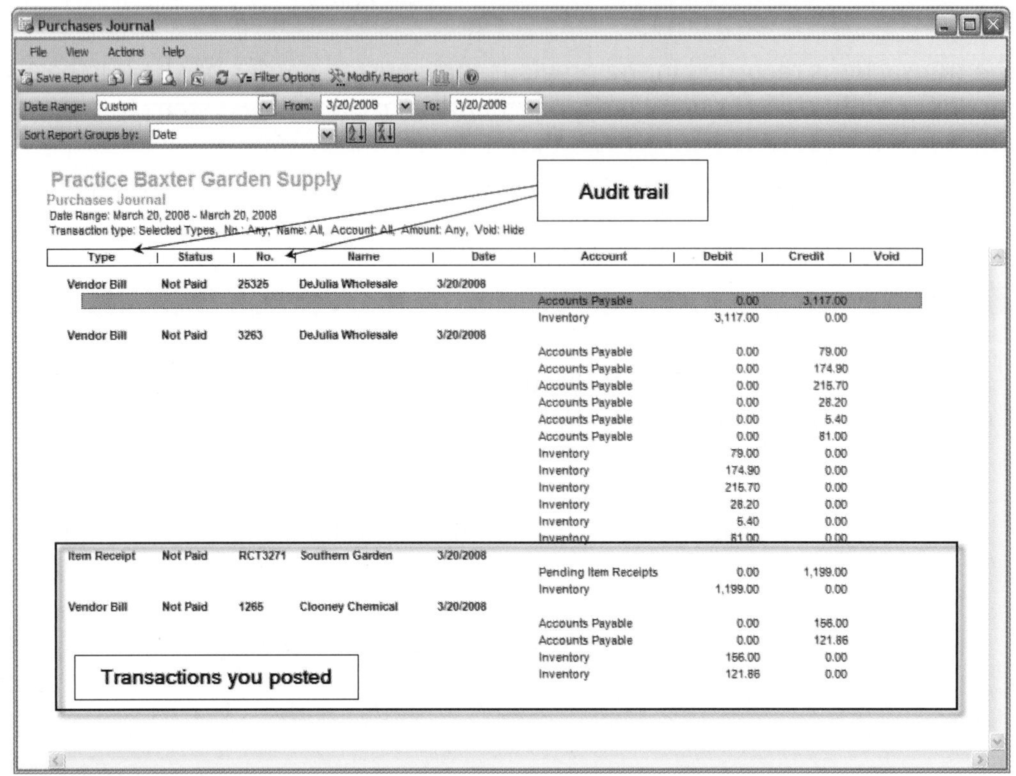

Figure 9:22

Notice that OAP posted the vendor receipt entry to the Pending Item Receipts liability account instead of the Accounts Payable account (Figure 9:22). When you post Southern Garden's bill in a subsequent exercise, OAP will reclassify the receipt liability into Accounts Payable.

4. Close the report and now trace the entries to the vendor accounts.

Select ***Reports>>Vendors and Payables>>Vendor Transaction History*** on the main menu and filter for the date range of **From** "3/20/2008" **To** "3/20/2008."

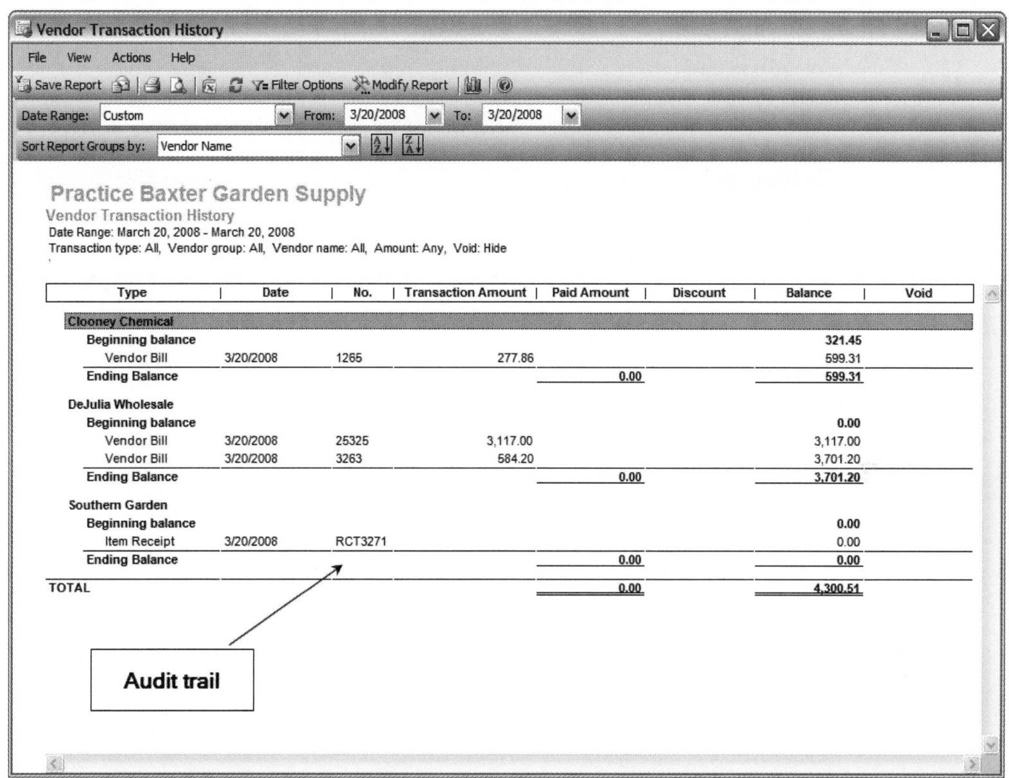

Practice Baxter Garden Supply
Vendor Transaction History
Date Range: March 20, 2008 - March 20, 2008
Transaction type: All, Vendor group: All, Vendor name: All, Amount: Any, Void: Hide

Type	Date	No.	Transaction Amount	Paid Amount	Discount	Balance	Void
Clooney Chemical							
Beginning balance						321.45	
Vendor Bill	3/20/2008	1265	277.86			599.31	
Ending Balance				0.00		599.31	
DeJulia Wholesale							
Beginning balance						0.00	
Vendor Bill	3/20/2008	25325	3,117.00			3,117.00	
Vendor Bill	3/20/2008	3263	584.20			3,701.20	
Ending Balance				0.00		3,701.20	
Southern Garden							
Beginning balance						0.00	
Item Receipt	3/20/2008	RCT3271				0.00	
Ending Balance				0.00		0.00	
TOTAL				0.00		4,300.51	

Figure 9:23

Notice that Southern Garden's receipt has no entry under the Transaction Amount column and the account balance remains unchanged, explaining why OAP did not post Southern Garden's receipt to Accounts Payable. Southern Garden cannot be paid for this transaction until the bill arrives so the transaction in not an account that is payable. Furthermore, you will see later in the chapter that the Accounts Payable account must reconcile to the total outstanding balance on vendor accounts so OAP had to record the receipt transaction to a liability account other than Accounts Payable.

Close this report.

5. Finally, verify OAP's entries to general ledger accounts.

   Select ***Reports>>Company and Financial>>Transaction Detail by Account*** on the main menu. Enter "3/20/2008" as the date range. By now you are able to trace the audit trail to locate the accounts affected by these transactions.

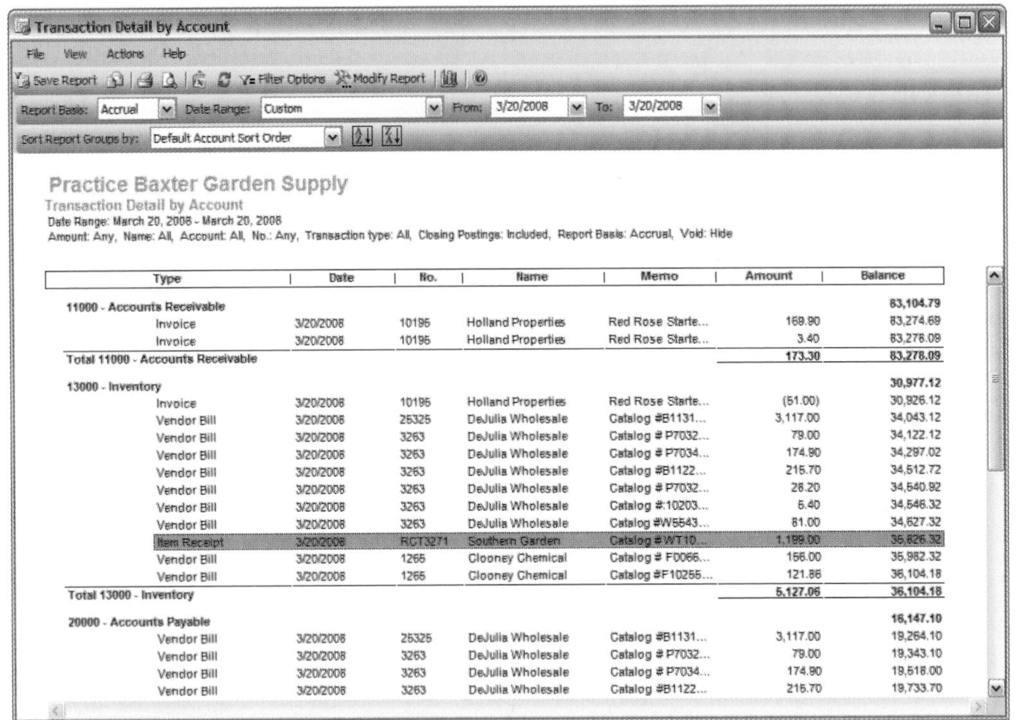

Practice Baxter Garden Supply
Transaction Detail by Account
Date Range: March 20, 2008 - March 20, 2008
Amount: Any, Name: All, Account: All, No.: Any, Transaction type: All, Closing Postings: Included, Report Basis: Accrual, Void: Hide

Type	Date	No.	Name	Memo	Amount	Balance
11000 - Accounts Receivable						83,104.79
Invoice	3/20/2008	10195	Holland Properties	Red Rose Starte...	169.90	83,274.69
Invoice	3/20/2008	10195	Holland Properties	Red Rose Starte...	3.40	83,278.09
Total 11000 - Accounts Receivable					173.30	83,278.09
13000 - Inventory						30,977.12
Invoice	3/20/2008	10195	Holland Properties	Red Rose Starte...	(51.00)	30,926.12
Vendor Bill	3/20/2008	25325	DeJulia Wholesale	Catalog #B1131...	3,117.00	34,043.12
Vendor Bill	3/20/2008	3263	DeJulia Wholesale	Catalog # P7032...	79.00	34,122.12
Vendor Bill	3/20/2008	3263	DeJulia Wholesale	Catalog # P7034...	174.90	34,297.02
Vendor Bill	3/20/2008	3263	DeJulia Wholesale	Catalog #B1122...	215.70	34,512.72
Vendor Bill	3/20/2008	3263	DeJulia Wholesale	Catalog # P7032...	28.20	34,540.92
Vendor Bill	3/20/2008	3263	DeJulia Wholesale	Catalog #:10203...	5.40	34,546.32
Vendor Bill	3/20/2008	3263	DeJulia Wholesale	Catalog #W5543...	81.00	34,627.32
Item Receipt	3/20/2008	RCT3271	Southern Garden	Catalog # WT10...	1,199.00	35,826.32
Vendor Bill	3/20/2008	1265	Clooney Chemical	Catalog # F0066...	156.00	35,982.32
Vendor Bill	3/20/2008	1265	Clooney Chemical	Catalog #F10255...	121.86	36,104.18
Total 13000 - Inventory					5,127.06	36,104.18
20000 - Accounts Payable						16,147.10
Vendor Bill	3/20/2008	25325	DeJulia Wholesale	Catalog #B1131...	3,117.00	19,264.10
Vendor Bill	3/20/2008	3263	DeJulia Wholesale	Catalog # P7032...	79.00	19,343.10
Vendor Bill	3/20/2008	3263	DeJulia Wholesale	Catalog # P7034...	174.90	19,518.00
Vendor Bill	3/20/2008	3263	DeJulia Wholesale	Catalog #B1122...	215.70	19,733.70

Figure 9:24

Close the report. You have completed tracing the entries.

CORRECTING A VENDOR RECEIPT AND BILL

You can modify vendor receipts and ***unpaid*** vendor bills. Vendor receipts and bills with the **Not Paid** status are listed on the Open view of the Bill/Item Receipt List. Click the **Bill and Item Receipts** link under **Find** and verify that the Current View reads Open (Figure 9:25).

Bill/Item Receipt List — Current View: Open

Type	Due Date	No.	Vendor Name	Original Amount	Balance
Add a new Bill					
Vendor Bill	4/1/2008	1006	Miles Maintenance	$400.00	$400.00
Vendor Bill	4/1/2008	3253	Daniel Lawn Pro	$7,532.00	$7,532.00
Vendor Bill	4/2/2008	1000	Abney and Son	$75.00	$75.00
Vendor Bill	4/2/2008	1003	Hubbard Wholesale	$76.50	$76.50
Vendor Bill	4/2/2008	1021	Clooney Chemical	$23.85	$23.85
Vendor Bill	4/3/2008	2456	Jackson Advertising	$650.00	$650.00
Vendor Bill	4/4/2008	14223	Sulley Printing	$675.00	$675.00
Vendor Bill	4/4/2008	32659	Abney and Son	$2,349.00	$2,349.00
Vendor Bill	4/5/2008	9823	Cline Construction	$55.65	$55.65
Vendor Bill	4/5/2008	32987	Stanley Shipping	$253.95	$253.95
Vendor Bill	4/9/2008	2351	Office Maxter	$1,500.00	$1,500.00
Vendor Bill	4/11/2008	116655	Clooney Chemical	$297.60	$297.60
Vendor Bill	4/13/2008	7891	Hubbard Wholesale	$795.00	$795.00
Vendor Bill	4/16/2008	10045	Office Maxter	$150.00	$150.00
Vendor Bill	4/16/2008	10046	Jackson Advertising	$50.00	$50.00
Vendor Bill	4/17/2008	4587	Cline Construction	$1,517.50	$1,517.50
Vendor Bill	4/19/2008	1265	Clooney Chemical	$277.86	$277.86
Vendor Bill	4/19/2008	3263	DeJulia Wholesale	$584.20	$584.20
Vendor Bill	4/18/2008	25325	DeJulia Wholesale	$3,117.00	$3,117.00
Item Receipt	4/19/2008	RCT3271	Southern Garden	$1,199.00	$1,199.00
Vendor Bill	4/20/2008	29099	Southern Garden	$727.50	$727.50
Vendor Bill	4/23/2008	6326	Southern Garden	$150.00	$150.00
Vendor Bill	4/24/2008	9864	Caldwell Tools	$167.20	$167.20
Vendor Bill	4/24/2008	72633	Clooney Chemical	$628.99	$628.99
Vendor Bill	4/25/2008	3253	DeJulia Wholesale	$3,003.55	$3,003.55
Vendor Bill	4/27/2008	7285	Southern Garden	$358.65	$358.65

Figure 9:25

There are several unpaid bills as well as the Item Receipt from Southern Garden. Double click the Vendor Bill from Daniel Lawn Pro to open it (Figure 9:26).

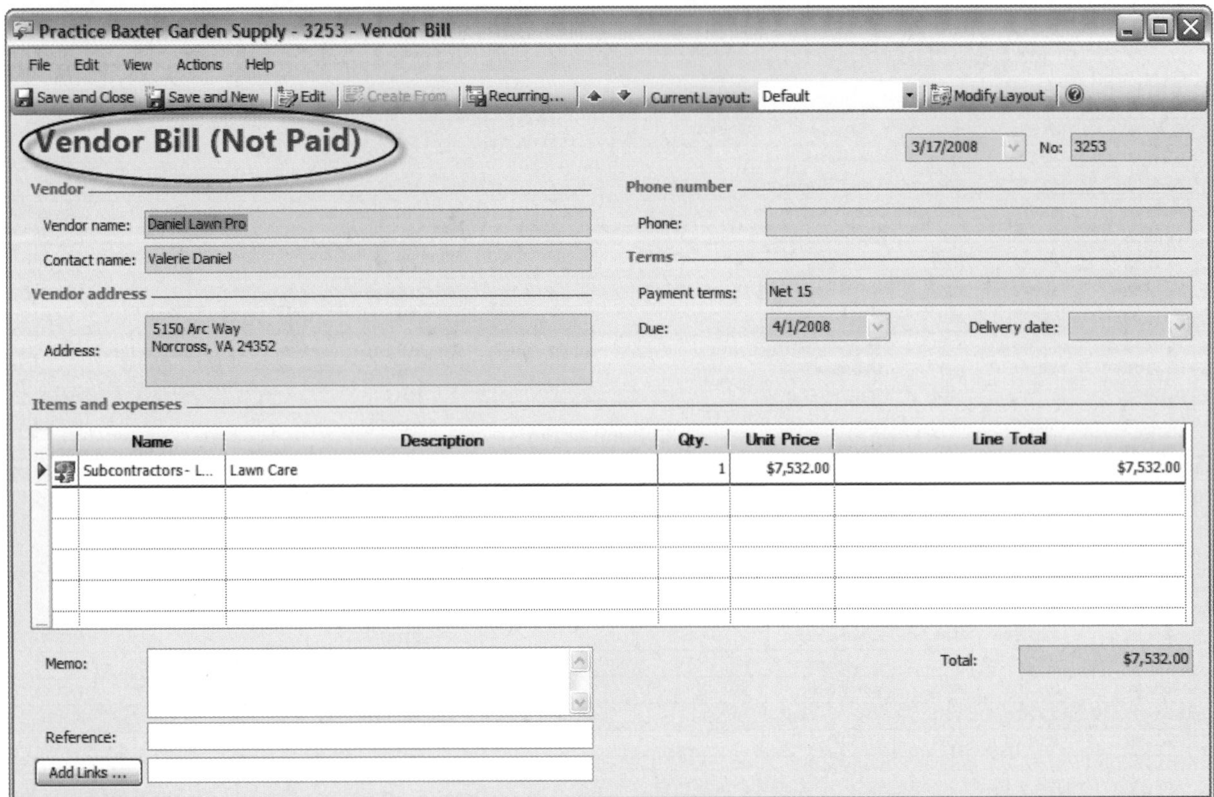

Figure 9:26

This bill is Not Paid so it can be modified. Clicking **Edit** on the toolbar will reopen the bill for editing. After changing, **Save and Close** causes OAP to void the original transaction by posting reversing entries for the original transaction and new entries for modified transaction.

You cannot delete vendor bills or receipts. Instead, you must void these transactions by selecting ***Actions>>Void*** on the menu. *(Note: This menu selection is not available if you already clicked Edit. Exit the transaction to make the menu available. You can then right click the transaction on the list and select Void.)* After voiding a transaction OAP releases the PO used to create the transaction so you can again receive the items.

Click **X** to close Daniel's transaction.

A bill's status changes to **Paid** after paying the bill. Toggle the Current View on the Bill/Item Receipt List to All (Figure 9:27). Bills with zero under the Balance column are paid.

Bill/Item Receipt List Current View: All

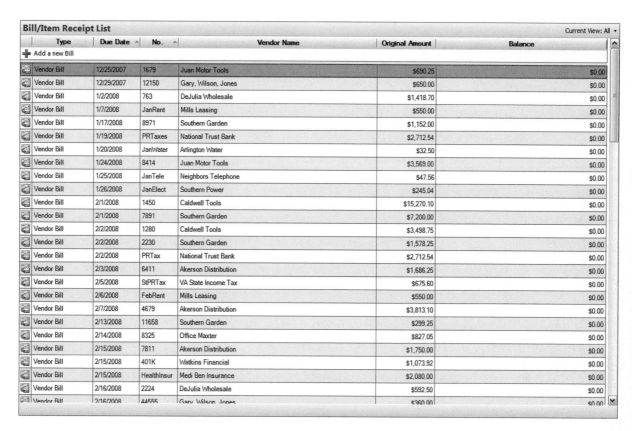

Type	Due Date	No.	Vendor Name	Original Amount	Balance
Add a new Bill					
Vendor Bill	12/25/2007	1679	Juan Motor Tools	$690.25	$0.00
Vendor Bill	12/29/2007	12150	Gary, Wilson, Jones	$650.00	$0.00
Vendor Bill	1/2/2008	763	DeJulia Wholesale	$1,418.70	$0.00
Vendor Bill	1/7/2008	JanRent	Mills Leasing	$550.00	$0.00
Vendor Bill	1/17/2008	8971	Southern Garden	$1,152.00	$0.00
Vendor Bill	1/19/2008	PRTaxes	National Trust Bank	$2,712.54	$0.00
Vendor Bill	1/20/2008	JanWater	Arlington Water	$32.50	$0.00
Vendor Bill	1/24/2008	8414	Juan Motor Tools	$3,569.00	$0.00
Vendor Bill	1/25/2008	JanTele	Neighbors Telephone	$47.56	$0.00
Vendor Bill	1/26/2008	JanElect	Southern Power	$245.04	$0.00
Vendor Bill	2/1/2008	1450	Caldwell Tools	$15,270.10	$0.00
Vendor Bill	2/1/2008	7891	Southern Garden	$7,200.00	$0.00
Vendor Bill	2/2/2008	1280	Caldwell Tools	$3,498.75	$0.00
Vendor Bill	2/2/2008	2230	Southern Garden	$1,578.25	$0.00
Vendor Bill	2/2/2008	PRTax	National Trust Bank	$2,712.54	$0.00
Vendor Bill	2/3/2008	6411	Akerson Distribution	$1,686.25	$0.00
Vendor Bill	2/5/2008	StPRTax	VA State Income Tax	$675.60	$0.00
Vendor Bill	2/6/2008	FebRent	Mills Leasing	$550.00	$0.00
Vendor Bill	2/7/2008	4679	Akerson Distribution	$3,813.10	$0.00
Vendor Bill	2/13/2008	11658	Southern Garden	$299.25	$0.00
Vendor Bill	2/14/2008	8325	Office Maxter	$827.05	$0.00
Vendor Bill	2/15/2008	7811	Akerson Distribution	$1,750.00	$0.00
Vendor Bill	2/15/2008	401K	Watkins Financial	$1,073.92	$0.00
Vendor Bill	2/15/2008	HealthInsur	Medi Ben Insurance	$2,080.00	$0.00
Vendor Bill	2/16/2008	2224	DeJulia Wholesale	$592.50	$0.00
Vendor Bill	2/16/2008	44555	Gary, Wilson, Jones	$360.00	$0.00

Figure 9:27

Double click to open bill 8971 from Southern Garden (Figure 9:28).

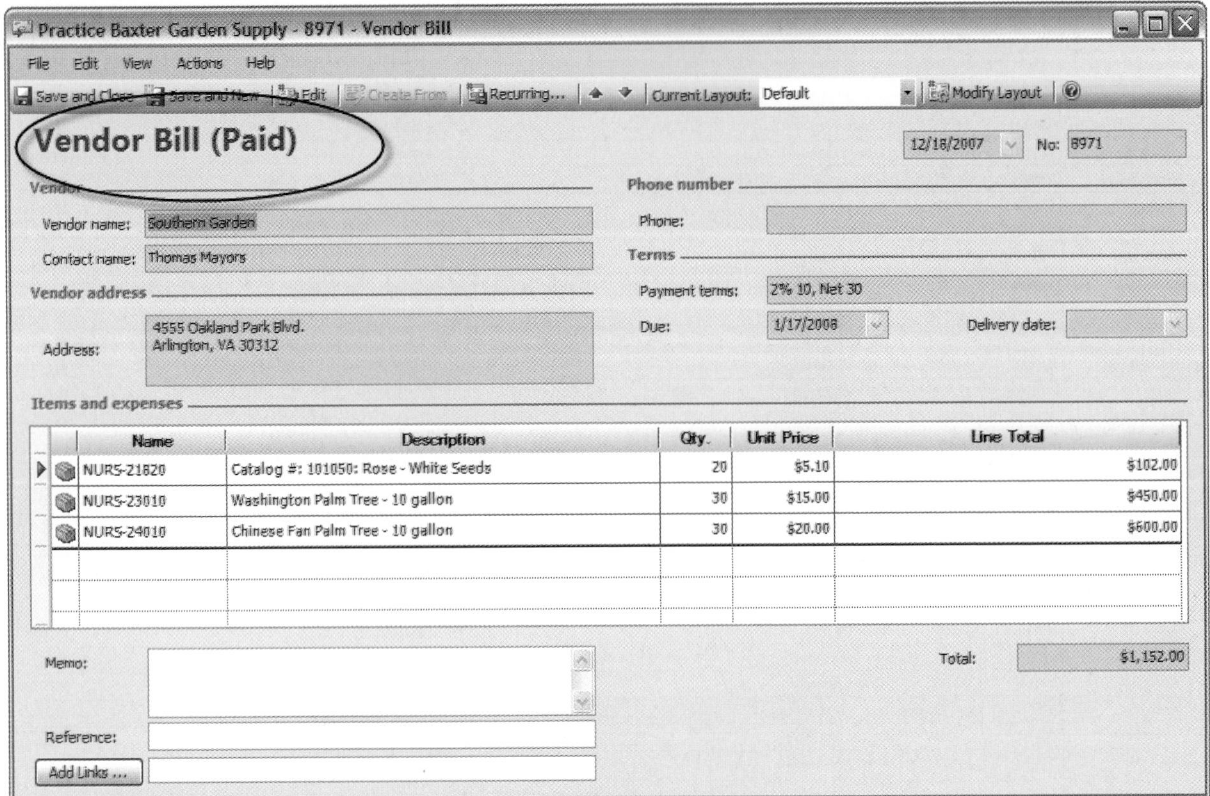

Figure 9:28

This bill is Paid and, although OAP will let you Edit it, the bill should not be modified because the payment will no longer match the bill. Instead, you should void the payment before modifying the bill. We will illustrate voiding a vendor payment later in the chapter. In addition, Appendix B provides complete instructions on correcting transactions.

Click <u>**X**</u> to close the transaction.

2. Click **Create Bill** on the toolbar, change the transaction date to "3/20/2008," and enter Southern Garden's invoice number of "97325." Notice that the transaction type changed from Item Receipt (Figure 9:29) to Vendor Bill (Figure 9:30).

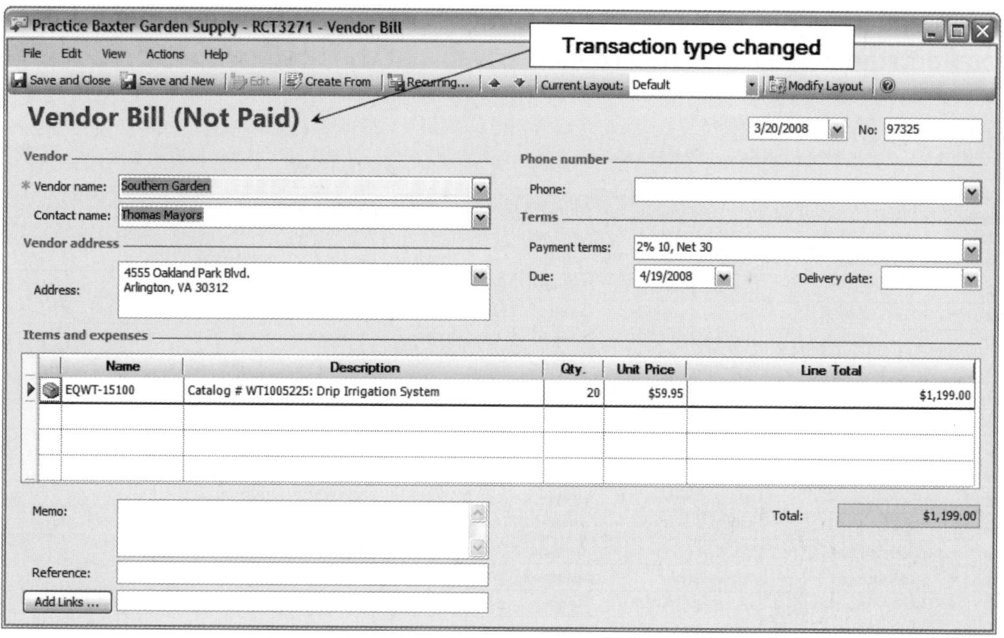

Figure 9:30

3. Click **Save and Close**. Return to the Bill/Item Receipt List and note that the Type has changed to Vendor Bill.

ENTER VENDOR BILL FOR VENDOR RECEIPT

On March 30, 2008, Baxter received Invoice 7631 for $188.00 from DeJulia Wholesale for RCT0808. The bill is dated March 27, 2008. Record this transaction and print the Purchases Journal for March 27.

Vendor Accounts

This topic explains creating, editing, and deleting vendor accounts.

Click **Vendors** under **Find** to open the Vendor List. As on the Customer list, OAP reports the total outstanding balance for accounts payable at the bottom.

Vendor List — Current View: Active

Add a new Vendor

Active	Vendor Name	Address	City	State	Zip Code	Phone	Fax	Balance
✓	Abney and Son	3280 Park Lane	Arlington	VA	23047	770-555-0000	770-555-00...	$2,499.00
✓	Akerson Distribution	24 Bethany Drive	Salem	VA	23076	678-555-1279	770-555-77...	$0.00
✓	Arlington Water	Box 4551	Arlington	VA	30303	770-555-0177	770-555-01...	$0.00
✓	Caldwell Tools	2356 Steve Reynolds Place	Norpoint	VA	23531	770-555-7130	770-555-58...	$167.20
✓	Cline Construction	2207 King Spring Road	Arlington	VA	23503	770-555-8546	770-555-65...	$1,573.15
✓	Clooney Chemical	3099 Weston Blvd.	Arlington	VA	26301	404-555-0899	404-555-10...	$1,228.30
✓	Cloudet Property	1898 Myers Avenue	Arlington	VA	23607	404-555-9699	404-555-80...	$0.00
✓	Daniel Lawn Pro	5150 Arc Way	Norcross	VA	24352	770-555-1126	770-555-11...	$7,532.00
✓	DeJulia Wholesale	4800 Peachtree Ind. Blvd.	Duluth	VA	33252	404-555-1500	404-555-15...	$6,892.75
✓	Gary, Wilson, Jones	One Tower Square	Arlington	VA	32352	404-555-8000	404-555-81...	$0.00
✓	Hawkins Web Design	7030 State Street	Arlington	VA	33252	770-555-4221	770-555-42...	$0.00
✓	Hubbard Wholesale	1500 Pavilion Place	Arlington	VA	30093	770-555-7155	770-555-71...	$871.50
✓	Jackson Advertising	1458 Chaseway Circle	Arlington	VA	30308	404-555-5855	404-555-57...	$700.00
✓	Juan Motor Tools	1085 Pleasant Hill Road	Darlington	VA	30093	770-555-0188	770-555-01...	$0.00
✓	Kidd Computers	111 Main Street	Woodstock	VA	30188	770-555-5827	770-555-58...	$0.00
✓	Medi Ben Insurance	311 State Bridge Road	Arlington	VA	30136	770-555-1136	770-555-86...	$0.00
✓	Miles Maintenance	2536 Satellite Road	Arlington	VA	30093	770-555-7117	770-555-70...	$400.00
✓	Mills Leasing	3012 Perimeter Way Suite 2...	Dunby	VA	30120	404-555-1901	404-555-24...	$0.00
✓	National Trust Bank	1201 Piedmont Place	Arlington	VA	30312	404-555-0799	404-555-10...	$0.00
✓	Neighbors Telephone	PO Box 9010	Arliington	VA	30303	404-555-1022	404-555-10...	$0.00
✓	Office Maxter	238 Abigail Drive	Arlington	VA	30001	800-555-9090		$1,650.00
✓	Paris Brothers	8572 Halcyon Way	Arlington	VA	30044	770-555-4154	770-555-21...	$0.00
✓	Petty Cash							$0.00
✓	Safe State Insurance	1875 Engle Rd	Arlington	VA	23793			$0.00
✓	Southern Garden	4555 Oakland Park Blvd.	Arlington	VA	30312	404-555-9668	404-555-15...	$15,468.58

Total outstanding balance: $42,248.53

Figure 9:31

Double click **Southern Garden** to open the account and follow below as we describe the tabs on the vendor account.

General Tab

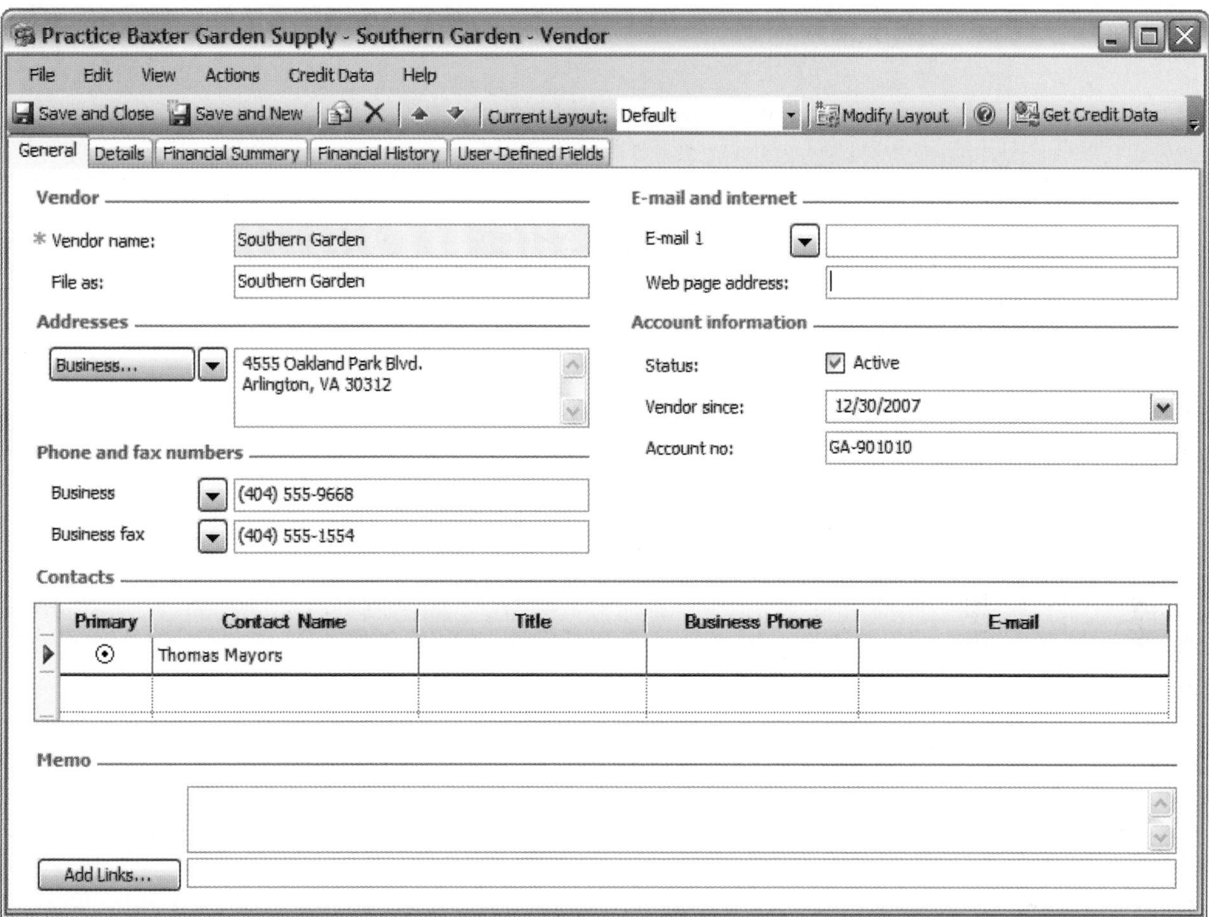

Figure 9:32

This tab stores basic information such as address, phone numbers, and contacts. When **Active** is not checked, OAP denies posting future purchases and bills for the vendor. This option is important when companies need to control purchases for reasons such as poor vendor performance but cannot delete the account because it contains transaction history.

Details Tab

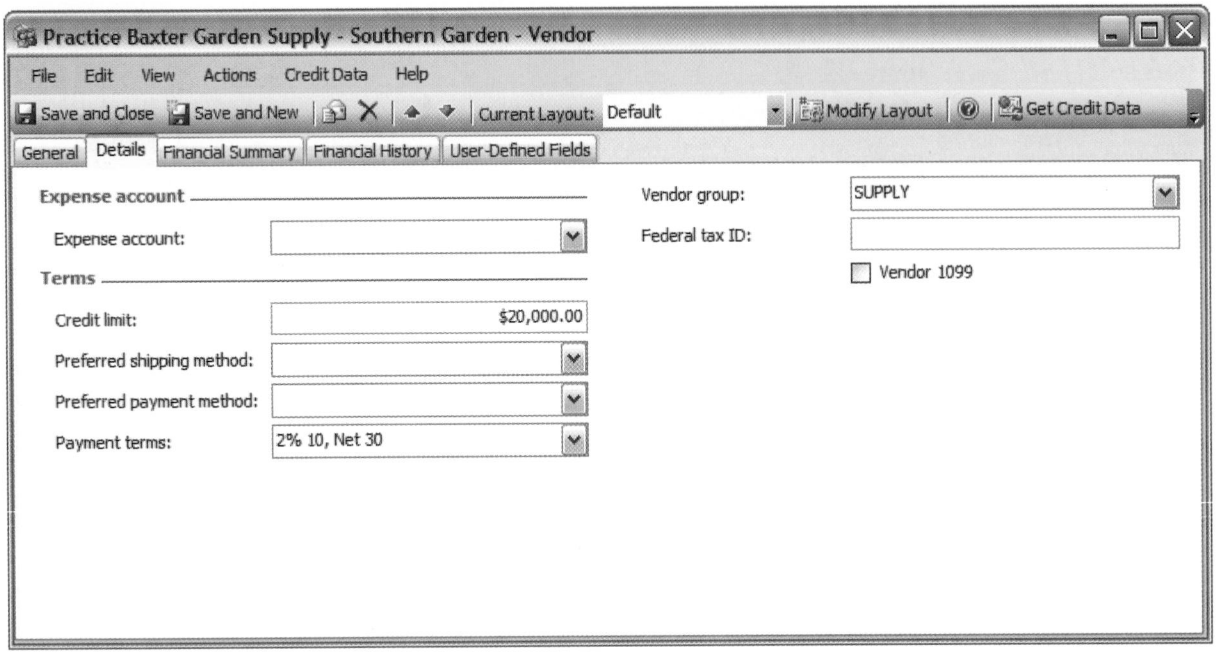

Figure 9:33

This tab stores defaults to be used on vendor transactions and reporting.

Expense account stores the general ledger account to be used when posting a vendor bill for expenses (i.e., line items using the expense icon). Vendors that are inventory suppliers will not have an account in this field because purchases from these vendors are for inventory items (i.e., line items with the inventory icon) and OAP posts the transaction to the general ledger asset account stored on the item.

Credit limit instructs OAP to warn when saving a vendor bill that causes the account balance to exceed the credit limit.

Payment terms function like customer payment terms by controlling vendor bill due dates and early payment discount terms.

Vendor group is optional and used on reports to analyze purchases by vendor characteristics. You can click the dropdown list to view the types used by Baxter.

Federal tax ID stores a vendor's social security number or federal ID number used when preparing Form 1099.

Vendor 1099 triggers a vendor account for IRS tax reporting. If selected, OAP tracks annual payments to the vendor for reporting on Form 1099. *(Note: The IRS requires an annual filing of Form 1099 for payments made to subcontractors that exceed $600. Information on 1099 reporting requirements is available at www.irs.gov.)*

Financial Summary Tab

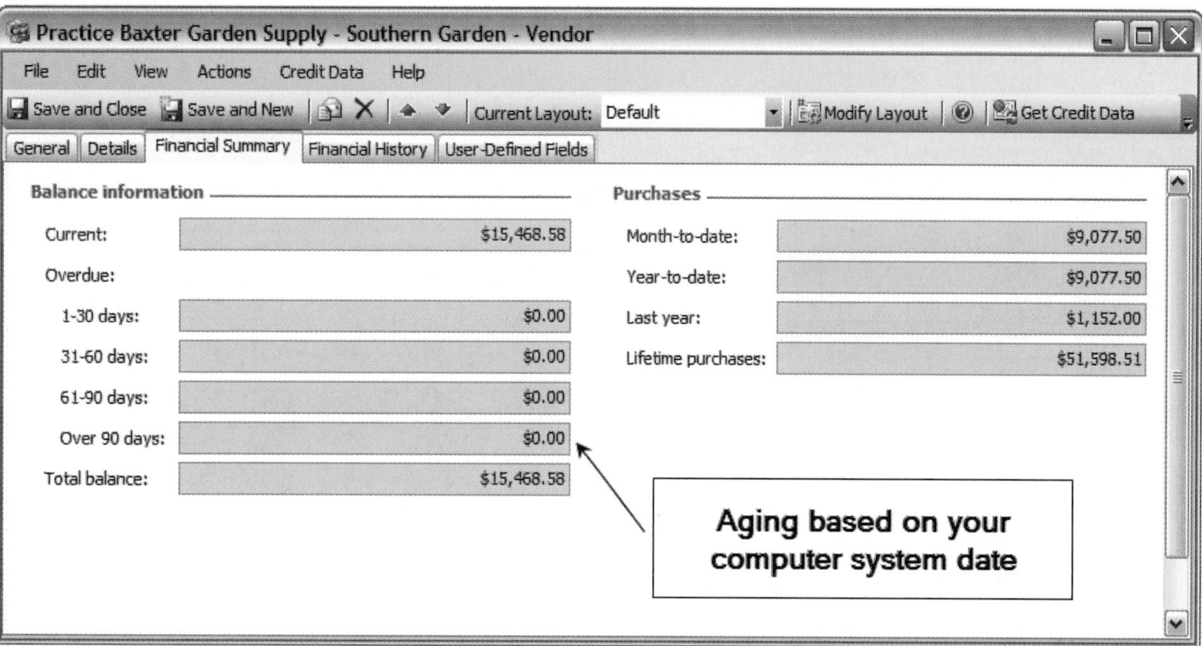

Figure 9:34

This tab provides a quick snapshot on the age of the vendor balance and purchasing totals. OAP uses your computer's system date to calculate aging categories.

Financial History Tab

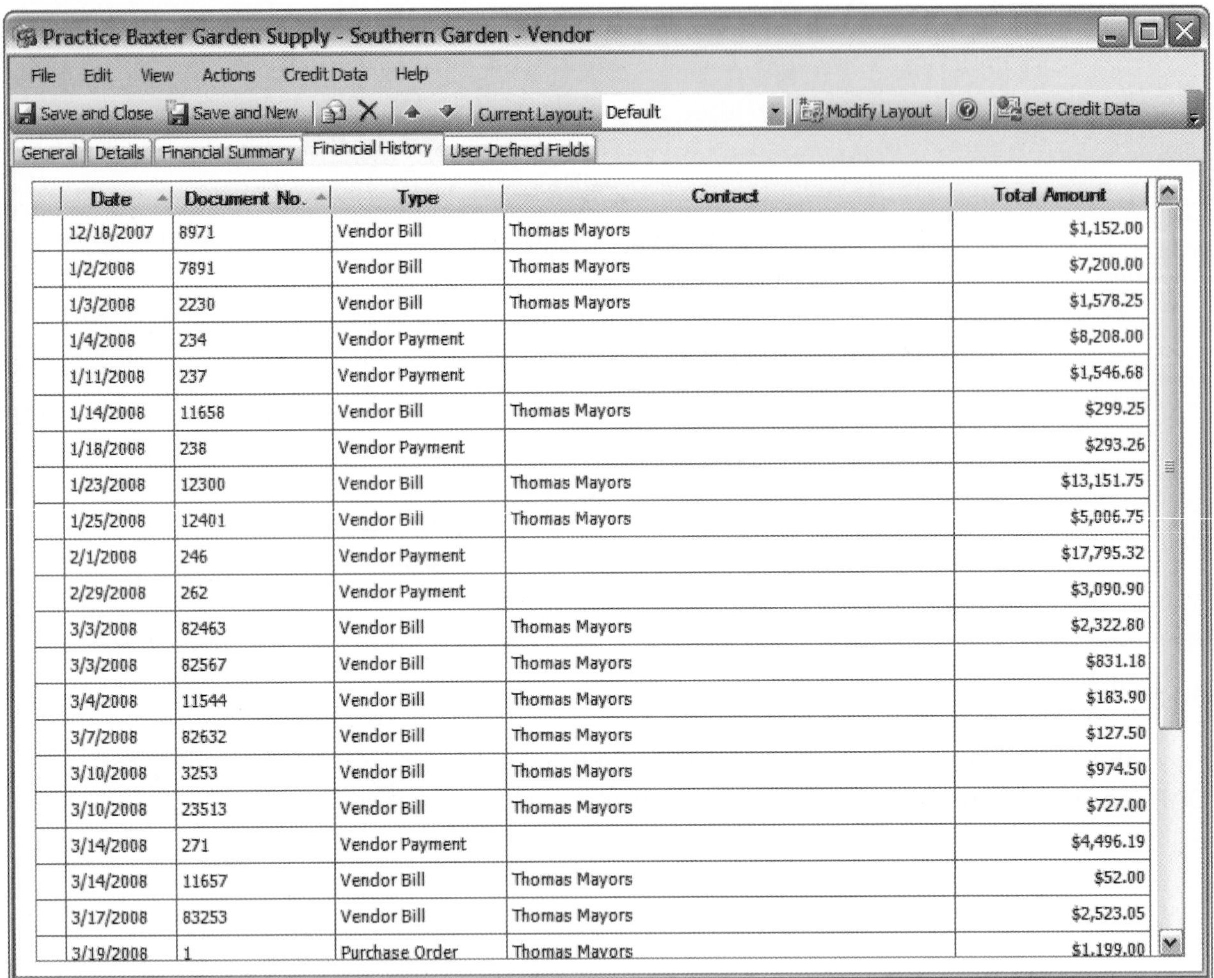

Date	Document No.	Type	Contact	Total Amount
12/18/2007	8971	Vendor Bill	Thomas Mayors	$1,152.00
1/2/2008	7891	Vendor Bill	Thomas Mayors	$7,200.00
1/3/2008	2230	Vendor Bill	Thomas Mayors	$1,578.25
1/4/2008	234	Vendor Payment		$8,208.00
1/11/2008	237	Vendor Payment		$1,546.68
1/14/2008	11658	Vendor Bill	Thomas Mayors	$299.25
1/18/2008	238	Vendor Payment		$293.26
1/23/2008	12300	Vendor Bill	Thomas Mayors	$13,151.75
1/25/2008	12401	Vendor Bill	Thomas Mayors	$5,006.75
2/1/2008	246	Vendor Payment		$17,795.32
2/29/2008	262	Vendor Payment		$3,090.90
3/3/2008	82463	Vendor Bill	Thomas Mayors	$2,322.80
3/3/2008	82567	Vendor Bill	Thomas Mayors	$831.18
3/4/2008	11544	Vendor Bill	Thomas Mayors	$183.90
3/7/2008	82632	Vendor Bill	Thomas Mayors	$127.50
3/10/2008	3253	Vendor Bill	Thomas Mayors	$974.50
3/10/2008	23513	Vendor Bill	Thomas Mayors	$727.00
3/14/2008	271	Vendor Payment		$4,496.19
3/14/2008	11657	Vendor Bill	Thomas Mayors	$52.00
3/17/2008	83253	Vendor Bill	Thomas Mayors	$2,523.05
3/19/2008	1	Purchase Order	Thomas Mayors	$1,199.00

Figure 9:35

This tab lists vendor transactions. You can drill down to original entries by double clicking a transaction, which facilitates answering vendor inquiries.

Click **X** to close Southern Garden's account and **No.** if prompted to save changes. Now practice editing vendor accounts by completing the next exercise.

Steps to Edit Vendor Account Information

1. Open **Daniel Lawn Pro's** account. Select the **Details** tab and change the **Credit Limit** from $5,000.00 to $7,000.00.

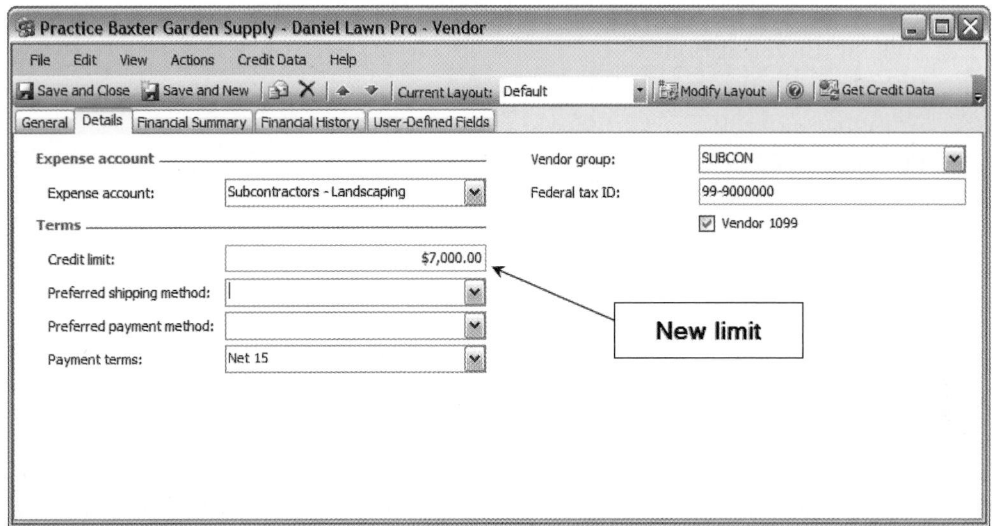

Figure 9:36

2. Click **Save and Close**.

You can delete a vendor by highlighting the account on the list and clicking X on the toolbar. Like customers, you cannot delete accounts with transaction history so change the Active option to deny future transactions.

Adding vendors is similar to adding customers. Practice creating a new vendor in the exercise that follows.

CREATE A NEW VENDOR

Baxter is adding the following new vendor account on March 14, 2008.

Sullivan Buyer Supplies
P.O. Box 1732
Arlington, VA 30022
Phone: 701 555-6723
Fax: 701 555-8723
Contact: Susan Calley
Email: SCalley@bbsupply.com

Expense account: Office Supplies Expense
Payment terms: Net 30
Vendor group: Office

Create the account and print the Vendor List filtered to display only the new vendor.

Vendor Bills for Expenses

In addition to bills for inventory purchases, Baxter receives bills for expenses such as office supplies, utilities, and insurance. These bills generally do not originate on POs.

On March 28, Baxter receives a bill for advertising expense. Complete the next exercise to record the transaction.

Steps for Entering Vendor Bills for Expenses

1. Click **Enter Bills** and enter "3/28/2008" as the transaction date. Enter 5701 as the vendor invoice **No.** and look up "Jackson Advertising" as the **Vendor name**. (See Figure 9:37.)

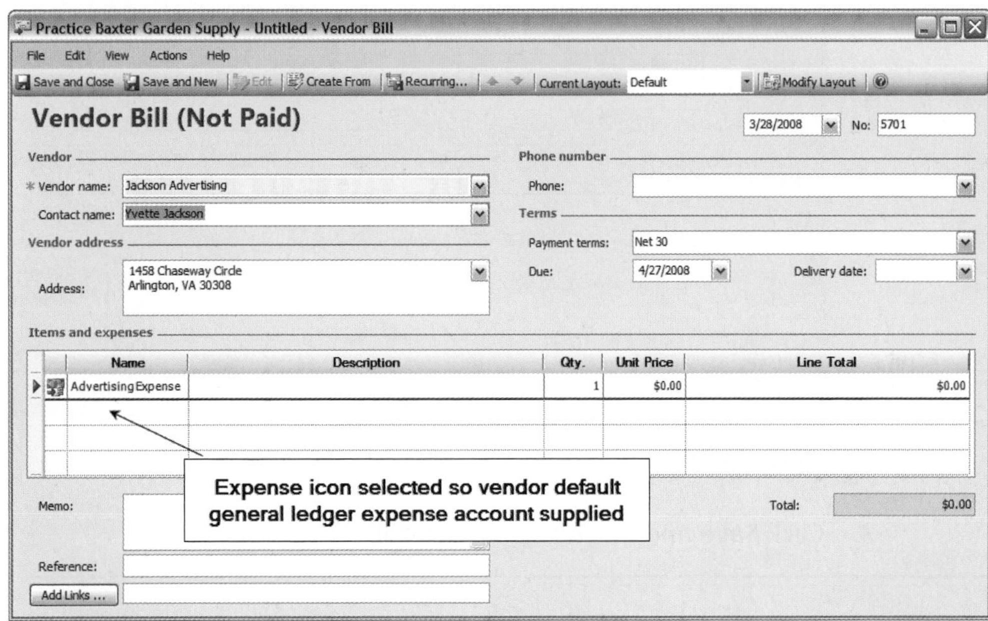

Figure 9:37

Notice that the **Icon** defaulted to **Expense** because this vendor's account stores **Advertising Expense** as the default account for transactions.

2. Tab to **Description** and type "Advertising flyers." Tab to **Unit Price** and enter "250.00." (See Figure 9:38.)

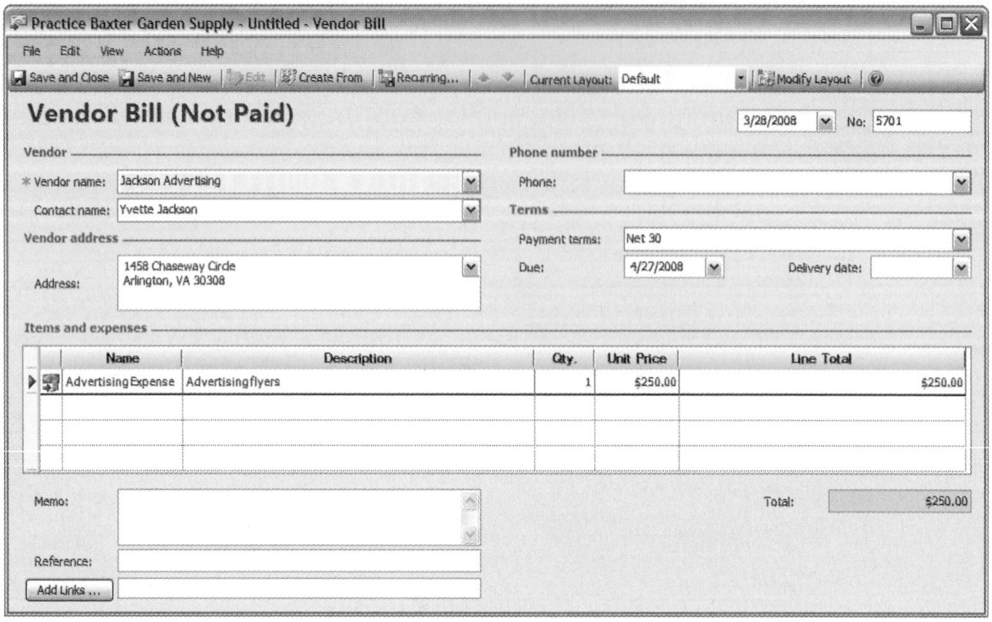

Figure 9:38

3. Click **Save and Close** to post the bill.

The next exercise provides more practice on entering vendor bills for expenses.

ENTER VENDOR BILLS FOR EXPENSES

On March 31, 2008, Baxter received the following bills.

Juan Motor Tools Invoice 73434 for $603.25 dated March 28, 2008 for repairing vehicle transmission.

Neighbors Telephone bill for $216.00 dated March 24, 2008 for March telephone.

Hints:
There are a couple of points to this exercise. First, the invoice date, not the date you received the bill, is always the transaction date. Generally, bills will not be received on the same date as the invoice date.

Second, Neighbors' transaction did not provide an invoice number. You will often encounter bills without an invoice number, particularly bills for utility and professional service expense. Therefore, you must create an invoice number and create it in such a way as to later identify the transaction. For instance, you can use "MarTeleph" as the invoice number for March telephone.

Recurring Vendor Bills

OAP will memorize vendor bills, which is especially useful for repeating bills such as rent. You can memorize bills while posting a new bill or open a posted bill to memorize it.

The accountant has just signed a contract with Miles Maintenance for monthly office cleaning. The first payment is due by March 16. In the following exercise you will enter the March bill and turn it into a recurring bill.

STEPS TO CREATE A RECURRING VENDOR BILL

1. Click **Enter Bills** on the home page and enter the information shown in Figure 9:39.

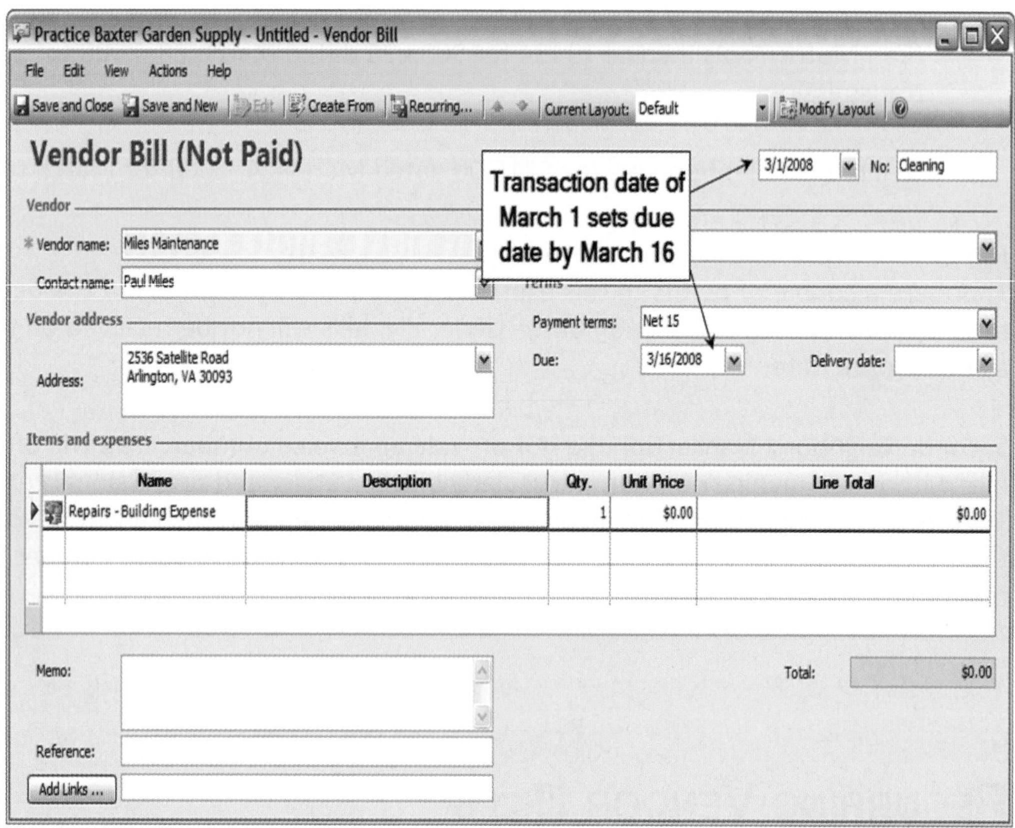

Figure 9:39

2. Tab to **Name** so you can create a new general ledger account for this expense.

   Click the dropdown list and then scroll to the top and select **Add a new Financial Account**.

   Select the **Expense** type and click **OK**. Create the account using the information in Figure 9:40 and then click **Save and Close**. You have just added a general ledger account "on the fly."

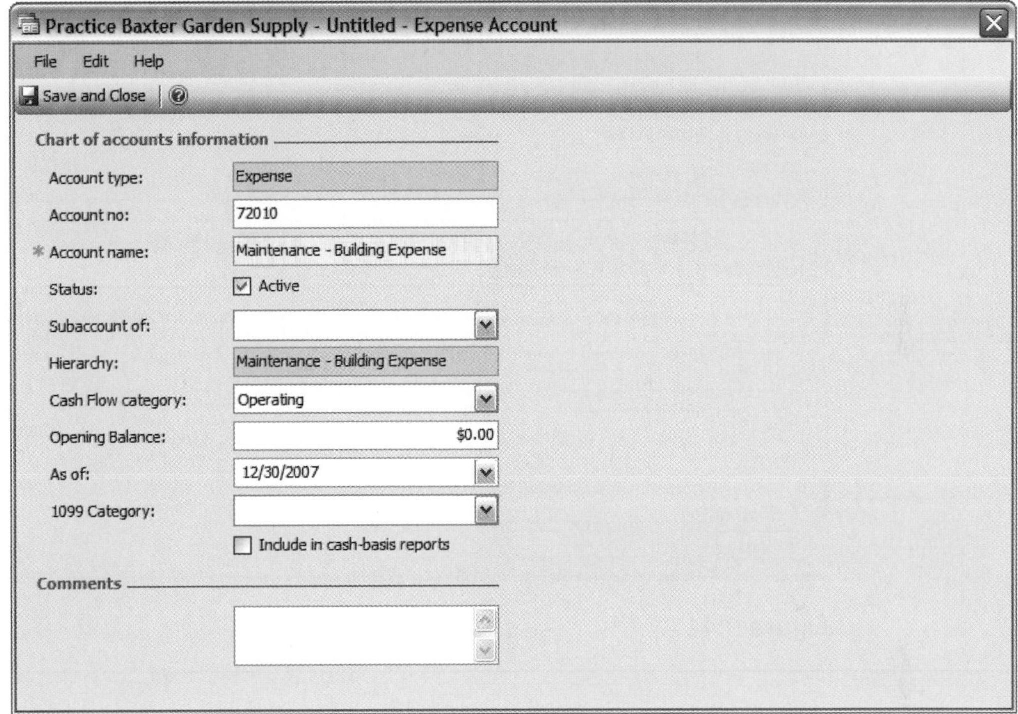

Figure 9:40

3. Return to the transaction and enter "Monthly cleaning" as the **Description** and "$175.00" as the **Unit Price**. (See Figure 9:41.)

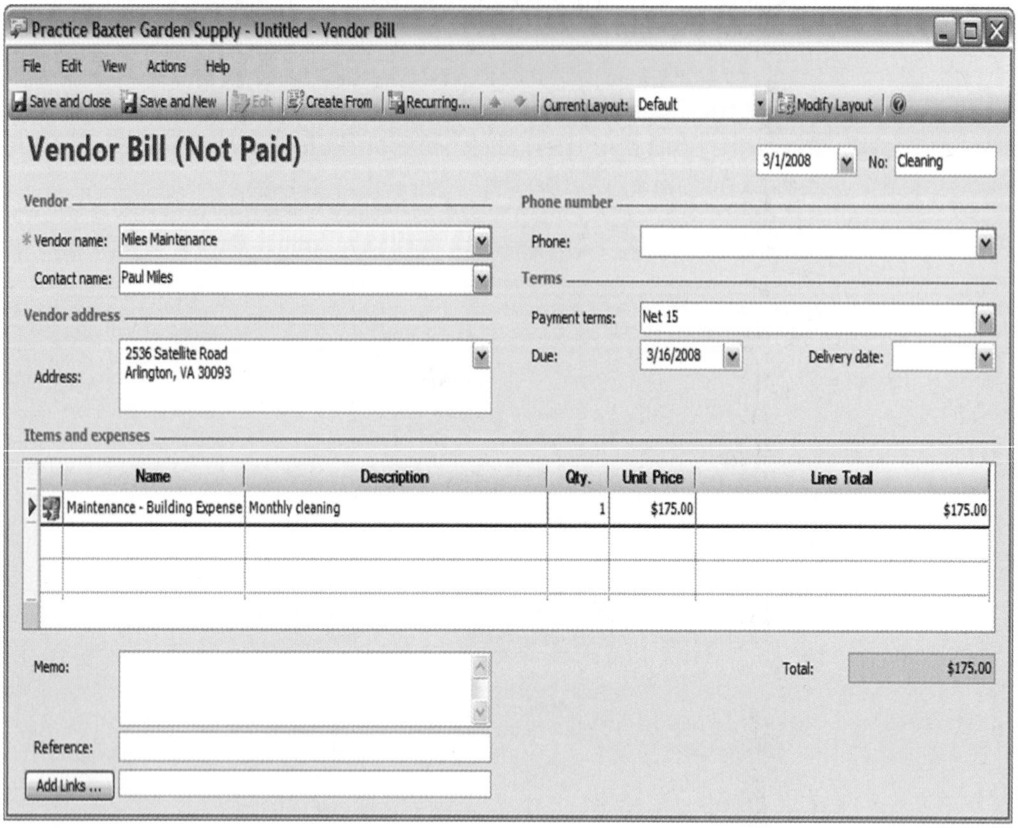

Figure 9:41

4. Click **Recurring** on the toolbar and complete the window as illustrated next.

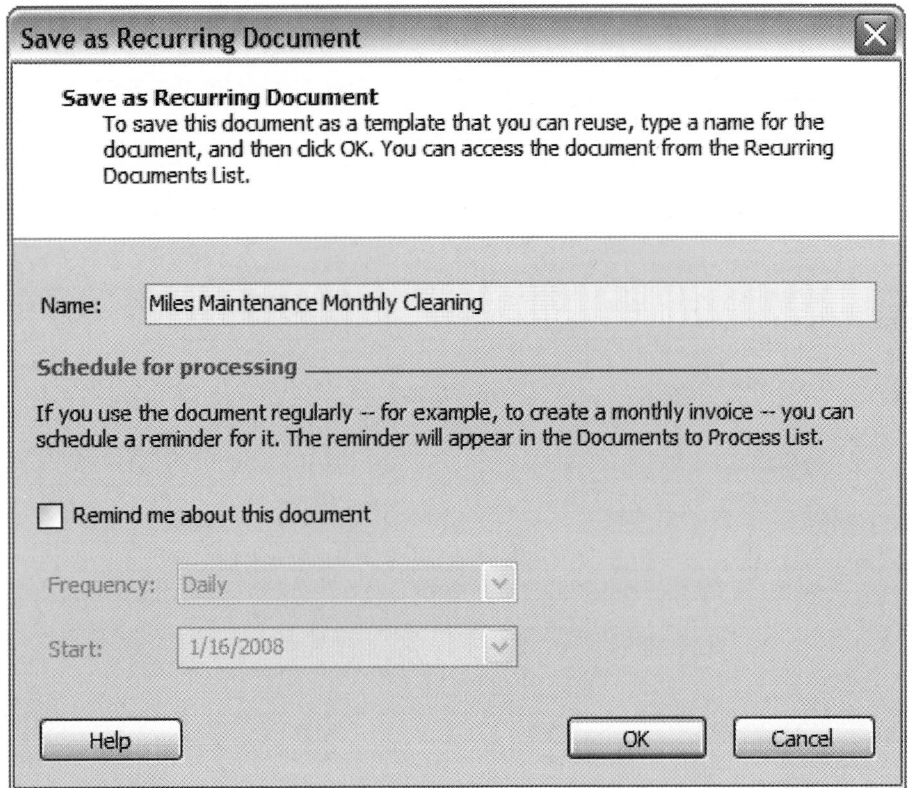

Figure 9:42

Note: Normally you would choose the Remind me about this document option and set the Frequency to Monthly. OAP would then remind you to post this transaction on the first of every month; however; these reminders would pile up considering you are working exercises months after the company's current accounting period.

Click **OK** to save the recurring transaction. Click **Save and Close** to post the March transaction.

5. You will now locate the recurring transaction. Click the **Recurring Documents** link under **Find** or select ***Company>>Company Lists>>Recurring Documents*** on the main menu. Click the Type column to sort the list (Figure 9:43).

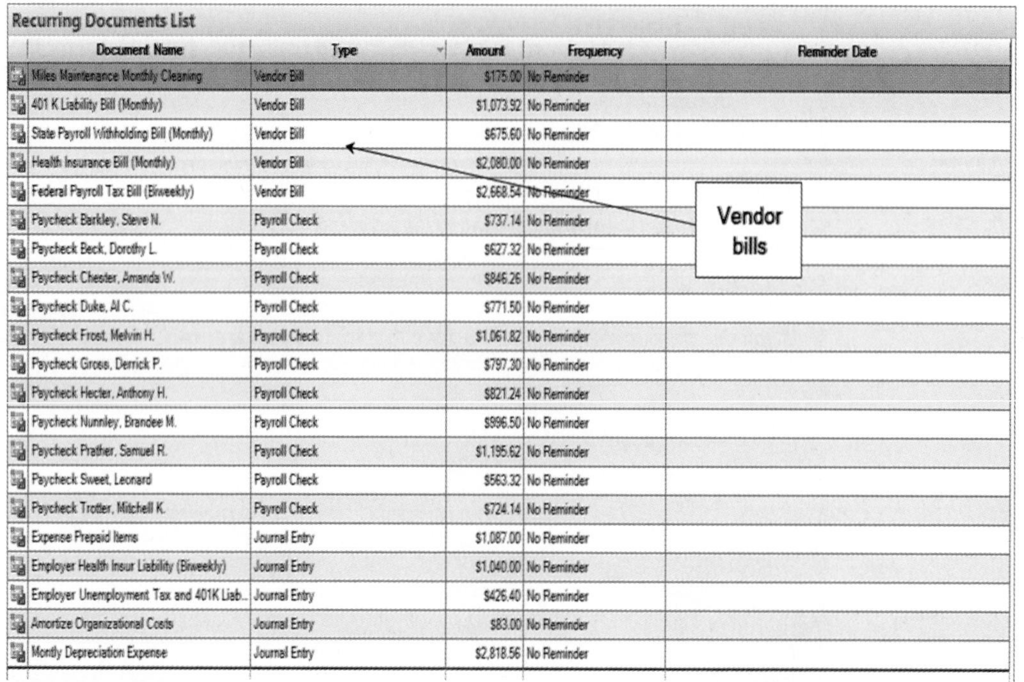

Recurring Documents List

Document Name	Type	Amount	Frequency	Reminder Date
Miles Maintenance Monthly Cleaning	Vendor Bill	$175.00	No Reminder	
401 K Liability Bill (Monthly)	Vendor Bill	$1,073.92	No Reminder	
State Payroll Withholding Bill (Monthly)	Vendor Bill	$675.60	No Reminder	
Health Insurance Bill (Monthly)	Vendor Bill	$2,080.00	No Reminder	
Federal Payroll Tax Bill (Biweekly)	Vendor Bill	$2,668.54	No Reminder	
Paycheck Barkley, Steve N.	Payroll Check	$737.14	No Reminder	
Paycheck Beck, Dorothy L.	Payroll Check	$627.32	No Reminder	
Paycheck Chester, Amanda W.	Payroll Check	$846.26	No Reminder	
Paycheck Duke, Al C.	Payroll Check	$771.50	No Reminder	
Paycheck Frost, Melvin H.	Payroll Check	$1,061.82	No Reminder	
Paycheck Gross, Derrick P.	Payroll Check	$797.30	No Reminder	
Paycheck Hecter, Anthony H.	Payroll Check	$821.24	No Reminder	
Paycheck Nunnley, Brandee M.	Payroll Check	$996.50	No Reminder	
Paycheck Prather, Samuel R.	Payroll Check	$1,195.62	No Reminder	
Paycheck Sweet, Leonard	Payroll Check	$563.32	No Reminder	
Paycheck Trotter, Mitchell K.	Payroll Check	$724.14	No Reminder	
Expense Prepaid Items	Journal Entry	$1,087.00	No Reminder	
Employer Health Insur Liability (Biweekly)	Journal Entry	$1,040.00	No Reminder	
Employer Unemployment Tax and 401K Liab...	Journal Entry	$426.40	No Reminder	
Amortize Organizational Costs	Journal Entry	$83.00	No Reminder	
Montly Depreciation Expense	Journal Entry	$2,818.56	No Reminder	

Figure 9:43

Baxter has several recurring transactions. In the next chapter you will use the payroll check transactions to pay employees.

Recurring transactions are posted by double clicking a transaction to reopen, making any necessary changes, and then saving the transaction.

You can modify the scheduling and name of the transaction by right clicking it and selecting **Edit Recurring Document**.

6. Let's post the cleaning bill for April. Double click **Miles Maintenance Monthly Cleaning**. Enter "4/1/2008" as the transaction date and "Cleaning" as the **No.** Click **Save and Close** to post the transaction.

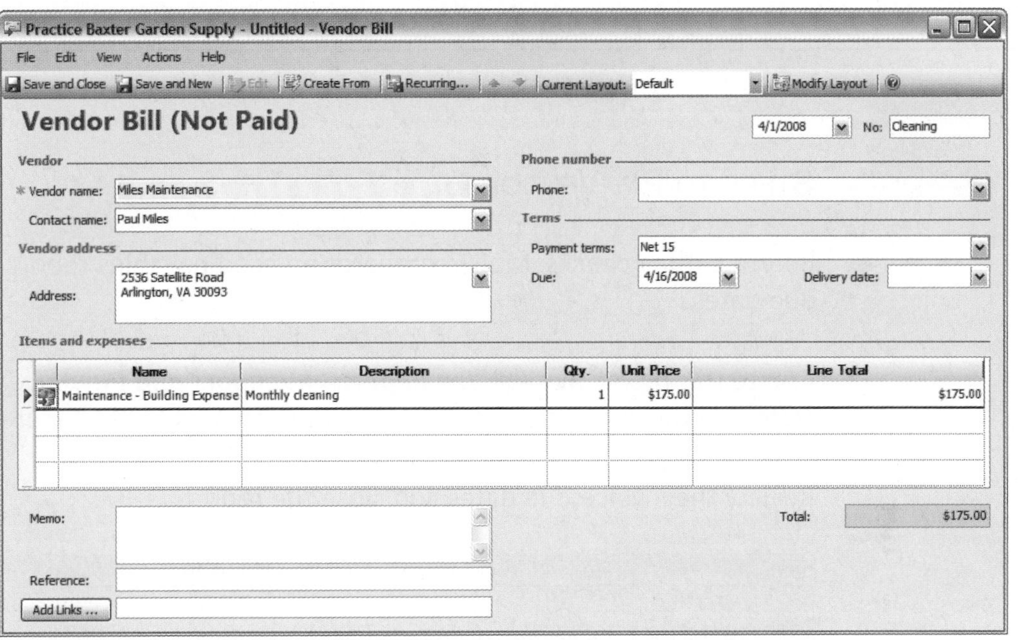

Figure 9:44

Vendor Payments

In this topic, you focus on paying vendor bills. In the exercise that follows you create checks dated March 21, 2008 to pay vendor bills due by April 2, 2008.

Steps to Pay Vendors

1. Before cutting checks, Melvin prepares an aged payables report to review bill due dates.

   Create this report by selecting ***Reports>>Vendors and Payables>>A/P Aging Detail*** on the main menu. Change the Date to 3/21/2008 (Figure 9:45).

   Review the invoice due dates and close the report.

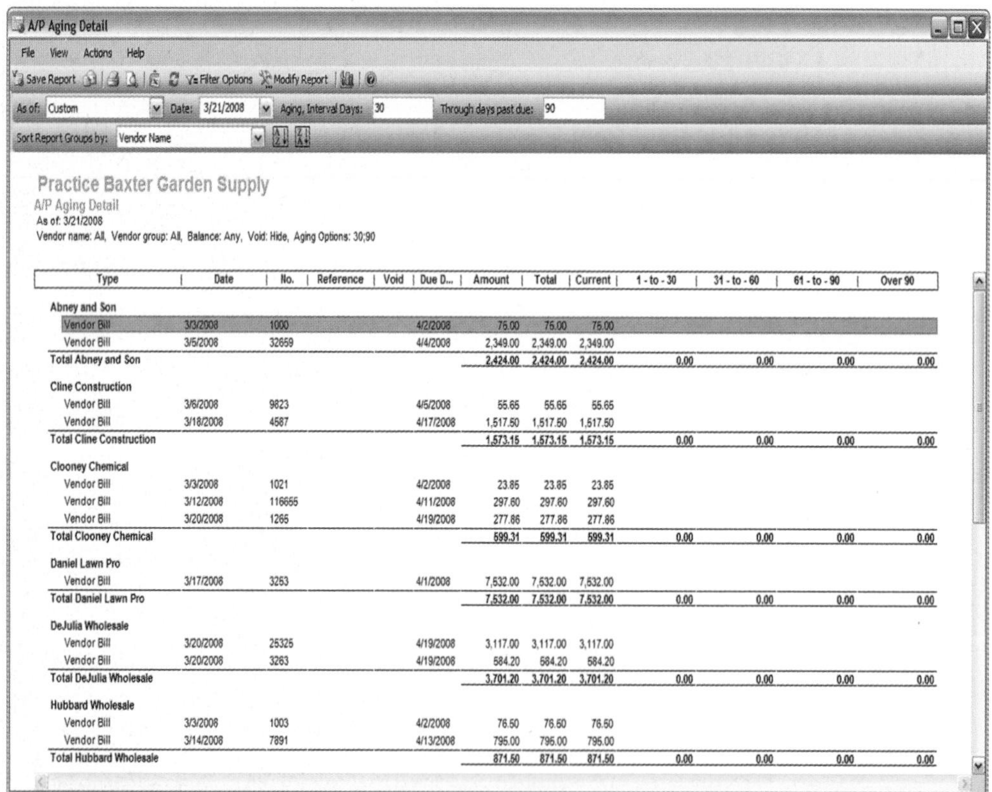

Practice Baxter Garden Supply
A/P Aging Detail
As of: 3/21/2008
Vendor name: All, Vendor group: All, Balance: Any, Void: Hide, Aging Options: 30;90

Type	Date	No.	Reference	Void	Due D...	Amount	Total	Current	1 - to - 30	31 - to - 60	61 - to - 90	Over 90
Abney and Son												
Vendor Bill	3/3/2008	1000			4/2/2008	75.00	75.00	75.00				
Vendor Bill	3/5/2008	32659			4/4/2008	2,349.00	2,349.00	2,349.00				
Total Abney and Son						2,424.00	2,424.00	2,424.00	0.00	0.00	0.00	0.00
Cline Construction												
Vendor Bill	3/6/2008	9823			4/5/2008	55.65	55.65	55.65				
Vendor Bill	3/18/2008	4587			4/17/2008	1,517.50	1,517.50	1,517.50				
Total Cline Construction						1,573.15	1,573.15	1,573.15	0.00	0.00	0.00	0.00
Clooney Chemical												
Vendor Bill	3/3/2008	1021			4/2/2008	23.85	23.85	23.85				
Vendor Bill	3/12/2008	116665			4/11/2008	297.60	297.60	297.60				
Vendor Bill	3/20/2008	1265			4/19/2008	277.86	277.86	277.86				
Total Clooney Chemical						599.31	599.31	599.31	0.00	0.00	0.00	0.00
Daniel Lawn Pro												
Vendor Bill	3/17/2008	3253			4/1/2008	7,532.00	7,532.00	7,532.00				
Total Daniel Lawn Pro						7,532.00	7,532.00	7,532.00	0.00	0.00	0.00	0.00
DeJulia Wholesale												
Vendor Bill	3/20/2008	25325			4/19/2008	3,117.00	3,117.00	3,117.00				
Vendor Bill	3/20/2008	3263			4/19/2008	584.20	584.20	584.20				
Total DeJulia Wholesale						3,701.20	3,701.20	3,701.20	0.00	0.00	0.00	0.00
Hubbard Wholesale												
Vendor Bill	3/3/2008	1003			4/2/2008	76.50	76.50	76.50				
Vendor Bill	3/14/2008	7891			4/13/2008	795.00	795.00	795.00				
Total Hubbard Wholesale						871.50	871.50	871.50	0.00	0.00	0.00	0.00

Figure 9:45

2. Click **Pay Bills** under **Start a Task** and enter the information in Figure 9:46 to the top of the form.

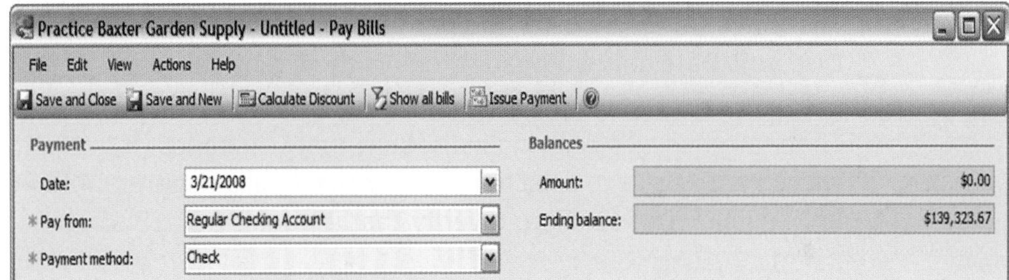

Figure 9:46

Date is the date that will print on checks. **Pay from** is the general ledger account to be credited by the payments.

3. You will now go through two steps to select bills for payment. First, you will select all bills with a due date on or before April 2, 2008, by entering 4/2/2008 in the **Bill due on or before** field (Figure 9:47).

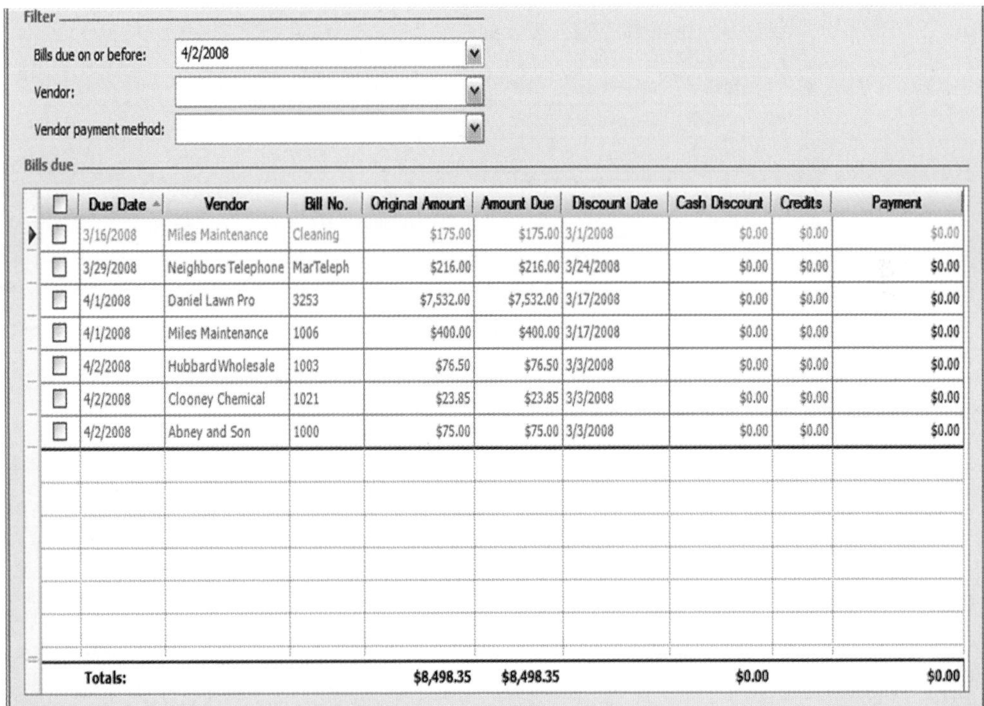

☐	Due Date	Vendor	Bill No.	Original Amount	Amount Due	Discount Date	Cash Discount	Credits	Payment
☐	3/16/2008	Miles Maintenance	Cleaning	$175.00	$175.00	3/1/2008	$0.00	$0.00	$0.00
☐	3/29/2008	Neighbors Telephone	MarTeleph	$216.00	$216.00	3/24/2008	$0.00	$0.00	$0.00
☐	4/1/2008	Daniel Lawn Pro	3253	$7,532.00	$7,532.00	3/17/2008	$0.00	$0.00	$0.00
☐	4/1/2008	Miles Maintenance	1006	$400.00	$400.00	3/17/2008	$0.00	$0.00	$0.00
☐	4/2/2008	Hubbard Wholesale	1003	$76.50	$76.50	3/3/2008	$0.00	$0.00	$0.00
☐	4/2/2008	Clooney Chemical	1021	$23.85	$23.85	3/3/2008	$0.00	$0.00	$0.00
☐	4/2/2008	Abney and Son	1000	$75.00	$75.00	3/3/2008	$0.00	$0.00	$0.00
	Totals:			$8,498.35	$8,498.35		$0.00		$0.00

Figure 9:47

4. The list sorts to view bills meeting the filter criteria. Click the selection box in the header row to select these bills for payment.

5. For the second step, you will select bills carrying a discount that expires by April 2, 2008.

   Click **Show all bills** on the toolbar and then click **Calculate Discount**. Click the **Discount Date** column header to sort the list by this date.

   There are five bills carrying a discount that will be lost if not paid with this check run. Click the selection box for these bills (Figure 9:48). Review the total in the Payment column and verify that it equals $14,188.50.

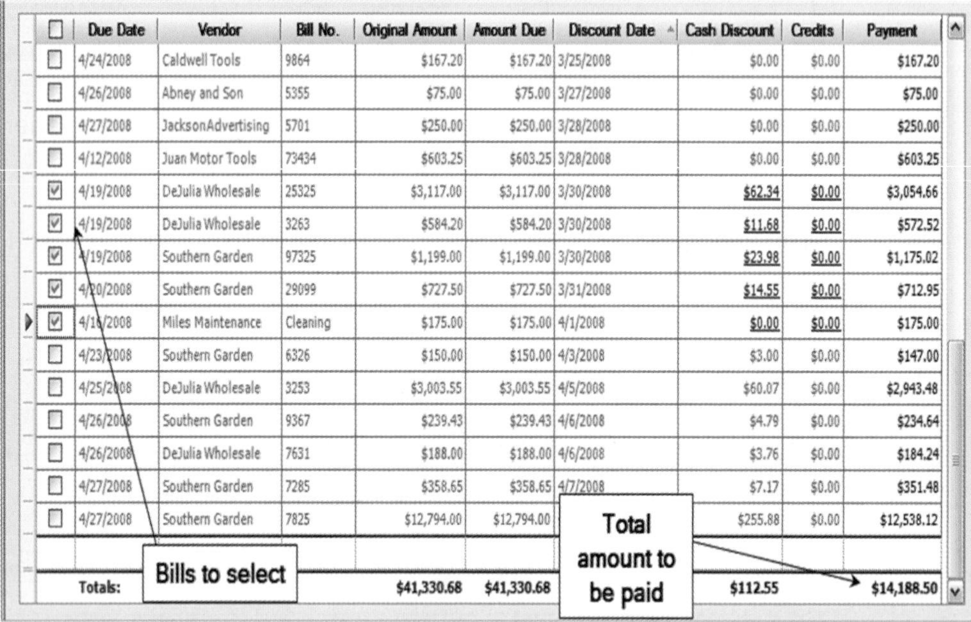

☐	Due Date	Vendor	Bill No.	Original Amount	Amount Due	Discount Date	Cash Discount	Credits	Payment
☐	4/24/2008	Caldwell Tools	9864	$167.20	$167.20	3/25/2008	$0.00	$0.00	$167.20
☐	4/26/2008	Abney and Son	5355	$75.00	$75.00	3/27/2008	$0.00	$0.00	$75.00
☐	4/27/2008	JacksonAdvertising	5701	$250.00	$250.00	3/28/2008	$0.00	$0.00	$250.00
☐	4/12/2008	Juan Motor Tools	73434	$603.25	$603.25	3/28/2008	$0.00	$0.00	$603.25
☑	4/19/2008	DeJulia Wholesale	25325	$3,117.00	$3,117.00	3/30/2008	$62.34	$0.00	$3,054.66
☑	4/19/2008	DeJulia Wholesale	3263	$584.20	$584.20	3/30/2008	$11.68	$0.00	$572.52
☑	4/19/2008	Southern Garden	97325	$1,199.00	$1,199.00	3/30/2008	$23.98	$0.00	$1,175.02
☑	4/20/2008	Southern Garden	29099	$727.50	$727.50	3/31/2008	$14.55	$0.00	$712.95
☑	4/1[illegible]/2008	Miles Maintenance	Cleaning	$175.00	$175.00	4/1/2008	$0.00	$0.00	$175.00
☐	4/23/2008	Southern Garden	6326	$150.00	$150.00	4/3/2008	$3.00	$0.00	$147.00
☐	4/25/2008	DeJulia Wholesale	3253	$3,003.55	$3,003.55	4/5/2008	$60.07	$0.00	$2,943.48
☐	4/26/2008	Southern Garden	9367	$239.43	$239.43	4/6/2008	$4.79	$0.00	$234.64
☐	4/26/2008	DeJulia Wholesale	7631	$188.00	$188.00	4/6/2008	$3.76	$0.00	$184.24
☐	4/27/2008	Southern Garden	7285	$358.65	$358.65	4/7/2008	$7.17	$0.00	$351.48
☐	4/27/2008	Southern Garden	7825	$12,794.00	$12,794.00	[illegible]	$255.88	$0.00	$12,538.12
	Totals:			$41,330.68	$41,330.68		$112.55		$14,188.50

Figure 9:48

6. Click **Issue Payment** on the toolbar and click **OK** to save your selections. *(Note: You can also click Save and Close to keep your selections and then use the Issue Payment icon on the home page to return to printing checks.)*

   Figure 9:49 illustrates the window that opens to list the checks that will print and the total for the checks. The first check will print on check number 286.

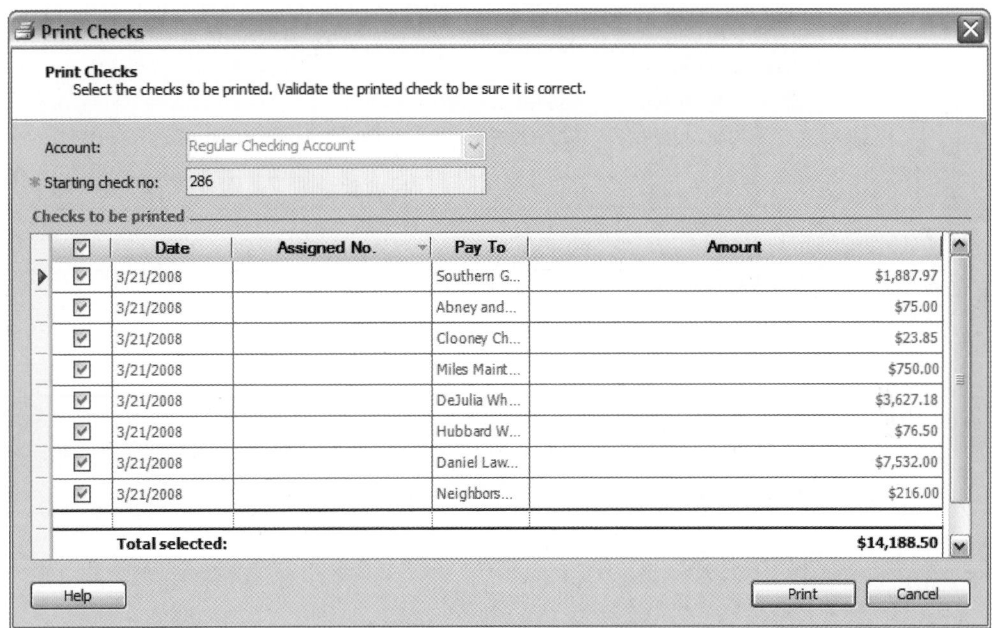

Figure 9:49

Note: You can click Cancel at this step and return to printing checks later by using the Issue Payments icon on the home page.

7. Click **Print** and the printer selection window opens. Select a printer and click **OK.**

8. OAP returns to the Print Checks window to confirm that checks printed correctly. Click **Close** and OAP assigns the check numbers and post the payments.

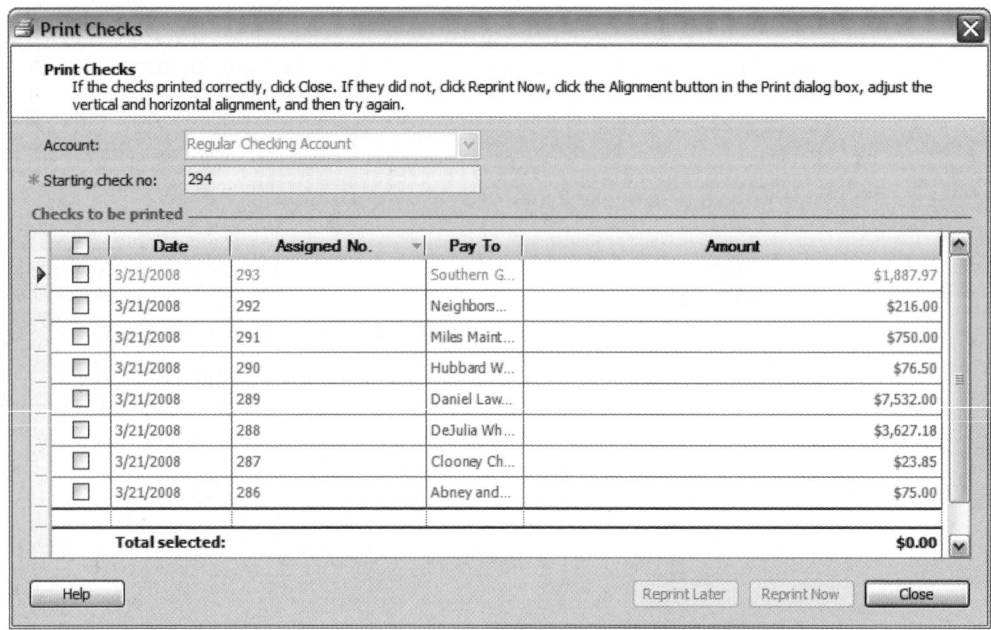

Figure 9:50

Note: If a printer error occurs, click the selection box on checks with errors and the Reprint Later and Reprint Now buttons activate. You can then reprint the checks by clicking one of the buttons.

9. OAP confirms nine payments were issued. Click **OK** and then click **X** to close the Pay Bills window.

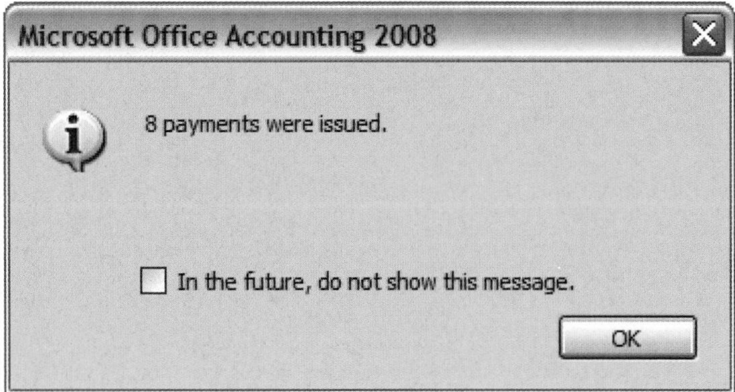

Figure 9:51

BEHIND THE KEYS OF A POSTED VENDOR PAYMENT

Now trace the audit trail for the checks printed in the last topic. On the main menu, select ***Reports>>Company and Financial>>Transaction Journal***. Change the date range to "3/21/2008" and filter the report for the **Vendor Payment** transaction type. Finally, change the report title to Cash Disbursements Journal and save the report.

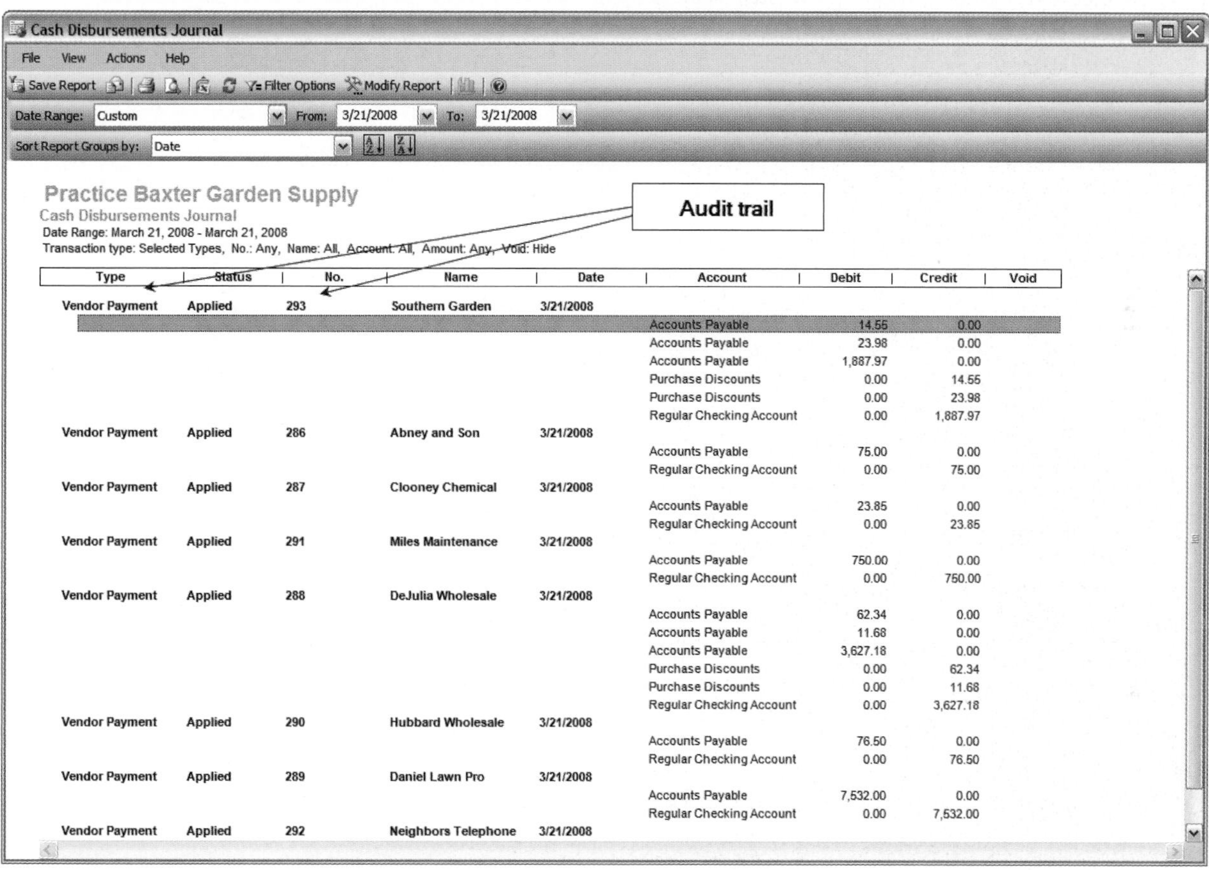

Type	Status	No.	Name	Date	Account	Debit	Credit	Void
Vendor Payment	Applied	293	Southern Garden	3/21/2008				
					Accounts Payable	14.55	0.00	
					Accounts Payable	23.98	0.00	
					Accounts Payable	1,887.97	0.00	
					Purchase Discounts	0.00	14.55	
					Purchase Discounts	0.00	23.98	
					Regular Checking Account	0.00	1,887.97	
Vendor Payment	Applied	286	Abney and Son	3/21/2008				
					Accounts Payable	75.00	0.00	
					Regular Checking Account	0.00	75.00	
Vendor Payment	Applied	287	Clooney Chemical	3/21/2008				
					Accounts Payable	23.85	0.00	
					Regular Checking Account	0.00	23.85	
Vendor Payment	Applied	291	Miles Maintenance	3/21/2008				
					Accounts Payable	750.00	0.00	
					Regular Checking Account	0.00	750.00	
Vendor Payment	Applied	288	DeJulia Wholesale	3/21/2008				
					Accounts Payable	62.34	0.00	
					Accounts Payable	11.68	0.00	
					Accounts Payable	3,627.18	0.00	
					Purchase Discounts	0.00	62.34	
					Purchase Discounts	0.00	11.68	
					Regular Checking Account	0.00	3,627.18	
Vendor Payment	Applied	290	Hubbard Wholesale	3/21/2008				
					Accounts Payable	76.50	0.00	
					Regular Checking Account	0.00	76.50	
Vendor Payment	Applied	289	Daniel Lawn Pro	3/21/2008				
					Accounts Payable	7,532.00	0.00	
					Regular Checking Account	0.00	7,532.00	
Vendor Payment	Applied	292	Neighbors Telephone	3/21/2008				

Figure 9:52

The report shows that checks debited Accounts Payable and credited the Regular Checking Account. In addition, bills carrying a discount posted the discount amount as a credit to Purchase Discounts. Close the report.

Select ***Reports>>Vendors and Payables>>Vendor Transaction History*** on the main menu to trace the payments to the vendor accounts. Enter "3/21/2008" as the date range and filter the report to display the transaction type of **Vendor Payment** (Figure 9:53).

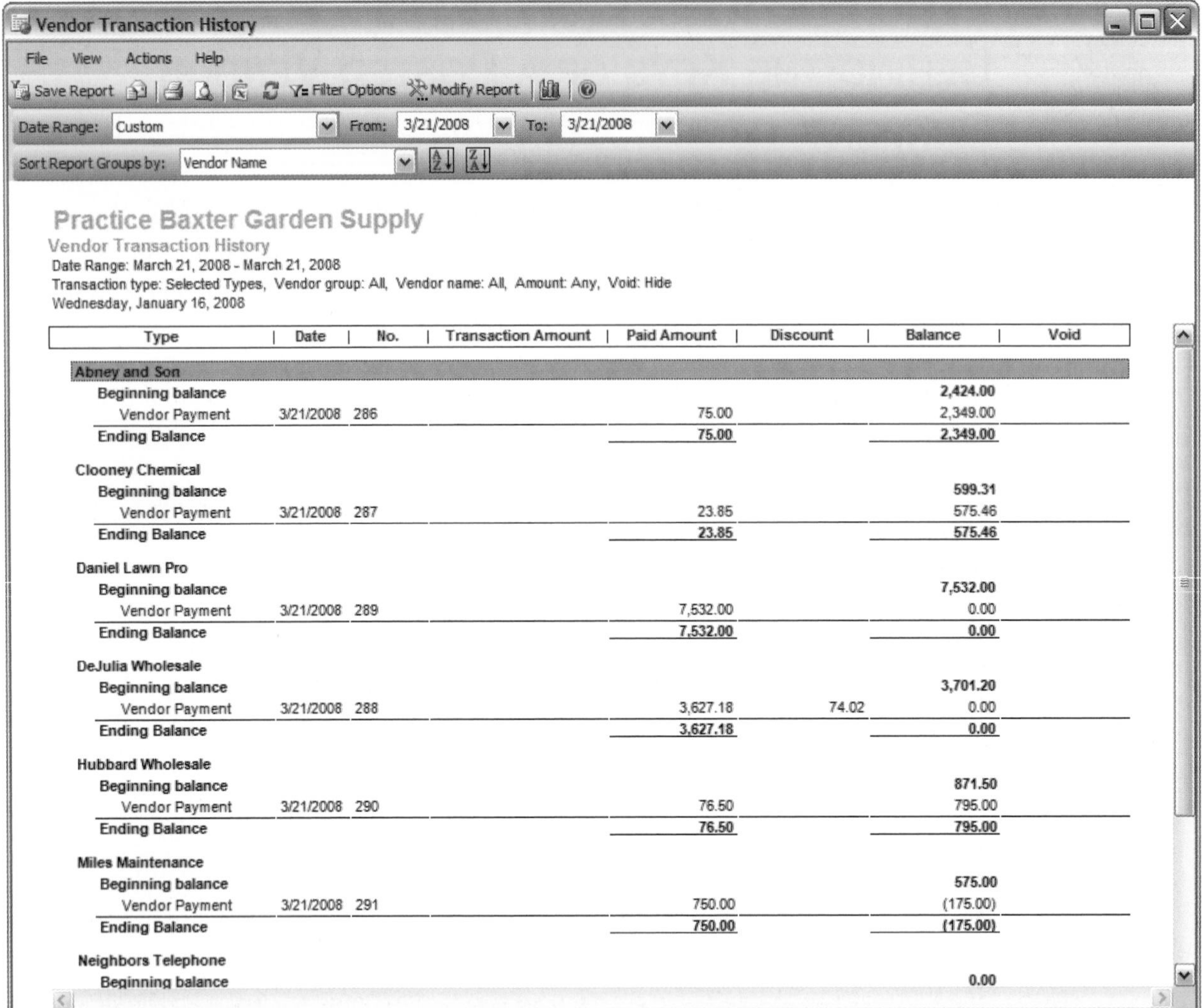

Vendor Transaction History

File View Actions Help

Save Report | Filter Options | Modify Report

Date Range: Custom From: 3/21/2008 To: 3/21/2008

Sort Report Groups by: Vendor Name

Practice Baxter Garden Supply

Vendor Transaction History

Date Range: March 21, 2008 - March 21, 2008

Transaction type: Selected Types, Vendor group: All, Vendor name: All, Amount: Any, Void: Hide

Wednesday, January 16, 2008

Type	Date	No.	Transaction Amount	Paid Amount	Discount	Balance	Void
Abney and Son							
Beginning balance						**2,424.00**	
Vendor Payment	3/21/2008	286		75.00		2,349.00	
Ending Balance				**75.00**		**2,349.00**	
Clooney Chemical							
Beginning balance						**599.31**	
Vendor Payment	3/21/2008	287		23.85		575.46	
Ending Balance				**23.85**		**575.46**	
Daniel Lawn Pro							
Beginning balance						**7,532.00**	
Vendor Payment	3/21/2008	289		7,532.00		0.00	
Ending Balance				**7,532.00**		**0.00**	
DeJulia Wholesale							
Beginning balance						**3,701.20**	
Vendor Payment	3/21/2008	288		3,627.18	74.02	0.00	
Ending Balance				**3,627.18**		**0.00**	
Hubbard Wholesale							
Beginning balance						**871.50**	
Vendor Payment	3/21/2008	290		76.50		795.00	
Ending Balance				**76.50**		**795.00**	
Miles Maintenance							
Beginning balance						**575.00**	
Vendor Payment	3/21/2008	291		750.00		(175.00)	
Ending Balance				**750.00**		**(175.00)**	
Neighbors Telephone							
Beginning balance						**0.00**	

Figure 9:53

Close this report and complete tracing entries by opening the **Transaction Detail by Account** report. Locate your entries to Accounts Payable, Regular Checking Account, and Purchase Discounts (not illustrated).

Writing Checks Without a Vendor Bill

OAP also allows you to write checks without entering a vendor bill first. For instance, you may need to write a check to a local grocer for office party food. Sometimes the vendor account is new so it needs to be created "on the fly." *(Note: Remember "on the fly" means creating a new account while entering a transaction.)*

Complete the next exercise to write a check that replenishes petty cash.

STEPS TO WRITING A CHECK WITHOUT A VENDOR BILL

1. Select ***Banking>>Write Checks*** on the main menu. Select "Regular Checking Account" as the **Bank account** and enter "3/31/2008" as the **Date**. Select Petty Cash as the Pay to and enter $375.15 as the Amount. (See Figure 9:54.)

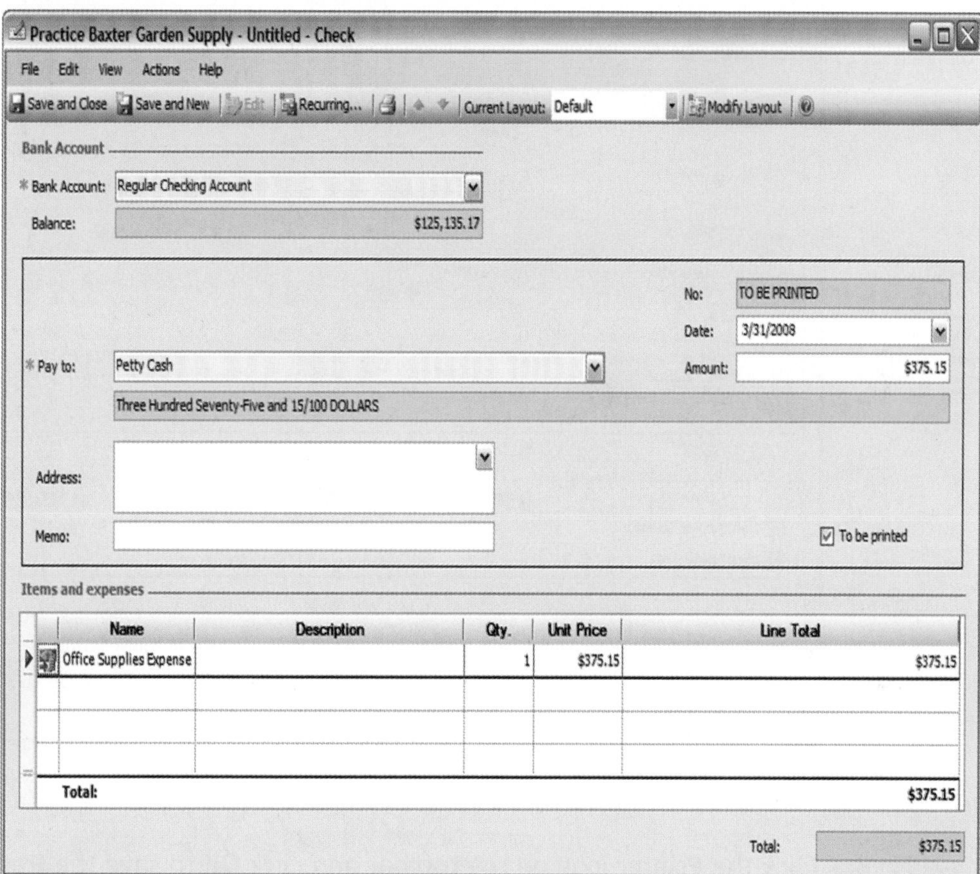

Figure 9:54

2. The first line item contains the Office Supplies Expense account. Tab to **Unit Price** and change the amount to $223.00. Tab to the next line item and select the expense icon. Tab to **Name** and select **Travel Expense**. Tab to **Unit Price** and enter $152.15. (See Figure 9:55.)

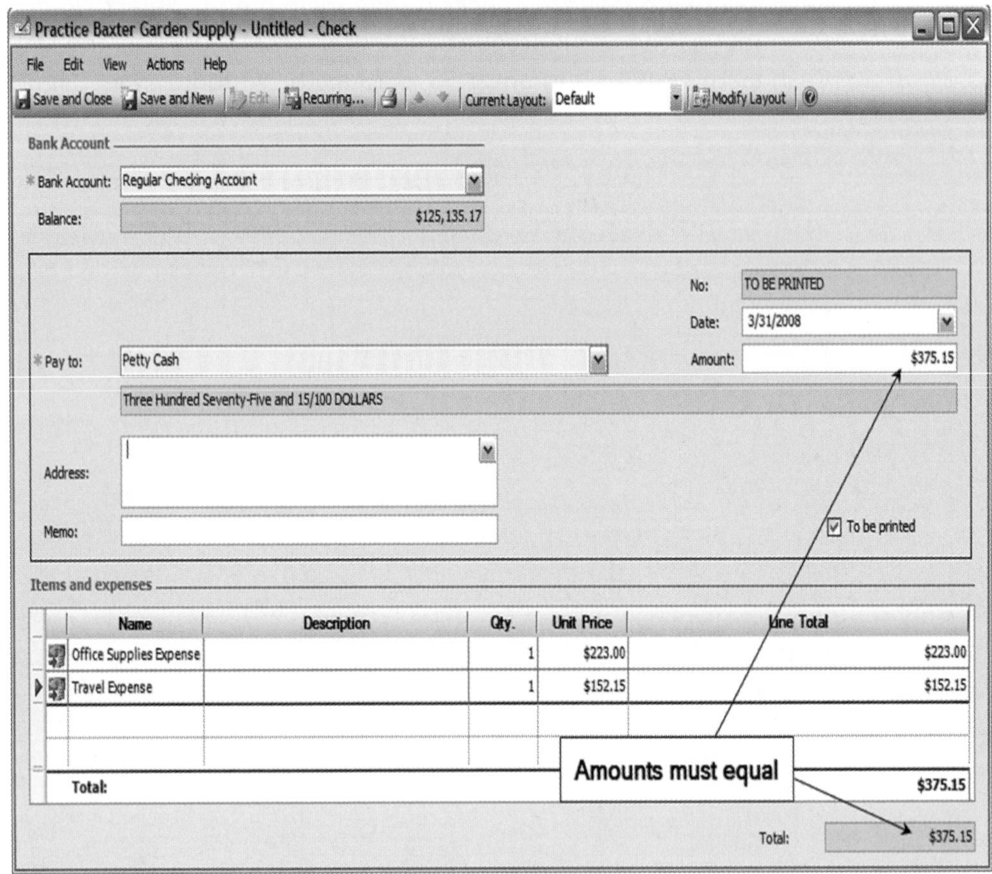

Figure 9:55

3. Click the **Printer** icon on the toolbar and click **OK** to save the transaction. When the Print Checks window opens the Starting check no will be 294. Click **Print** and then click **OK** in the printer selection window.

   Return to the Print Checks window and click **Close**.

4. Return to the transaction window and notice that the check number has been assigned (Figure 9:56). Click **Save and Close.**

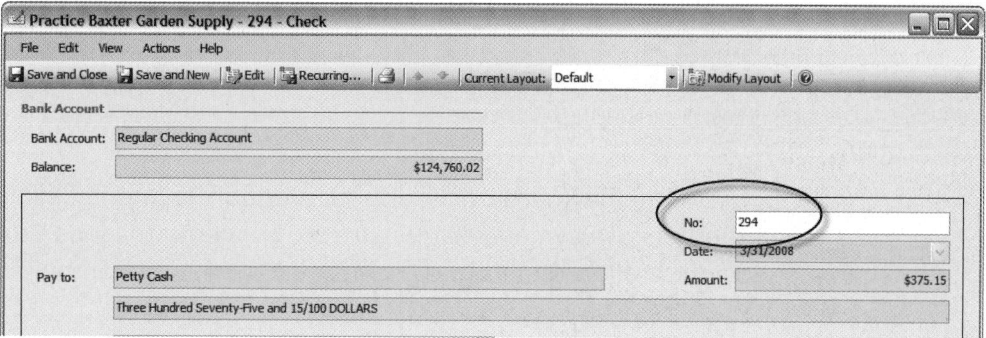

Figure 9:56

VOIDING VENDOR PAYMENTS

OAP does not permit editing payments; therefore, you must void checks and reissue the payments to make corrections. Practice performing these steps in the exercise that follows.

Steps to Voiding a Vendor Payment

1. In this exercise you will void check number "286" issued to Abney and Son on March 21.

   First, locate the payment by clicking the **Vendor Payments** link under **Find** to open the Vendor Payments list (Figure 9:57). Verify that the **Current View** is **Issued** and scroll to the bottom and locate the transaction by referring to the Payment No. column.

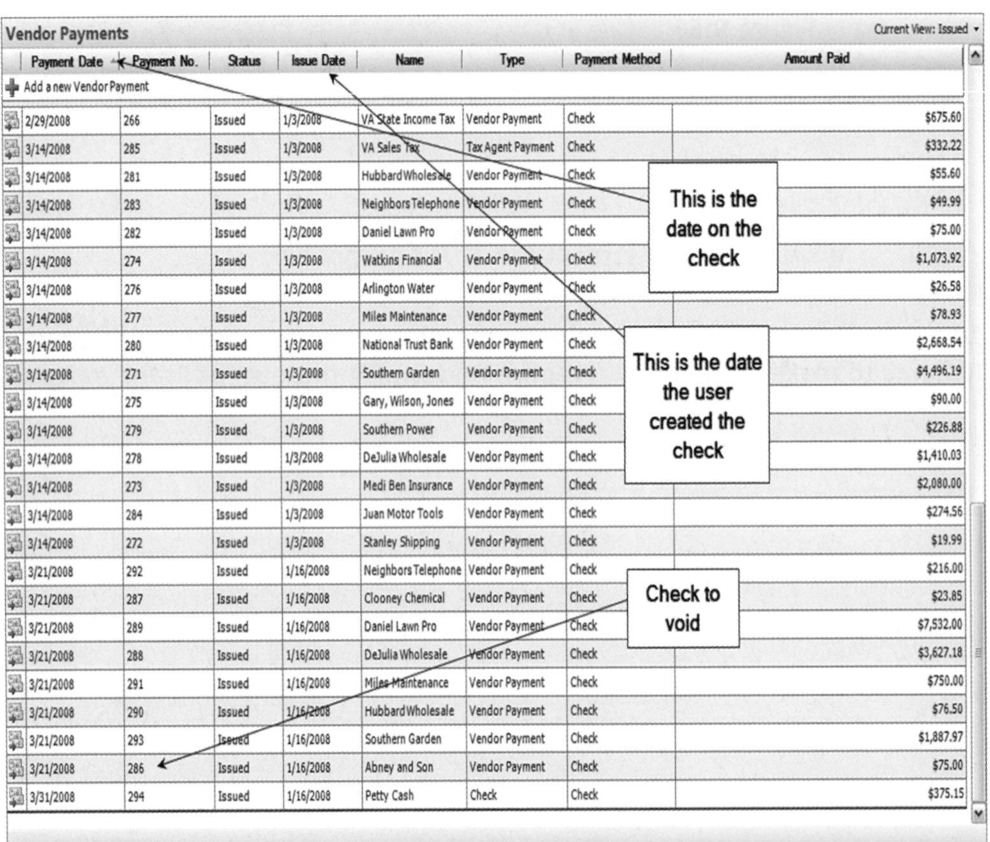

Vendor Payments — Current View: Issued

Add a new Vendor Payment

Payment Date	Payment No.	Status	Issue Date	Name	Type	Payment Method	Amount Paid
2/29/2008	266	Issued	1/3/2008	VA State Income Tax	Vendor Payment	Check	$675.60
3/14/2008	285	Issued	1/3/2008	VA Sales Tax	Tax Agent Payment	Check	$332.22
3/14/2008	281	Issued	1/3/2008	Hubbard Wholesale	Vendor Payment	Check	$55.60
3/14/2008	283	Issued	1/3/2008	Neighbors Telephone	Vendor Payment	Check	$49.99
3/14/2008	282	Issued	1/3/2008	Daniel Lawn Pro	Vendor Payment	Check	$75.00
3/14/2008	274	Issued	1/3/2008	Watkins Financial	Vendor Payment	Check	$1,073.92
3/14/2008	276	Issued	1/3/2008	Arlington Water	Vendor Payment	Check	$26.58
3/14/2008	277	Issued	1/3/2008	Miles Maintenance	Vendor Payment	Check	$78.93
3/14/2008	280	Issued	1/3/2008	National Trust Bank	Vendor Payment	Check	$2,668.54
3/14/2008	271	Issued	1/3/2008	Southern Garden	Vendor Payment	Check	$4,496.19
3/14/2008	275	Issued	1/3/2008	Gary, Wilson, Jones	Vendor Payment	Check	$90.00
3/14/2008	279	Issued	1/3/2008	Southern Power	Vendor Payment	Check	$226.88
3/14/2008	278	Issued	1/3/2008	DeJulia Wholesale	Vendor Payment	Check	$1,410.03
3/14/2008	273	Issued	1/3/2008	Medi Ben Insurance	Vendor Payment	Check	$2,080.00
3/14/2008	284	Issued	1/3/2008	Juan Motor Tools	Vendor Payment	Check	$274.56
3/14/2008	272	Issued	1/3/2008	Stanley Shipping	Vendor Payment	Check	$19.99
3/21/2008	292	Issued	1/16/2008	Neighbors Telephone	Vendor Payment	Check	$216.00
3/21/2008	287	Issued	1/16/2008	Clooney Chemical	Vendor Payment	Check	$23.85
3/21/2008	289	Issued	1/16/2008	Daniel Lawn Pro	Vendor Payment	Check	$7,532.00
3/21/2008	288	Issued	1/16/2008	DeJulia Wholesale	Vendor Payment	Check	$3,627.18
3/21/2008	291	Issued	1/16/2008	Miles Maintenance	Vendor Payment	Check	$750.00
3/21/2008	290	Issued	1/16/2008	Hubbard Wholesale	Vendor Payment	Check	$76.50
3/21/2008	293	Issued	1/16/2008	Southern Garden	Vendor Payment	Check	$1,887.97
3/21/2008	286	Issued	1/16/2008	Abney and Son	Vendor Payment	Check	$75.00
3/31/2008	294	Issued	1/16/2008	Petty Cash	Check	Check	$375.15

Figure 9:57

2. Right click the transaction and select **Void**. When OAP confirms the action, click **Yes**. Notice the payment is removed from the Vendor Payments list. You must toggle the Current View to Voided to find it.

3. Now view the entries posted by your action. Select ***Reports>>Company and Financial>>Transaction Detail by Account*** on the main menu. Filter the report to Show void transactions and display only the Regular Checking Account and Accounts Payable account. Enter "3/21/2008" (i.e., date on the check) as the date range.

   Notice that OAP voided the check as of the check date. Close the report.

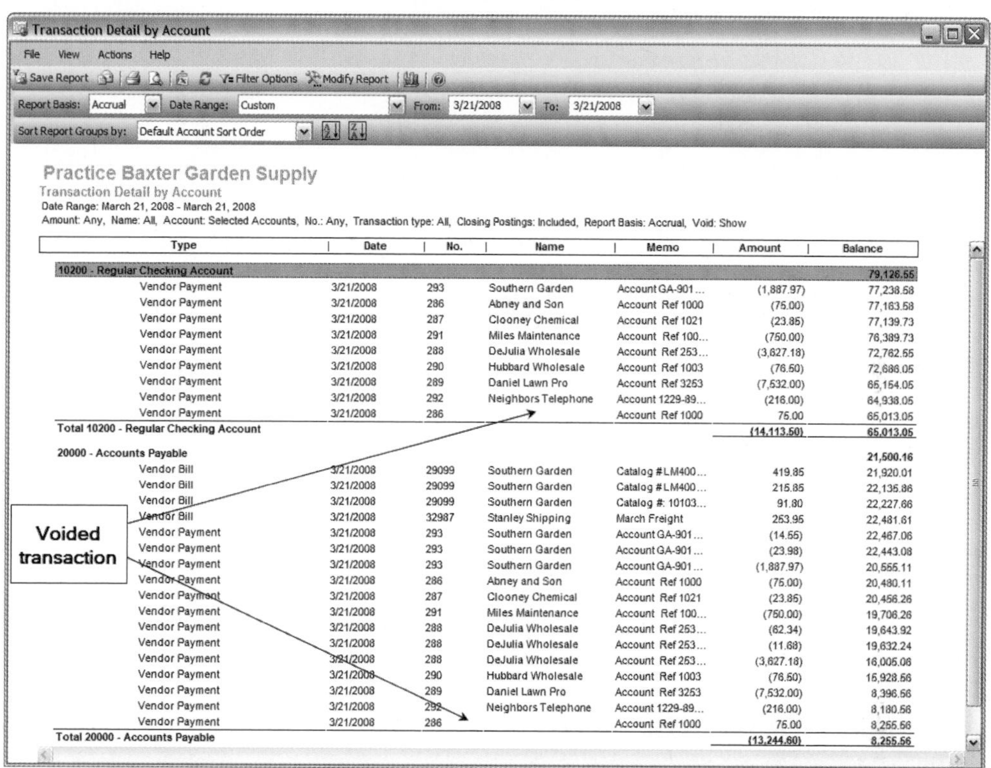

Practice Baxter Garden Supply
Transaction Detail by Account
Date Range: March 21, 2008 - March 21, 2008
Amount: Any, Name: All, Account: Selected Accounts, No.: Any, Transaction type: All, Closing Postings: Included, Report Basis: Accrual, Void: Show

Type	Date	No.	Name	Memo	Amount	Balance
10200 - Regular Checking Account						79,126.55
Vendor Payment	3/21/2008	293	Southern Garden	Account GA-901...	(1,887.97)	77,238.58
Vendor Payment	3/21/2008	286	Abney and Son	Account Ref 1000	(75.00)	77,163.58
Vendor Payment	3/21/2008	287	Clooney Chemical	Account Ref 1021	(23.85)	77,139.73
Vendor Payment	3/21/2008	291	Miles Maintenance	Account Ref 100...	(750.00)	76,389.73
Vendor Payment	3/21/2008	288	DeJulia Wholesale	Account Ref 253...	(3,627.18)	72,762.55
Vendor Payment	3/21/2008	290	Hubbard Wholesale	Account Ref 1003	(76.50)	72,686.05
Vendor Payment	3/21/2008	289	Daniel Lawn Pro	Account Ref 3253	(7,532.00)	65,154.05
Vendor Payment	3/21/2008	292	Neighbors Telephone	Account 1229-89...	(216.00)	64,938.05
Vendor Payment	3/21/2008	286		Account Ref 1000	75.00	65,013.05
Total 10200 - Regular Checking Account					(14,113.50)	65,013.05
20000 - Accounts Payable						21,500.16
Vendor Bill	3/21/2008	29099	Southern Garden	Catalog #LM400...	419.85	21,920.01
Vendor Bill	3/21/2008	29099	Southern Garden	Catalog #LM400...	215.85	22,135.86
Vendor Bill	3/21/2008	29099	Southern Garden	Catalog #: 10103...	91.80	22,227.66
Vendor Bill	3/21/2008	32987	Stanley Shipping	March Freight	253.95	22,481.61
Vendor Payment	3/21/2008	293	Southern Garden	Account GA-901...	(14.55)	22,467.06
Vendor Payment	3/21/2008	293	Southern Garden	Account GA-901...	(23.98)	22,443.08
Vendor Payment	3/21/2008	293	Southern Garden	Account GA-901...	(1,887.97)	20,555.11
Vendor Payment	3/21/2008	286	Abney and Son	Account Ref 1000	(75.00)	20,480.11
Vendor Payment	3/21/2008	287	Clooney Chemical	Account Ref 1021	(23.85)	20,456.26
Vendor Payment	3/21/2008	291	Miles Maintenance	Account Ref 100...	(750.00)	19,706.26
Vendor Payment	3/21/2008	288	DeJulia Wholesale	Account Ref 253...	(62.34)	19,643.92
Vendor Payment	3/21/2008	288	DeJulia Wholesale	Account Ref 253...	(11.68)	19,632.24
Vendor Payment	3/21/2008	288	DeJulia Wholesale	Account Ref 253...	(3,627.18)	16,005.06
Vendor Payment	3/21/2008	290	Hubbard Wholesale	Account Ref 1003	(76.50)	15,928.56
Vendor Payment	3/21/2008	289	Daniel Lawn Pro	Account Ref 3253	(7,532.00)	8,396.56
Vendor Payment	3/21/2008	292	Neighbors Telephone	Account 1229-89...	(216.00)	8,180.56
Vendor Payment	3/21/2008	286		Account Ref 1000	75.00	8,255.56
Total 20000 - Accounts Payable					(13,244.60)	8,255.56

Figure 9:58

4. Now open the Vendor List and double click to open Abney and Son's account. Click the **Financial History** tab. The voided payment released the March bill so that it can be repaid. You will pay this bill in the next exercise.

   Close the vendor's account.

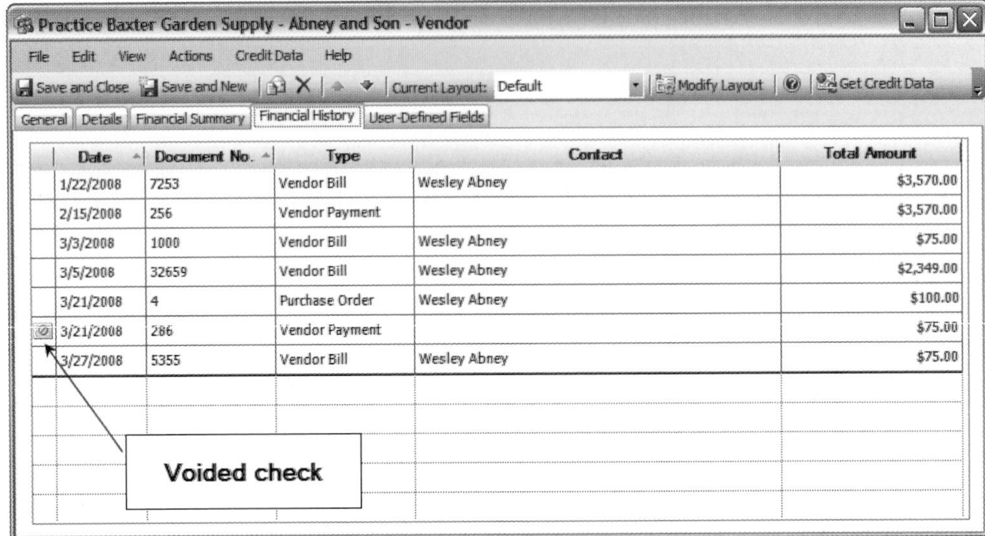

Figure 9:59

PAY VENDORS

In this exercise you create vendor checks dated April 1, 2008 that pay bills due by 4/12/2008 and bills carrying a discount that expires by 4/12/2008.

Click the Payment field for Sully Printing and reduce the payment to $600.00.

Total payments are $22,783.41. Print the checks on starting check number 295.

Select ***Reports>>Banking>>Payments*** on the main menu and enter "4/1/2008" as the report range. Modify the report and remove the Issue date, No., Status detail, Memo, and Reference number columns. Print the report to document the payments.

PAYING SALES TAX

At the end of every month, Baxter must remit the sales tax collected from customers. OAP tracks the sales tax collected and the following shows you how to remit the tax.

STEPS TO PAYING SALES TAX

1. First, we will view the Sales Tax Liability report. Select ***Company>>Sales Tax>>View Sales Tax Liability*** on the main menu. Enter the date range of "3/1/2008" to "3/31/2008."

   Baxter owes sales tax on the cash basis, meaning the company owes the tax after collecting it from the customer, (i.e., the customer pays the invoice). Therefore, change the **Report Basis** to **Cash** and the total in the Tax Collected column reports the sales tax due by April 15, 2008 (Figure 9:60). *(Note: Your report will differ if you have not completed all previous exercises.)*

   Close the report.

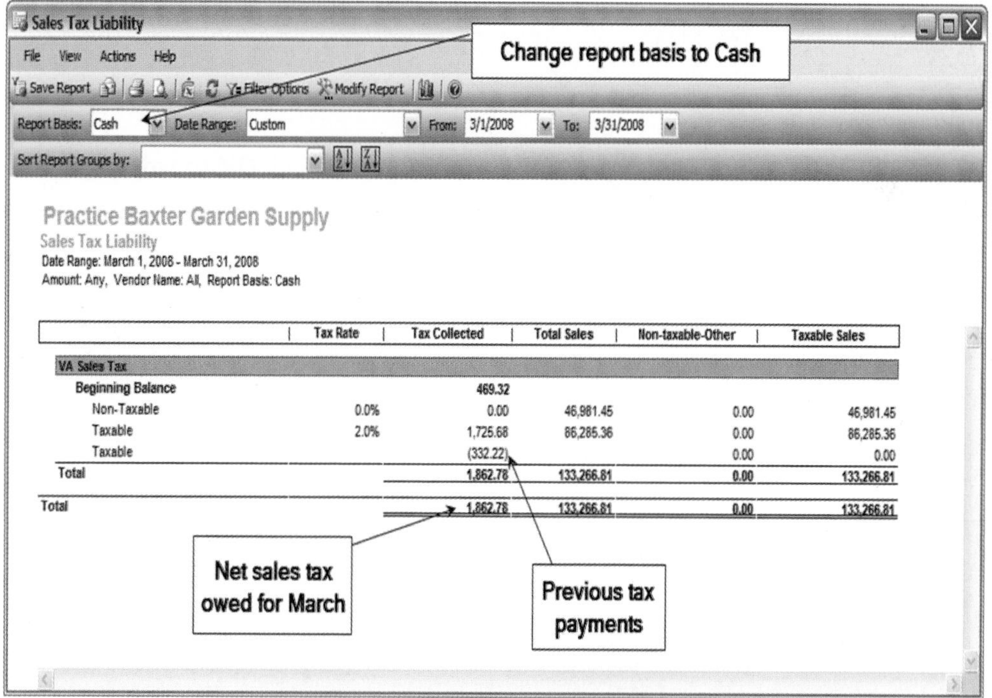

Practice Baxter Garden Supply
Sales Tax Liability
Date Range: March 1, 2008 - March 31, 2008
Amount: Any, Vendor Name: All, Report Basis: Cash

	Tax Rate	Tax Collected	Total Sales	Non-taxable-Other	Taxable Sales
VA Sales Tax					
Beginning Balance		469.32			
Non-Taxable	0.0%	0.00	46,981.45	0.00	46,981.45
Taxable	2.0%	1,725.68	86,285.36	0.00	86,285.36
Taxable		(332.22)		0.00	0.00
Total		1,862.78	133,266.81	0.00	133,266.81
Total		1,862.78	133,266.81	0.00	133,266.81

Figure 9:60

2. You will now process the tax payment. Select ***Company>>Sales Tax>>Pay Sales Tax*** on the main menu and enter the information provided in Figure 9:61. *(Note: You have entered 4/15/2008 as the Filter because Baxter owes sales tax collected in March by the 15th day of the following month.)*

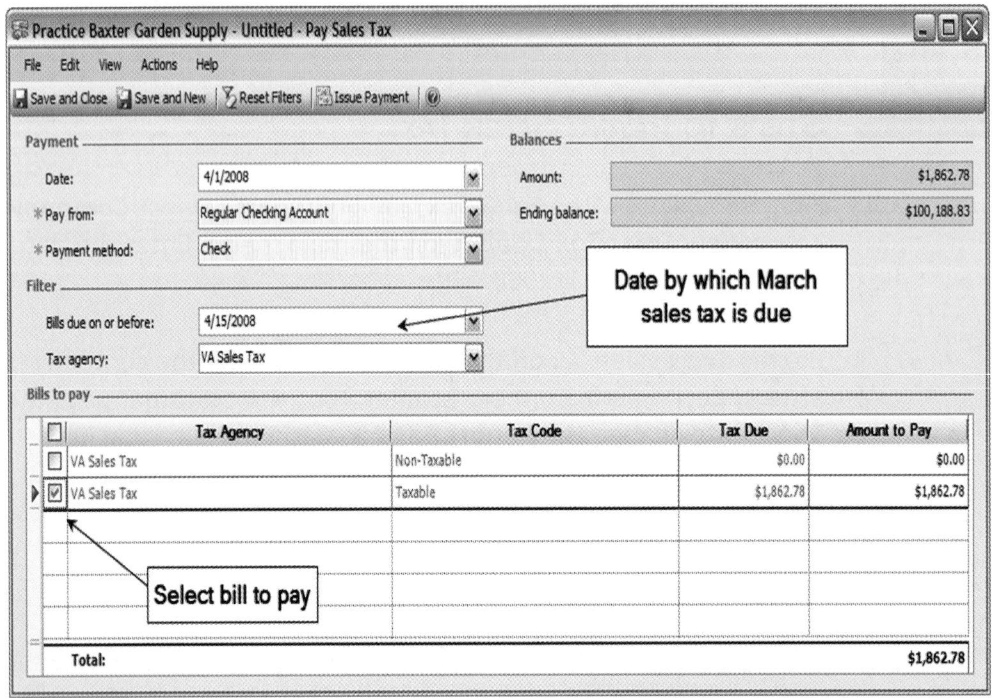

Figure 9:61

3. Click **Issue Payment** on the toolbar and click **OK** to save the selected payment.

4. The Starting check no is 305 (Figure 9:62). Click **Print**, choose a printer, and click **OK**.

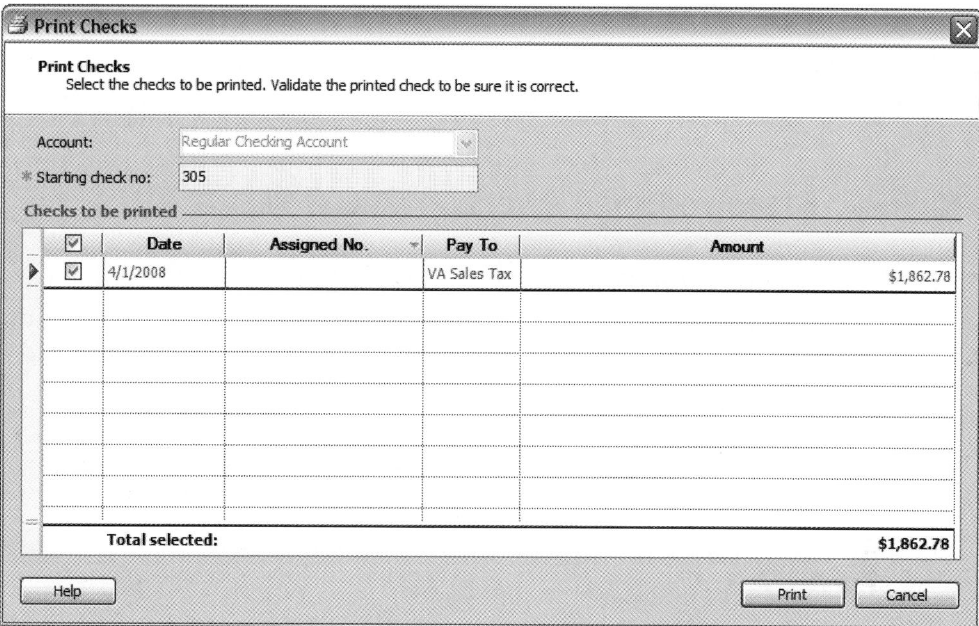

Figure 9:62

5. Click **Close** on the Print Checks window and click **OK** on the payment message.

Vendor Credits

Just as Baxter issues credits to customers, vendors may issue credits to Baxter. Complete the next exercise to record Baxter's credits from vendors.

Steps to Enter a Vendor Credit Memo

1. Click **New Credit Memo** under **Start a Task** or on the home page. Baxter received a credit memo dated March 27 from Cline Construction for returning 3 items of AVRY-10200-4ft-RD billed on Invoice 4587. Enter the information as illustrated in Figure 9:63.

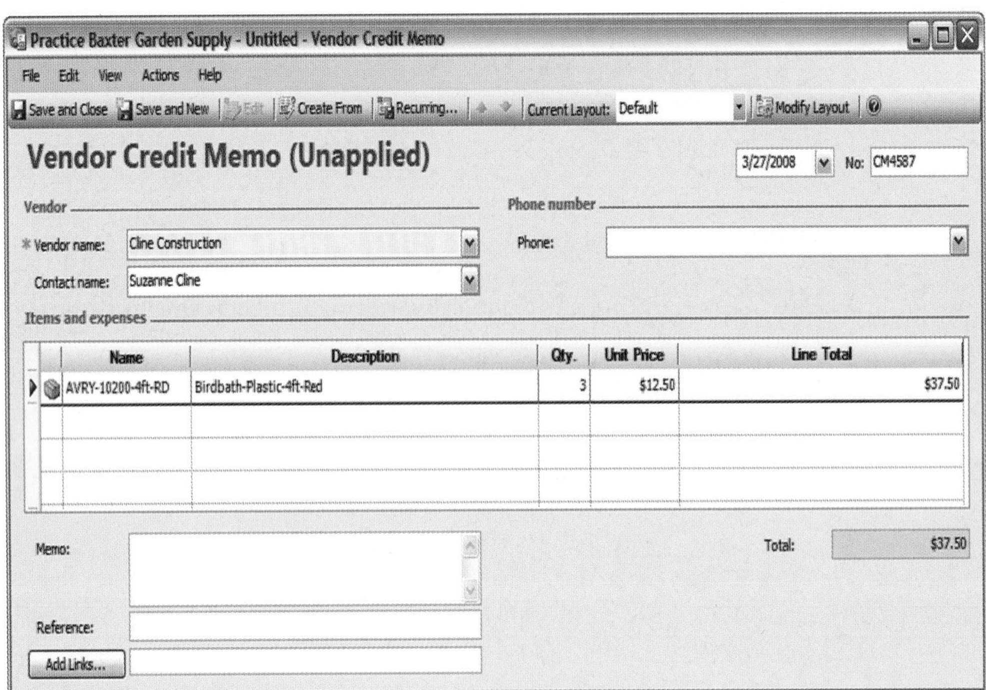

Figure 9:63

2. Click **Save and New** so we can demonstrate another method of entering credit memos.

3. Baxter received credit memo CM5355 dated March 27 from Abney and Son for returning 2 items of AVRY-10050-SM-EFL billed on Invoice 5355.

   Select **Abney and Son** as the vendor and then click **Create From** on the toolbar. Highlight the outstanding bill and click **OK** (Figure 9:64).

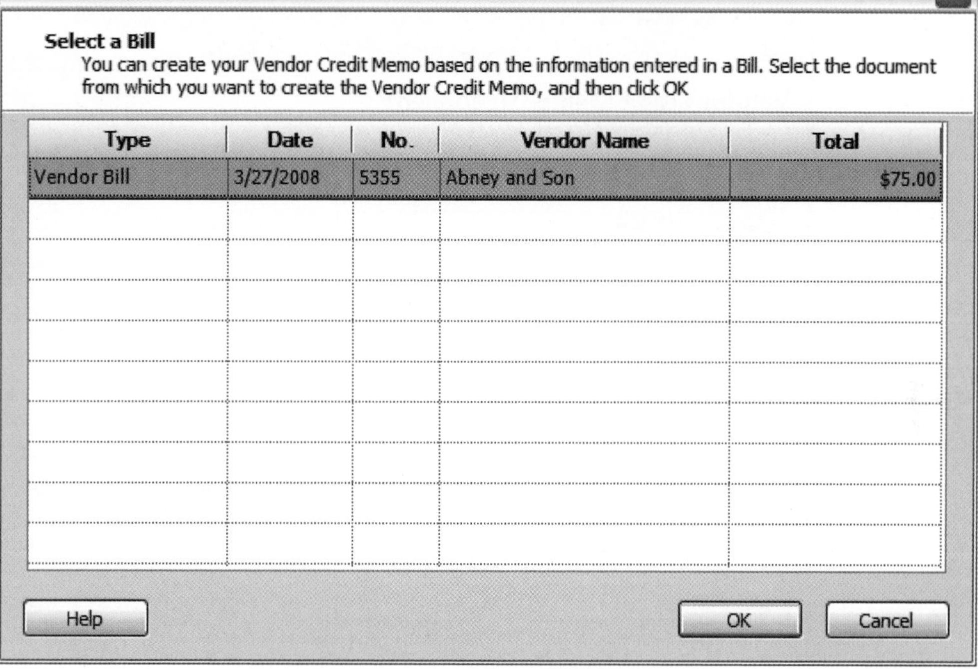

Figure 9:64

4. The Vendor Credit Memo window now displays line items on the original bill. Change the date to 3/27/2008 and enter the credit memo number. Adjust the **Qty** on the line item to 2. (See Figure 9:65.)

   Click **Save and Close**.

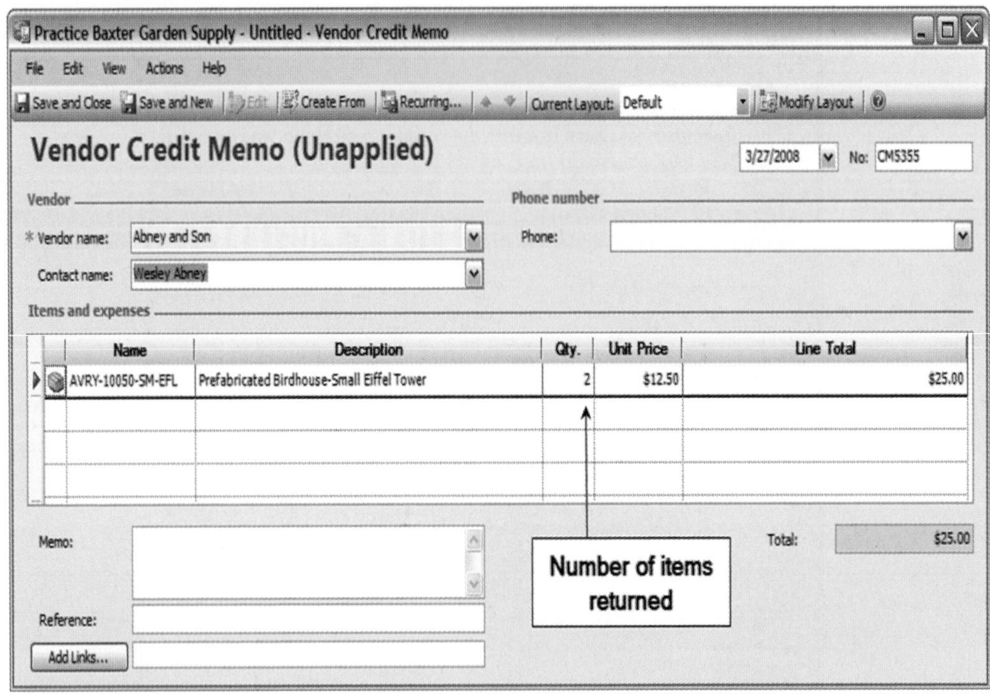

Figure 9:65

5. You will now view the affect of these credit memos in the Pay Bills window. Click **Pay Bills** and enter "4/7/2008" as the check date.

   First, check the status of the credit memo from Cline Construction for Invoice 4587. Select this invoice and click the **hyperlink** under the **Credits** column (Figure 9:66).

   The credit memo must be applied to the invoice before the amount owed on the invoice is reduced. Select the credit in the Apply Credits and Payments window and click **Adjust**.

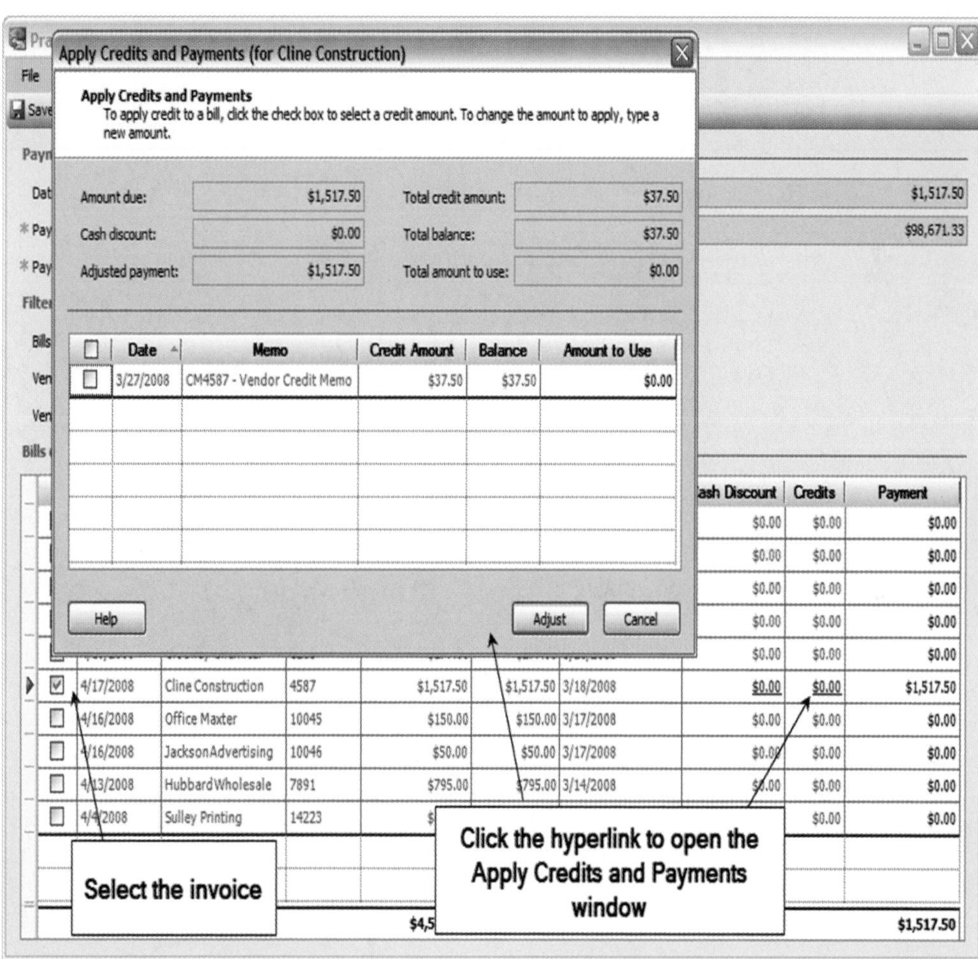

Figure 9:66

6. The Pay Bills window now displays the credit amount for this invoice (Figure 9:67).

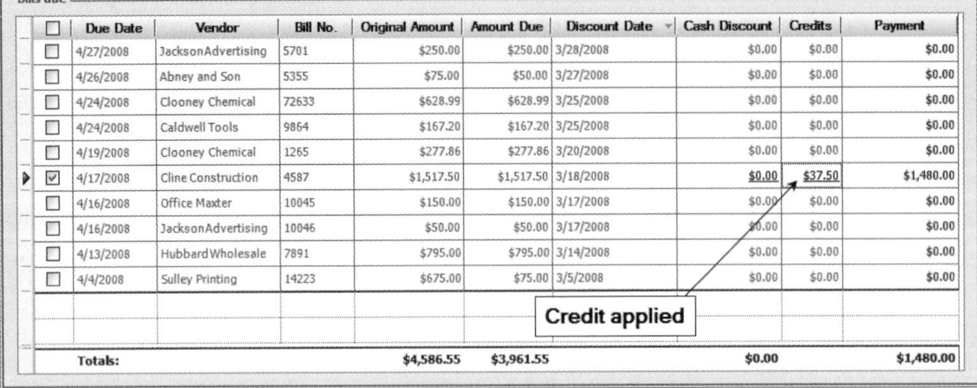

☐	Due Date	Vendor	Bill No.	Original Amount	Amount Due	Discount Date	Cash Discount	Credits	Payment
☐	4/27/2008	JacksonAdvertising	5701	$250.00	$250.00	3/28/2008	$0.00	$0.00	$0.00
☐	4/26/2008	Abney and Son	5355	$75.00	$50.00	3/27/2008	$0.00	$0.00	$0.00
☐	4/24/2008	Clooney Chemical	72633	$628.99	$628.99	3/25/2008	$0.00	$0.00	$0.00
☐	4/24/2008	Caldwell Tools	9864	$167.20	$167.20	3/25/2008	$0.00	$0.00	$0.00
☐	4/19/2008	Clooney Chemical	1265	$277.86	$277.86	3/20/2008	$0.00	$0.00	$0.00
☑	4/17/2008	Cline Construction	4587	$1,517.50	$1,517.50	3/18/2008	$0.00	$37.50	$1,480.00
☐	4/16/2008	Office Maxter	10045	$150.00	$150.00	3/17/2008	$0.00	$0.00	$0.00
☐	4/16/2008	JacksonAdvertising	10046	$50.00	$50.00	3/17/2008	$0.00	$0.00	$0.00
☐	4/13/2008	HubbardWholesale	7891	$795.00	$795.00	3/14/2008	$0.00	$0.00	$0.00
☐	4/4/2008	Sulley Printing	14223	$675.00	$75.00	3/5/2008	$0.00	$0.00	$0.00
	Totals:			$4,586.55	$3,961.55		$0.00		$1,480.00

Figure 9:67

7. What about the status of the credit memo from Abney and Son for Invoice 5355. Select this invoice and again click the **Credit hyperlink**.

   You find no credits for this invoice because the credit memo was applied when posted in Step 4. This is verified by noting that the Original Amount on the invoice was $75.00 whereas the Amount Due is $50.00.

   Click **Cancel** to close the Apply Credits and Payments window.

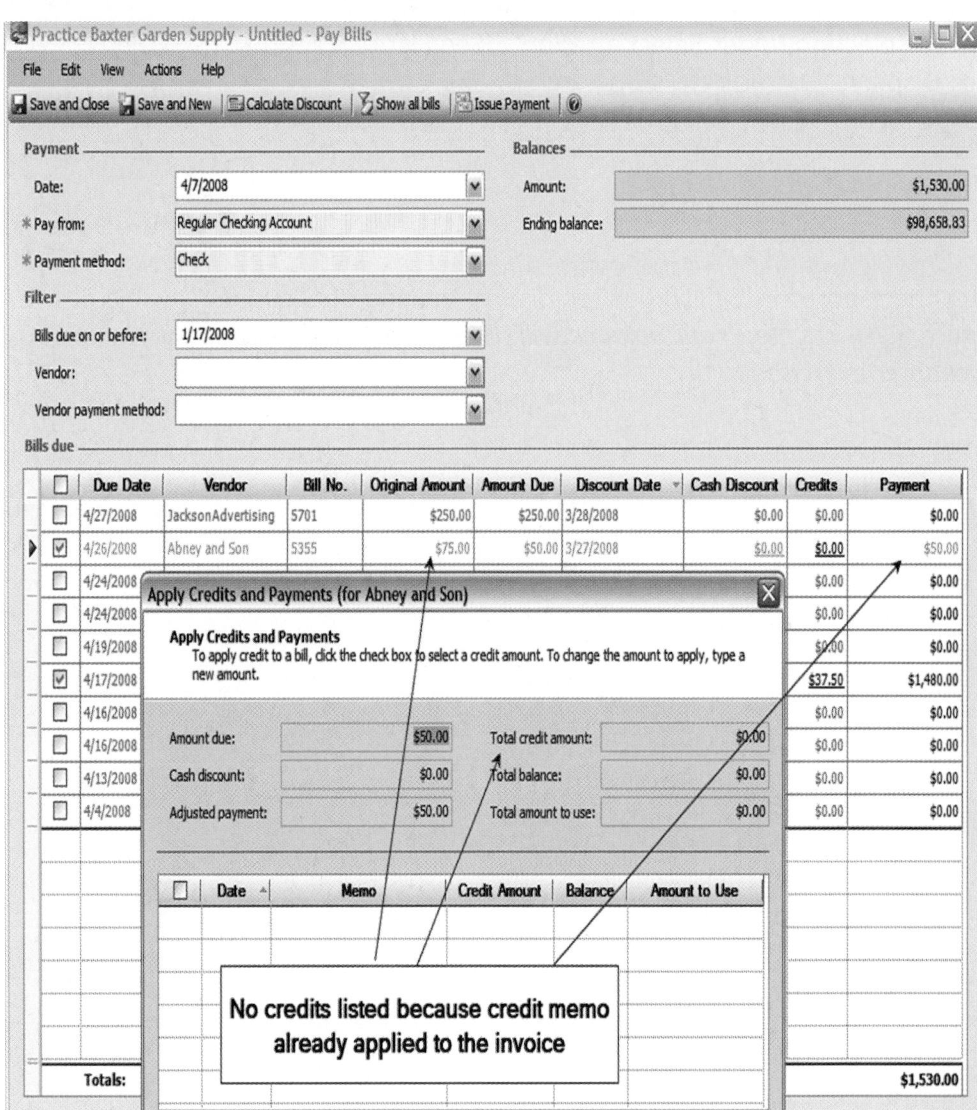

Figure 9:68

8. You will not issue these payments so click **X** and click **No** to exit the window without saving the changes.

Vendor Reporting and Reconciling Vendor Activities

OAP offers a variety of vendor reports that can be run from the ***Reports>>Purchases*** *or* ***Reports>>Vendors and Payables*** menus. In addition, you can run these reports using the Reports section on the right of the Vendors Home page.

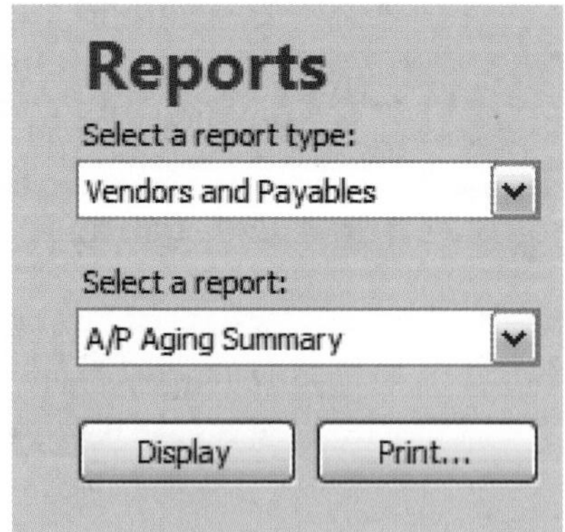

Figure 9:69

Let's run the A/P Aging Summary first because it is the current selection under **Select a report**. (See Figure 9:69.) Click **Display**.

Filter the report for "3/31/2008" to display the age of accounts payable at the end of March (Figure 9:70). *(Note: Your balance will differ from the illustration if you have not completed all chapter exercises.)*

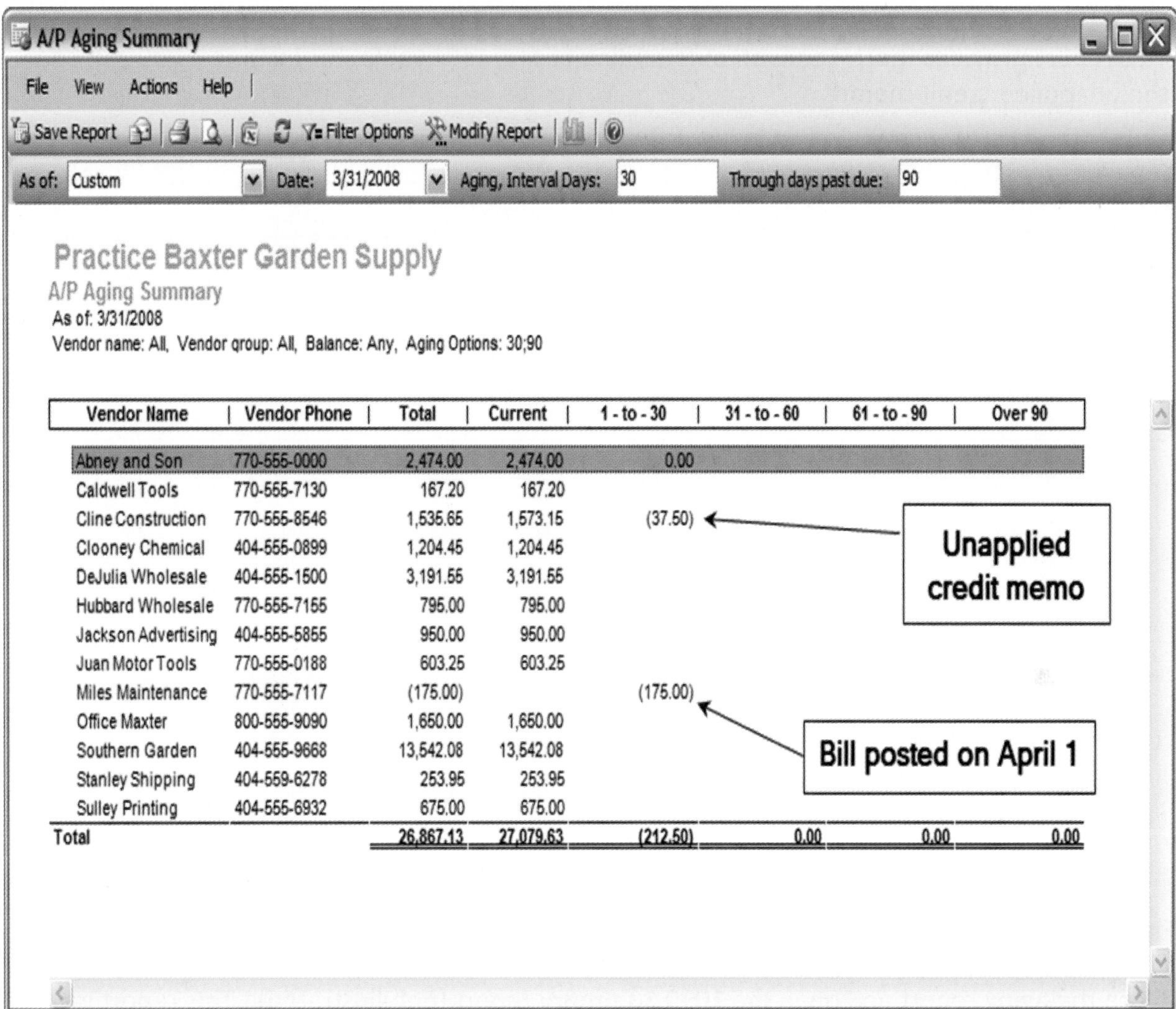

Practice Baxter Garden Supply
A/P Aging Summary
As of: 3/31/2008
Vendor name: All, Vendor group: All, Balance: Any, Aging Options: 30;90

Vendor Name	Vendor Phone	Total	Current	1 - to - 30	31 - to - 60	61 - to - 90	Over 90
Abney and Son	770-555-0000	2,474.00	2,474.00	0.00			
Caldwell Tools	770-555-7130	167.20	167.20				
Cline Construction	770-555-8546	1,535.65	1,573.15	(37.50)			
Clooney Chemical	404-555-0899	1,204.45	1,204.45				
DeJulia Wholesale	404-555-1500	3,191.55	3,191.55				
Hubbard Wholesale	770-555-7155	795.00	795.00				
Jackson Advertising	404-555-5855	950.00	950.00				
Juan Motor Tools	770-555-0188	603.25	603.25				
Miles Maintenance	770-555-7117	(175.00)		(175.00)			
Office Maxter	800-555-9090	1,650.00	1,650.00				
Southern Garden	404-555-9668	13,542.08	13,542.08				
Stanley Shipping	404-559-6278	253.95	253.95				
Sulley Printing	404-555-6932	675.00	675.00				
Total		26,867.13	27,079.63	(212.50)	0.00	0.00	0.00

Figure 9:70

This report is a condensed version of accounts payable and serves several purposes. First, Baxter can quickly monitor the age of vendor balances to manage cash flow. The report can also point out unapplied credit memos or other vendor balance issues as illustrated above.

Second, the report is used to reconcile vendor activities with the accounts payable control account. This task is performed by comparing the aging report Total with the March ending balance in accounts payable. You can view your March ending balance in accounts payable by selecting ***Reports>>Company and Financial>>Trial Balance*** on the main menu and filtering the report for 3/31/2008 (not illustrated). Scroll to the Accounts Payable account and compare the balance on this report with the total on your aging report. The two amounts must agree to confirm proper recording of vendor activities.

Vendor activities can become out of balance when you improperly correct vendor transactions. Therefore, you should always refer to the instructions in this chapter or Appendix B when correcting transactions. You should reconcile the aged payables report to the accounts payable balance at the end of every month and prior to issuing financial reports.

Close this report and open the **Detail A/P Aging** report filtered for "3/31/2008" (Figure 9:71). This report provides more detail on outstanding accounts payable, for instance, you can see the unapplied credit memo.

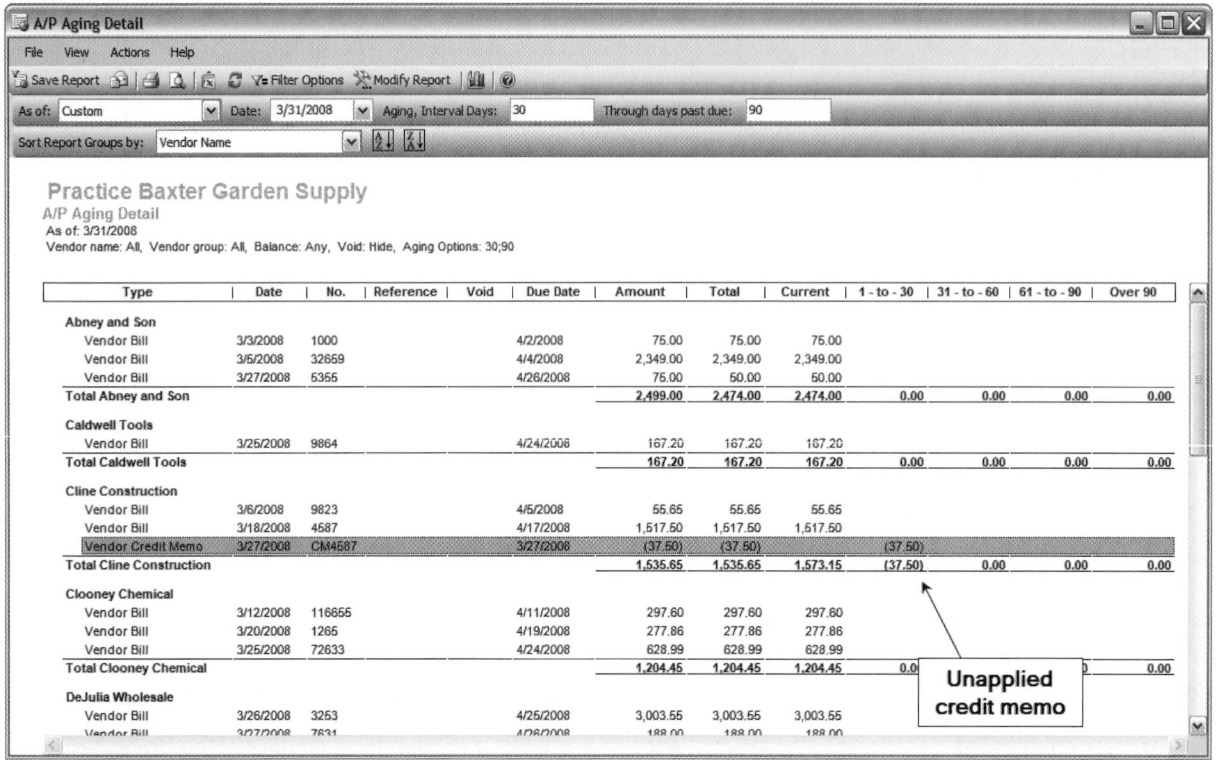

Practice Baxter Garden Supply
A/P Aging Detail
As of: 3/31/2008
Vendor name: All, Vendor group: All, Balance: Any, Void: Hide, Aging Options: 30;90

Type	Date	No.	Reference	Void	Due Date	Amount	Total	Current	1 - to - 30	31 - to - 60	61 - to - 90	Over 90
Abney and Son												
Vendor Bill	3/3/2008	1000			4/2/2008	75.00	75.00	75.00				
Vendor Bill	3/5/2008	32659			4/4/2008	2,349.00	2,349.00	2,349.00				
Vendor Bill	3/27/2008	5355			4/26/2008	75.00	50.00	50.00				
Total Abney and Son						2,499.00	2,474.00	2,474.00	0.00	0.00	0.00	0.00
Caldwell Tools												
Vendor Bill	3/25/2008	9864			4/24/2008	167.20	167.20	167.20				
Total Caldwell Tools						167.20	167.20	167.20	0.00	0.00	0.00	0.00
Cline Construction												
Vendor Bill	3/6/2008	9823			4/5/2008	55.65	55.65	55.65				
Vendor Bill	3/18/2008	4587			4/17/2008	1,517.50	1,517.50	1,517.50				
Vendor Credit Memo	3/27/2008	CM4587			3/27/2008	(37.50)	(37.50)		(37.50)			
Total Cline Construction						1,535.65	1,535.65	1,573.15	(37.50)	0.00	0.00	0.00
Clooney Chemical												
Vendor Bill	3/12/2008	116655			4/11/2008	297.60	297.60	297.60				
Vendor Bill	3/20/2008	1265			4/19/2008	277.86	277.86	277.86				
Vendor Bill	3/25/2008	72633			4/24/2008	628.99	628.99	628.99				
Total Clooney Chemical						1,204.45	1,204.45	1,204.45	0.0			0.00
DeJulia Wholesale												
Vendor Bill	3/26/2008	3253			4/25/2008	3,003.55	3,003.55	3,003.55				

Figure 9:71

Close the aging report and open the **1099 Summary** report (not illustrated). This report will list payments to vendors marked for 1099 reporting when payments to the vendor equal or exceed the $600 reporting threshold. Remember 1099 reporting requirements are set by the IRS.

Close the report.

Purchase and Inventory Activity Reporting

In addition to monitoring accounts payable, companies also analyze purchasing activities and inventory turnover. On the Vendors Home page, change the reporting category to **Purchases** and click the dropdown list on **Select a report** to view purchasing reports that can be printed to analyze vendor purchases.

The Purchases by Vendor report will help analyze the volume of items purchased from vendors. If a company finds large volumes of purchases with specific vendors then it can possibly negotiate more favorable discount terms or preferred pricing discounts.

Now change the report type to **Inventory**. These reports analyze inventory turnover and stock status. In addition, Chapter 8 illustrated using inventory reports to reconcile inventory activities to the general ledger inventory control account.

Remember that OAP reports can be exported to Excel. After exporting, financial data can be further analyzed such as calculating inventory turnover ratios.

The key point to remember is reports form the basis for analyzing company performance. Take time to open each inventory and purchase report to understand the wide range of information available through reports.

You have now completed the chapter. ***Make a backup of the Practice Baxter Garden Supply data file to a backup file named "practicebaxtergardensupply Chpt 9." In the next chapter, you will build on the work completed in this chapter.***

Summary

You began the chapter by learning to post transactions in a manual accounting system and then posted the *MAPS* transactions in OAP. After each posting exercise, you were taken *Behind the Keys* to trace the effect of these transactions on financial accounts. You also learned to use the Vendors Home page for processing vendor activities.

You have recorded POs and receipts of items on a PO. You have posted vendor bills for receipts and vendor bills for expenses. You also paid vendors, voided payments, and recorded vendor credits.

Finally, you reconciled vendor transactions to the general ledger and were exposed to a variety of accounts payable, purchasing, and inventory reports that analyze activities. You are now ready to focus on the payroll activities covered in Chapter 10.

END-OF-CHAPTER QUESTIONS

TRUE/FALSE

_____ 1. A posted vendor receipt can be located on the Purchase Order List.

_____ 2. You can enter a receipt for vendor shipments by selecting the purchase order.

_____ 3. You can correct a vendor bill that has been paid.

_____ 4. Vendor bills for expenses are entered as item receipts.

_____ 5. When recording an item receipt, you first verify that quantities ordered were received.

_____ 6. OAP marks a PO as Received when you transfer it to a receipt.

_____ 7. After posting a vendor bill for an item receipt, the receipt is replaced by the vendor bill.

_____ 8. You can reopen a vendor transaction using the vendor account.

_____ 9. A PO list can be exported to Excel.

_____ 10. You must delete the check transaction to correct paying the wrong vendor.

MULTIPLE CHOICE

_____ 1. OAP posts entries for an item receipt as a _____.

a. debit to inventory and credit to accounts payable
b. debit to inventory, credit to accounts payable, and debit to cost of goods sold
c. debit to inventory and credit to pending item receipts
d. debit to pending item receipts and credit to accounts payable

_____ 2. OAP posts entries for vendor payments as a_____.

a. debit to inventory and credit to cash
b. debit to cash and credit to accounts payable
c. credit to cash and debit to accounts payable
d. credit to cash and debit to pending item receipts

_____ 3. OAP posts entries for a PO as a _____.
   a. credit to inventory and debit to accounts payable
   b. debit to inventory and credit to accounts payable
   c. debit to inventory and credit to pending items receipts
   d. none of the above

_____ 4. You can locate inventory items that need to be reordered by reviewing the _____.
   a. Item List
   b. Inventory Stock Status by Item report
   c. Inventory Valuation report
   d. both a and b

_____ 5. Payments to vendors can be reduced in the _____ window.
   a. Payments
   b. Pay Bills
   c. Print Checks
   d. all of the above

_____ 6. Recurring transactions are located under _____.
   a. ***Reports>>>Recurring Documents***
   b. Recurring Documents link under Find
   c. ***View>>Recurring Documents***
   d. Recurring Documents link under Find

_____ 7. Purchase orders that are marked as Received are found _____.
   a. on the Purchase Order List filtered for All
   b. on the Purchase Order List filtered for Received
   c. on a vendor's account
   d. all of the above

Practice Set

In this Practice Set you will be using the **Graded Baxter Garden Supply** data file with the tasks completed in the Practice Set at the end of Chapter 8. ***When this data file is not loaded on your computer, restore it using the "gradedbaxtergardensupply Chpt 8" backup file created after completing the Chapter 8 Practice Set.***

1. Open **Graded Baxter Garden Supply**. Print documents only when instructed. All reports will be printed in Step 2.

2008

Apr 1 Post a bill for $600.00 to Mills Leasing for monthly office rent. Turn this bill into a recurring transaction.

Post a bill from Safe State Insurance dated April 1 for $600.00 for 6 months of prepaid vehicle insurance.

Apr 4 Create and print the following POs. Do not use the Inventory Reorder feature so click Cancel if prompted with the window.

PO 1 for $602.25 to Cline Construction for the following items.

Item	Short Description	Qty	Unit Price
AVRY-10200-2ft-GRN	Birdbath 2ft Green	25	$ 12.50
AVRY-10200-2ft-WHTE	Birdbath 2ft White	25	$ 11.59

PO 2 for $1,035.00 to Abney and Son for the following items.

Item	Short Description	Qty	Unit Price
AVRY-10050-LG-CSL	Birdhouse-Large Castle	30	$ 17.25
AVRY-10050-LG-HTL	Birdhouse-Large Hotel	30	$ 17.25

PO 3 for $557.25 to DeJulia Wholesale for the following items.

Item	Short Description	Qty	Unit Price
TOOL-35520	Hedge Shears	25	$ 7.95
TOOL-35530	Pruning Shears	30	$ 11.95

PO 4 for $935.00 to Clooney Chemical for the following items *Note: Price may have changed.*

Item	Short Description	Qty	Unit Price
EQFF-13100	Fertilizer Pump Sprayer	20	$ 17.00
EQFF-13110	Fertilizer Comp. Sprayer	35	$ 17.00

Apr 9 Post the following receipts and bills.

DeJulia Wholesale receipt number RCT6932, $557.25, for all items on PO 3 issued April 4.

Abney and Son Invoice INV871 dated April 7, $1,035.00, for all items on PO 2 issued April 4.

Apr 10 Post the following receipts and bills.

DeJulia Wholesale Invoice INV3030 dated April 10, $557.25, for receipt number RCT6932

Clooney Chemical Invoice INV3031 dated April 10, $850.00, for the following items received on PO 4 issued April 4. *Note: Not all items received.*

Item	Short Description	Qty	Unit Price
EQFF-13100	Fertilizer Pump Sprayer	15	$ 17.00
EQFF-13110	Fertilizer Comp. Sprayer	35	$ 17.00

Cline Construction receipt number RCT321, $602.25, for all items on PO 1 issued April 4.

Apr 14 Post Cline Construction Invoice 1315 dated April 11, $602.25, for receipt number RCT321.

Post Cline Construction credit memo CM1315 dated April 13, $62.50, for returning 5 AVRY-10200-2ft-GRN on Invoice 1315.

Apr 15 Post Clooney Chemical Invoice 2351 dated April 14, $85.00, for the 5 remaining items of EQFF-13100 on PO 4 issued April 5.

Apr 16 Pay vendors for bills due by April 23 plus pay DeJulia Wholesale Invoice INV3030 carrying a discount. Remember to click Calculate Discount. Total payments equal $22,725.85. Print on first check number 286.

Apr 18 Post the following bills for expenses dated April 18.

Southern Power	April electricity	$153.00
Neighbors Telephone	April telephone	$205.00
Arlington Water	April water	$125.00

Apr 22 Write and print check number 300 to Postmaster for postage expense, $250.00. You can add this account "on the fly" using the following information.

Address:	317 W. Main St, Arlington, VA 23135
Expense account:	Postage Expense
Vendor group:	Admin

Apr 23 Issue PO 5 for $679.50 to Southern Garden for the following items.

Item	Short Description	Qty	Unit Price
EQWT-15120	Garden Hose 75 ft.	20	$ 15.95
EQWT-15130	Hose Hanger-Wall Mount	15	$ 7.95
EQWT-15170	Sprinkler Oscillating	25	$ 9.65

PO 6 for $856.50 to Clooney Chemical for the following items.

Item	Short Description	Qty	Unit Price
NURS-21810	Rose – Yellow Seeds	40	$ 5.10
NURS-21820	Rose – White Seeds	25	$ 5.10
NURS-22000	Ginko Tree 14-16 ft.	30	$ 17.50

PO 7 for $78.00 to DeJulia Wholesale for the following items.

Item	Short Description	Qty	Unit Price
TOOL-35280	Garden Hand Trowel	15	$ 5.20

Pay vendors for bills with a due date on or before May 3 plus Cline Construction Invoice 1315 reduced for the outstanding credit memo. Total payments equal $17,975.14. Print on first check number is 301.

Apr 24 Create the following new vendor account.

Wilmort Hotel
173 E. Rutherford St.
Newport, RI 32653
Telephone: (800) 555-1353

Expense account: Travel Expense
Payment terms: Net 15
Vendor group: Admin

Post the following bills dated April 23.

Wilmort Hotel, Invoice 2353	April travel expense	$ 225.00
Office Maxter, Invoice IV3131	Office supply expense	$ 108.00
Juan Motor Tools, Invoice 3089	Auto repairs	$ 325.00
Kidd Computers, Invoice IVB431	Repair computer	$ 178.25

Apr 25 Post DeJulia Wholesale receipt number RCT8032, $78.00, for all items on PO 7 issued April 23.

Apr 28 Post Southern Garden Invoice IVC686 dated April 28, $615.70 for the following items on PO 5 issued April 23. *Note: Not all items received.*

Item	Short Description	Qty	Unit Price
EQWT-15120	Garden Hose 75 ft.	16	$ 15.95
EQWT-15130	Hose Hanger-Wall Mount	15	$ 7.95
EQWT-15170	Sprinkler Oscillating	25	$ 9.65

Apr 30 Print check number 309 for $1,758.41 for sales tax due through May 1.

2. Print the following reports to document April vendor transactions.

   a. Transaction Journal listing April 1 through April 30 transactions and filtered for the transaction types of Item Receipt, Purchase Order, Vendor Bill, Vendor Credit Memo, and Vendor Payment.

   b. Detailed A/P Aging report at April 30, 2008. Explain how you would use this report.

   c. Vendor Payments report for April 1 through April 30 modified to remove the Issue Date, Status Detail, Reference number, and Void columns.

3. ***Back up the Graded Baxter Garden Supply data file to a backup file named "gradedbaxtergardensupply Chpt 9." The Practice Set for the next chapter will build on the work completed in this chapter.***

CHAPTER 10 PAYROLL ACTIVITIES FOR A MERCHANDISING BUSINESS

LEARNING OBJECTIVES

This chapter works with the **Practice Baxter Garden Supply** data file containing the tasks completed in Chapter 9. ***When this data file is not loaded on your computer, restore it using the "practicebaxtergardensupply Chpt 9" backup file created after reading Chapter 9.***

In this chapter, you will process Baxter's payroll and:

1. Learn *MAPS* for employee paychecks before processing paychecks in OAP
2. Use the Employee Home page to manage employees and process paychecks
3. Calculate, print, and post employee paychecks
4. Go *Behind the Keys* of posted paychecks
5. Correct a posted paycheck
6. Remit payroll tax liabilities to government taxing agencies

Launch OAP and open **Practice Baxter Garden Supply**.

MANUAL ACCOUNTING PROCEDURES

Baxter pays employees biweekly (every two weeks) so the number of pay periods for the year is 26 (i.e., 52 weeks divided by 2). Employees are paid either an annual salary or an hourly wage. Salaried employees receive the same gross pay amount each pay period, which is calculated by dividing the annual salary by the number of pay periods in the year. Hourly employees are paid for the hours worked during the pay period and these employees turn in timesheets to document those hours.

You will soon learn that payroll in a manual accounting system is tedious and time consuming. You must first calculate each hourly employee's gross pay by totaling timesheet hours for the pay period and multiplying total hours by the hourly pay rate. As explained above, salaried employees receive the same gross pay each pay period.

After calculating gross pay, you then calculate each employee's net pay. Net pay equals gross pay minus total payroll tax withholdings and voluntary deductions. The following tables explain payroll tax withholdings and voluntary deductions.

Employee Tax Withholdings	**Description**
Federal Income Tax	Employee federal income taxes withheld on taxable wages. Taxable wages exclude employee contributions to a 401K or IRA retirement plan. IRS Circular E sets the guidelines for withholding federal income taxes (explained below).
Social Security (FICA)	Employee taxes withheld on gross wages and paid to the federal government to fund Social Security retirement. Gross wages include employee contributions to a 401K or IRA retirement plan. The IRS currently taxes gross wages at 6.2 percent (0.062) until wages paid during the year exceed an annual cap. For 2007, the annual cap was $97,500. This cap is increased each year and the 2008 cap was not available at the time of publishing the text.
Medicare	Employee taxes withheld on gross wages and paid to the federal government to fund Medicare health insurance. Gross wages include employee contributions to a 401K or IRA retirement plan. The IRS taxes gross wages at 1.45 percent (0.0145) and there is no annual wage cap.
State Income Tax	Employee state income taxes withheld on taxable wages (i.e., gross wages minus contributions to a 401K or IRA retirement plan). Each state publishes guidelines for withholding state income taxes. ***Baxter withholds 3 percent (0.03) of gross wages.***

Employee Voluntary Deductions	Description
Retirement Plans	Employee voluntary contributions to an employer-sponsored retirement plan. Retirement plans include 401K and IRA plans. These contributions are deducted from gross wages to determine federal and state taxable wages. ***Baxter sponsors a 401K retirement plan and employees may elect to participate.***
Health Insurance	Health insurance premiums deducted from net pay when the employer requires its employees to pay for a portion of health insurance costs. ***Baxter does not require employees to share this cost.***
Contributions	Deductions from net pay for charitable contributions made by the employee.

Baxter also pays taxes on employee compensation and provides additional compensation by paying the full cost of health insurance and matching employee contributions to a company sponsored 401K plan. The next tables explain typical employer tax liabilities and other forms of additional employee compensation.

Employer Payroll Taxes	Description
Social Security (FICA) and Medicare	Employer portion of Social Security and Medicare taxes paid on gross wages. The employer tax equals the tax paid by employees.
Federal Unemployment (FUTA)	Employer tax on gross wages paid to the federal government for subsidizing state unemployment compensation funds. Typically, employers pay 0.08 percent (0.008) on the first $7,000 of annual gross wages paid to each employee.
State Unemployment (SUTA)	Employer tax on gross wages paid to the state for funding compensation for unemployed workers. Typically the tax rate is based on an employer's unemployment history and/or business type and will be capped after reaching an annual limit on gross wages. ***For Baxter the rate is 1.5 percent (0.015) of the first $8,000 of annual wages paid to each employee.***
Worker's Compensation	Employer tax paid to the state to fund compensating injured workers. Typically, states set the tax rates based on risk factors in an employee's job. ***The text does not illustrate worker's compensation tax.***

Additional Compensation	Description
Retirement Plans	Employer contributions to a company-sponsored 401K or IRA retirement plan. Typically companies match contributions based on employee participation in the plan. ***Baxter's matches employee 401K contributions $.50 for every dollar contributed by the employee, up to a maximum of 5 percent (0.05) of the employee's annual pay.***
Health Insurance	Employer premiums for health insurance. Employers may pay all premiums or require employees to share in this cost. ***Baxter pays all health insurance premiums for employees eligible to participate in the plan.***

Each pay period the accountant prepares the following Excel spreadsheet called the Payroll Register. The register illustrated in Figure 10:1 covers the pay period of February 25 to March 9, 2008.

	A	B	C	D	E	F	G	H	I	J	K	L	M	N	O	P
1	**Baxter Garden Supply**															
2	**Pay Period 2/25/2008 thru 3/09/2008**															
3																
4	**Check No.**	**Employee**	**Filing Status**	**Allow**	**Pay Type**	**Pay Rate**	**Regular Hrs**	**OT Hrs**	**Gross Pay**	**Taxable Pay**	**Federal Income Tax**	**Soc. Sec. (FICA) Tax**	**Medicare Tax**	**VA State Tax**	**401K Deduc.**	**Net Pay**
5	1180	Barkley, Steve N.	Married	3	Hourly wage	11.00	80.00		880.00	844.80	15.00	54.56	12.76	25.34	35.20	737.14
6	1181	Beck, Dorothy L.	Married	2	Hourly wage	9.00	80.00		720.00	720.00	16.00	44.64	10.44	21.60	0.00	627.32
7	1182	Chester, Amanda W.	Single	1	Hourly wage	14.00	80.00		1,120.00	1,075.20	111.00	69.44	16.24	32.26	44.80	846.26
8	1183	Duke, Al C.	Single	0	Hourly wage	12.50	80.00		1,000.00	1,000.00	122.00	62.00	14.50	30.00	0.00	771.50
9	1184	Frost, Melvin H.	Single	1	Salary	1,461.54			1,461.54	1,373.85	159.00	90.62	21.19	41.22	87.69	1,061.82
10	1185	Gross, Derrick P.	Married	2	Salary	1,000.00			1,000.00	940.00	38.00	62.00	14.50	28.20	60.00	797.30
11	1186	Hecter, Anthony H.	Single	1	Hourly wage	13.00	80.00		1,040.00	1,040.00	108.00	64.48	15.08	31.20	0.00	821.24
12	1187	Nunnley, Brandee M.	Married	1	Salary	1,211.54			1,211.54	1,211.54	86.00	75.12	17.57	36.35	0.00	996.50
13	1188	Prather, Samuel R.	Married	1	Salary	1,584.62			1,584.62	1,489.54	128.00	98.25	22.98	44.69	95.08	1,195.62
14	1189	Sweet, Leonard	Single	0	Hourly wage	9.00	80.00		720.00	720.00	80.00	44.64	10.44	21.60	0.00	563.32
15	1190	Trotter, Mitchell K.	Married	2	Hourly wage	11.00	80.00		880.00	844.80	28.00	54.56	12.76	25.34	35.20	724.14
16																
17		**Totals**					**560.00**	**0.00**	**11,617.70**		**891.00**	**720.31**	**168.46**	**337.80**	**357.97**	**9,142.16**
18																
19		**Tax Basis**									**Circular E**	**6.20%**	**1.45%**	**3.00%**		
20																
21		**G/L Accounts**							**60000**		**23400**	**23400**	**23400**	**23600**	**23300**	**10300**
22																

Figure 10:1

The Payroll Register shows that Amanda Chester claims the Single (S) federal filing status with one withholding allowance. To calculate Amanda's federal income tax withholding for this pay period look to the 2007 IRS Circular E tax table in Figure 10:2. *(Note: IRS tables for 2008 were not available at the time of publishing the text.)*

SINGLE Persons—BIWEEKLY Payroll Period
(For Wages Paid in 2007)

f the wages are–		And the number of withholding allowances claimed is—										
At least	But less than	0	1	2	3	4	5	6	7	8	9	10
		The amount of income tax to be withheld is—										
$800	$820	$92	$72	$53	$33	$19	$5	$0	$0	$0	$0	$0
820	840	95	75	56	36	21	7	0	0	0	0	0
840	860	98	78	59	39	23	9	0	0	0	0	0
860	880	101	81	62	42	25	11	0	0	0	0	0
880	900	104	84	65	45	27	13	0	0	0	0	0
900	920	107	87	68	48	29	15	2	0	0	0	0
920	940	110	90	71	51	31	17	4	0	0	0	0
940	960	113	93	74	54	34	19	6	0	0	0	0
960	980	116	96	77	57	37	21	8	0	0	0	0
980	1,000	119	99	80	60	40	23	10	0	0	0	0
1,000	1,020	122	102	83	63	43	25	12	0	0	0	0
1,020	1,040	125	105	86	66	46	27	14	1	0	0	0
1,040	1,060	128	108	89	69	49	30	16	3	0	0	0
1,060	1,080	131	111	92	72	52	33	18	5	0	0	0
1,080	1,100	134	114	95	75	55	36	20	7	0	0	0
1,100	1,120	137	117	98	78	58	39	22	9	0	0	0
1,120	1,140	140	120	101	81	61	42	24	11	0	0	0
1,140	1,160	143	123	104	84	64	45	26	13	0	0	0
1,160	1,180	146	126	107	87	67	48	28	15	2	0	0
1,180	1,200	149	129	110	90	70	51	31	17	4	0	0
1,200	1,220	152	132	113	93	73	54	34	19	6	0	0
1,220	1,240	155	135	116	96	76	57	37	21	8	0	0
1,240	1,260	158	138	119	99	79	60	40	23	10	0	0
1,260	1,280	161	141	122	102	82	63	43	25	12	0	0
1,280	1,300	164	144	125	105	85	66	46	27	14	1	0
1,300	1,320	169	147	128	108	88	69	49	30	16	3	0
1,320	1,340	174	150	131	111	91	72	52	33	18	5	0
1,340	1,360	179	153	134	114	94	75	55	36	20	7	0
1,360	1,380	184	156	137	117	97	78	58	39	22	9	0
1,380	1,400	189	159	140	120	100	81	61	42	24	11	0

Figure 10:2

Figure 10:2 is the IRS table for employees paid biweekly and claiming the Single (S) filing status. There are separate IRS tables for employees claiming the Married (M) filing status and separate tables for married and single employees paid on a weekly or monthly basis.

Amanda's $111.00 federal income tax withholding amount is found at the point where her taxable pay of $1,075.20 intersects with her one claimed withholding allowance. Federal income taxes are calculated on taxable pay, which is equal to gross pay minus 401K deductions.

Amanda's FICA tax withholding of $69.44 equals her gross pay times 6.2 percent (.062). Her Medicare tax withholding of $16.24 equals gross pay times 1.45 percent (.0145). *(Note: 401K contributions are not deducted from FICA and Medicare tax calculations.)*

The state tax withholding amount of $32.26 is based on state tax rates of 3 percent (.03) of taxable pay. 401K contributions are deducted from gross pay to determine taxable pay for state purposes.

Baxter sponsors a 401K retirement plan that allows employees to elect participation by contributing a percentage of gross pay. Employees can choose to contribute any percentage up to 11 percent of gross pay and Baxter will match contributions by the same percentage up to 5 percent of gross pay. Amanda has chosen to contribute 4 percent (.04) of gross pay each pay period.

Amanda has no deductions for health insurance premiums or charitable contributions. In fact, premiums are not deducted from any employee's paycheck because Baxter pays the full cost of health insurance. Finally, there are no employees making charitable contributions through payroll.

Accordingly, Amanda's net pay of $846.26 equals her gross pay of $1,120.00 minus the sum of her tax withholdings and voluntary deductions.

In addition to preparing the payroll register, the accountant computes the following employer payroll tax liabilities for the pay period.

	R	S	T	U	V	W	X
1	**Baxter Garden Supply**						
2	**Employer Costs for Period 2/25/2008 thru 3/09/2008**						
3							
4	**Employee**	**401K Match**	**ER Soc. Sec. (FICA)**	**ER Medicare**	**ER FUTA**	**ER SUTA**	**Health Insurance**
5	Barkley, Steve N.	17.60	54.56	12.76	7.04	13.20	125.00
6	Beck, Dorothy L.	0.00	44.64	10.44	5.76	10.80	0.00
7	Chester, Amanda W.	22.40	69.44	16.24	8.96	16.80	90.00
8	Duke, Al C.	0.00	62.00	14.50	8.00	15.00	90.00
9	Frost, Melvin H.	43.85	90.62	21.19	4.58	21.92	125.00
10	Gross, Derrick P.	30.00	62.00	14.50	8.00	15.00	90.00
11	Hecter, Anthony H.	0.00	64.48	15.08	8.32	15.60	90.00
12	Nunnley, Brandee M.	0.00	75.12	17.57	9.69	18.17	125.00
13	Prather, Samuel R.	47.54	98.25	22.98	0.00	23.77	125.00
14	Sweet, Leonard	0.00	44.64	10.44	5.76	10.80	90.00
15	Trotter, Mitchell K.	17.60	54.56	12.76	7.04	13.20	90.00
16							
17	**Totals**	**178.99**	**720.31**	**168.46**	**73.15**	**174.26**	**1,040.00**
18							
19	**Tax Basis**	**50% Match**	**6.20%**	**1.45%**	**0.8%**	**1.5%**	
20							
21	**G/L Accounts**	**23300 / 60500**	**23400 / 61000**	**23400 / 61000**	**23500 / 61000**	**23700 / 61000**	**23750 / 60600**

Figure 10:3

After computing employee pay and employer payroll tax expenses, the accountant creates paychecks and records the general journal entries illustrated in Figure 10:4.

Audit trail

Baxter Garden Supply
General Journal — Page 7

Date	Account Post Ref.	Description	Debit	Credit
3/10/2008	60000	Salaries and Wages Expense	11,617.70	
	23400	Federal Payroll Taxes Payable		1,779.77
	23600	State Payroll Taxes Payable		337.80
	23300	401K Deductions Payable		357.97
	10300	Payroll Checking Account		9,142.16
To record employee paychecks				
3/10/2008	61000	Payroll Tax Expense	1,136.18	
	60500	Pension/Profit-Sharing Expense	178.99	
	60600	Employee Benefits Expense	1,040.00	
	23400	Federal Payroll Taxes Payable		888.77
	23500	FUTA Tax Payable		73.15
	23700	SUTA Tax Payable		174.26
	23300	401K Deductions Payable		178.99
	23750	Health Insurance Payable		1,040.00
To record employer payroll tax and benefit expense				

Figure 10:4

These journal entries are then posted to the general ledger accounts illustrated next. *(Note: Only two general ledger accounts are illustrated.)* As explained in previous chapters, the audit trail is recorded while posting to general ledger accounts.

General Ledger					
Payroll Checking Account			**Account No. 10300**		
Date	**Description**	**Post Ref.**	**Debit**	**Credit**	**Balance**
3/07/2008	Balance Forward				12,097.97
3/10/2008		GJ 7		9,142.16	2,955.81

Audit trail

General Ledger					
Federal Payroll Taxes Payable			**Account No. 23400**		
Date	**Description**	**Post Ref.**	**Debit**	**Credit**	**Balance**
3/07/2008	Balance Forward				0.00
3/10/2008		GJ 7		1,779.77	1,779.77
3/10/2008		GJ 7		888.77	2,668.54

Figure 10:5

With an understanding of *MAPS* for paycheck activities, you are now ready to perform these activities in OAP.

EMPLOYEES MENU AND HOME PAGE

Before processing employee activities become familiar with the commands that initiate activities. The Employees menu is illustrated in Figure 10:6. The first menu choice opens the Employees Home page. There are separate menus for creating employees and timesheets and for entering manual payroll.

Click **Employees Home** on the menu to open the Employees Home page illustrated in Figure 10:7. This page serves as central command for processing employee activities. You can also click the Employees Home page icon to activate this page.

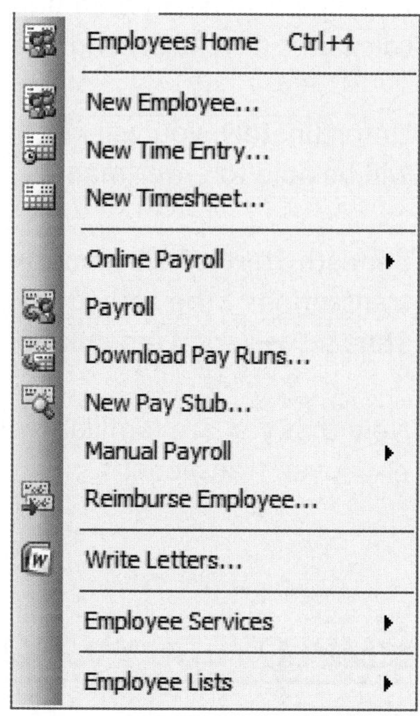

Figure 10:6

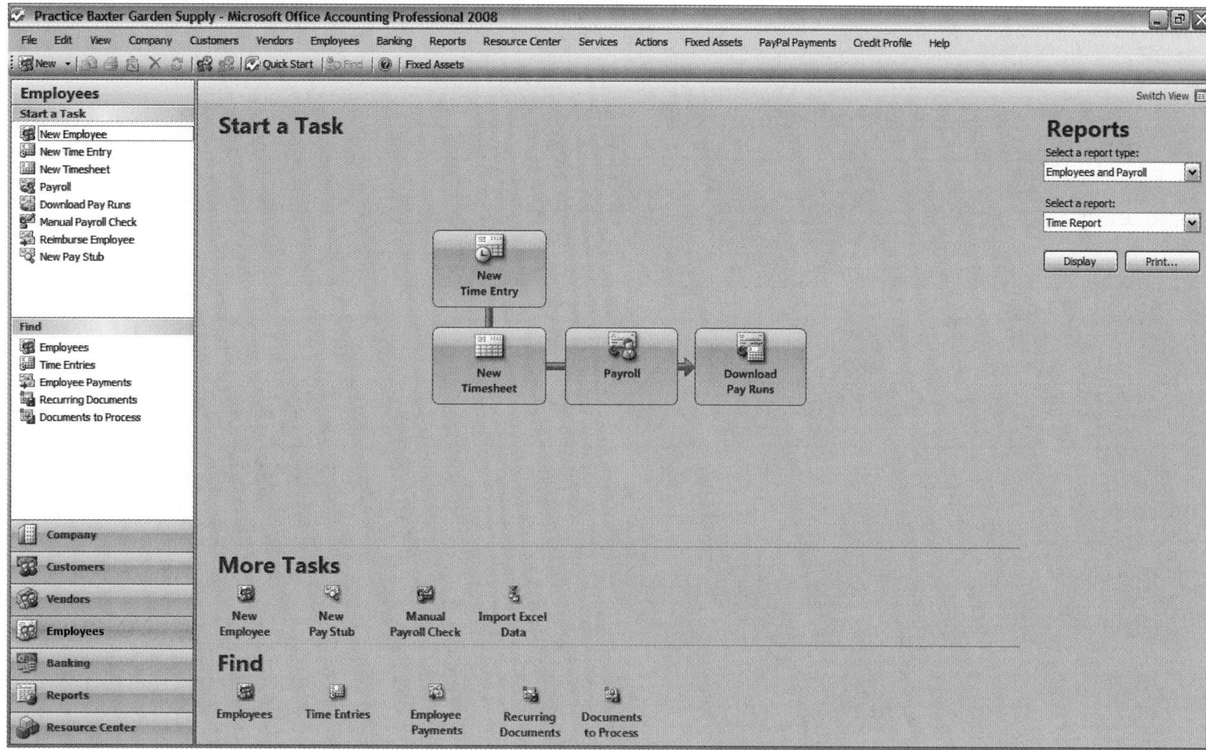

Figure 10:7

You will find that the home page contains links to many of the commands located on the Employees menu. **Start a Task** icons show that employee hours are entered through timesheets and can then be uploaded to ADP's online payroll service. Thereafter, ADP calculates paychecks and sends back pay information for downloading into OAP.

Unfortunately, you will not be able to use this service because it is fee based. However, you will be able to enter manual paycheck information to print paychecks.

Beneath Start a Task icons are the icons for **More Tasks** and opening lists that **Find** posted transactions. The activities located in the center of the home page are replicated under the **Start a Task** and **Find** links located to the left of the page.

Now that you are familiar with the Employees menu and home page let's begin recording employee transactions.

Employees Accounts

Click the **Employees** link under **Find** to open the following Employee List.

Employee List — Current View: Active

	Active	Employee Name	Job Title	Home Phone	Business Phone	Mobile Phone
Add a new Employee						
	✓	Barkley, Steve N.	Warehouse	(770) 555-4547		
	✓	Beck, Dorothy L.	Retail Clerk	(404) 555-5668		
	✓	Chester, Amanda W.	OfficeAdministration	(404) 555-7447		
	✓	Duke, Al C.	Inventory Clerk	(770) 555-3349		
	✓	Frost, Melvin H.	Accountant	(404) 555-4558		
	✓	Gross, Derrick P.	Asst Sales Manager	(770) 555-1392		
	✓	Hecter, Anthony H.	Retail Clerk	(770) 555-4558		
	✓	Nunnley, Brandee M.	Sales Manager	(770) 555-0027		
	✓	Prather, Samuel R.	Owner	(770) 555-0791		
	✓	Sweet, Leonard	Retail Clerk	(770) 555-0005		
	✓	Trotter, Mitchell K.	Shipping	(404) 555-8551		

Figure 10:8

Double click to open Amanda Chester's account and follow below as we explain the fields on an employee account.

General Tab

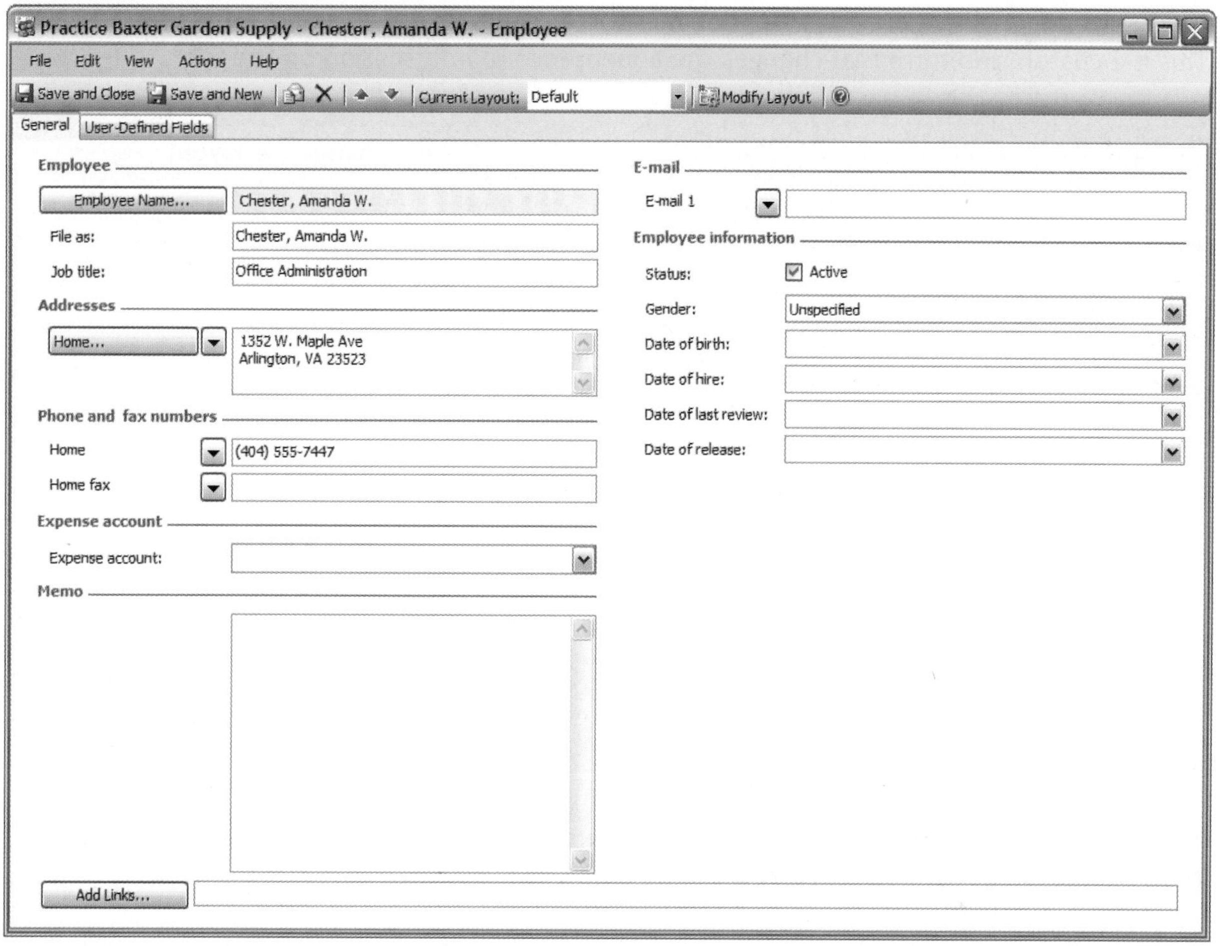

Figure 10:9

This tab stores employee contact information as well as hire, review, and release dates.

User-Defined Fields

After selecting this tab, click the dropdown list on **Current Layout** to select **Employee Form**. This is a customized form that changes the appearance of information on the tab.

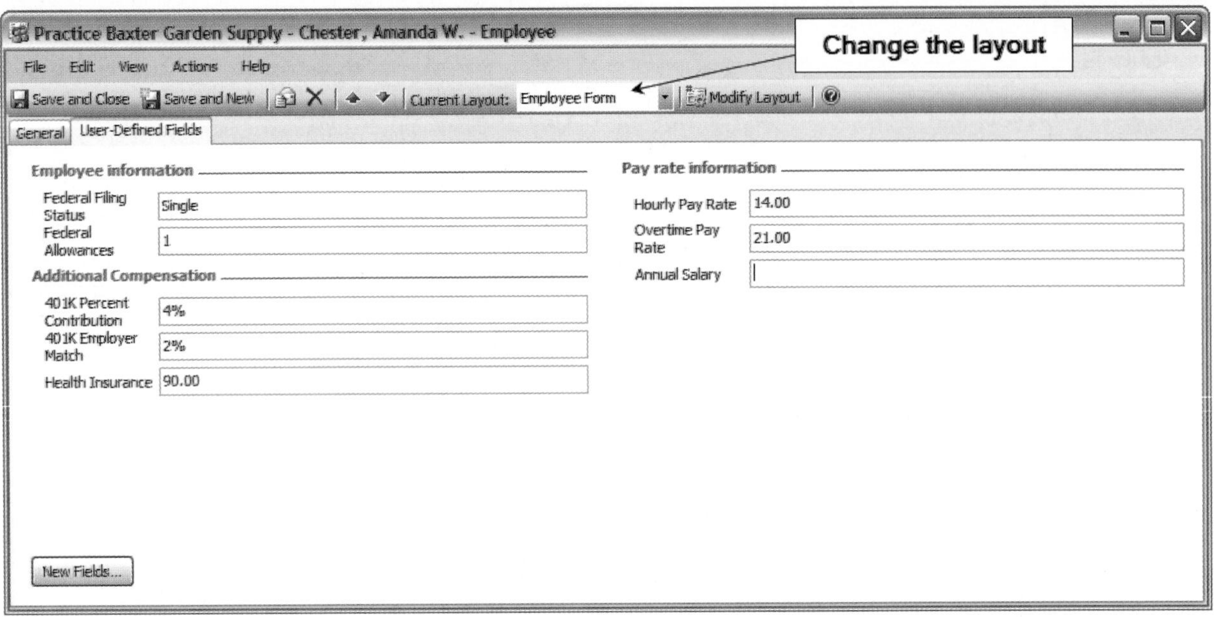

Figure 10:10

These fields are user defined and have been created to store additional payroll information that OAP does not provide for storing on the employee account.

The tab shows that Amanda is paid a regular hourly rate of $14.00 and $21.00 per hour for overtime. She claims the Single federal filing status with one allowance, contributes to the company sponsored 401K plan, and receives employer health insurance benefits.

Click **X** to close Amanda's account and click **No** to saving changes. OAP always issues this prompt even when no changes were made to the account.

Now open Brandee Nunnley's account and activate the User-Defined Fields tab (Figure 10:11).

Practice Baxter Garden Supply - Nunnley, Brandee M. - Employee

File Edit View Actions Help

Save and Close Save and New Current Layout: Employee Form Modify Layout

General User-Defined Fields

Employee information

Federal Filing Status: Married

Federal Allowances: 1

Additional Compensation

401K Percent Contribution:

401K Employer Match:

Health Insurance: 125.00

Pay rate information

Hourly Pay Rate:

Overtime Pay Rate:

Annual Salary: 31,500.00

New Fields...

Figure 10:11

The tab shows that Brandee is a salaried employee and claims the Married federal filing status with one allowance. Click **X** to close the account and **No** to saving changes.

You can delete employee accounts by highlighting an account on the Employee List and clicking X on the toolbar; however, you cannot delete employees with transaction history. If attempting to delete an employee account with history, you will receive the message in Figure 10:12 reminding you to change the account's active status in lieu of deleting.

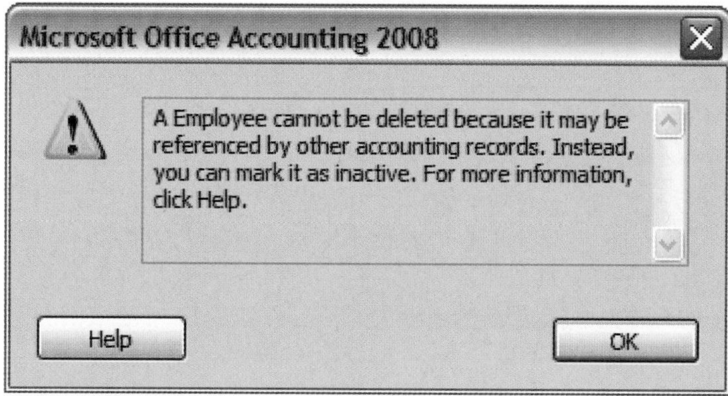

Figure 10:12

MANAGING EMPLOYEES

In this topic you learn to create and terminate employees. Click the **New Employee** link under Start a Task or the **Add a new Employee** link at the top of the Employee List. Baxter has hired Susan Sharpton to work as a retail clerk. Complete the next steps to create the account.

Complete the **General** tab by referring to Figure 10:13.

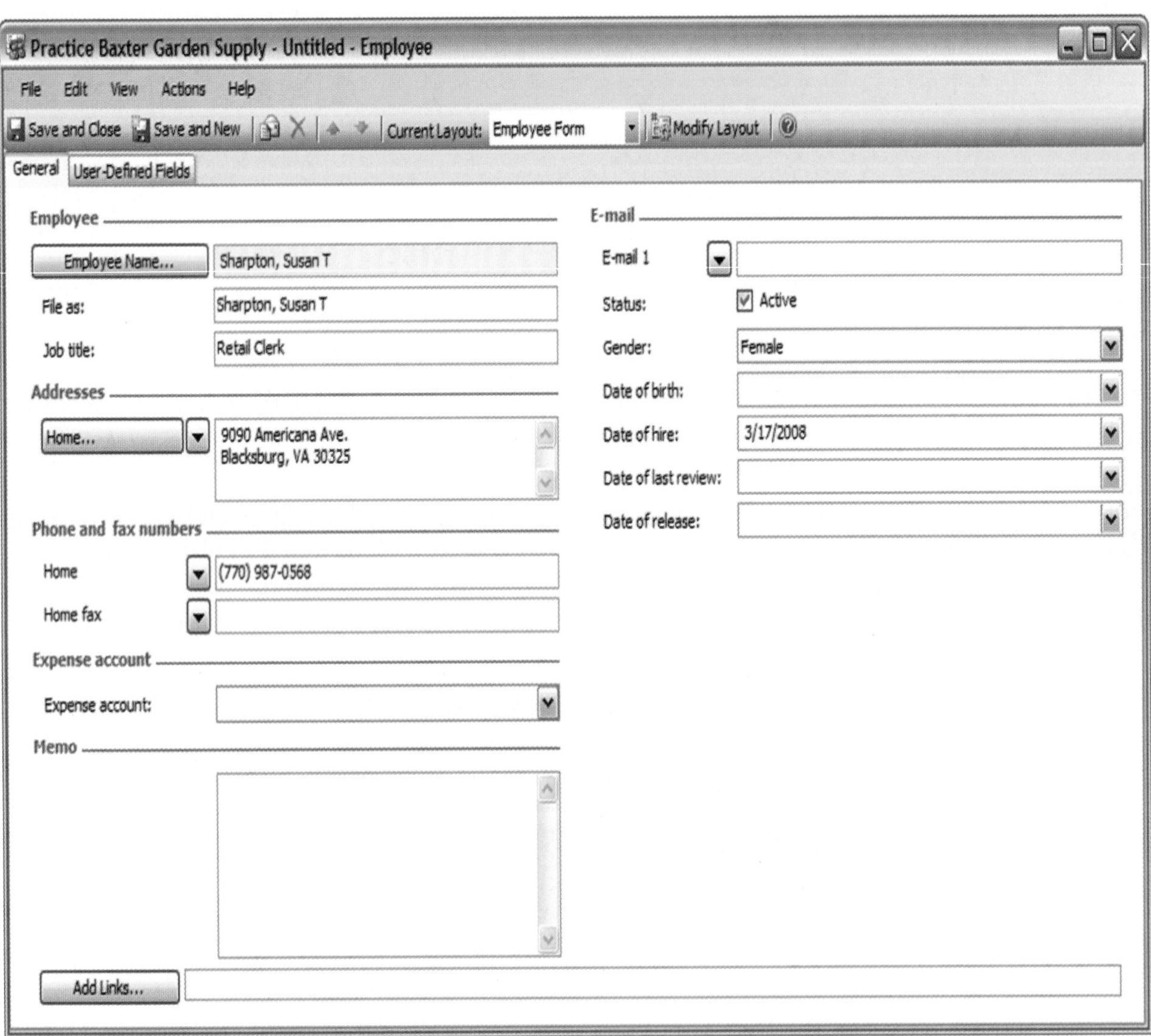

Figure 10:13

Baxter Garden Supply
Pay Period 3/10/2008 thru 3/23/2008

Check No.	Employee	Filing Status	Allow	Pay Type	Pay Rate	Regular Hrs	OT Hrs	Gross Pay	Taxable Pay	Federal Income Tax	Soc. Sec. (FICA) Tax	Medicare Tax	VA State Tax	401K Deduc.	Net Pay
1191	Barkley, Steve N.	Married	3	Hourly wage	11.00	80.00	2.00	913.00	876.48	17.00	56.61	13.24	26.29	36.52	763.34
1192	Beck, Dorothy L.	Married	2	Hourly wage	9.00	80.00		720.00	720.00	16.00	44.64	10.44	21.60	0.00	627.32
1193	Chester, Amanda W.	Single	1	Hourly wage	14.00	80.00		1,120.00	1,075.20	111.00	69.44	16.24	32.26	44.80	846.26
1194	Duke, Al C.	Single	0	Hourly wage	12.50	78.00		975.00	975.00	116.00	60.45	14.14	29.25	0.00	755.16
1195	Frost, Melvin H.	Single	1	Salary	1,461.54			1,461.54	1,373.85	159.00	90.62	21.19	41.22	87.69	1,061.82
1196	Gross, Derrick P.	Married	2	Salary	1,000.00			1,000.00	940.00	38.00	62.00	14.50	28.20	60.00	797.30
1197	Hecter, Anthony H.	Single	1	Hourly wage	13.00	80.00		1,040.00	1,040.00	108.00	64.48	15.08	31.20	0.00	821.24
1198	Nunnley, Brandee M.	Married	1	Salary	1,211.54			1,211.54	1,211.54	86.00	75.12	17.57	36.35	0.00	996.50
1199	Prather, Samuel R.	Married	1	Salary	1,584.62			1,584.62	1,489.54	128.00	98.25	22.98	44.69	95.08	1,195.62
1200	Sharpton, Susan T.	Married	0	Hourly wage	10.50	40.00		420.00	411.60	11.00	26.04	6.09	12.35	8.40	356.12
1201	Sweet, Leonard	Single	0	Hourly wage	9.00	80.00		720.00	720.00	80.00	44.64	10.44	21.60	0.00	563.32
1202	Trotter, Mitchell K.	Married	2	Hourly wage	11.00	80.00		880.00	844.80	28.00	54.56	12.76	25.34	35.20	724.14
	Totals					**598.00**	**2.00**	**12,045.70**		**898.00**	**746.85**	**174.67**	**350.35**	**367.69**	**9,508.14**
	Tax Basis									**Circular E**	**6.20%**	**1.45%**	**3.00%**		
	G/L Accounts							**60000**		**23400**	**23400**	**23400**	**23600**	**23300**	**10300**

Figure 10:15

Baxter Garden Supply
Employer Costs for Period 3/10/2008 thru 3/23/2008

Employee	401K Match	ER Soc. Sec. (FICA)	ER Medicare	ER FUTA	ER SUTA	Health Insurance
Barkley, Steve N.	18.26	56.61	13.24	7.30	13.70	125.00
Beck, Dorothy L.	0.00	44.64	10.44	5.76	10.80	0.00
Chester, Amanda W.	22.40	69.44	16.24	8.96	16.80	90.00
Duke, Al C.	0.00	60.45	14.14	7.80	14.63	90.00
Frost, Melvin H.	43.85	90.62	21.19	0.00	10.40	125.00
Gross, Derrick P.	30.00	62.00	14.50	8.00	15.00	90.00
Hecter, Anthony H.	0.00	64.48	15.08	8.32	15.60	90.00
Nunnley, Brandee M.	0.00	75.12	17.57	7.55	18.17	125.00
Prather, Samuel R.	47.54	98.25	22.98	0.00	1.15	125.00
Sharpton, Susan T.	4.20	26.04	6.09	3.36	6.30	0.00
Sweet, Leonard	0.00	44.64	10.44	5.76	10.80	90.00
Trotter, Mitchell K.	17.60	54.56	12.76	7.04	13.20	90.00
Totals	**183.85**	**746.85**	**174.67**	**69.85**	**146.55**	**1,040.00**
Tax Basis	**50% Match**	**6.20%**	**1.45%**	**0.8%**	**1.5%**	
G/L Accounts	**23300 / 60500**	**23400 / 61000**	**23400 / 61000**	**23500 / 61000**	**23700 / 61000**	**23750 / 60600**

Figure 10:16

Steps to Create Employee Paychecks

1. The accountant has already created recurring employee paychecks so click **Recurring Documents** under Find.

Recurring Documents List

Document Name	Type	Amount	Frequency	Reminder Date
Miles Maintenance Monthly Cleaning	Vendor Bill	$175.00	No Reminder	
401 K Liability Bill (Monthly)	Vendor Bill	$1,073.92	No Reminder	
State Payroll Withholding Bill (Monthly)	Vendor Bill	$675.60	No Reminder	
Health Insurance Bill (Monthly)	Vendor Bill	$2,080.00	No Reminder	
Federal Payroll Tax Bill (Biweekly)	Vendor Bill	$2,668.54	No Reminder	
Paycheck Barkley, Steve N.	Payroll Check	$737.14	No Reminder	
Paycheck Beck, Dorothy L.	Payroll Check	$627.32	No Reminder	
Paycheck Chester, Amanda W.	Payroll Check	$846.26	No Reminder	
Paycheck Duke, Al C.	Payroll Check	$771.50	No Reminder	
Paycheck Frost, Melvin H.	Payroll Check	$1,061.82	No Reminder	
Paycheck Gross, Derrick P.	Payroll Check	$797.30	No Reminder	
Paycheck Hecter, Anthony H.	Payroll Check	$821.24	No Reminder	
Paycheck Nunnley, Brandee M.	Payroll Check	$996.50	No Reminder	
Paycheck Prather, Samuel R.	Payroll Check	$1,195.62	No Reminder	
Paycheck Sweet, Leonard	Payroll Check	$563.32	No Reminder	
Paycheck Trotter, Mitchell K.	Payroll Check	$724.14	No Reminder	
Expense Prepaid Items	Journal Entry	$1,087.00	No Reminder	
Employer Health Insur Liability (Biweekly)	Journal Entry	$1,040.00	No Reminder	
Employer Unemployment Tax and 401K Liab...	Journal Entry	$426.40	No Reminder	
Amortize Organizational Costs	Journal Entry	$83.00	No Reminder	
Montly Depreciation Expense	Journal Entry	$2,818.56	No Reminder	

Recurring paychecks

Figure 10:17

2. Double click **Paycheck Barkley, Steve N.** to open his recurring paycheck.

   Change the **Date** to "3/24/2008" and the **Amount** to $763.34.

   Change the **Memo** to "Pay period Mar 10 to Mar 23, 2008" and click the **To be printed** option.

   Figure 10:18 illustrates the top portion of the check.

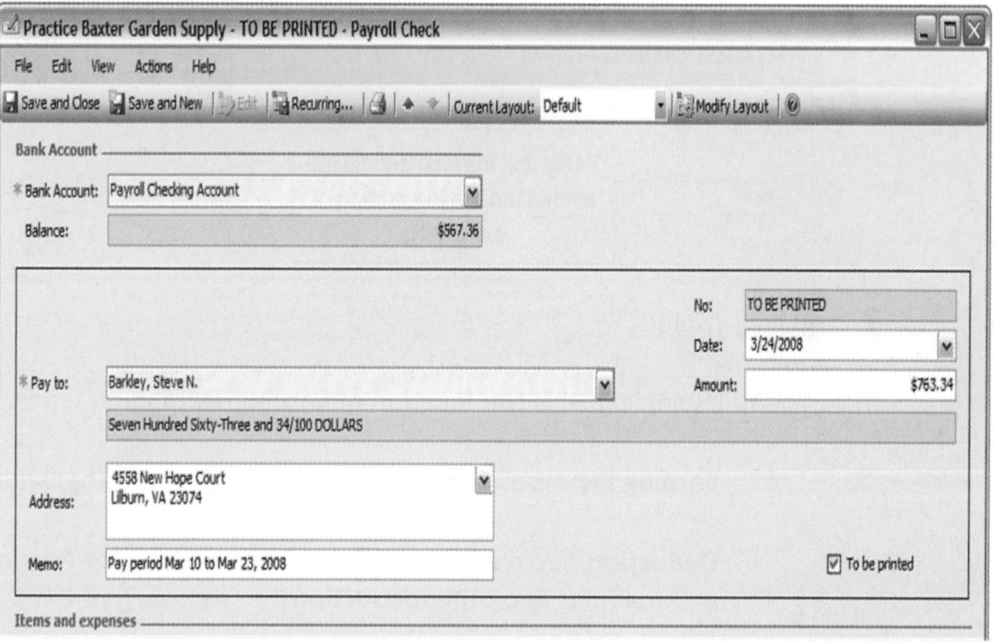

Figure 10:18

3. You will now change information on the bottom. Remember the data are gathered from the Excel spreadsheet. Complete the fields as illustrated in Figure 10:19.

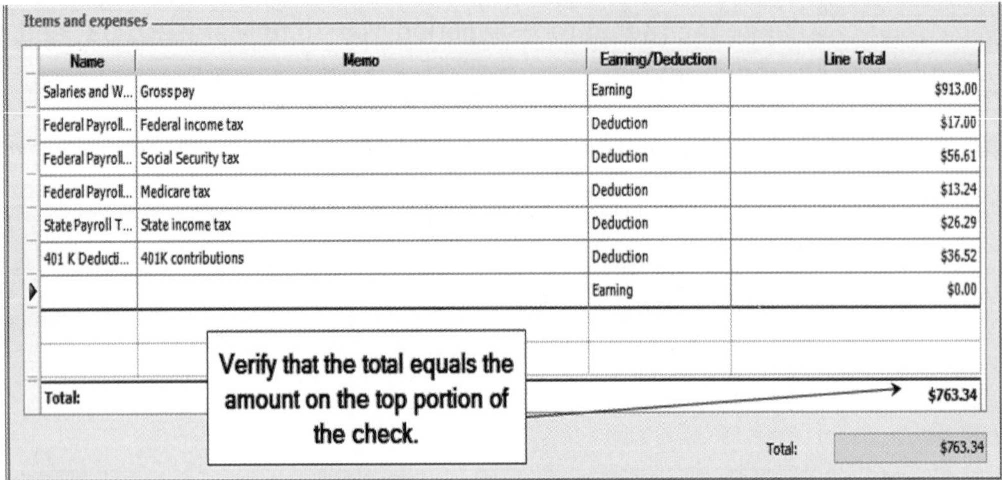
Items and expenses

Name	Memo	Earning/Deduction	Line Total
Salaries and W...	Gross pay	Earning	$913.00
Federal Payroll...	Federal income tax	Deduction	$17.00
Federal Payroll...	Social Security tax	Deduction	$56.61
Federal Payroll...	Medicare tax	Deduction	$13.24
State Payroll T...	State income tax	Deduction	$26.29
401 K Deducti...	401K contributions	Deduction	$36.52
		Earning	$0.00
Total:			$763.34

Total: $763.34

Figure 10:19

The following explains the function of Earning/Deduction types.

Earning increases the paycheck and is used for employee gross pay.

Deduction decreases the paycheck and is used for employee tax withholdings and other deductions.

Total must agree with **Amount** at the top.

4. Click **Save and Close**. You will print the check in a later step. If prompted that the check exceeds the bank balance, mark the option to turn off future messages and click Yes. You will transfer money to this account later in the text. Also, if prompted to link an employee account to an address, click the option to turn off future messages and click Yes.

5. Continue opening recurring paychecks and finish creating paychecks for this pay period by referring to the payroll register illustrated previously and the next series of paycheck illustrations. Some employees will receive the same pay amount as on the recurring check so you need only change the top portion of the check.

   Always remember to change the check date to "3/24/2008" and to confirm the amount. Also change the Memo description to "Pay period Mar 10 to Mar 23, 2008" and mark the **To be printed** option. *(Hint: You can copy and paste the memo description.)*

Paycheck Beck, Dorothy L.

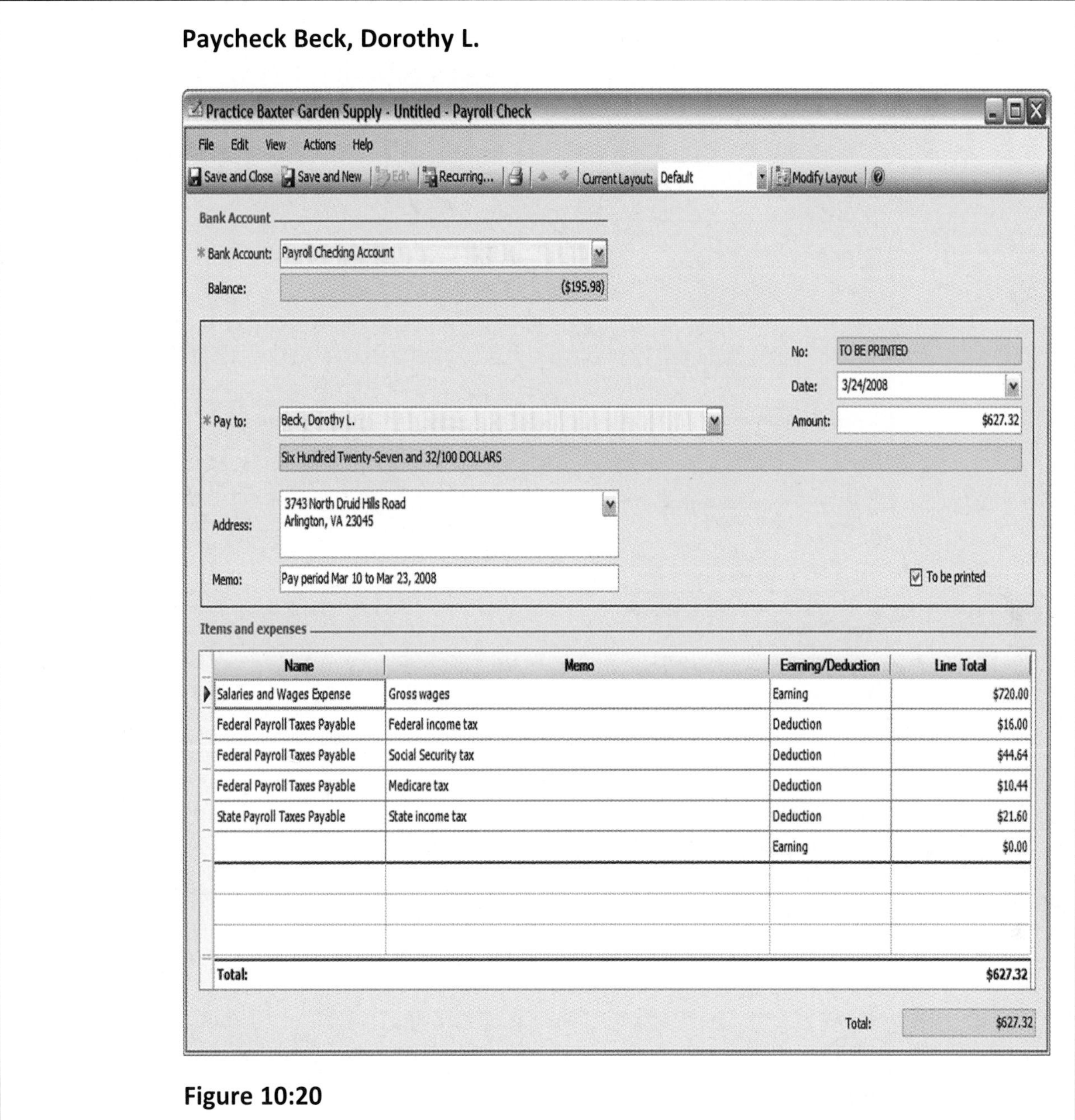

Name	Memo	Earning/Deduction	Line Total
Salaries and Wages Expense	Gross wages	Earning	$720.00
Federal Payroll Taxes Payable	Federal income tax	Deduction	$16.00
Federal Payroll Taxes Payable	Social Security tax	Deduction	$44.64
Federal Payroll Taxes Payable	Medicare tax	Deduction	$10.44
State Payroll Taxes Payable	State income tax	Deduction	$21.60
		Earning	$0.00
Total:			**$627.32**

Figure 10:20

Paycheck Chester, Amanda W.

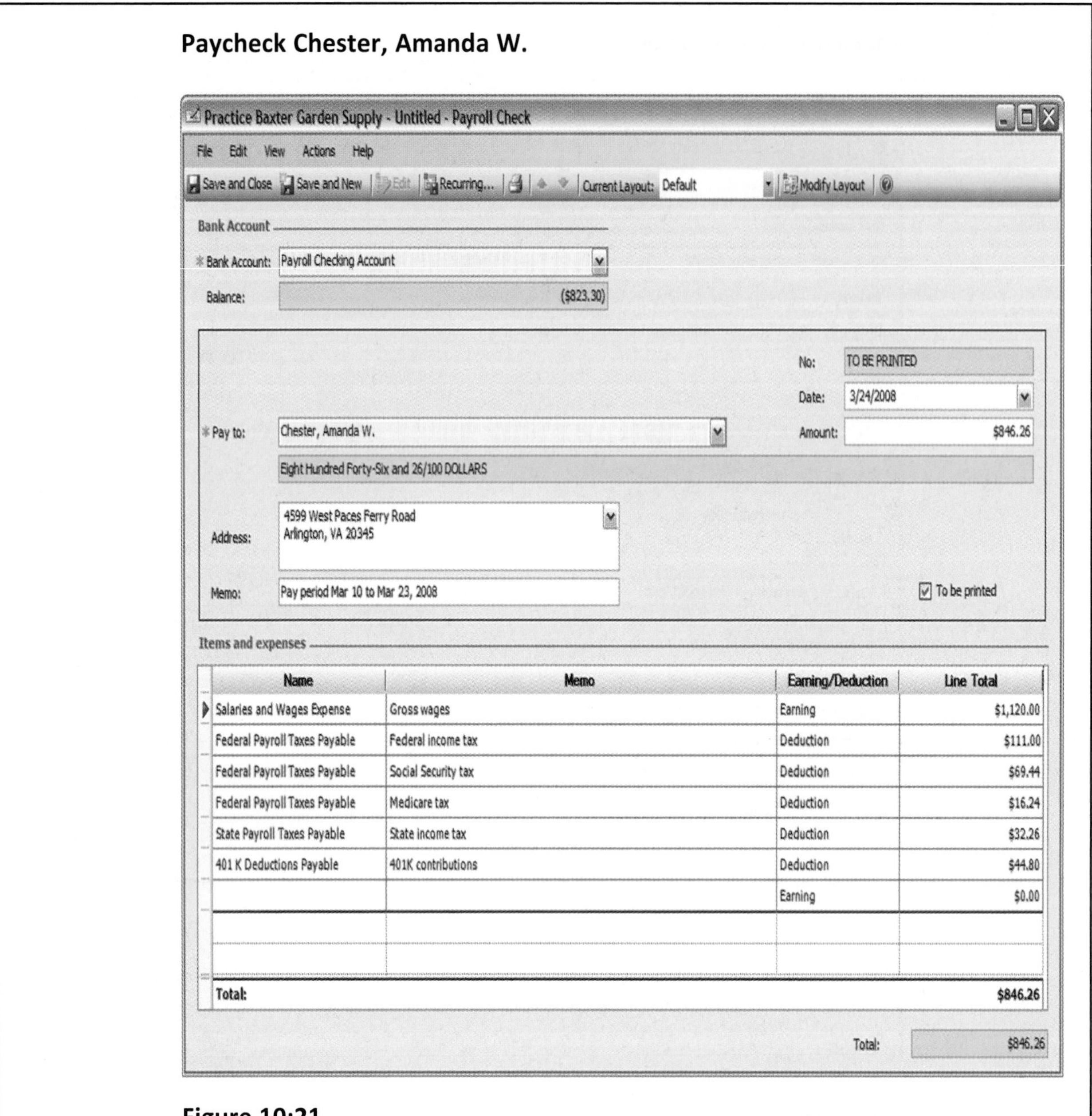

Practice Baxter Garden Supply - Untitled - Payroll Check

File Edit View Actions Help

Save and Close | Save and New | Edit | Recurring... | Current Layout: Default | Modify Layout

Bank Account

Bank Account: Payroll Checking Account

Balance: ($823.30)

No: TO BE PRINTED

Date: 3/24/2008

Pay to: Chester, Amanda W.

Amount: $846.26

Eight Hundred Forty-Six and 26/100 DOLLARS

Address: 4599 West Paces Ferry Road
Arlington, VA 20345

Memo: Pay period Mar 10 to Mar 23, 2008

To be printed

Items and expenses

Name	Memo	Earning/Deduction	Line Total
Salaries and Wages Expense	Gross wages	Earning	$1,120.00
Federal Payroll Taxes Payable	Federal income tax	Deduction	$111.00
Federal Payroll Taxes Payable	Social Security tax	Deduction	$69.44
Federal Payroll Taxes Payable	Medicare tax	Deduction	$16.24
State Payroll Taxes Payable	State income tax	Deduction	$32.26
401 K Deductions Payable	401K contributions	Deduction	$44.80
		Earning	$0.00
Total:			**$846.26**

Total: $846.26

Figure 10:21

Paycheck Duke, Al C.

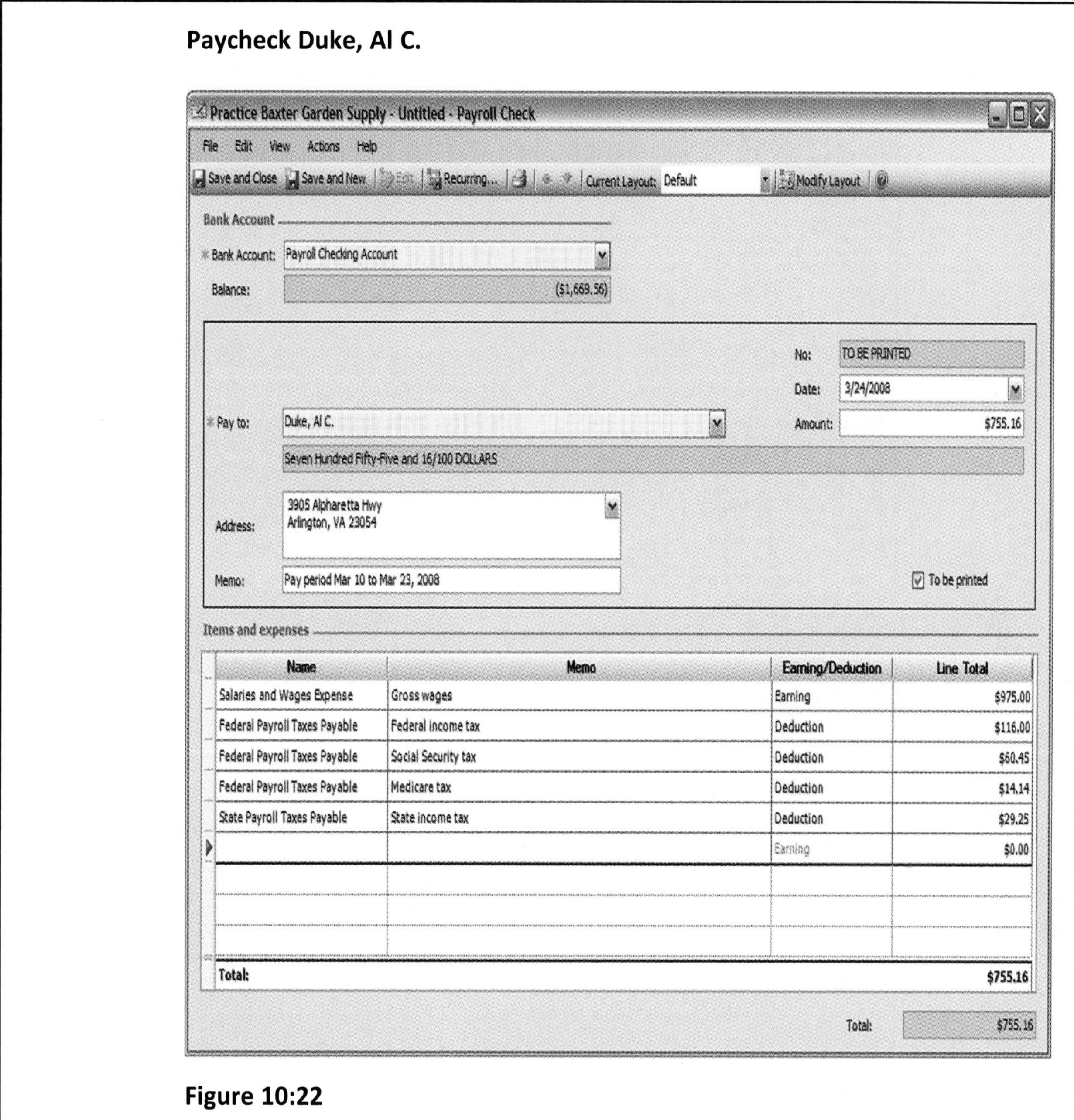

Name	Memo	Earning/Deduction	Line Total
Salaries and Wages Expense	Gross wages	Earning	$975.00
Federal Payroll Taxes Payable	Federal income tax	Deduction	$116.00
Federal Payroll Taxes Payable	Social Security tax	Deduction	$60.45
Federal Payroll Taxes Payable	Medicare tax	Deduction	$14.14
State Payroll Taxes Payable	State income tax	Deduction	$29.25
		Earning	$0.00
Total:			**$755.16**

Figure 10:22

Paycheck Frost, Melvin H.

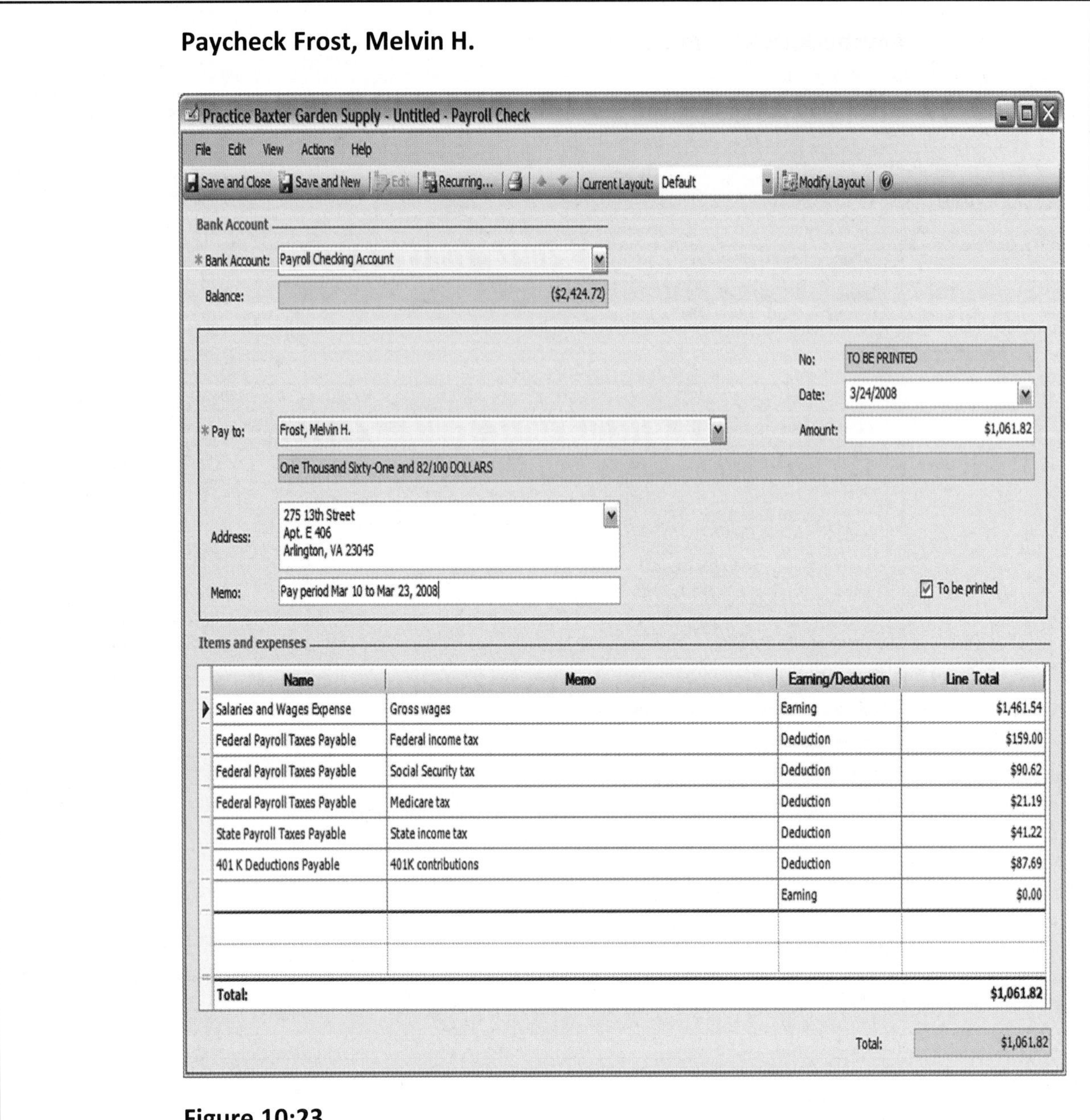

Name	Memo	Earning/Deduction	Line Total
Salaries and Wages Expense	Gross wages	Earning	$1,461.54
Federal Payroll Taxes Payable	Federal income tax	Deduction	$159.00
Federal Payroll Taxes Payable	Social Security tax	Deduction	$90.62
Federal Payroll Taxes Payable	Medicare tax	Deduction	$21.19
State Payroll Taxes Payable	State income tax	Deduction	$41.22
401 K Deductions Payable	401K contributions	Deduction	$87.69
		Earning	$0.00
Total:			$1,061.82

Figure 10:23

Paycheck Gross, Derrick P.

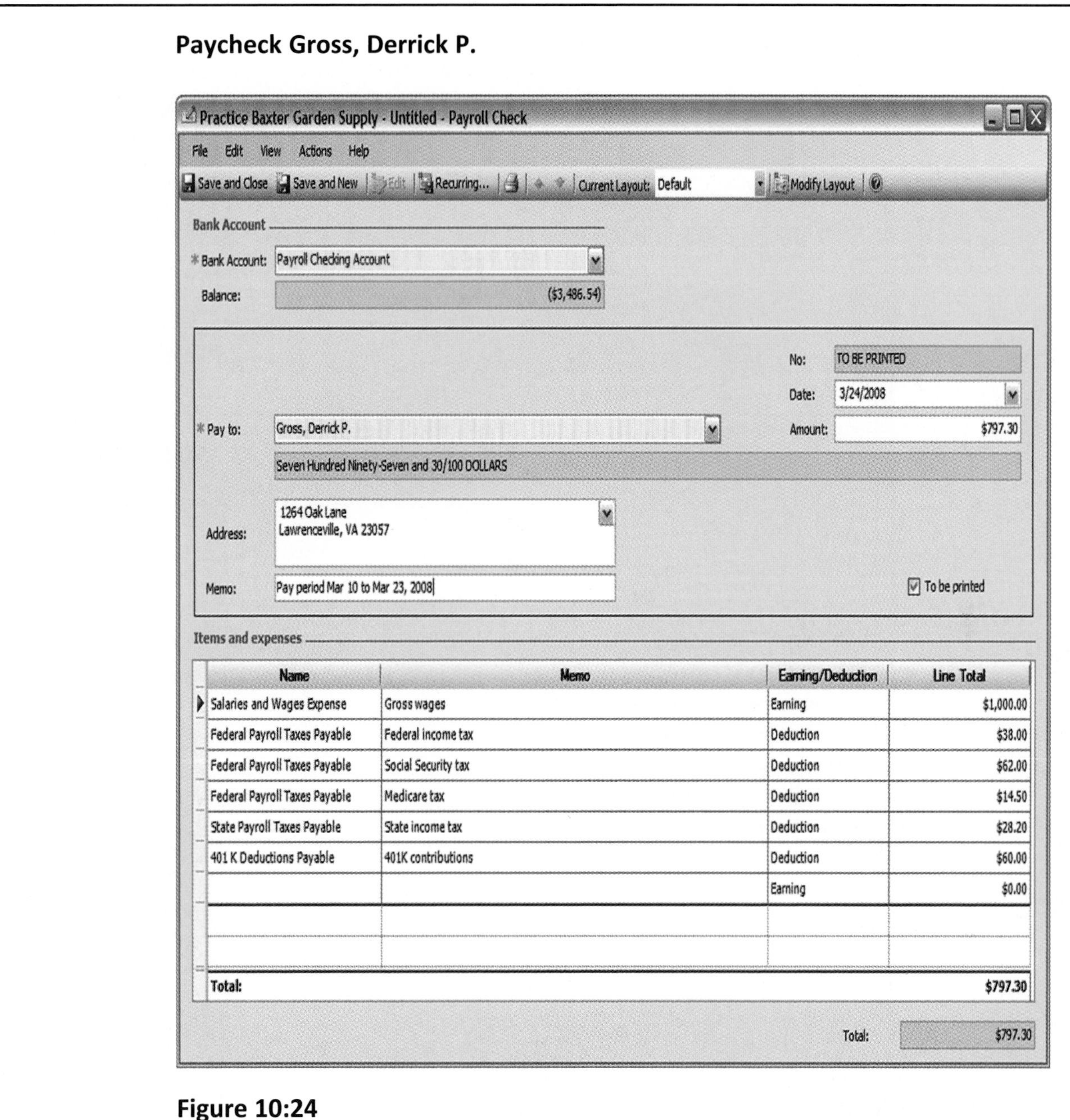

Figure 10:24

Paycheck Hecter, Anthony H.

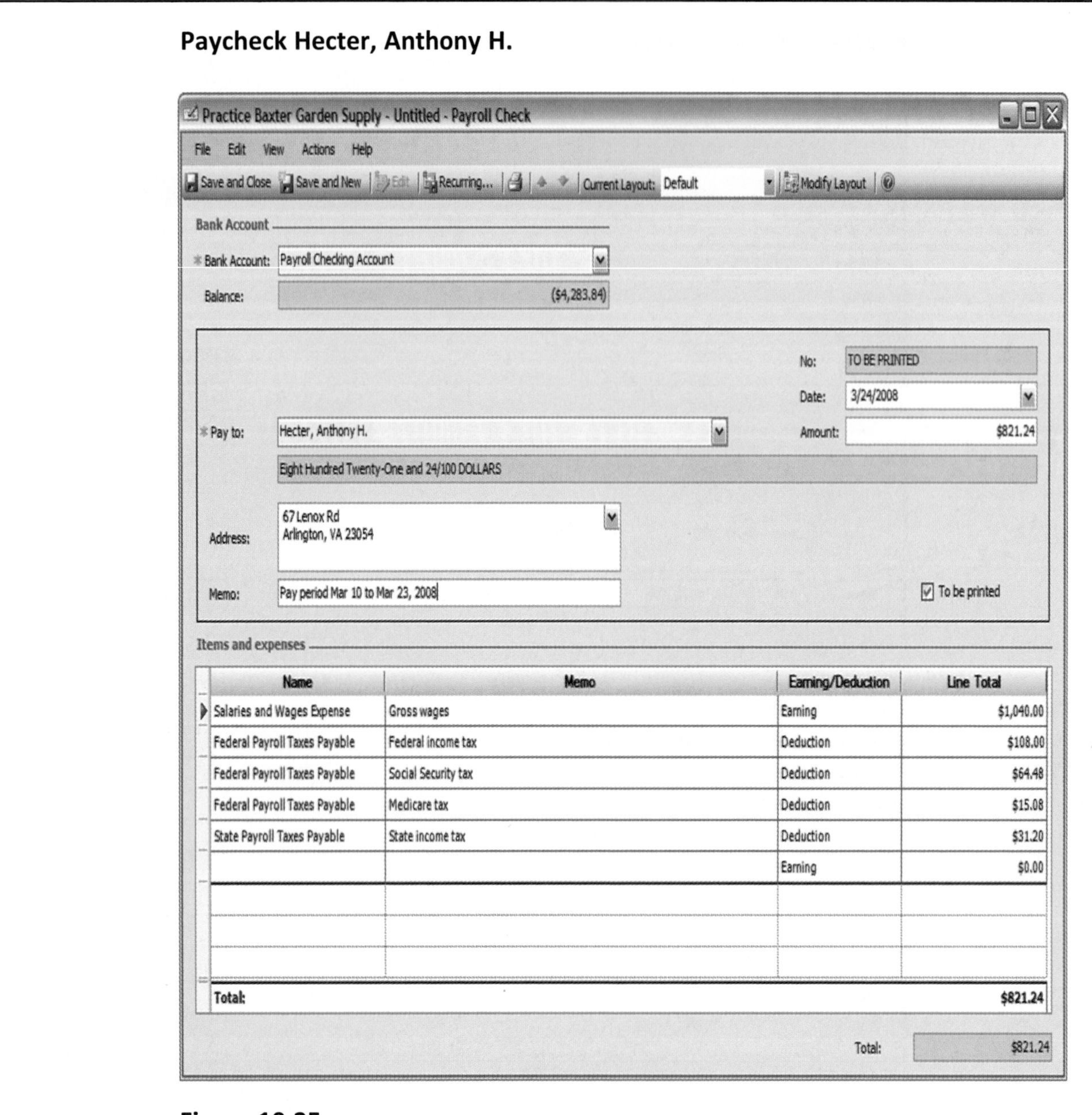

Figure 10:25

Paycheck Nunnley, Brandee M.

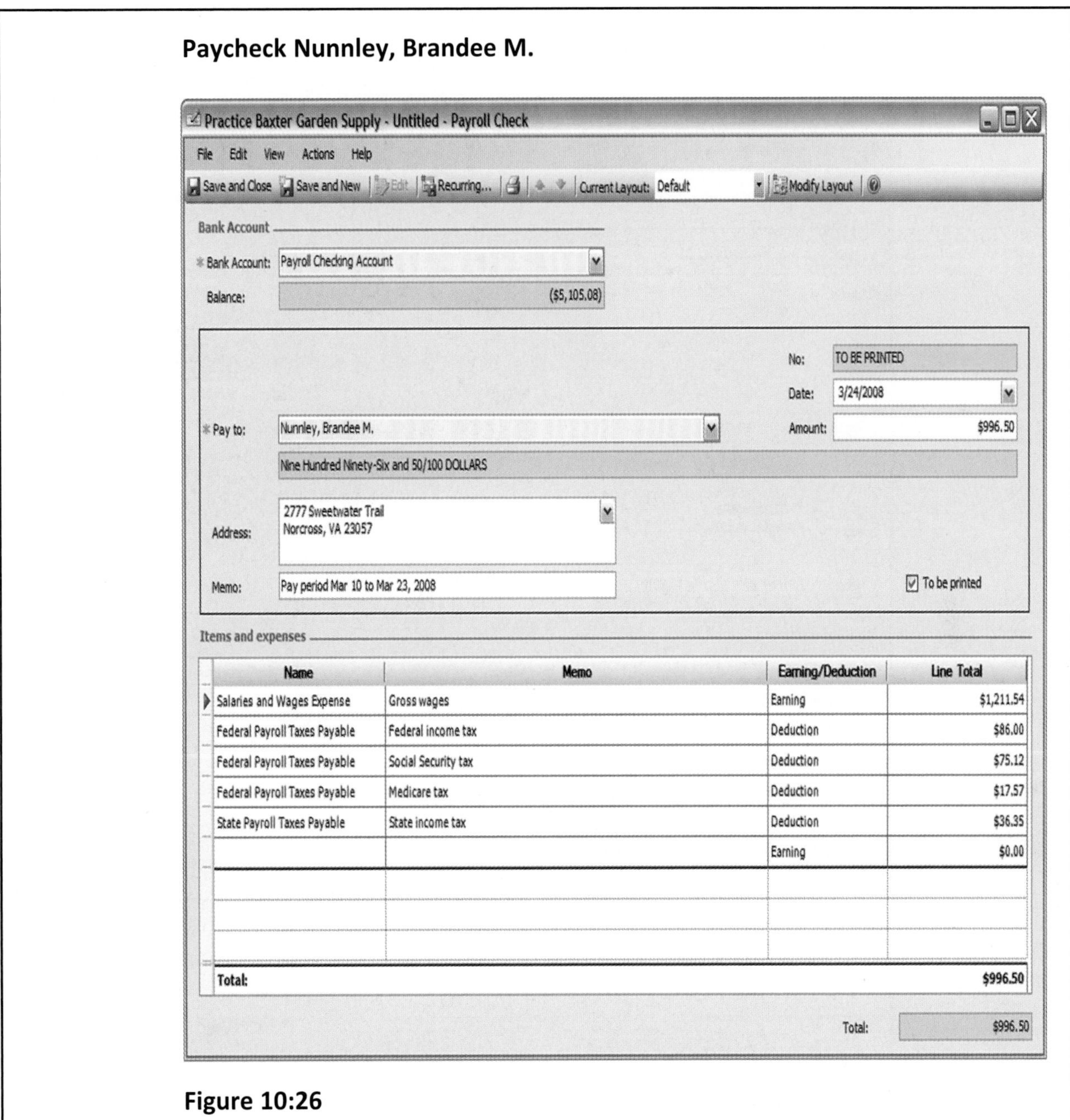

Name	Memo	Earning/Deduction	Line Total
Salaries and Wages Expense	Gross wages	Earning	$1,211.54
Federal Payroll Taxes Payable	Federal income tax	Deduction	$86.00
Federal Payroll Taxes Payable	Social Security tax	Deduction	$75.12
Federal Payroll Taxes Payable	Medicare tax	Deduction	$17.57
State Payroll Taxes Payable	State income tax	Deduction	$36.35
		Earning	$0.00
Total:			**$996.50**

Figure 10:26

Paycheck Prather, Samuel R.

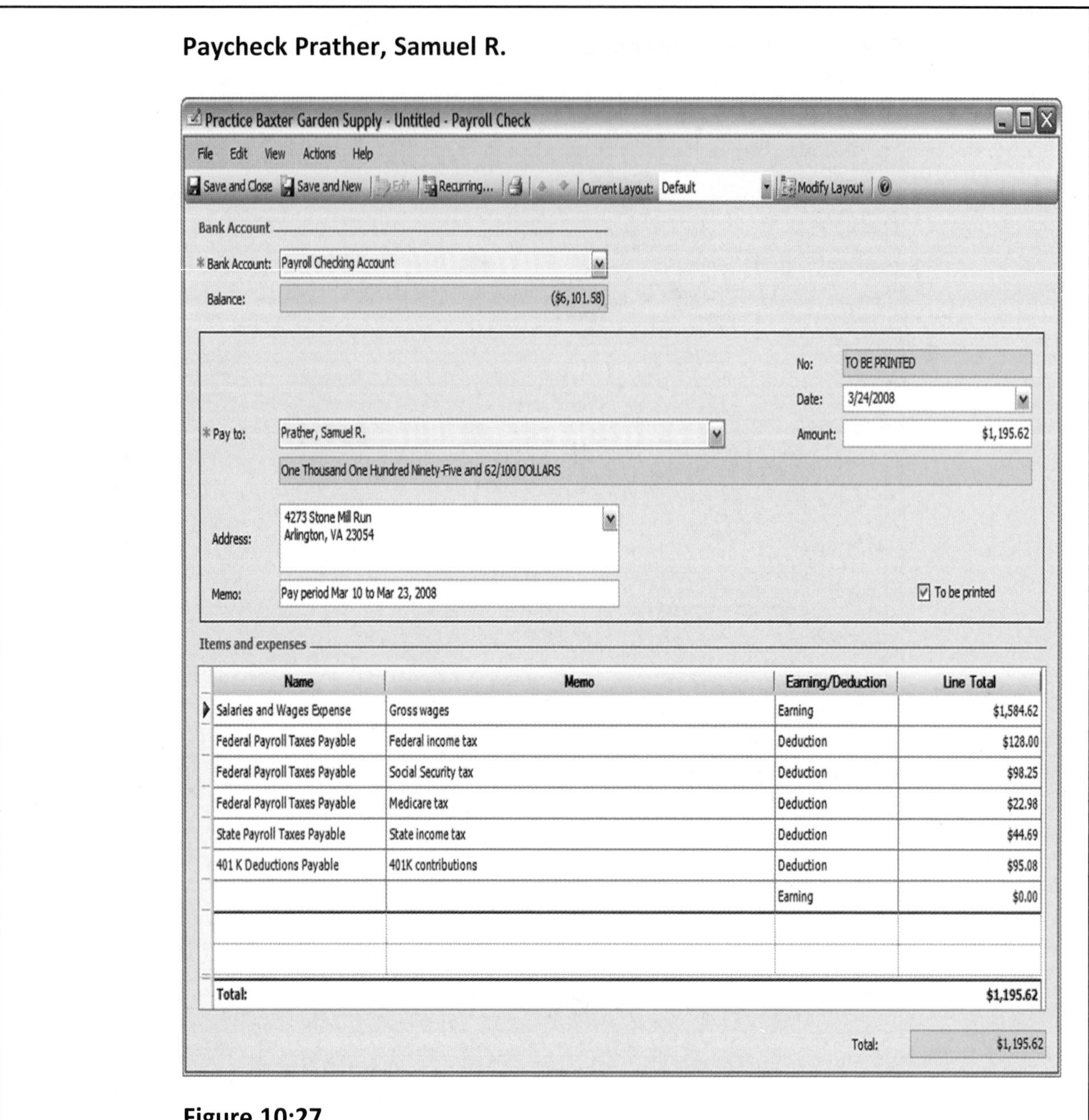
Practice Baxter Garden Supply - Untitled - Payroll Check

File Edit View Actions Help

Save and Close | Save and New | Edit | Recurring... | Current Layout: Default | Modify Layout

Bank Account

Bank Account: Payroll Checking Account

Balance: ($6,101.58)

No: TO BE PRINTED

Date: 3/24/2008

Pay to: Prather, Samuel R.

Amount: $1,195.62

One Thousand One Hundred Ninety-Five and 62/100 DOLLARS

Address: 4273 Stone Mill Run
Arlington, VA 23054

Memo: Pay period Mar 10 to Mar 23, 2008

To be printed

Items and expenses

Name	Memo	Earning/Deduction	Line Total
Salaries and Wages Expense	Gross wages	Earning	$1,584.62
Federal Payroll Taxes Payable	Federal income tax	Deduction	$128.00
Federal Payroll Taxes Payable	Social Security tax	Deduction	$98.25
Federal Payroll Taxes Payable	Medicare tax	Deduction	$22.98
State Payroll Taxes Payable	State income tax	Deduction	$44.69
401 K Deductions Payable	401K contributions	Deduction	$95.08
		Earning	$0.00
Total:			**$1,195.62**

Total: $1,195.62

Figure 10:27

Paycheck Sweet, Leonard

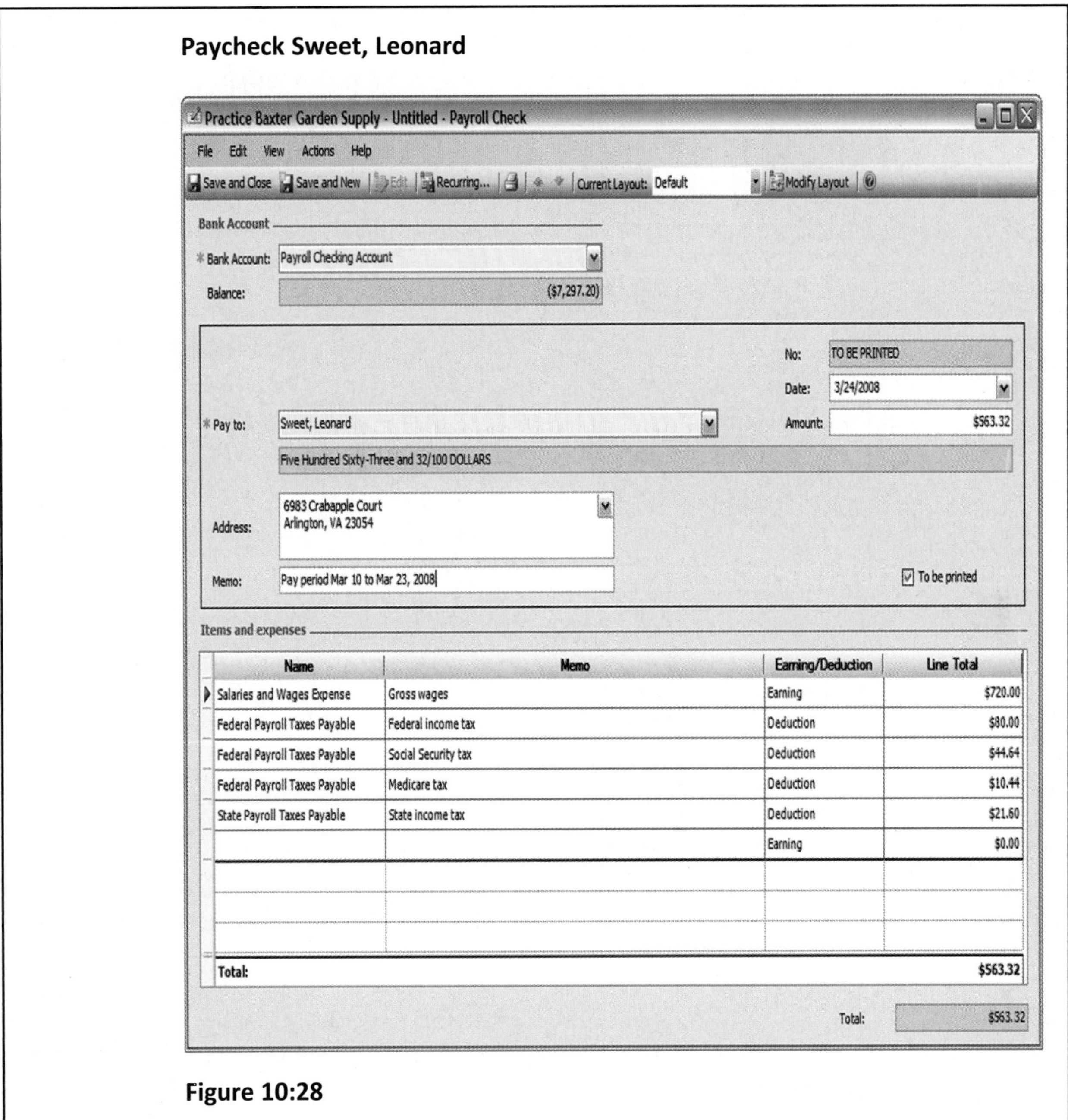

Practice Baxter Garden Supply - Untitled - Payroll Check

File Edit View Actions Help

Save and Close | Save and New | Edit | Recurring... | Current Layout: Default | Modify Layout

Bank Account

Bank Account: Payroll Checking Account

Balance: ($7,297.20)

No: TO BE PRINTED

Date: 3/24/2008

Pay to: Sweet, Leonard

Amount: $563.32

Five Hundred Sixty-Three and 32/100 DOLLARS

Address: 6983 Crabapple Court
Arlington, VA 23054

Memo: Pay period Mar 10 to Mar 23, 2008

To be printed

Items and expenses

Name	Memo	Earning/Deduction	Line Total
Salaries and Wages Expense	Gross wages	Earning	$720.00
Federal Payroll Taxes Payable	Federal income tax	Deduction	$80.00
Federal Payroll Taxes Payable	Social Security tax	Deduction	$44.64
Federal Payroll Taxes Payable	Medicare tax	Deduction	$10.44
State Payroll Taxes Payable	State income tax	Deduction	$21.60
		Earning	$0.00
Total:			$563.32

Total: $563.32

Figure 10:28

Paycheck Trotter, Mitchell K.

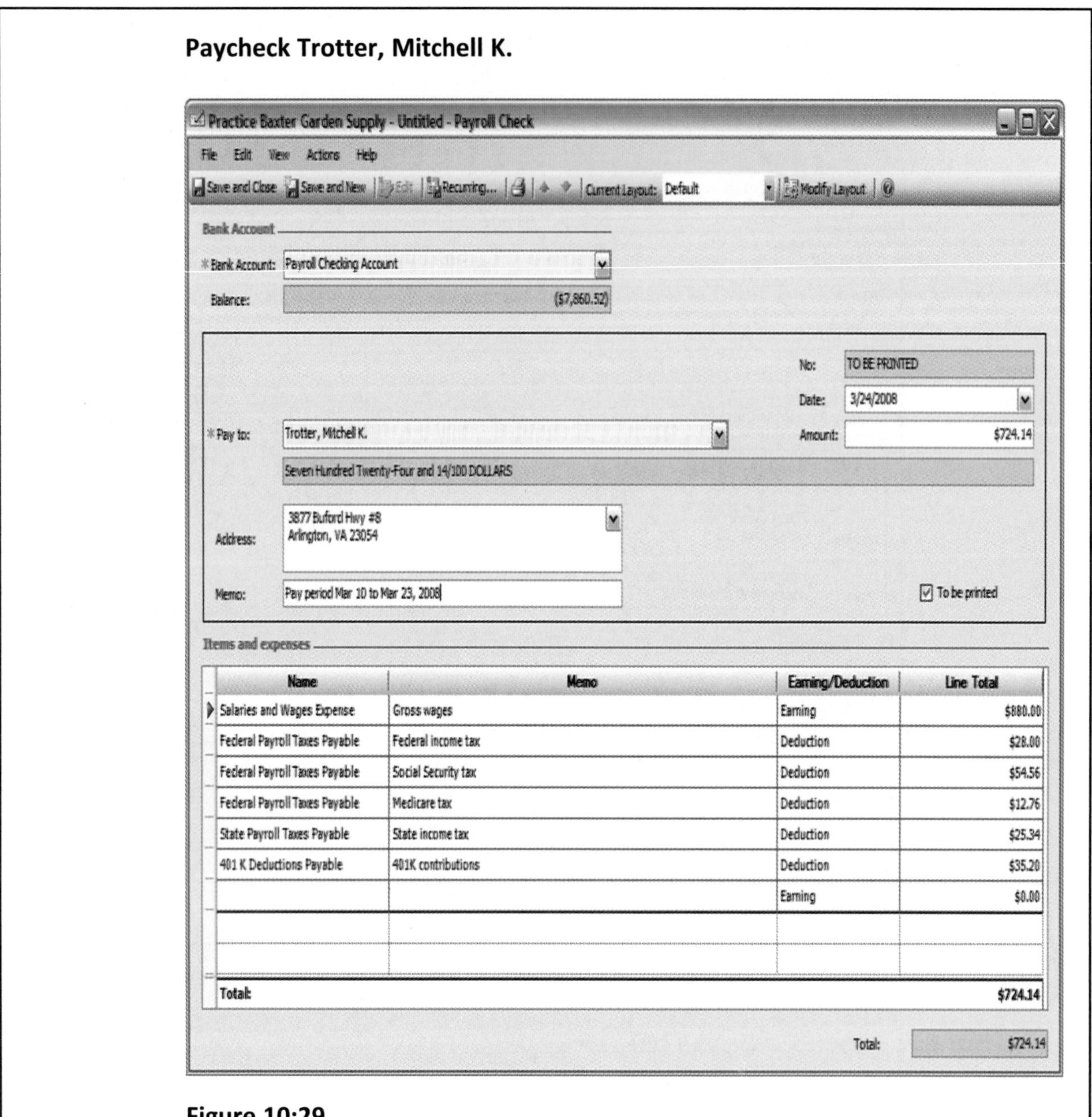

Practice Baxter Garden Supply - Untitled - Payroll Check

File Edit View Actions Help

Save and Close | Save and New | Edit | Recurring... | Current Layout: Default | Modify Layout

Bank Account

Bank Account: Payroll Checking Account

Balance: ($7,860.52)

No: TO BE PRINTED

Date: 3/24/2008

Pay to: Trotter, Mitchell K.

Amount: $724.14

Seven Hundred Twenty-Four and 14/100 DOLLARS

Address: 3877 Buford Hwy #8
Arlington, VA 23054

Memo: Pay period Mar 10 to Mar 23, 2008

To be printed

Items and expenses

Name	Memo	Earning/Deduction	Line Total
Salaries and Wages Expense	Gross wages	Earning	$880.00
Federal Payroll Taxes Payable	Federal income tax	Deduction	$28.00
Federal Payroll Taxes Payable	Social Security tax	Deduction	$54.56
Federal Payroll Taxes Payable	Medicare tax	Deduction	$12.76
State Payroll Taxes Payable	State income tax	Deduction	$25.34
401 K Deductions Payable	401K contributions	Deduction	$35.20
		Earning	$0.00
Total:			$724.14

Total: $724.14

Figure 10:29

6. You will now create a paycheck for the new employee. Click **Manual Payroll Check** under **Start a Task** and enter the following information. Be sure to select the Payroll Checking Account.

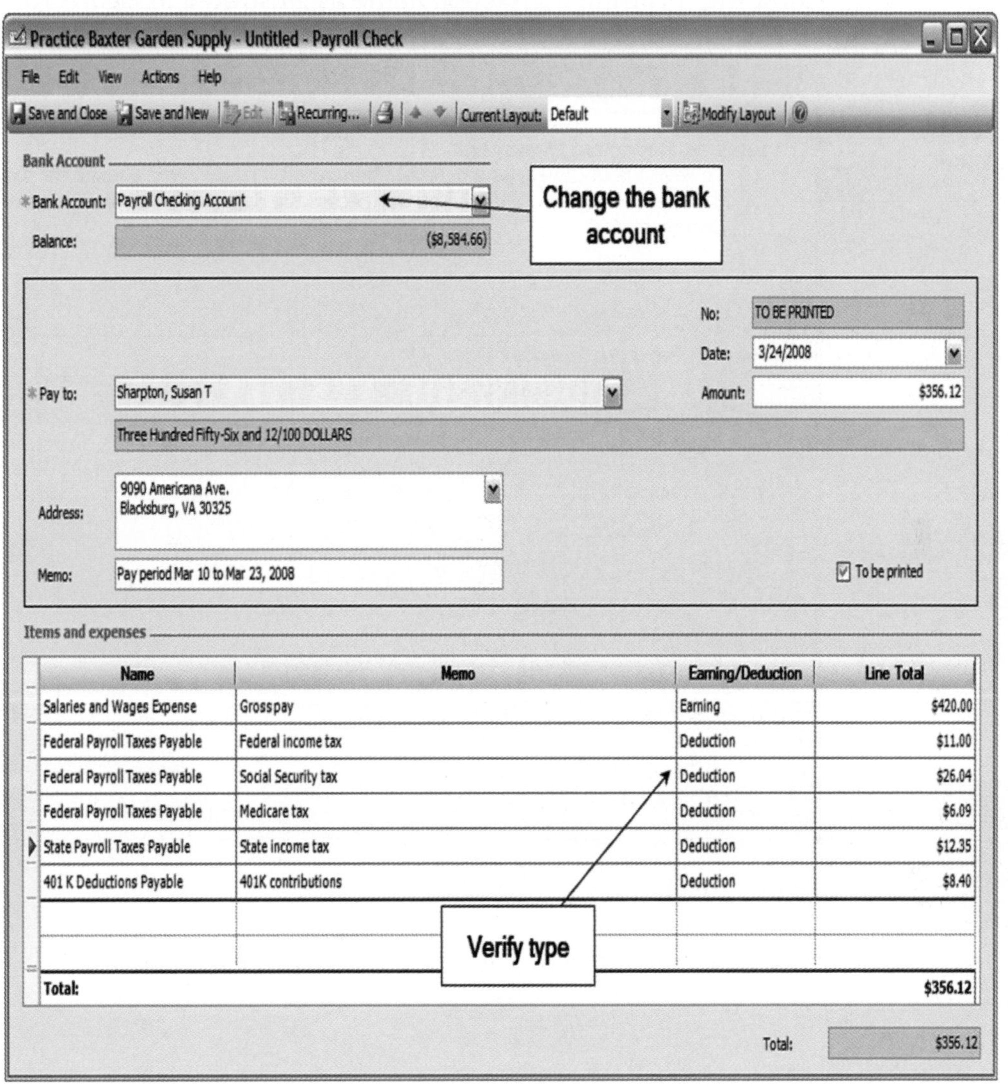

Figure 10:30

7. Click **Recurring** on the toolbar. This causes the transaction to be saved so OAP prompts to store the address. Click **Yes**.

   Enter the recurring transaction name as illustrated in Figure 10:31 and click **OK**.

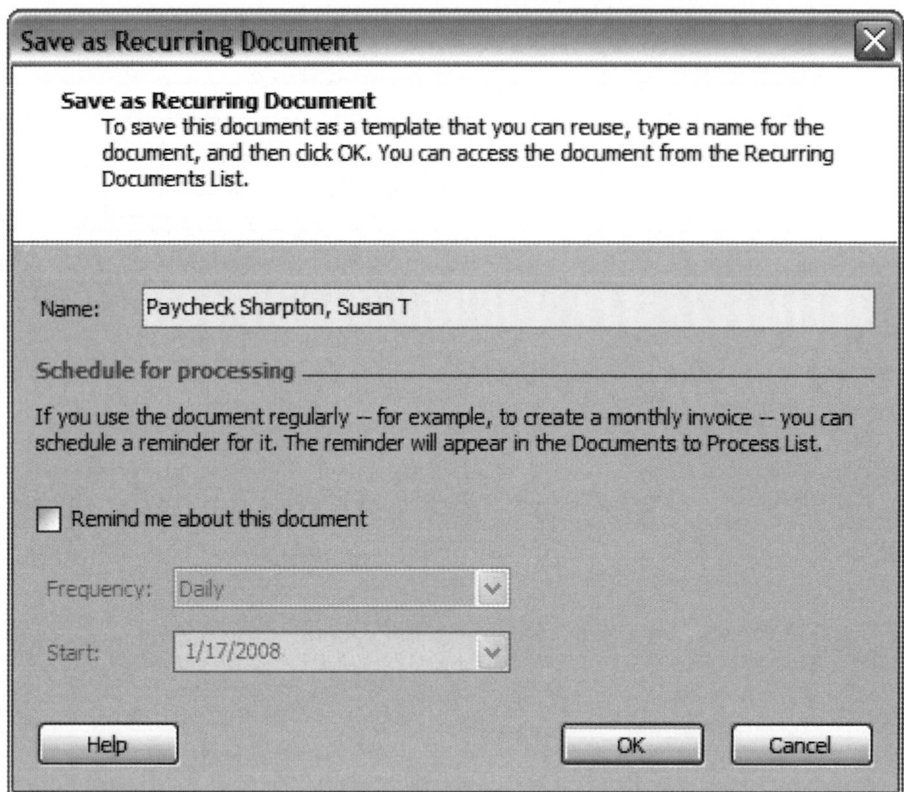

Figure 10:31

Click **Save and Close** to post the paycheck transaction.

8. You will next print the paychecks, but first verify your entries. Select ***Reports>>Employees and Payroll>>Employee Payments*** on the main menu. Filter the report for "3/24/2008" and remove the Issue date, No., Status detail, Memo, and Reference number columns (Figure 10:32).

   You can export the report to Excel to total the amount and compare to the Payroll Register illustrated previously. Should you find an error on a check, double click to reopen it, make changes, and resave the transaction.

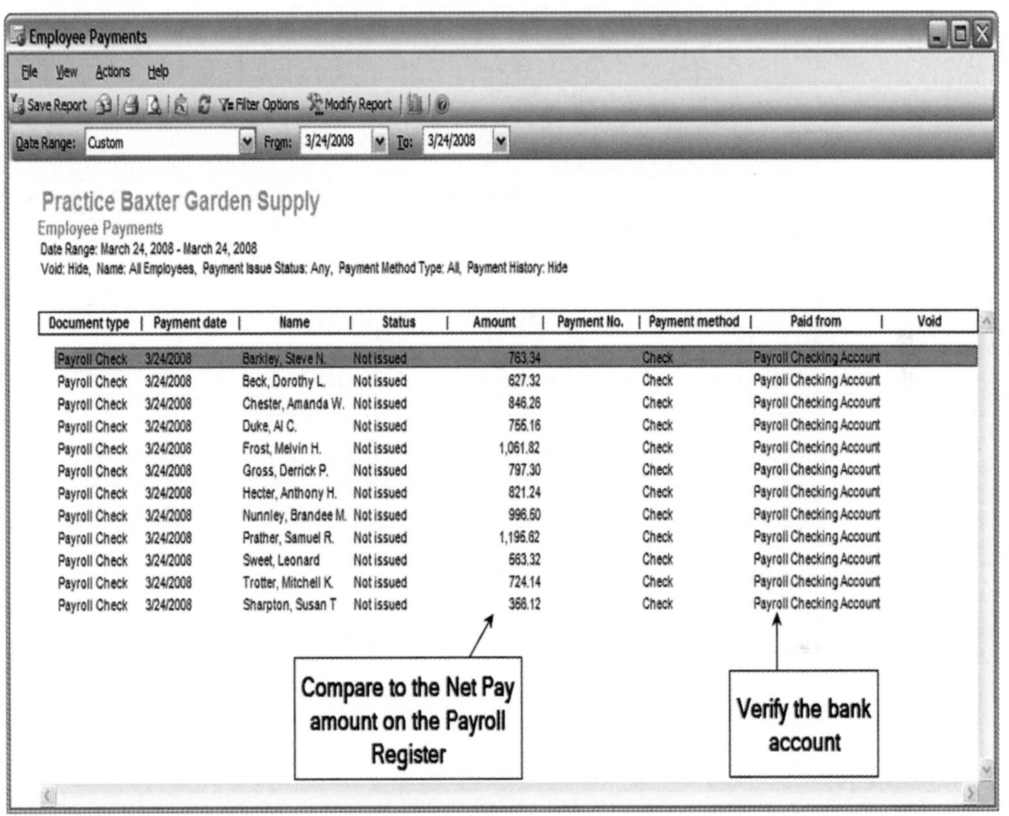

Practice Baxter Garden Supply
Employee Payments
Date Range: March 24, 2008 - March 24, 2008
Void: Hide, Name: All Employees, Payment Issue Status: Any, Payment Method Type: All, Payment History: Hide

Document type	Payment date	Name	Status	Amount	Payment No.	Payment method	Paid from	Void
Payroll Check	3/24/2008	Barkley, Steve N.	Not issued	763.34		Check	Payroll Checking Account	
Payroll Check	3/24/2008	Beck, Dorothy L.	Not issued	627.32		Check	Payroll Checking Account	
Payroll Check	3/24/2008	Chester, Amanda W.	Not issued	846.26		Check	Payroll Checking Account	
Payroll Check	3/24/2008	Duke, Al C.	Not issued	766.16		Check	Payroll Checking Account	
Payroll Check	3/24/2008	Frost, Melvin H.	Not issued	1,061.82		Check	Payroll Checking Account	
Payroll Check	3/24/2008	Gross, Derrick P.	Not issued	797.30		Check	Payroll Checking Account	
Payroll Check	3/24/2008	Hecter, Anthony H.	Not issued	821.24		Check	Payroll Checking Account	
Payroll Check	3/24/2008	Nunnley, Brandee M.	Not issued	996.60		Check	Payroll Checking Account	
Payroll Check	3/24/2008	Prather, Samuel R.	Not issued	1,196.62		Check	Payroll Checking Account	
Payroll Check	3/24/2008	Sweet, Leonard	Not issued	663.32		Check	Payroll Checking Account	
Payroll Check	3/24/2008	Trotter, Mitchell K.	Not issued	724.14		Check	Payroll Checking Account	
Payroll Check	3/24/2008	Sharpton, Susan T	Not issued	366.12		Check	Payroll Checking Account	

Figure 10:32

9. Close the report and print the paychecks. Select ***Employees>>Manual Payroll>>Print Payroll Checks*** on the main menu.

   Complete the window as illustrated in Figure 10:33. The total amount to pay should be $9,508.14, which agrees to the Net Pay total on the Payroll Register.

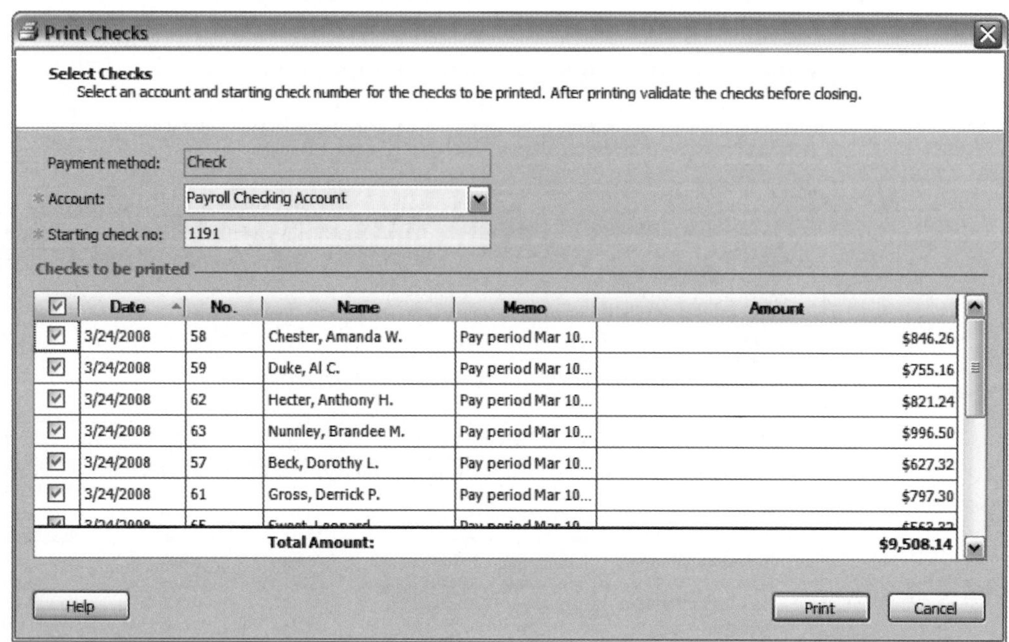

Figure 10:33

10. Click **Print**, select a printer, and click **OK**.

11. Click **Close** to exit the Print Checks window. Click **OK** when OAP displays payment information.

12. The last step is posting employer payroll tax liabilities. Baxter enters a bill for federal income tax withholdings and Social Security and Medicare taxes each pay date. The accountant has created a recurring vendor bill for this payment.

    Click **Recurring Documents** and open the **Federal Payroll Tax Bill (Biweekly)** recurring document. Enter the information illustrated in Figure 10:34. Again, this information comes from the Excel spreadsheets previously illustrated.

    Click **Save and Close** to post the bill.

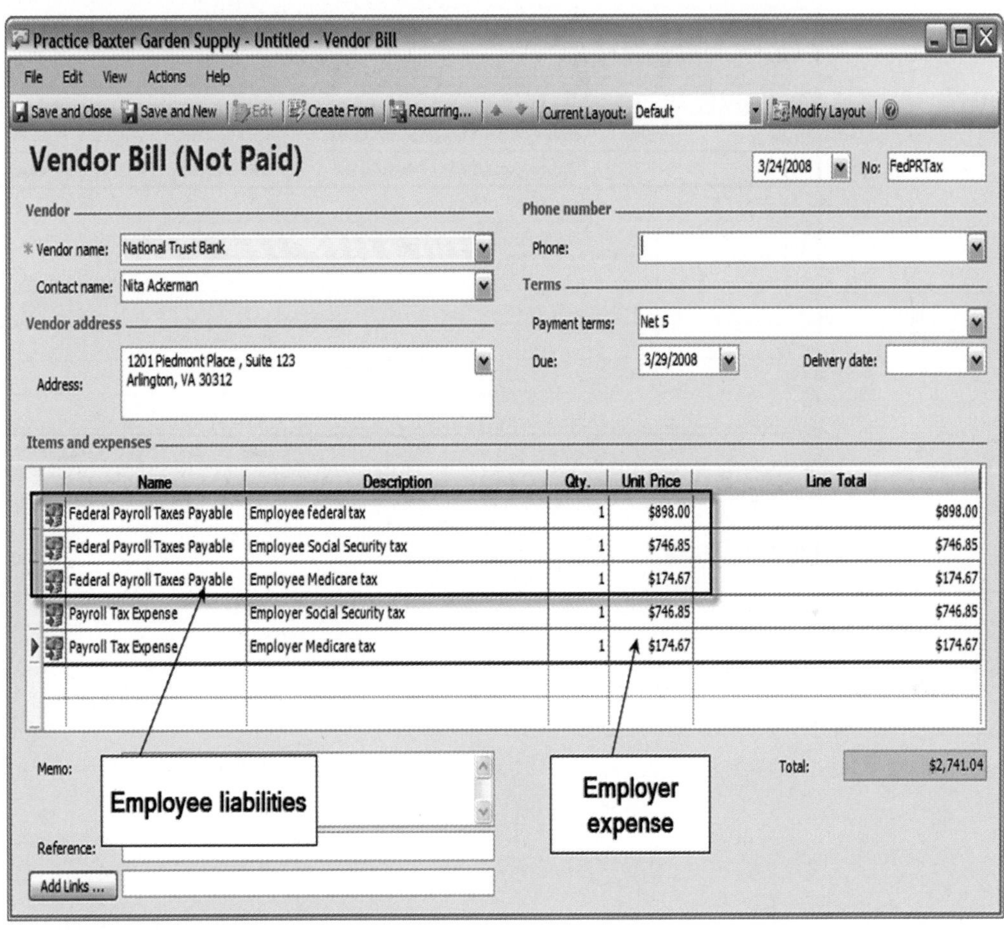

Figure 10:34

13. Next post a journal entry for health insurance liabilities. Open the **Employer Health Insur Liability (Biweekly)** recurring document and complete as illustrated (Figure 10:35). Click **Save and Close**.

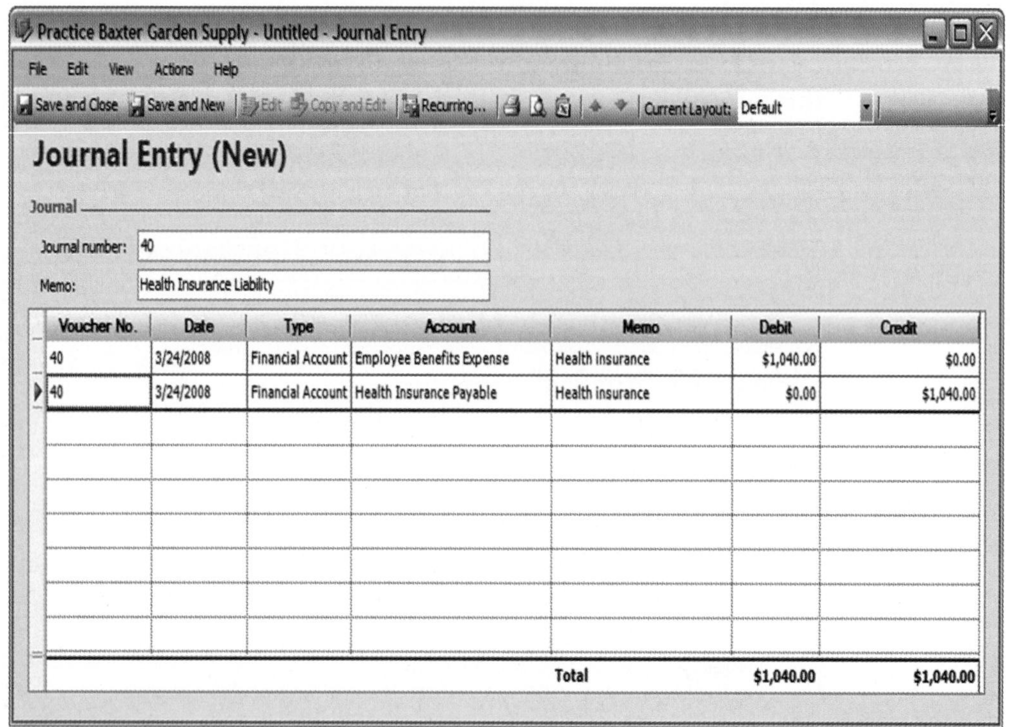

Figure 10:35

14. Finally, post a journal entry for 401K employer contributions and unemployment taxes. Open the **Employer Unemployment Tax and 401K Liability (Biweekly)** recurring document and complete as illustrated (Figure 10:36). Click **Save and Close**.

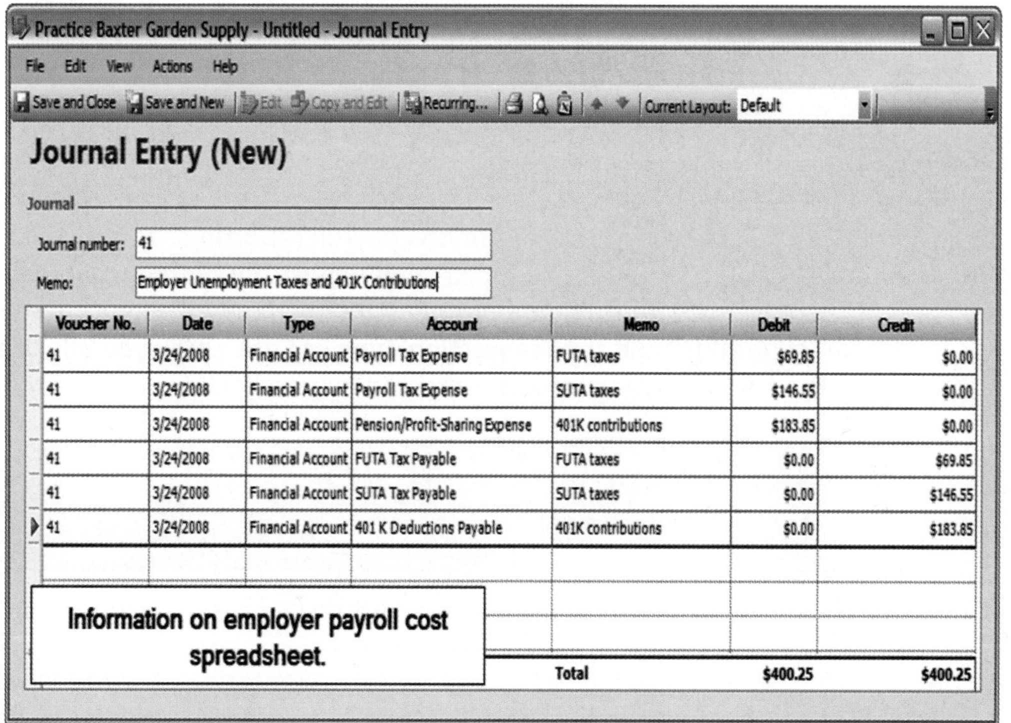

Voucher No.	Date	Type	Account	Memo	Debit	Credit
41	3/24/2008	Financial Account	Payroll Tax Expense	FUTA taxes	$69.85	$0.00
41	3/24/2008	Financial Account	Payroll Tax Expense	SUTA taxes	$146.55	$0.00
41	3/24/2008	Financial Account	Pension/Profit-Sharing Expense	401K contributions	$183.85	$0.00
41	3/24/2008	Financial Account	FUTA Tax Payable	FUTA taxes	$0.00	$69.85
41	3/24/2008	Financial Account	SUTA Tax Payable	SUTA taxes	$0.00	$146.55
41	3/24/2008	Financial Account	401 K Deductions Payable	401K contributions	$0.00	$183.85
				Total	$400.25	$400.25

Figure 10:36

You will next trace entries for these paychecks.

BEHIND THE KEYS OF A POSTED PAYCHECK

You will now trace the entries made when printing paychecks by completing the next steps.

STEPS TO TRACING PAYCHECK ENTRIES

1. You will find that OAP has limited payroll reporting. You can trace entries on the Transaction Journal by selecting ***Reports>>Company and Financial>>Transaction Journal*** on the main menu. Filter the report for "3/24/2008" and the **Transaction Type** of Cash Employee Bill. Figure 10:37 lists the general ledger accounts affected by paychecks.

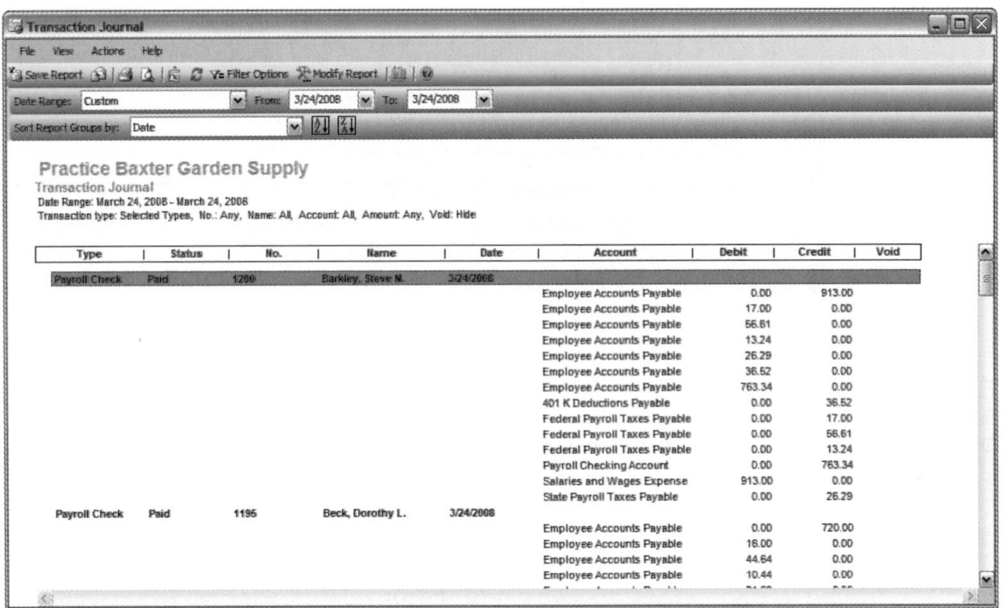

Practice Baxter Garden Supply
Transaction Journal
Date Range: March 24, 2008 - March 24, 2008
Transaction type: Selected Types, No.: Any, Name: All, Account: All, Amount: Any, Void: Hide

Type	Status	No.	Name	Date	Account	Debit	Credit	Void
Payroll Check	Paid	1200	Barkley, Steve N.	3/24/2008				
					Employee Accounts Payable	0.00	913.00	
					Employee Accounts Payable	17.00	0.00	
					Employee Accounts Payable	56.61	0.00	
					Employee Accounts Payable	13.24	0.00	
					Employee Accounts Payable	26.29	0.00	
					Employee Accounts Payable	36.52	0.00	
					Employee Accounts Payable	763.34	0.00	
					401 K Deductions Payable	0.00	36.52	
					Federal Payroll Taxes Payable	0.00	17.00	
					Federal Payroll Taxes Payable	0.00	56.61	
					Federal Payroll Taxes Payable	0.00	13.24	
					Payroll Checking Account	0.00	763.34	
					Salaries and Wages Expense	913.00	0.00	
					State Payroll Taxes Payable	0.00	26.29	
Payroll Check	Paid	1195	Beck, Dorothy L.	3/24/2008				
					Employee Accounts Payable	0.00	720.00	
					Employee Accounts Payable	16.00	0.00	
					Employee Accounts Payable	44.64	0.00	
					Employee Accounts Payable	10.44	0.00	

Figure 10:37

2. You can also print the ***Reports>>Employees and Payroll>>Employee Payments*** report printed earlier. Filter the report for "3/24/2008" and notice that this time the Status is Issued and the check number is listed under the Payment No. column (Figure 10:38). Close the report.

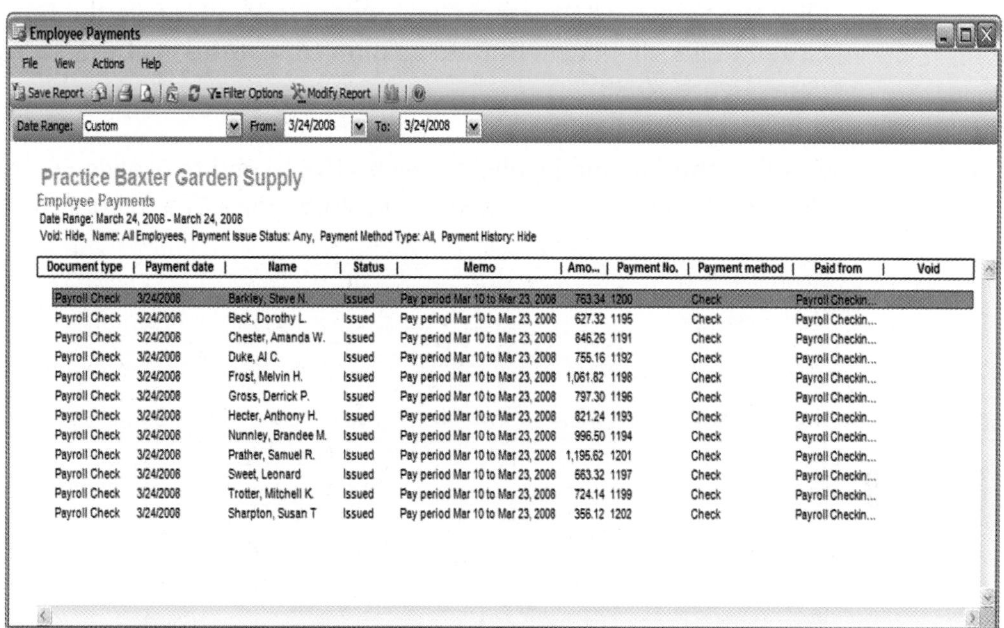

Practice Baxter Garden Supply
Employee Payments
Date Range: March 24, 2008 - March 24, 2008
Void: Hide, Name: All Employees, Payment Issue Status: Any, Payment Method Type: All, Payment History: Hide

Document type	Payment date	Name	Status	Memo	Amo...	Payment No.	Payment method	Paid from	Void
Payroll Check	3/24/2008	Barkley, Steve N.	Issued	Pay period Mar 10 to Mar 23, 2008	763.34	1200	Check	Payroll Checkin...	
Payroll Check	3/24/2008	Beck, Dorothy L.	Issued	Pay period Mar 10 to Mar 23, 2008	627.32	1195	Check	Payroll Checkin...	
Payroll Check	3/24/2008	Chester, Amanda W.	Issued	Pay period Mar 10 to Mar 23, 2008	846.26	1191	Check	Payroll Checkin...	
Payroll Check	3/24/2008	Duke, Al C.	Issued	Pay period Mar 10 to Mar 23, 2008	755.16	1192	Check	Payroll Checkin...	
Payroll Check	3/24/2008	Frost, Melvin H.	Issued	Pay period Mar 10 to Mar 23, 2008	1,061.82	1198	Check	Payroll Checkin...	
Payroll Check	3/24/2008	Gross, Derrick P.	Issued	Pay period Mar 10 to Mar 23, 2008	797.30	1196	Check	Payroll Checkin...	
Payroll Check	3/24/2008	Hecter, Anthony H.	Issued	Pay period Mar 10 to Mar 23, 2008	821.24	1193	Check	Payroll Checkin...	
Payroll Check	3/24/2008	Nunnley, Brandee M.	Issued	Pay period Mar 10 to Mar 23, 2008	996.50	1194	Check	Payroll Checkin...	
Payroll Check	3/24/2008	Prather, Samuel R.	Issued	Pay period Mar 10 to Mar 23, 2008	1,195.62	1201	Check	Payroll Checkin...	
Payroll Check	3/24/2008	Sweet, Leonard	Issued	Pay period Mar 10 to Mar 23, 2008	563.32	1197	Check	Payroll Checkin...	
Payroll Check	3/24/2008	Trotter, Mitchell K.	Issued	Pay period Mar 10 to Mar 23, 2008	724.14	1199	Check	Payroll Checkin...	
Payroll Check	3/24/2008	Sharpton, Susan T	Issued	Pay period Mar 10 to Mar 23, 2008	356.12	1202	Check	Payroll Checkin...	

Figure 10:38

3. You can also trace entries to the general ledger by printing the **Transaction Detail by Account** report (not illustrated).

VOIDING EMPLOYEE PAYCHECKS

When you were entering paycheck data we explained correcting a paycheck before printing it. What happens when you find an error after printing? The only solution is to void the paycheck and reissue it.

Practice voiding a printed paycheck by completing the next exercise.

Steps to Voiding a Printed Paycheck

1. Click the **Employee Payments** link under Find and toggle the **Current View** to **Issued**. Click the Payment Date column to sort the list by descending paycheck date (Figure 10:39).

   Scroll to the top and highlight Check 1198 issued to Melvin Frost on March 24. Right click the transaction and select **Void**. Click **Yes** to confirm.

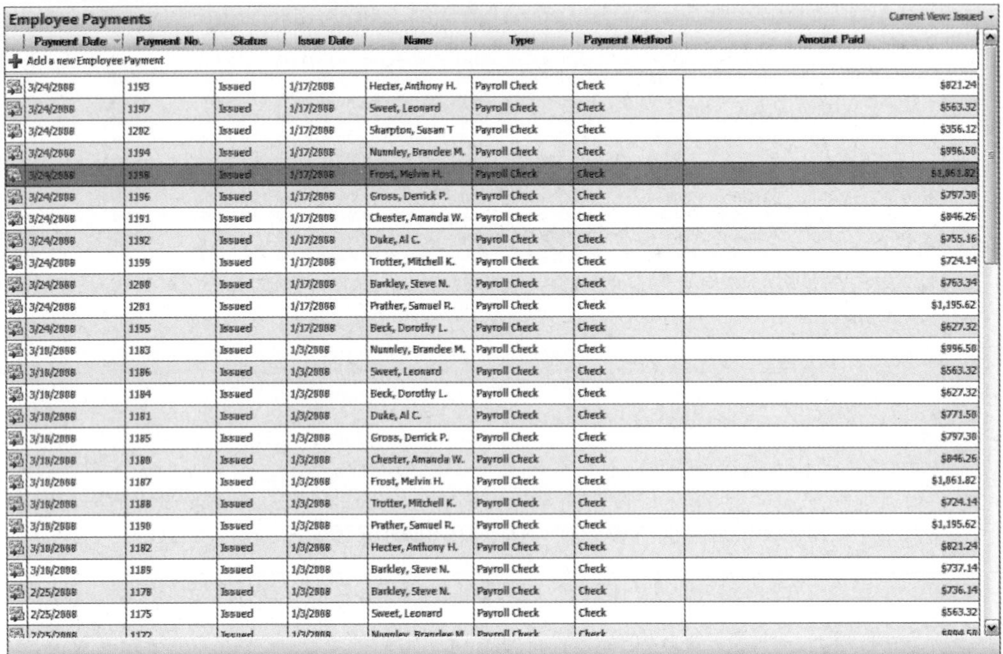

Employee Payments — Current View: Issued

Payment Date	Payment No.	Status	Issue Date	Name	Type	Payment Method	Amount Paid
3/24/2008	1193	Issued	1/17/2008	Hecter, Anthony H.	Payroll Check	Check	$821.24
3/24/2008	1197	Issued	1/17/2008	Sweet, Leonard	Payroll Check	Check	$563.32
3/24/2008	1202	Issued	1/17/2008	Sharpton, Susan T	Payroll Check	Check	$356.12
3/24/2008	1194	Issued	1/17/2008	Nunnley, Brandee M.	Payroll Check	Check	$996.50
3/24/2008	1198	Issued	1/17/2008	Frost, Melvin H.	Payroll Check	Check	$1,861.82
3/24/2008	1196	Issued	1/17/2008	Gross, Derrick P.	Payroll Check	Check	$797.30
3/24/2008	1191	Issued	1/17/2008	Chester, Amanda W.	Payroll Check	Check	$846.26
3/24/2008	1192	Issued	1/17/2008	Duke, Al C.	Payroll Check	Check	$755.16
3/24/2008	1199	Issued	1/17/2008	Trotter, Mitchell K.	Payroll Check	Check	$724.14
3/24/2008	1200	Issued	1/17/2008	Barkley, Steve N.	Payroll Check	Check	$763.34
3/24/2008	1201	Issued	1/17/2008	Prather, Samuel R.	Payroll Check	Check	$1,195.62
3/24/2008	1195	Issued	1/17/2008	Beck, Dorothy L.	Payroll Check	Check	$627.32
3/10/2008	1183	Issued	1/3/2008	Nunnley, Brandee M.	Payroll Check	Check	$996.50
3/10/2008	1186	Issued	1/3/2008	Sweet, Leonard	Payroll Check	Check	$563.32
3/10/2008	1184	Issued	1/3/2008	Beck, Dorothy L.	Payroll Check	Check	$627.32
3/10/2008	1181	Issued	1/3/2008	Duke, Al C.	Payroll Check	Check	$771.50
3/10/2008	1185	Issued	1/3/2008	Gross, Derrick P.	Payroll Check	Check	$797.30
3/10/2008	1180	Issued	1/3/2008	Chester, Amanda W.	Payroll Check	Check	$846.26
3/10/2008	1187	Issued	1/3/2008	Frost, Melvin H.	Payroll Check	Check	$1,861.82
3/10/2008	1188	Issued	1/3/2008	Trotter, Mitchell K.	Payroll Check	Check	$724.14
3/10/2008	1190	Issued	1/3/2008	Prather, Samuel R.	Payroll Check	Check	$1,195.62
3/10/2008	1182	Issued	1/3/2008	Hecter, Anthony H.	Payroll Check	Check	$821.24
3/10/2008	1189	Issued	1/3/2008	Barkley, Steve N.	Payroll Check	Check	$737.14
2/25/2008	1178	Issued	1/3/2008	Barkley, Steve N.	Payroll Check	Check	$736.14
2/25/2008	1175	Issued	1/3/2008	Sweet, Leonard	Payroll Check	Check	$563.32
2/25/2008	1172	Issued	1/3/2008	Nunnley, Brandee M	Payroll Check	Check	$996.50

Figure 10:39

2. Now reissue his paycheck. Click **Recurring Documents** under Find. Reopen Melvin's recurring paycheck document and enter the following information.

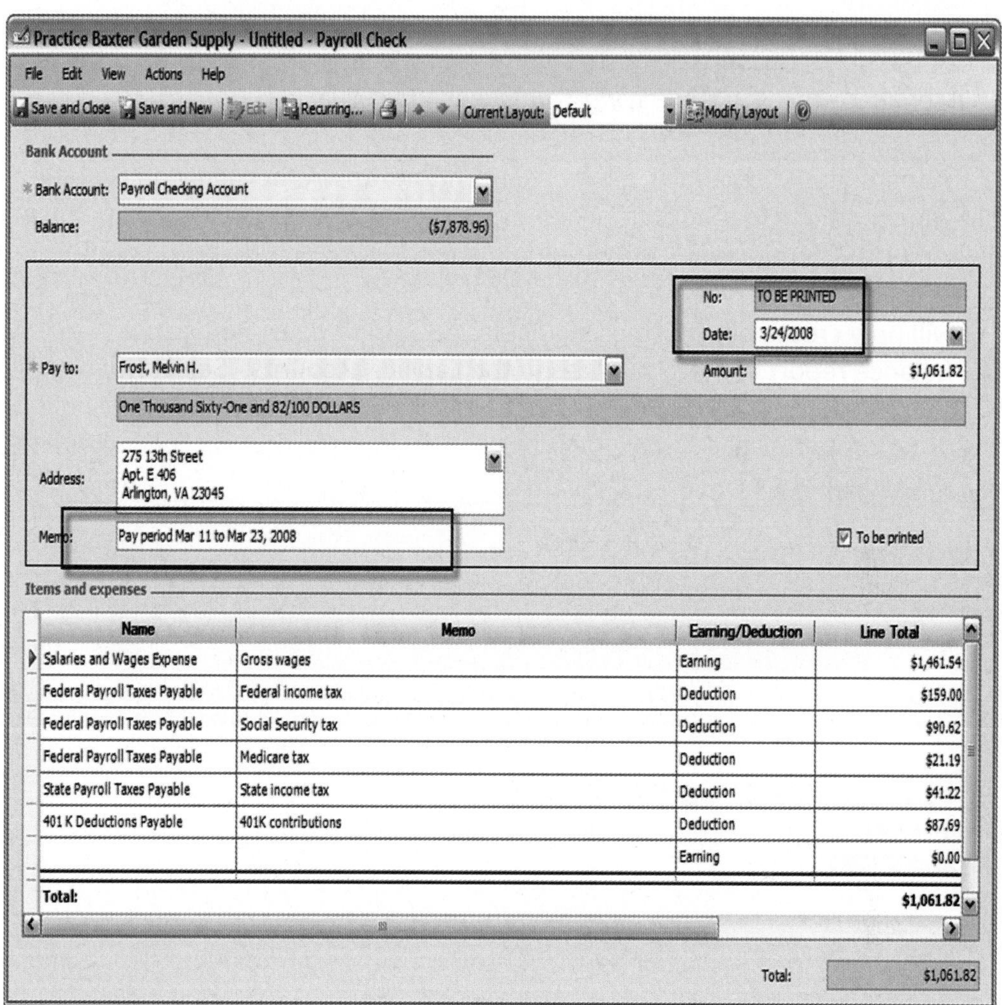

Figure 10:40

3. Click the **Printer** icon on the toolbar and click **OK** to save the entry.

   Enter **Starting check no.** "1203," click **Print**, select a printer, and click **OK**.

   Click **Close** to exit the Print Checks window.

4. Click **Save and Close** to exit Melvin's paycheck.

PAYING EMPLOYER AND EMPLOYEE PAYROLL TAXES

In this topic you remit employee tax withholdings and employer payroll tax liabilities. Payroll taxes are due on the dates set by the taxing agency. Normally federal tax, FICA, and Medicare taxes are due within three to five days after paying employees. This explains why you posted a bill for these taxes in the *Paying Employees* topic.

State income tax withholdings for the current month are normally due the first of the following month. Health insurance premiums and 401K contributions are also due the first of every month. Federal and state unemployment taxes are due at the end of every quarter.

You will now create bills for these liabilities. Before creating these bills, you should prepare a trial balance report to view balances in the liability accounts. Select ***Reports>>Company and Financial>>Trial Balance*** on the main menu. Filter the report for 3/31/2008 and scroll down to the accounts illustrated in Figure 10:41.

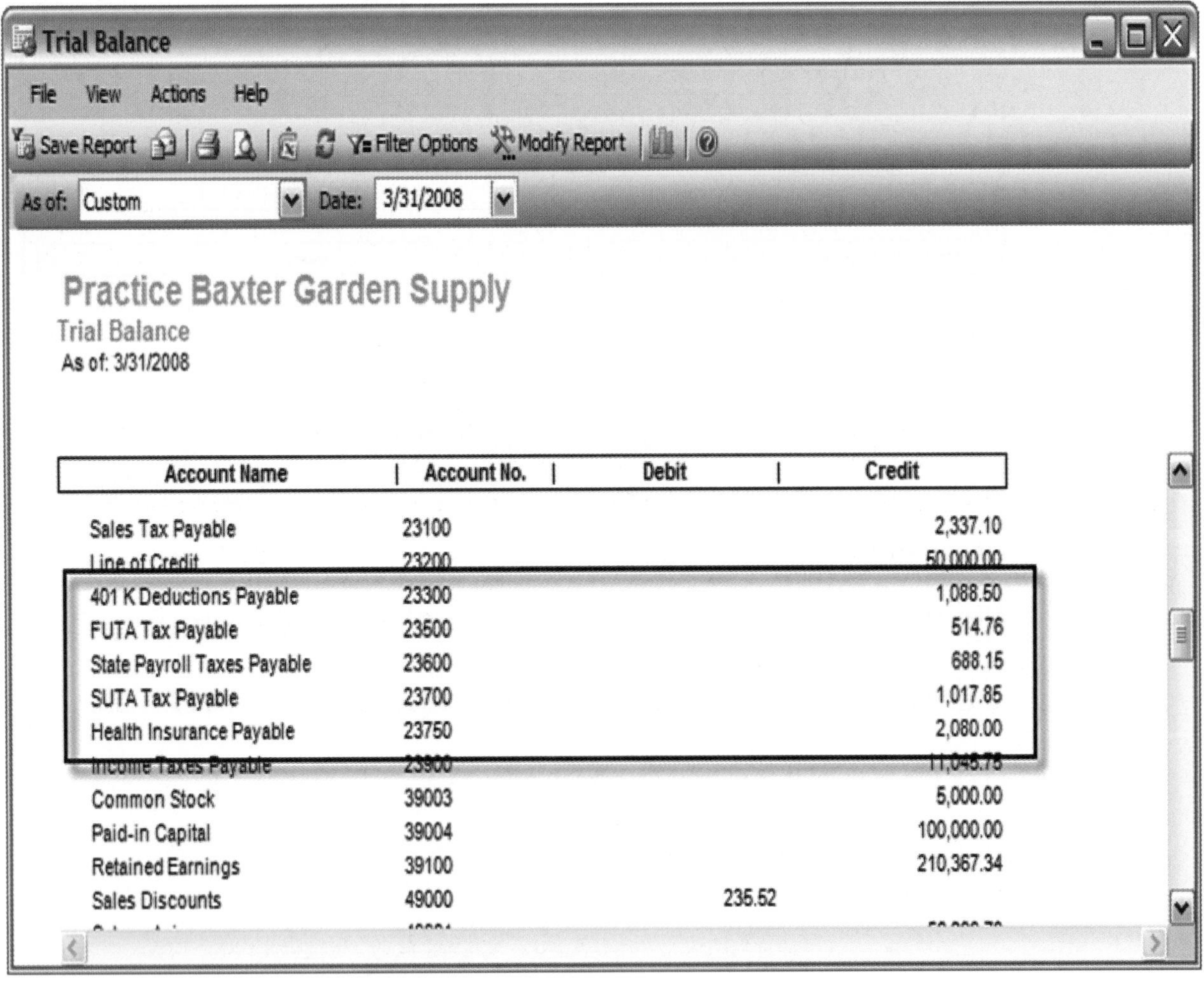

Account Name	Account No.	Debit	Credit
Sales Tax Payable	23100		2,337.10
Line of Credit	23200		50,000.00
401 K Deductions Payable	23300		1,088.50
FUTA Tax Payable	23500		514.76
State Payroll Taxes Payable	23600		688.15
SUTA Tax Payable	23700		1,017.85
Health Insurance Payable	23750		2,080.00
Income Taxes Payable	23900		11,048.75
Common Stock	39003		5,000.00
Paid-in Capital	39004		100,000.00
Retained Earnings	39100		210,367.34
Sales Discounts	49000	235.52	

Figure 10:41

In the next exercise you create bills for employer health insurance and unemployment liabilities. In the *You Try* that follows you create bills for state income taxes and 401K contributions.

STEPS TO PAYING PAYROLL TAXES

1. You will first pay the monthly health insurance premiums. Click **Recurring Documents** under Find and open the **Health Insurance Bill (Monthly)** recurring document. Complete the bill using the following information.

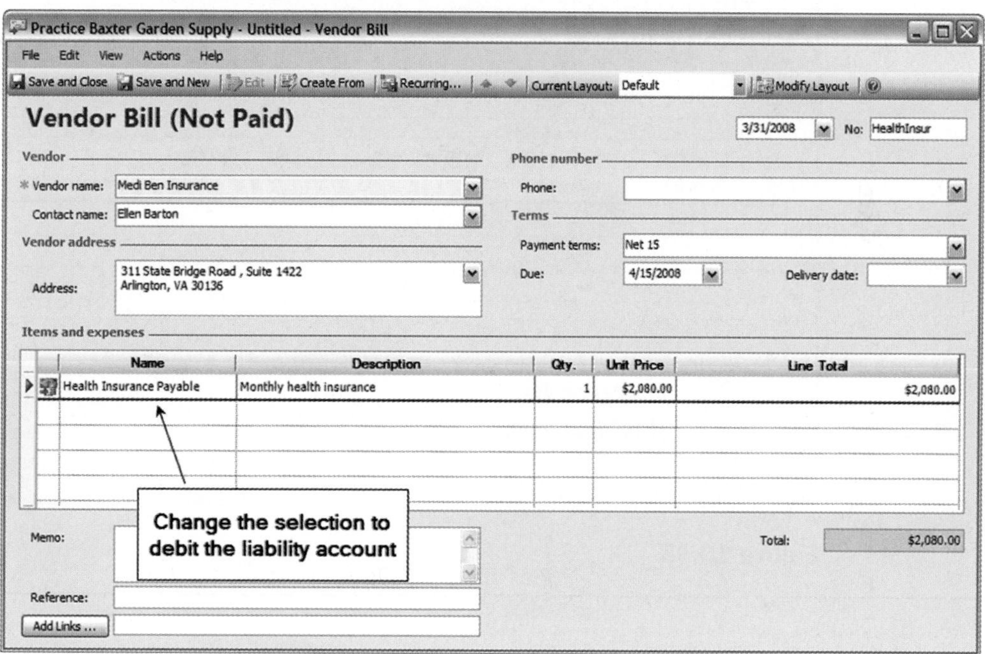

Figure 10:42

2. Click **Recurring** on the toolbar and select **Replace** to resave the recurring document with the new account. Click **Save and Close** to post the bill.

3. Now pay the unemployment taxes. The accountant has not created recurring documents for these bills so select ***Vendors>>Enter Bills*** on the main menu and enter the information illustrated in Figure 10:43.

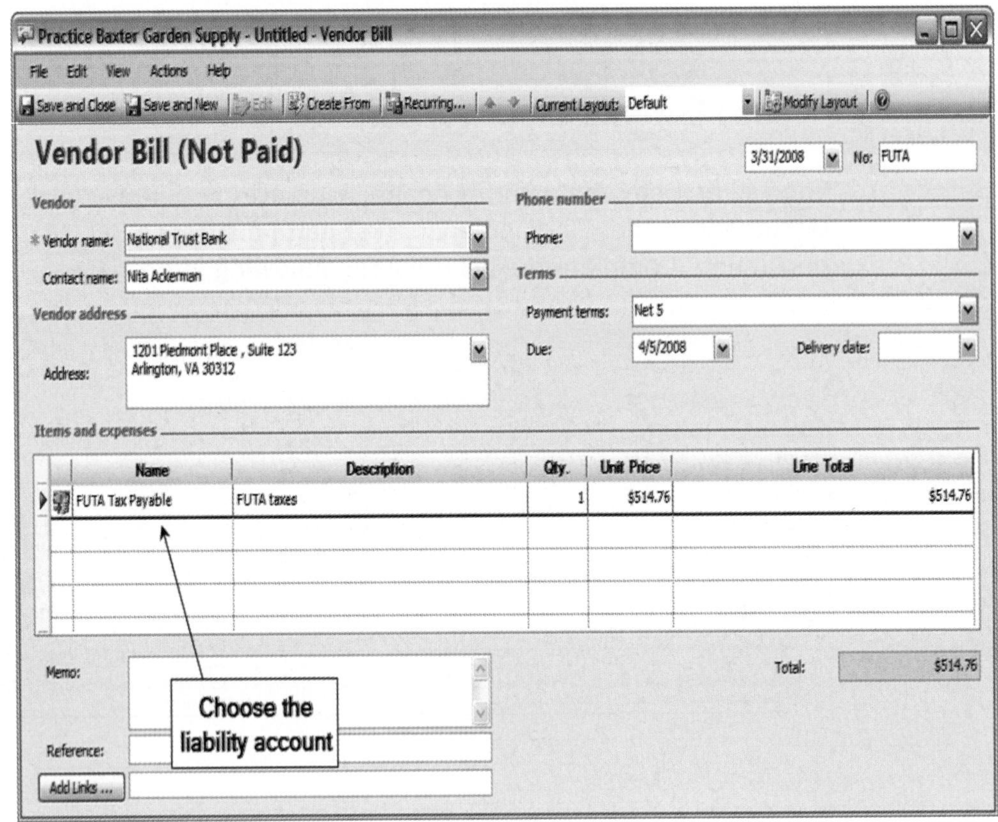

Figure 10:43

4. Click **Recurring** and name the document as shown in Figure 10:44. Click **OK.**

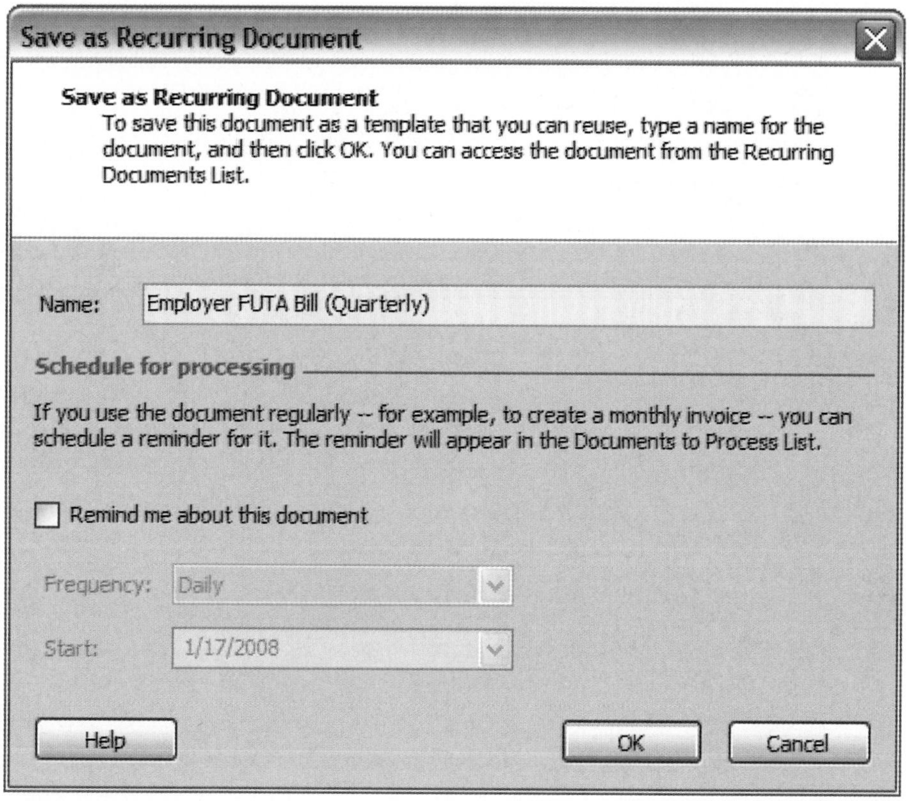

Save as Recurring Document

Save as Recurring Document
To save this document as a template that you can reuse, type a name for the document, and then click OK. You can access the document from the Recurring Documents List.

Name: Employer FUTA Bill (Quarterly)

Schedule for processing

If you use the document regularly -- for example, to create a monthly invoice -- you can schedule a reminder for it. The reminder will appear in the Documents to Process List.

Remind me about this document

Frequency: Daily

Start: 1/17/2008

Help OK Cancel

Figure 10:44

5. Click **Save and New** on the Vendor Bill window and create the bill for SUTA taxes as illustrated in Figure 10:45.

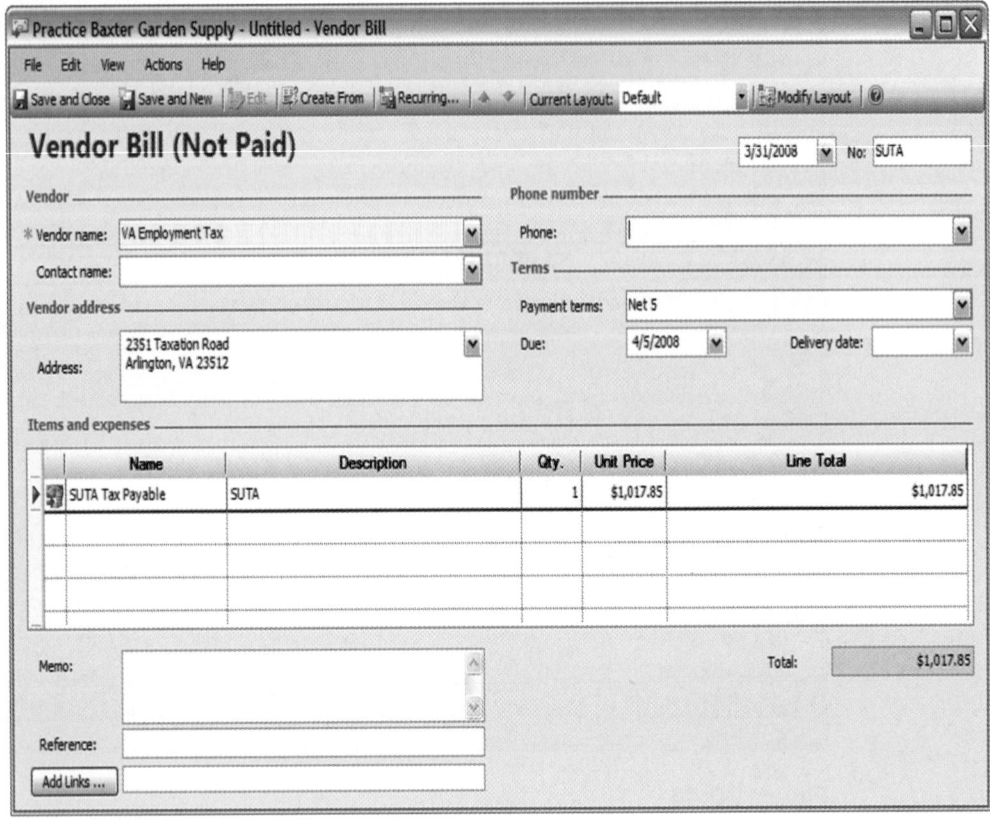

Figure 10:45

6. Click **Recurring** and save the document as illustrated in Figure 10:46. Click **OK** and then click **Save and Close** on the Vendor Bill window.

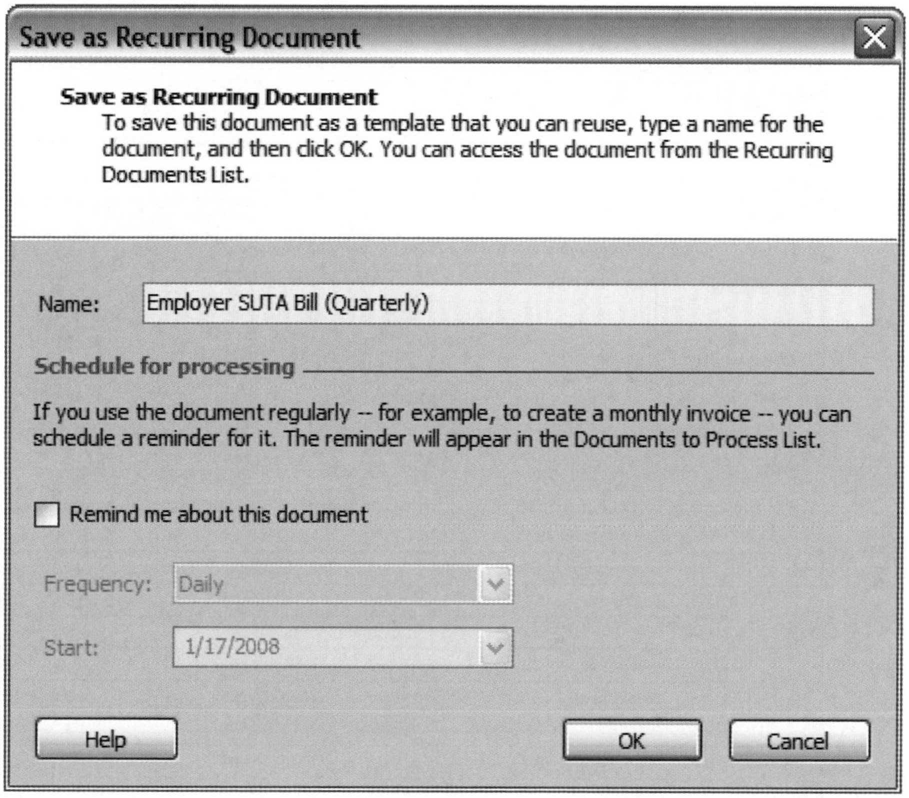

Save as Recurring Document

Save as Recurring Document
To save this document as a template that you can reuse, type a name for the document, and then click OK. You can access the document from the Recurring Documents List.

Name: Employer SUTA Bill (Quarterly)

Schedule for processing

If you use the document regularly -- for example, to create a monthly invoice -- you can schedule a reminder for it. The reminder will appear in the Documents to Process List.

Remind me about this document

Frequency: Daily

Start: 1/17/2008

Help OK Cancel

Figure 10:46

7. Now cut the checks to the vendors. Click **Pay Bills** on the Vendors Home page. Enter 3/31/2008 as the payment date and select the four bills illustrated in Figure 10:47.

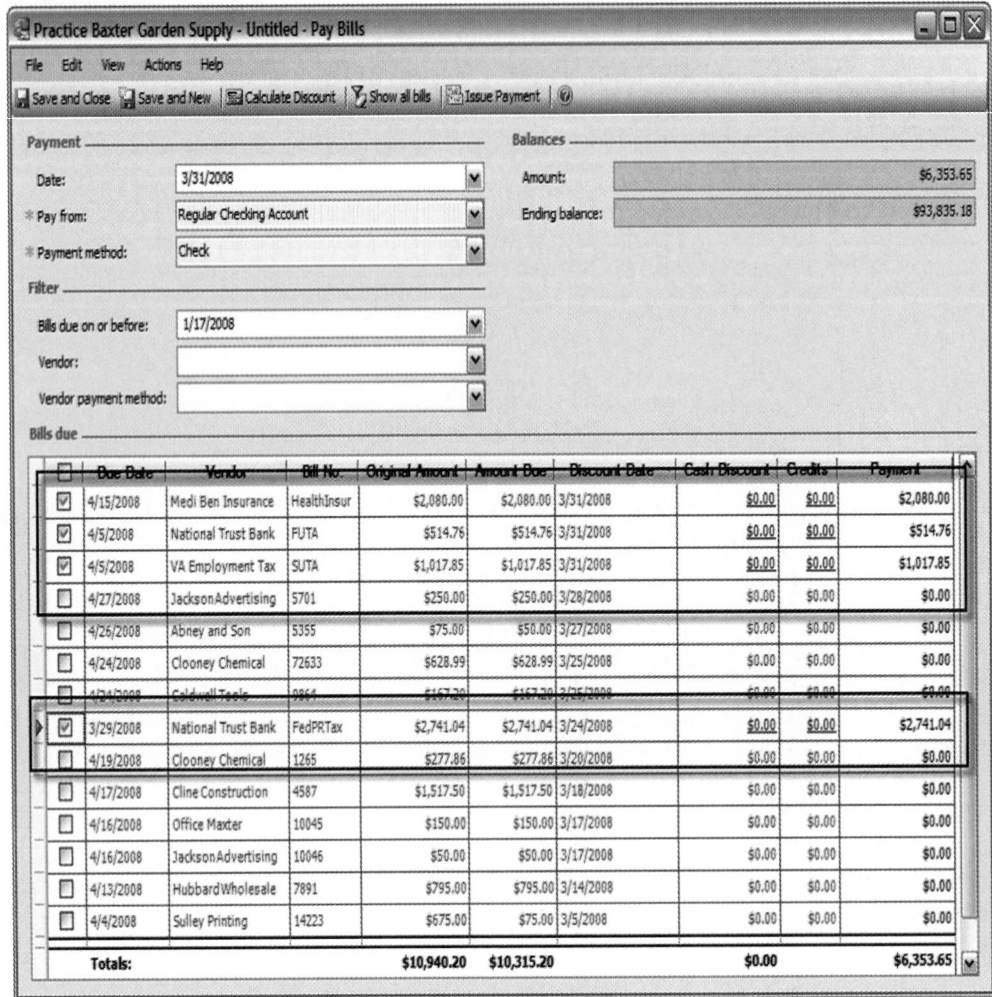

Figure 10:47

8. Click **Issue Payment** and complete the steps that print the checks. The first check number is 306.

CREATE CHECKS FOR PAYROLL TAXES

In this exercise you create and pay the bills for March state income tax liabilities and 401K contributions. Create the bills using the recurring documents listed below. All bills are dated 3/31/2008.

401 K Liability Bill (Monthly)
State Payroll Withholding Bill (Monthly)

Print the checks dated April 2, 2008 using 309 as the first check number. Also print the Payment report for April 2, 2008.

You have now completed the chapter. ***Make a backup of the Practice Baxter Garden Supply data file to a backup file named "practicebaxtergardensupply Chpt 10." In the next chapter, you will build on the work completed in this chapter.***

SUMMARY

You began this chapter with a *MAPS* overview on payroll processing. We first explained types of employee withholdings and voluntary deductions as well as types of employer payroll taxes and additional compensation. You also learned to calculate payroll tax withholdings.

You created a new employee and learned the procedures for terminating employees. With this knowledge, you were ready to process paychecks. You used recurring documents to create employee paychecks and printed the checks. After printing, you went *Behind the Keys* to trace entries posted to the general ledger. Finally, you recorded payroll tax liabilities and printed checks for these liabilities.

In the next chapter you focus on finalizing Baxter's March accounting period by recording adjusting entries, printing financial statements, and closing the period.

END-OF-CHAPTER QUESTIONS

TRUE/FALSE

______ 1. The Check Detail report lists employee paychecks.

______ 2. Employers pay Social Security and Medicare taxes in an amount equal to that withheld from employee paychecks.

______ 3. Employer payroll taxes can be entered as vendor bills.

______ 4. You can modify an employee's paycheck after the check has been printed.

______ 5. Employer tax expense includes unemployment taxes.

______ 6. Worker's compensation taxes are withheld from employee paychecks.

______ 7. Gross pay for a salaried employee equals hours worked in the pay period times the pay rate.

______ 8. You should contribute to a 401K plan when possible to reduce your federal and state taxes while saving for the future.

MULTIPLE CHOICE

______ 1. The ______ report lists all paycheck entries posted to the general ledger.
   a. GL Report
   b. Transaction Detail by Account
   c. Check Detail
   d. both a and b

______ 2. The ______ link will display a list of employee paychecks waiting to be printed.
   a. Vendor Payments
   b. Employee Payments
   c. Time Entries
   d. Memorized Documents

______ 3. Medicare withholdings are calculated as ______ of an employee's wages.
   a. 1.45 percent
   b. 6.2 percent
   c. both a and b
   d. none of the above

_____ 4. Per the IRS tax table, an employee must withhold _____ for federal taxes when paid biweekly for taxable pay of $960 and claiming Single with 2 allowances. *(Note: See Appendix D for complete payroll tax withholding tables.)*

a. 74
b. 77
c. 96
d. None of the above

_____ 5. An employee with gross pay of $1,295 will have a net pay of _____. Assume the employee is paid biweekly, claims Single with 0 allowances, contributed $35 to a 401K plan, and pays state taxes at 3 percent of net pay.

a. 958.08
b. 962.13
c. 997.13
d. 976.86

Practice Set

In this Practice Set you will be using the **Graded Baxter Garden Supply** data file with the tasks completed in the Practice Set at the end of Chapter 9. ***When this data file is not loaded on your computer, restore it using the "gradedbaxtergardensupply Chpt 9" backup file created after completing the Chapter 9 Practice Set.***

1. Open **Graded Baxter Garden Supply** and complete the March and April payroll activities that follow.

<u>**2008**</u>

Mar 24 Create the following paychecks for the Pay Period ending 3/23/2008. Print the paychecks on starting check number 1191.

Baxter Garden Supply

Pay Period 3/10/2008 thru 3/23/2008

Check No.	Employee	Filing Status	Allow	Pay Type	Pay Rate	Regular Hrs	OT Hrs	Gross Pay	Taxable Pay	Federal Income Tax	Soc. Sec. (FICA) Tax	Medicare Tax	VA State Tax	401K Deduc.	Net Pay
1191	Barkley, Steve N.	Married	3	Hourly wage	11.00	80.00		880.00	844.80	15.00	54.56	12.76	25.34	35.20	737.14
1192	Beck, Dorothy L.	Married	2	Hourly wage	9.00	80.00		720.00	720.00	16.00	44.64	10.44	21.60	0.00	627.32
1193	Chester, Amanda W.	Single	1	Hourly wage	14.00	80.00		1,120.00	1,075.20	111.00	69.44	16.24	32.26	44.80	846.26
1194	Duke, Al C.	Single	0	Hourly wage	12.50	80.00		1,000.00	1,000.00	122.00	62.00	14.50	30.00	0.00	771.50
1195	Frost, Melvin H.	Single	1	Salary	1,461.54			1,461.54	1,373.85	159.00	90.62	21.19	41.22	87.69	1,061.82
1196	Gross, Derrick P.	Married	2	Salary	1,000.00			1,000.00	940.00	38.00	62.00	14.50	28.20	60.00	797.30
1197	Hecter, Anthony H.	Single	1	Hourly wage	13.00	80.00	5.00	1,137.50	1,137.50	120.00	70.53	16.49	34.13	0.00	896.35
1198	Nunnley, Brandee M.	Married	1	Salary	1,211.54			1,211.54	1,211.54	86.00	75.12	17.57	36.35	0.00	996.50
1199	Prather, Samuel R.	Married	1	Salary	1,584.62			1,584.62	1,489.54	128.00	98.25	22.98	44.69	95.08	1,195.62
1200	Sweet, Leonard	Single	0	Hourly wage	9.00	80.00		720.00	720.00	80.00	44.64	10.44	21.60	0.00	563.32
1201	Trotter, Mitchell K.	Married	2	Hourly wage	11.00	80.00		880.00	844.80	28.00	54.56	12.76	25.34	35.20	724.14
	Totals					560.00	5.00	11,715.20		903.00	726.36	169.87	340.73	357.97	9,217.27
	Tax Basis									Circular E	6.20%	1.45%	3.00%		
	G/L Accounts							60000		23400	23400	23400	23600	23300	10300

Mar 24 Post recurring journal entries for the following 401K, FUTA, SUTA, and health insurance liabilities.

Post the recurring bill to National Trust Bank for the following employer FICA and Medicare taxes plus employee federal, FICA, and Medicare tax withholdings. Print check 310 for $2,695.46.

Baxter Garden Supply						
Employer Costs for Period 3/10/2008 thru 3/23/2008						
Employee	**401K Match**	**ER Soc. Sec. (FICA)**	**ER Medicare**	**ER FUTA**	**ER SUTA**	**Health Insurance**
Barkley, Steve N.	17.60	54.56	12.76	7.04	13.20	125.00
Beck, Dorothy L.	0.00	44.64	10.44	5.76	10.80	0.00
Chester, Amanda W.	22.40	69.44	16.24	8.96	16.80	90.00
Duke, Al C.	0.00	62.00	14.50	8.00	15.00	90.00
Frost, Melvin H.	43.85	90.62	21.19	4.66	10.40	125.00
Gross, Derrick P.	30.00	62.00	14.50	8.00	15.00	90.00
Hecter, Anthony H.	0.00	70.53	16.49	9.10	17.06	90.00
Nunnley, Brandee M.	0.00	75.12	17.57	7.55	18.17	125.00
Prather, Samuel R.	47.54	98.25	22.98	5.28	1.15	125.00
Sweet, Leonard	0.00	44.64	10.44	5.76	10.80	90.00
Trotter, Mitchell K.	17.60	54.56	12.76	7.04	13.20	90.00
Totals	**178.99**	**726.36**	**169.87**	**77.15**	**141.58**	**1,040.00**
Tax Basis	**50% Match**	**6.20%**	**1.45%**	**0.8%**	**1.5%**	
G/L Accounts	**23300 / 60500**	**23400 / 61000**	**23400 / 61000**	**23500 / 61000**	**23700 / 61000**	**23750 / 60300**

<u>2008</u>

Apr 2 Post recurring bills for the following payroll liabilities. All bills affect liability accounts.

Medi Ben Insurance	March health insurance	$2,080.00
VA State Income Tax	March state taxes	$ 678.53
Watkins Financial	March 401K liabilities	$1,073.92

Create bills for the following payroll liabilities.

National Trust Bank	First Qtr. FUTA taxes	$ 522.06
VA Employment Tax	First Qtr. SUTA taxes	$1,012.88

Print checks for the above bills totaling $5,367.39 on starting check number 311.

Apr 7 Create the following paychecks for the Pay Period ending 4/6/2008. Print paychecks on starting check number 1202.

Baxter Garden Supply
Pay Period 3/24/2008 thru 4/6/2008

Check No.	Employee	Filing Status	Allow	Pay Type	Pay Rate	Regular Hrs	OT Hrs	Gross Pay	Taxable Pay	Federal Income Tax	Soc. Sec. (FICA) Tax	Medicare Tax	VA State Tax	401K Deduc.	Net Pay
1202	Barkley, Steve N.	Married	3	Hourly wage	11.00	80.00		880.00	844.80	15.00	54.56	12.76	25.34	35.20	737.14
1203	Beck, Dorothy L.	Married	2	Hourly wage	9.00	80.00		720.00	720.00	16.00	44.64	10.44	21.60	0.00	627.32
1204	Chester, Amanda W.	Single	1	Hourly wage	14.00	80.00		1,120.00	1,075.20	111.00	69.44	16.24	32.26	44.80	846.26
1205	Duke, Al C.	Single	0	Hourly wage	12.50	80.00		1,000.00	1,000.00	122.00	62.00	14.50	30.00	0.00	771.50
1206	Frost, Melvin H.	Single	1	Salary	1,461.54			1,461.54	1,373.85	159.00	90.62	21.19	41.22	87.69	1,061.82
1207	Gross, Derrick P.	Married	2	Salary	1,000.00			1,000.00	940.00	38.00	62.00	14.50	28.20	60.00	797.30
1208	Hecter, Anthony H.	Single	1	Hourly wage	13.00	80.00		1,040.00	1,040.00	108.00	64.48	15.08	31.20	0.00	821.24
1209	Nunnley, Brandee M.	Married	1	Salary	1,211.54			1,211.54	1,211.54	86.00	75.12	17.57	36.35	0.00	996.50
1210	Prather, Samuel R.	Married	1	Salary	1,584.62			1,584.62	1,489.54	128.00	98.25	22.98	44.69	95.08	1,195.62
1211	Sweet, Leonard	Single	0	Hourly wage	9.00	75.00		675.00	675.00	71.00	41.85	9.79	20.25	0.00	532.11
1212	Trotter, Mitchell K.	Married	2	Hourly wage	11.00	80.00		880.00	844.80	28.00	54.56	12.76	25.34	35.20	724.14
	Totals					555.00	0.00	11,572.70		882.00	717.52	167.81	336.45	357.97	9,110.95
	Tax Basis									Circular E	6.20%	1.45%	3.00%		
	G/L Accounts							60000		23400	23400	23400	23600	23300	10300

Apr 7 Post recurring journal entries for the following 401K, FUTA, SUTA, and health insurance liabilities.

Post the recurring bill to National Trust Bank for the following employer FICA and Medicare taxes plus employee federal, FICA, and Medicare tax withholdings.
Print check 316 to National Trust Bank for $2,652.66.

Baxter Garden Supply **Employer Costs for Period 3/24/2008 thru 4/6/2008**						
Employee	**401K Match**	**ER Soc. Sec. (FICA)**	**ER Medicare**	**ER FUTA**	**ER SUTA**	**Health Insurance**
Barkley, Steve N.	17.60	54.56	12.76	7.04	13.20	125.00
Beck, Dorothy L.	0.00	44.64	10.44	5.76	10.80	0.00
Chester, Amanda W.	22.40	69.44	16.24	2.24	16.80	90.00
Duke, Al C.	0.00	62.00	14.50	8.00	15.00	90.00
Frost, Melvin H.	43.85	90.62	21.19	0.00	0.00	125.00
Gross, Derrick P.	30.00	62.00	14.50	8.00	15.00	90.00
Hecter, Anthony H.	0.00	64.48	15.08	5.30	15.60	90.00
Nunnley, Brandee M.	0.00	75.12	17.57	0.00	10.98	125.00
Prather, Samuel R.	47.54	98.25	22.98	0.00	0.00	125.00
Sweet, Leonard	0.00	41.85	9.79	5.40	10.13	90.00
Trotter, Mitchell K.	17.60	54.56	12.76	7.04	13.20	90.00
Totals	**178.99**	**717.52**	**167.81**	**48.78**	**120.71**	**1,040.00**
Tax Basis	**50% Match**	**6.20%**	**1.45%**	**0.8%**	**1.5%**	
G/L Accounts	**23300 / 60500**	**23400 / 61000**	**23400 / 61000**	**23500 / 61000**	**23700 / 61000**	**23750 / 60300**

Apr 14 Add the following new employee. Remember to choose Employee Form as the Current Layout.

Name:	Arthur C. Parker
Address:	782 Sewickly Blvd, Arlington, VA 30025
Job title:	Sales Manager
Telephone:	770-987-7109
Hired:	4/14/2008
Federal filing status:	Single
Allowances:	0
401K:	4% with employer match of 2%
Annual salary:	$27,690.00

Terminate Brandee M. Nunnley. Release date is April 14, 2008.

Apr 21 Create the following paychecks for the Pay Period ending 4/20/2008. Print the paychecks on starting check number 1213.

Note: When creating Arthur Parker's check verify that the Bank Account is Payroll Checking Account.

Baxter Garden Supply
Pay Period 4/7/2008 thru 4/20/2008

Check No.	Employee	Filing Status	Allow	Pay Type	Pay Rate	Regular Hrs	OT Hrs	Gross Pay	Taxable Pay	Federal Income Tax	Soc. Sec. (FICA) Tax	Medicare Tax	VA State Tax	401K Deduc.	Net Pay
1213	Barkley, Steve N.	Married	3	Hourly wage	11.00	80.00		880.00	844.80	15.00	54.56	12.76	25.34	35.20	737.14
1214	Beck, Dorothy L.	Married	2	Hourly wage	9.00	80.00		720.00	720.00	16.00	44.64	10.44	21.60	0.00	627.32
1215	Chester, Amanda W.	Single	1	Hourly wage	14.00	80.00		1,120.00	1,075.20	111.00	69.44	16.24	32.26	44.80	846.26
1216	Duke, Al C.	Single	0	Hourly wage	12.50	80.00		1,000.00	1,000.00	122.00	62.00	14.50	30.00	0.00	771.50
1217	Frost, Melvin H.	Single	1	Salary	1,461.54			1,461.54	1,373.85	159.00	90.62	21.19	41.22	87.69	1,061.82
1218	Gross, Derrick P.	Married	2	Salary	1,000.00			1,000.00	940.00	38.00	62.00	14.50	28.20	60.00	797.30
1219	Hecter, Anthony H.	Single	1	Hourly wage	13.00	80.00		1,040.00	1,040.00	108.00	64.48	15.08	31.20	0.00	821.24
1220	Nunnley, Brandee M.	Married	1	Salary	605.77			605.77	605.77	17.00	37.56	8.78	18.17	0.00	524.26
1221	Parker, Arthur C.	Married	0	Salary	537.50			537.50	516.00	20.00	33.33	7.79	15.48	21.50	439.40
1222	Prather, Samuel R.	Married	1	Salary	1,584.62			1,584.62	1,489.54	128.00	98.25	22.98	44.69	95.08	1,195.62
1223	Sweet, Leonard	Single	0	Hourly wage	9.00	75.00		675.00	675.00	71.00	41.85	9.79	20.25	0.00	532.11
1224	Trotter, Mitchell K.	Married	2	Hourly wage	11.00	80.00		880.00	844.80	28.00	54.56	12.76	25.34	35.20	724.14
	Totals					**555.00**	**0.00**	**11,504.43**		**833.00**	**713.29**	**166.81**	**333.75**	**379.47**	**9,078.11**
	Tax Basis									**Circular E**	**6.20%**	**1.45%**	**3.00%**		
	G/L Accounts							**60000**		**23400**	**23400**	**23400**	**23600**	**23300**	**10300**

Apr 21 Post recurring journal entries for the following 401K, FUTA, SUTA, and health insurance liabilities.

Post the recurring bill to National Trust Bank for the following employer FICA and Medicare taxes plus employee federal, FICA, and Medicare tax withholdings. Print check 317 to National Trust Bank for $2,593.20.

Baxter Garden Supply
Employer Costs for Period 4/7/2008 thru 4/20/2008

Employee	401K Match	ER Soc. Sec. (FICA)	ER Medicare	ER FUTA	ER SUTA	Health Insurance
Barkley, Steve N.	17.60	54.56	12.76	6.72	13.20	125.00
Beck, Dorothy L.	0.00	44.64	10.44	5.76	10.80	0.00
Chester, Amanda W.	22.40	69.44	16.24	0.00	2.40	90.00
Duke, Al C.	0.00	62.00	14.50	0.00	15.00	90.00
Frost, Melvin H.	43.85	90.62	21.19	0.00	0.00	125.00
Gross, Derrick P.	30.00	62.00	14.50	0.00	15.00	90.00
Hecter, Anthony H.	0.00	64.48	15.08	0.00	9.34	90.00
Nunnley, Brandee M.	0.00	37.56	8.78	0.00	0.00	125.00
Parker, Arthur C.	10.75	33.33	7.79	4.30	8.06	0.00
Prather, Samuel R.	47.54	98.25	22.98	0.00	0.00	125.00
Sweet, Leonard	0.00	41.85	9.79	5.40	10.13	90.00
Trotter, Mitchell K.	17.60	54.56	12.76	6.72	13.20	90.00
Totals	**189.74**	**713.29**	**166.81**	**28.90**	**97.13**	**1,040.00**
Tax Basis	**50% Match**	**6.20%**	**1.45%**	**0.8%**	**1.5%**	
G/L Accounts	**23300 / 60500**	**23400 / 61000**	**23400 / 61000**	**23500 / 61000**	**23700 / 61000**	**23750 / 60300**

Apr 30 Post recurring bills for the following payroll liabilities. All bills affect liability accounts.

Medi Ben Insurance	April health insurance	$2,080.00
VA State Income Tax	April state taxes	$ 670.20
Watkins Financial	April 401K liabilities	$1,106.17

2. Print the following reports to document activities.

    a. Employee Payments report filtered for 3/24/2008 to 4/21/2008. Modify the report to remove the Issue date, Status detail, Reference number, and Void columns.

    b. Check Detail report filtered for 3/24/2008 to 4/30/2008 and for the Name of the following vendors.
    Medi Ben Insurance Company
    National Trust Bank
    VA Department of Taxation
    VA Employment Tax
    Watkins Financial Planning

3. ***Back up the Graded Baxter Garden Supply data file to a backup file named "gradedbaxtergardensupply Chpt 10." The Practice Set for the next chapter will build on the work completed in this chapter.***

CHAPTER 11 CLOSE THE ACCOUNTING PERIOD FOR A MERCHANDISING BUSINESS

LEARNING OBJECTIVES

This chapter works with the **Practice Baxter Garden Supply** data file containing the tasks completed in Chapter 10. ***When this data file is not loaded on your computer, restore it using the "practicebaxtergardensupply Chpt 10" backup file created after reading Chapter 10.***

In this chapter you complete Baxter's accounting transactions for March 2008 by:

1. Analyzing transactions posted in March
2. Posting adjusting entries
3. Reconciling bank statements
4. Printing financial reports
5. Closing the accounting period

Launch OAP an open **Practice Baxter Garden Supply**.

ANALYZE TRANSACTIONS

In Chapters 3 and 7 you posted general journal entries. In this chapter, you again post journal entries to adjust account balances and accrue expenses. You will then print financial statements for March and close the accounting period.

It is important to analyze posted transactions before closing an accounting period. You begin this analysis by reviewing the **GL Report**.

Open the report by selecting ***Reports>>Company and Financial>>GL Report*** on the main menu. *(Note: You can also access this report from the Reports section of the Company Home page and from the Reports Home page.)*

Enter the date range of 3/1/2008 to 3/31/2008 (Figure 11:1).

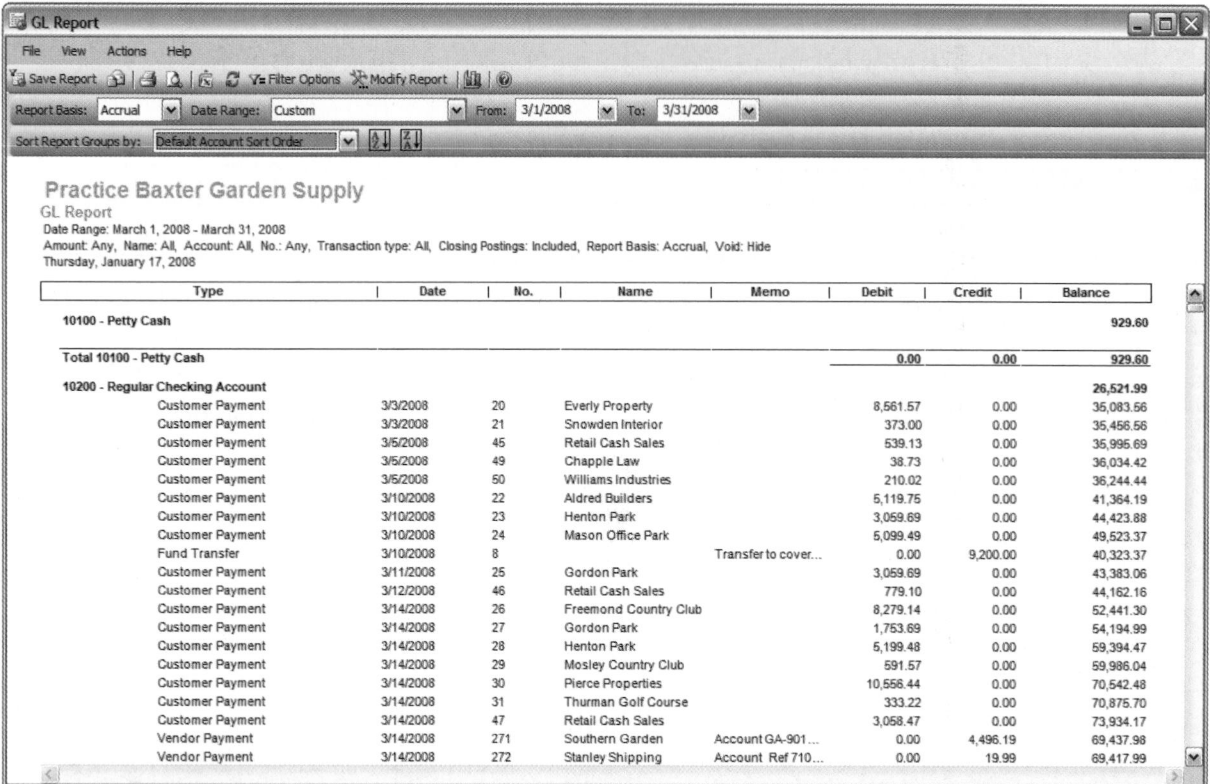

Practice Baxter Garden Supply
GL Report
Date Range: March 1, 2008 - March 31, 2008
Amount: Any, Name: All, Account: All, No.: Any, Transaction type: All, Closing Postings: Included, Report Basis: Accrual, Void: Hide
Thursday, January 17, 2008

Type	Date	No.	Name	Memo	Debit	Credit	Balance
10100 - Petty Cash							**929.60**
Total 10100 - Petty Cash					**0.00**	**0.00**	**929.60**
10200 - Regular Checking Account							**26,521.99**
Customer Payment	3/3/2008	20	Everly Property		8,561.57	0.00	35,083.56
Customer Payment	3/3/2008	21	Snowden Interior		373.00	0.00	35,456.56
Customer Payment	3/5/2008	45	Retail Cash Sales		539.13	0.00	35,995.69
Customer Payment	3/5/2008	49	Chapple Law		38.73	0.00	36,034.42
Customer Payment	3/5/2008	50	Williams Industries		210.02	0.00	36,244.44
Customer Payment	3/10/2008	22	Aldred Builders		5,119.75	0.00	41,364.19
Customer Payment	3/10/2008	23	Henton Park		3,059.69	0.00	44,423.88
Customer Payment	3/10/2008	24	Mason Office Park		5,099.49	0.00	49,523.37
Fund Transfer	3/10/2008	8		Transfer to cover...	0.00	9,200.00	40,323.37
Customer Payment	3/11/2008	25	Gordon Park		3,059.69	0.00	43,383.06
Customer Payment	3/12/2008	46	Retail Cash Sales		779.10	0.00	44,162.16
Customer Payment	3/14/2008	26	Freemond Country Club		8,279.14	0.00	52,441.30
Customer Payment	3/14/2008	27	Gordon Park		1,753.69	0.00	54,194.99
Customer Payment	3/14/2008	28	Henton Park		5,199.48	0.00	59,394.47
Customer Payment	3/14/2008	29	Mosley Country Club		591.57	0.00	59,986.04
Customer Payment	3/14/2008	30	Pierce Properties		10,556.44	0.00	70,542.48
Customer Payment	3/14/2008	31	Thurman Golf Course		333.22	0.00	70,875.70
Customer Payment	3/14/2008	47	Retail Cash Sales		3,058.47	0.00	73,934.17
Vendor Payment	3/14/2008	271	Southern Garden	Account GA-901...	0.00	4,496.19	69,437.98
Vendor Payment	3/14/2008	272	Stanley Shipping	Account Ref 710...	0.00	19.99	69,417.99

Figure 11:1

This report differs from the Transaction Detail by Account report because it breaks transactions into Debit and Credit columns along with listing ending account balances. The following explains steps to perform when analyzing this report.

First, scroll through the report looking for transactions that may indicate a posting error. In particular, scroll down to 72100 Repairs - Equipment Expense and locate the entry for shipping. The accountant recalls this transaction as shipping a package to a customer so it should have been posted to 57500 Freight.

You will now reclassify the expense. Double click the entry to reopen and click Edit. In **Name**, change the account to **Freight** (Figure 11:2).

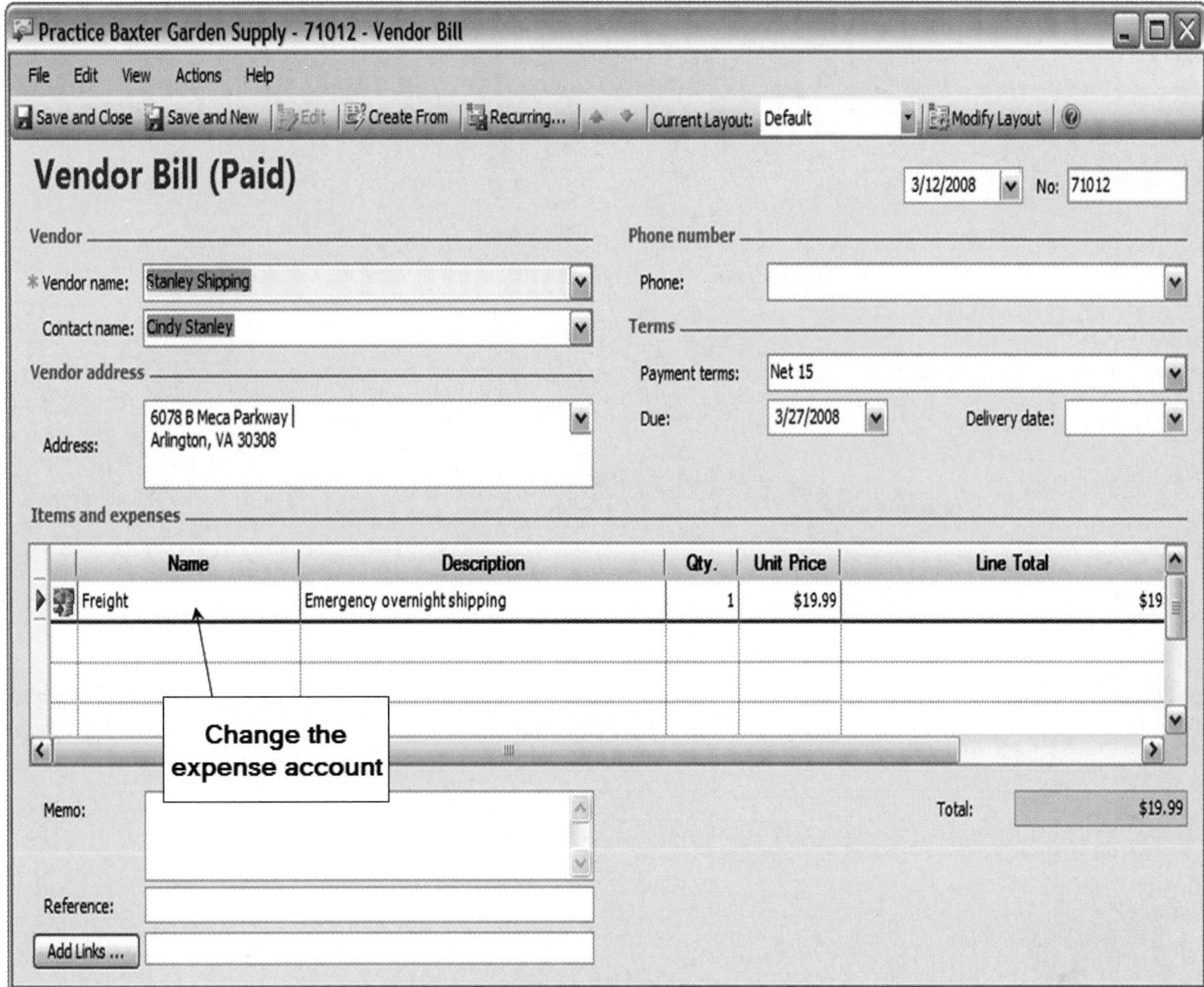

Figure 11:2

Click **Save and Close**. Return to the GL Report, which refreshes, and scroll down to view the change. That is how easy it is to reclassify a posting error for a transaction linked to a general ledger account.

However, it is not as easy to correct a posting error when the posting account is linked to a transaction from another record such as an inventory item. We will now simulate this type of error.

Let us assume that the accountant noticed item AVRY-10050-LG-CSL has been posting revenue to 40002 Sales – Books and not to 40001 Sales – Aviary. Figure 11:3 shows an invoice containing this item. Notice that you cannot change the general ledger account on the transaction.

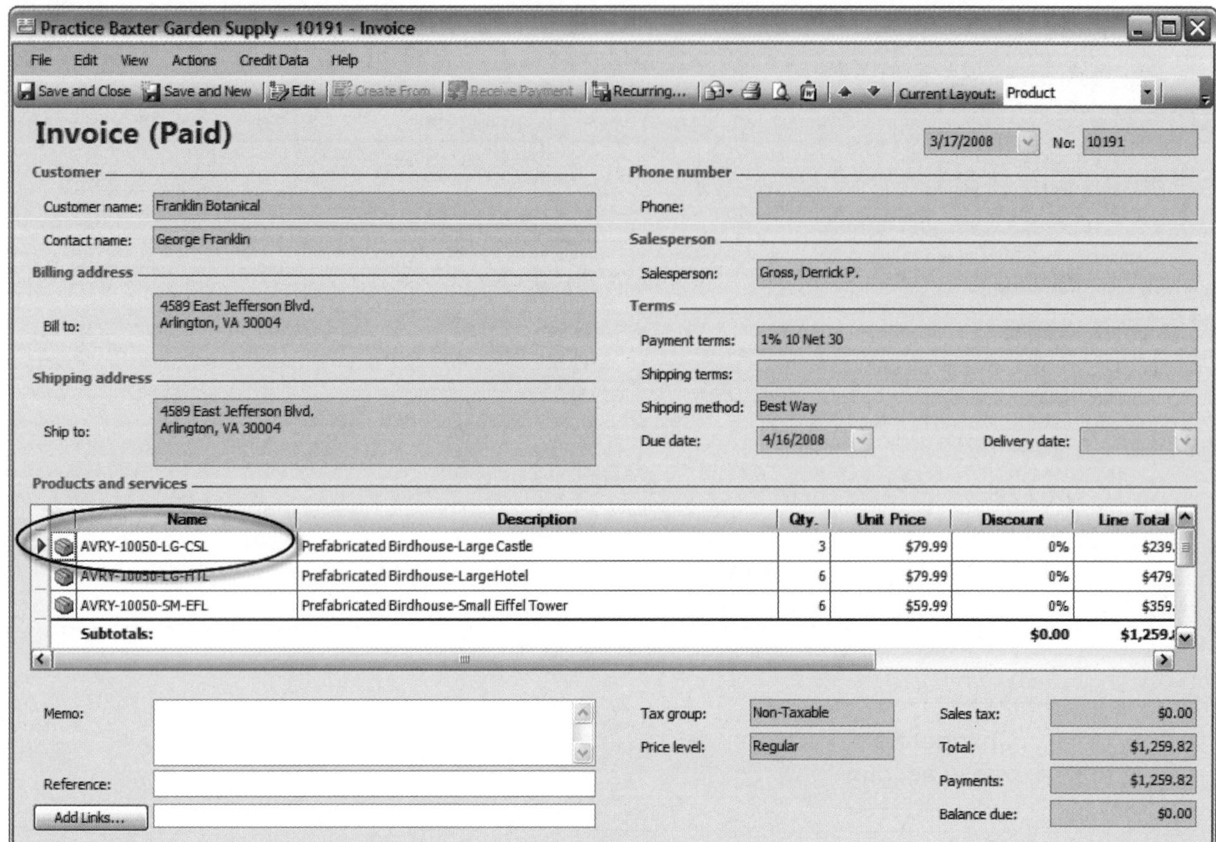

Figure 11:3

To correct an error of this type you would have to change the default income account on the inventory item. However, this only corrects future postings. To reclassify existing income, you need to run an inventory items sales report and post a journal entry to reclassify all previously posted amounts. You can see why it is important to review general ledger postings monthly so you can catch errors as early as possible.

The next step in analyzing the GL Report involves reviewing it for missing transactions. In particular, scroll to account 10300 Payroll Checking to see that the March 24 bank transfer covering payroll checks has not been recorded.

Scroll to 14000 Prepaid Insurance. The entry recognizing this month's expired prepaid insurance also needs to be recorded.

Finally, scroll to 15010 Accum Depreciation – Furniture. You can confirm that the depreciation entries for this month have been posted.

You will finish recording adjusting entries in the exercises that follow.

You have finished reviewing the report so close it.

Now is a good time to talk about using a suspense account. Scroll to the bottom of the General Ledger report to locate the **99999 Suspense** account. This account is used when you need to post an entry but do not have all the information necessary to complete it.

For instance, assume the company sold a vehicle costing $3,000 and received $500 in cash. You cannot delay recording cash on the sale; however, you do not have final depreciation on the vehicle to finalize gain or loss on the sale. This is where the entry can be posted using the suspense account. The following illustrates the journal entry to post the transaction using the suspense account.

	Debit	Credit
10200 Regular Checking Account	$ 500	
99999 Suspense	$2,500	
15200 Vehicles		$3,000

When you later calculate that $1,000 was previously recorded to the accumulated vehicle depreciation account and that final depreciation is $1,200, the following journal entry records the depreciation adjustment.

	Debit	Credit
75000 Depreciation Expense	$ 200	
15210 Accum. Depreciation – Vehicles		$ 200

You are now ready to reclassify the earlier suspense account entry by recording the next journal entry.

	Debit	Credit
15210 Accum. Depreciation – Vehicles	$1,200	
90000 Gain/Loss on Sale of Assets	$1,300	
99999 Suspense		$2,500

Thus, the suspense account becomes a useful tool for recording entries when you are unsure of all the accounts affected by a transaction. However, you must diligently review the balance in the suspense account to make sure entries are finalized.

There are a variety of procedures to be followed before closing an accounting period. Some of these were explained in previous chapters. Additional procedures vary based on a company's accounting transactions. It is not possible to simulate the variety of reconciling procedures you may encounter in practice. Instead, we have prepared the following preclosing checklist to help guide you in the future.

Preclosing Checklist	
Review Pending Transactions	Review pending sales to verify all sales income has been recognized.
	Review pending purchases to verify all expenses have been recognized.
	Review payroll tax liability accounts to ensure timely payment.
Reconciliation Procedures	Reconcile all bank statements.
	Reconcile the A/R aging report to the accounts receivable control account. (Performed in Chapters 4 and 8.)
	Reconcile the inventory valuation report to the inventory control account. (Performed in Chapter 8.)
	Reconcile fixed asset reports to fixed asset control accounts. Often fixed asset costs and depreciation will be tracked outside the software. OAP can track fixed asset costs and calculate depreciation, but this feature is not illustrated.
	Reconcile the A/P aging report to the accounts payable control account. (Performed in Chapter 5 and 9.)
Adjusting Entries	Post petty cash transactions.
	Review prepaid expenses for expired costs.
	Review accrued liability accounts such as wages and taxes payable.
	Review expenses in the prior period to identify expenses that need to be recognized in the current period. For example, missing utility bills or recurring rent transactions.
	Review posted expenses for prepaid costs and for fixed assets expensed to office supplies.

Post Adjusting Entries

In this topic you post Baxter's remaining adjusting entries for March. The accountant has already posted depreciation expense. When posting depreciation, keep in mind that this is an estimate of expense based on ending assets held in the prior year. Actual depreciation expense is then adjusted at year-end to take into account asset additions and deletions during the year.

All that remains are entries recording the transfer of funds from the regular checking account to the payroll checking, the expensing of expired prepaid expense, and the accrual of wage expense. In the next exercise you post the bank transfer and accrue wage expense. In the *You Try* that follows you expense expired prepaid expense.

Steps to Enter Adjusting Entries

1. You will record the payroll transfer first. Select ***Banking>>Transfer Funds*** on the main menu and enter the information in Figure 11:4. Click **Transfer** to post the entry.

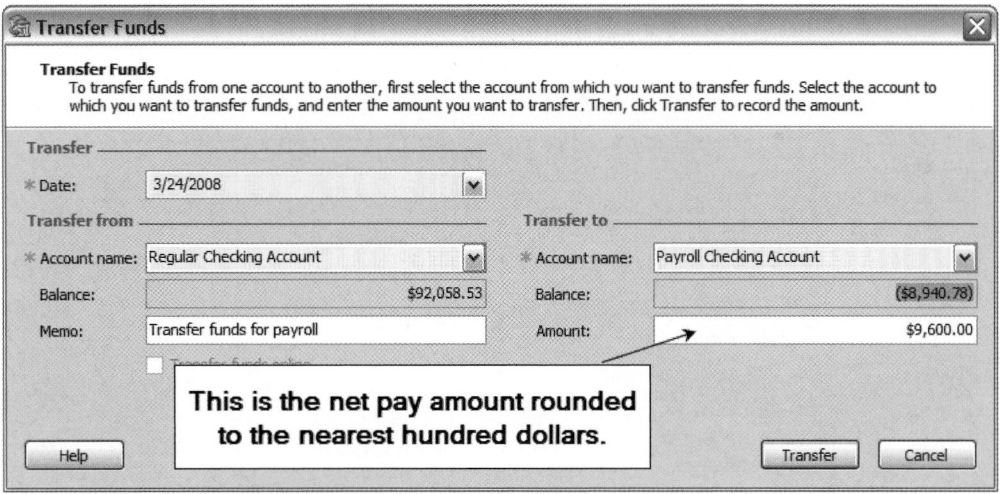

Figure 11:4

2. You will now post the accrued wage entry. You must first calculate the amount to accrue using the next steps.

   a. ***Compute the daily wage rate:*** Open the GL report for the month of March and look at the total debit to 60000 Salaries and Wages Expense. The total, rounded to the nearest hundred dollars, is $23,700. Divide the total by 4 (i.e., the number of weeks covered by the report) to calculate that the average weekly wage was $5,925. This then makes the average daily wage rate equal to $1,185 (i.e., $5,925 / 5).

   b. ***Compute the number of days to accrue:*** The last pay period ended on March 23 and there are 31 days in March. This means that there are 6 days of wages to accrue (i.e., March 24 through March 28 and March 31).

   c. ***Multiply the daily wage rate by the number of dates to accrue:*** The daily wage multiplied by the accrual days makes the accrued wage amount equal to $7,110 (i.e., $1,185 times 6 days).

3. You are now ready to post the entry. Click **New Journal Entry** under Find and enter the transaction as illustrated in Figure 11:5. The first two lines book the accrual for March and the next two lines reverse the accrual in April.

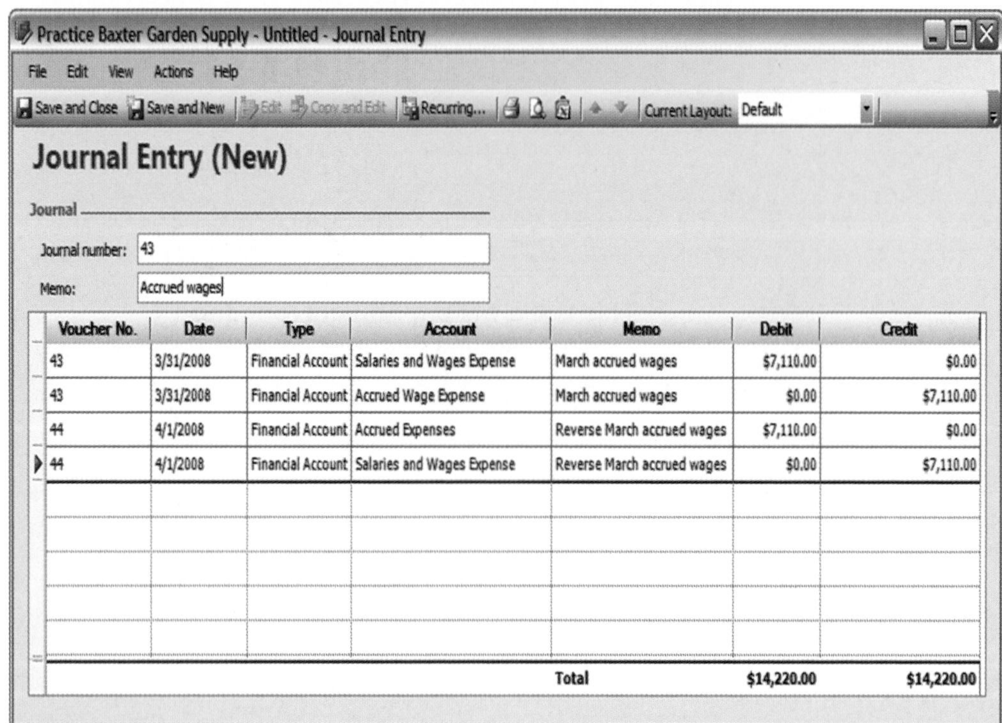

Practice Baxter Garden Supply - Untitled - Journal Entry

File Edit View Actions Help

Save and Close | Save and New | Edit | Copy and Edit | Recurring... | Current Layout: Default

Journal Entry (New)

Journal

Journal number: 43

Memo: Accrued wages

Voucher No.	Date	Type	Account	Memo	Debit	Credit
43	3/31/2008	Financial Account	Salaries and Wages Expense	March accrued wages	$7,110.00	$0.00
43	3/31/2008	Financial Account	Accrued Wage Expense	March accrued wages	$0.00	$7,110.00
44	4/1/2008	Financial Account	Accrued Expenses	Reverse March accrued wages	$7,110.00	$0.00
44	4/1/2008	Financial Account	Salaries and Wages Expense	Reverse March accrued wages	$0.00	$7,110.00
				Total	$14,220.00	$14,220.00

Figure 11:5

4. Click **Save and Close** to post the entry.

FINISH RECORDING MARCH ADJUSTING ENTRIES

In this exercise you reclassify the expired portion of prepaid expense.

a. On March 31 the accountant determined that $400.00 of prepaid auto insurance and $687.00 of prepaid business insurance have expired. Post the entry.

RECONCILE BANK ACCOUNTS

After posting adjusting entries, you are ready to reconcile Baxter's bank accounts. The accountant has already reconciled the savings account. Baxter has received the March bank statement for the Regular Checking Account (Figure 11:6) and you will next reconcile this account in the exercise that follows.

Baxter Garden Supply
Bank Statement March 31, 2008

February Statement Balance				$ 45,243.25
March Deposits	Mar 3, 2008		8,561.57	
	Mar 3, 2008		373.00	
	Mar 5, 2008		539.13	
	Mar 5, 2008		38.73	
	Mar 5, 2008		210.02	
	Mar 10, 2008		5,119.75	
	Mar 10, 2008		3,059.69	
	Mar 10, 2008		5,099.49	
	Mar 11, 2008		3,059.69	
	Mar 12, 2008		779.10	
	Mar 14, 2008		8,279.14	
	Mar 14, 2008		1,753.69	
	Mar 14, 2008		5,199.48	
	Mar 14, 2008		591.57	
	Mar 14, 2008		10,556.44	
	Mar 14, 2008		333.22	
	Mar 14, 2008		3,058.47	
	Mar 17, 2008		326.34	
	Mar 17, 2008		489.58	
	Mar 17, 2008		693.19	
	Mar 17, 2008		2,194.38	
	Mar 17, 2008		10,046.90	
	Mar 17, 2008		3,915.23	
	Mar 18, 2008		485.19	
	Mar 24, 2008		6,957.25	
	Mar 24, 2008		12,196.95	
	Mar 24, 2008		4,588.03	
	Mar 24, 2008		7,257.10	
	Mar 24, 2008		2,497.93	
	Mar 24, 2008		3,117.73	
	Mar 25, 2008		183.58	
	Mar 27, 2008		213.89	
	Mar 28, 2008		611.91	
	Mar 31, 2008		7,258.99	
	Mar 31, 2008		285.56	
	Mar 31, 2008		14,969.20	
	Mar 31, 2008		59.00	
Total Deposits for March				134,960.11
March Checks Cleared				
	Mar 3, 2008	262	3,090.90	
	Mar 4, 2008	263	2,445.25	
	Mar 4, 2008	264	124.68	
	Mar 4, 2008	265	550.00	
	Mar 3, 2008	266	675.60	
	Mar 3, 2008	267	434.73	
	Mar 3, 2008	269	5,962.50	
	Mar 3, 2008	270	5,437.60	
	Mar 17, 2008	271	4,496.19	
	Mar 17, 2008	272	19.99	
	Mar 16, 2007	273	2,080.00	
	Mar 16, 2007	274	1,073.92	
	Mar 18, 2008	275	90.00	
	Mar 18, 2008	276	26.58	
	Mar 18, 2008	277	78.93	
	Mar 18, 2008	278	1,410.03	
	Mar 21, 2008	279	226.88	
	Mar 21, 2008	280	2,668.54	
	Mar 21, 2008	281	55.60	
	Mar 21, 2008	282	75.00	
	Mar 21, 2008	283	49.99	
	Mar 28, 2008	284	274.56	
	Mar 26, 2008	285	332.22	
	Mar 26, 2008	287	23.85	
	Mar 28, 2008	288	3,627.18	
	Mar 26, 2008	289	7,532.00	
	Mar 28, 2008	290	76.50	
	Mar 28, 2008	291	750.00	
	Mar 28, 2008	293	1,887.97	
Total Cleared Checks for March				45,577.19
Less Bank Transfers				
	Mar 10, 2008		9,200.00	
	Mar 24, 2008		9,600.00	
Total March Transfers				18,800.00
March Service Charges				83.20
March 31 Ending Bank Balance				$115,742.97

Figure 11:6

STEPS TO RECONCILE THE CHECKING ACCOUNT

1. Click **Banking** to open the Banking Home page and then click **Reconcile Account.** *(Note: You can also select **Banking>>Reconcile Account** on the main menu.)*

   Select the **Regular Checking Account**. Enter the **Statement date** and **Ending balance** listed on the bank statement.

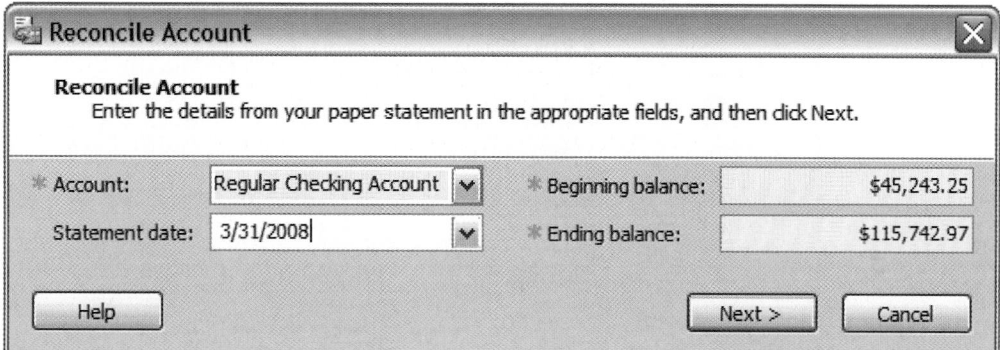

Figure 11:7

2. Click **Next** to open the window for selecting deposits and checks that have cleared the March statement (Figure 11:8).

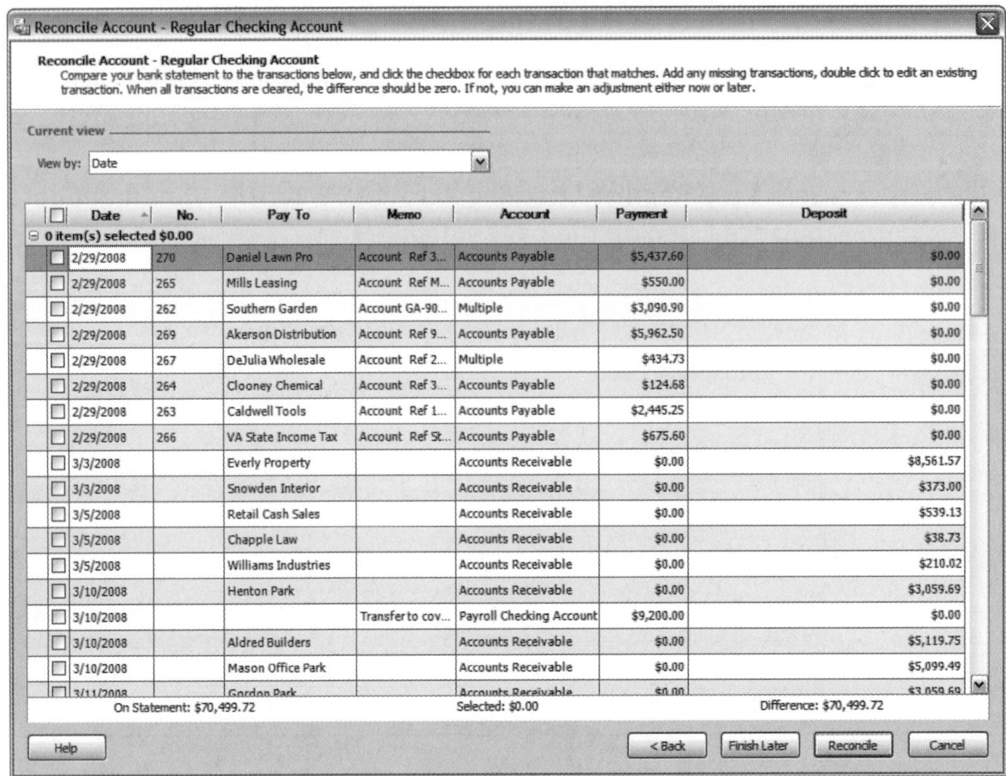

Figure 11:8

3. The following explanations help identify and select transactions in the window.

   Individual items are selected by clicking the item's selection box. Clicking the box in the header row selects all items.

   Outstanding checks display a check number in the No. column and an amount under the Payment column.

   Outstanding deposits display an amount under the Deposit column.

   Bank transfers display a bank account name in the Account column.

   The list can be sorted by clicking a column header. You can also change the view by selecting an option from the dropdown list on View by.

4. You will first enter the bank service charge for March. Scroll to the bottom of the list and click the link **Click here to add a new Transaction**.

   Select **Enter bank fee** and click **OK**. Enter the following information and click **OK**.

Figure 11:9

5. Click the selection box in the header row to select all items. It is often easier to mark all items as cleared and then scroll through to remove uncleared items.

6. Refer back to the bank statement and click to deselect checks that have not cleared in March. *(Note: All deposits have cleared.)* You can click the **No.** column header to sort by check number. When finished, the reconciliation window appears as illustrated in Figure 11:10.

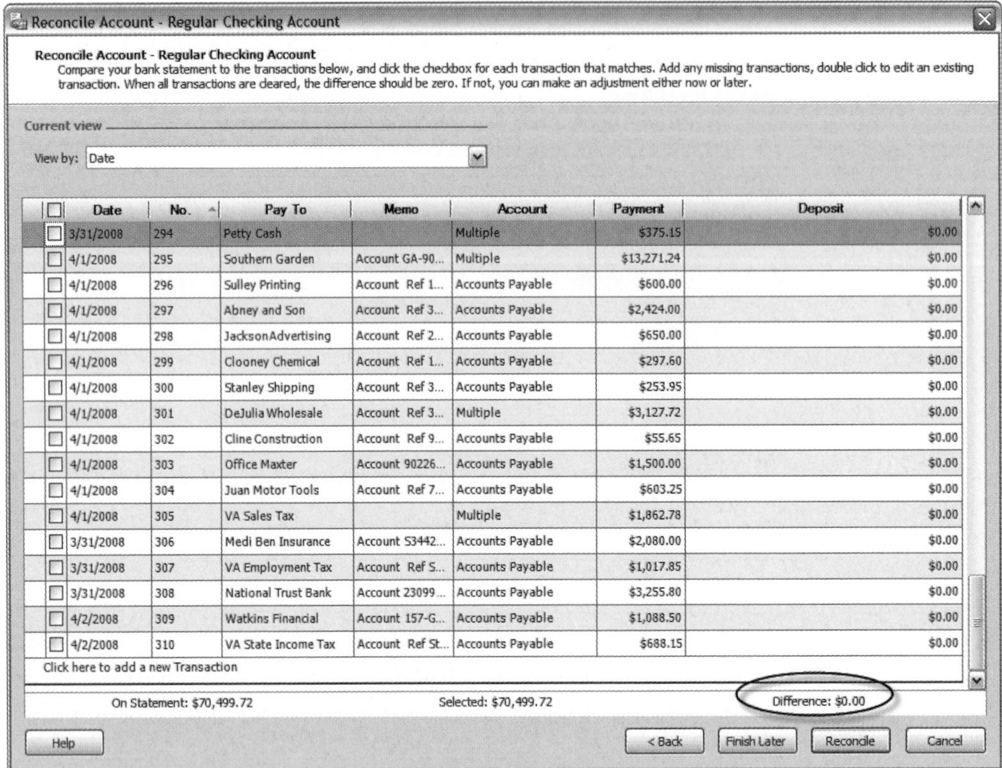

Figure 11:10

You cannot complete the next step until the **Difference** equals zero.

When you have difficulty reconciling an account, the Finish Later button will save your work and close the reconciliation window. You can then return later to complete the reconciliation.

7. Click **Reconcile** and then click **Display Report**.

   Total Cleared Deposits will equal the total deposits on the bank statement (Figure 11:11).

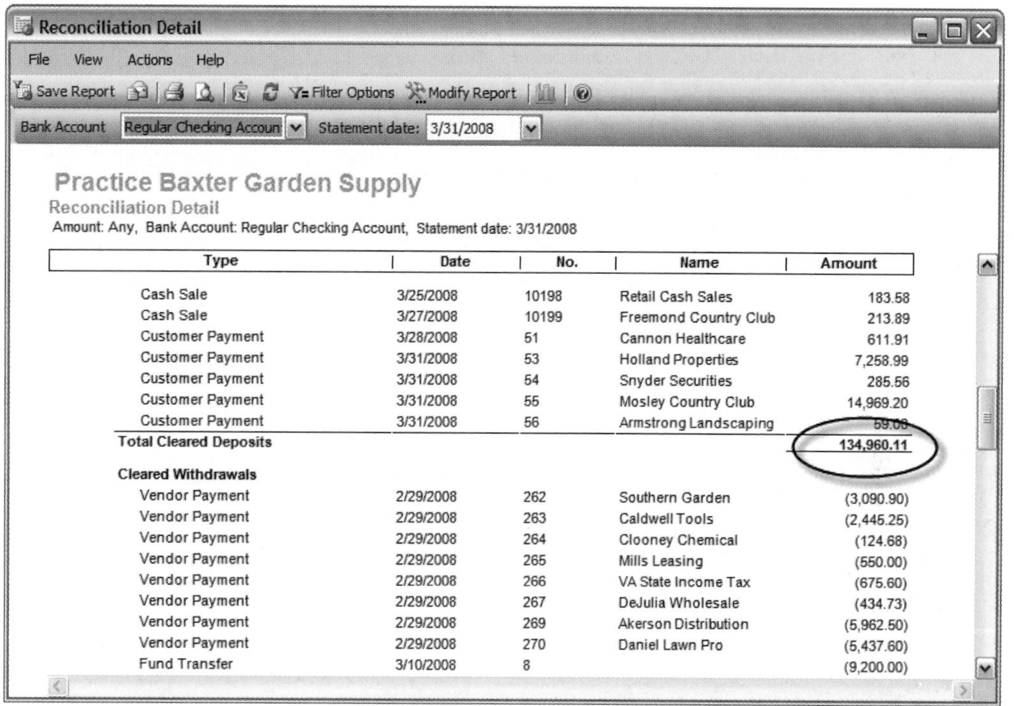

Practice Baxter Garden Supply

Reconciliation Detail

Amount: Any, Bank Account: Regular Checking Account, Statement date: 3/31/2008

Type	Date	No.	Name	Amount
Cash Sale	3/25/2008	10198	Retail Cash Sales	183.58
Cash Sale	3/27/2008	10199	Freemond Country Club	213.89
Customer Payment	3/28/2008	51	Cannon Healthcare	611.91
Customer Payment	3/31/2008	53	Holland Properties	7,258.99
Customer Payment	3/31/2008	54	Snyder Securities	285.56
Customer Payment	3/31/2008	55	Mosley Country Club	14,969.20
Customer Payment	3/31/2008	56	Armstrong Landscaping	59.0[illegible]
Total Cleared Deposits				**134,960.11**
Cleared Withdrawals				
Vendor Payment	2/29/2008	262	Southern Garden	(3,090.90)
Vendor Payment	2/29/2008	263	Caldwell Tools	(2,445.25)
Vendor Payment	2/29/2008	264	Clooney Chemical	(124.68)
Vendor Payment	2/29/2008	265	Mills Leasing	(550.00)
Vendor Payment	2/29/2008	266	VA State Income Tax	(675.60)
Vendor Payment	2/29/2008	267	DeJulia Wholesale	(434.73)
Vendor Payment	2/29/2008	269	Akerson Distribution	(5,962.50)
Vendor Payment	2/29/2008	270	Daniel Lawn Pro	(5,437.60)
Fund Transfer	3/10/2008	8		(9,200.00)

Figure 11:11

Total Cleared Withdrawals will match the sum of total cleared checks, bank transfers, and bank fees on the bank statement. The Reconciled Balance As Of Statement Date will match the ending balance on the bank statement. (See Figure 11:12.)

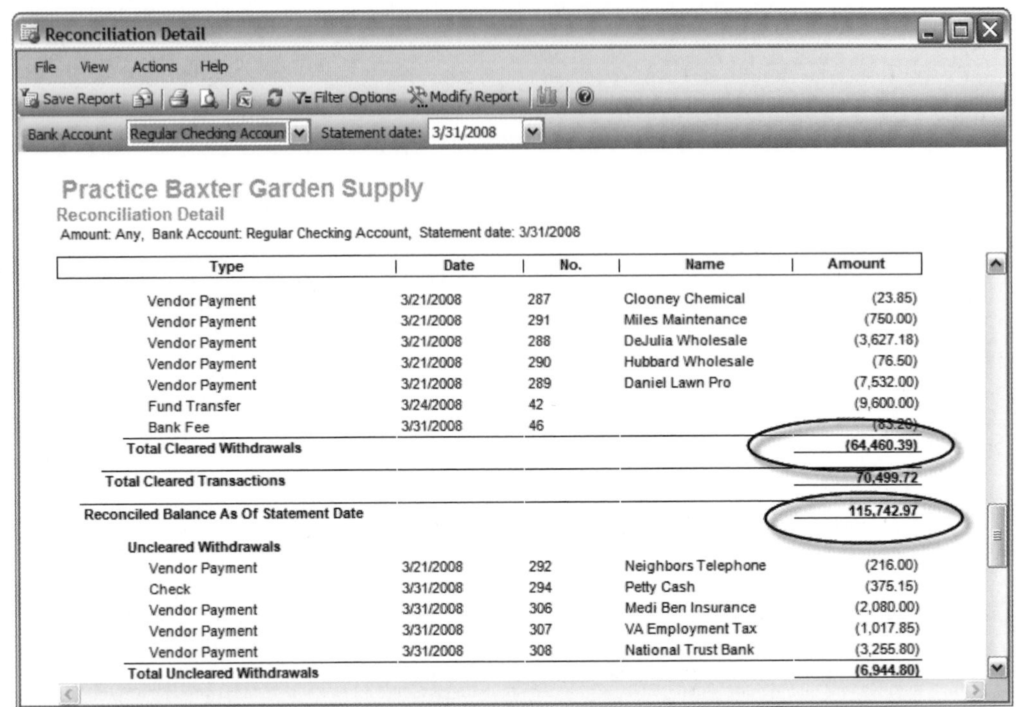

Reconciliation Detail

File View Actions Help

Save Report | Filter Options | Modify Report

Bank Account: Regular Checking Account | Statement date: 3/31/2008

Practice Baxter Garden Supply
Reconciliation Detail
Amount: Any, Bank Account: Regular Checking Account, Statement date: 3/31/2008

Type	Date	No.	Name	Amount
Vendor Payment	3/21/2008	287	Clooney Chemical	(23.85)
Vendor Payment	3/21/2008	291	Miles Maintenance	(750.00)
Vendor Payment	3/21/2008	288	DeJulia Wholesale	(3,627.18)
Vendor Payment	3/21/2008	290	Hubbard Wholesale	(76.50)
Vendor Payment	3/21/2008	289	Daniel Lawn Pro	(7,532.00)
Fund Transfer	3/24/2008	42		(9,600.00)
Bank Fee	3/31/2008	46		(83.20)
Total Cleared Withdrawals				(64,460.39)
Total Cleared Transactions				70,499.72
Reconciled Balance As Of Statement Date				115,742.97
Uncleared Withdrawals				
Vendor Payment	3/21/2008	292	Neighbors Telephone	(216.00)
Check	3/31/2008	294	Petty Cash	(375.15)
Vendor Payment	3/31/2008	306	Medi Ben Insurance	(2,080.00)
Vendor Payment	3/31/2008	307	VA Employment Tax	(1,017.85)
Vendor Payment	3/31/2008	308	National Trust Bank	(3,255.80)
Total Uncleared Withdrawals				(6,944.80)

Figure 11:12

8. Print the report by clicking the Printer icon and then click **X** to close it.

Note: You can reprint the Reconciliation Detail Report by selecting ***Reports>>Banking >>Reconciliation Detail*** *on the main menu.*

RECONCILE THE PAYROLL CHECKING ACCOUNT

The March bank statement for the Payroll Checking Account has arrived. All paychecks and deposits have cleared. Bank charges for March are $32.75 and the ending bank statement balance is $626.47.

Reconcile the statement and print the Reconciliation Detail report.

FINANCIAL REPORTS

You have now completed the preclosing checklist and are ready to print the trial balance and financial statements.

The trial balance is printed first so that one final check of account balances can be performed. Select ***Reports>>Company and Financial>>Trial Balance*** on the main menu. Enter 3/31/2008 as the date and scroll to the bottom (Figure 11:13).

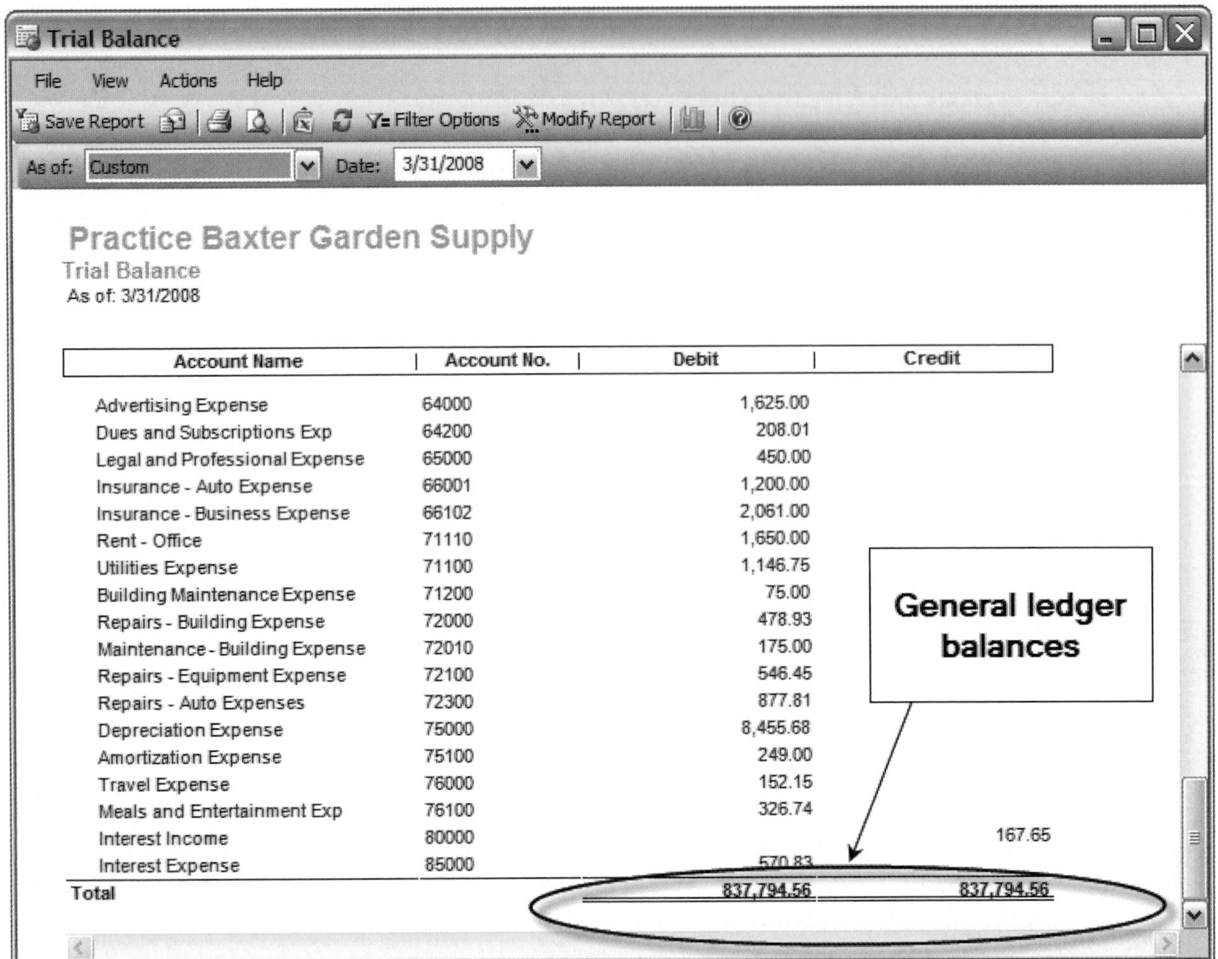

Practice Baxter Garden Supply
Trial Balance
As of: 3/31/2008

Account Name	Account No.	Debit	Credit
Advertising Expense	64000	1,625.00	
Dues and Subscriptions Exp	64200	208.01	
Legal and Professional Expense	65000	450.00	
Insurance - Auto Expense	66001	1,200.00	
Insurance - Business Expense	66102	2,061.00	
Rent - Office	71110	1,650.00	
Utilities Expense	71100	1,146.75	
Building Maintenance Expense	71200	75.00	
Repairs - Building Expense	72000	478.93	
Maintenance - Building Expense	72010	175.00	
Repairs - Equipment Expense	72100	546.45	
Repairs - Auto Expenses	72300	877.81	
Depreciation Expense	75000	8,455.68	
Amortization Expense	75100	249.00	
Travel Expense	76000	152.15	
Meals and Entertainment Exp	76100	326.74	
Interest Income	80000		167.65
Interest Expense	85000	570.83	
Total		837,794.56	837,794.56

Figure 11:13

In a manual accounting system this report was critical to proving that debits equaled credits (i.e., general ledger accounts balance) before preparing financial statements. You will recall Chapter 8 illustrations on cross-footing manual Sales Journal transactions before posting Sales Journal totals to general ledger accounts. This calculation was performed to prove that transactions balanced before posting column totals to general ledger accounts. However, this calculation did not prevent posting a total backwards (i.e., a debit as a credit) on the account or transposing numbers when posting.

Remember that a manual system not only involved posting entries from the Sales Journal but also the Purchase Journal illustrated in Chapter 9, Payroll Register illustrated in Chapter 10, and General Journal illustrated in Chapter 3. Imagine how easy it would be to post a transaction incorrectly, thus causing general ledger accounts to be out of balance. You now understand how the "trial" balance garnered its name. Imagine the number of trials it could take before the books balanced in a manual system. In fact, accounts would prepare a preclosing trial balance before posting adjusting entries and then a post closing trial balance before preparing financial statements.

All that work is eliminated with accounting software. Although a computerized trial balance still verifies that general ledger accounts balance, this report more likely functions as a tool for reconciling account balances to external source documents and other software reports. In fact, you used this report in Chapter 8 to tie the balance on the A/R aging report back to the balance in Accounts Receivable to prove that customer activities reconciled to the general ledger.

Close the trial balance so we can now focus on financial statements.

Select ***Reports>>Company and Financial>>Profit and Loss*** on the main menu and filter the report for 1/1/2008 to 3/31/2008 (Figure 11:14).

Practice Baxter Garden Supply
Profit and Loss
Date Range: January 1, 2008 - March 31, 2008
Account: All, Report Basis: Accrual, Name: All, Closing Postings: Not Included

	1/1/08 - 3/31/08
Ordinary Income/Expense	
Income	
49000 - Sales Discounts	(235.52)
40000 - Sales	
40001 - Sales - Aviary	56,290.70
40002 - Sales - Books	7,283.21
40003 - Sales - Equipment	64,284.46
40004 - Sales - Food/Fert	5,216.69
40005 - Sales - Hand Tools	7,068.11
40008 - Sales - Nursery	68,303.03
40009 - Sales - Pots	5,537.37
40010 - Sales - Seeds	9,013.46
40011 - Sales - Soil	8,784.02
Total 40000 - Sales	231,781.05
48000 - Sales Returns and Allowances	(0.90)
Total Income	231,544.63
Cost of Goods Sold	
59500 - Purchase Discounts	(903.08)
50000 - Product Cost	
50001 - Product Cost - Aviary	19,118.70
50002 - Product Cost - Books	2,378.30
50003 - Product Cost - Equipment	26,555.05
50004 - Product Cost - Food/Fert	2,051.61
50005 - Product Cost - Hand Tools	2,829.05
50007 - Product Cost - Miscellaneous	183.90
50008 - Product Cost - Nursery	12,966.60
50009 - Product Cost - Pots	2,135.85
50010 - Product Cost - Seeds	3,447.50
50011 - Product Cost - Soil	3,921.94
Total 50000 - Product Cost	75,588.50
57300 - Subcontractors	
57306 - Subcontractors - Landscaping	12,969.60
Total 57300 - Subcontractors	12,969.60
Total COGS	87,655.02
Gross Profit	143,889.61
Expense	
73000 - Bank Charges	310.20
57500 - Freight	398.94
58500 - Inventory Adjustments	15.90
60000 - Salaries and Wages Expense	74,923.90
60500 - Pension/Profit-Sharing Expense	1,078.80
60600 - Employee Benefits Expense	6,240.00
61000 - Payroll Tax Expense	6,897.98
63000 - Office Supplies Expense	2,876.43
63100 - Postage Expense	309.72
64000 - Advertising Expense	1,625.00
64200 - Dues and Subscriptions Exp	208.01
65000 - Legal and Professional Expense	450.00
66000 - Insurance Expense	
66001 - Insurance - Auto Expense	1,200.00
66102 - Insurance - Business Expense	2,061.00
Total 66000 - Insurance Expense	3,261.00
71000 - Rent Expense	
71110 - Rent - Office	1,650.00
Total 71000 - Rent Expense	1,650.00
71100 - Utilities Expense	1,146.75
71200 - Building Maintenance Expense	75.00
72000 - Repairs - Building Expense	478.93
72010 - Maintenance - Building Expense	175.00
72100 - Repairs - Equipment Expense	546.45
72300 - Repairs - Auto Expenses	877.81
75000 - Depreciation Expense	8,455.68
75100 - Amortization Expense	249.00
76000 - Travel Expense	152.15
76100 - Meals and Entertainment Exp	326.74
Total Expense	112,729.39
Net Ordinary Income	31,160.22
Other Income/Expense	
Other Income	
80000 - Interest Income	167.65
Total Other Income	167.65
Other Expense	
85000 - Interest Expense	570.83
Total Other Expense	570.83
Net Other Income	(403.18)
Net Income	30,757.04

Figure 11:14

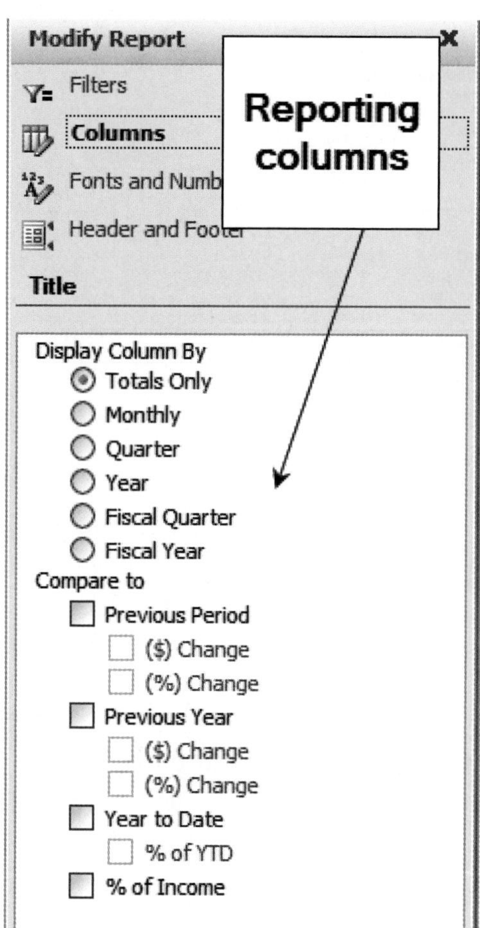

Figure 11:15

Figure 11:14 is also called the Income Statement and we will refer to it as such. The Income Statement you produced displays only year-to-date net income. We will next modify it to display financial results that compare multiple time periods.

Click **Modify Report** and select **Columns** (Figure 11:15). Select the **Monthly** column and close the Modify Report pane. Scroll to the bottom to view Net Income by month (Figure 11:16).

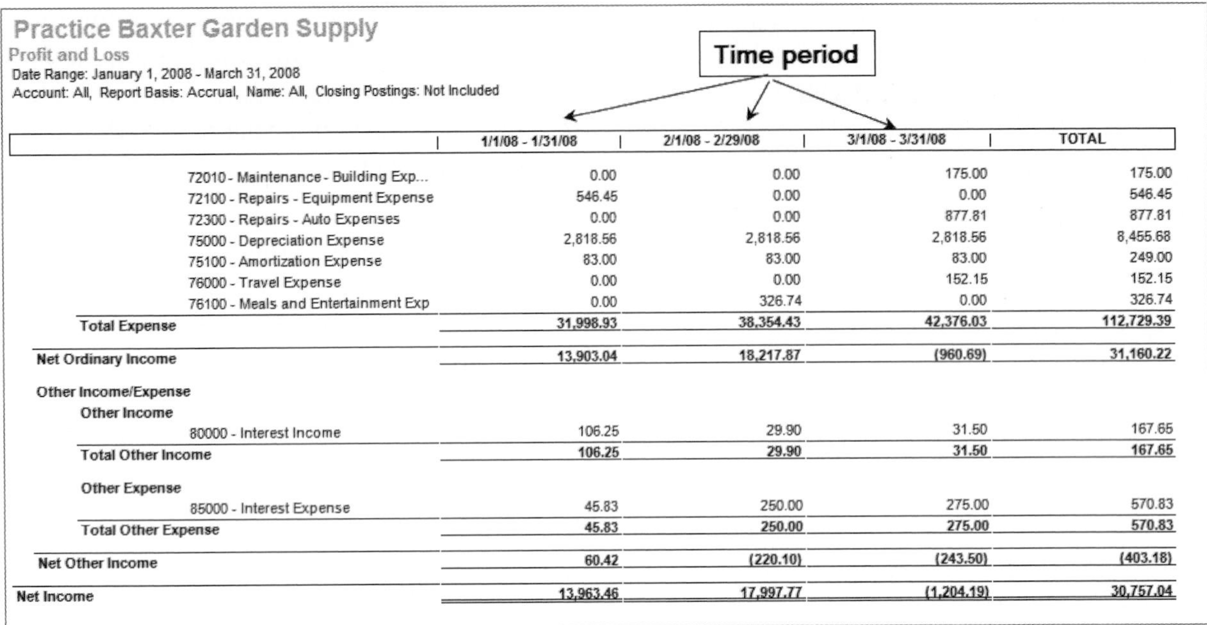

Practice Baxter Garden Supply
Profit and Loss
Date Range: January 1, 2008 - March 31, 2008
Account: All, Report Basis: Accrual, Name: All, Closing Postings: Not Included

	1/1/08 - 1/31/08	2/1/08 - 2/29/08	3/1/08 - 3/31/08	TOTAL
72010 - Maintenance - Building Exp...	0.00	0.00	175.00	175.00
72100 - Repairs - Equipment Expense	546.45	0.00	0.00	546.45
72300 - Repairs - Auto Expenses	0.00	0.00	877.81	877.81
75000 - Depreciation Expense	2,818.56	2,818.56	2,818.56	8,455.68
75100 - Amortization Expense	83.00	83.00	83.00	249.00
76000 - Travel Expense	0.00	0.00	152.15	152.15
76100 - Meals and Entertainment Exp	0.00	326.74	0.00	326.74
Total Expense	31,998.93	38,354.43	42,376.03	112,729.39
Net Ordinary Income	13,903.04	18,217.87	(960.69)	31,160.22
Other Income/Expense				
Other Income				
80000 - Interest Income	106.25	29.90	31.50	167.65
Total Other Income	106.25	29.90	31.50	167.65
Other Expense				
85000 - Interest Expense	45.83	250.00	275.00	570.83
Total Other Expense	45.83	250.00	275.00	570.83
Net Other Income	60.42	(220.10)	(243.50)	(403.18)
Net Income	13,963.46	17,997.77	(1,204.19)	30,757.04

Figure 11:16

You already know that the Income Statement paints a company's financial picture over a period of time and this report tells Baxter's owners that February produced the highest net income whereas March actually produced a net loss. Therefore, the time period comparison revealed better information on company performance.

OAP uses general ledger account types to create the Income Statement. You will recall choosing an account type when creating general ledger accounts. You will now see how types are mapped to the Income Statement.

Press **Ctrl + Shift + A** on the keyboard to open the **Chart of Accounts** and refer back to the Income Statement illustrated in Figure 11:14 as we discuss the account types displayed on the Chart of Accounts.

Scroll down the Chart of Accounts until you reach account 40000 Sales. This account is assigned the Income type; therefore, it appears under the Income category of the Income Statement. Cost of Goods Sold account types appear under Cost of Goods Sold and so forth. Individual account balances are listed within each category and subaccounts are grouped with the main account.

Account types serve the same purpose on the Balance Sheet. Close the Income Statement and open the **Balance Sheet** filtered for 3/31/2008 (Figure 11:17).

Practice Baxter Garden Supply
Balance Sheet
As of: 3/31/2008
Report Basis: Accrual

	As of 3/31/08
Assets	
Current Assets	
Cash	
10100 - Petty Cash	929.60
10200 - Regular Checking Account	108,798.17
10300 - Payroll Checking Account	626.47
10400 - Savings Account	7,592.65
Total Cash	**117,946.89**
Accounts Receivable	
11000 - Accounts Receivable	24,734.00
Total Accounts Receivable	**24,734.00**
Other Current Assets	
11100 - Allowance for Doubtful Acc...	(5,000.00)
14000 - Prepaid Expenses	9,783.00
Inventory Assets	
13000 - Inventory	53,925.89
Total Inventory Assets	**53,925.89**
Total Other Current Assets	**58,708.89**
Total Current Assets	**201,389.78**
Fixed Assets	
15000 - Furniture and Fixtures	62,769.25
15010 - Accum. Depreciation-Furniture	(54,680.61)
15100 - Equipment	38,738.33
15110 - Accum. Depreciation-Equipment	(33,199.85)
15200 - Vehicles	86,273.40
15210 - Accum. Depreciation-Vehicles	(51,585.26)
15300 - Other Depreciable Property	6,200.96
15310 - Accum. Depreciation-Other	(3,788.84)
15500 - Buildings	145,500.00
15510 - Accum. Depreciation-Buildings	(34,483.98)
15600 - Building Improvements	26,500.00
15610 - Accum. Depreciation-Bldg Imp	(4,926.27)
16900 - Land	40,000.00
Total Fixed Assets	**223,317.13**
Other Assets	
19000 - Deposits	15,000.00
19100 - Organization Costs	4,995.10
19110 - Accum Amortiz - Organiz Costs	(2,249.00)
19900 - Other Noncurrent Assets	3,333.00
Total Other Assets	**21,079.10**
Total Assets	**445,786.01**
Liabilities & Equity	
Liabilities	
Current Liabilities	
Accounts Payable	
20000 - Accounts Payable	28,643.78
Total Accounts Payable	**28,643.78**
Other Current Liabilities	
23010 - Accrued Interest Expense	525.00
23020 - Accrued Wage Expense	7,110.00
23100 - Sales Tax Payable	2,337.10
23200 - Line of Credit	50,000.00
23900 - Income Taxes Payable	11,045.75
Total Other Current Liabilities	**71,017.85**
Total Current Liabilities	**99,661.63**
Total Liabilities	**99,661.63**
Equity	
39003 - Common Stock	5,000.00
39004 - Paid-in Capital	100,000.00
39100 - Retained Earnings	210,367.34
Net Income	30,757.04
Total Equity	**346,124.38**
Total Liabilities & Equity	**445,786.01**

Figure 11:17

Unlike the Income Statement, the Balance Sheet reports a company's financial position as of a specific point in time. Take the time to scroll through the Balance Sheet and the Chart of Accounts to understand type mapping on the statement.

Close all open reports and open the **Cash Flow Statement**. Enter the date range of 3/1/2008 to 3/31/2008 (Figure 11:18).

Practice Baxter Garden Supply
Cash Flow Statement
Date Range: March 1, 2008 - March 31, 2008
Closing Postings: Not Included

	3/1/08 - 3/31/08
OPERATING ACTIVITIES	
Net Income	**(1,204.19)**
Adjustments to reconcile net income to net cash provided by Operating Activities	
11000 - Accounts Receivable	62,972.06
14000 - Prepaid Expenses	1,087.00
13000 - Inventory	(16,129.33)
20000 - Accounts Payable	29,581.84
23010 - Accrued Interest Expense	275.00
23020 - Accrued Wage Expense	3,110.00
23100 - Sales Tax Payable	899.49
23500 - FUTA Tax Payable	(371.76)
23700 - SUTA Tax Payable	(697.04)
Net Cash provided by Operating Activities	**79,523.07**
INVESTING ACTIVITIES	
15010 - Accum. Depreciation-Furniture	420.80
15110 - Accum. Depreciation-Equipment	442.31
15210 - Accum. Depreciation-Vehicles	1,437.89
15310 - Accum. Depreciation-Other	64.57
15510 - Accum. Depreciation-Buildings	396.37
15610 - Accum. Depreciation-Bldg Imp	56.62
19110 - Accum Amortiz - Organiz Costs	83.00
Net Cash provided by Investing Activities	**2,901.56**
Net cash change for the Period	**82,424.63**
Cash at beginning of the period	**35,522.26**
Cash at end of the Period	**117,946.89**

Figure 11:18

This may be your first exposure to the Cash Flow Statement so we will spend some time explaining its importance. This statement reports changes in cash produced by operating, investing, and financing activities. Net Cash provided by Operating Activities is cash generated by day-to-day activities such as selling collecting accounts receivable and reducing accounts payable. Net Cash provided by Investing Activities is the cash effect of buying or selling company assets such as equipment or buildings. Finally, Net Cash provided by Financing Activities is the cash effect of borrowing or repaying loans. *(Note: Baxter does not have any financing activities for March.)*

After reviewing the report, the accountant notices that accumulated depreciation accounts are appearing under financing activities and should appear under operating activities because depreciation is a noncash activity added back to Net Income to determine cash from operations.

Return to the Chart of Accounts. Scroll to **15010 Accum. Depreciation-Furniture** and right click to select **Open Selected Items**. Change the **Cash Flow category** to **Operating** (Figure 11:19).

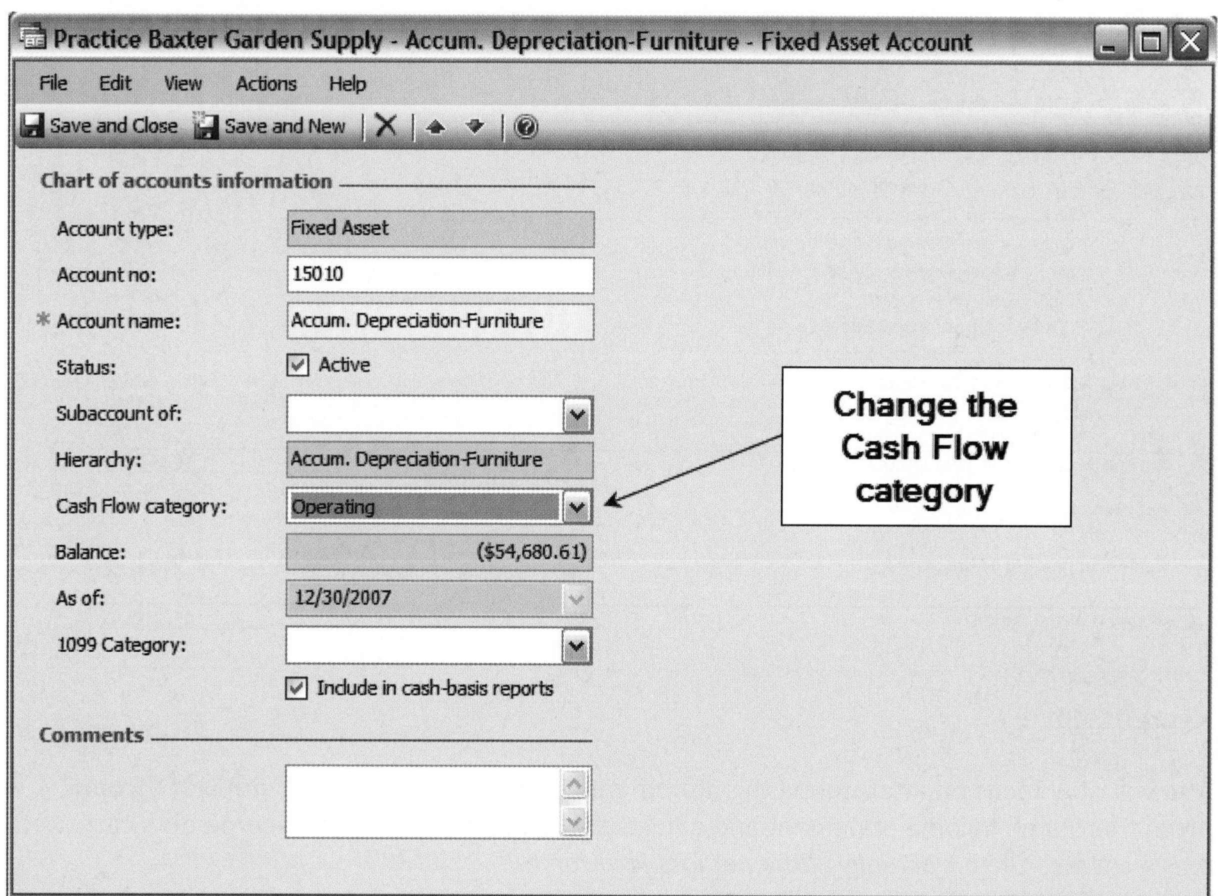

Figure 11:19

Use this record scroll button to move to the next accumulated depreciation account, clicking **OK** when prompted to save changes. Continue changing the cash flow category on remaining accumulated depreciation accounts as well as the accumulated amortization account. When finished, return to the Cash Flow Statement and click **Yes** to refresh the report (Figure 11:20).

Practice Baxter Garden Supply
Cash Flow Statement
Date Range: March 1, 2008 - March 31, 2008
Closing Postings: Not Included

	3/1/08 - 3/31/08
OPERATING ACTIVITIES	
Net Income	**(1,204.19)**
Adjustments to reconcile net income to net cash provided by Operating Activities	
11000 - Accounts Receivable	62,972.06
14000 - Prepaid Expenses	1,087.00
13000 - Inventory	(16,129.33)
15010 - Accum. Depreciation-Furniture	420.80
15110 - Accum. Depreciation-Equipment	442.31
15210 - Accum. Depreciation-Vehicles	1,437.89
15310 - Accum. Depreciation-Other	64.57
15510 - Accum. Depreciation-Buildings	396.37
15610 - Accum. Depreciation-Bldg Imp	56.62
19110 - Accum Amortiz - Organiz Costs	83.00
20000 - Accounts Payable	29,581.84
23010 - Accrued Interest Expense	275.00
23020 - Accrued Wage Expense	3,110.00
23100 - Sales Tax Payable	899.49
23500 - FUTA Tax Payable	(371.76)
23700 - SUTA Tax Payable	(697.04)
Net Cash provided by Operating Activities	**82,424.63**
Net cash change for the Period	**82,424.63**
Cash at beginning of the period	**35,522.26**
Cash at end of the Period	117,946.89

Figure 11:20

We will now focus on interpreting this statement. The statement begins with **Net Income** from the March Income Statement and adjusts this number to arrive at income on a cash basis. *(Note: Baxter actually had a net loss for March.)*

Noncash items (i.e., depreciation) are added back to net income and cash increases and decreases for operating assets and liabilities (i.e., accounts receivable, accounts payable, etc.) are factored in to obtain **Net Cash provided by Operating Activities**. Positive net cash flow from operations is a critical point of analysis. Companies that continually fail to generate cash from operations will eventually need to borrow to fund day-to-day operations, such as paying employees and vendors. Continued borrowing eventually places a company in the position of closure when they no longer have the cash flow to pay back the debt.

The Net Cash provided by Operating Activities is then adjusted for any cash increases and decreases in investing or financing activities to arrive at the **Net cash change for the Period**. Notice that Baxter has a large positive net cash increase for the period whereas it actually generated a net income loss for the period. This result, in large part, was due to collecting more cash from accounts receivable and using less cash to pay accounts payable.

Focus now on cash at the beginning and ending of the period. **Cash at the beginning of the period** equals the total for all cash accounts listed on the Balance Sheet for February 29.

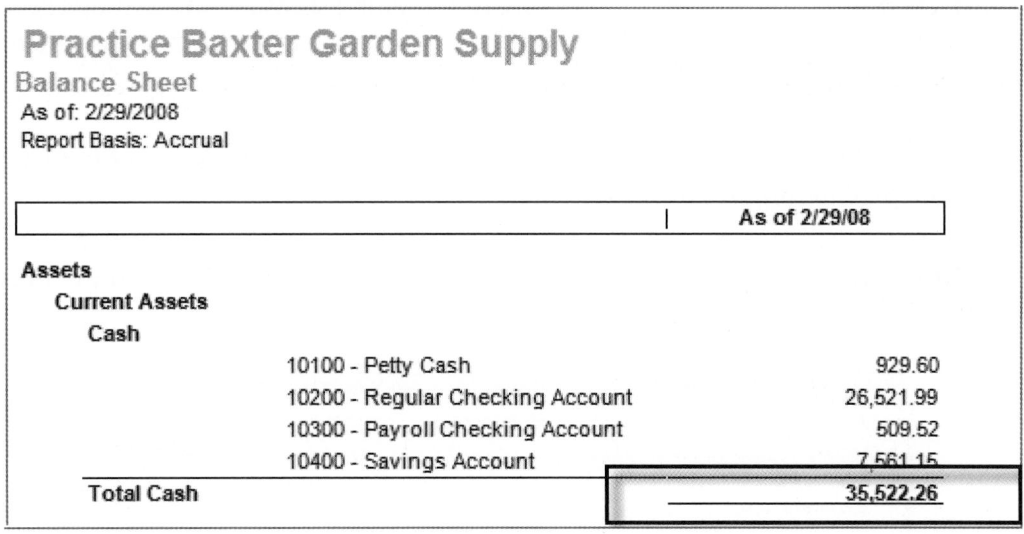

Practice Baxter Garden Supply
Balance Sheet
As of: 2/29/2008
Report Basis: Accrual

	As of 2/29/08
Assets	
Current Assets	
Cash	
10100 - Petty Cash	929.60
10200 - Regular Checking Account	26,521.99
10300 - Payroll Checking Account	509.52
10400 - Savings Account	7,561.15
Total Cash	**35,522.26**

Figure 11:21

Cash at the end of Period equals the total for all cash accounts listed on the Balance Sheet for March 31.

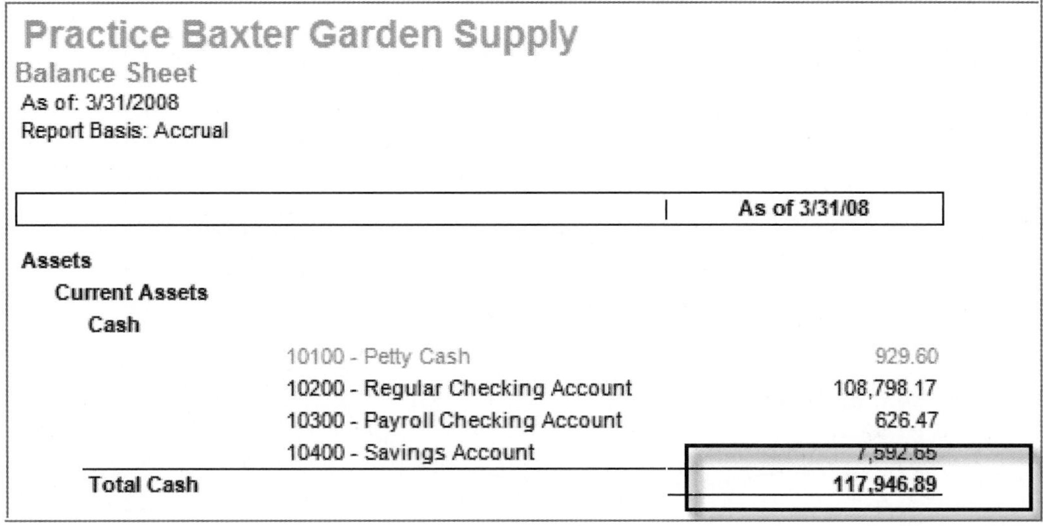

Practice Baxter Garden Supply
Balance Sheet
As of: 3/31/2008
Report Basis: Accrual

	As of 3/31/08
Assets	
Current Assets	
Cash	
10100 - Petty Cash	929.60
10200 - Regular Checking Account	108,798.17
10300 - Payroll Checking Account	626.47
10400 - Savings Account	7,592.65
Total Cash	**117,946.89**

Figure 11:22

The difference between the two matches the **Net cash change for the Period**.

Close this statement. After printing financial statements, you are ready to close the accounting period.

Close the Accounting Period

Closing the accounting period is important to prevent posting transactions that affect issued financial statements. You do not want to send March financial statements to owners or the bank and subsequently have an entry erroneously posted to March.

Before closing the March accounting period, create a ***backup of Baxter's data file to a backup file named "practicebaxtergardensupply Chpt 11."***

Now select ***Company>>Preferences*** on the main menu and enter "4/1/2008" in the **Prevent posting before** field (Figure 11:23).

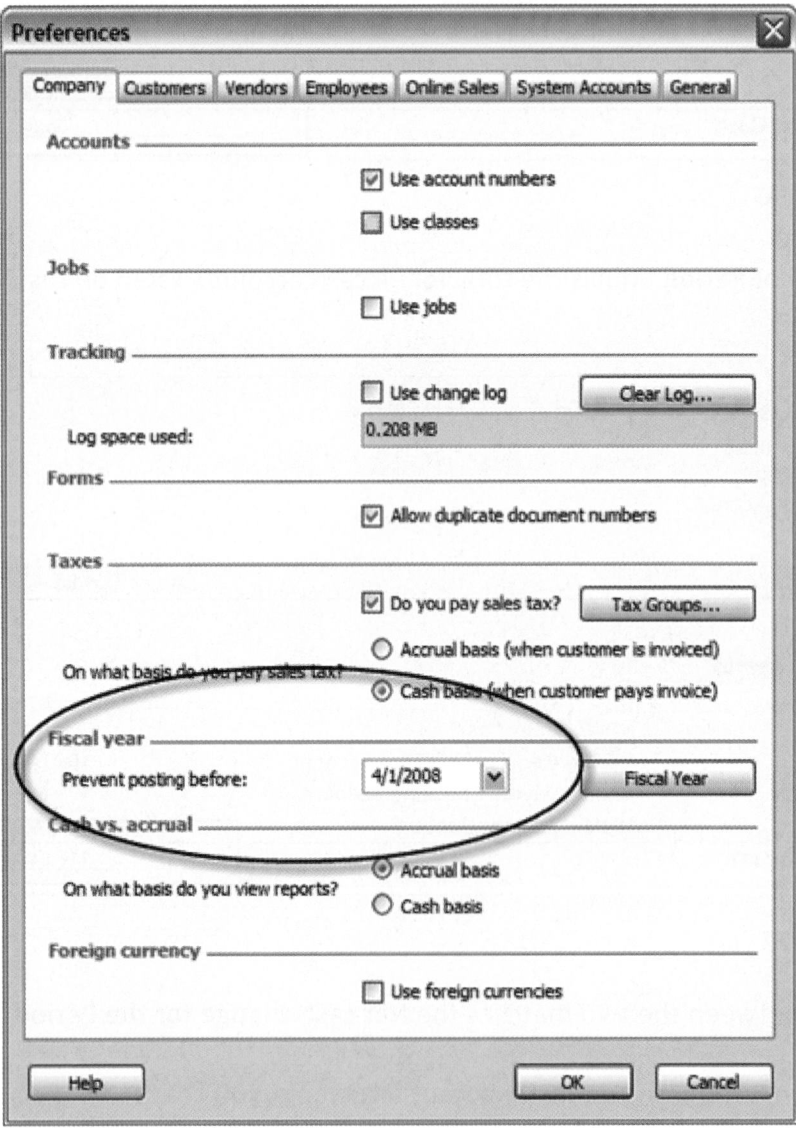

Figure 11:23

Click **OK** to save the changes and close the window.

Closing the year is different from closing the period. When closing a year you click the **Fiscal Year** button on the Preferences window or select ***Company>>Manage Fiscal Year*** on the main menu.

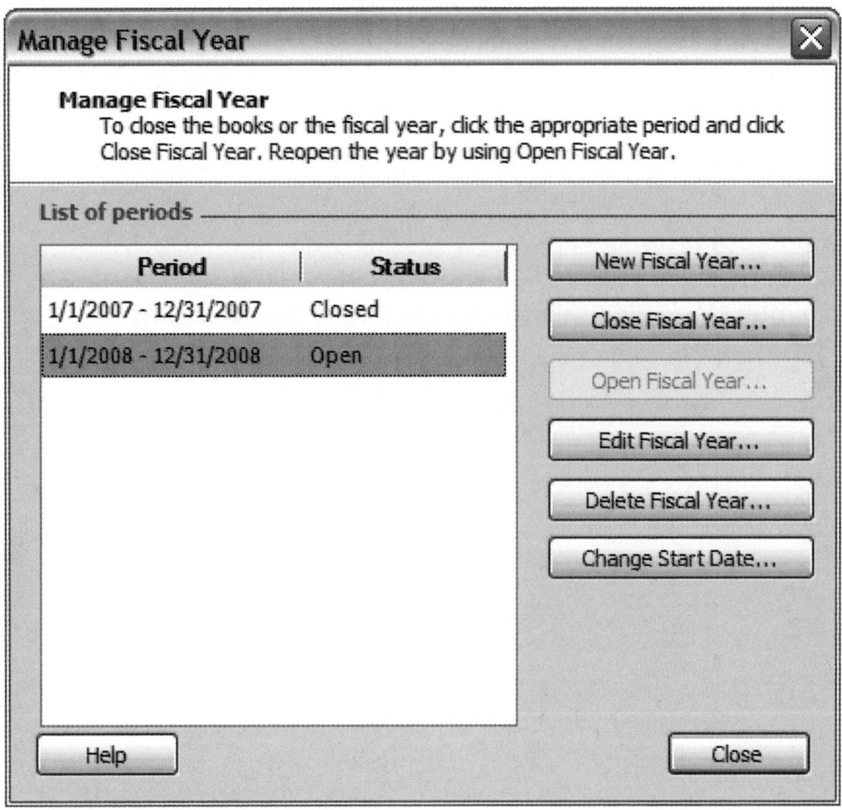

Figure 11:24

You then highlight the year to close and the **Close Fiscal Year** button activates. When closing a year, OAP posts closing entries. Closing entries zero out balances in income and expense accounts by posting these balances into retained earnings.

Click **X** to close the Manage Fiscal Year window. You have completed the chapter and have already backed up the data file.

SUMMARY

In this chapter, you finalized Baxter's March accounting period. You began by reviewing the GL Report for missing transactions and posting errors. You corrected posting errors and posted adjusting entries. You then reconciled bank statements and printed financial statements.

Finally, you backed up the Practice Baxter Garden data file and closed the March accounting period.

Congratulations! You have completed an entire accounting cycle for a merchandising business. The chapter that follows illustrates creating a new company.

END-OF-CHAPTER QUESTIONS

TRUE/FALSE

_____ 1. Closing the period prevents inadvertently altering financial statements from a prior month.

_____ 2. Adjusting entries are used to record transactions not posted through customer, vendor, and employee activities.

_____ 3. The last line on the Cash Flow Statement reconciles to total cash on the Balance Sheet for the same reporting period.

_____ 4. Adjusting entries are routine, so these transactions are memorized to save data entry time.

_____ 5. Closing the fiscal year is the same as closing the accounting period.

MULTIPLE CHOICE

_____ 1. Which statement reports a company's financial position at a specific point in time?
- a. Statement of Cash Flows
- b. Balance Sheet
- c. Statement of Retained Earnings
- d. Income Statement

_____ 2. Which report would you use to spot missing or out-of-sequence accounts payable checks?
- a. Missing Checks
- b. Check Detail
- c. Bank Transactions
- d. All of the above

_____ 3. Net income/net loss for March will affect the _____.
- a. Balance Sheet
- b. Income Statement
- c. Cash Flow Statement
- d. all of the above

_____ 4. Which report demonstrates that the inventory general ledger account reconciles to the value held in inventory?

   a. Inventory Stock Status by Item
   b. Inventory Valuation
   c. Both a and b
   d. None of the above

_____ 5. Which report verifies that the general ledger is “in balance”?

   a. Balance Sheet
   b. Trial Balance
   c. Cash Flow Statement
   d. Income Statement

Practice Set

In this Practice Set you will be using the **Graded Baxter Garden Supply** data file with the tasks competed in the Practice Set at the end of Chapter 10. ***When this data file is not loaded on your computer, restore it using the "gradedbaxtergardensupply Chpt 10" backup file created after completing the Chapter 10 Practice Set.***

1. Open **Graded Baxter Garden Supply** and perform the accounting activities that follow to close the March accounting period.

<u>**2008**</u>

Mar 24 Post the transfer of $10,000 from the Regular Checking Account to the Payroll Checking Account to cover March 24 paychecks.

EOM Reconcile the Regular Checking Account for March 31 using the statement that follows. *(Note: This statement is different from the statement illustrated in the chapter.)* Print the Reconciliation Detail report.

Reconcile the Payroll Checking Account for March 31. The March ending statement balance is $1,333.29. All March checks and deposits have cleared and the monthly bank charge is $16.80. Print the Reconciliation Detail report. *(Remember that April paychecks are in this account.)*

Post an entry that expenses the following prepaid insurance.

Insurance - Auto Expense	$200.00
Insurance - Business Expense	$800.00

Accrue $5,000 for Salaries expense and then reverse the entry on April 1.

Print the Trial Balance as of 3/31/2008.

Print the Balance Sheet, Profit and Loss, and Cash Flow Statement for March. *(Note: Your professor may have you change the cash flow category on accumulated depreciation and amortization accounts.)*

Create a backup file named "gradedbaxtergardensupply March Close" and then close the March accounting period.

Baxter Garden Supply
Bank Statement March 31, 2008

Beginning Balance from February Statement				**$ 45,243.25**
March Deposits				
	Mar 3, 2008		8,561.57	
	Mar 3, 2008		373.00	
	Mar 5, 2008		539.13	
	Mar 5, 2008		38.73	
	Mar 5, 2008		210.02	
	Mar 10, 2008		5,119.75	
	Mar 10, 2008		3,059.69	
	Mar 10, 2008		5,099.49	
	Mar 11, 2008		3,059.69	
	Mar 12, 2008		779.10	
	Mar 14, 2008		3,058.47	
	Mar 14, 2008		8,279.14	
	Mar 14, 2008		1,753.69	
	Mar 14, 2008		5,199.48	
	Mar 14, 2008		591.57	
	Mar 14, 2008		10,556.44	
	Mar 14, 2008		333.22	
	Mar 17, 2008		326.34	
	Mar 17, 2008		489.58	
	Mar 17, 2008		693.19	
	Mar 17, 2008		2,194.38	
	Mar 17, 2008		10,046.90	
	Mar 17, 2008		3,915.23	
	Mar 18, 2008		485.19	
	Mar 24, 2008		6,957.25	
	Mar 24, 2008		12,196.95	
	Mar 24, 2008		4,588.03	
	Mar 24, 2008		7,257.10	
	Mar 24, 2008		2,497.93	
Total Deposits for March				108,260.25
March Checks Cleared				
	Feb 29, 2008	262	3,090.90	
	Feb 29, 2008	263	2,445.25	
	Feb 29, 2008	264	124.68	
	Feb 29, 2008	265	550.00	
	Feb 29, 2008	266	675.60	
	Feb 29, 2008	267	434.73	
	Feb 29, 2008	269	5,962.50	
	Feb 29, 2008	270	5,437.60	
	Mar 14, 2008	271	4,496.19	
	Mar 14, 2008	274	1,073.92	
	Mar 14, 2008	275	90.00	
	Mar 14, 2008	276	26.58	
	Mar 14, 2008	277	78.93	
	Mar 14, 2008	278	1,410.03	
	Mar 14, 2008	279	226.88	
	Mar 14, 2008	280	2,668.54	
	Mar 14, 2008	281	55.60	
	Mar 14, 2008	282	75.00	
	Mar 14, 2008	283	49.99	
	Mar 14, 2008	284	274.56	
	Mar 14, 2008	285	332.22	
	Mar 24, 2008	310	2,695.46	
Total Cleared Checks for March				32,275.16
Less Bank Transfers				
	Mar 10, 2008		9,200.00	
	Mar 24, 2008		10,000.00	
Total March Transfers				19,200.00
March Service Charges				76.80
Ending Bank Balance March 31, 2008				**$ 101,951.54**

2. Perform the accounting activities that follow to close the April accounting period.

2008

Apr 7	Post the transfer of $8,500.00 from the Regular Checking Account to the Payroll Checking Account to cover paychecks printed on April 7.	
Apr 21	Post the transfer of $9,000.00 from the Regular Checking Account to the Payroll Checking Account to cover paychecks printed on April 21.	
Apr 24	Journal entry for the sale of a vehicle:	
	Vehicle cost:	$13,500
	Accumulated Depreciation on vehicles:	$10,700
	Cash deposited to Regular Checking Account	$ 1,000
Apr 30	Adjusting journal entries:	
	Accrue 8 days of wages and reverse on May 1	$ 9,230
	Prepaid auto insurance	$ 200
	Prepaid business insurance	$ 800
	Accrue Interest Expense	$ 300

Post the memorized depreciation entry

Reconcile the Regular Checking Account using the statement that follows. Print the Reconciliation Detail report.

Reconcile the Payroll Checking Account. The ending statement balance is $625.48. All April checks and deposits have cleared and the monthly bank charge is $18.75. Print the Reconciliation Detail report.

Reconcile the Savings Account. Interest income is $37.50 and the ending statement balance is $7,630.15. Do not print the reconciliation report.

Print the Trial Balance for 4/30/2008.

Print the Balance Sheet, Profit and Loss, and Cash Flow Statement for April.

Create a backup file named "gradedbaxtergardensupply April Close" and then close the April accounting period.

Baxter Garden Supply
Bank Statement April 30, 2008

Beginning Balance from March Statement				**$ 101,951.54**
April Deposits				
	Apr 2, 2008		59.90	
	Apr 9, 2008		15,091.57	
	Apr 9, 2008		3,108.45	
	Apr 17, 2008		203.90	
	Apr 21, 2008		7,137.17	
	Apr 21, 2008		2,276.95	
	Apr 21, 2008		5,129.04	
	Apr 22, 2008		159.97	
	Apr 22, 2008		7,432.29	
	Apr 22, 2008		9,281.08	
	Apr 24, 2008		1,000.00	
	Apr 30, 2008		1,911.29	
	Apr 30, 2008		4,429.20	
Total Deposits for April				57,220.81
April Checks Cleared				
	Mar 14, 2008	272	19.99	
	Mar 14, 2008	273	2,080.00	
	Apr 2, 2008	311	2,080.00	
	Apr 2, 2008	312	1,012.88	
	Apr 2, 2008	313	522.06	
	Apr 2, 2008	314	1,073.92	
	Apr 2, 2008	315	678.53	
	Apr 7, 2008	316	2,652.66	
	Apr 16, 2008	295	877.50	
	Apr 16, 2008	297	675.00	
	Apr 16, 2008	286	2,424.00	
	Apr 16, 2008	292	700.00	
	Apr 16, 2008	287	321.45	
	Apr 16, 2008	296	253.95	
	Apr 16, 2008	288	1,573.15	
	Apr 16, 2008	299	600.00	
	Apr 16, 2008	293	400.00	
	Apr 16, 2008	289	4,247.30	
	Apr 16, 2008	294	600.00	
	Apr 16, 2008	291	871.50	
	Apr 16, 2008	298	1,650.00	
	Apr 16, 2008	290	7,532.00	
	Apr 21, 2008	317	2,593.20	
	Apr 22, 2008	300	250.00	
	Apr 23, 2008	304	125.00	
	Apr 23, 2008	305	3,003.55	
	Apr 23, 2008	306	153.00	
	Apr 23, 2008	307	539.75	
	Apr 23, 2008	308	205.00	
Total Cleared Checks for April				39,715.39
Less Bank Transfers				
	Apr 7, 2008		8,500.00	
	Apr 21, 2008		9,000.00	
Total April Transfers				17,500.00
April Service Charges				87.50
Ending Bank Balance April 30, 2008				**$ 101,869.46**

PROJECT 2 COMPREHENSIVE EXAM FOR A MERCHANDISING BUSINESS

You begin this exam by opening the **olsenofficefurnitureproject** sample company. *(Note: This file was copied to your computer and attached to the software in Chapter 1.)* Add your initials to the **Company name** and **Legal name** using the main menu path of ***Company>>Company Information***.

The following are February 2008 transactions for Olsen Office Furniture. Olsen specializes in selling midrange office furniture to wholesale distributors and also sells furniture directly to businesses for use in their offices. You will be entering all transactions for the month of February, including month-end adjusting entries.

All checks received on account are deposited to the Regular Checking Account.

<table>
<tr><td>Feb 1</td><td>Issue and print the following sales invoices.

Invoice 1790 to Winetraub Office Furniture for $2,999.80.
<u>Qty</u> <u>Item</u> <u>Unit Price</u>
20 SmallDesk $149.99

Invoice 1791 to Anderson & Anderson, Attorneys at Law for $9,523.00.
<u>Qty</u> <u>Item</u> <u>Unit Price</u>
10 ChairClothBlack $185.00
12 ChairLeatherBlack $375.00
3 ConfTableOak $850.00</td></tr>
<tr><td></td><td>Received the following checks. (Note: Verify that checks will deposit into the Regular Checking Account.)

Check number 1835 for $8,774.88 from Arbrook Office Supply for Invoice 1783.
Check number 3078 for $30,575.25 from Parker Office Building for Invoice 1784.</td></tr>
<tr><td></td><td>New vendor:
Pearson Property Management
3075 W. 7th Street
Forth Worth, TX 76022
Terms: Net 3
Expense account: 74000 Rent or Lease Expense

Enter a rent bill for $800.00 to Pearson Property Management for February office and warehouse rental.</td></tr>
<tr><td></td><td>Print checks for all bills due on or before February 8. First check number is 8937.</td></tr>
</table>

Feb 4

You will use OAP's reorder inventory feature in this project. Open the Item List and select the Reorder Inventory toolbar icon to open the window illustrated below. Always change the Qty. to Order amount so that it equals the Restock Level when using this feature and verify that the option is marked for creating separate POs.

Create the POs. Set the PO dates. Set Brothers Furniture Mfg's PO number to 1040 and Planter Interiors PO number to 1041. *(Note: Both POs will be open for you to set the PO number.)* Print the POs.

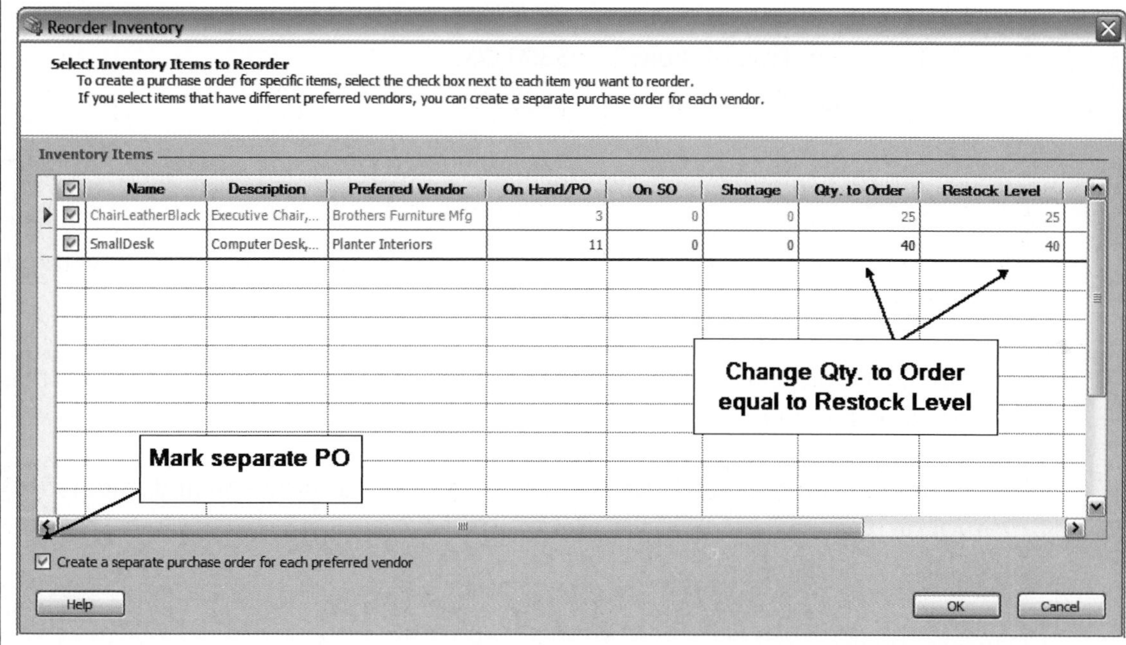

Received bills for the following inventory.

All items on PO 1038 to Tollman Table Manufacturing. Invoice 68534 for $5,500.00 dated Feb. 4.

All items on PO 1039 to Willis Office Supplies. Invoice 2378 for $1,910.00 dated Feb. 4.

Received the following checks.

Check number 8053 for $34,595.00 from Ernst Furniture for Invoice 1785.

Check number 3478 for $5,403.50 from Poseiden Landscaping for Invoice 1786.

<table>
<tr><td>Feb 4</td><td>Issue and print the following sales orders.

Sales Order 1 to Arbrook Office Supply for $3,599.78.
Qty Item Unit Price
15 ChairErgo $169.99
7 SmallDesk $149.99

Sales Order 2 to Parker Office Building for $11,425.00 before tax.
Qty Item Unit Price
8 ConfTableMaple $850.00
5 ExecDeskMaple $925.00</td></tr>
<tr><td>Feb 6</td><td>Issue and print the following sales invoices.

Invoice 1792 for Sales Order 1 to Arbrook Office Supply for $3,599.78. All items were shipped.

Invoice 1793 for Sales Order 2 to Parker Office Building for $12,224.75 with tax. All items were shipped.</td></tr>
<tr><td></td><td>Issue Credit Memo CM1787 for $4,012.50 with tax to Anderson and Anderson for the return of 10 ChairLeatherBrown on Invoice 1787.</td></tr>
<tr><td></td><td>Received check number 5768 for $4,825.57 from Anderson and Anderson for balance due on Invoice 1787.</td></tr>
</table>

Feb 8

Issue and print the following sales invoices.

Invoice 1794 to Wellman and Wellman, CPA for $27,017.50 with tax. *(You checked with Mr. Olsen and he approved exceeding the customer's credit limit.)*

Qty	Item	Unit Price
20	ChairLeatherBrown	$375.00
10	ExecDeskAsh	$925.00
10	ConfTableAsh	$850.00

Invoice 1795 Ernst Furniture for $11,799.85.

Qty	Item	Unit Price
15	ChairErgo	$169.99
10	ExecDeskOak	$925.00

Issue the following POs. Make sure to change the date and set the Qty. to Order as indicated. Set PO numbers equal to:

Brothers furniture Mfg	1042
Oregon Oak Furniture	1043
Planter Interiors	1044
Tollman Table Manufacturing	1045

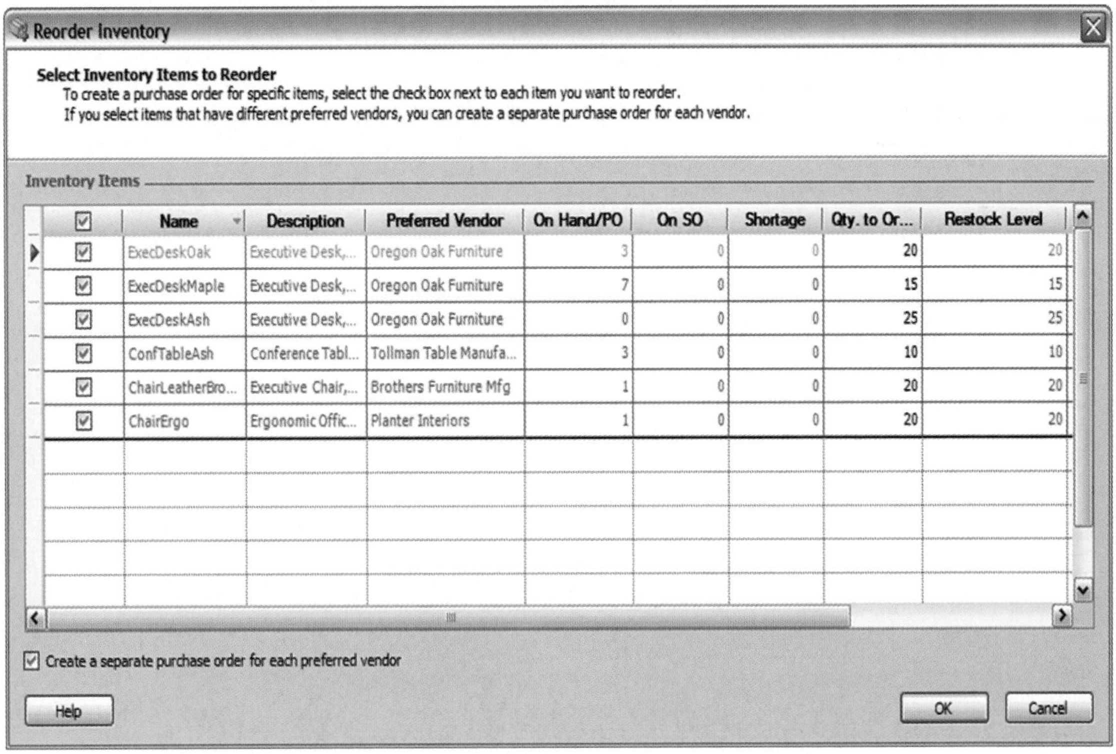

Reorder Inventory

Select Inventory Items to Reorder

To create a purchase order for specific items, select the check box next to each item you want to reorder.
If you select items that have different preferred vendors, you can create a separate purchase order for each vendor.

Inventory Items

☑	Name	Description	Preferred Vendor	On Hand/PO	On SO	Shortage	Qty. to Or...	Restock Level
☑	ExecDeskOak	Executive Desk,...	Oregon Oak Furniture	3	0	0	20	20
☑	ExecDeskMaple	Executive Desk,...	Oregon Oak Furniture	7	0	0	15	15
☑	ExecDeskAsh	Executive Desk,...	Oregon Oak Furniture	0	0	0	25	25
☑	ConfTableAsh	Conference Tabl...	Tollman Table Manufa...	3	0	0	10	10
☑	ChairLeatherBro...	Executive Chair,...	Brothers Furniture Mfg	1	0	0	20	20
☑	ChairErgo	Ergonomic Offic...	Planter Interiors	1	0	0	20	20

☑ Create a separate purchase order for each preferred vendor

Help | OK | Cancel

Feb 8	Received the following inventory. Invoice 3479 dated Feb. 8 from Brothers Furniture for $1,125.00 for 15 of the ChairLeatherBlack items on PO 1040. All items on PO 1041 to Planter Interiors. Invoice not included. Receipt number RCT89007 dated Feb. 8.
Feb 11	Prepare payroll for the biweekly pay period ended Feb. 10 based on the following spreadsheets. Recurring paychecks already exist. Print the paychecks on beginning check number 1109. Post the recurring vendor bill for employee federal withholding, Medicare, and Social Security taxes and company Medicare and Social Security taxes. Print check number 8942 for $2,199.42 from the Regular Checking Account. Post the recurring journal entry for the FUTA and SUTA employer taxes listed on the spreadsheet. Transfer $8,533.29 from the Regular Checking Account to the Payroll Checking Account to cover the Net Pay listed on the spreadsheet.
	Enter Invoice 100378 for $2,600.00 dated Feb. 8 from Planter Interiors for receipt number RCT89007.

Olsen Office Furniture
Pay Period 1/28/2008 thru 2/10/2008

Employee	Filing Status	Allow	Pay Type	Pay Rate	Regular Hrs	OT Hrs	Gross Pay	Federal Income Tax	Soc. Sec. (FICA) Tax	Medicare Tax	Net Pay
Anderson, Daniel	Married	3	Hourly	15.00	80.00	4.00	1,290.00	59.00	79.98	18.71	1,132.31
Jenkins, Charles	Married	2	Hourly	15.00	80.00		1,200.00	67.00	74.40	17.40	1,041.20
Olsen, David	Married	4	Salary	2,500.00			2,500.00	222.00	155.00	36.25	2,086.75
Olsen James	Married	3	Salary	2,500.00			2,500.00	242.00	155.00	36.25	2,066.75
Vavra, Wesley	Married	4	Hourly	16.00	80.00		1,280.00	46.00	79.36	18.56	1,136.08
Wilson, Brian	Married	4	Hourly	15.00	80.00		1,200.00	38.00	74.40	17.40	1,070.20
Totals					**320.00**	**4.00**	**9,970.00**	**674.00**	**618.14**	**144.57**	**8,533.29**
Tax Basis								**Circular E**	**6.20%**	**1.45%**	
G/L Accounts							**60000**	**23400**	**23400**	**23400**	**10300**

Olsen Office Furniture
Employer Costs for Period 1/28/2008 thru 2/10/2008

Employee	ER Soc. Sec. (FICA)	ER Medicare	ER FUTA	ER SUTA
Anderson, Daniel	79.98	18.71	10.32	38.70
Jenkins, Charles	74.40	17.40	9.60	36.00
Olsen, David	155.00	36.25	20.00	75.00
Olsen James	155.00	36.25	20.00	75.00
Vavra, Wesley	79.36	18.56	10.24	38.40
Wilson, Brian	74.40	17.40	9.60	36.00
Totals	**618.14**	**144.57**	**79.76**	**299.10**
Tax Basis	**6.20%**	**1.45%**	**0.8%**	**3.0%**
G/L Accounts	**23400 / 60100**	**23400 / 60100**	**23500 / 60100**	**23700 / 60100**

<table>
<tr><td>Feb 14</td><td>Issue and print sales invoice 1796 to Baker Hardware for $7,998.25 with tax for the following items.

Qty | Item | Unit Price
10 | ChairClothBlack | $185.00
15 | ChairLeatherBlack | $375.00</td></tr>
<tr><td></td><td>Received the following inventory.

The remaining items on PO 1040 to Brothers Furniture. Invoice 3501 for $750.00 dated Feb. 14

All items on PO 1044 to Planter Interiors. Invoice 100425 for $700.00 dated Feb. 14.

All items on PO 1042 issued to Brothers Furniture. Invoice 3502 for $1,500.00 dated Feb. 14.</td></tr>
<tr><td>Feb 15</td><td>New vendor:
DFW Equipment
3300 Camp Bowie Blvd.
Fort Worth, TX 76022
Terms: Net 3 Days
Expense account: 74500 Repairs Expense

Enter Invoice 5663 dated Feb. 15 for $859.87 from DFW Equipment for repair of equipment.

Pay bill on check number 8943.</td></tr>
<tr><td></td><td>Received the following inventory.

All items on PO 1045 issued to Tollman Tables Manufacturing. Invoice 68578 for $2,500.00 dated Feb. 15.

All items on PO 1043 issued to Oregon Oak Furniture. Invoice 98873 for $21,000.00 dated Feb. 15.</td></tr>
</table>

Feb 18

Mr. Olsen sent a memo instructing you to raise the credit limit for Art Decoraters and Arbrook Office Supply to $85,000.

Issue and print the following Sales Invoices.

Invoice 1797 to Art Decoraters for $37,824.70.

Qty	Item	Unit Price
30	SmallDesk	$149.99
25	ExecDeskAsh	$925.00
12	ConfTableAsh	$850.00

Invoice 1798 to Arbrook Office Supply for $35,774.80.

Qty	Item	Unit Price
20	ExecDeskOak	$925.00
15	ExecDeskMaple	$925.00
20	ChairErgo	$169.99

Issue the following POs.

PO 1046 to Oregon Oak Furniture for $21,000.00 for the following items.

Item	Qty	Price
ExecDeskAsh	25	$350.00
ExecDeskMaple	15	$350.00
ExecDeskOak	20	$350.00

PO 1047 to Planter Interiors for $3,300.00 for the following items.

Item	Qty	Price
ChairErgo	20	$35.00
SmallDesk	40	$65.00

PO 1048 to Tollman Table Manufacturing for $2,500.00 for the following item.

Item	Qty	Price
ConfTableAsh	10	$250.00

Received the following checks.

Check number 2057 for $5,950.00 from Art Decoraters for Invoice 1788.
Check number 90087 for $2,549.85 from Winetraub Office Furniture for Invoice 1789.

<table>
<tr><td>Feb 18</td><td>Issue the following Sales Orders.

Sales Order 3 to Ernst Furniture for $36,250.00.
<u>Qty</u> <u>Item</u> <u>Unit Price</u>
30 ExecDeskAsh $925.00
10 ConfTableOak $850.00

Sales Order 4 to Winetraub Office Furniture for $13,599.25.
<u>Qty</u> <u>Item</u> <u>Unit Price</u>
25 ChairErgo $169.99
10 ChairClothBlack $185.00
50 SmallDesk $149.99</td></tr>
<tr><td>Feb 20</td><td>Received the following inventory.

All items on PO 1046 to Oregon Oak Furniture. Invoice 98899 for $21,000.00 dated Feb. 20.

All items on PO 1047 to Planter Interiors. Invoice 100863 for $3,300.00 dated Feb. 19.</td></tr>
<tr><td></td><td>Mr. Olsen sent a memo instructing you to raise the credit limit for Ernst Furniture to $50,000.</td></tr>
<tr><td></td><td>Issue the following Sales Invoices.

Invoice 1799 for Sales Order 3 to Ernst Furniture for $36,250.00. All items shipped.

Invoice 1800 for Sales Order 4 to Winetraub Office Furniture for $12,749.30. Only 20 units of Chair Ergo were shipped.</td></tr>
</table>

<table>
<tr><td>Feb 22</td><td>Received all items on PO 1048 to Tollman Tables Manufacturing. Invoice 68883 for $2,500.00 dated Feb. 22.</td></tr>
<tr><td></td><td>Issue the following POs.

PO 1049 to Brothers Furniture Mfg for $1,300.00 for the following item.
<u>Item</u> <u>Qty</u> <u>Price</u>
ChairClothBlack 20 $65.00

PO 1050 to Oregon Oak Furniture for $8,870.00 for the following item.
<u>Item</u> <u>Qty</u> <u>Price</u>
ExecDeskAsh 25 $350.00

PO 1051 to Planter Interiors for $3,300.00 for the following items.
<u>Item</u> <u>Qty</u> <u>Price</u>
ChairErgo 20 $35.00
SmallDesk 40 $65.00

PO 1052 to Tollman Table Manufacturing for $2,500.00 for the following item.
<u>Item</u> <u>Qty</u> <u>Price</u>
ConfTableOak 10 $250.00</td></tr>
<tr><td>Feb 25</td><td>Prepare payroll for the biweekly pay period ended Feb. 24 based on the following spreadsheets. Print the paychecks on beginning check number 1115.

Post the recurring vendor bill for employee federal withholding, Medicare, and Social Security taxes and company Medicare and Social Security taxes. Print check number 8944 for $2,177.64 from the Regular Checking Account.

Post the recurring journal entry for the FUTA and SUTA employer taxes listed on the spreadsheet.

Transfer $8,458.18 from the Regular Checking Account to the Payroll Checking Account to cover the Net Pay amount listed on the spreadsheet.</td></tr>
<tr><td></td><td>Pay all vendor invoices due on or before March 9. Print checks on beginning check number 8945.</td></tr>
</table>

Olsen Office Furniture
Pay Period 2/11/2008 thru 2/24/2008

Employee	Filing Status	Allow	Pay Type	Pay Rate	Regular Hrs	OT Hrs	Gross Pay	Federal Income Tax	Soc. Sec. (FICA) Tax	Medicare Tax	Net Pay
Anderson, Daniel	Married	3	Hourly	15.00	80.00		1,200.00	51.00	74.40	17.40	1,057.20
Jenkins, Charles	Married	2	Hourly	15.00	80.00		1,200.00	67.00	74.40	17.40	1,041.20
Olsen, David	Married	4	Salary	2,500.00			2,500.00	222.00	155.00	36.25	2,086.75
Olsen James	Married	3	Salary	2,500.00			2,500.00	242.00	155.00	36.25	2,066.75
Vavra, Wesley	Married	4	Hourly	16.00	80.00		1,280.00	46.00	79.36	18.56	1,136.08
Wilson, Brian	Married	4	Hourly	15.00	80.00		1,200.00	38.00	74.40	17.40	1,070.20
Totals					**320.00**	**0.00**	**9,880.00**	**666.00**	**612.56**	**143.26**	**8,458.18**
Tax Basis								**Circular E**	**6.20%**	**1.45%**	
G/L Accounts							**60000**	**23400**	**23400**	**23400**	**10300**

Olsen Office Furniture
Employer Costs for Period 2/11/2008 thru 2/24/2008

Employee	ER Soc. Sec. (FICA)	ER Medicare	ER FUTA	ER SUTA
Anderson, Daniel	74.40	17.40	9.60	36.00
Jenkins, Charles	74.40	17.40	9.60	36.00
Olsen, David	155.00	36.25	4.00	45.00
Olsen James	155.00	36.25	4.00	45.00
Vavra, Wesley	79.36	18.56	10.24	38.40
Wilson, Brian	74.40	17.40	9.60	36.00
Totals	**612.56**	**143.26**	**47.04**	**236.40**
Tax Basis	**6.20%**	**1.45%**	**0.8%**	**3.0%**
G/L Accounts	**23400 / 60100**	**23400 / 60100**	**23500 / 60100**	**23700 / 60100**

Feb. 27	Received the following checks. Check number 90133 for $2,999.80 from Winetraub Office Furniture for Invoice 1790. Check number 5773 for $9,523.00 from Anderson & Anderson for Invoice 1791.
Feb 28	Received the following inventory. 20 ExecDeskAsh items on PO 1050 to Oregon Oak Furniture. Invoice 98903 for $7,000.00 dated Feb. 28. All items on PO 1051 to Planter Interiors. Invoice 100984 for $3,300.00 dated Feb. 28. All items on PO 1052 to Tollman Table Manufacturing. Invoice 68885 for $2,500.00 dated Feb. 27.
	Pay February sales tax liability due on March 1, 2008 to Texas Comptroller and print on check number 8949.
	Write check number 8950 for $625.00 to Reliant Electric for the February electricity bill. Write check number 8951 for $237.50 to Fort Worth Water Utilities for the February water bill.

EOM	Prepare the following end-of-month adjusting entries. Post the recurring journal entry for depreciation expense. Accrue 5 days of wages and make it a reversing entry. Post the liability to Wages Payable. Calculate the accrual using the gross pay for all employees for the month of February divided by 4 weeks. Reverse this entry on Mar 1. Write and print check number 8952 to Cash for $154.50 to replenish petty cash fund. Debit the following expense accounts. Office Supplies $ 27.50 Meals and Entertainment $127.00 Expense one month of Prepaid expenses to insurance expense, $300.00. Prepare the following bank reconciliations and print the detail reconciliation report. Regular Checking Account statement balance using the statement that follows. Payroll Checking Account statement balance is $333.64. All items have cleared. Print the following reports for February. General Ledger Trial Balance report. Review for accuracy. Aged Receivables and Aged Payables detail reports as of February 28 and Inventory Valuation report for month of February. Reconcile these reports to the appropriate account balances on the Trial Balance report. Print the following February financial statements. Profit & Loss Balance Sheet Cash Flow Statement
Backup the company data file to a backup file named **OlsenProj2.QBB**.	

Olsen Office Furniture
Bank Statement February 29, 2008

Beginning Balance from January Statement				$ 89,267.36
February Deposits				
	Feb 1, 2008		8,774.88	
	Feb 1, 2008		30,575.25	
	Feb 4, 2008		5,403.50	
	Feb 4, 2008		34,595.00	
	Feb 6, 2008		4,825.57	
	Feb 18, 2008		2,549.85	
	Feb 18, 2008		5,950.00	
	Feb 27, 2008		2,999.80	
	Feb 27, 2008		9,523.00	
Total Deposits for February				105,196.85
February Checks Cleared				
	Jan 30, 2008	8936	2,177.64	
	Feb 1, 2008	8937	5,500.00	
	Feb 1, 2008	8938	1,875.00	
	Feb 1, 2008	8939	147.58	
	Feb 1, 2008	8940	575.00	
	Feb 1, 2008	8941	800.00	
	Feb 11, 2008	8942	2,199.42	
	Feb 15, 2008	8943	859.87	
	Feb 25, 2008	8944	2,177.64	
	Feb 25, 2008	8945	5,500.00	
	Feb 25, 2008	8946	1,910.00	
	Feb 25, 2008	8947	1,125.00	
	Feb 25, 2008	8948	2,600.00	
Total Cleared Checks for February				27,447.15
Less Bank Transfers				
	Feb 11, 2008		8,533.29	
	Feb 25, 2008		8,458.18	
Total February Transfers				16,991.47
February Service Charges				75.00
Ending Bank Balance February 29, 2008				$ 149,950.59

CHAPTER 12 CREATE A NEW COMPANY

LEARNING OBJECTIVES

In this chapter you create a new data file for a merchandising business named Electronics Supply. This task is completed using the following steps.

1. Create a new company data file.
2. Create an Excel spreadsheet using OAP's template to import the new company's chart of accounts and beginning balances. *(Note: You will need to have Microsoft Excel installed on the machine.)*
3. Import the chart of accounts from the spreadsheet.
4. Create customers, vendors, inventory, and employees for the new company.

You are then asked to complete a Practice Set at the end of the chapter. This Practice Set contains Electronics Supply's January accounting transactions.

NEW COMPANY DATA FILE

Launch OAP and select ***File>>New Company*** on the main menu. Click **Yes** when prompted to close the open company.

You begin at the Company and Preferences screen illustrated in Figure 12:1. Enter the information as illustrated and click **Next.**

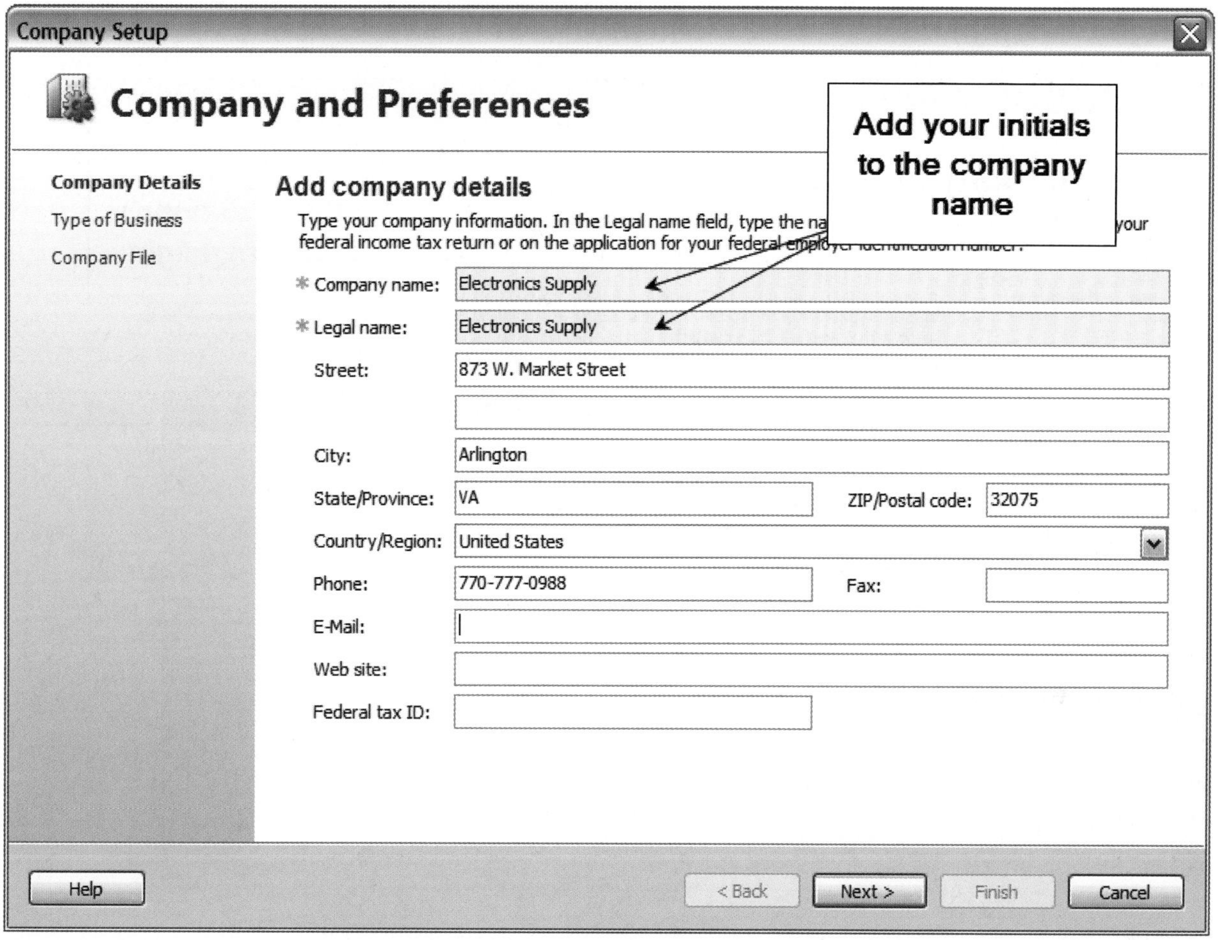

Company Setup

Company and Preferences

Add your initials to the company name

Company Details
Type of Business
Company File

Add company details

Type your company information. In the Legal name field, type the na... your federal income tax return or on the application for your federal employer identification number.

* Company name: Electronics Supply
* Legal name: Electronics Supply
Street: 873 W. Market Street
City: Arlington
State/Province: VA ZIP/Postal code: 32075
Country/Region: United States
Phone: 770-777-0988 Fax:
E-Mail:
Web site:
Federal tax ID:

Help < Back Next > Finish Cancel

Figure 12:1

You next select the company's business type. (See Figure 12:2.) Choose **Basic** and click **Next**.

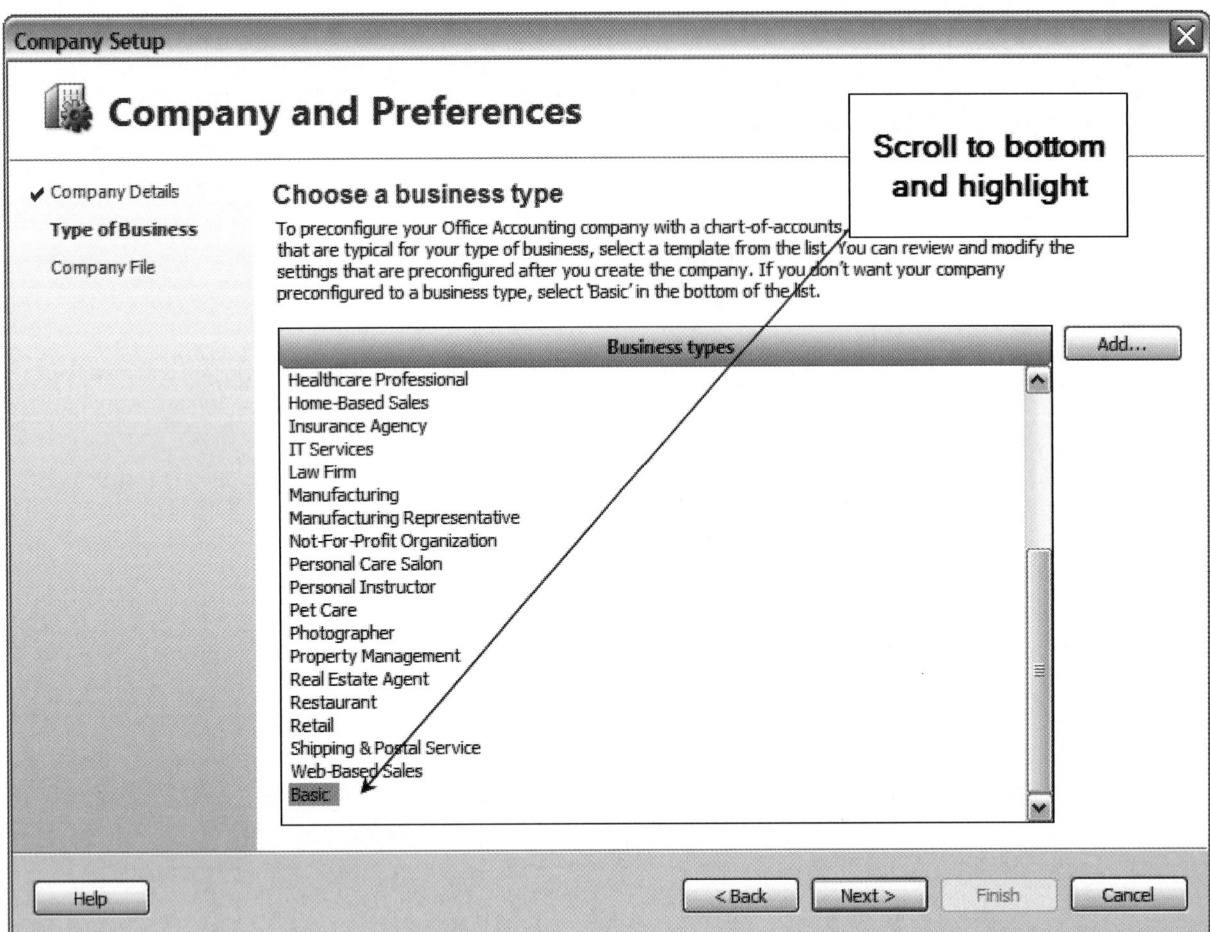

Figure 12:2

Click **Finish** to create the data file (Figure 12:3). It will take a few minutes to complete the process.

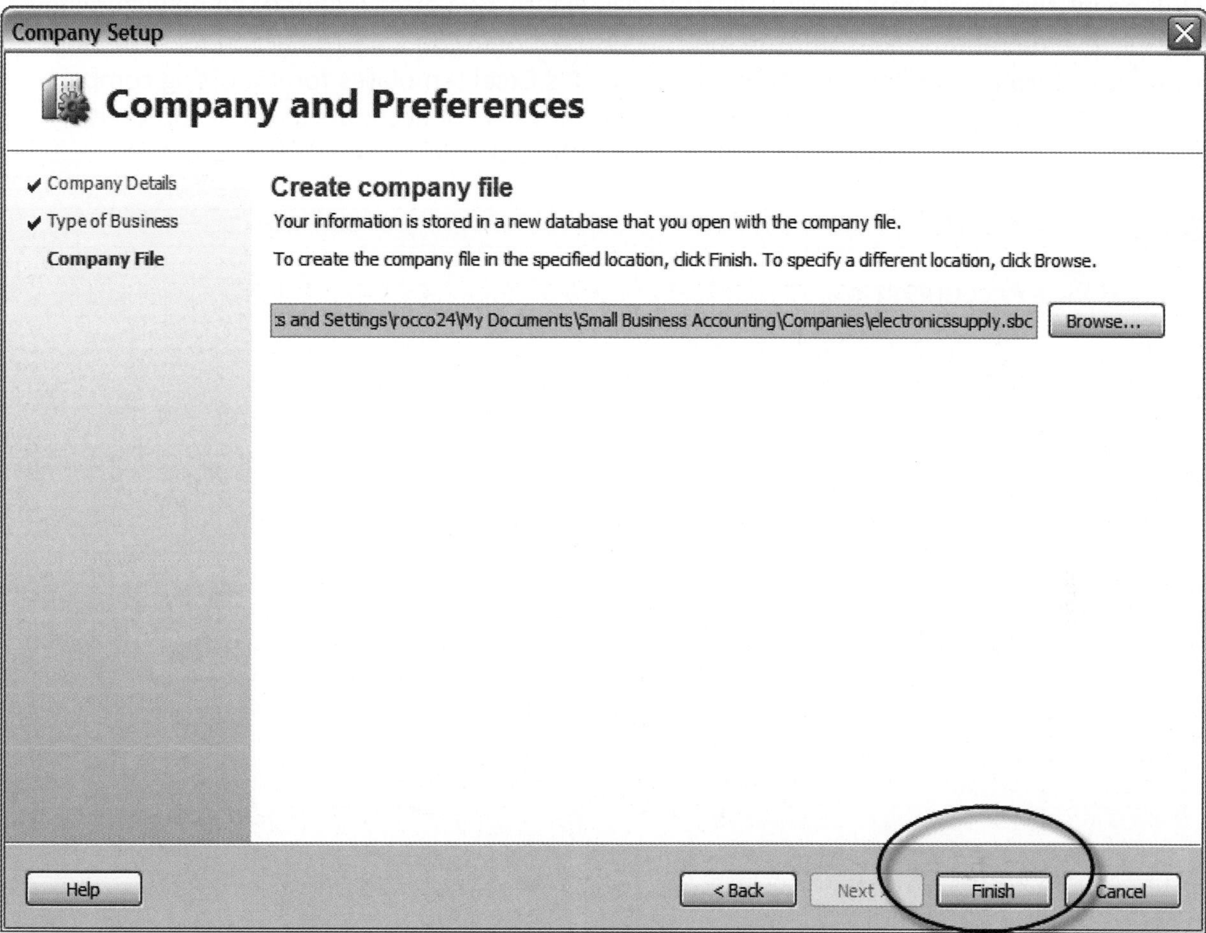

Figure 12:3

With the company data file created you are now ready to create the chart of accounts.

CREATE THE CHART OF ACCOUNTS

OAP opens the Quick Start window illustrated in Figure 12:4 after creating the new company. We will use the Add Business Information section to create the chart of accounts. The Add Business Information section contains links to OAP's Excel templates for importing company records. We will use the Accounts link to create the chart of accounts in Excel and then import the accounts and beginning balances into the data file.

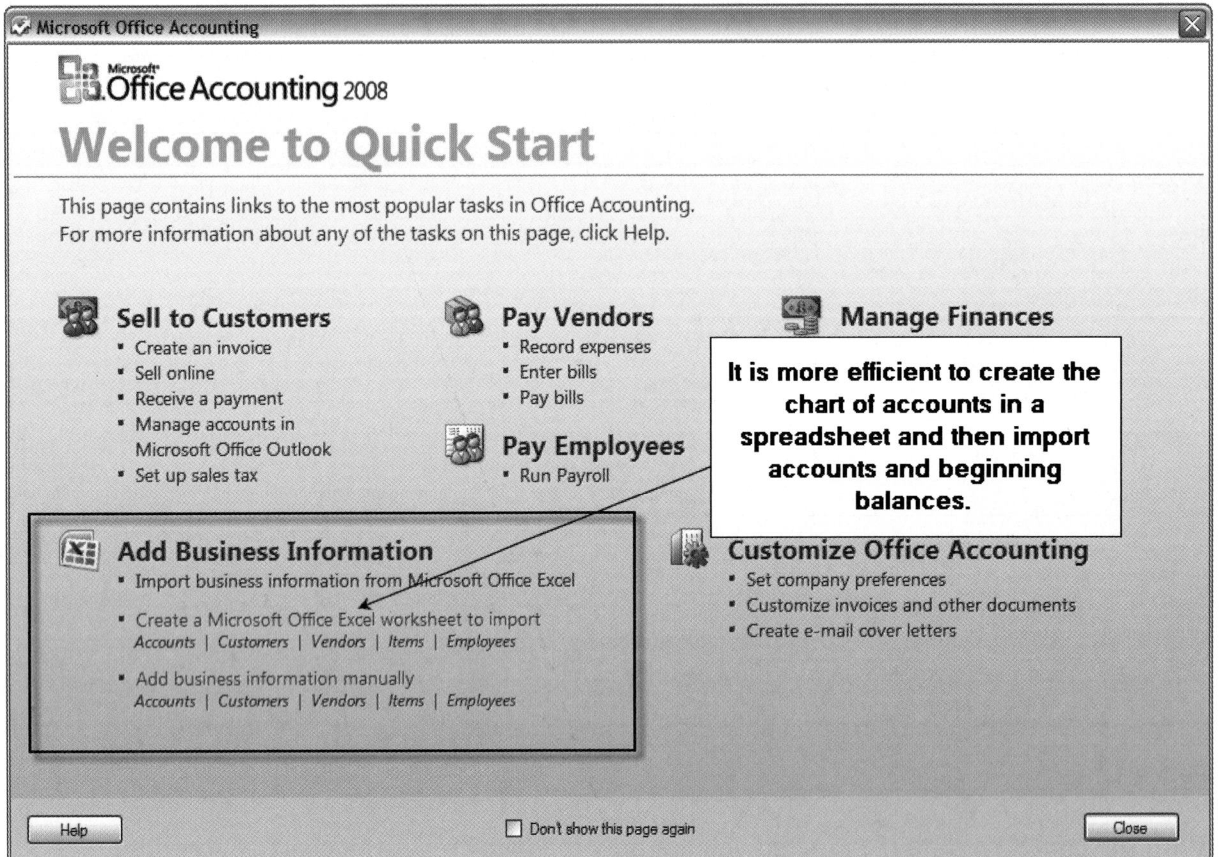

Figure 12:4

Click the **Accounts** link and a template opens with the Instructions tab active (Figure 12:5). *(Note: We are using Excel 2007; therefore, your spreadsheet will appear different if using an earlier version of Excel. We will provide the Excel commands for earlier versions of the software.)*

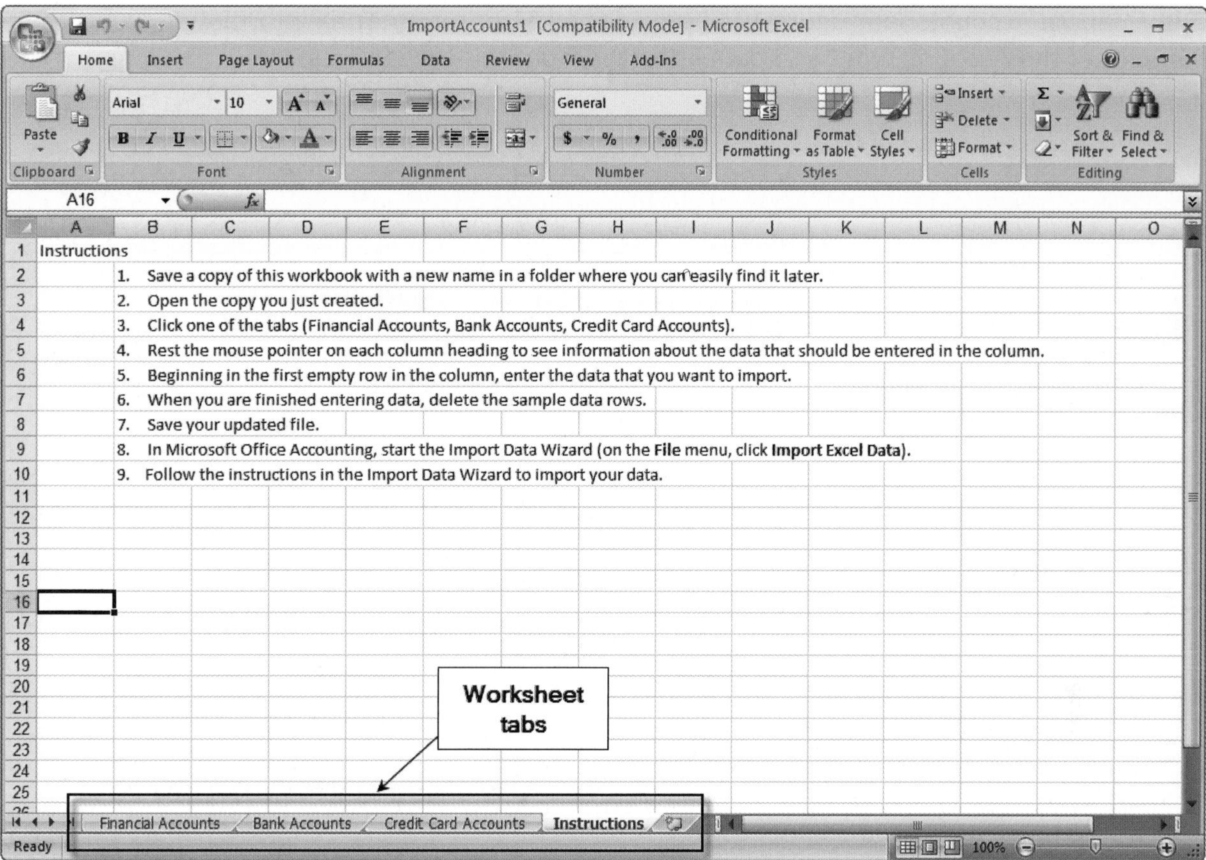

Figure 12:5

Select the **Financial Accounts** tab.

The Financial Accounts tab (Figure 12:6) provides a layout for entering information along with samples of the Account Types and data imported from this spreadsheet.

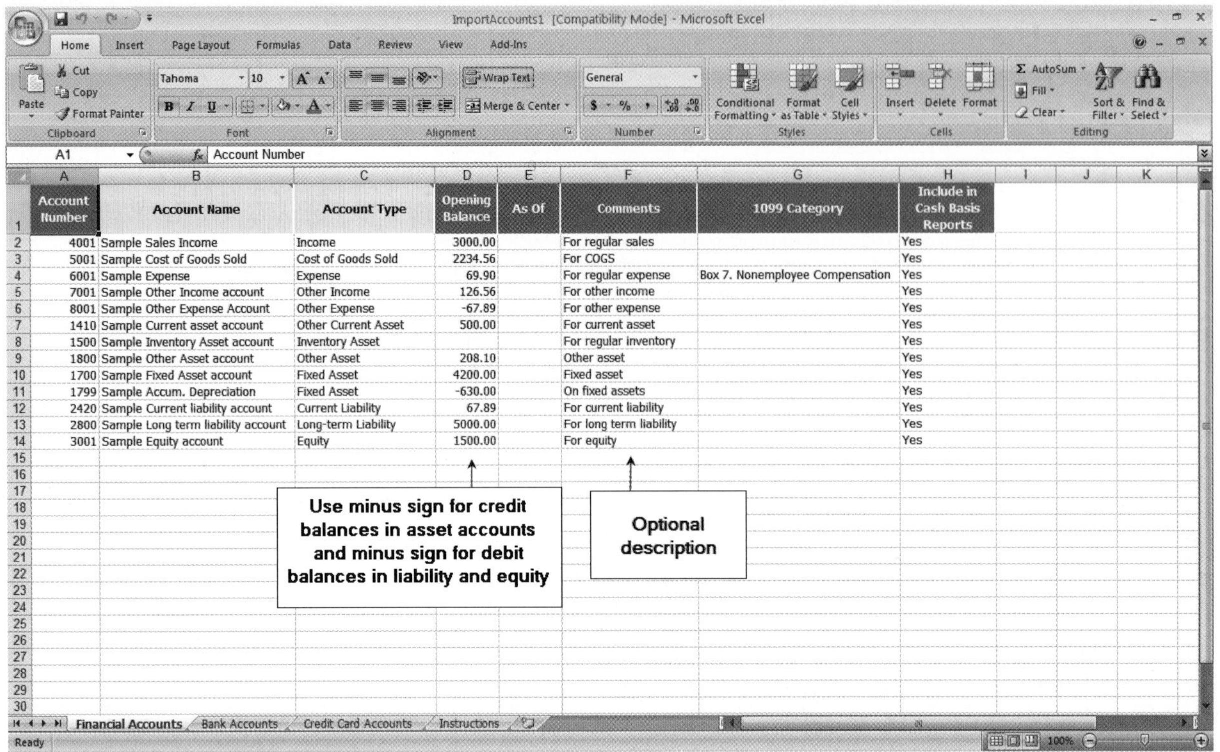

Account Number	Account Name	Account Type	Opening Balance	As Of	Comments	1099 Category	Include in Cash Basis Reports
4001	Sample Sales Income	Income	3000.00		For regular sales		Yes
5001	Sample Cost of Goods Sold	Cost of Goods Sold	2234.56		For COGS		Yes
6001	Sample Expense	Expense	69.90		For regular expense	Box 7. Nonemployee Compensation	Yes
7001	Sample Other Income account	Other Income	126.56		For other income		Yes
8001	Sample Other Expense Account	Other Expense	-67.89		For other expense		Yes
1410	Sample Current asset account	Other Current Asset	500.00		For current asset		Yes
1500	Sample Inventory Asset account	Inventory Asset			For regular inventory		Yes
1800	Sample Other Asset account	Other Asset	208.10		Other asset		Yes
1700	Sample Fixed Asset account	Fixed Asset	4200.00		Fixed asset		Yes
1799	Sample Accum. Depreciation	Fixed Asset	-630.00		On fixed assets		Yes
2420	Sample Current liability account	Current Liability	67.89		For current liability		Yes
2800	Sample Long term liability account	Long-term Liability	5000.00		For long term liability		Yes
3001	Sample Equity account	Equity	1500.00		For equity		Yes

Figure 12:6

Delete rows 2 through 14 containing sample data so you can enter the chart of accounts illustrated in Figure 12:8.

Notice that you are not entering bank accounts because these accounts are imported from the Bank Accounts worksheet. You are also not entering a beginning balance for inventory because this balance is established when importing items from a different workbook illustrated later. Finally, you are not creating accounts that the software has already created. (See Figure 12:7.) *(Note: These accounts can be viewed by opening the Chart of Accounts list from the main menu.)*

Chart of Accounts

Active	No.	Name	Type	Balance
✔	1000	Undeposited Funds	Cash Account	$0.00
✔	1200	Accounts Receivable	Accounts Receivable	$0.00
✔	2000	Accounts Payable	Accounts Payable	$0.00
✔	2010	Pending Item Receipts	Current Liability	$0.00
✔	2050	Sales Tax Payable	Current Liability	$0.00
✔	2110	Employee Payroll Liabilities	Payroll Liability	$0.00
✔	3000	Opening Balances	Equity	$0.00
✔	3100	Retained Earnings	Equity	$0.00
✔	4100	Cash Discount Given	Income	$0.00
✔	4200	Write Off	Income	$0.00
✔	5100	Cash Discount Taken	Cost of Goods Sold	$0.00
✔	6250	Bank Charge	Expense	$0.00

Add a new Account

Accounts OAP created when establishing the company

Figure 12:7

Account Number	Account Name	Account Type	Opening Balance	As Of	Comments	1099 Category	Include in Cash Basis Reports
1010	Petty Cash	Cash Account	500.00	01/01/08			Yes
1250	Allowance for Doubtful Accounts	Other Current Asset	-3000.00	01/01/08			Yes
1300	Inventory	Inventory Asset	0.00	01/01/08			Yes
1400	Prepaid Expenses	Other Current Asset	900.00	01/01/08			Yes
1500	Furniture and Fixtures	Fixed Asset	30000.00	01/01/08			Yes
1501	Accum Depr - Furn and Fixt	Fixed Asset	-4286.00	01/01/08			Yes
1510	Equipment	Fixed Asset	27000.00	01/01/08			Yes
1511	Accum Depr - Equipment	Fixed Asset	-5400.00	01/01/08			Yes
1520	Vehicles	Fixed Asset	35000.00	01/01/08			Yes
1521	Accum Depr - Vehicles	Fixed Asset	-11667.00	01/01/08			Yes
2200	Accrued Wages	Current Liability	0.00	01/01/08			Yes
2330	Federal Payroll Taxes Payable	Payroll Liability	0.00	01/01/08			Yes
2340	FUTA Payable	Payroll Liability	0.00	01/01/08			Yes
2350	State Payroll Taxes Payable	Payroll Liability	0.00	01/01/08			Yes
2360	SUTA Payable	Payroll Liability	0.00	01/01/08			Yes
2370	Health Insurance Payable	Current Liability	0.00	01/01/08			Yes
2380	Income Taxes Payable	Current Liability	0.00	01/01/08			Yes
3910	Capital Stock	Equity	1000.00	01/01/08			Yes
3920	Paid In Capital	Equity	150000.00	01/01/08			Yes
3940	Dividends Paid	Equity	0.00	01/01/08			Yes
4000	Sales Income	Income	0.00	01/01/08			Yes
5000	Cost of Goods Sold	Cost of Goods Sold	0.00	01/01/08			Yes
5200	Purchase Returns and Allowances	Cost of Goods Sold	0.00	01/01/08			Yes
5900	Inventory Adjustments	Cost of Goods Sold	0.00	01/01/08			Yes
6000	Wages Expense	Expense	0.00	01/01/08			Yes
6100	Payroll Tax Expense	Expense	0.00	01/01/08			Yes
6110	Employee Benefit Expense	Expense	0.00	01/01/08			Yes
6200	Rent Expense	Expense	0.00	01/01/08			Yes
6210	Maintenance and Repairs Expense	Expense	0.00	01/01/08			Yes
6220	Utilities Expense	Expense	0.00	01/01/08			Yes
6300	Office Supplies Expense	Expense	0.00	01/01/08			Yes
6310	Telephone Expense	Expense	0.00	01/01/08			Yes
6320	Advertising Expense	Expense	0.00	01/01/08			Yes
6330	Postage Expense	Expense	0.00	01/01/08			Yes
6400	Travel Expense	Expense	0.00	01/01/08			Yes
6410	Meals and Entertainment Expense	Expense	0.00	01/01/08			Yes
6600	Insurance Expense	Expense	0.00	01/01/08			Yes
6800	Depreciation Expense	Expense	0.00	01/01/08			Yes
6810	Bad Debt Expense	Expense	0.00	01/01/08			Yes
8000	Interest Income	Other Income	0.00	01/01/08			Yes
8100	Other Income	Other Income	0.00	01/01/08			Yes
8500	Interest Expense	Other Expense	0.00	01/01/08			Yes
8600	Gain or Loss - Sale of Assets	Other Expense	0.00	01/01/08			Yes
9500	Income Tax Expense	Other Expense	0.00	01/01/08			Yes
9999	Suspense Account	Other Expense	0.00	01/01/08			Yes

Figure 12:8

After completing the Financial Accounts tab, click the Bank Accounts tab and enter the information provided in Figure 12:9. Remember to delete sample data.

Account Number	Account Name	Opening Balance	As Of	Comments	Include in Cash Basis Reports	Bank Name	Bank Account Type	Bank Account Number
1020	Checking Account	162000.00	01/01/08		Yes		Checking	
1030	Payroll Checking Account	5000.00	01/01/08		Yes		Checking	

Figure 12:9

You are now ready to save the workbook. If using Excel 2007, click the **Office icon** and select **Save As Excel 98-2008 Workbook**. If using an earlier version of Excel, click ***File>>Save As*** on the main menu.

Choose **My Documents** as the **Save in** location and name the workbook **Electronics COA** (Figure 12:10). Click **Save** and then close the workbook.

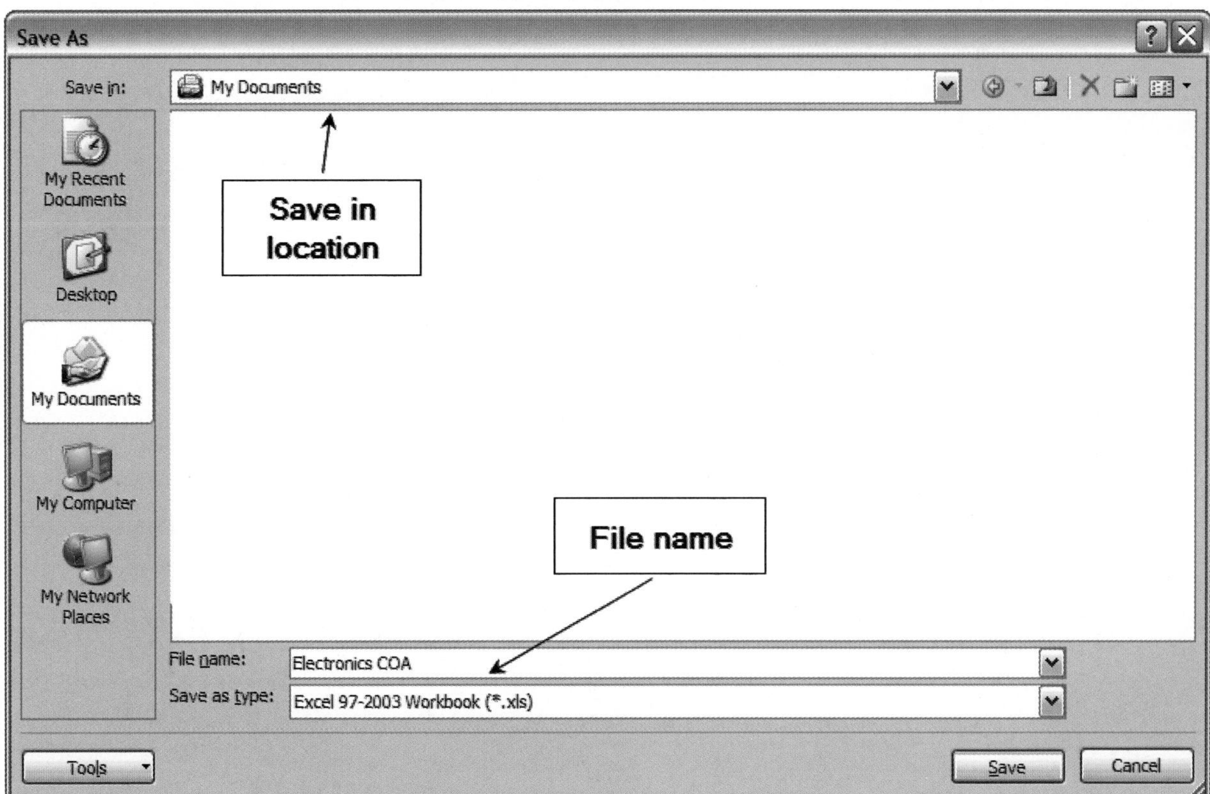

Figure 12:10

You are now ready to import the chart of accounts and beginning balances. Return to OAP and select ***File>>Import Excel Data*** on the main menu. Keep the option to import **Accounts,** uncheck the option to create a backup before importing, and click the **Browse** button. (See Figure 12:11.)

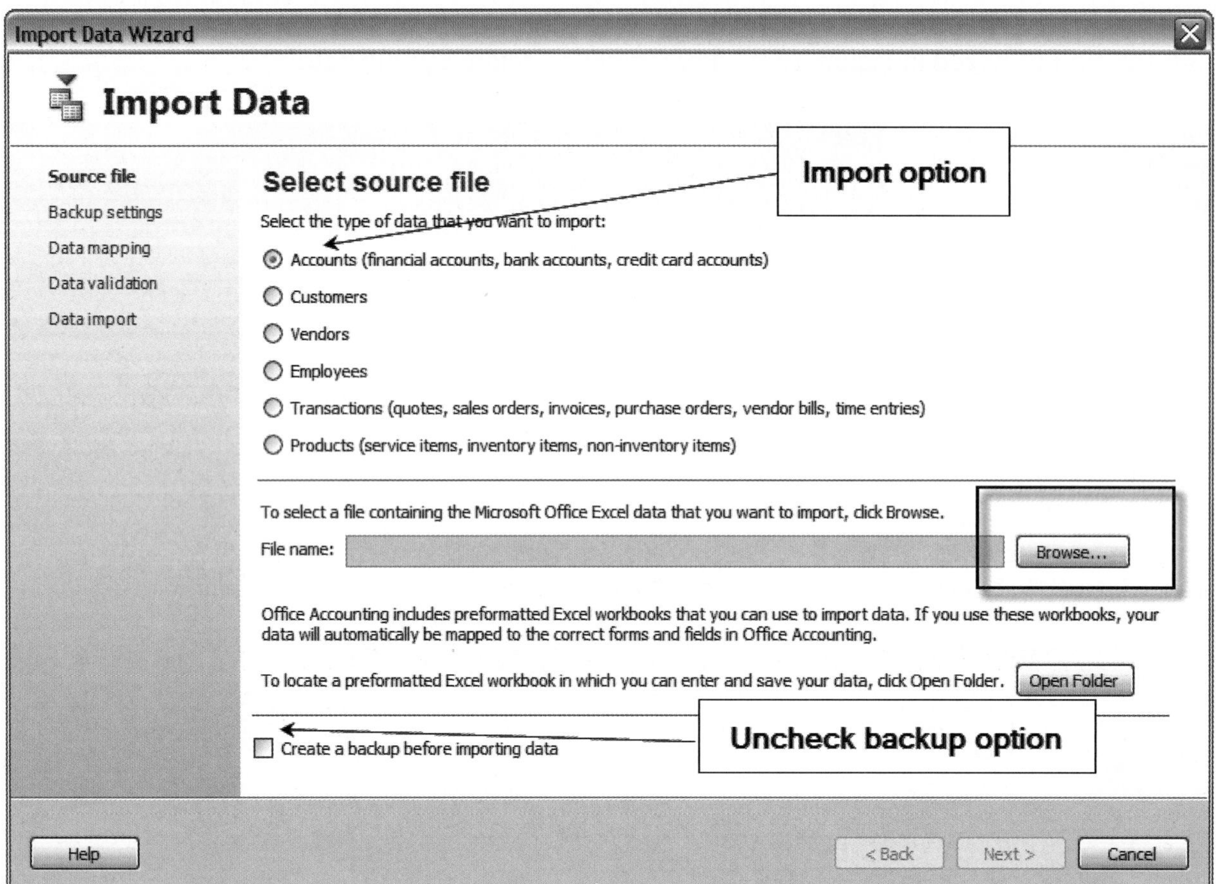
Import Data Wizard
Import Data
Source file
Backup settings
Data mapping
Data validation
Data import
Select source file
Import option
Select the type of data that you want to import:
Accounts (financial accounts, bank accounts, credit card accounts)
Customers
Vendors
Employees
Transactions (quotes, sales orders, invoices, purchase orders, vendor bills, time entries)
Products (service items, inventory items, non-inventory items)
To select a file containing the Microsoft Office Excel data that you want to import, click Browse.
File name:
Browse...
Office Accounting includes preformatted Excel workbooks that you can use to import data. If you use these workbooks, your data will automatically be mapped to the correct forms and fields in Office Accounting.
To locate a preformatted Excel workbook in which you can enter and save your data, click Open Folder.
Open Folder
Uncheck backup option
Create a backup before importing data
Help
< Back
Next >
Cancel

Figure 12:11

Change the **Look in** location to **My Documents**, select **Electronics COA**, and click **Open** (Figure 12:12).

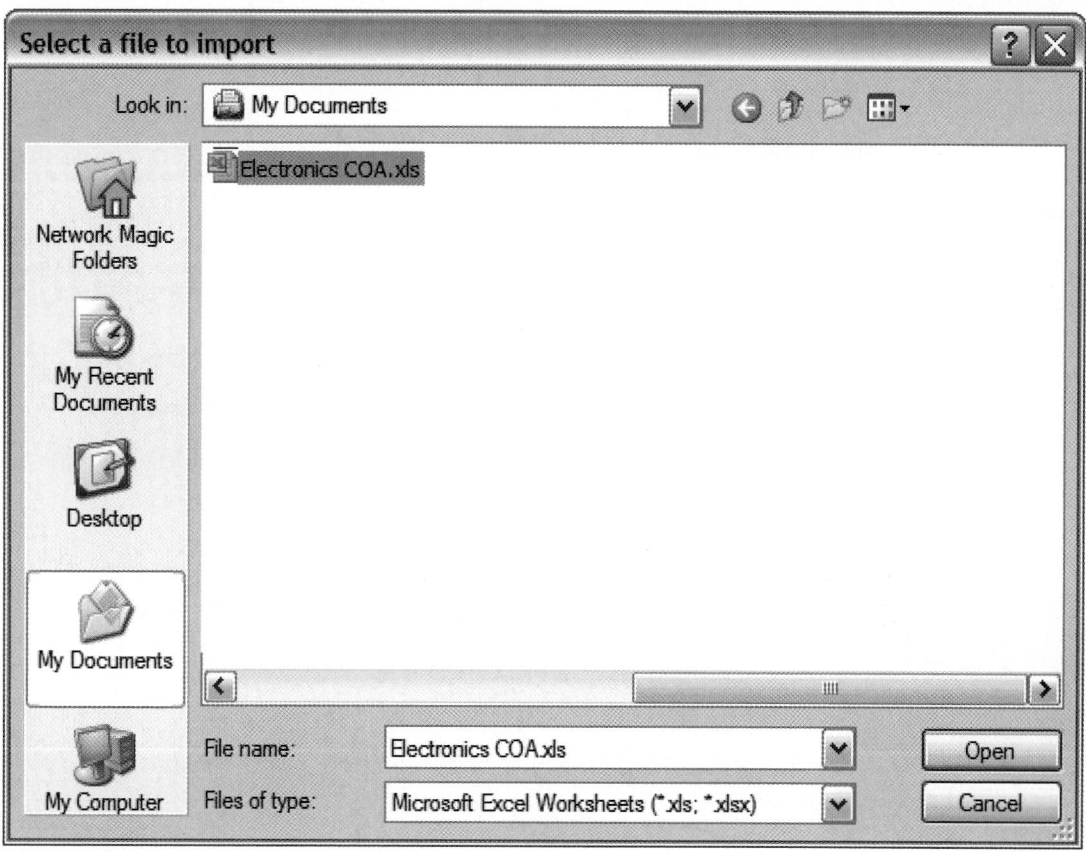

Figure 12:12

Click **Next** and select the worksheets to import (Figure 12:13).

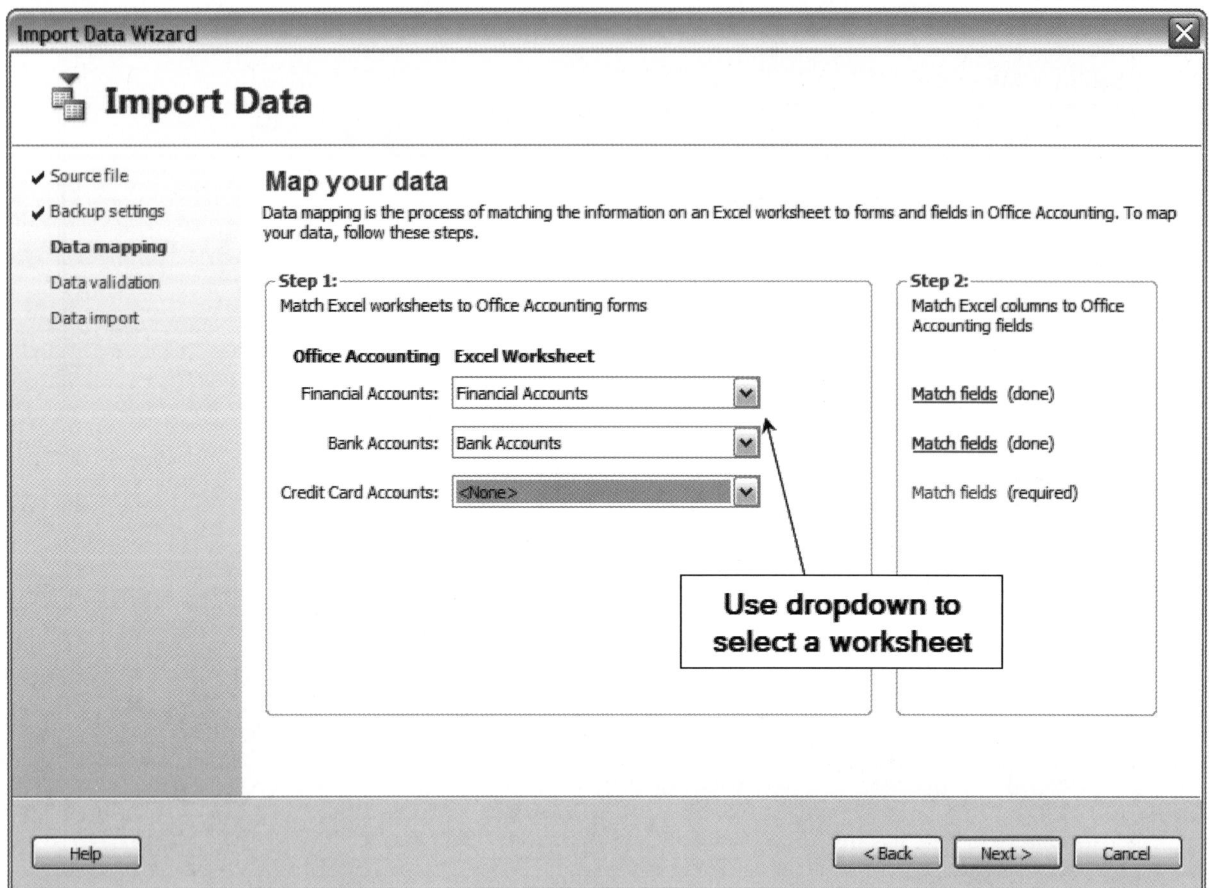

Figure 12:13

OAP validates the data before importing. We created an error on our worksheet to illustrate correcting and revalidating the import. (See Figure 12:14.)

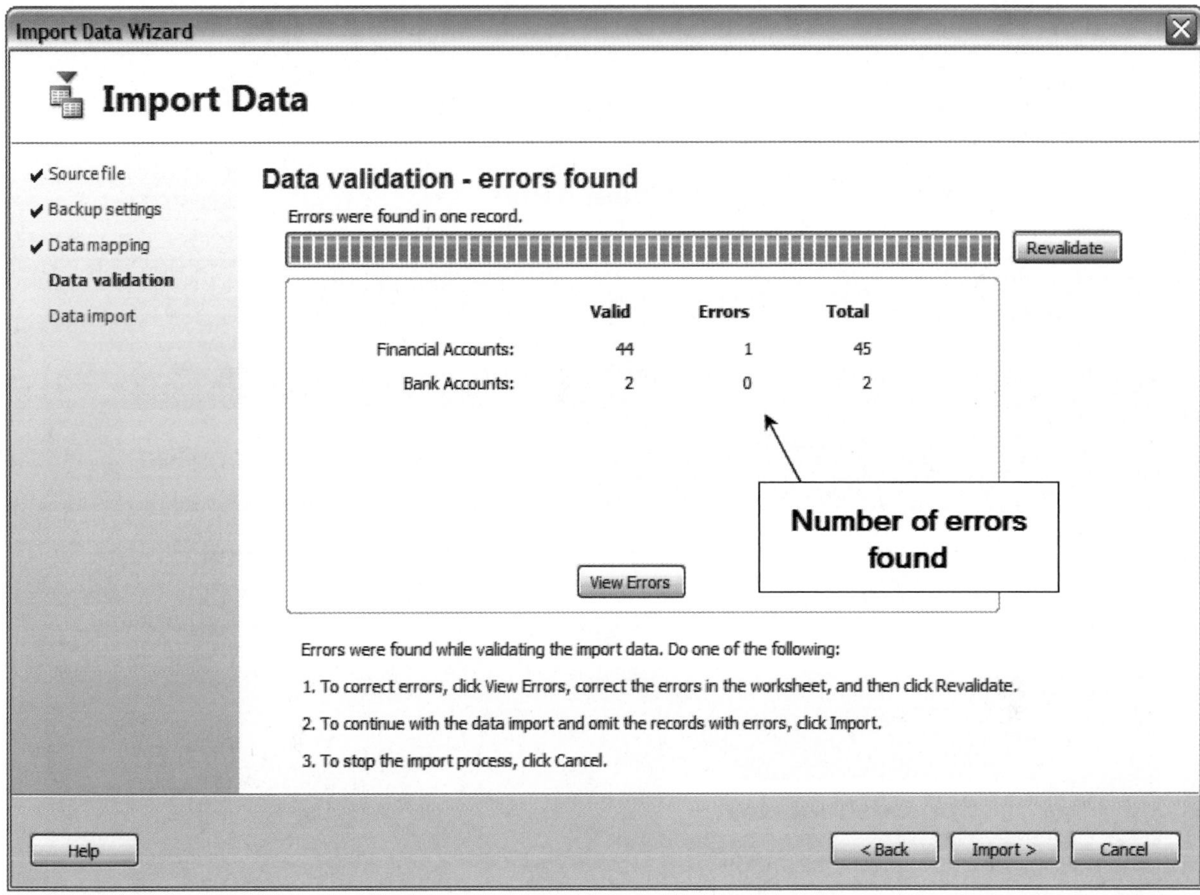

Figure 12:14

When errors are found, click **View Errors** to identify the type of error and the spreadsheet rows containing the error. (See Figure 12:15.)

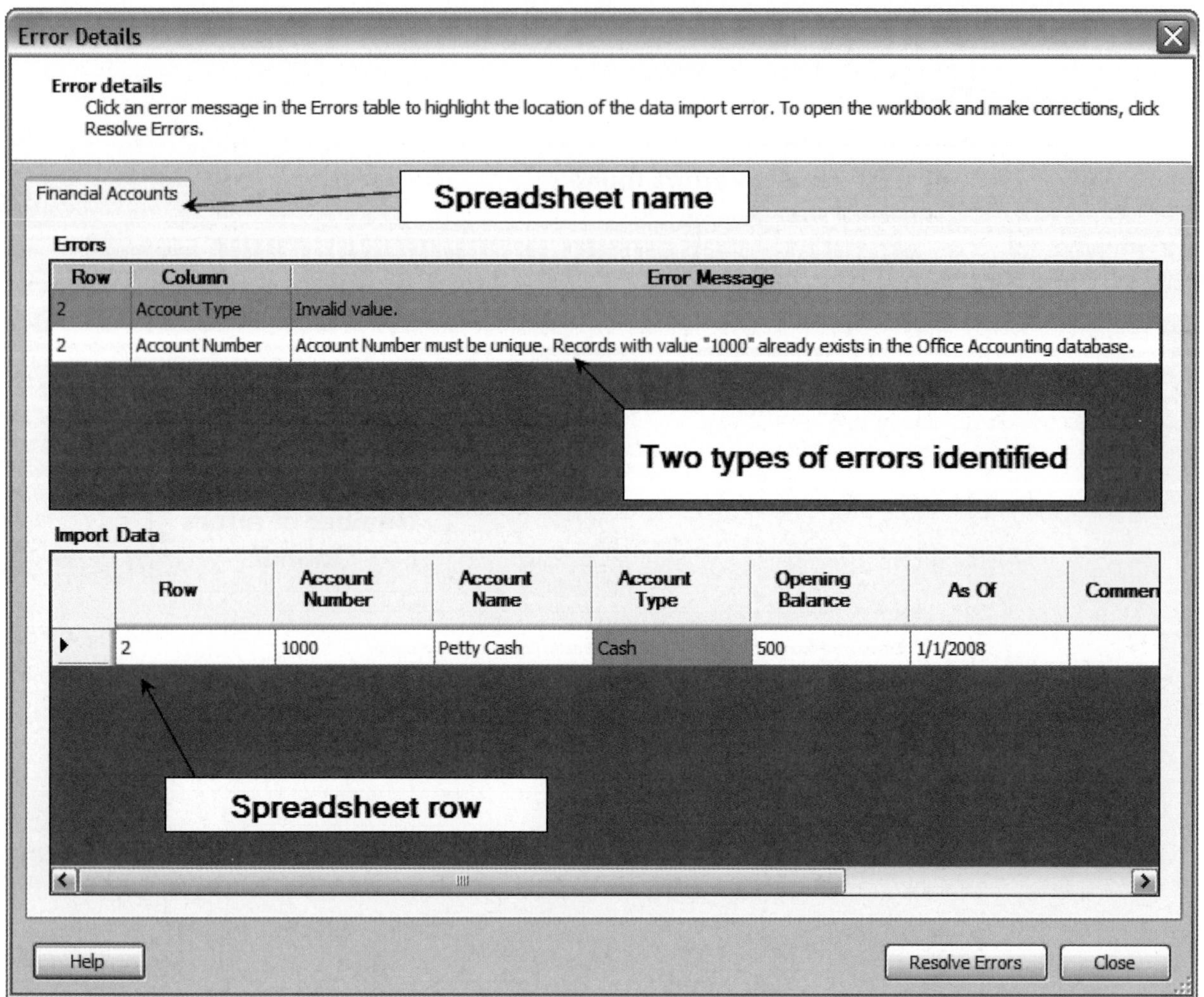

Figure 12:15

After identifying the rows with errors and the types of errors, click **Resolve Errors** to reopen the worksheet, make corrections, resave the workbook, and close it.

After resolving errors, return to the Error Details window and click **Close**. Upon returning to the Import Data Wizard window click **Revalidate**.

Do not import records until no errors are found. (See Figure 12:16.)

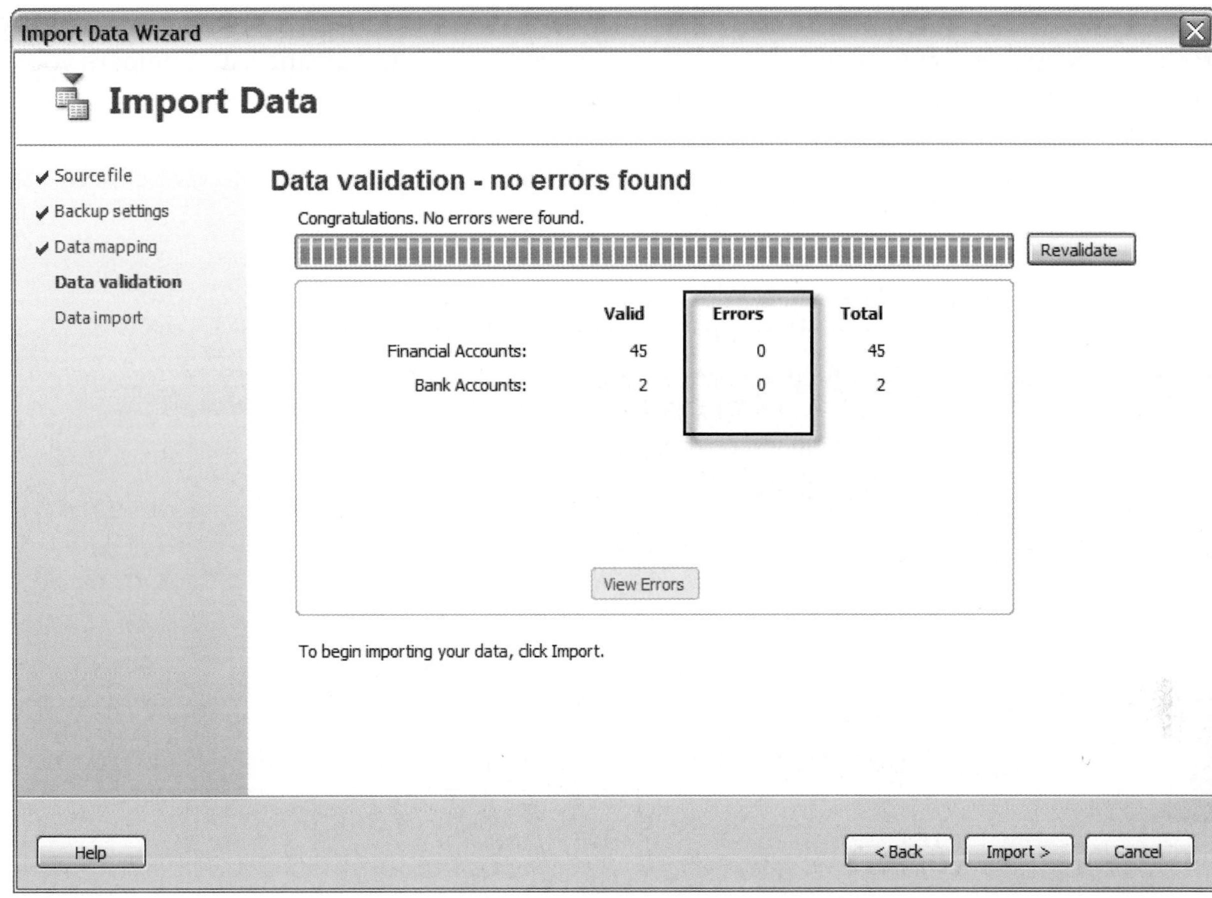

Figure 12:16

Click **Import** and then **Finish**. We next check our results. Select ***Company>>Company Lists>>Chart of Accounts*** on the main menu or use shortcut key **Ctrl+Shift+A** to open the Chart of Accounts.

We still need to finish the chart of accounts by modifying the accounts OAP created.

First, right click the **1000 Undeposited Funds** account and select **Open Selected Items**. Remove the checkmark from the **Active** field and click **Save and Close**.

Next open the **2110 Employee Payroll Liabilities** account and again remove the **Active** checkmark.

Next open the accounts listed next and change the names as indicated.

Account	**Change Account Name to**
4100 Cash Discount Given	Sales Discounts
4200 Write OffSales	Returns and Allowances
5100 Cash Discount Taken	Purchase Discounts

Finally, open the accumulated depreciation accounts and change the **Cash Flow category** to **Operating**.

Now print the Chart of Accounts report. Using **Filter Options**, modify the **Active Status** to display only **Active** accounts and click the Name column header to sort the list. Compare your results with those illustrated in Figure 12:18.

If you find a mistake on an account name, return to the Chart of Accounts list, right click to open the account, and make the changes.

If you find a mistake on a beginning balance, double click the account on the Chart of Accounts list to open the Account Register. Double click the transaction to open the entry, make changes, and resave. (See Figure 12:17.)

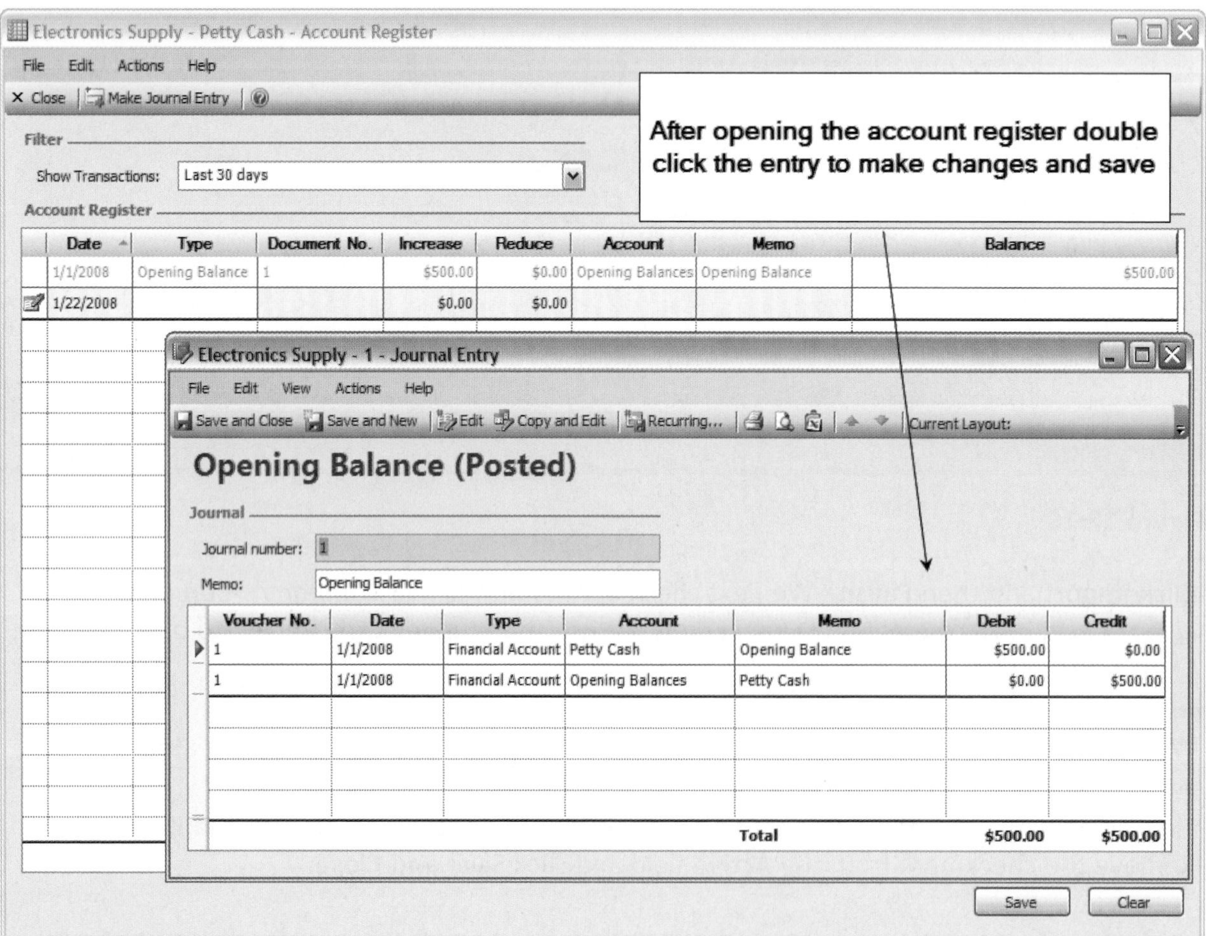

Figure 12:17

Electronics Supply
Chart of Accounts
Active Status: Active, Account: All

Name	Type	Balance
1010 - Petty Cash	Cash Account	500.00
1020 - Checking Account	Bank	162,000.00
1030 - Payroll Checking Account	Bank	5,000.00
1200 - Accounts Receivable	Accounts Receivable	0.00
1250 - Allowance for Doubtful Accounts	Other Current Asset	(3,000.00)
1300 - Inventory	Inventory Asset	0.00
1400 - Prepaid Expenses	Other Current Asset	900.00
1500 - Furniture and Fixtures	Fixed Asset	30,000.00
1501 - Accum Depr - Furn and Fixt	Fixed Asset	(4,286.00)
1510 - Equipment	Fixed Asset	27,000.00
1511 - Accum Depr - Equipment	Fixed Asset	(5,400.00)
1520 - Vehicles	Fixed Asset	35,000.00
1521 - Accum Depr - Vehicles	Fixed Asset	(11,667.00)
2000 - Accounts Payable	Accounts Payable	0.00
2010 - Pending Item Receipts	Current Liability	0.00
2050 - Sales Tax Payable	Current Liability	0.00
2200 - Accrued Wages	Current Liability	0.00
2330 - Federal Payroll Taxes Payable	Payroll Liability	0.00
2340 - FUTA Payable	Payroll Liability	0.00
2350 - State Payroll Taxes Payable	Payroll Liability	0.00
2360 - SUTA Payable	Payroll Liability	0.00
2370 - Health Insurance Payable	Current Liability	0.00
2380 - Income Taxes Payable	Current Liability	0.00
3000 - Opening Balances	Equity	85,047.00
3100 - Retained Earnings	Equity	0.00
3910 - Capital Stock	Equity	1,000.00
3920 - Paid In Capital	Equity	150,000.00
3940 - Dividends Paid	Equity	0.00
4000 - Sales Income	Income	0.00
4100 - Sales Discounts	Income	0.00
4200 - Sales Returns and Allowances	Income	0.00
5000 - Cost of Goods Sold	Cost of Goods Sold	0.00
5100 - Purchase Discounts	Cost of Goods Sold	0.00
5200 - Purchase Returns and Allowances	Cost of Goods Sold	0.00
5900 - Inventory Adjustments	Cost of Goods Sold	0.00
6000 - Wages Expense	Expense	0.00
6100 - Payroll Tax Expense	Expense	0.00
6110 - Employee Benefit Expense	Expense	0.00
6200 - Rent Expense	Expense	0.00
6210 - Maintenance and Repairs Expense	Expense	0.00
6220 - Utilities Expense	Expense	0.00
6250 - Bank Charge	Expense	0.00
6300 - Office Supplies Expense	Expense	0.00
6310 - Telephone Expense	Expense	0.00
6320 - Advertising Expense	Expense	0.00
6330 - Postage Expense	Expense	0.00
6400 - Travel Expense	Expense	0.00
6410 - Meals and Entertainment Expense	Expense	0.00
6600 - Insurance Expense	Expense	0.00
6800 - Depreciation Expense	Expense	0.00
6810 - Bad Debt Expense	Expense	0.00
8000 - Interest Income	Other Income	0.00
8100 - Other Income	Other Income	0.00
8500 - Interest Expense	Other Expense	0.00
8600 - Gain or Loss - Sale of Assets	Other Expense	0.00
9500 - Income Tax Expense	Other Expense	0.00
9999 - Suspense Account	Other Expense	0.00

Figure 12:18

Close the Trial Balance report. You will next check company preferences by selecting ***Company>>Preferences*** on the main menu to open the preference window.

Select the **Vendors** tab and mark the option to **Update cost automatically**.

Select the **System Accounts** tab and set the following general ledger accounts as the default system account.

Opening balances	3100 Retained Earnings
Undeposited funds	1020 Checking Account
Write off account	1250 Allowance for Doubtful Accounts

Click **OK** to save your changes.

Finally, make the following journal entry to reclassify imported opening balances to the retained earnings account. Then open the Opening Balances account and mark it inactive.

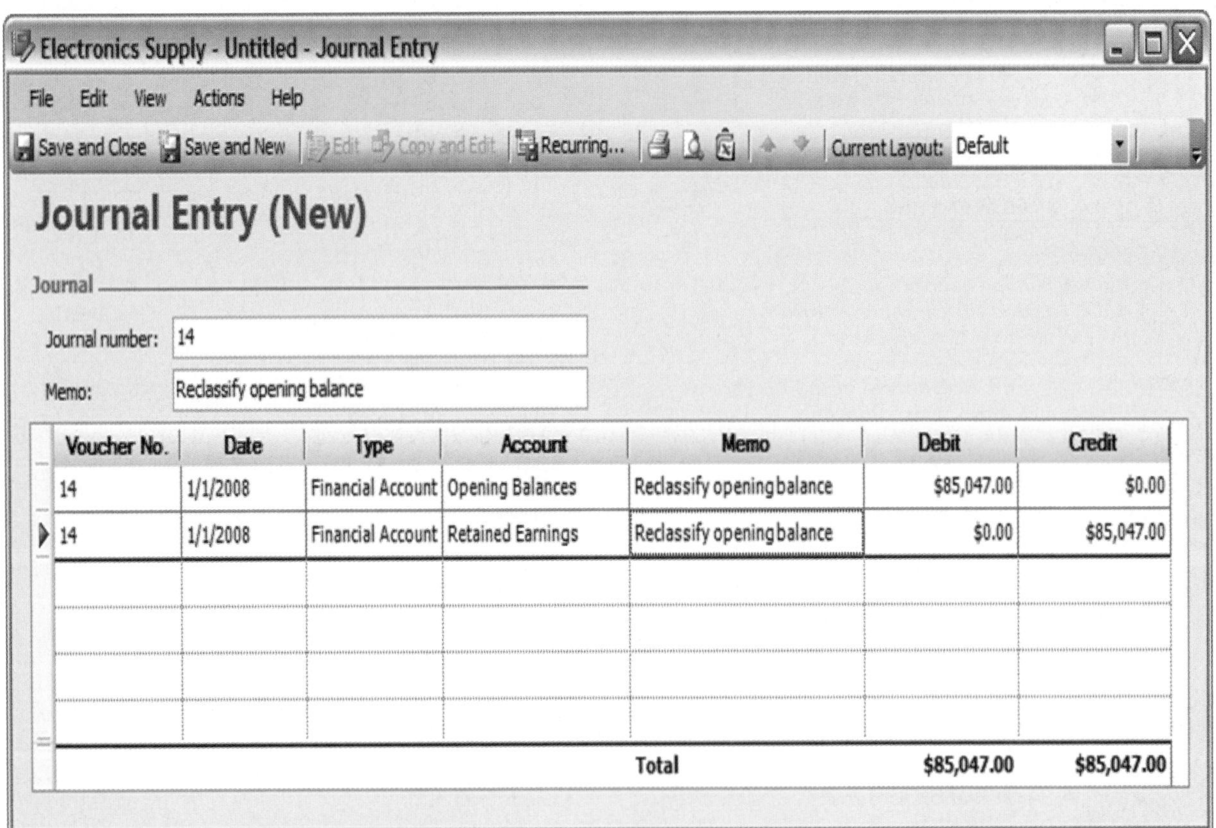

Figure 12:19

You are now ready to create customer accounts.

Create Customers

Return to the Quick Start window by selecting it from the computer task bar. We will not use OAP's import feature to create Electronics Supply's remaining records because there are fewer records so it is more efficient to just enter information in the software.

Click the **Customers** link under **Add business information manually** to open the Customer window. Electronic Supply's customer accounts and beginning balances are illustrated in Figure 12:21. Complete the **General** tab on the first account by referring to Figure 12:20 and then enter the customer's terms and credit limit on the Details tab. *Note: Electronics Supply is a wholesaler and does not collect sales tax from customers so keep None as the Tax group.)*

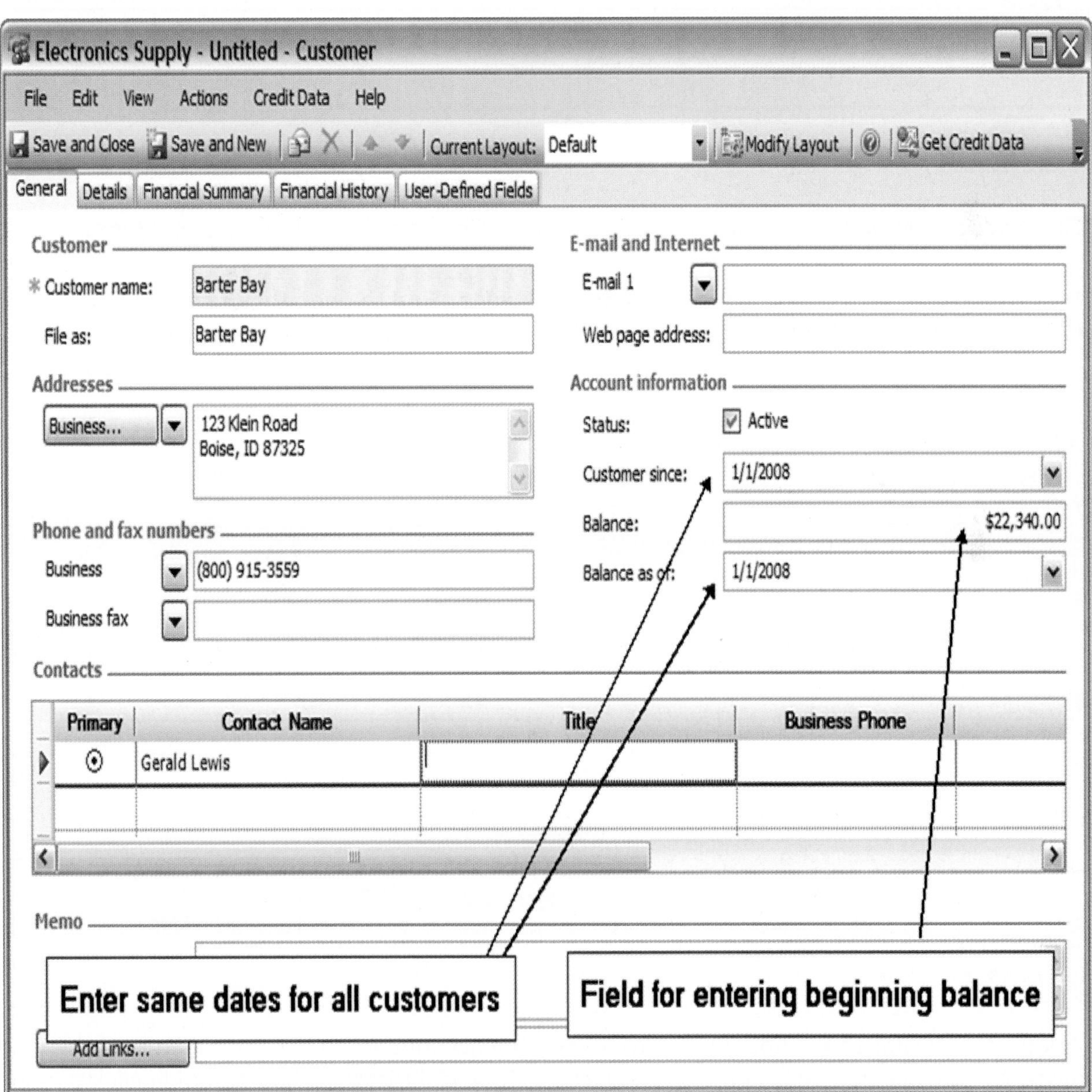

Figure 12:20

Electronics Supply									
Customer List									
Customer	Contact	Telephone	Address	City	State	Zip	Terms	Credit Limit	Beginning Balance
Barter Bay	Gerald Lewis	800-915-3559	123 Klein Road	Boise	ID	87325	Net 30	30,000.00	22,340.00
Better Buy	Jeremy Michael	800-924-4766	825 W. Exchange St	Chicago	IL	60609	2% 10 Net 30	50,000.00	27,000.00
Discount Electronics	Jamie Foxtrot	800-940-9594	33 Rodeo Drive	Berstow	CA	65841	Net 30	30,000.00	9,670.00
Electronic Town	Clarice Tompson	800-945-1080	3454 Broadway Ave	Aliquippa	PA	42251	Net 30	30,000.00	23,500.00
GG Hregg Stores	Trevor Logan	800-958-1442	454 Sanford St	Lansing	MI	60543	Net 30	30,000.00	9,600.00
Television World	Tina Filmore	800-997-3373	25 Saturday Ave	New York	NY	36544	Net 30	30,000.00	0.00

Figure 12:21

Click **Save and New** to continue creating accounts. When finished, click **Save and Close**.

Next, verify your entries. Click the **Customers** link under **Find** to open the Customer List. Select ***View>>Add/Remove Content*** on the main menu to add the **Credit Limit** and **Account Since** fields and remove the **Fax** field. Now compare your results those illustrated in Figure 12:22.

Customer List — Current View: Active

	Active	Customer Name	Address	City	State	Zip Code	Phone	Balance	Credit Limit	Account Since
	Add a new Customer									
	✓	Barter Bay	123 Klein Road	Boise	ID	87325	800-915-3559	$22,340.00	$30,000.00	1/1/2008
	✓	Better Buy	825 W. Exchange St	Chicago	IL	60609	800-924-4766	$27,000.00	$50,000.00	1/1/2008
	✓	Discount Electronics	33 Rodeo Drive	Berstow	CA	65841	800-940-9594	$9,670.00	$30,000.00	1/1/2008
	✓	Electronic Town	3454 Broadway Ave	Aliquippa	PA	42251	800-945-1080	$23,500.00	$30,000.00	1/1/2008
	✓	GG Hregg Stores	454 Sanford St	Lansing	MI	60543	800-958-1442	$9,600.00	$30,000.00	1/1/2008
	✓	Television World	25 Saturday Ave	New York	NY	36544	800-997-3373	$0.00	$30,000.00	1/1/2008

Balance in accounts receivable

Total outstanding balance: $92,110.00

Figure 12:22

If you find a mistake then double click to reopen the account and make corrections. If the mistake is on a beginning balance then select the Financial History tab and double click the Opening Balance transaction to correct the journal entry. Click Save and Close to post the change.

CREATE VENDORS

You are now ready to create vendor accounts. First, create two additional payment terms. Select ***Company>>Manage Support Lists>>Payment Terms List*** on the main menu and, using ***Add***, create the following terms. Close the terms Manage Payment Term window when finished.

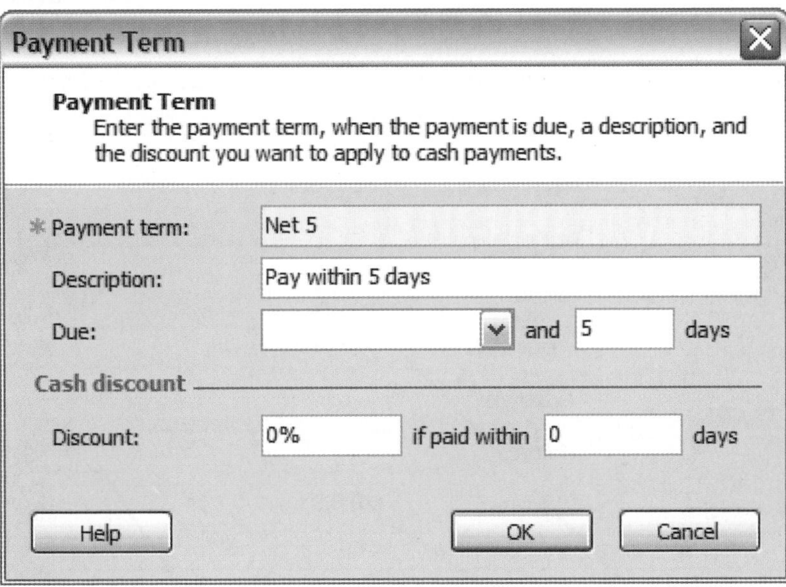

Figure 12:23

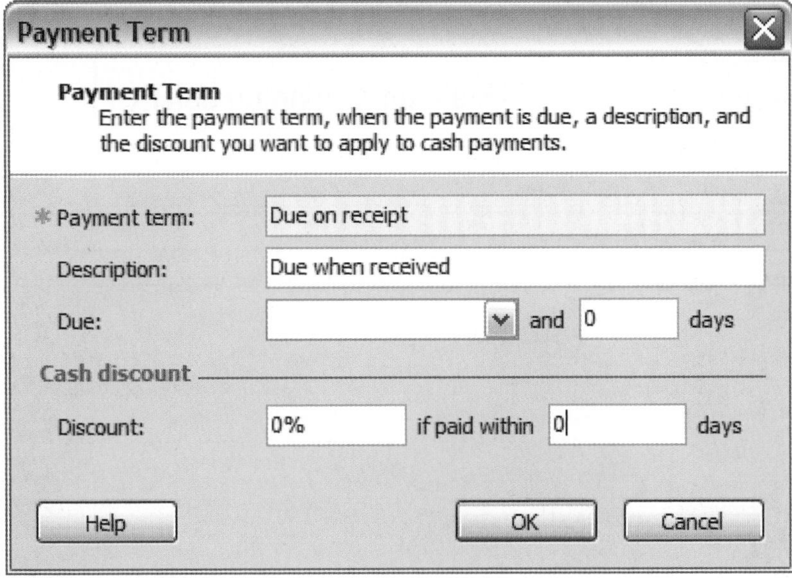

Figure 12:24

Electronics Supply's vendor accounts and beginning balances are illustrated in Figure 12:26. Return to the Quick Start window and click the **Vendors** link under **Add business information manually**. Figure 12:25 illustrates completing the General tab for the first vendor. Remember to enter the Expense account and Payment terms on the Details tab. Click **Save and New** to continue adding accounts and **Save and Close** when finished.

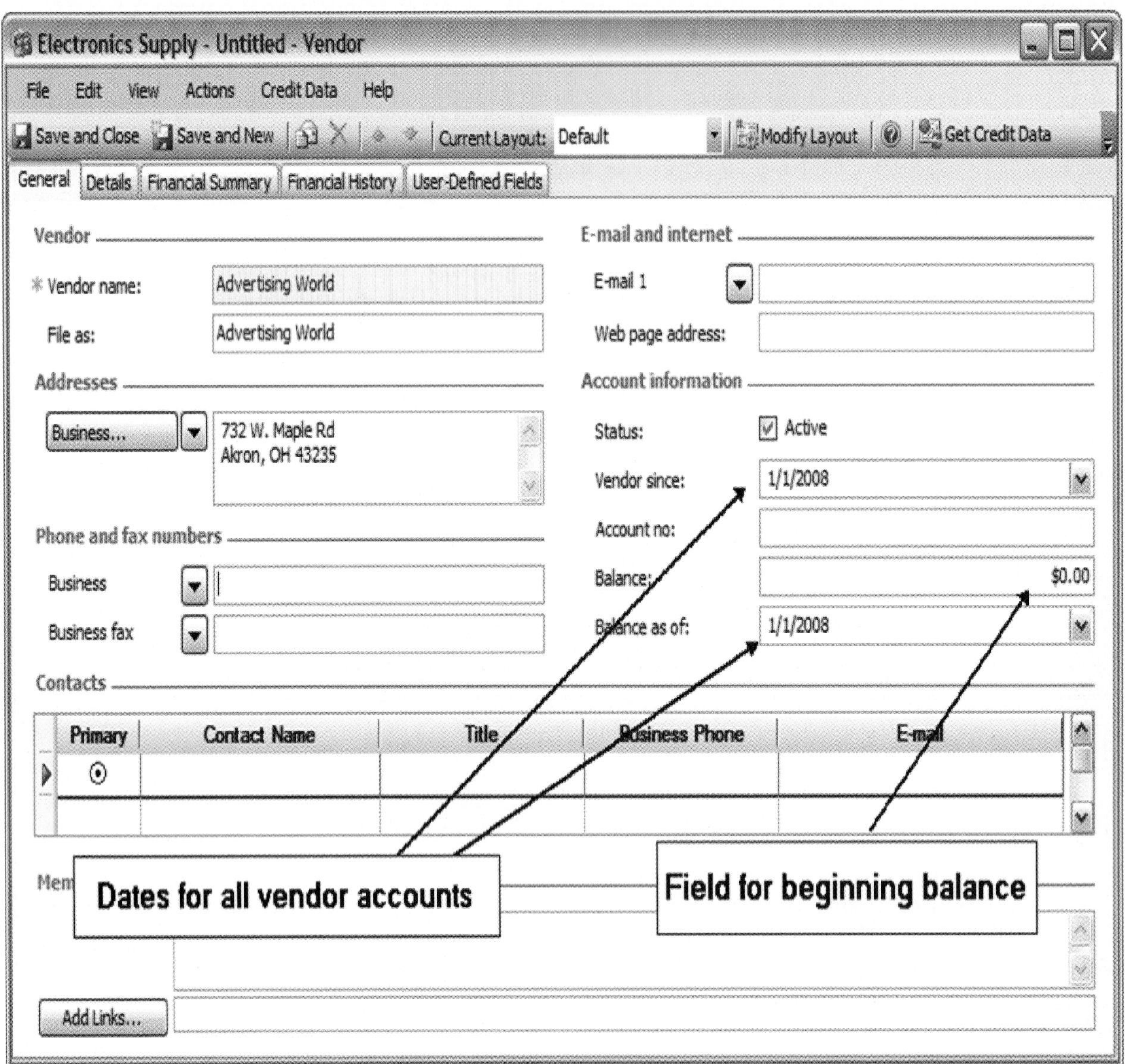

Figure 12:25

Electronics Supply							
Vendor List							
Vendor	**Address**	**City**	**State**	**Zip**	**Expense Account**	**Terms**	**Beginning Balance**
Advertising World	732 W. Maple Rd	Akron	OH	43235	6320 Advertising Expense	Net 30	0.00
Bank Amerex	2332 Arlington Dr	Arlington	VA	23532	2330 Federal Payroll Taxes Payable	Net 5	0.00
Canyon Cam	8754 Anthony Lane	Harrisburg	PA	15237		2% 10 Net 30	7,740.00
Cooleys Repair	8 Ripley Ave	Blacksburg	VA	43253	6210 Maintenance & Repairs Expense	Net 30	0.00
CSB Telephone	2 Rich St	Arlington	VA	45325	6310 Telephone Expense	Net 15	0.00
Federal Xpert	903 Mulberry Ave	Montpelier	NH	17325	6330 Postage Expense	Net 15	0.00
Javix Cam	898 Main St	Albany	NY	09325		Net 30	7,760.00
Mutual Health Insurance	7542 Golf Way	Concord	NH	45789	2370 Health Insurance Payable	Net 15	0.00
Neer Pio	896 Angel Rd	Salem	OR	23456		Net 30	41,400.00
Office Rex	105 Curl Ave	Arlington	VA	44333	6300 Office Supplies Expense	Net 30	0.00
Petty Cash					6300 Office Supplies Expense	Due on receipt	0.00
Rental Experts	872 Alum St	Arlington	VA	36544	6200 Rent Expense	Net 5	0.00
SumSang Corporation	78123 Mulberry Ave	Santa Anita	CA	09827		Net 30	0.00
Travelor's Insurance	7895 Cat Drive	Salem	OR	78453	1400 Prepaid Expenses	Net 15	0.00
VA Depart. of Taxation	PO Box 8721	Arlington	VA	32513	2350 State Payroll Taxes Payable	Net 5	0.00
VA Employment Commission	PO Box 8181	Arlington	VA	32513	2360 SUTA Payable	Net 5	0.00
Virginia Electric	41 Cala Road	Arlington	VA	42353	6220 Utilities Expense	Net 15	0.00

Figure 12:26

Next, compare your results to those illustrated in Figure 12:27. Click the **Vendors** link under **Find** to open the Vendor List and then select ***View>>Add/Remove Content*** on the main menu to add the **Account Since** field to the list and remove the Fax field.

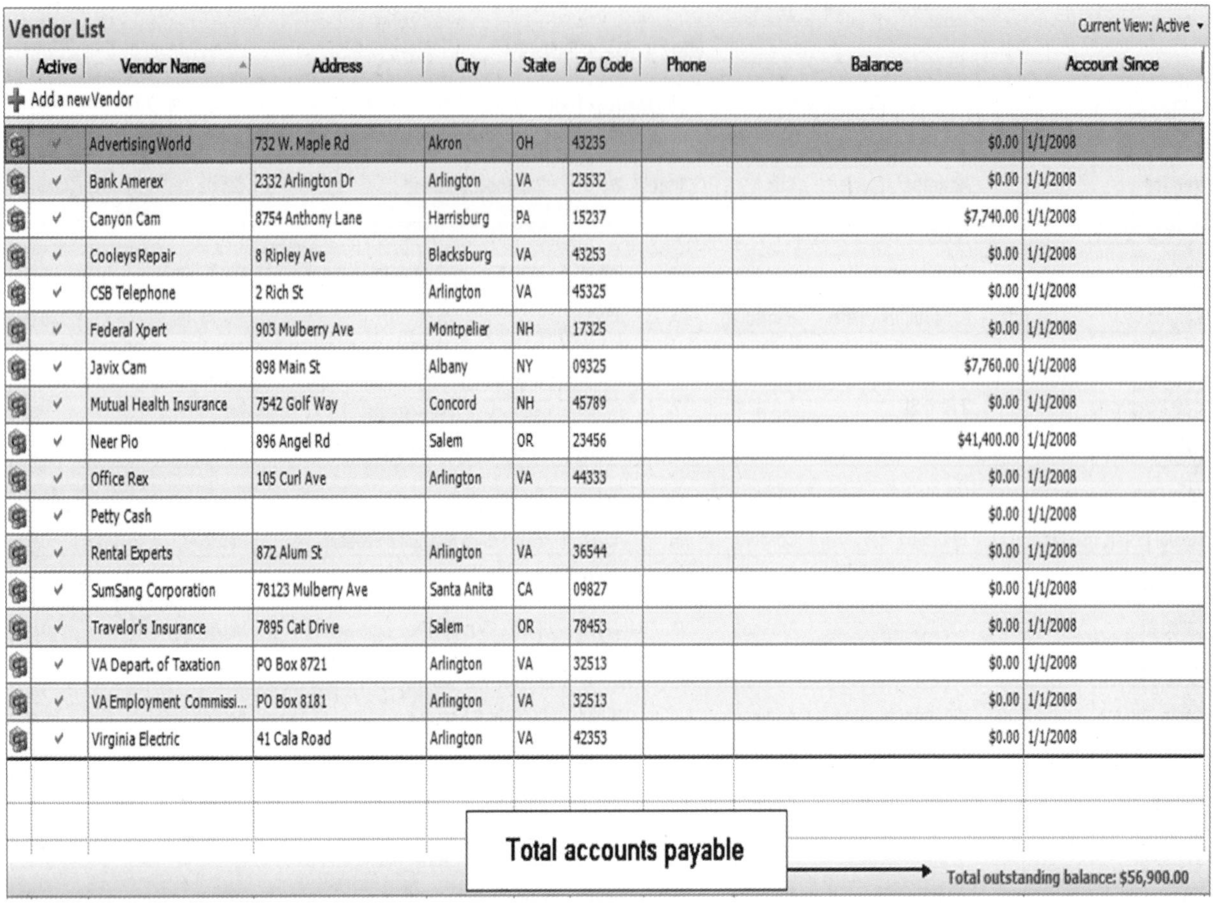

Vendor List

Current View: Active

Add a new Vendor

Active	Vendor Name	Address	City	State	Zip Code	Phone	Balance	Account Since
✓	Advertising World	732 W. Maple Rd	Akron	OH	43235		$0.00	1/1/2008
✓	Bank Amerex	2332 Arlington Dr	Arlington	VA	23532		$0.00	1/1/2008
✓	Canyon Cam	8754 Anthony Lane	Harrisburg	PA	15237		$7,740.00	1/1/2008
✓	Cooleys Repair	8 Ripley Ave	Blacksburg	VA	43253		$0.00	1/1/2008
✓	CSB Telephone	2 Rich St	Arlington	VA	45325		$0.00	1/1/2008
✓	Federal Xpert	903 Mulberry Ave	Montpelier	NH	17325		$0.00	1/1/2008
✓	Javix Cam	898 Main St	Albany	NY	09325		$7,760.00	1/1/2008
✓	Mutual Health Insurance	7542 Golf Way	Concord	NH	45789		$0.00	1/1/2008
✓	Neer Pio	896 Angel Rd	Salem	OR	23456		$41,400.00	1/1/2008
✓	Office Rex	105 Curl Ave	Arlington	VA	44333		$0.00	1/1/2008
✓	Petty Cash						$0.00	1/1/2008
✓	Rental Experts	872 Alum St	Arlington	VA	36544		$0.00	1/1/2008
✓	SumSang Corporation	78123 Mulberry Ave	Santa Anita	CA	09827		$0.00	1/1/2008
✓	Travelor's Insurance	7895 Cat Drive	Salem	OR	78453		$0.00	1/1/2008
✓	VA Depart. of Taxation	PO Box 8721	Arlington	VA	32513		$0.00	1/1/2008
✓	VA Employment Commissi...	PO Box 8181	Arlington	VA	32513		$0.00	1/1/2008
✓	Virginia Electric	41 Cala Road	Arlington	VA	42353		$0.00	1/1/2008

Total accounts payable → Total outstanding balance: $56,900.00

Figure 12:27

If you find a mistake then double click to reopen the account and make corrections. If the mistake is on a beginning balance then select the Financial History tab and double click the Opening Balance transaction to correct the journal entry. Click Save and Close to post the change.

Create Inventory Items

You are now ready to create the inventory items illustrated in Figure 12:29. Return to the Quick Start window and click **Items** under **Add business information manually**. Select **Inventory** as the Item Type and enter the following information. *(Note: All items you will create are of the Inventory type.)*

Refer to Figure 12:28 to create the first item. After entering the Income account, choose the option to **Always update the default account** and click **Yes** when prompted. Click Save and New to continue creating items and Save and Close when finished.

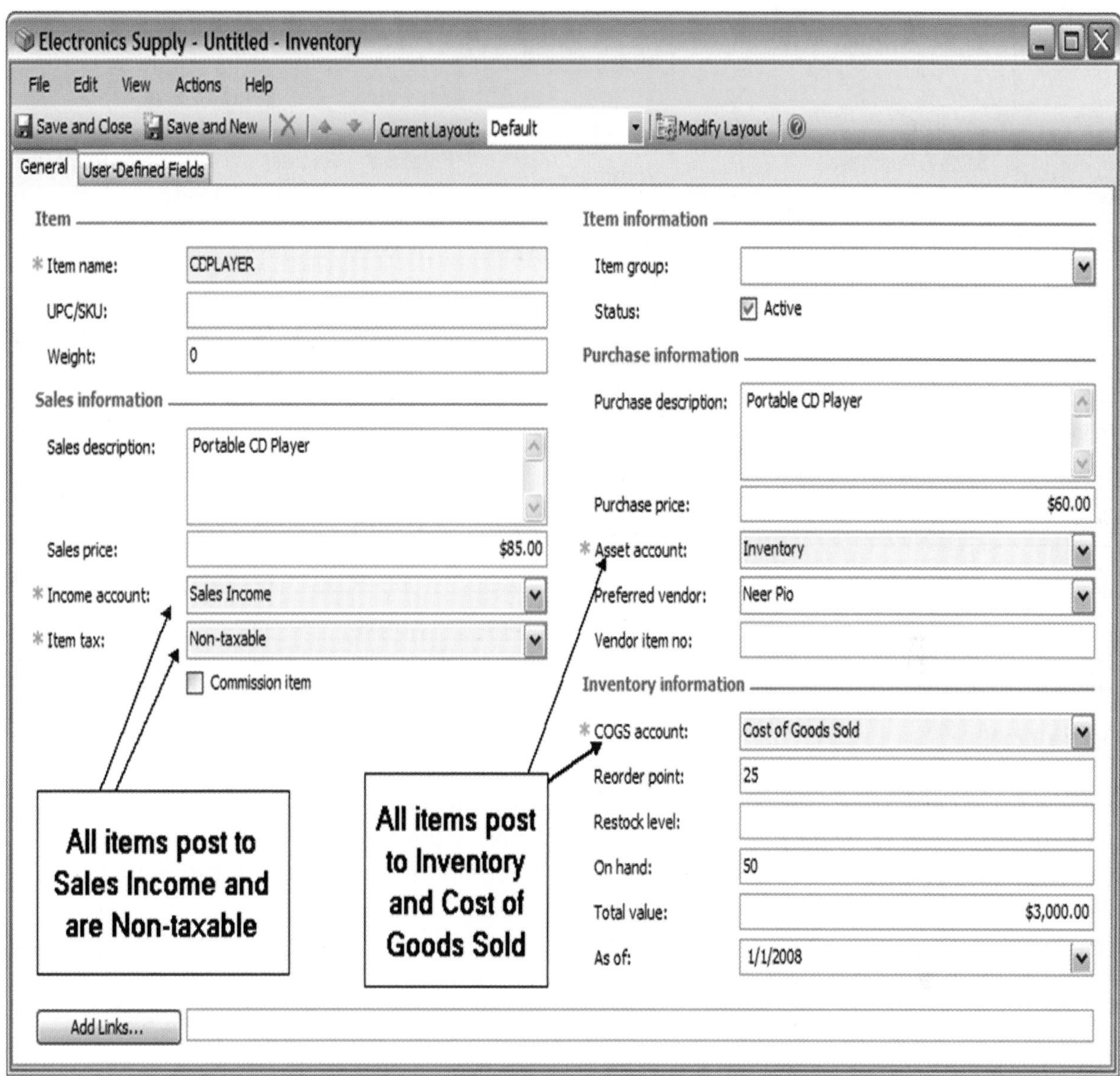
Electronics Supply - Untitled - Inventory
File Edit View Actions Help
Save and Close
Save and New
Current Layout: Default
Modify Layout
General
User-Defined Fields
Item
* Item name: CDPLAYER
UPC/SKU:
Weight: 0
Sales information
Sales description: Portable CD Player
Sales price: $85.00
* Income account: Sales Income
* Item tax: Non-taxable
Commission item
Item information
Item group:
Status: Active
Purchase information
Purchase description: Portable CD Player
Purchase price: $60.00
* Asset account: Inventory
Preferred vendor: Neer Pio
Vendor item no:
Inventory information
* COGS account: Cost of Goods Sold
Reorder point: 25
Restock level:
On hand: 50
Total value: $3,000.00
As of: 1/1/2008
Add Links...
All items post to Sales Income and are Non-taxable
All items post to Inventory and Cost of Goods Sold

Figure 12:28

Electronics Supply							
Item List							
Item Name	Sales & Purchase Description	Sales Price	Preferred Vendor	Purchase Price	Reorder Point	On Hand	Beginning Balance
CDPLAYER	Portable CD Player	85.00	Neer Pio	60.00	25	50	3,000.00
DIGCAM	Digital Camera	285.00	Canyon Cam	191.00	25	50	9,550.00
DIGCORD	Digital Camcorder	588.00	Javix Cam	394.00	20	60	23,640.00
DVDPLAYER	DVD Player	195.00	SumSang Corporation	131.00	25	50	6,550.00
DVRREC	DVR Recorder	95.00	SumSang Corporation	67.00	30	80	5,360.00
ENTSYS	Dolby Surround System	1,350.00	Neer Pio	837.00	15	25	20,925.00
HDTV	HD Television	2,700.00	SumSang Corporation	1,620.00	15	20	32,400.00
HOMSTER	Home Stereo	895.00	Neer Pio	600.00	25	30	18,000.00
LCDTV	LCD Television	4,500.00	SumSang Corporation	2,700.00	15	20	54,000.00
PRINTER	Color Printer	250.00	SumSang Corporation	175.00	20	90	15,750.00

Figure 12:29

Now verify your entries. Select ***Reports>>Inventory>>Inventory Stock Status by Item*** on the main menu. Filter to display January 1, 2008 and modify the report to remove the Place Order, Next Delivery, and Next Shipment columns. Compare your results to the report illustrated next.

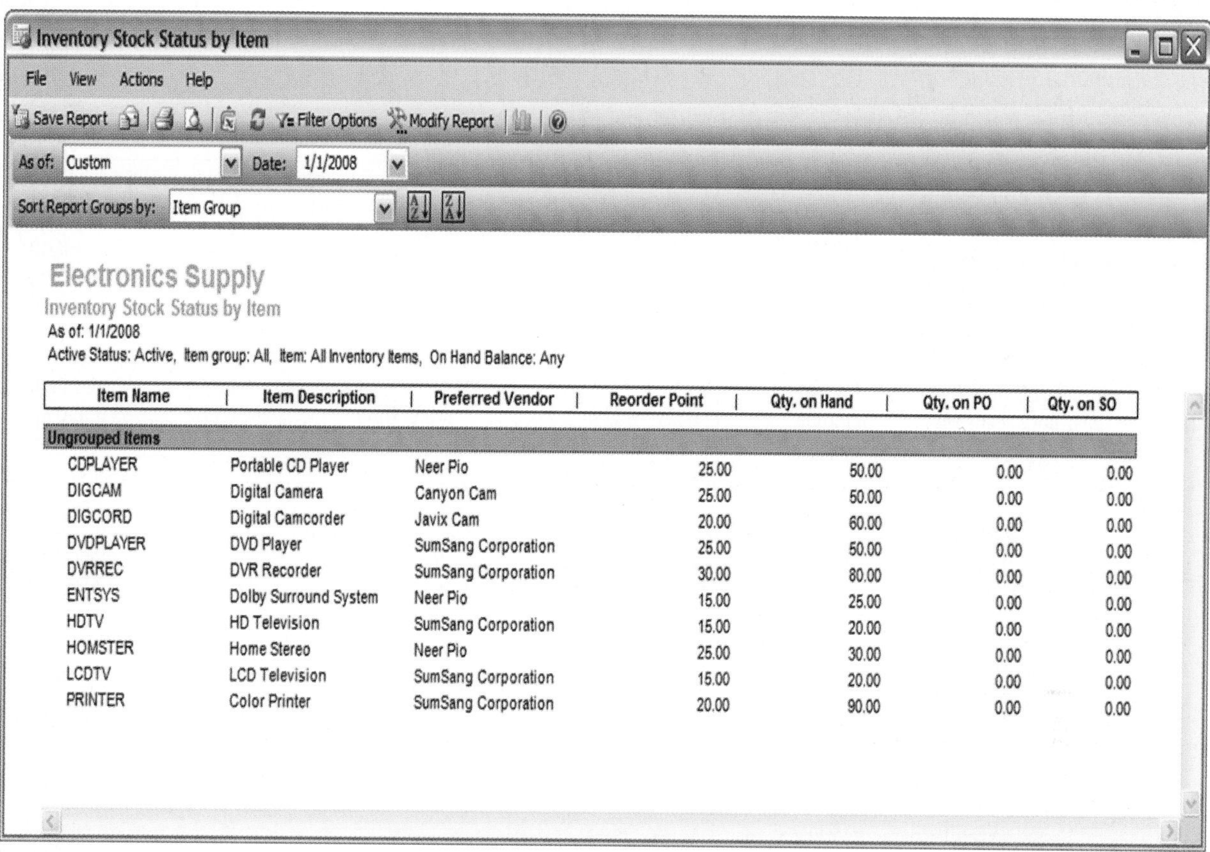
Inventory Stock Status by Item

File View Actions Help

Save Report | Filter Options | Modify Report

As of: Custom Date: 1/1/2008

Sort Report Groups by: Item Group

Electronics Supply
Inventory Stock Status by Item
As of: 1/1/2008
Active Status: Active, Item group: All, Item: All Inventory Items, On Hand Balance: Any

Item Name	Item Description	Preferred Vendor	Reorder Point	Qty. on Hand	Qty. on PO	Qty. on SO
Ungrouped Items						
CDPLAYER	Portable CD Player	Neer Pio	25.00	50.00	0.00	0.00
DIGCAM	Digital Camera	Canyon Cam	25.00	50.00	0.00	0.00
DIGCORD	Digital Camcorder	Javix Cam	20.00	60.00	0.00	0.00
DVDPLAYER	DVD Player	SumSang Corporation	25.00	50.00	0.00	0.00
DVRREC	DVR Recorder	SumSang Corporation	30.00	80.00	0.00	0.00
ENTSYS	Dolby Surround System	Neer Pio	15.00	25.00	0.00	0.00
HDTV	HD Television	SumSang Corporation	15.00	20.00	0.00	0.00
HOMSTER	Home Stereo	Neer Pio	25.00	30.00	0.00	0.00
LCDTV	LCD Television	SumSang Corporation	15.00	20.00	0.00	0.00
PRINTER	Color Printer	SumSang Corporation	20.00	90.00	0.00	0.00

Figure 12:30

If you find a mistake then double click to open the item and make corrections.

Next verify your inventory value. Select ***Reports>>Inventory>>Inventory Valuation*** on the main menu. Filter the report to display the value as of January 1, 2008 and remove the Entry Date, Name, and No. columns. Compare your results to those illustrated next.

Electronics Supply
Inventory Valuation
Date Range: January 1, 2008 - January 1, 2008
Active Status: Active, Item group: All, Item: All, Void: Hide

Type	Transaction Date	Qty.	Transaction Value	Qty. on Hand	Balance Value
CDPLAYER					
Beginning Balance				**0.00**	**0.00**
Inventory Adjustment	1/1/2008	50.00	3,000.00	50.00	3,000.00
Ending Balance				**50.00**	**3,000.00**
DIGCAM					
Beginning Balance				**0.00**	**0.00**
Inventory Adjustment	1/1/2008	50.00	9,550.00	50.00	9,550.00
Ending Balance				**50.00**	**9,550.00**
DIGCORD					
Beginning Balance				**0.00**	**0.00**
Inventory Adjustment	1/1/2008	60.00	23,640.00	60.00	23,640.00
Ending Balance				**60.00**	**23,640.00**
DVDPLAYER					
Beginning Balance				**0.00**	**0.00**
Inventory Adjustment	1/1/2008	50.00	6,550.00	50.00	6,550.00
Ending Balance				**50.00**	**6,550.00**
DVRREC					
Beginning Balance				**0.00**	**0.00**
Inventory Adjustment	1/1/2008	80.00	5,360.00	80.00	5,360.00
Ending Balance				**80.00**	**5,360.00**
ENTSYS					
Beginning Balance				**0.00**	**0.00**
Inventory Adjustment	1/1/2008	25.00	20,925.00	25.00	20,925.00
Ending Balance				**25.00**	**20,925.00**
HDTV					
Beginning Balance				**0.00**	**0.00**
Inventory Adjustment	1/1/2008	20.00	32,400.00	20.00	32,400.00
Ending Balance				**20.00**	**32,400.00**
HOMSTER					
Beginning Balance				**0.00**	**0.00**
Inventory Adjustment	1/1/2008	30.00	18,000.00	30.00	18,000.00
Ending Balance				**30.00**	**18,000.00**
LCDTV					
Beginning Balance				**0.00**	**0.00**
Inventory Adjustment	1/1/2008	20.00	54,000.00	20.00	54,000.00
Ending Balance				**20.00**	**54,000.00**
PRINTER					
Beginning Balance				**0.00**	**0.00**
Inventory Adjustment	1/1/2008	90.00	15,750.00	90.00	15,750.00
Ending Balance				**90.00**	**15,750.00**
TOTAL				475.00	189,175.00

Figure 12:31

If you find a mistake then first reconfirm that the Purchase price on the item is correct. Next, double click on the report to open the transaction. Click Edit to reopen the Adjusted Inventory transaction and correct the Qty Difference. Click Save and Close to post the change.

Create Employees

Finally, you will create Electronics Supply's employees. Return to the Quick Start window and click **Employees** under **Add business information manually**. Figure 12:32 illustrates creating the first employee listed in Figure 12:33. Click **Save and New** to continue adding employees and **Save and Close** when finished.

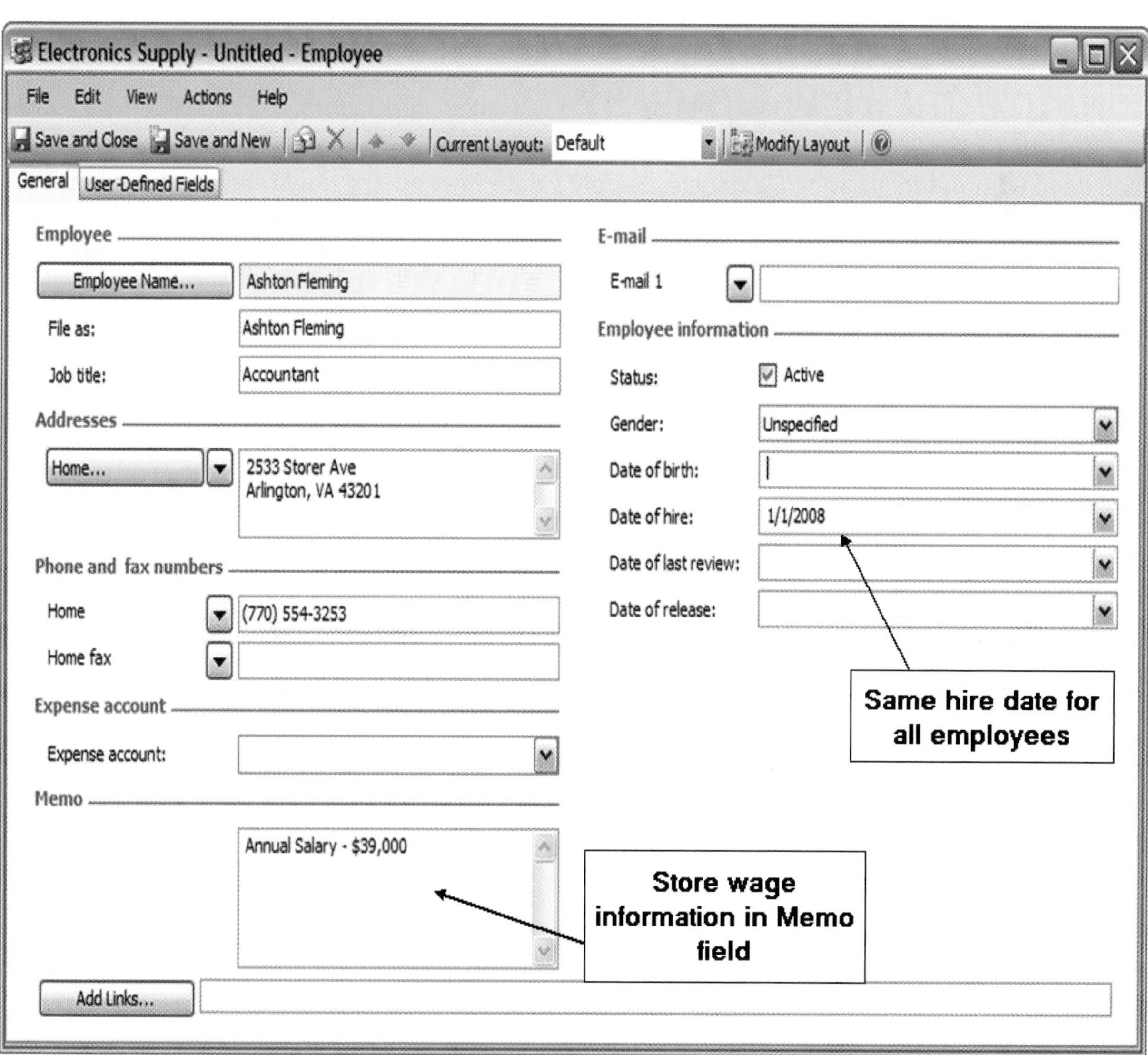

Figure 12:32

Electronics Supply Employee Information								
Employee	**Address**	**City**	**State**	**Zip**	**Position**	**Telephone**	**Annual Salary**	**Hourly Rate**
Ashton Fleming	2533 Storer Ave	Arlington	VA	43201	Accountant	770-554-3253	39,000.00	
Susan Gonzales	18 Birdlane Dr	Blacksburg	VA	43231	President	770-555-1144	67,600.00	
Lebron Johns	873 Star Ave	Arlington	VA	43232	Shipping	770-555-8923		12.50
April Levine	998 Maplewood Dr	Gunther	VA	43235	Sales	770-783-8323		18.00

Figure 12:33

Return to the Quick Start window and select the **Don't show this page again** option. Click **Close** to exit the window and **OK** to confirm.

Finalize the New Company

You have completed creating Electronics Supply's data file and are now ready to review the final Trial Balance. Click ***Reports>>Company and Financial>>Trial Balance*** on the main menu and filter for January 1, 2008. Click the Account No. column to sort the report and compare your results those illustrated next.

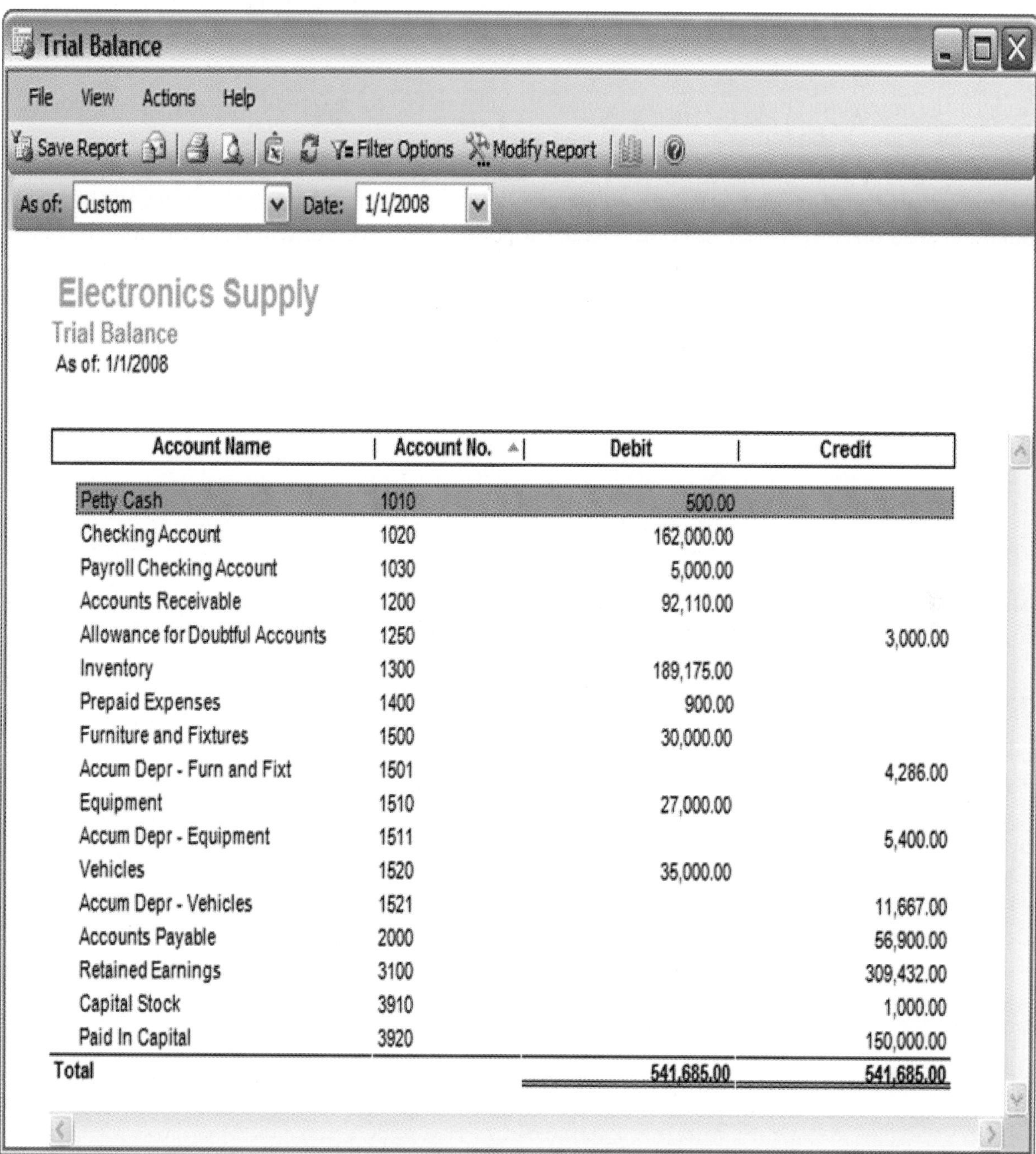

Trial Balance

File View Actions Help

Save Report | Filter Options | Modify Report

As of: Custom Date: 1/1/2008

Electronics Supply
Trial Balance
As of: 1/1/2008

Account Name	Account No.	Debit	Credit
Petty Cash	1010	500.00	
Checking Account	1020	162,000.00	
Payroll Checking Account	1030	5,000.00	
Accounts Receivable	1200	92,110.00	
Allowance for Doubtful Accounts	1250		3,000.00
Inventory	1300	189,175.00	
Prepaid Expenses	1400	900.00	
Furniture and Fixtures	1500	30,000.00	
Accum Depr - Furn and Fixt	1501		4,286.00
Equipment	1510	27,000.00	
Accum Depr - Equipment	1511		5,400.00
Vehicles	1520	35,000.00	
Accum Depr - Vehicles	1521		11,667.00
Accounts Payable	2000		56,900.00
Retained Earnings	3100		309,432.00
Capital Stock	3910		1,000.00
Paid In Capital	3920		150,000.00
Total		541,685.00	541,685.00

Figure 12:34

Finish the chapter by ***creating a backup of the Electronics Supply data file. Name the backup file "electronicssupply Original."***

SUMMARY

Congratulations! You have completed all the steps needed to create a new company. You began by creating the data file and then imported the chart of accounts and beginning balances. From there you created customers, vendors, and inventory items, making sure to verify opening balances after creating. Finally, you created employees and reviewed the Trial Balance. You are now ready to complete the following Practice Set where you record Electronics Supply's accounting transactions for January.

PRACTICE SET

1. Enter the following January 2008 accounting transactions for Electronics Supply. Click OK whenever OAP warns that a transaction exceeds a customer's credit limit because the owner has approved these transactions. Print transactions only when instructed. Reports are printed in Steps 2 and 3.

Jan. 2	Sales Invoice 2000 for $11,400 to Barter Bay for 40 items of DIGCAM, unit sales price $285. *(Note: Change the No field to 2000.)* Print the invoice.
	Sales Order 1 for $90,000 to Television World for 20 items of LCDTV, unit sales price $4,500.
	Check number 783 from Discount Electronics for $9,670 paying opening balance in full. *(Note: Click Yes when prompted to save the payment method.)*
	PO 101 for $41,850 to Neer Pio for 50 items of ENTSYS, unit price $837. PO 102 for $48,600 to SumSang Corporation for 30 items of HDTV, unit price $1,620. Print both POs.
	Vendor Invoice 1235 for $3,000 from Travelor's Insurance; $1,200 for 6 months of prepaid auto insurance and $1,800 for 6 months of prepaid business insurance.
Jan. 4	Check number 132 from GG Hregg Stores for $9,600 that pays the opening balance in full.
	Sales Invoice 2001 for $90,000 to Television World for all items on Sales Order 1.
	PO 103 for $108,000 to SumSang Corporation for 40 items of LCDTV, unit price $2,700. *(Note: Click Cancel to close the Reorder Inventory feature.)*
	Vendor Invoice 3729 for $48,600 for all items on SumSang Corporation PO 102.

Date	Transaction
Jan. 8	Vendor Invoice 3733 for $108,000 for all items on SumSang Corporation PO 103.
	Sales Invoice 2002 for $38,500 to Better Buy for 50 items of DVRREC, unit sales price $95, and 25 units of ENTSYS, unit sales price $1,350.
	Check number 0888 from Electronic Town for $23,500 that pays the opening balance in full. Check number 632 from Better Buy for $27,000 that pays the opening balance in full.
Jan. 9	Vendor Receipt RCT3253 from Neer Pio for all items on PO 101.
	Check number 772 from Barter Bay for $22,340 that pays the opening balance in full.
Jan. 10	Vendor Invoice 7333 for $41,850 from Neer Pio for Receipt RCT3253. Vendor Invoice 45 for $350 from Advertising World for January advertising expense.
	Credit Memo CM2000 for $1,425 to Barter Bay for returning 5 items of DIGCAM on Invoice 2000.

Jan. 14	Create the following payroll checks for the biweekly pay period ended January 13. Memorize each paycheck without a reminder for use on the next pay date. *(Note: Turn off future warnings and click Yes when prompted about liability accounts. Also click Yes when prompted to save the home address.)* Print checks from the Payroll Checking Account on starting check number 1236.

Electronics Supply
Pay Period 12/31/2007 thru 1/13/2008

Check No.	Employee	Filing Status	Allow	Pay Type	Pay Rate	Regular Hrs	OT Hrs	Gross Pay	Federal Income Tax	Soc. Sec. (FICA) Tax	Medicare Tax	VA State Tax	Net Pay
1236	Fleming, Ashton	Single	0	Salary	1,500.00			1,500.00	219.00	93.00	21.75	60.00	1,106.25
1237	Gonzalez, Susan	Married	2	Salary	2,600.00			2,600.00	265.00	161.20	37.70	104.00	2,032.10
1238	Johns, Lebron	Single	1	Hourly	12.50	80.00		1,000.00	102.00	62.00	14.50	40.00	781.50
1239	Levine, April	Married	0	Hourly	18.00	80.00		1,440.00	142.00	89.28	20.88	57.60	1,130.24
	Totals					**160.00**	**0.00**	**6,540.00**	**728.00**	**405.48**	**94.83**	**261.60**	**5,050.09**
	Tax Basis								**Circular E**	**6.20%**	**1.45%**	**4.00%**	
	G/L Accounts							**6000**	**2330**	**2330**	**2330**	**2350**	**1030**

Jan. 14	Create and post a recurring journal entry for the following FUTA, SUTA, and health insurance liabilities.
	Create and post a recurring bill to Bank Amerex for the following employer FICA and Medicare taxes plus employee federal, FICA, and Medicare tax withholdings.

Electronics Supply
Employer Costs for Period 12/31/2007 thru 1/13/2008

Employee	ER Soc. Sec. (FICA)	ER Medicare	ER FUTA	ER SUTA	Health Insurance
Fleming, Ashton	93.00	21.75	12.00	30.00	109.00
Gonzalez, Susan	161.20	37.70	20.80	52.00	109.00
Johns, Lebron	62.00	14.50	8.00	20.00	109.00
Levine, April	89.28	20.88	11.52	28.80	109.00
Totals	**405.48**	**94.83**	**52.32**	**130.80**	**436.00**
Tax Basis	**6.20%**	**1.45%**	**0.8%**	**2.0%**	
G/L Accounts	**2330 / 6100**	**2330 / 6100**	**2340 / 6100**	**2360 / 6100**	**2370 / 6110**

	Transfer $1,000.00 from 1020 Checking Account to 1030 Payroll Checking Account.
	PO 104 for $8,650 to SumSang Corporation for 50 units of DVDPLAYER, unit price $131, and 30 units of DVRREC, unit price $70. Unit price on last item has increased.
Jan. 16	Print checks from the 1020 Checking Account paying vendors for bills due before January 30. Starting check number is 239. Four bills selected totaling $61,628.62.
	Sales Order 2 for $112,500 to GG Hregg Stores for 25 units of LCDTV, unit sales price $4,500.
	PO 105 for $1,500 to Neer Pio for 25 units of CDPLAYER, unit price $60.
	Check number 6323 from Better Buy for $37,730 paying Invoice 2002 in full. *(Hint: Invoice carries a discount.)* Check number 2223 from Barter Bay for $9,975 paying Invoice 2000 in full. *(Hint: Customer has unused credits.)*

Date	Transaction
Jan. 18	Sales Invoice 2003 for $112,500 to GG Hregg Stores for all items on Sales Order 2.
	Vendor Receipt RCT332 for all items on Neer Pio PO 105.
	Vendor Invoice 88395 for $8,650 for all items on SumSang Corporation PO 104.
	Check number 7325 from Television World for $90,000 paying Invoice 2001.
Jan. 22	PO 106 for $9,550 to Javix Cam for 50 units of DIGICAM, unit price $191.
	Post the following vendor bills dated January 22. CSB Telephone for January telephone, $230 Virginia Electric for January electric, $370 Cooleys Repair, Invoice 7722 for $275 for furnace repair expense Office Rex, Invoice 4234 for $673 for office supplies expense
Jan. 23	PO 107 for $24,000 to Neer Pio for 40 units of HOMSTER, unit price $600.
	Sales Invoice 2004 for $53,850 to Electronic Town for 30 of HOMSTER, unit sales price $895 and 10 units of HDTV, unit sales price $2,700.
	Vendor Receipt RCT55533 for all items on Javix Cam PO 106.
	Vendor Invoice 7395 for $1,500 from Neer Pio for Receipt RCT332.
Jan. 25	Sales Invoice 2005 for $33,270 to Discount Electronics for 40 units of DIGCORD, unit sales price $588, and 50 units of DVDPLAYER, unit sales price $195. Sales Invoice 2006 for $20,000 to Barter Bay for 80 units of PRINTER, unit sales price $250. Sales Invoice 2008 for $14,310 to Better Buy for 30 units of CDPLAYER, unit sales price $85, and 20 units of DIGCORD, unit sales price of $588.
	PO 108 for $15,760 to Canyon Cam for 40 units of DIGCORD, unit price $394.

Jan. 28	Create the following payroll checks for the biweekly pay period ended January 27. Print checks from Payroll Checking Account on starting check number 1240.

Electronics Supply
Pay Period 1/14/2008 thru 1/27/2008

Check No.	Employee	Filing Status	Allow	Pay Type	Pay Rate	Regular Hrs	OT Hrs	Gross Pay	Federal Income Tax	Soc. Sec. (FICA) Tax	Medicare Tax	VA State Tax	Net Pay
1240	Fleming, Ashton	Single	0	Salary	1,500.00			1,500.00	219.00	93.00	21.75	60.00	1,106.25
1241	Gonzalez, Susan	Married	2	Salary	2,600.00			2,600.00	265.00	161.20	37.70	104.00	2,032.10
1242	Johns, Lebron	Single	1	Hourly	12.50	80.00	2.00	1,037.50	105.00	64.33	15.04	41.50	811.63
1243	Levine, April	Married	0	Hourly	18.00	80.00		1,440.00	142.00	89.28	20.88	57.60	1,130.24
	Totals					**160.00**	**2.00**	**6,577.50**	**731.00**	**407.81**	**95.37**	**263.10**	**5,080.22**
	Tax Basis								**Circular E**	**6.20%**	**1.45%**	**4.00%**	
	G/L Accounts							**6000**	**2330**	**2330**	**2330**	**2350**	**1030**

<table>
<tr><td>Jan. 28</td><td>Post the recurring journal entry for the following FUTA, SUTA, and health insurance liabilities.</td></tr>
<tr><td></td><td>Post the recurring bill to Bank Amerex for the following employer FICA and Medicare taxes plus employee federal, FICA, and Medicare tax withholdings.

<table>
<tr><th colspan="6">Electronics Supply
Employer Costs for Period 1/14/2008 thru 1/27/2008</th></tr>
<tr><th>Employee</th><th>ER Soc. Sec. (FICA)</th><th>ER Medicare</th><th>ER FUTA</th><th>ER SUTA</th><th>Health Insurance</th></tr>
<tr><td>Fleming, Ashton</td><td>93.00</td><td>21.75</td><td>12.00</td><td>30.00</td><td>109.00</td></tr>
<tr><td>Gonzalez, Susan</td><td>161.20</td><td>37.70</td><td>20.80</td><td>52.00</td><td>109.00</td></tr>
<tr><td>Johns, Lebron</td><td>64.33</td><td>15.04</td><td>8.30</td><td>20.75</td><td>109.00</td></tr>
<tr><td>Levine, April</td><td>89.28</td><td>20.88</td><td>11.52</td><td>28.80</td><td>109.00</td></tr>
<tr><td>Totals</td><td>407.81</td><td>95.37</td><td>52.62</td><td>131.55</td><td>436.00</td></tr>
<tr><td>Tax Basis</td><td>6.20%</td><td>1.45%</td><td>0.8%</td><td>2.0%</td><td></td></tr>
<tr><td>G/L Accounts</td><td>2330 / 6100</td><td>2330 / 6100</td><td>2340 / 6100</td><td>2360 / 6100</td><td>2370 / 6110</td></tr>
</table>
</td></tr>
<tr><td></td><td>Transfer $6,000.00 from 1020 Checking Account to 1030 Payroll Checking Account.</td></tr>
<tr><td></td><td>Create bills for the following payroll liabilities.

Mutual Health Insurance, $872.00 paying January health insurance

VA Depart. of Taxation, $524.70 paying January state tax withholding</td></tr>
<tr><td></td><td>PO 109 for $118,500 to SumSang Corporation for 60 units of PRINTER, unit price $175, and 40 units of LCDTV, unit price $2,700.</td></tr>
<tr><td>Jan. 30</td><td>Vendor Invoice 89323 for $18,000 for only 30 units of HOMSTER on Neer Pio PO 107.

Vendor Invoice 2232 for $15,760 for all items on Canyon Cam PO 108.</td></tr>
<tr><td></td><td>Print checks out of 1020 Checking Account paying vendor bills due before or carrying a discount that expires before February 15. Starting check number is 244. Ten bills selected totaling $217,978.86.</td></tr>
</table>

Jan. 31	Vendor Invoice for $1,000 from Rental Experts for February rent on storage warehouse.
	Vendor Invoice 66323 for $500 from Federal Xpert for postage expense.
	Sales Order 3 for $5,850 to Electronic Town for 30 units of DVDPLAYER, unit price $195.
	Write check number 253 for $450 from 1020 Checking Account to Petty Cash, expensed as follows. Travel $210 Meals and Entertainment $240

EOM	Record January depreciation of $1,779. Accum Depr - Equipment $450 Accum Depr - Furn and Fixt $357 Accum Depr - Vehicle $972
	Accrue $3,300 for 4 days of payroll and reverse the entry on February 1.
	Record expired prepaid insurance. Auto insurance $200 Business insurance $300

2. Reconcile the January 31 bank statements and print detail reconciliation reports for each account.

   Reconcile the Checking Account using the bank statement appearing on the next page.

   The Payroll Checking Account beginning balance is $5,000 and the ending statement balance is $1,842.69. All January checks and deposits have cleared and bank service charges are $27.00.

Electronics Supply, Inc.
Bank Statement Date: January 31, 2008

Beginning Balance from December Statement				$ 162,000.00
January Deposits				
	Jan 2, 2008		9,670.00	
	Jan 4, 2008		9,600.00	
	Jan 8, 2008		23,500.00	
	Jan 8, 2008		27,000.00	
	Jan 9, 2008		22,340.00	
	Jan 16, 2008		37,730.00	
	Jan 16, 2008		9,975.00	
	Jan 18, 2008		90,000.00	
Total Deposits for January				229,815.00
January Checks Cleared				
	Jan 16, 2008	239	1,728.62	
	Jan 16, 2008	240	7,740.00	
	Jan 16, 2008	241	7,760.00	
	Jan 16, 2008	242	41,400.00	
	Jan 16, 2008	243	3,000.00	
Total Cleared Checks for January				61,628.62
Less Bank Transfers				
	Jan 14, 2008		1,000.00	
	Jan 28, 2008		6,000.00	
Total January Transfers				7,000.00
January Service Charges				102.00
Ending Bank Balance January 31, 2008				$ 323,084.38

3. Print the following reports.

   a. Trial Balance as of January 31, 2008, sorted by Account No.

   b. Sales by Customer Detail for the month of January.

   c. Deposit Detail for the month of January.

   d. A/R Aging Detail as of January 31.

   e. Purchases by Vendor Detail for the month of January.

   f. Purchases by Item Detail for the month of January modified to add the PO No. column.

   g. Payments report for the month of January, sorted by Payment No. and modified to remove the Issued date, No., Status detail, Reference number, Payment method, and Void columns.

   h. A/P Aging Detail as of January 31.

   i. Inventory Valuation for the month of January, modified to remove the Entry Date column.

   j. Profit and Loss for the month of January.

   k. Balance Sheet as of January 31.

   l. Cash Flow Statement for the month of January.

4. ***Back up the Electronics Supply data file to a backup file named "electronicssupply Chpt 12."***

APPENDIX A INSTALLING OFFICE ACCOUNTING PROFESSIONAL

Before installing OAP, verify that your computer meets the following minimum system requirements for a single user installation.

Hardware/Software	Minimum Requirements
Computer processor	1 gigahertz (GHz) processor or higher
Memory	512 MB or higher
Hard disk	2 gigabyte (GB)
Drive	CD-ROM or DVD drive
Display	1024 x 768 or higher resolution monitor
Internet functionality	Dial-up or broadband service with Internet Explorer 6.0 or later
Operating system	Windows XP with Service Pack (SP) 2, Windows Server 2003 with SP1 or later operating systems
Additional Software	Microsoft Office XP and Microsoft Office Outlook 2003 with Business Contact Manager SP2 or later is required to share financial data

To locate your computer's processor, RAM information, and operating system version, right click the **My Computer** icon on your desktop and select the **Properties** menu (Figure: A:1).

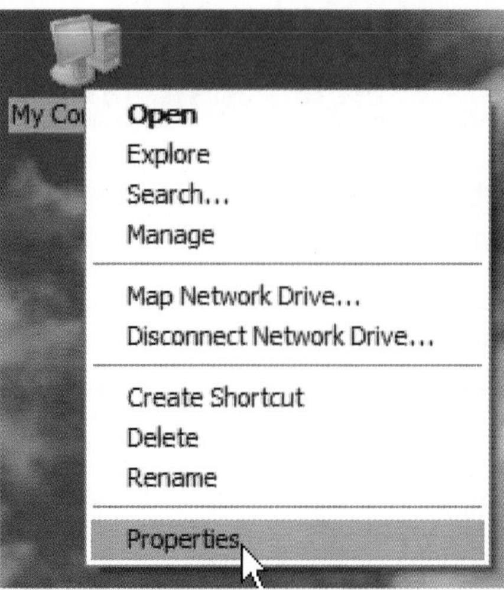

Figure A:1

Click to select the **General** tab (Figure: A:2) listing your computer's system information. *(Note: The window view is based on the computer operating system; therefore, your view may vary from the illustration.)* After reviewing, click **OK** to close the System Properties window.

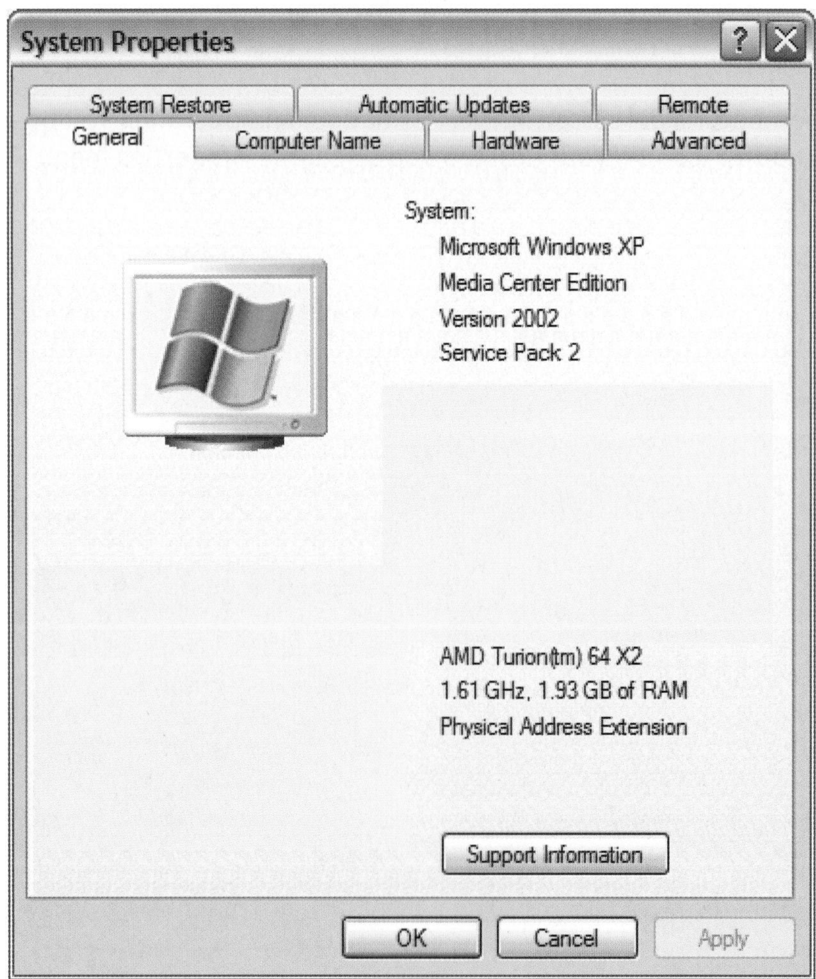

Figure A:2

To review your computer's available hard disk space, double click the **My Computer** icon and locate the drive labeled **C** (Figure: A:3). *(Note: Your window may list folder contents differently than illustrated. You can click the icon noted to change the view.)*

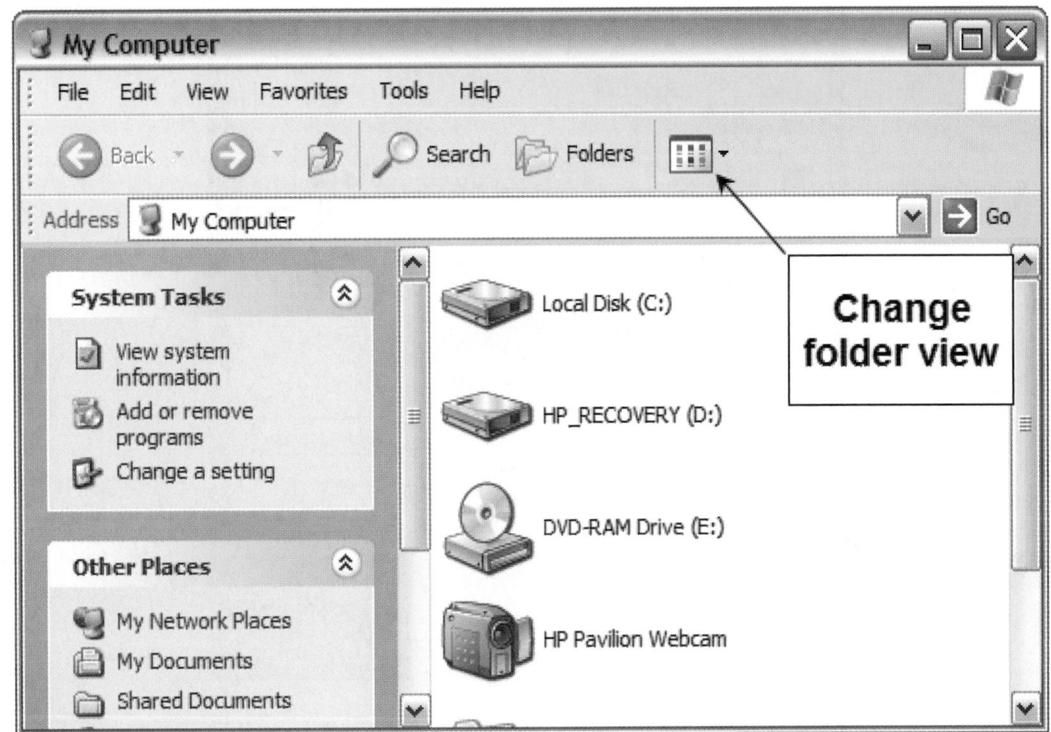

Figure A:3

Right click the drive labeled **C** and select **Properties** to view the free space on your drive (Figure: A:4). When finished, close the Local Disk Properties and the My Computer windows by clicking **X**.

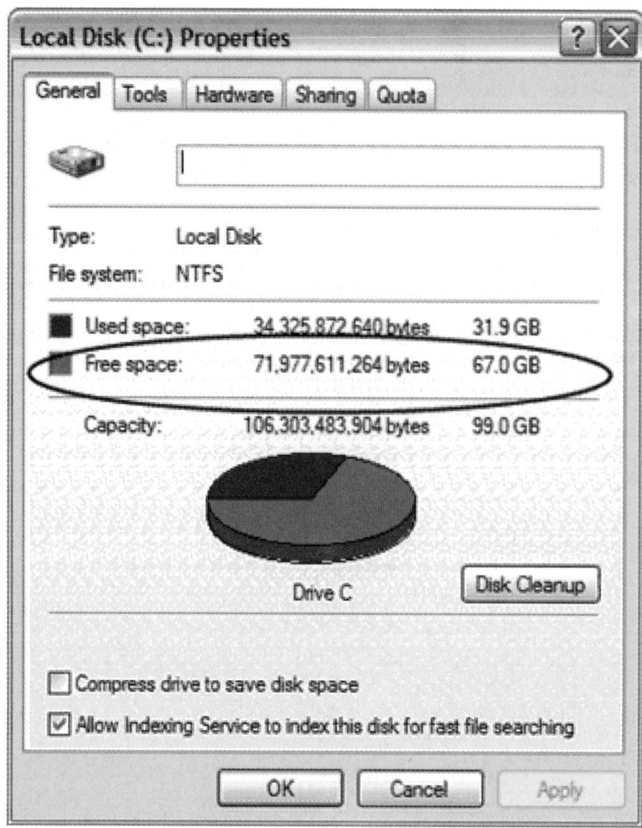

Figure A:4

After confirming that your computer meets minimum system requirements, close all programs currently running and insert the CD labeled **Microsoft Office Accounting Professional 2008** into your computer's disk drive. After inserting, installation activates.

> *Note: Sometimes a CD will not automatically begin installation. If you encounter this situation, click* start *and select* Run... *. In the window that opens, click the* ***Browse*** *button. Use the* ***Look in*** *box* Look in: *to select the CD drive. (Note: This drive is normally labeled D.) Click the file named* ***SETUP.EXE*** *and then click* ***Open****.*

Click **OK** if you receive a prompt to install the .NET Framework (not illustrated). *(Note: When installing this component, OAP will prompt you to reboot the computer before continuing with installation.)*

Click **Yes** if prompted to access information on the Internet. Continue clicking Next until you reach the screen containing the option of **Install Now**. Select **Install Now** and click the **Install** button. Do not interrupt the installation process. OAP will notify you when the process has completed (Figure: A:5).

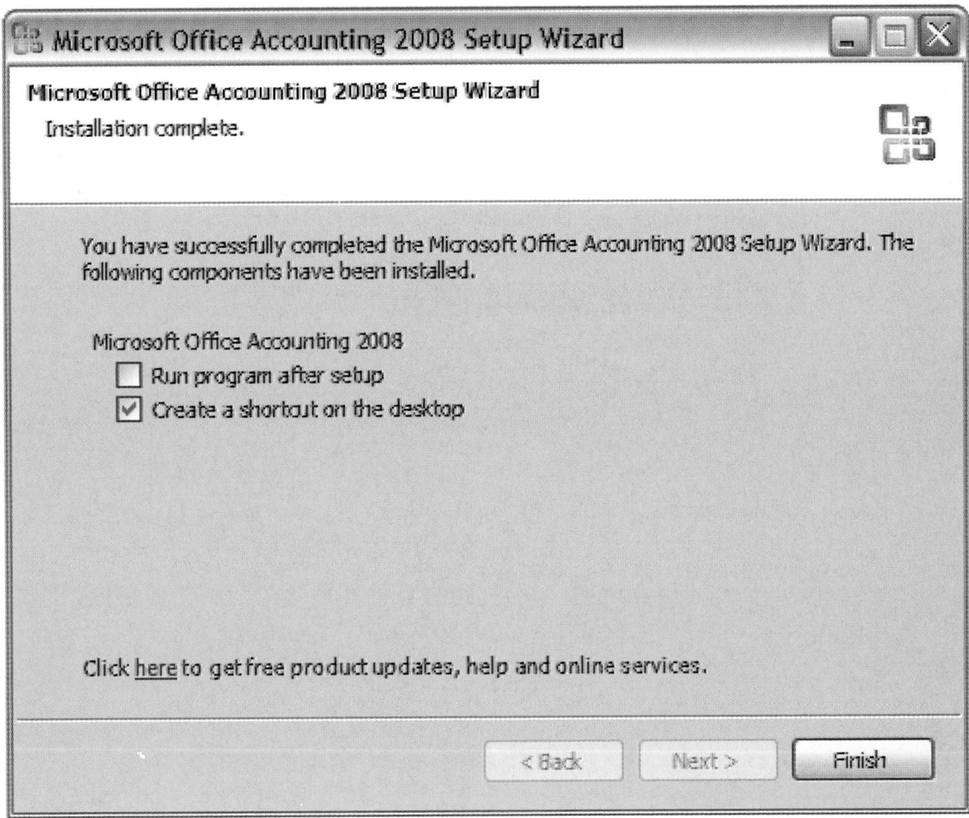

Figure A:5

Choose the option illustrated in Figure: A:5 and click **Finish**. You can now safely remove the software CD.

❖ ***Register the Software***

Figure A:6

After installing, you must register OAP to begin using it. Locate the shortcut icon on your desktop illustrated in Figure: A:6. *(Note: If you cannot locate a shortcut on the desktop, click the **Start** menu and then click either **Programs** or **All** Programs. Next, point to the **Microsoft Office** folder and click **Microsoft Office Accounting 2008**.)*

Locate the software's product key on the inside cover of your software disk and enter it into the fields illustrated in Figure: A:7.

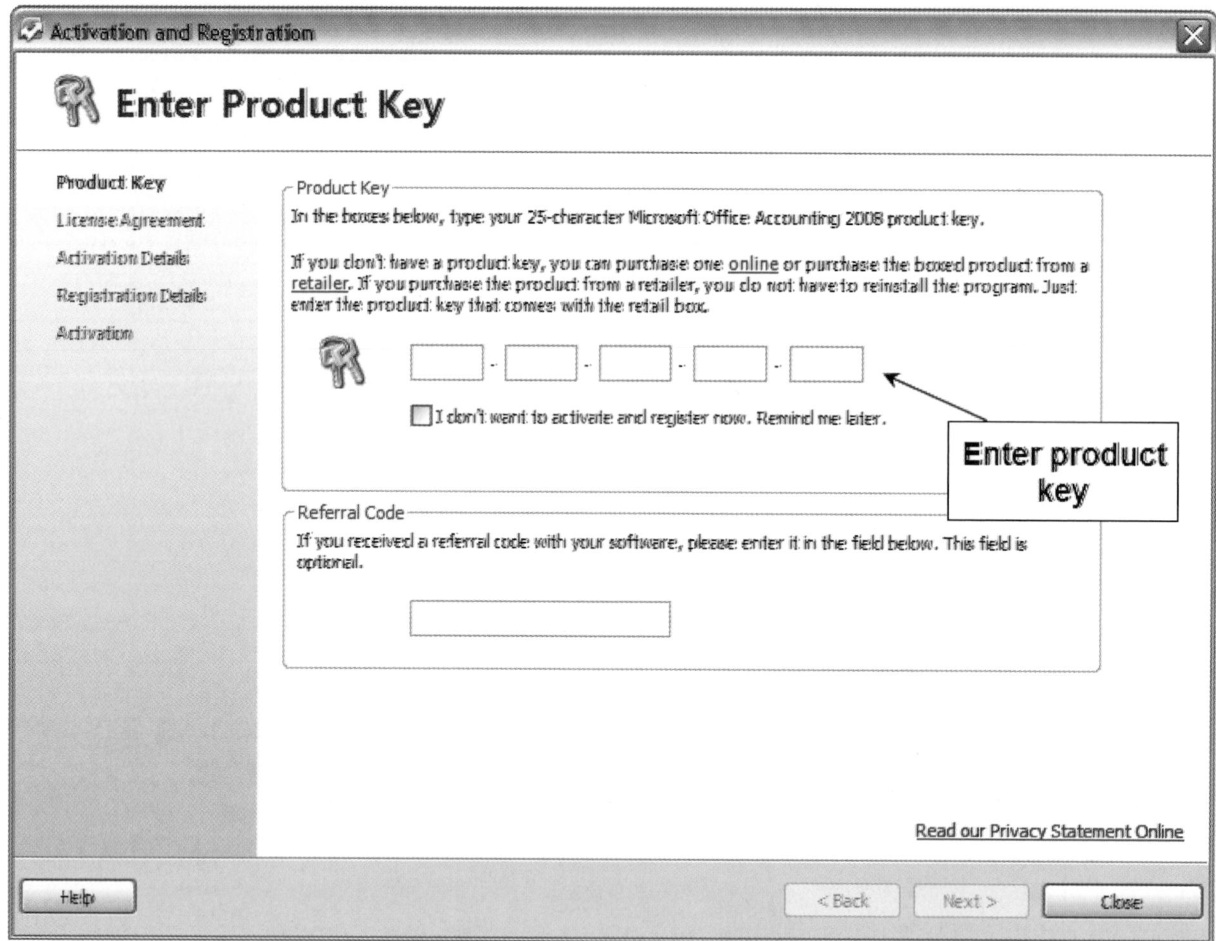

Figure A:7

Click **Next** when finished and OAP's license agreement appears (Figure: A:8). *(Note: If the Next button is unavailable verify that the product key was correctly entered.)*

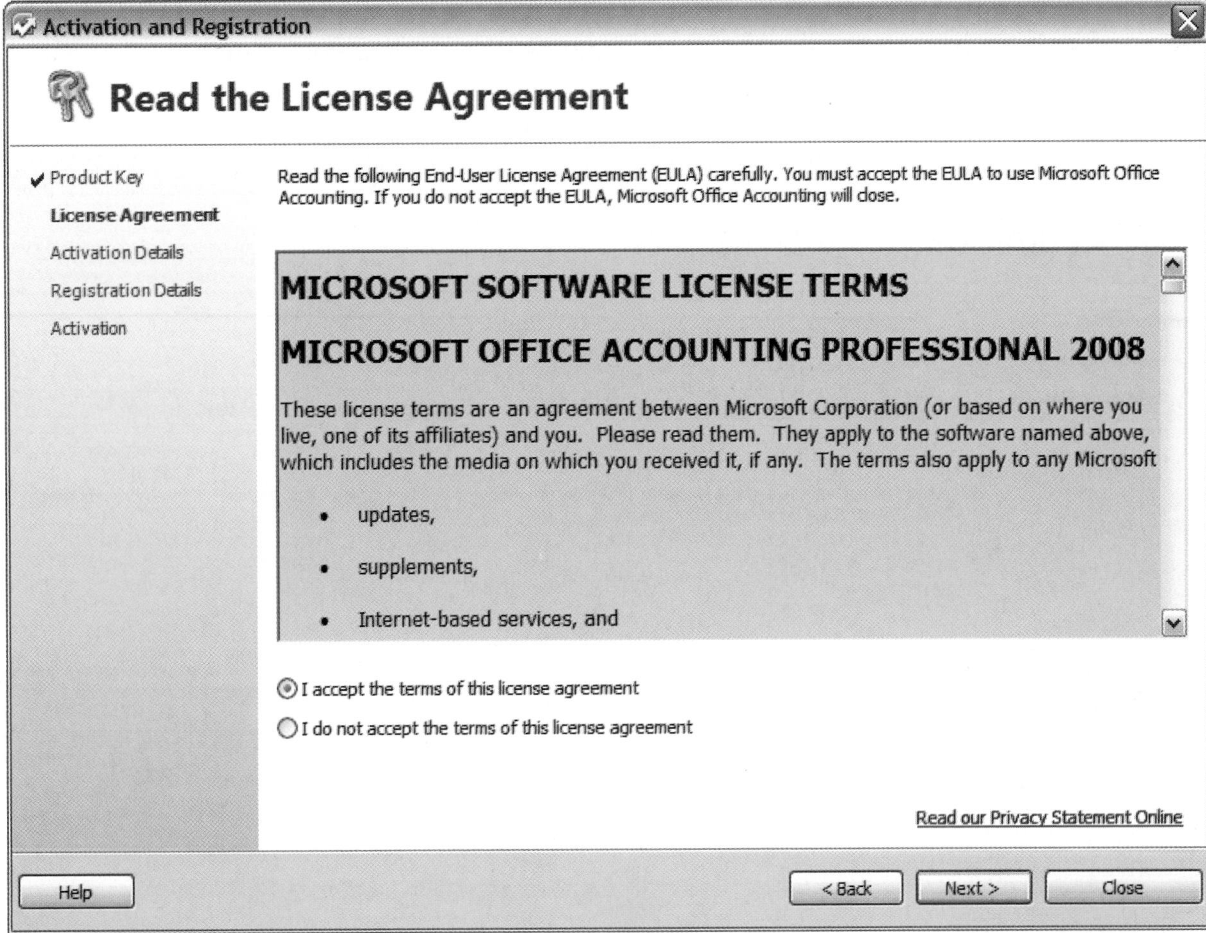

Figure A:8

All purchased software comes with a license agreement setting forth a purchaser's permitted use of the software. You do not own the software you buy; instead, you license the right to use it. On the licensing window, you are promising Microsoft that your copy of OAP will be used on a single computer and that you will not make copies of OAP for sale or distribution to other users. You are also promising to not "loan" your copy of OAP to others so that they can install the software. This is a legally binding agreement and failure to abide by its terms constitutes software piracy.

Take a few minutes to read the license agreement and then select "I accept the terms of this license agreement." After making this selection, click **Next**.

In Figure: A:9 you are choosing the method of activating the software. Select "I want to activate the software over the Internet (Recommended)" as long as you computer is connected to the Internet. Click **Next**.

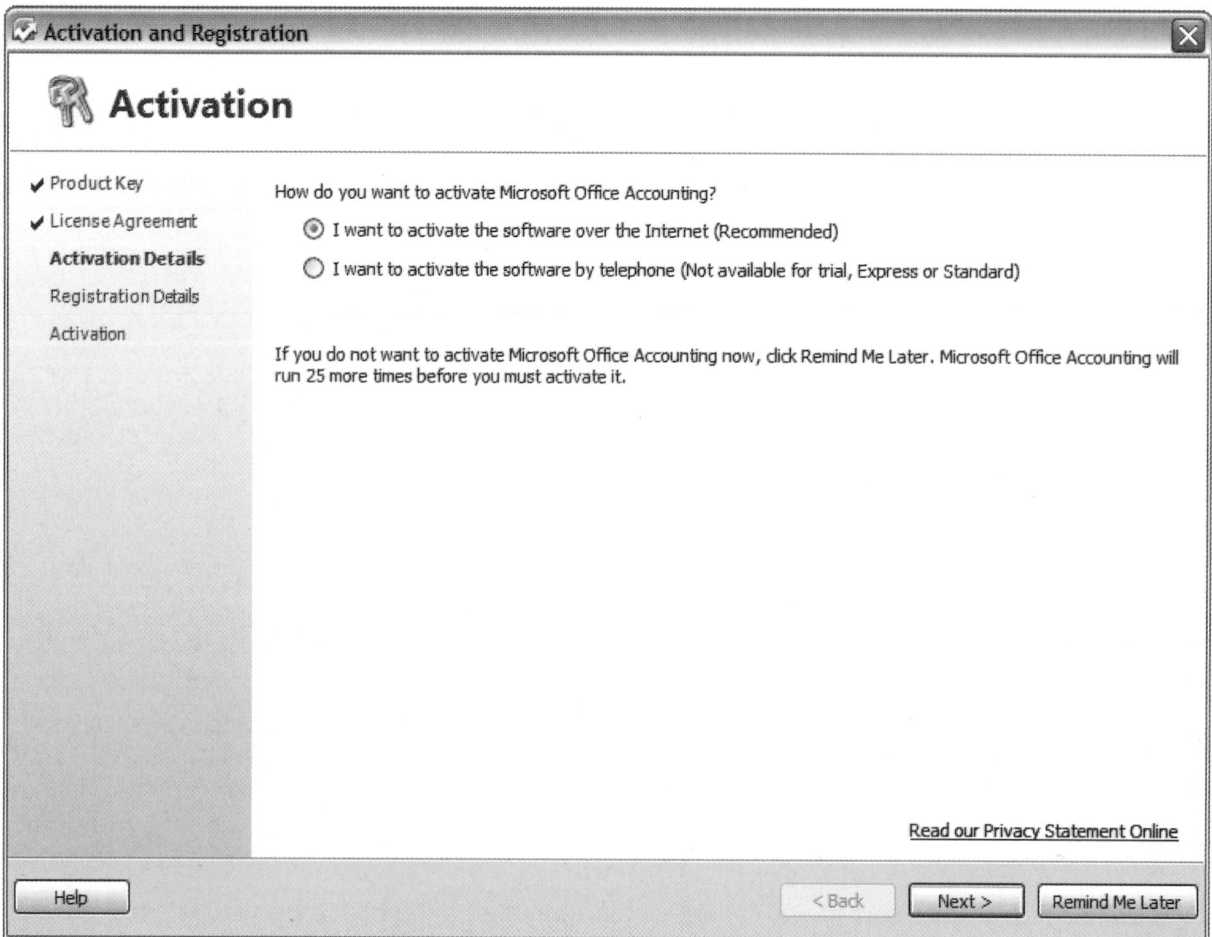

Figure A:9

Follow the onscreen prompts to complete registration and then click **Close**.

When the screen illustrated in Figure: A:10 opens click the **Exit** button. Return to Chapter 1 where you will load the sample databases.

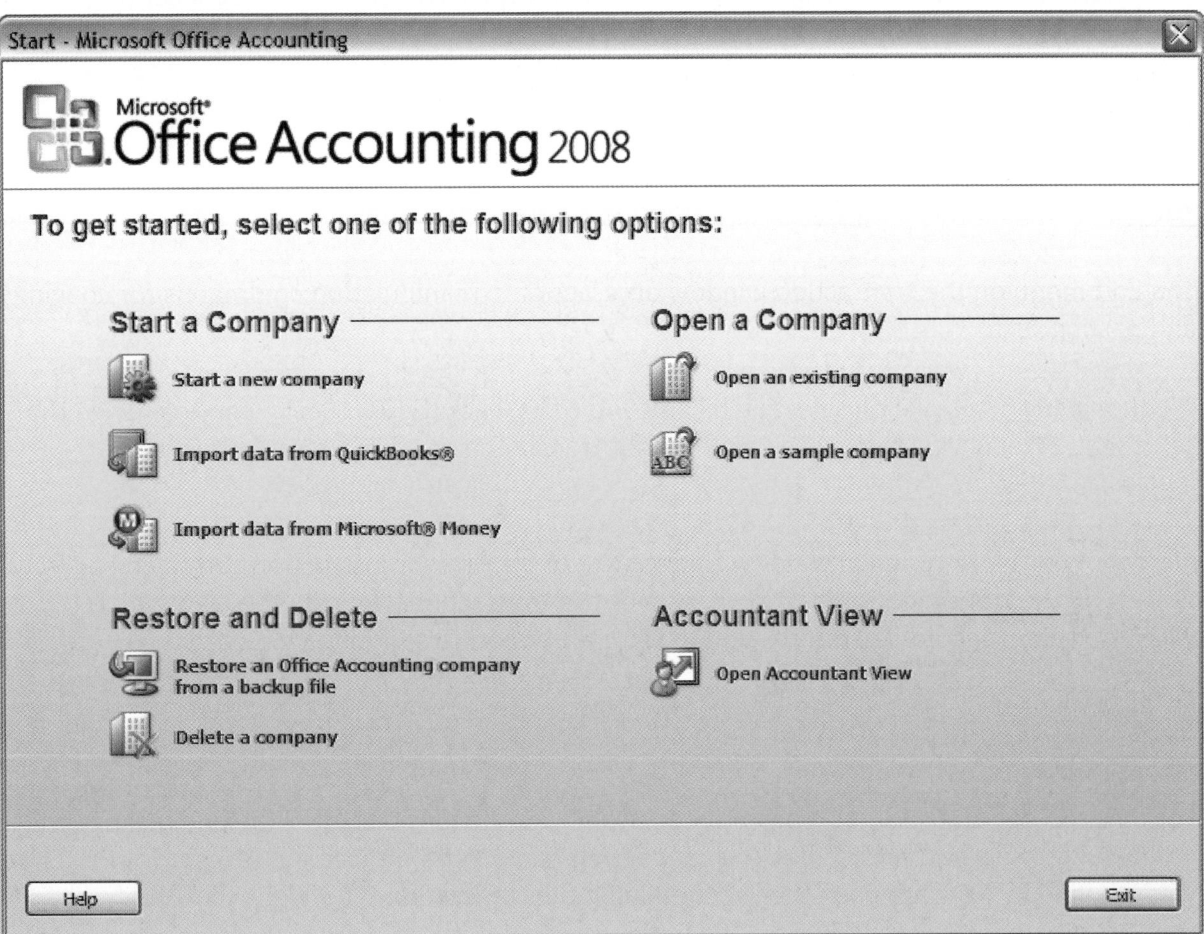

Figure A:10

APPENDIX B CORRECTING TRANSACTIONS

This information appears throughout the text and is repeated here to provide a central location for instructions on correcting transactions.

New Transactions

You can change data in any field while entering a new transaction.

The Edit menu on the transaction window accesses data manipulation commands for copying and pasting text.

When making a mistake on selecting billable job costs, click the **Job Costs** icon to change the selection. After saving the invoice, you cannot transfer costs again unless you void the invoice.

Clicking **X** on the transaction window causes OAP to prompt for instructions on saving or discarding the transaction. Selecting Yes saves the transaction, No exits the transaction without saving; and Cancel returns you to the transaction to continue working.

Posted Transactions

For most posted transactions, you can reopen the transaction, click the Edit icon, change the data, and resave the transaction. You cannot delete a posted transaction (except for POs) but you can void it. To void, open the list containing the transaction type, right click the transaction, and then select **Void**.

The transaction categories below provide additional guidance on correcting posted transactions.

- Sales Invoices

  You can modify or void a posted sales invoice ***as long as you have not posted a customer payment against the invoice***. The first step is locating the posted invoice on the Invoice List. You double click to reopen the transaction and then click Edit to enter your changes. You repost the transaction by clicking **Save and Close**.

  Invoices are voided by highlighting the transaction on the Invoice List, right clicking, and selecting Void. You can also void an invoice after reopening it by selecting ***Action>>Void*** on the transaction menu.

  Voiding an invoice causes OAP to enter a reversing entry on the customer account and general ledger. If the invoice was created from a Quote or Sales Order, OAP will reinstate the status of the original document so you can reinvoice it. Voided transactions are listed on account registers with the Void symbol.

When the posted invoice involves employee time or job materials, OAP will reinstate the invoiced time and materials so you can reinvoice the customer.

After posting a customer payment against an invoice you should not alter the invoice without first voiding the customer payment. *(Note: Read the instructions that follow to void a customer payment.)*

❖ Customer Payments

You cannot modify or delete a posted customer payment. Therefore, you must void the payment and reenter it. To void, locate the transaction on the Received Payment List, right click, and select Void.

❖ Purchase Orders

Purchase orders do not post so these transactions do not interact with other vendor transactions ***until after you apply a vendor bill or receipt***. You can modify or delete a PO with the Not Received status. First, locate the transaction on the Purchase Order List. To modify the PO, double click to reopen, enter the changes, and click Save and Close. To delete the PO, open the transaction and click this delete on the toolbar. You can delete without opening the PO by right clicking it on the PO list and selecting Delete.

After matching inventory receipts with the PO, the status will change to Received or Partially Received. You can no longer modify POs with the Received status unless you void the vendor bill or receipt. You can only change the outstanding items on a Partially Received PO. Furthermore, you will have to toggle the Current View on the Purchase Order List to Received or All to locate these POs.

If you need to modify a Received or Partially Received PO, then follow the next instructions and void the vendor bill or receipt. This will reinstate the PO status to Not Received.

❖ Vendor Bills and Receipts

Vendor receipts can be modified and voided. Vendor bills can also be modified and voided ***as long as you have not paid the bill*** (i.e., bills with the Not Paid status). To modify, reopen the bill or receipt on the Bill/Item Receipt List, click Edit on the toolbar, enter the changes, and then click Save and Close. To void, you can reopen the transaction and select ***Actions>>Void*** on the transaction window menu or highlight the transaction on the list, right click, and select Void.

After paying a vendor bill, you should not modify data on the transactions without first voiding the vendor payment. (Note: The instructions that follow explain voiding vendor payments.) After voiding the payment, the bill will be reinstated so you can repay the vendor.

- Vendor Payments

  You cannot modify or delete vendor payments; therefore, you must void checks with an error. To void, locate the transaction on the Vendor Payments List, right click, and then select Void. (Note: Verify that the View option on the list equals Issued.) After voiding, you can reselect the bill for payment.

- Employee Time and Paychecks

  You can correct employee timesheets ***as long as you have not invoiced the time to the customer***. Although you can reopen a time entry using the Time Report, you will find it easier to correct a timesheet by clicking the New Timesheet icon on the Employee Home page. After opening the Timesheet entry window, look up the employee and select the week.

  If you find an error on a paycheck prior to printing it, then open the Employee Payments List and change the view to Not Issued. Double click to reopen the transaction, enter changes and then click Save and Close. Remember to always run the Employee Payments report prior to printing paychecks so you can identify errors.

  If you find an error on a paycheck after printing it, you must void the paycheck and reissue it. To void a paycheck, highlight the transaction on the Employee Payments list, right click, and select Void. (Remember to toggle the list's Current View to Issued.)

- General Journal Entries

  You can modify a posted journal entry by reopening it on the Journal Entry List, clicking the Edit button, entering changes, and then clicking Save and Close to repost the entry. Journal entries are voided by right clicking the entry on the list and selecting Void.

APPENDIX C BACKING UP AND RESTORING DATA FILES

For your convenience, the instructions in Chapter 1 for backing up and restoring company data files are repeated below. You must still refer to Chapter 1 to attach and detach data files. The following procedures not only protect your work but allow you to move work between home and school.

Backup Procedures

Data files should be backed up each time you finish working in a company because the backup file can be used to restore your work should a problem occur with your computer. OAP's backup utility performs a back up on the company currently open in the software. The following instructions assume that company is Practice Baxter Garden Supply.

❖ *Backup Step 1*

Open the company to be backed up and select ***File>>Utilities>>Data Utilities*** on the main menu to open the window illustrated in Figure: C:1. Click **Backup**.

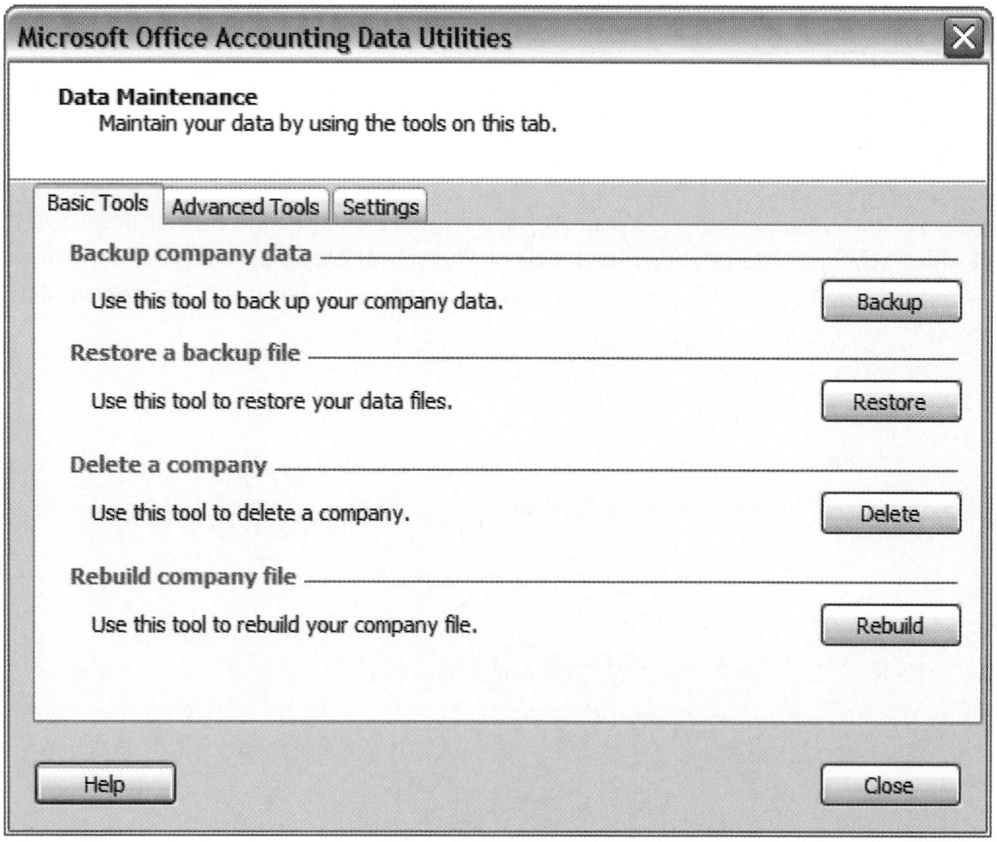

Microsoft Office Accounting Data Utilities

Data Maintenance
Maintain your data by using the tools on this tab.

Basic Tools | Advanced Tools | Settings

Backup company data
Use this tool to back up your company data. [Backup]

Restore a backup file
Use this tool to restore your data files. [Restore]

Delete a company
Use this tool to delete a company. [Delete]

Rebuild company file
Use this tool to rebuild your company file. [Rebuild]

[Help] [Close]

Figure C:1

❖ ***Backup Step 2***

The Backup window opens with the **Backup file name** defaulted to the company name plus the computer's system date (Figure: C:2).

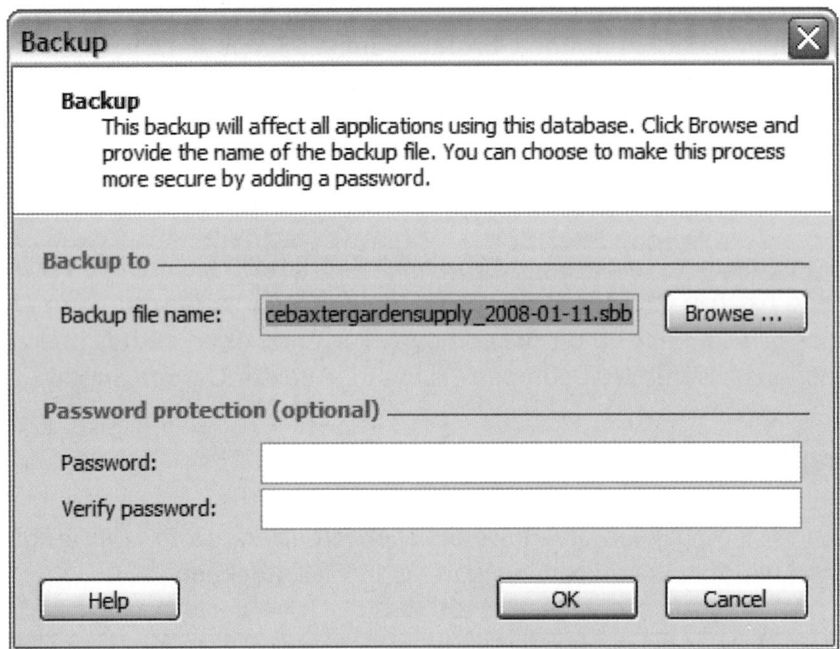

Figure C:2

❖ ***Backup Step 3***

Click **Browse** so that you can select a path for storing the backup file and change the name of the backup file. OAP stores backups in the default path of ***Desktop>>My Documents>>Small Business Accounting>>Backups***. You can trace this path by clicking the dropdown list on the **Save in** box (Figure: C:3).

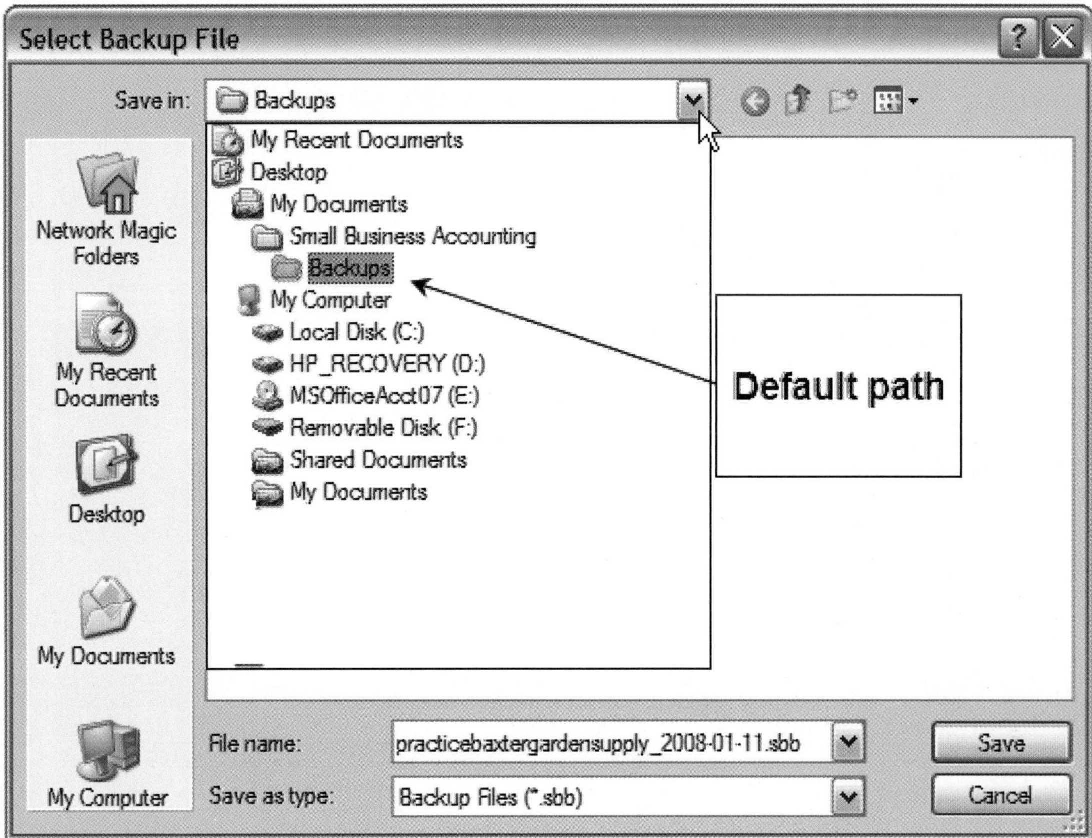

Figure C:3

Note: You can copy data files to a removable storage drive by changing the path to that location. A CD drive is normally labeled "D" and a USB drive normally labeled "E". Just remember where you stored the backup file should you need to restore it later.

❖ ***Backup Step 4***

Keep the current path but you will change the backup file name. We recommend that you replace the date portion of the file name with the chapter name you are currently working on. Thus, change the **File name** to ***practicebaxtergardensupply Chpt 1*** (Figure: C:4)and click **Save**.

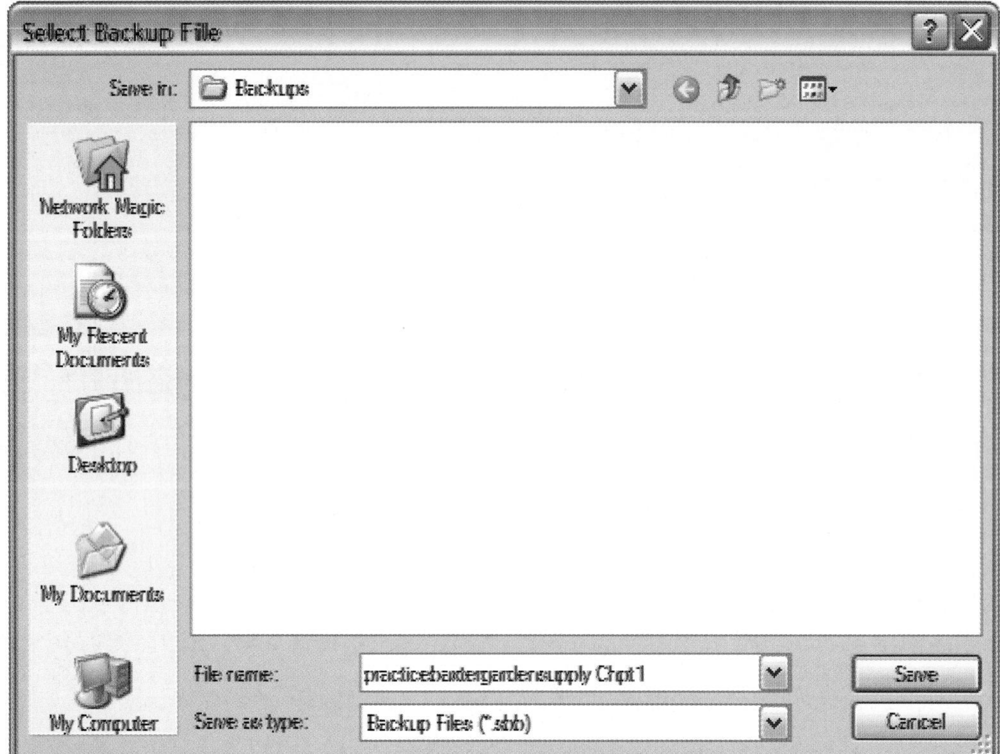

Figure C:4

❖ ***Backup Step 5***

You are returned to the Backup window (Figure: C:5). Click **OK** to create the backup file and **OK** when OAP prompts that backup is complete. Click **Close** to exit the utility window.

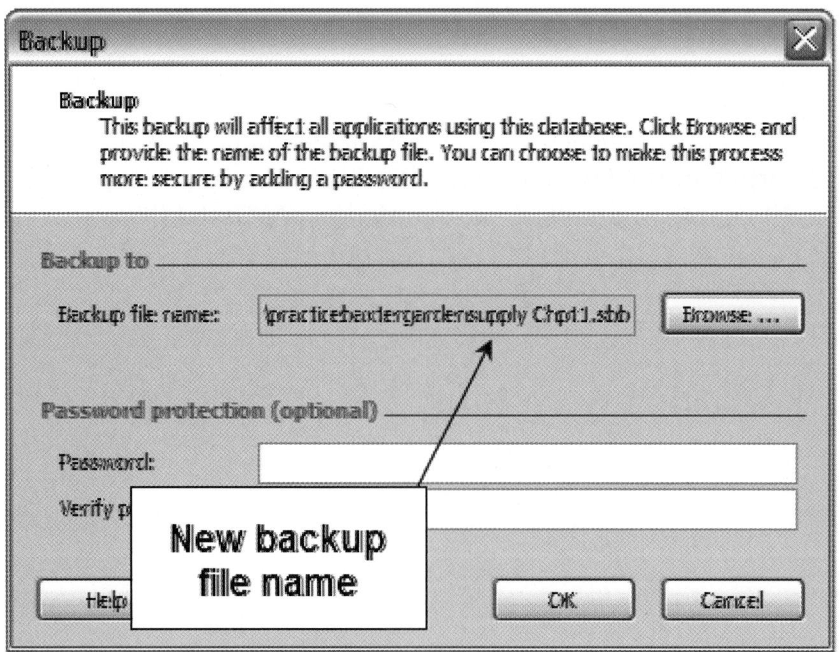

Figure C:5

Restore Procedures

You will need these instructions should you need to restore previous work due to a computer problem or want to move data files between school and home. The illustrations that follow assume Practice Baxter Garden Supply is the company being restored.

Note: You cannot restore previous work unless you have created a backup file; however, you can always reload the original data from the Student CD.

Note: Restoring a backup file overwrites all existing data. Therefore, you should backup the current data to a unique file name before restoring a backup file.

❖ ***Restore Step 1***

The easiest method for restoring data is to restore a backup file while in the software. First, you have to close the current company or open a different company from the one you want to restore. We will close the current company so click ***File>>Close Company*** on the main menu to open the **Start** window and click the icon marked in Figure: C:6.

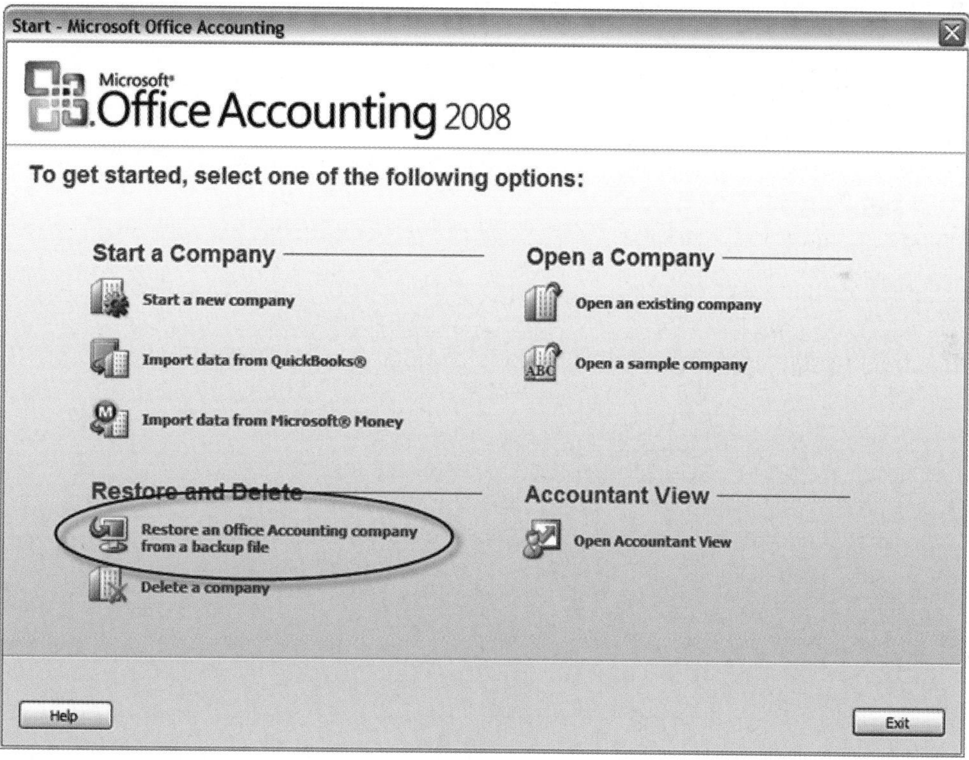

Figure C:6

❖ *Restore Step 2*

When the **Database Restore** window opens (Figure: C:7), click **Browse** on the **Backup filename** to select the location and name of the backup file to restore.

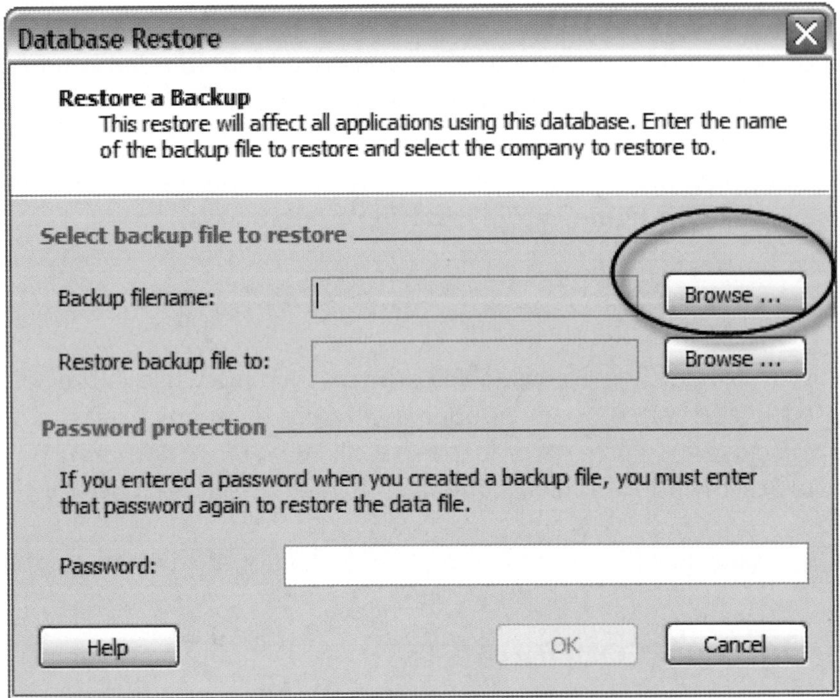

Figure C:7

❖ *Restore Step 3*

Highlight the backup file created in the previous topic and click **Open** (Figure: C:8).

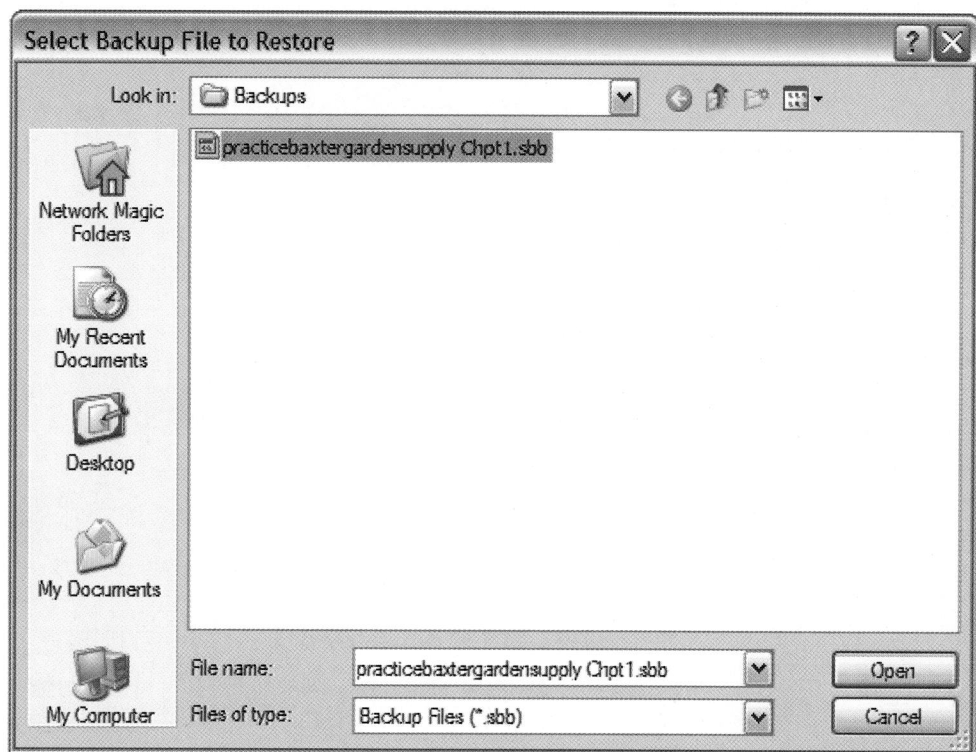

Figure C:8

❖ ***Restore Step 4***

When you return to the Database Restore window, click **Browse** on **Restore backup file to**. Highlight the company name being restored (Figure: C:9) and click **Save**. Click **Yes** to confirm replacing the file.

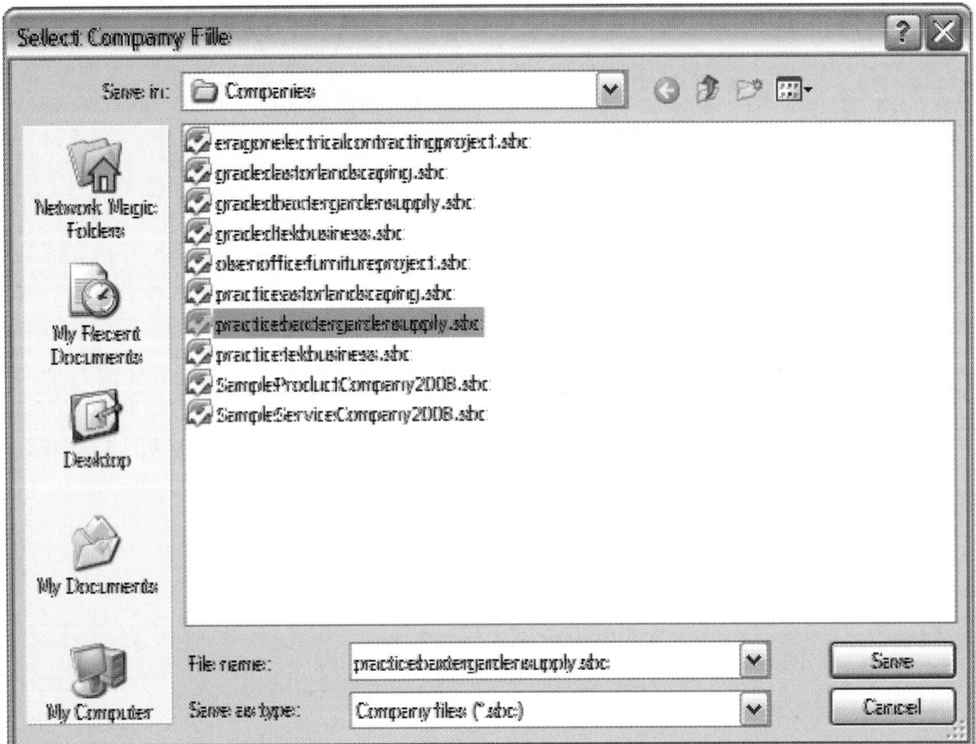

Figure C:9

❖ ***Restore Step 5***

When you have returned to the Database Restore window, click **OK** and OAP overwrites the existing file with the backup file. Click **OK** when the restore completes.

Click **Open an existing company** on the Start screen to reopen a company file.

*Note: You can also restore a data file by selecting **File>>Utilities>>Data Utilities** on OAP's main menu; however, you must make sure to open a different company file from the one you are restoring.*

Moving Data Between Home and School

You can use the backup and restore procedures previously illustrated to copy work between school and a home computer by following the next steps.

1. On the current machine, open the company to be copied to the new machine and follow the steps listed in the *Backup Procedures* above. For Backup Step 3, change the Look in location to your USB or CD drive.

2. On the second machine, follow the steps outlined in the *Restore Procedures* above. *(Note: You must have previously attached the data file to the software.)* In Restore Step 3, change the Look in location to your USB or CD drive.

APPENDIX D IRS CIRCULAR E TAX TABLES

The IRS tax tables used in the text begin on the next page. These tables are from IRS's Circular E publication for 2007 because the 2008 tables were not available at the time of publishing the text.

SINGLE Persons—BIWEEKLY Payroll Period

(For Wages Paid in 2007)

If the wages are–		And the number of withholding allowances claimed is—										
At least	But less than	0	1	2	3	4	5	6	7	8	9	10
		The amount of income tax to be withheld is—										
$0	$105	$0	$0	$0	$0	$0	$0	$0	$0	$0	$0	$0
105	110	1	0	0	0	0	0	0	0	0	0	0
110	115	1	0	0	0	0	0	0	0	0	0	0
115	120	2	0	0	0	0	0	0	0	0	0	0
120	125	2	0	0	0	0	0	0	0	0	0	0
125	130	3	0	0	0	0	0	0	0	0	0	0
130	135	3	0	0	0	0	0	0	0	0	0	0
135	140	4	0	0	0	0	0	0	0	0	0	0
140	145	4	0	0	0	0	0	0	0	0	0	0
145	150	5	0	0	0	0	0	0	0	0	0	0
150	155	5	0	0	0	0	0	0	0	0	0	0
155	160	6	0	0	0	0	0	0	0	0	0	0
160	165	6	0	0	0	0	0	0	0	0	0	0
165	170	7	0	0	0	0	0	0	0	0	0	0
170	175	7	0	0	0	0	0	0	0	0	0	0
175	180	8	0	0	0	0	0	0	0	0	0	0
180	185	8	0	0	0	0	0	0	0	0	0	0
185	190	9	0	0	0	0	0	0	0	0	0	0
190	195	9	0	0	0	0	0	0	0	0	0	0
195	200	10	0	0	0	0	0	0	0	0	0	0
200	205	10	0	0	0	0	0	0	0	0	0	0
205	210	11	0	0	0	0	0	0	0	0	0	0
210	215	11	0	0	0	0	0	0	0	0	0	0
215	220	12	0	0	0	0	0	0	0	0	0	0
220	225	12	0	0	0	0	0	0	0	0	0	0
225	230	13	0	0	0	0	0	0	0	0	0	0
230	235	13	0	0	0	0	0	0	0	0	0	0
235	240	14	0	0	0	0	0	0	0	0	0	0
240	245	14	1	0	0	0	0	0	0	0	0	0
245	250	15	1	0	0	0	0	0	0	0	0	0
250	260	15	2	0	0	0	0	0	0	0	0	0
260	270	16	3	0	0	0	0	0	0	0	0	0
270	280	17	4	0	0	0	0	0	0	0	0	0
280	290	18	5	0	0	0	0	0	0	0	0	0
290	300	19	6	0	0	0	0	0	0	0	0	0
300	310	20	7	0	0	0	0	0	0	0	0	0
310	320	21	8	0	0	0	0	0	0	0	0	0
320	330	22	9	0	0	0	0	0	0	0	0	0
330	340	23	10	0	0	0	0	0	0	0	0	0
340	350	24	11	0	0	0	0	0	0	0	0	0
350	360	25	12	0	0	0	0	0	0	0	0	0
360	370	26	13	0	0	0	0	0	0	0	0	0
370	380	27	14	1	0	0	0	0	0	0	0	0
380	390	28	15	2	0	0	0	0	0	0	0	0
390	400	30	16	3	0	0	0	0	0	0	0	0
400	410	31	17	4	0	0	0	0	0	0	0	0
410	420	33	18	5	0	0	0	0	0	0	0	0
420	430	34	19	6	0	0	0	0	0	0	0	0
430	440	36	20	7	0	0	0	0	0	0	0	0
440	450	37	21	8	0	0	0	0	0	0	0	0
450	460	39	22	9	0	0	0	0	0	0	0	0
460	470	40	23	10	0	0	0	0	0	0	0	0
470	480	42	24	11	0	0	0	0	0	0	0	0
480	490	43	25	12	0	0	0	0	0	0	0	0
490	500	45	26	13	0	0	0	0	0	0	0	0
500	520	47	28	15	2	0	0	0	0	0	0	0
520	540	50	30	17	4	0	0	0	0	0	0	0
540	560	53	33	19	6	0	0	0	0	0	0	0
560	580	56	36	21	8	0	0	0	0	0	0	0
580	600	59	39	23	10	0	0	0	0	0	0	0
600	620	62	42	25	12	0	0	0	0	0	0	0
620	640	65	45	27	14	1	0	0	0	0	0	0
640	660	68	48	29	16	3	0	0	0	0	0	0
660	680	71	51	32	18	5	0	0	0	0	0	0
680	700	74	54	35	20	7	0	0	0	0	0	0
700	720	77	57	38	22	9	0	0	0	0	0	0
720	740	80	60	41	24	11	0	0	0	0	0	0
740	760	83	63	44	26	13	0	0	0	0	0	0
760	780	86	66	47	28	15	1	0	0	0	0	0
780	800	89	69	50	30	17	3	0	0	0	0	0

SINGLE Persons—BIWEEKLY Payroll Period

(For Wages Paid in 2007)

If the wages are–		And the number of withholding allowances claimed is—										
At least	But less than	0	1	2	3	4	5	6	7	8	9	10
		The amount of income tax to be withheld is—										
$800	$820	$92	$72	$53	$33	$19	$5	$0	$0	$0	$0	$0
820	840	95	75	56	36	21	7	0	0	0	0	0
840	860	98	78	59	39	23	9	0	0	0	0	0
860	880	101	81	62	42	25	11	0	0	0	0	0
880	900	104	84	65	45	27	13	0	0	0	0	0
900	920	107	87	68	48	29	15	2	0	0	0	0
920	940	110	90	71	51	31	17	4	0	0	0	0
940	960	113	93	74	54	34	19	6	0	0	0	0
960	980	116	96	77	57	37	21	8	0	0	0	0
980	1,000	119	99	80	60	40	23	10	0	0	0	0
1,000	1,020	122	102	83	63	43	25	12	0	0	0	0
1,020	1,040	125	105	86	66	46	27	14	1	0	0	0
1,040	1,060	128	108	89	69	49	30	16	3	0	0	0
1,060	1,080	131	111	92	72	52	33	18	5	0	0	0
1,080	1,100	134	114	95	75	55	36	20	7	0	0	0
1,100	1,120	137	117	98	78	58	39	22	9	0	0	0
1,120	1,140	140	120	101	81	61	42	24	11	0	0	0
1,140	1,160	143	123	104	84	64	45	26	13	0	0	0
1,160	1,180	146	126	107	87	67	48	28	15	2	0	0
1,180	1,200	149	129	110	90	70	51	31	17	4	0	0
1,200	1,220	152	132	113	93	73	54	34	19	6	0	0
1,220	1,240	155	135	116	96	76	57	37	21	8	0	0
1,240	1,260	158	138	119	99	79	60	40	23	10	0	0
1,260	1,280	161	141	122	102	82	63	43	25	12	0	0
1,280	1,300	164	144	125	105	85	66	46	27	14	1	0
1,300	1,320	169	147	128	108	88	69	49	30	16	3	0
1,320	1,340	174	150	131	111	91	72	52	33	18	5	0
1,340	1,360	179	153	134	114	94	75	55	36	20	7	0
1,360	1,380	184	156	137	117	97	78	58	39	22	9	0
1,380	1,400	189	159	140	120	100	81	61	42	24	11	0
1,400	1,420	194	162	143	123	103	84	64	45	26	13	0
1,420	1,440	199	166	146	126	106	87	67	48	28	15	2
1,440	1,460	204	171	149	129	109	90	70	51	31	17	4
1,460	1,480	209	176	152	132	112	93	73	54	34	19	6
1,480	1,500	214	181	155	135	115	96	76	57	37	21	8
1,500	1,520	219	186	158	138	118	99	79	60	40	23	10
1,520	1,540	224	191	161	141	121	102	82	63	43	25	12
1,540	1,560	229	196	164	144	124	105	85	66	46	27	14
1,560	1,580	234	201	169	147	127	108	88	69	49	29	16
1,580	1,600	239	206	174	150	130	111	91	72	52	32	18
1,600	1,620	244	211	179	153	133	114	94	75	55	35	20
1,620	1,640	249	216	184	156	136	117	97	78	58	38	22
1,640	1,660	254	221	189	159	139	120	100	81	61	41	24
1,660	1,680	259	226	194	162	142	123	103	84	64	44	26
1,680	1,700	264	231	199	166	145	126	106	87	67	47	28
1,700	1,720	269	236	204	171	148	129	109	90	70	50	31
1,720	1,740	274	241	209	176	151	132	112	93	73	53	34
1,740	1,760	279	246	214	181	154	135	115	96	76	56	37
1,760	1,780	284	251	219	186	157	138	118	99	79	59	40
1,780	1,800	289	256	224	191	160	141	121	102	82	62	43
1,800	1,820	294	261	229	196	163	144	124	105	85	65	46
1,820	1,840	299	266	234	201	168	147	127	108	88	68	49
1,840	1,860	304	271	239	206	173	150	130	111	91	71	52
1,860	1,880	309	276	244	211	178	153	133	114	94	74	55
1,880	1,900	314	281	249	216	183	156	136	117	97	77	58
1,900	1,920	319	286	254	221	188	159	139	120	100	80	61
1,920	1,940	324	291	259	226	193	162	142	123	103	83	64
1,940	1,960	329	296	264	231	198	165	145	126	106	86	67
1,960	1,980	334	301	269	236	203	170	148	129	109	89	70
1,980	2,000	339	306	274	241	208	175	151	132	112	92	73
2,000	2,020	344	311	279	246	213	180	154	135	115	95	76
2,020	2,040	349	316	284	251	218	185	157	138	118	98	79
2,040	2,060	354	321	289	256	223	190	160	141	121	101	82
2,060	2,080	359	326	294	261	228	195	163	144	124	104	85
2,080	2,100	364	331	299	266	233	200	168	147	127	107	88
$2,100 and over		Use Table 2(a) for a **SINGLE person** on page 37. Also see the instructions on page 35.										

MARRIED Persons—**BIWEEKLY** Payroll Period

(For Wages Paid in 2007)

If the wages are–		And the number of withholding allowances claimed is—										
At least	But less than	0	1	2	3	4	5	6	7	8	9	10
		The amount of income tax to be withheld is—										
$0	$250	$0	$0	$0	$0	$0	$0	$0	$0	$0	$0	$0
250	260	0	0	0	0	0	0	0	0	0	0	0
260	270	0	0	0	0	0	0	0	0	0	0	0
270	280	0	0	0	0	0	0	0	0	0	0	0
280	290	0	0	0	0	0	0	0	0	0	0	0
290	300	0	0	0	0	0	0	0	0	0	0	0
300	310	0	0	0	0	0	0	0	0	0	0	0
310	320	1	0	0	0	0	0	0	0	0	0	0
320	330	2	0	0	0	0	0	0	0	0	0	0
330	340	3	0	0	0	0	0	0	0	0	0	0
340	350	4	0	0	0	0	0	0	0	0	0	0
350	360	5	0	0	0	0	0	0	0	0	0	0
360	370	6	0	0	0	0	0	0	0	0	0	0
370	380	7	0	0	0	0	0	0	0	0	0	0
380	390	8	0	0	0	0	0	0	0	0	0	0
390	400	9	0	0	0	0	0	0	0	0	0	0
400	410	10	0	0	0	0	0	0	0	0	0	0
410	420	11	0	0	0	0	0	0	0	0	0	0
420	430	12	0	0	0	0	0	0	0	0	0	0
430	440	13	0	0	0	0	0	0	0	0	0	0
440	450	14	1	0	0	0	0	0	0	0	0	0
450	460	15	2	0	0	0	0	0	0	0	0	0
460	470	16	3	0	0	0	0	0	0	0	0	0
470	480	17	4	0	0	0	0	0	0	0	0	0
480	490	18	5	0	0	0	0	0	0	0	0	0
490	500	19	6	0	0	0	0	0	0	0	0	0
500	520	20	7	0	0	0	0	0	0	0	0	0
520	540	22	9	0	0	0	0	0	0	0	0	0
540	560	24	11	0	0	0	0	0	0	0	0	0
560	580	26	13	0	0	0	0	0	0	0	0	0
580	600	28	15	2	0	0	0	0	0	0	0	0
600	620	30	17	4	0	0	0	0	0	0	0	0
620	640	32	19	6	0	0	0	0	0	0	0	0
640	660	34	21	8	0	0	0	0	0	0	0	0
660	680	36	23	10	0	0	0	0	0	0	0	0
680	700	38	25	12	0	0	0	0	0	0	0	0
700	720	40	27	14	1	0	0	0	0	0	0	0
720	740	42	29	16	3	0	0	0	0	0	0	0
740	760	44	31	18	5	0	0	0	0	0	0	0
760	780	46	33	20	7	0	0	0	0	0	0	0
780	800	48	35	22	9	0	0	0	0	0	0	0
800	820	50	37	24	11	0	0	0	0	0	0	0
820	840	52	39	26	13	0	0	0	0	0	0	0
840	860	54	41	28	15	2	0	0	0	0	0	0
860	880	56	43	30	17	4	0	0	0	0	0	0
880	900	58	45	32	19	6	0	0	0	0	0	0
900	920	61	47	34	21	8	0	0	0	0	0	0
920	940	64	49	36	23	10	0	0	0	0	0	0
940	960	67	51	38	25	12	0	0	0	0	0	0
960	980	70	53	40	27	14	1	0	0	0	0	0
980	1,000	73	55	42	29	16	3	0	0	0	0	0
1,000	1,020	76	57	44	31	18	5	0	0	0	0	0
1,020	1,040	79	59	46	33	20	7	0	0	0	0	0
1,040	1,060	82	62	48	35	22	9	0	0	0	0	0
1,060	1,080	85	65	50	37	24	11	0	0	0	0	0
1,080	1,100	88	68	52	39	26	13	0	0	0	0	0
1,100	1,120	91	71	54	41	28	15	2	0	0	0	0
1,120	1,140	94	74	56	43	30	17	4	0	0	0	0
1,140	1,160	97	77	58	45	32	19	6	0	0	0	0
1,160	1,180	100	80	61	47	34	21	8	0	0	0	0
1,180	1,200	103	83	64	49	36	23	10	0	0	0	0
1,200	1,220	106	86	67	51	38	25	12	0	0	0	0
1,220	1,240	109	89	70	53	40	27	14	1	0	0	0
1,240	1,260	112	92	73	55	42	29	16	3	0	0	0
1,260	1,280	115	95	76	57	44	31	18	5	0	0	0
1,280	1,300	118	98	79	59	46	33	20	7	0	0	0
1,300	1,320	121	101	82	62	48	35	22	9	0	0	0
1,320	1,340	124	104	85	65	50	37	24	11	0	0	0
1,340	1,360	127	107	88	68	52	39	26	13	0	0	0
1,360	1,380	130	110	91	71	54	41	28	15	2	0	0

MARRIED Persons—**BIWEEKLY** Payroll Period

(For Wages Paid in 2007)

If the wages are–		And the number of withholding allowances claimed is—										
At least	But less than	0	1	2	3	4	5	6	7	8	9	10
		The amount of income tax to be withheld is—										
$1,380	$1,400	$133	$113	$94	$74	$56	$43	$30	$17	$4	$0	$0
1,400	1,420	136	116	97	77	58	45	32	19	6	0	0
1,420	1,440	139	119	100	80	60	47	34	21	8	0	0
1,440	1,460	142	122	103	83	63	49	36	23	10	0	0
1,460	1,480	145	125	106	86	66	51	38	25	12	0	0
1,480	1,500	148	128	109	89	69	53	40	27	14	1	0
1,500	1,520	151	131	112	92	72	55	42	29	16	3	0
1,520	1,540	154	134	115	95	75	57	44	31	18	5	0
1,540	1,560	157	137	118	98	78	59	46	33	20	7	0
1,560	1,580	160	140	121	101	81	62	48	35	22	9	0
1,580	1,600	163	143	124	104	84	65	50	37	24	11	0
1,600	1,620	166	146	127	107	87	68	52	39	26	13	0
1,620	1,640	169	149	130	110	90	71	54	41	28	15	1
1,640	1,660	172	152	133	113	93	74	56	43	30	17	3
1,660	1,680	175	155	136	116	96	77	58	45	32	19	5
1,680	1,700	178	158	139	119	99	80	60	47	34	21	7
1,700	1,720	181	161	142	122	102	83	63	49	36	23	9
1,720	1,740	184	164	145	125	105	86	66	51	38	25	11
1,740	1,760	187	167	148	128	108	89	69	53	40	27	13
1,760	1,780	190	170	151	131	111	92	72	55	42	29	15
1,780	1,800	193	173	154	134	114	95	75	57	44	31	17
1,800	1,820	196	176	157	137	117	98	78	59	46	33	19
1,820	1,840	199	179	160	140	120	101	81	62	48	35	21
1,840	1,860	202	182	163	143	123	104	84	65	50	37	23
1,860	1,880	205	185	166	146	126	107	87	68	52	39	25
1,880	1,900	208	188	169	149	129	110	90	71	54	41	27
1,900	1,920	211	191	172	152	132	113	93	74	56	43	29
1,920	1,940	214	194	175	155	135	116	96	77	58	45	31
1,940	1,960	217	197	178	158	138	119	99	80	60	47	33
1,960	1,980	220	200	181	161	141	122	102	83	63	49	35
1,980	2,000	223	203	184	164	144	125	105	86	66	51	37
2,000	2,020	226	206	187	167	147	128	108	89	69	53	39
2,020	2,040	229	209	190	170	150	131	111	92	72	55	41
2,040	2,060	232	212	193	173	153	134	114	95	75	57	43
2,060	2,080	235	215	196	176	156	137	117	98	78	59	45
2,080	2,100	238	218	199	179	159	140	120	101	81	61	47
2,100	2,120	241	221	202	182	162	143	123	104	84	64	49
2,120	2,140	244	224	205	185	165	146	126	107	87	67	51
2,140	2,160	247	227	208	188	168	149	129	110	90	70	53
2,160	2,180	250	230	211	191	171	152	132	113	93	73	55
2,180	2,200	253	233	214	194	174	155	135	116	96	76	57
2,200	2,220	256	236	217	197	177	158	138	119	99	79	60
2,220	2,240	259	239	220	200	180	161	141	122	102	82	63
2,240	2,260	262	242	223	203	183	164	144	125	105	85	66
2,260	2,280	265	245	226	206	186	167	147	128	108	88	69
2,280	2,300	268	248	229	209	189	170	150	131	111	91	72
2,300	2,320	271	251	232	212	192	173	153	134	114	94	75
2,320	2,340	274	254	235	215	195	176	156	137	117	97	78
2,340	2,360	277	257	238	218	198	179	159	140	120	100	81
2,360	2,380	280	260	241	221	201	182	162	143	123	103	84
2,380	2,400	283	263	244	224	204	185	165	146	126	106	87
2,400	2,420	286	266	247	227	207	188	168	149	129	109	90
2,420	2,440	289	269	250	230	210	191	171	152	132	112	93
2,440	2,460	292	272	253	233	213	194	174	155	135	115	96
2,460	2,480	295	275	256	236	216	197	177	158	138	118	99
2,480	2,500	298	278	259	239	219	200	180	161	141	121	102
2,500	2,520	301	281	262	242	222	203	183	164	144	124	105
2,520	2,540	304	284	265	245	225	206	186	167	147	127	108
2,540	2,560	307	287	268	248	228	209	189	170	150	130	111
2,560	2,580	310	290	271	251	231	212	192	173	153	133	114
2,580	2,600	313	293	274	254	234	215	195	176	156	136	117
2,600	2,620	316	296	277	257	237	218	198	179	159	139	120
2,620	2,640	319	299	280	260	240	221	201	182	162	142	123
2,640	2,660	322	302	283	263	243	224	204	185	165	145	126
2,660	2,680	325	305	286	266	246	227	207	188	168	148	129
2,680	2,700	328	308	289	269	249	230	210	191	171	151	132
$2,700 and over		Use Table 2(b) for a **MARRIED person** on page 37. Also see the instructions on page 35.										

APPENDIX E SOLUTIONS FOR "YOU TRY" EXERCISES

CHAPTER 1

No in-chapter exercises were presented.

CHAPTER 2

No in-chapter exercises were presented.

CHAPTER 3

RECORD TEK'S JANUARY TRANSACTIONS

Journal Entry window.

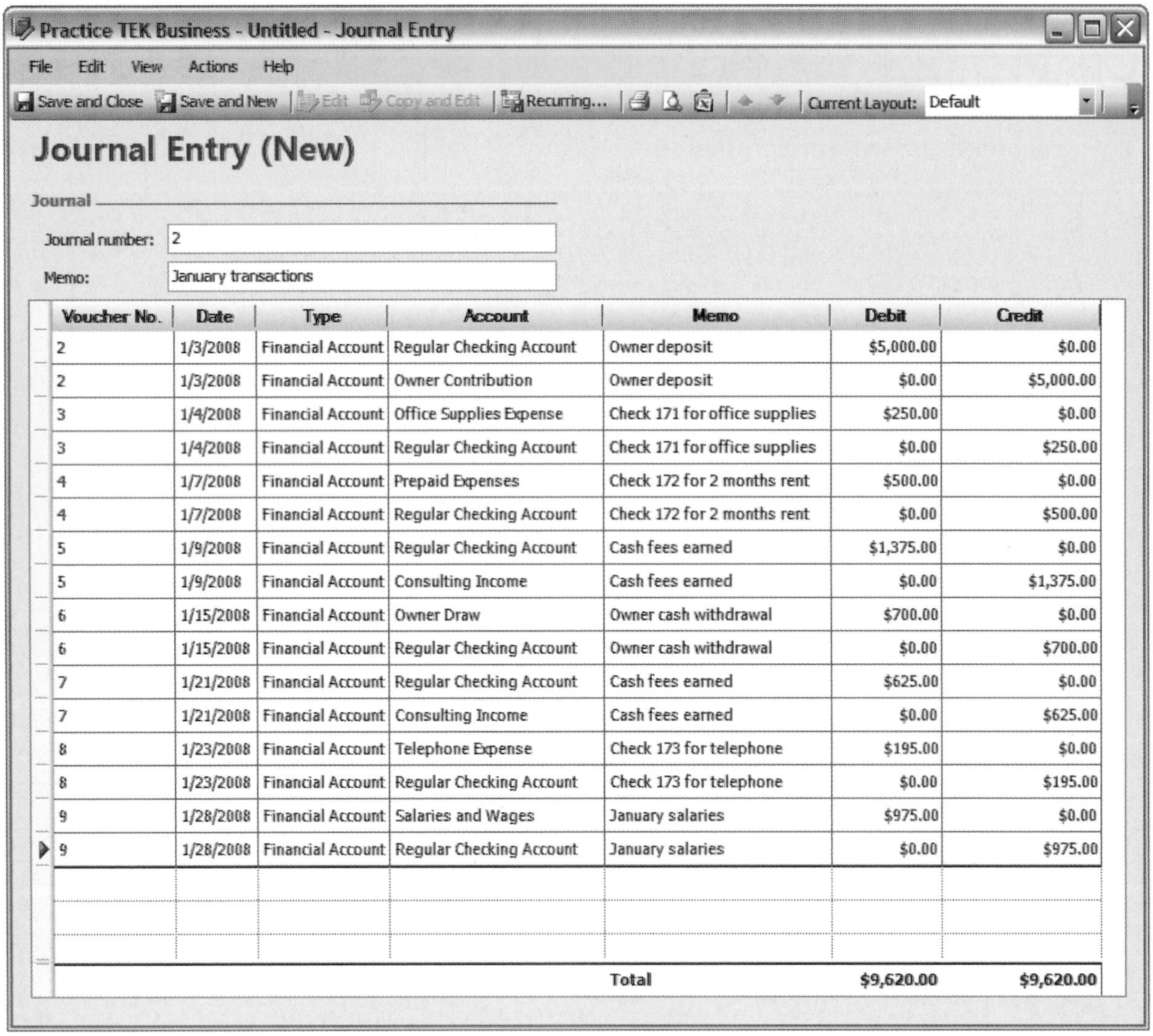

Practice TEK Business - Untitled - Journal Entry

File Edit View Actions Help

Save and Close | Save and New | Edit | Copy and Edit | Recurring... | Current Layout: Default

Journal Entry (New)

Journal

Journal number: 2

Memo: January transactions

Voucher No.	Date	Type	Account	Memo	Debit	Credit
2	1/3/2008	Financial Account	Regular Checking Account	Owner deposit	$5,000.00	$0.00
2	1/3/2008	Financial Account	Owner Contribution	Owner deposit	$0.00	$5,000.00
3	1/4/2008	Financial Account	Office Supplies Expense	Check 171 for office supplies	$250.00	$0.00
3	1/4/2008	Financial Account	Regular Checking Account	Check 171 for office supplies	$0.00	$250.00
4	1/7/2008	Financial Account	Prepaid Expenses	Check 172 for 2 months rent	$500.00	$0.00
4	1/7/2008	Financial Account	Regular Checking Account	Check 172 for 2 months rent	$0.00	$500.00
5	1/9/2008	Financial Account	Regular Checking Account	Cash fees earned	$1,375.00	$0.00
5	1/9/2008	Financial Account	Consulting Income	Cash fees earned	$0.00	$1,375.00
6	1/15/2008	Financial Account	Owner Draw	Owner cash withdrawal	$700.00	$0.00
6	1/15/2008	Financial Account	Regular Checking Account	Owner cash withdrawal	$0.00	$700.00
7	1/21/2008	Financial Account	Regular Checking Account	Cash fees earned	$625.00	$0.00
7	1/21/2008	Financial Account	Consulting Income	Cash fees earned	$0.00	$625.00
8	1/23/2008	Financial Account	Telephone Expense	Check 173 for telephone	$195.00	$0.00
8	1/23/2008	Financial Account	Regular Checking Account	Check 173 for telephone	$0.00	$195.00
9	1/28/2008	Financial Account	Salaries and Wages	January salaries	$975.00	$0.00
9	1/28/2008	Financial Account	Regular Checking Account	January salaries	$0.00	$975.00
				Total	**$9,620.00**	**$9,620.00**

Figure E:1

Transaction Journal report for the date range of 1/3/2008 to 1/31/2008. (Note: Entry line items were posted in debit / credit order; however, OAP will not always display entries as such.)

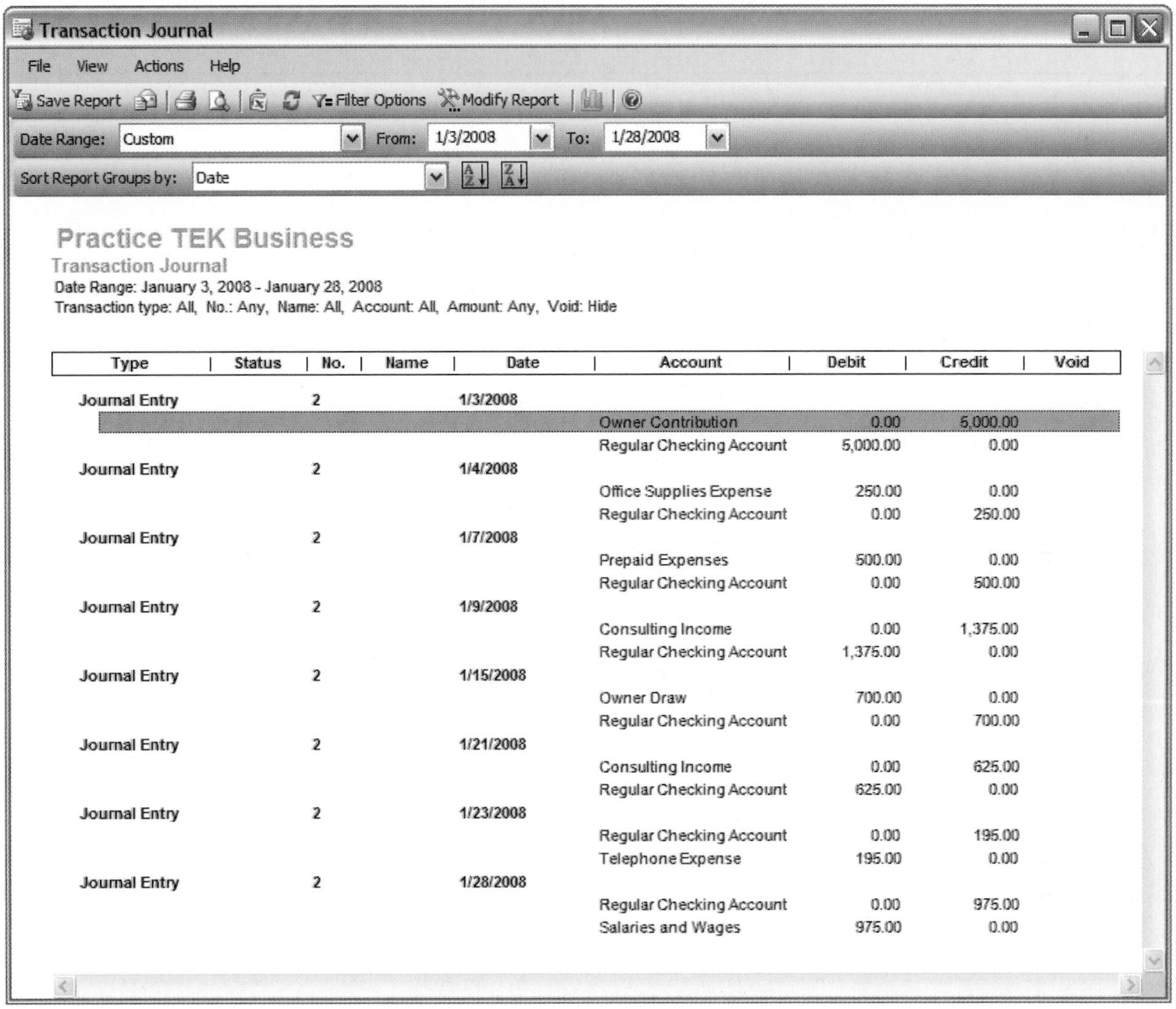

Transaction Journal

File View Actions Help

Save Report | Filter Options | Modify Report

Date Range: Custom From: 1/3/2008 To: 1/28/2008

Sort Report Groups by: Date

Practice TEK Business

Transaction Journal

Date Range: January 3, 2008 - January 28, 2008

Transaction type: All, No.: Any, Name: All, Account: All, Amount: Any, Void: Hide

Type	Status	No.	Name	Date	Account	Debit	Credit	Void
Journal Entry		2		1/3/2008				
					Owner Contribution	0.00	5,000.00	
					Regular Checking Account	5,000.00	0.00	
Journal Entry		2		1/4/2008				
					Office Supplies Expense	250.00	0.00	
					Regular Checking Account	0.00	250.00	
Journal Entry		2		1/7/2008				
					Prepaid Expenses	500.00	0.00	
					Regular Checking Account	0.00	500.00	
Journal Entry		2		1/9/2008				
					Consulting Income	0.00	1,375.00	
					Regular Checking Account	1,375.00	0.00	
Journal Entry		2		1/15/2008				
					Owner Draw	700.00	0.00	
					Regular Checking Account	0.00	700.00	
Journal Entry		2		1/21/2008				
					Consulting Income	0.00	625.00	
					Regular Checking Account	625.00	0.00	
Journal Entry		2		1/23/2008				
					Regular Checking Account	0.00	195.00	
					Telephone Expense	195.00	0.00	
Journal Entry		2		1/28/2008				
					Regular Checking Account	0.00	975.00	
					Salaries and Wages	975.00	0.00	

Figure E:2

RECORD ADDITIONAL JOURNAL ENTRIES

Journal Entry window.

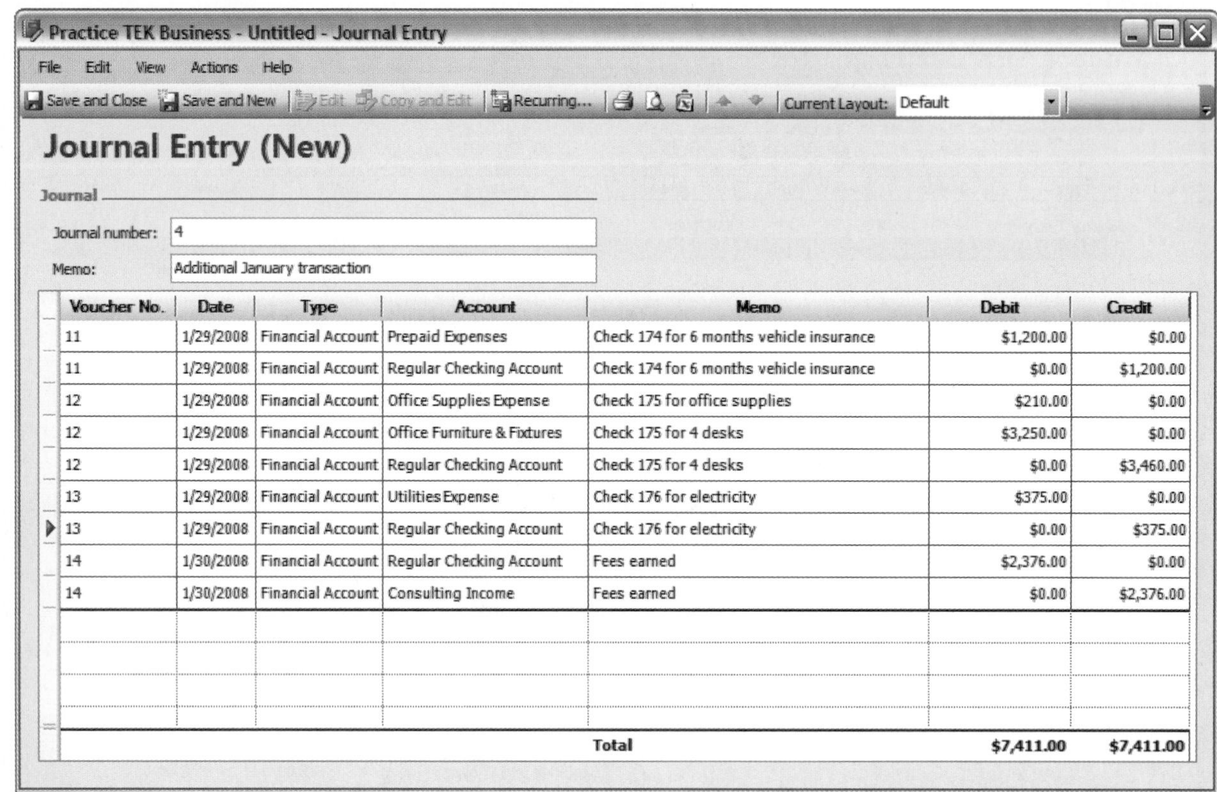

Voucher No.	Date	Type	Account	Memo	Debit	Credit
11	1/29/2008	Financial Account	Prepaid Expenses	Check 174 for 6 months vehicle insurance	$1,200.00	$0.00
11	1/29/2008	Financial Account	Regular Checking Account	Check 174 for 6 months vehicle insurance	$0.00	$1,200.00
12	1/29/2008	Financial Account	Office Supplies Expense	Check 175 for office supplies	$210.00	$0.00
12	1/29/2008	Financial Account	Office Furniture & Fixtures	Check 175 for 4 desks	$3,250.00	$0.00
12	1/29/2008	Financial Account	Regular Checking Account	Check 175 for 4 desks	$0.00	$3,460.00
13	1/29/2008	Financial Account	Utilities Expense	Check 176 for electricity	$375.00	$0.00
13	1/29/2008	Financial Account	Regular Checking Account	Check 176 for electricity	$0.00	$375.00
14	1/30/2008	Financial Account	Regular Checking Account	Fees earned	$2,376.00	$0.00
14	1/30/2008	Financial Account	Consulting Income	Fees earned	$0.00	$2,376.00
				Total	**$7,411.00**	**$7,411.00**

Figure E:3

Transaction Journal report for the date range of 1/27/2008 to 1/30/2008.

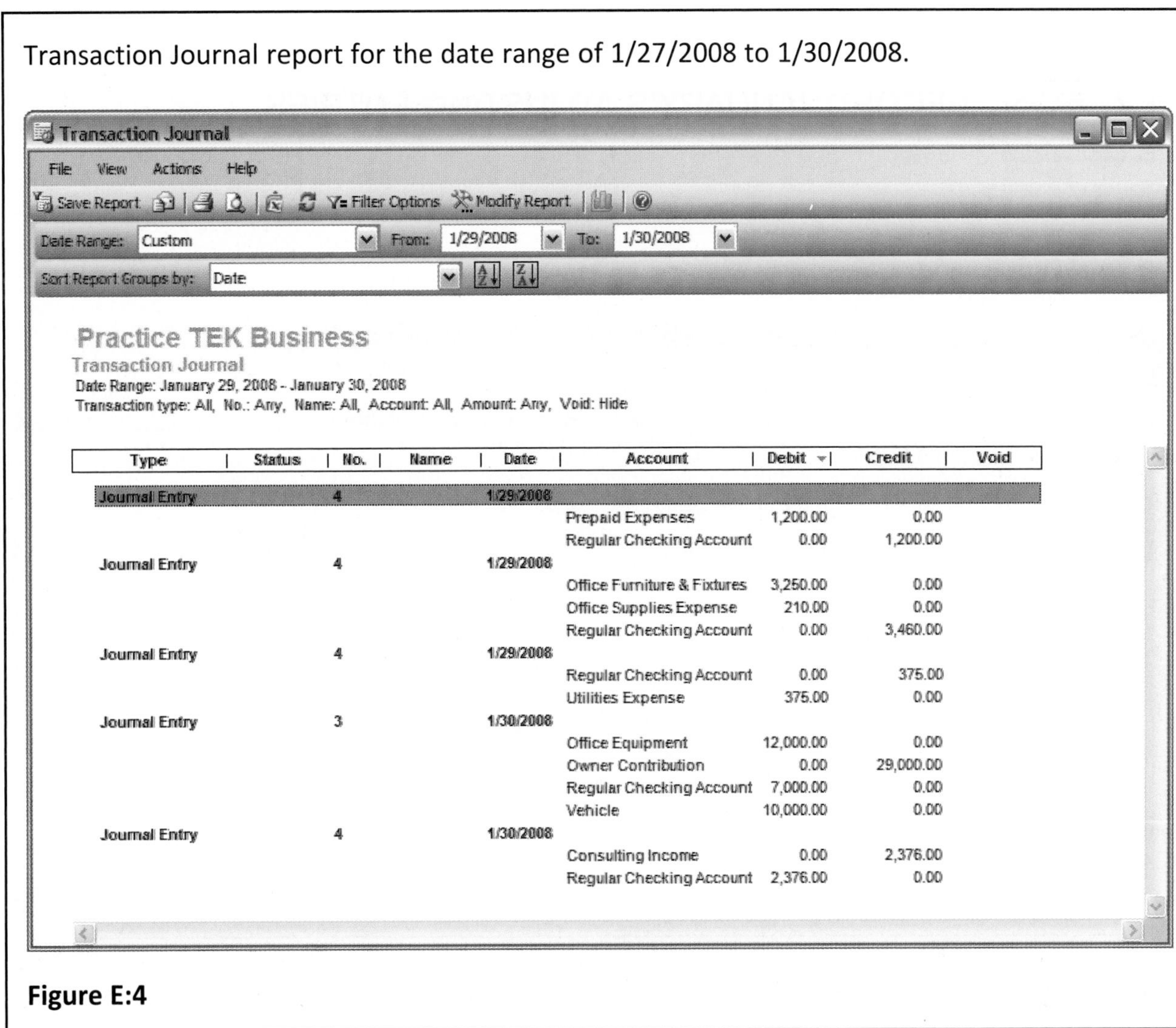

Practice TEK Business
Transaction Journal
Date Range: January 29, 2008 - January 30, 2008
Transaction type: All, No.: Any, Name: All, Account: All, Amount: Any, Void: Hide

Type	Status	No.	Name	Date	Account	Debit	Credit	Void
Journal Entry		4		1/29/2008				
					Prepaid Expenses	1,200.00	0.00	
					Regular Checking Account	0.00	1,200.00	
Journal Entry		4		1/29/2008				
					Office Furniture & Fixtures	3,250.00	0.00	
					Office Supplies Expense	210.00	0.00	
					Regular Checking Account	0.00	3,460.00	
Journal Entry		4		1/29/2008				
					Regular Checking Account	0.00	375.00	
					Utilities Expense	375.00	0.00	
Journal Entry		3		1/30/2008				
					Office Equipment	12,000.00	0.00	
					Owner Contribution	0.00	29,000.00	
					Regular Checking Account	7,000.00	0.00	
					Vehicle	10,000.00	0.00	
Journal Entry		4		1/30/2008				
					Consulting Income	0.00	2,376.00	
					Regular Checking Account	2,376.00	0.00	

Figure E:4

RECORD JANUARY'S ADJUSTING ENTRIES

Journal Entry window.

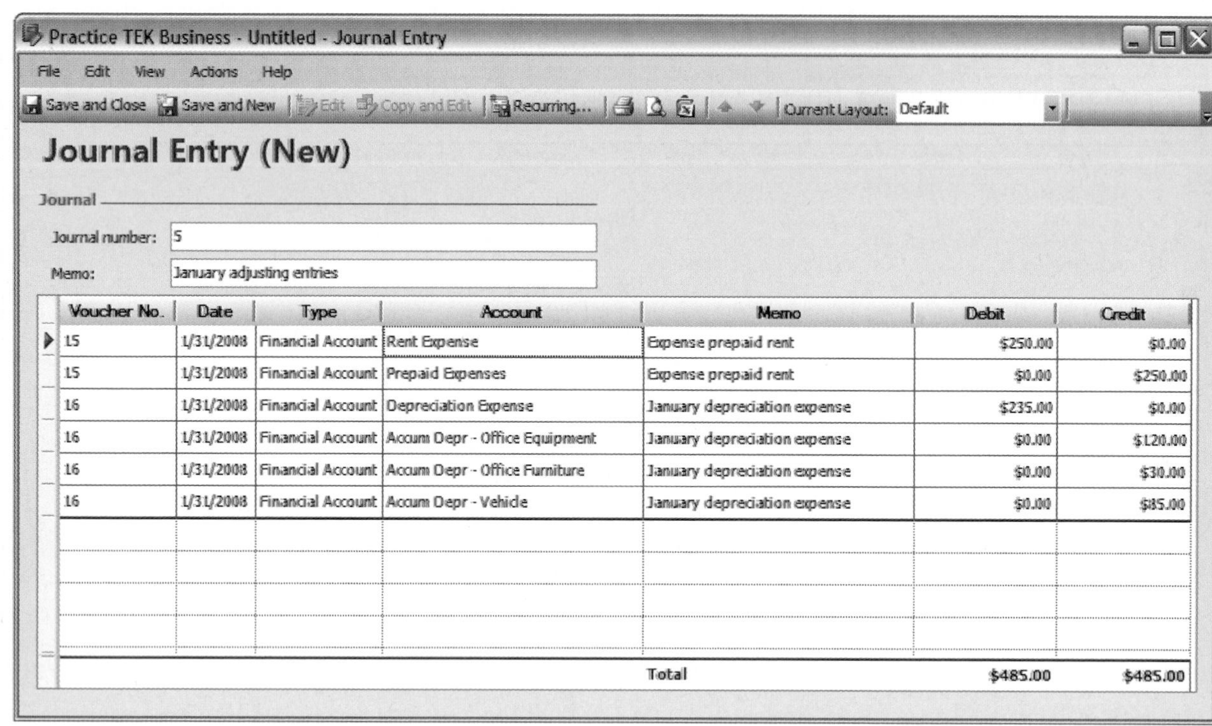

Voucher No.	Date	Type	Account	Memo	Debit	Credit
15	1/31/2008	Financial Account	Rent Expense	Expense prepaid rent	$250.00	$0.00
15	1/31/2008	Financial Account	Prepaid Expenses	Expense prepaid rent	$0.00	$250.00
16	1/31/2008	Financial Account	Depreciation Expense	January depreciation expense	$235.00	$0.00
16	1/31/2008	Financial Account	Accum Depr - Office Equipment	January depreciation expense	$0.00	$120.00
16	1/31/2008	Financial Account	Accum Depr - Office Furniture	January depreciation expense	$0.00	$30.00
16	1/31/2008	Financial Account	Accum Depr - Vehicle	January depreciation expense	$0.00	$85.00
				Total	$485.00	$485.00

Figure E:5

Transaction Journal report for January 31, 2008.

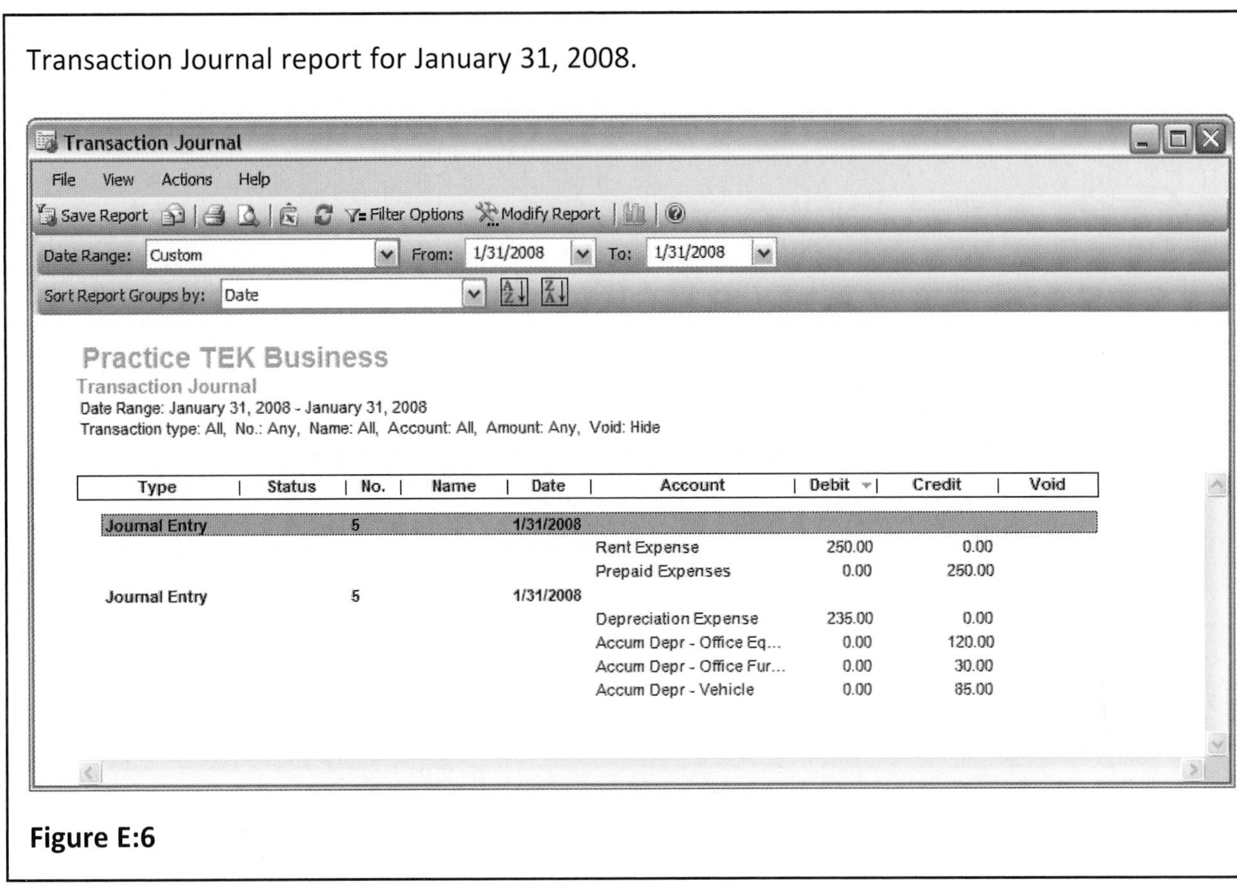
Transaction Journal

File View Actions Help

Save Report | Filter Options | Modify Report

Date Range: Custom From: 1/31/2008 To: 1/31/2008

Sort Report Groups by: Date

Practice TEK Business

Transaction Journal

Date Range: January 31, 2008 - January 31, 2008

Transaction type: All, No.: Any, Name: All, Account: All, Amount: Any, Void: Hide

Type	Status	No.	Name	Date	Account	Debit	Credit	Void
Journal Entry		5		1/31/2008				
					Rent Expense	250.00	0.00	
					Prepaid Expenses	0.00	250.00	
Journal Entry		5		1/31/2008				
					Depreciation Expense	235.00	0.00	
					Accum Depr - Office Eq...	0.00	120.00	
					Accum Depr - Office Fur...	0.00	30.00	
					Accum Depr - Vehicle	0.00	85.00	

Figure E:6

CHAPTER 4

ENTER A NEW SALES QUOTE

Job information.

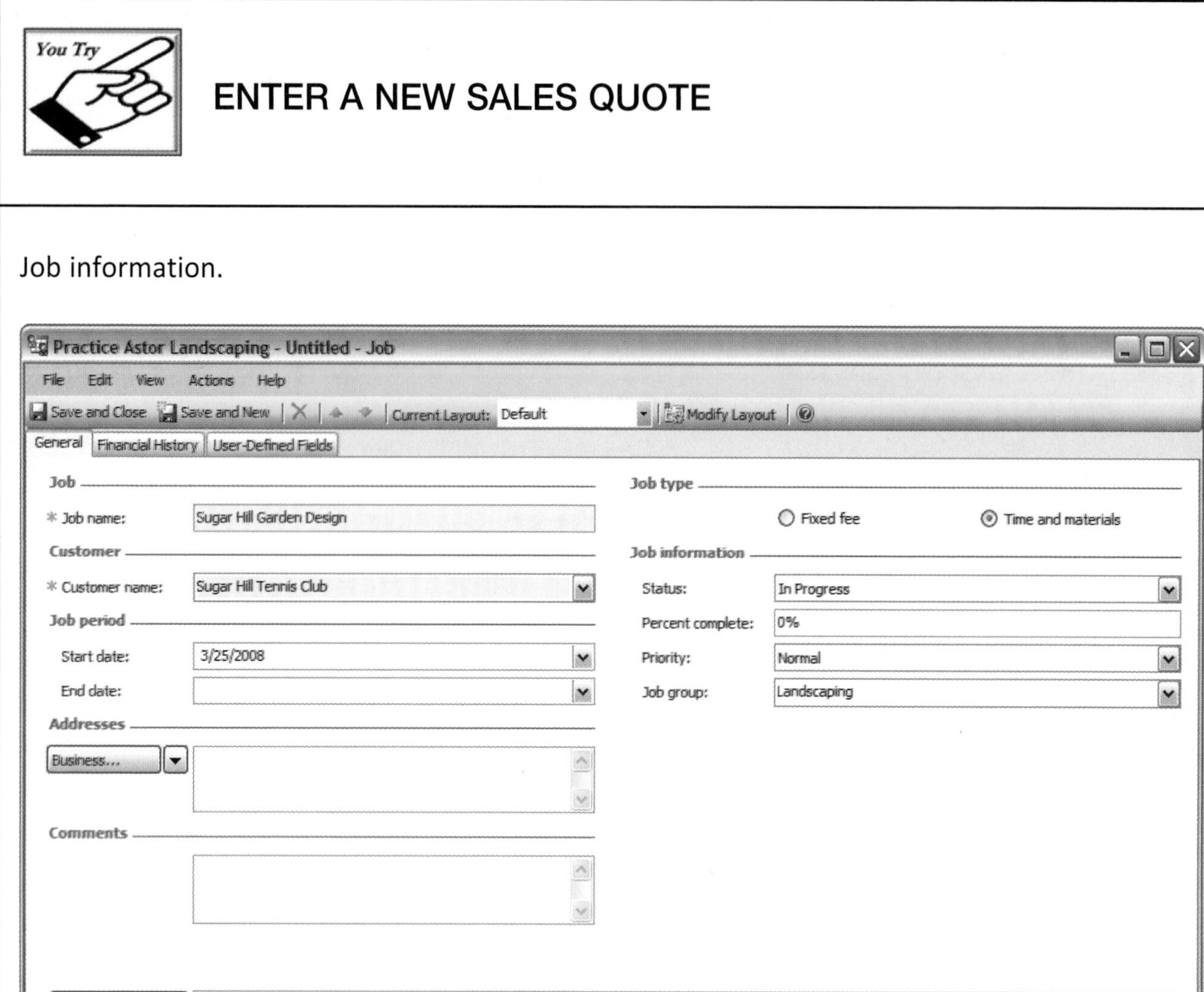

Figure E:7

Quote transaction window.

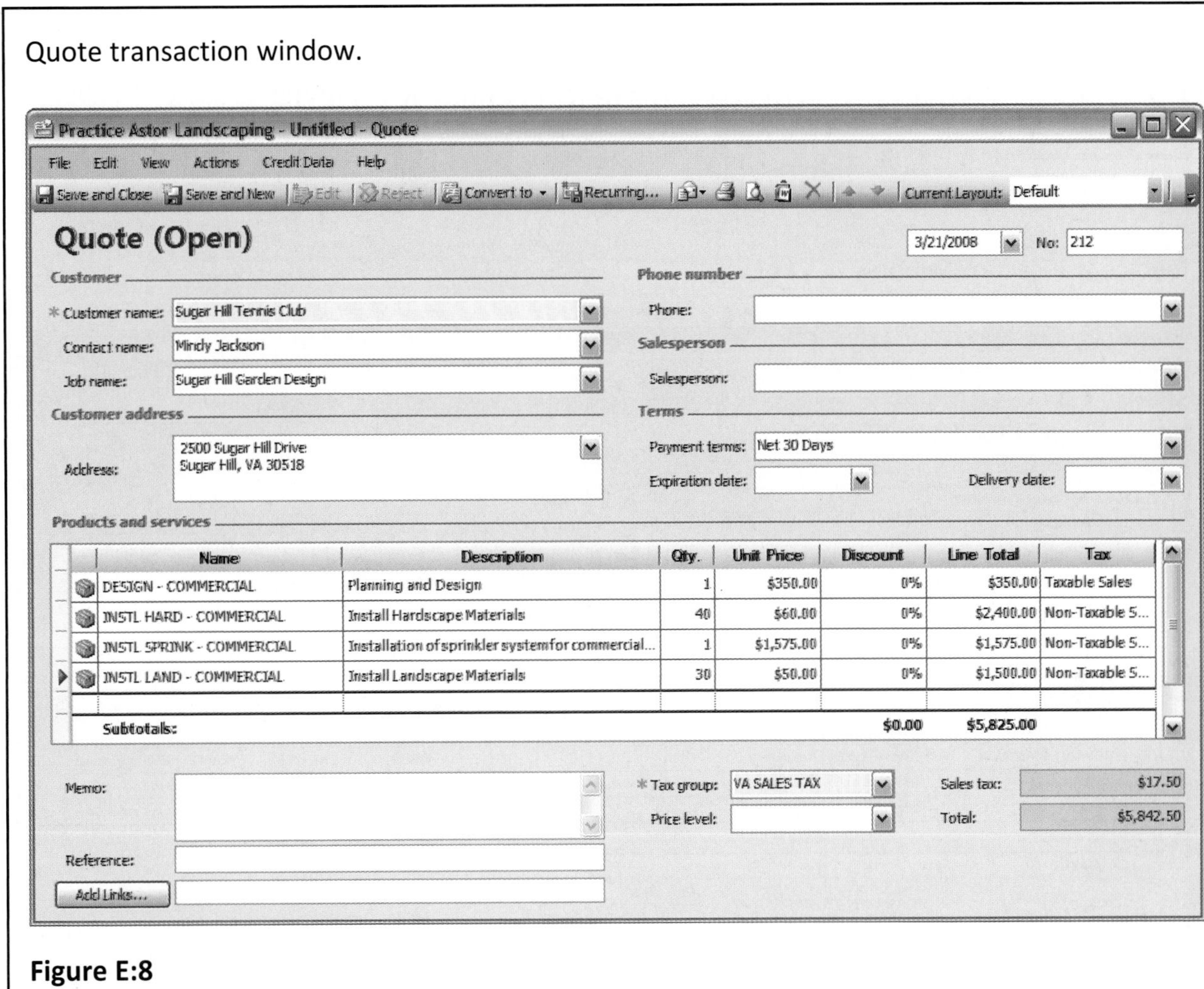

Figure E:8

CREATE A SALES INVOICE USING A QUOTE

Invoice transaction window.

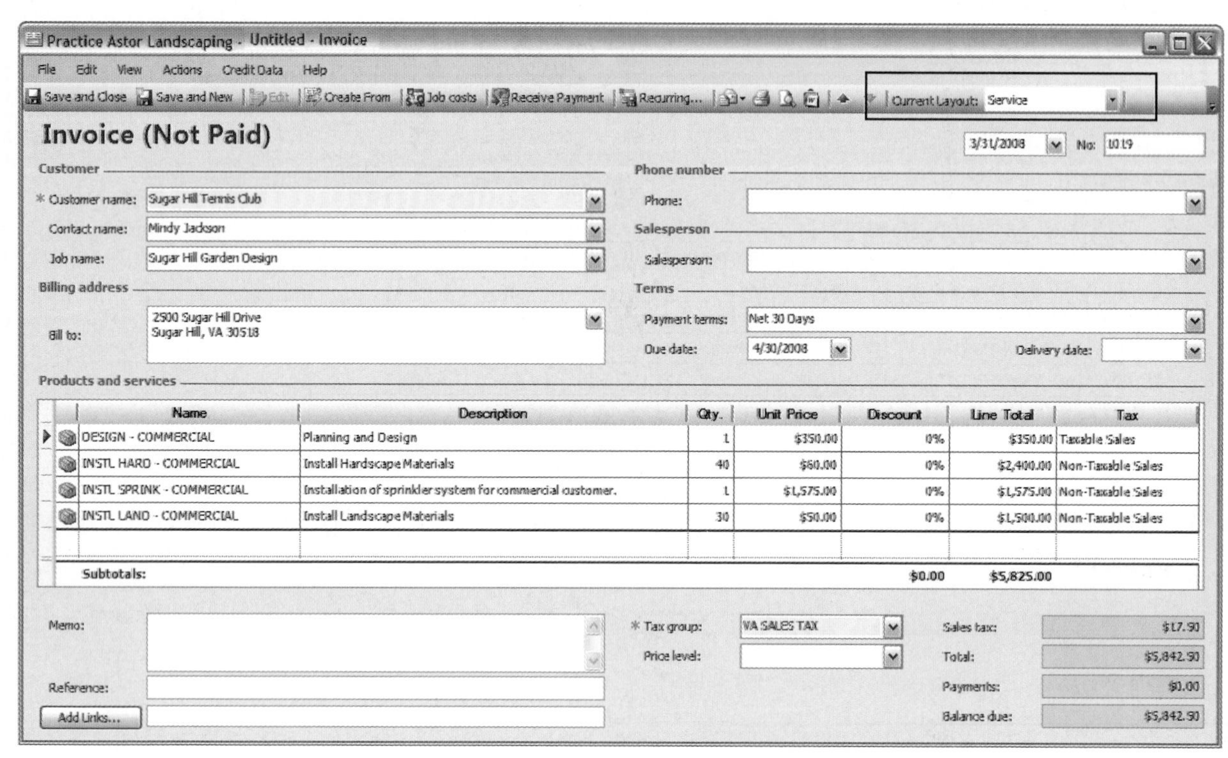

Figure E:9

Updated job.

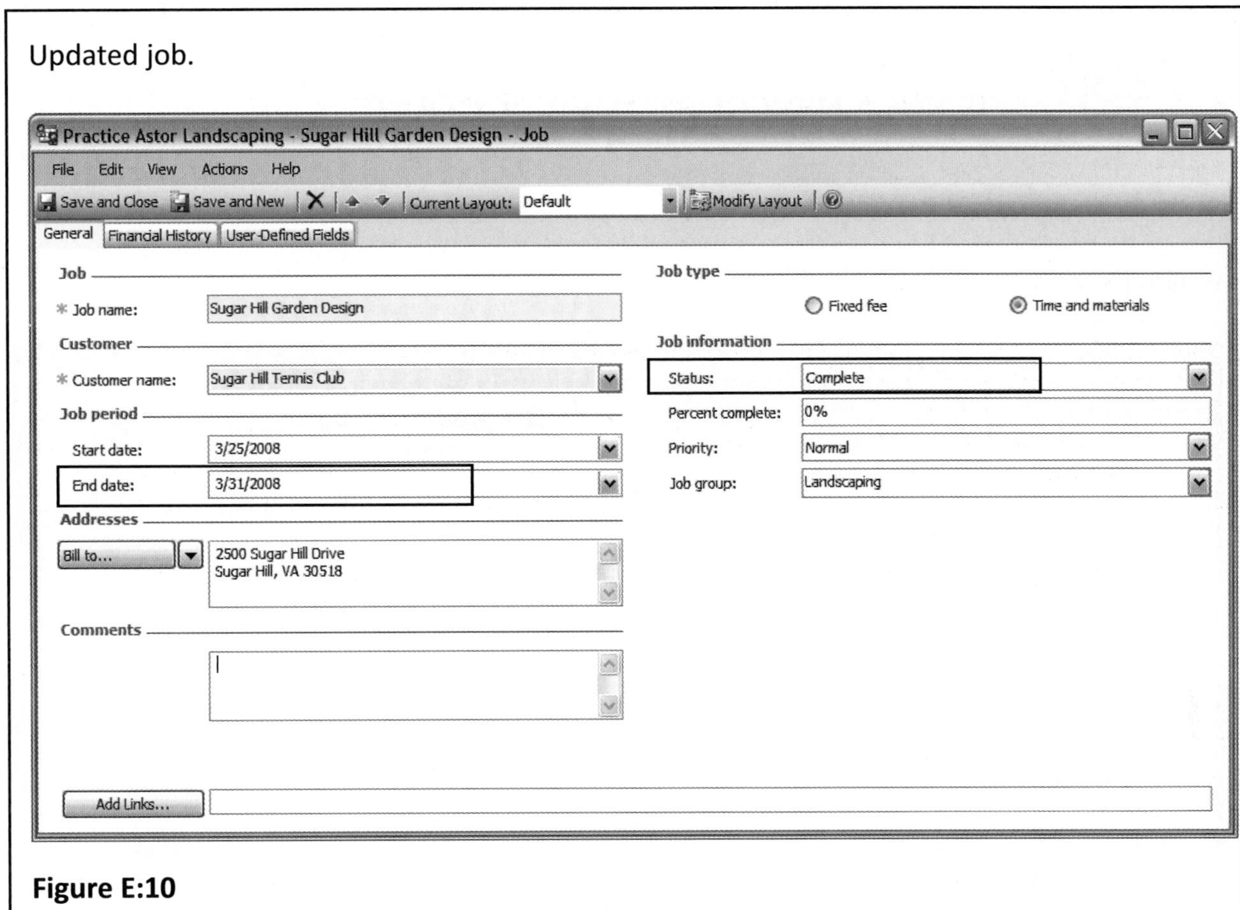

Figure E:10

CREATE A NEW CUSTOMER ACCOUNT

General information.

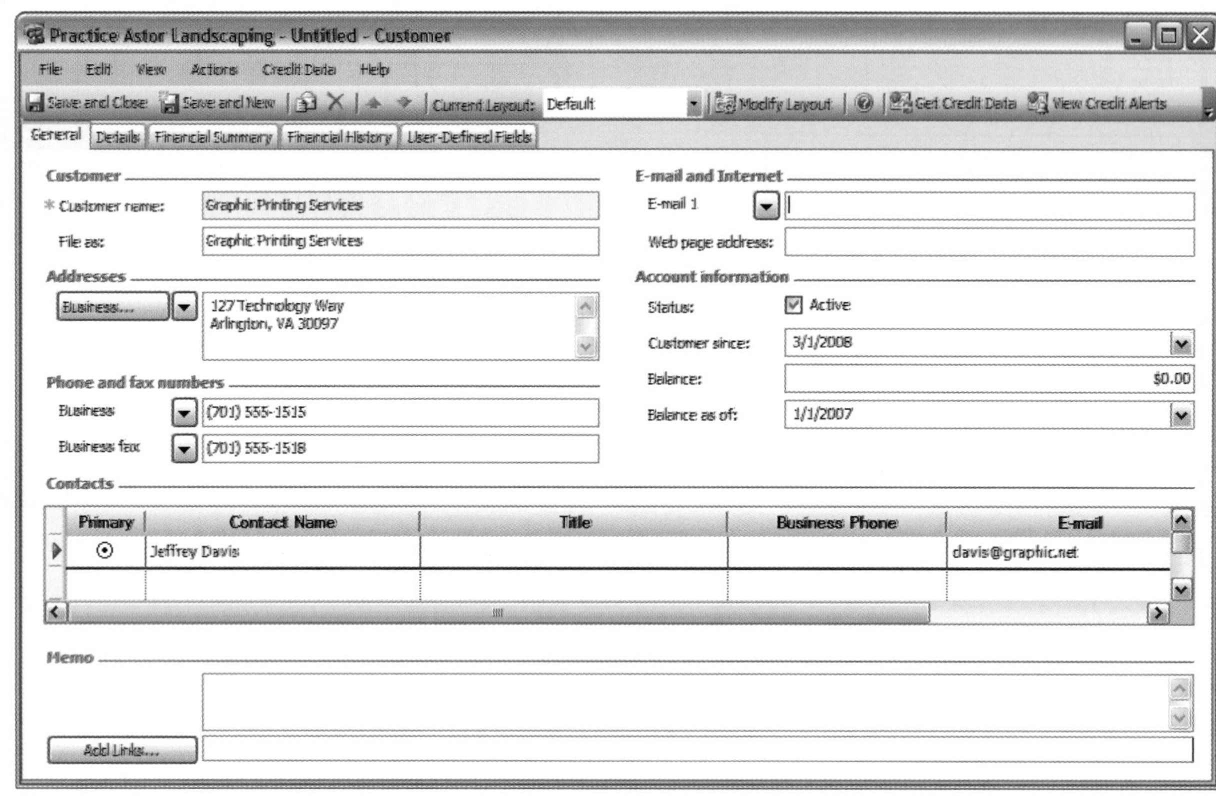

Figure E:11

Details information.

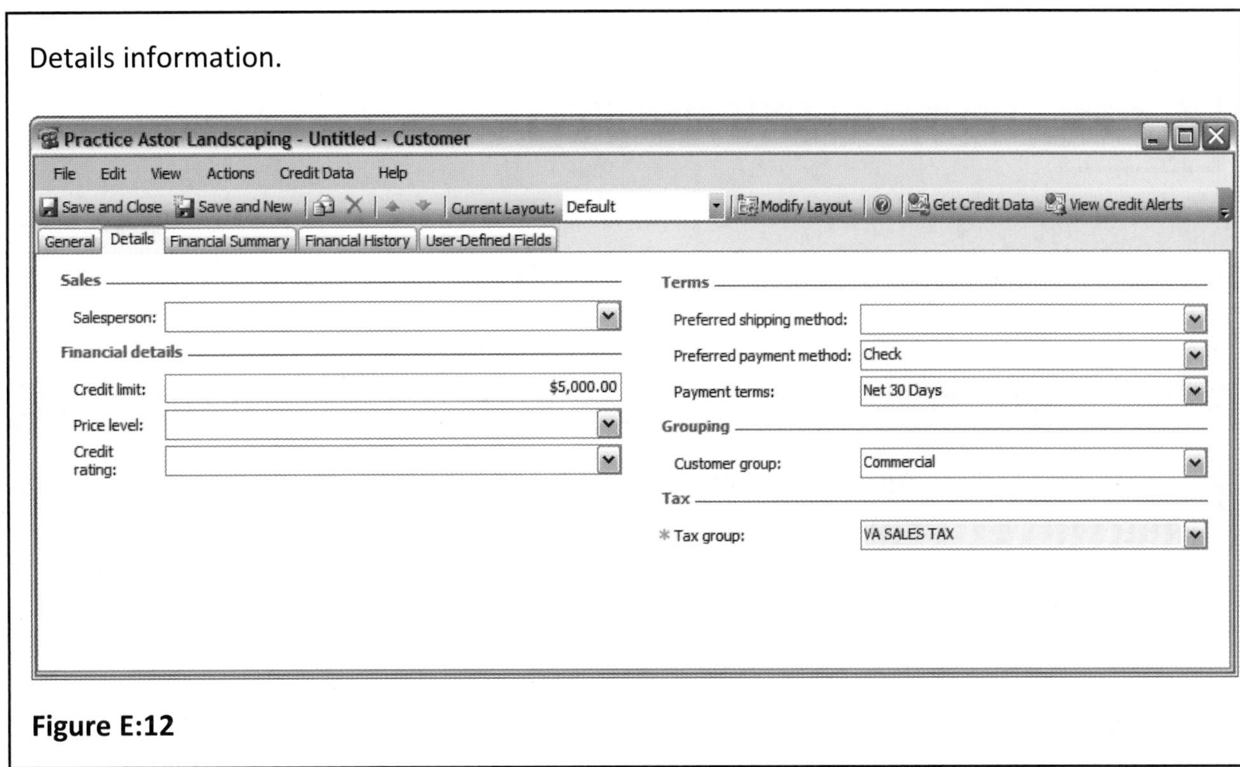

Figure E:12

INVOICE A CUSTOMER JOB

You select only Jeff Henderson's hours in the Time and Materials window to create the following invoice.

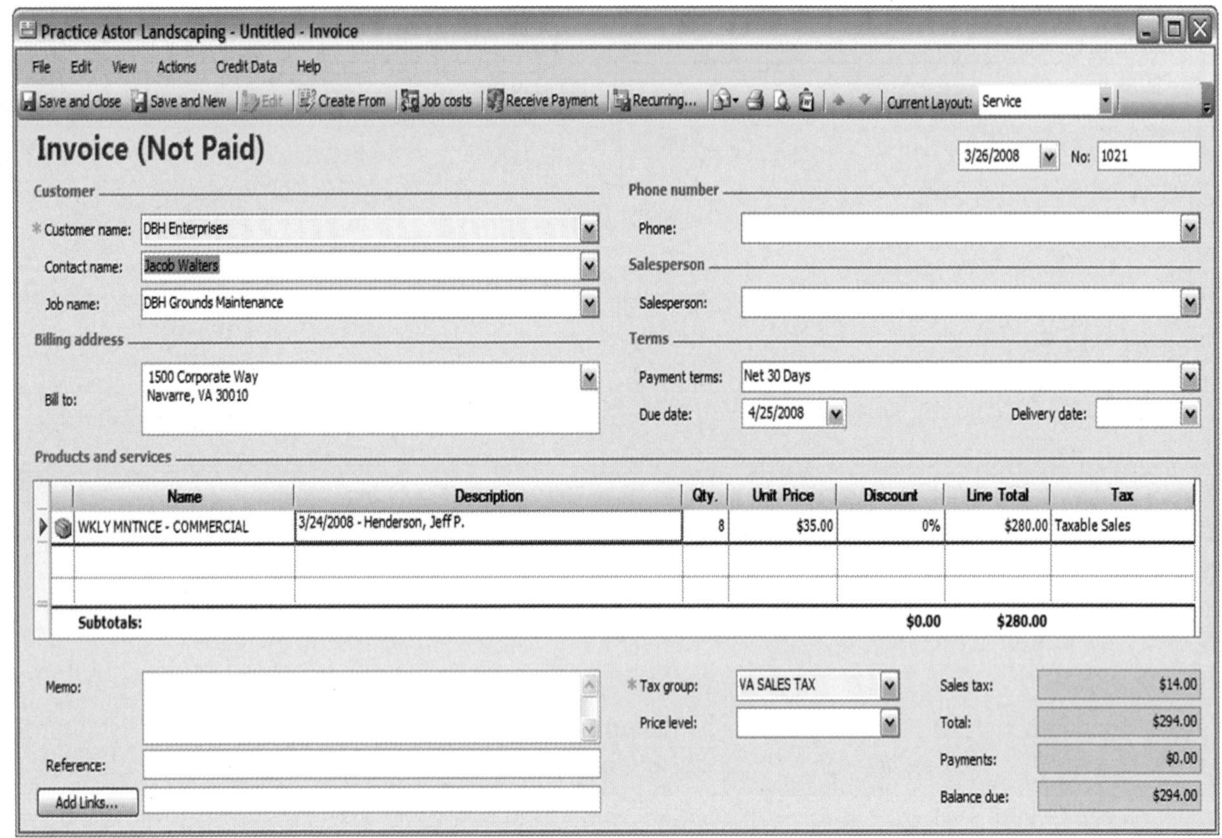

Figure E:13

CREATE A JOB REPORT

Profitability by Job Detail for Silver Homes. This report shows that all costs have been billed and that the company had a profit margin of 59.12 percent, assuming that standard costs reflect actual wages paid to employees.

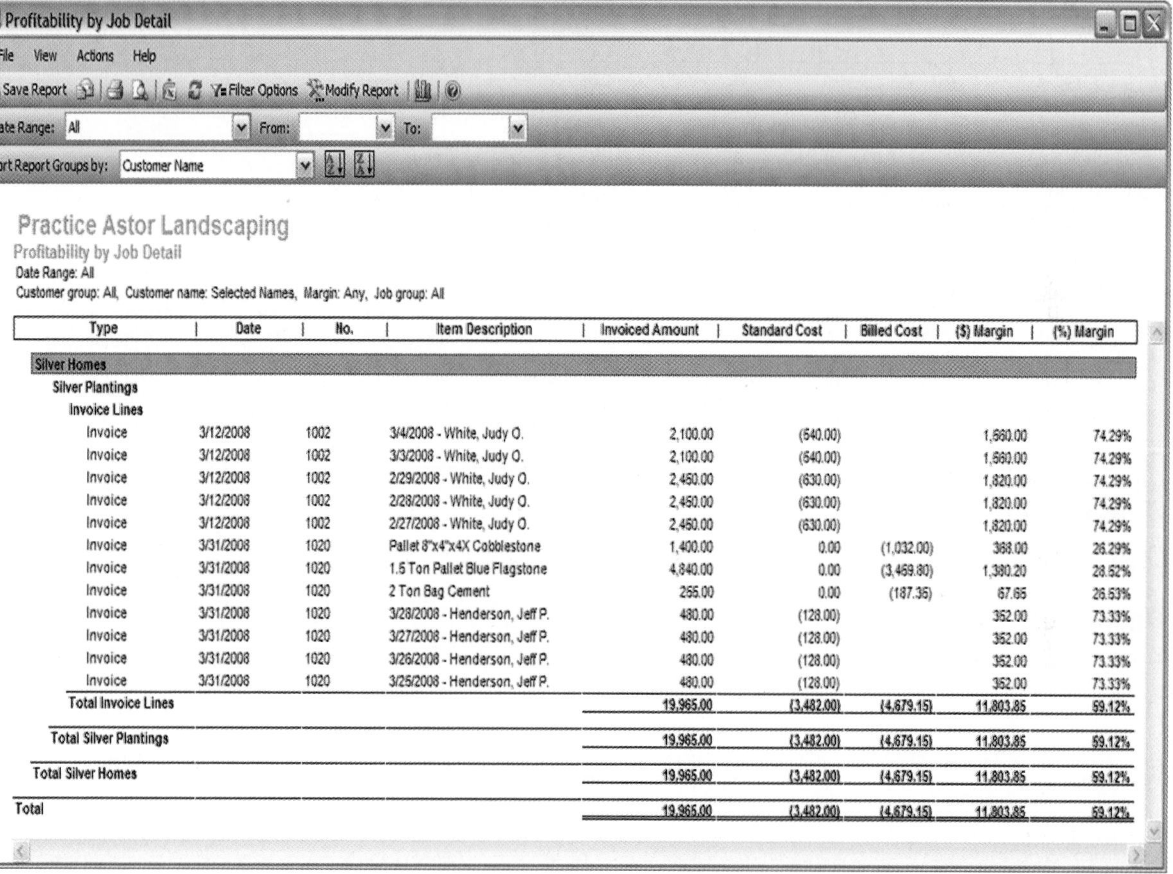

Practice Astor Landscaping
Profitability by Job Detail
Date Range: All
Customer group: All, Customer name: Selected Names, Margin: Any, Job group: All

Type	Date	No.	Item Description	Invoiced Amount	Standard Cost	Billed Cost	($) Margin	(%) Margin
Silver Homes								
Silver Plantings								
Invoice Lines								
Invoice	3/12/2008	1002	3/4/2008 - White, Judy O.	2,100.00	(540.00)		1,560.00	74.29%
Invoice	3/12/2008	1002	3/3/2008 - White, Judy O.	2,100.00	(640.00)		1,560.00	74.29%
Invoice	3/12/2008	1002	2/29/2008 - White, Judy O.	2,460.00	(630.00)		1,820.00	74.29%
Invoice	3/12/2008	1002	2/28/2008 - White, Judy O.	2,460.00	(630.00)		1,820.00	74.29%
Invoice	3/12/2008	1002	2/27/2008 - White, Judy O.	2,460.00	(630.00)		1,820.00	74.29%
Invoice	3/31/2008	1020	Pallet 8"x4"x4X Cobblestone	1,400.00	0.00	(1,032.00)	368.00	26.29%
Invoice	3/31/2008	1020	1.5 Ton Pallet Blue Flagstone	4,840.00	0.00	(3,469.80)	1,380.20	28.52%
Invoice	3/31/2008	1020	2 Ton Bag Cement	255.00	0.00	(187.35)	67.65	26.53%
Invoice	3/31/2008	1020	3/28/2008 - Henderson, Jeff P.	480.00	(128.00)		352.00	73.33%
Invoice	3/31/2008	1020	3/27/2008 - Henderson, Jeff P.	480.00	(128.00)		352.00	73.33%
Invoice	3/31/2008	1020	3/26/2008 - Henderson, Jeff P.	480.00	(128.00)		352.00	73.33%
Invoice	3/31/2008	1020	3/25/2008 - Henderson, Jeff P.	480.00	(128.00)		352.00	73.33%
Total Invoice Lines				19,965.00	(3,482.00)	(4,679.15)	11,803.85	59.12%
Total Silver Plantings				19,965.00	(3,482.00)	(4,679.15)	11,803.85	59.12%
Total Silver Homes				19,965.00	(3,482.00)	(4,679.15)	11,803.85	59.12%
Total				19,965.00	(3,482.00)	(4,679.15)	11,803.85	59.12%

Figure E:14

Job Estimates vs. Actuals Detail for Silver Homes. This report shows that the estimated job costs came close to the actual costs.

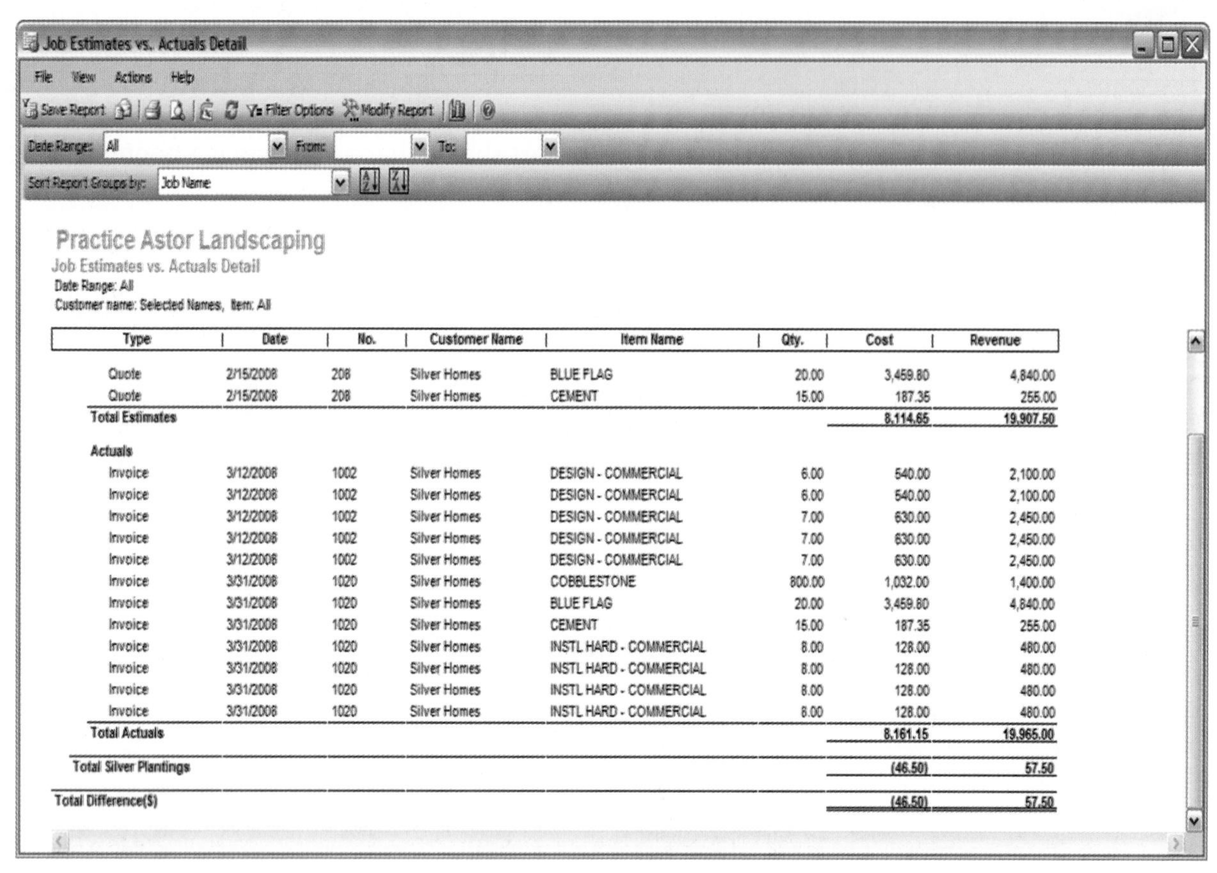

Practice Astor Landscaping
Job Estimates vs. Actuals Detail
Date Range: All
Customer name: Selected Names, Item: All

Type	Date	No.	Customer Name	Item Name	Qty.	Cost	Revenue
Quote	2/15/2008	208	Silver Homes	BLUE FLAG	20.00	3,459.80	4,840.00
Quote	2/15/2008	208	Silver Homes	CEMENT	15.00	187.35	255.00
Total Estimates						8,114.65	19,907.50
Actuals							
Invoice	3/12/2008	1002	Silver Homes	DESIGN - COMMERCIAL	6.00	540.00	2,100.00
Invoice	3/12/2008	1002	Silver Homes	DESIGN - COMMERCIAL	6.00	540.00	2,100.00
Invoice	3/12/2008	1002	Silver Homes	DESIGN - COMMERCIAL	7.00	630.00	2,450.00
Invoice	3/12/2008	1002	Silver Homes	DESIGN - COMMERCIAL	7.00	630.00	2,450.00
Invoice	3/12/2008	1002	Silver Homes	DESIGN - COMMERCIAL	7.00	630.00	2,450.00
Invoice	3/31/2008	1020	Silver Homes	COBBLESTONE	800.00	1,032.00	1,400.00
Invoice	3/31/2008	1020	Silver Homes	BLUE FLAG	20.00	3,459.80	4,840.00
Invoice	3/31/2008	1020	Silver Homes	CEMENT	15.00	187.35	255.00
Invoice	3/31/2008	1020	Silver Homes	INSTL HARD - COMMERCIAL	8.00	128.00	480.00
Invoice	3/31/2008	1020	Silver Homes	INSTL HARD - COMMERCIAL	8.00	128.00	480.00
Invoice	3/31/2008	1020	Silver Homes	INSTL HARD - COMMERCIAL	8.00	128.00	480.00
Invoice	3/31/2008	1020	Silver Homes	INSTL HARD - COMMERCIAL	8.00	128.00	480.00
Total Actuals						8,161.15	19,965.00
Total Silver Plantings						(46.50)	57.50
Total Difference($)						(46.50)	57.50

Figure E:15

RECORD CUSTOMER PAYMENTS

Transaction Journal filtered to become a Cash Receipts Journal.

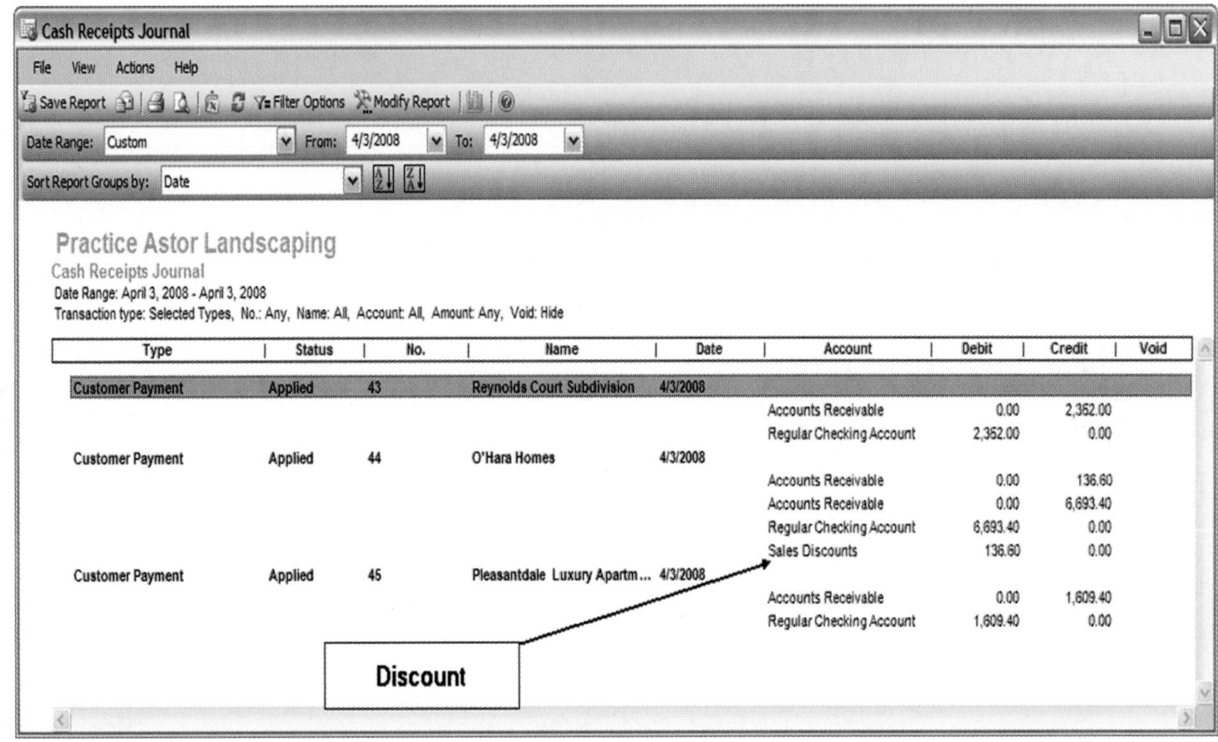

Practice Astor Landscaping
Cash Receipts Journal
Date Range: April 3, 2008 - April 3, 2008
Transaction type: Selected Types, No.: Any, Name: All, Account: All, Amount: Any, Void: Hide

Type	Status	No.	Name	Date	Account	Debit	Credit	Void
Customer Payment	Applied	43	Reynolds Court Subdivision	4/3/2008				
					Accounts Receivable	0.00	2,362.00	
					Regular Checking Account	2,362.00	0.00	
Customer Payment	Applied	44	O'Hara Homes	4/3/2008				
					Accounts Receivable	0.00	136.60	
					Accounts Receivable	0.00	6,693.40	
					Regular Checking Account	6,693.40	0.00	
					Sales Discounts	136.60	0.00	
Customer Payment	Applied	45	Pleasantdale Luxury Apartm...	4/3/2008				
					Accounts Receivable	0.00	1,609.40	
					Regular Checking Account	1,609.40	0.00	

Figure E:16

CHAPTER 5

ENTER PURCHASE ORDERS

PO to Calvert Stone Supplies.

Practice Astor Landscaping - Untitled - Purchase Order

File Edit View Actions Help

Save and Close | Save and New | Receive Items | Recurring... | Reorder Inventory | Current Layout: Default | Modify Layout

Purchase Order (Not Received)

3/25/2008 No: 3

Vendor

Vendor name: Calvert Stone Supplies

Contact name: Brenda Calvert

Vendor address

Address: 554 Ashford Ctr. N
Arlington, VA 30301

Shipping address

Ship to: 1505 Pavilion Place, Suite C
Arlington, VA 30093

Phone number

Phone:

Terms

Payment terms: 2% 10 Net 30 Days

Shipping terms:

Shipping method:

Delivery date:

Items and expenses

Name	Description	On Hand	Qty.	Unit Price	Line Total	Job Name	Billable
MULCH	6 Cu Ft Bags Mulch		40	$4.99	$199.60	Sugar Grounds Maintenance	☑

Memo:

Reference:

Add Links...

Total: $199.60

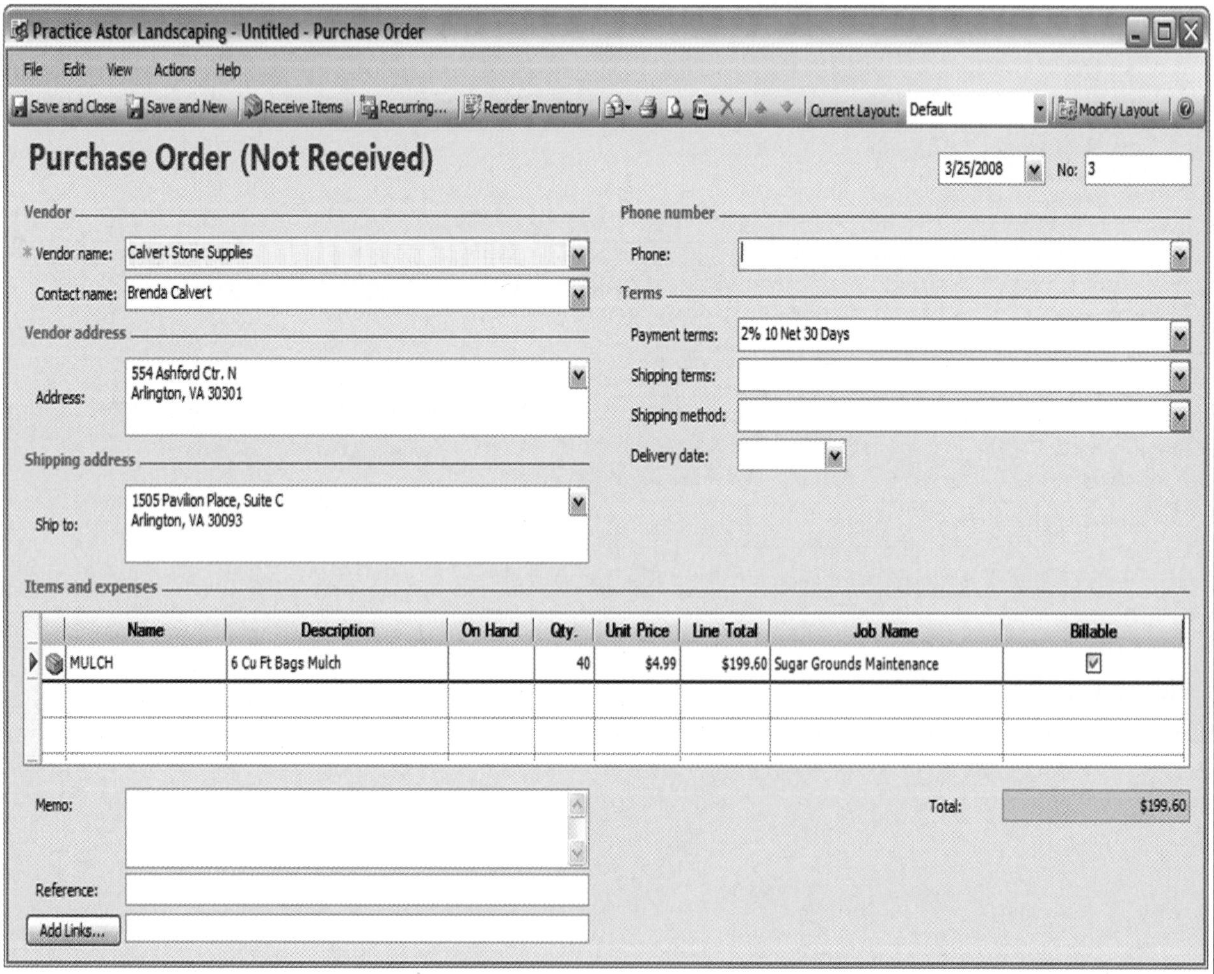

Figure E:17

PO to Southern Garden Wholesale. Printed POs are not illustrated.

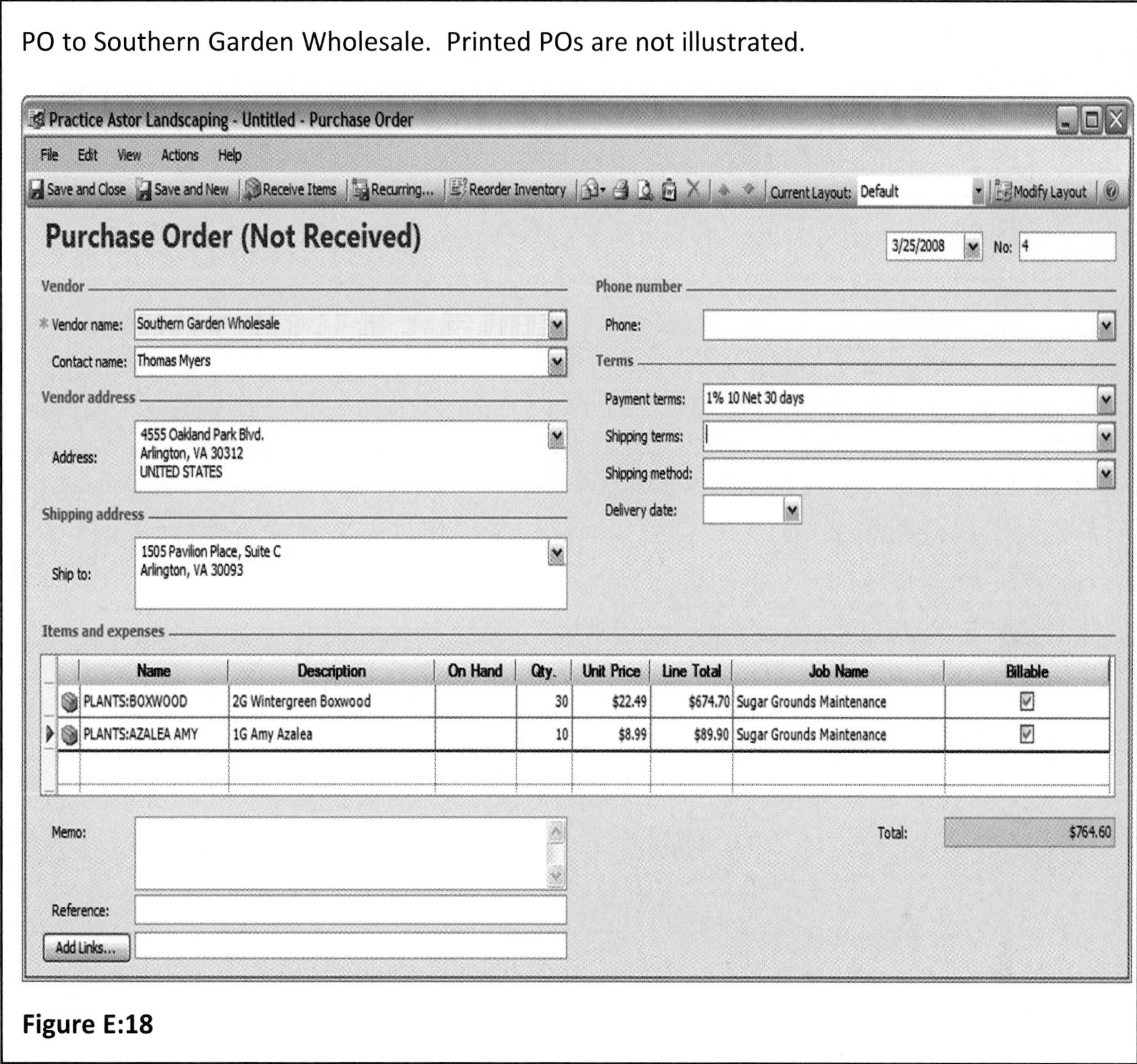

Figure E:18

ENTER VENDOR RECEIPTS AND BILLS FOR PURCHASE ORDERS

Purchases Journal for March 27, 2008.

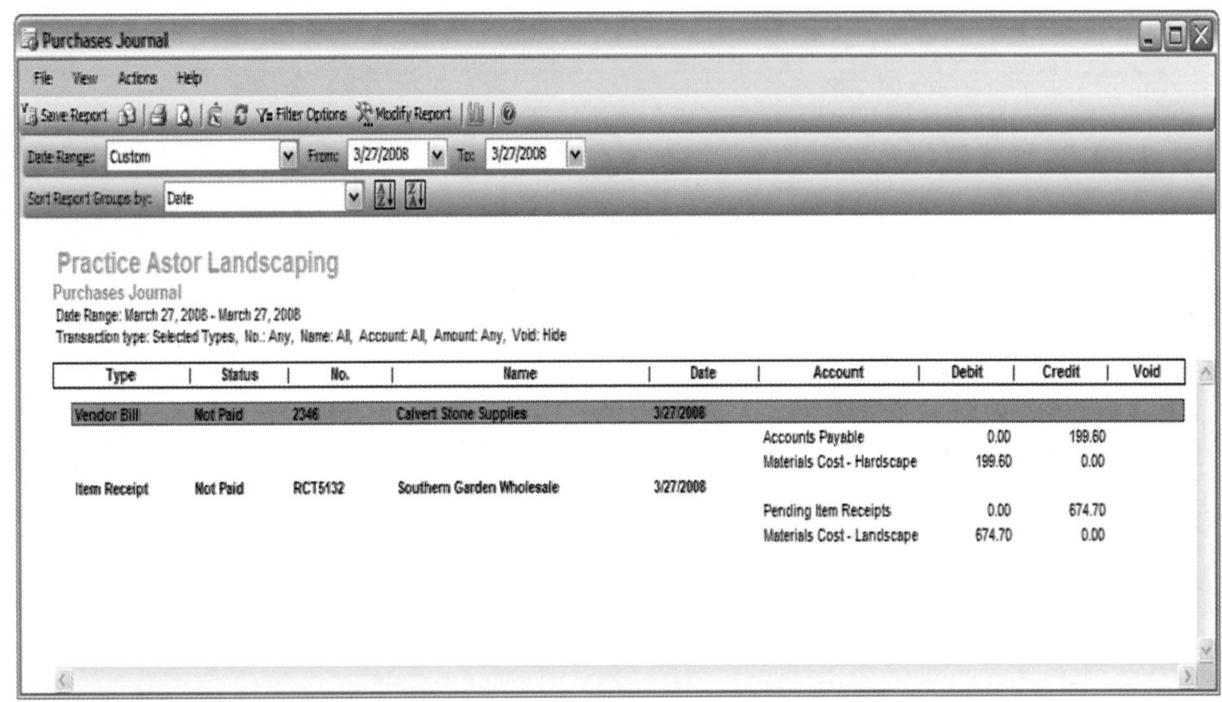

Practice Astor Landscaping
Purchases Journal
Date Range: March 27, 2008 - March 27, 2008
Transaction type: Selected Types, No.: Any, Name: All, Account: All, Amount: Any, Void: Hide

Type	Status	No.	Name	Date	Account	Debit	Credit	Void
Vendor Bill	Not Paid	2346	Calvert Stone Supplies	3/27/2008				
					Accounts Payable	0.00	199.60	
					Materials Cost - Hardscape	199.60	0.00	
Item Receipt	Not Paid	RCT5132	Southern Garden Wholesale	3/27/2008				
					Pending Item Receipts	0.00	674.70	
					Materials Cost - Landscape	674.70	0.00	

Figure E:19

ENTER VENDOR BILL FOR VENDOR RECEIPT

Purchases Journal for March 28.

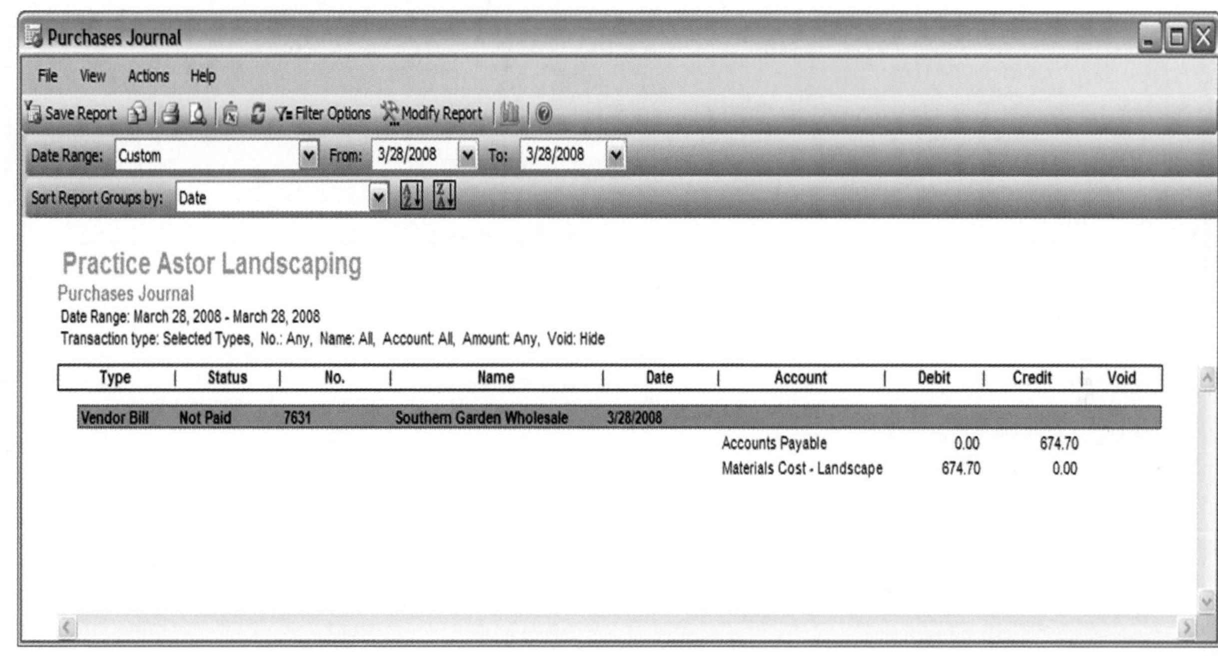

Figure E:20

CREATE A NEW VENDOR

General information for Jackson Hyland Tax Service.

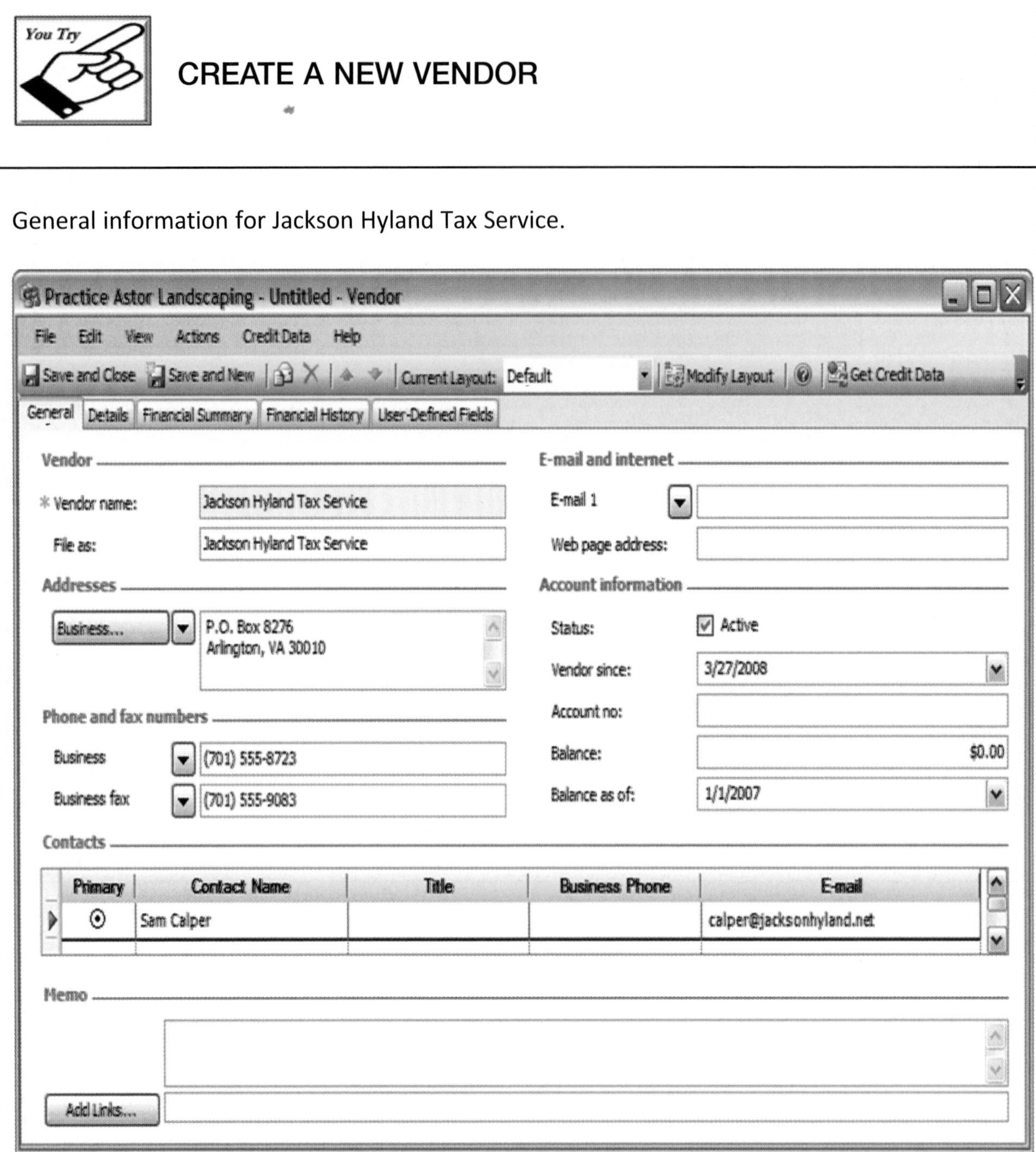

Figure E:21

Details for Jackson Hyland Tax Service.

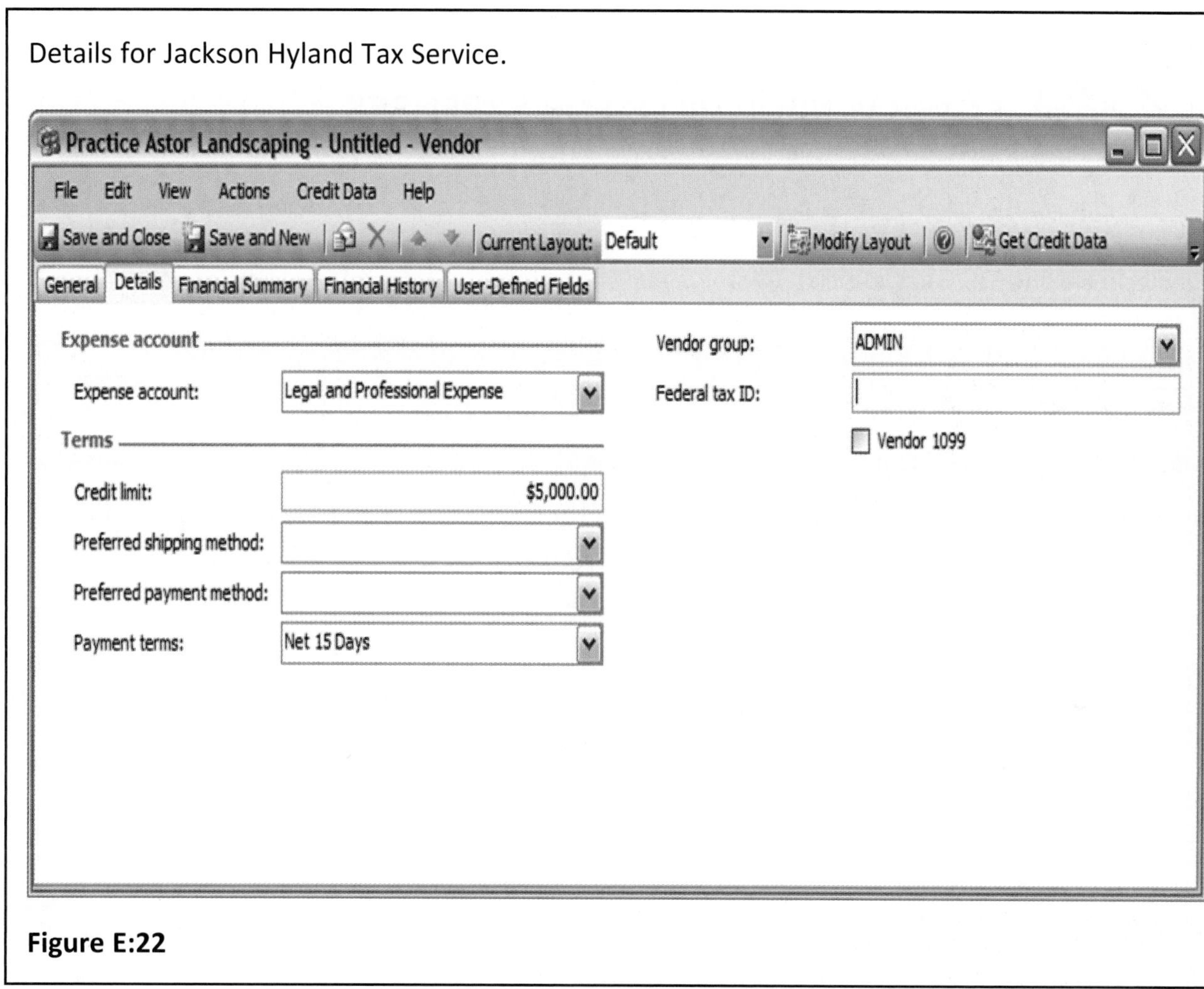

Figure E:22

ENTER VENDOR BILLS FOR EXPENSES

Jackson Hyland Tax Service bill.

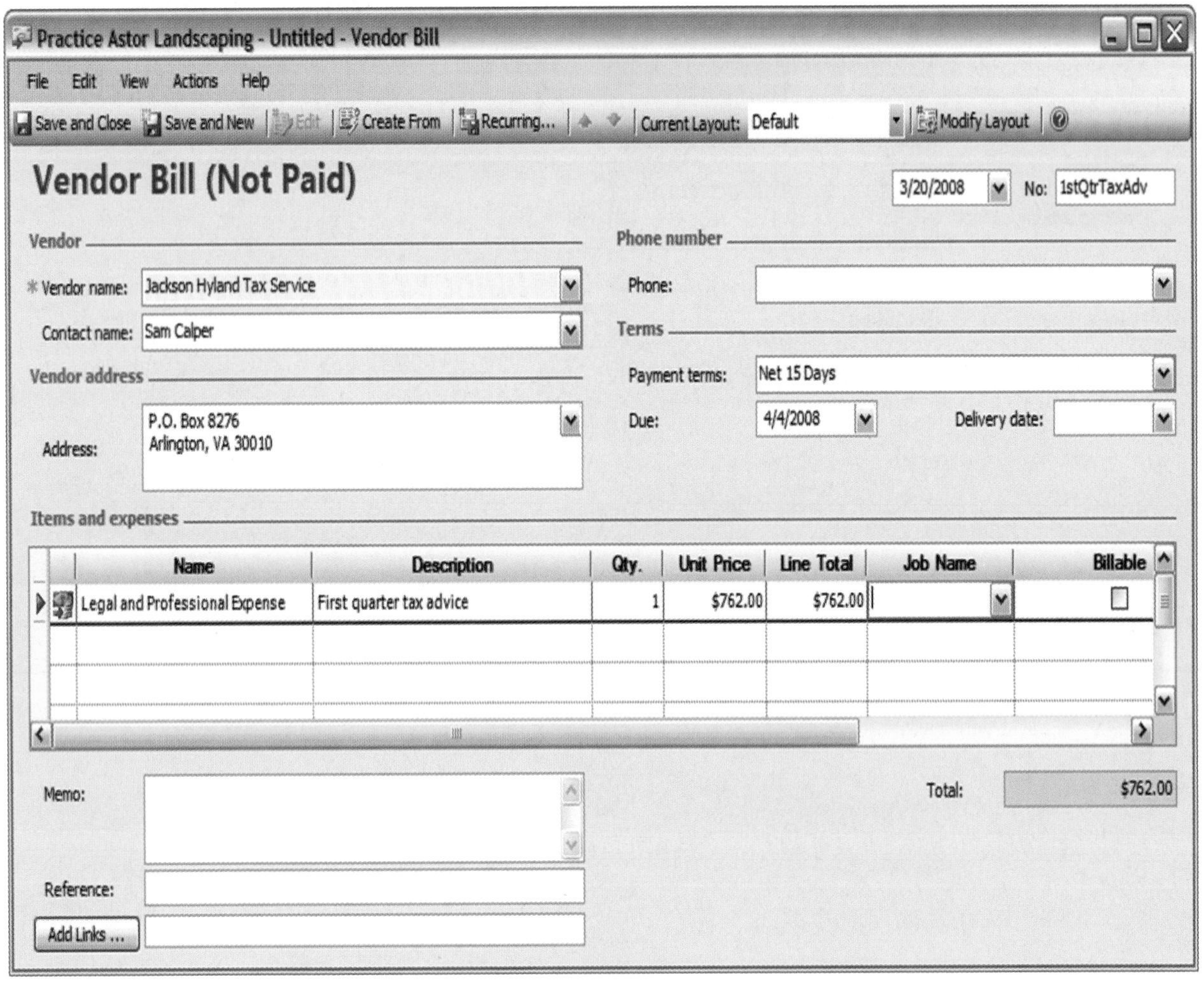

Practice Astor Landscaping - Untitled - Vendor Bill

File Edit View Actions Help

Save and Close | Save and New | Edit | Create From | Recurring... | Current Layout: Default | Modify Layout

Vendor Bill (Not Paid) 3/20/2008 No: 1stQtrTaxAdv

Vendor

* Vendor name: Jackson Hyland Tax Service
Contact name: Sam Calper

Vendor address

Address: P.O. Box 8276
Arlington, VA 30010

Phone number

Phone:

Terms

Payment terms: Net 15 Days
Due: 4/4/2008 Delivery date:

Items and expenses

Name	Description	Qty.	Unit Price	Line Total	Job Name	Billable
Legal and Professional Expense	First quarter tax advice	1	$762.00	$762.00		☐

Memo:

Total: $762.00

Reference:

Add Links ...

Figure E:23

You Try

PAY VENDORS

Payments report.

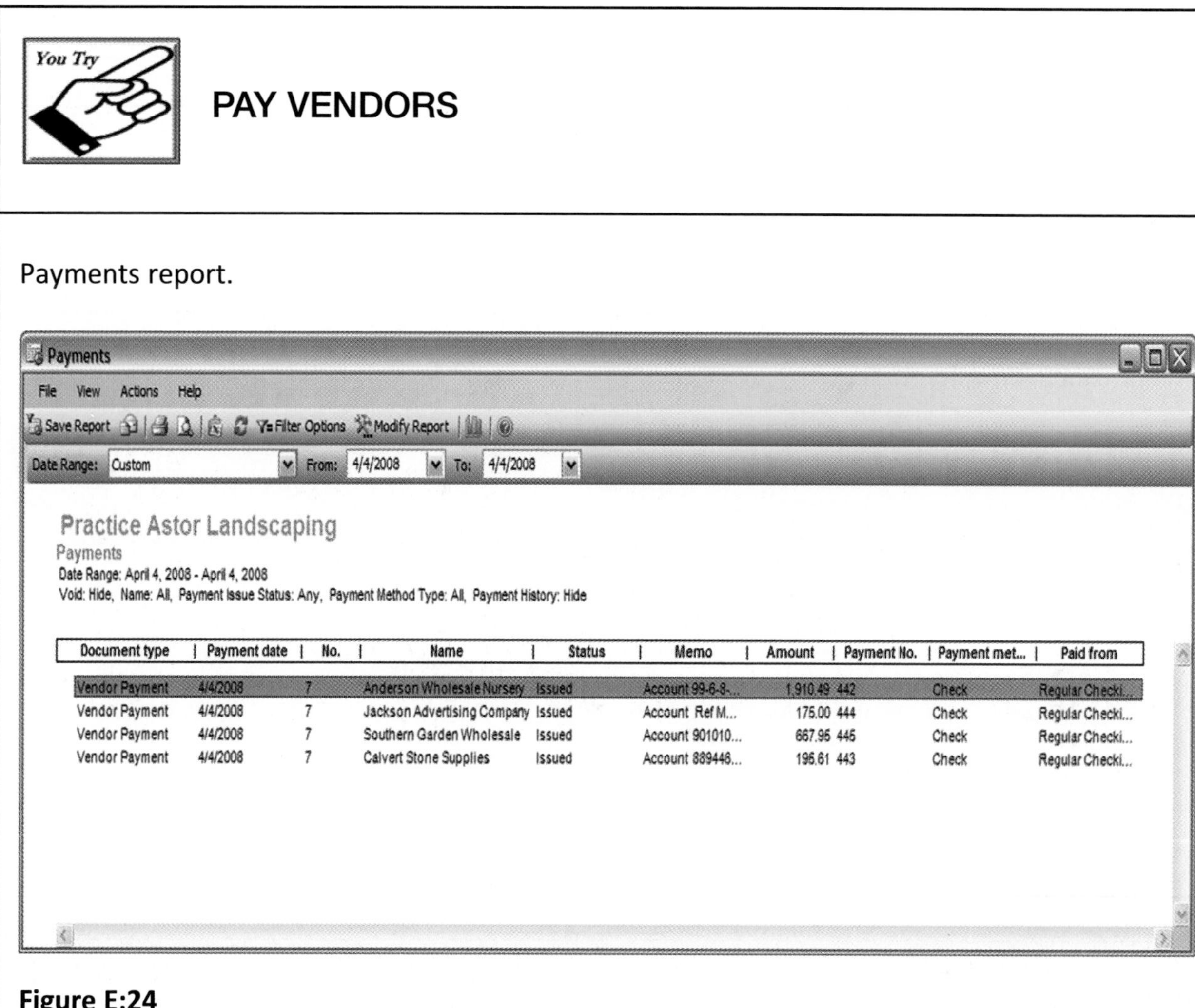

Practice Astor Landscaping

Payments

Date Range: April 4, 2008 - April 4, 2008

Void: Hide, Name: All, Payment Issue Status: Any, Payment Method Type: All, Payment History: Hide

Document type	Payment date	No.	Name	Status	Memo	Amount	Payment No.	Payment met...	Paid from
Vendor Payment	4/4/2008	7	Anderson Wholesale Nursery	Issued	Account 99-6-8-...	1,910.49	442	Check	Regular Checki...
Vendor Payment	4/4/2008	7	Jackson Advertising Company	Issued	Account Ref M...	175.00	444	Check	Regular Checki...
Vendor Payment	4/4/2008	7	Southern Garden Wholesale	Issued	Account 901010...	667.95	445	Check	Regular Checki...
Vendor Payment	4/4/2008	7	Calvert Stone Supplies	Issued	Account 889446...	196.61	443	Check	Regular Checki...

Figure E:24

CHAPTER 6

WORKING WITH TIMESHEETS

Roy Dillion's timesheet.

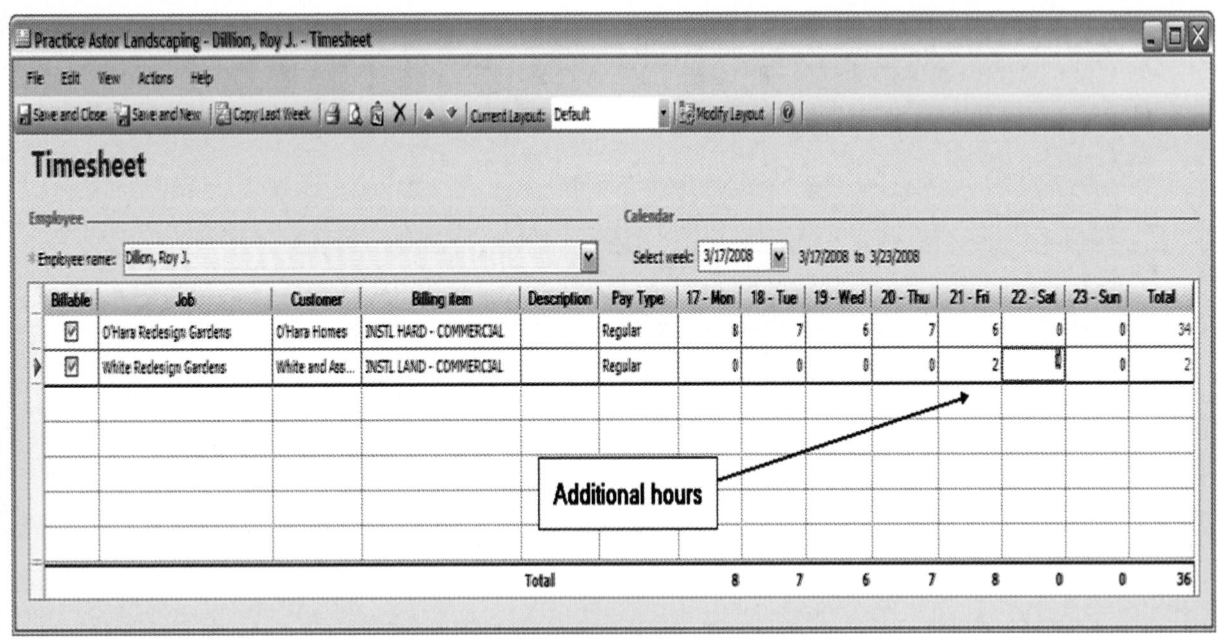

Figure E:25

CREATE CHECKS FOR PAYROLL TAXES

Payments report for April 2, 2008.

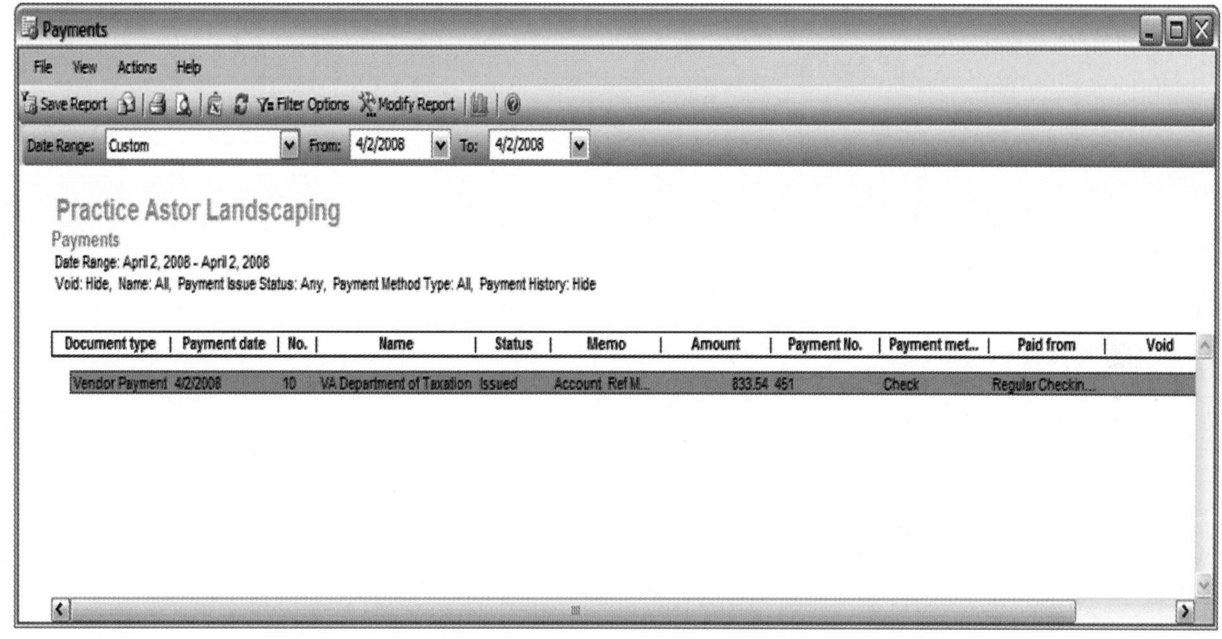

Figure E:26

CHAPTER 7

FINISH RECORDING MARCH ADJUSTING ENTRIES

Entry that accrues wages and reverses the accrual. You probably posted two separate entries because we haven't emphasized the feature that lets you enter multiple transactions with different dates.

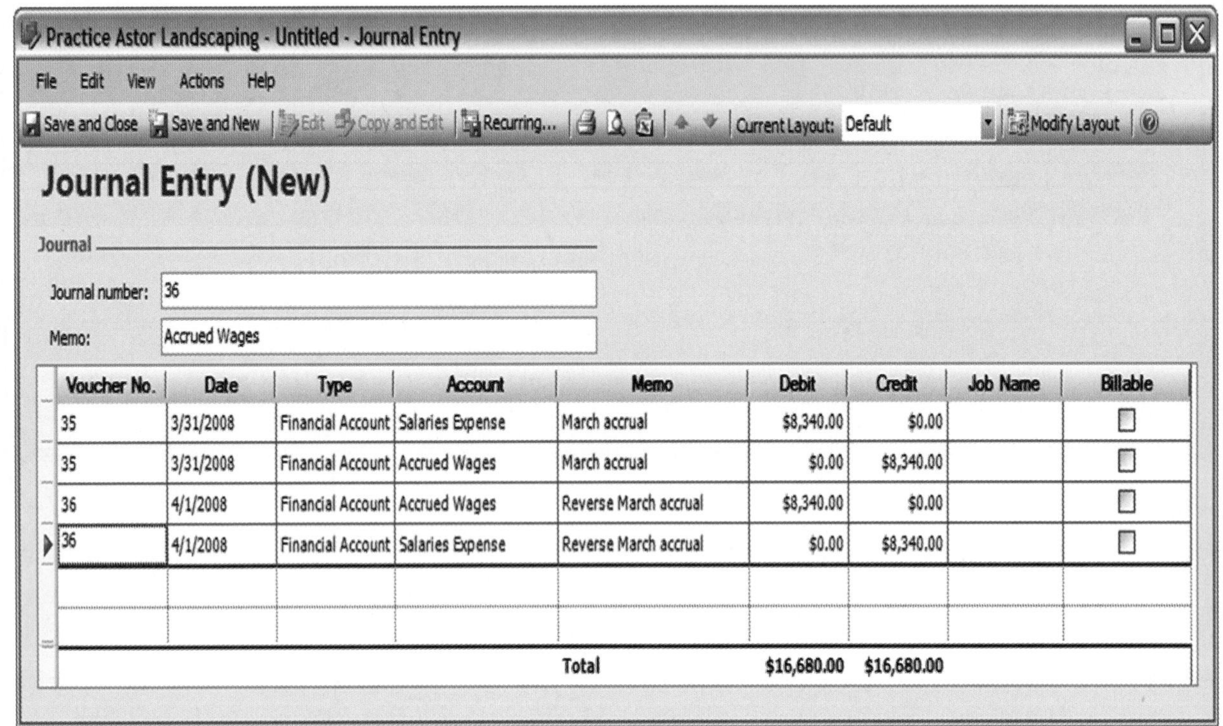

Figure E:27

RECONCILE THE PAYROLL CHECKING ACCOUNT

Payroll Reconciliation Detail report.

Practice Astor Landscaping
Reconciliation Detail
Amount: Any, Bank Account: Payroll Checking Account, Statement date: 3/31/2008

Type	Date	No.	Name	Amount
Payroll Checking Account				
Opening Balance				**447.53**
Cleared Deposits				
Fund Transfer	3/10/2008	20		10,800.00
Fund Transfer	3/24/2008	34		12,000.00
Total Cleared Deposits				**22,800.00**
Cleared Withdrawals				
Payroll Check	3/10/2008	721	Dillion, Roy J.	(793.93)
Payroll Check	3/10/2008	722	Folse, Jan B.	(642.80)
Payroll Check	3/10/2008	723	Greene, Kellie I.	(1,839.29)
Payroll Check	3/10/2008	724	Hardman, Alan	(843.81)
Payroll Check	3/10/2008	725	Hayes, Mike E.	(328.10)
Payroll Check	3/10/2008	726	Henderson, Jeff P.	(804.76)
Payroll Check	3/10/2008	727	Murray, Monica D.	(950.50)
Payroll Check	3/10/2008	728	Ramez, Victor M.	(587.12)
Payroll Check	3/10/2008	729	Ruland, Seth N.	(2,344.28)
Payroll Check	3/10/2008	730	White, Judy O.	(1,663.60)
Payroll Check	3/24/2008	738	Dillion, Roy J.	(717.15)
Payroll Check	3/24/2008	732	Folse, Jan B.	(642.80)
Payroll Check	3/24/2008	731	Hardman, Alan	(765.32)
Payroll Check	3/24/2008	736	Hayes, Mike E.	(530.98)
Payroll Check	3/24/2008	733	Henderson, Jeff P.	(728.98)
Payroll Check	3/24/2008	737	Murray, Monica D.	(950.50)
Payroll Check	3/24/2008	740	Ramez, Victor M.	(607.93)
Payroll Check	3/24/2008	739	Ruland, Seth N.	(2,344.28)
Payroll Check	3/24/2008	734	White, Judy O.	(1,663.60)
Payroll Check	3/24/2008	742	Greene, Kellie I.	(1,839.29)
Payroll Check	3/24/2008	741	Zickefoose, Jack A.	(384.20)
Bank Fee	3/31/2008	38		(28.30)
Total Cleared Withdrawals				**(22,001.52)**
Total Cleared Transactions				**798.48**
Reconciled Balance As Of Statement Date				**1,246.01**
Ending Balance				**1,246.01**

Figure E:28

CHAPTER 8

ENTER A NEW SALES ORDER

Chapple Law Offices sales order transaction. The printed order is not illustrated.

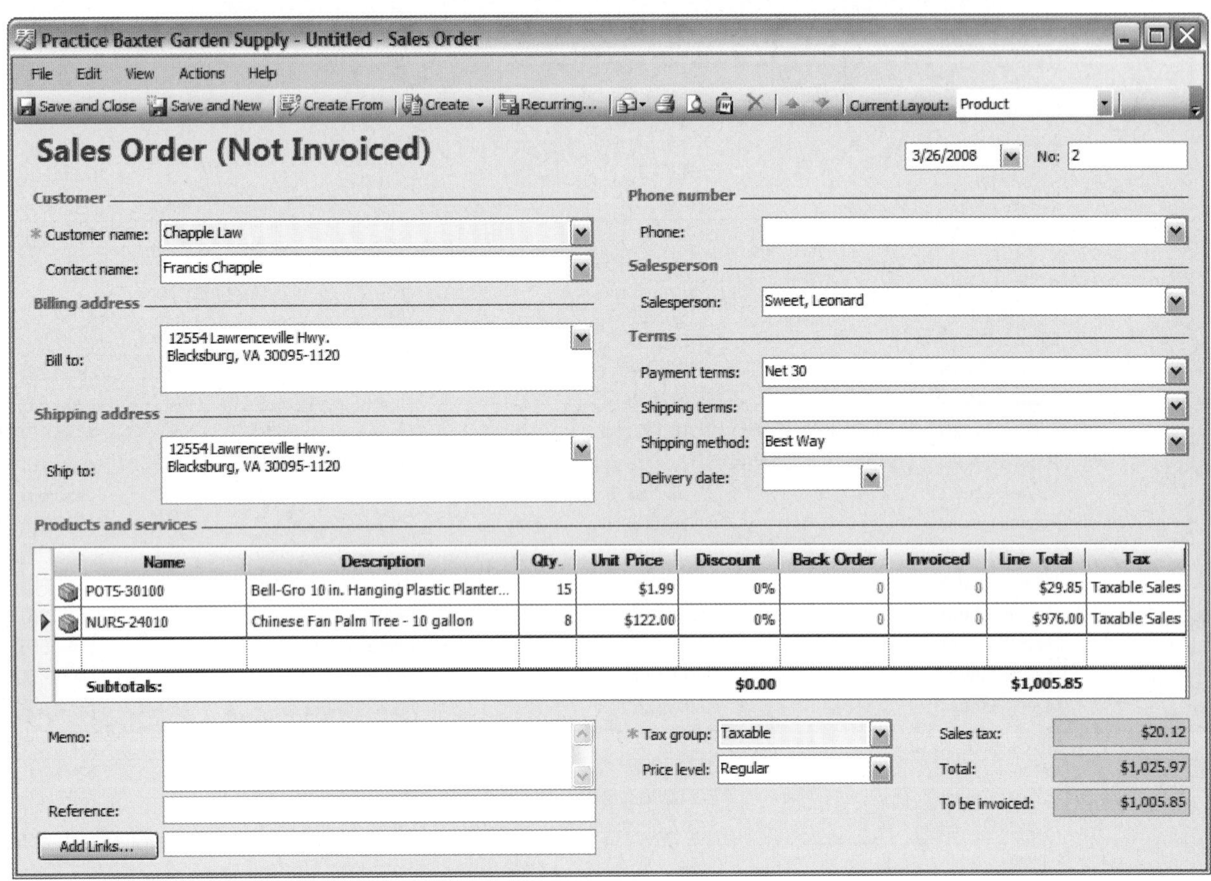

Figure E:29

CREATE A SALES INVOICE USING A SALES ORDER

Chapple Law invoice. The printed invoice is not illustrated.

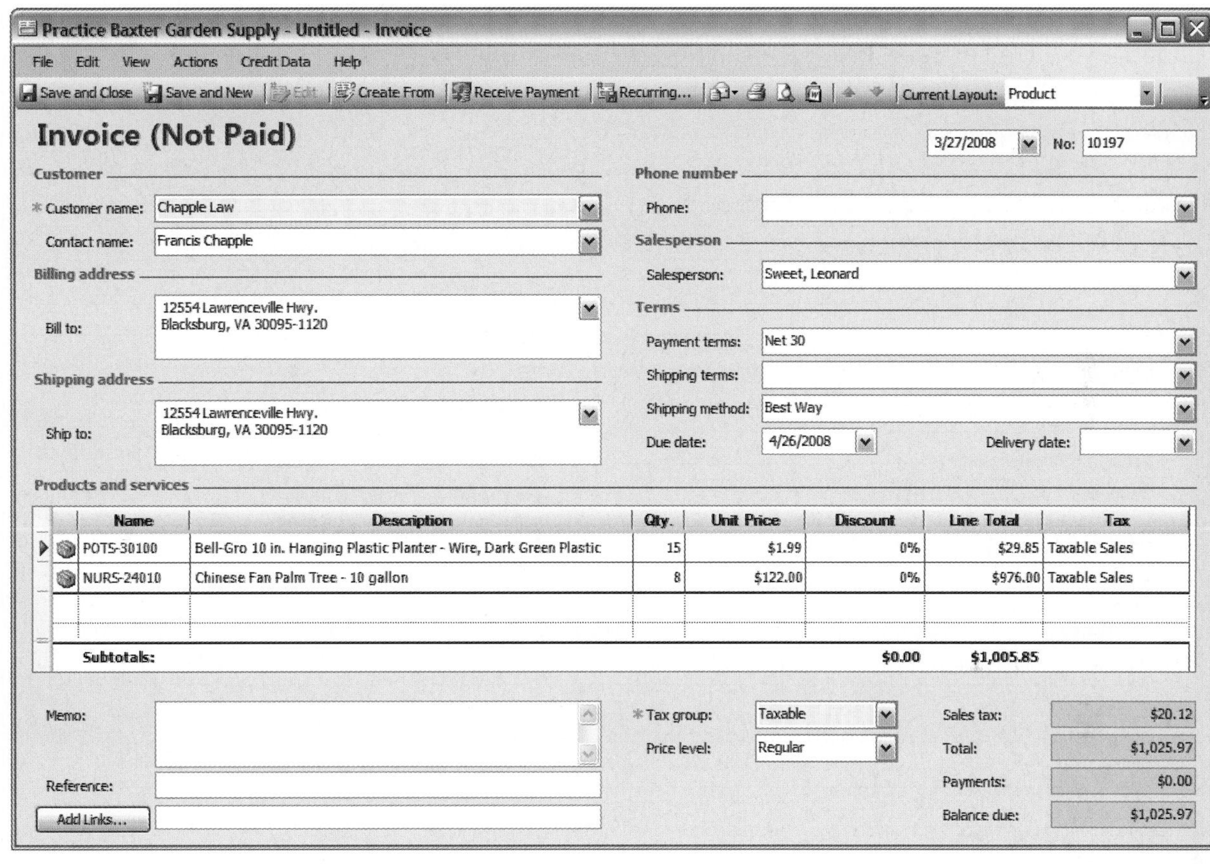

Figure E:30

CREATE A NEW CUSTOMER ACCOUNT

Frost Garden Center General tab.

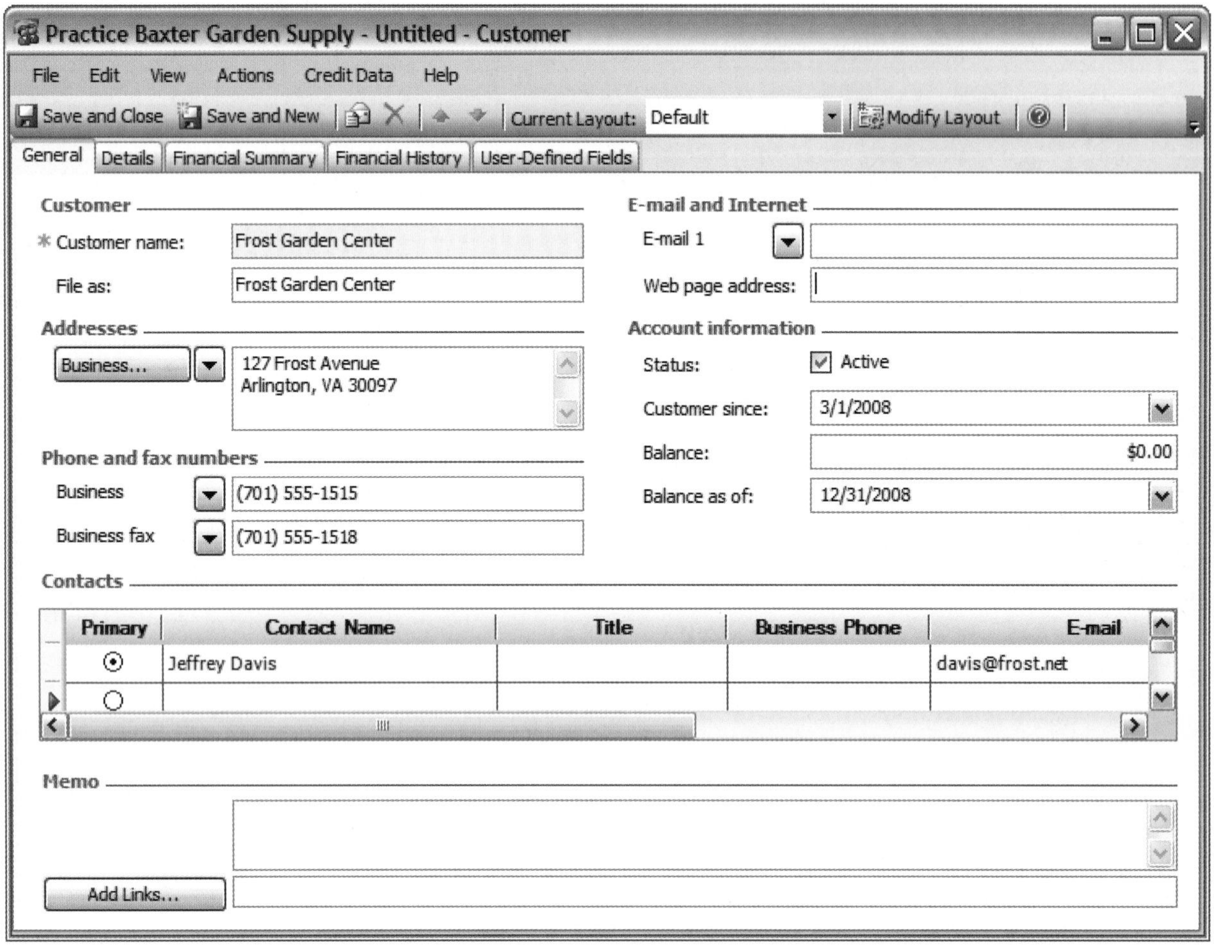

Practice Baxter Garden Supply - Untitled - Customer

File Edit View Actions Credit Data Help

Save and Close | Save and New | Current Layout: Default | Modify Layout

General | Details | Financial Summary | Financial History | User-Defined Fields

Customer

* Customer name: Frost Garden Center

File as: Frost Garden Center

Addresses

Business... 127 Frost Avenue
Arlington, VA 30097

Phone and fax numbers

Business (701) 555-1515

Business fax (701) 555-1518

E-mail and Internet

E-mail 1

Web page address:

Account information

Status: Active

Customer since: 3/1/2008

Balance: $0.00

Balance as of: 12/31/2008

Contacts

Primary	Contact Name	Title	Business Phone	E-mail
⦿	Jeffrey Davis			davis@frost.net
○				

Memo

Add Links...

Figure E:31

Frost Garden Center Details tab.

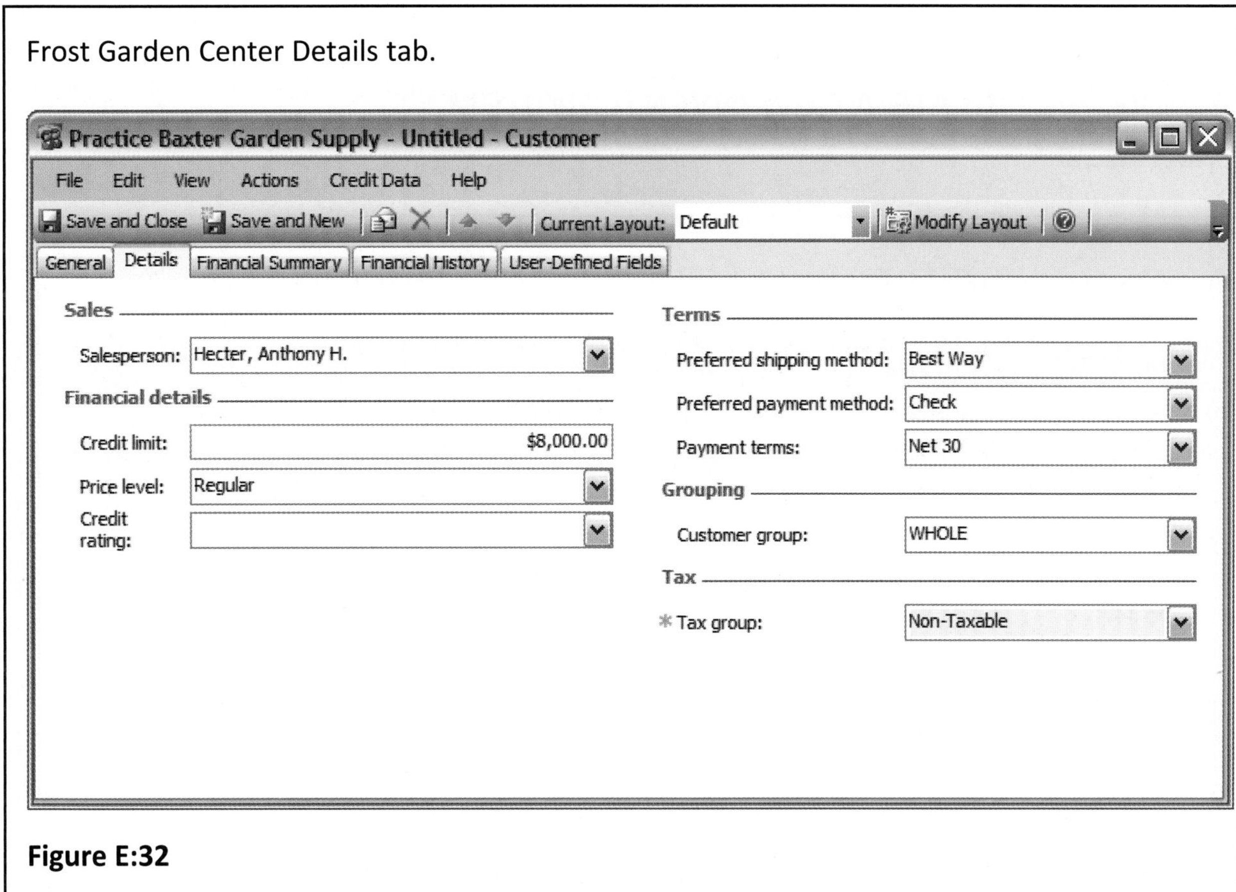

Figure E:32

CREATE A NEW INVENTORY ITEM

Inventory item EQWT-15175.

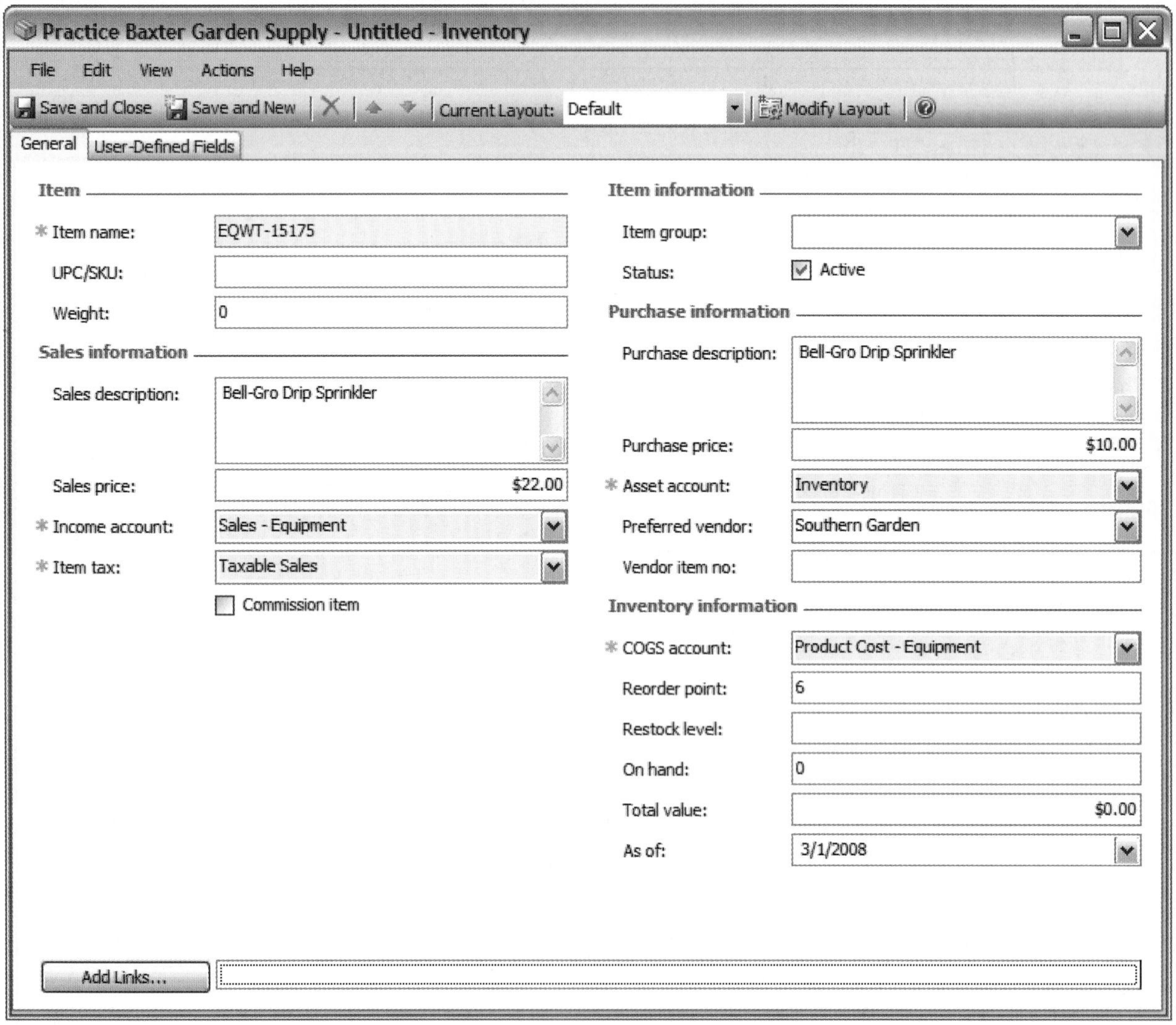

Practice Baxter Garden Supply - Untitled - Inventory

File Edit View Actions Help

Save and Close | Save and New | Current Layout: Default | Modify Layout

General | User-Defined Fields

Item

* Item name:	EQWT-15175
UPC/SKU:	
Weight:	0

Sales information

Sales description:	Bell-Gro Drip Sprinkler
Sales price:	$22.00
* Income account:	Sales - Equipment
* Item tax:	Taxable Sales
	☐ Commission item

Item information

Item group:	
Status:	☑ Active

Purchase information

Purchase description:	Bell-Gro Drip Sprinkler
Purchase price:	$10.00
* Asset account:	Inventory
Preferred vendor:	Southern Garden
Vendor item no:	

Inventory information

* COGS account:	Product Cost - Equipment
Reorder point:	6
Restock level:	
On hand:	0
Total value:	$0.00
As of:	3/1/2008

Add Links...

Figure E:33

Inventory Stock Status by Item report.

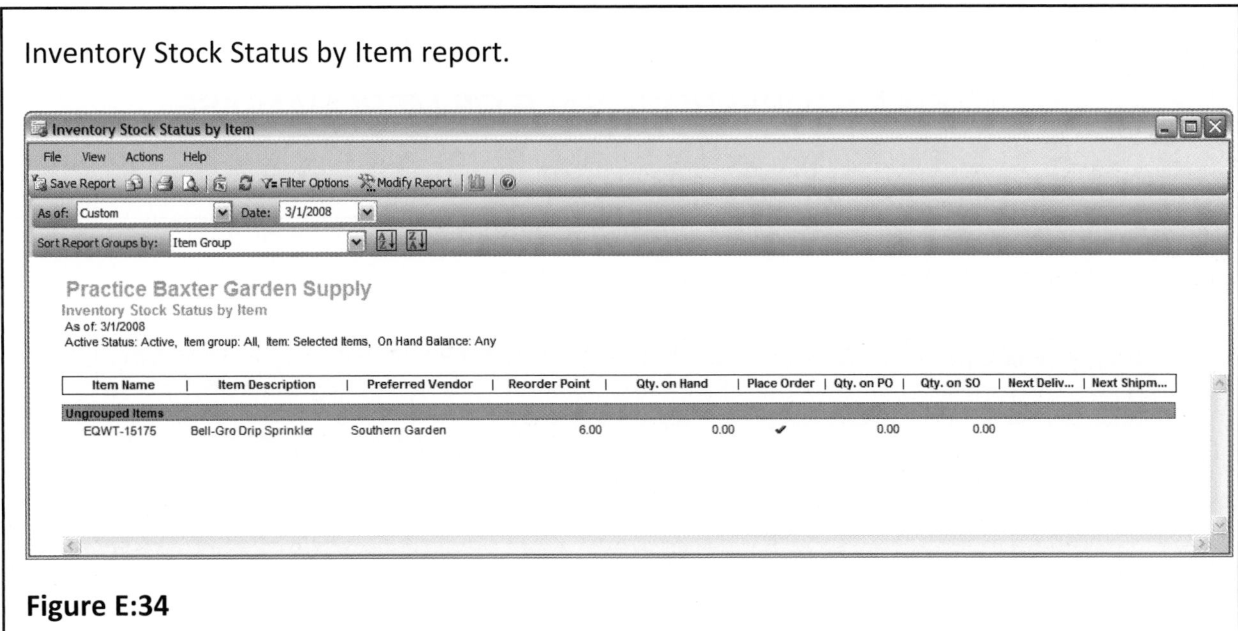

Item Name	Item Description	Preferred Vendor	Reorder Point	Qty. on Hand	Place Order	Qty. on PO	Qty. on SO	Next Deliv...	Next Shipm...
Ungrouped Items									
EQWT-15175	Bell-Gro Drip Sprinkler	Southern Garden	6.00	0.00	✔	0.00	0.00		

Figure E:34

ENTER A STOREFRONT SALE OF MERCHANDISE

Freemond Country Club sale (printed receipt not illustrated).

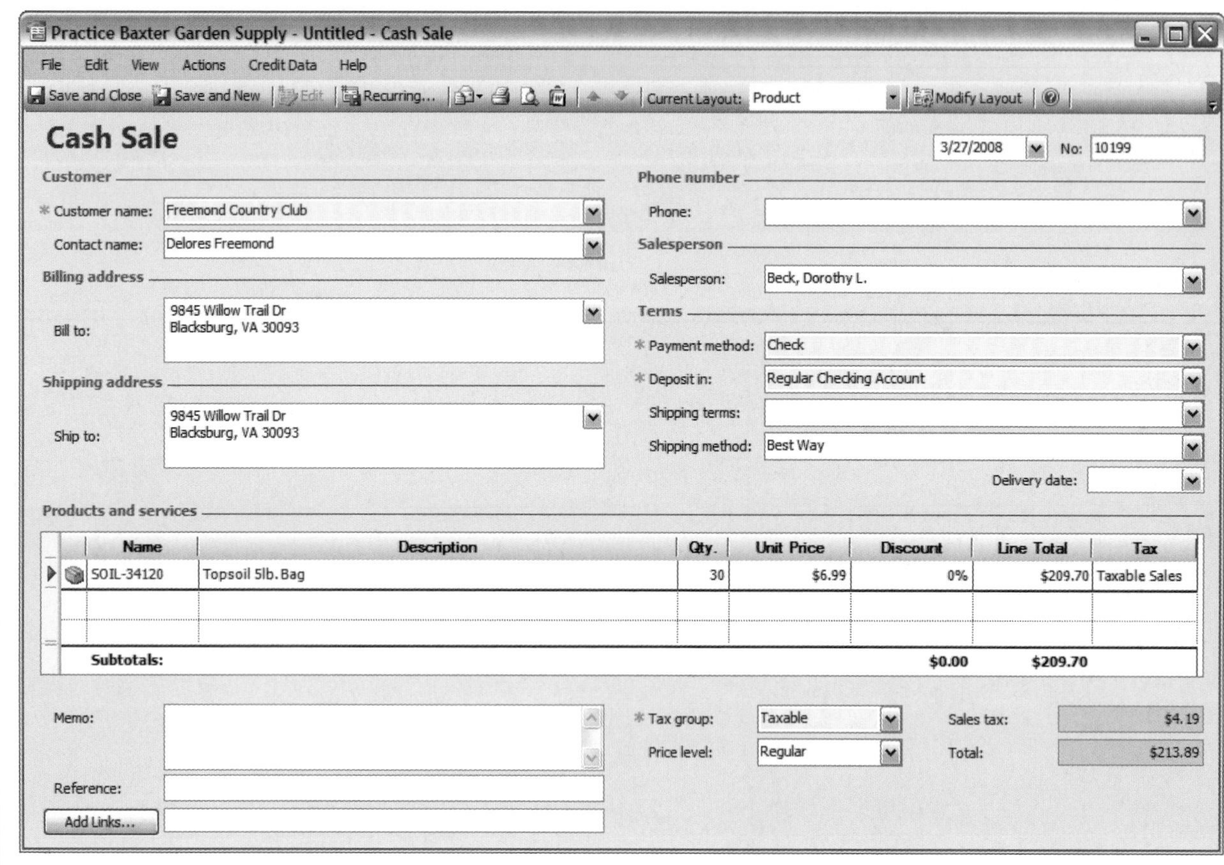

Figure E:35

RECORD CUSTOMER PAYMENTS

Transaction Journal filtered to become a Cash Receipts Journal.

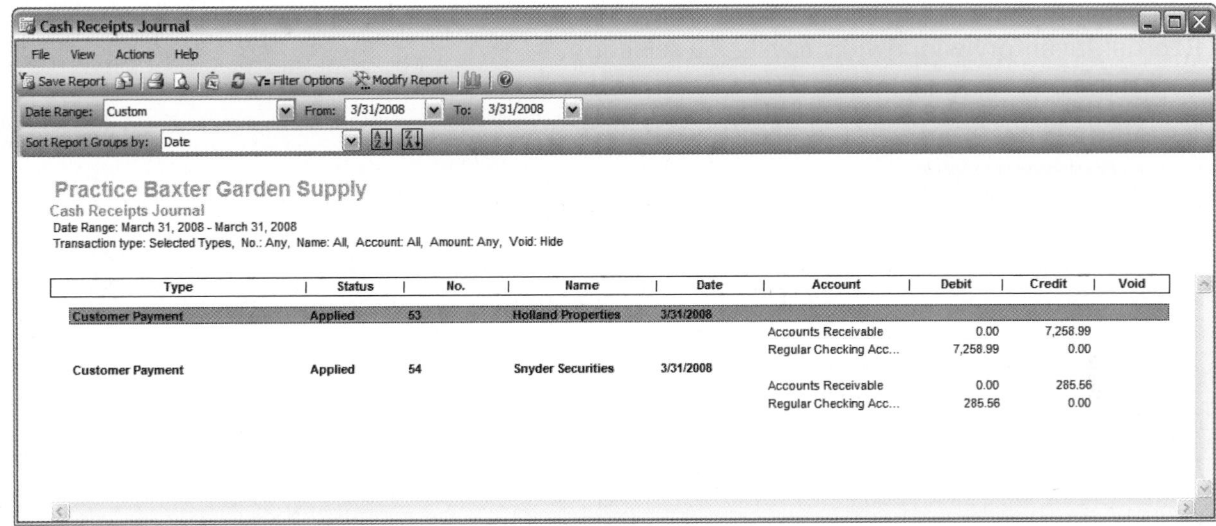

Type	Status	No.	Name	Date	Account	Debit	Credit	Void
Customer Payment	Applied	53	Holland Properties	3/31/2008				
					Accounts Receivable	0.00	7,258.99	
					Regular Checking Acc...	7,258.99	0.00	
Customer Payment	Applied	54	Snyder Securities	3/31/2008				
					Accounts Receivable	0.00	285.56	
					Regular Checking Acc...	285.56	0.00	

Figure E:36

CHAPTER 9

ENTER PURCHASE ORDERS

Reorder Inventory window displaying PO selections.

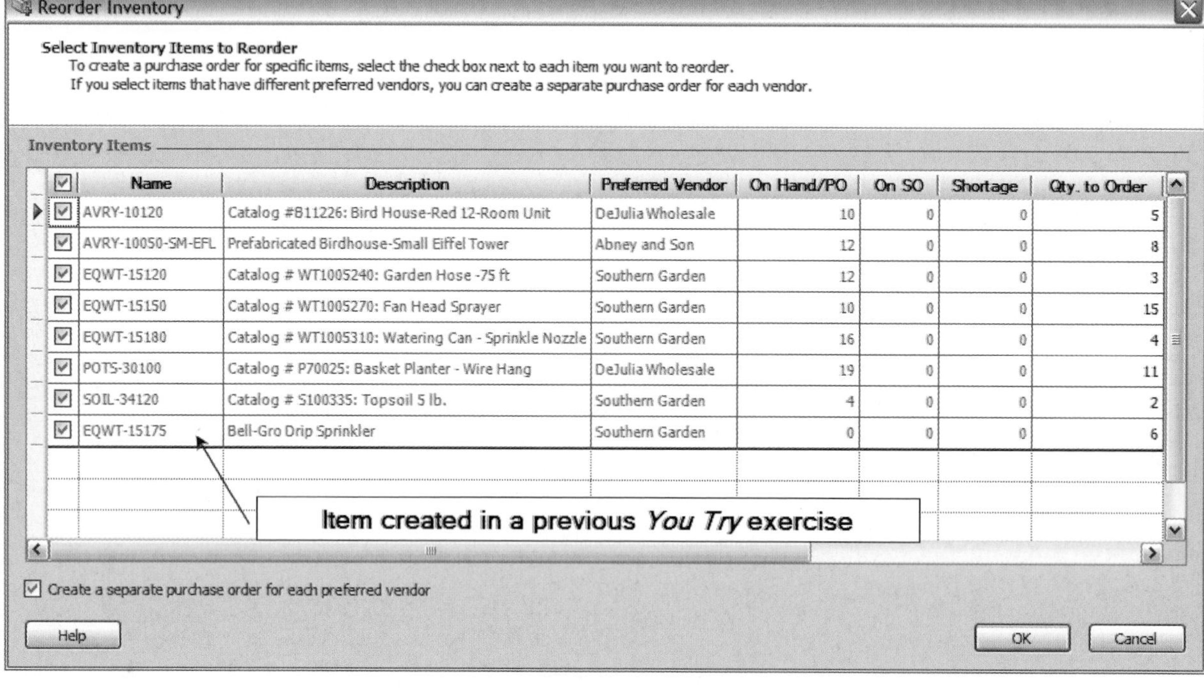

☑	Name	Description	Preferred Vendor	On Hand/PO	On SO	Shortage	Qty. to Order
☑	AVRY-10120	Catalog #B11226: Bird House-Red 12-Room Unit	DeJulia Wholesale	10	0	0	5
☑	AVRY-10050-SM-EFL	Prefabricated Birdhouse-Small Eiffel Tower	Abney and Son	12	0	0	8
☑	EQWT-15120	Catalog # WT1005240: Garden Hose -75 ft	Southern Garden	12	0	0	3
☑	EQWT-15150	Catalog # WT1005270: Fan Head Sprayer	Southern Garden	10	0	0	15
☑	EQWT-15180	Catalog # WT1005310: Watering Can - Sprinkle Nozzle	Southern Garden	16	0	0	4
☑	POTS-30100	Catalog # P70025: Basket Planter - Wire Hang	DeJulia Wholesale	19	0	0	11
☑	SOIL-34120	Catalog # S100335: Topsoil 5 lb.	Southern Garden	4	0	0	2
☑	EQWT-15175	Bell-Gro Drip Sprinkler	Southern Garden	0	0	0	6

Figure E:37

DeJulia Wholesale Suppliers PO. *(Note: Printed POs are not illustrated.)*

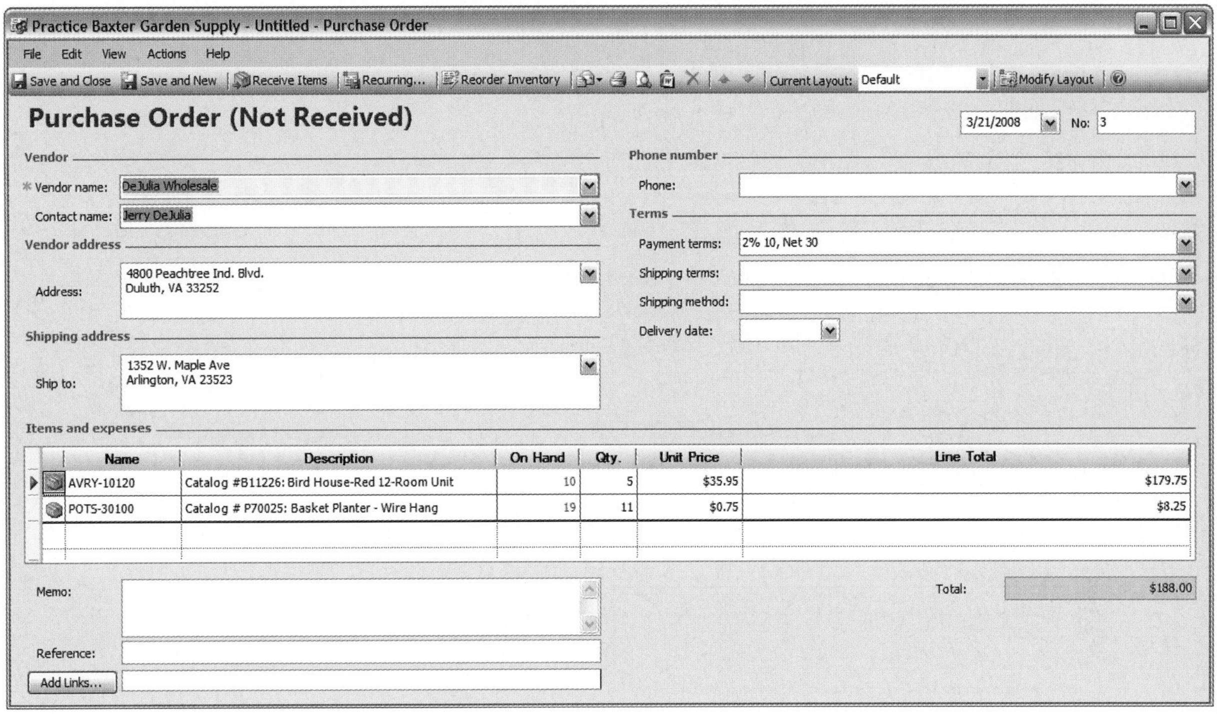

Practice Baxter Garden Supply - Untitled - Purchase Order

File Edit View Actions Help

Save and Close | Save and New | Receive Items | Recurring... | Reorder Inventory | Current Layout: Default | Modify Layout

Purchase Order (Not Received) 3/21/2008 No: 3

Vendor

Vendor name: DeJulia Wholesale

Contact name: Jerry DeJulia

Vendor address

Address: 4800 Peachtree Ind. Blvd.
Duluth, VA 33252

Shipping address

Ship to: 1352 W. Maple Ave
Arlington, VA 23523

Phone number

Phone:

Terms

Payment terms: 2% 10, Net 30

Shipping terms:

Shipping method:

Delivery date:

Items and expenses

Name	Description	On Hand	Qty.	Unit Price	Line Total
AVRY-10120	Catalog #B11226: Bird House-Red 12-Room Unit	10	5	$35.95	$179.75
POTS-30100	Catalog # P70025: Basket Planter - Wire Hang	19	11	$0.75	$8.25

Memo:

Total: $188.00

Reference:

Add Links...

Figure E:38

Abney and Son Contractors PO.

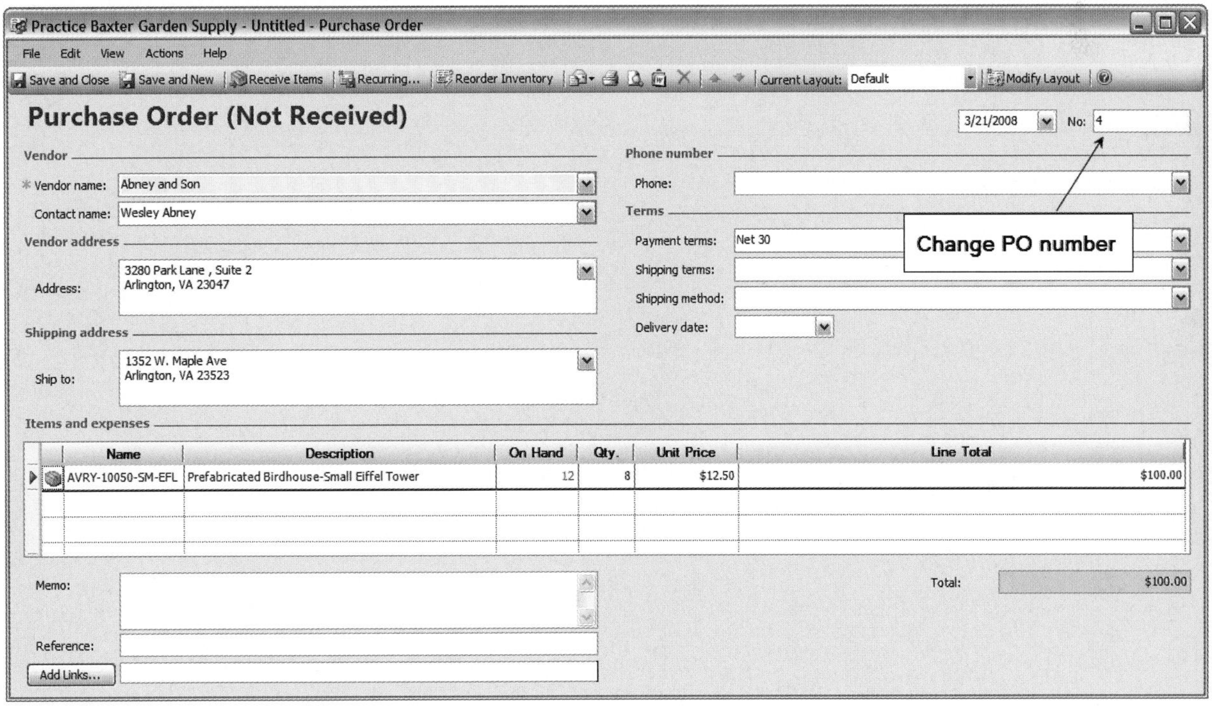

Practice Baxter Garden Supply - Untitled - Purchase Order

File Edit View Actions Help

Save and Close | Save and New | Receive Items | Recurring... | Reorder Inventory | Current Layout: Default | Modify Layout

Purchase Order (Not Received) 3/21/2008 No: 4

Change PO number

Vendor

Vendor name: Abney and Son

Contact name: Wesley Abney

Vendor address

Address: 3280 Park Lane , Suite 2
Arlington, VA 23047

Shipping address

Ship to: 1352 W. Maple Ave
Arlington, VA 23523

Phone number

Phone:

Terms

Payment terms: Net 30

Shipping terms:

Shipping method:

Delivery date:

Items and expenses

Name	Description	On Hand	Qty.	Unit Price	Line Total
AVRY-10050-SM-EFL	Prefabricated Birdhouse-Small Eiffel Tower	12	8	$12.50	$100.00

Memo:

Total: $100.00

Reference:

Add Links...

Figure E:39

Southern Garden PO.

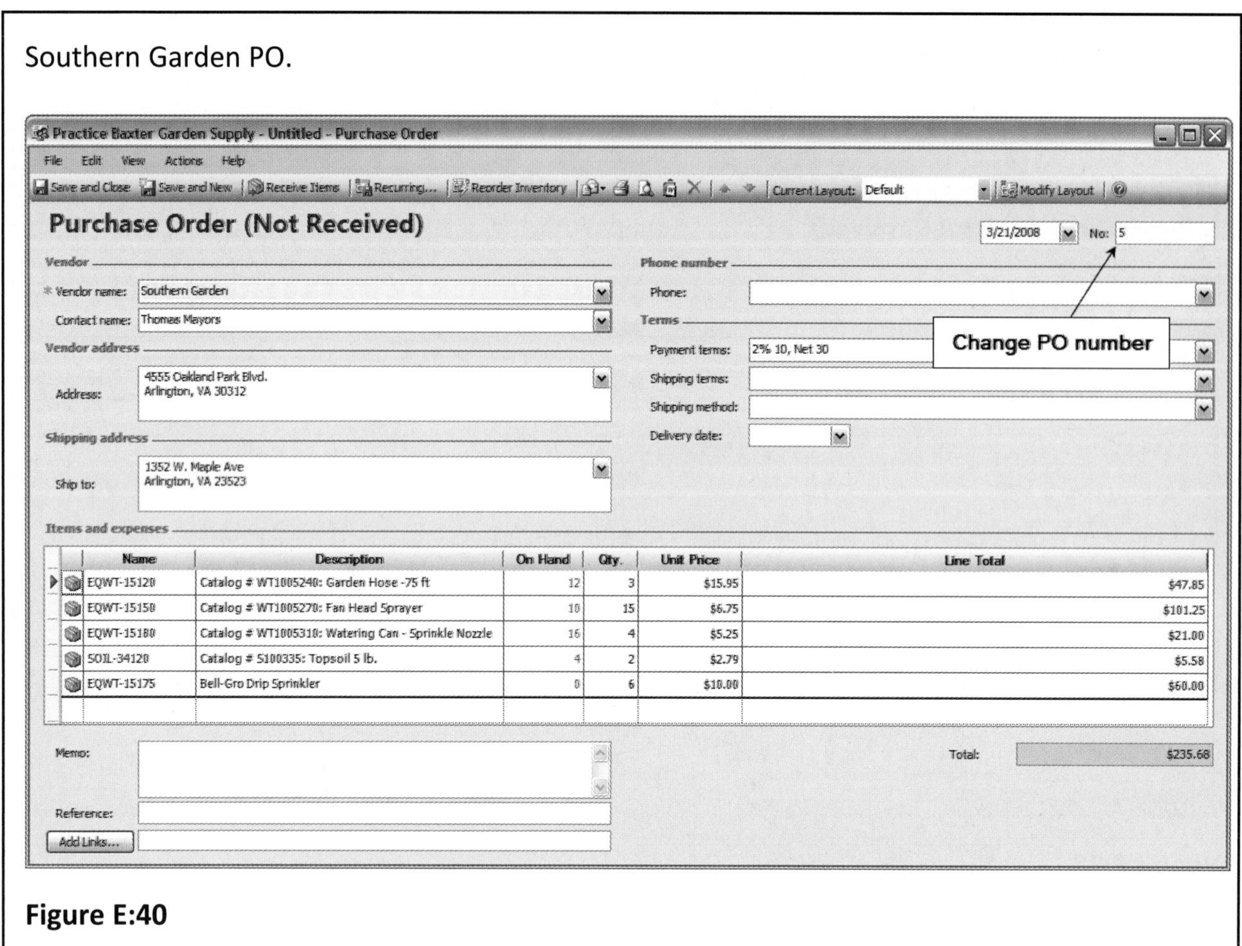

Figure E:40

You Try

ENTER VENDOR RECEIPTS AND BILLS FOR PURCHASE ORDERS

DeJulia Wholesale receipt.

Figure E:41

Abney and Son bill.

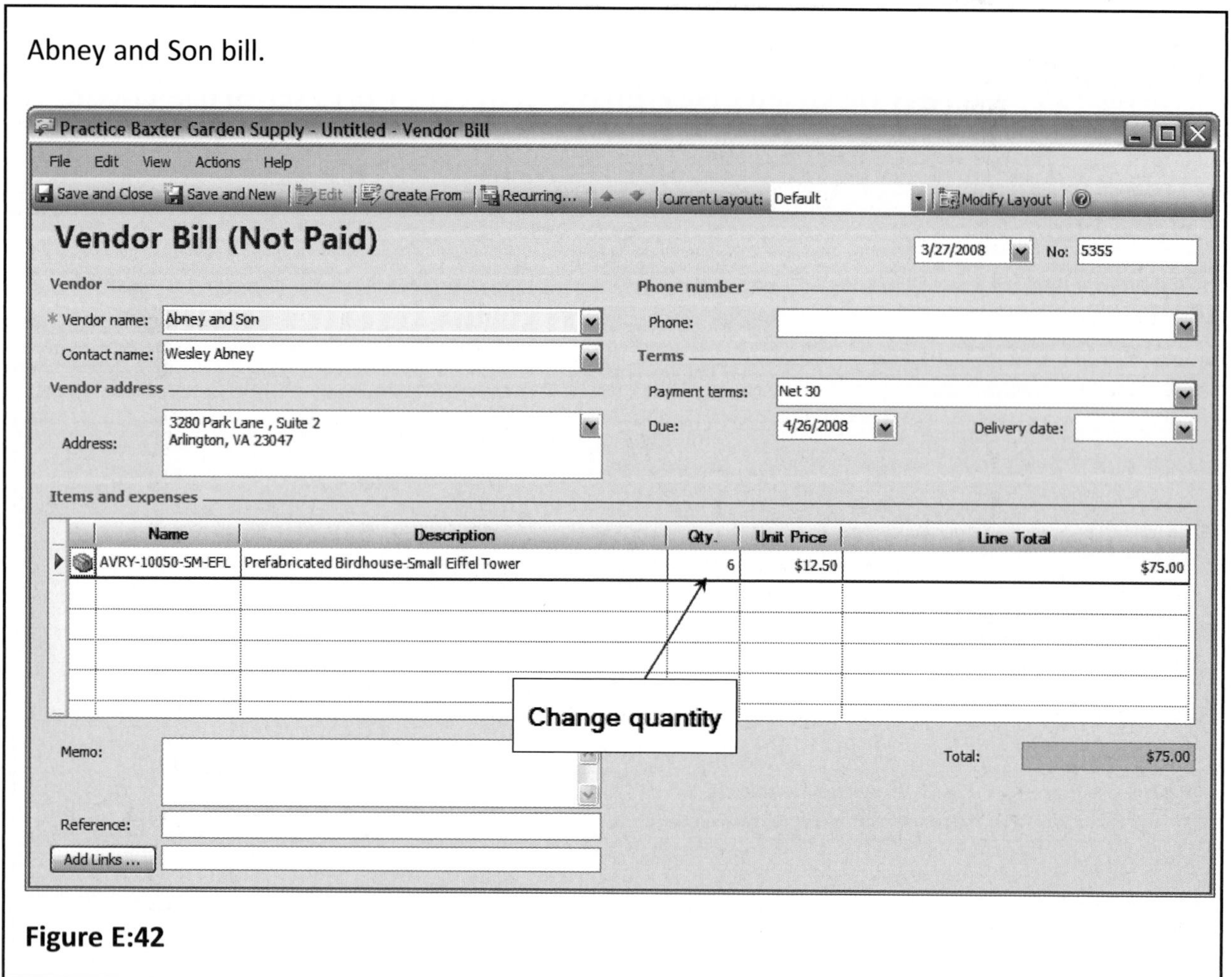

Figure E:42

Southern Garden bill.

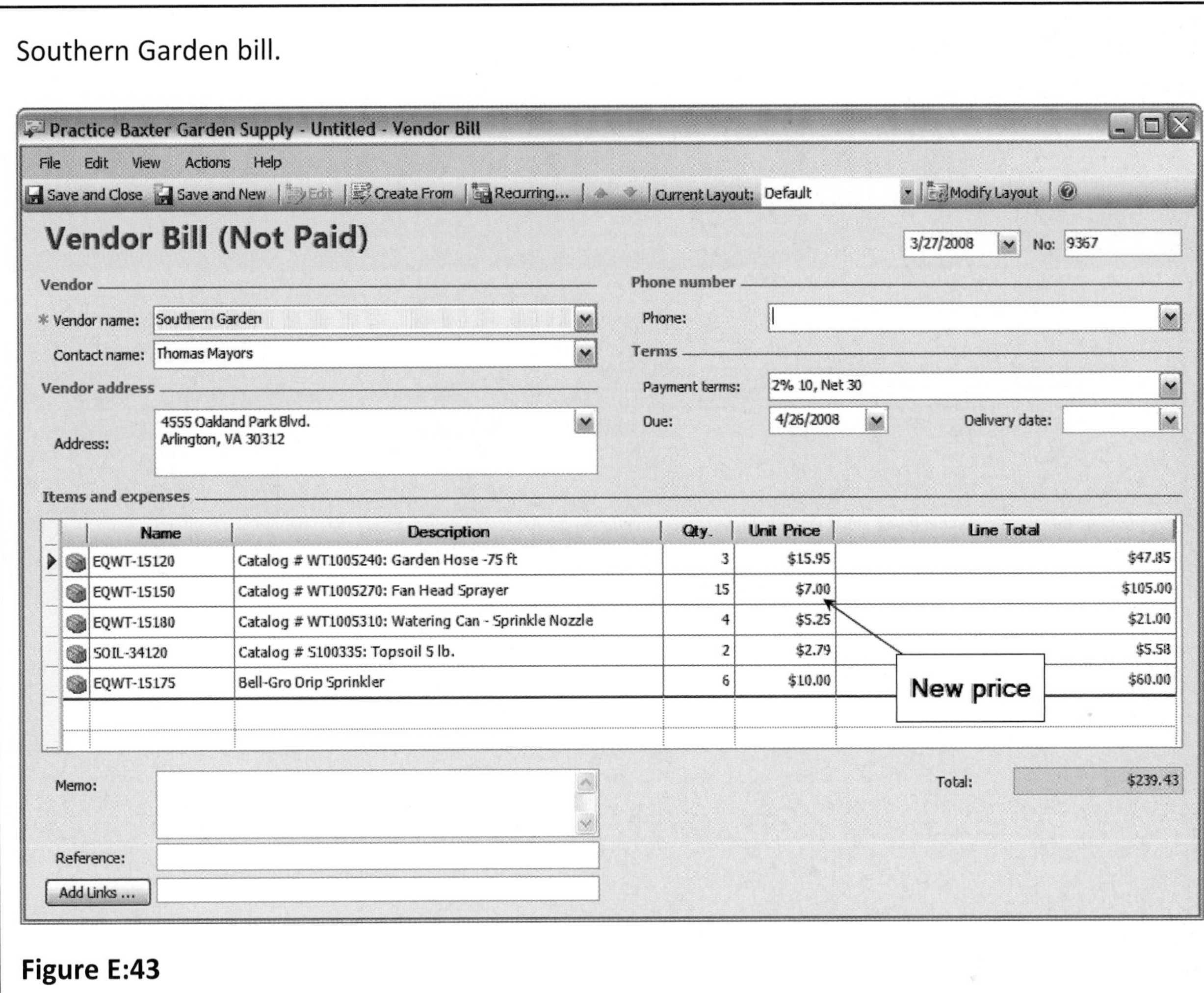

Practice Baxter Garden Supply - Untitled - Vendor Bill

File Edit View Actions Help

Save and Close | Save and New | Edit | Create From | Recurring... | Current Layout: Default | Modify Layout

Vendor Bill (Not Paid)

3/27/2008 No: 9367

Vendor

* Vendor name: Southern Garden

Contact name: Thomas Mayors

Vendor address

Address: 4555 Oakland Park Blvd.
Arlington, VA 30312

Phone number

Phone:

Terms

Payment terms: 2% 10, Net 30

Due: 4/26/2008 Delivery date:

Items and expenses

Name	Description	Qty.	Unit Price	Line Total
EQWT-15120	Catalog # WT1005240: Garden Hose -75 ft	3	$15.95	$47.85
EQWT-15150	Catalog # WT1005270: Fan Head Sprayer	15	$7.00	$105.00
EQWT-15180	Catalog # WT1005310: Watering Can - Sprinkle Nozzle	4	$5.25	$21.00
SOIL-34120	Catalog # S100335: Topsoil 5 lb.	2	$2.79	$5.58
EQWT-15175	Bell-Gro Drip Sprinkler	6	$10.00	$60.00

Memo:

Total: $239.43

Reference:

Add Links ...

Figure E:43

Purchases Journal for March 27.

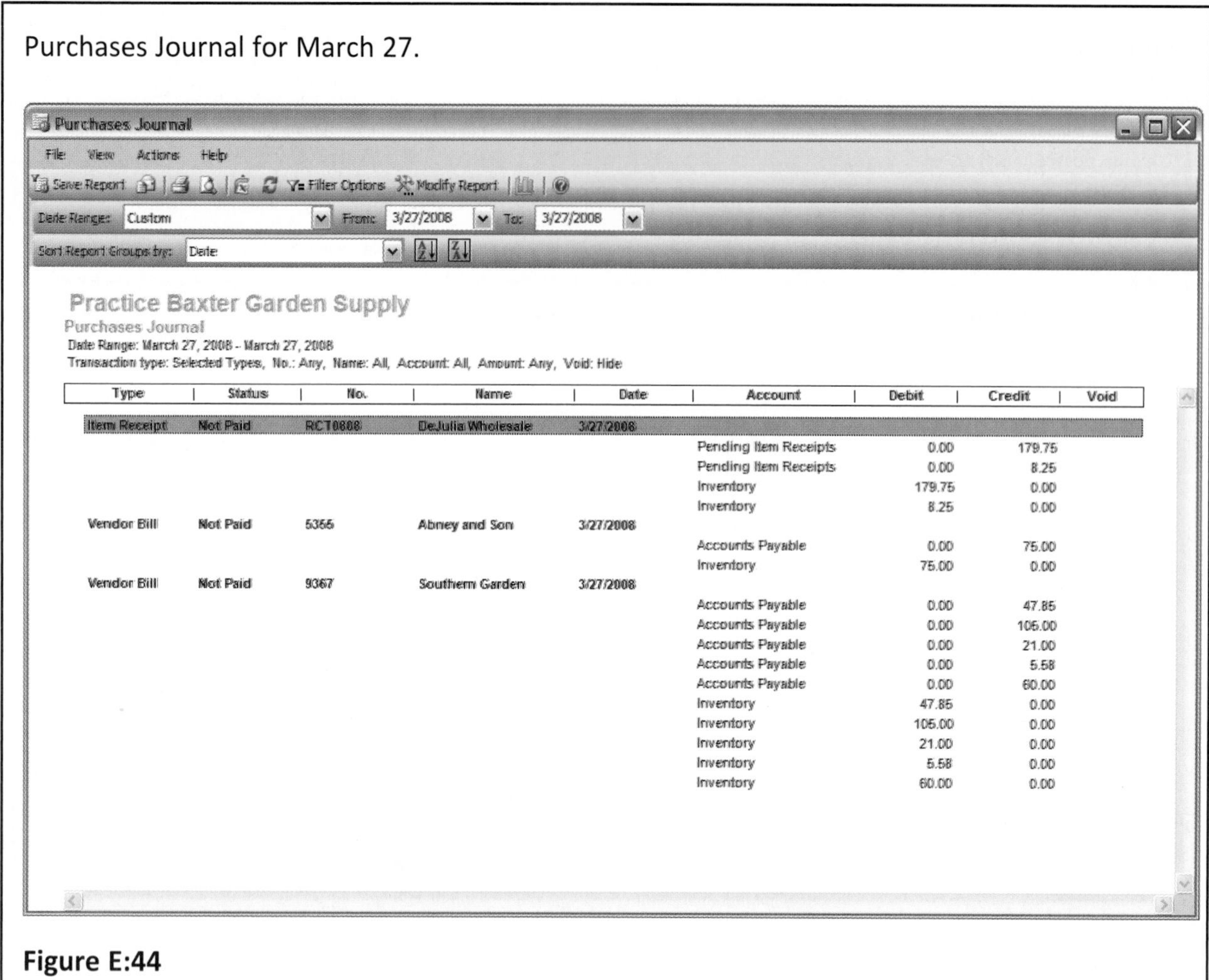
Purchases Journal

File View Actions Help

Save Report | Filter Options | Modify Report

Date Range: Custom From: 3/27/2008 To: 3/27/2008

Sort Report Groups by: Date

Practice Baxter Garden Supply

Purchases Journal

Date Range: March 27, 2008 - March 27, 2008

Transaction type: Selected Types, No.: Any, Name: All, Account: All, Amount: Any, Void: Hide

Type	Status	No.	Name	Date	Account	Debit	Credit	Void
Item Receipt	Not Paid	RCT0008	DeJulia Wholesale	3/27/2008				
					Pending Item Receipts	0.00	179.75	
					Pending Item Receipts	0.00	8.25	
					Inventory	179.75	0.00	
					Inventory	8.25	0.00	
Vendor Bill	Not Paid	5366	Abney and Son	3/27/2008				
					Accounts Payable	0.00	75.00	
					Inventory	75.00	0.00	
Vendor Bill	Not Paid	9367	Southern Garden	3/27/2008				
					Accounts Payable	0.00	47.85	
					Accounts Payable	0.00	105.00	
					Accounts Payable	0.00	21.00	
					Accounts Payable	0.00	5.58	
					Accounts Payable	0.00	60.00	
					Inventory	47.85	0.00	
					Inventory	105.00	0.00	
					Inventory	21.00	0.00	
					Inventory	5.58	0.00	
					Inventory	60.00	0.00	

Figure E:44

ENTER VENDOR BILL FOR VENDOR RECEIPT

DeJulia Wholesale bill.

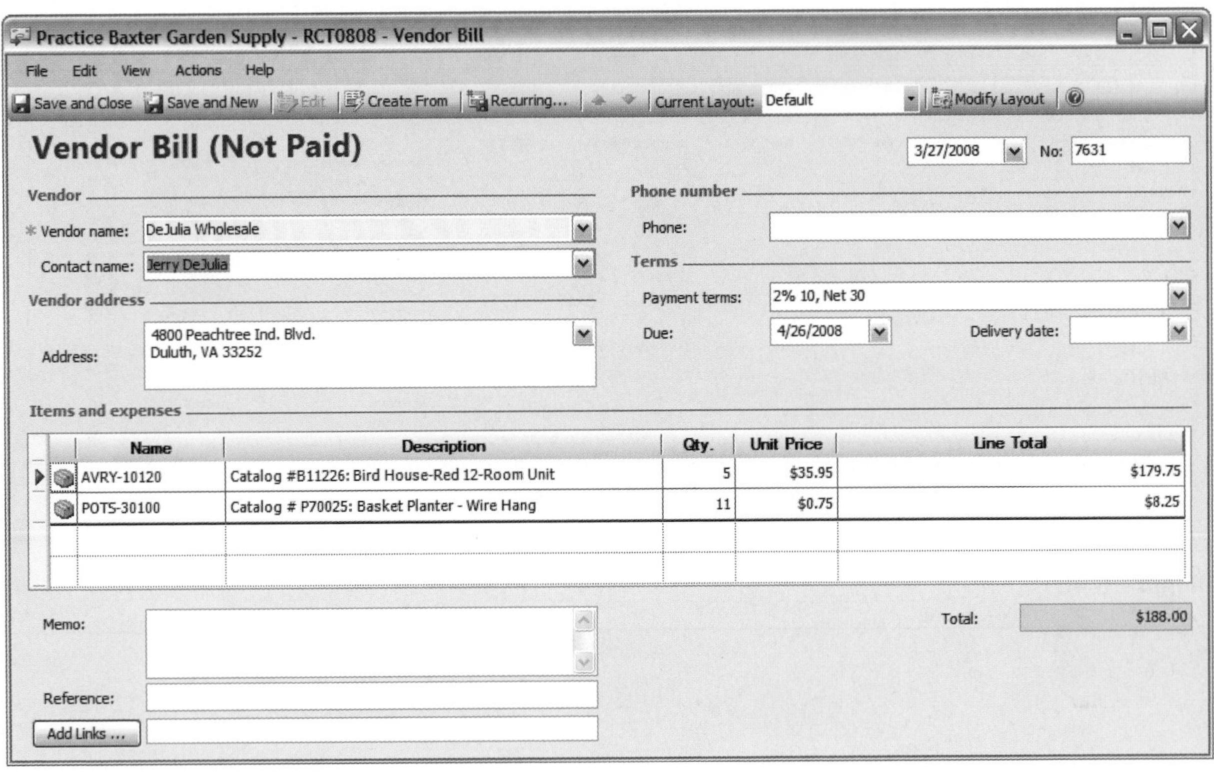
Practice Baxter Garden Supply - RCT0808 - Vendor Bill

File Edit View Actions Help

Save and Close | Save and New | Edit | Create From | Recurring... | Current Layout: Default | Modify Layout

Vendor Bill (Not Paid)

3/27/2008 No: 7631

Vendor

Vendor name: DeJulia Wholesale

Contact name: Jerry DeJulia

Vendor address

Address: 4800 Peachtree Ind. Blvd.
Duluth, VA 33252

Phone number

Phone:

Terms

Payment terms: 2% 10, Net 30

Due: 4/26/2008 Delivery date:

Items and expenses

Name	Description	Qty.	Unit Price	Line Total
AVRY-10120	Catalog #B11226: Bird House-Red 12-Room Unit	5	$35.95	$179.75
POTS-30100	Catalog # P70025: Basket Planter - Wire Hang	11	$0.75	$8.25

Total: $188.00

Memo:

Reference:

Add Links ...

Figure E:45

Purchases Journal for March 27.

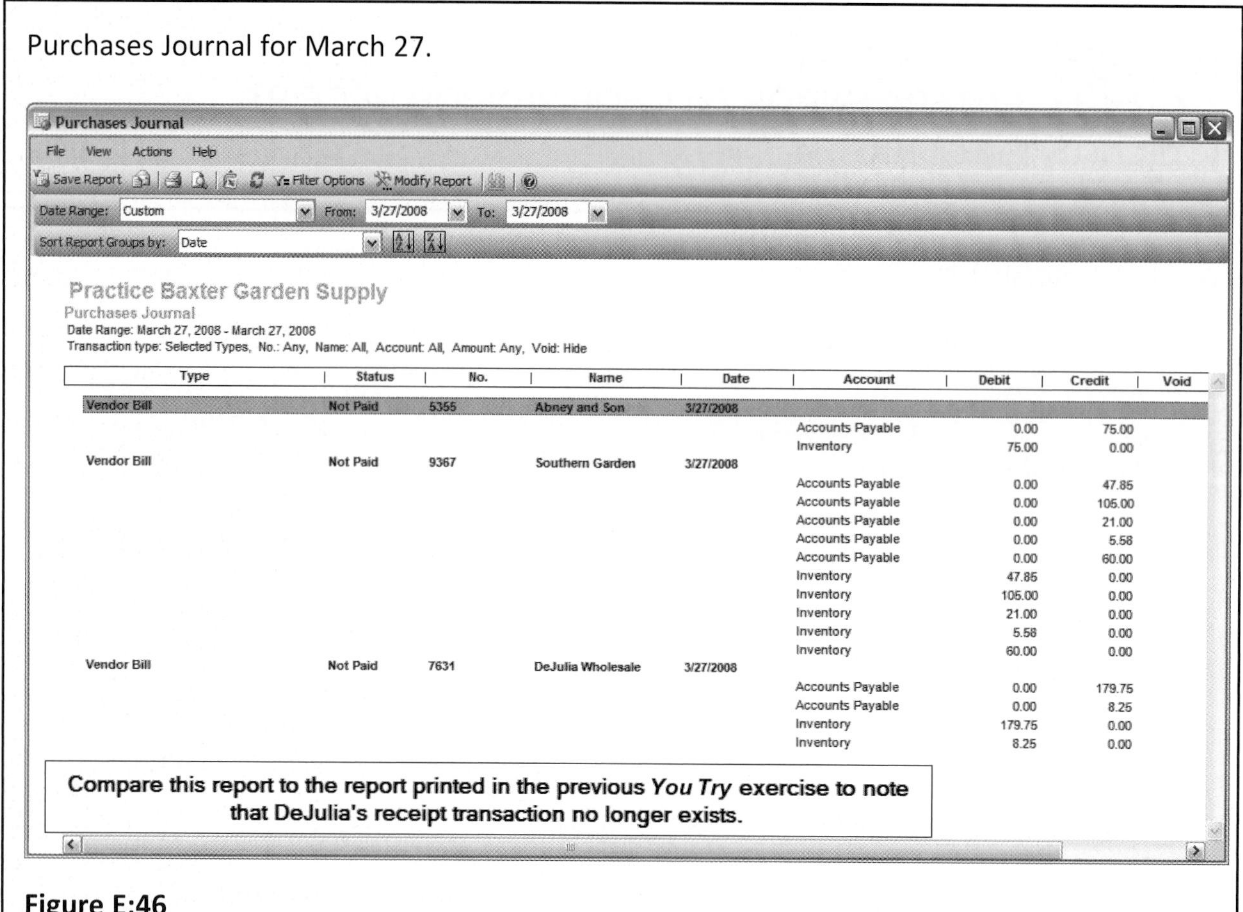

Purchases Journal

File View Actions Help

Save Report | Filter Options | Modify Report

Date Range: Custom From: 3/27/2008 To: 3/27/2008

Sort Report Groups by: Date

Practice Baxter Garden Supply

Purchases Journal

Date Range: March 27, 2008 - March 27, 2008

Transaction type: Selected Types, No.: Any, Name: All, Account: All, Amount: Any, Void: Hide

Type	Status	No.	Name	Date	Account	Debit	Credit	Void
Vendor Bill	Not Paid	5355	Abney and Son	3/27/2008				
					Accounts Payable	0.00	75.00	
					Inventory	75.00	0.00	
Vendor Bill	Not Paid	9367	Southern Garden	3/27/2008				
					Accounts Payable	0.00	47.85	
					Accounts Payable	0.00	105.00	
					Accounts Payable	0.00	21.00	
					Accounts Payable	0.00	5.58	
					Accounts Payable	0.00	60.00	
					Inventory	47.85	0.00	
					Inventory	105.00	0.00	
					Inventory	21.00	0.00	
					Inventory	5.58	0.00	
					Inventory	60.00	0.00	
Vendor Bill	Not Paid	7631	DeJulia Wholesale	3/27/2008				
					Accounts Payable	0.00	179.75	
					Accounts Payable	0.00	8.25	
					Inventory	179.75	0.00	
					Inventory	8.25	0.00	

Compare this report to the report printed in the previous *You Try* exercise to note that DeJulia's receipt transaction no longer exists.

Figure E:46

You Try

CREATE A NEW VENDOR

Sullivan Buyer Supplies General tab.

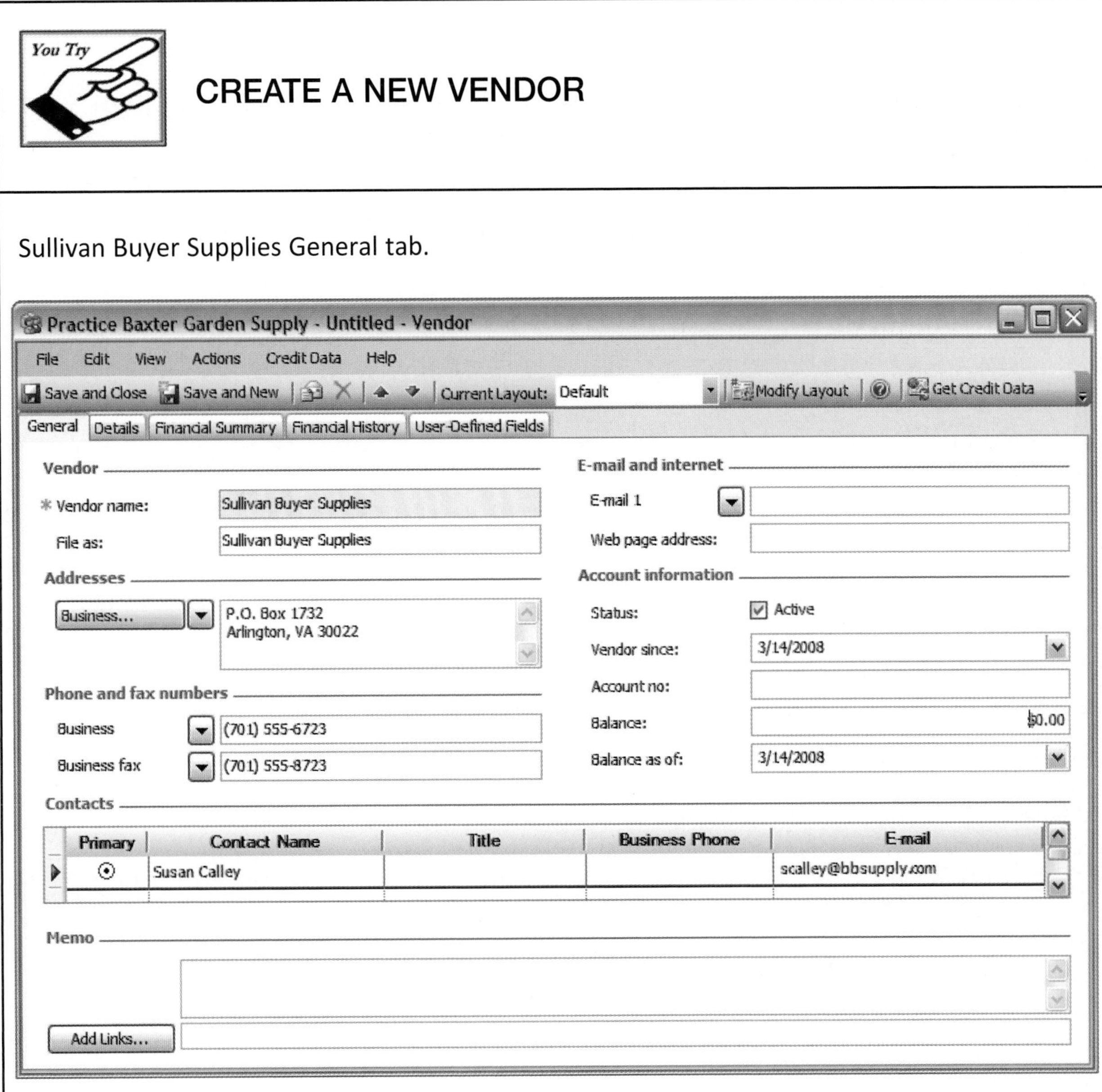

Figure E:47

Sullivan Buyer Supplies Details tab.

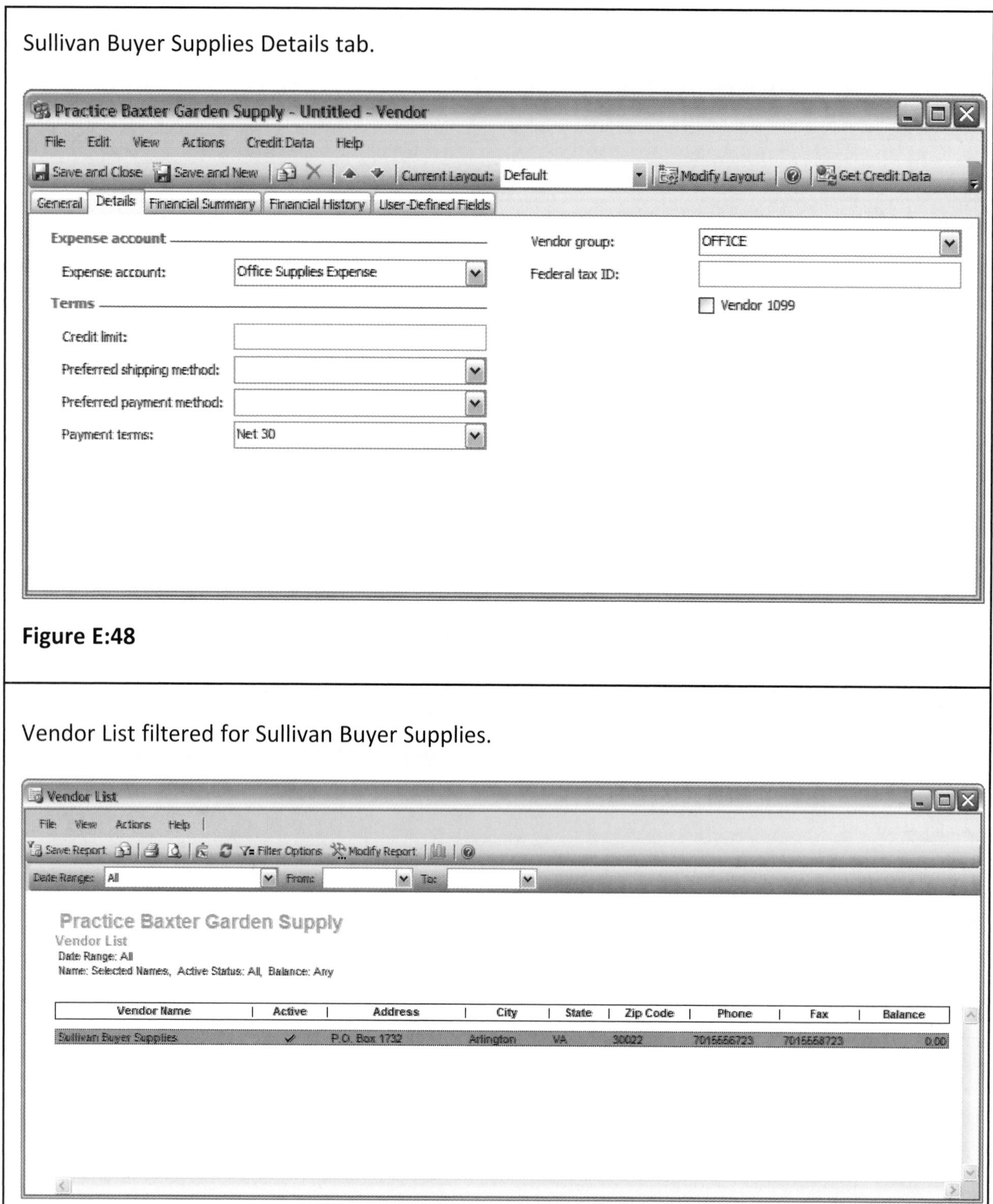

Figure E:48

Vendor List filtered for Sullivan Buyer Supplies.

Figure E:49

ENTER VENDOR BILLS FOR EXPENSES

Juan Motor Tools bill.

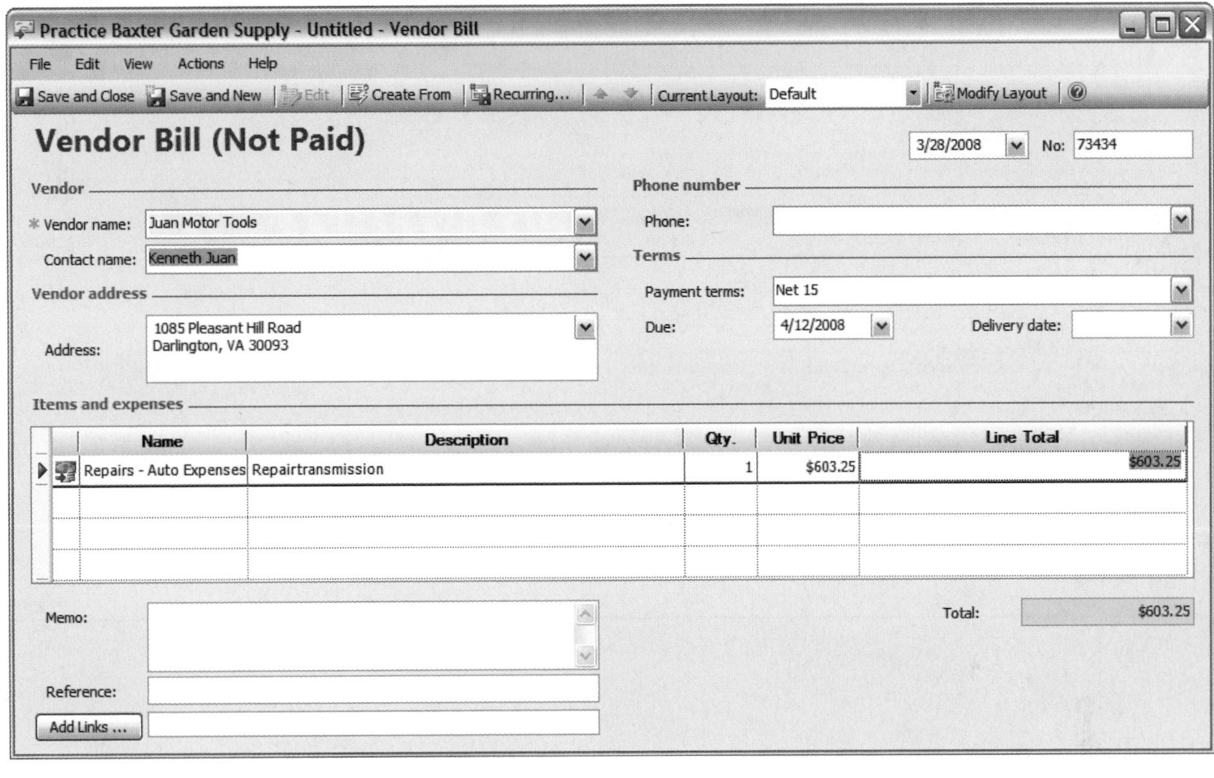

Figure E:50

Neighbors Telephone bill.

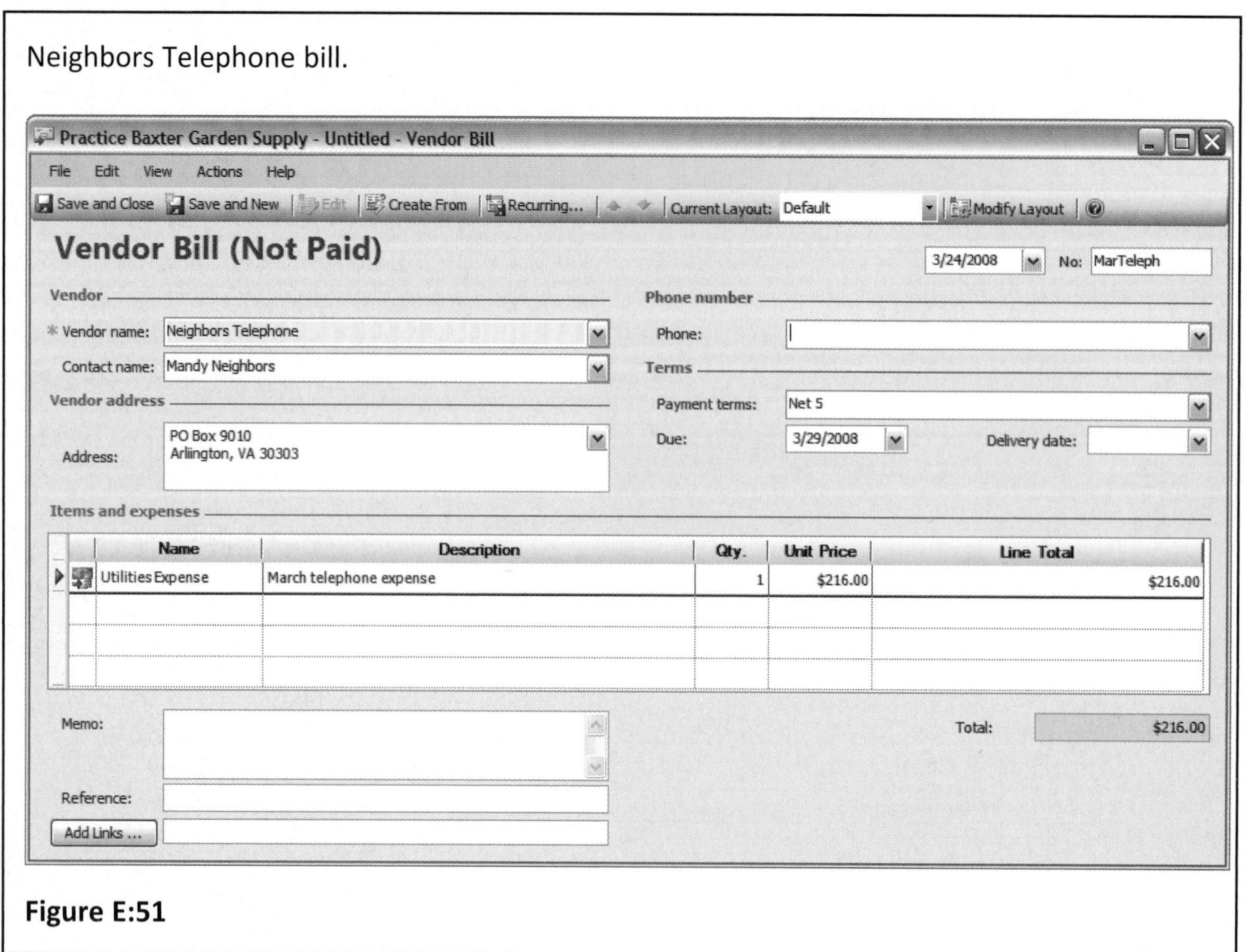

Figure E:51

PAY VENDORS

Pay Bills window when selecting bills due by 4/12/2008.

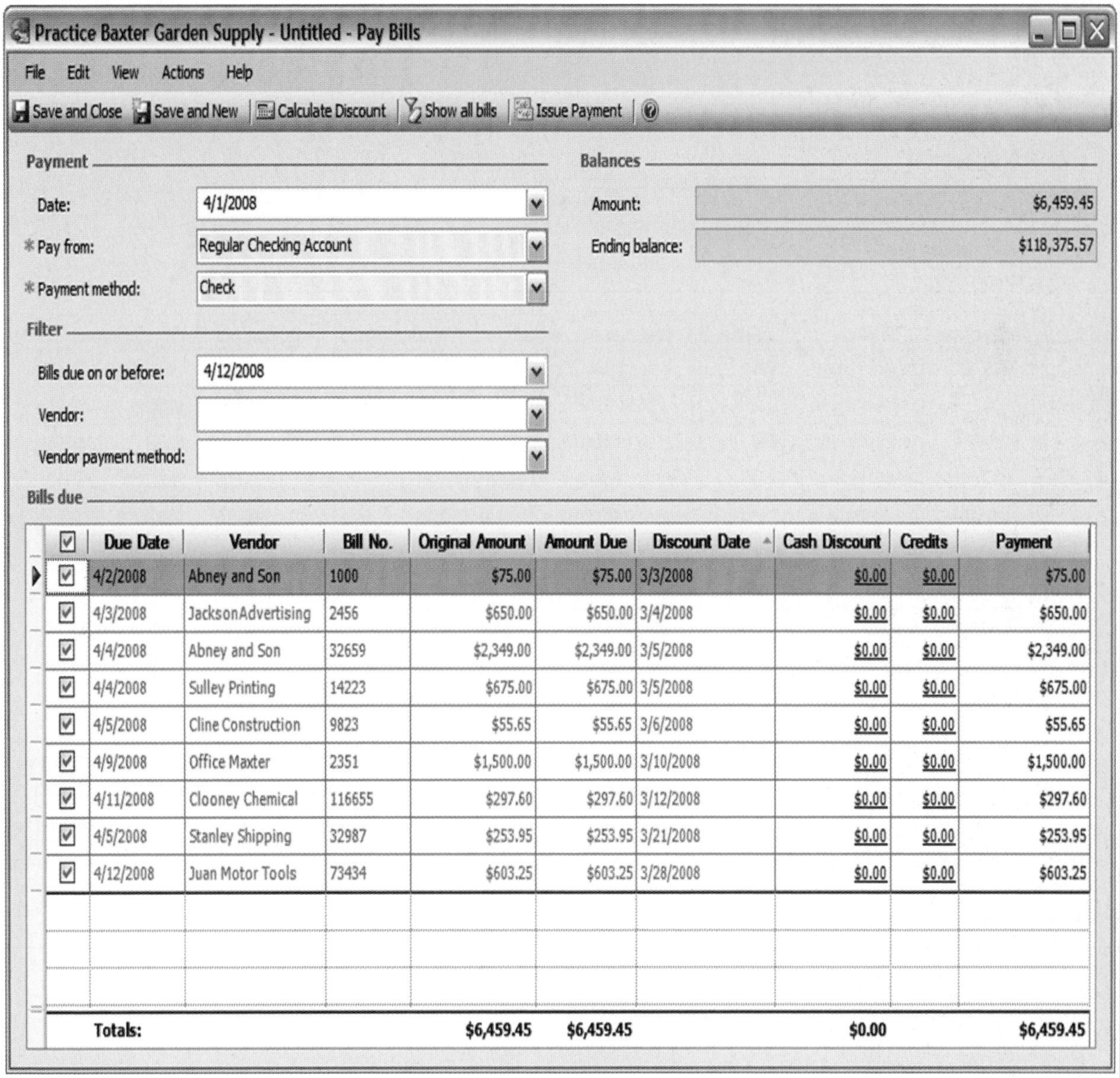

Practice Baxter Garden Supply - Untitled - Pay Bills

File Edit View Actions Help

Save and Close | Save and New | Calculate Discount | Show all bills | Issue Payment

Payment

Date: 4/1/2008

* Pay from: Regular Checking Account

* Payment method: Check

Balances

Amount: $6,459.45

Ending balance: $118,375.57

Filter

Bills due on or before: 4/12/2008

Vendor:

Vendor payment method:

Bills due

☑	Due Date	Vendor	Bill No.	Original Amount	Amount Due	Discount Date	Cash Discount	Credits	Payment
☑	4/2/2008	Abney and Son	1000	$75.00	$75.00	3/3/2008	$0.00	$0.00	$75.00
☑	4/3/2008	JacksonAdvertising	2456	$650.00	$650.00	3/4/2008	$0.00	$0.00	$650.00
☑	4/4/2008	Abney and Son	32659	$2,349.00	$2,349.00	3/5/2008	$0.00	$0.00	$2,349.00
☑	4/4/2008	Sulley Printing	14223	$675.00	$675.00	3/5/2008	$0.00	$0.00	$675.00
☑	4/5/2008	Cline Construction	9823	$55.65	$55.65	3/6/2008	$0.00	$0.00	$55.65
☑	4/9/2008	Office Maxter	2351	$1,500.00	$1,500.00	3/10/2008	$0.00	$0.00	$1,500.00
☑	4/11/2008	Clooney Chemical	116655	$297.60	$297.60	3/12/2008	$0.00	$0.00	$297.60
☑	4/5/2008	Stanley Shipping	32987	$253.95	$253.95	3/21/2008	$0.00	$0.00	$253.95
☑	4/12/2008	Juan Motor Tools	73434	$603.25	$603.25	3/28/2008	$0.00	$0.00	$603.25
	Totals:			**$6,459.45**	**$6,459.45**		**$0.00**		**$6,459.45**

Figure E:52

Pay Bills window selecting bills with a discount expiring by 4/12/2008.

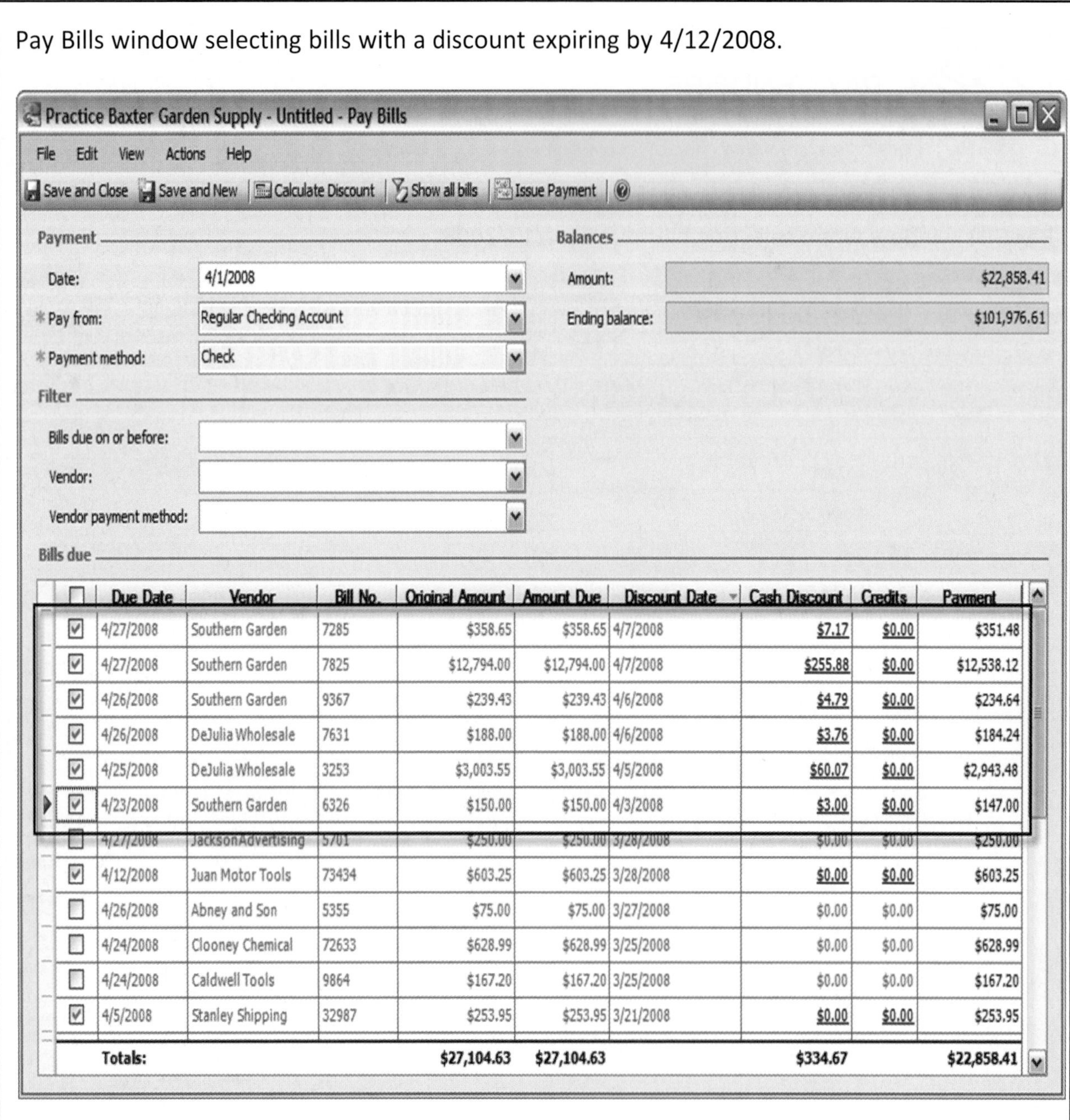

Practice Baxter Garden Supply - Untitled - Pay Bills
File Edit View Actions Help
Save and Close Save and New Calculate Discount Show all bills Issue Payment
Payment
Date: 4/1/2008
*Pay from: Regular Checking Account
*Payment method: Check
Balances
Amount: $22,858.41
Ending balance: $101,976.61
Filter
Bills due on or before:
Vendor:
Vendor payment method:
Bills due
Due Date Vendor Bill No. Original Amount Amount Due Discount Date Cash Discount Credits Payment
4/27/2008 Southern Garden 7285 $358.65 $358.65 4/7/2008 $7.17 $0.00 $351.48
4/27/2008 Southern Garden 7825 $12,794.00 $12,794.00 4/7/2008 $255.88 $0.00 $12,538.12
4/26/2008 Southern Garden 9367 $239.43 $239.43 4/6/2008 $4.79 $0.00 $234.64
4/26/2008 DeJulia Wholesale 7631 $188.00 $188.00 4/6/2008 $3.76 $0.00 $184.24
4/25/2008 DeJulia Wholesale 3253 $3,003.55 $3,003.55 4/5/2008 $60.07 $0.00 $2,943.48
4/23/2008 Southern Garden 6326 $150.00 $150.00 4/3/2008 $3.00 $0.00 $147.00
4/27/2008 Jackson Advertising 5701 $250.00 $250.00 3/28/2008 $0.00 $0.00 $250.00
4/12/2008 Juan Motor Tools 73434 $603.25 $603.25 3/28/2008 $0.00 $0.00 $603.25
4/26/2008 Abney and Son 5355 $75.00 $75.00 3/27/2008 $0.00 $0.00 $75.00
4/24/2008 Clooney Chemical 72633 $628.99 $628.99 3/25/2008 $0.00 $0.00 $628.99
4/24/2008 Caldwell Tools 9864 $167.20 $167.20 3/25/2008 $0.00 $0.00 $167.20
4/5/2008 Stanley Shipping 32987 $253.95 $253.95 3/21/2008 $0.00 $0.00 $253.95
Totals: $27,104.63 $27,104.63 $334.67 $22,858.41

Figure E:53

Pay Bills window after reducing payment to Sully Printing.

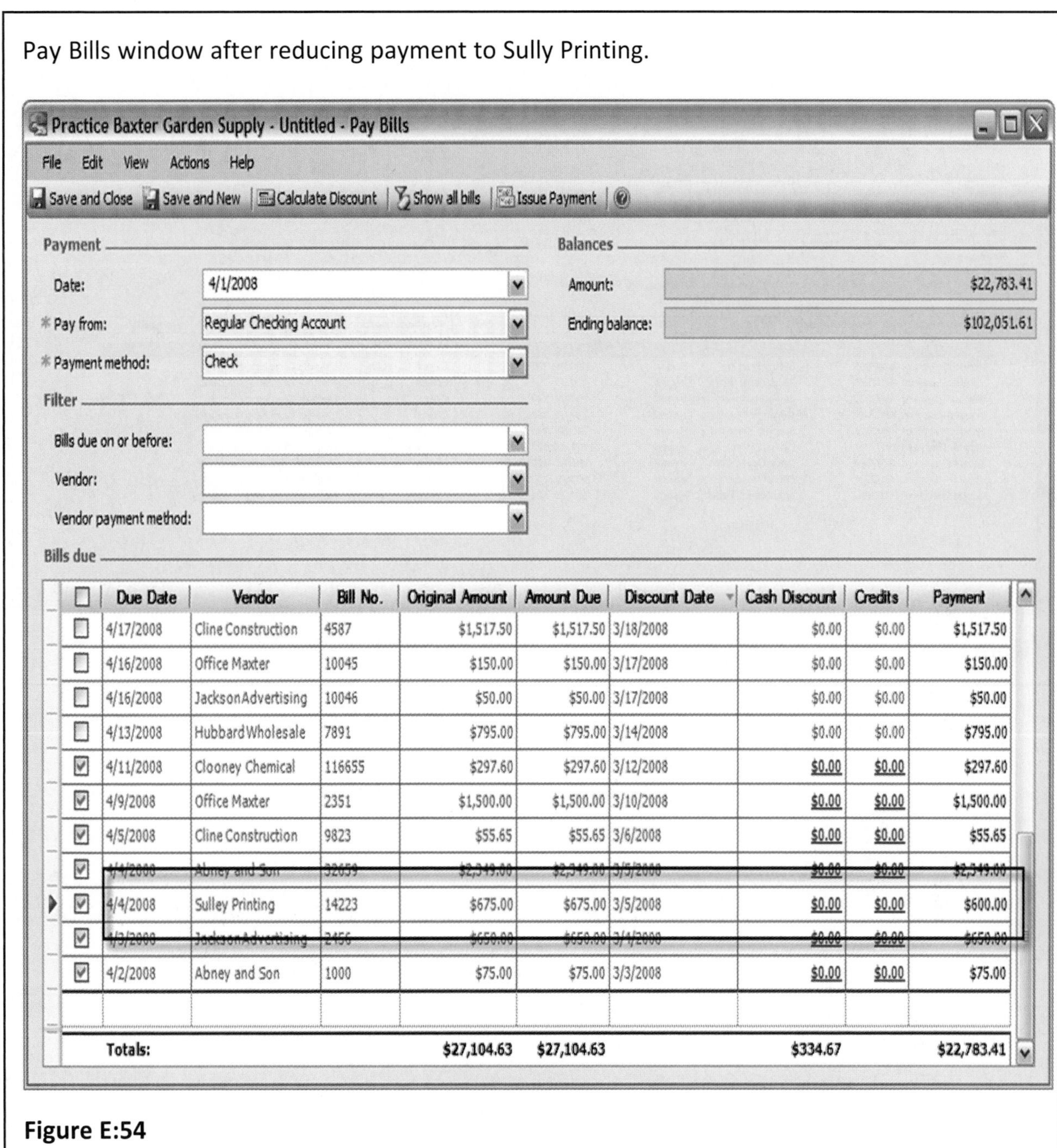

Practice Baxter Garden Supply - Untitled - Pay Bills
File Edit View Actions Help
Save and Close Save and New Calculate Discount Show all bills Issue Payment
Payment
Date: 4/1/2008
Pay from: Regular Checking Account
Payment method: Check
Balances
Amount: $22,783.41
Ending balance: $102,051.61
Filter
Bills due on or before:
Vendor:
Vendor payment method:
Bills due
Due Date Vendor Bill No. Original Amount Amount Due Discount Date Cash Discount Credits Payment
4/17/2008 Cline Construction 4587 $1,517.50 $1,517.50 3/18/2008 $0.00 $0.00 $1,517.50
4/16/2008 Office Maxter 10045 $150.00 $150.00 3/17/2008 $0.00 $0.00 $150.00
4/16/2008 JacksonAdvertising 10046 $50.00 $50.00 3/17/2008 $0.00 $0.00 $50.00
4/13/2008 HubbardWholesale 7891 $795.00 $795.00 3/14/2008 $0.00 $0.00 $795.00
4/11/2008 Clooney Chemical 116655 $297.60 $297.60 3/12/2008 $0.00 $0.00 $297.60
4/9/2008 Office Maxter 2351 $1,500.00 $1,500.00 3/10/2008 $0.00 $0.00 $1,500.00
4/5/2008 Cline Construction 9823 $55.65 $55.65 3/6/2008 $0.00 $0.00 $55.65
4/4/2008 Sulley Printing 14223 $675.00 $675.00 3/5/2008 $0.00 $0.00 $600.00
4/2/2008 Abney and Son 1000 $75.00 $75.00 3/3/2008 $0.00 $0.00 $75.00
Totals: $27,104.63 $27,104.63 $334.67 $22,783.41

Figure E:54

Payments report for April 1.

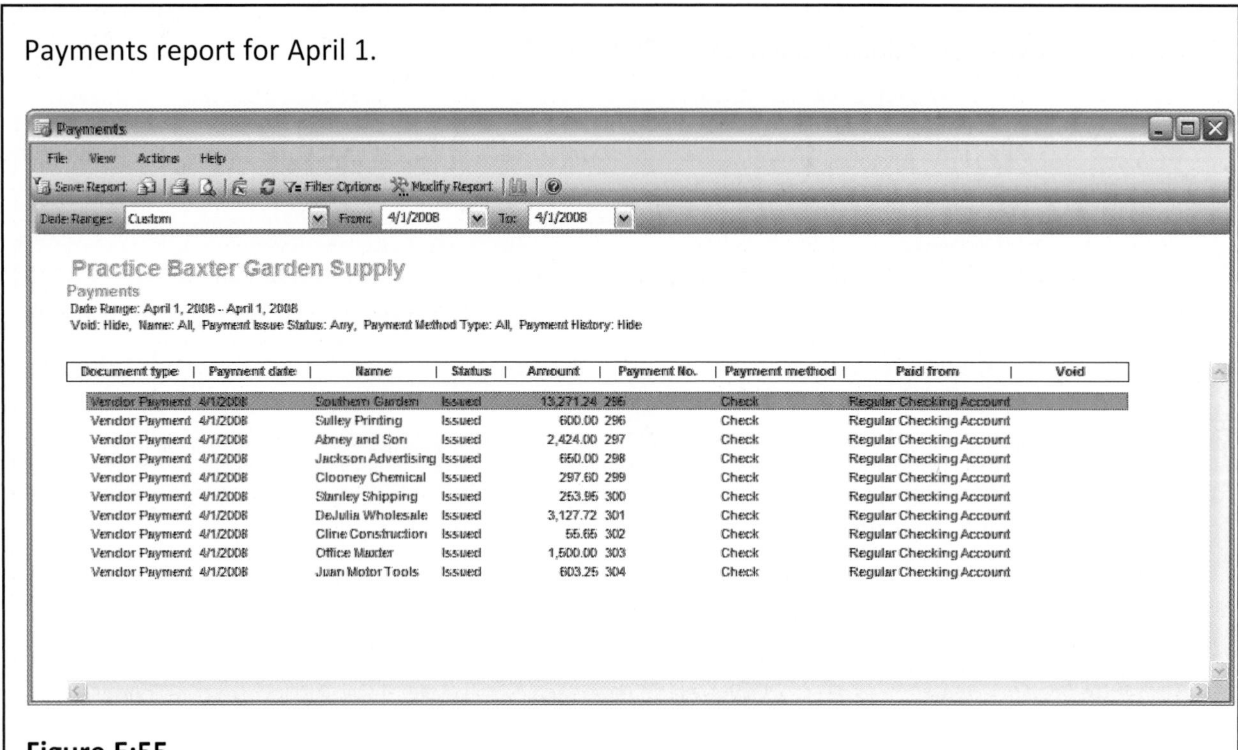

Practice Baxter Garden Supply
Payments
Date Range: April 1, 2008 - April 1, 2008
Void: Hide, Name: All, Payment Issue Status: Any, Payment Method Type: All, Payment History: Hide

Document type	Payment date	Name	Status	Amount	Payment No.	Payment method	Paid from	Void
Vendor Payment	4/1/2008	Southern Garden	Issued	13,271.24	295	Check	Regular Checking Account	
Vendor Payment	4/1/2008	Sulley Printing	Issued	600.00	296	Check	Regular Checking Account	
Vendor Payment	4/1/2008	Abney and Son	Issued	2,424.00	297	Check	Regular Checking Account	
Vendor Payment	4/1/2008	Jackson Advertising	Issued	650.00	298	Check	Regular Checking Account	
Vendor Payment	4/1/2008	Clooney Chemical	Issued	297.60	299	Check	Regular Checking Account	
Vendor Payment	4/1/2008	Stanley Shipping	Issued	253.95	300	Check	Regular Checking Account	
Vendor Payment	4/1/2008	DeJulia Wholesale	Issued	3,127.72	301	Check	Regular Checking Account	
Vendor Payment	4/1/2008	Cline Construction	Issued	55.65	302	Check	Regular Checking Account	
Vendor Payment	4/1/2008	Office Maxder	Issued	1,500.00	303	Check	Regular Checking Account	
Vendor Payment	4/1/2008	Juan Motor Tools	Issued	603.25	304	Check	Regular Checking Account	

Figure E:55

CHAPTER 10

CREATE CHECKS FOR PAYROLL TAXES

401K bill.

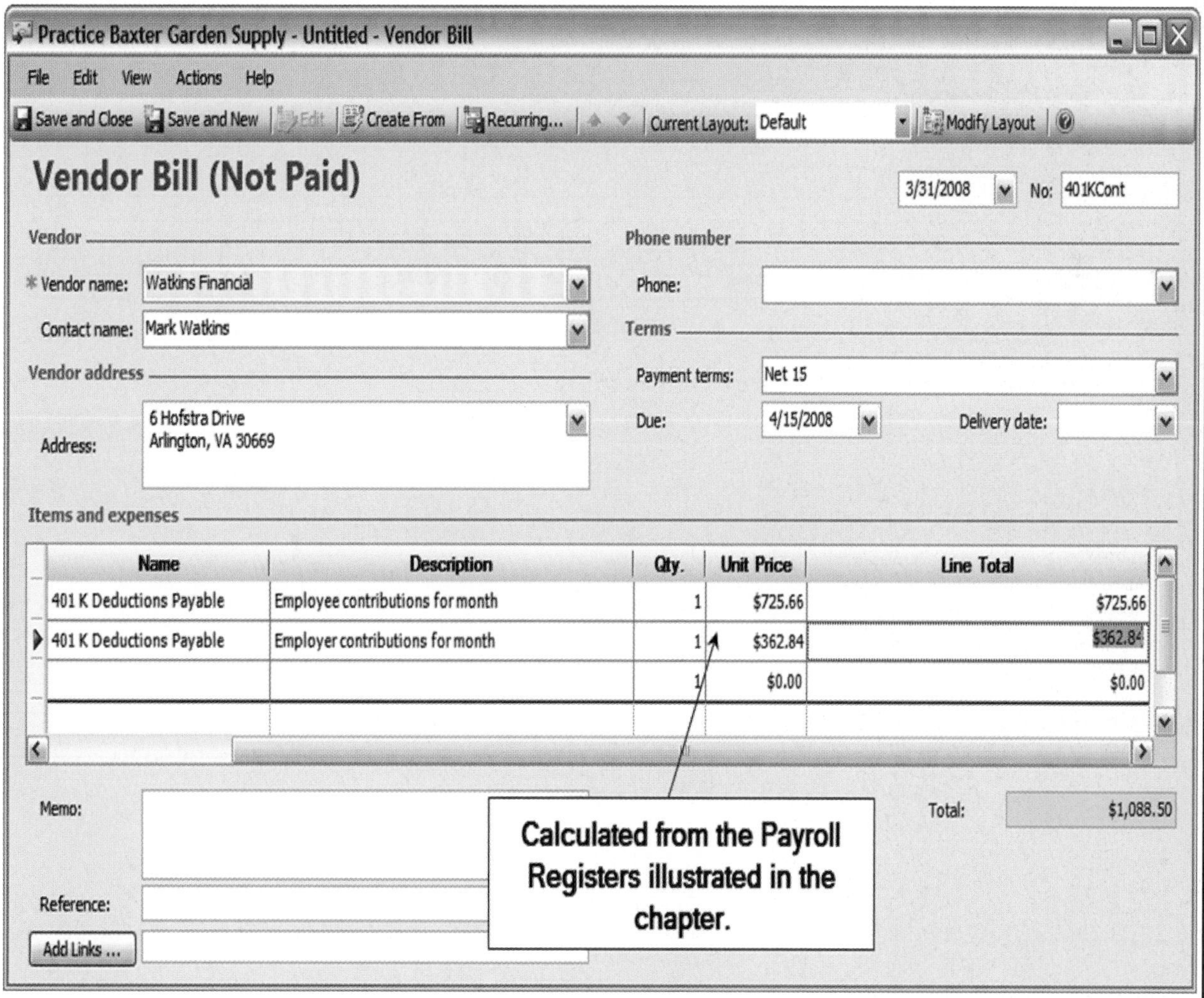

Practice Baxter Garden Supply - Untitled - Vendor Bill

File Edit View Actions Help

Save and Close | Save and New | Edit | Create From | Recurring... | Current Layout: Default | Modify Layout

Vendor Bill (Not Paid)

3/31/2008 No: 401KCont

Vendor

Vendor name: Watkins Financial

Contact name: Mark Watkins

Vendor address

Address: 6 Hofstra Drive
Arlington, VA 30669

Phone number

Phone:

Terms

Payment terms: Net 15

Due: 4/15/2008 Delivery date:

Items and expenses

Name	Description	Qty.	Unit Price	Line Total
401 K Deductions Payable	Employee contributions for month	1	$725.66	$725.66
401 K Deductions Payable	Employer contributions for month	1	$362.84	$362.84
		1	$0.00	$0.00

Memo:

Reference:

Add Links ...

Total: $1,088.50

Calculated from the Payroll Registers illustrated in the chapter.

Figure E:56

State payroll tax liability bill.

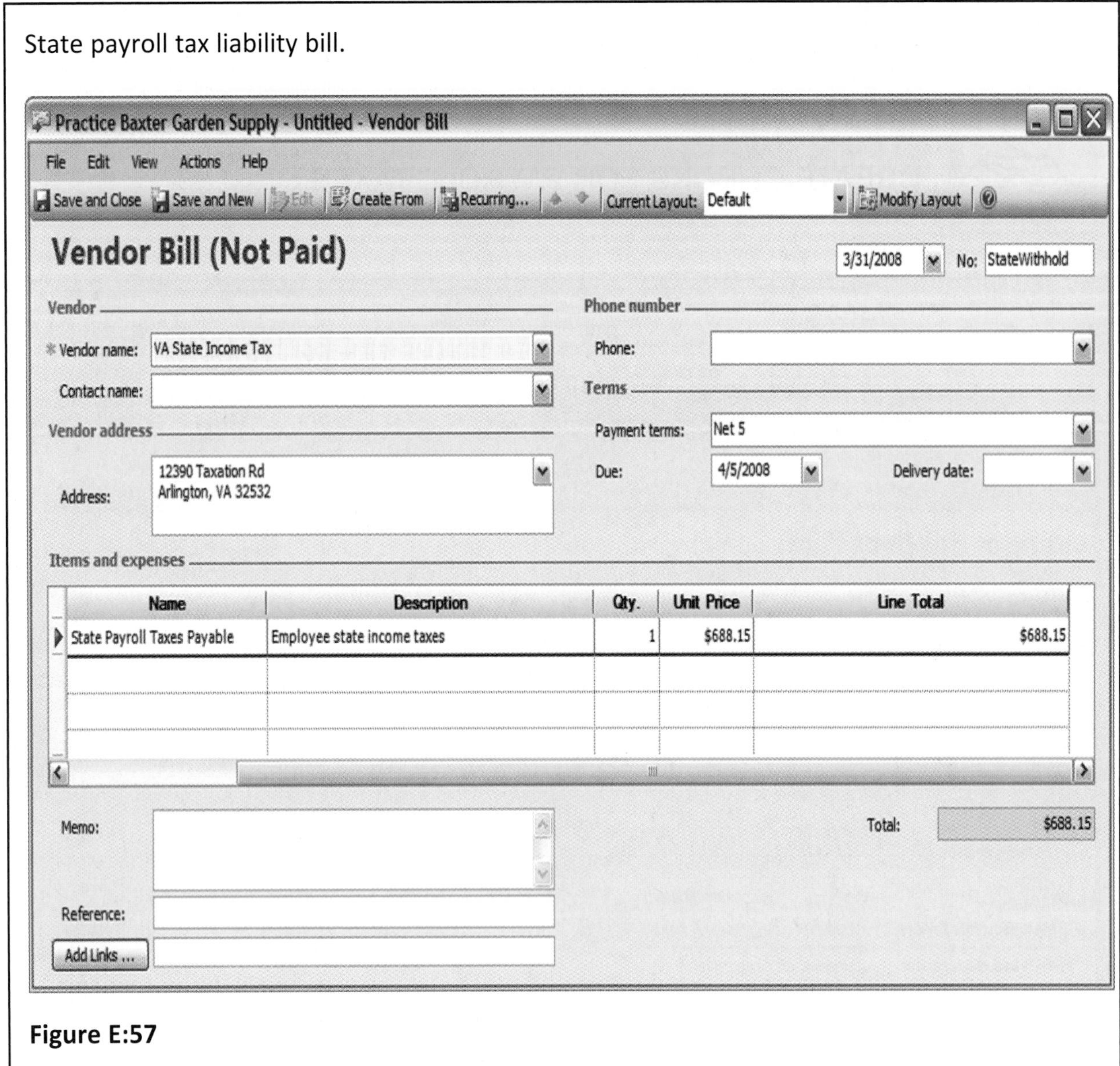

Figure E:57

Payments report for April 2, 2008.

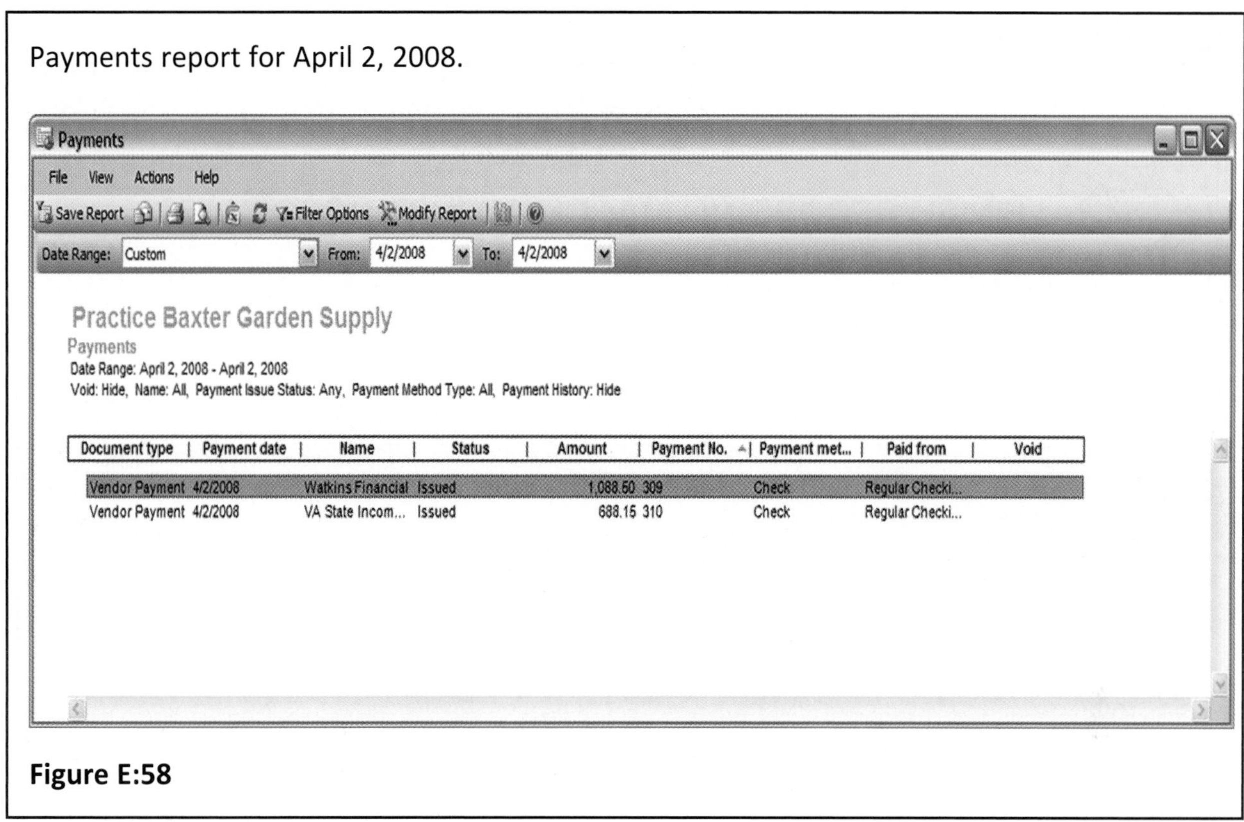

Figure E:58

CHAPTER 11

FINISH RECORDING MARCH ADJUSTING ENTRIES

Prepaid expense entry.

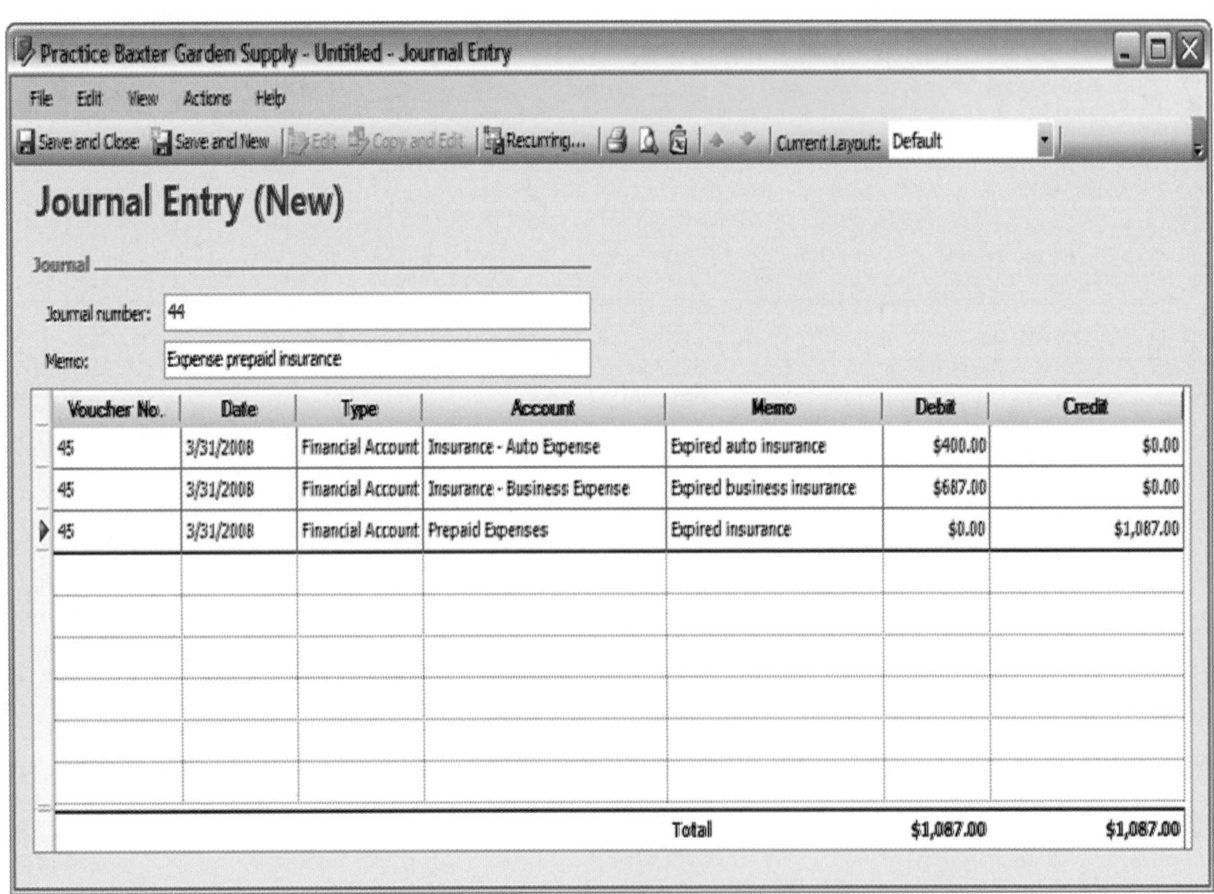

Voucher No.	Date	Type	Account	Memo	Debit	Credit
45	3/31/2008	Financial Account	Insurance - Auto Expense	Expired auto insurance	$400.00	$0.00
45	3/31/2008	Financial Account	Insurance - Business Expense	Expired business insurance	$687.00	$0.00
45	3/31/2008	Financial Account	Prepaid Expenses	Expired insurance	$0.00	$1,087.00
				Total	$1,087.00	$1,087.00

Figure E:59

RECONCILE THE PAYROLL CHECKING ACCOUNT

Payroll Reconciliation Detail report.

Practice Baxter Garden Supply
Reconciliation Detail
Amount: Any, Bank Account: Payroll Checking Account, Statement date: 3/31/2008

Type	Date	No.	Name	Amount
Payroll Checking Account				
Opening Balance				**509.52**
Cleared Deposits				
Fund Transfer	3/10/2008	8		9,200.00
Fund Transfer	3/24/2008	42		9,600.00
Total Cleared Deposits				**18,800.00**
Cleared Withdrawals				
Payroll Check	3/10/2008	1189	Barkley, Steve N.	(737.14)
Payroll Check	3/10/2008	1184	Beck, Dorothy L.	(627.32)
Payroll Check	3/10/2008	1190	Prather, Samuel R.	(1,195.62)
Payroll Check	3/10/2008	1186	Sweet, Leonard	(563.32)
Payroll Check	3/10/2008	1188	Trotter, Mitchell K.	(724.14)
Payroll Check	3/10/2008	1180	Chester, Amanda W.	(846.26)
Payroll Check	3/10/2008	1181	Duke, Al C.	(771.50)
Payroll Check	3/10/2008	1187	Frost, Melvin H.	(1,061.82)
Payroll Check	3/10/2008	1185	Gross, Derrick P.	(797.30)
Payroll Check	3/10/2008	1182	Hecter, Anthony H.	(821.24)
Payroll Check	3/10/2008	1183	Nunnley, Brandee M.	(996.50)
Payroll Check	3/24/2008	1200	Barkley, Steve N.	(763.34)
Payroll Check	3/24/2008	1195	Beck, Dorothy L.	(627.32)
Payroll Check	3/24/2008	1191	Chester, Amanda W.	(846.26)
Payroll Check	3/24/2008	1192	Duke, Al C.	(755.16)
Payroll Check	3/24/2008	1196	Gross, Derrick P.	(797.30)
Payroll Check	3/24/2008	1193	Hecter, Anthony H.	(821.24)
Payroll Check	3/24/2008	1194	Nunnley, Brandee M.	(996.50)
Payroll Check	3/24/2008	1201	Prather, Samuel R.	(1,195.62)
Payroll Check	3/24/2008	1197	Sweet, Leonard	(563.32)
Payroll Check	3/24/2008	1199	Trotter, Mitchell K.	(724.14)
Payroll Check	3/24/2008	1202	Sharpton, Susan T	(356.12)
Payroll Check	3/24/2008	1203	Frost, Melvin H.	(1,061.82)
Bank Fee	3/31/2008	47		(32.75)
Total Cleared Withdrawals				**(18,683.05)**
Total Cleared Transactions				**116.95**
Reconciled Balance As Of Statement Date				**626.47**
Ending Balance				**626.47**

Figure E:60

INDEX

D

E

F

G

H

S

T

U

V

W

Y